LBC CASEBOOKS

REAL PROPERTY
COMMENTARY AND MATERIALS

CANADA AND U.S.A.

The Carswell Company Ltd
Agincourt, Ontario

HONG KONG

Bloomsbury Books Ltd

NEW ZEALAND

University Bookshop (Auckland) Ltd
The University Bookshop, Christchurch
Bell's Techbooks Ltd, Wellington

UNITED KINGDOM

Sweet & Maxwell Ltd
London

REAL PROPERTY
Commentary and Materials

by

C. M. SAPPIDEEN
LL.B. (Melb.), LL.M. (Syd.)
Senior Lecturer in Law, Faculty of Law,
University of Queensland,
Barrister and Solicitor of the Supreme Court of Victoria

R. T. J. STEIN
LL.B. (A.N.U.), LL.M. (Dalhousie), A.Mus.A. (A.M.E.B.)
Senior Lecturer in Law, Faculty of Law,
University of Sydney,
Barrister-at-Law of the Supreme Court of New South Wales

P. J. BUTT
B.A., LL.M. (Syd.)
Associate Professor of Law, Faculty of Law,
University of Sydney,
Solicitor of the Supreme Court of New South Wales

G. L. CERTOMA
Dott. Giur. (Florence), B.A., LL.M. (Syd.)
Sometime Senior Lecturer in Law, Faculty of Law,
University of Sydney,
Solicitor of the Supreme Court of New South Wales

THIRD EDITION

THE LAW BOOK COMPANY LIMITED
1990

Published in Sydney by

The Law Book Company Limited
  44-50 Waterloo Road, North Ryde, N.S.W.
  490 Bourke Street, Melbourne, Victoria
  40 Queen Street, Brisbane, Queensland
  81 St George's Terrace, Perth, W.A.

First edition 1980
Second edition 1985
Third edition 1990

National Library of Australia
  Cataloguing-in-Publication entry

Real property, commentary and materials.

  3rd ed.
  Includes index.
  ISBN 0 455 20960 X.
  ISBN 0 455 20961 8 (pbk.).

  1. Real property—Australia. 2. Real property—
  Australia—Cases. I. Sappideen, C. (Carolyn).

346.94043

Typeset in Times Roman, 10 on 11 point, by Mercier Typesetters Pty Ltd,
    Granville, N.S.W.
Printed by Hogbin Poole (Printers) Pty Ltd, Redfern, N.S.W.

EXTRACTS FROM PREFACE TO THE FIRST EDITION

The subject of real property traditionally has evoked a love-hate relationship among students and practitioners alike. For some, it "appears to come almost as near to perfection as can be expected in any human institution" (Royal Commission on Real Property, First Report, 1829, p. 6). For others, it "offers no intellectual entertainment and . . . is scarcely a subject worthy of study for its own sake" (*Cheshire's Modern Law of Real Property* (11th ed., 1972), p. 3). We have approached our task as a labour of love.

Our aim in selecting the materials included in the text has been to cover the major substantive parts of the law of real property which form the basis of land law courses taught in law schools in this country. We have not sought to include the whole range of areas which are often subsumed under the heading of real property (and so areas such as the rule against perpetuities, planning law and the sale of land have been excluded) but have concentrated on eight main topics, each represented by a separate chapter in the book. As well as extracting leading cases and relevant statutory materials, we have included notes and commentary designed to encourage a close study of the law. In addition, in selected areas we have provided further references and materials for students who may wish to delve deeper into the intricacies of those areas; we hope that these may prove useful to reseachers and practitioners also.

We would like gratefully to acknowledge the assistance of Professor R. A. Woodman, of the University of Sydney, Faculty of Law, who read large sections of the manuscript and made many helpful suggestions.

No doubt the book will be found to contain some defects, but perhaps with due humility we might conclude by echoing the sentiments of Dr Cheshire who, in the Introduction to the first edition of his now classic *Modern Law of Real Property*, hoped that there were no defects which could not be "readily eradicated should sufficient support be forthcoming to justify the publication of a second edition".

P. J. BUTT
G. L. CERTOMA
C. M. SAPPIDEEN
R. T. J. STEIN

Sydney,
July 1980

PREFACE TO THE THIRD EDITION

In this third edition we have attempted to incorporate the many significant developments which have occurred in the law of real property since 1985. This has necessitated an increase in the size of the text, particularly to take account of new decisions in the Torrens system and in leases. The general structure of the book, however, remains unchanged.

As with the second edition, for reasons of space we have generally restricted statutory references to those of New South Wales, our aim being to elucidate general principles of law rather than to catalogue statutory divergences throughout the country. In any case, we would anticipate that students using the book will be doing so in the context of a university or college course on real property and will be directed by their lecturers to the relevant statutory provisions applying in their particular jurisdiction.

C. M. SAPPIDEEN

R. T. J. STEIN

P. J. BUTT

G. L. CERTOMA

Sydney,
March 1990

ACKNOWLEDGMENTS

The authors acknowledge with gratitude permission by the following publishers to reproduce extracts from cases in this book:

Butterworths Pty Ltd: cases from *Australian Law Reports* and *All England Reports*.

Council of Law Reporting for New South Wales: cases from *New South Wales Law Reports* and *New South Wales Reports*.

Council of Law Reporting for Victoria: cases from *Victorian Reports*.

Incorporated Council of Law Reporting for England and Wales: cases from *Law Reports* and *Weekly Law Reports*.

The Law Book Company Limited: cases from *Commonwealth Law Reports* and *South Australian State Reports*.

TABLE OF CONTENTS

Preface to the First Edition v

Preface to the Third Edition vii

Acknowledgments ix

Table of Cases xvii

Table of Statutes xxxiii

Chapter 1   **PHYSICAL LIMITS OF LAND** 1

     A.   Cujus est Solum ejus est Usque ad Coelum et ad Inferos 1

     B.   Quicquid Plantatur Solo, Solo Cedit 12

         1.   What constitutes a fixture? 12

         2.   Right to remove fixtures 13

Chapter 2   **CONCURRENT OWNERSHIP** 44

     A.   Concept and Characteristics 44

         1.   Right of survivorship 45

         2.   The four unities 50

     B.   Creation 50

     C.   Determination 51

         1.   Joint tenancy 51

         2.   Tenancy in common 85

     D.   Rights of Joint Tenants and Tenants in Common inter se 86

Chapter 3   **OLD SYSTEM TITLE AND REGISTRATION OF DEEDS LEGISLATION** 106

     A.   Priorities—General Principles 106

         1.   Two legal estates 106

         2.   Two equitable estates 106

         3.   Legal and equitable estates 109

     B.   Registration of Deeds Legislation 110

Chapter 4   **THE TORRENS SYSTEM** 125

     A.   Objects of Registration 125

     B.   Indefeasibility of Title 127

     C.   The Register 130

     D.   Unregistered Interests 133

     E.   Caveats 137

         1.   Effect of a caveat 138

         2.   Duty to caveat 140

Chapter 4 **THE TORRENS SYSTEM**—*continued*

F. Settlement of Registration 152

G. Exceptions to Indefeasibility of Title 165
   1. Fraud 166
   2. Estates interests and such entries 187
   3. Omission or misdescription of easements 190
   4. Short term tenancies 190
   5. Personal equities 196
   6. Correction of errors 200
   7. Statutory charges 201

H. Volunteers 204

I. Adverse Possession 209

J. The Assurance Fund 210

Chapter 5 **EASEMENTS AND PROFITS À PRENDRE** 214

A. Introduction 214

B. The Essential Requirements of an Easement 216
   1. Requirement of dominant and servient tenements 221
   2. Accommodation of the dominant tenement 222
   3. The dominant and servient tenements must not be owned and
      occupied by the same person 227
   4. The easement or profit must be capable of forming the subject
      matter of a grant 227

C. Creation of Easements 239
   1. By express grant 239
   2. By express reservation 241
   3. By statute 241
   4. By implied grant or reservation 242
   5. By prescription 258
   6. By estoppel 273

D. Extent and Duration of User 273
   1. Express grant or reservation 274
   2. Implied grant or reservation 279
   3. Prescription 279

E. Easements, Profits and the Torrens System 280

F. Extinguishment of Easements and Profits 294
   1. Express release 294
   2. Implied release 294
   3. Operation of law 295
   4. Order of the court 296

G. Remedies 301

Chapter 6 **COVENANTS CONSTITUTING AN INTEREST IN LAND** 303

A. Introduction 303

B. Enforcing Covenants at Common Law 308
   1. The burden of a covenant 308
   2. The benefit of a covenant 320

Chapter 6 **COVENANTS CONSTITUTING AN INTEREST IN LAND**—*continued*

    C. Enforcing Covenants in Equity 340
      1. The burden of a covenant 340
      2. The benefit of a covenant 346
        (a) Original covenantee 346
        (b) Successor in title to the covenantee 347
        (c) Express assignment 347
        (d) Benefit annexed to the land 349
        (e) Schemes of development 351

    D. Restrictive Covenants—Creation—Conveyancing Act 1919 (N.S.W.)
        Requirements 361
      1. Section 88(1) 361
        (a) Clear indication of land benefited and land burdened 362
        (b) Rights to release, vary or modify covenants 363
      2. Section 88B 364

    E. Restrictive Covenants and Torrens Title 364

    F. Modification and Extinguishment of Covenants 376
      1. Express release 376
      2. Operation of law 376
      3. Implied release 378
      4. Order of court 378
        (a) General considerations 380
        (b) Obsolescence 381
        (c) Impedes reasonable user without securing practical benefit 382
        (d) Express or implied release 382
        (e) No substantial injury 383

Chapter 7 **MORTGAGES** 389

    I. The Nature of a Mortgage 389

    II. Creation of Mortgages 393
      A. Legal Mortgage of Freehold Land Under Old System Title .. 393
      B. Legal Mortgage of Leaseholds Under Old System Title 394
        1. By assignment 394
        2. By sub-lease 394
      C. Equitable Mortgages 394
        1. Mortgage of the equity of redemption in old system land 394
        2. Executory agreement to grant a legal mortgage 395
        3. Mortgage by deposit of title deeds 399
      D. Mortgages of Land Under Torrens Title 401

    III. Clogs on the Equity of Redemption 404
      A. Power to Extinguish Equity of Redemption 404
      B. Time Limits on Right to Redeem 407
      C. Collateral Advantages 411
      D. Miscellaneous Matters 419
        1. Covenant to repay a greater amount than that advanced 419
        2. Covenant to pay a higher rate of interest upon default 422
        3. Covenant to pay whole of principal and interest
          immediately upon default 423
        4. Unconscionable dealing 426
        5. Early redemption of mortgages 427
        6. Late redemption—"the six months rule" 432
      E. Modern Statutory Provisions 434
        1. Trade Practices Act 1974 (Cth) 434
        2. Contracts Review Act 1980 (N.S.W.) 435

Chapter 7 **MORTGAGES**—*continued*

  III. Clogs on the Equity of Redemption—*continued*

      E. Modern Statutory Provisions—*continued*
          3. Credit Act 1984 (N.S.W.) 436
          4. Industrial Arbitration Act 1940 (N.S.W.) 437

  IV. Remedies of the Mortgagee 438
      A. Right to Sue on the Personal Covenant 438
          1. Credit Act 1984 (N.S.W.) 439
      B. Right to Possession 439
          1. Old system title 439
          2. Torrens title 440
          3. Credit Act 1984 440
          4. Liability of mortgagee in possession 440
          5. Right to improve the property 443
      C. Right to Lease 445
          1. Old system title 445
          2. Torrens title 445
      D. Right to Appoint a Receiver 446
      E. Foreclosure 447
          1. General 447
          2. Old system title 448
          3. Torrens title 451
      F. Power of Sale 452
          1. Manner of exercise of power 453
          2. Injunction to restrain sale 479
          3. Protection of purchaser 481
          4. Application of proceeds of sale 483

  V. Priorities 484
      A. General 484
          1. Old system title 484
          2. Torrens title 484
      B. Tacking 484
          1. Tabula in naufragio 485
          2. Further advances 486

Chapter 8 **LEASEHOLDS** 501

  I. Essential Requirements of a Leasehold Interest 501
      1. The right to exclusive possession 501
      2. Duration of the lease 533

  II. Types of Tenancies 537
      1. Tenancy at sufferance 537
      2. Tenancy at will 540
      3. Tenancy from year to year 547
      4. Tenancies under section 127 of the Conveyancing Act 554
      5. Other periodical tenancies 558
      6. Tenancies for a fixed term of years 559
      7. Concurrent leases 559
      8. Reversionary leases 559
      9. Agreements for a lease: Walsh v. Lonsdale 560
    10. Leases by estoppel 563

  III. Formal Requirements for the Creation of Leases 567
      1. Statutory requirements 567
      2. Entry 572

Chapter 8 **LEASEHOLDS**—*continued*

IV. Rights and Obligations of Lessor and Lessee: Covenants in Leases 572
    A. Covenants Implied by the General Law 572
        1. For quiet enjoyment 573
        2. Not to derogate from grant 579
        3. That furnished premises are reasonably fit for human habitation at the commencement of the term 582
        4. To use the premises in a tenant-like manner 584
        5. To yield up possession to the lessor at the end of the tenancy 586
        6. To cultivate in a husband-like manner 586
    B. Covenants Implied by Statute 588
        1. Covenant to pay rent 589
        2. Covenant to repair 589
    C. Usual Covenants 601
    D. Covenants Implied by Construction 603
    E. Short Form Covenants 604
    F. Statutory Provisions Affecting Covenants 604

V. Assignments and Sub-Leases 604
    A. The Right to Assign or Sub-Lease 604
    B. Covenants Against Assigning or Sub-Leasing 605
        1. Absolute covenants 605
        2. Qualified covenants 606
        3. Unreasonably withholding consent 607
        4. Effect of breach of covenant against assigning 619
    C. The Enforcement of Covenants Against Assignees and Sub-Lessees 619
        1. Privity of contract 619
        2. Privity of estate 620
        3. Covenants which "touch and concern" the land 621
        4. Assignment of the lease 625
        5. Assignment of the reversion 627
        6. Land under the Real Property Act 628

VI. Remedies 629
    A. Distress for Rent 629
    B. Action for Compensation for the Use of the Land 629
    C. Damages and Injunction 630
    D. Forfeiture by Re-Entry 630
        1. The right to forfeit 630
        2. Exercise of the right 631
        3. Formal requirements 633
        4. Waiver 639
        5. Relief against forfeiture 645

VII. Rent Control and Security of Tenure 646

Index 659

TABLE OF CASES

Where an extract from a case is reproduced, the name of the case and the page on which the reproduction commences appear in **heavy type**.

A.G. Securities v. Vaughan **527**, 531
AMEV-UDC Finance Ltd v. Austin 426
Abbeyfield (Harpenden) Society Ltd v. Woods 519, 524
Abbey National Building Society v. Maybeech Ltd 650, 655
Abela v. Public Trustee 75
Abigail v. Lapin 107, 138, **144**, 147, 148, 149, 150, 151, 152, 155, 476, 499
Abrahams v. Shaw 593
Abson v. Fenton 275
Achatz v. De Reuver 170, 177
Ackroyd v. Smith 221, 223, 274
Adams v. Bank of New South Wales 483
Adams v. Cairns 551
Addiscombe Garden Estates Ltd v. Crabbe 505, 507, 509, 513, 518
Adler v. Blackman 553
Aglionby v. Cohen 630
Agra Bank v. Barry 113
Albert, Re 48, 49
Alderson v. White 392
Aldin v. Latimer Clark, Muirhead & Co. 257, 581
Aldred's Case 228, 229, 302
Aldridge v. Wright 251
Aldrington Garages Ltd v. Fielder 513, 520
Alexandra, Re 382, 383
Alexandre v. New Zealand Breweries Ltd 479
Alfred F. Beckett Ltd v. Lyons 214
Allan v. Liverpool Overseers 516
Allcock v. Moorhouse 604
Allen v. Greenwood 228
Allen v. Lawson 306, 330
Allingham, Re 67
American Express International Banking Corp. v. Hurley 446, 447, 468
Amoco Australia Pty Ltd v. Rocca Bros Motor Engineers Co. Pty Ltd 604
Amory Pty Ltd, Application of, Re 360, 375
Anderson v. Bostock 223
Anderson v. Bowles 538
Anderson v. Lidell 403
Anderson v. Midland Railway Co. 548
Anderson v. Toohey's Ltd 605
Anderson, Ex parte; Re Green 628
Anderton and Milner's Contract, Re 602
Angus v. Dalton 268, 270, 272
Anning v. Anning 52
Anstruther-Gough-Calthorpe v. McOscar .. 593, 598
Anthony v. Commonwealth 270

Antoniades v. Villiers 528, 529, 531
Antovic v. Volker 435
Arcade Hotel Pty Ltd, Re 335, 337, 338, 339, 349
Argyle Art Centre Pty Ltd v. Argyle Bond & Free Stores Co. Pty Ltd 630, 643
Armour v. Penrith Project Pty Ltd 213
Armstrong, Re 55
Armstrong v. Wilkins 205
Army, Minister of State for v. Dalziel 523
Ashburn Anstalt v. Arnold 505, 535
Ashton v. Corrigan 396
Aspen v. Seddon 316
Aspen v. Seddon (No. 2) 316
Assaf v. Fuwa 110
Assets Co. Ltd v. Mere Roihi 128, 129, 143, 166, 172, 176, 186, 196, 288, 290, 291
Attorney-General v. Antrobus 220
Attorney-General v. De Keyser's Royal Hotel Ltd 629
Attorney-General (N.S.W.) v. Dickson 234
Attorney-General v. Horner (No. 2) 275
Attorney-General v. Magdalen College 104
Attorney-General (Southern Nigeria) v. John Holt v. Co. (Liverpool) Ltd 233, 239, 272
Auerbach v. Bech 245, 256, 296
Austerberry v. Corp. of Oldham 308, **309**, 314, 324, 328, 344
Australia and New Zealand Banking Group Ltd v. Greig **402**, 404
Australian and New Zealand Banking Group Ltd v. Bangadilly Pastoral Co. Pty Ltd 455, 478
Australian Express Pty Ltd v. Pejovic 444
Australian Hi-fi Publications Pty Ltd v. Gehl **280**, 286
Australian Provincial Assurance Assoc. Ltd v. Rogers 557, 629
Australian Provincial Assurance Co. Ltd v. Coroneo 12, **23**

Badcock and Badcock 79
Bahr v. Nicolay (No. 2) 170, 200, 287
Bailey v. Barnes 482, **485**
Bailey v. John Paynter (Mayfield) Pty Ltd 590
Bailey v. Stephens 275
Bain v. Brand 13, 28, **31**
Baker v. Gostling 565
Baker v. Wind 392
Balcairn Guest House Ltd v. Weir 583

Ballard's Conveyance, Re 331, **332**,
336, 339, 349
Bambury v. Chapman 608
Bank of Cyprus (London) Ltd v. Gill 468
Bank of New South Wales v. O'Connor ... 399
Bank of Victoria v. M'Hutchison 550, 551,
552, 553
Banner v. Berridge 431, 483
Bannerman Brydone Folster & Co. v.
Murray 406
Bannister v. Bannister 173
Bannister; Binions v. Evans 175, 180
Barclay's Bank Ltd v. Bird 439
Barina Properties Pty Ltd v. Bernard Hastie
(Aust.) Pty Ltd 604, 612
Barlow v. Rhodes 255
Barnes v. Barratt 513
Barnes v. James 142
Barns v. Queensland National Bank Ltd
469, 473, 474, 477, 478
Barrow v. Isaacs & Son 606
Barrow's Case 163, 164
Barry v. Hasseldine 250
Barry v. Heider 134, 144, 155, 171, 180,
182, 198, 199, 200, 282, 288, 293
Barry and the Conveyancing Act, Re 348
Bashir v. Commissioner for Lands 631
Bass v. Gregory 228
Bates v. Casey and Milne 622
Bates v. Donaldson 614, 617
Bathurst (Earl) v. Fine 655
Baxter v. Four Oaks Properties Ltd ... 356, 357,
358, 359
Baxton v. Kara 562
Bayley v. Bradley 538
Baynes & Co. v. Lloyd & Sons 572, 575, 576
Bayview Properties Pty Ltd v. Attorney-
General (Vic.) 214
Beard v. Baulkham Hills Shire Council 221
Beattie v. Fine 550
Beck v. Auerback 286
Beckett v. Tower Assets Co. 392
Bedford (Duke of) v. Trustees of the British
Museum 341
Belajev, Re 559
Belgravia Insurance Co. v. Meah 649
Belmont (C.J.) Pty Ltd v. A.G.C. (General
Finance) Ltd 423
Belton v. Bass, Ratcliffe and Gretton Ltd 456
Benger v. Quatermain 23
Bennett v. Excelsior Land etc., Co. Ltd ... 602
Berndt (J.C.) Pty Ltd v. Walsh **577**
Bernstein (Lord) v. Skyviews & General Ltd 1, 5
Berrey v. Lindley 554
Beswick v. Beswick 321, 397, 398
Beswicke v. Alner 10
Bettyes v. Maynard 457
Bibby v. Carter 302
Bickel v. Duke of Westminster 608, 612, 617, 618
Bicknell v. Hood 560
Biggs v. Hoddinott 408, 414, 417
Biggs v. McEllister 206
Biggs v. Peacock 84
Bird v. Trustees, Executors & Agency Co.
Ltd 321

Birmingham and District Land Co. and
Allday 352
Birmingham Citizens Permanent Building
Society v. Caunt 440
Birmingham, Dudley and District Banking
Co. v. Ross 247, 254, 579, 580
Bishop v. Taylor 534
Biss, Re 93
Bland v. Moseley 229
Blaxland v. Grattan 113, 118
Blomley v. Ryan 427
Bloomfield v. Bloomfield 550
Blundell v. Associated Securities Ltd 480
Bogdanovic v. Koteff **206**
Bognuda v. Upton and Shearer Ltd 273
Bohn v. Miller Bros Pty Ltd 337
Bolton v. Clutterbuck 249
Bond v. Rosling 558
Bonner's Case 398
Bonnin v. Andrews 168
Bonomi v. Backhouse 261
Booker v. Palmer 503, 510, 517, 518
Booth v. Salvation Army Building
Association Ltd 419, 422
Borman v. Griffith 227, 248
Boroughe's Case 634
Borthwick-Norton v. Romney Warwick
Estates Ltd 654
Boulter v. Boulter 97, 98, 103
Bower v. Peate 579
Bowser v. Colby 647
Box v. Attfield 550, 551, 553
Boyce v. Beckman 113, **118**
Boyd v. Mayor of Wellington 129, 130,
132, 196, 197, 198, 199
Boyd v. Shorrock 17, 19
Boyer v. Warbey 589, 627
Brace v. Duchess of Marlborough 486
Bradford Banking Co. Ltd v. Henry Briggs
Son & Co. Ltd 489, 490, 491, 496
Bradley v. Carritt 415, 416, 417, 418
Bradley v. McBride 289
Bramwell v. Bramwell 503
Brand v. Chris Building Co. Pty Ltd 3
Branwood Park Pastoral Co. Pty Ltd v.
Willing & Sons Pty Ltd 430, 432
Braythwayte v. Hitchcock 549, 554
Breams Property Investment Co. Ltd v.
Strougler 622
Bresking v. Wall 476
Breskvar v. Wall .. 127, 130, 171, 178, 180, 182,
197, 198, 208, 282, 284
Brew Bros Ltd v. Snax (Ross) Ltd 599
Brewster v. Kidgill 225
Brickom Investments Ltd v. Carr 645
Brickwood v. Young 94, **97**, 101, 103
Bridle v. Ruby 272
Brigers v. Orr 482
Brighty v. Norton 434
British Equitable Assurance Co. Ltd v.
Baily 471
British Railways Board v. Glass 234, 279
Brocklesby v. Temperance Permanent
Building Society 146

Bromley Park Garden Estates Ltd v.
Moss 607, **612**, 617, 618
Brook, Ex parte; Re Roberts 14, **38**
Broomfield v. Williams 256
Brown v. Alabaster 248
Brown v. Raindle 56
Browne v. Cranfield 402
Browne v. Flower 228, 257, 576, 579
Browne v. Lockhart 433
Brunker v. Perpetual Trustee Co. Ltd 52, 205, 206
Brunner v. Greenslade 340, 352,
                        353, 360, 376, 378
Brutan Investments Pty Ltd v. Underwriting
and Insurance Ltd 478
Bryant v. Foot 258
Bryant v. Lefever 228
Bryen v. Reus 606
Budd-Scott v. Daniell 575
Bull v. Bull 90
Bullen v. A'Beckett 111
Bulkey v. Wilford 119
Bulstrode v. Lambert 234, 235, 237, 279
Burfort Financial Investments v. Chotard 603
Burgess v. Rawnsley 59, **69**, 74, 78, 79
Burgh v. Legge 194
Burgis v. Constantine 147
Burkinshaw v. Nicholls 292
Burnham v. Carroll Musgrove Theatres Ltd 555,
                                            556
Burrows v. Crimp 112, 114
Burrows v. Lang 254
Bursill Enterprises Pty Ltd v. Berger Bros
Trading Co. Pty Ltd 187, 233, 235, 238
Butcher v. Bowen 512
Butler v. Fairclough 138, 140, 145, 147,
148, 149, 150, 151, 152, 166, 172, 176, 499
Butts v. O'Dwyer 557
Byrne, Re 94, 96

Cable v. Bryant 228, 258
Cachalot Nominees Pty Ltd v. Prime
Nominees Pty Ltd 478
Cadogan v. Dimovic 656
Cadwell v. Fellowes 56
Calabar Properties Ltd v. Seagull Autos Ltd 633
Calabar Properties Ltd v. Stitcher 601
Calabrese v. Miuccio 82
Caldwell v. Rural Bank of New South Wales 131,
                                            199
Caledonian Railway Co. v. Sprot 261
California (People of) v. Nogarr 65, 66
Camden v. Batterbury 626
Cameron v. Dalgety 225
Campbell v. Bank of New South Wales 452
Campbell v. Holyland **448**
Campden Hill Towers Ltd v. Gardner 583
Canas Property Co. Ltd v. K. L. Television
Services Ltd 629, 633
Canham v. Fisk 295
Cannon v. Villars 276, 279
Cannon Enterprises Ltd v. Ranchhod 656
Cantanzariti v. Whitehouse 44
Carberry v. Gardiner 557, **568**

Cardiothoracic Institute v. Shrewdcrest Ltd 559
Cargill v. Gotts 272, 280
Carmody v. Delehunt 50
Caroline Chisholm Village Pty Ltd, Re 321, 353
Carter v. Carter 486
Casborne v. Scarfe 62
Catholic Supplies Ltd and Jones, Re 648
Cave v. Cave 112
Celsteel Ltd v. Alton House Holdings Ltd
(No. 2) 573
Centaploy Ltd v. Matlodge Ltd 535
Central Estates (Belgravia) Ltd v. Woolgar
(No. 2) 643, **652**
Central Mortgage Registry of Australia Ltd
v. Donemore Pty Ltd 487, **495**
Centrax Trustees Ltd v. Ross 432
Chamberlain and the Conveyancing Act,
Re 304, 380, 382, 385
Chambers v. Randall 348
Chandless-Chandless v. Nicholson 645
Chaplin v. Young 440
Charalambous v. Ktori 602
Charmelyn Enterprises Pty Ltd v. Klonis .. 422
Charrington v. Simmons & Co. Ltd 10
Chasemore v. Richards 266, 271
Chastey v. Ackland 228
Chatsworth Estate Co. v. Fewell 378
Chatsworth Properties Ltd v. Effiom 445
Chelsea and Walham Green v. Armstrong 321
Chelsea Investments Pty Ltd v.
Commissioner of Taxation 512
Chelsea Waterworks Co. v. Bowley 239
Cherry v. Heming 553
Chester v. Buckinham Travel Ltd 603
Chester v. Willan 54
Chesterfield v. Harris 215, 222, 223
Child v. Douglas 329
Cholmondeley v. Clinton 455
Christopoulos v. Kells 204, 286
Chronopoulos v. Caltex Oil (Aust.) Pty Ltd 605
Church v. Brown 601, 605
Church of England Building Society v.
Piskor 567
Citicorp Australia Ltd v. McLoughney 478
Cityland and Property (Holdings) Ltd v.
Dabrah 420, 422
City Mutual Life Assurance Society Ltd v.
Smith 160
Civil Service Co-op Society Ltd v.
McGrigor's Trustees 644
Clarke v. Raymor (Brisbane) Pty Ltd
(No. 2) 151
Claude Neon Ltd v. Melbourne and
Metropolitan Board of Works 512
Clayton v. Corby 90
Clements v. Ellis 127, 129, 132, 185
Clemow v. Cook 562
Clem Smith Nominees Pty Ltd v. Farrelly 306,
                                            330, 334
Clifton v. Viscount Bury 4
Climie v. Wood 16
Clore v. Theatrical Properties Ltd 505
Clyne v. Lowe 192
Coatsworth v. Johnson 554, 562

Cobb v. Lane 504, 512, 518
Cochrane v. Entwhistle 399
Cochrane v. Verner 229
Codelfa Construction Pty Ltd v. S.R.A. of
    N.S.W. 174, 181, 525
Coggan v. Warwicker 541
Cole v. Kelly 554
Cole v. Stewart 26
Coleman v. De Lissa 118, 404
Coles v. Simms 358
Coles (G. J.) & Co. Pty Ltd v. Commissioner
    of Taxation 604
Colin D. Young Pty Ltd v. Commercial and
    General Acceptance Ltd 482
Colledge v. H.C. Curlett Construction Co.
    Ltd 23
Collen v. Wright 586
Collins v. Flynn 599
Collins v. Hopkins **582**
Colls v. Home & Colonial Store Ltd 228
Colvin v. Bowen 608
Commercial and General Acceptance Ltd v.
    Nixon 468, 478
Commercial Bank of Australia v. Amadio   426
Commonwealth v. New South Wales 130
Commonwealth v. Registrar of Titles (Vic.) 228,
                                                230
Commonwealth Bank of Australia v. Cohen   436
**Commonwealth   Life   (Amalgamated)
    Assurance Ltd v. Anderson** **546**, 604
Commonwealth of Australia v. K. N. Harris
    Pty Ltd 512
Compton v. Richards 244
Concord Municipal Council v. Coles   215, 221,
                                                233
Congleton Corp. v. Pattison 328, 623
Connellan Nominees Pty Ltd v. Cameron   271
Connolly v. Noone and Cairns Timber Ltd   287
Conquest v. Ebbets 600
Conroy v. Knox 456
Consolidated Development Pty Ltd v. Holt   633,
                                                655
Cook, Re 383, 395
Cook v. Bank of New South Wales 436
Cook v. Mayor & Corp. of Bath 295
Cook v. Shoesmith 606
Cooke v. Chilcott 341
Cooke v. Ingram 293
Cook's   Mortgage,   Re;   Lawledge   v.
    Tyndall 98, 99
Cooper, Re; Cooper v. Vesey 112, **114**
Copeland v. Greenhalf   222, 227, 233, 234, 238,
                                                239
Cordell v. Second Clanfield Properties Ltd   234
Cordingley (Deceased), Re 83, 84, 85
Corin v. Patton 52
Cornish v. Book Green Laundry Ltd 562
Cornish v. Lloyd 512
Corporate   Affairs,   Commissioner   for,
    (W.A.) v. Nut Farms (Aust.) Pty Ltd   214
Corporation of London v. Riggs **248**,
                                                273, 279
Corry and Corry 75, **80**

Cottage Holiday Associates Ltd v. Customs
    and Excise Commissioners 559
Coulls v. Bagot's Executor & Trustee Co.
    Ltd 397, 398
Countess of Shrewsbury's Case 585
Courtenay v. Austin 153, 191
Cowper v. Fletcher 55
Cox v. Hoban 603
Crabb v. Arun District Council 273
Craddock v. Scottish Provident Institution   395
Cram v. Bellambi Coal Co. Ltd 555
Credland v. Potter 123, 124, 487
Creelam's Case 290
Creer v. P & O Lines (Aust.) Pty Ltd 606
Creery v. Summersell and Flowerdew &
    Co. Ltd 643
Croft v. Lumley 641
Croft v. Powell 393
Cromwell Property Investment Co. Ltd v.
    Western and Toovey 434
Crossley v. Lee 14
Crossley & Sons Ltd v. Lightowler 252
Crow v. Wood 227, 257, 303, 307
Crowley v. Templeton 132
Cruse v. Mount 583
**Cuckmere Brick Co. Ltd v. Mutual Finance
    Ltd** 458, **461**, 468, 473,
                     474, 477, 478, 479, 480, 481
Cunningham v. National Australia Bank
    Ltd 479
Cunningham, Ex parte; Re McCarthy 293
Currey v. Federal Building Society 144, 159
Cuthbertson v. Swan 136, 137

Dabbs v. Seaman 256, 273, **287**, 294
Dalegrove Pty Ltd v. Isles Parking Station
    Pty Ltd 628
Dally-Watkins, Ex parte; Re Wilson 638
Dalton v. Angus 229, 259, **260**, 268, 272
Daly v. Edwardes 505
Dampier Mining Co. Ltd v. Commissioner
    of Taxation (Cth) 512
Danby v. Read 393
Dand v. Kingscote 275, 276
Daniher v. Fitzgerald 570
Danita Investments Pty Ltd v. Rockstrom   512
Darling v. Clue 259
Davenport Central Service Station Ltd v.
    O'Connell 622
Davey v. Durrant 456, 458, 468
David Blackstone Ltd v. Burnetts (West
    End) Ltd 644
David Jones Ltd v. Leventhal 655
Davies v. Bennison 1, 12
Davies v. Du Paver 270
Davies v. Marshall 294
Davis v. McConochie 570
Davis v. Symons 409, 410
Dawson, Re 19
Deanshaw and Deanshaw v. Marshall 279
Deeley v. Lloyds Bank Ltd 489, 490
De Falbe, Re 20, 34, 35, 36
De Lassalle v. Guildford 181

Delehunt v. Carmody 50
Delohery v. Permanent Trustee Co. (N.S.W.) 259
Dennerstein, Re 375
Dennis v. McDonald 86
Derry v. Peek 469, 475
Deventer Pty Ltd v. B. P. Australia Ltd .. 30
Dewhirst v. Edwards 223, 273, 286, 287
D'Eyncourt v. Gregory 16
Diment v. Foot 270, 271
Dimmick v. Pearce Investments Pty Ltd ... 478
Direct Food Supplies (Victoria) Pty Ltd v. D.L.V. Pty Ltd 648
Dixon, In the Estate of 48, 49
Dixon v. Muckleston 145
Dockrill v. Cavanagh ... 553, 554, **555**, 559, 571
Doe v. Chamberlaine 502
Doe v. David 621
Doe v. Ingleby 621
Doe d. Ambler v. Woodbridge 641
Doe d. Bennett v. Turner 538
Doe d. Bromfield v. Smith 548
Doe d. Cheny v. Batten 643
Doe d. Davenish v. Moffatt 548, 554
Doe d. Dixie v. Davies 551
Doe d. Edney v. Benham 543
Doe d. Jones v. Jones 545
Doe d. King v. Grafton 543
Doe d. Lockwood v. Clarke 534
Doe d. Martin and Jones v. Watts 543, 550
Doe d. Nicholl v. M'Kaeg 545, 546
Doe d. Oldershaw v. Breach 548
Doe d. Pennington v. Taniere 551
Doe d. Rigge v. Bell 552, 554
Doe d. Shore v. Porter 554
Doe d. Thomson v. Amey ... 549, 551, 552, 554
Doe d. Tilt v. Stratton 548, 556
Doherty v. Allman 346
Dollar v. Winston 609
Dolling, Re 49
Dolphin's Conveyance, Re ... 352, 353, **355**, 359
Donnelly v. Adams 292
Donoghue v. Stevenson 468
Douglas v. Culverwell 391, 392
Douglas v. Lock 234
Downes v. Grazebrook 454
Dowse v. Wynyard Holdings Ltd 576, 578
Drake v. Gray 335, 337, 350
Drake v. Templeton 132
Drane v. Evangelou 576
Draper's Conveyance, Re 70, 72, 73, 76, 77, 78, 79
Driscoll v. Church Commissioners for England 298, 385
Drive Yourself Hire Co. (London) Ltd v. Strutt 321
Dudgeon v. Chie 302
Dudley and District Benefit Building Society v. Emerson 445
Dukart v. District of Surrey 221
Duke v. Robson 468
Dumpor's Case 605, 645
Duncan v. Louch 220
Dunn Pty Ltd v. L. M. Ericsson Pty Ltd 13

Durham and Sunderland Railway Co. v. Walker 234
Durkowyak v. Durkowyak 396
Dynevor (Lord) v. Tennant 256
Dyson v. Forster 623

Eardley v. Granville 11
Eastern Telegraph Co. Ltd v. Dent 606
Easton v. Ardizzone 138
Easton v. Isted 228
Eastwood v. Ashton 282
Ecclesiastical Commissioners for Englands Conveyance, Re 321, 336
Edge v. Boileau 573
Edler v. Auerbach 583
Edward Keller (Aust.) Pty Ltd v. Hennelly 436
Edwardes v. Barrington 505
Edwards v. McDowell 456
Edwards v. Sims 1
Efstratiou v. Glantschnig 170
Egerton v. Esplanade Hotels, London, Ltd 653
Elibank-Murray v. Dunne 240
Ellenborough Park, Re **216**, 222, 223, 225, 227, 231, 233
Elliot, Re 118, 404
Ellis v. Loftus Iron Co. 7, 12
Ellis v. Rowbotham 641, 642
Ellison v. O'Neill **335**, 339, 340, 349
Ellison v. Vukicevic 240
Elliston v. Reacher 314, 315, 352, **353**, 357, 358, 359, 360, 377, 378
Elwes v. Maw 14
Errington v. Errington **501**, 504, 505, 507, 508, 509, 513, 518, 547
Esanda Finance Corp. Ltd v. Plessing 426
Escott v. Newport Corp. 239
Esdaile v. Lewis 606
Espley v. Wilkes 289, 292
Esso Petroleum v. Kingswood Motors 346
Esso Petroleum Co. Ltd v. Harper's Garage (Stourport) Ltd 305, 435, 604
Esther Investments Pty Ltd v. Cherrywood Park Pty Ltd 650
Eustace v. Scawen 54
Evans v. Davis 632
Expo International Pty Ltd v. Chant 447, 468, 478
Eyre v. McDowall 395
Ezekiel v. Orakpo 645

Facchini v. Bryson 505, 507, 509, 518
Fairclough v. Swan Brewery Co. 407, 410, 411, 418
Falcke v. Scottish Imperial Insurance Co. 3
Farnham v. Orrell 436
Farquharson Bros & Co. v. King & Co. ... 292
Farrar v. Farrars Ltd 453, 457, 463, 464, 465, 467, 470
Farrington v. Forrester 87
Farrow's Bank Ltd, Re 606
Fawkes v. Attorney-General (Ontario) 211

Federated Homes v. Mill Lodge 322, 324, 326, 339, 349, 350, 351
Fels v. Knowles 133
Fenn v. Smart 632, 633
Ferguson v. Anon. 585
Fettel, Re 84, 85
Fink v. McIntosh 559
Fink v. Robertson 452
Finn v. London Bank of Australia 446
Fireproof Door Ltd, Re 56
Fisher v. Dixon 32, 38
Fitzgerald's Trustee v. Mellersh **432**
Fletcher v. Nokes 637
Flexman v. Corbett 602
Ford v. Heathwood 230
Formby v. Barker 321, 345, 346
Forrest, Re 64
Forrest Trust, Re 403
Forster v. Elvet Colliery Co. Ltd 321
Forsyth v. Blundell **472**, 478, **479**, 480, 482
Foster v. Robinson 503
Four Maids Ltd v. Dudley Marshall (Properties) Ltd 439
Fox v. Hunter-Paterson 541
Fox v. Jolly **634**
Fox, Application of, Re 332, 340, 353, 375
Francis, Re 60
Franklin v. Ind 136
Frank Warr & Co. v. London County Council 505
Frater v. Finlay **223**, 227, 304, 307, 320, 342
Frazer v. Walker 126, 127, 128, 129, 130, 159, 160, 161, 162, 180, 182, 184, 185, **196**, 197, 198, 199, **200**, 203, 207, 208, 211, 282, 285
Frederick Berry Ltd v. Royal Bank of Scotland 606
Free Church of Scotland (General Assembly of) v. Overtoun (Lord) 471
Freed v. Taffel 51
Freemantle Trades Hall Industrial Assoc. v. Victor Motor Co. Ltd 633
Friedman v. Barrett 182
Friedman, Ex parte 182
Friend v. Mayer 434
Frieze v. Unger 60, **66**, 512
Fry v. Lane 427
Fuller v. Goodwin 113, 116, 118, 121
Fuller's Theatre & Vaudeville Co. v. Rofe 640
Furness Railway Co. v. Cumberland Co-op. Building Society 288, 292
Fyfe v. Smith **441**

Gabolinscy v. Hamilton City Corp 583
Gas & Fuel Corp. (Vic.) v. Barba 221
Gayford v. Moffatt 248
Geddes v. Frase 563
Gemmell Holdings, Re. 339, 340
General Finance Agency etc. Co. v. Perpetual Executors & Trustees Assoc. (Aust.) Ltd 142
Gentle v. Faulkner 606

George v. Commercial Union Assurance Co. (Aust.) Ltd 480
Gerraty v. McGavin 638
Gesmundo v. Anastasiou 3
Ghey and Galton's Application, Re ... 298, 381, 382, 385
Gibbs v. Messer 127, 129, 143, 166, 167, 171, 179, 182
Gibbs and Houlder Bros & Co. Ltd's Lease, Re; Houlder Bros & Co. Ltd v. Gibbs 607, 608, 609, 611, 612, 614, 616, 617
Gibons v. Kirk 629
Gifford v. Dent 4, 5, 6
Gilbert v. Spoor 382
Gill v. Lewis **645**, 648
Glenwood Lumber Co. Ltd v. Phillips 515, 523
Godfrey v. Poole 118
Goff v. O'Connor 26
Goldberg v. Edwards 256
Goldcel Nominees Pty Ltd v. Network Finance Ltd 479
Goldsworthy Mining Ltd v. Federal Commissioner of Taxation 523
Goodtitle v. Herbert 553
Goodtitle v. Tombs 87
Goodwin v. Papadopoulos 362, 363
Goodwin v. Waghorn 401
Governors of Bridewell Hospital v. Fawkner 619
Graham v. K. D. Morris & Sons Pty Ltd 1, 8
Graham v. Markets Hotel Pty Ltd 597, 598, 601
Graham v. Philcox 257, 273
Great Northern Railway Co. v. Arnold 534
Great Western Permanent Loan Co. v. Friesen 144, 155
Green v. Ashco Horticulturist Ltd 257
Greenwood Village Pty Ltd v. Tom the Cheap (W.A.) Pty Ltd 648
Greig v. Watson 402
Griffies v. Griffies 89
Grigsby v. Melville 233, 234, 239
Grimwood v. Moss 644
Groongal Pastoral Co. Ltd (in liq.) v. Falkiner 132, 159, 438
Grosvenor Hotel Co. v. Hamilton 257, 572, 581
Grundy v. Ley 439
Guppys (Bridport) Ltd v. Brookling 576
Gurfinkel v. Bentley Pty Ltd **390**
Gurfinkel v. Panizza **390**
Guth v. Robinson 223
Gutteridge v. Munyard 596

Haddelsey v. Adams 45
Hadjiloucas v. Crean 530
Hagee (London) Ltd v. Erikson and Larson 541
Halbert v. Mynar 46, **48**
Hall v. Busst 176
Halliard Property Co. Ltd v. Jack Segal Ltd 638
Halsall v. Brizell 226, 304, 307, 308, 313, 315, 316, 318, 342
Hamerton v. Stead 548
Hamilton v. Joyce 269, 271, 272
Hamilton's Estate 123

Hamlyn & Co. v. Wood & Co. 603
Hampshire v. Wickens **601**
Hansford v. Jago 248, 250, 256
Harada v. Registrar of Titles 221, 239
Harding v. Crethorn 586
Hardwick v. Johnson 505
Harmer v. Jumbil (Nigeria) Tin Areas Ltd 258,
579, 581
Harris v. Da Pinna 228
Harris v. Earl of Chesterfield 222
Harris v. Walker 69
Harrison v. Wells 563, 565
Harrison Ainslie & Co. v. Muncaster .. 578, 579
Hart v. Hart 397, 398
Hart v. Windsor 583
Hartley v. Humphris 468
Harty v. Kolman 555
Harvey v. McWatters 479, 480
Harvey v. Walker 606
Haskell v. Marlow **599**, 600
Hawkesley v. May 70, 76, 77
Hayes v. Seymour-Johns 512
Hayes Estate, Re 67
Hayward v. Skinner 84
Haywood v. Brunswick Permanent Benefit
    Building Society 310, 341, 344
Healey v. Hawkins 269
Health, Minister of v. Belotti 503, 546
Heath v. Pugh 447
Heaton v. Loblay 382, 383
Heffield v. Meadows 594
Heglibiston Establishment v. Heyman 655
Hellawell v. Eastwood 17, 18, 19, 36
Hemmings v. Stoke Poges Golf Club 630
Henderson v. Astwood 444, 455
Henderson v. Eason 87, 89, 90, **91**, 102
Henderson v. Hay 601
Henderson v. Squire **586**
Henderson's Conveyance, Re 381, 382
Henry, Ex parte; Commissioner of Stamp
    Duties, Re 214
Henry Roach (Petroleum) Pty Ltd v. Credit
    House (Vic.) Pty Ltd 479
Hermann v. Hodges 396
Herz v. Union Bank of London 257
Heslop v. Burns 512, 519, 547
Hewett, Re; Hewett v. Hallett 51
Heydon's Case 121
Heyman v. Darwins Ltd 558
Hickley v. Hickley 454
Hickman v. Peacey **46**, 48
Higgins v. Betts 302
Hill v. Grange 256
Hill v. Harris 583
Hill v. Hickin 87, 88
Hill v. Tupper 215, 221, 222, 223, 227
Hindmarsh v. Quinn 214, 302
Hindson v. Ashby 301
Hinton v. Fawcett 644
Hobson v. Gorringe 13, 24, **27**
Hodgkinson v. Crowe 602
Hodson v. Deans 483
Hodson v. Sharp 565
Hoffman v. Fineberg 653

Hogan v. Howard Finance Ltd 436
Holden v. Blaiklock 638
Holland v. Hodgson .. 12, **15**, 23, 24, 25, 28, 29
Hollins v. Verney 271
Holohan v. Friends Provident and Century
    Life Office 474, 477, 479
Hope v. R.C.A. Photophone of Australia
    Pty Ltd 173
Hopgood v. Brown 316
Hopkinson v. Rolt 123, 487, 489, 490,
                          491, 496, 497, 498
Horne v. Horne 133
Horsefall v. Mather 584
Horsey Estate Ltd v. Steiger and Petrifite
    Co. Ltd **621**, 637
Hosking (R. M.) Properties Pty Ltd v.
    Barnes 170, 177
Housing Commission (N.S.W.) v. Allen ... 630
Howard v. Fanshawe 645
Howard v. Harris 413
Howard v. Penrith Municipal Council 131
Howard v. Shaw 502
Howe v. Botwood 598
Hoyt's Pty Ltd v. Spencer 557, 569
Hudson v. Cripps 575
Hughes v. Mockbell 570
Hulley v. Silverspring Bleaching & Dyeing
    Co. Ltd 272
Humphries v. Brogden 261
Hunt v. Luck 192, 193, **194**, 196, 562
Hunter's Lease, Re; Giles v. Hutchings 628
Hutchinson v. Lemon 190
Hyde Management Services Pty Ltd v.
    F.A.I. Insurances Ltd 427, 434
Hyman v. Rose **650**, 655

I.A.C. (Finance) Pty Ltd v. Courtenay 149,
                    153, 158, 159, 161, 164, 191
I.A.C. (Leasing) Ltd v. Humphrey 424
I.C.I. Alkali (Aust.) Pty Ltd (in liq.) v.
    Commissioner of Taxation 513, 553
Imray v. Oakshette 656
Industrial Properties (Barton Hill) Ltd v.
    Associated Electrical Industries Ltd ... **563**
Inglis v. Commonwealth Trading Bank of
    Australia 479, 480
Inner City Businessmen's Club Ltd v. James
    Kirkpatrick Ltd 644, 648
International Drilling Fluids Ltd v.
    Louisville Investments (Uxbridge) Ltd 608,
                                         616
International Tea Stores Co. v. Hobbs 220,
                                      253, 254
Irving v. Commercial Banking Co. (Syd.) 458
Isaac v. Hotel de Paris Ltd 504, 518
Isherwood v. Butler Pollnow Pty Ltd 447
Ives (E. R.) Investment Ltd v. High .. 287, 316,
                                      318, 320

Jackson v. Jackson 70, 73, 78
James v. Dean 547

James v. Registrar-General 201, 284, 286
James v. Stevenson 284, 294
Jelbert v. Davis 273, 277
Jenkins v. Jackson 575
Jeffries v. Williams 302
Jeff's Transfer, Re 338
Jeff's Transfer, Rogers v. Astley (No. 2),
    Re 326, 349
Jenkins v. Jones **481**
Jennings v. Ward 411, 414
Jennison v. Traficante 222
Jobson v. Nankervis 284, 285, 294
John v. Holmes 343
Johnson v. Senes and Berger 638
John Trenberth Ltd v. National Westminster
    Bank Ltd 1, 12
Johnston v. Krakowski 69
Johnstone, Re **68**
Johnstone v. Holdway 221
Jones, Re; Farrington v. Forrester 98,
                                        101, 103
Jones v. Carter 631, 632, 633
Jones v. Jones 90
Jones v. Lavington 576
Jones v. Mills 542, 543
Jones v. Price 231
Jones v. Pritchard 246, 252
Jones v. Sherwood Hills Pty Ltd 360,
                                        363, 375
**Jonray (Sydney) Pty Ltd v. Partridge Bros
    Pty Ltd** **158**, 163
Joseph Abraham Pty Ltd v. Emelin 512
Josephson v. Mason 136, 191, 570
Joyner v. Weeks 600
Junghenn v. Wood 589
**Just (J. & H.) (Holdings) Pty Ltd v. Bank of
    New South Wales** **147**, 151,
                                    399, 401, 499

Kalmac Property Consultants Ltd v.
    Delicious Foods Ltd 577
Karaggianis v. Malltown Pty Ltd 582, 603
Keates v. Lyon 358
Kebewar Pty Ltd v. Harkin 247, 258,
                                        273, 286
Keegan v. Young 302
Keeves v. Dean 604
Keewatin Power Co. Ltd v. Lake of the
    Woods Milling Co. Ltd 246
**Kelsen v. Imperial Tobacco Co. (of Great
    Britain and Ireland) Ltd** 1, 3, 6, 9
Kemp v. Derrett 536
Kemp v. Lumeah Investments Pty Ltd 562
Kennedy v. De Trafford 93, **459**, 461,
                462, 463, 464, 465, 466, 467,
                469, 470, 471, 473, 474, 475, 478
Kennedy v. General Credits Ltd 441
Kenny v. Preen **573**, 576
Kensington (Lord) v. Bouverie 441
Kenyon v. Hart 4
Keppel v. Bailey 223, 227, 341
Kerley v. Moule 116
Kerridge v. Foley 330, 332, 349, 352, 362, 363, 376

Kighly v. Bulkly 543
King v. A.G.C. (Advances) Ltd 151
King v. David Allen & Sons (Billposting) Ltd   505
King v. Eversfield 536
King v. King 81, 146
King v. Smail **204**, 207
Knight v. Simmond 377
**Knightsbridge Estates Trust Ltd v.
    Byrne** **407**, 420, 421
Kotis v. Devitt 3
**Kreglinger G. & C. New Patagonia Meat &
    Cold Storage Co. Ltd** 62, 389, 393,
            406, 409, 410, **412**, 418, 420, 421
Krell v. Henry 603
Kumar v. Dunning 623, 625, 628

Lace v. Chandler 133
Lace v. Chantler **533**, 534, 535, 536
Ladies' Hosiery and Underwear Ltd v.
    Parker 554
Lam Kee Ying Sdn. Bd. v. Lam Shes Tong   655
Lamos Pty Ltd v. Hutchinson 286
Lamson Store Service Co. Ltd v. Russell
    Wilkins & Sons Ltd 424, 426
Landale v. Menzies 524, 540, **541**,
                                546, 547, 551
Land Settlement Association Ltd v. Carr ..   558
Lander and Bagley's Contract, Re 602
Lane Cove Municipal Council v. Hurdis ...   345
Langdale Pty Ltd v. Sollas 332, 337, 339
Lange v. Ruwoldt 136, 137
Lapham v. Orange City Council (No. 2) ...   512
Lapin v. Abigail 147, 148, 155
Larke Hoskins & Co. Ltd v. Icher   556, 569, 572
**Latec Investments Ltd v. Hotel Terrigal Pty
    Ltd (in liq.)** **107**, 172, 177,
                                475, 476, 478, 480
Lavender v. Betts 576
Lawrence v. South County Freeholds Ltd   359, 378
Leader v. Homewood 39
Lee v. K. Carter Ltd 608, 609, 611
Lee v. Smith 549
Leech v. Schweder 229
Leeward Securities Ltd v. Lilyheath
    Properties Ltd 617
Lehmann v. McArthur 613
Lehrer and the Real Property Act, Re   130
Leicester (Earl of) v. Wells-in-the-Sea
    U.D.C. 334
Leigh v. Dickeson 88, 93, **94**, 98, 99,
                        101, 103, 104, 105, 538
Leigh v. Taylor 13, 35, 36
Leitz Leeholme Stud Pty Ltd v. Robinson   556
Le Neve v. Le Neve 198
Lend Lease Development Pty Ltd v.
    Zemlicka 582
Leonida v. Scotson Pty Ltd 538
Lepla v. Rogers 607
Leschallas v. Woolf 42
Levet v. Gas Light & Coke Co. 228
Lewis v. Baker 543, 572
Lewis v. Bell 522

Lidsdale Nominees Pty Ltd v. Elkharadly .. 629, 643, 644

Lincoln v. Wright 393

Lister v. Lane and Nesham 596, 597, 598

Little v. Dardier 289, 290, 292

Liverpool City Council v. Irwin 525, 603

Lloyd's Bank v. Dalton 269

Lloyd's Bank Ltd v. Bullock 107

Loan Investment Corp. (Aust.) Ltd v. Bonner 396

Lock v. Abercester 273

Lock v. Pearce 636, 655

Lock (S.H.) (Aust.) Ltd v. Kennedy 436

Logue v. Shoalhaven Shire Council 171, 180, **196**

Loke Yew v. Port Swettenham Rubber Co. Ltd **168**, 170, 172, 177, 178

London and County (A. & D.) Ltd v. Wilfred Sportsman Ltd 589

London and County Banking Co. v. Goddard 394

London and County Banking Co. Ltd v. Ratcliffe 489

London County Council v. Allen 320, **343**

London and South Western Railway Co. v. Gomm 304, 310, 328, 329, 343

Long v. Gowlett 256, 257

Longbottom v. Berry 19

Louinder v. Stuckey 631

Louis and the Conveyancing Act, Re 332, 360, 363, 364, **365**, 373, 374, 375, 376

Low v. Adams 550

Lowe (Inspector of Taxes) v. J. W. Ashmore Ltd 215

Lowenthal v. Vanhoute 645

Lowther v. Heaver 562

Lukass Investment Pty Ltd v. Makaroff 480, 482

Luke v. Luke **86**, 102

Lurcott v. Wakeley and Wheeler **595**, 598

Lyme Valley Squash Club v. Newcastle under Lyme Borough Council 242

Lynes v. Snaith 502, 503, 546

Lyon v. Greenhow 598

Lyons v. Imperial Land Co. 113, 114, 122

Lyons v. Lyons 60, **63**

Lyttleton Times Co. Ltd v. Warners Ltd .. 246, 252, 580

Lyus v. Prowsa Ltd 175, 178, 180, 321

M.R.A. Engineering Ltd v. Trimster Co. Ltd 249, 251, 256

McCall v. Abelesz 576, 577

McCauley v. Federal Commissioner of Taxation 214

McCormick v. McCormick 88, 89, 102

McEacharn v. Colton 607

McGinnis v. Union Bank of Australia Ltd 482

McGuigan Investments Pty Ltd v. Dalwood Vineyards Pty Ltd 306, 330, 334

McHugh v. Union Bank of Canada ... 462, 465, 466, 467, 468, 473, 474

McIlraith v. Grady 237

McIntyre v. Porter 294

McKee v. McKee 75

MacKenzie v. Childers 352

McKenzie v. McAllum 608

Mackintosh v. Trotter 39

McMahon v. Burchell 88, 90, 92

McMahon v. Docker 606

McMahon v. Public Curator (Qld.) 94, 101, 103

McNab v. Earle 52, **58**

McPherson v. Temiskaming Lumber Co. Ltd 523

Mack and the Conveyancing Act, Re .. 360, 375

Main Roads, Commissioner of v. B.P. Australia 345

Majala Pty Ltd v. Ellas 644

Malden Farms Ltd v. Nicholson 278

Malzy v. Eichholz 572, 576

Manchester Brewery Co. v. Coombs ... 562, 566

Manchester, Sheffield and Lincolnshire Railway Co. v. North Central Wagon Co. 391

Mander v. Falcke 343

Manly Properties Pty Ltd v. Castrisos 383

Mann v. Stephens 358

Manning v. Wasdale 215

Mantania v. National Provincial Bank Ltd 576

Maori Trustee v. Bolton 630

March v. Neumann 538

Marchant v. Charters 519

Marcroft Wagons Ltd v. Smith 503, 517

Margil Pty Ltd v. Stegul Pastoral Pty Ltd 248, 250, 287, 295, 296, 362

Markham v. Paget 575, 579

Marks v. Warren 605, 606

Marriott v. Anchor Reversionary Co. Ltd 464

Marsden v. Campbell 111, **113**

Marsden v. Edward Heyes Ltd 584, 585

Marshall v. Coupon Furnishing Co. 550

Marten v. Flight Refuelling Ltd 334, 335, 348, 350

Martin v. Smith 552

Martins Camera Corner Pty Ltd v. Hotel Mayfair Ltd 576

Martinson v. Clowes 454, 456

Martyn, Re 359, 364, 374, 375

Mason v. Clarke 214, 234, 302

Mason v. Island Air Pty Ltd 393

Mason and the Conveyancing Act, Re 381, 382, 383, 387

Massart v. Blight 619

Master v. Hansard 358

Masters v. Cameron 175

Mather v. Fraser 18, 19, 28

Matthews v. Smallwood 639, 640, 643

Matzner v. Clyde Securities Ltd 111, 124, 443, 486, **487**, 496

Maughan, Re 562

Maurice Toltz Pty Ltd v. Macy's Emporium Pty Ltd 227

May v. Belleville 234

Mayer v. Coe 129, 165, 208

Mayfair Trading Co. Pty Ltd v. Dreyer ... 10

Mayhew v. Suttle 517

Mayner v. Payne 363

Mayor of Congleton v. Pattison 621, 622

Mayor, etc., of Dunedin v. Searl 645

Mayor, etc., of Thetford v. Tyler 629
Mears v. Callender 14
Measures v. McFadyen 628
Mediservices International Pty Ltd v. Stocks
    & Realty (Security Finance) Pty Ltd .. 481
Mellor v. Lees 405
Mellor v. Walmesley 288, 292
Mendl v. Smith 401
Mercantile Credits Ltd v. Shell Co. of
    Australia 133, 190
Mercantile General Life Reassurance Co.
    (Aust.) Ltd v. Permanent Trustee
    Australia Ltd 231, 241, **279**
Meriton Apartments Pty Ltd v. McLaurin
    and Tait (Developments) Pty Ltd 158
Merten v. Shoalhaven Shire Council 197
Metcalf v. Campion 442
Metropolitan Railway Co. v. Fowler 227,
                                       235, 295
Metropolitan Trade Finance Co. Pty Ltd v.
    Coumbis 605
Meye v. Electric Transmission Ltd 540, 554
Middleton v. Baldock 503
Midland Credit Ltd v. Hallad 441
Midland Railway Co.'s Agreement, Re 535, 536,
                                            537
Miliangos v. George Frank (Textiles) Ltd 397
Millbourn v. Lyons 345
Miller v. Emcer Products Ltd 233, 238
Miller v. Jackson 258
Miller v. Minister of Mines 203, 284
Mills v. Lewis 439
Mills v. Renwick 486
Mills v. Stokman 159, 171, 177, 182, 214
Milner's Safe Co. Ltd v. Great Northern &
    City Railway 279
Milroy v. Lord 52
Ministry of Agriculture v. Matthews 503
Miscamble's Application, Re 337, 338, 382
Mitchinson v. Carter 604
Mock v. Thomson and Mel Studios Pty Ltd 170
Mole v. Ross 50, 51
Molton Finance Ltd, Re 399
Moore v. Dimond 547, 554, 560, 569
Moore v. Rawson 295
Moore v. Ullcoats Mining Co. Ltd 631
Morgan v. Coulson 437
Morgan v. Hardy 594, 595
Morgan v. Jeffreys 409
Morison v. Edmiston 550
Morland v. Cook 309, 314
Mouat v. Ross 570
Moule v. Garrett **625**
Mount Cook National Park Board v. Mount
    Cook Motels Ltd 581
Mount Tomah Blue Metals Ltd (in liq.), Re 396
Mountnoy v. Collier 564
Multiservice Bookbinding Ltd v. Marden .. 419
Mumford v. Stohwasser 486
Munro v. Stuart ... 169, 174, 181, 182, 191, **192**
Murdoch and Barry, Re 59
Murdock v. Kennedy 629
Murphy, Ex parte 550
Murry Bull & Co. Ltd v. Murray 518

Murray v. Hall 90
Murrell, Re 483
Muttyloll Seal v. Annundochunder Sandle 393

N.G.L. Properties Pty Ltd v. Harlington Pty
    Ltd 629, 633
Nash v. Eads 458
National Australia Bank Ltd v. Nobile 434
National Bank (A/asia) v. United Hand-in-
    Hand and Band of Hope Co. . 64, 440, 462
National Carriers Ltd v. Panalpina
    (Northern) Ltd 588
National Mutual Life Assoc. v. Benjamin 448
National Provincial Bank Ltd v. Ainsworth 505
National Provincial Bank Ltd v. Hastings
    Car Mart Ltd 505
National Westminister Bank Ltd v. Hart .. 566
Nationwide Building Society v. Registry of
    Friendly Societies 422
Natural Gas and Oil Corp. Ltd (in liq.) v.
    Byrne **538**
Neaverson v. Peterborough 272
Neeta (Epping) Pty Ltd v. Phillips 163
Nelson v. Walker 247
Newbolt v. Bingham 647
Newnham v. Willison 269
Newsome v. Graham 564
Newtown Abbot Co-op. Society Ltd v.
    Williamson and Treadgold Ltd 306, 330, 348,
                                       350, 372
New Zealand Government Property Corp. v.
    H. M. & S. Ltd **15, 40**
Nicholls v. Lovell 214
Nickerson v. Barraclough 246, 251
Nielson-Jones v. Fedden .. 70, 72, 73, 76, 77, 78
Nisbet and Potts Contract, Re 304, 342,
                                       343, 345
Noack v. Noack 94, 101, 103
Noakes & Co. v. Rice 345, 404, 405,
                                411, 415, 417, 418
Nocton v. Lord Ashburton 199
Norfolk Capital Group Ltd v. Kitway Ltd 612
Northampton (Marquess of) v. Salt 393
Northbourne (Lord) v. Johnston & Sons 334, 335
North Sydney Printing Pty Ltd v. Sabemo
    Investment Corp. Pty Ltd 246, 251
Norris v. Wilkinson 401
Northern Counties Fire Insurance Co. v.
    Whipp 109, 484
Norton v. Kilduff 304
Nottingham Patent Brick and Tile Co. v.
    Butler 358
Nutt v. Easton 468

O'Byrne's Estate, Re 111, **122**, 487, 497
O'Cedar Ltd v. Slough Trading Co. Ltd .. 582
O'Dea v. Allstates Leasing System (W.A.)
    Pty Ltd 426
O'Keefe v. Malone 524
O'Keefe v. Williams 579
O'Rorke v. Bolingbroke 427

Oak Property Co. Ltd v. Chapman 640, 643
Oertel v. Hordern 170, 177, 182
Official Trustee in Bankruptcy, (ex parte) 60
Old Gate Estates v. Alexander 503
Old Grovebury Manor Farm Ltd v.
W. Seymour Plant Sales & Hire Ltd
(No. 2) 619, 639
Onehunga Sawmilling Co. Ltd v. Official
Assignee of King 406
Osborne v. Bradley 332, 350
Osmanoski v. Rose 151, 152
Otter v. Lord Vaux 456
Outram v. Maude 269
Owen v. Gadd 573, 576, 578
Owendale Pty Ltd v. Anthony 644

Paine & Co. v. St Neots Gas & Coke Co. 302
Palm Beach Lands Pty Ltd v. Marshall 346
Palmer v. Fletcher 579
Palmer v. Hendrie 438
Palmer v. Wiley 138
Pampris v. Thanos 583
Pannell v. City of Londond Brewery Co. 638
Paoro Torotoro v. Sutton 136
Papadopoulos v. Goodwin 280, 286
Pargeter v. Pargeter 503
Parimax (S.A.) Pty Ltd, Re 386
Parker v. Housefield 401
Parker v. Jones 656
Parker v. Registrar-General 210
Parker v. Taswell 56, 562, 570
Parker v. Webb 624
Parker d. Walker v. Constable 542
Parkin v. Thorold 558
Parkinson v. Hanbury 440
Parkinson v. Reid 316
Parish v. Kelly 250, 286
Pascoe v. Swan 87, 88
Patridge v. McIntosh & Sons Ltd 401
Patzak v. Lytton 52, 75
Payne v. Haine 588, **590**, 593
Peabody Donation Fund v. Higgins 619
Peakin v. Peakin 502
Pearse; Ex parte 113, 122
Pegge v. Neath and District Tramways Co.
Ltd 396
Pembery v. Lamdin 598
**Pendlebury v. Colonial Mutual Life
Assurance Society Ltd** 469, 473,
474, 475, 477, 478, 480
Penton v. Barnett 637
Penton v. Robart 41
Perera v. Vandiyar 576
Perpetual Executors & Trustees Association
(Aust.) Ltd v. Hosken 55, 132
Perpetual Trustee Co. v. Crawshaw 46
Perry v. Rolfe 402
Perry Herrick v. Attwood 146
Perth Brewery Co. Ltd v. Simms 419
Perth Construction Pty Ltd v. Mount
Lawley Pty Ltd 382
Pertsoulis and Pertsoulis 75, 80
Pesic v. South Sydney Municipal Council 2

Phene's Trust, Re 49
Phillips v. McLachan 290
Phillips v. Phillips 107, 108, 155
Phipps v. Pears **228**, 257
Pickering v. Rudd 4, 5, 6, 7, 12
Picone v. Grocery & General Merchants Ltd 605
Pieper v. Edwards 301, 383
Pierce v. Canada Permanent Loan & Savings
Co. 498, 499
Pike v. Venables 375, 382
Pilcher v. Rawlins 110, 486
Pimms Ltd v. Tallow Chandlers Co. 608,
611, 617
Pinewood Estate, Farnborough, Re 360, 373
Pinhorn v. Souster 547
Pinnington v. Galland 246
Pioneer Gravels (Qld) Pty Ltd v. T. & T.
Mining Corp. Pty Ltd 655
Pirie v. Registrar-General 201, 364, 369, 373, 376
Pirie v. Saunders 534
Pirie and the Real Property Act, Re .. 364, 369,
372, 373
Piromalli v. Di Masi 271
Plaister, Re 46
Platt v. Ong 649, 655
Plowden v. Hyde 62
Plumpton v. Plumpton 136
Plymouth Corp. v. Harvey 638
Pole-Carew v. Western Counties & General
Manure Co. Ltd 42
Pollard's Estate, Re 60
Poltava Pty Ltd, Application of, Re 375, 380, 382
Pomfret v. Ricroft 225
Poole's Case 38
Port v. Griffith 581
Porter v. Associated Securities Ltd 478
Post Office v. Aquarius Properties Ltd 599
Potter v. Edwards 419
Powel v. Hemsley 342
Powley v. Walker 587
Pratten v. Warringah Shire Council **202**, 286
Premier Confectionery (London) Co. Ltd v.
London Commercial Sale Rooms Ltd 612,
615
Price v. Mayman 633
Prior's Case (The) 323, 333
Progressive Mailing House Pty Ltd v. Tabali
Pty Ltd 631
Property & Bloodstock Ltd v. Emerton 476,
477, 619
Proprietors of "Averil Court" Building
Units Plan No. 2001 383
Proprietors of the Centre Building Units
Plan No. 343 v. Bourne 44
Proprietors Strata Plan No. 9968 v.
Proprietors Strata Plan No. 11173 295
Prosser v. Rice 483
Protector Endowment Loan and Annuity
Co. v. Grice 423, 425, 426
Proudfoot v. Hart 590, **591**, 593,
594, 595, 596, 597
Pryce v. Bury 401
Pryce and Irving v. McGuiness 250, 284

Public Transport Commission of New South
Wales v. J. Murray-More (N.S.W.) Pty
Ltd 480
Public Trustee v. Evans 85
Public Trustee v. Grivas 75, 79, 80
Pugh v. Savage 271
Puhi Maihi v. McLeod 590
Pukuweka Sawmills Ltd v. Winger 24
Pwllbach Colliery Co. Ltd v. Woodman ... 246,
                                         250
Pyer v. Carter 243, 244, 247, 248

Quadramain Pty Ltd v. Sevastapol
Investments Pty Ltd 305, 306, 330
Quarrell v. Beckford 443
Queensland Brewery Ltd v. Baker 419
Queensland Insurance v. A.M.F. Insurance 173
Queensland Land & Coal Co., Re; Davis v.
Martin 396
Queensland Trustees Ltd v. Registrar of
Titles 498
Queensway Marketing Ltd v. Associated
Restaurants Ltd 576
Quennell v. Maltby 439
Quesnel Forks Gold Mining Co. Ltd v.
Ward 631
Quick v. Taff Ely Borough Council 599
Quicke v. Chapman 256
Quint v. Robertson 404

R. v. Earsman 282
R. v. Herstmonceaux 543
R. v. Morrish 542
R. v. Paulson 644
R. v. Phillips 281
R. v. Registrar of Titles; Ex parte Watson 456
R.P.C. Holdings Ltd v. Rogers 273, 279
Radaich v. Smith 505, 512, 521,
                     523, 524, 525, 526, 537
Railways, Commissioner of v. Valuer-
General 7
Rallason v. Leon 558
Ramsden v. Dyson 3
Rasheed v. Burns Philp Trustee Co. Ltd .. 644
Ratcliffe v. Watters 129, 130, 184, 208
Ravenseft Properties Ltd v. Davstone
(Holdings) Ltd 598
Reardon Smith Line v. Hansen-Tangen 174
Rees v. Guardian Trust & Executors Co. of
New Zealand Ltd 393
Rees v. Rees 93, 102
Reeve v. Lisle 406
Regent Oil Co. Ltd v. J. A. Gregory (Hatch
End) Ltd 440
Regis Property Co. Ltd v. Dudley 600
Regis Property Co. Ltd v. Redman 231, 257
Register (A Bankrupt), Re; Ex parte Official
Assignee 645
Registrar-General, Ex parte; Re Council of
Municipality of Randwick 203
Registrar-General v. Behn 213
Registrar of Titles (W.A.) v. Franzon 211

Reid v. Bickerstaff 359, 360
Reid v. Moreland Timber Co. Pty Ltd 214,
                                        302
Reid v. Smith 13, 24
Reilly v. Booth 233, 235
Reliance Finance Corp. Pty Ltd v. Heid ... 151
Reliance Permanent Building Society v.
Harwood-Stamper 462, 468
Remon v. City of London Real Property
Co. Ltd 537, 539
Renals v. Cowlishaw 328, 329, 330,
                          350, 354, 357, 358
Reynolds v. Ashby & Son 23
Rich v. Miles 290
Richard Clarke & Co. Ltd v. Widnall 645
Richards v. Morgan 441
Richards v. Rose 243, 244, 246, 252
Richardson v. Gifford 571
Richardson v. Graham 295
Richardson v. Landecker 524, 559
Richardson v. Langridge 549, 554
Rice v. Rice 107, 147
Rider v. Smith 225
Ridgeway and Smith's Contract, Re 132
Ridley v. Lee 359
Ridley v. Taylor 383
Riley and the Real Property Act v. Pentilla 221,
                              233, 273, 295
Rimmer v. Webster 146, 147
Road Chalets Pty Ltd v. Thornton Motors
Pty Ltd 393
Roads v. Overseers of Trumpington 511
Roake v. Chadha 326, 351
Robert John Pty Ltd v. Fostar's Shoes Pty
Ltd 512
Robert Reid & Co. v. Minister for Public
Works 401
Roberts v. Karr 288, 289, 290, 292
Robertson, Re 45
Robertson v. Norris 454, 457
Robinson, Re 380
Robinson v. Bailey 277
Roche, Re 338, 339
Rodwell v. Evans 271
Roe v. Prideaux 550
Roe v. Sales 621
Rogers v. Challis 395
Rogers v. Hosegood 325, 327, 333,
                          348, 349, 372, 623
Rogers v. Rice 655
Rookes v. Barnard 576
Rose Bay Bowling and Recreation Club Ltd,
Re 298
Rosling v. Pinnegar 278
Rouse's Case 538
Rowe v. Oades 392
Rowston v. Sydney County Council 555
Royal Victorian Pavilion Ramsgate, Re 342
Rudd v. Bowles 292
Rafa Pty Ltd v. Cross 226, 320
Rugby Joint Water Board v. Walters 280
Rugby Schools (Governors) v. Tannahill ... 649,
                                          653

Rush and Hazell and the Real Property Act,
Re 138
Russell v. Archdale 338, 349
Russell v. Beecham 605
Ryan v. Nothelfer 151
Ryan v. O'Sullivan 401

SEDAC Investments Ltd v. Tanner 639
Sacher Investments Pty Ltd v. Forma Stereo
    Consultants Pty Ltd 628
Saint v. Pilley 39
Salt v. Marquess of Northampton 411
Salter v. Kidgly 315
Sammon, Re 59
Sampson v. Hodson-Pressinger 575
Samuel v. Jarrah Timber and Wood Paving
Corp. Ltd 404
Sander v. Twigg 136
Sanders v. Cooper 629
Sanderson v. Mayor of Berwick-on-Tweed 578
Sandon v. Hooper 441
Sangster v. Burns 605
Santley v. Wilde 411, 416, 418
Sarat Chunder Dey v. Gopal Chunder Laha 292
Sarson v. Roberts 583
Saunders v. Dehew 486
Saunders v. Smith 6
Savage & Sons (J.J.) Pty Ltd v. Blakney .. 181
Saviane v. Stauffer Chemical Co. (Aust.)
    Pty Ltd 588
Savill Bros Ltd v. Bethell 234
Scapinello v. Scapinello 102
Schalit v. Joseph Nadler Ltd 566
Schebsman, Re; Official Receiver v. Cargo
    Superintendents (London), Ltd and
    Schebsman 174
Schmeling v. Stankovic 60
Scholes v. Blunt 112, 114
Schultz v. Corwill Properties Pty Ltd 112,
    130, **184**
Schwann v. Cotton 247, 248
Scott-Whitehead v. National Coal Board ... 228,
    271, 272
Secured Income Real Estate (Aust.) Ltd v. St
    Martin's Investments Pty Ltd 607
Seftons v. Tophams Ltd 326
Segal Securities Ltd v. Thoseby 639, 643
Seidler v. Schallhofer 655
Selous, Re 51
Selwyn v. Garfitt 482
Selwyn's Conveyance, Re 335, 337
Serjeant v. Nash, Field & Co. 605
Serle, Re 637
Seton v. Slade 404
Sevastopol Investments Pty Ltd 306
Sewell v. Agricultural Bank of Western
    Australia 456
Sexton v. Horton 338
Shanly v. Ward 617
Shannon Ltd v. Venner Ltd 221
Shayler v. Woolf 324
Shell Mex and B.P. Ltd v. Manchester
    Garages Ltd 513, 519

Shepard v. Jones 444
Sheppard v. Hong Kong and Shanghai
    Banking Corp. 617
Shepherd Homes Ltd v. Sandham 10
Shevill v. Builders Licensing Board 631
Shiloh Spinners Ltd v. Harding ... 309, 649, 650
Shropshire Union Railways and Canal Co. v.
    The Queen 147, 148
Silovi Pty Ltd v. Barbaro 214, 240, 287
Simm v. Anglo-American Telegraph Co. .. 289
Simms v. Lee 539
Simpson v. Forrester 403, 438
Sims and Sims 80
Simultaneous Colour Printing Syndicate v.
    Foweraker 396
Sinclair v. Hope Investments Pty Ltd 481
Slough Picture Hall Co. Ltd v. Wade 42
Smallman v. Agborow 67
Smallwood v. Sheppards 559
Smith v. Australian Real Estate and Invest-
    ment Co. Ltd 381
Smith v. Deane 118, 121
Smith v. Gronow 621
Smith v. Jones 196
Smith v. Kemp 301
Smith v. Smith 432, 433
Smith v. Widlake 551
Smith and Snipes Hall Farm Ltd v. River
Douglas Catchment Board 321, 323,
    325, 327, 350
Snedeker v. Warring 26
Somma v. Hazelhurst ... 513, 520, 528, 530, 531
Sotheby v. Grundy 599
South African Territories Ltd v. Wallington 396
South-Eastern Drainage Board (South
    Australia) v. Savings Bank of South
    Australia 202, 203
Southgate Borough Council v. Watson 503
Southwell v. Roberts 443, 444
Sovmots Investments Ltd v. Secretary of
    State for the Environment 7
Spark's Lease, Re 619
Spencer's Case 323, 333, 344, 351
Spicer v. Martin 354, 355, 357
Spooner v. Sandilands 395
Sporle v. Whayman 401
Spurgin v. White 545, 546
Spyer v. Phillipson 15, 24, 33, 36
Squarey v. Harris-Smith 242
Squire v. Rogers 91, 94, **101**
St Edmundsbury and Ipswich Diocesan
    Board of Finance v. Clark (No. 2) 241, 276
Stack v. Cameron 608, 612
Staffordshire & Worcestershire Canal Navi-
    gation v. Bradley 223
Standard Chartered Bank Ltd v. Walker . 446,
    447, 468
Standard Portland Cement Co. Pty Ltd v.
    Good 13
Stanhope v. Haworth 648
Stannard v. Issa 382
Standwell Park Hotel Co. Ltd v. Leslie 422
Stapleford Colliery Co. (Barrow's Case), Re 163,
    164

State Savings Bank v. Kircheval 26
Steiper v. Deviot Pty Ltd **648**
Stephens, Ex parte 38
Sterne v. Beck 424
Stevens v. Allan 279, 284
Stevenson v. Lambard 570
Stillwell v. Blackman 347, 348, 349
Stocks and Enterprises Pty Ltd v. McBurney
427, 432
Stoneman v. Lyons 273
Story v. Johnson 88
Stoyles v. Job 606
Strand Music Hall Co., Re 396
Street v. Mountford **513, 528, 529,**
530, 532, 537
Strode v. Parker 422
Stromdale and Ball Ltd v. Burden 321
Stuart v. Joy 620
Stuart v. Kingston 166, 172, 176, 178, 198
Sturges v. Bridgman 266, 269, 270
Sturolson & Co. v. Weniz 520
Sturton v. Richardson 91
Stuy. v. B. C. Ronalds Pty Ltd 287
Styles & Co. v. Richardson 550
Suffield v. Brown 252
Sunset Properties Pty Ltd v. Johnston 242,
248, 273, 279
Supreme Court Registrar to Alexander
Dawson Inc., Re 406
Sutherland (Duke of) v. Heathcote 214, 302
Sutherland Shire Council v. Moir 130
Sutherland v. Peel 116
Swain v. Ayres 560, 562
Swan v. Sinclair 294
Swan v. Swan 88, 98, 104
Swanley Coal Co. v. Denton **399**
Swansborough v. Coventry 242, 244, 248
Swanson v. Forton 608, 609
Sweet v. Southcote 164
Sweet and Maxwell Ltd v. Universal News
Service Ltd 605
Swift Investments (P. & A.) v. Combined
English Stores Group PLC **622**
Swordheath Properties Ltd v. Tabet 630
Sydie v. Saskatchewan and Battle River
Land and Development Co. 170
Sydney and Suburban Land Assoc. v. Lyons 122
Syndicate (G.M.S.) Ltd v. Gary Elliott Ltd 655

Taff Vale Railway Co. v. Cardiff Railway
Co. 239
Talbot v. Blindell 655
Talga Investments Pty Ltd v. Tweed Canal
Estates Pty Ltd 239
Tall-Bennett & Co. Ltd v. Sadot Holdings
Pty Ltd 589
Tarn v. Turner 62
Tarrant v. Zandstra 248, 250, 284, 287
Tataurangi Tairuakena v. Mua Carr ... 196, 198
Tattersall's Hotel Penrith Pty Ltd v.
Permanent Trustee Co. of New South
Wales Ltd 633
Taxes, Commissioner of (Qld) v. Camphin 175

Taylor v. Caldwell 516
Taylor v. Needham 292
Taylor v. Russell 110, 486
Taylor v. Webb 600
Taylor v. Wheeler 395
Taylor v. Whitehead 224
Teaff v. Hewitt 26
Teasdale v. Sanderson 86, 88, 89, 100
Tehidy Minerals Ltd v. Norman 272, 294
Telex (Australasia) Pty Ltd v. Thomas Cook
& Sons (Australasia) Pty Ltd 579
Templeton v. Leviathan Pty Ltd 132, 155
Texaco Antilles Ltd v. Kernochan 347,
359, 360, 376
Thomas v. Owen 255
Thomas v. Sorrell 502, 510
Thomas v. Thomas 44, 296
Thomas Bookman Ltd v. Nathan 609
Thomas Guaranty Ltd v. Campbell 401
Thompson v. Hudson 424
Thompson v. Park 503
Thompson v. Trafford 41
Thornhill v. Manning 450
Thorton v. Thompson 626
Thorpe v. Brumfitt 223, 274
Threlfall, Re 536, 546
Thurlow v. Mackeson 457
Thwaites v. Brahe 272
Tidey v. Mollett 558
Tiltwood, Sussex; Barrett v. Bond, Re ... 376
Titchmarsh v. Royston Water Co. Ltd 249
Tito v. Waddell (No. 2) 309, **311**, 320
Todrick v. Western National Omnibus 223,
273, **274**, 278
Toleman v. Portbury 645
Tolman's Estate; Re 93
Tomlin v. Luce 461, 462, 463, 464, 465, 467
Toms v. Wilson 434
Toohey v. Gunther 418
Tooker v. Smith 554
Toomes v. Conset 405
Tooth & Co. v. Parkes 419
Tophams Ltd v. Earl of Sefton ... 310, 326, 342
Torrens v. Walker 597
Torrisi v. Magame Pty Ltd 286, 287
Toscano v. Holland Securities Pty Ltd 436
Trade Practices Commission (Cth) and A-G
for the Commonwealth v. Tooth & Co.
Ltd and Tooheys Ltd 604
Tredegar (Viscount) v. Harwood .. 608, 609, 618
Treloar v. Bigge 606
Tress v. Savage 552
Treweeke v. 36 Wolseley Road Pty Ltd 295,
296, 380, 383
Trieste Investments Pty Ltd v. Watson 281
Trimelston (Lord) v. Hamill 442
Truman, Hanbury, Buxton & Co. Ltd's
Application, Re 381, 385
Trustees Executors & Agency Co. Ltd v.
Anson 64
Tsang Chuen v. Li Po Kwai 147
Tse Kwong Lam v. Wong Chit Sen 455, 468
Tucker v. Coleman 58
Tuckett v. Brice 272

Tulk v. Moxhay 134, 137, 303, 305, 308, 310, 327, **340**, 341, 342, 343, 344, 345, 346, 348, 366, 368, 370, 371
Turner v. Bladin 397
Turner v. Cameron 17
Turner v. Morgan 88
Turner v. Walsh 62
Turner v. York Motors Pty Ltd 541, 555
Twentieth Century Banking Corp. Ltd v. Wilkinson 448
Tyson v. Tyson 78

Umney v. The Company 56
Underwood v. Lord Courtown 498
Unimin Pty Ltd v. Commonwealth (Aust.) 214
Union Bank of Australia v. Atkins 438
Union Bank of Scotland v. National Bank of Scotland 489, 490, 492
United Starr-Bowkett Co-op. Building Society (No. 11) Ltd v. Clyne 158, 162, **190**, 193
Union Lighterage Co. v. London Graving Dock Co. 249, 269
Union of London and Smith's Bank Ltd's Conveyance; Re, Miles v. Easter 322, 339, **347**, 348
Upper Hutt Arcade Ltd v. Burrell 562

Vallee v. Dumergue 194
Vandeventer v. Dale Construction Co. 398
Van Kempen v. Finance & Investments Pty Ltd 431
Varella v. Mariscovetere 513
Varley v. Coppard 621
Vassiliou v. Criterion Holdings Ltd 576
Vaudeville Electric Cinema Ltd v. Muriset 23, 24
Vernon v. Bethell 406
Vickery v. Municipality of Strathfield 202
Victor Leggo (A.) & Co. Pty Ltd v. Aerosols (Aust.) Pty Ltd 221
Vukicevic v. Alliance Acceptance Co. Ltd 214
Vyse v. Foster 104
Vyvyan v. Arthur 623

Waimiha Sawmilling Co. Ltd v. Waione Timber Co. Ltd 166, 171, 176, 177, 179
Walker v. Linom 107
Walker v. Lovell 78
Wall v. Australian Real Estate Investment Co. Ltd 382
Wallis and Simmonds (Builders) Ltd, Re .. 401
Walmsley v. Milne 18, 19, 28
Walsh v. Griffiths-Jones 513
Walsh v. Lonsdale 294, 376, **560**, 562, 563, 566
Walton v. Forsyth 51
Wandsworth District Board of Works v. United Telephone Co. Ltd 4, 5, 6, 7

Wanner v. Caruana **423**, 431
Warburton v. Loveland 117, 121
Ward v. Kirkland 237, 245, 246, 256, 257, 258, 287
Ward v. Ward 294, 298
Waring v. Ward 438
Waring (Lord) v. London and Manchester Assurance Co. Ltd 476, 477
Warmington v. Miller 562
Warner v. Jacob 455, 471, 474
Warren v. Keen **584**, 585
Waters v. Mynn 393
Waterlow v. Bacon 294
Watkinson, Re 49
Watson, Re 393
Watson v. Lane 564
Watts v. Kelson 248
Webb v. Bevis 15, **37**, 38
Webb v. Bird 228, 229, 266, 270
Webb v. Russell 329, 656
Webb's Lease, Re 251
Webb Ltd v. Webb 503
Webster v. Strong 295
Wedd v. Porter 584
Weeton v. Woodcock 38, 39, 41
Weigall & Dawes' Lease, Re 554
Wellington City Corp. v. Public Trustee, McDonald, and District Land Registrar, Wellington 56, 570
West v. A.G.C. (Advances) Ltd 435, 436
West v. Williams .. 487, 489, 490, 491, 492, 493
West Kanmantoo Mining Co. v. English Scottish, and Australian Chartered Bank 113
West Layton Ltd v. Ford 612, 614, 615, 616, 618
West London Commercial Bank v. Reliance Permanent Building Society 483
Western v. Macdermott 358
Western Bank Ltd v. Schindler 443
Westhoughton Urban District Council v. Wigan Coal & Iron Co. Ltd 316, 324
Westminster (Duke of) v. Swinton 655
Westpac Banking Corp v. Sugden 436
Wettern Electric Ltd v. Welsh Development Agency 583
Wheaton v. Maple & Co. 271
Wheelan, ex parte 633
Wheeldon v. Burrows 242, **243**, 245, 246, 247, 251, 256, 257, 273, 280, 281, 282, 283, 285, 286, 287
Wheeler v. Horne 91
Wheeler v. Mercer 538, 541
Whitcomb v. Minchin 454
White, Re; Ex parte Goggs 456
White v. Bijou Mansions 321
White v. Grand Hotel, Eastbourne, Ltd .. 273, 277
White v. Taylor (No. 2) 227, 248, 253, 260, 272, 296
White v. Williams 253
Wickham v. Hawker 234
Whitehouse v. Hugh 363
Wickens, Ex parte 432

Wicks v. Bennett; Friedman v. Barrett; Ex
  parte Friedman 177
Wight v. Haberdan Pty Ltd **396**
Wilcox Mofflin Ltd v. Commissioner of
  Stamp Duties 389
Wilde v. Waters 16
Wilkes v. Spooner **164**, 165, 343
Wilks, Re; Child v. Bulmer ... 59, 71, 72, 77, 79
Wilkinson v. Haygarth 90
Wilkinson v. Spooner 269, 281, 284
William Brandt's Sons & Co. v. Dunlop
  Rubber Co. 322, 347
Williams, Re 205
Williams v. Earle 621, 622
Williams v. Lewis **586**
Williams v. Morgan 409, 448
Williams v. Owen 392, 393
Williams (P. M.) and the Conveyancing Act 382
Williams v. Hensman 58, 69, 72, 73,
                                  74, 75, 76, 77, 82
Williams v. Williams 99, 103
Willoughby D'Eresby (Baroness), Ex parte   42
Wilson (A. R.) and the Conveyancing Act   382
Wilson v. Anderton 564
Wilson v. Bell 70, 71, 73, 78
Wilson v. Darling Island Stevedoring &
  Lighterage Co. Ltd 175
Wiltshear v. Cottrel 16, 18, 19, 26, 28
Windmill Investment (London) Ltd v.
  Milano Restaurant Ltd 643
Wing v. Angrave 48
Wiscot's Case 85
Wolfe v. Freijah's Holdings Pty Ltd 294
Wolff v. Vanderzee 462, 464, 465, 466, 467
Wolfson v. Registrar-General (N.S.W.) ... 134,
                                           201

Wollerton & Wilson Ltd v. Richard Costain
  Ltd 1, 9, 10, 11
Wong v. Beaumont Property Trust Ltd ... 246,
                                           250
Wood v. Leadbitter 503
Wood v. Seely 292
Woodall v. Clifton 622
Wood Factory Pty Ltd v. Kiritos Pty Ltd 631
Woodhouse & Co. Ltd v. Kirkland (Derby)
  Ltd 258, 279
Woodhouse v. Ah Peck 629
Woodifield v. Bond 590
Worthington v. Gimson 255
Wright v. Gibbons 51, **52**, 59, 62, 66, 75
Wright v. Lawson 596
Wright v. MacAdam 233, 239, **253**, 256
Wright v. New Zealand Farmers Co-op.
  Assoc. of Canterbury Ltd 458
Wrigley v. Gill 441
Wrotham Park Estate Co. v. Parkside
  Homes Ltd 334
Wynne v. Moore 455

Yates v. Morris 654
York House Proprietary Ltd v. Federal
  Commissioner of Taxation 570
Young, Re; Brickwood v. Young .. 98, 256, 296

Zegir v. Woop 538
Zenere v. Leate 237
Zetland (Earl of) v. Hislop 345
Zetland (Marquess of) v. Driver 326, 333,
                                          339, 349
Zimbler v. Abrahams 56

TABLE OF STATUTES

Commonwealth

Bankruptcy Act 1924
 s. 103(4): 205
 s. 192: 205
 s. 193: 205
 Pt XII: 205

Civil Aviation (Damage by Aircraft) Act 1958: 1

Family Law Act 1975: 80, 82
 s. 79: 68, 75, 81
 s. 86: 82

Lands Acquisition Act 1906: 230

Matrimonial Causes Act 1959: 80, 82
 s. 71: 68
 s. 86: 81
 s. 86(1): 68, 79, 81
 Pt VIII: 80

National Security (Fair Rents) Regulations 1939: 656

National Security (Fair Rents) Regulations 1941: 656

National Security (Landlord and Tenant) Regulations 1941: 656

Trade Practices Act 1974: 304, 306, 411, 419, 434, 435, 604
 s. 45: 305, 434
 s. 45B: 304, 305, 306, 434, 604
 s. 45B(9): 306
 s. 45C: 304, 305, 306
 s. 47: 604
 s. 47(9): 604
 s. 52: 434
 s. 82: 434
 s. 87: 434

New South Wales

Agricultural Holdings Act 1941: 587
 s. 4(1): 587
 s. 7: 14
 s. 15(2): 587
 s. 21: 14

Companies (N.S.W.) Code 1981
 s. 5(1): 410
 s. 150: 410

Contracts Review Act 1980: 411, 419, 435, 436, 437, 604
 s. 4(1): 435
 s. 6(1): 435

s. 6(2): 435
s. 7: 436
s. 7(1): 435
s. 9: 437
s. 9(1): 435
s. 9(2): 435

Conveyancing Act 1919: 110, 111, 131, 364, 365, 373, 439
 s. 7: 605
 s. 12: 322, 347
 s. 23B: 393, 567, 568, 569, 571, 605
 s. 23B(1): 239, 294, 376
 s. 23B(3): 568, 605
 s. 23C: 239, 567, 569, 605
 s. 23C(1): 294
 s. 23C(1)(a): 394, 571
 s. 23C(1)(c): 394
 s. 23D: 567-568, 569, 570, 571
 s. 23D(2): 555, 571
 s. 23E: 568
 s. 23E(c): 571
 s. 24: 51
 s. 25: 45
 s. 26: 50, 61, 63
 s. 27: 51
 s. 35: 45
 s. 36C: 303, 321, 332, 346, 353
 s. 43: 393
 s. 45(1): 241
 s. 45A: 234, 241
 s. 54A: 563, 569
 s. 66F: 83
 s. 66G: 83, 84, 85
 s. 66G(1): 83, 84
 s. 66G(4): 83, 84, 85
 s. 66G(7): 85
 s. 66H: 83
 s. 66I: 83
 s. 67: 252-253, 255, 256, 257, 293
 s. 67(2): 253
 s. 67(3): 256
 s. 70: 322, 343, 346, 348, 349, 351
 s. 70(1): 324, 327, 350, 351
 s. 70A: 310, 342, 343, 625
 s. 74: 631
 s. 74(2): 588
 s. 78(1)(c): 393
 s. 78(1)(D): 626
 s. 84: 589, 603
 s. 84(1): 585, 588
 s. 84(1)(b): 588
 s. 84A: 589
 s. 85: 603
 s. 85(1): 588
 s. 85(1)(d): 603, 631, 634
 s. 86: 604

Conveyancing Act 1919—*continued*
s. 87A: 215, 307
s. 88: 222, 331, 336, 366-373
s. 88(1): 240, 241, 327, 332, 348, 349, 351, 353, 360-376
s. 88(1)(a): 369
s. 88(1)(c): 363
s. 88(1)(d): 363
s. 88(2): 371
s. 88(3): 201, 364, 365-376
s. 88(3)(a): 373, 374
s. 88(3)(b): 369, 370, 375
s. 88(3)(c): 370, 374
s. 88(4): 240, 361, 371
s. 88A: 221
s. 88A(1)(a): 222
s. 88A(1)(b): 221
s. 88A(3): 222
s. 88AA: 222, 240, 241
s. 88AB: 215
s. 88B: 240, 241, 286, 361, 364, 373, 376, 378
s. 88B(2)(c): 240, 241
s. 88B(3): 364
s. 88B(3)(c): 227, 240, 241, 296
s. 88B(3)(c)(i): 286
s. 88B(3A): 241-242
s. 88D: 307, 322, 345
s. 88D(1): 307
s. 88E: 307, 322, 345
s. 88EA: 215, 307
s. 88EA(4): 215
s. 88EA(8): 215
s. 88F: 307
s. 89 (now rep.): 365, 366-367, 371, 373
s. 89(1) (now rep.): 361
s. 89: 296, 297, 299, 301, 305, 378-379, 380, 381, 383, 385
s. 89(1): 297, 298, 300, 301, 383
s. 89(1)(a): 383, 385
s. 89(1)(b): 297, 298, 300, 301, 383
s. 89(1)(c): 383, 385, 386
s. 89(3): 297, 298, 300, 301, 335, 366
s. 89(8): 297, 299
s. 91: 61
s. 91(3)(a): 61
s. 93: 411, 425, 426, 429, 430, 431
s. 93(1): 427, 429, 430
s. 93(3): 427
s. 100: 438, 448
s. 100(2): 452
s. 101: 452
s. 102: 438
s. 103(2): 448
s. 106: 445
s. 106(17): 445
s. 107: 446
s. 109: 452
s. 109(1)(a): 452, 455
s. 109(1)(c): 446
s. 109(3): 446, 452
s. 109(5): 446, 452, 455
s. 110: 452
s. 111: 452
s. 112(2): 394

s. 112(3): 481
s. 112(4): 483
s. 112(7): 479
s. 115: 446
s. 115(2): 446
s. 115(3): 446
s. 115A(2): 447
s. 115A(2)(a): 446
s. 115A(2)(c): 447
s. 117: 623, 627, 628
s. 117(1): 627
s. 117(2): 627
s. 118: 627, 628
s. 120: 605, 645
s. 120A(1): 572
s. 120A(2): 572
s. 120A(3): 560
s. 120A(5): 559
s. 121: 656
s. 122: 656
s. 123: 605, 645
s. 127: 546, 555, 556, 557, 569, 570, 571, 585, 605
s. 127(1): 554, 555
s. 129: 638, 639
s. 129(1): 634, 638
s. 129(2): 650, 656
s. 129(2A): 650
s. 129(8): 634
s. 129(10): 634
s. 130: 656
s. 132: 612
s. 133: 606
s. 133A(1): 600-601
s. 133B(1): 606, 608
s. 134: 308, 559
s. 164: 112, 189
s. 178: 272
s. 179: 259
s. 181A: 222
s. 184B: 111
s. 184D(1): 111
s. 184G: 111, 152
s. 196: 131
s. 196(2): 130
s. 196(6): 131
s. 196(8): 131
s. 196(15): 131
Pt IV, Div. 6: 85
Pt XXIII, Div. 1: 106, 110
Pt XXIII, Div. 3: 241
Sched. 2: 393
Sched. 4, Pt II: 604
Sched. 8: 222

Conveyancing (Amendment) Act 1930: 149, 153, 310
Sched., s. 2: 571

Conveyancing (Amendment) Act 1972: 299, 374

Conveyancing (Forestry Rights) Amendment Act 1987: 215, 240

Conveyancing (Strata Titles) Act 1961: 232

Credit Act 1984: 436, 437, 447, 448, 452
s. 5(1): 436
s. 13: 30-31
s. 18(1): 436
s. 18(2): 436
s. 19: 436
s. 30(2): 436
s. 74: 437, 439
s. 89: 436
s. 107: 439, 440, 447, 448
s. 107(2): 439
s. 107(3): 439
s. 145: 437
s. 146: 436
s. 146(2): 437
s. 147: 437
s. 168: 439
s. 171: 437

Credit (Home Finance Contracts) Act 1984: 437, 448, 452
s. 4: 437
s. 5: 437
s. 7: 440, 447, 448
s. 7(1): 439
s. 7(2): 439
s. 7(4): 439

Crown Lands Consolidation Act 1913
s. 235: 1

Damage by Aircraft Act 1952: 1

Deeds Registration Act 1825: 116

Dividing Fences Act 1951: 342

Encroachment of Buildings Act 1922: 2, 3
s. 2: 2
s. 3: 2
s. 4(1): 2

Environmental Planning and Assessment Act 1979
s. 28: 304-305, 307, 381

Fair Rents Act 1915: 656

Imperial Acts Application Act 1969: 44, 90, 585
s. 8: 241
s. 18: 630
s. 19: 630
s. 20: 630
s. 32(1): 585
s. 32(3): 585

Industrial Arbitration Act 1940: 411, 419, 437, 604
s. 88F: 437, 604

Judgment Creditors' Remedies Act 1901
s. 27(1)(b): 402, 404

Landlord and Tenant Act 1899 s. 2AA: 630, 631
s. 8: 645
s. 8(1): 634
s. 8(2): 634
s. 8(3): 645
s. 9: 645
s. 10: 645

s. 22A(a): 541
s. 22A(b): 541

Landlord and Tenant (Amendment) Act 1948:
190, 192, 506, 508, 656
s. 2: 630
s. 8(1A): 583
s. 39: 583
s. 62B: 605
s. 80: 643

Landlord and Tenant Amendment (Distress Abolition) Act 1930
s. 2: 629

Limitation Act 1969
s. 25: 648

Local Government Act 1919: 131
s. 147: 93, 94
s. 152: 284
s. 327: 131
s. 327(2): 130
s. 331(2): 131
s. 338(2): 130
s. 398: 202, 203
s. 602(1): 196
s. 602(2)(b): 197
s. 602(5A): 196
s. 604: 197

Local Government and Conveyancing (Amendment) Act 1964: 364

Partition Act 1900: 85, 103
s. 4(1): 83

Pastures Protection Act 1902: 543

Public Health Act 1902
s. 57: 584
s. 58: 584

Public Works Act 1900: 98
s. 56: 99

Public Works Act 1912
s. 4A: 241

Rabbit Act 1890: 541

Real Property Act 1862
s. 42: 187
s. 49: 187
s. 54: 188

Real Property Act 1900: 106, 111, 125, 135, 144,
155, 159, 163, 177, 185, 191, 203, 208, 251,
403, 418, 439, 452, 483, 494
s. 2: 135
s. 2(4): 134
s. 3: 256, 293
s. 3(a): 628
s. 4: 201
s. 12: 200
s. 12(1)(d): 201
s. 12(1)(f): 201
s. 12(3): 200, 201
s. 32: 201

Real Property Act 1900—*continued*
s. 32(1): 151
s. 33A(5): 158
s. 35: 132
s. 36(1): 156
s. 36(3): 156
s. 36(4): 132, 159
s. 36(6): 164
s. 36(9): 484, 494
s. 37: 187
s. 39: 131, 569
s. 39(3): 165
s. 40: 151, 184, 201, 284, 289
s. 40(1): 288
s. 40(3): 628
s. 41: 134-135, 154, 155, 209, 401, 557, 570
s. 41(1): 126, 154
s. 42: 127, 129, 154, 158, 159, 161, 162, 163,
    184, 186, 189, 193, 197, 198, 199, 200, 201,
    207, 208, 247, 281, 282, 283, 284, 285, 293,
    369, 374, 375, 494
s. 42(a): 282
s. 42(b): 281, 282, 284
s. 42(c): 282
s. 42(d): 157, 191, 192, 193, 194
s. 42(1): 165, 287
s. 42(1)(b): 201, 247, 280, 286
s. 42(1)(c): 207
s. 42(1)(d): 170, 190, 568
s. 43: 139, 153, 154, 155, 156, 157, 158, 159,
    160, 161, 162, 166, 169, 185, 191, 193, 194,
    201, 207, 209
s. 43(2): 150
s. 43A: 59, 140, 149, 150, 155, 156, 157, 158,
    159, 160, 161, 162, 163, 191, 192, 193
s. 43A(1): 139, 152, 153, 154, 155, 157, 164, 193
s. 43A(2): 157
s. 43A(3): 157
s. 44: 136
s. 45B(1): 209
s. 45C: 286
s. 45D(1): 209
s. 45D(2): 209
s. 45D(3): 209
s. 45D(4): 209
s. 45D(6): 209
s. 45E(1): 209
s. 45E(3): 209
s. 45E(4): 209
s. 45H(1): 209
s. 45I(2): 209
s. 45K: 209
s. 46: 159, 215, 240, 241, 280, 291
s. 47: 215, 240, 280, 288, 293
s. 47(1): 280
s. 47(5): 280
s. 47(6): 294
s. 47(6A): 294
s. 47(7): 227, 296, 378
s. 47(8): 296
s. 51: 256, 628
s. 52: 628
s. 53: 570, 571
s. 53(1): 568

s. 53(2): 131
s. 53(4): 446
s. 56A: 484, 494
s. 57: 160, 402, 451, 452, 471, 476
s. 57(1): 401
s. 58(1): 455
s. 58(2): 483
s. 58(3): 483
s. 58A: 452
s. 60: 440
s. 61: 451
s. 62: 451, 452
s. 62(2): 403
s. 63: 443
s. 64: 443
s. 65: 160
s. 72: 135
s. 74: 138-139, 153
s. 74F(1): 138
s. 74F(2): 151, 481
s. 74F(5): 138
s. 74H(4): 138
s. 74L: 138
s. 78M: 137
s. 82: 135
s. 84: 45
s. 86: 135
s. 96: 207
s. 103: 159
s. 111: 149
s. 121: 201
s. 124: 184, 207
s. 124(d): 207
s. 124(e): 207
s. 126: 132, 210, 212
s. 126(1)(a): 212
s. 126(1)(b): 211
s. 126(1)(c): 211
s. 126(1)(d): 211
s. 126(2): 212
s. 126(2)(c): 211, 213
s. 126(5): 211, 212, 213
s. 127: 132, 210
s. 130: 210
s. 131: 210
s. 132: 210
s. 133: 210, 212
s. 133(a): 212
s. 135: 132, 200, 207, 210
s. 136: 200
s. 137: 200
Pt IVA: 137
Pt IVB: 137
Pt VIA: 209, 286
Pt IX: 45, 135
Sched. 5: 159
Reg. 6B: 138

Real Property (Amendment) Act 1921
s. 14: 203

Real Property (Amendment) Act 1970: 296

Real Property (Forestry Rights) Amendment Act
    1987: 215, 240

Reduction of Rents Act 1931: 656

Registration Act 1843: 116, 119, 120
  s. 11: 119

Registration Amendment Act 1861: 116

Registration of Deeds Act 1897: 106, 110, 111, 114, 118
  s. 12: 152

Residential Tenancies Act 1987: 588, 657
  s. 4: 577
  s. 15: 589
  s. 18: 588
  s. 22(1): 577
  s. 24: 588
  s. 25: 583, 588
  s. 26: 588
  s. 28: 588
  s. 53: 631
  s. 57: 631
  s. 61: 588
  s. 72: 631
  s. 78: 589

Restraints of Trade Act 1976: 604

Strata Titles Act 1973: 44, 342
  s. 39: 152
  s. 80(a)(i): 230

Suitors Fund Act 1951: 198

Supreme Court Act 1970
  s. 67: 447
  s. 75: 606

Supreme Court Rules
  Pt 48: 44, 90
  Pt 49: 44, 90

Titles to Land Act 1858
  s. 18: 116

Trustee Act 1925
  s. 70: 394
  s. 71: 394

Wills, Probate and Administration Act 1898
  s. 58: 86

Queensland

Property Law Act 1974
  s. 18(2): 380
  s. 85(1): 478

Real Property Act 1861: 128
  s. 123: 128
  s. 124: 128

Real Property Act 1877: 208
  s. 48: 136

Stamp Act 1894
  s. 53(5): 127

South Australia

Law of Property Act 1936: 79

Real Property Act 1861: 208

Real Property Act 1886: 202, 203
  s. 3: 203
  s. 6: 202
  s. 10: 202
  s. 67: 203
  s. 69: 203
  s. 70: 203
  s. 71: 203

South-Eastern Drainage Act 1931: 202

Tasmania

Conveyancing and Law of Property Act 1884
  s. 84C: 380
  s. 84C(1)(b): 380

Real Property Act 1862: 52, 54, 55
  s. 3: 55
  s. 34(3): 55
  s. 35(2): 54
  s. 37: 55
  s. 39: 54, 58
  s. 39(1): 54
  s. 42: 54, 55, 58
  s. 87: 55, 58
  s. 88: 55
  Form IV: 55

Victoria

Property Law Act 1958
  s. 79A: 337

Transfer of Land Act 1890
  s. 114: 471

Transfer of Land Act 1915: 375
  s. 72: 143
  s. 183: 140
  s. 184: 140, 141, 143
  s. 185: 140, 143

Transfer of Land Act 1928: 64, 65

Transfer of Land Act 1954: 205, 206
  s. 3(1): 206
  s. 43: 206

Transfer of Land Act 1958: 207, 479
  s. 77(1): 479

Western Australia

Transfer of Land Act 1893: 176, 183
  s. 4: 285
  s. 68: 171, 172, 173, 176, 177, 178, 179, 180, 182, 184

Transfer of Land Act 1893—*continued*
 s. 82: 285
 s. 134: 171, 176, 177, 178, 180, 182
 s. 199: 178, 180
 s. 199(iv): 178

Australian Capital Territory

Real Property Ordinance 1925
 s. 94(2): 477
 s. 94(3): 477
 s. 94(4): 477
 s. 99(1): 476

Northern Territory

Supreme Court Rules
 O. 36: 102

United Kingdom

Air Navigation Act 1920
 s. 9: 4
 s. 9(1): 6

Apportionment Act 1870: 641

Australian Courts Act 1828: 259

Bankruptcy Act 1869
 s. 23: 38, 39
 s. 125: 38

Bills of Sale Act 1878
 s. 4: 400

Bills of Sale Act 1893: 25

Civil Aviation Act 1949: 6
 s. 40(1): 4, 5, 6, 7, 8

Companies Act 1929
 s. 74: 410

Conveyancing and Law of Property Act 1881: 634, 635
 s. 6: 253, 254
 s. 14: 635, 637, 638
 s. 14(1): 635
 s. 58(1): 325

Conveyancing Act 1882: 195

Grantees of Reversions Act 1540: 623, 627, 628

Judicature Act 1873: 558, 560, 561, 627

Land Drainage Act 1930: 323

Landlord and Tenant Act 1954: 40, 43, 541
 s. 34: 43

Lands Clauses Consolidation Act 1845: 239

Law of Property Act 1925: 53, 183
 s. 36(2): 59, 70, 72, 74, 75, 76, 77, 78, 79
 s. 40: 71
 s. 56: 321, 332
 s. 62: 230, 245, 253, 254, 255, 256, 257
 s. 62(1): 253
 s. 78: 324, 325, 326, 327
 s. 78(1): 325, 327
 s. 78(2): 325
 s. 79: 326
 s. 84: 379, 380
 s. 84(1): 298
 s. 84(1)(a): 381
 s. 84(1B): 379
 s. 84(1c): 379
 s. 115: 409
 s. 141: 623
 s. 146: 326, 639, 640, 642, 653, 654
 s. 184: 48, 49

Law of Property Act 1969
 s. 1: 43

Leasehold Reform Act 1967: 608, 609, 610, 653

Limitation Act 1939: 502, 512

Prescription Act 1832: 271
 s. 2: 263, 271

Rent Act 1974: 612, 615, 617, 618

Settled Land Act 1925: 332

Statute of Anne: 4 Anne c. 16 (1705): 44, 91
 s. 27: 87, 89, 90, 91

Statute of Frauds 1677: 183, 395, 399, 504, 550, 554, 563, 569, 629
 s. 1: 553, 571
 s. 2: 553, 571
 s. 3: 569
 s. 4: 553, 569

Statute of Marlborough 1267: 585

Statute of Uses 1535: 57, 58, 241, 572

Statute of Westminster 1275 c. 39: 258

Usury Laws Repeal Act 1854: 411

Validation of War Time Leases Act 1944: 534

New Zealand

Land Transfer Act 1870
 s. 46: 166
 s. 119: 166
 s. 129: 166
 s. 130: 166

Land Transfer Act 1885
 s. 55: 166
 s. 56: 166
 s. 189: 166
 s. 190: 166

Land Transfer Act 1952: 65, 133, 196, 203, 204
   s. 62: 129, 180, 196, 200
   s. 63: 180, 196, 200
   s. 80: 200
   s. 81: 200
   s. 85: 128, 200
   s. 183: 200

Mining Act 1926: 203
   s. 58: 203
   s. 179: 203
   s. 180: 203
   s. 185: 203

ONE

PHYSICAL LIMITS OF LAND

Two Latin maxims are traditionally referred to as defining the physical limits of land: cujus est solum, ejus est usque ad coelum et ad inferos and quicquid plantatur solo, solo cedit.

A. "CUJUS EST SOLUM, EJUS EST USQUE AD COELUM ET AD INFEROS"

This means that the owner of the soil is presumed to own everything "up to the sky and down to the centre of the earth". In other words, land extends upwards indefinitely into space and downwards to the centre of the earth, like an open-ended, inverted pyramid. Consequently, an invasion of the airspace at any height whatsoever above the soil will constitute a trespass. The legislature, apparently recognising this theoretical position, has enacted the *Damage by Aircraft Act* 1952 (N.S.W.), which provides that no action shall lie in respect of trespass or nuisance by reason only of the flight of aircraft at a reasonable height, provided that air navigation regulations are observed. However, the Act imposes a strict liability in cases of material damage caused to property by aircraft: see also the *Civil Aviation (Damage by Aircraft) Act* 1958 (Cth).

It appears that the maxim has not as yet found a literal application, and trespass to airspace has been limited to that height at which it is contemplated an owner might be expected to make use of the air column above the land as a natural incident of the user of the land: see Fleming, *The Law of Torts* (7th ed.), p. 42; Richardson, "Private Property Rights in Airspace at Common Law" (1953) 31 Can. B.R. 117; *Davies v. Bennison* (1927) 22 Tas. L.R. 52; *Kelsen v. Imperial Tobacco Co. (of Great Britain and Ireland) Ltd* [1957] 2 Q.B. 334; *Woollerton and Wilson Ltd v. Richard Costain Ltd* [1970] 1 W.L.R. 411; *Graham v. K. D. Morris & Sons Pty Ltd* [1975] Qd R. 1; *Lord Bernstein of Leigh v. Skyviews & General Ltd* [1978] Q.B. 479; *John Trenberth Ltd v. National Westminster Bank Ltd* (1979) 39 P. & C.R. 104.

Similarly, under the general law, land includes all substrata (*Edwards v. Sims* (1929 Ky) 24 S.W. 2d 619) and minerals unless the Crown grant specifically reserves them or they are excluded by statute: see now s. 235 of the *Crown Lands Consolidation Act* 1913 (N.S.W.).

A permanent trespass may arise where a structure encroaches upon neighbouring land: see McKenzie, "The Conveyancer" (1941) 15 A.L.J. 81 at 84. A strict application of the maxim in such cases could result in a demand for the demolition

1

of the offending encroachment. The problem is dealt with now by the *Encroachment of Buildings Act* 1922 (N.S.W.), which empowers either the adjacent or encroaching owner to approach the court in the case of an encroachment by a "substantial building of a permanent character", including a wall:

> 2. . . . .
>
> "Encroachment" means encroachment by a building, and includes encroachment by overhang of any part as well as encroachment by intrusion of any part in or upon the soil.
>
> 3. (1) Either an adjacent owner or an encroaching owner may apply to the court for relief under this Act in respect of any encroachment.
>
> (2) On the application the court may make such orders as it may deem just with respect to—
>
> (a) the payment of compensation to the adjacent owner;
>
> (b) the conveyance transfer or lease of the subject land to the encroaching owner, or the grant to him of any estate or interest therein or any easement right or privilege in relation thereto;
>
> (c) the removal of the encroachment.
>
> (3) The court may grant or refuse the relief of any part thereof as it deems proper in the circumstances of the case, and in the exercise of this discretion may consider amongst other matters—
>
> (a) the fact that the application is made by the adjacent owner or by the encroaching owner, as the case may be;
>
> (b) the situation and value of the subject land, and the nature and extent of the encroachment;
>
> (c) the character of the encroaching building, and the purposes for which it may be used;
>
> (d) the loss and damage which has been or will be incurred by the adjacent owner;
>
> (e) the loss and damage which would be incurred by the encroaching owner if he were required to remove the encroachment;
>
> (f) the circumstances in which the encroachment was made.
>
> (4) The court may refer any question involved to a licensed surveyor or a valuer.
>
> (5) This section applies to encroachments made either before or after the commencement of this Act.

But the Act does not extend to an encroachment upon a public road; neither the encroaching owner nor a council in which the public road is vested are entitled to make any application under the Act: *Pesic v. South Sydney Municipal Council* [1978] 1 N.S.W.L.R. 135.

According to s. 4(1) of the *Encroachment of Buildings Act* 1922 (N.S.W.), the minimum compensation payable by an encroaching owner for the conveyance, transfer, lease or grant of any estate or interest in the land encroached upon shall be, if the encroaching owner satisfies the court that the encroachment was not intentional and did not arise from negligence, the unimproved capital value of the land; otherwise it shall be three times that amount. The intention or negligence contemplated by the subsection is referable to the erection of the encroaching building and not, for instance, to a subsequent subdivision of land resulting in an encroachment by an existing building: *Gesmundo v. Anastasiou* (1975) 1 B.P.R. 9297. Moreover, the person whose intention or negligence is relevant is that of the owner (or builder) at the time when the encroachment was brought about and not that of a subsequent owner of the encroachment: *Kotis v. Devitt* (1979) 1 B.P.R. 9231.

The *Encroachment of Buildings Act* is, moreover, not applicable where a building is erected entirely on the wrong land. In *Ramsden v. Dyson* (1886) L.R. 1 H.L. 129 at 140-141, Lord Cranworth said:

> If a stranger begins to build on my land supposing it to be his own, and I, perceiving his mistake, abstain from setting him right, and leave him to persevere in his error, a court of equity will not allow me afterwards to assert my title to the land on which he had expended money on the supposition that the land was his own . . . but if a stranger builds on my land knowing it to be mine, there is no principle of equity which would prevent my claiming the land with the benefit of all the expenditure made on it.

Where, however, a stranger builds on land, not knowing it to be the property of another, and the true owner is unaware of what is being done, there is a general rule that there is no lien in favour of a person who has expended money on property in which he or she has no interest or for the benefit of another: *Falcke v. Scottish Imperial Insurance Co.* (1886) 34 Ch.D. 234. This principle was applied in *Brand v. Chris Building Co. Pty Ltd* [1957] V.R. 625 at 628 in which Hudson J. said:

> I think the correct statement of the position is as set out in *Halsbury's Laws of England* (3rd ed.), Vol. 14, para. 1179: "When A stands by while his right is being infringed by B, the following circumstances must as a general rule be present in order that the estoppel may be raised against A: (1) B must be mistaken as to his own legal rights; if he is aware that he is infringing the rights of another, he takes the risk of those rights being asserted; (2) B must expend money, or do some act, on the faith of his mistaken belief; otherwise, he does not suffer by A's subsequent assertion of his rights; (3) acquiescence is founded on contract with a knowledge of one's legal rights, and hence A must know of his own rights; (4) A must know of B's mistaken belief; with that knowledge it is inequitable for him to keep silence and allow B to proceed on his mistake; (5) A must encourage B in his expenditure of money or other act, either directly or by abstaining from asserting his legal right."

KELSEN v. IMPERIAL TOBACCO CO. (OF GREAT BRITAIN AND IRELAND) LTD

Queen's Bench Division [1957] 2 Q.B. 334 at 343

[The plaintiff alleged that the defendants, by affixing an advertising sign which projected into the airspace above the plaintiff's single-storey shop, had trespassed on his airspace, and sought a mandatory injunction for the removal of the sign.]

McNAIR J. That leads me to the next and in some ways most interesting point of the case, namely, whether an invasion of an airspace by a sign of this nature does give rise to an action in trespass or whether the rights, if any, of the owner of the airspace are not limited to complaining of nuisance; for if his rights are so limited it is clear on the facts of this case that no nuisance was created since the presence of this sign in the position where it was on this wall caused no inconvenience and no interference with the plaintiff's use of his airspace. This question of trespass by invasion of the airspace has been the subject of considerable controversy. One starts with the decision of Lord Ellenborough in *Pickering v. Rudd* (1815) 4 Camp. 219; 171 E.R. 70, where the trespass alleged was that the defendant had broken and entered the plaintiff's close by nailing on the defendant's own house a board which projected several inches from the wall and so far overhung the garden. Lord Ellenborough, in 1815, quite clearly said (at 220; at 70-71): "I do not think it is a trespass to interfere with the column of air superincumbent on the close. I once had occasion to rule upon the circuit, that a man who, from the outside of a field, discharged a gun into it, so as that the shot must have struck the soil, was guilty of breaking and entering it. A very learned judge, who went the circuit with me, at first doubted the decision, but I believe he afterwards approved of it, and that it met with the general concurrence of those to whom it was mentioned. But I am by no means prepared to say, that firing across a field in vacuo, no part of the contents touching it, amounts to a clausum fregit. Nay, if this board overhanging the plaintiff's garden be a trespass, it would follow that an aeronaut is liable to an action of trespass quare clausum fregit, at the suit of the occupier of every field over which his balloon passes in the course of his voyage. Whether the action may be maintained cannot depend upon the length of time for which the superincumbent air is invaded. If any damage arises from the object which overhangs the close, the remedy is by an action on the case."

Hawkins J. followed that decision and took the same view in *Clifton v. Viscount Bury* (1887) 4 T.L.R. 8, where he was dealing with the passage of bullets fired from a musketry range, the bullets passing some 75 ft above the surface of the land and not striking the land. He again held that that was not trespass, but, if anything, was nuisance.

There was an early doubt as to the correctness of Lord Ellenborough's statement expressed by Blackburn J. in *Kenyon v. Hart* (1865) 6 B. & S. 249 at 252; 122 E.R. 1188 at 1189; it seems to me that since that date there has been a consistent line of authority to the contrary. For instance, in *Wandsworth District Board of Works v. United Telephone Co. Ltd* (1884) 13 Q.B.D. 904 one of the questions at issue was whether a telephone line running across a street constituted a trespass as against the local authority in whom the street was vested. The main contest in the case was as to the extent of the vesting in the local authority, the conclusion being reached that they did not have vested in them the airspace above this street beyond what was necessary for its use as a street; but I think each of the Lords Justices in that case was quite clear in his conclusion that if the street and the airspace above it had been vested in the local authority the passage of a telephone line through that airspace would have constituted a trespass and not a mere nuisance. I need not elaborate my judgment by citing the passages from the three judgments.

In the case to which I have already referred, namely, the decision of Romer J. in *Gifford v. Dent* [1926] W.N. 336, the judge quite clearly took the view that a sign which was erected on the wall above the ground floor premises which had been demised to the plaintiff and projected some 4 ft 8 ins from the wall did constitute a trespass over the plaintiff's airspace, that airspace being the column of air above the basement which projected out into the pavement. The report of *Gifford's* case reads: "If he"—that is, the judge—"was right in the conclusion to which he had come that the plaintiffs were tenants of the forecourt and were accordingly tenants of the space above the forecourt usque ad coelum, it seemed to him that the projection was clearly a trespass upon the property of the plaintiffs." That decision, I think, has been recognised by the textbook writers, and in particular by the late Professor Winfield, as stating the true law. It is not without significance that the legislature in the *Air Navigation Act* 1920 (U.K.), s. 9 (replaced by s. 40(1) of the

Civil Aviation Act 1949 (U.K.)), found it necessary expressly to negative the action of trespass or nuisance arising from the mere fact of an aeroplane passing through the air above the land. It seems to me clearly to indicate that the legislature at least were not taking the same view of the matter as Lord Ellenborough in *Pickering v. Rudd* (1815) 4 Camp. 219; 171 E.R. 70, but rather taking the view accepted in the later cases, such as the *Wandsworth District* case (1884) 13 Q.B.D. 904, subsequently followed by Romer J. in *Gifford v. Dent* [1926] W.N. 336. Accordingly, I reach the conclusion that a trespass and not a mere nuisance was created by the invasion of the plaintiff's airspace by this sign.

Injunction granted.

LORD BERNSTEIN OF LEIGH v. SKYVIEWS AND GENERAL LTD

Queen's Bench Division [1978] Q.B. 479 at 485

[The plaintiff was the owner of and resident at premises comprising a country house and surrounding land in Kent. The defendants, whose business was to take aerial photographs of properties and then offer them for sale to the owners, took a single aerial photograph of the plaintiff's premises from a height of several hundred feet. The plaintiff objected to the photograph being taken without his permission and demanded that the defendants hand over or destroy all negatives and prints of the photograph. The defendants did not do so. The plaintiff brought an action against the defendants, alleging that they had wrongfully entered the airspace above the plaintiff's premises to take the photograph and were guilty of trespass and actionable invasion of the plaintiff's right to privacy. The plaintiff claimed damages for trespass and injunctions to restrain the defendants from entering the airspace and from invading the plaintiff's right to privacy. The plaintiff further contended that the defendants were not entitled to rely on the statutory defence under s. 40(1) of the *Civil Aviation Act* 1949 (U.K.), since that section was limited to a bare right of passage over land and did not permit the use of airspace for the purpose of photography.]

GRIFFITHS J. I turn now to the law. The plaintiff claims that as owner of the land he is also owner of the airspace above the land, or at least has the right to exclude any entry into the airspace above his land. He relies on the old Latin maxim, *cujus est solum ejus est usque ad coelum et ad inferos*, a colourful phrase often on the lips of lawyers since it was first coined by Accursius in Bologna in the 13th century. There are a number of cases in which the maxim has been used by English judges but an examination of those cases shows that they have all been concerned with structures attached to the adjoining land, such as overhanging buildings, signs or telegraph wires, and for their solution it has not been necessary for the judge to cast his eyes towards the heavens; he has been concerned with the rights of the owner in the airspace immediately adjacent to the surface of the land.

That an owner has certain rights in the airspace above his land is well established by authority. He has the right to lop the branches of trees that may overhang his boundary, although this right seems to be founded in nuisance rather than trespass.
. . .

In *Gifford v. Dent* [1926] W.N. 336 Romer J. held that it was a trespass to erect a sign that projected 4 ft 8 ins over the plaintiff's forecourt and ordered it to be removed. He invoked the old maxim in his judgment. The report reads: "the plaintiffs were tenants of the forecourt and were accordingly tenants of the space above the forecourt usque ad coelum, it seemed to him that the projection was clearly a trespass upon the property of the plaintiffs".

That decision was followed by McNair J. in *Kelsen v. Imperial Tobacco Co. Ltd*
[1957] 2 Q.B. 334, in which he granted a mandatory injunction ordering the
defendants to remove a sign which projected only 8 ins over the plaintiff's property.
The plaintiff relies strongly on this case, and in particular on the following passage
when, after citing the judgment of Romer J. to which I have already referred,
McNair J. continued (at 345): "That decision, I think, has been recognised by the
textbook writers, and, in particular, by the later Professor Winfield (*Winfield on
Tort* (6th ed.), p. 379), as stating the true law. It is not without significance that in
the *Air Navigation Act* 1920 (U.K.), s. 9(1), which was replaced by s. 40(1) of the
Civil Aviation Act 1949 (U.K.), the legislature found it necessary expressly to
negative the action of trespass or nuisance arising from the mere fact of an
aeroplane passing through the air above the land. It seems to me clearly to indicate
that the legislature were not taking the same view of the matter as Lord
Ellenborough in *Pickering v. Rudd* (1815) 4 Camp. 219; 171 E.R. 70, but were
taking the view accepted in the later cases, such as *Wandsworth Board of Works
v. United Telephone Co.* (1884) 13 Q.B.D. 904, subsequently followed by Romer J.
in *Gifford v. Dent* [1926] W.N. 336. Accordingly, I reach the conclusion that a
trespass, and not a mere nuisance, was created by the invasion of the plaintiff's
airspace by this sign."

I very much doubt if in that passage McNair J. was intending to hold that the
plaintiff's rights in the airspace continued to an unlimited height or "ad coelum"
as counsel for the plaintiff submits. The point that the judge was considering was
whether the sign was a trespass or a nuisance at the very low level at which it
projected. This to my mind is clearly indicated by his reference to *Winfield on Tort*
(6th ed.), p. 380 in which the text reads: "it is submitted that trespass will be
committed by [aircraft] to the airspace if they fly so low as to come within the area
of ordinary user." The author in that passage is careful to limit the trespass to the
height at which it is contemplated an owner might be expected to make use of the
airspace as a natural incident of the user of his land. If, however, the learned judge
was by his reference to the *Civil Aviation Act* 1949, and his disapproval of the views
of Lord Ellenborough in *Pickering v. Rudd* (1815) 4 Camp. 219; 171 E.R. 70,
indicating the opinion that the flight of an aircraft at whatever height constituted
a trespass at common law, I must respectfully disagree.

I do not wish to cast any doubts on the correctness of the decision on its own
particular facts. It may be a sound and practical rule to regard any incursion into
the airspace at a height which may interfere with the ordinary user of the land as
a trespass rather than a nuisance. Adjoining owners then know where they stand;
they have no right to erect structures overhanging or passing over their neighbours'
land and there is no room for argument whether they are thereby causing damage
or annoyance to their neighbours about which there may be much room for
argument and uncertainty. But wholly different considerations arise when
considering the passage of aircraft at a height which in no way affects the user of
the land.

There is no direct authority on this question but as long ago as 1815 Lord
Ellenborough in *Pickering v. Rudd* (1815) 4 Camp. 219 at 221; 171 E.R. 70 at 71
expressed the view that it would not be a trespass to pass over a man's land in a
balloon; and in *Saunders v. Smith* (1838) 2 Jur. 491 at 492 Shadwell V.-C. said:
"Thus, upon the maxim of law 'Cujus est solum ejus est usque ad coelum,' an
injunction might be granted for cutting timber and severing crops: but, suppose a
person should apply to restrain an aerial wrong, as by sailing through the air over
a person's freehold in a balloon; this surely would be too contemptible to be taken
notice of."

In *Commissioner for Railways v. Valuer-General* [1974] A.C. 328 at 351, 352 Lord Wilberforce had this to say of the maxim: "There are a number of examples of its use in judgments of the 19th century, by which time mineral values had drawn attention to downwards extent as well as, or more than, extent upwards. But its use, whether with reference to mineral rights, or trespass in the airspace by projections, animals or wires, is imprecise and it is mainly serviceable as dispensing with analysis: cf. *Pickering v. Rudd* (1815) 4 Camp. 219; 171 E.R. 70; *Ellis v. Loftus Iron Co.* (1874) L.R. 10 C.P. 10. In none of these cases is there an authoritative pronouncement that 'land' means the whole of the space from the centre of the earth to the heavens: so sweeping, unscientific and unpractical a doctrine is unlikely to appeal to the common law mind."

In *Sovmots Investments Ltd v. Secretary of State for the Environment* [1976] 3 W.L.R. 597 at 608 Browne L.J. said of counsel's submission that land in its ordinary legal sense meant from the centre of the earth to the sky: "We therefore do not think it necessary to consider whether counsel's contention as to the 'ordinary legal meaning' of 'land' is right: we will only say that what Lord Wilberforce said in giving the opinion of the Privy Council in *Comr for Railways v. Valuer-General* [1974] A.C. 328 seems to us to throw great doubt on it."

I can find no support in authority for the view that a landowner's rights in the airspace above his property extend to an unlimited height. In *Wandsworth Board of Works v. United Telephone Co.* (1884) 13 Q.B.D. 904 Bowen L.J. described the maxim, usque ad coelum, as a fanciful phrase, to which I would add that if applied literally it is a fanciful notion leading to the absurdity of a trespass at common law being committed by a satellite every time it passes over a suburban garden. The academic writers speak with one voice in rejecting the uncritical and literal application of the maxim: see, by way of example only, *Winfield and Jolowicz on Tort* (10th ed.), p. 305; *Salmond on Tort* (16th ed.), p. 44; *Shawcross and Beaumont on Air Law* (3rd ed.), Vol. 1, p. 536; *McNair on the Law of the Air* (3rd ed.), p. 97 and *Halsbury's Laws of England* (4th ed.), Vol. 2, paras 1422-1500. I accept their collective approach as correct. The problem is to balance the rights of an owner to enjoy the use of his land against the rights of the general public to take advantage of all that science now offers in the use of airspace. This balance is in my judgment best struck in our present society by restricting the rights of an owner in the airspace above his land to such height as is necessary for the ordinary use and enjoyment of his land and the structures on it, and declaring that above that height he has no greater rights in the airspace than any other member of the public.

Applying this test to the facts of this case, I find that the defendants' aircraft did not infringe any rights in the plaintiff's airspace, and thus no trespass was committed. It was on any view of the evidence flying many hundreds of feet above the ground and it is not suggested that by its mere presence in the airspace it caused any interference with any use to which the plaintiff put or might wish to put his land. The plaintiff's complaint is not that the aircraft interfered with the use of his land but that a photograph was taken from it. There is, however, no law against taking a photograph, and the mere taking of a photograph cannot turn an act which is not a trespass into the plaintiff's airspace into one that is a trespass. . . .

My finding that no trespass at common law has been established is sufficient to determine this case in the defendants' favour. I should, however, deal with a further defence under the *Civil Aviation Act* 1949 (U.K.), s. 40(1) of which provides: "No action shall lie in respect of trespass or in respect of nuisance, by reason only of the flight of an aircraft over any property at a height above the ground, which, having regard to wind, weather, and all the circumstances of the case is reasonable, or the ordinary incidents of such flight so long as the provisions of Part II and this Part of this Act and any Order in Council or order made under Part II of this Part of this Act are duly complied with.''

It is agreed that all the statutory provisions have been complied with by the defendants, nor is there any suggestion that the aircraft was not flying at a reasonable height; but it is submitted by the plaintiff that the protection given by the subsection is limited to a bare right of passage over land analogous to the limited right of a member of the public to pass over the surface of a highway, and my attention has been drawn to a passage in *Shawcross and Beaumont on Air Law* (3rd ed.), Vol. 1, p. 561 in which the editors express this view: I see nothing in the language of the section to invite such a restricted reading which would withdraw from its protection many very beneficial activities carried on from aircraft. . . .

It is, however, to be observed that the protection given is limited by the words ''by reason only of the flight'', so although an owner can found no action in trespass or nuisance if he relies solely on the flight of the aircraft above his property as founding his cause of action, the section will not preclude him from bringing an action if he can point to some activity carried on by or from the aircraft that can properly be considered a trespass or nuisance, or some other tort. For example, the section would give no protection against the deliberate emission of vast quantities of smoke that polluted the atmosphere and seriously interfered with the plaintiff's use and enjoyment of his property; such behaviour remains an actionable nuisance. Nor would I wish this judgment to be understood as deciding that in no circumstances could a successful action be brought against an aerial photographer to restrain his activities. The present action is not founded in nuisance for no court would regard the taking of a single photograph as an actionable nuisance. But if the circumstances were such that a plaintiff was subjected to the harassment of constant surveillance of his house from the air, accompanied by the photographing of his every activity, I am far from saying that the court would not regard such a monstrous invasion of his privacy as an actionable nuisance for which they would give relief. However, that question does not fall for decision in this case and will be decided if and when it arises.

On the facts of this case even if contrary to my view the defendants' aircraft committed a trespass at common law in flying over the plaintiff's land, the plaintiff is prevented from bringing any action in respect of that trespass by the terms of s. 40(1) of the *Civil Aviation Act* 1949.

For these reasons the plaintiff's action fails and there will be judgment for the defendants.

Judgment for the defendants.

GRAHAM v. K. D. MORRIS & SONS PTY LTD

Supreme Court of Queensland [1974] Qd R. 1 at 4

[The plaintiff was owner and occupier of a house. Adjoining the land on its northern boundary was a parcel of land owned by the Commonwealth on which the defendant was constructing a substantial building. The defendant caused a crane to be erected almost centrally upon the building under construction. When the crane was not in operation the jib was left free to rotate such that, when the wind was in the north or north-east, the jib encroached 62 ft over the plaintiff's land and was suspended above the roof of her house; this frequently happened. A week after the plaintiff sought an injunction to restrain the trespass and a notice of motion seeking an interlocutory injunction, the defendant's solicitors wrote to the plaintiff's solicitors "formally" seeking permission to the encroachment and offering to pay "reasonable compensation in respect of such encroachment". The defendant had not previously sought permission.]

CAMPBELL J. In my opinion, the invasion of the plaintiff's airspace by the projection of the crane jib is a trespass by the defendant and not a mere nuisance. I am not prepared to take a view of this issue which differs from that expressed by McNair J. in *Kelsen v. Imperial Tobacco Co. (of Great Britain and Ireland) Ltd* [1957] 2 Q.B. 334. I am persuaded that the overhanging crane which, as the plaintiff says and I accept, is both an unsightly feature of her land and a cause of nervousness and apprehension to her, interferes with that part of the airspace above her land which is requisite for the proper use and enjoyment of that land.

Mr Callinan submitted that damages would be an adequate remedy and that an injunction would be extremely oppressive to the defendant. He also argued that, should I be disposed to grant an injunction, I should suspend it for a period sufficient to enable the works to be completed by the defendant, as was done by Stamp J. in *Woollerton and Wilson Ltd v. Richard Costain Ltd* [1970] 1 W.L.R. 411. The facts in that case correspond very closely to the facts before me. Stamp J. held that neither the absence of any damage caused by the trespass, either present or apprehended, or the principle known as "the balance of convenience" was an answer to the claim for an injunction. The question before me is similar to that before his Lordship who, when considering whether the balance of convenience was material to a case where an interlocutory injunction to restrain a trespass is sought, said (at 414): "The question, therefore, as I see it is not whether the plaintiffs ought to have an injunction until the trial but whether they ought to have an injunction."

Any order I make will stand only until the trial of the action but, for reasons stated by Stamp J., I will not refuse the injunction because of the hardship of the defendant. In any event, any hardship which the defendant will suffer has been brought about by its own negligence and its cavalier attitude.

I do not think that damages would be an appropriate remedy in the circumstances of this case. Mr Callinan argued that the court could assess real and not merely nominal damages although such an assessment presented many difficulties. Professor Dworkin has suggested (33 M.L.R. 556) that damages in the case of the projecting crane should be: "more than nominal and should reflect a payment by the defendants for the use of the plaintiffs' airspace".

This may well be so, but the point that has impressed me here is that the defendant did not seek prior permission and did not seek to negotiate until after the writ was issued. I think this illustrates a high-handed attitude on its part. Were I to refuse an injunction on the ground that the plaintiff could be adequately compensated in damages I would in effect be permitting a deliberate act of trespass to continue not for a short time but for about another 18 months upon payment to the plaintiff of an uncertain sum to be calculated at some future time. In such event, what would be the situation if the plaintiff wished in the near future to sell or to lease her house? What effect will this infringement of her right of property have on the price a purchaser may be willing to pay? There are many pertinent factors other than the consideration of damages as a possibly sufficient remedy which have led me to conclude that I should not refuse an injunction. I am persuaded by "the rule that where the plaintiff has established the invasion of a common law right, and there is ground for believing that without an injunction there is likely to be a repetition of the wrong, he is, in the absence of special circumstances, entitled to an injunction against such repetition'': per Cussen J. in *Beswicke v. Alner* [1926] V.L.R. 72 at 72, 76; cited with approval by Dixon C.J. in *Mayfair Trading Co. Pty Ltd v. Dreyer* (1958) 101 C.L.R. 428 at 451.

In *Charrington v. Simons & Co. Ltd* [1970] 1 W.L.R. 725 Buckley J. made an order for a mandatory injunction to remedy a clear breach of contract but suspended it for three years in order to allow the defendant to carry out certain ameliorative works. However, the Court of Appeal, [1971] 1 W.L.R. 598, held that the judge did not properly exercise his judicial discretion in suspending the injunction: "For in effect he sought to force upon a reluctant plaintiff something very like a settlement involving operations by the defendant on the plaintiff's land which must lead to greatly increased harm to his business, as a condition or term of his obtaining a mandatory injunction should the works not prove a satisfactory solution."

The following passage also occurs in the judgment of the court (at 603): "We have already explained why we do not think it necessary to discuss authorities and principles generally. We would however say that we share with counsel for both parties doubts as to the usefulness of the phrase used by the judge 'a fair result'—a phrase echoed in *Shepherd Homes Ltd v. Sandham* [1970] 3 W.L.R. 348. Further, we wish to reserve our opinion whether the decision in *Woollerton and Wilson Ltd v. Richard Costain Ltd* [1970] 1 W.L.R. 411 was correct. Neither counsel seemed to think it was."

Should I, in the exercise of my discretion, refuse to grant an injunction? I have already said that I do not consider damages an adequate remedy. Further, the defendant made no offer of monetary compensation to the plaintiff even after complaints were made, and in fact even now has merely offered to negotiate for reasonable compensation. At no time has the defendant admitted that its acts constituted a trespass and at no time has it apologised to the plaintiff for the overhanging of its crane, and I find it difficult to accept that, until receipt of the letter dated 24 December 1973, the defendant did not appreciate that any action of trespass could arise. Why did not the defendant seek the plaintiff's permission to the encroachment prior to commencing the work of building? Why now does it, in the letter of 25 February 1974, merely seek "formal" permission? It is said that cranes of this type (tower cranes) have been in operation for some 12 years and that many hundreds of them are in use. Are the manufacturers (Favelle Mort Ltd) and the defendant unaware of the decision in Woollerton's case which was given on 19 November 1969? On that day Stamp J. said (at 416): "A contractor in the future will be warned not to enter into a building contract involving the erection of one of these cranes in such a position as to swing upon the land of an adjoining owner without first obtaining permission from that adjoining owner. Much has been made in this case of the importance of work being done by the defendants; but if I had thought that the defendants in this case had deliberately proceeded upon the footing that the importance of the work would prevent the court from granting an injunction, I would have made an order different from that which I will make."

Why did not the defendant, as a matter of urgency, seek legal advice on the real issue at the very latest after 24 December 1973, instead of attempting to rely on the technical views of certain experts and to raise an excuse akin to the plea of necessity?

In all the circumstances I consider that I cannot allow the defendant to continue to commit this unlawful trespass. If I did not grant the injunction I would be condoning a clear breach by the defendant of the plaintiff's proprietary rights. I consider it should be stopped now and that no special factors exist which would justify my refusing to grant an injunction or to suspend it for any length of time.

The time to seek permission and for negotiation was prior to the commencement of the work. It is not for me at this stage to act as an arbitrator or to conduct some form of negotiations between the parties with a view to obtaining the plaintiff's permission to the tort on the basis of the interests of the public, fairness to the defendant or otherwise. Why should I bring pressure upon the plaintiff to hamper her legal rights for monetary compensation of any amount?

Upon the plaintiff giving the usual undertaking as to damages I propose to order that the defendant by itself its servants and agents be restrained until the trial of this action from continuing to trespass on the plaintiff's land by virtue of its crane jib. As this may involve the dismantling of the crane or the taking of other remedial steps in order to prevent the jib from swinging free in all weather conditions, I will hear submissions from counsel as to what time, if any, should be allowed to the defendant to comply with the injunction.

Injunction granted.

NOTES

1. In *Woollerton and Wilson Ltd v. Richard Costain Ltd* [1970] 1 W.L.R. 411, referred to in the principal case, the intrusion of a crane jib into the plaintiff's airspace 50 ft above roof level was held to constitute a trespass but the court postponed the operation of the injunction to prevent such trespass until the anticipated completion of the building under construction:

> It is no part of the plaintiffs' case that the crane incommodes them or their servants in the slightest degree or is in any way a nuisance. The plaintiffs do not claim that they are in any fear or apprehension. But they claim an interlocutory injunction to restrain what is conceded to be an invasion of their airspace and a trespass.
>
> The plaintiffs, while not complaining of any damage, apprehension or inconvenience have, so they would have the court believe, only one object in these proceedings, namely, to prevent the jib of the crane swinging over their premises; and something more than £250 which the defendants have offered would have been required to induce them to change their mind.
>
> It is the plaintiffs' case that the absence of any damage caused by the trespass, either present or apprehended, is no reason for refusing the injunction for which they ask. It is their further contention that since the tort of trespass is admitted and is threatened to be continued there is no good reason for refusing interlocutory relief on the ground of balance of convenience. In my judgment both these submissions are well founded.
>
> It is in my judgment well established that it is no answer to a claim for an injunction to restrain a trespass that the trespass does no harm to the plaintiff. Indeed, the very fact that no harm is done is a reason for rather than against the granting of an injunction: for if there is no damage done the damage recovered in the action will be nominal and if the injunction is refused the result will be no more nor less than a licence to continue the tort of trespass in return for a nominal payment. . . .
>
> Mr Harman referred me to a number of cases the effect of which, he submitted, was to modify the principle or rule so stated in *Eardley v. Granville* (1876) 3 Ch.D. 826 and to justify the court in refusing an injunction in a case such as the present. These were cases in which the claim was based on nuisance, not on trespass. The gist of an action for nuisance is damage. And since the tort of nuisance can only exist if there be damage, in an action for nuisance damage can be obtained which will be measured by the extent of the nuisance and the plaintiff in such a case is not in a situation of a plaintiff in an action for trespass who may recover only nominal damages. In an action of nuisance the licence which the court by refusing an injunction may be said to give the defendant to continue the nuisance will be compensated by the damage which the plaintiff will receive on his claim for damages. . . . Taking all the factors to which I have called attention into consideration, I conclude that I ought in the exercise of my discretion to grant the injunction which the plaintiffs seek until trial of the action, but to postpone its operation until the end of November of next year. I am conscious that by so doing I am giving with one hand and taking away with the other. But by so doing I give effect to the process by which I have come to my conclusion that in principle there ought to be an injunction but on the particular facts of this case not until the defendants have had a proper opportunity of finishing the job.

2. The approach taken in the principal case was also followed in *John Trenberth Ltd v. Westminster Bank Ltd* (1979) 39 P. & C.R. 104. In this case the defendant's contractors, after protracted and fruitless negotiations by the defendant to obtain the plaintiff's permission, erected scaffolding on the plaintiff's property in order to carry out repairs, pursuant to a statutory duty, on the adjoining building owned by the defendant. The court said (at 107): "People are not to infringe the property rights of others and then say, 'And I am entitled to go on doing it because I am really doing you no tangible harm, and fivepence will amply compensate you for that harm.' "

3. It appears clear that actual contact with the soil or a chattel on the land will constitute trespass. In *Davies v. Bennison* (1927) 22 Tas. L.R. 52 the defendant shot and killed the plaintiff's cat which was on the roof of a shed in the plaintiff's yard. The plaintiff succeeded in an action for trespass and nervous shock. The Chief Justice said (at 55):

> A man who walks from his roof on to that of his neighbour is clearly guilty of trespass. The neighbour's house is part of his freehold. But when the intrusion consists of sending something such as a balloon, a bird, a kite, or a missile over another's land without touching it or anything built or growing upon it, important fundamental and subtle questions arise. The only direct dictum upon the point is that of Lord Ellenborough in *Pickering v. Rudd* (1815) 4 Camp. 219; 177 E.R. 70. . . .
>
> So far as the ability to use land, and the air above it, exists, mechanically speaking, to my mind any intrusion above land is a direct physical breach of the negative duty not to interfere with the owner's use of his land, and is in principle a trespass. At any rate, I can see no doubt whatever that an owner's rights extend to a height sufficient to cover the facts of this case.

See also *Ellis v. Loftus Iron Co.* (1874) L.R. 10 C.P. 10.

B. QUICQUID PLANTATUR SOLO, SOLO CEDIT

According to this maxim, whatever is attached to the soil becomes part of it; in this maxim is embodied the law relating to fixtures. Accordingly, a building erected on land or objects which are permanently attached to a building on the land become in law "land". Therefore, the materials of which a house is constructed and the objects permanently attached to it cease to have the character of chattels, and the owner of the soil becomes their owner.

1. What constitutes a fixture?

To determine whether an object constitutes a fixture is often difficult. In principle it depends upon two tests: first, the degree of annexation, and secondly, the purpose of annexation. The former, however, is only a prima facie test and may be expressed as follows: objects not attached to the land other than by their own weight are prima facie chattels, with the onus of proving the contrary resting upon those who assert that they have become fixtures; and conversely, objects affixed to the land even slightly are prima facie fixtures, with the onus of proving the contrary resting upon those who assert that they are chattels: *Holland v. Hodgson* (1872) L.R. 8 C.P. 328, extracted below p. 15. It is the latter test, the purpose of annexation, which will be the decisive test. Thus even where an object is physically attached to the land, it will remain a chattel if the purpose of the annexation was not to effect a permanent improvement in the land, but merely for the temporary and more convenient use or enyoyment of the object as a chattel. Sir Frederick Jordan, in *Australian Provincial Assurance Co. Ltd v. Coroneo* (1938) 38 S.R. (N.S.W.) 700, extracted below p. 23, stated the test to be whether the object is affixed with the "intention that it shall remain in position permanently or for an indefinite or substantial period . . . or whether it has been fixed with the intent that it shall remain in position only for some temporary purpose", although this may be an oversimplification of the "purpose of annexation" test which would seem to extend beyond a mere temporal aspect of the terms "permanent" and "temporary" as various other circumstances may also go to determine the purpose of annexation:

see *N. H. Dunn Pty Ltd v. L. M. Ericsson Pty Ltd* (unreported, N.S.W. Court of Appeal, 6 December 1979). In any event, the intent or purpose of annexation is an objective intent, which must be ascertained by investigating not the subjective intent of the person making the affixation but external factors patent for all to see (*Hobson v. Gorringe* [1897] 1 Ch. 182, extracted below p. 27), although this is not to say that a subjective intent is never relevant; for example, actual intent may affect the status of an item where there is an express agreement between the owner of the chattel and the owner of the realty. Factors indicative of the intent or purpose of annexation include, for example, injury to the object or the fabric of the freehold on removal, the nature of the object itself, the taste and fashion of the day, whether the object forms an essential part of a general scheme or design, and local custom: *Leigh v. Taylor* [1902] A.C. 157, extracted below p. 19; *Reid v. Smith* (1906) 3 C.L.R. 656, extracted below p. 24.

If, according to these two tests, an object is found to be a chattel, generally it can be removed by the person bringing it onto the freehold or by the person's successors in title at any time. If, on the other hand, it is held that the object has become a fixture, prima facie, it cannot be removed. However, the rule that a fixture cannot be severed from the inheritance has been relaxed in favour of "limited owners".

2. Right to remove fixtures

An affixation may be made either by the owner of an estate of inheritance or, on the other hand, by limited owners, that is, life tenants or tenants under a lease. In the former case, that is, where the affixation is made by a person not a limited owner, the right of severance may arise in the case of the following relationships:

(i) Vendor and purchaser. Here, without exception, all objects which are fixtures at the date of contract pass to the purchaser, subject to any special provision to the contrary in the contract for sale. Thus, if a fixture is excepted by contract from a sale of the land, it remains the property of the vendor: see, for example, *Standard Portland Cement Co. Pty Ltd v. Good* (1982) 57 A.L.J.R. 151.

(ii) Mortgagor and mortgagee. Here again, without exception (and subject only to any special provision to the contrary in the mortgage), all fixtures, whether attached before or after the date of mortgage, form part of the security and enure for the benefit of the mortgagee.

(iii) Devisee and other beneficiaries under a will. All fixtures, without exception, pass under the devise to the beneficiary of the real estate.

Where the affixation has been made by a "limited owner" and it has been determined that the object is a fixture, a second question will arise, namely, is it a fixture of a kind which may be removed by the "limited owner"? That these are two separate and independent questions is emphasised clearly in *Bain v. Brand* (1876) 1 App. Cas. 762, extracted below p. 31; the second question does not arise until it is first determined in accordance with the above tests that the object in question has become a fixture. This issue will arise in the following relationships:

(a) Landlord and tenant

All fixtures attached by a tenant prima facie form part of the inheritance for the benefit of the landlord. However, important exceptions have been established enabling the removal of "tenant's fixtures", that is, fixtures attached by a tenant for trade, domestic and ornamental purposes, and, to a lesser extent, agricultural purposes. Formerly the agricultural fixtures of market gardeners, but not farmers, could be removed, for only the former were regarded as being engaged in trade: see *Elwes v. Maw* (1802) 3 East. 38; 102 E.R. 510 (affixations by a farmer) and *Mears v. Callender* [1901] 2 Ch. 388 (glasshouses affixed by a market gardener). Now legislation enables a tenant to remove agricultural fixtures (see *Agricultural Holdings Act* 1941 (N.S.W.), s. 21), although the definition of "agricultural holding" is such that only certain farmer-tenants are covered by the legislation. Moreover, agricultural tenants have the right to compensation from the landlord on quitting their holding at the determination of the tenancy for given improvements: *Agricultural Holdings Act* 1941 (N.S.W.), ss 7 et seq.

Section 21 of the *Agricultural Holdings Act* 1941 (N.S.W.) provides:

21. Any engine, machinery, fencing or other fixture affixed to a holding by a tenant before or after the commencement of this Act, and any building erected by him thereon for which he is not under this Act or otherwise entitled to compensation and which is not so affixed or erected in pursuance of some obligation in that behalf or instead of some fixture or building belonging to the landlord, shall be the property of and be removable by the tenant before or within a reasonable time after the termination of the tenancy:

Provided that—

(a) before the removal of any fixture or building the tenant shall pay all rent owing by him, and shall perform or satisfy all other his obligations to the landlord in respect of the holding;

(b) in the removal of any fixture or building the tenant shall not do any avoidable damage to any other building or other part of the holding;

(c) immediately after the removal of any fixture or building the tenant shall make good all damage occasioned to any other building or other part of the holding by the removal;

(d) the tenant shall not remove any fixture or building without giving one month's previous notice in writing to the landlord of his intention to remove it;

(e) at any time before the expiration of the notice of removal the landlord, by notice in writing given by him to the tenant, may elect to purchase any fixture or building comprised in the notice of removal, and any fixture or building comprised in the notice of removal, and any fixture or building thus elected to be purchased shall be left by the tenant, and shall become the property of the landlord, who shall pay to the tenant the fair value thereof to an incoming tenant of the holding and any dispute as to value shall be determined by arbitration under this Act.

However, the title to the fixture remains in the landlord until the tenant exercises the power to sever: *Crossley v. Lee* [1908] 1 K.B. 86. Generally the tenant must remove her or his fixtures during the currency of the tenancy where the tenancy is for a fixed term. Where the tenant herself or himself brings the term to an end by surrender, she or he may possibly be allowed a reasonable time thereafter to remove her or his fixtures if the court is of the opinion that the tenant does not have sufficient time to remove them: see *Ex parte Brook* (1878) 10 Ch. D. 100, extracted below p. 38 (disclaimer of lease by the trustee in bankruptcy of the lessee). Where the lease is forfeited for breach of covenant by the tenant, it is not clear whether the tenant will be given a further period in which to remove her or his fixtures.

Where the tenant surrenders the lease and vacates the property without removing her or his fixtures, then it is clear that the tenant has abandoned them and they remain the property of the landlord. On the other hand, if a tenant surrenders the lease, either expressly or by operation of law, but remains in possession, it is prima facie a question of construing the instrument of surrender to determine whether or not the tenant has given up the right to remove her or his fixtures. If the instrument is silent, then the tenant retains the right to remove the fixtures for so long as the tenant continues in possession as a tenant, whether by holding over, statutory tenancy, extension of lease or new lease: see *New Zealand Government Property Corp. v. H.M. & S. Ltd* [1982] 1 Q.B. 1145, extracted below p. 40.

(b) Life tenant and remainderman

Here, as with the landlord and tenant relationship, all fixtures prima facie pass with the inheritance to the remainderman, with the exception of trade, ornamental and domestic fixtures which are removable by the personal representative of a deceased life tenant within a reasonable time after the life tenant's death. The statutory exception regarding agricultural fixtures does not apply in the case of a life tenant.

Where there has been an affixation by a limited owner, the test of "purpose of annexation" will apply again, but this time to decide whether the trade, domestic, ornamental or agricultural fixture has been affixed for a permanent, indefinite or substantial period. If answered affirmatively, it is a "landlord's fixture" and cannot be removed notwithstanding its trade, domestic, ornamental or agricultural nature. If answered negatively, it may be removed as a "tenant's fixture". An important factor in resolving the matter will be the extent of injury to the inheritance and the object upon removal: necessary destruction of the object by removal is indicative of an intent that it remain permanently for the benefit of the inheritance: *Webb v. Bevis* [1940] 1 All E.R. 247, extracted below p. 37. On the other hand, mere damage to the inheritance on removal, thereby rendering the limited owner liable in waste, will not necessarily be conclusive. The limited owner may still be entitled to remove the fixture notwithstanding her or his liability to reinstate the premises: *Spyer v. Phillipson* [1931] 2 Ch. 183, extracted below p. 33.

HOLLAND v. HODGSON

Exchequer Chamber (1872) L.R. 7 C.P. 328

[Mason, the owner in fee of a worsted mill, mortgaged to the plaintiffs the mill, various engines and "all other fixtures whatever which now or at any time hereafter during the continuance of this security shall be set up and affixed to the said hereditaments".

Subsequently, Mason assigned all his estate and effects to the defendants as trustees, to be administered as under a bankruptcy. The defendants took possession of the mill, including 436 looms installed therein. The plaintiff claimed that the looms passed to them under the mortgage.

The looms were driven by a steam engine. In order to keep them steady and in a proper position for working, the looms on the ground floor were fastened to the floor by nails driven through holes in the feet of the looms into wooden plugs in the stone floor. The upper rooms of the mill were built and arranged specially to receive the looms, which were kept in position by being nailed—similarly to the looms in the ground floor rooms—into beams of wood built into the floor. The looms could easily be removed by drawing the nails from the wooden plugs or beams without serious injury to the floors.

The question was whether the looms constituted fixtures, in which case they passed to the plaintiffs as part of the mortgage security.]

BLACKBURN J. . . . Since the decision of this court in *Climie v. Wood* (1869) L.R. 4 Exch. 328 it must be considered as settled law (except perhaps in the House of Lords) that what are commonly known as trade or tenant's fixtures form part of the land, and pass by a conveyance of it; and that though if the person who erected those fixtures was the tenant with a limited interest in the land he has a right, as against the freeholder, to sever the fixtures from the land, yet if he be a mortgagor in fee he has no such right as against his mortgagee. Trade and tenant's fixtures are, in the judgment in that case, accurately defined as "things which are annexed to the land for the purposes of trade or of domestic convenience or ornament in so permanent a manner as to become part of the land, and yet the tenant who has erected them is entitled to remove them during his term, or it may be within a reasonable time after its expiration". It was not disputed at the bar that such was the law; and it was admitted, and we think properly admitted, that where there is a conveyance of the land the fixtures are transferred, not as fixtures, but as part of the land. . . . There is no doubt that the general maxim of the law is, that what is annexed to the land becomes part of the land; but it is very difficult, if not impossible, to say with precision what constitutes an annexation sufficient for this purpose. It is a question which must depend on the circumstances of each case, and mainly on two circumstances, as indicating the intention, viz., the degree of annexation and the object of the annexation. When the article in question is no further attached to the land, then by its own weight it is generally to be considered a mere chattel: see *Wiltshear v. Cottrell* (1853) 1 El. & Bl. 674; 118 E.R. 589 and the cases there cited. But even in such a case, if the intention is apparent to make the articles part of the land, they do become part of the land: see *D'Eyncourt v. Gregory* (1866) L.R. 3 Eq. 382. Thus blocks of stone placed one on the top of another without any mortar or cement for the purpose of forming a dry stone wall would become part of the land, though the same stones, if deposited in a builder's yard and for convenience sake stacked on the top of each other in the form of a wall, would remain chattels. On the other hand, an article may be very firmly fixed to the land, and yet the circumstances may be such as to shew that it was never intended to be part of the land, and then it does not become part of the land. The anchor of a large ship must be very firmly fixed in the ground in order to bear the strain of the cable, yet no one could suppose that it became part of the land, even though it should chance that the shipowner was also the owner of the fee of the spot where the anchor was dropped. An anchor similarly fixed in the soil for the purpose of bearing the strain of the chain of a suspension bridge would be part of the land. Perhaps the true rule is, that articles not otherwise attached to the land than by their own weight are not to be considered as part of the land, unless the circumstances are such as to shew that they were intended to be part of the land, the onus of shewing that they were so intended lying on those who assert that they have ceased to be chattels, and that, on the contrary, an article which is affixed to the land even slightly is to be considered as part of the land, unless the circumstances are such as to shew that it was intended all along to continue a chattel, the onus lying on those who contend that it is a chattel. This last proposition seems to be in effect the basis of the judgment of the Court of Common Pleas delivered by Maule J. in *Wilde v. Waters* (1855) 16 C.B. 637; 139 E.R. 909. This, however, only removes the difficulty one step, for it still remains a question in each case whether the circumstances are sufficient to satisfy the onus. In some cases, such as the anchor of the ship or the ordinary instance given of a carpet nailed to the floor of a room, the nature of the thing sufficiently shews it is only fastened as a chattel temporarily, and not affixed permanently as part of the land. But ordinary trade or tenant fixtures which are put up with the intention that they should be removed by the tenant (and so are put up for a purpose in one sense only temporary, and certainly not for the purpose of improving the reversionary interest of the landlord) have always been considered as part of the land, though severable by the tenant. In most, if not all, of such cases the reason why the articles are considered fixtures is probably that indicated by Wood V.-C. in *Boyd v. Shorrock* (1867) L.R. 5 Eq. 72 at 78, that the tenant indicates by the mode in which he puts them up that he regards them as attached to the property during his interest in the property. What we have now to decide is as to the application of these rules to looms put up by the owner of the fee in the manner described in the case. In *Hellawell v. Eastwood* (1851) 6 Ex. 295; 155 E.R. 554 (decided in 1851) the facts as stated in the report are, that the plaintiff held the premises in question as tenant of the defendants, and that a distress for rent had been put in by the defendants under which a seizure was made of cotton-spinning machinery called "mules", some of which were fixed by screws to the wooden floor, and some by screws which had been sunk in the stone floor, and secured by molten lead poured into them. It may be inferred that the plaintiff being the tenant only had put up those mules; and from the large sum for which the distress appears to have been levied (£2,000) it seems probable that he was the tenant of the whole mill. It does not appear what admissions, if any, were made at the trial, nor whether the court had or had not by the reservation power to draw inferences of fact, though it seems assumed in the judgment that they had such a power. Parke B., in delivering the judgment of the court, says, "This is a question of fact depending on the circumstances of each case, and principally on two considerations; first, the mode of annexation to the soil or fabric of the house, and the extent to which it is united to them, whether it can easily be removed integrè salve et commode or not without injury to itself or the fabric of the building; secondly, on the object and purpose of the annexation, whether it was for the permanent and substantial improvement of the dwelling, in the language of the civil law, perpetui usûs causâ, or in that of the year book, pour un profit del inheritance, or merely for a temporary purpose and the more complete enjoyment and use of it as a chattel." It was contended by Mr Field [for the defendants] that the decision in *Hellawell v. Eastwood* (1851) 6 Ex. 295 had been approved in the Queen's Bench in the case of *Turner v. Cameron* (1870) L.R. 5 Q.B. 306. It is quite true that the court in that case said that it afforded a true exposition of the law as applicable to the particular facts upon which the judgment proceeded; but the court expressly guarded their approval by citing from the judgment delivered by Parke B., the facts upon which they considered it to have proceeded: "They were attached slightly so as to be capable of removal without the least injury to the fabric of the building or to themselves, and the object of the annexation was not to improve the inheritance, but merely to render the machines steadier and more capable of convenient use as chattels." As we have already observed, trade or tenant fixtures might in one sense be said to be fixed "merely for a temporary purpose"; but we cannot suppose that the Court of Exchequer meant to decide that they were not part of the land, though liable to be severed by the tenant.

The words "merely for a temporary purpose" must be understood as applying to such a case as we have supposed, of the anchor dropped for the temporary purpose of mooring the ship, or the instance immediately afterwards given by Parke B., of the carpet tacked to the floor for the purpose of keeping it stretched whilst it was there used, and not to a case such as that of a tenant who, for example, affixes a shop counter for the purpose (in one sense temporary) of more effectually enjoying the shop whilst he continues to sell his wares there. Subject to this observation, we think that the passage in the judgment in *Hellawell v. Eastwood* does state the true principles, though it may be questioned if they were in that case correctly applied to the facts. The court in their judgment determine what they have just declared to be a question of fact thus: "The object and purpose of the connection was not to improve the inheritance, but merely to render the machines steadier and more capable of convenient use as chattels." Mr Field was justified in saying, as he did in his argument, that as far as the facts are stated in the report they are very like those in the present case, except that the tenant who put the mules up cannot have been supposed to intend to improve the inheritance (if by that is meant his landlord's reversion), but only at most to improve the property whilst he continued tenant thereof; and he argued with great force that we ought not to act on a sumise that there were any special facts or findings not stated in the report, but to meet the case, as shewing that the judges who decided *Hellawell v. Eastwood* (1851) 6 Ex. 295; 155 E.R. 554 thought that articles fixed in a manner very like those in the case before us remained chattels; and this is felt by some of us at least to be a weighty argument. But that case was decided in 1851. In 1853 the Court of Queen's Bench had, in *Wiltshear v. Cotterill* (1853) 1 El. & Bl. 674; 118 E.R. 589, to consider what articles passed by the conveyance in a fee of a farm. Among the articles in dispute was a threshing machine, which is described in the report thus: "The threshing machine was placed inside one of the barns (the machinery for the horse being on the outside), and there fixed by screws and bolts to four posts which were let into the earth." *Hellawell v. Eastwood* was cited in the argument. The court (without, however, noticing that case) decided that the threshing machine, being so annexed to the land, passed by the conveyance. It seems difficult to point out how the threshing machine was more for the improvement of the inheritance of the farm than the present looms were for the improvement of the manufactory; and in *Mather v. Fraser* (1856) 2 K. & J. 536; 69 E.R. 595 Wood V.-C., who was there judged both of the fact and the law, came to the conclusion that machinery affixed not more firmly than the articles in question by the owner of the fee to land, for the purpose of carrying on a trade there, became part of the land. This was decided in 1856. And in *Walmsley v. Milne* (1859) 7 C.B. (N.S.) 115; 141 E.R. 759 the Court of Common Pleas, after having their attention called to a slight misapprehension by Wood V.-C., of the effect of *Hellawell v. Eastwood* (1851) 6 Ex. 295; 155 E.R. 554, came to the conclusion, as is stated by them (at 131), "that we are of opinion, as a matter of fact, that they were all firmly annexed to the freehold for the purpose of improving the inheritance, and not for any temporary purpose. The bankrupt was the real owner of the premises, subject only to a mortgage which vested the legal title in the mortgagee until the repayment of the money borrowed. The mortgagor first erected baths, stables and a coach-house, and other buildings, and then supplied them with the fixtures in question for their permanent improvement. As to the steam engine and boiler, they were necessary for the use of the baths. The hay-cutter was fixed into a building adjoining the stable as an important adjunct to it, and to improve its usefulness as a stable. The malt-mill and grinding-stones were also permanent erections, intended by the owner to add to the value of the premises. They therefore resemble in no particular (except being fixed to the building by screws) the mules put up by the tenant in *Hellawell v. Eastwood*." It is stated in a note to the report of the case that, on a subsequent day, it was intimated by the court that Willes J. entertained serious doubts as to whether the articles in question were not chattels. The reason of his doubt is not stated, but probably it was from a doubt whether the Exchequer had not, in *Hellawell v. Eastwood*, shewn that they would have thought that the articles were not put up for the purpose of improving the inheritance, and from deference to that authority. The doubt of this learned judge in one view weakens the authority of *Walmsley v. Milne*, but in another view it strengthens it, as it shews that the opinion of the majority, that as a matter of fact the hay-cutter, which was not more firmly fixed than the mules in *Hellawell v. Eastwood*, must be taken to form part of the land, because it was "put up as an adjunct to the stable, and to improve its usefulness as a stable," was deliberately adopted as the basis of the judgment; and it is to be observed that Willes J., though doubting, did not dissent. *Walmsley v. Milne* was decided in 1859. This case and that of *Wiltshear v. Cotterill* (1853) 1 El. & Bl. 674; 118 E.R. 589 seem authorities for this principle, that where an article is affixed by the owner of the fee, though only affixed by bolts and screws, it is to be considered as part of the land, at all events where the object of setting up the articles is to enhance the value of the premises to which it is annexed for the purposes to which those premises are applied. The threshing machine in *Wiltshear v. Cotterill* was affixed by the owner of the fee to the barn as an adjunct to the barn, and to improve its usefulness as a barn, in much the same sense as the hay-cutter in *Walmsley v. Milne* was affixed to the stable as an adjunct to it, and to improve its usefulness as a stable. And it seems difficult to say that the machinery in *Mather v. Fraser* (1856) 2 K. & J. 536; 69 E.R. 595 was not as much affixed to the mill as an adjunct to it and to improve the usefulness of the mill as such, as either the threshing machine or the hay-cutter. If, therefore, the matter were to be decided on principle, without reference to what has since been done on the faith of the decisions, we should be much inclined, notwithstanding the profound respect we feel for everything that was decided by Parke B., to hold that the looms now in question were, as a matter of fact, part of the land. But there is another view of the matter which weighs strongly with us. *Hellawell v. Eastwood* was a decision between landlord and tenant, not so likely to influence those who advance money on mortgage as *Mather v. Fraser*, which was a decision directly between mortgagor and mortgagee. We find that *Mather v. Fraser*, which was decided in 1856, has been acted upon in *Boyd v. Shorrock* (1867) L.R. 5 Eq. 72 by the Court of Queen's Bench in *Longbottom v. Berry* (1869) L.R. 5 Q.B. 123, and in Ireland in *Re Dawson* (1868) Ir. Law Rep. 2 Eq. 218. These cases are too recent to have been themselves much acted upon, but they shew that *Mather v. Fraser* (1856) 2 K. & J. 536; 69 E.R. 595 has been generally adopted as the ruling case. We cannot, therefore, doubt that much money has, during the last 16 years, been advanced on the faith of the decision in *Mather v. Fraser*. It is of great importance that the law as to what is the security of a mortgagee should be settled; and without going so far as to say that a decision only 16 years old should be upheld, right or wrong, on the principle that communis error facit jus, we feel that it should not be reversed unless we clearly see that it is wrong. As already said, we are rather inclined to think that, if it were res integra we should find the same way. We think, therefore, that the judgment below should be affirmed.

LEIGH v. TAYLOR

House of Lords [1902] A.C. 157 at 158

[Madame de Falbe, tenant for life of certain estates, hung in the drawing room of the mansion-house valuable tapestries belonging to her. Strips of wood were placed over the paper which covered the walls and were fastened by nails to the walls. Canvas was stretched over the strips of wood and nailed to them, and the tapestries were stretched over the canvas and fastened by tacks to it and the pieces of wood. Mouldings, resting on the surface of the wall and fastened to it, were placed round each piece of tapestry. The question was whether the tapestries passed to the estate of the life tenant or passed with the inheritance for the benefit of the remainderman.

Byrne J., at first instance, held that the tapestries had become attached to the freehold and passed with it to the remainderman. This decision was reversed by the Court of Appeal, which made an order declaring that the tapestries were chattels belonging to the estate of Madame de Falbe: *Re De Falbe* [1901] 1 Ch. 523. Against this decision an appeal was brought by those representing the remainderman.]

EARL OF HALSBURY L.C. One principle, I think, has been established from the earliest period of the law down to the present time, namely, that if something has been made part of the house it must necessarily go to the heir, because the house goes to the heir and it is part of the house. That seems logical enough. Another principle appears to be equally clear, namely, that where it is something which, although it may be attached in some form or another (I will say a word in a moment about the degree of attachment) to the walls of the house, yet, having regard to the nature of the thing itself, and the purpose of its being placed there, is not intended to form part of the realty, but is only a mode of enjoyment of the thing while the person is temporarily there, and is there for the purpose of his or her enjoyment, then it is removable and goes to the executor.

My Lords, we have heard something about a suggested alteration of the law; but those two principles appear to have been established from the earliest times, and they are principles still in force. But the moment one comes to deal with the facts of each particular case, I quite agree that something has changed very much: I suspect it is not the law or any principle of law, but it is a change in the mode of life, the degree in which certain things have seemed susceptible of being put up as mere ornament, whereas at an earlier period the ruder constructions rendered it impossible sometimes to sever the thing which was put up from the realty. If that is true, it is manifest that you can lay down no rule which will in itself solve the question; you must apply yourself to the facts of each particular case; and I am content here to apply myself to the facts of this case. Here are tapestries which, it is admitted, are worth a great deal of money. I put the case: Suppose this had been a tenant from year to year, and she put up these things, is it conceivable that a person would for the purpose of a tenancy from year to year put up these things exactly in this way if thereby they made a present of £7,000 to the landlord? . . .

[I]n logic I am unable to sever the two sets of facts which I suggest. It is all very well to say that there is a difference between the cases of an heir and an executor on the one hand, and a landlord and a tenant on the other; but if you grant the proposition that it must depend upon the purpose of the annexation, and you must attend to the degree of the annexation, I am wholly unable to frame a hypothesis of a state of things in which these two principles will not decide the question, whether you are dealing with a landlord and tenant, or whether you are dealing with a tenant for life and a remainderman, or with people standing in any other relation to these things. . . .

My Lords, we come then, in my view, to the determination of the question upon the principles I have pointed out, applying them to the particular facts of this case. What are they? Here we have objects of ornamentation of very great value. Undoubtedly their only function in life, if it may be so called, is the decoration of a room. Suppose the person had intended to remove them the next month or the next year or what not, I do not know . . . in what other way they could have been fastened than they were. We have seen the hard matchboard to which they were fastened in the first instance; then canvass was stretched on it, and the decoration of the wall as it originally stood was perfectly preserved except to the extent to which the nails were driven into the wall; they were necessarily driven into the wall, because otherwise the tapestry could not have been stretched out firm, as it was. I do not know any other mode by which the large one, for example, 14 ft long, could have been placed there as it was. One has immediately before one's mind's eye cases of pictures of another sort, and after all, although this tapestry is very valuable, as I understand, and very beautiful, it is only a picture made in a particular form—it is a picture, whether woven or worked or what not, made for the purpose of ornamentation. When one looks at it and sees what it is, I should have thought, if ever there was an extreme case in which it would have been impossible to suppose that the person intended to dedicate it to the house, it was the case of these tapestries, which can be, and in fact have been, removed without anything but the most trifling disturbance of the material of the wall.

Therefore I come to the conclusion that this thing, put up for ornamentation and for the enjoyment of the person while occupying the house, is not under such circumstances as these part of the house. That is the problem one has to solve in each of these cases. If it is not part of the house, it falls under the rule now laid down for some centuries, that it is a sort of ornamental fixture and can be removed by whoever has the right to the chattel—whose it was when it was originally put up. . . .

LORD MACNAGHTEN. My Lords, I am quite of the same opinion.

It seems to me that the only question is, have these tapestries become part of the freehold? I think they were purely matter of ornament, and not part of the freehold at all. Mr Levett has spoken of the courts changing the law. I do not think the law has changed. The change I should say is rather in our habits and mode of life. The question is still as it always was, has the thing in controversy become parcel of the freehold? To determine that question you must have regard to all the circumstances of the particular case—to the taste and fashion of the day as well as to the position in regard to the freehold of the person who is supposed to have made that which was once a mere chattel part of the realty. The mode of annexation is only one of the circumstances of the case, and not always the most important—and its relative importance is probably not what it was in ruder or simpler times. I think the judgments in the Court of Appeal covered the whole ground.

LORD SHAND. My Lords, I am also of opinion that the decision by the Court of Appeal ought to be affirmed.

It may be true, as has been observed by my noble and learned friend on the Woolsack and by my noble and learned friend opposite (Lord Macnaghten), that there has been no change of the law; but I rather think that in the progress of time the law has been developed in the direction of holding what would at one time have been held to be parts of a building to be now temporary fixtures only, removable by the person who attached them to the building or his personal representative, and I think that this later view should be maintained.

It appears to me to be a sound principle, and to be the result of the later cases (whatever may have been the older law), that where a tenant for a time or a tenant for life has purchased tapestries or pictures and affixed them to the walls for the purposes of ornamentation, he is entitled to remove them, and his executor has the same right. That principle, as it seems to me, is decisive of this case.

My Lords, there has been an attempt to shew that there was here such a degree or character of annexation as to make these tapestries permanent additions to the house. I doubt whether there could have been such annexation by a tenant where the purpose of the annexation is ornamental. However firmly a tenant may put up such ornaments as pictures or tapestries upon the walls, I confess I think he is

entitled to remove them, if during his tenancy he desires to do so, in order it may
be to substitute others in their place, or to take them away altogether, and the same
would be true at the end of his tenancy, at least where they are not built in, so as
to be really parts of the permanent building. His position is that of a temporary
occupant, having put up things for temporary purposes. He will be bound to take
care that no damage occurs to the walls which he does not put right; but that is a
different matter from an obligation to leave chattels which have not been build in
as additions to the house, and which remain so when his tenancy ends.

Here, in fact, I think there was no permanent attachment, and I need not repeat
what has been said by my noble and learned friend the Lord Chancellor as to the
character of the attachments.

I entirely agree with the judgment of the Court of Appeal, and with the grounds
upon which the learned judges unanimously proceeded in giving their judgment.

LORD BRAMPTON. My Lords, I am of the same opinion. I entirely agree with the
exhaustive judgments in the Court of Appeal, and I agree also with all the
observations the Lord Chancellor has made with respect to this case.

I confess I see no difficulty about the case myself, and I cannot see in the least
how it can be said that these tapestries could ever have formed a portion of the
house. It is not as if they had been pictures painted upon the walls of the house as
a fresco that could not have been removed. There I can thoroughly understand that
it could not be removed, because you could not remove it without removing part
of the wall itself—in which case you would probably destroy the fresco and injure
the house. But there is no sense in which these tapestries can be said to have been
part of the house, nor do I see how any structural injury to the house could really
be caused by their removal.

LORD ROBERTSON. My Lords, I also concur.

My view is completely represented by the judgment of Stirling L.J.

LORD LINDLEY. My Lords, I am entirely of the same opinion. I can not bring
myself to believe that Madame de Falbe when she put up these tapestries intended
so to fix them as to make them part of the mansion for the benefit of the
remainderman. They remained chattels from first to last.

Order of the Court of Appeal affirmed.

NOTES AND QUESTIONS

1. Were the tapestries held to be removable as chattels or tenants' fixtures? Was the court adopting a
   subjective rather than an objective approach when considering the intent of the life tenant in affixing
   the tapestries? How decisive was it that the tapestries were ornamental? Does the fact that an object
   is ornamental necessarily mean that it has been affixed only for a temporary purpose and consequently
   never passes with the inheritance?

2. Suppose that a testator in his lifetime bought a house in which the former owner had fitted and
   decorated the dining room as a perfect specimen of an Elizabethan room. As part of this scheme of
   decoration, certain pieces of tapestry had been fixed to the walls by being nailed upon wooden frames
   which were kept in their place by mouldings above it which were fastened to the wall by screws. A
   valuable picture of Queen Elizabeth I, painted on wood, was similarly fixed in its place over the
   fireplace by mouldings which had been constructed specially for the picture. The picture and tapestries
   were bought by the testator as part of the house and included in its price. Neither the tapestries nor
   the picture were fastened to the freehold in such a way as to make them irremovable without injury
   to the building. The testator by his will gave his wife all the furniture and chattels in the house and
   devised the house to others. Does the picture and tapestry pass under the gift of chattels to the wife
   or under the devise of the house?

Suppose further that there were, in other rooms in the house, certain ornamental wood carvings which were in place for 200 years. These carvings were affixed to the walls of various rooms by nails or pegs driven through them into stiles built into the walls. However, they were entirely independent of the construction of the house and could be removed without making any difference to the completeness of the panelling in the rooms. Do these carvings pass as part of the gift of chattels or do they form part of the inheritance? See *Re Whaley* [1908] 1 Ch. 615 and *Re Lord Chesterfield's Settled Estates* [1911] 1 Ch. 237.

AUSTRALIAN PROVINCIAL ASSURANCE CO. LTD v. CORONEO

Supreme Court of New South Wales (Full Court) (1938) 38 S.R. (N.S.W.) 700 at 712

[This case involved, inter alia, certain theatre seats in respect of which conversion was complained of by the plaintiff. The plaintiff had the burden of establishing first, that the seats were chattels and secondly, that his common law right to the immediate possession of these chattels was interfered with by reason of certain acts on the part of the defendant company.

When the building had been erected, the plaintiff proceeded to equip it so that it could be used for the display of moving pictures. For this purpose he installed the necessary apparatus, most of which was to a greater or less extent fixed to the building. He also provided a large number of chairs. During his occupancy of the theatre, he used it two days a week for moving pictures, and for the rest of the time it was used for such purposes as concerts, meetings, boxing contests and euchre parties, as opportunity offered. The chairs, which were of two sorts, were fastened together in rows, and these rows were fixed to the floor when the chairs were in use. They were unfixed and moved about as occasion required. For example, when moving pictures were displayed, the best were put at the back and the others at the front, and this order was reversed in the case of concerts. When the euchre parties were given, a large number of the chairs were removed from the body of the hall and stacked at the sides to make room for tables. Sometimes, also, some of the chairs were hired out, which involved their absence from the hall during the period of hire.]

JORDAN C.J. A fixture is a thing once a chattel which has become in law land through having been fixed to land. The question whether a chattel has become a fixture depends upon whether it has been fixed to land, and if so for what purpose. If a chattel is actually fixed to land to any extent, by any means other than its own weight, then prima facie it is a fixture; and the burden of proof is upon anyone who asserts that it is not: if it is not otherwise fixed but is kept in position by its own weight, then prima facie it is not a fixture; and the burden of proof is on anyone who asserts that it is: *Holland v. Hodgson* (1872) L.R. 7 C.P. 328 at 335. The test of whether a chattel which has been to some extent fixed to land is a fixture is whether it has been fixed with the intention that it shall remain in position permanantly or for an indefinite or substantial period (*Holland v. Hodgson* at 336), or whether it has been fixed with the intent that it shall remain in position only for some temporary purpose: *Vaudeville Electric Cinema Ltd v. Muriset* [1923] 2 Ch. 74 at 87. In the former case, it is a fixture, whether it has been fixed for the better enjoyment of the land or building, or fixed merely to steady the thing itself, for the better use or enjoyment of the thing fixed: *Holland v. Hodgson* (1872) L.R. 7 C.P. 328; *Reynolds v. Ashby & Son* [1904] A.C. 466; *Colledge v. H. C. Curlett Construction Co. Ltd* [1932] N.Z.L.R. 1060; *Benger v. Quartermain* [1934] N.Z.L.R. 13. If it is proved to have been fixed merely for a temporary purpose it is not a fixture: *Holland v. Hodgson* at 337; *Vaudeville Electric Cinema Ltd v. Muriset.* The intention of the person fixing it must be gathered from the purpose for which and the time during which user in the fixed position is contemplated: *Hobson v. Gorringe* [1897] 1 Ch. 182; *Pukuweka Sawmills Ltd v. Winger* [1917] N.Z.L.R. 81. If a thing has been securely fixed, and in particular if it has been so fixed that it cannot be detached without substantial injury to the thing itself or to that to which it is attached, this supplies strong but not necessarily conclusive evidence that a permanent fixing was intended: *Holland v. Hodgson*; *Spyer v. Phillipson* [1931] 2 Ch. 183 at 209-210. On the other hand, the fact that the fixing is very slight helps to support an inference that it was not intended to be permanent. But each case depends on its own facts. . . .

In the present case there was evidence that at all relevant times the building in which the alleged chattels had been placed had been used for miscellaneous purposes. At no time since the end of the year 1926 was it used as a picture theatre. Prior to that it was used on some occasions as a picture threatre and on others for purposes which necessitated its being to some extent dismantled as a picture theatre. It appears from evidence which was unchallenged that some articles, the secure and permanent fixing of which was necessary in order that the place could be used for moving pictures at all, were fixed with the evident intention that they should remain in position indefinitely, so as to admit of the use of the place for moving picture purposes as and when occasion might require. To take two instances, there was a switchboard which was admittedly screwed to the wall, and a Crompton generating set, which was admittedly fastened to a concrete bed by means of bolts that went through the concrete. These were evidently intended to remain in position permanently, and have in fact remained in position through all the vicissitudes which the theatre has experienced. A verdict that these are not fixtures cannot be supported. The chairs are in a somewhat different position; and having regard to the evidence as to the purposes for which they were provided and used, and the extent and reason of their fixation on the occasions when they were fixed, I do not think that a verdict that they did not become fixtures is incapable of being supported.

REID v. SMITH

High Court of Australia (1906) 3 C.L.R. 656 at 660

[Smith, the respondent in this appeal from the Supreme Court of Queensland, was the transferee of a lease, granted by the appellant's predecessor in title, which contained a covenant by the lessees to erect on the land a building of a value not less than £50. In pursuance of this covenant, the lessee had already erected on the land a small wooden building, actually affixed to the soil, before the respondent became the transferee. To his he attached another wooden building which he used as a dwelling-house, and on another part of the land he erected another wooden building, also used as a dwelling-house. Both dwelling-houses rested by their own weight on piers or piles. A flight of steps was nailed to the verandah of each building, the bottom tread of which rested on a piece of timber sunk into the ground. In order to check the ravages of white ants, it is the practice in Northern Queensland to build houses upon piers or piles, with iron plates to break the continuity between the superstructure and the ground. The question as to whether the buildings were fixtures arose out of a suit for an injunction by the appellant to restrain the respondent from removing the buildings at the termination of the tenancy.]

GRIFFITH C.J. Now, the rule relied upon by the defendant in support of his claim to remove the buildings is a rule of common law. He contends that it is a rule that chattels of any kind placed upon the soil, but not annexed to it, remain chattels. . . . In the present case the original building was erected under a building lease, and it is not disputed that it must be regarded as having become annexed to the freehold. It happens that there were only one or two nails driven into the stumps, but, apart from that, it is conceded that, having been put there with the intention that it should become part of the freehold, it did become part of the freehold. In front of this building, which was of comparatively small value, a dwelling-house was erected afterwards, which was attached to the original building. The mode of attachment is not clear, but it is found that it was attached; so that, prima facie, this building is also attached to the freehold, although, as a matter of fact, it is not nailed to the supports on which it rests. That building may be said, from one point of view, to be attached in part to the freehold, and in part to be not attached. The other dwelling-house only differs in that it all rests on its own weight on the piers. It is not distinguishable from the first by the passer-by. We have, then, two similar buildings on the same piece of land, and anyone on passing would take them to be houses of the same kind, but one of them, it is said, belongs in part only to the freehold, and the other not at all; and, in order to discover whether it does or does not, according to the suggested rule you must disturb the house, because you cannot tell whether there is any annexation of the wooden structure to the piers without taking down the structure, or taking away the pier, or making some investigation of that sort. It would be a singular thing if the question whether a building is part of the freehold or not should depend upon a fact which can only be ascertained by a partial destruction of the building itself. Again, suppose in such a case the owner made a devise of his real estate to one person, and of his personal estate to another—according to the suggested rule, the legatee of the personal estate might remove the buildings, and if the owner had demised them in his lifetime, the tenant would have two lessors, one his landlord as to the land, and another his landlord with respect to the buildings. Again, if the property remains a chattel, and, apparently, subject to the *Bills of Sale Act* 1893 (U.K.), it could not pass under a real property mortgage. It would have a singularly disturbing effect on the securities of a great number of institutions established for the purpose of encouraging the erection of houses—most of which in Queensland are wooden houses—if it were declared that such houses are only chattels. I may remark in passing that the reason in Queensland why wooden buildings of this sort are frequently not fixed by spikes or nails to the piers or stumps, is in order to break the continuity between the ground and the woodwork, so that white ants may not be able to reach the wood. Generally iron plates are placed on the top of the piers or stumps, and if there is any hole made in them at all there is a danger that the white ants may get through and get at the building itself. These considerations make me hesitate to hold that a structure of this sort is not part of the freehold. . . .

Very few cases have arisen, as I said, where the question was as to things that were not fixed to the ground. It was supposed at one time that that was an imperative condition. The first doubt perhaps, to be found in any recorded case is suggested in the well-known passage from the judgment of Blackburn J., in the case of *Holland v. Hodgson* (1872) L.R. 7 C.P. 328 at 334. That was a decision of the Court of Exchequer Chamber, and it is binding in England upon all the courts, until it is overruled by the House of Lords, which, I think, is extremely unlikely to happen. He said, in a passage quoted by Chubb J.: "There is no doubt that the general maxim of the law is, that what is annexed to the land becomes part of the land; but it is very difficult, if not impossible, to say with precision what constitutes an annexation sufficient for this purpose. It is a question which must depend on the circumstances of each case, and mainly on two circumstances, as indicating the intention, viz., the degree of annexation and the object of the annexation. When the article in question is no further attached to the land than by its own weight, it is generally to be considered a mere chattel: see *Wiltshear v. Cottrell* (1853) 1 El. & Bl. 674; 118 E.R. 589 and the cases there cited. But even in such a case, if the intention is apparent to make the articles part of the land, they do become part of the land.'' That is a distinct recognition of the possibility that property might become part of the freehold, without being actually annexed to the land. . . .

The earliest forms of structure, or some of the earliest familiar to us in this country, are what are called slab buildings. They are fixed to the freehold, because the slabs are let into the ground. There is, perhaps, an earlier form of structure—a structure consisting of rough saplings let into the ground side by side. I have seen many structures of that kind, which were undoubtedly fixtures; and, as civilization advanced, a more comfortable and more permanent style of building was adopted; yet, according to the contention in this case, that would not be a fixture, but remains a mere chattel. In the present case, the original building was spoken of by the learned judge as if it was obviously part of the freehold, and as if it was quite sufficient to show that a thing was attached to the house to show that it also becomes part of the freehold. Of course, that is not conclusive. In America, the law appears to be in accordance with what one would expect it to be. We were referred to the *State Savings Bank v. Kircheval* 27 Am. Rep. 310 at 312, which is a decision of the Supreme Court of Missouri. That is valuable as containing a statement of what, in the American States, is the law on this subject. The learned judge, in delivering the judgment of the court, quotes from the decisions of other courts. He first quotes this passage: ''The destination which gives a movable object an immovable character, results from facts and circumstances determined by the law itself, and could neither be established nor taken away by the simple declaration of the proprietor, whether oral or written.'' After mentioning *Snedeker v. Warring* 2 Kernan 178, he said: ''In *Goff v. O'Connor* 16 Ill. 422 the court said: 'Houses in common intendment of the law are not fixtures but part of the land. . . . This does not depend, in the case of houses, so much upon the particular mode of attaching, or fixing and connecting them with the land, upon which they stand or rest, as upon the uses and purposes for which they are erected and designed.' In *Cole v. Stewart* 11 Cush. 182 the building was intended by the owner to be temporary, and was built with a view to ultimate removal. In a contest between the mortgagee, whose mortgage was executed subsequent to the erection of the house, and a purchaser of the building from the mortgagor, it was held to be a fixture. In the light of these cases, and many others which we have examined, we do not regard the fact that the building in question was erected as a temporary building, and with an intention of ultimate removal, at all decisive as to whether it became a part of the realty or not. The manner in which a building is placed upon land whether upon wooden posts, or a rock, or brick foundation, does not determine its character. As was said by Parker J., in *Snedeker v. Warring* above cited: 'A thing may be as firmly fixed to the land by gravitation as by clamps or cement. Its character may depend upon the object of its erection.' In *Teaff v. Hewitt* 1 Ohio St. 511 it was held that: 'The intention of the party making the annexation to make the article a permanent accession to the freehold, this intention to be inferred from the nature of the article affixed, the relation and situation of the party making the annexation, the structure and mode of annexation, and the purpose and use of which the annexation has been made,' is a controlling circumstance in determining whether the structure is to be regarded as a fixture or not.''

I agree, therefore, in the conclusion the learned judge came to, that, the question being as stated by Blackburn J., there is a general principle that, if buildings are not actually annexed to the freehold, the onus may probably lie upon the person claiming them as real property to show affirmatively that they were erected with the intention that they should become part of the land. I differ from the learned judge in thinking that it is not sufficient to show that the thing in question is a dwelling-house—an ordinary dwelling-house, on a town allotment, in an inhabited town. In the case of a similar building in another part of the country, erected under entirely different circumstances, a different conclusion might be drawn. For instance, in the case of a manager's house, erected on a gold-mining lease, the same conclusion might not necessarily follow. But in the present case, it appears to me that the proper inference to be drawn from the facts is that these houses became part of the freehold. I think, indeed, this case might be rested even on narrower grounds. This was, as I said, a building lease, and although the tenant, of whom the defendant is the assignee, was bound by the covenants of the lease only to erect a building of £50 in value, I think it ought to be inferred from the lease itself that the intention was that any dwelling-house put on the land should be considered annexed to the freehold. For these reasons I think that the conclusion of the learned judge was erroneous, and that the appeal must be allowed.

[Barton and O'Connor JJ. delivered separate but concurring judgments.]

QUESTION

The lessee under a lease for five years of a station property erects a manager's house. The house, a prefabricated structure, is erected in two hours, rests on brick piers by its own weight, and is completely detachable from its plumbing and electrical connections. The lessee, at the end of the lease, wishes to remove the house. It was always his intention to remove the house when the lease terminated. Is he entitled to remove it?

HOBSON v. GORRINGE

Court of Appeal [1897] 1 Ch. 182 at 188

[Hobson let a gas engine to King, the owner of a mill, on hire-purchase. The terms of the hiring agreement were that King would pay the price of the gas engine by instalments, upon completion of which the ownership of the engine would pass to King, with the proviso that should King fail to pay the instalments, Hobson should be at liberty to repossess and remove the engine. The engine was brought onto the premises and bolted onto iron plates which were set into a concrete bed; the purpose was to prevent the engine from rocking and shifting when in use. Subsequently, King mortgaged the premises to Gorringe. King defaulted under both the hiring agreement and the mortgage. The mortgagee entered and took possession of the mortgaged premises together with the gas engine. Kekewich J. held that Gorringe, the mortgagee, was entitled to the proceeds of the sale of the engine. Hobson appealed.]

SMITH L.J. (delivering the judgment of the court). The question is whether Mr Gorringe is entitled, under the above circumstances, to the gas engine. It is not disputed that he is entitled to the land; but the plaintiff, Mr Hobson, denies that he is entitled to the gas engine upon the ground that it had never become King's, and had always remained a chattel belonging to him, Hobson. There can be no doubt, upon a mortgage in fee of the land, that, as between the mortgagor and mortgagee, the mortgagee is entitled to all fixtures which may be upon the land, whether placed there before or after the mortgage. . . . It is said that this gas engine never was a fixture, but always remained a chattel, and consequently never passed to Gorringe as mortgagee of the land. It obviously did not pass to him as a chattel under the mortgage to him of "fixed machinery", for, if a chattel, it ever remained Hobson's, and never was the property of King; and unless Mr Gorringe takes the engine as part of the land mortgaged to him he does not take it at all. Now, leaving out of consideration for the present the hire and purchase agreement of 7 January 1895, there is a sequence of authorities which established that the gas engine, affixed as it was and for the purpose for which it was to King's freehold, ceased to be a chattel and become part of the freehold.

[His Lordship then referred, inter alia, to *Wiltshear v. Cottrell* (1853) 1 El. & Bl. 674 at 688; 118 E.R. 589 at 694-695; *Mather v. Fraser* (1856) 2 K. & J. 536; 69 E.R. 595; *Walmsley v. Milne* (1859) 7 C.B. (N.S.) 115; 141 E.R. 759; see above p. 16 et seq.]

But it was argued that the terms of the hiring and purchase agreement caused this engine to remain a chattel, notwithstanding its annexation to the soil, for it was said that the intention of the parties who placed it where it was must be considered, and if this consideration shewed that the intention was that the chattel was not to be a fixture, though actually fixed to the freehold, it still remained a chattel. In support of this argument a passage in the judgment of Lord Blackburn (then Blackburn J.), when delivering the judgment of the Exchequer Chamber in *Holland v. Hodgson* (1872) L.R. 7 C.P. 328, was quoted. That learned judge, when dealing with what were or were not fixtures, says (at 335): "Perhaps the true rule is, that articles not otherwise attached to the land than by their own weight are not to be considered as part of the land, unless the circumstances are such as to shew that they were intended to be part of the land, the onus of shewing that they were so intended lying on those who assert that they have ceased to be chattels, and that, on the contrary, an article which is affixed to the land even slightly is to be considered as part of the land, unless the circumstances are such as to shew that it was intended all along to continue a chattel, the onus lying on those who contend that it is a chattel." The question in each case is whether the circumstances are sufficient to satisfy the onus.

It is said on behalf of the plaintiff that the hire and purchase agreement shews an intention on Mr Hobson's part, as also on King's part, that the gas engine should remain a chattel until King had paid the stipulated instalments, which he never did. Now, if the engine had been a trade fixture, erected by King as tenant, with a limited interest, we apprehend that when affixed to the soil, as it was, it would have become a fixture—that is, part of the soil, and would immediately have vested in the owner of the soil, subject to the right of King to remove it during his term. "Such," says Lord Chelmsford, in *Bain v. Brand* (1876) 1 App. Cas. 762 at 772, "is the general law. But an exception has been long established in favour of a tenant erecting fixtures for the purposes of trade, allowing him the privilege of removing them during the continuance of the term. When he brings any chattel to be used in his trade and annexes it to the ground it becomes a part of the freehold, but with a power as between himself and his landlord of bringing it back to the state of a chattel again by severing it from the soil. As the personal character of the chattel ceases when it is fixed to the freehold, it can never be revived as long as it continues so annexed."

It seems to us that the true view of the hiring and purchase agreement, coupled with the annexation of the engine to the soil which took place in this case, is that the engine became a fixture—that is, part of the soil—when it was annexed to the soil by screws and bolts, subject as between Hobson and King to this, that Hobson had the right by contract to unfix it and take possession of it if King failed to pay him the stipulated monthly instalments. In our opinion, the engine became a fixture—that is, part of the soil—subject to this right of Hobson which was given him by contract. But this right was not an easement created by deed, nor was it conferred by a covenant running with the land. The right, therefore, to remove the fixture imposed no legal obligation on any grantee from King of the land. Neither could the right be enforced in equity against any purchaser of the land without notice of the right, and the defendant Gorringe is such a purchaser. The plaintiff's right to remove the chattel if not paid for cannot be enforced against the defendant, who is not bound either at law or in equity by King's contract. The plaintiff's remedy for the price or for damages for the loss of the chattel is by action against King, or, he being bankrupt, by proof against his estate.

This, in our judgment, is sufficient to determine this case in favour of the defendant: but as another point has been stoutly argued on behalf of the plaintiff, we will deal with it. It is said that the intention that the gas engine was not to become a fixture might be got out of the hire and purchase agreement, and, if so, it never became a fixture and part of the soil, and it was said that the case of *Holland v. Hodgson* (1872) L.R. 7 C.P. 328 had so decided. For this point it must be assumed that such intention is manifested by the hiring and purchase agreement, though, as before stated, we think it is not. Now, in *Holland v. Hodgson*, Lord Blackburn, when dealing with the "circumstances to shew intention," was contemplating and referring to circumstances which shewed the degree of annexation and the object of such annexation which were patent for all to see, and not to the circumstances of a chance agreement that might or might not exist between an owner of a chattel and a hirer thereof. This is made clear by the examples that Lord Blackburn alludes to to shew his meaning. He takes as instances (a) blocks of stone placed in position as a dry stone wall or stacked in a builder's yard; (b) a ship's anchor affixed to the soil, whether to hold a ship riding thereto or to hold a suspension bridge. In each of these instances it will be seen that the circumstance to shew intention is the degree and object of the annexation which is in itself apparent, and thus manifested the intention. Lord Blackburn in his proposed rule was not contemplating a hire and purchase agreement between the owner of a chattel and a hirer or any other agreement unknown to either a vendee or mortgagee in fee of land, and the argument that such a consideration was to be entertained, in our judgment, is not well founded.

. . . That a person can agree to affix a chattel to the soil of another so that it becomes part of that other's freehold upon the terms that the one shall be at liberty in certain events to retake possession we do not doubt, but how a de facto fixture becomes not a fixture or is not a fixture as regards a purchaser of land for value without notice by reason of some bargain between the affixers we do not understand, nor has any authority to support this contention been adduced. For the above reasons in our judgment the gas engine became affixed to and was part of King's freehold, and thus passed to Mr Gorringe as mortgagee in fee of King's land.

Appeal dismissed.

NOTES AND QUESTIONS

1. Is the nature of the intention which determines whether a chattel has become a fixture identical to that required in the case of an affixation by a limited owner? What factors are considered in determining an objective intention?

2. Suppose that X, an owner of a service station, enters into an agreement for the loan of a petrol storage tank which is buried in the ground under a concrete slab and that under the loan agreement, the lender, Y, is to retain ownership of the tank with a right to enter onto the land at the expiration of the loan agreement to remove the tank. Suppose further that X enters into a short term lease with Z and that during that lease the lender of the tank, Y, becomes entitled under the agreement with X to enter the land and remove the tank. Is the law of fixtures relevant to this problem? If so, could the tenant, Z, argue that the tank is a fixture so that, as against Z, the lender, Y, cannot remove the

tank? In that event does it matter that Z was aware of the terms of the agreement between X and Y? Consider *Deventer Pty Ltd v. B.P. Australia Ltd* (1983) Q. Conv. R. 54-104 at 56,600. Do you agree with the decision in that case?

3. How is s. 13 of the *Credit Act* 1984 (N.S.W.) relevant to whether a chattel passes with the land to which it has become annexed?

    The section provides as follows:

    13. (1) A contract for the hiring of goods shall be deemed to be a credit sale contract if—

    (a) the cash price of the goods at the time when the contract for the hiring is made is not more than $20,000 or the goods are, or include, a commercial vehicle or farm machinery in relation to which the cash price is more than $20,000; and

    (b) under the contract the person to whom the goods are hired has a right, obligation or option to purchase the goods.

    (2) A contract for the hiring of goods shall be deemed to be a credit sale contract if the cash price of the goods at the time the contract is made is not more than $20,000 or the goods are a commercial vehicle or farm machinery and—

    (a) the contract provides, or it is reasonably likely having regard to the nature of the goods that the goods are, or are to be, affixed to land or to other goods and the goods are not, or when so affixed would not be, reasonably capable of being re-delivered to the supplier;

    (b) before the contract is made, the supplier—

      (i) acts in such a manner that the person to whom the goods are hired ought reasonably to infer that the supplier is willing, whether during or within a reasonable time after the period during which the contract is in force, to negotiate the sale to him of the goods or of goods of a value and description similar to the value and description of the goods to which the contract relates (being a value and description as at the time the contract is made); and

      (ii) expects, or in the circumstances ought reasonably to expect, that the person to whom the goods are hired will negotiate the purchase by him of the goods or of goods of such a similar value and description; or

    (c) before the contract is made, it is agreed that the person to whom the goods are hired may continue the contract for a nominal consideration for a period that exceeds, or for two or more periods that together exceed, the period of two years after the expiration of the original term of the contract for the hiring.

    (3) Where a contract for the hiring of goods is by this section deemed to be a credit sale contract—

    (a) the person from whom the goods are hired is the credit provider under the credit sale contract;

    (b) the person to whom the goods are hired is the debtor under the credit sale contract;

    (c) the cash price of the goods for the purposes of the credit sale contract is the cash price in relation to the contract for the hiring;

    (d) the instalments payable under the contract for the hiring are instalments payable under the credit sale contract;

    (e) the property of the supplier in the goods passes under the contract to the person to whom the goods are hired upon delivery of the goods or the making of the contract whichever last occurs;

    (f) a mortgage containing the prescribed terms and conditions shall be deemed to have been entered into in writing between the person to whom the goods are hired and the supplier as security for payment to the supplier of the amount payable to him by the person to whom the goods are hired under the contract; and

    (g) any provision in the contract for hiring by virtue of which the supplier is empowered to take possession, or dispose of, the goods to which the contract relates is void.

    (4) Subsection (2) does not apply to a contract for the hiring of goods that are or might reasonably be expected to be used by the person to whom they are hired for the purpose of a business carried on by him or by him and another person or other persons, where the whole or the greater part of the amount payable under the contract is, or might reasonably be expected to be, a loss or outgoing necessarily incurred in carrying on the business.

(5) In this section—

    (a) a reference to a contract for the hiring of goods does not include—

        (i) a reference to a contract for the hiring of goods to a body corporate; or

        (ii) a reference to a contract for the hiring of goods to the extent that the financial accommodation provided in relation to the goods is not credit within the meaning of this Act; and

    (b) "cash price", in relation to a contract for the hiring of goods—

        (i) where at the time the contract is made the goods are available for purchase for cash from the person from whom the goods are hired—means the lowest price at which the person to whom the goods are hired might have bought the goods from the first-mentioned person for cash;

        (ii) where at the time the contract is made the goods are reasonably available for purchase for cash but are not reasonably available for purchase for cash from the person from whom the goods are hired—means the price at which, at that time, the person to whom the goods are hired might reasonably have bought goods of that kind for cash; or

        (iii) where at the time the contract is made the goods are not reasonably available for purchase for cash—means the amount that is the reasonable value of the goods at that time.

BAIN v. BRAND

House of Lords (1876) 1 App. Cas. 762 at 766

[Certain machinery was erected and used by a lessee of a colliery. The lessee died and, under the law of Scotland, the balance of the term in the lease passed to the heir. The question was whether the machinery passed to the heir or whether it could be severed and taken by the executors of the personal estate of the deceased tenant. The machinery was annexed to the land for the purpose of working the colliery and was capable of being removed either in its entire state or by being taken to pieces without material injury.]

THE LORD CHANCELLOR. My Lords, the case therefore being, in my opinion, uncovered by any decision which has settled the law upon the subject, I have to proceed to look at it in point of principle. Looking at it in that way, I would remind your Lordships that there are, with regard to matters of this kind, which are included under the comprehensive term of "fixtures", two general rules, a correct appreciation of which will, as it seems to me, go far to solve the whole difficulty in this case. My Lords, one of those rules is the general well-known rule that whatever is fixed to the freehold of land becomes part of the freehold or inheritance. The other is quite a different and separate rule—whatever once becomes part of the inheritance cannot be severed by a limited owner, whether he be owner for life or for years, without the commission of that which, in the law of England, is called waste, and which, according to the law both of England and Scotland, is undoubtedly an offence which can be restrained. Those, my Lords, are two rules, not one by way of exception to the other, but two rules standing consistently together. My Lords, an exception indeed, and a very important exception, has been made, not to the first of these rules, but to the second. To the first rule which I have stated to your Lordships there is, so far as I am aware, no exception whatever. That which is fixed to the inheritance becomes a part of the inheritance at the present day as much as it did in the earliest times. But to the second rule, namely, the irremoveability of things fixed to the inheritance, there is undoubtedly ground for a very important exception. That exception has been established in favour of fixtures which have been attached to the inheritance for the purposes of trade, and perhaps in a minor degree for the purpose of agriculture. Under that exception a tenant who has fixed to the inheritance things for the purpose of trade has a certain power of severance and removal during the tenancy. What extent of removal the executor of one who is not a tenant, but is a complete owner of the inheritance, may have as against the heir, whether in point of fact he has any right of removal at all, or any right to take more than that which really and properly considered was never fixed to the inheritance in a definite way, I need not stop to consider, because the case of *Fisher v. Dixon* (1845) 5 Dunlop 775 has clearly decided by the authority of your Lordships that fixtures of the kind now before your Lordships cannot be removed by the executor of one who is complete owner of the inheritance.

Therefore your Lordships have upon the one hand the rule as laid down in the case of *Fisher v. Dixon*, that fixtures of the present kind cannot be removed by the executor as against the heir of the complete owner of the inheritance, and you have on the other hand the exception to which I have referred, that fixtures of this kind can be removed by the executor of a tenant, or by the tenant himself as against the landlord during the course of the tenancy. But your Lordships have here to consider an intermediate case between those two. You have not to consider the case of the person who represents the entire inheritance, but you have to consider the case not of the whole inheritance but of a heritable subject, namely, a lease which is heritable according to Scottish law, upon the ground included in which fixtures of the kind I have referred to have been erected: and you have to determine whether, the tenant having died, and the lease still continuing, and the lease having passed to the heir, the executor has as against that heir a right to remove those fixtures. There is certainly no authority for saying that the executor can remove these fixtures as against the heir. In my opinion there is no principle in the rules which I have endeavoured to express which can warrant that right of removal. These things which I have termed fixtures are ex hypothesi annexed to the inheritance at the time of the death of the tenant. Thereupon the heritable subject, namely, the lease, at once passes to his heir. What right has the executor, or how is that right founded, to come upon the heritable subject which has passed to the heir, and to strip it of those things which have become fixed to it? There is no doubt, ex hypothesi, a right to remove these fixtures as against the landlord, but who is the person to exercise that right? It is not a right in gross, it is not a right collateral to the ownership of the subject, it is a right which of necessity must be annexed to the ownership of the subject, and must be exercised by him who is the owner of the subject. But the owner of the subject is not the executor. The owner of the subject is the heir, and therefore, as it seems to me, your Lordships are obliged to consider the person to whom the subject itself has passed, and to hold the right which is annexed to that subject to be exercisable by that person, and by that person only. . . .

Therefore, my Lords, without pursuing the subject further, I submit to your Lordships that upon principle it is impossible to justify the right of the executors in this case. . . .

Lord Gifford [in the Court of Session] appears to assume that you are to determine at the moment the fixture is placed in the soil what is to be its destiny during the whole of the lease, and he asserts that it never becomes attached to the inheritance so as to be capable of being called a part of the inheritance—that it remains quoad omnia moveable and amongst the moveables of the tenant. My Lords, it appears to me that that is an error; it does become attached to the inheritance. The fixture does become part of the inheritance; it does not remain a moveable quoad omnia; there does exist on the part of the tenant a right to remove that which has been thus fixed, but if he does not exercise that right it continues to be that which it became when it was first fixed, a part of the inheritance.

[Similar judgments were delivered by Lords Chelmsford, O'Hagan and Selbourne.]

NOTE

The result was that the machinery affixed to the leasehold property passed as fixtures to the heir of the lessee, and not to the executors of the lessee; the question of the removability of the machinery as trade fixtures could only arise as between the heir of the lessee and the owner of the freehold and not, as in this case, as between the heir (devisee) and the other beneficiaries of the deceased lessee.

SPYER v. PHILLIPSON

Court of Appeal [1931] 2 Ch. 183 at 204

[The lessee of a flat, which he held for a term of 21 years, without the consent of the lessor, installed in some of the rooms certain valuable antique panelling, ornamental chimney pieces and so-called "period" fireplaces. No portion of the structure of these rooms was altered in order to fix the panelling, but it was placed in position by inserting into the walls wooden plugs to which it was attached by screws. Some slight structural alteration was effected in fixing the new chimney pieces and fireplaces.

Expert witnesses said that the method stated to be employed was the ordinary way of affixing panelling to rooms already built, whether it was to be fixed permanently or for a temporary purpose. The lessee having died during the currency of the term, his executors claimed the right to remove the panelling, chimney pieces and fireplaces, alleging that these installations were tenant's fixtures, and as such removable by them. The lessor, on the other hand, contended that the panelling and chimney pieces had been fixed and installed in such a way as to become part of the structure of the demised premises; that their removal would cause damage to the structure; that the installations by the lessee constituted landlord's fixtures, and that his executors were not entitled to remove them. Luxmoore J. at first instance held that the panelling, chimney pieces and fireplaces were removable by the defendants. The plaintiff appealed.]

LORD HANWORTH M.R. After reading the judgment of Luxmoore J. I should be prepared really to leave the matter where he has left it; he has recounted the facts and given, if I may respectfully say so, a lucid judgment upon the law to which it seems unnecessary to add anything. In deference, however, to the arguments that we have had from Mr Macaskie and from Mr Slade, I will venture to add a few remarks in support of the judgment which we are now affirming. It is a mere truism to say that in our law anything that is affixed to the freehold passes with the freehold and cannot, as a rule, be removed or severed from the freehold. But upon that there have been engrafted a number of exceptions, relating to fixtures which have been put in either by the craftsman who has been working in the house, the tenant who has been occupying it, or by a tenant for life. In all those cases a number of exceptions have been engrafted, enabling the tenant to remove what has been put into the premises, not for the purpose of final inclusion in their structure, but in order that the tenant might enjoy them more freely. The question that we have to determine in this case is, do the facts which are before us compel the inference that this panelling was fixed, so that the removal of it was no longer contemplated; that the panelling had been finally made an integral part of the dwelling-rooms; or is the right inference that the panelling had been put up with the intention on the part of the tenant of removing it as and when he was minded so to do, and that the affixing of the panelling was only for the purpose of the complete enjoyment by the tenant of that expensive panelling? It is to be remembered that this claim on the part of the representatives of the tenant is made during the currency of the term. Different considerations apply where the tenant has not attempted to exercise his right until after the expiration of the term.

We have had our attention called to a number of cases, but those cases are illustrations of how the law upon this subject has gradually been relaxed in favour of the tradesman and certainly largely in favour of the tenant. When we look at the cases themselves it will be found that tenants have been allowed to remove matters of ornament which for their enjoyment required very considerable affixture to the premises. In particular, going as far back as 1703, we find a catalogue of such matters as chimney pieces, wainscots, chimney glasses, pier glasses, hangings and the like, which have been allowed to be taken away. I pause for a moment at chimney pieces, because certainly for the safe enjoyment of such structures it is necessary that very substantial attachment of them should be provided. Here we have this panelling fixed in the rooms, and it has been fixed, as appears from the evidence, in the only way that it could be properly fixed, whether it was set up for permanence or whether it was set up with a view to its removal. Attention has been rightly called to the fact that not only has the panelling been set up, but there have been structural alterations made to the aperture for the fireplaces and chimney pieces, that the furnishings of the windows have been removed, and also that there have been ceilings attached to the original ceilings, so as to make them more in keeping with the proper period to which the panelling belonged. One little point arises upon that to which I think it is worth while calling attention, a point which I made in the course of the argument. That is, that if, in the report of Mr Head, an examination be made of his little sketch, whereby, I think it is in room A, it is seen how the panelling is set up and the frieze above it attached to the wall, it will be observed that instead of attaching that frieze to the substance of the wall itself care was taken to make a temporary structure of framed canvas, bringing that forward, so that the wall as it stood was allowed to remain in its original condition behind the frieze. It is said that that was necessary in order that the frieze might be as nearly as may be in a vertical line with the panelling, but again I am by no means satisfied that what I have called the bracket which runs round the top of the panelling was a part of the original panelling, or whether that was not a part which had necessarily to be superimposed in order to fit the old panelling together. But in any event it seems to me that that structure for the purpose of carrying the frieze was of the nature of a temporary structure, faithfully preserving the moulding behind it, whereas a simpler, a more durable, and possibly less expensive method might have been adopted, unless a marked intention had been revealed to make the totality of the structure one which could be afterwards taken down.

I do not think we need go back in the cases beyond the tapestries case of *Re De Falbe* [1901] 1 Ch. 523. In that case it is quite right to observe that there was a much lighter method of affixing than has been here adopted, but when one looks at the judgment of Vaughan Williams L.J. he says (at 534): "There is this amount of consistency" in the cases, "that, starting with the absolutely rigid rule, 'Quicquid plantatur solo solo cedit,' there has been a consistent progress towards relaxation of that rule, and in my view there has never been any substantial intermission of that relaxation". An obvious observation falls to be made. He is speaking in 1901, I am speaking in 1931, a generation later. If therefore this case is not, perhaps, exactly within the decision or the rule in the *De Falbe* case (though I think it is), yet it would only be another illustration that there has been a consistent progress towards the relaxation of the rule against tenants being required to hand over their fitments to the landlord. He says (at 536): "In dealing with the question of fixtures it sometimes becomes material to consider the object and purpose of the annexation, by which I do not mean that there must be an inquiry into the motive of the person who annexed them, but a consideration of the object and purpose of the annexation as it is to be inferred from the circumstances of the case." Then he adds (at 536): "That being so, it is impossible to say that the only matter to be taken into consideration is the quantum of fixture." The observation there made is approved and followed by Lord Macnaghten in his speech in that same case when it was before the House of Lords, sub nom. *Leigh v. Taylor* [1902] A.C. 157. He says this (at 162): "The mode of annexation is only one of the circumstances of the case, and not always the most important—and its relative importance is probably not what it was in ruder or simpler times." We have therefore a rule showing that the tenant's right has been consistently, steadily and progressively enlarged, that the quantum of attachment is a factor, but not more than a factor, and not always the most important factor for decision. Then what are the other factors to consider? I think one must consider: Why was the article or ornament ever brought into the flat at all? Was it for the permanent enhancement of the building itself, or was it for the enjoyment of the ornament itself? In the same case Lord Halsbury says (at 161): "The principle appears to me to be the same today as it was in the early times, and the broad principle is that, unless it has become part of the house in any intelligible sense, it is not a thing which passes to the heir. I am of opinion that this tapestry has not become part of the house, and was never intended in any way to become part of the house; and I am, therefore, of opinion that this appeal ought to be dismissed", and he says that the rule, whether it be between tenant for life and remainderman, or whether it be between landlord and tenant concerning the attachment and so on of these factors is practically the same. With that guidance before us, and with the definition of "fixtures" which Stirling L.J. in *Re De Falbe* [1901] 1 Ch. 523 at 538 gives in that case, which is also quoted, I observe, by Luxmoore J., " 'they are articles which were originally personal chattels, and which, although they have been annexed to the freehold by a temporary occupier, are nevertheless removable, and of course saleable, at the will of the person who has annexed them,' " I ask myself the question: Is there any evidence such as to compel one to come to the conclusion that this expensive panelling was put up some ten or a dozen years before the expiration of the lease in order that the value of the flat might be enhanced for the benefit of the landlord, rather than put up for the purpose of the enjoyment of those ornaments by the tenant himself? Ornaments may vary from one generation to another, but it would appear that at the present time devices are resorted to to make a room look as our ancestors 100 or 200 or 300 years ago would have liked it to look. That is still a matter of ornament at the present time.

The criticism that has been made, and quite fairly made, by Mr Macaskie that you find the tenant doing very considerable injury to the premises by abstracting the skirting boards and the fitments of the windows and the like, has, to my mind, but little bearing upon the problem. Quite true it is that the tenant thereby exposed himself to a liability for breach of covenant, and involved himself in a liability of replacement to a value which may be not inconsiderable; yet all those are matters of detail, detailed risks which the tenant might be prepared to run in order to be able to set up this ornament that he wanted to enjoy. He may have been quite conscious that he was committing a breach of covenant in cutting away these details, but ready to run the risk, for at any time he could, of course, on terms have obtained relief from the proviso for re-entry, which was the safeguard against his committing this breach of the covenant. On these grounds it appears to me that the tenant has not lost his right of removal, that although he is liable to reinstate the premises you cannot deduce from that an intention on his part—or rather, to use the words of

Vaughan Williams L.J., you cannot infer that the object and purpose of the annexation was to benefit the premises and the landlord rather than for the purposes of his own temporary enjoyment. . . .

ROMER L.J. I agree. I merely desire to say this. Luxmoore J., in the course of his judgment and after referring to the well-known passage in Parke B.'s judgment in *Hellawell v. Eastwood* (1851) 6 Ex. 295 at 312; 155 E.R. 554 at 561, said: "I think in fact, that these are not two considerations, but really only one consideration; what was the object and purpose of the annexation?; and that among the matters which have to be considered in coming to a conclusion in answer to the question, what was the object and purpose of the annexation, are first the mode of annexation, and secondly, what would happen if the mode of annexation were severed, and it is sought to take the particular things away." Speaking for myself, I think that that is a correct statement of the law. So long as the article can be removed without doing irreparable damage to the demised premises I do not think that either the method of annexation or the degree of annexation, or the quantum of damage that would be done to the article itself or to the demised premises by its removal, has really any bearing upon the question of the tenant's rights to remove, except in so far as they throw light upon the question of the intention with which the chattel was affixed by him to the demised premises. That, I think, is entirely consistent with the view that was expressed by Vaughan Williams L.J. in his judgment in *Re De Falbe* [1901] 1 Ch. 523.

[Lawrence J. was of the same view.]

Appeal dismissed.

NOTES AND QUESTIONS

1. Did the court in *Spyer v. Phillipson* adopt the correct approach in determining the removability of the items? Do you see an alternative and preferable approach which would have resulted in the same conclusion? The court referred to annexure for the better enjoyment of the thing itself and annexure for a temporary purpose. Are these to be regarded as tests for determining whether a fixture is a tenant's fixture?

2. Lord Halsbury in *Leigh v. Taylor* [1902] A.C. 157, see above p. 20, said:

   Suppose this had been a tenant from year to year, and she put up these things, is it conceivable that a person would for the purpose of a tenancy from year to year put up these things exactly in this way if thereby she made a present of £7,000 to the landlord?

   This was cited by Luxmoore J. at first instance in *Spyer v. Phillipson* and approved by the Court of Appeal. Furthermore, Luxmoore J. said, in considering the object and purpose of annexation:

   Again I have to consider the interest of the person who puts the particular chattel into the property and bear that in mind in answering the question, what was the object and purpose of the annexation? As I pointed out Mr Phillipson was a tenant for a term of years. It would be a little surprising if this gentleman were to spend £5,000 in purchasing panelling and have it put in on the footing that he would only enjoy it for 11 or 13 years, and at the end of that time he would lose all interest in it, and it would belong to a complete stranger, that is, the landlord of the premises.

   Do these statements indicate that the intent in determining the purpose of annexation is a subjective intent?

3. Did the court in *Spyer v. Phillipson* consider either damage to the object or inheritance as a relevant or conclusive consideration in determining the tenant's right of removal? Consider also the following extract:

WEBB v. FRANK BEVIS LTD

Court of Appeal [1940] 1 All E.R. 247 at 250

[The respondent had leased certain land from the War Office and had covenanted in his lease that he would, at the end of the term, at his own expense remove all buildings and erections and restore the site to its original state and condition. The appellant company which carried on business as manufacturers of breeze and cement products was allowed to occupy part of the land as a tenant at will and, for the purpose of housing their machinery and warehousing their plant and materials, they erected on the land a shed 135 ft long and 50 ft wide. It was built of corrugated iron and was laid upon a concrete floor. The roof rested upon solid timber posts, which in turn rested on the concrete floor, but they were not embedded in it. Each post was tied to the concrete floor by wrought iron straps on the opposite sides, and was held in position by a bolt which ran horizontally through each post. The straps, which were fixed in and protruded from the concrete floor, were fastened tightly by a nut screwed on one end of the bolt. There was no other attachment to the soil. In the shed, there were three heavy pieces of machinery similarly attached to the concrete floor.

Once the roof and sides, which were capable of being taken down in panels, had been removed, the posts could easily be removed by undoing the bolts and, if need be, the upstanding straps left behind could be cut off level with the surface of the concrete floor.

It was held at first instance that the superstructure of the shed must be regarded as one with the concrete floor, and as constituting a single unit affixed to the soil to the same extent as the floor itself. Accordingly, it was a landlord's, and not a tenant's fixture. The appellant appealed against this decision. On appeal.]

SCOTT L.J. (delivering the judgment of the court). That the concrete floor was so affixed to the ground as to become part of the soil is obvious. It was completely and permanently attached to the ground, and, secondly, it could not be detached except by being broken up and ceasing to exist either as a concrete floor or as the cement and rubble out of which it had been made. Does that fact of itself prevent the superstructure from being a tenant's fixture? I do not think so. If it had been erected on concrete blocks, one under each post, the top level with the surface of the ground, and the attachment of post to block had been plainly removable at ground level, "the object and purpose" of the attachment would have been obvious—namely, to erect a mere tenant's fixture. In my opinion, it was equally so in the actual construction adopted for holding the posts in position on their concrete supports. The photographs proved below, and shown to us, demonstrate the simplicity of this method of detachment, once the upper parts and walls had been taken down.

The judge held, and I think rightly held, that the superstructure was "to a very. large extent" a "temporary" building, by which I understand him to mean that the object and purpose for which the company erected it were its use for such time as they might need it. That view goes a long way, if not all the way, towards the conclusion that, regarded apart from the floor, the shed was in law removable. The very uncertainty of the company's tenure of the site ultimately of necessity determined "the purpose and object" of the erection, and, when the judge found as a fact, as he did, that "it could be taken away, no doubt piecemeal," and re-erected elsewhere, I think he consciously decided that, apart from the floor, it was a tenant's trade fixture, and removable by the tenant as such. His only ground for taking the opposite view was that he thought himself bound to regard the two as one unit, and thought that the floor compelled him to treat the whole as a landlord's fixture. In my respectful judgment, this reasoning rested on a fallacy. If the respondent had already made the concrete floor, as well he might for the purposes of his own business, and the company had then become his tenant at will and put up the self-same superstructure, what relevance would the floor have had? In my view, none. It would not have had any more relevance than would any flat, rigid and unbreakable surface already existing when some heavy superstructure is put upon it, such as a windmill of a century or two ago, or the actual machines in the present case.

To my mind, it is inconceivable that the tenant at will should go to the expense of putting up such a structure unless it was for "the purpose and object," first, of himself using it, and, secondly, of taking it away if he ceased to be tenant.

The condition of the legal quality of removability—namely, that the subject matter should not, by the process of removal, lose its essential character or value (see *Fisher v. Dixon* (1845) 5 Dunlop 775)—was plainly satisfied by the judge's own finding to which I have referred, and I see nothing in the evidence to raise a doubt as to the propriety of that finding. For these reasons, I think that the appeal should be allowed on the issue as to the shed.

QUESTION

What do you think would have been the result in *Webb v. Frank Bevis Ltd* if the superstructure could have been removed only by the separation of component boards rather than removal of whole panels?

EX PARTE BROOK; RE ROBERTS

Court of Appeal (1878) 10 Ch. D. 100 at 108

[The question before the court involved the entitlement of a landlord to possession of his tenant's fixtures through the tenant's trustee in bankruptcy consequent upon a disclaimer by the trustee of the lease formerly held by the bankrupt.]

THESIGER L.J. (delivering the judgment of the court). Where the trustee in a liquidation disclaims, there, by the joint operation of the disclaimer and the provisions of ss 23 and 125 of the Act, the term is to be deemed for all purposes to have come to an end on the day of the appointment of the trustee. In other words, the trustee is placed in the position of never having had any estate at all. . . . [T]he logical and legal conclusion is, not merely that a severance by the trustee of fixtures after the disclaimer is wrongful, although that is included, and was all that was necessary to be decided in *Ex parte Stephens* (1877) 7 Ch. D. 127, but that any severance which has taken place after the date when the term is put an end to for all purposes, and by a person who, like a trustee, is in the position of never having had any interest in the term, must necessarily be wrongful.

Apart, however, from the authority of *Ex parte Stephens*, we arrive at the conclusion that the landlords' claim in the present case is a well-founded one. The general presumption of law with reference to tenants' fixtures remaining affixed to the freehold when a term comes to an end is, that "they become a gift in law to him in reversion," and are, therefore, not removable: per Lord Holt in *Poole's Case* (1703) 1 Salk. 368; 91 E.R. 320. That general presumption has, however, been made subject to a qualification which is expressed in the proposition laid down by the Court of Exchequer in *Weeton v. Woodcock* (1840) 7 M. & W. 14 at 19; 151 E.R. 659 at 661-662 in these terms—viz., "that the tenant's right to remove fixtures continues during his original term, and during such further period of possession by him as he holds the premises under a right still to consider himself as tenant," or, in the language of Parke B. in *Mackintosh v. Trotter* (1838) 3 M. & W. 184; 150 E.R. 1108, "that the tenant has the right to remove fixtures of this nature during his term, or during what may for this purpose be considered as an excrescence on the term". Much reliance has been placed in argument on the part of the respondent upon this qualification of the general presumption of law, and it has been urged upon us that in this case the period between the appointment of the trustee and the disclaimer was such an "excrescence" on the term, and that the respondent had during that period a right to consider himself as tenant. We cannot accede to that argument. It is not easy to define precisely what was meant by the propositions to which we have just referred, and we observe, that as regards the rule laid down in *Weeton v. Woodcock*, the difficulty which we feel in understanding its exact meaning was shared in by the Court of Common Pleas, as stated by Willes J. in delivering the judgment of that court in *Leader v. Homewood* (1858) 5 C.B. (N.S.) 546 at 553; 141 E.R. 221 at 223-224. It may be that in cases where a tenant holds over after the expiration of a term certain under a reasonable supposition of consent on the part of his landlord, or in the case where an interest of uncertain duration comes suddenly to an end, and the tenant keeps possession for such reasonable time only as would enable him to sever his fixtures and to remove them with his goods and chattels off the demised premises, or even in cases where the landlord exercises a right of forfeiture, and the tenant remains on the premises for such reasonable time as last referred to, the law would presume a right to remove tenant's fixtures after the expiration or determination of the tenancy. But, however that may be, we are clearly of opinion that the case of a surrender of a lease by a tenant, while tenant's fixtures remain affixed to the freehold, does not, either upon principle or the authority of decided cases, give any right to the tenant subsequently to remove such fixtures. At the date of the surrender they form part of the freehold, and the law has no right to limit the effect of the surrender by excluding from it that which legally passes by it, and which has not been excluded from it by the bargain of the parties. If that be so, then when the legislature, by s. 23 of the *Bankruptcy Act* 1869 (U.K.), says that a lease disclaimed shall be deemed to be surrendered, are we justified in attributing to the language used any meaning other than that which is its natural meaning—viz., that the ordinary consequences of a surrender shall follow the disclaimer? No doubt difficulties will always arise when courts are called upon to treat a thing as being in law that which in fact it is not: and if in this case the strict carrying out in all points of the analogy of an ordinary surrender were to lead to consequences manifestly absurd or unjust, it would be the duty of the court to find, if possible, some construction of the section in question which would not entail such consequences. In the present instance no such consequences are the result of the construction which the language of the section naturally requires. Extreme cases may, it is true, be put in which it would work a hardship upon the creditors, and the present case is, perhaps, an example; for, if the trustee had kept the property on for a year, he might, at the expense of the small payment of £40, have obtained the fixtures in dispute. But in a vastly greater number of cases any different construction would work a considerable hardship upon the landlord. Indeed, in *Saint v. Pilley* (1875) L.R. 10 Ex. 137, Amphlett B. appears to have considered the dismantling of a house by severance of tenant's fixtures inconsistent with the exercise of the right of disclaimer, and to have been disposed, as stated by him (at 141), to agree with the view taken in *Amos on Fixtures* (2nd ed.), p. 239, that after the sale of fixtures a trustee could not disclaim. When, too, it is remembered that the section under consideration is one which, upon any construction of it, favours the interests of the creditors at the expense of the landlord, we think that it would be unreasonable to allow possible cases of hardship upon the creditors to weight against an interpretation of it which gives to the analogy of a surrender its natural and proper effect. . . .

The effect, therefore, of a disclaimer generally being such as we have laid down, and there being in the agreement before the debtor and his landlords no special stipulations as regards fixtures which make this case in any way exceptional, the necessary conclusion must be that the respondent, by disclaiming the property to which the fixtures were attached after his sale of those fixtures, constituted himself by relation a wrongdoer in respect of that sale, and is liable to pay over to the appellants the whole of the moneys which by his wrongful act he has realised. The appeal must be allowed. . . .

NEW ZEALAND GOVERNMENT PROPERTY CORP. v. H.M. & S. LTD

Court of Appeal [1982] 1 Q.B. 1145

LORD DENNING M.R. . . . Her Majesty's Theatre is one of the most famous in London. It was built in 1898 by that great actor Sir Herbert Beerbohm Tree. The landlords were the Carlton Hotel Ltd. They leased it to him and his company, Playhouse Ltd, for 72 years from 10 October 1898 to 30 September 1970, at a rent of £3,700 a year. The lessees covenanted to use it as and for a first-class theatre only, to keep the demised premises (including landlord's fixtures) in good repair and so to deliver it up at the end of the term.

Many years ago the lease became vested in a company called H.M. & S. Ltd, of which the leading figure is Mr Prince Littler. The ownership has become vested in the New Zealand government.

The theatre was occupied "for the purpose of business". So the tenancy came within the *Landlord and Tenant Act* 1954 (U.K.). It meant that before the old lease came to an end, the lessees were entitled to, and did, apply for a new lease under that Act. The landlords conceded that the tenants were entitled to a new lease. The only question was as to the terms of it. There were negotiations between the parties about the terms. They started early in 1970 (before the old lease expired) and continued through the next two or three years. Meanwhile, pending all the negotiations under the statute, the old lease continued in existence automatically. It did not determine on 30 September 1970. It continued until 8 February 1973, when the parties executed a new lease.

It is under that new lease of 8 February 1973, that the question arises. It was for 21 years from 1 October 1970, at a rent for the first seven years of £25,000 a year: and for the next seven years at the "open market rental of the demised premises". That is the point at issue. What is the "open market rental" for the second seven years? The first seven years were to end on 30 September 1977. In anticipation of this, the parties negotiated for the new rental for the second seven years of the term. The landlords' surveyor put it at £55,000 a year. The tenants' surveyor did not agree. The matter went to arbitration before an official referee (Judge Lewis Hawser Q.C.), sitting as an arbitrator. In the course of the arbitration a point of law arose about tenant's fixtures. There were many of them in the theatre. The tenants had put them in over many years. Typical were the seats in the stalls and auditorium. Were they to be included as part of the "demised premises" on which the tenants were to pay rent? Were the tenants to pay rent for them on the basis that they belonged to the landlords? Or were the tenants free from paying any rent on them because they belonged to them, the tenants?

Now, before I go any further, I must observe that it is clear that a tenant has a right to remove "tenant's fixtures" before the term comes to an end. So the tenants here have a right to remove them, not only during the old lease itself, but also at any time before the old lease as extended came to an end on 8 February 1973. The old lease, as extended, was surrendered "by operation of law" on 8 February 1973, when the new lease was granted. That had been clear for centuries: see *Thompson v. Trafford* (1593) Pop. 8; 79 E.R. 1131.

WHAT WAS THE EFFECT OF THE SURRENDER?

What then was the effect of the surrender? The landlords say that, when the old lease was surrendered in 1973, the tenants lost their right to remove the tenants' fixtures. They became a gift to the landlords. They became part of the "demised premises". So that in 1977 the new rental was to be paid on the basis that they belonged to the landlords and the tenants were to pay rent for them just as if they were part of the structure itself.

But the tenants say that the surrender in 1973 did not have that effect. They say that so long as they continued in possession—whether under the old lease or an extension of it, or on a new lease—they retained their right to remove them. . . .

THE CORRECT RULE

In the present case the question arises: If the term expires by effluence of time or by surrender—and the tenants remain in possession by virtue of a new tenancy express or implied—can they still remove the "tenant's fixtures" during their extended time of possession? Or did they lose them irretrievably when their original term came to an end? There are many statements in the text books to the effect that the tenant loses them when his original term comes to an end. Woolf J. quotes the text books at length. I think those text books are wrong. In my opinion the tenant remains entitled to remove the "tenant's fixtures" so long as he remains in possession. That was decided in *Penton v. Robart* (1801) 2 East 88; 102 E.R. 302. Robart was under-tenant of a yard and buildings at Battlebridge. During his sub-tenancy he erected a wooden shed for the purpose of making varnish. It had a brick foundation. The original term expired at Michaelmas 1800. He remained in possession *for some time afterwards*, and during that time he pulled down the wooden superstructure of the shed and carried away the utensils. The head landlord claimed that they belonged to him. The Court of King's Bench held that the tenant was entitled to remove them. Lord Kenyon C.J. said (at 90-91; at 303): "The old cases upon this subject leant to consider as realty whatever was annexed to the freehold by the occupier: but in modern times the leaning has always been the other way in favour of the tenant, in support of the interests of trade which is become the pillar of the state. What tenant will lay out his money in costly improvements of the land, if he must leave everything behind him which can be said to be annexed to it. . . . Here the defendant did no more than he had a right to do; *he was in fact still in possession of the premises at the time the things were taken away, and therefore there is no pretence to say that he had abandoned his right to them.*" (Emphasis added.)

That case was distinguished in *Weeton v. Woodcock* (1840) 7 M. & W. 14; 151 E.R. 659, but not doubted. The landlords let a cotton factory to Taylor for seven years. Taylor installed a steam engine boiler, firmly fixed to the floor and walls of the engine house. Taylor became bankrupt. His property vested in his assignees, Woodcock and others. They entered into possession of the factory. The landlords then forfeited the lease for breach of covenant by Taylor. So it came to an end. The assignees then sold the boiler and removed it. The landlords claimed that the assignees had no right to sell the boiler: because the term had already come to an end, and the tenant no longer remained in possession. The Court of Exchequer held that the assignees were not entitled to remove the boiler. After the lease was forfeited, they held on—not as tenants nor by agreement with the landlords—but as trespassers. So they had no right to remove the boiler. Alderson B. in giving the reserved judgment of a strong court, said (at 19; at 661): "The rule to be collected from the several cases decided on this subject seems to be this, that the tenant's right to remove fixtures continues during his original term, *and during such further period of possession by him, as he holds the premises under a right still to consider himself as tenant.*" (Emphasis added.)

THE CONTRARY VIEW

I think that is the correct rule. But I have to recognise that there are later observations which throw doubt on it. It is said that when the tenant surrenders his existing term and takes a new tenancy, without reserving his right to remove tenant's fixtures, he loses that right altogether, even though he still remained in possession as a tenant. In the case of an express surrender, there is this dictum by Parker J. in *Leschallas v. Woolf* [1908] 1 Ch. 641 at 652: "In my opinion, however, if the tenant upon the surrender of his lease in order that a new lease may be granted makes no stipulation to the contrary, he does lose his right to remove tenant's fixtures." And in the case of a surrender by operation of law, there seems to be a decision by Scrutton J. in *Slough Picture Hall Co. Ltd v. Wade* (1916) 32 T.L.R. 542.

To which I would add the dictum of Warrington L.J. in *Pole-Carew v. Western Counties & General Manure Co. Ltd* [1920] 2 Ch. 97 at 122: "I think it is clear that after a surrender of the term in the land to which tenant's fixtures are attached and a subsequent lease to the same tenant the latter can no longer remove the tenant's fixtures unless his existing right to remove them is reserved expressly or by necessary implication."

OPINION RESERVED

But as against all these statements, it is to be observed that on two separate occasions the Court of Appeal has expressly left it open. In 1881 in *Ex parte Baroness Willoughby D'Eresby* (1881) 44 L.T. 781 the Court of Appeal, consisting of James, Cotton and Lush L.JJ., said (at 785): "If, and when the simple case shall arise of a tenant, having removable fixtures, continuing his possession under a new or extended term, we desire to hold ourselves perfectly free as to the question whether he retains his right of removal during such continuous possession, unfettered by anything said in this case." Likewise in *Pole-Carew v. Western Counties & General Manure Co. Ltd* [1920] 2 Ch. 97 at 119 per Lord Sterndale M.R.; and at 123 per Younger L.J.

CONSIDER ON PRINCIPLE

This means that in this court we can consider the point upon principle. I would test it by taking these illustrations:

First, a tenant takes a lease of business premises for five years, and puts in a valuable machine fixed to the floor for use in his trade. After the five years are at an end, he holds over with the consent of his landlord as tenant from year to year. Nothing is said about the machine. Then after three more years he moves out and goes elsewhere. Surely he can remove his machine and take it with him. It would be most unjust if he could not do so.

Secondly, the tenant does not hold over with nothing said. At the end of the five years, he takes a new lease from his landlord for another three years to run from the expiry of the first term. But nothing is said about the machine. Then, at the end of the next three years, he moves out and goes elsewhere. Surely he can take the machine with him. There is no difference between a new lease and holding over.

Thirdly, the tenant takes a new lease for three years from his landlord, but it is back-dated so that it starts after the first four years, and not after five. Nothing is said about the machine. The first lease is then surrendered by operation of law at the end of the fourth year. But surely at the end of the new lease, he can take the machine with him.

Fourthly, the same as the last, but the tenant at the end of the fourth year expressly surrenders the first lease and takes a grant of a new lease. Nothing is said about the machine. Surely at the end of the new lease he can take away the machine. Is it really necessary to say to him: "Did you tell the landlord that you reserved your right to take away the machine?" He would answer: "No, I did not do so, because it did not occur to me. It was my machine and I assumed I could take it away when I left."

These illustrations convince me that all the statements in the text books are erroneous. I hold that when an existing lease expires or is surrendered and is followed immediately by another, to the same tenant remaining in possession, the tenant does not lose his right to remove tenant's fixtures. He is entitled to remove them at the end of his new tenancy.

IMPROVEMENTS

But then it is said that s. 34 of the *Landlord and Tenant Act* 1954 (U.K.), as amended by s. 1 of the *Law of Property Act* 1969 (U.K.), shows that Parliament proceeded on a different course. That section says that in fixing the rent payable under a new tenancy, there is to be taken into account any "improvements" carried out within the last 21 years, but not those carried out more than 21 years past. But the answer is that that applies to improvements made by the tenant which are "landlord's fixtures"—which the tenant is never able to remove. It does not apply to "tenant's fixtures".

TIME OF FIXING RENT

Finally, coming back to our present case, the rent to be assessed for the second seven years was, and would have to be, fixed by agreement or by the judge during the period when the original lease was automatically extended by the *Landlord and Tenant Act* 1954. During that automatic extension the tenant would certainly have a right to remove the tenant's fixtures. So the new rent should be assessed on that basis.

CONCLUSION

After this long discussion, I think that in this court we should free ourselves from the shackles of the past. It is time that the law about removal of tenant's fixtures was brought up to date. This case gives this court the opportunity to do so. I think the rent of the Haymarket Theatre should be assessed on the basis that the tenant's fixtures could have been removed by the tenant if he wished—and that they should not be regarded as part of the "demised premises" for the purpose of fixing the rent.

I would therefore dismiss the appeal.

[Dunn and Fox L.JJ. delivered separate but concurring judgments.]

TWO

CONCURRENT OWNERSHIP

A.   CONCEPT AND CHARACTERISTICS

Co-ownership exists where two or more persons simultaneously, and not in succession, hold an interest in the same parcel of land. There are four types of co-ownership, the first two of which are now obsolete: coparcenary, tenancy by entireties, joint tenancy and tenancy in common. The basic feature of all forms of co-ownership is that each co-owner is entitled to the possession of the whole of the land, although not to any part of it exclusively. Thus, no co-owner can point to any part of the land as her or his own to the exclusion of the other co-owners and, conversely, no co-owner can be guilty of trespass unless she or he commits an act which amounts to an actual ouster or dispossession of her or his co-owners: *Thomas v. Thomas* (1850) 5 Exch. 28; 155 E.R. 13; and see, for example, *Proprietors of the Centre Building Units Plan No. 343 v. Bourne* [1984] 1 Qd R. 613 with respect to the co-ownership of individual unit proprietors, or their tenants, in common property under the Queensland equivalent of the *Strata Titles Act* 1973 (N.S.W.). Similarly, if one co-owner leases her or his share or interest, the tenant cannot exclude the lessor's co-owner or the co-owner's separate lessee from such use and enjoyment of the land as co-ownership authorises: *Catanzariti v. Whitehouse* (1981) 55 F.L.R. 426 and the authorities cited therein. This characteristic is called the unity of possession. One result of this characteristic at common law was that since each co-owner was entitled to the whole just as much as any other, if one co-owner obtained a larger share than was her or his due of the rents and profits, there was no remedy against that co-owner in trespass, money had and received, or account. The common law, however, was later altered by statute: 4 Anne c. 16. Equity also recognised a right of account. The statute 4 Anne c.16 is not applicable in New South Wales: *Imperial Acts Application Act* 1969 (N.S.W.); but see *Supreme Court Rules* (N.S.W.) Pts 48 and 49.

Joint tenants, with respect to all persons other than themselves, are in the position of a single owner. They are jointly seised of the whole estate. They are said to be seised "per mie et per tout". Tenants in common, like joint tenants, enjoy unity of possession, but each tenant in common has a distinct share in the property in its entirety.

The two basic characteristics of a joint tenancy are: (1) the right of survivorship, or the "jus accrescendi", and (2) the four unities.

1. Right of survivorship

Upon the death of one joint tenant, that tenant's interest in the land accrues for the benefit of the remaining joint tenants, and this process continues until there is only one survivor who becomes single owner. The right of survivorship is not defeated by a contrary provision contained in the will of a deceased joint tenant nor by the provisions relating to distribution of intestate estates where a deceased joint tenant dies intestate. The right of survivorship does not apply to tenancies in common. The undivided share of a deceased tenant in common passes according to the terms of that person's will or on intestacy. It is possible, however, to create expressly a tenancy in common with a right of survivorship. Nonetheless, such a tenancy in common is still distinct from a joint tenancy because whilst an express right of survivorship cannot be defeated by alienation to a third party by one of the tenants in common (*Haddelsey v. Adams* (1856) 22 B. 266; 52 E.R. 1110), the right of survivorship in a joint tenancy can be defeated by alienation to a third party by one of the joint tenants.

Before the 1970 amendments to the *Real Property Act* 1900 (N.S.W.), s. 84 of the Act permitted the entry of the words "no survivorship" upon the transfer of any land, estate or interest in the case where two or more joint proprietors were to take as trustees. The section simply imposed upon the proprietors who remained after one of their co-proprietors had died, the obligation of approaching the Supreme Court for an order enabling the survivors to deal with the land:

> [T]he use of the words "no survivorship" in s. 84 was not intended to prevent the estate surviving on the death of one of the joint proprietors and so to create a new estate in land, which is not a joint tenancy at all . . . the effect of the entry is confined to the effect expressly given to it by s. 84, namely, that it shall not be lawful for any less number of joint proprietors than the number registered when the entry was made to transfer or otherwise deal with the land without obtaining the sanction of the Court: *Re Robertson* (1943) 44 S.R. (N.S.W.) 103 at 105.

The effect of the words "no survivorship" was not to destroy the element of survivorship in a joint tenancy nor to convert it into a tenancy in common. Section 84 was among those sections in Pt IX of the New South Wales *Real Property Act* headed "Trusts". Whilst one aim of the Act is to keep title untrammelled by equitable interests, s. 84 "was designed to provide some protection in favour of cestuis que trust without entering notice of the trusts on the register book. It does provide some measure of protection but the devise is inconvenient and little used": *Re Robertson* at 104-105.

Unless there exists the right of survivorship and the uncertainty as to who shall survive, there cannot be a joint tenancy. Accordingly, at common law, a corporation, because it could never die, could not be a joint tenant. Now, by legislation, a corporation may be a joint tenant: *Conveyancing Act* 1919 (N.S.W.), s. 25. The right of survivorship, however, does not preclude a joint tenant making an inter vivos disposition of her or his interest in the land but this will result in the severance of the joint tenancy converting that interest into a tenancy in common.

The application of the doctrine of survivorship at first presented difficulties in those cases where joint tenants perished in a common disaster. The problem was overcome initially by allowing the respective heirs of the joint tenants to hold in joint tenancy so that survivorship did not apply. The present position is set out in s. 35 of the *Conveyancing Act* 1919 (N.S.W.):

In all cases where two or more persons have died under circumstances rendering it uncertain which of them survived, the deaths shall for all purposes affecting the title to any property be presumed to have taken place in order of seniority, and the younger shall be deemed to have survived the elder.

The statutory presumption, however, is inapplicable where there is evidence by which the order or death can be ascertained: *Re Plaister; Perpetual Trustee Co. v. Crawshaw* (1934) 34 S.R. (N.S.W.) 547. It is only if the order of death cannot be proved that the "uncertainty" required by the section subsists and the statutory presumption is applicable: it does not matter that the deaths may have been simultaneous (*Hickman v. Peacey* [1945] A.C. 305, extracted below) or that the deaths did not arise out of the same accident or upon the same occasion unless one of the deaths is presumed under the common law: *Halbert v. Mynar* [1981] 2 N.S.W.L.R. 659, extracted below p. 48.

HICKMAN v. PEACEY

House of Lords [1945] A.C. 305 at 321

[Four persons, two of whom had made wills benefiting some of the others, were killed by a bomb which burst in a London dwelling-house during the war. The house was demolished by the bomb and the bodies were buried in the ruins. There was no evidence to show whether any of the deceased had survived the others.]

LORD MACMILLAN. Two views have been advanced as to its meaning and effect. According to one view, which is the view of Lord Greene M.R. and Goddard L.J., the statutory presumption is strictly limited in its application to cases in which "the court is satisfied as to two things—one that the proper inference from the circumstances is that the deaths took place consecutively, the other, that the circumstances leave the court in uncertainty as to which death took place first": *Re Grosvenor* [1944] Ch. 138 at 146. That is to say, all that the statute does is to fix artificially the order of sequence among consecutive deaths, where that order cannot in fact be ascertained. If the circumstances are such as to justify an inference that all the parties concerned died simultaneously then the circumstances are not such as to render it uncertain which of them survived the other or others, for it is certain that none survived the other or others. This according to Goddard L.J. . . . is the literal construction of the plain words of the enactment. The other view is that when the circumstances are such that it cannot be ascertained that one of the deceased survived the other then the uncertainty which the section postulates exists and the statutory presumption applies. One reason why it cannot be ascertained that one survived the other may well be that the deaths occurred so closely in time that there is a high probability that they were practically simultaneous. I say "practically" for reasons which will appear later. Having carefully weighed the arguments in support of each of these rival constructions I pronounce unhesitatingly in favour of the latter. . . .

I prefer to read the enactment as meaning that where the circumstances are such that it is not possible to say with certainty that one of the victims survived the other there is then uncertainty as to which survived the other. . . .

I prefer, therefore, to judge the language of the present enactment by a more commonplace standard. I think that it poses a practical question—Can you say for certain which of these two dead persons died first? If you cannot say for certain, then you must presume the older to have died first. It is immaterial that the reason for your inability to say for certain which died first is either because you think they both died simultaneously or because you think they died consecutively but you do not know in what sequence. . . .

I would only add a few words regarding the term "uncertain" which occurs in the enactment and which was so much canvassed in the course of the argument. The basis of belief may range from mere conjecture through all degrees of probability to absolute demonstration—possibility, probability, certainty. In seeking to arrive at a conclusion in fact in ordinarily human affairs the law rejects mere possibility as an insufficient basis of proof, but on the other hand it does not exact absolute or mathematical proof. It is content to proceed on probability, if it is sufficient, and the test of sufficient probability is that the direct evidence, with all legitimate inferences, is such as ought to satisfy the mind of a person of reasonable intelligence. But the result of a decision on a question of fact by a judge or a jury is not certainty. It is finality, not certainty. Your Lordships in considering a verdict of a jury on a question of fact have often declared that it is not to be disturbed because there was evidence on which a reasonable person could so find but that it is not to be taken that your Lordships would have reached the same conclusion. Can it be said that in such circumstances the fact found by the jury has been ascertained with certainty? It has been determined with finality in law, but not with certainty in fact. In my opinion the legislature in employing the word "uncertain" in the section which the House has to construe was not thinking of the kind of certainty with which the law has to be content but was using the word in its ordinary acceptation as denoting a reasonable element of doubt.

So, coming at last to the facts of the present case so far as known, I put the question thus: Can it be said for certain of any of the five persons involved in this tragic occurrence that one did or did not survive the other? All that is certain is that a high explosive bomb fell on a small house, No. 5, Upper Cheyne Row, Chelsea, on 14 September 1940 about 6.30 o'clock, that it exploded within the house and reduced it to a heap of ruins, that five dead bodies, severely mutilated, were subsequently recovered from the debris, and that there was a shelter in the basement of the house to which the deceased were in the habit of resorting when there was an air raid. No technical evidence was led on the action of blast from high explosives or its effect on the human body. Now I do not for the purposes of my argument need to say that, if a judge or jury had to try the issue whether in these circumstances all the victims of the calamity perished at precisely the same instant, and were to find as a matter of fact that this was so, the finding would on appeal be set aside on the ground that there was no evidence on which a reasonable man could reach that conclusion—pace Lord Cranworth L.C., who thought that the simultaneous death of two human beings was insusceptible of proof. Two most eminent and most reasonable judges have so found in this case. But, with all respect, that is not an issue which the statute requires to be determined in order to bring it into operation or exclude its operation. All that is necessary, in order to invoke the statutory presumption, is the presence in the circumstances of an element of uncertainty as to which of the deceased survived the other or others. I can imagine a juryman saying "I really cannot answer this question. It may be that they died one after the other or it may be that they all died at the same moment, but in any case I cannot say for certain which, if any, was the survivor." That is also my state of mind on the facts of the present case. Without resorting to fantastic or far-fetched conjectures it is perfectly possible that the blast of the explosion did not annihilate the whole of these five victims at the same instant. Thus, one of them may quite well have been out of the shelter in another part of the house at the moment of the impact of the shell and the blast, though by an infinitesimal interval, may have struck him sooner or later than the others. I simply do not know. Nobody can know. Where everything depends, as Lord Cranworth said in *Wing v. Angrave* (1860) 8 H.L.C. 183 at 207; 11 E.R. 397 at 406-407, on "survivorship for a second" I cannot accept the view that in the circumstances of this case there was no element of uncertainty, legal or other, on the cardinal issue.

My opinion accordingly is that the statutory presumption applies and that the appeal should be allowed.

[Lords Porter and Simonds agreed, Viscount Simon L.C. and Lord Wright dissented.]

HALBERT v. MYNAR

Supreme Court of New South Wales [1981] 2 N.S.W.L.R. 659 at 666

WADDELL J. I turn now to the application of the *Conveyancing Act* 1919 (N.S.W.), s. 35, which provides: "In all cases where two or more persons have died under circumstances rendering it uncertain which of them survived, the deaths shall for all purposes affecting the title to any property be presumed to have taken place in order of seniority, and the younger be deemed to have survived the elder." . . .

The first [question] is whether the section, on its true interpretation, is confined to persons who die by the same accident or upon the same occasion. Such persons are referred to in the decisions as commorientes. The third defendant submits that the section is so confined. As a matter of construction the question is whether each of the persons must have died under the same "circumstances" or whether that word is to be read distributably as relating to each death in question. In a decision of the House of Lords, *Hickman v. Peacey* [1945] A.C. 304 at 314, 315, Viscount Simon L.C. said of the English section: "It is to be observed that, whatever may be the case in similar provisions in the Roman law, s. 184 is not limited to multiple deaths arising out of a 'common disaster'. For example, if a husband goes on a long voyage and the ship completely disappears in circumstances where his death has to be presumed to have occurred, but there is no material to indicate on what date he was drowned, and if his wife was in a nursing home when he started and subsequently died under an operation, there may be absolutely no means of ascertaining which of them died first. Yet in such a case there is no 'common disaster' at all. It is therefore a useful provision of the statute law which requires the question of survivorship in such a case, which otherwise remains insoluble, to be determined by asking which of them was the younger. No one in such an instance would suggest that there were grounds for believing that they both died at the same moment of time. But it is in connection with a 'common disaster' that these problems more usually present themselves."

This expression of opinion was not necessary for the purposes of the case before the court. The question was whether the section applied to determine the order of death of four persons who were killed by a direct hit from a high explosive bomb on the house in which they were sheltering during the Battle of Britain. It has, however, been adopted in two later cases; by Lush J. in *Re Albert* [1967] V.R. 875; and by Helsham J., as he then was, in *In the Estate of Dixon* (1969) 90 W.N. (Pt 1) (N.S.W.) 469. I think that I should do likewise.

The second question is whether the section can be applied where one of the deaths is presumed under the common law. As to this there is a conflict of authority. In *Re Albert* [1967] V.R. 875, it was held that it did not. In *In the Estate of Dixon* it was held that it did but in this case, *Re Albert* was not cited or considered and as the application was ex parte the court did not have the advantage of argument on both sides and, in particular, of considering the argument which found favour with Lush J.

In *Re Albert* [1967] V.R. 875, the question was whether a nephew, who had last been heard of in 1928, should be deemed, pursuant to the section, to have survived his aunt who died intestate in 1958, she being his senior. Lush J. expressed his views as follows (at 880): "Ultimately the question must depend upon the construction of s. 184 itself. The argument contended for by the last-named defendant in the present case gives the section the same meaning as if it read, 'in all cases where two or more persons have died and it is uncertain which of them survived the other or others'. If this is what the section means, the words, 'in circumstances rendering', are either superfluous or clumsy. In my opinion, however, these words supply the key to the present problem. They indicate that the section applies where two or more persons have died, where the circumstances of the death of each is known and where those circumstances render it uncertain which of them survived the other or others. If this is the correct construction of the section, it covers the hypothetical case used by Viscount Simon (which is, I think, not a case of presumption of death but a case in which it could be left to a jury to infer death—compare *Taylor on Evidence* (12th ed.), para. 201 and cases there cited), but it does not cover cases such as *Re Phene's Trusts* (1869) 5 Ch. App. 139, *Re Watkinson* [1952] V.L.R 123, *Re Dolling* [1956] V.L.R. 535 or the present case. In these cases, nothing is known of the circumstances of the death of one of the persons concerned, and the uncertainty which exists is, therefore, not one which arises from the circumstances in which that party died but from the fact that none of the circumstances of death—time, place or cause—of one of the relevant persons is known at all. The condition of the operation of the section is that the circumstances of the two deaths, whether occurring together or separately, produce the uncertainty. The condition is not satisfied if the circumstances of one death are unknown."

In *In the Estate of Dixon* (1969) 90 W.N. (Pt 1) (N.S.W.) 469, an application was made for letters of administration of the estate of the deceased upon presumption of his death. He had been last seen alive on 27 October 1961 and had not been seen or heard of since then. The question was whether the applicant, a brother, was one of the next of kin of the deceased. This depended on whether the deceased had survived his father who died on 18 November 1964. Helsham J. said (at 473): "Death which is presumed by reason of unexplainable absence is no less a fact because it arises by a presumption of law, and in my view is just as much a death falling within the terms of the section as any other death. I therefore hold that s. 35 includes the case of death presumed from an absence of seven years, where the common law presumption of death applies."

With the greatest of respect to his Honour, I find myself in agreement with the reasoning of Lush J. I adopt the conclusion which he reached. He gives a number of examples of the undesirable consequences of applying the section to the case of a death presumed under the common law. These are the consequence of the position that in the case of such a presumed death the deceased must, as a matter of law, be considered to have died at some unspecified time during a period which is not less than seven years and may be much longer depending on when the proceedings in which it is sought to apply the presumption commenced. If the construction proposed by Lush J. is adopted the practical consequence is that the deaths in question will inevitably have taken place within a short space of time. It is unlikely that the legislature intended the section to determine arbitrarily the order of death of persons whose deaths may have been separated by many years.

2. The four unities

The four unities, namely, unity of possession, interest, title and time, must be present in a joint tenancy. Although in a particular tenancy in common the four unities may be present, only the unity of possession is essential. The unity of interest requires that the interest of each joint tenant be the same in nature, extent and duration as, in theory, joint tenants are jointly seised of the one estate. Unity of title requires that each joint tenant derive her or his title from the same document or by simultaneous acts of adverse possession. Unity of time requires that the interest of each joint tenant must have vested at the same time subject to two exceptions: a conveyance to uses and gifts by will. Thus in a conveyance "to F and his heirs to the use of X and any wife he may marry", upon the marriage of X, X and his wife held as joint tenants. Again, in a gift by will "to A for life with remainder to the children of B and their heirs", all the children of B born during A's lifetime would take as joint tentants notwithstanding that they may have acquired vested interests at different points in time. Quaere, whether the first exception now overrides the requirement of unity of interest itself as a consequence of the legislative provisions enabling the creation by direct conveyance of interests which could formerly be created by means of uses.

B.   CREATION

At common law there was a presumption in favour of a joint tenancy; thus a conveyance to two or more persons created a joint tenancy, rather than a tenancy in common, provided that none of the unities was absent and that no "words of severance" (which indicated that each tenant was to take a distinct share in the land) were expressed in the instrument. However, equity preferred the certainty and equality of a tenancy in common as against the chance of "all or nothing" which arose from the right of survivorship in the case of a joint tenancy; in particular it presumed a tenancy in common in three situations where persons held as joint tenants at common law: namely, where two or more persons purchased property and provided the purchase money in unequal shares; where two or more mortgagees advanced money on mortgage in equal or unequal shares; and where land was acquired by partners for use as partnership assets.

The *Conveyancing Act* 1919 (N.S.W.), s. 26 reverses the common law presumption; now, any disposition of a beneficial interest in any property, whether with or without the legal estate to or for two or more persons together beneficially, is deemed to be made to or for them as tenants in common and not as joint tenants; but the section does not extend to persons who take as executors, administrators, trustees or mortgagees, nor does it apply where the instrument expressly provides that the persons are to take as joint tenants. Section 26 applies irrespective of whether or not the "disposition" arises directly out of an "instrument" and irrespective of whether the parties contributed to the purchase price in equal or unequal shares: *Carmody v. Delehunt* [1984] 1 N.S.W.L.R. 667; affirmed by the High Court in *Delehunt v. Carmody* (1986) 61 A.L.J.R. 54, where the co-ownership arose out of a resulting trust. In *Mole v. Ross* (1951) 24 A.L.J. 356 it was said that it is not necessary to use the precise words "as joint tenants" to create a joint tenancy, but that any clear and plain language expressing an intention to do so will suffice. However, on construction of the particular instrument, in *Mole v. Ross* the words "as joint legatees" were held not to create a joint tenancy.

The *Conveyancing Act* 1919, s. 27 brought about yet another change in respect of co-ownership. Before the *Conveyancing Act* if persons, entitled in equity as tenants in common became legal joint tenants, the equitable interest merged in the legal estate and they became joint tenants both at law and in equity. This often defeated the intention of the parties and led to unjust results: see, for instance, *Re Selous* [1901] Ch. 921. Now s. 27 of the *Conveyancing Act* 1919 (N.S.W.) provides that in the absence of a contrary agreement "where two or more persons entitled beneficially as tenants in common to an equitable estate in any property are or become entitled in their own right whether as joint tenants or tenants in common to the legal estate in such property equal to and co-extensive with such equitable estate both the legal and equitable estates shall be held by them as tenants in common".

C. DETERMINATION

1. Joint tenancy

A joint tenancy may be determined in a number of ways: survivorship, alienation, agreement or conduct, partition and merger. It is apparent that as the continued existence of a joint tenancy requires the presence of the four unities and the right of survivorship, each of the methods of determination result from the destruction of one or more of these essential requirements.

(a) Survivorship

As already explained, survivorship will ultimately result in sole ownership, at which point the co-ownership ceases.

(b) Alienation

Although a joint tenant is precluded from alienating her or his interest by will, no such prohibition exists in the case of inter vivos transactions. However, if a joint tenant alienates her or his interest inter vivos the joint tenancy is severed and a tenancy in common will result between the person to whom the interest is conveyed and the other co-tenant: *Wright v. Gibbons* (1949) 78 C.L.R. 313, extracted below p. 52. Moreover, in principle, there is no reason why, nowadays, a unilateral transfer or conveyance by a joint tenant to herself or himself should not operate to sever a joint tenancy: s. 24 of the *Conveyancing Act* 1919 (N.S.W.).

There has to be an actual alienation or a binding and enforceable contract, which is tantamount to an actual alienation, before severance of a joint tenancy can occur. "[A] binding and enforceable contract entered into by one joint tenant will have the same effect as an actual alienation of the interest. The reason is put succinctly by North J. in *Re Hewett* [1894] 1 Ch. 362 at 367, where his Lordship said it had this effect 'because it is quite clear that any agreement to sever made by a joint tenant, if it binds the parties, if it is made for value, is just as effectual as if the intention of the parties expressed in the agreement had actually been carried out by a conveyance of the property'. The severance occurs in equity, and can be enforced": *Freed v. Taffel* [1984] 2 N.S.W.L.R. 322 at 325; see also *Walton v. Forsyth* (1984) N.S.W. Conv. R. 55-214.

In the case of land under the *Real Property Act* 1900 (N.S.W.), a transfer by a joint tenant must be registered before it can sever the joint tenancy: *McNab v. Earle* [1981] 2 N.S.W.L.R. 673 extracted below p. 58. The traditional statement with respect to a voluntary alienation is that of Turner L.J. in *Milroy v. Lord* (1862) 4 De G. F. & J. 264 at 274; 45 E.R. 1185 at 1189:

> I take the law of this court to be well settled, that, in order to render a voluntary settlement valid and effectual, the settler must have done everything which, according to the nature of the property comprised in the settlement, was necessary to be done in order to transfer the property and render the settlement binding upon him. He may of course do this by actually transferring the property to the persons for whom he intends to provide, and the provision will then be effectual, and it will be equally effectual if he transfers the property to a trustee for the purposes of the settlement, or declares that he himself holds it in trust for those purposes; and if the property be personal, the trust may, as I apprehend, be declared either in writing or by parol; but, in order to render the settlement binding, one or other of these modes must, as I understand the law of this court, be resorted to, for there is no equity in this court to perfect an imperfect gift. The cases I think go further to this extent, that if the settlement is intended to be effectuated by one of the modes to which I have referred, the court will not give effect to it by applying another of those modes. If it is intended to take effect by transfer, the court will not hold the intended transfer to operate as a declaration of trust, for then every imperfect instrument would be made effectual by being converted into a perfect trust. These are the principles by which, as I conceive, this case must be tried.

This statement of principle was considered and applied in *Anning v. Anning* (1907) 4 C.L.R. 1049 and, with respect to a transfer of land under the provisions of the *Real Property Act*, in *Brunker v. Perpetual Trustee Co. Ltd* (1937) 57 C.L.R. 555; *Corin v. Patton* (1988) 13 N.S.W.L.R. 15; and *Patzak v. Lytton* (1984) F.L.C. 91-550.

WRIGHT v. GIBBONS

High Court of Australia (1949) 78 C.L.R. 313 at 322

[Olinda Gibbons, Ethel Rose Gibbons and Bessie Melba Gibbons were registered as joint tenants for an estate in fee simple in land under the provisions of the *Real Property Act* 1862 (Tas.). By single instrument of transfer, Olinda Gibbons purported to transfer to Ethel Rose Gibbons her interest in the land and Ethel Rose Gibbons purported to tranfer to Olinda Gibbons her interest in the land with intent that all three co-owners should be tenants in common in equal shares. On registration, the appropiate certificate of title was indorsed with a memorial of the memorandum of transfer as a result of which the former joint tenants were registered as tenants in common in equal shares. Bessie Melba Gibbons, who survived the two other tenants, sought a declaration in the Supreme Court of Tasmania that the memorandum of transfer did not effect a severance of the joint tenancy, and consequently that she, as survivor of the three, became solely entitled to an estate in fee simple, the defendants being Reginald Charles Wright (the executor of the wills of Ethel Rose Gibbons, who died on 26 January 1946, and Olinda Gibbons, who died on 30 November 1946) and the Recorder of Titles.

Pursuant to an order for the determination of the question before trial, Clark J. held that the joint tenancy had not been severed by reason of the memorandum of transfer. On appeal.]

LATHAM C.J. I do think that the defendant's case can be supported upon the basis that the sisters simply exchanged their interests. When an exchange of interests in land takes place the result is that what was previously the interest of B becomes the interest of A and vice versa. But in the present case the essence of the defendant's contention is that the transferees each got an interest, namely as tenant in common, which was different from the interest which the transferors had—namely an interest as joint tenant.

It has always been the law that a joint tenancy may be severed and converted into a tenancy in common by an agreement. This doctrine, however, does not help the defendants in the present case because the third joint tenant, Bessie Melba Gibbons, was not a party to the transaction between her co-tenants. There is no authority that some only of a number of joint tenants can bring about a severance of a joint tenancy inter se, though it is clear that all the joint tenants can bring about that result by an agreement to which they are all parties. But, further, the document upon which the defendants rely is a transfer and not an agreement. It is effective as a transfer or as nothing.

All the authorities concur in stating that alienation of his interest by a joint tenant to a stranger severs the joint tenancy so as to produce the result stated: see, for example, Lyttleton, *Treatise of Tenures* (1841), ss 292, 304; *Williams on the Law of Real Property* (1st ed.), pp. 132, 133, repeated in subsequent editions; *Halsbury's Laws of England* (1st ed.), Vol. 24, p. 204 (before the *Law of Property Act* 1925 (U.K.)). But in the present case two of the three joint tenants have attempted to alienate their interests to one another. The learned trial judge held that there was no true alienation, but that the cross-transfers left the two parties to that transaction just as they were. His Honour said: "It seems to me that such a transfer could operate nothing. Each party would be at once giving and receiving the same thing. It would be a futility." But this statement, with all respect to the learned judge, assumes rather than proves the proposition which is in question. If the transfer leaves A and B as they were, that is as joint tenants, with the same interests, then there is obviously no creation of a tenancy in common. But the question whether the transfer does so leave them, or whether it operates so as to make the joint tenants tenants in common is just the question to be decided. It is true that if one joint tenant A successfully transferred to another joint tenant B his interest as a joint tenant and B successfully transferred to A his interest as a joint tenant, the parties would be left just where they were, because the interest of each joint tenant is absolutely identical. But no transfer of an interest as a joint tenant so as to make the transferee a joint tenant with other joint tenants is possible when the transferee is a stranger to the joint tenancy. The transfer, if it could be effective, would destroy unity of time and unity of title so far as the interest of the transferee was concerned. Therefore he could not be a joint tenant with the other original joint tenants. No joint tenant can alienate to a stanger so as to make that person joint tenant with his co-tenants, but he can alienate so as to make that person a tenant in common with his co-tenants. In the present case the question is whether such an alienation to another joint tenant is possible.

The interests of each joint tenant in the land held are always the same in respect of possession, interest, title and time. No distinction can be drawn between the interest of any one tenant and that of any other tenant. If one joint tenant dies his interest is extinguished. He falls out, and the interest of the surviving joint tenant or joint tenants is correspondingly enlarged.

Where a joint tenant alienates his interest to a stranger the joint tenancy is severed and the alienee becomes a tenant in common as to an undivided share of the land. If there were only one other joint tenant, then the alienee and the continuing joint tenant hold as tenants in common. If, however, there were three joint tenants A, B and C, and A transferred his interest to a stranger, D, then D would own a one third interest as tenant in common with B and C, and B and C would hold a two thirds interest as between themselves as joint tenants. The survivor of B and C would take the whole of the two thirds interest, but D would not either gain or lose by the survivorship of any person.

When one joint tenant transfers his interest to another joint tenant the transfer (which at common law was effected by release because each joint tenant is conceived as holding every part and the whole of the land—"per my et per tout") does not operate by way of extinguishment of the estate. A mere extinguishment would enure in favour of B and C, and not only in favour of B in accordance with the intention of the parties. Accordingly such a transfer is said to pass (mitter) the estate. See Coke's note upon *Littleton* (18th ed., 1823), Vol. 2, p. 193a., s. 304. Section 304 is as follows: "And, if three joyntenants be, and the one release by his deed to one of his companions all the right which he hath in the land, then hath he to whom the release is made, the third part of the lands by force of the said release, and he and his companion shall hold the other two parts in joynture (et il et son companion teigneront les auters deux parts en joynture). And as to the third part, which he hath by force of the release, he holdeth that third part with himself and his companion in common." Coke's note is: "Upon this case these two things are to be observed. First, that in this case this release doth enure by way of mitter l'estate, and not by way of extinguishment, for then the release should enure to his companion also, and he is in the per by him that maketh the release."

But although such a transaction should be carried out by release, a grant is interpreted as being a release: see *Eustace v. Scawen* (1624) Cro. Jac. 696; 79 E.R. 604; *Chester v. Willan* (1670) 2 Wms. Saund. 96; 85 E.R. 768.

The *Real Property Act* 1862 (Tas.) does not alter the law with respect to joint tenancy. It leaves the incidents of joint tenancy standing as they are determined by the common law and any other relevant statute. But it requires that documents transferring interests in land under the Act should be in a particular form and should be registered: ss 42, 39.

If there are three joint tenants, A, B and C, and one joint tenant A transfers his interest to another joint tenant B, the result is that A then has no interest in the land, B becomes a tenant in common as to one third interest in the land, and remains a joint tenant with C as to a two thirds interest. If subsequently B transfers to A the interest which he still has as a joint tenant (A then having become a stranger to the title, his interest having passed to B), there is a further and complete severance. A becomes a tenant in common as to one third interest with B and C, the transfer working a severance of the joint tenancy between B and C in the two thirds interest in the land. The final result is that A, B and C become tenants in common, each having a one third interest.

If the transfer by B to A were made on a day subsequent to the transfer by A to B, as I have assumed in what has just been said there would be no doubt as to the result. The difficulty in the present case arises from the fact that there was only one document which came into operation at a particular moment of time, namely upon registration: see *Real Property Act* 1862 (Tas.), ss 35(2), 39(1). But if the document is construed in accordance with the principle ut res magis valeat quam pereat, the transaction can be upheld by regarding the words of transfer by A to B as equivalent to a release and by regarding the words of transfer by B to A as constituting a grant. The transfer by A to B made B a tenant in common with C as to a one third interest, leaving B and C as joint tenants in respect of a two thirds interest. That joint tenancy of B and C was severed when B transferred his interest as joint tenant to A. If the document is so interpreted effect is given to the plain intention of the parties so that A, B and C became tenants in common of the land, each owning a one third interest.

In my opinion the appeals should be allowed and the point of law determined by declaring that the joint tenancy in the land under the *Real Property Act* was severed by the registration of the transfer dated 6 December 1945.

RICH J. . . . I think that some confusion has occurred by concentrating attention on the principles of common law conveyancing and not observing the innovation effected by the new or Torrens system. The Torrens system, which is in use in all the States and in New Zealand, originated in two statutes passed in 1858 by the Parliament of South Australia prompted by Sir Robert Torrens whose name the system commemorates. Its basal features are that transactions in land should be carried out by their registration in a government office, thus guaranteeing ownership of an absolute and indefeasible title to realty and that by the exclusive use of a transfer in the statutory form conveyances and assurances which under the old system had become cumbersome and intricate should be simplified.

An examination of the relevant Act—the *Real Property Act* 1862 (Tas.) as originally enacted—shows how the system works. "Land" includes every estate and interest in land, and "transfer" means the passing of any estate or interest in land under this Act, whether for valuable consideration or otherwise: s. 3. "Joint tenants", by the statutory fiction "deemed", are treated as joint proprietors or co-proprietors: ss 87, 88. Registration is provided for in ss 34(3), 37, 42 and Form IV. in the first schedule. The scheme of transfer and registration is the only method by which any alienation or disposition of a share or interest in land may be made.

The ownership by two or more persons of real property with the requisites of unity of possession, interest, title and time confers on each such person a share or right severable and capable of alienation. The instrument in question is an adaption of the form provided in the schedule which is the appropriate and only form by which any share in land registered under the Act can be disposed of. In the instant case the fact that there is only one document and not separate transfers does not, in my opinion, result in a "futility" but is effective and operates as a severance.

The statutory forms "may be used with such alterations as the character of the parties or the circumstances of the case may render necessary": s. 3, concluding provision; cf. *Perpetual Executors & Trustees Association (Aust.) Ltd v. Hosken* (1912) 14 C.L.R. 286. Under the old system severance may be effected by alienation to a stranger or by release (operating as an extinguishment of right) or by grant from one joint tenant to another. Even the grant of a lease by one joint tenant to another has been considered to effect a severance: *Cowper v. Fletcher* (1865) 6 B. & S. 465 at 472; 122 E.R. 1267 at 1270; *Re Armstrong* (1920) 1 I.R. 239. Having regard to the acts of the parties, I would give effect to their intention and construe the transfer as constituting a severance.

I would add that, even assuming that the form used by the parties could be regarded as so vitally irregular as to be incapable, upon registration, of producing the result which it was obviously intended to produce—that of vesting the legal estate in Ethel Rose Gibbons and Olinda Gibbons as to one third each as tenants in common—nevertheless it is clear that it would operate in equity as an agreement for valuable consideration by each to vest in the other a one third interest as tenant in common, an agreement which would in equity be specifically enforceable by an order directing the execution of whatever might be the proper form of instrument, and would, pending such execution, operate in equity to sever the joint tenancy and

create equitable interests as tenants in common: *Brown v. Raindle* (1796) 3 Ves. Jun.
256; 30 E.R. 998; *Parker v. Taswell* (1858) 2 De G. & J. 559 at 570, 571; 44 E.R.
1106 at 1110, 1111; *Cadwell v. Fellowes* (1870) L.R. 9 Eq. 410; *Re Hewett; Hewett
v. Hallett* (1894) 1 Ch. 362 at 367; *Zimbler v. Abrahams* (1903) 1 K.B. 577 at 588;
Re Fireproof Doors Ltd; Umney v. the Company (1916) 2 Ch. 142 at 150, 151;
*Wellington City Corp. v. Public Trustee, McDonald, and District Land Registrar,
Wellington* [1921] N.Z.L.R. 1086.

For these reasons I would allow the appeal.

DIXON J. . . . The case can, on this footing, be stated in an abstract way. A, B
and C are joint tenants for an estate in fee simple in land under the Real Property
Acts. By one instrument of transfer A purports to transfer to B his undivided
interest in the land and B purports to transfer to A his undivided interest in the land
to the intent that they shall all three be tenants in common in equal shares. Upon
registration of the transfer is there a severance so that they become tenants in
common in equal shares? Clark J. answered this question in the negative. The full
force of his Honour's reasons for this conclusion can only be understood from a
study of the judgment and the learning it contains. The foundation of the decision
may, I believe, nevertheless be stated almost in a sentence. It is that in contemplation
of law joint tenants are jointly seised for the whole estate they take in land and no
one of them has a distinct or separate title, interest or possesssion. It follows that
an attempt on the part of two of three joint tenants mutually to assure each to the
other his or her undivided share in the hope that each of their two shares will be
taken by a new title and so enure as a several undivided interest, must fail because
it can accomplish nothing. An alienation by a joint tenant of an undivided interest
to a stranger, upon this view, imparts a several interest because such a power is
incident to joint tenancy; but that is very different from identifying the respective
interests of joint tenants and transposing them. . . . In two places Richard Preston
summed up the result: "Joint tenants are said to be seised per my et per tout. They
are in under the same feudal contract or investiture. Hence livery of seisin from one
to another is not sufficient. For all purposes of alienation, each is seised of, and has
a power of alienation over that share only which is his aliquot part": *Essay on
Abstracts of Title* (2nd ed.), Vol. 2, p. 62. "The real distinction is, joint tenants have
the whole for the purpose of tenure and survivorship, while, for the purpose of
immediate alienation, each has only a particular part"; *On Estates* (2nd ed.), Vol. 1,
p. 136. An alienation by one joint tenant to a stranger might be made by the
appropriate means of assurance and in respect of the aliquot share of the alienor
the stranger would come in with the remaining co-tenant or co-tenants as a tenant
in common.

But with respect to the alienation of the share of a joint tenant to a companion,
special rules applied. Because the alienee was regarded as already in by the
infeudation creating the joint tenancy the proper means of assuring the share of the
alienor to him was release. The release operated as a discharge of the benefit of the
infeudation or feudal contract from one joint tenant to another: Watkins,
Conveyancing (9th ed.), Coote's note, p. 167. "But though this release will, for all
purposes of conveyance, pass the moiety of the releasing joint tenant to his
companion, yet the usual practice was to take a conveyance by lease and release":
Watkins, op. cit., p. 167. "The proper assurance between joint tenants is a release.
One may release to all. Several may release to the others. One or more may release
to some or one of the others: and if they convey by lease and release or by
feoffment, such lease and release or feoffment will operate as a release; but then
there must be a deed": Preston, op. cit., Vol. 2, p. 61. "If one of three or more

joint tenants release to another of them, the share so released will be held in severalty; and as to the remaining shares the parties will continue joint tenants. The releasee is in by way of conveyance or title as an assignee and not under the original feudal contract": Preston, op. cit., Vol. 2, p. 61.

Take then the present case, A, B and C are joint tenants. A might release or grant (and a grant would be given effect as a release) his aliquot share to B and B would take that share as tenant in common with C. B would retain his own original aliquot share as joint tenant with C. B's two aliquot shares would be distinguishable by their different incidents. A has become a stranger to the jointure. Surely B could by an appropriate assurance impart B's original aliquot share to A. If so he would come in as a tenant in common. He would then "be in by way of conveyance or title as an assignee". If the two assurances were made separately and in proper succession it would not matter how short a time elapsed between them. The result would be that A, B and C, having been joint tenants up to the execution of the first assurance, that is up to the release or its equivalent, would upon the execution of the second assurance become tenants in common in equal shares. What is an appropriate assurance for the second transfer or assignment (that of B's original share to A) has of course differed at different times, feoffment, lease and release and grant, but that is immaterial.

Suppose again that A, B and C being joint tenants for an estate in fee simple, A and B joined in an assurance, let us say a grant, of their two aliquot shares to X, as a grantee to uses, to the use of A and B and their respective heirs as tenants in common in equal shares. Would that not have operated to make them tenants in common not only between themselves but also with C? I have not seen a precedent for nor a reference to such an assurance, but I can see no objection to it, unless it be on the alleged ground that, for the purposes of the *Statute of Uses,* the feoffor, any more than the person seised, cannot be identical with the person entitled to the use. But that has never been the rule where the person entitled to the use takes a different estate or interest or under different limitations or in another right.

While these two instances may show that, independently of the Torrens system, by the use of appropriate assurances, A and B could have severed the jointure between C and themselves as well as between one another, the objection still remains that they could not have done so by mutual releases one to another nor by mutual grants one at least of which must have operated, if at all, as a release. That objection is probably a good one. The strength of the objection will be seen by taking one of the two mutual attempts to transfer the interests. As a release the attempt by A to transfer his share to B cannot operate unless B continues in his position in the jointure. But as a grant it cannot operate unless B has already ceased to occupy his position in the jointure. For him to attempt to change it eo instanti with the operation of the grant or release by himself to A therefore would appear to be inconsistent with both alternatives.

The foregoing shows that under the general law the question depended upon the conveyance or assurance used to effect the mutual transfers of the aliquot shares of the two joint tenants who desired to bring about a severance of the jointure with their companion as well as between themselves. This conclusion, to my mind, reduces the matter to a question of the operation of the Real Property Acts. It does so for two reasons. In the first place the conclusion must mean that not only for the purpose of alienations to strangers but also for the purpose of alienation of a share by one joint tenant to another, the aliquot share of each existed in contemplation of law as a distinct and ascertained proprietary interest.

The second reason is that it shows that the obstacle to concurrent cross-transfers of interests was that, except by employing the *Statute of Uses,* no assurance existed capable of effecting the transfers simultaneously but only by successive steps.

In approaching the Real Property Acts, it must be borne in mind that the interests of each joint tenant fell within the general statutory principle that all lands and all interests therein lie in grant.

Section 39 of the *Real Property Act* 1862 (Tas.) provides that upon registration of an instrument the estate or interest specified in the instrument shall pass in the manner set forth and specified in the instrument. Section 42 says that when land is to be transferred (and that must mean an interest therein) the registered proprietor shall execute a memorandum of transfer in the prescribed form containing an accurate statement of the estate or interest intended to be transferred. Section 87 provides that two or more persons who may be registered as joint proprietors of an estate or interest in the land shall be deemed to be entitled to the same as joint tenants. These provisions result in each joint proprietor being entitled as a registered proprietor to transfer his interest by a memorandum of transfer presented for registration: see *Tucker v. Coleman* (1885) 4 N.Z.L.R. 128. When this system for the conveyance of distinct legal proprietary interests is applied to the common law conceptions of the interests of joint tenants it appears to me to follow that an exclusive method of assuring the aliquot share of a joint tenant is provided and that all the consequences ensue which at common law followed the transfer or legal assignment of such a share. Moreover it supplies a method of assurance of general application, that is to say one that will be apt and effective to impart any transferable interest. It is of course subject to the law of capacity or law of persons. But if it is a legal interest, as opposed to equitable, in property and is alienable the system enables the transfer thereof to be made. It is of course true that this train of reasoning still falls short by one step of establishing that the transfer by one joint tenant of his interest may be made to his companion and e converso of the companion's share to him. But in my opinion the considerations that have preceded the discussion of the Real Property Acts are enough to make good that step. For those considerations appear to show first that there is no incapacity in one of three joint tenants to take as a tenant in common a transfer of a companion's share; secondly that the companion's share is in contemplation of law a distinct and ascertained proprietary interest; thirdly that by a means of conveyancing that is superseded the result might have been brought about.

The consequence is that if A, B and C are joint tenants, in my opinion cross-transfers may be made at the same time of the respective aliquot interests of A and B to one another and the result is to produce a tenancy in common among A, B and C.

It follows that I think that the appeal should be allowed.

Appeal allowed.

McNAB v. EARLE

Supreme Court of New South Wales [1981] 2 N.S.W.L.R. 673 at 676

NEEDHAM J. In the present case the severance relied upon by the defendant is of the first class referred to by Page Wood V.-C. (*Williams v. Hensman* (1861) 1 J. & H. 546 at 557; 70 E.R. 862 at 867) that is, "an act of any one of the persons interested operating upon his own share". It is clear that "if the act of a joint tenant (is to amount) to a severance it must be such as to preclude him from claiming by survivorship any interest in the subject matter of the joint tenancy": *Re Wilks* [1891] 3 Ch. 59 at 62. In that case the severance claimed was based upon the issue by one joint tenant of a summons for payment out to him of one third of the fund. It happened that the applicant died before the case came on for hearing and Stirling J. held there had been no severance because the applicant was at liberty to abandon the summons or amend it. Whether the actual decision in that case is correct or not (Lord Denning M.R. in *Burgess v. Rawnsley* [1975] Ch. 429 at 440 doubted it, while Browne L.J. (at 444) and Sir John Pennycuick (at 447) merely said that it had to be read in the light of s. 36(2) of the *Law of Property Act* 1925 (U.K)), nobody has questioned the statement of Stirling J. (in *Re Wilks* at 61, 62) that a joint tenancy may be severed "by a disposition made by one of the joint owners amounting at law or in equity to an assignment of the share of that owner". The assignment could be to another joint tenant and severance could follow assignments to each other of two out of three joint tenants: *Wright v. Gibbons* (1949) 78 C.L.R. 313.

The question, then, is whether the transfer in this case comes within the statement of principle by Stirling J. or Page Wood V.-C. Did Mrs McNab's action in executing the transfer to herself, an act not communicated to the other joint tenant and not perfected at law by registration, amount to "an assignment . . . of (her) share" or to an "act . . . operating upon (her) own share".

Two Canadian cases are of interest. I have already referred to *Re Murdoch and Barry* (1975) 64 D.L.R. (3d) 222, a decision of Goodman J. in the Ontario High Court. In that case, it was held that a conveyance by one joint tenant to herself, once registered, effected a severance. The principle applied was that the execution of the deed together with an act constituting delivery was sufficient to effect a severance, and that delivery must have taken place at least by the time of registration. It is clear from the judgment that it was not considered a sufficient act of severance merely to execute the deed.

Similarly, in *Re Sammon* (1979) 94 D.L.R. (3d) 594, a decision of the Ontario Court of Appeal, it was held that the execution of a deed "to uses" by one joint tenant to himself and physical delivery of the deed to his solicitor did not effect severance. There the joint tenant executing the deed instructed his solicitor not to register it until after his death for fear that his wife, the other joint tenant, should discover his action. The court said that the question was whether there had been, in law, a delivery of the deed. The deed, as in the present case, was part of a procedure in which the "assignor" made a will on the basis that the deed was effective. The court held that there was no evidence that the assignor-testator intended to be immediately and unconditionally bound by the deed, or that he looked upon the deed as less "ambulatory" than the will. The court rejected an argument that it would have been improper for the assignor to destroy the deed. The argument was circular, because if the deed was not effective to sever the tenancy, it was a mere piece of paper.

There is, of course, in respect of *Real Property Act* land, no act which equates with delivery of a deed. Apart from equities or protection against notice by virtue of s. 43A of the *Real Property Act* 1900 (N.S.W.), a transfer has no operation prior to registration. In the present case no equity can arise nor can protection be required or acquired against notice. The transfer, in my opinion, being inoperative, was at all times revocable, just as the will was, and, if Mrs McNab had directed Mr Edwards to destroy one or other or both of them he would have been under a duty to comply with such an instruction.

Those being, in my opinion, the principles applicable to this transfer, the point in issue has to be decided in favour of the plaintiff, that is, the proper conclusion is that no severance was effected by what took place.

An involuntary alienation, likewise, operates to sever a joint tenancy so that, for example, the bankruptcy of a joint tenant operates to sever the joint tenancy by statutory alienation: see, for example, *Re Francis; Ex parte Official Trustee in Bankruptcy* (1988) 82 A.L.R. 335.

Severance may arise also from a partial alienation of the joint tenant's interest, but only where the partial alienation in fact constitutes the grant of an estate and not a mere incumbrance. For example, the grant of a first mortgage over old system title land constitutes an alienation of the legal estate in the land to the mortgagee and, accordingly, severs the joint tenancy (*Re Pollard's Estate* (1863) 3 De G.J. & S. 541; 46 E.R. 746), but this does not sever the beneficial estate of the mortgagors, with which the legal estate merges on reconveyance or discharge of the mortgage, so that upon reconveyance a surviving joint mortgagor will be solely entitled to the legal estate as the person to whom the equity of redemption has passed by survivorship: *Schmeling v. Stankovic* (1984) 3 B.P.R. N.S.W. (S.C.) 97, 191. Quaere the effect of a grant of a mortgage by a joint tenant of Torrens title land, where the mortgage does not effect a transfer of an interest in the land but only creates a statutory charge. The preferred view is that the grant of a mortgage over Torrens title land by a joint tenant does not sever the joint tenancy: see (1936) 9 A.L.J. 322 at 431; Baalman, *The Torrens System in New South Wales* (2nd ed.), p. 351; Mendes De Costa, "Co-ownership Under Victorian Land Law" (1962) 3 M.U.L.R. 433 at 447; and *Lyons v. Lyons* [1967] V.R. 169, extracted below p. 63.

Similarly, the question arises whether a lease by a joint tenant effects a severance of the joint tenancy. The preferable view appears to be that there is no severance, and that "at most it effects a 'severance for the time', or 'suspends' the joint tenancy pro tem": see *Frieze v. Unger* [1960] V.R. 230, extracted below p. 66.

SCHMELING v. STANKOVIC

Supreme Court of New South Wales (1984) 3 B.P.R. 9325

COHEN J. The plaintiff seeks a declaration that he and the defendant are beneficial owners as tenants in common of certain land situated at Orange, and consequential orders.

The land is held under the old system of registration and was conveyed to the defendant and his wife, Elsa Stankovic, as joint tenants, by deed of conveyance dated 27 May 1960. On 17 April 1961 they mortgaged the land to the Commercial Bank of Australia Ltd. The deed of mortgage was in a common form. It recited the consideration of advances being made and stated that the mortgagor as beneficial owner conveyed the land to the mortgagee to be held in fee simple subject to the proviso for redemption which followed thereafter.

The proviso set out the requirements for repayment and then provided that on those being met the mortgagor "will at the request and cost of the mortgagor execute a statutory discharge of mortgage or will reconvey the mortgaged property or such part thereof as is then vested in the mortgagee unto the mortgagor or as he shall direct".

Elsa Stankovic died on 18 August 1983, while the mortgage was still undischarged. By her will she appointed her son, who is the plaintiff, to be her executor and she gave to him the whole of her estate. The plaintiff claims that the equity of redemption was held by the defendant and his wife as tenants in common, and accordingly that he is entitled to the one half share of the deceased. The bank has, since the commencement of these proceeding, executed a discharge, but this has no effect on the claim being made.

Counsel for the plaintiff has submitted that upon the execution of the mortgage the land was conveyed to the bank and the joint tenancy in the legal estate was converted into a tenancy in severalty. The interest of the defendant and his wife derived its source from the proviso in the mortgage, and that was a disposition of the property to them. Accordingly, s. 26 of the *Conveyancing Act* 1919 (N.S.W.) applies and there is a presumption that the disposition is to them as tenants in common, in the absence of any express provision that they take as joint tenants. This would apply whether there was a reconveyance or a statutory discharge.

It is further pointed out that the definition of "mortgagor" in the mortgage includes each of them and their respective executors, administrators and assigns. Thus, it is submitted, the interest of the deceased as a tenant in common in the equity of redemption, passed to the plaintiff on her death.

Section 26 of the *Conveyancing Act* states:

"26. (1) In the construction of any instrument coming into operation after the commencement of this Act a disposition of the beneficial interest in any property whether with or without the legal estate to or for two or more persons together beneficially shall be deemed to be made to or for them as tenants in common, and not as joint tenants.

(2) This section does not apply to persons who by the terms or by the tenor of the instrument are executors, administrators, trustees, or mortgagees, nor in any case where the instrument expressly provides that persons are to take as joint tenants or tenants by entireties."

The provision for statutory discharge of a mortgage is s. 91 of the same Act. This allows for the mortgage being discharged by a memorandum indorsed on, or annexed to, the mortgage. The effect of that memorandum is set out in subs. (3)(a), which states: "Every such memorandum of discharge, upon registration, but as from the date of such memorandum, shall, unless a contrary intention appears in the memorandum, vacate the mortgage debt, and shall operate as a deed of conveyance of the estate and interest of the mortgagee of and in the mortgaged property to the person for the time being entitled to the equity of redemption to the uses and for the estates and interests, and subject to the powers and trusts to, for, and subject to which, the equity of redemption at the date of such memorandum stood limited or subject discharged from all moneys secured by the mortgage: Provided that in case there is any subsequent subsisting mortgage on the property at the date of such memorandum, the legal estate in the property under the discharged mortgage shall vest in the person in whom the subsequent mortgage is vested, or in the event of there being more than one such mortgage then in the person who has the prior right to call for a conveyance of such legal estate."

Although the plaintiff's submission would seem to produce hitherto unforeseen consequences, his counsel submits that a prudent conveyancer, on the repayment of the mortgage moneys, would have the property reconveyed to the mortgagors as joint tenants, thus overcoming the effect which it is said follows from the agreement to reconvey. Indeed, on the plaintiff's argument, that prudent conveyancer, in order to protect the joint tenancy, would have to persuade the mortgagee to amend the form of mortgage so as to provide for a reconveyance to the mortgagors specifically as joint tenants.

The plaintiff's argument depends entirely on the contractual basis of the equity of redemption, as contained in the terms of the mortgage. It is first necessary to consider what are the interests of the parties at the time of the giving of a mortgage over old system land to secure a loan.

A mortgage of common law title land is a transfer of the legal title for the purpose of providing to the mortgagee a security or pledge for the debt: *Casborne v. Scarfe* (1737) 1 Atk. 603; 26 E.R. 377; *Turner v. Walsh* [1909] 2 K.B. 484 at 494. The equity of redemption which remains in the mortgagor is an equitable estate in the land, a concept which was first put forward by Lord Hardwicke in *Casborne v. Scarfe*. This was the modern view which was thereafter supported by the courts: see Turner, *The Equity of Redemption*, Ch. 4.

The person having that equity of redemption is considered as the beneficial owner of the land, subject only to the mortgagee's security, and that ownership remains in the mortgagor until foreclosure. "The mortgagor has an estate in the land, and he can deal with that estate just as much as if he had never made a mortgage, and can sell it, settle it, create charges upon it in favour of his wife or children, or demise it; he can do anything he pleases with it, as if he had the estate in fee unencumbered, but always subject to the mortgage": per Kekewich J. in *Tarn v. Turner* (1888) 39 Ch.D. 456 at 460.

On the other hand a mortgagee's interest is, in equity, not a right to the mortgage property, but to the mortgage debt, and his beneficial interest in the security is only as a means for enforcing his right to the debt: see Waldock, *The Law of Mortgages*, (2nd ed.), p. 202.

The equitable interest or estate of the mortgagor arises on the execution of the mortgage. In addition, on default there arises an equity to redeem, quite apart from the contractual right to redeem on a particular date: *G. and C. Kreglinger v. New Patagonia Meat & Cold Storage Co. Ltd* [1914] A.C. 25 at 48 per Lord Parker.

Whether the right be a contractual one or an equitable one, it is a right to have the legal title restored to the beneficial owner, so that the legal and equitable estates are merged. In *Plowden v. Hyde* (1852) 2 De G.M. & G. 684; 42 E.R. 1040, it was said by Lord Cranworth (at 696; at 1044) that the mortgagor takes a conveyance to the same uses to which it had stood previously to the mortgage. The mortgagor is "bringing home the legal interest, or . . . clothing the equitable with the legal estate".

Where the legal estate before the granting of the mortgage was held in joint tenancy, then upon that mortgage being entered into, there immediately arose an equitable estate. This was not dependent on the proviso as to the reconveyance or discharge but came into existence on the principles set out above. That estate was held in the same way that the legal and beneficial estate had been previously held, namely on joint tenancy. Although there had been a conveyance in form, that had not severed the whole of the joint tenancy but merely the legal estate by converting it into a severality. The equitable owners retained as joint tenants the powers of selling, devising or otherwise dealing with their equitable estate, and there had been no step taken which would have brought about an alteration in the nature of their holding.

If one of the joint tenants were to enter into a mortgage of his or her interest, then that would have effected a severance of the joint tenancy. In *Wright v. Gibbons* (1949) 78 C.L.R. 313, where considerable discussion of the principles of joint tenancies took place, there had been mortgages executed by two of three joint tenants of land held under common law title. The court at first instance had held that the mortgages had severed the joint tenancy in respect of that part of the land.

This was not disputed on appeal: see at 320. That severance comes about because there has been a destruction of the unity of title by an assignment of the interest of one of the joint tenants. See Francis, *Mortgages and Securities* (2nd ed.), pp. 54-55.

In the present case there has been no interference with the unity of title, except as already referred to. The proviso in the mortgage does no more than set out the rights of a mortgagor, that is to have a restoral of the legal title upon the payment of capital, interest and charges. If a statutory discharge were to be executed then its effect would be that of a conveyance of the legal interest to the mortgagors to the uses and for the estates and interests to which the equity of redemption stood at the date of the memorandum. That estate or interest, had Mrs Stankovic still been alive, would have been a joint tenancy in the equitable estate.

The plaintiff then must rely upon the further part of the proviso which, as an alternative, requires a reconveyance to the mortgagor or as he shall direct. This, as expanded by the definition in cl. 23, means to the mortgagors and their respective executors, administrators and assigns, or as they shall direct.

In my view, this does not amount to a disposition of the beneficial interest in the property as referred to in s. 26. It is the mechanics by which the legal estate is to be dealt with, depending on what may be the ownership of the equity of redemption at the time when all moneys due to the mortgage and costs and charges, have been repaid. No time for that repayment is stipulated. The conveyance is to be to whomsoever is at that time the person entitled to the equity of redemption or as the mortgagor at the time shall direct. The person entitled may by then be an assignee or devisee, or, as in the present case, it may be the joint tenant to whom the equity of redemption has passed by survivorship.

The beneficial interest in the property at all times remained in the mortgagors. It was not conveyed to the mortgagee and it was therefore not to be reconveyed. All that the reconveyance would do was, in the words of Lord Cranworth, to bring home the legal interest. It could not alter the existing equitable interest which would still have been held on a joint tenancy, assuming both tenants were still alive.

In the present case it does not seem necessary to consider what would have happened if a reconveyance had been executed. The plaintiff's claim was based on a contractual term of the mortgage, namely that the proviso was, by virtue of s. 26 an agreement to convey to the mortgagors and that this conveyance when it occurred, would be to them as tenants in common. It had to assume that this was the only way in which the mortgagors acquired their equity of redemption. In fact, at the time of the death of Mrs Stankovic, she and the defendant held the equity of redemption as an equitable estate as joint tenants, not by virtue of the proviso, but for the reasons I have already set out. The identification of the document as a mortgage gave rise, on its execution, to the equitable estate of the mortgagors.

Thus, on the death of Mrs Stankovic that equitable estate vested in the defendant by survivorship. There was nothing which passed to the executor of Mrs Stankovic's estate.

I therefore order that the summons be dismissed with costs.

LYONS v. LYONS

Supreme Court of Victoria [1967] V.R. 169 at 173

McINERNEY A.J. It becomes, therefore, necessary to consider whether the joint tenancy was severed by the execution by William Patrick Lyons of a mortgage of his interest to Adelaide Mary Gray.

In the case of land under the general law it is clear that a mortgage by one joint tenant of his interest in the land to a stranger to the tenancy effects a severance of the joint tenancy. . . .

The reason is plain: under the general law the mortgagor conveys his estate in the mortgaged land to the mortgagee. There is thus vested in the mortgagee all the estate and interest formerly vested in the joint tenant mortgagor: but the mortgagee obtains that estate and interest under a different instrument or judicial act than the other joint tenant or tenants, and there is thus no unity of title between the mortgagee and them.

. . . Challis writes: "But in order that a grant by one joint tenant may bind his fellows, it must be the grant of an estate and not the grant of a mere incumbrance or burden of the estate, such as a rent-charge or a right of common." . . .

The justification for the different result would seem, therefore, to lie in the more technical reason that in the one case (the mortgage by conveyance of the fee simple to the mortgagee) the unity of title is destroyed by that conveyance, while in the other (the grant of a rent-charge, or profit à prendre, or easement), where the fee simple is not conveyed away, the unity of title is not destroyed.

What, then, is the effect of a mortgage under the Torrens system by one joint tenant to a stranger to the tenancy?

The accepted view of the Torrens system under a mortgage is that it has effect as a security only and does not operate as a transfer or the estate or interest charged. . . .

[In] *Re Forrest; Trustees Executors & Agency Co. Ltd v. Anson* [1953] V.L.R. 246 at 256 Herring C.J. said: "When the legislature introduced the statutory mortgage under the *Transfer of Land Act* 1928 (Vic.), it took the final step in the movement towards hypotheca that the Court of Chancery was unable, by reason of its limited jurisdiction, to take, and introduced what was practically the Roman hypotheca with the addition of registration. For it introduced a registered charge to take effect as a security, which conferred on the creditor merely a group of powers to secure the money lent, such as to sell, to take possession, etc., whilst leaving the owner what he is meant to be, owner subject to his fulfilling his obligation."

Against the view of Herring C.J., just quoted, there must however be set the view expressed in the same case by Gavan Duffy and Dean JJ., in their joint judgment at 271: "But the significant thing is that, whether the mortgage be one under the general law or under the *Transfer of Land Act*, the real beneficial owner is the mortgagor, not the mortgagee, and the transaction is simply one by way of security. Upon payment of the amount due by him the mortgagor is entitled to have his property released from the security. It is of little importance from a practical point of view where the legal title resides. The formalities of the transaction differ in the two cases, but all the realities are the same. It, therefore, seems appropriate enough to describe the right of the mortgagor, as Parliament has described it, as an equity of redemption in each case, and equally appropriate to describe the proceeding whereby a mortgagor enforces such right as a suit to redeem the mortgage. It is a right derived from the general principle of equity where property is charged to secure a debt. The relief claimed by a mortgagor of land under the *Transfer of Land Act* differs from an ordinary redemption action only in that, instead of a direction to reconvey the land, the court orders the execution of a discharge having the same effect in freeing the land from the charge upon it. In *National Bank (A/asia) v. United Hand-in-Hand and Band of Hope Co.* (1879) 4 App. Cas. 391, Molesworth J., the Full Court and the Privy Council treated an action by a mortgagor of land under the Act as an ordinary redemption action.

What has been said supports the view that the formal changes effected by the *Transfer of Land Act* in the case of a mortgage effected and registered under that Act are more apparent than real. If substance and effect be regarded, and not form (and equity has always so regarded mortgages), it appears that, as between mortgagor and mortgagee, and subject to the express provisions of the Act, the differences are not great. . . .''

To say that the mortgage has an interest in the land does not solve the present problem. The grantee of a rent-charge or of an easement of way or common or of a profit à prendre, has an interest in land, yet the creation of such an interest in land by one joint tenant does not sever the joint tenancy under the general law.

The industry of counsel and my own research have not discovered any Australian or New Zealand case law on the point I have to decide. There is a respectable body of conveyancing opinion, however, that a mortgage under the Torrens system by one joint tenant does not sever the joint tenancy. Thus in New Zealand a former Registrar-General of Land (Mr E. C. Adams) in his book on the *Land Transfer Act*, at para. 213, wrote in 1958: "A mortgage of land under the *Land Transfer Act* by one or two or more joint tenants, does not break or cause the severance of the joint tenancy. Therefore, if the joint tenant who has mortgaged dies before the other joint tenant or tenants, the land will vest in the surviving joint tenant or tenants free of the mortgage. It is for this reason that the conveyancer should never advise a mortgage by one joint tenant as an adequate security.

If, however, the joint tenant who has mortgaged is the ultimate survivor, then the mortgage becomes an effective security against the *whole* estate. But where one joint tenant mortgages to a stranger and subsequently transfers his estate or interest in the land to the other joint tenant, the transferee is bound by the mortgage, whether or not he survives the transferor; this is because he claims under the transfer and not by survivorship.''

The last passage is obviously based on the reasoning of the court in *Lord Abergavenny's Case* 6 Co. Rep. 78(b) at 79(b); 77 E.R. 373 at 373-374.

The same writer, as editor of *Garrow's Law of Real Property* (5th ed.), p. 65, note (q) wrote: "Under the general law the tenancy is severed, if a joint tenant mortgages his interest to a stranger, but it is submitted that this cannot apply to a mortgage of land subject to the *Land Transfer Act*, because under that Act a mortgage operates not as a transfer of the property but as a charge merely. A mortgage of his interest by a joint tenant under the *Land Transfer Act* is a very risky transaction: see Practical Note No. 4 in (1945) 21 N.Z.L.J. 274.'' The view put by Mr Adams has been expressed also in New South Wales: see Baalman, *The Torrens System in New South Wales*, p. 331; and Helmore, *The Law of Real Property in New South Wales* (2nd ed.), p. 273.

. . . I am disposed to agree with the comments of Nourse J., in *People of California v. Nogarr* 67 Am. L.R. (2nd) 992 at 999 (1958): "There is nothing inequitable in holding that the lien of the respondent's mortgage did not survive the death of the mortgagor. Their note was payable upon demand and they could have enforced the lien and mortgage by foreclosure and sale prior to the death of the mortgagor and thus have severed the joint tenancy. If they chose not to do so but to await the contingency of which joint tenant died first they did so at their own risk. Under that event the lien that they had expired. If the event had been otherwise and the mortgagor had been the survivor the security of their lien would have been doubled.'' . . .

I do not, therefore, find persuasive Dr Mendes Da Costa's arguments in support of the view that the mortgage effects a severance. Futhermore, it seems to me that if the transaction does not effect a severance (because it does not destroy any of the four unities) there is no real ground for holding that its effect is to suspend the joint tenancy. I therefore accept as correct the reasoning and the conclusion in *People v. Nogarr*, according as it does with what I understand to be long-standing conveyancing opinion both in Australia and New Zealand, as expressed for instance by Dr Kerr and Mr Adams in the passages cited earlier in this judgment.

FRIEZE v. UNGER

Supreme Court of Victoria [1960] V.R. 230 at 242

SHOLL J. In their interesting and able written submissions in the present case, which were filed by leave after the argument of 14 and 15 May, Professor Derham and Mr Wilson have shown by an analysis of the authorities that the question of severance or no severance apparently depended, and still depends, upon (a) the nature of the grantor's estate, and (b) the quantum of the interest granted; and also that there are three possible views as to the nature and extent of any severance effected. To take the last point first, they cite the following passage from a modern American commentator, Lawrence F. Kuechler, in (1937) 25 Calif. L. Rev. 203 at 207: "Assume that A and B were joint tenants in fee, and that A leased his interest to C for a term. If the lease did not effect a severance except in so far as it was necessary to protect the lessee, the survivor would take the entire estate subject to the rights of the lessee; for the rights of the survivor, having accrued at the time of conveyance to A and B, have not been divested. On the other hand, if the lease effected a complete and final severance, the survivor would take no part of the deceased's interest, which would descend to the latter's heirs; for by this hypothesis the joint tenancy became a tenancy in common, and the right of survivorship was extinguished. A third possibility would make the result depend upon the date of A's death. Assuming that A is survived by B, and that A died while the lease was still in force, it might be reasoned that A's heirs would take by inheritance, since the existence of the lease at the time when the right of survivorship would otherwise have been affected, would operate as a severance permanently extinguishing such right. If, however, A died after C's term had expired, it might be held that B took the entire premises as survivor; for it could be reasoned, that, as soon as the lease expired both A and B being still alive, they stood in their orginal relationship as joint tenants."

If joint tenants hold in fee, the grant by one of a life estate or of a lease for life or lives, effects, according to what is now considered the "better opinion", a severance of the entire fee simple, so that the remainder or reversion will descend to the heir of the grantor; see Co. Litt. 191b; and the text writers above cited; and see also per Dixon J. (as he then was), in *Wright v. Gibbons* (1949) 78 C.L.R. 313 at 330.

But a demise for a term of years by one of two joint tenants in fee does not, according to the preferable view, work a severance of the whole fee; at most it effects a "severance for the time", or "suspends" the joint tenancy pro tem. This is the view of Dixon J. in *Wright v. Gibbons*; and see Co. Litt. 185a, 318a and Megarry and Wade, *Law of Real Property*, n. 23, commenting on Coke's doctrine. It is not altogether apparent what is meant by a temporary severance or suspension; but at all events, it is clear that the doctrine involves the proposition that the reversion expectant on the term will pass to the survivor of the joint tenants, so that any "severance" or "suspension" is such only as is necessary to procure for the lessee the enjoyment during the term of the grantor's moiety both after as well as before the grantor's death: cf. Co. Litt 186a; and Rolle's Abr., 1668, Vol. 2, p. 89, in a note on *Smallman v. Agborow* (1617) Cro. Jac. 417; 79 E.R. 356. Even in such a case, however, Megarry and Wade, op. cit., consider that the severance is of the whole estate of the joint tenants; but they do not distinguish between the case of joint tenants in fee, and the case of joint tenants for lives, as to which see below. On the other hand, Cheshire, *Real Property* (7th ed.) says "no severance is effected". And in *Preston on Abstracts* (2nd ed.), Vol. 2, pp. 56-63, it is said that a partial alienation, as for life, only suspends the jointure, but that a lease for years does not either sever or suspend it. At all events, notwithstanding these differing opinions, this much should now be taken to be clear, that in the case of a lease for a term of years by one joint tenant in fee, the term survives the death of the grantor, but the reversion passes to the survivor: and see Com. Dig. IV, 112, tit. Estates, (K5). It would seem that if and so far as in such a case there is a suspension of the jointure during the term, the result is that the lessee for years and the lessor's co-tenant hold as would tenants in common: cf. Litt. ss 300, 301, 302, referring to the cases of leases for life. Whether the survivor in such a case would be entitled to the rent as such, was once questioned, and it was held that he was not; see *Anon.* (1560) 2 Dyer 187a; 73 E.R. 412. It was also Coke's view that he would not: see Co. Litt. 185a, 318a; and so it was also said by Preston, op. cit., Vol. 2, p. 64.

In the case of joint tenants for lives the grant of a term of years by one joint tenant probably severs the joint tenancy at any rate temporarily during the term; at all events the lease binds the survivor: see Com. Dig., IV, 112, tit. Estates, (K5); referring to *Anon.* and *Smallman v. Agborow* which are simply authorities for the view that the lease in such a case binds the survivor. The opinion of Megarry and Wade, op. cit., and the submission advanced by Professor Derham and Mr Wilson in the present proceedings, is that there is in such a case a complete severance of the whole jointure, both during and after the term, but the decisions which they cite, though expressed in general language, are not necessarily inconsistent with the notion of a temporary severance only. On the other hand, Preston, op. cit., considered that in such a case there was no severance or even suspension of the joint tenancy at all, though the lease nevertheless bound the survivor.

In the case of joint tenants of a term of years, a grant by one of a term of years to a stranger has always been held wholly to sever the jointure, and to exclude survivorship: see Co. Litt. 192a; Preston, op. cit., Vol. 2, p. 60; and all the modern textbooks.

There will be no severance of the joint tenancy where all the joint tenants act together in the alienation of the jointly held property. Therefore, if all the joint tenants together contract to sell the jointly held property there will be no severance of the joint tenancy: *Re Hayes Estate* [1920] 1 Ir. R. 207; *Re Allingham* [1932] V.L.R. 469. In the latter case both joint tenants joined in the sale of the land under an open contract. Lowe J. said (at 472):

> I see no reason why a change in the form of the property should in itself effect an alteration in the nature of the ownership. The law permits a joint tenancy in personal property no less than in realty. Neither can I see that a contract to sell the property will be any more effective to work that change, that is, to work a severance, if nothing more appears. In my opinion the joint tenants of the land became the joint tenants of the proceeds of the sale of the land. But, of course, the joint tenants may effect a severance of their interest in the proceeds of the sale, as, for instance, by dividing the proceeds of sale equally between themselves.

A resumption of land held by joint tenants does not of itself operate to sever the joint tenancy, but rather converts it into a joint claim for compensation: see *Ex parte Railway Commissioners (N.S.W.)* (1941) 41 S.R. (N.S.W.) 92 where Roper J. said (at 95):

> It was also argued that the resumption itself had effected a severance by changing the interests of the two joint tenants into claims for compensation, but their claims for compensation could in my opinion only be regarded as a joint claim. . . . Here a joint estate in land is converted into a joint claim for compensation, and on that claim being met by payment into court into a joint interest in the fund in court.

A specifically enforceable contract to alienate creates an equitable interest in the land in favour of the purchaser and this will effect severance in equity, though not at law since the legal act of alienation has not taken place. Similarly, it may be that an order made by the court pursuant to s. 86(1) of the *Matrimonial Causes Act* 1959 (Cth) (see now s. 79 of the *Family Law Act* 1975 (Cth)) as respects a property settlement of jointly held land may have the effect of severing the joint tenancy in equity: see *Re Johnstone* [1973] Qd R. 347 at 350 et seq.:

> In the present case no transfer of any interest in the land to the former husband had been effected at the date of his death; no such transfer could have been effected because the Director [of War Service Homes], up to that time, had not given his consent in writing. The order made at the time of the decree nisi imposed an obligation upon the applicant to transfer her interest in the land, subject to the consent of the Director. She was bound to take all necessary steps to perfect the transfer, including, no doubt, whatever steps were proper in an attempt to obtain the Director's consent. But what was the effect upon this obligation of the former husband's death? At the time at which that happened the parties were still registered as joint tenants, and, if they were still at that time to be regarded as holding the land in that capacity, the effect of his death was to vest the whole estate in it in the wife by survivorship, unless there had in the meantime been a severance. If there was a severance, what was the event which produced it?
>
> The order made in relation to the matrimonial home seems to contemplate a state of affairs quite inconsistent with the continued existence of a joint tenancy, or at all events with that incident of it which provides for one of two joint tenants to succeed to the other's interest by survivorship. The order was made in the exercise of the court's powers under s. 86(1) of the *Matrimonial Causes Act* 1959 (Cth); it was an order which, to adapt the words of that subsection, required the applicant to make, for the benefit of her husband, or possibly for the benefit of both of them, since there were no children to whom s. 71 applied, a "settlement of property" which was considered just and equitable in the circumstances. It seems to me to be quite inconsistent with the intention of the order that, if for any reason no transfer had been executed by the wife at the husband's death, its operation should be defeated by the incident of succession by survivorship arising out of the existence of the joint tenancy. It was a provision of a "once and for all" nature, to be contrasted with, for example, a provision for the payment of maintenance by weekly sums, although there was also in this case a provision of the latter kind. I am not aware of any authority on the matter, but it seems to me that there is no reason in principle why a severance, in certain circumstances, should not be effected by an order of the court, if that is necessary in order to ensure that the order may be perfected. That an order of this general nature, that is an order which makes a provision which is intended to have effect once and for all, may be enforced

by or against a party's personal representative is shown by *Harris v. Walker* (1969) 14 F.L.R. 167, in which McLelland C.J. in Eq. followed the ratio of certain English decisions, although he recognised that what was said by Kitto J. in *Johnston v. Krakowski* (1965) 113 C.L.R. 552 may have been inconsistent with those decisions. But I respectfully agree with the reasons which McLelland C.J. in Eq. gave for deciding that he was at liberty to follow the English decisions. The reasoning of the learned judge, applied to the facts of the present case, would lead to the conclusion that the late Mr Johnstone, as soon as the order was made, was entitled in equity to an estate in fee simple in the land, subject to the consent of the Director. Of course it would not be necessary to consider the question of severance if Mr Johnstone had not died, but that is the event which has led to the difficulty in the present case. In my opinion, the effect of the court's order was, since the $300 stipulated by the order had been paid, to effect a severance of the joint tenancy upon the death of Mr Johnstone. It follows that immediately after his death the parties should be regarded in equity as tenants in common, and, leaving aside for the moment the question of the Director's consent, the applicant could now be compelled to execute whatever documents were necessary to pass her interest in the land to Mr Johnstone's administrator, and the Registrar of Titles would be required to register the administrator as proprietor of an estate in fee simple in the land.

(c) Agreement or conduct

BURGESS v. RAWNSLEY

Court of Appeal [1975] Ch. 429 at 438

[Honick, a widower, and the defendant, a widow, met and became friendly. Honick was the tenant of a house in which he lived in the downstairs flat, the upstairs flat being vacant. In 1967 Honick and the defendant bought the house in their joint names "as joint tenants", each providing half of the purchase price of £850. Honick bought the house as a matrimonial home in contemplation of marriage to the defendant. The defendant was minded to live in the upstairs flat and said that Honick never mentioned marriage to her. They did not marry and the defendant did not move into the house. There was evidence accepted by the county court judge of an oral agreement between Honick and the defendant in 1968 whereby she agreed to sell her share in the house to him for £750, but that she subsequently refused to sell. Honick died in 1971 leaving the plaintiff, his daughter, as his administratrix.

The plaintiff claimed that there was a resulting trust or, alternatively, that the joint tenancy had been severed in equity. The defendant claimed that the house was hers by survivorship. It was held at first instance that the defendant held the house on trust for the plaintiff and herself in equal shares. On appeal.]

LORD DENNING M.R. [T]here was an agreement that [the defendant] would sell her share to [Honick] for £750. Almost immediately afterwards she went back upon it. Is that conduct sufficient to effect a severance? . . .

Nowadays everyone starts with the judgment of Sir William Page Wood V.-C. in *Williams v. Hensman* (1861) 1 J. & H. 546 at 557; 70 E.R. 862 at 866-867, where he said: "A joint tenancy may be severed in three ways: in the first place, an act of any one of the persons interested operating upon his own share may create a severance as to that share. . . . Secondly, a joint tenancy may be severed by mutual agreement. And, in the third place, there may be a severance by any course of dealing sufficient to intimate that the interests of all were mutually treated as constituting a tenancy in common. When the severance depends on an inference of this kind without any express act of severance, it will not suffice to rely on an intention, with respect to the particular share, declared only behind the backs of the other persons interested. You must find in this class of cases a course of dealing by which the shares of all the parties to the contest have been effected, as happened in the cases of *Wilson v. Bell* (1843) 5 Ir.Eq.R. 501 and *Jackson v. Jackson* (1804) 9 Ves. Jun. 591; 32 E.R. 732.'' In that passage Page Wood V.-C. distinguished between severance "by mutual agreement" and severance by a "course of dealing". That shows that a "course of dealing" need not amount to an agreement, expressed or implied, for severance. It is sufficient if there is a course of dealing in which one party makes clear to the other that he desires that their shares should no longer be held jointly but be held in common. I emphasise that it must be made clear to the other party. That is implicit in the sentence in which Page Wood V.-C. says: "it will not suffice to rely on an intention, with respect to the particular share, declared only behind the backs of the other persons interested."

Similarly it is sufficient if both parties enter on a course of dealing which evinces an intention by both of them that their shares shall henceforth be held in common and not jointly. As appears from the two cases to which Page Wood V.-C. referred of *Wilson v. Bell* (1843) 5 Ir.Eq.R. 501 and *Jackson v. Jackson* (1804) 9 Ves. Jun. 591; 32 E.R. 732.

I come now to the question of notice. Suppose that one party gives a notice in writing to the other saying that he desires to sever the joint tenancy. Is that sufficient to effect a severance? I think it is. It was certainly the view of Sir Benjamin Cherry when he drafted s. 36(2) of the *Law of Property Act* 1925 (U.K.). It says in relation to real estates: "where a legal estate (not being settled land) is vested in joint tenants beneficially, and any tenant desires to sever the joint tenancy in equity, he shall give to the other joint tenants *a notice in writing of such desire or do such other acts or things as would, in the case of personal estate, have been effectual* to sever the tenancy in equity, and thereupon under the trust for sale affecting the land the net proceeds of sale, and the net rents and profits until sale, shall be held upon the trusts which would have been requisite for giving effect to the beneficial interests if there had been an actual severance."

I have italicised the important words. The word "other" is most illuminating. It shows quite plainly that, in the case of personal estate one of the things which is effective in equity to sever a joint tenancy is "a notice in writing" of a desire to sever. So also in regard to real estate.

Taking this view, I find myself in agreement with Havers J. in *Hawkesley v. May* [1956] 1 Q.B. 304 at 313-314, and of Plowman J. in *Re Draper's Conveyance* [1969] 1 Ch. 486. I cannot agree with Walton J. in *Nielson-Jones v. Fedden* [1974] 3 W.L.R. 583 at 594-595, that those cases were wrongly decided. It would be absurd that there should be a difference between real estate and personal estate in this respect. Suppose real estate is held on a joint tenancy on a trust for sale and is sold and converted into personal property. Before sale, it is severable by notice in writing. It would be ridiculous if it could not be severed afterwards in like manner. I look upon s. 36(2) as declaratory of the law as to severance by notice and not as a new provision confined to real estate. A joint tenancy in personal estate can be severed by notice just as a joint tenancy in real estate.

It remains to consider *Nielson-Jones v. Fedden* [1974] 3 W.L.R. 583. In my view it was not correctly decided. The husband and wife entered upon a course of dealing sufficient to sever the joint tenancy. They entered into negotiations that the property should be sold. Each received £200 out of the deposit paid by the purchaser. That was sufficient. Furthermore there was disclosed in correspondence a declaration by the husband that he wished to sever the joint tenancy: and this was made clear by the wife. That too was sufficient.

I doubt whether *Re Wilks; Child v. Bulmer* [1891] 3 Ch. 59 can be supported. A young man who had just become 21 applied to the court to have one third of a joint fund paid out to him. He died just before the application was heard. Stirling J. held that, if he had died just after, there would have been a severance: but, as he died just before, there was not. Ironically enough too, the delay was not on his side. It was the delay of the court. Nowadays I think it should have been decided differently. The application was a clear declaration of his intention to sever. It was made clear to all concerned. There was enough to effect a severance.

It remains to apply these principles to the present case. I think there was evidence that Mr Honick and Mrs Rawnsley did come to an agreement that he would buy her share for £750. That agreement was not in writing and it was not specifically enforceable. Yet it was sufficient to effect a severance. Even if there was not any firm agreement but only a course of dealing, it clearly evinced an intention by both parties that the property should henceforth be held in common and not jointly.

On these grounds I would dismiss the appeal.

BROWNE L.J. I agree that this appeal should be dismissed, but only on the second of the two grounds on which the county court judge based his decision. . . .

As to the second point, that is the severance point, the county court judge dealt with this point in one sentence in his judgment, and we are told that, according to the shorthand notes taken by both solicitors, a substantial part of that sentence was not included in his judgment as delivered orally. The one sentence as it appears in his written judgment was: "I hold that there has been a severance of the joint tenancy brought about by the conduct of the defendant in asking £750 for her share which was agreed to. . . ." The words which we are told did not appear in the shorthand note are "in asking £750 for her share which was agreed to". But I think we must take it that the county court judge found as a fact that Mrs Rawnsley did agree to sell share to Mr Honick for £750 and then went back on it. . . .

Mr Levy conceded, as is clearly right, that if there had been an enforceable agreement by Mrs Rawnsley to sell her share to Mr Honick, that would produce a severance of the joint tenancy; but he says that an oral agreement, unenforceable because of s. 40 of the *Law of Property Act* 1925 (U.K.), is not enough. Section 40 merely makes a contract for the disposition of an interest in land unenforceable by action in the absence of writing. It does not make it void. But here the plaintiff is not seeking to enforce by action the agreement by Mrs Rawnsley to sell her share to Mr Honick. She relies upon it as effecting the severance in equity of the joint tenancy. An agreement to sever can be inferred from a course of dealing (see Lefroy B. in *Wilson v. Bell* (1843) 5 Ir.Eq.R. 501 at 507 and Stirling J. in *Re Wilks; Child v. Bulmer* [1891] 3 Ch. 59) and there would in such a case ex hypothesi be no express agreement but only an inferred, tacit agreement, in respect of which there would seldom if ever be writing sufficient to satisfy s. 40. It seems to me that the point is that the agreement establishes that the parties no longer intend the tenancy to operate as a joint tenancy and that automatically effects a severance. I think the reference in Megarry and Wade, *The Law of Real Property* (3rd ed.), pp. 418, 419 to specifically enforceable contracts only applies where the suggestion is that the joint tenancy has been severed by an alienation by one joint tenant to a third party, and does not apply to severance by agreement between the joint tenants. . . .

The result is that I would uphold the county court judge's judgment on his second ground, namely, that the joint tenancy was severed by a agreement between Mrs Rawnsley and Mr Honick that she would sell her share to him for £750. In my view her subsequent repudiation of that agreement makes no difference. I would dismiss the appeal on this ground.

This conclusion makes it unnecessary to consider the important and difficult questions of what the effect of negotiations not resulting in an agreement or of a mere declaration would have been and, in particular, the problem raised by the decision of Plowman J. in *Re Draper's Conveyance* [1969] 1 Ch. 486 and Walton J. in *Nielson-Jones v. Fedden* [1974] 3 W.L.R. 583. Further, if the evidence and the conclusion that there was an agreement in this case are rejected, I doubt whether there was enough evidence in this particular case as to a course of dealing to raise the question of the application of Page Wood V.-C.'s third category, *Williams v. Hensman* (1861) 1 J. & H. 546 at 557; 70 E.R. 862 at 866-867. I therefore prefer not to express any final opinion on these points. Lord Denning M.R. has dealt with them in his judgment and I have the advantage of knowing what Sir John Pennycuick is going to say about that aspect of the case. I agree with both of them that Page Wood V.-C.'s third category is a separate category from his second category. I agree also that the proviso to s. 36(2) of the *Law of Property Act* 1925 (U.K.) seems to imply that notice in writing would, before 1925, have been effective to sever a joint tenancy in personal property. It is clear that s. 36(2), as Sir John Pennycuick is going to point out, made a radical alteration in the previous law by introducing the new method of severance by notice in writing, and that cases before 1925, in particular *Re Wilks; Child v. Bulmer* [1891] 3 Ch. 59, must now be read in the light of this alteration. I agree that an uncommunicated declaration by one joint tenant cannot operate as a severance.

In my judgment, the appeal should be dismissed on the second ground relied on by the county court judge.

SIR JOHN PENNYCUICK. I agree that this appeal should be dismissed. The county court judge based his conclusions upon two grounds, namely, (1) that the property was conveyed to Mr Honick and Mrs Rawnsley in the contemplation by Mr Honick (but not communicated to or agreed by Mrs Rawnsley) that they would marry; (2) that the joint tenancy if created was severed by agreement between Mr Honick and Mrs Rawnsley whereby Mr Honick was to buy her out for £750. I shall consider these two grounds in the same order. . . .

(2) It seems to me, however, that the judge's second ground was a valid one. It is not in dispute that an agreement for severance between joint tenants effects a severance. This is the rule two propounded by Sir William Page Wood V.-C. in *Williams v. Hensman* (1861) 1 J. & H. 546 at 557; 70 E.R. 862 at 866-867. The words he uses are contained in one sentence: "Secondly, a joint tenancy may be severed by mutual agreement." For a clear and full general statement as to severance of a joint tenancy, see *Halsbury's Laws of England* (3rd ed.), Vol. 32, p. 335. In the present case the judge found as a fact that Mr Honick and Mrs Rawnsley at the beginning of July 1968 agreed upon the sale by her to him of her share at the price of £750. . . . Once that finding of facts is accepted, the case falls squarely within rule two of Page Wood V.-C. It is not contended that it is material that the parties by mutual consent did not proceed to carry out the agreement. Rule two applies equally, I think, whether the agreement between the two joint tenants is expressly to sever or is to deal with the property in a manner which involves severance. Mr Levy contended that in order that rule two should apply, the agreement must be specifically enforceable. I do not see any sufficient reason for importing this

qualification. The significance of an agreement is not that it binds the parties; but that it serves as an indication of a common intention to sever, something which it was indisputably within their power to do. It will be observed that Page Wood V.-C. in his rule two makes no mention of specific enforceability. Contrast this position where severance is claimed under his rule one by reason of alienation by one joint tenant in favour of a third party. We were referred to a sentence in Megarry and Wade, op. cit., p. 418, where, under the heading of "Alienation in equity," it is said: "In equity, . . . a specifically enforceable contract to alienate creates an equitable interest in the property even though the legal act of alienation has not taken place." That statement has, I think, no application to an agreement between the two joint tenants themselves. The only other authority relied on by Mr Levy on this point is a sentence in the old Irish case of *Wilson v. Bell* (1843) 5 Ir.Eq.R. 501 at 507, where it is said: "it is settled, that an agreement to sever will in equity amount to a severance: and as this is personal property, there is no doubt that even a parol agreement would be sufficient for that purpose." I think that sentence is altogether inadequate to support Mr Levy's contention.

Mr Mummery advanced an alternative argument to the effect that even if there were no agreement by Mr Honick to purchase Mrs Rawnsley's share, nevertheless the mere proposal by Mr Honick to purchase her share would operate as a severance under the rule three in *Williams v. Hensman* (1861) 1 J. & H. 546 at 557; 70 E.R. 862 at 866-867. That rule is stated by Page Wood V.-C. in the following terms: "And, in the third place, there may be a severance by any course of dealing sufficient to intimate that the interests of all were mutually treated as constituting a tenancy in common. When the severance depends on an inference of this kind without any express act of severance, it will not suffice to rely on intention, with respect to the particular share, declared only behind the backs of the other persons interested. You must find in this class of cases a course of dealing by which the shares of all the parties to the contest have been effected, as happened in the cases of *Wilson v. Bell* (1843) 5 Ir.Eq.R. 501 and *Jackson v. Jackson* (1801) 9 Ves. Jun. 591; 32 E.R. 732."

I do not doubt myself that where one tenant negotiates with another for some rearrangement of interest, it may be possible to infer from the particular facts a common intention to sever even though the negotiations break down. Whether such an inference can be drawn must I think depend upon the particular facts. In the present case the negotiations between Mr Honick and Mrs Rawnsley, if they can be properly described as negotiations at all, fall, it seems to me, far short of warranting an inference. One could not ascribe to joint tenants an intention to sever merely because one offers to buy out the other for £X and the other makes a counter-offer of £Y.

We were referred to a long series of authorities going back to *Partriche v. Powlet* (1740) 2 Atk. 54; 26 E.R. 430 and culminating in the conflicting decisions of Plowman J. in *Re Draper's Conveyance* [1969] 1 Ch. 486; and Walton J. in *Nielson-Jones v. Fedden* [1974] 3 W.L.R. 582. Once it has been determined that an agreement was made, as in the present case, anything more one may say on this line of authorities must necessarily be obiter; but I think it may be helpful to state very shortly certain views which I have formed in the light of the authorities.

(1) I do not think rule three in Page Wood V.-C.'s statement in *Williams v. Hensman* (1861) 1 J. & H. 546 at 557; 70 E.R. 862 at 866-867 is a mere subheading of rule two. It covers only acts of the parties, including, it seems to me, negotiations which, although not otherwise resulting in any agreement, indicate a common intention that the joint tenancy should be regarded as severed.

I do not overlook the words which I have read from Page Wood V.-C.'s statement, namely, that you must find a course of dealing by which the shares of all the parties to the contract have been affected. But I do not think those words are sufficient to import a binding agreement.

(2) Section 36(2) of the *Law of Property Act* 1925 (U.K.) has radically altered the law in respect of severance by introducing an entirely new method of severance as regards land, namely, notice in writing given by one joint tenant to the other.

(3) Pre-1925 judicial statements, in particular that of Stirling J. in *Re Wilks; Child v. Bulmer* [1891] 3 Ch. 59, must be read in the light of this alteration in the law; and, in particular, I do not see why the commencement of legal proceedings by writ or orginating summons or the swearing of an affidavit in those proceedings, should not in appropriate circumstances constitute notice in writing within the meaning of s. 36(2). The fact that the plaintiff is not obliged to prosecute the proceedings is I think irrelevant in regard to notice.

(4) Perhaps in parenthesis because the point does not arise, the language of s. 36(2) appears to contemplate that even under the existing law notice in writing would be effective to sever a joint tenancy in personalty: see the words "such other act or thing". The authorities to the contrary are rather meagre and I am not sure how far this point was ever really considered in relation to personalty before 1925. If this anomaly does exist, and I am afraid I am not prepared to say positively that it does not exist, the anomaly is quite indefensible and should be put right as soon as possible.

(6) An uncommunicated declaration by one party to the other or indeed a mere verbal notice by one party to another clearly cannot operate as a severance.

(7) The policy of the law as it stands today, having regard particularly to s. 36(2), is to facilitate severance at the instance of either party, and I do not think the court should be over zealous in drawing a fine distinction from the pre-1925 authorities.

(8) The foregoing statement of principles involves criticism of certain passages in the judgments of Plowman J. and Walton J. in the two cases cited. Those cases, like all other cases, depend on their own particular facts, and I do not myself wish to go on to apply these obiter statements of principle to the actual decisions in these cases.

Appeal dismissed.

NOTES AND QUESTIONS

1. Did the Court in *Burgess v. Rawnsley* hold that the joint tenancy in question was severed by "mutual agreement" or a "course of dealing"?

2. The applicability of *Burgess v. Rawnsley* in New South Wales is subject to the absence of a New South Wales equivalent to s. 36(2) of the *Law of Property Act* 1925 (U.K.). One effect of the English provision is that an equitable joint tenancy may be severed by any of the methods previously effective or by notice in writing given to the other joint tenant, a method which is, according to Sir John Pennycuick in *Burgess v. Rawnsley,* an entirely new method of severance as regards land. This method is, therefore, not available in New South Wales, nor could it be regarded as a "course of dealing" as such conduct must show a common intention that the joint tenancy be severed.

3. Although the third rule enunciated in *Williams v. Hensman* (1861) 1 J. & H. 546 at 557; 70 E.R. 862 at 866-867 (severance by a "course of dealing") is separate to and not merely a subrule of the second rule in that case (severance by "mutual agreement"), that is to say, the third rule covers negotiations which do not result in any agreement but are indicative of an intention that the joint tenancy should be severed, nonetheless, it is swallowed up by the second rule where there is evidence of an agreement. Moreover, it does not matter that such agreement is not specifically enforceable because the significance of the agreement is not that it binds the parties but only that it serves as an indication of a common intention to sever. This is applicable in New South Wales.

The matter is conveniently summarised in the judgment of Rath J. in *Abela v. Public Trustee* [1983] 1 N.S.W.L.R. 308. The facts of the case are that a husband and wife were joint tenants of the matrimonial home. After their separation, the wife commenced negotiations with the husband to sell the home and divide the proceeds of sale between them. In subsequent matrimonial proceedings, a consent order was made that the parties join in the sale of the home and that the net proceeds not be released to the parties until authorised by the parties or order of the court. There was then the dissolution of the marriage and the sale of the property but the husband died before any agreement was reached as to the respective shares of the net proceeds of the sale. The wife sought a declaration that as at the date of death of her former husband the joint tenancy had not been severed. His Honour stated at 315 et seq.:

> The conclusions as to severance of a joint tenancy by agreement and conduct that I draw from the authorities are as follows:
>
> 1. Severance is effected by an agreement to sever the joint tenancy.
>
> 2. The agreement need not be specifically enforceable or even binding as a contract at law.
>
> 3. Subsequent repudiation of the agreement does not effect its operation of severance.
>
> 4. Severance may also be effected by conduct of the joint tenants not evidencing an agreement to sever but showing a common intention that the joint tenancy shall be severed.
>
> In the present case, the parties in my opinion agreed upon the severance of the joint tenancy at the time of the terms of settlement. It was submitted on behalf of the plaintiff that the agreement to sever was not complete because it did not define the shares of the parties. It did however provide a mechanism for defining the shares, which it may be presumed the parties thought would be efficacious. The mechanism failed expressly to provide for the death of a joint tenant before agreement had been reached on the shares to be taken, but that failure cannot alter the fact the parties had agreed upon the severance of the joint tenancy. In my view the agreement should not be construed as an agreement that the joint tenancy be severed in the future upon resolution of the question of the share of each party. The proper inference is that the parties agreed upon an immediate severance of their joint tenancy, leaving to the future only a decision as to their shares. The mechanism for that decision having failed, the parties have their particular interest: see *Wright v. Gibbons* (1949) 78 C.L.R. 313 at 330, 331, in this case their equal shares.
>
> Thus I regard the case, so far as the proceeds of sale are concerned, as falling into the second category referred to in *Williams v. Hensman* (1861) 1 J. & H. 546 at 557; 70 E.R. 862 at 866-867. If this is not the proper analysis, the same result would be reached, by way of the third category, from the consideration of the course of conduct of the parties, including, but not limited to, the agreement embodied in the terms of settlement.

4. In order to sever a joint tenancy, a "course of dealing" must be irrevocable. Thus, merely filing and serving an application under s. 79 of the *Family Law Act* 1975 (Cth), which concerns property settlements, with the accompanying affidavits in support does not constitute conduct which would sever a joint tenancy: see, for example, *Patzak v. Lytton* (1984) F.L.C. 91-550 at 79, 458. Rather, severance arises at the point at which an order is made by the court: *Pertsoulis and Pertsoulis* (1980) F.L.C. 90-832, extracted below; *Public Trustee v. Grivas* [1974] 2 N.S.W.L.R. 316; *McKee v. McKee* (1986) 10 Fam L.R. 754 in which a court order whose operation was postponed to the future neverless effected an immediate severance of the joint tenancy. Where, however, the property order is subject to certain conditions precedent, other than mere procedural steps, the order is not a final order because it cannot be enforced until there has been a compliance with the conditions: *Corry and Corry* (1983) F.L.C. 91-343, extracted below p. 80.

PERTSOULIS AND PERTSOULIS

Family Court of Australia (1980) F.L.C. 75,265 at 75,269

PAWLEY S.J. The question is: Does the filing of an application under s. 79 of the *Family Law Act* 1975 (Cth) by one party or by both parties to a joint tenancy operate to bring about the severance of that tenancy?

The English authorities bearing on this question are in conflict. It must, of course, be remembered that since 1925 the position in England is different from that in Australia by reason of the provisions of s. 36(2) of the *Law of Property Act* 1925 (U.K.). That section, which has no counterpart in New South Wales, reads as follows: "where a legal estate (not being the settled land) is vested in joint tenants beneficially, and any tenant decides to sever the joint tenancy in equity, he shall give to the other joint tenants a notice in writing of such desire or do such other acts and things as would, in the case of personal estate, have been effectual to sever the tenancy in equity, and thereupon under the trust for sale affecting the land the net proceeds of sale, and the net rents and profits until sale, shall be held upon the trusts which would have been requisite for giving effect to the benefical interests if there had been an actual severance."

Apart from statutory provisions the ways in which a joint tenancy may be severed were discussed by Sir William Page Wood V.-C. in *Williams v. Hensman* (1861) 1 J. & H. 546 at 557; 70 E.R. 862 at 866-867 where he said: "A joint tenancy may be severed in three ways: in the first place, an act of any one of the persons interested operating upon his own share may create a severance as to that share. . . . Secondly, a joint tenancy may be severed by mutual agreement. And, in the third place, there may be a severance by any course of dealing sufficient to intimate that the interests of all were mutually treated as constituting a tenancy in common. When the severance depends on an inference of this kind without any express act of severance, it will not suffice to rely on an intention, with respect to the particular share, declared only behind the backs of other persons interested."

It seems to me that the law as thus expressed is the law which must be applied to the facts of this particular case.

As I have said, the decisions in England seem to be in conflict. *Re Draper's Conveyance* [1969] 1 Ch. 486 was a case where the relevant facts were as follows:

Prior to 17 November 1965 a husband and wife owned a certain property as joint tenants. On that date the wife obtained a decree nisi of divorce which was made absolute on 3 March 1966. On 11 February 1966 the wife issued a summons in the Probate, Divorce and Admiralty Division seeking an order that the house be sold and the proceeds of sale be distributed in accordance with the parties' respective interests. This application was supported by affidavit. An order was made for the sale of the property and a declaration was made that she was entitled to a half interest. On 6 January 1967 the husband died intestate prior to the property having been sold. The wife then brought a summons to determine whether she held the property for herself absolutely or for herself and the estate of the husband as tenants in common in equal shares. It was argued before the learned trial judge that the joint tenancy had been severed and Plowman J. (at 492) said: "it seems to me that Mr Cooke's submissions are right whether they are based on the new provision in s. 36(2) of the *Law of Property Act* 1925 (U.K.), or whether they are based on the old law which applied to severing a joint tenancy in the case of a personal estate. It seems to me that that summons, coupled with the affidavit in support of it, clearly evinced an intention on the part of the wife that she wished the property to be sold and the proceeds distributed, a half to her and a half to the husband. And if that is right then it seems to me that that is wholly inconsistent with the notion that a beneficial joint tenancy in that property is to continue, and therefore, . . . I feel little doubt that in one way or the other this joint tenancy was severed in equity before the end of February 1966, as a result of the summons which was served on the husband and as a result of what the wife stated in her affidavit in support of the summons."

In coming to the conclusion referred to his Honour had relied upon the judgment of Havers J. In *Hawkesley v. May* [1956] 1 Q.B. 304. However, in *Nielson-Jones v. Fedden* [1975] 1 Ch. 222 Walton J. was critical of the decision in *Hawkesley v. May* and went on to deal with *Re Draper's Conveyance* [1969] 1 Ch. 486. He said: "Since I have already concluded above that Haver J.'s dictum was wholly unwarranted, I can place no greater reliance upon it when blandly repeated in *Re Draper's Conveyance*. I am also troubled about the suggestion that the mere issue of the originating summons, coupled with the affidavit in support, could amount to a notice in writing under s. 36(2). It appears to me that the reasons so cogently stated by Stirling J. in *Re Wilks; Child v. Bulmer* [1891] 3 Ch. 59 apply with equal force: Until any order had been made the wife was domina litis, and entitled to withdraw the proceedings entirely. In other words, it appears to me that s. 36(2) contemplates an irrevocable notice, and that the issue of proceedings is the very reverse of an irrevocable act. If the proceedings are, indeed, to constitute a severance, it must, I think, follow as a consequence that they themselves become irrevocable, and this I find difficult to appreciate."

In *Re Wilks; Child v. Bulmer*, Stirling J. had said: "In the present case all that was done by or on behalf of Wilks Child was to take out and prosecute a summons for payment of one third of the fund to himself: but no order was made. Until an order was made on that summons Wilks Child was completely master of the proceedings; he was at liberty, if he thought fit, to discontinue them at any moment, paying of course the costs incurred by the other parties. . . . If an order had been made on the summons the position would not have been the same; Wilks Child would no longer have been at liberty as of right either to abandon the summons, or to amend it. It is not necessary to decide the point, but he would then appear to me to have carried his acts to such a point as to preclude him from claiming any further right by survivorship."

Leaving aside any consideration of the effect of s. 36(2) of the *Law of Property Act 1925* (U.K.) it would seem to me that if one were to rely on a particular course of dealing by one of the parties to a joint tenancy as constituting a severance on the authority of *Re Wilks; Child v. Bulmer*, that course of dealing must be such as to preclude him from claiming by survivorship any interest in the subject matter of the joint tenancy, that is to say, the course of dealing must be irrevocable.

For the purposes of this case that proposition, if correct, would be sufficient to end the matter. There would not have been any severance.

However, following *Nielson-Jones v. Fedden* the problem soon arose again, this time before the Court of Appeal in *Burgess v. Rawnsley* [1975] 1 Ch. 429. Referring to the decision in *Nielson-Jones v. Fedden* Lord Denning said (at 438): "Walton J. founded himself on the decision of Stirling J. in *Re Wilks; Child v. Bulmer* [1891] 3 Ch. 59. He criticised *Hawkesley v. May* [1956] 1 Q.B. 304 and *Re Draper's Conveyance* [1969] 1 Ch. 486, and said that they were clearly contrary to the existing and established law. He went back to *Coke upon Littleton* and to *Blackstone's Commentaries*. Those old writers were dealing with legal joint tenancies. . . . Now that is all very well when you are considering how a legal joint tenancy can be severed. But it is of no application today when there can be no severance of a legal joint tenancy; and you are only considering how a beneficial joint tenancy can be severed. The thing to remember today is that equity leans against joint tenants and favours tenancies in common."

His Lordship then went on to quote the passage from *Williams v. Hensman* (1861) 1 J. & H. 546 at 557; 70 E.R. 862 at 866 to which I have already referred and he continued: "In that passage Page Wood V.-C. distinguished between severance 'by mutual agreement' and severance by a 'course of dealing'. That shows that a 'course of dealing' need not amount to an agreement, expressed or implied, for severance. It is sufficient if there is a course of dealing in which one party makes clear to the other that he desires that their shares should no longer be held jointly but be held in common. I emphasise that it must be made clear to the other party. . . . Similarly it is sufficient if both parties enter on a course of dealing which evinces an intention by both of them that their shares shall henceforth be held in common and not jointly."

Browne L.J., however, found that the appeal went off on other points and, therefore, that it was not necessary to deal with the questions raised in *Nielson-Jones v. Fedden* [1975] 1 Ch. 222 and in *Re Draper's Conveyance* [1969] 1 Ch. 486 and Sir John Pennycuick, the third member of the court, dealt more particularly with the law as provided by the statute rather than the general law.

If Lord Denning's remarks are to be taken as applying to the position as it is under the general law it may be argued that in this particular case, although there was no agreement about how the property was to be disposed of, there was a claim evidenced by the application of the husband in the Supreme Court, Family Law Division, and the application of the wife in the Family Court that the property be dealt with in ways in which it could not be dealt with if it were to be held in joint tenancy and, consequently, that the joint tenancy had been severed. However, Lord Denning's remarks have not been left without criticism, although there would not appear to be any further English decisions dealing directly with the problem confronting us.

In a note contained in the (1976) 50 A.L.J. 249 and which discusses the decision in *Burgess v. Rawnsley* [1975] 1 Ch. 429 the learned author wrote: "Unhappily, that is where the matter rests. The judgment of Lord Denning, with respect, cannot be said to have solved the issue as to whether one joint tenant can effect a severance by unilateral declaration communicated to, but against the wishes of, the other or others. It appears to the writer, with respect, that Walton J. was correct in saying that neither Havers J. nor Plowman J. had had, the benefit of examining the authorities and that their decisions ought to be regarded as given per incuriam. Moreover, it is clear that Page Wood V.-C., in formulating the three categories (with which, as Lord Denning put it, 'nowadays everyone starts') regarded the first class as applying where there is an express act of severance, such as alienation, so that a mere declaration could not fall within the first class, and must, unless it forms part of an agreement, fall into the third class; and in the third class, to return to the words of the Vice-Chancellor, one must find 'a course of dealing by which the shares of all the parties to the contest have been effected, as happened in the cases of *Wilson v. Bell* (1843) 5 Ir. Eq. R. 501 and *Jackson v. Jackson* (1804) 9 Ves. Jun. 591; 32 E.R. 732'. Next, if one party can unilaterally effect severance by a mere expression of intention why should communication to the other be necessary? It must be the expression, or formation, of intention that effects the severance, not the communication, because the unwilling co-owner, if Lord Denning's proposition is correct, has no way of preventing the severance taking place, whether he knows about it or not. Moreover, it should be noted again that Lord Denning was the only member of the court to raise this matter, Browne L.J. and Sir John Pennycuick not expressing any opinion except to agree that an uncommunicated declaration by one joint tenant cannot operate as a severance (*Walker v. Lovell* [1975] 3 W.L.R. 107 at 110 and 113 respectively)—and those statements must be read in the context of the "notice" provision of s. 36(2) of the *Law of Property Act* 1925 (U.K.), which provision has no New South Wales equivalent: see *Tyson v. Tyson* [1969] N.S.W.R. 177 at 181. Finally, as another commentator has pointed out, if a unilateral declaration suffices to sever a joint tenancy why, on the one hand, is a will insufficient for the purpose, and why, on the other, is there any need for a category of severance by agreement: (1968) 84 L.Q.R. 463?"

Moreover, as was pointed out in an article in (1968) 84 L.Q.R. 463, although Plowman J. in *Re Draper's Conveyance* [1969] 1 Ch. 486 had held that severance had been effected by the issue of the summons, in fact when the matter came on for hearing before him an order for sale had already been made and the wife could no longer abandon or amend the summons and would then appear to have carried her acts to such a point as to preclude her from claiming any right by survivorship and that the conditions referred to in *Re Wilks* [1891] 3 Ch. 59 had to that extent been fulfilled.

In New South Wales a similar question was considered by Bowen C.J. in Eq. (as he then was) in *Public Trustee v. Grivas* (1975) 25 F.L.R. 1. There both parties to a marriage had sought an order under s. 86(1) of the *Matrimonial Causes Act* 1959 (Cth) that the former matrimonial home which they had owned as joint tenants be sold and the net proceeds of sale be equally divided between them. A decree nisi was pronounced and the order in respect of the property made by consent. After the decree had become absolute the husband remarried and before the property had been sold he died intestate. His Honour held that the effect of that order was that the joint tenancy had been severed and his Honour said: "Although it would, of course, have been clearer if there had been an express order that the parties should thenceforth hold the property as tenants in common, I do not think that the absence of these express words should lead me to the opposite conclusion, that they were not to do so. Rather, I think that the whole thrust and effect of the order is that it was a final division of the property between them equally.

If I am wrong in the view which I have just expressed, it appears to me, at least from the form of the order, which was by consent, and founded upon the pleadings, there is evidenced an agreement between the parties that, in respect of the former matrimonial home, there should be a final division of it or the benefit of it between them in the finalisation of the matrimonial affairs. I, therefore, find in the present case that there was an agreement such that it had the effect, at the time the order was made, of bringing about a severance."

In the present case it seems to me that those words have particular application to the problem before me. Of course, it was not argued before his Honour that the mere issue of a summons was sufficient conduct on the part of a joint tenant to sever the joint tenancy and, of course, his Honour's decision came before the decision of the Court of Appeal in *Burgess v. Rawnsley* [1975] 1 Ch. 429. However, taking into account what has been said in criticism of the decision of Lord Denning in that case, and remembering the difference of law in England and in New South Wales, I do not think it appropriate to hold that the mere filing and service of an application and affidavits in support constitute the kind of conduct which would have the effect of severing a joint tenancy, nor do I think that in this particular case it could be argued that an agreement to sever had come about by reason of both parties filing applications. I would, with respect, agree with what was said by Murray J. in *Badcock and Babcock* (1979) F.L.C. 90-723 at 78,897: "I would not be prepared to go so far as to say that the summons issued by Mrs Babcock for partition in the Supreme Court amounted to a severance of the beneficial joint tenancy, for two reasons:

(a) our *Law of Property Act* 1936 (S.A.) does not contain a section similar to that of s. 36(2) of the English *Law of Property Act* 1925, and

(b) the wife could withdraw the partition proceedings at any time prior to judgment leaving her competent to claim by survivorship."

At any time prior to an order being made the parties could have withdrawn their applications and although an order was, in fact, made in favour of the husband this order has been set aside and any effect that it had has, therefore, become null and void. It seems to me, on all the authorities, that where applications are made under the *Family Law Act* 1975 (Cth) for settlement of property requiring the severance of a joint tenancy such severance can only take place, as was implied by the decision of Bowen C.J. in Eq., at the time an order is made.

It follows, therefore, that until she constituted herself a tenant in common beneficially with the estate of her deceased husband the wife in this matter held the whole of the property (as indeed she still does at law) by reason of survivorship.

Nevertheless, although the question, as I have already said, may be an important one in certain cases, I do not think that in the particular case it constitutes in any way a deciding factor.

It is clear from the evidence before me that the applicant made substantial contribution to the acquisition of the matrimonial home and it seems to me in justice and in equity that had the matter been litigated between the two parties prior to the husband's death it is likely that it would have resulted in an order that the property be sold and the proceeds equally divided. It does not seem to me that anything that has happened since should affect that position.

CORRY AND CORRY

Family Court of Australia (1983) F.L.C. 78,311 at 78,313

BAKER J. It was submitted by the solicitor for the wife that the effect of the orders of 14 January 1983 was to sever the joint tenancy and he relied upon the decision of Bowen C.J. in *Public Trustee v. Grivas* [1974] 2 N.S.W.L.R. 316.

The wife's solicitor further submitted that because the orders of 14 January 1983 were in fact final orders the wife's right to have those orders enforced did not abate upon the husband's death and sought to rely upon the decisions of the Family Court in *Pertsoulis and Pertsoulis* (1979) F.L.C. 90-613 and *Sims and Sims* (1981) F.L.C. 91-072.

The facts in the case of *Public Trustee v. Grivas* are not dissimilar to the facts in the present case in that in the former case a decree nisi for dissolution of marriage was pronounced by the Supreme Court of New South Wales pursuant to the *Matrimonial Causes Act* 1959 (N.S.W.) on the wife's petition and on the same day an order was made in relation to the former matrimonial home of the parties. The latter order was in the following terms: "That by consent the property at one hundred and sixty two (162) Victoria Street Kingswood in the State of New South Wales being the land comprised in Certificate of Title Volume 9555 Folio 15 be sold and the net proceeds of such sale be equally divided between the petitioner and the respondent."

The said decree nisi became absolute and the husband then remarried. Some steps were taken to sell the property after the decree nisi and in fact an offer to purchase was made but before acceptance the husband died. Bowen C.J. came to the conclusion that the order of the court effectively severed the joint tenancy and (at 321) said: "The order, in my view, being an indivisible provision for a settlement between the parties, it would be inconsistent with the order for the joint tenancy to survive and be effective so as to render the order abortive. In other words, it appears to me that inherent in the order is involved a severance of the joint tenancy between the parties. I do not accept the argument that the powers of the Family Law Division under Pt VIII are in all respects limited, as a matter of jurisdiction, to the making of orders which have no operation beyond the joint lives of the parties. In my view the power of the court under s. 86(1) is not so limited as a matter of jurisdiction. In addition, it appears to me that in the exercise of that jurisdiction in the present case the Family Law Division has evidenced an intention to divide the property in question between the parties without any limitation as to the length of the life of either of them. It would, of course, be in the highest degree inconvenient if an order such as that made in the present case would fall to the ground upon the death of either party where, as here, it is the division of a capital asset and an order which no doubt furnished some basis for the other orders which were limited to the life of the parties. It appears to me the parties were entitled to order their affairs on the basis it was a final settlement. It would be a matter of chance which of them might die first and suffer the results of the order being rendered ineffectual, if the rule of survivorship should be held to continue to apply. Although it would, of course, have been clearer, if there had been an express order that the parties should henceforth hold the property as tenants in common, I do not think that the absence of these express words should lead me to the opposite conclusion, that they were not to do so. Rather, I think that the whole thrust and effect of the order is that it was a final division of the property between them equally.''

With that conclusion I respectfully agree. Although his Honour was considering an order made under the provisions of s. 86 of the *Matrimonial Causes Act* 1959, I am firmly of the view that a final order in similar terms made pursuant to the provisions of s. 79 of the *Family Law Act* 1975 (Cth) has the effect of severing the joint tenancy.

The facts in the case before me however differ in a material respect with the facts which were before his Honour. The orders of 14 January 1983 were not by consent and were made in the absence of the husband. Although the husband had previously been served with the original application and the wife's affidavits in support and had been given due notice of the date of the hearing of the proceedings he did not appear at the trial nor was he legally represented.

The orders which I made required the husband within 28 days after the service upon him of a copy of the said orders to execute a memorandum of transfer of his interests as joint tenant in the former matrimonial home to the wife and granted the husband liberty to apply to set aside such orders within a period of 28 days after the service of a copy of such orders upon him.

The clear intention of the orders was firstly, that the husband be given due notice of the making of them and, secondly, that he have liberty to apply to set aside such orders as he may be advised. Therefore there existed two conditions which must have been fulfilled before the orders could be said to be final orders. Firstly, that the husband be served with a copy of the orders and, secondly, that no action be taken by him within 28 days of such service to set the orders aside.

The husband was never served personally with a copy of the orders and on 5 April 1983 as I have said an order was made dispensing with the service of the said orders in the terms which I have already indicated.

The husband died, as I have said, on 29 April 1983 and it is clear on the evidence before me that on that day the orders above referred to could not have been enforced by the wife as the orders dispensing with the service of same upon the husband had not been complied with. Therefore, as at 29 April 1983 the orders of 14 January 1983 remained subject to a condition precedent to such orders having full and final effect and they could not be said at that date to be final orders capable of immediate enforcement.

In *King v. King* (1973) 24 F.L.R. 269 the petitioning wife was granted a decree nisi for the dissolution of her marriage with the respondent husband pursuant to the provisions of the *Matrimonial Causes Act* 1959 (N.S.W.). By the same decree the husband was ordered to transfer to the wife all his right title and interest in the jointly owned matrimonial home. The wife died before the time had arrived for the decree to become absolute and nothing had been done to effect a transfer of the husband's interest in the property to her in the meantime.

Lucas J. held that as a result of the abatement by death of the suit the husband was no longer obliged to comply with the order for the transfer of the matrimonial home.

My understanding of the authorities leads me to the conclusion that an order is not a final order if some further step must be taken other than a procedural step before such order can be enforced or the party required to comply with its terms.

On the facts before me the husband, had he received due notice of the terms of the order granting him liberty to apply to set the order aside, could have made the appropriate application. Clearly this option was never open to him as his death intervened prior to the service of a copy of the order upon him or due notice of such order having been given.

In the end result the fact that the husband pursuant to order 6 of 14 January 1983 had liberty to apply to set aside the said orders within a period of 28 days after the service of a copy thereof upon him leads me to conclude that the said orders were not final orders incapable of alteration, amendment or variation.

I conclude therefore that there is no severance of the joint tenancy for the reasons stated and I further conclude that the wife's application abates due to the death of the husband.

What then is the present legal situation as far as the wife is concerned? I am of the view that the husband's death entitles her to become registered as the sole proprietor in fee simple of the matrimonial home by survivorship. In this respect therefore the wife is in precisely the same situation on the facts before me as was the husband in the case of *King v. King* (1973) 24 F.L.R. 269.

NOTES AND QUESTIONS

1. It has been held that a maintenance agreement which dealt with property matters and registered under s. 86 of the *Family Law Act* 1975 (Cth) together with the events that had happened, effected a severance of a joint tenancy: *Re Pozzi* [1982] Qd R. 449. Which rule or rules enunciated by Sir William Page V.-C. in *Williams v. Hensman* (1861) 1 J. & H. 546 at 557; 70 E.R. 862 at 866-867 do you consider relevent to the issue of a severance of a joint tenancy by a maintenance agreement under s. 86 of the *Family Law Act* 1975 (Cth)?

2. Although an agreement is ineffective for the purposes of the *Family Law Act* 1975 (Cth) because it was not approved by the Family Court, the agreement may nevertheless be effective for other purposes under the general law and thereby sever a joint tenancy: *Calabrese v. Miuccio (No. 2)* [1985] 1 Qd R. 17.

(d) Partition

Partition is another method by which both joint tenancies and tenancies in common may be brought to an end. All the co-owners may agree to a voluntary partition and thus each becomes sole owner of the parcel of land allotted to her or him. At common law there was no right for one co-owner to compel a partition. This right was given by statute in 1539 and 1540, no matter how inconvenient a partition might have been to the others. The Partition Acts of 1868 and 1876 empowered the court to order a sale as an alternative to partition in certain circumstances, and this has remained the approach taken in most Australian States. However, in New South Wales the opposite approach, namely, sale as the primary right and partition in special circumstances, has been adopted: see the *Conveyancing Act* 1919 (N.S.W.), Pt IV, Div. 6, ss 66F to 66I inclusive, which provides in s. 66G:

(1) Where any property (other than chattels) is held in co-ownership the court may, on the application of any one or more of the co-owners, appoint trustees of the property and vest the same in such trustees, subject to incumbrances affecting the entirety, but free from incumbrances affecting any undivided shares, to be held by them on the statutory trust for sale or on the statutory trust for partition. . . .

(4) If, on an application for the appointment of trustees on the statutory trust for sale, any of the co-owners satisfies the court that partition of the property would be more beneficial for the co-owners interested to the extent of upwards of a moiety in value than sale, the court may, with the consent of the incumbrancers of the entirety (if any), appoint trustees of the property on the statutory trust for partition, or as to part of the property on the statutory trust for sale, and as to part on the statutory trust for partition, but a purchaser shall not be concerned to see or inquire whether any such consent as aforesaid has been given.

In *Re B. Cordingley (decd)* (1948) 48 S.R. (N.S.W.) 248 at 249-251, Sugerman J. described the New South Wales provisions as follows:

. . . reference to the earlier law must not be pressed too far. The provisions of the Conveyancing Acts cannot be regarded as merely creating new machinery. To give an important and relevant illustration, they alter the relationship between partition and sale which existed under the earlier law. The right which was an incident of an undivided share was partition. The power of the court to order sale in lieu of partition in any of the cases mentioned in s. 4(1) of the *Partition Act* 1900 (N.S.W.), arose only where "but for this Act . . . a decree for partition might have been made". The three cases set out in paras (a), (b) and (c) of s. 4(1) contemplate partition as the primary right; the power to order sale in lieu thereof depended upon the matter being brought within one of those paragraphs. The position is different under the Conveyancing Acts provisions.

Under s. 66G(1) the court may, on the application of one or more co-owners, appoint trustees and vest the property in them on the statutory trust for sale *or* the statutory trust for partition. Sale and partition, that is to say, are true alternatives; there is no longer the dependence of the power to order the one on the power to order the other. And it may perhaps be suggested, although it is unnecessary to express a concluded opinion on the point, that the emphasis has in another way been shifted from partition as the primary right, with sale in particular cases, to sale as the primary right with partition in special circumstances—as is perhaps to be expected of legislation which appears to have been inspired by the treatment of co-ownership under the English property legislation of 1925. Subsection (4) empowers the court on an application for appointment of trustees on the statutory trust for sale to appoint trustees on the statutory trust for partition where a co-owner satisfies it that partition would be more beneficial than sale to a majority in value of co-owners. There is no corresponding provision for the case of an application for appointment on the statutory trust for partition. Perhaps the reason is that such an application may be met by a counter-application for appointment on the statutory trust for sale, and that thereupon the question: "Sale or partition?" would be answered by reference to subs. (4).

The alteration which I have mentioned shows, I think, that, even where there is a subsisting trust for sale, *Biggs v. Peacock* (1882) 22 Ch.D. 284 cannot be relied upon as authority for the proposition that an application for appointment of trustees on the statutory trust for sale should on that account be refused. For power to order sale is no longer conditional on power to order partition, and *Biggs v. Peacock* is only authority that the subsistence of a trust for sale excludes partition—for reasons which are peculiar to partition. "But here the estate is converted into personalty, and the cestuis que trust are only entitled to shares of the proceeds. Although no doubt if all are of age and sui juris they could call upon the trustee to convey the estate to them, yet none of them has a right in opposition to the others, to insist upon partition being made of it, which would be dealing with it as if it were real estate": *Biggs v. Peacock* at 286 per Jessel M.R. . . .

Although in my view the decision in *Biggs v. Peacock* does not exclude appointment of trustees on the statutory trust for sale on the mere ground of the subsistence of a trust for sale under the trust instrument, it may be that no order should be made in cases where it is clear that there is a subsisting trust for sale under the trust instrument and it appears that such trust is as effective as would be the statutory trust for sale. If an order should be refused in such a case, it would not be for the reasons stated in *Biggs v. Peacock*, but for the reason that an order would be plainly unnecessary. However that may be, I am not satisfied on the facts and the arguments that the present is such a case. Whether there is a trust for sale is not altogether clear and has not been at all fully argued; and one, and perhaps two or all, of the trustees seems to have proceeded upon the view that there is a mere power. Some proceedings were necessary to define the position, and an application under s. 66G was not inappropriate.

Although a co-owner is entitled as of right to an order for either sale or partition under s. 66G(1) of the *Conveyancing Act* 1919 (N.S.W.), the power to order partition in lieu of sale under s. 66G(4) of the Act remains, however, a matter of true discretion in the court. In *Hayward v. Skinner* [1981] 1 N.S.W.L.R. 590 at 593, Kearney J. described the powers of the court under these subsections as follows:

The defendants further submit that if partition is shown to be more beneficial to the majority of co-owners, then the order for partition must follow because the word "may" as used in subs. (4) should have the same mandatory effect as that word bears in subs. (1). On this point I have been referred of course, to the decision in *Re Fettell* (1952) 52 S.R. (N.S.W.) 221 and also to *Re Cordingley (decd)* (1948) 48 S.R. (N.S.W.) 248. Mandatory effect is given to the word "may" in subs. (1) because sale or partition are now the rights inherent in co-ownership. Thus, the right to partition has always been treated as an incident of the property of a co-owner, and the alternative of sale has been engrafted upon it by statute. Section 66G confers the choice of partition or sale, but it is an entitlement of a co-owner to have one or the other. Hence the word "may" as used in subs. (1) has the same effect as the word "shall".

In subs. (4) the court is concerned with the preferment of partition over sale in the circumstances mentioned. Both the above-mentioned authorities suggest that s. 66G renders the alternative of sale the primary right, with partition in special circumstances. Moreover, Sugerman J.'s remark in *Re Cordingley (decd)* (1948) 48 S.R. (N.S.W.) 248 that subs. (4) "empowers the court to order partition when duly satisfied", and McLelland J.'s comment in *Re Fettell* (1952) 52 S.R. (N.S.W.) 221 at 228 that the circumstances mentioned in subs. (4) "are the only ones in which the court has a discretion" tend to support the view that under subs. (4) there is truly a discretion vested in the court as to the choice to be made.

As sale and partition are under s. 66G "true alternatives" (*Re Cordingley (decd)* at 250) the mere establishment of the ground for partition does not, in my view, extinguish the right to sale so as to enable it to be said of subs. (4) that "the object of the power is to effectuate a legal right" (see *Re Fettell* at 227), with the consequence that the power must then be exercised. Rather, I consider that upon the court being satisfied under subs. (4), a condition is fulfilled enabling the court to prefer partition to sale if it sees fit in the exercise of a discretion based upon consideration of all the circumstances of the case. This view derives support from the power in subs. (4) extending to the grant of mixed relief comprising part sale and part partition.

Hence it does not follow from the fact that it is shown to be more beneficial to the majority of co-owners, that partition must necessarily follow. If this were so, it would leave out of account consideration of any countervailing circumstances. There may, for example, be circumstances imposing considerable hardship on a minority of co-owners if the greater benefit to the majority should prevail.

In light of the foregoing factors and of the terminology of the *Partition Act* 1900 (N.S.W.), which s. 66G replaced, it seems to me that if the legislature had intended that greater benefit to the majority of the co-owners should automatically result in partition despite the existence of the alternative right to sale, it would have expressed such intention by unambiguously mandatory wording.

It should, moreover, be observed that by s. 66G(7) of the *Conveyancing Act* 1919 (N.S.W.) neither the appointment of trustees for sale nor a sale made pursuant to a statutory trust for sale under s. 66G of itself effects a severance of the joint tenancy.

(e) Merger

A Joint tenancy will be severed where a joint tenant acquires an interest greater in quantum than that of the other joint tenants; the acquisition of the further estate in land merges with the initial interest to destroy the unity of interest, and thereby severs the joint tenancy. However, there is no severance if at the time of creation of the joint tenancy, one of the joint tenants is given some further interest in the land beyond her or his interest as joint tenant: *Wiscot's Case* (1599) 2 Co. Rep. 60b; 76 E.R. 555.

(f) Unlawful killing

Public policy requires that a person guilty of unlawful killing cannot benefit from the principle of survivorship. However, strictly speaking, this rule, which is not without exception (see *Public Trustee v. Evans* (1985) 2 N.S.W.L.R. 188), does not operate to sever the joint tenancy but, rather, the slayer will hold the victim's share as constructive trustee for the estate of the victim so that the effect is similar to a severance in equity.

2. Tenancy in common

Tenancies in common may be determined first, where the whole of the land becomes solely vested in one tenant, and secondly, by partition, which, in New South Wales may be effected either in accordance with Pt IV, Div. 6 of the

Conveyancing Act 1919 (see above) or, in the case of next of kin on intestacy, in accordance with s. 58 of the *Wills, Probate and Administration Act* 1898, where the partition is effected by an arbitrator appointed by the court.

D. RIGHTS OF JOINT TENANTS AND TENANTS IN COMMON INTER SE

(a) Occupation rent

Since co-owners have equal rights of enjoyment and possession over the whole of the land, if one co-owner alone chooses to exercise the common law right to occupy the land, that co-owner is under no obligation to pay an occupation rent at the instance of the co-owner not exercising the like right: *Luke v. Luke* (1936) 36 S.R. (N.S.W.) 310. The latter will only be entitled to an occupation rent if he or she has either been excluded by the co-owner in occupation, for example where one co-owner leaves the co-owned property as a result of the violence of the co-owner in occupation (*Dennis v. McDonald* [1982] 2 W.L.R. 275), or where the co-owner in occupation makes a claim for an allowance in respect of expenditure made by her or him on repairs or improvements on the property, in which case the court may, in accordance with the equitable maxim "he who seeks equity must do equity", require the co-owner in occupation to offset against this claim an occupation rent: *Luke v. Luke*; *Teasdale v. Sanderson* (1864) 33 Beav. 534; 55 E.R. 476.

LUKE v. LUKE

Supreme Court of New South Wales (1936) 36 S.R. (N.S.W.) 310 at 313

[Pursuant to the provisions of the will of the testator, John Luke, a certain residence came to be jointly occupied by two tenants in common, Laura Luke and the defendant Ada Luke, until the death of the former.

Laura Luke died intestate, leaving three sisters, three brothers, and five nephews and nieces, children of a deceased sister, entitled to her estate as her next of kin. Letters of administration to her estate were duly granted to the plaintiff Reuben James Luke and the defendant Ada Luke.

Since the death of Laura Luke the defendant Ada Luke continued to occupy the said residence, without any exclusion by her of any of the next of kin of her deceased sister Laura or any attempt on the part of any of them to exercise a right of residence.

This was a motion by the plaintiffs for an order that the Public Trustee (who had the administration of the estate) be authorised to sell the real estate of the testator, including his residence, for purposes of distribution, and that the defendant Ada Luke should be charged with an occupation rent.]

LONG INNES C.J. IN EQ. This motion raises for determination the question whether in a suit for administration, a defendant tenant in common, who has exercised his common law right to occupy the property the subject of the tenancy in common, which property is ordered to be sold by the court, is liable to be charged with an occupation rent in a case in which he has not excluded his co-tenants in common from the subject property and is making no claim for any allowance in respect of expenditure on his part in repairs or improvements to the property in question.

In *Teasdale v. Sanderson* (1864) 33 Beav. 534; 55 E.R. 476 it was held that a tenant in common who has been in occupation of part of the common property, and who claims an allowance for improvements effected to any part of the common property, will only be granted such allowance on submitting to be charged with an occupation rent. This case was, as explained by North J. in *Re Jones; Farrington v. Forrester* [1893] 2 Ch. 461 at 478, an application of the equitable maxim that he who seeks equity must do equity. Commenting on the statement of Sir J. Romilly M.R.: "I think that these accounts must be reciprocal, and, unless the defendant is charged with an occupation rent, he is not entitled to any account of substantial repairs and lasting improvements on any part of the property", North J. said: "That seems to me to show that he was not to be allowed to have the equitable assistance of the court to get any part of his expenditure repaid, unless he was willing to be charged with what he could not by the rules of law, as distinguished from equity, be made liable for. It was merely a case of imposing terms: a man who comes into equity must do equity."

It is also well settled that a tenant in common who has occupied the common property and also excluded his co-tenant in common therefrom can not only be sued at law for ejectment and for mesne profits (*Goodtitle v. Tombs* (1770) 3 Wils. K.B. 118; 95 E.R. 965), but is also liable in a partition suit to be charged with an occupation rent: *Pascoe v. Swan* (1859) 27 Beav. 508; 54 E.R. 201.

These exceptions to the general rule that a tenant in common is entitled to exercise acts of ownership over the whole of the common property without liability to be called upon to account in respect thereof, appear to me to be based on well-established principles; in the first class of cases, upon the maxim that he who seeks equity must do equity; and in the exclusion cases upon the fact that by excluding his co-owner from the exercise of his legal rights the tenant in common who so excluded his co-owner had committed a legal wrong. It appears to me, however, to be difficult to find any satisfactory principle on which a further exception should be engrafted on that general rule in a case, such as the present, where the person whom it is sought to charge with an occupation rent has committed no legal wrong, and who does not come into equity seeking equity, or asking equitable relief, but who, when brought unwillingly into this court, takes no active part in the proceedings, and merely submits to such decree as the court may think proper to make.

It was, however, contended that this court, when administering a fund, the proceeds of conversion of land belonging to tenants in common, and of which it has complete control, will in every case compel a co-owner who has been in occupation of the whole or part of the common property to account for an occupation rent to his co-owner who has been out of possession.

In support of this contention, reliance was principally placed upon the statement in *Halsbury's Laws of England*, Vol. 21, para. 1594, in the Article upon Partition: "Where one party has been in exclusive occupation, the court, if desired, will order that he shall be charged with an occupation rent"; and upon the language of Stirling J. (as he then was) in *Hill v. Hickin* [1897] 2 Ch. 579 at 580, 581 where he said, in reference to the question whether in a partition action an occupation rent, which had been certified to be due from one co-owner, could be set off against his share to the prejudice of his mortgagee: "The defendant James Hickin not having been tenant or bailiff of his co-owners, nothing could have been recovered from him at law; nor does the Statute of Anne, 4 Anne c. 16, s. 27, apply: see *Henderson v. Eason* (1851) 17 Q.B. 701; 117 E.R. 1451. It has, however, long been the practice of the Court of Chancery and of the Chancery Division to direct such inquiries as have been directed in the present case: see as to occupation rent, *Turner v. Morgan* (1863) 8 Ves. Jun. 143 at 145; 32 E.R. 307 at 308; and as to expenditure on improvements, *Swan v. Swan* (1820) 8 Price 518; 146 E.R. 1281. The principle on which the allowance for improvements is made is stated by Cotton L.J. in *Leigh v. Dickeson* (1884) 15 Q.B.D. 60.''

The language of Stirling J. in that excerpt from his judgment in that case is somewhat cryptic. In *McCormick v. McCormick* [1921] N.Z.L.R. 384 at 386 Salmond J. seems to have regarded it as intended to be of general application; he says: "So in *Hill v. Hickin*, Stirling J. apparently considered that in a partition suit an occupation rent would be charged against an occupying owner as a matter of course, and without proof of any special circumstances such as wrongful exclusion or tenancy." I am, however, by no means clear that such was the case. *Hill v. Hickin* is not satisfactorily reported; the statement of facts states that "one of the inquiries" directed by the judgment was "what sum was due from the defendant James Hickin in respect of his occupation of the hereditaments since 29 September 1890 (he having been in occupation during that period without payment of rent)", but omits to state what other inquiries were directed. From the reference made by Stirling J. to the practice of the Court of Chancery to direct an inquiry as to expenditure on improvements, in regard to which he referred to *Swan v. Swan* and *Leigh v. Dickeson*, it appears to me to be at least possible, and even probable, that in that case the defendant James Hickin was claiming an allowance in respect of such expenditure on his part; in which case the language of Stirling J. cannot be read as stating that the practice of the Court of Chancery was to charge an occupation rent in every case. If, however, it can properly be so read, it is significant that *Turner v. Morgan* (1803) 8 Ves. Jun. 143; 32 E.R. 307, the only case cited by him in respect of an occupation rent, was a case of exclusion, and I have not been referred to any other case in which an occupation rent was charged except under special circumstances. It was in any case an obiter dictum.

The three cases cited by the editors of *Halsbury's Laws of England* in the footnote to the passage already quoted are not, in my opinion, authority for the proposition stated by them in general terms.

Of these, *Story v. Johnson* (1837) 2 Y. & C. Ex. 586; 160 E.R. 529 does not appear to me to be in point, it was not a case of one tenant in common being in personal occupation of the common property at all; *Pascoe v. Swan* (1859) 27 Beav. 508; 54 E.R. 201 was a case of exclusion; and *Teasedale v. Sanderson* (1864) 33 Beav. 534; 55 E.R. 476 was, as I have already said, a case in which the defendant, who was claiming an allowance in respect of expenditure on repairs and improvements, was required to do equity by submitting to be charged with an occupation rent.

I am of opinion, therefore, that the proposition is not supported by authority; and there is, on the other hand, a considerable body of authority to the contrary.

In *M'Mahon v. Burchell* (1846) 5 Hare. 322; 67 E.R. 936, in proceedings instituted to obtain payment of certain legacies, the executors claimed a set-off in respect of an occupation rent alleged to be due by the plaintiff William M'Mahon in regard to property of which he was tenant in common, and an inquiry had been directed to ascertain what rent, if any, was due. The Master reported that the plaintiff ought to be charged with certain occupation rent, and to this report no exception was taken. A reference had also been directed to ascertain what amount ought to be allowed to the plaintiff William M'Mahon in respect of repairs and out-goings, and the Master reported the sum which ought to be allowed. To this report also no exception was taken. On the case coming on for further directions, Wigram V.-C. said (at 324; at 936-937): "I was of opinion upon the case in evidence before the Master, whatever the grounds might be on which the Master's opinion was founded, that the plaintiff William was entitled to be considered as tenant in common, occupying the Lower House under that title, admitting some, and not excluding any other members of the family from residing there if they thought fit; and that, in that character, he was not chargeable to them in respect of his occupation of the Lower House. I remain of the same opinion now." In the same case on appeal ((1846) 2 Ph. 127 at 134, 135; 41 E.R. 889 at 892-893) Lord Cottenham L.C. said: "There is this direct issue between the parties; the plaintiff says, I occupied the house as tenant in common the defendant only says, you did occupy, and in respect of such occupation, rent became due. . . . I must, therefore, take it that he means to raise this proposition, that the fact of the plaintiff having occupied the house not in entirety, but as a tenant in common, makes him liable to his co-tenants. A case has been referred to (*Henderson v. Eason* (1851) 10 Jur. 821; 117 E.R. 1451) in which the Vice-Chancellor of England is represented to have so decided; but I cannot think that the Vice-Chancellor can have laid down any such doctrine; for the effect would be, that one tenant in common, by keeping out of the actual occupation of the premises, might convert the other into his bailiff; in other words, prevent the other from occupying them, except upon the terms of paying him rent. There is nothing in the Acts of Parliament (4 Anne c. 16, s. 27; and 3 & 4 W. 4c. 27, s. 12) to lead to that conclusion, which is contrary to the law as clearly established from the time of Lord Coke downwards. I cannot think, therefore, that the Vice-Chancellor intended to lay down such a proposition. Indeed, it has hardly been contended for at the Bar."

In passing I may state that, by reason of the claim which was apparently being made by the plaintiff William M'Mahon for an allowance in respect of repairs and outgoings, an occupation rent might possibly have been properly charged in that case on the ground that a plaintiff seeking equity must do equity: *Teasdale v. Sanderson* (1864) 33 Beav. 534; 55 E.R. 476.

Again in *Griffies v. Griffies* (1863) 8 L.T. 758 Kindersely V.-C. held, in a suit for partition, that where one of the tenants in common was in occupation of the estate, he could not be made liable either for rent or for waste; in the course of his judgment the Vice-Chancellor said: "As each party is entitled to enter upon the whole property, there can be no claim by one tenant in common against another for an occupation rent. As to cutting down trees, and the other acts of waste alleged in the bill, each tenant in common has a right to exercise acts of ownership over the whole property, and no charge can therefore be sustained in respect of such an act."

Finally in *McCormick v. McCormick* [1921] N.Z.L.R. 384 Salmond J. concluded a considered judgment, in the course of which he reviewed most of the cases to which I have referred, by saying (at 387, 388): "In this state of the authorities I prefer to follow the express and definite decision in *Griffies v. Griffies* (1863) 8 L.T. 758 that there is no general right even in a partition suit to charge an occupying owner with an occupation rent. I think that the obligations of co-owners to account to each other are the same in equity as at law, and are the same in a partition suit as in other proceedings, save only that in a partition suit, if an occupying owner claims an allowance for his expenditure, he can obtain it only if he consents to be charged with an occupation rent." To this statement of the position I would only add that, for my part, I can see no reason why the application of the maxim, he who seeks equity must do equity, should be limited to suits for partition, and I think it improbable that Salmond J. was of a different opinion.

The conclusion to which I have come is that the contention that the defendant Ada Luke should be charged with an occupation rent in this case is neither supportable on principle, nor established by authority, and that, in fact, the balance of authority is to the contrary.

I make the order for sale as asked, and declare that the defendant Ada Luke is not chargeable with an occupation rent.

NOTES

1. In *Jones v. Jones* [1977] 1 W.L.R. 438 a son and his stepmother held a one quarter and three quarter share respectively as tenants in common in a house. The plaintiff stepmother claimed rental from the defendant stepson who was in sole occupation of the property. It was held by the Court of Appeal that the plaintiff was not entitled to rent from the defendant for his occupation of the house. Lord Denning M.R. said:

> It is quite plain that these two people were in equity tenants in common having a three quarter and one quarter share respectively. One was in occupation of the house. The other not. Now the common law said clearly that one tenant in common is not entitled to rent from another tenant in common, even though that other occupies the whole. That appears from *M'Mahon v. Burchell* (1846) 2 Ph. 127 at 134; 41 E.R. 889 at 892 per Lord Cottenham L.C., and *Henderson v. Eason* (1851) 17 Q.B. 701 at 720; 117 E.R. 1451 at 1458. Of course if one of the tenants let the premises at a rent to a stranger and received the rent, there would have to be an account, but the mere fact that one tenant was in possession and the other out of possession did not give the one that was out any claim for rent. It did not do so in the old days of legal tenants in common. Nor does it in modern times of equitable tenants in common. In *Bull v. Bull* [1955] 1 Q.B. 234 at 239 I said: "the son, although he is the legal owner of the house, has no right to turn his mother out. She has an equitable interest which entitles her to remain in the house as tenant in common with him until the house is sold." As between tenants in common, they both equally entitled to occupation and one cannot claim rent from the other. Of course, if there was an ouster, that would be another matter; or if there was a letting to a stranger for rent that would be different, but there can be no claim for rent by one tenant in common against the other whether at law or in equity.

2. The equal rights of enjoyment and possession shared by co-owners do not entitle one co-owner to destroy the co-owned property. Where the co-owner in occupation destroys the property his co-owners may have a remedy in trespass (*Wilkinson v. Haygarth* (1847) 12 Q.B. 837; 116 E.R. 1085), or waste. In the case of a partial destruction, a co-owner is liable for waste (*Murray v. Hall* (1849) 7 C.B. 441; 137 E.R. 175) and, moreover, it is sometimes suggested that destructive waste constitutes ouster thereby giving rise to trespass: thus, in *Wilkinson v. Haygarth* the defendant pleaded to a declaration in trespass for breaking the plaintiffs' close and digging and carrying away the turf, that he did so under licence from W who owned the close with others as tenants in common. It was held that the plea was bad because the tenant in common could not himself have done the act which amounted to a destruction and, therefore he could not authorise another to do it:

> The turf is composed of the grass and soil on which it grows, as peat is the vegetable and the soil of which it has become a part. The turf does not so grow as to become part of the accruing profits which are the subject of enjoyment by the tenants in common. It is admitted that, if there has been an ouster, the present action will lie; that taking a chattel away constitutes an ouster; and that in all cases the destruction of the property is also an ouster. In *Clayton v. Corby* (1843) 5 Q.B. 415; 114 E.R. 1306 a prescription, in a plea, to take in alieno solo as much clay for making bricks at defendant's brick-kiln as he required was held bad; the principle of that case was that such a taking destroyed the subject matter. I consider this, therefore, an ouster effected by means of the destruction of the property: at 845 per Lord Denman C.J.

> It must be admitted, on the part of the plaintiff, that the tenant might license the doing of whatever he might do himself: and, on the other hand, the defendant must admit that this does not include acts of destruction. Now taking turf is not like taking the vestura terrae, or other growing profits. Were we to hold that a tenant in common could take away the turf, we must say also that one tenant in common could carry all the brick earth from the surface; and it is impossible to say where we could stop: at 845-846 per Coleridge J.

(b) Liability to account

At common law, as a result of the inherent nature of co-ownership, there was no remedy if one co-owner obtained a larger share of the rents and profits than was her or his due. However, an action for an account was given both by statute, 4 Anne c. 16, s. 27 (1705), and in equity. The statute 4 Anne c. 16 is not applicable in New South Wales: *Imperial Acts Application Act* 1969; but see the *Supreme Court Rules*, Pts 48 and 49. The right to an account extends only to benefits received from third parties or the natural and necessary working out of the co-owned property (such as a coal mine) where the working out is regarded as rightfully taken for the benefit of all co-owners, and not to profits received by a co-owner in occupation as a result of her or his own labours. "The receipts . . . liable to account . . . are limited to those receipts which can properly be regarded as rents and revenue of the common property itself as distinct from profits . . . [resulting from the] use and occupation of the common property (e.g., fees for services and for use of items of equipment).": *Squire v. Rogers* (1979) 27 A.L.R. 330 at 345, extracted below p. 101.

HENDERSON v. EASON

Exchequer Chamber (1851) 17 Q.B. 701; 117 E.R. 1451 at 1457

PARKE B. [This] is an action of account founded on the Statute 4 Anne c. 16, by Robert Eason against the executor of his co-tenant in common Edward Eason. . . . There is an averment that Eason in his lifetime received more than his just share and proportion of the rents, issues and profits of the said tenancy, that is to say the whole of the rents, issues and profits, and had not rendered an account to the plaintiff.

. . . Evidence was given that two Easons were tenants in common in fee of a messuage and farm of above 133 acres of land from November 1833 to November 1838, during which time Eward Eason occupied the whole on his own account, the plaintiff occupying no part: that he cultivated the same on his own account solely, and appropriated the produce to his own use; and that he cropped the farm in the usual way, kept the usual quantity of live and dead stock, and farmed well; and that he received all the produce of the farm, and sold it on his own account.

. . .

There is no doubt as to the law before the Statute of 4 Anne c. 16. If one tenant in common occupied, and took the whole profits, the other had no remedy against him whilst the tenancy in common continued, unless he was put out of possession, when he might have his ejectment, or unless he appointed the other to be his bailiff as to his undivided moiety, and the other accepted that appointment, when an action of account would lie, as against a bailiff of the owner of the entirety of an estate.

Until the Statute of Anne this state of the law continued. That statute provides by s. 27, that an action of account may be brought and maintained by one joint tenant and tenant in common, his executors and administrators, against the other, for receiving more than comes to his just share or proportion, and against the executor and administrator of such joint tenant or tenant in common; and the auditors are authorised to administer an oath.

Declarations framed on this statute vary from those at common law, as it is an essential averment in them that the defendant has received more than his share. This was held in the case of *Wheeler v. Horne* (1851) Willes 208; 125 E.R. 1135, and in *Sturton v. Richardson* (1860) 13 M. & W. 17; 158 E.R. 7.

Under the Statute of Anne he is bailiff only by virtue of his receiving more than his just share, and as soon as he does so, and is answerable only for so much as he actually receives, as is fully explained by Lord Chief Justice Willes in the case above cited. He is not responsible, as a bailiff at common law, for what he might have made without his wilful default.

It is to be observed that the statute does not mention lands or tenements, or any particular subject. Every case in which a tenant in common receives more than his share is within the statute; and account will lie when he does receive, but not otherwise. It is to be observed, also, that the receipt of issues and profits is not mentioned, but simply the receipt of more than comes to his just share; and, further, he is to account when he receives, not takes, more than comes to his just share. What, then, is a "receiving" of more than comes to his just share, within the meaning of that provision in the Statute of Anne?

It appears to us that, construing the Act according to the ordinary meaning of the words, this provision of the statute was meant to apply only to cases where the tenant in common receives money or something else, where another person gives or pays it, which the co-tenants are entitled to simply by reason of their being tenants in common, and in proportion to their interests as such, and of which one receives and keeps more than his just share according to that proportion.

The statute, therefore, includes all cases in which one of two tenants in common of lands leased at a rent payable to both, or of a rent charge, or any money payment or payment in kind, due to them from another person, receives the whole or more than his proportionate share according to his interest in the subject of the tenancy. There is no difficulty in ascertaining the share of each, and determining when one has received more than his just share: and he becomes, as to that excess, the bailiff of the other, and must account.

But when we seek to extend the operation of the statute beyond the ordinary meaning of its words, and to apply it to cases in which one has enjoyed more of the benefit of the subject, or made more by its occupation, than the other, we have insuperable difficulties to encounter.

There are obviously many cases in which a tenant in common may occupy and enjoy the land or other subject of tenancy in common solely, and have all the advantage to be derived from it, and yet it would be most unjust to make him pay anything. For instance, if a dwelling-house, or barn, or room, is solely occupied by one tenant in common, without ousting the other, or a chattel is used by one co-tenant in common, nothing is received; and it would be most inequitable to hold that he thereby, by the simple act of occupation or use, without any agreement, should be liable to pay a rent or anything in the nature of compensation to his co-tenants for that occupation or use to which to the full extent to which he enjoyed it he had a perfect right. It appears impossible to hold that such a case could be within the statute; and an opinion to that effect was expressed by Lord Cottenham in *M'Mahon v. Burchell* 2 Ph. 127 at 134; 41 E.R. 889 at 892. Such cases are clearly out of the operation of the statute.

Again, there are many cases where profits are made, and are actually taken, by one co-tenant, and yet it is impossible to say that he has received more than comes to his just share. For instance, one tenant employs his capital and industry in cultivating the whole of a piece of land, the subject of the tenancy, in a mode in which the money and labour expended greatly exceed the value of the rent or compensation for the mere occupation of the land; in raising hops, for example, which is a very hazardous adventure. He takes the whole of the crops: and is he to be accountable for any of the profits in such a case, when it is clear that, if the speculation had been a losing one altogether, he could not have called for a moiety of the losses, as he would have been enabled to do had it been so cultivated by the mutual agreement of the co-tenants? The risk of the cultivation, and the profits and loss, are his own; and what is just with respect to the very uncertain and expensive crop of hops is just also with respect to all the produce of the land, the *fructus* industriales, which are raised by the capital and industry of the occupier, and would not exist without it. In taking all that produce he cannot be said to receive more than his just share and proportion to which he is entitled as a tenant in common. He receives in truth the return for his own labour and capital, to which his co-tenant has no right.

In the case before Lord North in Skinner [Anonymous in Chancery, Skinn. 230.], in which it is said that, if one of four tenants in common stock land and manage it, the rest shall have an account of the profits, but if a loss come, as of the sheep, they shall bear a part, it is evident, from the context, Lord North is speaking of a case where one tenant in common manages by the mutual agreement of all for their common benefit; for he gives it as an illustration of the rights of a part owner of a ship to an account when the voyage is undertaken by his consent, expressed or implied.

Where the natural produce of the land is augmented by the capital and industry of the tenant, grass, for instance, by manuring and draining, and the tenant takes and sells it, or where, by feeding it with his cattle, he makes a profit by it, the case seems to us to be neither within the words or spirit of the Act, though these are not cases of fructus industriales in either case.

It may be observed, however, that the evidence stated in the bill of exceptions does not raise either of these points.

We therefore think that, upon the evidence set out in this case, there was nothing to warrant the jury in coming to the conclusion that the defendant received more than his just share within the meaning of the Act; and that the direction of the learned judge as to the second issue was therefore wrong. And we also think that there was no conclusive or sufficient, or indeed any, evidence that he had the care and management of the farm for their common profit, as averred in the declaration. We therefore think that there should be.

Judgment to reverse the judgment of Q.B., and for a venire de novo.

NOTES

1. The principal case was followed in South Australia (*Rees v. Rees* [1931] S.A.S.R. 78) and in Tasmania: *Re Tolman's Estate* (1928) 23 Tas. L.R. 29.

2. Co-owners do not stand in a fiduciary relation to each other and, accordingly, a co-owner in occupation is not a trustee for herself or himself and her or his co-owners with respect to the proceeds derived from the property as a result of her or his own labour and capital: *Rees v. Rees* [1931] S.A.S.R. 78 at 81. Richards J. there said:

> The point raised by the defence in the present action; that in farming the land the plaintiffs did so as trustees for themselves and the defendants, is dealt with in the note in Lindley on p. 37: "nor can one co-owner, by leaving the management of the property in the hands of the other, impose upon him an obligation of a fiduciary character." The authority cited for this proposition is *Kennedy v. De Trafford* [1897] A.C. 180 (see especially at 189 per Lord Herchell), which is cited by Collins M.R. in *Re Biss* [1903] 2 Ch. 40 at 57, for the statement that "tenants in common do not stand in a fiduciary relation to each other". There is nothing in the circumstances of the present case giving rise to any such relationship concerning the management of the farm or the produce thereof.

(c) Improvements and repairs

A claim for an allowance for repairs, improvements or outgoings is a "passive" or "defensive" equity, that is, a claim which can only be made on partition or in an administration suit, unless the expenditure is required by law (*Leigh v. Dickeson* (1884) 15 Q.B.D. 60), as, for example, by s. 147 of the *Local Government Act* 1919 (N.S.W.):

147. (1) Where the land is owned or held jointly by two or more ratable persons, such persons shall be jointly and severally liable to the council for the rate, but as between themselves each shall only be liable for such part of the rate as is proportionate to his interest in the land and in the improvements thereon.

(2) If any of such persons pays to the council more than his proportionate part, he may recover the excess by way of contribution from the others.

The benefit of a claim for repairs, improvements or outgoings will run with the land so as to be enforceable by a successor in title of the co-owner making the improvements. The High Court has proceeded on the assumption that the quantum allowed as compensation will be the amount by which the value of the land has been increased as a result of the improvements (*Brickwood v. Young* (1905) 2 C.L.R. 387; See also *Leigh v. Dickeson* (1884) 15 Q.B.D. 60; *Re Byrne* (1906) 6 S.R. (N.S.W.) 532; and *Noack v. Noack* [1959] V.R. 137), although it has been held elsewhere that the compensation allowed will be limited to the actual cost of the improvements or the present value of the increment to the property, whichever is the lesser: *McMahon v. Public Curator (Qld)* [1952] St. R. Qd 197. Compensation cannot be recovered for repairs in the nature of maintenance such that its value would be exhausted when renewed (for example, periodic painting of a house: *McMahon v. Public Curator (Qld)*), for repairs required to be made by the co-owner in occupation pursuant to a contractual obligation, or where the improvement is a gift to the other co-owner.

Where a co-owner not in possession claims in a partition suit a share in the rents and profits resulting from the use of improvements made by the co-owner in possession, the former must make an allowance in respect of the improvements that is not restricted to the lesser of the cost of the improvements or the present enhancement of the value of the land but of an amount which is equal to the expenditure on the improvements actually made by the co-owner in possession, to the extent that the proceeds of sale allow: *Squire v. Rogers* (1979) 27 A.L.R. 330, extracted below p. 101.

LEIGH v. DICKESON

Court of Appeal (1884) 15 Q.B.D. 60 at 63

[The plaintiffs were trustees of a lady named Eyles who was entitled to an undivided three fourths of a house as tenant in common with another.

Eyles then leased to one Prebble for 21 years her interest at the rate of £33 5s. per annum. In 1865 the lease was assigned by Prebble to the defendant, who entered and paid rent. In 1871 the defendant purchased the one fourth interest of the other tenant in common. On 6 January 1881, the lease expired, but the defendant continued in possession. A correspondence then took place between the plaintiffs and the defendant and their solicitors with a view to continue the tenancy; but on the plaintiffs asking for an advanced rent which the defendant was unwilling to pay, no further agreement was arrived at. Upon the facts Pollock B. came to the conclusion that the occupation by the defendant, which occurred after the expiration of the lease in question on 6 January 1881, must be referred, not to his right as tenant in common, but to his continuing in occupation as tenant at sufferance. He therefore gave judgment for the plaintiffs for £24 9s. 6d., the amount claimed for use and occupation: (1883) 12 Q.B.D. 194 at 196.

The defendant, by way of set-off and counterclaim, sought to recover from the plaintiffs £80, which, he alleged, he had laid out and expended in substantial and other proper repairs and improvements upon the premises since the expiration of the lease. Pollock B. was of opinion that the set-off and counterclaim could not be sustained in law, and gave judgment upon it for the plaintiffs: 12 Q.B.D. 194 at 200. The defendant appealed.]

BRETT M.R. The cestui que trust of the plaintiffs and the defendant were tenants in common of a house: the defendant has done certain repairs which may be taken to have been reasonable and proper: he has paid for, or at least become liable to pay for, those repairs. An action having been brought against him, he seeks by a counterclaim to recover that money which he has paid or is liable to pay. The cestui que trust of the plaintiffs has derived benefit from the expenditure incurred by the defendant, and the defendant seeks to reimburse himself for the cost of the repairs in proportion to the benefit which the tenant in common with him has received. Does this counterclaim fall within any legal and recognised principle? There was no express request by the tenant in common with him that he should expend the money. . . .

[I]t has been always clear that a purely voluntary payment cannot be recovered back. Voluntary payments may be divided into two classes. Sometimes money has been expended for the benefit of another person under such circumstances that an option is allowed to him to adopt or decline the benefit: in this case, if he exercises his option to adopt the benefit, he will be liable to repay the money expended; but if he declines the benefit he will not be liable. But sometimes the money is expended for the benefit of another person under such circumstances, that he cannot help accepting the benefit, in fact that he is bound to accept it: in this case he has no opportunity of exercising any option, and he will be under no liability. Under which class does this case come? Tenants in common are not partners, and it has been so held; one of them is not an agent for another. The cost of the repairs to the house was a voluntary payment by the defendant, partly for the benefit of himself and partly for the benefit of his co-owner; but the co-owner cannot reject the benefit of the repairs, and if she is held to be liable for a proportionate share of the cost, the defendant will get the advantage of the repairs without allowing his co-owner any liberty to decide whether she will refuse or adopt them. The defendant cannot recover at common law; he cannot recover for money paid in equity, for that is a legal remedy: there is no remedy in this case for money paid. But it is said that there is a remedy in equity: a suit for a partition may be maintained in equity: that is a remedy which is known and recognised in a court of equity: in a suit in the Chancery Division expenditure between tenants in common would be taken into account. Reference has been made during the argument to an old form of writ; it looks to be a writ of a mandatory nature: but it has proved to be wholly unworkable in a court of common law. Therefore the rights of tenants in common went into Chancery, where a suit for a partition might be maintained. That is the only remedy which exists either at law or in equity. No such claim as that put forward in the present counterclaim can be found to have been upheld either at law or in equity. If the law were otherwise, a part owner might be compelled to incur expense against his will: a house might be situate in a decaying borough, and it might be thought by one co-owner that it would be better not to repair it. The refusal of a tenant in common to bear any part of the cost of proper repair may be unreasonable: nevertheless, the law allows him to refuse, and no action will lie against him. The judgment of Pollock B. was right, and this appeal must be dismissed.

COTTON L.J. I am of the same opinion. The plaintiffs have brought an action to recover rent, and the defendant by his counterclaim raises the question whether one tenant in common is liable to another for the cost of repairs.

I think that the plaintiffs are entitled to succeed in their claim for rent. It has been urged that one tenant in common cannot recover against another for rent, for either of them may enjoy the possession. But in the present case the defendant, although he himself was tenant in common, had possession of the whole of the house by virtue of a lease from his co-tenant in common. A correspondence ensued, as to the terms under which he should remain in occupation of the house. Under these circumstances, I think that the defendant must be considered as holding exclusive possession of the house upon the terms of the lease, and therefore, that he is liable for rent at the same rate as was reserved by the lease.

Then a question is raised as to repairs, and the objection is taken upon demurrer to the counterclaim. I think that it must be assumed that the house was in a bad state of repair, and that the repairs executed by the defendant were necessary. As to the claim for improvements, it has been urged that no tenant in common is entitled to execute improvements upon the property held in common, and then to charge his co-tenant in common with the cost. This seems to me the true view, and I need not further discuss the question as to improvements. As to the question of repairs, it is to be observed that when two persons are under a common obligation, one of them can recover from the other the amount expended in discharge or fulfilment of the common obligation; but that is not the position of affairs here: one tenant in common cannot charge another with the cost of repairs without a request, and in the present case it is impossible even to imply a request. No action for money paid will lie at common law; and in equity there is no remedy against a co-tenant in common, except in the case which I will presently mention. . . . Therefore, no remedy exists for money expended in repairs by one tenant in common, so long as the property is enjoyed in common; but in a suit for a partition it is usual to have an enquiry as to those expenses of which nothing could be recovered so long as the parties enjoyed their property in common; when it is desired to put an end to that state of things, it is then necessary to consider what has been expended in improvements or repairs: the property held in common has been increased in value by the improvements and repairs; and whether the property is divided or sold by the decree of the court, one party cannot take the increase in value, without making an allowance for what has been expended in order to obtain that increased value: in fact, the execution of the repairs and improvements is adopted and sanctioned by accepting the increased value. There is, therefore, a mode by which money expended by one tenant in common for repairs can be recovered, but the procedure is confined to suits for partition. Tenancy in common is an inconvenient kind of tenure; but if tenants in common disagree, there is always a remedy by a suit for a partition, and in this case it is the only remedy.

[Lindley J. came to the same conclusion.]

Appeal dismissed.

NOTE

In *Re Byrne* (1906) 6 S.R. (N.S.W.) 532 one of the joint tenants in remainder, Byrne, during the lifetime of the tenant for life, expended out of his own moneys a sum of £975 in erecting a house upon certain property. The improvements increased the value of the property by £900. The property was resumed and the money paid into court. The life tenant having died, Byrne claimed to be entitled to the sum of £900 out of the resumption moneys prior to distribution among the joint tenants. At the time Byrne built the house, his mother, the life tenant, was living and was in occupation of the property. Byrne, therefore, was entitled in remainder, and was not in possession. Walker J. found in respect of the two points raised by the respondent:

> Mr Maughan's first point was that the claim must fail, because no case could be cited where this claim, which has been termed a defensive equity, has been allowed except where the persons effecting the improvements were in possession either under a lease or some other circumstances. . . .

It has been held, as I understand the decision in *Boulter v. Boulter* (1898) 19 L.R. (N.S.W.) Eq. 135, that the equity can be enforced by a tenant in common who at the time of the expenditure was out of possession. It is true that in that case the claimant was in occupation of the property as lessee at the time he made the improvements, but as I read the judgment the learned judge distinguished between his dual capacities and held that the fact of his being also a lessee made no difference. This is borne out by what Sir Samuel Griffith C.J. says in *Brickwood v. Young* (1905) 2 C.L.R. 387 at 395: "In *Boulter v. Boulter* the same learned judge from whose decision this appeal is brought held that the rule applies in suits for administration as well as in suits for partition, and when the improvements are made while the estate of the tenant in common is only an estate in remainder, as well as when his estate is an estate in possession." Therefore he must have understood that Simpson C.J. in Eq. in *Boulter v. Boulter* held that the equity could be enforced where the expenditure was made by a tenant in common out of possession. Then why ought I not to enforce it in this case? What is the ground of the rule? I imagine that it must be that it is unjust and inequitable that the other co-owners should get the benefit of the improvement without contributing to the cost. If for that reason this equity is enforced in the case of a tenant in common who while in possession effects an improvement, still more and with greater reason should the equity be allowed in cases where the tenant in common effected the improvement while out of possession, for in the former case the tenant in common in possession might be held to have been sufficiently recouped by the enjoyment of the property in its improved condition. . . .

Mr Maughan's second point was that this equity has never yet been allowed in cases of joint tenancy, but only in cases of tenancy in common. No doubt that is so according to the reported cases; but that argument ought not to be pressed too far. The point has never been taken until now, perhaps, because joint tenancy is a comparatively rare estate. I, however, have had to deal with this question on principle and apart from authority; and if the principle underlying the decisions is that stated by me, why should it not apply to a joint tenancy? . . .

I hold, therefore, that Mr W. A. Byrne is entitled to the relief he asks.

BRICKWOOD v. YOUNG

High Court of Australia (1905) 2 C.L.R. 387 at 388

[The following statement of the facts is taken from the judgment of Griffiths C.J.

This appeal relates to the distribution of a sum of money paid into court by the Minister for Public Works, representing the value of land resumed by the Crown for public purposes. On 18 May 1869, the appellant's predecessor in title, one Gannon, purchased the land in question, and took a conveyance of it from six persons, Elizabeth Young and her five children, who were all of full age. Elizabeth Young was tenant for life of the land under her deceased husband's will, and it appears to have been assumed that the other five vendors were tenants in common in remainder. In fact, however, they had only executory interests, the actual trusts of the will having been for the use of the wife for life, and after her death for such of the testator's children as should be living at her decease, but the testator directed that, in case any of them should die in the lifetime of his wife leaving issue, the share that would have belonged to any deceased child should go to his children. The fee was vested in the trustees of the will, so that the interests were equitable interests. One of the children died unmarried. Three of the others died in the lifetime of the tenant for life, leaving issue, who consequently took the shares of their deceased parents. One of the children survived the tenant for life, who died in 1890.

The result was that the deed of 18 May 1869 only operated as a conveyance of the life estate and of the undivided fourth share in remainder of the son who survived her. Upon her death the appellant, who had by the effect of several mesne conveyances acquired Gannon's title, became an equitable tenant in common with the respondents other than the Minister, who are the children of those children of the testator who predeceased the tenant for life, his share being one fourth.

One of his predecessors in title, one Porter, had in 1872 erected houses upon the land, by which it was alleged that its value was considerably increased. The appellant continued in possession of the land and in receipt of the rents and profits until the resumption.

When the amount of compensation had been settled, he, in the first instance, claimed the whole of the money, alleging that the title of the respondents other than the Minister was barred by adverse possession. This fact being disputed by these respondents, the appellant asked for and received payment of the one fourth to which he was admittedly entitled, and asked that the other three fourths might be paid into court under the *Public Works Act* 1900 (N.S.W.) which was done.

A petition was then presented by the respondents, other than the Minister for Public Works, for payment of the fund to them. The appellant first claimed the whole fund on the ground above stated, but failed to establish his claim. He then claimed to be entitled to be recouped out of the fund to an amount equal to three fourths of that by which the purchase money was increased by reason of the improvements by his predecessor in title.

Simpson C.J. in Eq. rejected this claim on the grounds, (1) that there was no instance in which the court had given effect to the equity relied on when it was not administering the whole fund, (2) that the appellant had not himself made the expenditure of which he claimed the benefit: *Re Young; Brickwood v. Young* (1904) 4 S.R. (N.S.W.) 743. He thought that the appellant's predecessor in title, Porter, who actually made the expenditure, had received the benefit of it on his sale to his successor in title; that he could not keep the whole purchase money as owner in fee and at the same time set up an equity as tenant in common; that, if he claimed as tenant in common, he must bring into account the purchase money he received; and that as the appellant could not do this, his claim must fail.

From this decision the present appeal was brought.]

GRIFFITH C.J. . . . . The doctrine relied upon by the appellant is of comparatively recent development. The earliest reported case is *Swan v. Swan* (1819) 8 Price 518; 146 E.R. 1281; and as late as 1883 so learned a judge as Fry J. expressed doubts as to the validity of the doctrine. In *Leigh v. Dickeson* (1884) 15 Q.B.D. 60, however, decided in the following year, it is asserted by Cotton L.J. as follows (at 67): "No remedy exists for money expended in repairs by one tenant in common, so long as the property is enjoyed in common; but in a suit for partition it is usual to have an inquiry as to those expenses of which nothing could be recovered so long as the parties enjoyed their property in common; when it is desired to put an end to that state of things, it is then necessary to consider what has been expended in improvements or repairs: the property held in common has been increased in value by the improvements and repairs; and whether the property is divided or sold by the decree of the court, one party cannot take the increase in value, without making an allowance for what has been expended in order to obtain that increased value. . . . There is, therefore, a mode by which money expended by one tenant in common for repairs can be recovered, but the procedure is confined to suits for partition." The application of the doctrine was extended in *Re Jones; Farrington v. Forrester* [1893] 2 Ch. 461 to a case of an expenditure by a tenant for life in entirety, who was also owner in remainder of a moiety in fee; and in *Re Cook's Mortgage; Lawledge v. Tyndall* [1896] 1 Ch. 923, to a case of division of funds in an administration suit. In *Boulter v. Boulter* (1898) 19 L.R. (N.S.W.) Eq. 135 the same learned judge from whose decision this appeal is brought held that the rule applies in suits for administration as well as in suits for partition, and when the improvements are made while the estate of the tenant in common is only an estate in remainder, as well as when his estate is an estate in possession. In the present case the person who made the improvements was tenant pur autre vie of the whole, and also tenant in remainder of an undivided fourth. It appears from the case of *Leigh v. Dickeson* that the equity in question is not one which can be asserted actively, except in a suit for partition or administration, in which all the parties are equally regarded as actors, but is what was called in argument a defensive equity. And this point was relied on by Mr Knox for the respondents, who contended that the appellant, having accepted his own fourth of the purchase money payable on the resumption, must be considered as an actor in respect of the other three fourths paid into court. He also contended that this payment to the appellant operated as a partition of the land and an allotment to the appellant his one fourth share, so that the fund in court represents only the other three fourths to which he has no title.

With regard to the second ground of the learned judge's decision, I cannot regard the equitable right of a tenant in common to compensation as against his co-tenants as merely personal to the individual tenant who effects the improvements. The principle appears to be that the making of permanent improvements by one tenant in common in sole occupation gives rise to an equity attaching to the land, analogous to an equitable charge created by the owners for the time being, but enforceable only in the event of partition or a distribution of the value of the land amongst the tenants in common. There can be no reason why such a charge should not run with the land in favour of purchasers from the person orginally entitled to it. It is clearly a right incidental to the possession of the land, and cannot be asserted until that possession is disturbed. It appears to me, therefore, that the equity passes with the land, and may be asserted by the possessor for the time being, who, I think, may claim the benefit of the improvements effected by his predecessor in title. It is true that Porter, who made the improvements, has been paid for them, but not by the respondents. The purchase money which the appellant paid for the land prima facie included the enhanced value, and I can see no reason why he should not stand in the place of Porter, whose rights he acquired for valuable consideration. This view was acted on without objection in *Re Jones; Farrington v. Forrester* [1893] 2 Ch. 461, where the claim to compensation was successfully asserted by the heir-at-law of the person who made the improvements. And in *Williams v. Williams* (1891) 81 L.T. N.S. 163, mentioned in *Seton's Judgments and Orders* (6th ed.), Vol. 2, p. 1860, the right of the tenant in common in possession to take advantage of the expenditure of his predecessors in title was allowed, apparently as a matter of course. In my opinion this objection fails. With regard to the other objection, regard must be had to the substance rather than to the form of the matter. When the land was resumed, the appellant was in possession as tenant in common, and the respondents could only have asserted their title against him by a suit for partition, in which he could have set up his equity to compensation for the improvements. Upon the resumption the land was represented by the purchase money. By s. 56 of the *Public Works Act* 1900 (N.S.W.) the appellant, as the person in possession of the land, is to be deemed to have been lawfully entitled to the land until the contrary is shown. It is the respondents, therefore, who are in the position of actors, asserting a claim to that which prima facie is the property of the appellant. The equity set up by him is, therefore, a "defensive" equity, namely, to claim compensation before effect is given to the better title of the respondents. Having regard to the principle of the doctrine invoked by the appellant, it seems quite immaterial that he has already received without objection part of the property to the whole of which he is prima facie entitled. The parties asserting the adverse claim are in either case equally bound to do equity. Nor, in my judgment, can the payment of one fourth of the purchase money to the appellant affect his right to set up this equity. No one disputed his right to receive it, and his solicitor's letter to the Crown Solicitor of 13 October 1903, which asked for payment of the one fourth, and contained a request that the other three fourths should be paid into court, added "upon which I would made application for payment out". It is clear that under these circumstances no abandonment of the appellant's right to the three fourths or any part of it can be inferred, any more than if, on an application for payment of part of a fund in court to a person admittedly entitled to it, it were ordered to be paid to him without prejudice to his right to claim the residue, he could be said to have abandoned his claim to the residue.

For these reasons it appears to me, both on principle and authority, that the appellant, who is defending his prima facie claim to the fund representing the three fourths, is entitled to assert his lien upon it for the value of the improvements. It was, however, contended that he is debarred from doing so, because it may turn out that he is indebted to the respondents, in respect of three fourths of the rents and profits received by him since the death of the tenant for life, in an amount greater than that which he is entitled to claim under his lien, and that in that event the respondents ought to be in a position to take the difference out of his fourth share which he has already received. The indebtedness is not disputed. The claim to recover from him three fourths of the rents and profits existed before the resumption, and is not affected by it. The respondents had no lien for it upon the land, and the payment into court of the three fourths did not give them any lien upon the sum paid in, and, a fortiori, gave them none upon the other fourth. No doubt the court may, and I think ought to, impose as a condition of allowing the appellant to assert his equity in respect of the improvements that he shall account for the rents and profits so far as they may exhaust the amount of his charge: see *Teasdale v. Sanderson* (1864) 33 Beav. 534; 55 E.R. 476. I doubt whether in this proceeding any more onerous terms could be imposed upon him without his consent; but, as he is willing to submit to pay any amount that may be found due from him upon a balance of accounts, it is not necessary to express any opinion on the point.

In my opinion, therefore, the learned judge ought to have directed an account of the money expended by the appellant or his predecessors in title in permanent improvements on the land since the deed of 18 May 1869, and an inquiry as to the extent to which the compensation money paid on resumption was increased by such expenditure, and there should have been a declaration that the appellant is entitled to a lien upon the fund in court for an amount equal to three fourths of the amount of such increase. There should then have been directed an inquiry, prefixed by the appellant's submission, as to what sum is due by the appellant to the respondents, in respect of three fourths of the rents and profits of the land received by him since the death of the tenant for life, with a direction that the amount so found due shall be set off against the amount found due to him in respect of the improvements, and that the resulting balance, if in his favour, shall be paid to him out of the fund in court, and, if against him, be paid by him into court in augmentation of the fund before any claim is made by him to receive costs out of the fund. The order for payment of costs by the appellant must be omitted, and an order substituted for payment of his costs and those of the Minister occasioned by adverse litigation between adverse claimants out of the fund. The order appealed from must be varied accordingly. The appellant's costs should be paid out of the fund.

[Barton and O'Connor JJ., in separate judgments, concurred.]

NOTES

1. The principle that a co-owner who makes improvements to the common property is entitled on partition to compensation to the extent to which the expenditure on the improvements has enhanced the value of the property has found expression in several cases. However, this principle does not apply where the intent of the co-owner making the improvements is to confer a gift upon the other co-owner. Thus in *Noack v. Noack* [1959] V.R. 137 at 146, the court said:

> The appellant's claim to be entitled to be allowed expenses and outgoings in respect of improvements effected by him to the lands in question in the adjustment of the rights of the parties upon a sale or partition rested upon principles of equity enunciated in such cases as *Leigh v. Dickeson* (1884) 15 Q.B.D. 60; *Brickwood v. Young* (1905) 2 C.L.R. 387. According to these principles a co-owner who improves the common property at his own expense is, in general, entitled upon a partition or sale of the property to an allowance to the extent to which by his expenditure he has enhanced the value of the property. The fairness of this gives rise to an equity. This equitable principle, however, can have no application where the intention of one co-owner in making the improvements is to confer the full benefit thereof on his companion as well, or to use the expression of the learned trial judge, "to make the improvements part of the common property". No principle of equity can be invoked to recall a gift once made.

> In *Noack v. Noack* the court found that the husband made a gift of the improvements to his wife by way of advancement.

2. It is apparent from *Brickwood v. Young* that because the court ordered accounts to be taken, both of the money expended in making the permanent improvements and the extent by which the compensation paid on the resumption of the property was increased by such expenditure, the court considered these matters relevant in ascertaining the quantum of compensation due to the co-owner making the improvements. However, the court did not indicate the relationship between the increase in value of the property and the actual amount expended in making the improvements. See the following comments by Macrossan CJ. in *McMahon v. Public Curator (Qld)* [1952] Q.S.R. 197:

> At 479 North J. [in *Re Jones; Farrington v. Forrester* [1893] 2 Ch. 461] expressed the order to which the representatives of the deceased co-owner were entitled as follows: He said "they are entitled to an inquiry to what extent the present value of the property has been increased by the expenditure made in 1870. It may turn out that the present value of the increase is £1,200, and in that case the charge account cannot be for more than £900. It may be that the present value of the increase is less than that—for example only £600—and in that case only £600 can be allowed out of the proceeds of sale." It is clear, I think from this, that the amount to which a co-owner making improvements may be entitled against another co-owner in taking the accounts in a partition action, is limited to the actual cost of the improvements, and if the present value of the increment to the property is less than the actual cost of the improvements, he is further limited to that present value. . . .

> I am not prepared to direct that the cost of periodical painting of the house on more than one occasion be taken into account as part of the improvements. . . . This expenditure, of which Michael McMahon was the beneficiary, and the value of which in any instance would be exhausted when painting was renewed, appears to me to be in the nature of ordinary maintenance.

> As it was admitted that the amount by which the improvements . . . have enhanced the present value of the lands is in excess of the actual cost of the improvements, there will be no inquiry as to the amount of that enhancement.

SQUIRE v. ROGERS

Federal Court of Australia (1979) 27 A.L.R. 330 at 343

[The defendant-appellant, Squire, and plaintiff-respondent, Rogers, were joint lessees of land. The plaintiff left Australia and returned to the United States. The lease contained a covenant, requiring that certain works and repairs be carried out on the land, with which the defendant alone complied. The improvements and the land were used by the defendant for the conduct of the business of providing accommodation in flats, rooms, and caravans. The plaintiff had made no contribution to the improvements and all outgoings had been paid by the defendant. Upon an application by the plaintiff for an order for the sale of the said leasehold

land and for an account, the Supreme Court of the Northern Territory ordered the
sale; that accounts be taken of the rents and profits; and that there be an adjustment
on the sale in favour of the defendant to the extent to which the value of the land
had been increased by the defendant's expenditure on improvements. The evidence
was that the defendant expended some $100,000 on improvements and the total
increment in value of the land as a result of the improvements did not exceed
$15,000. The grounds of appeal included, inter alia, the question of the account.]

DEANE J. . . . There remains for consideration the defendant's attack on the
order for an account. That order was that: "pursuant to O. 36 of the *Supreme Court
Rules* the Master to take an account of the rent and profits received by the defendant
in respect of the said land since 5 September 1961".

. . .

The cases in which one co-owner can obtain an account of receipts from another
co-owner who has had the sole use of the joint property are, except where the sole
use has been the result of agreement (whether express, implied or imputed), holding
over or actual exclusion, limited to those cases where one co-owner has received
more than his share of the rents or other revenues of the common property: see
McCormick v. McCormick [1921] N.Z.L.R. 384 at 385; *Henderson v. Eason* (1851)
17 Q.B. 701; *Rees v. Rees* [1931] S.A.S.R. 78 at 81; *Luke v. Luke* (1936) 36 S.R.
(N.S.W.) 310 at 313-314; *Scapinello v. Scapinello* [1968] S.A.S.R. 316 at 320 et seq.
The plaintiff does not allege any relevant agreement between the defendant and
herself. The statement of claim did no more than allege that the defendant was, and
for some years had been, carrying on the business of permitting persons to occupy
cabins and to park caravans on the land for reward to himself. The evidence
indicated that "the business" in question consisted of the business of "a caravan
and cabin park" and that occupation fees were obtained for the use (to use neutral
terms) of furnished flats, single rooms and caravans as well as for the use of parking
and associated facilities for caravans. The receipts for which the defendant would
be liable to account on the plaintiff's claim are limited to those receipts which can
properly be regarded as rents and revenue of the common property itself as distinct
from profits which the defendant may have made by his use and occupation of the
common property (for example, fees for services and for use of items of equipment).
Plainly, the identification of what properly constituted rents and revenue of the
common property in that sense required further evidence as to the precise nature of
the receipts of the business which the defendant carried on on the land and could
involve disputed questions of fact and law. In the absence of agreement between the
parties, the case should be remitted to the Supreme Court for the ascertainment of
the relevant facts and the determination of any such disputed questions. The
question of what outgoings should be allowed to the defendant on the taking of the
account can only be resolved in the light of whether the appropriate order for an
account embraced all or some only (and if so which) of the defendant's receipts from
his activities on, and in respect of, the land. The question of outgoings also raises
the question of what, if any, allowance should be made to the defendant in respect
of expenditure on capital improvements.

Senior counsel who appeared for the defendant on the hearing of the appeal
directed the attention of the court to a number of passages in the evidence which
are relevant to the determination of the entitlement of the defendant to an allowance
for capital expenditure upon the taking of an account of rents and receipts received
by the defendant from the joint property. The plaintiff gave evidence that there was
no question in her mind that there was any danger that the lease would be forfeited
by reason of a failure to comply with the covenant requiring the erection of
buildings on the land for the reason that she knew that the defendant "would be

continuing with improvements and so on''. She added that, during her absence: ''I was in constant contact with others in the Territory and I did know that improvements were being made and so on.'' She also gave evidence that it was the practice between the defendant and herself that ''while one person was managing the property, living there, and the other was away, to use the funds to improve the property, and take care of maintenance, etc.''. This evidence, which was largely left unexplored, plainly supported the inference that, if some ''rents and profits'' received by the defendant were, as would seem likely, applied in the making of improvements, they were so applied with the authority of the plaintiff. If this were the case, the defendant was, on the taking of an account, entitled to an allowance for any ''rents and profits'' which had been so applied. There remains for consideration the question of the defendant's entitlement to any additional allowance in respect of his expenditure on improvements on the subject land.

As a general rule, capital expenditure upon permanent improvements to land by one joint owner without the authority of his co-owner creates a passive equity which attaches to the land. The joint owner making the improvements is not entitled to bring proceedings for contribution against his co-owner. In circumstances where his co-owner (or a successor in title of his co-owner other than a purchaser for value without notice) would otherwise unfairly benefit under an order in equity (including partition or sale of the property), he is entitled to an allowance for his expenditure on such improvements to the extent to which they result in the present enhancement of the value (or the price on sale) of the land: see, generally, *Leigh v. Dickeson* (1884) 15 Q.B.D. 60; *Williams v. Williams* (1899) 81 L.T. (N.S.) 163; *Re Jones; Farrington v. Forrester* [1892] 2 Ch. 461; *Brickwood v. Young* (1905) 2 C.L.R. 387; *Re Byrne* (1906) 6 S.R. (N.S.W.) 532; *McMahon v. Public Curator (Qld)* [1952] St. R. Qd. 197; *Noack v. Noack* [1959] V.R. 137 and Mendes da Costa, ''Co-ownership under Victorian Land Law'', 3 M.U.L.R. 137 at 138 et seq. The operation of these principles, on a sale under the *Partition Act* 1900 (N.S.W.), was succinctly stated by Simpson C.J. in Eq. in *Boulter v. Boulter* (1898) 19 L.R. (N.S.W.) Eq. 135 at 137 in the following passage: ''Where an owner of an undivided interest in land spends money in improving the property so that on a sale under the *Partition Act* it fetches an enhanced price, a court of equity in dividing the proceeds of sale will not allow the other co-owners to take their shares of the increased price without making an allowance for what has been expended to obtain that increased value: *Leigh v. Dickeson*. This course of action cannot inflict any injustice on the other co-owners, for it takes nothing out of their pockets, it only prevents them putting into their pockets moneys obtained by the expenditure of another person, unless they recoup him such expenditure. In no case can the co-owner who has improved the property obtain more than his outlay, though such outlay may have trebled the value of the property. And, on the other hand, the increase in the price obtained is the limit of what he can receive, though his actual outlay may be far larger.''

The applicability of this general rule was conceded, on the hearing, by counsel for the plaintiff and his Honour directed that there should be paid to the defendant from the proceeds of sale ''that sum, if any, which is properly attributable to the improvements effected on the said land by the defendant''. It is clear, in the context of his Honour's reasons for judgment in which the above passage from *Boulter v. Boulter* (1898) L.R. (N.S.W.) Eq.135 is quoted with approval, that the order related to the amount by which the sale price could be seen to have been increased by the improvements effected by the defendant. No other order or allowance was made or directed in the defendant's favour in respect of his capital expenditure upon improvements. The evidence indicated that, on the basis of the orders made, the defendant would receive no allowance in respect of the major part of the money which he had spent on improvements on the subject land. A valuation which was placed in evidence by the plaintiff indicated that the total increment in value of the land as a result of the improvements did not exceed $15,000. It was, no doubt, for that reason thought unnecessary to limit the amount representing the increment in the price received to be allowed in the defendant's favour to the amount actually expended in effecting the improvements.

Senior counsel for the defendant on the appeal expressly disclaimed any suggestion that the defendant was entitled to assert any independent claim for contribution to the cost of capital improvements beyond the amount which the learned judge ordered to be paid from the proceeds of sale. It appears from the evidence that, with the possible exception of any occupation fees received in respect of the hut erected by the plaintiff and subsequently improved by the defendant and in respect of the use of the site by caravans, any rents and profits received by the defendant in respect of the land were received as a consequence of the use of improvements effected by him. A question arises whether the equitable principles underlying the defendant's entitlement to a limited allowance from the proceeds of sale of his expenditure on improvements (to the extent that they result in an increased price on sale) are, in the circumstances of the case, also applicable to preclude the plaintiff from being entitled, upon accounts upon partition or sale, to receive a one half share of any rents and profits resulting from the use of the improvements without making a full allowance in favour of the defendant in respect of his expenditure upon those improvements. In my view those principles do so apply.

In *Leigh v. Dickeson* (1884) 15 Q.B.D. 60 at 67 Cotton L.J. explained the right of the co-owner to receive a limited allowance for capital expenditure upon sale or partition as follows: "in a suit for a partition it is usual to have an inquiry as to those expenses of which nothing could be recovered so long as the parties enjoyed their property in common; when it is desired to put an end to that state of things, it is then necessary to consider what has been expended in improvements or repairs: the property held in common has been increased in value by the improvements and repairs; and whether the property is divided or sold by the decree of the court, one party cannot take the increase in value, without making an allowance for what has been expended in order to obtain that increased value; in fact, the execution of the repairs and improvements is adopted and sanctioned by accepting the increased value."

Again, in *Swan v. Swan* (1820) 8 Price 518 at 519; 146 E.R. 1281 at 1282 the Court of Exchequer Chamber similarly explained the right of one joint owner ("the defendant") to such an allowance for capital expenditure against another joint owner ("the plaintiff"): "Although, in point of law, the defendant may not, strictly speaking, have any lien on the premises, yet if he has been at expense in improving them, as stated, beneficially for the plaintiff, the plaintiff has clearly no right to take advantage of that expenditure, without making any allowance": see also *Attorney-General v. Magdalen College, Oxford* (1854) 18 Beav. 223 at 255; 52 E.R. 88 at 100; *Vyse v. Foster* (1872) L.R. 8 Ch. App. 309 at 336-337.

In the present case, there is no suggestion that the plaintiff was excluded from the subject land against her will. She voluntarily left it in the occupation of the defendant in the expectation that the defendant would spend money on improvements and, by so spending it, preserve their joint leasehold interest in the land by complying with the covenant requiring the making of improvements. She was aware of the defendant's activities on the land and the fact that he was effecting improvements and made no complaint in that respect. In the circumstances, the plaintiff is not entitled to a one half share of the rents and profits which the defendant received in respect of the subject land as a result of the use of the

improvements which he had effected while denying the defendant's entitlement to
an allowance in respect of their cost. In my view, she is, in the circumstar
entitled voluntarily to adopt the benefit of the improvements by clair
receiving one half of any profit resulting from their use at the price of be
to contribute to, or make an allowance in respect of, their cost over and
amount included in the restricted allowance to which the defenc
independently entitled on partition or sale. If she accepts the benefit of
earned, she must bear her share of the burden of earning it. The case is o
referred to by Sir William Brett M.R. in *Leigh v. Dickeson* (1884) 15 C
when he said at 64-65: "Sometimes money has been expended for the
another person under such circumstances that an option is allowed to him
or decline the benefit: in this case, if he exercises his option to adopt th
he will be liable to repay the money expended; but if he declines the bene
not be liable."

In the result, the order for an account made by the Supreme Court should be set
aside. In the absence of agreement between the parties as to appropriate orders, the
matter should be remitted to the Supreme Court for the hearing of further evidence
to enable the definition, with some precision, of the receipts and outgoings to be
included and allowed on the taking of the account. In view of the concessions made
by the plaintiff, any account ordered by the Supreme Court should be limited to the
period of six years prior to 14 December 1976 and the defendant should, on the
taking of the account, be allowed an amount as recompense for his work and labour
in deriving any receipts included in the amount. The Supreme Court should
determine whether any receipts to be included in the account ordered had been
applied to the making of improvements in accordance with a general arrangement
between the plaintiff and defendant. If so the defendant should, on the taking of
any such account, be entitled to an allowance in respect of any receipts included in
the account which had been so applied. In the event that the plaintiff persisted in
seeking an account of receipts which had been derived by the defendant as a result
of the use of the improvements which he had effected, the orders made for
distribution of the proceeds of sale should be varied so as to allow the full
reimbursement of the defendant (to the extent that the proceeds of sale allow) of
all expenditure upon capital improvements whose use has contributed to the receipts
the subject of the account, to the extent that a credit for such expenditure had not
already been allowed upon the taking of an account. In the circumstances of the
case, the sale of the property should await the outcome of any such further hearing
before the Supreme Court (but not the actual taking of the account) so that the
respective rights and obligations of the parties might be sufficiently defined to
enable each of them to make an informed decision on any questions which might
arise on, or in relation to, any auction or other disposition of the joint property.

At the conclusion of argument on the appeal, counsel for the parties informed the
court that, in the event that the court came to the conclusion to which I have come
as to the appropriate orders to be made for disposing of the appeal and that that
conclusion was sustained in the event of an appeal from this court, the parties were
in agreement on orders which would, if made, avoid any need for the matter to be
remitted to the Supreme Court. Those orders were reduced to writing by the parties
as "Short Minutes of Proposed Orders".

I would dismiss the appeal in so far as it relates to the orders for sale made by
the Supreme Court and allow the appeal in so far as it relates to the order for an
account. I would vary the orders made by the Supreme Court by substituting for
them the orders set out in the "Short Minutes of Proposed Orders" submitted by
the parties.

[Forster and Brennan JJ. agreed.]

THREE

OLD SYSTEM TITLE AND REGISTRATION OF DEEDS LEGISLATION

A. PRIORITIES—GENERAL PRINCIPLES

The question of priorities will arise where two or more persons claim inconsistent interests in the same parcel of land. The law has developed various general rules to rank the competing claims in order. These rules, as will be seen later, have been modified by statute: in the case of Old System title land, by Div. 1 of Pt XXIII of the *Conveyancing Act* 1919 (N.S.W.) which in 1984 replaced, with substantially no alteration, the *Registration of Deeds Act* 1897 (N.S.W.); and in the case of Torrens title land, by the *Real Property Act* 1900 (N.S.W.). However, any understanding of this area of the law must commence with a brief introduction to the general rules of priorities.

It is apparent that because our legal system distinguishes between legal and equitable interests, there are four possible situations in which a conflict may arise: (1) between two legal interests; (2) between two equitable interests; (3) between a prior legal and a subsequent equitable interest; and (4) between a prior equitable and a subsequent legal interest. In relation to each of these situations the law has developed certain rules as to priorities.

1. Two legal estates

The general rule of priority here is non dat quod non habet, that is, a person cannot give that which he or she does not own. Thus, priority depends upon the respective dates at which the relevant interest is created, usually the date of execution of the relevant instrument, so that the prior interest prevails. Where the two interests are totally inconsistent, the latter disposition is a complete nullity; but there may be circumstances in which the two interests may stand with each other, in which case the later would take subject to the earlier, for example, a prior legal lease followed by a later conveyance of the fee simple.

2. Two equitable estates

The general rule in the case of two competing equitable interests is qui prior est tempore potior est jure, that is, he or she who is earlier in time is stronger in law. Thus, equitable interests rank in priority according to the date of their creation.

However, equity, because it looks to the conscience of the parties, is free to look beyond the maxim to the conduct of the interest holders and, accordingly, if there is anything making it inequitable for the first interest holder to maintain her or his prima facie priority, the first interest holder will be postponed to the holder of the later interest. Vice-Chancellor Kindersley in *Rice v. Rice* (1853) 2 Drew. 73; 61 E.R. 646 put the matter thus:

> To lay down the rule . . . with perfect accuracy, I think it should be stated in some such form as this: "As between persons having only equitable interests, if their equities are in all other respects equal, priority of time gives the better equity; or, Qui prior est tempore potior est jure."

At the close of his judgment his Lordship said of the competing claims of the vendor (who had a lien for unpaid purchase-money) and the equitable mortgagee in question:

> Their equitable interests, abstractedly considered, are of equal value in respect of their nature and quality; but whether their equities are in other respects equal, or whether the one or the other has acquired the better equity, must depend upon all the circumstances of each particular case, and especially the conduct of the respective parties. And among the circumstances which may give to the one the better equity, the possession of the title deeds is a very material one. But if after close examination of all these matters, there appears nothing to give to the one a better equity than the other, then, and then only, resort must be had to the maxim qui prior est tempore potior est jure, and priority of time then gives the better equity.

It is difficult to define exhaustively the conduct which will be sufficient to postpone the earlier interest. However, instances which have given rise to postponing conduct include: a principal who entrusts indicia of title to her or his agent (*Abigail v. Lapin* [1934] A.C. 491); a trustee for sale who fails to obtain the purchase-money but inserts the usual receipt in the conveyance (*Lloyd's Bank Ltd v. Bullock* [1896] 2 Ch. 192); and an equitable mortgagee who leaves the title deeds with the mortgagor: *Walker v. Linom* [1907] 2 Ch. 104.

The special position of a cestui que trust should be noted. Whilst in general a cestui que trust is not postponed as a result of improper conduct on the part of the trustee, this is not the case where the trustee has negligently failed to get in the title deeds: *Walker v. Linom* at 118-119. It appears that a distinction must be drawn between improper conduct on the part of the trustee at the date of creation of the trust, in which case the cestui que trust is bound by the actions of the trustee, and improper conduct in the course of administration of the trust, in which case the cestui que trust is not bound by the improper conduct of the trustee: for a discussion of the special position of a cestui que trust, see Sykes, *The Law of Securities* (4th ed.), pp. 405 et seq.

Where, however, the earlier interest is a "mere equity", the later equitable estate will gain priority if it is purchased for value without notice of the earlier interest. This raises the distinction between a "mere equity" and an equitable interest. Consider the following extract on this distinction.

LATEC INVESTMENTS LTD v. HOTEL TERRIGAL PTY LTD

High Court of Australia (1965) 113 C.L.R. 265 at 277

KITTO J. [T]he cases to which his Lordship [Lord Westbury in *Phillips v. Phillips* (1861) 4 De G.F. & J. 208; 45 E.R. 1164] was referring were not only those in which there is an assertion of an equity unaccompanied by an equitable interest . . . —

indeed he may not have had them in mind at all—but those in which an equity is asserted which must be made good before an equitable interest can be held to exist. In the latter class of cases the equity is distinct from, because logically antecedent to, the equitable interest, and it is against the equity and not the consequential equitable interest that the defence must be set up. That the defence of purchase for value without notice (in the absence of the legal estate) is a good defence against the assertion of the equity in such a case had been established long before Lord Westbury's time. . . .

The reason of the matter, as I understand it, is that the purchaser who has relied upon the instrument as taking effect according to its terms and the party whose rights depend upon the instrument being denied that effect have equal merits, and the court, finding no reason for binding the conscience of either in favour of the other, declines to interfere between them. Consequently the party complaining of the fraud or mistake finds himself unable to set up as against the other the equitable interest he asserts; but the fact remains that it is against the preliminary equity, and not against the equitable interest itself, that the defence of purchase for value without notice has succeeded. The maxim qui prior est tempore is not applicable, for it applies only as between equitable interests, the logical basis of it being that in a competition between equitable interests the conveyance in virtue of which the later interest is claimed is considered, as Lord Westbury pointed out, to be innocent, in the sense of being intended to pass that which the conveyor is justly entitled to and no more: *Phillips v. Phillips* (1861) 4 De G.F. & J. 208, at 215; 45 E.R. 1164 at 1166. Where a claim to an earlier equitable interest is dependent for its success upon the setting aside or rectification of an instrument, and the court, notwithstanding that the fraud or mistake (or other cause) is established, leaves the instrument to take effect according to its terms in favour of a third party whose rights have intervened, the alleged earlier equitable interest is unprovable against the third party, and consequently, so far as the case against him discloses, there is no prior equitable interest to which his conveyance can be held to be subject.

TAYLOR J. . . . [W]here a grantor is entitled to set aside a conveyance for fraud he has, in every sense of the term, an equitable interest in the subject land and that if he is to be postponed to an equitable interest acquired without notice at some later time it is not because it can be said, in the sense in which the appellants use that expression, that he has a mere equity as distinguished from an equitable estate; if he is to be postponed then there must be some other reason.

. . . It cannot, of course, be disputed at the present time that the defence of purchaser for value without notice of a prior equitable interest cannot be generally maintained but it does appear that it has always—that is to say, both before and after *Phillips v. Phillips* (1861) 4 De G.F. & J. 208; 45 E.R. 1164—been allowed to prevail where the person entitled to the earlier interest required the assistance of a court of equity to remove an impediment to his title as a preliminary to asserting his interest. In such cases it seems that the court will not interfere and to me it does not seem to matter much whether it be said that this is because, as Lord Westbury's observations suggest, that a plaintiff seeking to set aside a deed for fraud or to reform it for mistake is, at that stage, asserting an equity as distinguished from an equitable estate, or, because a plaintiff in such cases will be denied the assistance of a court of equity to remove the impediment to his title if, before he seeks that assistance, an equitable interest in the subject property has passed to a purchaser for value without notice of the plaintiff's prior interest. I prefer the latter as a more precise statement of the law and, indeed, I think this is the true meaning of Lord

Westbury's observations. But either statement leads to the same result which in the present case means that the interest of the M.L.C. Nominees should be taken to prevail over that of Hotel Terrigal.

[Menzies J. appeared to favour the view of Kitto J.]

3. Legal and equitable estates

In cases of competition between legal and equitable estates, the general rule is "where the equities are equal the law prevails", that is, where the merits are equal, the legal estate has priority.

(a) Prior legal subsequent equitable estate

According to the general rule, the earlier legal estate has priority and the onus will be on the holder of the subsequent equitable estate to show that the legal estate is to be postponed. The legal estate may, however, be postponed by blameworthy conduct on the part of the legal holder or by estoppel. The Court of Appeal in *Northern Counties Fire Insurance Co. v. Whipp* (1884) 26 Ch. D. 482 at 484 said:

> The authorities which we have reviewed appear to us to justify the following conclusions:
>
> (1) That the court will postpone the prior legal estate to a subsequent equitable estate: (a), where the owner of the legal estate has assisted in or connived at the fraud which has led to the creation of a subsequent equitable estate, without notice of the prior legal estate; of which assistance or connivance, the omission to use ordinary care in inquiry after or keeping title deeds may be, and in some cases has been, held to be sufficient evidence, where such conduct cannot otherwise be explained; (b), where the owner of the legal estate has constituted the mortgagor his agent with authority to raise money, and the estate thus created has by the fraud or misconduct of the agent been represented as being the first estate.
>
> But (2) that the court will not postpone the prior legal estate to the subsequent equitable estate on the ground of any mere carelessness or want of prudence on the part of the legal owner.

Broadly speaking, according to Professor Sykes in Sykes, op. cit., p. 399, there appear to be four types of conduct which will postpone the prior legal estate: (1) fraud; (2) gross negligence in relation to dealings with title deeds; (3) lack of authority or undisclosed limitations of authority in the case of mortgages by agents, or, more generally, in the case of acts by an agent of the legal owner; and (4) representations on the part of the legal owner contained in some document purporting to deal with the title such that the legal owner becomes bound by any equities coming into existence by reason of a third party acting on the faith of the document. Moreover, it has been said that all forms of postponing conduct fall into either one or other of two categories which, as Sykes points out, may or may not be mutually exclusive: first, that the person postponed is estopped from denying certain facts which by express words or conduct he or she has represented to exist and upon the faith of which another has acted—the "estoppel" theory; secondly, that the party postponed by her or his fraudulent or grossly negligent acts has caused an innocent person to act to her or his detriment—the "innocent person" theory.

(b) Prior equitable subsequent legal estate

Again, the general rule is, where the merits are equal the law prevails. However, equity will hold that the merits are unequal only where the legal holder had notice of the prior equity or was a volunteer. This is the doctrine of the bona fide purchaser of the legal estate taking for value and without notice of the prior equitable estate. Therefore, in order to gain priority the subsequent interest holder must:

(1) possess the legal estate;

(2) have given valuable consideration; and

(3) not be affected with actual, constructive or imputed notice of the earlier equitable interest at the time when the consideration is given: *Pilcher v. Rawlins* (1872) L.R. 7 Ch. D. 259 at 267-269.

The rule that a purchaser must take a legal estate before receiving notice is subject to two qualifications:

(1) The doctrine of tabula in naufragio: see Sykes, op. cit., p. 324; *Taylor v. Russell* [1892] A.C. 244. Where there is a first legal interest followed by two equitable interests, a purchaser for value of the later equitable interest, without notice of the earlier equitable interest, can gain priority over the earlier equitable interest by acquiring the legal estate even if he or she then has notice of the earlier equitable interest.

(2) It has been held in *Assaf v. Fuwa* [1955] A.C. 215 that a purchaser of an equitable interest without notice of an earlier equitable interest can defeat the prior equitable interest upon acquiring a better right to call for the legal estate.

B. REGISTRATION OF DEEDS LEGISLATION

As already pointed out, Div. 1 of Pt XXIII of the *Conveyancing Act* 1919 (N.S.W.), which in 1984 replaced the *Registration of Deeds Act* 1897 (N.S.W.), has affected the general rules of priorities in relation to Old System title. Registration pursuant to the *Conveyancing Act* does not, however, necessarily cure defects in a purchaser's title. Generally speaking, title is acquired independently of registration.

The *Conveyancing Act* provides a system of registering instruments for the purpose of gaining or preserving priority over unregistered instruments or subsequently registered instruments. The mischief which the Registration Acts have attempted to overcome is the defeat of a bona fide purchaser for value by a prior dealing with the land of which he or she had no notice. As a general rule, registration is not necessary to perfect a purchaser's title. But this needs qualification in several respects. First, failure to register may lead to postponement or complete defeat of the unregistered interest. Secondly, registration is a necessary precondition for the operation of certain instruments: see Woodman, *Law of Real Property in New South Wales*, Vol. 1, p. 179 et seq. Thirdly, the registration provisions of the *Conveyancing Act* 1919 (N.S.W.) may constitute an exception to the nemo dat rule: see below p. 112. The only mandatory aspect of the Registration Acts is the negative one of gaining or maintaining priority.

Registration of an instrument is notice to persons subsequently dealing with the title of the existence of that instrument. There are, however, two exceptions:

(1) a mortgagor is entitled, in the absence of actual notice, to repay instalments and interest to her or his mortgagee notwithstanding that an assignment of the mortgage to a third party has been registered; and

(2) a mortgagee in the case of a registered mortgage which provides for further advances will take priority over subsequent registered mortgages of which the mortgagee has no actual notice for any further advances made to the mortgagor after the registration of the second mortgage: *Re O'Byrne's Estate* (1885) 15 L.R. (Ir) 189, extracted below p. 122.

In both of these exceptions there is no constructive notice of the registration of the subsequent instrument since there is no obligation to search the register before paying the instalments or making the further advance respectively. But quaere, whether the decision in *Matzner v. Clyde Securities Ltd* [1975] 2 N.S.W.L.R. 293, extracted below p. 443, affects the above position. If, however, a search of the register is in fact made, the searcher will be on notice of interests discoverable by search, whether he or she actually finds them or not.

In New South Wales, priority is determined in accordance with s. 184G of the *Conveyancing Act* 1919 which provides:

184G. (1) All instruments (wills excepted) affecting, or intended to affect, any lands in New South Wales which are executed or made bona fide, and for valuable consideration, and are duly registered under the provisions of this Division, the *Registration of Deeds Act*, 1897, or any Act repealed by the *Registration of Deeds Act*, 1897, shall have and take priority not according to their respective dates but according to the priority of the registration thereof only.

(2) No instrument registered under the provisions of this Division or the *Registration of Deeds Act*, 1897, shall lose any priority to which it would be entitled by virtue of registration thereunder by reason only of bad faith in the conveyancing party, if the party beneficially taking under the instrument acted bona fide, and there was valuable consideration given therefor.

By s. 184D (1) of the *Conveyancing Act* the Registrar-General may register any instrument whatever, whether it relates to land or not, but, except for those instruments coming within s. 184G of the Act, such registration has effect for the purposes of record only. Section 184B of the Act expressly excludes from the operation of s. 184G instruments which are registered or required to be registered under the provisions of the *Real Property Act* 1900 (N.S.W.) and therefore their registration under the *Conveyancing Act* or in the General Register of Deeds would have the effect of record only.

The Act only determines priorities in cases of conflict between a registered and an unregistered instrument, or between two registered instruments. The Act does not affect priorities in the case of a conflict with an interest created other than by writing; the conflict will be resolved by reference to the general rules of priorities. The Act applies to equitable as well as legal interests; that is, it determines priorities in accordance with the date of registration without discrimination between legal and equitable interests.

The instrument which seeks to obtain the advantages of s. 184G of the *Conveyancing Act* must be made for valuable consideration, not nominal consideration: *Bullen v. A'Beckett* (1863) 1 Moore P.C.N.S. 223; 15 E.R. 684. However, voluntary transactions ought to be registered so as to fix a subsequent person, dealing with title, with notice of the voluntary transaction.

The instrument claiming priority must be made bona fide. It is the bona fides of the person claiming priority, the conveyee, that is relevant; it is irrelevant that the conveyor has acted in bad faith. It has been clearly established that an instrument executed with notice of a prior unregistered interest will not be made bona fide: *Marsden v. Campbell* (1897) 18 L.R. (N.S.W.) Eq. 33, extracted below p. 113.

Notice of an adverse interest will be fatal if received on or before the payment of the balance of the purchase moneys and execution of the conveyance, that is, generally, at settlement: *Scholes v. Blunt* (1917) 17 S.R. (N.S.W.) 36; *Burrows v. Crimp* (1887) 8 L.R. (N.S.W.) 198. Notice in this context may be actual (that is, actual notice of the existence of the prior adverse interest, however that knowledge may have been acquired, although vague rumours are not sufficient); constructive (that is, notice of those interests which would have been discovered if the usual investigations in the transaction in question had been made with proper diligence); and imputed (that is, notice, actual or constructive, received by an agent employed by the purchaser in the transaction in question, although notice will not be imputed to the purchaser where the matter, of which it is sought to affect the purchaser with notice, is the agent's own fraud or arises out of such fraud: see *Cave v. Cave* (1880) 15 Ch. D. 639; *Schultz v. Corwill Properties Pty Ltd* (1969) 90 W.N. (Pt 1) (N.S.W.) 529). These rules as to notice have now been embodied in statutory form. Section 164 of the *Conveyancing Act* 1919 (N.S.W.) provides:

164. (1) A purchaser shall not be prejudicially affected by notice of any instrument, fact, or thing, unless—

(a) it is within his own knowledge, or would have come to his knowledge, if such searches as to instruments registered or deposited under any Act of Parliament, inquiries, and inspections had been made as ought reasonably to have been made by him; or

(b) in the same transaction with respect to which a question of notice to the purchaser arises, it has come to the knowledge of his counsel as such, or of his solicitor or other agent as such, or would have to come to the knowledge of his solicitor or other agent as such, if such searches, inquiries, and inspections had been made as ought reasonably to have been made by the solicitor or other agent.

(1A) Omission to search in any register or list kept by, or filed with, the Corporate Affairs Commission or the National Companies and Securities Commission, whether within New South Wales or elsewhere, shall not of itself affect a purchaser of land with notice of any mortgage or charge.

(2) This section shall not exempt a purchaser from any liability under or any obligation to perform or observe any covenant, condition, provision, or restriction contained in any instrument under which his title is derived, mediately or immediately, and such liability or obligation may be enforced in the same manner and to the same extent as if this section had not been enacted.

(3) A purchaser shall not by reason of anything in this section be affected by notice in any case where he would not have been so affected if this section had not been enacted.

(4) This section applies to purchases made either before or after the commencement of this Act, save that where an action is pending at the commencement of this Act the rights of the parties shall not be affected by this section.

Registration will not give any efficacy to instruments otherwise void for reasons such as fraud, forgery or mistake: *Re Cooper* (1882) 20 Ch. D. 611, extracted below p. 114. However, registration of an instrument which would be effectual but for a prior unregistered instrument will give priority to that instrument; indeed, registration will overcome the doctrine of nemo dat quod non habet, so that in a competition between two inconsistent legal interests in the same property, the later interest will attain priority if registered first. This will be the case even where the second conveyance is not made by the same transferor but by some other person purporting to convey the same property, such as the official receiver of the first grantor: *Fuller v. Goodwin* (1865) 4 S.C.R. (N.S.W.) 66, extracted below p. 116; cf. *Blaxland v. Grattan* (1887) 8 L.R. (N.S.W.) 287, discussed below p. 118.

Further, registration will confer priority only where the instruments are conflicting or inconsistent with each other. For example, in a competition between a prior *specific* conveyance and a subsequent *general* conveyance which by its terms includes the subject matter of the prior specific conveyance, the general conveyance, if registered first, will gain priority and defeat the unregistered or subsequently registered specific conveyance: *Boyce v. Beckman* (1890) 11 L.R. (N.S.W.) 139, extracted below p. 118. On the other hand, it may be that the purchaser under the subsequent conveyance only bargained for such interest as the vendor could properly dispose of, in which case the conveyances are not conflicting or inconsistent, and the prior unregistered specific conveyance will not lose its priority even if the subsequent general conveyance is registered first: *Lyons v. Imperial Land Co.* (1894) 15 L.R. (N.S.W.) (Eq.) 64. Further, it may be that the later general conveyance is expressly or impliedly made subject to the existence of incumbrances or other interests, in which case registration will not defeat those incumbrances or interests: *Ex parte Pearse* (1900) 16 W.N. (N.S.W.) 262; contrast *West Kanmantoo Mining Co. v. English Scottish, and Australian Chartered Bank* (1868) 2 S.A.L.R. 97; and see Hogg, *Deeds Registration in Australasia*, p. 130.

MARSDEN v. CAMPBELL

Supreme Court of New South Wales (1897) 18 L.R. (N.S.W.) Eq. 33 at 36

[In March 1888, Campbell leased certain land to Marsden for 15 years; this lease was unregistered. In June 1890, Campbell mortgaged the land to Marsden; this mortgage was registered in 1891. In June 1893, Campbell executed a transfer of the land to Byrnes; this transfer was registered in the following July. At the time Byrnes purchased the land from Campbell, he knew that Marsden had been in possession of the land for five years and was running sheep there.

The defendants Campbell and Byrnes did not dispute that the mortgage to the plaintiff had priority over the transfer to the defendant Byrnes, and neither of them raised any question as to the validity of the lease between Campbell and the plaintiff; but Byrnes contended that by virtue of the Registration Acts the transfer to him took priority over the lease to the plaintiff.]

SIMPSON J. As pointed out by Lord Selborne in the *Agra Bank v. Barry* (1874) L.R. 7 H.L. 135 at 148, the question of bona fides is one which must be decided with reference to the nature and circumstances of each particular case. In the case of *Lyons v. Imperial Land Co.* (1894) 15 L.R. (N.S.W.) Eq. 64 at 72 the vendors had subdivided an estate and contracted to sell some of the lots to the plaintiff, the contract being unregistered; they subsequently mortgaged the whole estate to the Sydney and Suburban Building Society, who registered their mortgage. The society was aware at the time of taking their mortgage that portion of the estate had been sold, but they were not aware what portion, nor who was the purchaser. The Privy Council held, affirming the decision of Manning J., that, as the mortgagees knew they could not be getting a title to the whole of the lands comprised in their mortgage, their mortgage was not bona fide against the plaintiff.

In the present case the defendant Byrnes was aware that the plaintiff was in possession of the land in question, and had been in possession some five years. Francis Byrnes, a brother of the defendant, and a partner with him at the time spoken of, says in cross-examination: "The plaintiff's sheep trespassed all over our paddocks; I cannot say where they came from; they came from Campbell's land and other paddocks; I served Marsden with a written notice in 1888 as to the sheep which came from Campbell's paddock; it was in October 1888; after that notice the sheep didn't trespass so much."

The plaintiff says that previously to November 1888, Byrnes' sheep were on the land, that they were removed about that time, and that ever since he had some 1,200 sheep running on the land, and that the defendant Byrnes knew of this. This evidence is uncontradicted. I must, therefore, hold that the defendant Byrnes had full knowledge of the plaintiff's possession. . . .

In the contract of sale, Campbell to Byrnes, dated 27 June 1893, it is agreed that the balance of the purchase money is to be paid so soon as the vendor put the purchaser "in actual and exclusive possession" of the property sold. This obviously points to some third person being in possession.

Under these circumstances I must hold that the defendant Byrnes knew that Marsden had some interest in the land, and that he was content to run the risk of what this interest might turn out to be. The case seems to be indistinguishable in principle from *Lyons v. Imperial Land Co.* (1894) 15 L.R. (N.S.W.) (Eq.) 64. In that case the purchasers knew that some of the land comprised in their mortgage had been contracted to be sold, and they refrained from inquiry; in this case Byrnes knew that an interest in the land comprised in his transfer was outstanding in the plaintiff, and he made no inquiry. I must, therefore, hold that the lease to the plaintiff takes priority over the transfer to Byrnes.

NOTE

In the principal case the purchaser had notice of the lease at the date of purchase. If a purchaser obtains notice of an adverse interest after signing the contract for sale, but before payment of the balance of the purchase moneys and execution of the conveyance (commonly referred to as "settlement"), subsequent registration of the conveyance under the Registration of Deeds Acts will not confer priority: see *Scholes v. Blunt* (1917) 17 S.R. (N.S.W.) 36. In that case there was a contract to buy land, but before settlement the purchaser received notice that a third party had a right of way over the land. Notwithstanding this, the purchaser proceeded to complete the purchase and then registered the conveyance under the *Registration of Deeds Act* 1897 (N.S.W.). The court said that registration in such circumstances is not bona fide within the meaning of the Act.

Scholes v. Blunt may be contrasted with *Burrows v. Crimp* (1887) 8 L.R. (N.S.W.) 198, which illustrates that where notice of an adverse interest is received after the payment of the balance of the purchase moneys and execution of the conveyance, but before registration under the registration of deeds legislation, the subsequent registration will be effective to defeat the adverse interest. Fawcett J. said (at 210):

> This deed being registered takes precedence over any former deed dealing with the same property. It is said, however, that this deed cannot take effect unless it were executed bona fide. But, . . . where a person has become owner of property, bona fide and honestly, and hears that there is a prior deed in existence relating to the same property, it is a perfectly honest thing for him to promptly register his conveyance. That is what the law intends. The object of the law of registration is to keep people awake, and make them alive to their duties. It will not disentitle the registering vendee to the benefit of the Act.

RE COOPER; COOPER v. VESEY

Court of Appeal (1882) 20 Ch. D. 611 at 629

[A testator appointed his son, whose name and description were identical with those of his father, as one of the executors and trustees of his will. The son, who had obtained possession of the title deeds, without the knowledge and consent of his co-executrixes and co-trustees, executed certain mortgages over property of the testator, purporting to be the absolute owner of the property. He applied the mortgage money for his own purposes. The will had not been registered and the son had not told the mortgagees about the testator's death. The mortgage was registered. After the son's death the fraud was discovered and the co-trustees of the will brought an action against the mortgagees, claiming the mortgages were void against them, and the delivery up of the title deeds. Kay J., at first instance, held that the mortgagees could have no claim to the title deeds and ordered that they be delivered to the plaintiffs. The mortgagees appealed.]

COTTON L.J. The question upon which this case turns is a very curious one. Thomas Frederick Cooper, the son, signed, sealed, and delivered a parchment, and the question is whether, signing, as he did, his own name, the deed is a forged deed. When one looks at it, it is clear that it purports to be, not the deed of Thomas Frederick Cooper, the son, who signed, sealed and delivered it, but the deed of his father, who bore the same name and had the same description. And the question we have to consider is, whether, at the time when the son signed his name and sealed and delivered the parchment, he intended to represent that it would thereby become the deed of his father. In my opinion, although I cannot but regret having to come to such a conclusion, we can on the facts before us come to no other conclusion. Now this is what was done. The property having been the father's, and having been dealt with by his will (there was both freehold and leasehold property), the son takes to the solicitor from whom he is going to borrow money an abstract of title antecedent to the conveyances to his father, and also the deeds of conveyances to his father, but no subsequent muniments of title. He does not take his father's will, and he makes no statement about the death of his father, and takes no document which shews it or shews that he was the heir-at-law of his father. When he took those documents to the solicitor, in my opinion, the reasonable conclusion which any one would draw from the fact that a person of the name of Thomas Frederick Cooper was bringing abstracts and deeds shewing a title in Thomas Frederick Cooper of the same description would be that the person claiming title to the property was the Thomas Frederick Cooper in whom a title was shewn by the instruments so produced. . . . Then coming in this way, and representing the title to be that which was shewn by the deeds which he brought, he subsequently signs, seals, and delivers the mortgage deeds. And, in my opinion, having brought to the solicitor documents which shew a title, not in himself, but in a person of the same name, when, without any further explanation, he executed the mortgage deeds, he must be taken to have done so, not as his own deeds, but as the deeds of the person in whom the title was shewn. If that be so, if in signing the deeds he represented them to be the deeds of his father, he undoubtedly committed a forgery; that is to say, he made and used a false, feigned instrument, and must be taken to have done so for fraudulent purposes. It is said, what object could he have had in doing this, he having previously obtained money from the trust estate with the consent of his mother and sister. But he was largely involved, he had taken shares in his own name in the Slate Company, and there is not the slightest evidence on which we can rely that any of his family knew that he was doing this, or that it was done with their consent or for their benefit. The evidence all points the other way. I regret that I have to come to the conclusion, especially after his death, that he did this fraudulently, but I cannot help coming to the conclusion that, having got the £1,200, he desired to keep secret the fact that he required a further sum out of the estate for these speculations, and that this was the motive for his doing what probably he thought was not forgery, but what he must have known to be a fraudulent act.

In my opinion, these deeds on which the appellants rely are forged deeds, and that puts an end to the case, and shews that the judgment of the court below was right. Any title under the *Middlesex Registry Act* must be out of the question, because, in the view which I take, the mortgage deeds were not in any way the deeds of their heir. They purported to be the deeds of the father, not the deeds of the heir executed by him as such, and therefore no title under the Registry Act can arise out of them. Another point taken was that, at any rate as regards the leaseholds, there was a deposit of the title deeds by the executor, and it is said, a court of equity will not interfere with the possession thus acquired. But here we have the owner of the legal title coming into a court of law and equity, and saying, there is an attempt to deprive me, not only of my property, but of my title deeds. The legal title is shewn to be in the plaintiffs, and then, not merely as a court of equity, but as a court of law, we ought to make the order which has been made in the court below for the delivery up of the title deeds to the legal owners of the property.

[Jessell M.R. and Lindley L.J. delivered substantially similar judgments.]

NOTES

1. In *Kerley v. Moule, Argus*, 1861, a registered conveyance in fee was held void where its execution was induced by the fraud of the grantee. Molesworth J. said:

   > The registration of a deed does not cure either its legal or equitable defects, and the registration of a conveyance from Duffy could not give it priority over the plaintiffs insisting that the conveyance to Duffy was procured by fraud.

2. In *Sutherland v. Peel* (1864) 1 W.W. & a'B. 18, two lots, numbers 139 and 140, were sold to two different purchasers; by mistake, lot 139 was conveyed to the purchaser of lot 140, and vice versa. The conveyances were registered. The defendant claimed the more valuable lot which was mistakenly conveyed to him and sought to eject the plaintiff. It was held that the action of ejectment could not be maintained. Molesworth J. said:

   > Registration is only important in deciding priority between inconsistent conveyances, each of which could be effectual but for the other, but gives no increased efficacy to conveyances impugned for fraud or mistake.

FULLER v. GOODWIN

Supreme Court of New South Wales (1865) 4 S.C.R. (N.S.W.) 66 at 67

STEPHEN C.J. (delivering the judgment of the court). In this case a person seized of certain land, executed a mortgage of it, and afterwards became insolvent. His assignee, having (it would seem) no knowledge of that transaction—although whether he had such knowledge or not is, we conceive, immaterial—executed a conveyance of the same land, for valuable consideration, to the plaintiff. The latter instrument was registered immediately; and it is conceded, or the fact must be taken to have been found, that the plaintiff purchased the property innocently, and in good faith. The first instrument was not registered at all. The question is, under these circumstances, whether the plaintiff's conveyance shall or not prevail over that of the mortgagee?

The Registration Act of 1843, following the words of the old enactment in 6 Geo. 4 No. 22, gives "priority" to all deeds affecting property, if executed bona fide, according to the time of their registration. But s. 18 of the *Titles to Land Act*, passed in 1858 (extended by 24 Vic. No. 7), enacts that no instrument shall, by reason of bad faith in the conveying party, lose any "priority" to which it might be entitled by registration, if the party beneficially taking under it acted in good faith, and there was valuable consideration for the same.

No amount of fraud, therefore, or bad faith, in a conveying party, will affect the efficacy or operation of a registered deed, where the taker is himself innocent, as here, and gives value for the property. The question is, in what manner does registration operate; for, where there is no conflict as to priority—in other words, where there arises no question between two or more deeds, executed by the same transferor, or some person in his right, and conveying or purporting to convey the same property—registration is of no value. Registration is, at any rate not necessary (certain special cases excepted) to give efficacy to any deed. It appears clearly to us, that, in favour of an innocent taker for value who registers his deed, the statute confers on the conveying party, notwithstanding his previous inconsistent conveyance, if not registered, a title as against the transferee named therein; and thus enables the person secondly taking, immediately upon registration, to acquire that title.

Whether the first transferee, therefore, shall afterwards register his conveyance or not, the second deed will operate effectually against him. If he does so register, the words of the statute will be strictly applicable. There will then be "priority" in registration; and, each deed taking effect according to such priority, not according to its date, the second taker's will prevail. But it would be an absurd construction, that, because the legislature has indiscreetly used this word "priority" in the enactment, a different result could be attained by the first taker's omitting to register at any time. This would be to give effect to the letter, in utter disregard of the substance and evident object of the statute; and to enable every transferee of an estate, concealing his title—created possibility for purposes of fraud—to defeat a subsequent meritorious purchaser at pleasure. By never registering the first conveyance, such a transferee would obtain more than impunity for his neglect; and no man could ever safely purchase property, whatever might be the precautions adopted.

But the objection was taken for the defendant, that the enactment applied only to cases of double transfer by the same individual; since, although bad faith in the conveying party was immaterial against an innocent purchaser for value, yet the question of its existence is still a matter for inquiry in every case—and there can be no such question, as affecting a second conveyance in disparagement of the first, where the second is by a different person. The assignee of the transferor, moreover, after the latter's insolvency, could not (it was urged) have any estate to convey as his; for no estate or title, after the conveyance, remained in the insolvent—and none descended to the assignee, therefore, in his right.

If the law were as thus contended for, it would follow that persons taking property by deed, from a transferor subsequently becoming insolvent, would be in a wholly different position as to registration—or the security to be gained by registering—from all other parties similarly acquiring property. The transferees would enjoy complete immunity from molestation, as to their titles; for, as these need not be registered, the transactions would rarely, if ever, be known. The insolvent, on the other hand, would be enabled to escape the consequences of making such transfers, however fraudulent; while the assignee, tracing title by the registry alone, would incur the risk in all cases of conveying, or assuming to convey property, which the purchasers might eventually not be able to retain. The Registration Acts, in short, or at least their priority clauses, would not apply at all to conveyances executed, under any circumstances, by men who afterwards, at any time, are declared insolvent. We are of opinion that such is not the law; and that, as in the case of the English Registry Acts, although the language certainly is different (see *Warburton v. Loveland* (1832) 2 Dow & Cl. 480; 6 E.R. 806) the non-registration of a conveyance makes it (in effect) void, as against a subsequent purchaser for value, under a deed duly registered, whether from the transferor himself, or from his assignee. *The Insolvent Act*, ss 53 and 54, and the amending Act of 1843, s. 14, vest in the assignees of an insolvent all his estates and rights of every kind; and it is declared that all powers vested in him, which he might have legally executed for his benefit, may be executed after sequestration by such assignees. The question of "bad faith" in an assignee, we conceive, in executing the conveyance of a property previously transferred by the insolvent, would not necessarily be excluded—in considering the validity or operation of the second conveyance. . . .

For these reasons we hold that the plaintiff claiming for value under the assignee is entitled to recover in this action; and there will be no rule, therefore, to set aside the verdict.

NOTE

Contrast *Blaxland v. Grattan* (1887) 8 L.R. (N.S.W.) 287 which held that a registered conveyance from the sheriff pursuant to seizure of the land under a writ of fi. fa. did not take priority over a prior unregistered conveyance by the debtor. The court distinguished *Fuller v. Goodwin* on the basis that "[a]t the time of the sale by the sheriff, Grattan, senior, had no right, title, or interest of any sort remaining in him. If he had had anything in him, the transfer from the sheriff to the plaintiff would by its registration have taken priority over Grattan's transfer to the defendant. The sheriff is merely a conduit-pipe, and can give no greater estate to a purchaser than was in the person whose estate he sells. If we were to hold otherwise, we should have to overrule *Re Elliott* (1886) 7 L.R. (N.S.W.) 271 which, as it seems to me, was most properly decided." *Blaxland v. Grattan* appears to be inconsistent with the approach taken in *Fuller v. Goodwin* with regard to the effect of the *Registration of Deeds Act* 1897 (N.S.W.) on the nemo dat rule. Hogg, op. cit., p. 124 et seq. doubts whether *Blaxland v. Grattan* can be supported either on principle or authority. However, in *Smith v. Deane* (1889) 10 L.R. (N.S.W.) (Eq.) 207, the Chief Justice drew a distinction between *Blaxland v. Grattan* and *Fuller v. Goodwin* on the basis that the former involved a sale by the sheriff and the latter a sale by the official receiver:

> It is, however, contended that the subsequent case of *Blaxland v. Grattan* (1887) 8 L.R. (N.S.W.) 287 is at variance with *Fuller v. Goodwin*, and that the court cannot decide in accordance with the latter without overruling the former; but in my view both cases are good law, and there is a broad distinction to be drawn between them, for the one was a case of sale by the official assignee, the other the case of a sale by the sheriff. Now, the whole property of the insolvent vests in the official assignee, while the sheriff is a mere conduit-pipe between the judgment debtor and the purchaser, and no property vests in him at all; it is the sheriff's duty to seize the property of the judgment debtor and to sell what he has seized, but in a case like the present there would, after the first conveyance, be nothing for him to seize, and, consequently, nothing for him to sell. In the cases of *Godfrey v. Poole* (1884) 5 L.R. (N.S.W.) Eq. 1, *Coleman v. De Lissa* (1885) 6 L.R. (N.S.W.) Eq. 104, *Re Elliott* (1886) 7 L.R. (N.S.W.) 271, it is laid down that the sheriff can take nothing but what is at the time beneficially vested in the judgment debtor, and I am, therefore, of opinion that *Fuller v. Goodwin* (1865) 4 S.C.R. (N.S.W.) 66 and *Blaxland v. Grattan* may stand side by side.

Hogg, op. cit., p. 126 argues that if the distinction drawn in *Smith v. Deane* between a conveyance by the official receiver on the one hand and the sheriff on the other is to be upheld, it would depend on the peculiar terms of the conveyance in *Blaxland v. Grattan* rather than the mere fact that a sheriff's conveyance is any less entitled to gain priority over unregistered conveyances by the debtor than is an assignment by an official receiver.

BOYCE v. BECKMAN

Supreme Court of New South Wales (1890) 11 L.R. (N.S.W.) 139 at 143

[The judgment of the court (Sir George Innes, Stephen and Foster JJ.) was delivered by Sir George Innes J. The facts are set out in the judgment.]

SIR GEORGE INNES J. The facts of the case, so far as they are material, are as follows. On 21 December 1834, the land in question was granted by the Crown to one William O'Donnell. On 4 January 1841, one William Sparke, by virtue of certain mesne assurances, had become seized of an estate in fee simple in the land. On 13 October 1845, Sparke, being still seized in fee, by deed conveyed the land to the plaintiff. In that deed the land was referred to as being "certain lots in accordance with a map or plan attached to the deed". This deed remained unregistered until after 5 January 1852. On 1 January 1852, Sparke executed a conveyance under seal to one John Hawker Valentine Turner, through whom the defendant claims. That deed contained a recital that Sparke had contracted with Turner "for the absolute sale to him of the pieces or parcels of land and hereditaments hereinafter mentioned and described or intended so to be, with the appurtenances, at or for the price or sum of £40". The operative words, which it is necessary to quote, are as follows: "This indenture witnesseth that he the said William Sparke doth grant, etc., unto the said J. H. V. Turner all that piece or parcel of land . . . being lots 10 and 11 on the original map or plan thereof . . . and also all that piece or parcel of land . . . being lots 19 and 20 on the said original map or plan thereof . . . and also all that piece or parcel of land . . . being lots 64, 65, 66, 67, 68, 69, and 70 on the said original map or plan thereof, the whole of which lots are a portion of the land originally granted to one William O'Donnell; and also all or any other lots forming a portion of the said grant to William O'Donnell to which he the said William Sparke is entitled either in possession, reversion, remainder, or otherwise, for an estate of freehold and inheritance, or in any way whatsoever . . . and all the estate, right, title, and interest, claim, and demand whatsoever, both legal and equitable, of him the said William Sparke therein and thereto." The three parcels of land described by metes and bounds, and specified as lots 11, 12, 19, 20, 64, 65, 66, 67, 68, 69, and 70, do not comprise any part of the land in dispute; but the defendant claims the land in dispute under the general words, "and also all or any other lots", etc. This deed of 1 January 1852, was on 5 January 1852, duly registered in compliance with the provisions of the *Registration Act* of 1843. Section 11 of that Act is in these words: "All deeds and other instruments wills excepted affecting any lands or hereditaments or any other property in New South Wales which shall be executed or made bona fide or for valuable consideration and which shall be duly registered under the provisions of this Act shall have and take priority not according to their respective dates but according to the priority of the registration thereof only." It is admitted that the deed of January 1852, was executed bona fide and for valuable consideration, as was also the prior deed of October 1845. There is no suggestion of notice, direct or indirect, express or constructive, to Turner of the sale in 1845. It is admitted, moreover, by the counsel for the plaintiff that if the deed of January 1852, had purported to convey in so many words the identical parcels of land—describing the land by metes and bounds or in any other way sufficient to place its identity beyond question—which had previously been conveyed by Sparke to the plaintiff, and which form the subject matter of this suit, then the plaintiff must fail, as it is conceded that in such case s. 11 of the *Registration Act* would be fatal to her claim. But it is contended on behalf of the plaintiff that on the proper construction of the deed of January 1852, that deed does not touch the lands in dispute, inasmuch as the words "all or any other lots forming a portion of the said grant to William O'Donnell, to which he the said William Sparke was then entitled," must be limited to such lots (if any) as he the said William Sparke had not theretofore parted with or conveyed away; in other words, that the fact being that Sparke had, in 1845, conveyed bona fide and for value the lands now in dispute to the plaintiff, and had never got them back, he could not be in 1852 in any sense "entitled" to them. It is further arued on behalf of the plaintiff that the effect of the recital in the deed of January 1852, was to limit the operative words of that deed to such lands as were specially described by metes and bounds, and therefore to render of no effect—even irrespectively of the existence of any prior deed and irrespectively of the effect of the *Registration Act*—the general words which follow the mention of the land so specially mentioned and described.

Leaving the latter branch of plaintiff's argument for the present and addressing ourselves to the consideration of the contention that, irrespective of any suggested restrictive operation of the recital, the land in dispute did not pass under the general words of description—that they were not and could not be included in those words—we must look at the facts. Sparke, up to the time of the execution by him of the deed of October 1845, was seized in fee of those lands. But for the deed of that date it is clear that he was entitled to them up to that time of the execution of the deed of 1 January 1852, and the lands, in any conveyance by him, would have been aptly and sufficiently described as "lots forming a portion of the grant to O'Donnell, to which I am entitled". The question, then, resolves itself into this: having regard to the *Registration Act*, which was in force both in 1845 and 1852, was Sparke, notwithstanding his having executed a conveyance in fee which remained unregistered, possessed of any interest in those lands which, not for his own benefit possibly, but for the benefit of a subsequent bona fide purchaser for value, could be described as a "title" to those lands? We are, of course, confining ourselves strictly to the arguments ingeniously conceived and forcibly urged by Mr Barton, that the general words of the deed of 1852 do not point to the land which Sparke had in 1845 conveyed to the plaintiff—that the identity of the parcels is not indicated by those general words. Mr Barton contends that the *Registration Act* (however much it may prefer, even contrary to their respective dates, that one of two deeds clearly dealing with the same land which is first registered) cannot alter the meaning of words, and that, inasmuch as Sparke knew he was not in 1852 entitled to the land which he had conveyed away in 1845, and as he must therefore be taken to have meant to exclude that land from the effect of general words used by him, the registration of the deed in which those general words occur could have no effect upon the meaning and intent of those words. But we are of opinion that the meaning and intention in the mind of a vendor which he may attach to words used in his conveyance is not, where it is a question of the proper construction of that deed in reference to the *Registration Act*, a matter for a court to consider. Although no doubt as between the vendor and the person who takes under a prior deed, even although unregistered, no title remains in the vendor, yet the question, as it seems to us, is—since the *Registration Act* has been in force, what has the subsequent bona fide purchaser for value a right to think the vendor meant, no matter what previous conveyance the vendor may have executed, and therefore no matter what the actual fact may be? And where a vendor who admittedly had been entitled in fee to land and is still, for aught that appears upon the register which the legislature has indicated as the place where an innocent and vigilant purchaser may search for dealings with the land which he buys, entitled in fee to that land says: "I sell and I hereby convey all the land comprised within a particular grant to which I am entitled," we think that by virtue of the *Registration Act* that purchaser, if he registers his conveyance before any other deed purporting to deal with that land is registered, becomes thereupon entitled to take priority over any previous unregistered conveyance of the same land. Such words, then, as "lands to which I am entitled", when used by a vendor, must be held to mean "such lands as I possess and am entitled to, whether included in any previous conveyance by me or not, if that conveyance remains unregistered", and cannot be held to except lands previously conveyed by him, so long as that conveyance remains unregistered. To hold otherwise would, in our opinion, be to defeat the very object of the Act. . . .

The cardinal rule in the construction of remedial statutes such as our *Registration Act* is so to construe them as to suppress the mischief and to advance the remedy—to give a broad and liberal, not a narrow and restricted, interpretation to the statute. To permit a bona fide purchaser for value to be defeated of his just expectations by his being told—"The vendor was not entitled to this land as he had sold it before; true, that as the conveyance executed by him on that previous sale had not been registered, and you had no other notice, direct or indirect, of the sale, you could not have found it out by the most diligent research, but as he only sold you in general terms the land in a particular grant to which he was entitled, he did not even purport to sell you this land, and therefore you have parted with your money for nothing" would be in our opinion to advance the mischief and to suppress the remedy. As it is said by Lord Coke on *Heydon's Case* (1584) 3 Co. Rep. 7d; 76 E.R. 637 "The office of all judges is always to make such construction as shall suppress the mischief and advance the remedy, and to suppress subtle inventions and evasions for continuance of the mischief, and pro privato commodo, and to add force and life to the cure and remedy, according to the true intent of the makers of the Act— pro bono publico." Applying the language of the judgment in *Warburton v. Loveland* 2 Dow. & Cl. 480 at 494; 6 E.R. 806 at 811 to this case, we say with their Lordships: "We think that it cannot be doubted but that the statute meant to afford an effectual remedy against the mischief arising to purchasers for a valuable consideration from the subsequent discovery of secret or concealed conveyances, or secret or concealed charges upon the estate. Now, it is obvious that no more effectual remedy can be devised than by requiring that every deed by which any interests in lands or tenements is transferred, or any charge created thereon, shall be put upon the register, under the peril that if it is not found thereon, the subsequent purchaser for a valuable consideration, and without notice, shall gain the priority over the former conveyance by the earlier registration of his subsequent deed." The case of *Warburton v. Loveland* was a case on the Irish *Registration Act*, and in that case much the same argument as has been addressed to us was pressed upon the court. It is met by Tindal C.J., as follows: "And it is further urged that as the fourth section, in declaring the effect and operation of registered conveyances, inter se, gives efficacy to the first registered deed in preference to the second, not absolutely, but only 'according to the right, title, and interest of the person conveying', a similar restriction must be understood to be imported into the fifth section also, and that the enactment which avoids altogether the prior unregistered as against the subsequent deed which is put upon the register must be understood with this tacit restriction, 'according to the right, title, and interest of the grantor in the second deed'. The meaning of those restrictive words in the fourth section appears to be 'according to what *would have been* the right, title, and interest of the person making the second conveyance had there been no deed but what appears upon the register'. For unless this be the meaning of those words in the fourth section, that clause of the statute affords no protection at all."

Our own cases have uniformly followed in the same direction, from *Fuller v. Goodwin* (1865) 4 S.C.R. (N.S.W.) 66 to *Smith v. Deane* (1889) 10 L.R. (N.S.W.) Eq. 207. In *Fuller v. Goodwin*, Stephen C.J., delivering the considered judgment of the court, says (at 68): "It appears clearly to us that, in favour of an innocent taker for value who registers his deed, the statute confers on the conveying party, notwithstanding his previous inconsistent conveyance, if not registered, a title as against the transferee named therein; and thus enables the person secondly taking immediately upon registration, to acquire that title." In *Smith v. Deane*, where again the same argument was used, viz., that the deeds were not inconsistent or "competitive", because the second deed purported to convey only the "right, title, and interest" remaining in the grantor after executing the first conveyance, the Chief Justice, following *Fuller v. Goodwin*, says: "The effect of registration is to vest the land again in the conveying party, in such a way as to feed the estate of the party who registers, and to give him priority over any previous unregistered purchaser." The result is that in such cases the prior unregistered deed is, as against the subsequent taker who is first to register, to be treated as if it had never existed. If, then, the previous deed—that of October 1845—had never existed, there can be no question that the land would have passed under the general words used in the deed of January 1852. For the reasons we have given, supported as they are by principle and authority, we think that on the proper construction of those words—it being impossible to put out of sight, as Mr Barton has urged us to do, the existence of the *Registration Act* and its bearing upon those words—the vendor must be taken to have intended, as between himself and Turner, the defendant's predecessor in title, to convey the same lands which he had previously, by the deed of October 1845, conveyed to the plaintiff.

With reference to the argument that the recitals must be held to restrict the operative words to the lands or lots specifically described by metes and bounds, we think that that argument is not sound, and that the cases cited in its support are not in point.

Verdict for the defendant.

NOTES AND QUESTIONS

1. In *Lyons v. Imperial Land Co.* (1894) 15 L.R. (N.S.W.) Eq. 64; sub nom. *Sydney and Suburban Land Assoc. v. Lyons* [1894] A.C. 260 the plaintiff purchased eight lots of the Henderson Estate from the defendant in October 1889, the purchase money being payable on instalments over 12 months. In June 1890 the defendant mortgaged the Henderson Estate to Sydney & Suburban Land Association in terms which included the land contracted to be sold to the plaintiff. The mortgage was registered. At the date of the mortgage, the mortgagee knew that some part of the estate had already been sold by the defendant but made no inquiries as to which part. It was held that "the real contract between the parties was for an advance to be made on the unsold portion of the estate and that the appellants [the mortgagee, Sydney & Suburban Land Association] took as security the Henderson Estate valeat quantum—subject to what it turned out to be".

2. In *Ex parte Pearse* (1900) 16 W.N. (N.S.W.) 262 it was held, applying *Lyons* case, that a general conveyance of "all the estate effects and assets real and personal of the Bank of Australia on 7 May 1855" and "which was or were not previously thereto sold or contracted to be sold to some person or persons other than the said Henry Osborne", which was registered did not take priority over a prior specific conveyance. The purchaser under such general conveyance by its very terms takes the property subject to what it turns out to be: the terminology of the general conveyance indicates of itself that some of the land subject of the general description may have been disposed of to some other party. Could it be argued that the same result would have transpired, in any event, in both *Lyons* case and *Ex parte Pearse* on the basis of the bona fides of the purchasers of the general conveyance?

RE O'BYRNE'S ESTATE

High Court of Chancery (Ireland) (1885) 15 L.R. Ir. 189

[O'Byrne executed a mortgage to the National Bank to secure past and future advances. This mortgage was duly registered under the Irish *Registry Act*, 6 Anne c. 2, s. 4. Subsequently, O'Byrne executed a mortgage over the same land to a third party who did not give notice to the Bank of this transaction. This instrument was also registered. Subsequent to this the National Bank from time to time made advances to O'Byrne without notice of the existence of the second mortgage, and the question before the court was whether the Bank was entitled to priority in respect of the advances made after the registration of the second mortgage.]

FLANAGAN J. . . . Mr Madden argued very forcibly and strongly that, on the construction of the fourth section of the *Registry Act* (6 Anne c. 2), which regulates priorities the moment a security is registered, the person registering it eo instanti acquires a right, not alone as against subsequent instruments, but even, as in the present case, against a prior registered instrument—a right not to be displaced; and it was argued before me that an addition to a sum of money secured by a mortgage is a "disposition" within the meaning of the fourth section, and that therefore a security, when registered, operates as a good and effectual deed against such advances made subsequently to it, and that therefore the Bank could not take priority against it. I confess I was rather startled by such a proposition. I do not mean to say that it may not be law; but it is undoubtedly a novel point, and it is a strange thing that it comes to be raised now, when the Act under which it arises has been in existence for a century and a half or more. I can only assume that the question was never raised before, because it was always taken for granted that a bank had the power of advancing sums of money under such a deed so long as there was no absolute notice of the registration of a subsequent deed.

In *Hopkinson v. Rolt* (1838) 9 H.L.C. 514; 48 E.R. 908 the House of Lords decided that where a first mortgage extends to future advances, further advances made by the first mortgagee after notice of the second mortgage, have no priority over such second mortgagee, even though the second mortgagee had notice of the nature of the first mortgage. But it is equally clear from that case that if no notice of the second mortgage had been given, the advances made subsequently to the registration would have been in priority to the second mortgage.

Independently of the provisions of the *Registry Act*, it is admitted on the authority of *Hopkinson v. Rolt*, that the Bank would be entitled to priority in respect of all advances made before notice to them of the subsequent agreement and mortgage. It is conceded, as I have said, that no such notice was ever given to the Bank; but it is contended that under the provisions of the fourth section of the *Registry Act*, each successive advance made by the Bank is a "disposition" within the meaning of that section, and therefore postponed to the agreement and mortgage—the priority being by that section regulated by the priority of the time of registration.

I am unable to accede to this view—the "disposition" in this case was, in my opinion, the original mortgage to the National Bank, and the subsequent advances under the provisions of that mortgage are not successive "dispositions", each as made requiring independent registration.

The mortgage is a "deed or conveyance" duly registered, the priority of which, and of all advances made under the contract incorporated in it, is determined by the date of the registration of the mortgage, save, according to the doctrine of *Hopkinson v. Rolt*, those advances made after notice of a subsequent mortgage.

Mr Madden argued that the Irish *Registry Act* excluded the doctrine of tacking, and that the future advances made were tacking within the meaning of that doctrine; and he specially relied on the case of *Credland v. Potter* (1874) L.R. 10 Ch. App. 12 in support of that view. *Credland v. Potter*, as I read it, decides only what was long before decided in this country in *Hamilton's Estate* (1905) 9 Ir. Ch. Rep. 512, that a charge created by an instrument in writing capable of registration and not registered, is void as against a subsequently duly registered mortgage without notice of the charge, and that persons claiming under that written instrument cannot tack that charge to a prior registered mortgage.

If Mr Madden's contention were law the results would be very startling—banking mortgages would become practically useless, as of necessity and almost de die in diem searches on the register should be made by banks to protect themselves from subsequent registered instruments which might claim priority over them. But, in my opinion, that proposition is not law.

There was another point, not much pressed nor apparently strongly entertained, namely, as to the effect of the registration of this matter as a lis pendens, and of course that is bound, so far as I am concerned, by my opinion on the other part of the case; and, as to the period of time when the Bank shall be deemed to have had notice, 11 September 1880, when the conditional order for sale was served on the Bank was the first time that the Bank was bound.

[The decision of the court was upheld on appeal on substantially the same grounds: see (1885) 15 L.R. Ir. 373.]

NOTES AND QUESTIONS

1. Compare Helmore, *The Law of Real Property in New South Wales* (2nd ed.), p. 337 where the view is taken that omission to search the Register in circumstances such as occurred in the principal case would amount to constructive notice of the second registered mortgage. This does not seem to be supported by the authorities. The position is different where the first registered mortgage makes no provision for further advances. In such case, a further advance by the first mortgagee is in effect the grant of a new and fresh interest in land, and if the first mortgagee fails to search the Register prior to making the further advance, he or she will be fixed with constructive notice of any subsequent registered mortgages and will be postponed accordingly: *Credland v. Potter* (1874) L.R. 10 Ch. 8.

2. Is the view put in the principal case affected in any way by the decision in *Matzner v. Clyde Securities Ltd*, dealt with in the chapter on mortgages, below p. 443?

FOUR

THE TORRENS SYSTEM

A. OBJECTS OF REGISTRATION

The growth in business activity in the 19th century brought an increase in the numbers of transfers of land. This produced a need for a system of land transfer which could handle adequately dealings with real property. The system of conveyancing then in operation, the "old" system, as it is now called, had numerous defects, such as duplication of documents and the requirement of searching the chain of title by skilled searchers. It also lent itself to the perpetration of frauds, particularly forgery. This led to a recognition that there must be a more satisfactory system of recording title supported by a form of registration. Two solutions were available: (1) registration of deeds, and (2) title by registration.

The first alternative operates on the principle that the deed, as registered, is evidence of title but that registration is not necessary to pass title. Under this system legal title is transferred by the deed of conveyance executed by the vendor in favour of the purchaser, and at common law this was the *only* requirement necessary to effect a disposition of the "legal" estate, registration of the deed of conveyance being largely to preserve existing priority between competing interests in property where such interests are represented by documents and to grant priority over competing unregistered instruments. Where there is no competition between instruments registration does not effect priority, although it does give notice of the transaction.

The second type of registration, title by registration, depends upon the theory that title is recorded in a Register which reveals information concerning the parcel and that the title is conferred upon registration. Registrations are effected by reference to the parcels themselves and not by reference to any index of the parties dealing with the property.

The two approaches exist side by side in New South Wales although the Torrens system aims to replace the "old" system completely. In the other States of Australia the "old" system has been replaced virtually by the transfer of all alienated lands to the Torrens system. The Torrens system has a number of principles, aims and hopes and the most important of these will be discussed below.

The first principle is that the title may be ascertained from an examination of the Register and the dealings with property are conducted by reference to the contents of the Register. This principle is found expressed in all States and is contained in the present New South Wales Act (the *Real Property Act* 1900):

125

[Section 41(1)] No dealing, until registered in the manner provided by this Act, shall be effectual to pass any estate or interest in any land under the provisions of this Act, or to render such land liable as security for the payment of money, but upon the registration of any dealing in the manner provided by this Act, the estate or interest specified in such dealing shall pass, or as the case may be the land shall become liable as security in manner and subject to the covenants, conditions, and contingencies set forth and specified in such dealing, or by this Act declared to be implied in instruments of a like nature.

Upon registration a proprietor's interest is not dependent upon her or his predecessor's title but it is taken subject to the exceptions specified in the Torrens statutes. This reflects the second aim of title by registration: "indefeasibility of title". Indefeasibility (see below) has received its settled interpretation in the advice of the Judicial Committee of the Privy Council in *Frazer v. Walker* [1967] 1 A.C. 569. Any person who obtains registration takes free of any defects in the title of the vendor which might have prevented the purchaser obtaining a good title under the "old" system. It is as though a new grant of title had been made by the Crown in favour of the current proprietor. Just as the Crown grant may not be challenged, neither may the interest of the registered proprietor subject, of course, to any statutory limitations (discussed below).

Thirdly, title is supported by the existence of an assurance fund which is used to compensate parties who suffer loss through the operation of the system of title by registration.

Fourthly, the system shows in the Register the location of the land, its proprietorship, and any encumbrances on the title. This should be compared with the "old" system in which title can be proved only by reference to all documents which affect it. There is no one document which sets out the title.

Fifthly, the curtain and mirror principles. These depend upon the view that the Register should present a clear and concise picture of the state of title uncluttered by trusts and equitable interests. (This approach, however, has not been adopted in all Torrens jurisdictions.) Special procedures exist for the protection of equitable and unregistered interests by the lodgment of caveats.

Sixthly, the various title deeds of the "old" system are replaced by one document, the certificate of title. One copy is kept at the Lands Title Office and one copy is issued to the registered proprietor.

These six principles or aims do not pretend to be an exhaustive list of the attributes of a system of title by registration, but they represent the major ones upon which the Torrens system is based.

The Torrens Acts of the various States recognise that the Register, unfortunately, cannot encompass all possible rights over land, a fact touched on already with reference to the exclusion of equitable interests from the Register. Some State Acts, however, allow the recording of a more wide-ranging category of interests than others. Further, all Acts make an exception from indefeasibility of title where a registered proprietor has acquired an interest through fraud. This and other exceptions will be discussed below.

ARTICLES

Moerlin Fox, P., "The Story Behind the Torrens System" (1950) 23 A.L.J. 489; Stein, R. T. J., "Sir Robert Richard Torrens and the Introduction of the Torrens System" (1981) 67 *Journal of the Royal Australian Historical Society* 119; Ruoff, T. B. F., "An Englishman Looks at the Torrens System" (1952) 26 A.L.J. 118, 162, 194, 228; Stein, R. T. J., "The Principles, Aims and Hopes of Title by Registration" (1983) 9 Adel. L.R. 267; Stein, R. T. J., "Torrens Title—A Case for the Registration of Trusts in New South Wales" (1982) 9 Syd. L.R. 605.

B. INDEFEASIBILITY OF TITLE

The relevant provisions are found in the *Real Property Act* 1900 (N.S.W.), s. 42: see below, p. 165.

The authorities show that there have been, in the past, two quite different concepts of indefeasibility. The first is "deferred indefeasibility" which is said to be advanced in *Gibbs v. Messer* [1891] A.C. 248. For example, if B forges a transfer from the registered proprietor A to a bona fide purchaser C, the Register may be rectified to restore A to the Register, but if C transfers to D who is a bona fide purchaser for value, A may not be returned to the Register. The general principle of this approach is that a registered proprietor may be removed from the Register to permit the restoration of a previous registered proprietor where that person has been removed wrongly as a result of an illegal transaction. However, such rectification is prevented if the registered proprietor has transferred her or his title to a bona fide purchaser for value. Under the second concept, "immediate indefeasibility", once a party obtains registration (subject to the exceptions specified in the Acts and the exception mentioned in *Frazer v. Walker* [1967] 1 A.C. 569, see below) and irrespective of fraud or forgery, save on the part of the person seeking registration, the Register cannot be impeached. This approach is supported by *Frazer v. Walker*. Under this principle of "immediate indefeasibility", the Register may not be rectified to restore A to title even while C remains as registered proprietor.

A recent statement of the principle of immediate indefeasibility is to be found in *Breskvar v. Wall* (1972) 126 C.L.R. 367 where the High Court of Australia expressly rejected the "deferred" approach. The court followed *Frazer v. Walker* and refused to indorse the opinions in favour of "deferred indefeasibility" which had been expressed by some members of the High Court in *Clements v. Ellis* (1934) 51 C.L.R. 217.

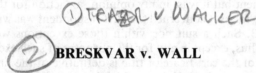

① FRAZER v WALKER

② BRESKVAR v. WALL

High Court of Australia (1972) 126 C.L.R. 376

[The Breskvars were registered proprietors of land. They executed a transfer to Petrie as security for a loan. The transfer left blank the name of the transferee. Because of this, the memorandum of transfer was void under the *Stamp Act* 1894 (Qld), s. 53(5). Petrie, in fraud, inserted the name of Wall, as transferee, into the void transfer. Petrie had the transfer registered. Wall sold the land to Alban Pty Ltd and executed a memorandum of transfer in the appropriate form which was handed over upon completion. Subsequent to this but before registration of the transfer to Alban the Breskvars became aware of the registration of the first fraudulent transfer. They lodged a caveat to protect their rights. Alban Pty Ltd claimed protection as a bona fide purchaser for value, even though it was not registered. The company argued that the Breskvars were guilty of postponing conduct in executing a transfer in blank and in failing to lodge a caveat. The court found in favour of Alban Pty Ltd on this argument.]

BARWICK C.J. The opinions held in some places in the past that the conclusive quality of the certificate of title did not enure for the benefit of a registered proprietor, other than the proprietor firstly registered on the land being brought under the provisions of the *Real Property Act* seem to me to be more difficult to maintain in the light of the provisions to which I have referred but, in any case, they were shown to be untenable by the decision of the Privy Council in *Assets Co. Ltd v. Mere Roihi* [1905] A.C. 176 where Lord Lindley pointed out that "the section making registered certificates conclusive evidence of title are too clear to be got over". "In dealing with actions between private individuals, their Lordships are unable to draw any distinction between the first registered owner and any other" (at 202). This is also made clear by the more recent decision of the Privy Council in *Frazer v. Walker* [1967] 1 A.C. 569 at 581, 584-585. Proceedings may of course be brought against the registered proprietor by the persons and for the causes described in the quoted sections of the Act or by persons setting up matters depending upon the acts of the registered proprietor himself. These may have as their terminal point orders binding the registered proprietor to divest himself wholly or partly of the estate or interest vested in him by registration and indorsement of the certificate of title: or in default of his compliance with such an order on his part, perhaps vesting orders may be made to effect the proper interest of the claimants in the land. Also, s. 124 gives the Supreme Court power to cancel an entry in the register book and to substitute another entry in the event of the recovery of any land by ejectment from a fraudulent proprietor or from any of the persons against whom an action of ejectment is not expressly barred by the Act. This is the only power of the Supreme Court to amend the Register: see *Assets Co. Ltd v. Mere Roihi* [1905] A.C. 176 at 195; *Frazer v. Walker* at 581. Section 85 of the *Land Transfer Act* 1952 (N.Z.) with which the last mentioned case was concerned gives the power of amendment upon the recovery of any land estate or interest by any proceedings whereas s. 124 of the Act deals only with the recovery of land by action of ejectment. The suit for declarations and orders for amendment of the Register brought by the appellant in *Frazer v. Walker* was held by the Privy Council in that case to be an action for the recovery of land: see at 586. The appellants' suit in this case was not an action of ejectment but it was, in my opinion, an action for the recovery of land and, in any case, so far as it concerned the first respondent was within the exceptions contained in s. 123. Such a suit not within those exceptions would be effectively barred by s. 123. Thus, except in and for the purposes of such excepted proceedings, the conclusiveness of the certificate of title is definitive of the title of the registered proprietor. That is to say, in the jargon which has had currency, there is immediate indefeasibility of title by the registration of the proprietor named in the Register. The stated exceptions to the prohibition on actions for recovery of land against a registered proprietor do not mean that that "indefeasibility" is not effective. It is really no impairment of the conclusiveness of the register that the proprietor remains liable to one of the excepted actions any more than his liability for "personal equities" derogates from that conclusiveness. So long as the certificate is unamended it is conclusive and of course when amended it is conclusive of the new particulars it contains.

The Torrens system of registered title of which the Act is a form is not a system of registration of title but a system of title by registration. That which the certificate of title describes is not the title which the registered proprietor formerly had, or which but for registration would have had. The title it certifies is not historical or derivative. It is the title which registration itself has vested in the proprietor. Consequently, a registration which results from a void instrument is effective according to the terms of the registration. It matters not what the cause or reason for which the instrument is void. The affirmation by the Privy Council in *Frazer v. Walker* of the decision of the Supreme Court of New Zealand in *Boyd v. Mayor of Wellington* [1924] N.Z.L.R. 1174 at 1223, now places that conclusion beyond question. Thus the effect of the *Stamp Act* upon the memorandum of transfer in this case is irrelevant to the question whether the certificate of title is conclusive of its particulars.

I have thus referred under the description, the Torrens system, to the various Acts of the States of the Commonwealth which provide for comparable systems of title by registration though these Acts are all not in identical terms and some do contain significant variations. It is I think a matter for regret that complete uniformity of this legislation has not been achieved, particularly as Australians now deal with each other in land transactions from State to State.

It follows, in my opinion, from the provisions of the Victorian Act which are counterpart to those of the Act to which I have referred and from the decisions of the Privy Council in *Frazer v. Walker* [1967] 1 A.C. 569 and in *Assets Co. Ltd v. Mere Roihi* [1905] A.C. 176 on comparable sections of the New Zealand Act that the appeal of the registered proprietor in the case of *Clements v. Ellis* (1934) 51 C.L.R. 217, ought to have been allowed. . . .

It follows in my opinion from *Frazer v. Walker* [1967] 1 A.C. 569 that *Clements v. Ellis* (1934) 51 C.L.R. 217 was not correctly decided. Further, in my opinion, *Mayer v. Coe* (1968) 88 W.N. (Pt 1) (N.S.W.) 549 and *Ratcliffe v. Watters* [1969] 2 N.S.W.R. 146 correctly applied *Frazer v. Walker* [1967] 1 A.C. 569.

[The remaining judgments of McTiernan, Menzies, Windeyer, Owen, Walsh and Gibbs JJ. have been omitted as they either come to the same result (based on priorities) or concur in the judgment of the Chief Justice.]

NOTES AND QUESTIONS

1. The result in the principal case would have been the same even if the court had adopted "deferred" indefeasibility. This is because Alban Pty Ltd had not been registered as proprietor and took priority according to the equitable rules governing priority. The Breskvars were guilty of postponing conduct in signing and entrusting the documents of title to Petrie and in their failure to lodge a caveat to protect their interest.

2. The principal case followed the advice of the Privy Council in *Frazer v. Walker* [1967] 1 A.C. 569. That case concerned the provisions of the *Land Transfer Act 1952* (N.Z.), s. 62, in terms similar to s. 42 of the New South Wales Act. Mrs Frazer, purporting to act for both herself and her husband in raising a mortgage over their already mortgaged property forged her husband's signature. The mortgage was registered but no repayments were made. The mortgagees, upon this default under the mortgage, exercised their power of sale and sold to Walker. The transfer was registered. Throughout, the mortgagees and Walker acted in good faith and without notice of the activities of Mrs Frazer. Mr Frazer claimed that he was not bound by the registration when Walker commenced an action for possession. The Board rejected the "deferred" indefeasibility theory and restricted the advice in *Gibbs v. Messer* (see note 3) to its special facts. Could the result in *Frazer's* case have been arrived at without a consideration of the question of "immediate" or "deferred" indefeasibility?

3. *Gibbs v. Messer* [1891] A.C. 248. A solicitor forged and registered a transfer to a fictitious person, Cameron. Purporting to act as Cameron's agent he arranged a mortgage; the mortgage was registered. Upon discovery of the mortgage, the former registered proprietor brought an action for rectification of the Register free from the encumbrance on the ground that registration would confer an indefeasible title only in favour of a bona fide purchaser who had not derived title immediately consequent upon the fraud. It was said that a person who deals with a fictitious person could not derive any benefit from his registration. Would this decision be the same today?

4. *Frazer v. Walker* has been followed in New South Wales in a number of cases. The first of these was *Mayer v. Coe* (1968) 88 W.N. (Pt 1) (N.S.W.) 549. Mrs Mayer instructed her solicitor to complete a purchase of land. This being done, he forged a mortgage over the land without her authority and then absconded with the proceeds. Mrs Mayer became aware of the true situation when Coe, the mortgagee, gave instructions for proceedings to be instituted against the mortgagor. Mrs Mayer

argued that she had title free of the mortgage. She based her argument upon "deferred" indefeasibility. The court said that it was bound to follow the advice of the Privy Council in *Frazer v. Walker*, even though indefeasibility was not a necessary basis for the decision. The title was subject to the interest of the mortgagee as his registration had secured an indefeasible title. This decision was approved in *Breskvar v. Wall*. See also *Schultz v. Corwill Properties Pty Ltd* (1969) 90 W.N. (Pt 1) (N.S.W.) 529 for a similar decision.

5. The plaintiff was the registered proprietor of lands which were resumed by the defendants for the purpose of a tramway. The resumption was effected by a proclamation which suffered from defects in form. This proclamation also vested the land in the defendants. Can the plaintiff upset the defendants' title? See *Boyd v. Mayor etc. of Wellington, District Land Registrar and The Attorney-General* (1924) 43 N.Z.L.R. 1174.

6. A was the registered proprietor of land, registered under the *Real Property Act* 1900 (N.S.W.). S, in fraud of A, obtained the certificate of title, forged the signature of S upon a memorandum of transfer and was registered as proprietor subject to a mortgage which she, S, had raised. A further registered mortgage was raised. The repayments were not met and the mortgagees proceeded in ejectment and A defended the proceedings. What are the rights of the mortgagees and what is the nature of A's interest? See *Ratcliffe v. Watters* (1969) 90 W.N. (Pt 1) (N.S.W.) 497.

7. A recent example of the extent of the principle of indefeasibility is found in *Sutherland Shire Council v. Moir* (1982) 49 L.G.R.A. 115. The Court of Appeal held that a forged plan of subdivision became effective upon registration to create the subdivision as shown on the plan.

ARTICLES

McCall, I., "Indefeasibility Re-examined: Frazer v. Walker and Some of its Consequences" (1970) 9 U.W.A.L.R. 321; Sackville, R., "Security Interests in Land—The Torrens System—Some Thoughts on Indefeasibility and Priorities" (1973) 47 A.L.J. 121; Taylor, W., "Scotching Frazer v. Walker" (1970) 44 A.L.J. 248; Teh, G. L., "Breskvar v. Wall: The End of Deferred Indefeasibility" (1974) 9 M.U.L.R. 381; Woodman, R. A., "The Torrens System in New South Wales: One Hundred Years of Indefeasibility of Title" (1970) 44 A.L.J. 96.

C. THE REGISTER

The Register is the record kept by the Registrar-General which reveals the state of the title. It is the fundamental key to systems of title by registration. A person recorded on the Register as the proprietor of an interest (unless he has committed actual fraud in obtaining his registration) holds that interest free of any other interests or encumbrances except those noted on the Register. In other words, he has "indefeasible" title. Title passes upon registration and by the act of the Crown: *Commonwealth v. New South Wales* (1918) 25 C.L.R. 325 at 342.

RE LEHRER AND THE REAL PROPERTY ACT 1900-1956

Supreme Court of New South Wales (1961) 61 S.R. (N.S.W.) 365

[The facts appear from the judgment.]

JACOBS J. I express my conclusion that the Registrar-General is bound to refuse to register a lease which effects an unapproved subdivision. Section 196(2) of the *Conveyancing Act* 1919, provides that every person who by any Act is required to procure the registration of a plan of a subdivision, shall lodge in the office of the Registrar-General a plan of that subdivision. Section 327(2) of the *Local Government Act* 1919, provides that land shall not be subdivided until a plan of the subdivision has been registered in the office of the Registrar-General. By the definition of subdivision a lease for more than five years is a subdivision but there cannot be a legal subdivision until the plan is registered. The Registrar-General is forbidden to register the plan by virtue of s. 338(2) of the *Local Government Act* 1919. I do not consider that he is bound to register the lease without a registered plan.

Section 196(15) of the *Conveyancing Act* 1919, gives the Registrar-General power to require the lodgment under that section of a plan before or in connection with the registration under the *Real Property Act* 1900 of any instrument. The position therefore would be that, in the case of an unapproved subdivision, the Registrar-General would no doubt require the lodgment of a plan under s. 196. If a plan were lodged the Registrar-General under subs. (8) would be required to satisfy himself that all the requirements of the *Conveyancing Act* 1919, in relation to the plan had been complied with. One of these requirements is in s. 196(6), namely, that the plan should comply with all statutory requirements relating to the plan. Therefore, unless the plan was approved as required by s. 327 of the *Local Government Act* 1919, it would not be a valid plan under s. 196. Such a plan, therefore, would not be "lodged" under that section and the Registrar-General would in my opinion be entitled to require the lodgment of a plan complying with all statutory requirements in connection with the registration of the lease. I therefore do not consider that the Registrar-General is bound to register a lease which does not comply with the requirements of the *Local Government Act* 1919 in regard to subdivision. . . .

Since I have held that a lease for more than five years of part of a building is not a subdivision within the meaning of the Act, I doubt whether in practice this question would arise. However, I express my view that there is no power in a council to impose such a term. Approval to a subdivision may by virtue of s. 331(2) be given subject to conditions. However, I do not consider that the addition of the term "for leasing purposes only" is truly a condition; rather, it is a qualification of the approval. I do not consider there is any power in the Act to qualify the approval in this manner. The matters which the council can take into account in deciding upon an application for approval of a subdivision are exhaustively set out in the Act: *Howard v. Penrith Municipal Council* (1958) 3 L.G.R.A. 260. None of these matters affect or deal with the title upon which the land will be held after the subdivision.

What is a sufficient description to satisfy s. 53(2) of the *Real Property Act* 1900?

In respect of this question and of the following question there has been argued before me the further question whether, if the description in a particular lease is inadequate or if the expression of the term in the lease is, or appears to be, uncertain, the Registrar-General should refuse registration. In regard to description, I am of opinion that the Act in s. 39 thereof makes it clear that the Registrar-General should not register a lease in which there is not a sufficient description. Section 39 provides that the Registrar-General shall not register any instrument purporting to transfer or otherwise to deal with or affect any estate or interest in land under the provision of the Act except in the manner therein provided, nor unless the instrument be in accordance with the provisions thereof. If there is presented to the Registrar-General a lease which for description of the land intended to be dealt with does not give such description as may be necessary to identify the land, I do not consider that the instrument is purporting to deal with an interest in the land in the manner provided in the Act, nor do I consider that the instrument is in accordance with the provisions of the Act. The requirements of s. 53(2) have not in that event been satisfied.

The position does not seem to me to be as simple when what is being considered is not the description of the land, a matter expressly provided for in the Act, but the term under the lease. There has been submitted to me a broad argument based upon the view that the Registrar-General does not in the ultimate analysis give to an instrument or dealing by registration any greater effect than it might otherwise have. Reliance has been placed upon the decision in *Caldwell v. Rural Bank of New South Wales* (1953) 53 S.R. (N.S.W.) 415, where it was held that the registration of the Minister as a registered proprietor of land purported to be acquired by means of an invalid resumption, did not give to him an indefeasible title. The court followed the minority view in *Boyd v. Mayor of Wellington* [1924] N.Z.L.R. 1174 and the view of Dixon J. in *Clements v. Ellis* (1934) 51 C.L.R. 217. It has been argued before me that since a title upon registration is not wholly indefeasible it is not the concern of the Registrar-General to satisfy himself in regard to legal validity of the dealing. It appears to me that this argument overlooks the fact that even if a title so registered is initially defeasible, it will become indefeasible in favour of a bona fide purchaser for value: see s. 135. I do not propose to attempt to analyse the many decisions which have dealt with the discretion or otherwise of the Registrar-General to refuse registration of a dealing: e.g. *Crowley v. Templeton* (1914) 17 C.L.R. 457; *Drake v. Templeton* (1913) 16 C.L.R. 153; *Perpetual Executors and Trustees Assoc. v. Hoshen* (1912) 14 C.L.R. 286; *Templeton v. Leviathan Pty Ltd* (1921) 30 C.L.R. 34. I summarise my view in the opinion that certainly in any case where an indefeasible title would be obtained by a bona fide purchaser, the Registrar-General has a duty to examine the validity of the dealing submitted and has a discretion to refuse to register the instrument. . . .

Is a lease expressed to be for the term during which shares in the capital of a certain company shall be personally held by the lessees void for uncertainty in the expression of the term?

In dealing with the last question I have referred to the broader question whether uncertainty in the expression of the term is a ground for refusal by the Registrar-General to register a lease. In relation to the description of the premises, I found that the matter was governed by the statute. However, this is not so in relation to the expression of the term. A conclusion which I expressed above is that the Registrar-General ought to refuse to register an instrument whereby he certifies a title which, even though defeasible in the first instance despite the registration, would become indefeasibile if transferred to a bona fide purchaser. By virtue of s. 35 of the *Real Property Act* 1900, a lease is deemed to be registered so soon as a memorial thereof as described in the Act has been entered in the register book upon the folium constituted by the existing certificate of title of such land. By s. 36(4) upon registration every instrument drawn in accordance with the Act is deemed to be embodied in the register book. To that extent the Registrar-General certifies the title of the lessee, and the lessee has the protection of those provisions of the Act which confer indefeasibility of title. However, when the Registrar-General registers a lease it is only the title which the parties by their words have themselves described which is thus registered and to which the Registrar-General thus gives his certificate. The Registrar-General by the registration cannot create a form of leasehold estate which is not known to the law: *Re Ridgeway and Smith's Contract* [1930] V.L.R. 111. The registration does not interfere with the ordinary effect of the instrument at law or in equity: *Groongal Pastoral Co. v. Faulkiner* (1924) 35 C.L.R. 157 at 163. It follows, therefore, that, if the Registrar-General registers a lease which is void for uncertainty of the term purported to be stated therein, no greater interest is conferred upon the purported lessee by the registration than he would have had apart from registration. If the lessee purports to transfer the lease to a bona fide purchaser, the purchaser takes no more than the registered interest of the lessee, which is nothing. I do not see how any person could by registration be deprived of any estate or interest in the land within the meaning of s. 126 of the Act, or could sustain any loss or damage within s. 127 of the Act.

Under these circumstances, I do not consider that the Registrar-General ought to refuse registration of an instrument because he forms the view that in law it is a void instrument, unless by registration some validity could be given to the instrument which it would not otherwise have, or some estate or interest could by registration be created beyond that purported to be dealt with in the instrument itself.

It would indeed be an onerous duty to impose upon the Registrar-General to require him to examine every instrument lodged for registration in order to determine not only whether it complied with the requirements of the Act as to form and whether it improperly affected the interest of any other person in the land but also the question whether it was effective in substantive law to create the interest which on the face of the instrument was purported thereby to be created. When there is taken into account the difficulty which can arise in determining whether particular limitations of interest or particular forms of interest purported to be created in real property are valid, it would hardly be expected that a determination of these matters would be thrown upon the Registrar-General except where the effect of the registration would be to validate that which would otherwise be invalid. Moreover, such a view would lead to the anomalous position that the determination of these matters by the Registrar-General or even upon case stated by the court would not bind any person. In the case of a lease, both lessor and lessee would be able to allege at any time that, despite the determination and despite the registration, the instrument was void.

When I apply this reasoning to the question whether the lease for a term during which shares in the capital of a certain company shall be personally held by the lessees ought to be registered, I conclude that the Registrar-General in such a case ought not to concern himself with the question whether the expression of the term is uncertain and therefore invalid under the general law. Though it would appear that in the present case the term does not found a valid lease—I would have difficulty distinguishing the case from that of *Lace v. Chandler* [1944] 1 All E.R. 306, to which I have been referred nevertheless, for the reasons which I have expressed, I do not consider that it is for me or for the Registrar-General to embark upon this question.

NOTES

1. See also *Fels v. Knowles* (1906) 26 N.Z.L.R. 604. In that case the defendants were trustees of property registered under the *Land Transfer Act* (N.Z.). A lease by the trustees of the lands for 14 years contained an option to purchase in favour of the lessee. The lease was registered. The lessees' executors, shortly before the expiration of the lease, sought to exercise the option to purchase. The defendants refused to transfer the property upon the grounds that they did not have power under the will to grant an option to purchase and that if they were to permit such a purchase they would be liable for breach of trust. The court held that this argument could not be accepted and that the defendants were bound by the option because the registration of the lease, containing the option, had given the lessees an indefeasible right to purchase according to the terms of the option. This was so even though it would involve a commission of breach of trust by the defendants. Compare *Horne v. Horne* (1906) 26 N.Z.L.R. 1208.

2. The respondent was registered proprietor of a lease which contained two options to renew. Between the exercise of the options a mortgage was granted and the mortgagee sought to exercise a power of sale. The lessee then endeavoured to register the extension of the lease unaffected by the rights of the mortgagee. It was held that the rights under the option were indefeasible and took priority over the mortgage because of the registration of the lease: see *Mercantile Credits Ltd v. Shell Co. of Australia* (1976) 136 C.L.R. 326.

D.   UNREGISTERED INTERESTS

Generally speaking unregistered interests are to be found in one of three situations: (1) where a transfer, mortgage, lease or other dealing has not been registered; (2) where an interest is of the type which is capable of registration, but is not embodied in a form suitable for registration; and (3) where an interest is of the sort in respect of which no provision is made for registration. All three categories of interests may be protected by caveat: see below.

The Torrens system does not permit or envisage the registration of all interests in land: see above. In a broad sense it may be said that registered interests correspond with "legal" interests at common law and that unregistered interests correspond with "equitable" interests at common law. The analogy cannot, however, be taken too far. For example, short term leases, which are discussed below, need not be registered but they may be "legal" interests. Moreover, some equitable interests may be registered. For example, a valid restrictive covenant under the principles in *Tulk v. Moxhay* (1848) 2 Ph. (Phil.) 774; 41 E.R. 1143 is an equitable interest capable of registration in some jurisdictions, as is the benefit of an option to purchase granted to a lessee. One type of equitable interest which is not registered is the interest of a beneficiary under a trust, the object being to ensure that the Register is not confused by a multiplicity of equitable rights: *Wolfson v. Registrar-General* (1934) 51 C.L.R. 300 at 308.

BARRY v. HEIDER

High Court of Australia (1914) 19 C.L.R. 197

[Barry executed a transfer of land in favour of Schmidt and the transfer, induced by fraud, was not registered. Schmidt then applied for a loan from Heider on the security of the land and provided the transfer together with an order from the transferor to the Registrar-General to deliver the certificate of title to Heider's solicitor. Subsequently, a caveat was lodged by Barry who claimed as unpaid vendor. Schmidt sought to raise a further mortgage from Gale, solicitor to Heider, who was aware of the caveat. During these negotiations the caveat was withdrawn, the purchase moneys remained unpaid and the advance was made by Gale. The caveat was withdrawn by the solicitor acting for Schmidt, and Gale was aware that the purchaser's solicitor was acting for both Barry and Schmidt.]

GRIFFITH C.J. The main contention for the appellant is that an unregistered instrument is inoperative to create any right with respect to the land itself. This argument is founded upon the provision in s. 2(4) of the Act that "All laws, statutes, Acts, ordinances, rules, regulations and practice whatsoever relating to freehold and other interests in land and operative on the first day of January one thousand eight hundred and sixty-three are, so far as inconsistent with the provisions of this Act, hereby repealed so far as regards their application to land under the provisions of this Act, or bringing of land under the operation of this Act," and upon s. 41, which enacts that

"(1) No instrument, until registered in manner hereinbefore prescribed, shall be effectual to pass any estate or interest in any land under the provisions of this Act, or to render such land liable as security for the payment of money, but upon the registration of any instrument in manner hereinbefore prescribed, the estate or interest specified in such instrument shall pass, or as the case may be the land shall become liable as security in manner and subject to the covenants, conditions and contingencies set forth and specified in such instrument, or by this Act declared to be implied in instruments of a like nature.

(2) Should two or more instruments executed by the same proprietor and purporting to transfer or encumber the same estate or interest in any land be at the same time presented to the Registrar-General for registration and endorsement, he shall register and endorse that instrument under which the person claims property

who shall present to him the grant or certificate of title of such land for that purpose." I note in passing that the second paragraph of this section treats the person presenting an instrument for registration as a person "claiming property" under it.

In my opinion the only relevant words of s. 2, "All laws . . . rules . . . practice", are not of themselves sufficient to embrace the body of law recognised and administered by courts of equity in respect of equitable claims to land arising out of contract or personal confidence. But it is said that the words of s. 41 "No instrument until registered . . . shall be effectual to pass any estate or interest in any land under the provisions of this Act" have that effect.

It is now more than half a century since the Australian colonies and New Zealand adopted, in substantially the same form but with some important variations, the system, sometimes called the "Torrens" system, which is now in New South Wales embodied in the *Real Property Act* 1900. With the exception of one decision in South Australia, soon afterwards overruled, the contention of the appellant has never been accepted in any of them.

I proceed to consider other provisions of the Act bearing on the question for the purpose of discovering whether equitable rights or claims with respect to land are recognised by it. PPA

Part IX of the Act deals with trusts. By s. 82 the Registrar-General is forbidden to make any entry of any notice of trusts, whether expressed, implied or constructive, in the register book. The section goes on to provide that trusts may be declared by any instrument, and that a duplicate or attested copy of the instrument may be deposited with him for safe custody and reference. The instrument itself is not to be registered, but the Registrar-General is required to enter on the register a caveat forbidding the registration of any instrument not in accordance with the trusts and provisions contained in the instrument so deposited. This is, in my opinion, an express recognition of the equitable rights or interests declared by that instrument. Section 86 provides that whenever any person "interested in land" under the Act appears to be a trustee within the meaning of any Trustee Act then in force, and a vesting order is made by the court, the Registrar-General shall enter the vesting order in the register book and on the instrument evidencing the registered title to the land, and that upon such entry being made the person in whom the order purports to vest the land shall be deemed to be registered proprietor. No restriction is made as to the cases in which the court may declare a trust. The jurisdiction recognised by this section clearly includes any case in which the court can make a vesting order under the Trustee Acts. That jurisdiction has always included cases in which specific performance of a contract to sell land has been decreed by the court. This, again, is an express recognition of an equitable claim or title to land as existing before and irrespective of registration.

The provisions of the Act relating to caveats embody a scheme expressly devised for the protection of equitable rights. The caveat required by s. 82 to be entered by the Registrar-General is one instance of the application of that scheme.

Section 72 provides that any person "claiming any estate or interest" in land under the Act "under any unregistered instrument" may by caveat forbid the registration of any interest affecting such land, estate or interest. This provision expressly recognises that an unregistered instrument may create a "claim" cognisable by a court of justice, and the caveat is the means devised for the protection of the right of the claimant pending proceedings in a competent court to enforce it.

Section 44 deals with the case of suits for specific performance brought by a registered proprietor against a purchaser without notice of any fraud or other circumstances which would affect the vendor's right, which can only be circumstances creating an equitable right in a third person. I cannot think that the jurisdiction of the court to grant specific performance as against a registered proprietor vendor is not equally recognised.

In South Australia the jurisdiction of the court to decree specific performance in such a case was affirmed by the Supreme Court in the case of *Cuthbertson v. Swan* (1877) 11 S.A.L.R. 102, overruling an earlier case of *Lange v. Ruwoldt* (1872) 6 S.A.L.R. 75. The judgment of the court (Way C.J. and Stow J.), which was delivered by Stow J., contains a very careful review of the provisions of the Act, entirely in accordance with the view I have expressed.

In 1877 the Queensland legislature gave express recognition to this view by the *Real Property Act Amendment Act* of that year, which provided (s. 48): "Every instrument signed by a proprietor or by others claiming through or under him purporting to pass an estate or interest in or security upon land for the registration of which provision is made by this Act shall until registered be deemed to confer upon the person intended to take under such instrument or other person claiming through or under him a right or claim to the registration of such estate or security."

This provision was adopted in South Australia in 1878. In the case of *Franklin v. Ind* (1883) 17 S.A.L.R. 133 at 164 the Supreme Court of that colony expressed the opinion that the new statute merely affirmed the law as declared in *Cuthbertson v. Swan* (1877) 11 S.A.L.R. 102.

Opinions to the same general effect were expressed by the Supreme Court of Victoria in the cases of *Plumpton v. Plumpton* (1886) 11 V.L.R. 733 and *Sander v. Twigg* (1887) 13 V.L.R. 765, by the Supreme Court of New Zealand in *Paoro Torotoro v. Sutton* (1875) 1 N.Z. Jur. (N.S.) S.C. 57, and by the Supreme Court of New South Wales in *Josephson v. Mason* (1912) 12 S.R. (N.S.W.) 249.

In my opinion equitable claims and interests in land are recognised by the Real Property Acts.

It follows that the transfer of 19 October, if valid as between the appellant and Schmidt, would have conferred upon the latter an equitable claim or right to the land in question recognised by the law. I think that it also follows that this claim or right was in its nature assignable by any means appropriate to the assignment of such an interest.

It further follows that the transfer operated as a representation, addressed to any person into whose hands it might lawfully come without notice of Barry's right to have it set aside, that Schmidt had such an assignable interest.

The respondent Heider's case is mainly based upon this representation, but does not entirely rest upon it. Barry's letter of 23 October authorising the delivery of the certificate of title to Messrs Gale and Gale, and delivered to them upon their request to Schmidt for its production, was, in my opinion, an even more emphatic representation that Schmidt had such an interest as entitled him to possession of the certificate of title. Mrs Heider thereupon became in a position to register the transfer from Barry to Schmidt, and consequent upon it to register Schmidt's mortgage to herself. Her right to do so was complete, although actual registration was formally impeded by the delay in the preparation of the new certificate. So far, therefore, as she is concerned, I think that Barry is not entitled to any relief against her except upon the terms of making good his representations. . . .

Gale, however, was not a mere stranger coming on the scene for the first time. He knew on 4 December that Peterson was acting as solicitor for Schmidt, the proposed borrower. The letter withdrawing the caveat was equivalent to an acknowledgment by Peterson, as agent for Barry, that the latter's lien for unpaid purchase money was satisfied. The case is, therefore, as if a person proposing to advance money on equitable mortgage were told by the solicitor for the proposed borrower, purporting also to act as solicitor for a prior equitable mortgagee, that the prior equitable mortgage had been satisfied. Can he safely act on such an assurance without further inquiry? After full consideration I have come to the conclusion that he cannot. In one sense it is not unreasonable in such a case, in the absence of any ground for suspecting fraud, to accept the assurance of the solicitor, but it would be more reasonable for the lender to ask for confirmation of the assurance from the prior equitable mortgagee himself or an independent agent. Under these circumstances I think that, in the absence of any positive evidence of Peterson's authority to make the assurance of satisfaction beyond that furnished by his having signed the caveat, Gale cannot rely on it. He is entitled to rely upon the previous representations already referred to, by which Barry is bound as against Mrs Heider, except so far as they were afterwards qualified by the caveat. But, not having established by positive evidence Peterson's authority to withdraw the caveat, he cannot rely upon the withdrawal as a further representation by Barry.

I think, therefore, that the rule qui prior est tempore potior est jure must prevail, and that Gale's mortgage must be postponed to Barry's vendor's lien.

[Barton J. concurred in the judgment of the Chief Justice and Isaacs J. expressed a similar opinion.]

NOTES AND QUESTIONS

1. Would the result in *Barry v. Heider* be any different in the light of the present provision allowing withdrawal by the lodging party's solicitor? See s. 78M.

2. Before his death K entered into a contract for the sale of his land to L. On his death the question arose for determination as to whether L held an interest in the property or whether it had passed to K's heir-at-law. It was held that L had no interest which could be enforced under the Torrens system: *Lange v. Ruwoldt* (1872) 6 S.A.L.R. 75. Although this view was rejected in *Cuthbertson v. Swan* (1877) 11 S.A.L.R. 102, which was followed in the principal case, the decision is instructive of the initial attitude taken to the system as one wholly different from the law as it had existed previously.

ARTICLES

Evatt, H. V., "Competing Equitable Interests in Torrens System Land" (1930) 4 A.L.J. 4; Sackville, R., "Competing Equitable Interests in Land Under the Torrens System" (1972) 45 A.L.J. 396; "Competing Equitable Interests in Land Under the Torrens System—A Postscript" (1972) 46 A.L.J. 344.

E. CAVEATS

In the main where there is a competition between unregistered interests priority will be resolved, where the equities are equal, by reference to the rule qui prior est tempore potior est jure (the first in time is the first in law). As a means of preserving the priority of an unregistered interest a caveat may be lodged. The word "caveat" means "beware". There are two principal kinds of caveat: caveats lodged by private persons, and those lodged by the Registrar-General. Private persons may lodge two chief kinds of caveat. The first is caveats against "primary applications", that is, when land is sought to be brought under the provisions of the Torrens system. (In this regard reference should be made to caveats and cautions arising upon the issue of qualified and limited certificates of title under Parts IVA and IVB of the Act.

These provisions have for their purpose the bringing of lands under the Torrens system where title was granted before title by registration was introduced.) The second kind is caveats relating to existing Torrens title land.

A caveat acts as a statutory injunction which prevents the alteration of the Register by the Registrar-General. The status quo is preserved until the rights of the parties are determined. Caveats ensure that if inconsistent interests are lodged for registration the caveator will be given the chance to commence proceedings to secure the right claimed. A caveat, to be enforceable, must claim some interest in the land to which it relates and must be in the approved form. The main provision for the lodgment of private caveats is found in s. 74F(1) of the *Real Property Act* 1900 (N.S.W.), as follows:

> Any person who, by virtue of any unregistered dealing or by devolution of law or otherwise, claims to be entitled to a legal or equitable estate or interest in land under the provisions of this Act may lodge with the Registrar-General a caveat prohibiting the recording of any dealing affecting the estate or interest to which the person claims to be entitled.

Failure to lodge a caveat may amount to postponing conduct in the situation where a prior interest has been created and a further interest is created in ignorance of the prior interest: *Butler v. Fairclough* (1917) 23 C.L.R. 78; *Abigail v. Lapin* [1934] A.C. 491. The failure of the prior interest holder in not lodging a caveat to protect his interest may result in that interest being postponed to the later interest. As the cases in this area show, this is not a universal rule.

As will be seen from *Re Rush and Hazell and the Real Property Act* [1963] N.S.W.R. 78, a caveat will protect an interest only if it is lodged before the lodgment for registration of some instrument evidencing competing rights. A caveat lodged after a competing instrument is lodged for registration will not affect the rights secured by the interest awaiting registration: confirmed in s. 74H(4).

A caveat should identify the caveator and his address, indicate the identity and address of the registered proprietor, indicate where notice may be served if an instrument is lodged which competes with the interest claimed in the caveat, specify the interest claimed, specify the title or registered dealing affected, specify the area of land affected by the caveat and be signed by the caveator or, where appropriate, his agent or attorney. It is most important that the interest claimed should be specified clearly and completely: *Palmer v. Wiley* (1906) 23 W.N. (N.S.W.) 90; *Easton v. Ardizzone* [1978] 2 N.S.W.L.R. 233; see ss 74F(5), 74L and reg. 6B.

1. Effect of a caveat

RE RUSH AND HAZELL AND THE REAL PROPERTY ACT

Supreme Court of New South Wales [1963] N.S.W.R. 78

[The circumstances were that a caveat had been lodged to protect an interest and this caveat was followed by the lodgment of a mortgage for registration. A further caveat was lodged to protect an interest. At this point notice was served upon the first caveator and the caveat lapsed because no action was taken upon the notice.]

McLELLAND C.J. IN EQ.
Section 74 of the Act is in the following terms:

> So long as any caveat remains in force prohibiting the transfer or other dealing with land, the Registrar-General shall not, except with the written consent of

the caveator or his agent, enter in the register-book any memorandum of transfer or other instrument purporting to transfer or otherwise deal with or affect the land, estate, or interest in respect to which such caveat is lodged:

Provided that nothing in this section shall prevent the entry in the register-book of a memorandum of transfer or other instrument presented for registration before and waiting registration at the time of the lodgment of the caveat and not afterwards withdrawn.

The short question is whether the memorandum of mortgage was, at the relevant times subsequent to 22 August 1961, an instrument awaiting registration within the meaning of the proviso.

It is not in dispute that the memorandum of mortgage was in a registrable form and that it was in order in a formal sense. On behalf of the Registrar-General it has been argued that in order to be described as "awaiting registration" it must, at the relevant time, be able to be registered and only awaiting, as it were, its turn in the queue with a clear run ahead of it and that in the present case that was not the position because caveat No. H842252 lodged prior to 22 August 1961, stood in the way. The correct description of the memorandum of mortgage, it was said, was an instrument awaiting rejection.

I am of opinion that this is too narrow a view of the proviso. The memorandum of mortgage was lodged in the Land Titles Office for registration. It was complete and in proper form for registration and I am of opinion that it answered the description of an instrument awaiting registration. It is true that whilst the caveat H842252 remained in force s. 74 prevented the memorandum of mortgage from being registered but that fact in my view did not prevent it within the ordinary meaning of the words from being properly described as an instrument "awaiting registration".

. . . [A] memorandum of transfer or other instrument awaiting registration cannot be denied registration by a caveat lodged after the date on which that instrument was presented for registration. It would appear reasonably plain that s. 43A(1) and the new proviso to s. 74 had a similar or related objective, that is, to ensure that a person taking a transfer or a mortgage of or other registrable instrument affecting land under the *Real Property Act* should not be prevented from obtaining registration of the instrument and thus obtaining the benefit of the provisions of s. 43 by reason of events, whether receipt of notice of an equitable interest or the lodgment of a caveat, occurring after the date of settlement, which would be the point of time at which the transfer, mortgage, or other instrument in registrable form would be handed over. Section 43A(1) in deeming the estate or interest taken under the unregistered but registrable instrument to be a legal estate, protects the transferee or mortgagee against the effect of notice, between the time of settlement and the time of registration, of outstanding equitable interests, that is, interests created before the date of settlement and brought to the notice of the transferee or mortgagee after settlement but before registration of the instrument in question. The proviso to s. 74 is supplemental to this provision in that it deprives a caveat lodged after the presentation for registration of a registrable instrument of any delaying or other effect upon such instrument. . . .

I direct the Registrar-General to register the memorandum of mortgage No. H864693.

In this case the instrument is in registrable form and otherwise in order in a formal way and when caveat H842252 lapsed could have been immediately registered.

The question relating to an instrument not in registrable form or not wholly in order in a formal sense, or which for some reason other than the existence of a caveat lodged prior in time, could not be registered immediately, I leave open for consideration when the question arises.

Order accordingly.

NOTE

See below for a consideration of s. 43A in New South Wales, which protects a "purchaser" in the period between completion and registration and which also involves an investigation of the nature of a dealing which may be said to be awaiting registration after it has been lodged for registration.

2. Duty to caveat

BUTLER v. FAIRCLOUGH

High Court of Australia (1917) 23 C.L.R. 78

[Good was the registered proprietor of a Crown lease which was subject to a mortgage. On 30 June he entered into an agreement, under seal, with Butler, whereby he agreed to charge the lease with a debt he owed to Butler and to execute a legal mortgage over the leasehold to the extent of the debt. Then, for valuable consideration, on 2 July 1915 Good agreed to sell the lease to the defendant, Fairclough, subject to the registered mortgage. Fairclough had no notice of Butler's unregistered mortgage. On 7 July 1915, the plaintiff, Butler, lodged a caveat to protect his equitable mortgage. On 12 July, Fairclough lodged the transfer for registration. On 23 July notice was served by the Registrar-General on the plaintiff caveator. On 6 October the parties conferred and it was agreed that Butler's unregistered mortgage had priority and that Fairclough should withdraw his transfer. On further advice, however, Fairclough relodged his transfer in March 1916. The Registrar-General did not give notice of the relodging to the caveator, as he thought, mistakenly, that Butler's caveat had lapsed when notice was given previously. Fairclough's transfer was registered. On appeal to the High Court.]

GRIFFITH C.J. Before dealing with these questions it will be convenient to consider the nature and effect of a caveat. That depends upon the provisions of ss 183-185 of the *Transfer of Land Act*. Section 183 provides that any beneficiary or person claiming any estate or interest in land under the operation of the Act under any unregistered instrument may lodge a caveat in the prescribed form forbidding the registration of any person as transferee of, and of any instrument affecting, such estate or interest either absolutely or conditionally. By s. 184 the Registrar of Titles is required on receipt of the caveat to notify it to the proprietor against whose title to deal with the estate or interest it has been lodged. Provisions then follow for the removal of the caveat by order of the Supreme Court at the suit of the registered proprietor or person claiming under him. The section proceeds: "Except in the case of a caveat lodged by or on behalf of a beneficiary claiming under any will or settlement or by the Registrar pursuant to the direction of the Commissioner every caveat lodged against a proprietor shall be deemed to have lapsed upon the expiration of fourteen days after notice given to the caveator that such proprietor has applied for the registration of a transfer or other dealing or the issue of a registration abstract. A caveat shall not be renewed by or on behalf of the same person in respect of the same estate or interest; but if before the expiration of the said period of fourteen days or such further period as is specified in any order made under this section the caveator or his agent appears before a Judge and gives such undertakings or security or lodges such sum in Court as such Judge considers sufficient to indemnify every person against any damage that may be sustained by reason of any disposition of the property being delayed, then and in such case such Judge may direct the Registrar to delay registering any dealing with the land lease mortgage or charge or issuing a registration abstract for a further period to be specified in such order, or may make such other order and in either case such order as to costs as is just.''

The effect of these provisions is not to enlarge or add to the existing proprietary rights of the caveator upon which the caveat is founded, but to protect those rights, if he has any. In the case of a caveat lodged by a beneficiary or equitable mortgagee its effect is to prevent the registration of any instrument the registration of which might have the effect of defeating his equitable interest in the land without giving him an opportunity of invoking the assistance of the court to give effect to that interest. But if he desires to do so he must take prompt action, that is, within 14 days, or the caveat will lapse, that is, the protection afforded by it will cease. In the case of such a caveat it might well happen that several instruments might be lodged by different persons, any of which, if registered, would pro tanto deprive the caveator of his equitable interest. It is suggested that the effect of the section is that the caveator must take proceedings to invoke the jurisdiction of the court within 14 days against the first of such persons who lodges an instrument for registration, and that, if for any reason he does not do so, the caveat is absolutely gone and can never be revived. It is obvious that the reasons which may induce such a caveator to refrain from taking action may be various. For instance, the instrument lodged for registration may be voluntarily withdrawn, or the caveator may not desire to prevent its registration. But it would be a singular result if the whole benefit of the system were in such a case lost to the beneficiary or equitable mortgagee unless he formally invoked the intervention of the court in a manner which would be either futile or contrary to his wishes. We are informed that until recently the Titles Office acted on the broader view, but that shortly before the re-lodging of the defendant's transfer the Registrar of Titles adopted the narrower view that a caveat absolutely and finally lapses if for any reason legal proceedings are not instituted by the caveator within 14 days after notice of the lodgment of the first instrument capable of affecting his title.

In my opinion the object of the provision was to give a permanent protection to such an equitable owner, subject only to the condition that he should take prompt action against any person who endeavoured to affect his rights prejudicially. The words of s. 184 are perhaps open to a wider construction, but the provision requiring the caveator to give security seems to me to imply that the sufficiency of the security is to be estimated with regard to the possible effect of delay upon some other known party, and not to the whole value of the caveator's interest, which would be the test if his security was to be given then, once for all, and for the benefit of all the world. I think, further, that in the sentence ''every caveat lodged against a proprietor shall be deemed to have lapsed upon the expiration of fourteen days etc.'' the words ''shall be deemed to have lapsed'' may be read as if transposed to follow the words ''upon the expiration of fourteen days etc.'' and should be read secundum materiam, that is to say, that the caveat shall be deemed to have lapsed so far as regards the attempted dealing of which notice has been given to the caveator. Another point of view which leads to the same result is to regard the specified term of 14 days as a period during which a right is maturing adversely to the caveator; so that if that inchoate right sooner comes to an end the 14 days cease to run. Applying the doctrine that in the case of ambiguity a document should be construed so as if possible to give effect to the obvious intention of the framers, I think that the construction I have indicated is the true one, and that when an instrument is withdrawn or the registered proprietor does not desire to prevent its registration such a caveat does not become inoperative except as against the instrument lodged, and that the former practice of the Titles Office was not only in conformity with, but prescribed by, the statute. . . . It must now be taken to be well settled that under the Australian system of registration of titles to land the courts will recognise equitable estates and rights except so far as they are precluded from doing so by the statutes. This recognition is, indeed, the foundation of the scheme of caveats which enable such rights to be temporarily protected in anticipation of legal proceedings. In dealing with such equitable rights the courts in general act upon the principles which are applicable to equitable interests in land which is not subject to the Acts. In the case of a contest between two equitable claimants the first in time, all other things being equal, is entitled to priority. But all other things must be equal, and the claimant who is first in time may lose his priority by any act or omission which had or might have had the effect of inducing a claimant later in time to act to his prejudice. Thus, if an equitable mortgagee of lands allows the mortgagor to retain possession of the title deeds, a person dealing with the mortgagor on the faith of that possession is entitled to priority in the absence of special circumstances to account for it.

Under the Australian system a clear title on the Register is, for some purposes at any rate, equivalent to possession of the title deeds. A person who has an equitable charge upon the land may protect it by lodging a caveat, which in my opinion operates as notice to all the world that the registered proprietor's title is subject to the equitable interest alleged in the caveat. In the present case the plaintiff might, if he had been sufficiently diligent, have registered his charge of 30 June on that day. The defendant, having before parting with the purchase money to Good found on searching the Register that Good had a clear title, and relying on the absence of any notice of defect in Good's title, paid the agreed price.

The question then seems to be: Had the plaintiff when the defendant acquired his equitable right taken or failed to take all reasonable steps to prevent Good from dealing with the land without notice of plaintiff's title? The cases of *Barnes v. James* (1902) 27 V.L.R. 749 and *General Finance Agency etc. Co. v. Perpetual Executors & Trustees Assoc. of Australia Ltd* (1902) 27 V.L.R. 739 are weighty pronouncements by a'Beckett and Holroyd JJ. to the effect that this is the decisive question.

It is contended that the holder of an equitable charge is entitled to a longer time than a day before protecting his title by a caveat. If a man having a registrable instrument neither lodges it for registration nor lodges a caveat to protect it, it is clear that a registrable instrument later in date, but lodged before his, will have precedence, notwithstanding notice of the earlier instrument received before lodging his own. That is by reason of the express provisions of the statute. But why should not the same principle apply in the case of equitable interests? The alternative view would in effect give as great validity to an unregistered equitable assignment unprotected by caveat as to a registrable instrument lodged for registration.

I feel unable to draw any line prescribing the time within which a caveat should be lodged. The person who does not act promptly loses the advantage which he would have gained by promptitude.

For these reasons I come to the conclusion that if a suit had been brought on 3 July between the plaintiff and defendant raising the question of priority the defendant would have been entitled to succeed. Nothing that has since happened can deprive him of this right unless the arrangement of 6 October had the effect of creating a new right in him. I have already dealt with that question. For even if the defendant obtained registration by fraud the plaintiff must recover on the strength of his own title, and if he had none he has not been prejudiced by the defendant's action.

The same consideration affords an answer to the suggested argument founded on s. 185 of the Act, which forbids an entry in the register of any dealing with land in respect of which a caveat has been lodged and remains in force. If the plaintiff is a stranger he cannot be heard to raise the question. But, in my opinion, this enactment does not bring a case in which the prohibition has been disregarded within the decision of the Judicial Committee in *Gibbs v. Messer* [1891] A.C. 248, or deprive a registered proprietor of the protection of s. 72.

ISAACS J. In my opinion, in the absence of some clear explanation justifying or excusing this failure it is one which, at all events in so simple a case as an equitable mortgage, postpones the mortgagee to the person bona fide misled by the result of a search as in the present case. The protection given by the Act to an unregistered and, perhaps, unregistrable transaction is coupled with the price of diligence in guarding others against loss arising through ignorance of the transaction. . . .

There remains the contention raised under s. 185, that that section constitutes a standing prohibition to the Registrar against registering a dealing so long as a caveat forbidding it is in force. The argument substantially is that the section creates an exception from the general authority of the Registrar to register a dealing, and any attempt on his part to register in such case is a nullity. The contention involves two assumptions: (1) that there was a caveat in force, and (2) that the registration notwithstanding the caveat was void.

As to the first assumption, though the legislature, by an amending Act, No. 2849, has placed the question beyond doubt for the future, it is necessary, in view of the possibilities arising out of the recently adopted practice in the Titles Office, to say that the caveat in this case was in force notwithstanding the events of October 1915.

Section 184 gives a caveator 14 days after notice to him that the proprietor had applied to register a dealing, to consider whether he will permit the dealing to pass unchallenged or will contest it. He has the whole 14 days to consider which course he will take. This necessarily contemplates a live application persisted in the whole time by the proprietor or the person whom the law regards as acting for the proprietor in so applying. If, however, the application is withdrawn within 14 days so that the caveator's right is acknowledged without a contest, the period of 14 days of inactivity contemplated by the section ceases to run. The Act is not so absurd as to insist on the caveator taking proceedings against a non-existent competitor. The view acted on in the Titles Office for many years previously was right, and in law the caveat still existed when the transfer was re-lodged in March 1916.

Then comes the second assumption as to nullity. It would be a strange result if a transferee, who possibly knew nothing of a caveat, and therefore nothing of the Registrar's omission, and who in due course, as he believed, became registered proprietor, and on the faith of his certificate and the guarantee given by s. 72, built on the land, should find that he owned nothing, that his certificate was a nullity, and, further, that he was unprovided for with regard to the assurance fund since he had been deprived of nothing. It would not only be strange, but it would not be in consonance with the central feature of the Act—the conclusiveness of a certificate based on a real and innocent transaction with the registered proprietor: see *Assets Co. Ltd v. Mere Roihi* [1905] A.C. at 211-212.

[Barton J. concurred in the judgment of Isaacs J. Gavan Duffy and Rich JJ. dissented.]

Appeal dismissed.

ABIGAIL v. LAPIN

Judicial Committee of the Privy Council [1934] A.C. 491

[The Lapins were the registered proprietors of land under the *Real Property Act*. As security for a loan they transferred their land to Mrs Heavener, who registered her transfer. The transfer was absolute in form and the Lapins did not lodge a caveat to protect their interest. Heavener, representing herself as absolute owner, mortgaged the land to Abigail in return for a loan. Abigail did not have notice of the Lapins' rights but had not searched the Register. Abigail's mortgage was unregistered when the Lapins lodged a caveat to protect their rights.]

LORD WRIGHT. The *Real Property Act* 1900 (N.S.W.), embodies what has been called, after the name of its originator, the Torrens system of the registration of title to land. It is a system which is in force throughout Australasia and in other parts as well. It is a system for the registration of title, not of deeds; the statutory form of transfer gives a title in equity until registration, but when registered it has the effect of a deed and is effective to pass the legal title; upon the registration of a transfer, the estate or interest of the transferor as set forth in such instrument with all rights, powers and privileges thereto belonging or appertaining is to pass to the transferee. No notice of trusts may be entered in the register book, but it has long been held that equitable claims and interests in land are recognised under the *Real Property Act*. This was held in *Barry v. Heider* (1914) 19 C.L.R. 197 and in *Great Western Permanent Loan Co. v. Friesen* [1925] A.C. 208; for the protection of such equitable interests or estates, the Act provides that a caveat may be lodged with the registrar by any person claiming as cestui que trust, or under any unregistered instrument or any other estate or interest; the effect of the caveat is that no instrument will be registered while the caveat is in force affecting the land, estate or interest until after a certain notice to the person lodging the caveat. Thus, though the legal interest is in general determined by the registered transfer, and is in law subject only to registered mortgages or other charges, the Register may bear on its face a notice of equitable claims, so as to warn persons dealing in respect of the land to enable the equitable claimant to protect his claim by enabling him to bring an action if his claim be disputed. In the Registry all statutory transfers are filed and duplicate certificates of title are kept and noted up from time to time with all registered dealings; the other duplicate certificate of title is held by the registered proprietor. The Register is open to inspection and search.

Provision is made by the Act for mortgages in statutory form, and for their registration; in such a case the legal estate remains in the registered proprietor of the fee simple, and the mortgage constitutes a charge of debt on the land; hence it may not be technically correct, though it is common, to speak of the mortgagor as having the equity of redemption, though the legal title remains in him. But a practice has sprung up of affecting [sic] what amounts to a mortgage by registering an instrument of transfer of the legal title from the mortgagor, and at the same time executing a document certifying that it was by way of security only. This is no doubt done for the purpose of facilitating dealings with the land by the transferee. Such a practice has been recognised in various decisions of the courts, and in particular in *Currey v. Federal Building Society* (1929) 42 C.L.R. 421. In the present case the same result was effected as the judge found as between the parties by an oral agreement; but all that appeared in the Registry was the absolute grant of transfer as for full consideration paid and received; no document of qualification was executed and no caveat was lodged. In the result the public register showed to all the world, that is, to any one who cared to inspect, that the fee simple was in the two estates vested in Mrs Heavener; the equity of redemption (if it is so to be called for convenience) was in no way indicated to any searcher of the register.

The Full Court of New South Wales regarded the present case as governed in principle by *Butler v. Fairclough* (1917) 23 C.L.R. 78 at 91, already mentioned, where there was a conflict of equities between a prior equitable incumbrancer who had lodged no caveat and a subsequent transferee who had, after a search of the register and without notice of the unregistered equitable charge, paid the purchase consideration. It was held that the former was to be postponed.

[His Lordship cited with approval the passage in the judgment of Griffith C.J. in *Butler v. Fairclough* beginning "It must now be taken" and ending "paid the agreed price", extracted above, p. 142 (second half of first paragraph to end second paragraph), and continued:]

Their Lordships think that case was rightly decided, though it may be that the statement as to retention of the title deeds needs some qualification. But the only distinction between *Butler v. Fairclough* (1917) 23 C.L.R. 78 at 91 and the present case appears to be that in the present case it was not proved that (though he had no notice of the prior charge) Abigail made any search before lending the money: he said he instructed his conveyancing clerk Harris to examine the title and left it to him. Though there is no reason why Harris should have neglected his duty, Harris was not called, it seems, because of the unfortunate course taken at the trial of raising fresh issues after the evidence was closed. That the question whether or not a search of the register had been made might be regarded as of decisive importance, does not emerge on the record or in any of the judgments until those in the High Court. The question is whether in such a case as this, where the title on the register was clear, the failure to prove a search by the second incumbrancer can make any difference. There is no reason to think that Heavener would have ventured to claim that Mrs Heavener was proprietor in fee simple unless she was so registered, and in that sense the grant of the transfer by the respondents to her did cause or contribute to Abigail's lending the money. A search by or on behalf of Abigail would merely have shown that the transfer purported to be for full consideration, thus excluding any idea of it being by way of security. . . .

But it may be that the majority judgment in the High Court laid emphasis on the absence of search of the register by Abigail because they were of opinion that there must be something in the nature of a direct representation by the respondents to Abigail. In fact, in this case the only documents under the hand of the respondents or either of them which a search would have revealed are the transfers, the terms of which embody a transfer out and out as for full consideration: and if these had been seen by or on behalf of Abigail they might in one sense be construed as a direct respresentation from them to him; but it seems that the transfers were put on the register by the Heaveners, not by the respondents: the transfers could thus only in an artificial sense be described as representations made by the respondents to Abigail. In truth, the essence of the matter was the conduct of the respondents in giving the transfers to Heavener: so far as there was any representation in any strict sense to Abigail, it was made by Heavener. In *Dixon v. Muckleston* (1872) L.R. 8 Ch. 155 at 160 Lord Selborne in terms distinguishes the case of an express representation from the case of acts or of negligence: a man, he says, "is not entitled to deny being bound by the natural consequence of his own acts, if it be a case of positive acts". He adds, in much the same language as that of Kindersley V.-C. quoted above: "By one or other of those means he may have armed another person with the power of going into the world under false colours; and if it be really and truly the case that by this act, or his improper omissions, such an apparent authority and power has been vested in that other person, he is bound upon equitable principles by the use made of that apparent authority and power." Lord Selborne also adds that the equitable charge will be good if there has been a positive statement honestly believed.

It is true that in cases of conflicting equities the decision is often expressed to turn on representations made by the party postponed, as for instance in *King v. King* [1931] 2 Ch. 294. But it is seldom that the conduct of the person whose equity is postponed takes or can take the form of a direct representation to the person whose equity is preferred: the actual representation is in general, as in the present case, by the third party, who has been placed by the conduct of the party postponed in a position to make the representation, most often, as here, because that party has vested in him a legal estate or has given him the indicia of a legal estate in excess of the interest which he was entitled in fact to have, so that he has in consequence been enabled to enter into the transaction with the third party on the faith of his possessing the larger estate. Such is the position here, which in their Lordships' judgment entitles the appellants to succeed in this appeal.

In the High Court Gavan Duffy and Starke JJ. also relied on a further or supplementary reasoning, based on the principle of an authority being acted upon to create the later equity, but acted upon either contrary to or in excess of the authority actually intended to be given. As they point out, the form of actual transfer was adopted "so that Olivia Sophia Heavener might deal with the lands as if they were her own and without the restrictions created by an instrument of mortgage under the Act of New South Wales": she was thus necessarily trusted by the respondents as to the time and method of realisation (that is, in order to pay the cash due to her husband) and not to exceed the limits of her security. On this view the case falls within the general principles laid down in *Brocklesby v. Temperance Permanent Building Society* [1895] A.C. 173 at 180. Lord Herschell L.C. thus sums up the rule: "Where a person has thus been entrusted with the possession of title deeds with authority to raise money upon them, the owner of the deeds cannot take advantage of any limitation in point of amount which he has placed upon the authority as against a lender who had no notice of it." The same principle, it was held, had been applied in equity in the case of *Perry Herrick v. Attwood* (1857) 2 De G. & J. 21. This decision of the House of Lords was followed in the later case of *Rimmer v. Webster* [1902] 2 Ch. 163 at 173, where certain stock had been transferred to a broker by the owner with instructions to sell it, but the broker abused his position as transferee of the stock in order to borrow money for his own purposes on its security: it was held by Farwell J. that the borrower's equity must prevail: Sir George Farwell thus stated the principle: "When . . . the owner is found to have given the vendor or borrower the means of representing himself as the beneficial owner, the case forms one of actual authority apparently equivalent to absolute ownership, and involving the right to deal with the property as owner, and any limitations on this generality must be proved to have been brought to the knowledge of the purchaser or mortgagee."

The foundation of the rule is that there has been an authority to deal with the property, as Gavan Duffy and Starke JJ. in the High Court have here found that there was; no doubt they have so found as an inference from all the facts, but their Lordships accept the finding. The case then becomes one of an agent exceeding the limits of his authority but acting within its apparent indicia. *Rimmer v. Webster*

[1902] 2 Ch. 163 at 173 has been approved by the Board in *Tsang Chuen v. Li Po Kwai* [1932] A.C. 715. *Burgis v. Constantine* [1908] 2 K.B. 484 contains nothing contrary to this rule; as Sir George Farwell there points out, the case before the court was to be distinguished from *Rimmer v. Webster* because it was one of trustee and cestui que trust, to which he thought the principles of the *Shropshire Union Railways and Canal Co.'s* case (1875) L.R. 7 H.L. 496 were applicable. Their Lordships agree with Gavan Duffy and Starke JJ. that on this ground also the appellants should succeed.

Appeal allowed.

NOTE

The majority of the High Court of Australia, sub nom. *Lapin v. Abigail* (1930) 44 C.L.R. 166 had taken a different approach to that adopted by the Judicial Committee. On the question of the effect upon equitable priorities of the failure to lodge a caveat, Dixon J. said:

> The view has sometimes been expressed that failure on the part of a prior equitable owner to lodge a caveat is a default sufficient to postpone his interest to a subsequent equity acquired by one who has searched the Register for caveats and, having found none, has thereupon acquired his interest: see *Butler v. Fairclough* (1917) 23 C.L.R. at 91-92 per Griffith C.J. It may be remarked that, if this view be correct, a curious consequence has arisen from the legislative attempt to provide a means of securing prior equitable rights from extinguishment by the registration of inconsistent dealings. Although it is registration which extinguishes the equity, and a caveat is therefore provided as a means of preventing registration, nevertheless, upon this view, failure to use that means affords a reason for defeating the equity or postponing it to the very interest, although unregistered, which, upon the terms of the statute requires registration in order to prevail. No doubt, if it were the settled practice for all owners of equitable interests to lodge caveats, failure to conform to the practice would naturally lead those who search to believe that there was no outstanding equity. It may well be doubted, however, whether such a regular practice has actually been established. But in this case the question need not be pursued because, although the appellants did not caveat, it does not appear that any search for caveats was made on Abigail's behalf or that he acted in the belief that there was no caveat. The default of the appellants—if default it be—therefore did not contribute directly to any assumption upon which Abigail may have dealt with the Heaveners.

J. & H. JUST (HOLDINGS) PTY LTD v. BANK OF NEW SOUTH WALES

High Court of Australia (1971) 125 C.L.R. 546

[The bank loaned money, by way of mortgage, to the registered proprietor of land, Josephson. As security for the loan the bank retained the certificate of title and a properly executed mortgage, in registrable form. The mortgage was not registered nor did the bank lodge a caveat to protect the mortgage. J. & H. Just (Holdings) advanced further moneys to Josephson on the security of the land. They did not sight the certificate of title but inquired as to its whereabouts and accepted the statement of the registered proprietor that it had been lodged with his banker for safe keeping. They lodged a caveat to protect their interest.]

BARWICK C.J. But it was the respondent's conduct in thus arming the mortgagee with the capacity to become the registered proprietor and able to deal with others as such and not any failure by them to lodge a caveat that was decisive in *Abigail v. Lapin* [1934] A.C. 491; 51 C.L.R. 58. Their Lordships' decision was an application of Kindersley V.-C.'s judgment in *Rice v. Rice* (1854) 2 Drew. 73; 61 E.R. 646, from which Lord Wright quotes a passage at 503-504 [of the report of *Abigail v. Lapin*]. A passage from the judgment of Knox C.J. in the case was adopted as setting out the relevant principles for resolving the competition of the parties' interest in the land. Ultimately "the case then becomes one of an agent exceeding the limits of his authority but acting within its apparent indicia" per Lord Wright at 72 of the report. I emphasise these aspects of the decision *Abigail v. Lapin* by the Privy Council because, once it is recognised that the respondents' conduct in handing over the memoranda of transfer and the duplicate certificates of title provided the ratio decidendi, much of what Lord Wright says about the consequences of a failure by a claimant to an equitable interest to lodge a caveat and particularly his comments on *Butler v. Fairclough* (1917) 23 C.L.R. 78, became, in my opinion, obiter.

Whilst it may be true in some instances that "the register may bear on its face a notice of equitable claims", this is not necessarily so and whilst in some instances a caveat of which the lodgment is noted in the certificate of title may be "notice to all the world" that the registered proprietor's title is subject to the equitable interest alleged in the caveat this, in my opinion, is not necessarily universally the case. To hold that a failure by a person entitled to an equitable estate or interest in land under the *Real Property Act* to lodge a caveat against dealings with the land must necessarily involve the loss of priority which the time of the creation of the equitable interest would otherwise give, is not merely in my opinion unwarranted by general principles or by any statutory provision but would in my opinion be subversive of the well recognised ability of parties to create or to maintain equitable interests in such lands. Sir Owen Dixon's remarks in *Lapin v. Abigail* (1930) 44 C.L.R. 166 at 205, with which I respectfully agree, point in this direction.

Of course, there may be situations in which such a failure may combine with other circumstances to justify the conclusion that "the act or omission proved against" the possessor of the prior equity "has conduced or contributed to a belief on the part of the holder of the subsequent equity, at the time when he acquired it, that the prior equity was not in existence": cf. per Knox C.J. in *Lapin v. Abigail* at 183-184. This is the relevant principle to apply if it is claimed that the priority of a prior equitable interest has been lost in competition with a subsequent equitable interest. "In general an earlier equity is not to be postponed to a later one unless because of some act or neglect of the prior equitable owner. In order to take away any pre-existing admitted title, that which is relied upon for such a purpose must be shown and proved by those upon whom the burden to show and prove it lies, and . . . it must amount to something tangible and distinct, something which can have the grave and strong effect to accomplish the purpose for which it is said to have been produced", per Lord Cairns L.C. in *Shropshire Union Railways and Canal Co. v. The Queen* (1875) L.R. 7 H.L. 496 at 507. "The act or default of the prior equitable owner must be such as to make it inequitable as between him and the subsequent equitable owner that he should retain his initial priority. This in effect means that his act or default must in some way have contributed to the assumption upon which the subsequent legal owner acted when acquiring his equity", per Dixon J. in *Lapin v. Abigail* at 204.

In my opinion, the failure to lodge a protective caveat cannot properly be said necessarily to be such an act or default. It could not properly be said to be so in the present case.

Mention should now be made of a second reason why in this case the failure to lodge a caveat could not be held to be privative of the bank's priority. The bank held the certificate of title and a memorandum of mortgage in registrable form. Whilst there is no express provision of the Act which forbids the registration of a dealing without the production of the duplicate certificate of title, it is the practice of the Registrar-General's office to refuse to accept an instrument of transfer or mortgage for registration without production of the duplicate certificate of title, unless the certificate is already in the Registrar-General's hands. See Baalman and

Wells, *Land Titles Office Practice* (3rd ed.), pp. 225-226. Thus a person in the situation of the bank could reasonably rely upon this practice and his possession of the duplicate certificate of title is a reasonably sufficient protection. Of course, a provisional certificate of title may be issued by the Registrar-General if the duplicate is lost, mislaid or destroyed: s. 111 of the Act. The stringency of proof required by the Registrar-General before issuing a provisional certificate may be gauged by a perusal of the departmental instructions set out in Baalman and Wells, p. 280. A person in the situation of the bank in this case does run the remote risk of a fraudulent claim being made to the Registrar-General by the borrower in order to obtain a provisional certificate. But, in my opinion, such a person is not to assume such criminal conduct on the part of the registered proprietor.

In any case the failure by such a person to lodge a protective caveat cannot of itself properly be held to be an act fulfilling the requirements to which I have referred of conduct which will deprive a prior equity of its priority. As I have said, the purpose of the caveat is protective: it is not to give notice. The holder of the subsequent equity in my opinion could not properly rely upon the absence of any notification in the register book of the lodgment of a caveat as a representation or as the basis for a conclusion that no equitable interest in the land existed in any person. In my opinion the conclusion and the reasoning of the Court of Appeal Division were correct on this aspect of the case.

The primary judge appears to have taken the view that s. 43A of the Act was a possible source of priority of the appellant's interest under its memorandum of mortgage. He thought the conduct of the appellant or rather that of his solicitor grossly negligent and such as to prevent the appellant having resort to the provision of s. 43A. The Court of Appeal indorsed the primary judge's view of the failure of the appellant's solicitor to obtain production of the duplicate certificate of title. I agree with these views in so far as they might affect the rights of the parties. But I am unable to see the relevance of the appellant's solicitor's conduct to the resolution of those rights. As I have pointed out, unless the priority which time gives to the bank's equitable interest in land is to be lost by reason of the bank's own conduct, there is no need in my opinion, to consider the conduct of the appellant. That conduct might be relevant if, after the bank's priority derived simply from earlier creation of its interest had been lost, a further question of the comparative claims of the holders of the equitable interests should arise. But in this case no such question, in my opinion, did arise.

Further, I have been unable to see the relevance of s. 43A to the problem raised by the case. No question of notice of the bank's interest was suggested to have been obtained by the appellant either at the time of making the loan to Josephson or subsequently until the Registrar-General informed him of the lodgment of the bank's dealing. I forbear therefore to discuss the nature and operation of the provision inserted by amendment in 1930 by No. 44 of that year. But in taking that course I would not wish to be thought to be differing from what was said by Taylor J. in *I.A.C. (Finance) Pty Ltd v. Courtenay* (1963) 110 C.L.R. 550.

MENZIES J. Like other members of the court, I do not find it necessary, in the resolution of this appeal, to consider s. 43A of the *Real Property Act* 1900 (N.S.W.). For the rest, I agree with the judgment of the Court of Appeal.

I would merely add that, in doing so, I am not, I think, differing at all from what was said by Griffith C.J. in *Butler v. Fairclough* (1917) 23 C.L.R. 78 at 91, or by Lord Wright in *Abigail v. Lapin* [1934] A.C. 491 at 502, about a caveat operating by way of notice to protect the equitable interest therein alleged. Furthermore, I see wisdom in using a caveat for this purpose. It is not to be disregarded that the form of caveat in the Sixteenth Schedule to the Act makes provision for a record to be made thereon of the entry of its particulars in the register book. This statutory form is not only ample warrant for the Registrar-General making such an entry; it is an indication from the Act itself that this should be done. The reason for such an entry must be to give notice of the caveat.

WINDEYER J. In my opinion the decision of the Supreme Court, Court of Appeal Division, was correct for the reasons that Jacobs J.A. there gave, except that I do not find it necessary to consider the effect of s. 43A of the *Real Property Act* 1900 (N.S.W.); for in the view that I take it has no direct bearing upon this case. I agree entirely in the judgment of the Chief Justice. Merely to emphasise my agreement I shall briefly state my view of the effect of the bank's not lodging a caveat against dealings, the matter in the forefront of the appellant's argument.

Too much has I think been read into the statement by Griffith C.J. in *Butler v. Fairclough* (1917) 23 C.L.R. 78 at 91—repeated by Lord Wright in the Privy Council in *Abigail v. Lapin* [1934] A.C. 491 at 502: "A person who has an equitable charge upon the land may protect it by lodging a caveat, which in my opinion operates as notice to all the world that the registered proprietor's title is subject to the equitable interest alleged in the caveat." It is the practice of the Registrar-General to note a caveat upon the relevant folium of the register book, although the Act does not require him to do so and a caveat is not a dealing. A caveat noted in the register book is no doubt a notice, to anyone who searches at the Registrar-General's Office, of the caveator's claim. I understand that the Registrar-General records all documents as they are lodged and that he lists caveats as if they were dealings and that this record is available for inspection. It is perhaps a register kept under the Act within the meaning of s. 43(2). However, the fact that a caveat discoverable by a search of the title is "notice to all the world" of the interest claimed does not mean that the absence of a caveat is a notice to all and sundry that no interest is claimed. To say that would, it seems, be to equate the noting of a caveat in the register book with the registration of a dealing: it would make competing equitable interests depend not upon priority of creation in time and other equitable considerations, but upon priority of the lodgment of caveats. After all, the primary purpose of a caveat against dealings is not to give notice to the world of an interest. It is to warn the Registrar-General of a claim. The word caveat has long been used in law to describe a notice given to an official not to take some step without giving the caveator an opportunity to oppose it. According to the *Oxford Dictionary* that sense of the word goes back to 1654. If a person intending to deal with a registered proprietor becomes aware of a caveat, it is notice to him of a claim that an interest is outstanding: and then: caveat emptor; qui ignorare non debuit quod jus alienum emit. But a caveat is not the only way in which a purchaser from the registered proprietor can be made aware of the prior equitable claims of another person. It is merely one way, and no doubt a very sure way, in which such a claimant may protect his interest against its subversion by the registered proprietor in favour of another person. As Jacobs J.A. said in this case—and I agree: "The particular way of protecting his interest and giving notice which was dealt with by Griffith C.J. was the lodging of a caveat but I cannot take his words to mean that that is the only way. His words did not touch the long-established practice of equitable mortgage or charge by deposit of that document or those documents without which no reasonable person dealing with an owner of land would proceed to the completion of the conveyancing transaction."

I can understand that a bank may, for good reasons, not wish to give notice to all the world that it has a charge over a customer's land to secure his overdraft. It may prefer to protect itself by obtaining and retaining possession of the duplicate certificate of title, without producing which no one can register a dealing with the land. I interpolate here that I use words "duplicate certificate of title" to denote the deed issued to the registered proprietor in distinction from the corresonding folium of the register book. That is the common usage of the term; and it is I think the sense of the words in s. 40; but I am aware that s. 32(1) states that "The Registrar-General shall keep a book, to be called the 'register book', and shall bind up therein the duplicates of all grants and certificates of title".

If, as I see the case, the equitable interest of the bank is not to be lost or postponed because the bank did not lodge a caveat, it seems to me irrelevant to enquire whether the appellant was prudent or imprudent in not prosecuting further enquiries before it lent money to the registered proprietor thinking it had the land as security. The conduct of the appellant would only be material if the bank, by some conduct on its part, had lost the priority in equity which arose from the priority of its transaction in point of time. The bank did not by not lodging a caveat warning the Registrar-General represent to the appellant that it had no claim. It relied upon its possession of a registrable instrument and a clean duplicate certificate of title. It is not to suffer because the registered proprietor made a statement to the appellant that was very far from frank in explanation of the bank's having his duplicate certificate of title.

[McTiernan and Owen JJ. concurred in the judgment of the Chief Justice.]

NOTES AND QUESTIONS

1. As to whether failure to caveat is a relevant consideration in determining "postponing conduct", particularly where there is a failure to obtain custody of the Certificate of Title, see also *Clarke v. Raymor (Brisbane) Pty Ltd (No. 2)* [1982] Qd R. 790. The judgment of Andrews S.P.J. suggests that it will be postponing conduct. However, the case is authority for a broader principle that the competition between unregistered interests is determined upon general principles of equity: the proper approach is to determine where the better equity lies after examination of all relevant facts and circumstances including the entire conduct of each equity holder in relation to his interest, and the fact that one interest is prior in point of time is a matter of last resort only.

2. The decision of the Court of Appeal in *Reliance Finance Corp. Pty Ltd v. Heid* [1982] 1 N.S.W.L.R. 466 suggests that, in line with the *Just* case, it will not be postponing conduct to fail to caveat where the Certificate of Title is handed by the registered proprietor to her or his solicitor for the purpose of dealing with the property. This point was not decided when the case went on appeal to the High Court of Australia (1983) 57 A.L.J.R. 683. However, it is submitted that this view is consistent with the *Just* case as well as *Butler* and *Abigail*. In addition, it should be also the case that depositing the Certificate of Title with a solicitor for safe keeping is, likewise, not postponing conduct where no caveat is recorded. Nevertheless, it is possible for a caveat to be lodged in such circumstances: s. 74F(2) permits the lodgment of a caveat by a registered proprietor who "fears an improper dealing" with her or his interest.

3. In *Ryan v. Nothelfer* (1983) N.S.W. Conv. R. 55-119, Needham J. held that failure to caveat was not postponing conduct. This decision is inconsistent with the general approach in all of the precedents which hold to the contrary, except where there is good reason, such as occurred in the *Just* case or in the circumstances explained in 2 above.

4. In *Person-to-Person Financial Services Ltd v. Sharari* [1984] 1 N.S.W.L.R. 745, McLelland J. refused to follow *Ryan v. Nothelfer*, holding it to be inconsistent with *Butler v. Fairclough*. His Honour said that failure to caveat would be postponing conduct on the facts and that there was considerable authority in this regard, since the decision of the High Court of Australia in *J. & H. Just (Holdings) Pty Ltd v. Bank of New South Wales*. The court quoted *Osmanoski v. Rose* [1974] V.R. 523, below, in support.

5. In *King v. A.G.C. (Advances) Ltd* [1983] V.R. 682, the registered proprietor charged his strata title property to secure repayment of an advance. The property comprised a home unit and a garage, with a separate title for each. The chargee lodged a caveat over the title to the home unit, but not over the title to the garage. The property was then sold to a purchaser, who claimed priority over the

chargee's interest in the garage because of failure to caveat in respect of the garage. Under the Victorian strata titles legislation, the home unit and the garage could not be dealt with separately. (A similar provision exists in New South Wales: s. 39 of the *Strata Titles Act* 1973 (N.S.W.).) The Victorian Full Court held that in view of this provision and since a caveat had been lodged in respect of the unit, the failure to lodge a caveat over the garage was not postponing conduct, with the result that the chargee's interest prevailed in respect of both titles.

6. In *Osmanoski v. Rose* [1974] V.R. 523 the registered proprietors executed a sale note (in effect, entered into a contract for sale) to the Osmanoskis who failed to caveat. Then the registered proprietors executed another sale note to Rose. The *Just Holdings* case was distinguished and *Butler* and *Abigail* were applied. Gowans J. held the failure to caveat to be postponing conduct on the part of the Osmanoskis.

ARTICLES

"Equitable Interests under the Torrens System—Caveats and Searches" (1935) 8 A.L.J. 413; Kerr, D., "The Drafting of a Caveat" (1927) 1 A.L.J. 73; Robinson, S., "Caveatable Interests—Their Nature and Priority" (1970) 44 A.L.J. 351.

F.   SETTLEMENT TO REGISTRATION

Special protection is advanced to a "purchaser" in the period from "settlement" to registration: see *Real Property Act* 1900, s. 43A(1).

"Settlement" or "completion" is the point in time in a conveyancing transaction when the purchaser, having been satisfied as to the title to the property, pays over the balance of the purchase price. If the land is under the provisions of the Torrens Act the purchaser will receive the Certificate of Title together with a memorandum of transfer. If the land is under "old" system title the purchaser will receive the title deeds together with a deed of conveyance transferring the property to him.

When the land is under "old" system title the deed of conveyance will pass the "legal" estate to the purchaser, and so a purchaser who buys bona fide for value without notice will take free of any outstanding equitable interests. If he does not acquire the legal estate upon completion, but only an equitable estate, he may be able to protect his purchase by virtue of the doctrine of tabula in naufragio: in essence this doctrine permits a holder of an equitable estate to take priority over a prior equitable estate if the holder of the subsequent equitable estate can acquire the legal estate without notice and without committing a breach of trust. Any purchaser, under the rule nemo dat quod non habet (one cannot sell that which he does not own), takes subject to a prior legal estate even if he does not have notice of it unless he is, by virtue of registration, entitled to the protection advanced by s. 184G of the *Conveyancing Act* 1919 (N.S.W.) (formerly, s. 12 of the *Registration of Deeds Act* 1897 (N.S.W.)).

Where the land is under the provisions of the various Torrens statutes all that the purchaser holds on settlement is an equitable interest. It is the act of registration which confers the statutory estate equivalent to the "legal" estate in the "old" system. In the intervening period it is possible for a person claiming a competing interest to seek an injunction restraining the Registrar-General from registering the transfer. If it can be shown that the applicant for injunctive relief has a better equity than the purchaser, he will take priority over the purchaser. It follows that a purchaser of land under the *Real Property Act* is not in as secure a position as is his counterpart who purchases land under "old" system title. It was to fill this lacuna that s. 43A(1) of the *Real Property Act* was passed. The subsection provides:

For the purpose only of protection against notice, the estate or interest in land under the provisions of this Act, taken by a person under a dealing registrable, or which when appropriately signed by or on behalf of that person would be registrable under this Act shall, before registration of that dealing, be deemed to be a legal estate.

The most important judicial interpretation of the effect of the subsection is contained in the extract following.

I.A.C. (FINANCE) PTY LTD v. COURTENAY

High Court of Australia (1963) 110 C.L.R. 550
(On appeal from the Supreme Court of New South Wales sub nom.
Courtenay v. Austin [1962] N.S.W.R. 296)

[Miss Austin, as registered proprietor, entered into a contract to sell land to the Courtenays. Later, on settlement, the executed memorandum of transfer and the Certificate of Title were retained by the vendor, as mortgagee. The transfer and mortgage were then lodged for registration by the vendor, but were later withdrawn by the vendor's solicitor. The vendor then entered into a contract to sell the land to Denton Subdivisions Pty Ltd. The sale was financed by mortgages including one to I.A.C. The transfer to Denton Subdivisions Pty Ltd and the mortgages were lodged for registration. Courtenay brought a suit to establish a right to be registered in preference to Denton Subdivisions Pty Ltd and I.A.C. Upon settlement of the sale to Denton Subdivisions Pty Ltd, the solicitor acting for Denton became aware of the transaction in favour of the Courtenays.]

HARDIE J. (at first instance) . . . I am of opinion that the introductory words of s. 43A(1) are to be construed as conferring protection, in the circumstances specified in the subsection, against unregistered estates or interests of which no notice was acquired before settlement but of which notice was or might be received after settlement and before registration of the particular dealing.

Some support for the construction of s. 43A(1) adopted above is derived from the fact that the amending Act of 1930 also introduced a proviso into s. 74, the section dealing with effect of a caveat. This new proviso alters the law so that a memorandum of transfer or other instrument awaiting registration cannot be denied registration by a caveat lodged after the date on which that instrument was presented for registration. It would appear reasonably plain that s. 43A(1) and the new proviso to s. 74 had a similar or related objective, that is, to ensure that a person taking a transfer or a mortgage of or other registrable instrument affecting land under the *Real Property Act* should not be prevented from obtaining registration of the instrument and thus obtaining the benefit of the provisions of s. 43 by reason of events, whether receipt of notice of an equitable interest or the lodgment of a caveat, occurring after the date of settlement, which would be the point of time at which the transfer, mortgage, or other instrument in registrable form would be handed over. Section 43A(1), in deeming the estate or interest taken under the unregistered but registrable instrument to be a legal estate, protects the transferee or mortgagee against the effect of notice, between the time of settlement and the time of registration, of outstanding equitable interests that is, interests created before the date of settlement and brought to the notice of the transferee or mortgagee after settlement but before registration of the instrument in question. The proviso to s. 74 is supplemental to this provision in that it deprives a caveat lodged after the presentation for registration of a registrable instrument of any delaying or other effect upon such instrument. It is not necessary in this case to consider the effect and operation of s. 43A(1) in relation to registrable instruments arising out of transactions not supported by valuable consideration, nor to consider what effect and operation the subsection has when a person who takes a registered [sic] instrument does not lodge it for registration until some time after its coming into his possession. The subsection undoubtedly assumes that lodgment for registration shall be effected immediately or at any event promptly; however, it does not so provide.

Section 43A(1) appears to be directed primarily to protecting a person taking under a registrable instrument against notice of equitable interests created by or arising out of instruments other than registrable instruments and also such interests arising out of transactions not embodied in any written document. No express provision is made in the section for the position where there are, as in the present case, two persons claiming, adversely to each other, to be entitled to be registered as proprietors of the same land pursuant to transfers from the same registered proprietor. A possible view of the section is that it has no application to such a case. However, for reasons which will appear later, it is not necessary to pursue the question. I will assume, without so deciding, that the section applied to the memorandum of transfer from Miss Austin to the Denton Company, notwithstanding the fact that there was a competing registrable instrument earlier in date and presented for registration at an earlier point of time.

Section 43A(1) provides that, for the purpose therein stated, the estate or interest taken by a person under a registrable instrument shall be deemed to be a legal estate. It does not say that it shall be deemed to be the statutory estate which would pass by virtue of s. 41(1) on registration of the instrument, nor in my view does the phrase "legal estate" in s. 43A(1) mean the statutory estate; it means a notional legal estate attracting the doctrine of a bona fide purchaser for value without notice, that is, an estate which prevails over and over-reaches outstanding equitable estates and interests of which the person taking the notional legal estate had no notice at the time of receipt of the unregistered but registrable instrument. The subsection thus means that the Denton Company, on receipt of its transfer, took a notional legal estate in the subject land freed from earlier equitable estates of which it had no notice at the relevant time but subject to such earlier equitable estates of which it had notice. The section does not protect the transferee against equitable estates of which it has notice not amounting to fraud, as does s. 43. On the foregoing view of the subsection it becomes material to consider whether the Denton Company had notice, at the time it took the transfer from Miss Austin, of the prior equitable estate or interest of the plaintiffs. . . .

[His honour upheld the Courtenay's claim.]

[On Appeal to High Court.]

KITTO J. The purpose and effect of s. 43A(1) have been the subject of controversy among legal writers, and they are not apparent until the provision is read, as its numbering suggests that it should be, as a supplement to the preceding provisions, and in particular ss 41, 42 and 43. Until registration, a person who has dealt with a registered proprietor cannot have more than an equitable interest, for until that event even a registrable instrument cannot pass the estate or interest which it specifies: s. 41. After registration, he holds, by virtue of s. 42, free from all encumbrances, liens, estates or interests not notified on his certificate of title (with immaterial exceptions); but this does not exlude equitable interests: *Barry v. Heider* (1914) 19 C.L.R. 197; *Great West Permanent Loan Co. v. Friesen* [1925] A.C. 208; *Abigail v. Lapin* [1934] A.C. 491 at 500; (1934) 51 C.L.R. 58 at 64, 65. Even as regards equitable interests he has a degree of immunity by virtue of s. 43. But the immunity under that section is limited: it is only such immunity as is created by exonerating him from the effect of notice of any trust or unregistered interest. "Except in the case of fraud," the section says, "no person contracting or dealing with or taking or proposing to take a transfer from the registered proprietor of any registered estate or interest shall be affected by notice, direct or constructive, of any trust or unregistered interest." It is settled law that the immunity thus conferred, upon a purchaser for example, is afforded to him if and when he becomes registered and not before: *Templeton v. Leviathan Pty Ltd* (1921) 30 C.L.R. 34 at 54, 55; *Lapin v. Abigail* (1930) 44 C.L.R. 166 at 182, 188, 196, 203 (cf. [1934] A.C. at 509; (1934) 51 C.L.R. at 73). In order to appreciate the nature of the addition which s. 43A enacts it is important to have in mind that this conclusion as to the operation of s. 43 is not reached by a process of interpretation. It is a conclusion not as to the meaning of the section but as to the way it works. A purchaser, his interest before registration being necessarily equitable only, derives no priority over the holder of a pre-existing equitable interest from absence of notice: *Phillips v. Phillips* (1861) 4 De G.F. & J. 208 at 215, 216; 45 E.R. 1164 at 1166; *Abigail v. Lapin* [1934] A.C. at 498, 499, 504; (1934) 51 C.L.R. at 63, 64, 68. Consequently, a provision that a person is not to be affected by notice of prior interests has no application to him so long as he remains unregistered. For the same reason, it has no application even to one who has become registered, if he acquired his estate or interest as a volunteer. It is only a person having a legal estate or legal interest acquired for value whose position is prejudiced by his having received, before paying his money, direct or constructive notice of an outstanding equitable interest. This is so even under the *Real Property Act*, for a registered interest is not (as was suggested in the course of the appellants' argument) some special kind of statutory interest—it is a legal interest, acquired by a statutory conveyancing procedure and protected from competition to the extent provided for by the Act, but having, subject to the Act, the nature and incidents provided by the general law. So all that the provision does which I have quoted from s. 43 is to protect against notice of any trust or unregistered interest a legal estate acquired for value. The statement that it has no operation in favour of a person before he becomes registered means, simply, before he acquires a legal estate by registration.

It is to this situation, as I understand the matter, that s. 43A(1) is addressed. Indeed, the introductory words by which its operation is limited, "For the purpose only of protection against notice", preclude, I think, any other view. Something which is less than a legal estate is to be deemed a legal estate for the purpose of the protection against notice which s. 43 provides for a legal estate. What is to receive this protection is the estate or interest in land "taken" by a person under an instrument which either is registrable or, if signed by or on behalf of that person, would be registrable. The word "taken" must be construed having regard to the provision in s. 41 that no instrument until registered shall be effectual to pass any estate or interest in land under the Act. The estate or interest "taken" under an unregistered instrument must therefore mean the estate or interest which the instrument on its true construction purports to confer, and upon its being registered will confer. That estate or interest is given by s. 43A the same immunity from the effect of notice as s. 43 provides for registered estates or interests in virtue of their being legal estates or interests. The result is that (fraud apart) a purchaser may pay his money to the registered proprietor in exchange for a registrable instrument (or one that will be registrable upon his signing it) without troubling about any notice that he may have received of a trust or unregistered interest. Provided that he lodges his instrument for registration before the holder of a competing prior interest renders the purchaser's instrument no longer registrable by lodging a registrable instrument for registration or entering a caveat, s. 36(1) will ensure that the purchaser obtains registration and thus obtains the protection of s. 43: see also s. 36(3). This is so because, by reason of a proviso added to s. 74 by the amending Act which inserted s. 43A, no caveat subsequently entered can defeat him, and the holder of the competing interest will not be entitled to the intervention of a court of equity on the ground that the purchaser acquired his right to registration with notice of that interest.

Accordingly in the present case Denton would be entitled by virtue of s. 43A, in my opinion, to have its transfer from Miss Austin registered, notwithstanding that before the settlement of its purchase it had express notice of the Courtenays' interest, if the Courtenays' prior application for registration had been effectually determined by the action that was taken by Miss Austin's solicitor. . . . In my opinion the proper conclusion in the present case is that the purported withdrawal of the transfer by Miss Austin's solicitor, being unauthorised, left the application for registration on foot notwithstanding the physical removal of the document from the Registrar-General's custody. . . .

TAYLOR J. . . . Clearly enough, the section was designed to deal with the position of the holder of a registrable instrument between the time of its receipt and the time of its registration. But its effect is by no means clear. No doubt it proceeds on the basis that under the law as settled at the date of its enactment s. 43 did not afford any degree of protection to a purchaser prior to registration and that any conflict between competing equitable interests prior to registration fell to be determined according to ordinary equitable principles. That is to say, that the earlier of two competing equitable interests must, in the ordinary course, be taken to prevail over the later. Of course, in any particular case, circumstances may be shown to have existed which will result in the earlier equitable interest being postponed. However, in the case where no such circumstances are shown to have existed, the question whether the second interest was acquired with notice of the earlier interest is completely irrelevant; the prior interest will prevail whether the later interest was acquired with or without notice of it. What use was it then for the section to stipulate "For the purpose only of protection against notice, the estate or interest in land . . . taken by a person under an instrument registrable . . . under this Act shall . . . be deemed to be a legal estate"? The section has been the subject of much professional discussion: see for example Baalman, *A Commentary on The Torrens System in New South Wales* (1951), pp. 176, 177; Kerr, *Australian Land Titles (Torrens) System* (1927), p. 28; and (1932) 6 A.L.J. 85. Various possibilities have been discussed but no really satisfactory answer appears as to the meaning of the section. Read literally it accomplishes nothing. If an intended transferee has paid his purchase money his position will not be worsened by notice, subsequently, of a prior equitable interest. It is, of course, true that his interest may be entirely defeated, in the absence of fraud, by prior registration of the earlier interest but if this occurs he will be defeated, not because he had notice of that interest at any stage, but by the transformation of that interest into the interest of a registered proprietor. On the other hand, if he secures registration first his interest will be likewise transformed into the estate of a registered proprietor and, in the absence of fraud, he will secure an indefeasible estate. Accordingly, a person who has paid his purchase money and who has secured a registrable memorandum of transfer needs no protection against notice received thereafter and a provision which purports, merely to protect him against the effects of notice will not confirm his title. It is, however, not unreasonable to assume that the section was intended to achieve some object. And that object, it seems, was to make some appropriate provision for "filling" what has been called the "gap" left in s. 43 by the "settled law" concerning that section: Baalman, p. 177. Does the section, then go further than merely to afford a so-called protection against notice and operate to give to the holder of a registrable memorandum of transfer priority over an earlier equitable interest where he has, without notice thereof, paid his purchase money and obtained his registrable instrument? The suggestion that it does is based upon the contention that the holder of a registrable instrument in such circumstances is enabled to assert, as against the prior equitable interest, that he has by virtue of the section a legal estate in the land acquired without notice of the earlier interest and that he is, therefore, entitled to perfect his title by registration. Such a construction, it is said, does some violence to the terms of the section but it is, it seems to me, the result, which notwithstanding its "ungainly approach" to the subject (see Baalman, above, p. 177), the section was intended to produce.

A further suggestion is that the section was intended to advance in point of time the protection afforded by s. 43 upon registration. That is to say, that the concluding words of the section—"legal estate"—should be understood to mean "the estate of a registered proprietor". But if it was intended so to advance the unqualified protection by s. 43 upon registration it would have been a simple matter to say so. To my mind the expression "a legal estate" was used advisedly and with a view to affording, at the most, the same measure of protection as that given at common law to a person who has acquired a legal estate in land without notice of some prior equitable interest. Some light is, I think, thrown on this particular problem by the provisions of s. 42(d) of the Act which, itself, was introduced into the Act at the same time as s. 43A. That subsection contains an exception from the conclusiveness of a registered proprietor's title in respect of any tenancy "whereunder the tenant is in possession or entitled to immediate possession . . . of which . . . the registered proprietor before he became registered as proprietor had *notice against which he was not protected*". The italicised expression, it seems to me, is intended as a reference to the measure of protection afforded by s. 43A. So read the provision acknowledges that the protection afforded by s. 43A is not unqualified and provides some indication that the expression in subs. (1) of the section—"legal estate"—is not to be understood as synonymous with "the estate of a registered proprietor". Further, if the other view as to the meaning of the expression "legal estate" were to be entertained, it would have been unnecessary for the purposes of the section to make the specific provisions contained in subss (2) and (3). Upon the stated hypothesis notice either before or after the acquisition of a registrable instrument would be quite irrelevant.

Once the contention that the expression "legal estate" in s. 43A(1) is synonymous with "the estate of a registered proprietor" be rejected—as I think it must—it is unnecessary for us to express any positive view as to the meaning of the subsection. I say this because it is clear upon the facts that Denton had express notice of Courtenays' interest before the contract of sale between Austin and Denton was carried to completion. This will appear from the facts to which I shall presently refer. In the circumstances of the case, therefore, the rights of the parties must, subject to one matter, be determined according to the ordinary principles upon which a court of equity would proceed. . . .

[Under the principles of the ordinary law of priorities, the interest of the Courtenays was held to prevail.

The judgment of Dixon C.J. has been omitted.]

Appeal dismissed.

NOTES AND QUESTIONS

1. Would Kitto J. have arrived at the same result if, as at present, there had been an equivalent to s. 33A(5), which was inserted in 1970? The provision is in the following terms:

> The Registrar-General may assume, and shall be deemed always to have been entitled to assume, that a person who lodges with him any dealing or other document has authority from all persons claiming under, or having an interest in, the dealing or other document—
>
> > (a) to lodge it with the Registrar-General;
> >
> > (b) to uplift it for amendment or to withdraw it from registration and, in either case, to give a receipt therefor;
> >
> > (c) to receive requisitions, communications and notices in respect thereof; and
> >
> > (d) to attend to all other matters which may arise in the course of registration thereof or in the course of any other action within the office of the Registrar-General with respect thereto.

2. The view of Taylor J. was adopted by the High Court of Australia in *Meriton Apartments Pty Ltd v. McLaurin and Tait (Developments) Pty Ltd* (1976) 50 A.L.J.R. 743 at 746, where the court (Barwick C.J., Mason and Jacobs JJ.) said:

> Indeed, there is an advantage to the purchaser in taking a transfer direct from the registered proprietor—the risk that intervening equitable interests will arise is diminished. And this procedure does not lessen the protection which s. 43A of the *Real Property Act* affords. The limited operation of that section is, we think, correctly explained by Taylor J. in *I.A.C. (Finance) Pty Ltd v. Courtenay* (1963) 110 C.L.R. 550 at 583-585; see also *United Starr-Bowkett Co-op. Building Society (No. 11) Ltd v. Clyne* (1967) 68 S.R. (N.S.W.) 331, esp. at 340-341; and *Jonray's* case [1969] 1 N.S.W.L.R. 621 at 627-628. The reasons given by Taylor J. indicate persuasively that the section confers upon a purchaser who has received a registrable instrument and paid the purchase money the same protection against notice as that achieved by a purchaser who acquires the legal estate at common law, rather than the larger degree of protection the purchaser would achieve if, in accordance with the view expressed by Kitto J. in the same case, the section advanced in time the protection which ss 42 and 43 give upon registration.

JONRAY (SYDNEY) PTY LTD v. PARTRIDGE BROS PTY LTD

Supreme Court of New South Wales (Court of Appeal)
(1969) 89 W.N. (Pt 1) (N.S.W.) 568

[A, the registered proprietor of land subject to a registered mortgage, entered into a contract to sell the land to M. Before the sale was completed M entered into a contract to sell the same land to Jonray. Upon settlement of the second sale, M proposed to hand to Jonray a memorandum of transfer by direction (that is to say, a transfer by A, as the current registered proprietor, to Jonray at the direction of M), together with an unregistered discharge of A's mortgage. Jonray refused to complete, arguing that upon completion M should be registered as proprietor free from the mortgage.]

THE COURT (HERRON C.J., JACOBS AND ASPREY JJ.A.) The provisions of the *Real Property Act* ensure that estates and interests in land under the general law are both acquired and protected by the statutory conveyancing procedure set forth in the Act: see *I.A.C. (Finance) Pty Ltd v. Courtenay* (1963) 110 C.L.R. 550 at 572 per Kitto J. A purchaser of an estate or interest in land under the Act is entitled to the benefit of the protection of the Act, and in the acquisition of that estate or interest he is entitled to insist upon his dealings being carried out in accordance with the conveyancing procedure which the Act provides so that he may obtain that protection. Accordingly, any conveyancing practice under the general law must be adapted to the provisions of the Act to enable the protection given by the Act to be retained and any conveyancing practice under the general law which operates to weaken that protection must be discarded on the ground that it is unreasonable. The *Real Property Act* makes no provision in terms for transfers by direction: see s. 46 and the Fifth Schedule. The practice of the Registrar-General is, we are told, to accept and register transfers by direction. The fact that the Act does not in terms refer to the interposition in a memorandum of transfer of a directing party does not, in our opinion, mean that, if such a party joins in and executes a memorandum of transfer, such instrument is invalidated as a registrable memorandum of transfer as contemplated by s. 46. Section 103 permits the form prescribed in the Fifth Schedule to be varied in appropriate circumstances to accord with some permissible conveyancing practice which is not in conflict with the provisions of the Act. Equitable interests are not excluded by the provisions of the Act: see *Groongal Pastoral Co. Ltd (in liq.) v. Falkiner* (1924) 35 C.L.R. 157 at 163-164; *I.A.C. (Finance) Pty Ltd v. Courtenay* at 571-573 per Kitto J. Cases may arise in which it is advisable for a directing party to be joined in a memorandum of transfer: see Stonham, *Vendor and Purchaser*, para. 1672. The equitable interests or personal rights of a directing party who joins in and executes a memorandum of transfer would be bound by his execution of the instrument (cf. *Currey v. Federal Building Society* (1929) 42 C.L.R. 431-432 per Knox C.J., Rich and Dixon JJ.) and "Upon registration, every instrument drawn in any of the several forms in the Schedule hereto, or in any form which, for the same purpose may be authorised in conformity with the provisions of this Act . . . shall have the effect of a deed duly executed by the parties signing the same": see ss 103 and 36(4). We are of opinion that the mere presence in a memorandum of transfer (which otherwise complies with the provisions of the Act) of a directing party does not affect the operation of the instrument as a registrable memorandum of transfer under the Act and that it is in order for the Registrar-General to accept and register the transfer in which a directing party has been joined.

If the transfer by direction be acceptable to the Registrar-General as a registrable instrument, it remains to consider what protection, to be expected from the provisions of the Act, has the transferee lost by accepting a transfer from the registered proprietor by the direction of the party with whom the transferee has entered into the contract of sale. The name of the transferor as registered proprietor is ascertainable by the usual searches; and the terms of the contract between the registered proprietor and the directing party do not concern the transferee, as both the registered proprietor and the directing party have joined in the transfer to him. Upon completion the transferee is bound only to pay the balance of the purchase price in cash to the directing party's solicitor or as the directing party's solicitor shall direct: cl. 1 of the contract. The transferee is taking, although at the request of the directing party, a transfer from the registered proprietor and, accordingly, will receive the benefits provided by ss 42 and 43 upon registration, and, so far as may be applicable (see *I.A.C. (Finance) Pty Ltd v. Courtenay* (1963) 110 C.L.R. 550), by s. 43A before registration. He may take steps to satisfy himself that the memorandum of transfer has been duly executed by the registered proprietor as transferor and that the person purporting to execute the document in that capacity is duly identified as the registered proprietor but, in the event of a forgery or some other fraud being practised in which he has not participated, his title becomes upon registration an indefeasible one: see s. 42; *Mills v. Stokman* (1967) 116 C.L.R. 61 at 78; *Frazer v. Walker* [1967] 1 A.C. 569. Due execution by and the true identity of the directing party are factors which also may be taken into account by the transferee but, inasmuch as the transferee is taking a transfer from the registered proprietor, any defects in one or both of those factors become irrelevant to the indefeasibility of the transferee's title upon registration. It has been suggested that, if the directing party were not the registered proprietor and thus not able as such to transfer the subject property to the transferee, the registered proprietor could, after settlement but before registration of the memorandum of transfer, restrain by injunction the registration thereof if there had been some unwarranted dealing with his estate or interest. That, however, is a risk which is always run by a transferee where fraud occurs, whether the transfer be direct to him from a person purporting to be the registered proprietor or from such a person at the direction of a third party. In either case, it is for the transferee to satisfy himself by the appropriate inquiry as to identity and due execution. The additional burden of inquiring as to the identity of and due execution by the registered proprietor comes about because the vendor to the transferee under the contract of sale is not the registered proprietor and, if a transferee wishes to avoid the additional work involved in making such inquiries of more than one party, he should ensure that the contract of sale contains an appropriate provision to the effect that the vendor is contracting to sell the subject property as the registered proprietor thereof or that the vendor will be the registered proprietor prior to settlement taking place. Accordingly, we take the view that the purchaser of an estate or interest in land under the Act has not lost the benefit of the protection of the Act merely by reason of the fact that the transfer is one in which the registered proprietor transfers to the transferee at the direction of the trasferee's immediate vendor. For these reasons we are of the opinion that in the present case the plaintiff was not entitled to object to the proposed memorandum of transfer.

We turn now to the question whether the plaintiff was bound to accept on settlement the discharged mortgage or was entitled to have the discharge of mortgage registered prior to settlement. Mr Gyles for the plaintiff relies upon the same submissions as he has made in respect of the transfer by direction, and it is not necessary to add anything on these arguments. But there are further features in respect of the discharge of mortgage. The first of these is based on the argument that a discharge of mortgage under s. 65 of the Act does not cause the mortgagor to take any estate or interest within the meaning of s. 43. We do not think that this submission can be correct. Although under s. 57 a mortgage is only security and does not operate as a transfer of the land charged, nevertheless such a charge is an interest in the land (*City Mutual Life Assurance Society Ltd v. Smith* (1932) 32 S.R. (N.S.W.) 332 at 335-336; 48 C.L.R. 532 at 539-540, 542-543). When it is discharged it seems to us that the charge as it were passes to and is merged in the estate of the mortgagor. Thereby the mortgagor takes the interest within the meaning of s. 43.

The second argument relies on the fact that a purchaser who takes on settlement a mortgage with discharge indorsed does not obtain the protection of s. 43 because he is not in respect of the mortgages a person contracting or dealing with or taking or proposing to take a transfer from the registered proprietor of the mortgage, namely, the mortgagee. Therefore, vis-à-vis the mortgage interest it is submitted that the ultimate purchaser, that is to say, the present appellant, gets no protection by virtue of s. 43. That the purchaser is not such a person in such circumstances seems to us to be clear, but it is then necessary to consider the practical effect which it has upon a purchaser that in such circumstances he is not able to claim the protection of s. 43 or, upon one view, of s. 43A. If there is no substantial effect, then the purchaser is in no significantly different position from the purchaser who takes a transfer by direction. Upon registration his title would be immediately indefeasible (*Frazer v. Walker* [1967] 1 A.C. 569).

Sections 43 and 43A are sections which deal with notice. It is necessary to consider the various ways in which notice may be relevant and to consider the operation of those sections in regard to such notice, at the same time considering whether registration will confer absolute indefeasibility.

If an instrument is void, notice is irrelevant.

(a) After registration there is immediate indefeasibility (*Frazer v. Walker* above).

(b) Before settlement notice may well amount to fraud by participatio criminis, if the reason for the voidness is a criminal act such as forgery.

(c) After settlement, but before registration, notice would not amount to fraud by participation and would not make the void instrument any more or less registrable. Therefore, the true proprietor could probably prevent registration of the forged instrument whether or not the transferee or proposed new proprietor of the interest had notice.

If the instrument is voidable in equity or if there is otherwise an outstanding equity or equitable interest, notice may be much more important than in a case where the instrument is void. The degree of its importance depends upon the answer given to a number of questions. First, are equitable interests dealt with only by s. 43 and thereby outside the purview of s. 42? Or are they caught up in the words "free from all other encumbrances, liens, estates, or interests whatsoever except . . ."? We do not here refer to personal equities which personally involve the new registered proprietor. We refer only to those equities of which the purchaser or new registered proprietor may have had notice. Secondly, what protection does s. 43A give after settlement and before registration?

If equitable interests fall within the words we have quoted from s. 42, then:

(a) after registration there is immediate indefeasibility (*Frazer v. Walker* [1967] 1 A.C. 569);

(b) before settlement notice may only be ignored provided that registration is obtained or provided that s. 43A protects against notice received both before and after settlement (see under (c) below). Of course if the holder of the prior equitable interest takes some step before settlement to assert his right he will have an interest earlier in time and ordinarily would have priority;

(c) after settlement but before registration,

(i) if the view of Kitto J. at 573 of *I.A.C. (Finance) Pty Ltd v. Courtenay* (above) is correct, the purchaser obtains the same protection from notice which s. 43 would or might give him on registration;

(ii) if the view of Taylor J. at 584 is correct, then he obtains the protection which an ordinary legal estate would give to a purchaser for value without notice.

The difference between these two views is that on the approach of Kitto J. notice received before settlement would be ineffectual after settlement (s. 43A), just as it would be after registration (s. 43), provided that in the latter case or, perhaps, in both cases the purchaser was contracting or dealing with or taking or proposing to take a transfer from the registered proprietor; whilst on the view of Taylor J. notice received before settlement could still affect the purchaser after settlement and before registration in the same way as such notice would affect a purchaser of the legal estate under the general law.

On the other hand, if equitable interests fall outside the purview of s. 42 and are wholly dealt with by s. 43 and s. 43A, there is no simple and immediate indefeasibility on registration as in *Frazer v. Walker* where the instrument was void.

The purchaser or transferee must be one who obtains the legal estate without notice or is deemed by s. 43A so to do or who falls within the words "person contracting or dealing with or taking or proposing to take a transfer from the registered proprietor of any registered estate or interest". If he is not such a person and as neither s. 42 nor s. 43 applies to him notice of an equitable interest received before settlement will bind him with that equitable interest (i) before settlement as a prior competing equitable interest; (ii) between settlement and registration because there is notice before obtaining the deemed legal estate (on the view of Taylor J.), or because s. 43 is inapplicable (on the view of Kitto J.); (iii) after registration because s. 43 is inapplicable.

In the light of these possibilities it is necessary to regard the area of risk of a purchaser who on settlement takes a discharged mortgage. If s. 42 is applicable to equitable interests the only possible area of risk is that between settlement and registration.

In our view s. 42 is applicable on registration not only to legal interests but also to equitable interests. We continue, of course, to leave aside personal equities. The section contains its own indication of this when it refers to "liens". This must refer to equitable liens because there are no such things as legal liens over real property. Legal liens are possessory liens, either general or particular. Equitable liens are in the nature of equitable charges and may exist over real or personal property. If therefore s. 42 refers to some kinds of equitable interest, there seems no good reason why it should not be taken to refer to all kinds of equitable interest (other than so-called personal equities). It is true that on this view there is little scope left, since *Frazer v. Walker* [1967] 1 A.C. 569, for the operation of s. 43, but it may be regarded as a clear direction by the legislature that even the doctrines of equity should give way to the new doctrine of indefeasibility. It may be regarded as a section of further assurance.

Therefore, on registration, the purchaser will obtain the protection of s. 42 in relation to all prior interests, even though he did not deal with the registered proprietor of all those interests and, accordingly, he will be protected against any defect in the discharge of mortgage once the discharge and the transfer to him are registered.

There still remains for consideraion the degree of protection given during the period between settlement and registration.

On the view of Kitto J. as to the operation of s. 43A, that section would not operate in the case of the discharge of mortgage because it is supplementary to s. 43 and the purchaser is not within the language of s. 43. On the view of Taylor J. it would still operate so as to give the purchaser common law protection as a purchaser of the legal estate provided no notice had been received before settlement. On this analysis it seems to us that if the view of Kitto J. is correct the proposed course would deprive the purchaser of the protection of s. 43A and this would be a material deprivation. On the other hand, if the view of Taylor J. is correct, s. 43A would still operate provided that the mortgagor had not received any notice of an equitable interest before settlement.

It seems to us in view of the decision in *United Starr-Bowkett Co-op. Building Society (No. 11) Ltd v. Clyne* (1967) 68 S.R. (N.S.W.) 331 we should adopt the construction of s. 43A which was adopted by Taylor J. The *Starr-Bowkett* case is not definitive upon the point but there are strong dicta (see at 332 per Herron C.J., at 339 per Sugerman J.A. and at 344 per Walsh J.A.). We are therefore of the opinion that s. 43A may protect the purchaser against a defect in the discharge of mortgage arising from an equity or equitable interest, provided no notice of the defect was possessed by the mortgagor when he took the registrable discharge of mortgage.

This involves the conclusion, contrary to the submission of Mr Gyles, that s. 43A operates not only to protect against notice the mortgagor who takes the discharge of mortgage but also any person claiming under the mortgagor, that is, the purchaser. It gives what has been described before us as a "successive" effect to s. 43A, but such an effect seems to us to accord with the general law. If A has the benefit of a defence of purchaser for value without notice all persons claiming under A have the same benefit whether or not they had notice and whether or not they were purchasers for value, provided they did not participate in an original breach of trust: *Re Stapleford Colliery Co. (Barrow's Case)* (1880) 14 Ch. D. 432 at 445.

It would therefore appear to us that the only areas of risk are (1) where the discharge of mortgage is void or (2) where notice of an equitable interest has been received before settlement. In both these cases there are risks of the same kind on the settlement of any transaction under the *Real Property Act*. It is true that the quantity of the risk is increased because there are two interests awaiting registration instead of one. It is also true that the purchaser has the added risk that the mortgagor unknown to the purchaser may have received some notice which has deprived him of the benefit of s. 43A. It seems to us that the nature of the risk remains substantially the same.

It may be said that the risk is there and that is a sufficient reason. However, the risk must inevitably be weighed against the gross conveyancing difficulties which would arise on a different view and these are practical difficulties which would not be readily solved by making some special provisions in the contract of sale.

NOTE

It would appear, at least in respect of leasehold interests, that unless all parties are present in person or represented at the settlement the result in the *Jonray* case will not apply. In *Neeta (Epping) Pty Ltd v. Phillips* (1974) 131 C.L.R. 286 at 303-304, Barwick C.J. and Jacobs J. said:

The vendor relied for her claim that prior registration of the surrender of lease was not necessary upon the decision in *Jonray (Sydney) Pty Ltd v. Partridge Bros Pty Ltd* (1969) 89 W.N. (Pt 1) (N.S.W.) 568, where it was held that a purchaser of land under the *Real Property Act* 1900 (N.S.W.) could not insist upon the prior registration of a discharge of a mortgage registered on the title but that the sale could be effectively completed by the vendor if he handed over to the purchaser on settlement a registrable discharge of mortgage. The New South Wales Court of Appeal discussed the question whether the transferee was put at any appreciable risk by such a course and concluded that it was not. On settlement the transferee would obtain the protection against notice of equitable interests given by ss 42 and 43A of the Act. However, in *Jonray (Sydney) Pty Ltd v. Partridge Bros Pty Ltd* (1969) 89 W.N. (Pt 1) (N.S.W.) 568 the court was dealing with the usual case where the mortgagee was to be represented on settlement and where the discharge of mortgage would be handed over in present payment of the mortgage debt either to the transferee or to a further distinct party, such as a new mortgagee from the proposed transferee. What was offered in the present case was something different. The surrender of lease was to be handed over but there was no suggestion that any representative of the lessee was to be present in order to receive present payment of the consideration for the surrender. The execution of the surrender had clearly been an execution conditional upon receipt of the consideration and if that consideration were not paid either before or at the time of settlement the surrender would not be effective on settlement even though it might be made so by lodgment and registration. On all these matters the purchaser was in the dark, and in these circumstances it was entitled to claim that the certificate of title be clear. If that did not suit the vendor then it was for her to suggest some other effective mode of settlement such as representation of the lessee on settlement so that the consideration could be paid over in return for delivery of the surrender or possibly settlement at the office of the Registrar-General and immediate lodgment for registration. But certainly the mere offer from the possession of the vendor of a form of surrender of lease purporting to be signed by the lessee, when it was known that the lessee was still in possession of the land, was not a sufficient protection to the purchaser.

WILKES v. SPOONER

Court of Appeal [1911] 2 K.B. 473

VAUGHAN WILLIAMS L.J. It cannot seriously be disputed that the proposition which I quoted from Ashburner's *Principles of Equity*, p. 75, is good law. It is as follows: "A purchaser for valuable consideration without notice can give a good title to a purchaser from him with notice. The only exception is that a trustee who has sold property in breach of trust, or a person who has acquired property by fraud, cannot protect himself by purchasing it from a bona fide purchaser for value without notice." The learned author cites as authorities for that proposition the cases of *Sweet v. Southcote* (1786) 2 Bro. C.C. 66; 29 E.R. 38 and *Barrow's Case* (1880) 14 Ch. D. 432. Those cases seem to me to be conclusive authorities for the proposition stated by the author in the text, the terms of which shew that he had in his mind the words used by Jessel M.R. in giving judgment in the latter case. The learned Master of the Rolls there said: "The only exception, and the well-known exception, to the rule which protects a purchaser with notice taking from a purchaser without notice is that which prevents a trustee buying back trust property which he has sold, or a fraudulent man who has acquired property by fraud saying he sold it to a bona fide purchaser without notice, and has got it back again. Those are cases to shew that a person shall not take advantage of his own wrong. But the present appellant had not done wrong: the shares had been sold for value. The appellant and his father were not trustees of the shares, and therefore they did no wrong in buying them back." Under these circumstances there is really to my mind only one question that we have to decide. So far as the landlord was concerned, if he had no notice, either actual or constructive, of the covenant entered into by the father in respect of No. 137, he became upon the surrender free to deal with the property unencumbered by any equity arising therefrom and, that being so, the only question really left to be decided is whether the landlord had notice, either actual or constructive.

It must not be inferred from anything which I have said that I do not think that any wrong was done to the plaintiff, who took the assignment of the general butcher's shop, being induced thereto by the covenant not to carry on anything beyond the business of a pork butcher on the other side of the street. I think that a wrong was plainly done to him by what occurred, but one cannot, because a wrong was done to him, and one might be glad to throw the loss occasioned to him upon those by whom the wrong was done, derogate from the plain rights of the landlord, who, when the surrender was made and the new lease granted, had no notice of the restrictive covenant.

FARWELL L.J. It is impossible for us or any court to upset law which has been settled for so many years. Therefore, when once the land got into the lessor's hands, he was free to deal with it, and to demise it free from any restrictive covenant to a person who wished to purchase or take a lease of it though such person had notice.

NOTES AND QUESTIONS

1. What would have been the position in *I.A.C. (Finance) v. Courtenay* and the application of s 43A(1) to that case if Denton had no notice of the interest of the Courtenays? Would it have mattered whether I.A.C. did or did not have notice of the Courtenays' interest?

2. A futher issue raised by s. 43A(1) is that there must be a "dealing registrable". According to the decisions in *I.A.C. (Finance) Pty Ltd v. Courtenay*, the dealing must be in order formally, received from and executed by the registered proprietor and accompanied by the grant or certificate of title or duplicate registered dealing. It may be that a dealing containing a patent error should be regarded as a "dealing registrable", notwithstanding the terms of s. 36(6), where the error has been corrected by the Registrar-General. The subsection provides:

For the purposes of this section—

(a) a dealing that is lodged in registrable form and is subsequently uplifted shall be deemed not to be in registrable form until re-lodged in the prescribed manner and in registrable form;

(b) a dealing shall be deemed not to be in registrable form—

    (i) if, notwithstanding anything done under section 39(3), the dealing requires a material correction, alteration or addition;

    (ii) unless the Registrar-General has authority to use, for the purpose of registering the dealing, the relevant certificate of title; or

    (iii) unless the dealing is in the approved form; and

(c) notwithstanding that it may have been accepted for lodgment by the Registrar-General, a dealing that is not in registrable form shall, where it is not uplifted, be deemed not to have been lodged with the Registrar-General until it is in registrable form.

3. Can a forged dealing be a "dealing registrable"? See *Mayer v. Coe* (1968) 88 W.N. (Pt 1) (N.S.W.) 549.

4. It should be noticed that *Wilkes v. Spooner* is a decision made under the old system. However, the principle it states has general application to a person claiming the "ongoing" effect of s. 43A(1).

G. EXCEPTIONS TO INDEFEASIBILITY OF TITLE

Section 42(1) of the *Real Property Act* 1900 (N.S.W.) provides:

Notwithstanding the existence in any other person of any estate or interest which but for this Act might be held to be paramount or to have priority, the registered proprietor for the time being of any estate or interest in land recorded in a folio of the Register shall, except in case of fraud, hold the same, subject to such other estates and interests and such entries, if any, as are recorded in that folio, but absolutely free from all other estates and interests that are not so recorded except—

(a) the estate or interest recorded in a prior folio of the Register by reason of which another proprietor claims the same land;

(b) in the case of the omission or misdescription of any easement or profit à prendre created in or existing upon any land;

(c) as to any portion of land that may by wrong description of parcels or of boundaries be included in the folio of the Register or registered dealing evidencing the title of such registered proprietor, not being a purchaser or mortgagee thereof for value, or deriving from or through a purchaser or mortgagee thereof for value; and

(d) a tenancy whereunder the tenant is in possession or entitled to immediate possession, and an agreement or option for the acquisition by such a tenant of a further term to commence at the expiration of such a tenancy, of which in either case the registered proprietor before he became registered as proprietor had notice against which he was not protected:

Provided that—

    (i) the term for which the tenancy was created does not exceed three years; and

    (ii) in the case of such an agreement or option, the additional term for which it provides would not, when added to the original term, exceed three years.

It has been indicated, at the outset of this chapter, that there are certain exceptions to the principle that the title of the registered proprietor is indefeasible. The main exceptions are those extracted above. The rights secured by those provisions take effect notwithstanding the general principles of the Torrens system and they take effect in the nature of "overriding" interests; that is, the exceptions in this sense, "ride over" the Register to the extent of their operation. They will be considered in the following order: (1) fraud; (2) encumbrances, liens, estates or interests recorded in the Register; (3) omission or misdescription of easements and profits; and (4) short term tenancies. In addition, there will be an analysis of (1) personal equities; (2) correction of errors; and (3) statutory interests not contained in the Torrens Acts but which ride over the Register. The position of the volunteer will be dealt with separately.

ARTICLE

Stein, R. T. J., "Preventing Riding Over the Register" (Legal Research Foundation (New Zealand), Publication No. 22 (1983)), 1.

1. Fraud

Fraud means something more than mere notice or disregard of the rights of another: it is in the nature of personal dishonesty or moral turpitude: *Stuart v. Kingston* (1923) 32 C.L.R. 309 at 329; *Waimiha Sawmilling Co. Ltd v. Waione Timber Co. Ltd* [1926] A.C. 101 at 106; *Butler v. Fairclough*, extracted above p. 140. Where an agent acts outside the scope of her or his authority, any fraud perpetrated for her or his own advancement will not be ascribed to the principal. Although notice of itself does not constitute fraud (s. 43), where is the line to be drawn? The authorities do not always provide clear answers. It must be remembered that many acts may amount to fraud, but the clearest example of fraud is forgery. This was brought out by the Judicial Committee of the Privy Council in *Gibbs v. Messer* [1891] A.C. 248 at 257, when it indicated that the usual consequence of forgery, in respect of a transfer of land, was that no interest was transferred. However, it is in this respect that the Torrens system differs from the "old" system of conveyancing, for a good title may be obtained through registration of a forged or fraudulent dealing under the principle of indefeasibility, subject to the observations made below.

ASSETS COMPANY LTD v. MERE ROIHI

Judicial Committee of the Privy Council [1905] A.C. 176

[The Assets Company became registered as a proprietor of former Maori land. The Maoris claimed that invalidities existed in the company's title, and that they remained entitled to the land despite the registration of the company. The title of the company was attacked on the bases of (1) fraud, and (2) invalidities in registration due to errors in the Land Court.]

LORD LINDLEY. Passing now to the question of fraud, their Lordships are unable to agree with the Court of Appeal. Sections 46, 119, 129 and 130 of the *Land Transfer Act* 1870, and the corresponding sections of the Act of 1885 (namely, ss 55, 56, 189, and 190) appear to their Lordships to shew that by fraud in these Acts is meant actual fraud, that is, dishonesty of some sort, not what is called constructive or equitable fraud—an unfortunate expression and one very apt to mislead, but often used, for want of a better term, to denote transactions having consequences in equity similar to those which flow from fraud. Further, it appears to their Lordships that the fraud which must be proved in order to invalidate the title of a registered purchaser for value, whether he buys from a prior registered owner or from a person claiming under a title certified under the Native Land Acts, must be brought home to the person whose registered title is impeached or to his agents. Fraud by persons for whom he claims does not affect him unless knowledge of it is brought home to him or his agents. The mere fact that he might have found out fraud if he had been more vigilant, and had made further inquiries which he omitted to make, does not of itself prove fraud on his part. But if it be shewn that his suspicions were aroused, and that he abstained from making inquiries for fear of learning the truth, the case is very different, and fraud may be properly ascribed to him. A person who presents for registration a document which is forged or has been fraudulently or improperly obtained is not guilty of fraud if he honestly believes it to be a genuine document which can be properly acted upon.

In dealing with colonial titles depending on the system of registration which they have adopted, it is most important that the foregoing principles should be borne in mind, for if they are lost sight of that system will be rendered unworkable. Their Lordships are keenly alive to the necessity of vigilance to protect natives against unfair and oppressive dealings on the part of Europeans; but on the other hand it is equally important not to disturb registered titles of bona fide purchasers, especially when accompanied by long possession and large outlays.

It was urged by counsel that the decision of this Board in *Gibbs v. Messer* [1891] A.C. 248 shews that it is not in all cases essential to bring fraud home to the registered owner. This is true; but the case is not really in point. As already explained, in *Gibbs v. Messer* [1891] A.C. 248 two bona fide purchasers were on the register, and the case turned on the non-existence of any real person to accept a transfer and get registered himself, and then to make a transfer to some one else. Moreover, forgery is more than fraud, and gives rise to considerations peculiar to itself.

In the first appeal, Waingaromia No. 3, the fraud charged is fraud by the Assets Company in obtaining a warrant from the Governor and a certificate of title from the district land registrar.

In the second appeal, Waingaromia No. 2, various frauds on the natives are charged against Cooper and the liquidators of the Glasgow Bank, who purchased from him. There is no definite charge of fraud by the Assets Company. The only charge against the company is that the company obtained from the district land registrar an indorsement of the transfer from the liquidators to the company, and that the obtaining of that indorsement was fraudulent and void as against the plaintiffs.

In the third appeal, Rangatira No. 2, the fraud charged is, again, that frauds were committed by other people, and that the obtaining and retaining by the company of a certificate of title from the district land Registrar was fraudulent and void as against the plaintiffs.

The evidence of fraud by the company entirely breaks down. The evidence shews that in all these cases the agents of the Assets Company in the colony took to the registrar and got him to register certain documents which according to their purport and effect entitled, and which they believed did in fact entitle, the company to be registered as owners. There is no evidence whatever of any fraudulent statement made by the company's agents to the Registrar, nor of any bribery, corruption, or dishonesty in the matter.

Their Lordships cannot help thinking that the equitable doctrines of constructive fraud have weighed too much with the Court of Appeal and have induced it to impute fraud to the Assets Company, although no dishonesty by the company or its agents, or by the liquidators of the City of Glasgow Bank, was really established.

Nor is there any proof whatever that the liquidators or the Assets Company dishonestly refrained from making inquiries which an honest purchaser would have made.

The conclusions thus arrived at dispose of all these appeals. Their Lordships do not, therefore, think it necessary to give any opinion on several other defences to these actions which were raised in the Court of Appeal, and relied upon by counsel for the appellants in their argument before this Board. Their Lordships refer to the defences based on the defective title in the plaintiffs, the absence of other parties, the *Statute of Limitations*, the effect of long possession and large outlays on the lands sought to be recovered, and the effect of decisions in former unsuccessful actions by natives suing on behalf of themselves and others. Their Lordships base their judgment on the conclusiveness of the registered title in the absence of fraud.

In upholding the title of the appellants on this broad ground it is satisfactory to find that their Lordships are not disturbing, but upholding, the views which had been until recently taken and acted upon in the colony for many years in actions brought against bona fide purchasers on the register. The same view has been taken in South Australia, as is shewn by *Bonnin v. Andrews* (1878) 12 S.A.L.R. 153.

[The Board held the title of the company to be indefeasible.]

Appeals allowed.

LOKE YEW v. PORT SWETTENHAM RUBBER CO. LTD

Judicial Committee of the Privy Council [1913] A.C. 491

[Land was owned by Eusope, granted to him by the Sultan of Selangor. Eusope sub-granted part of the land to Loke Yew, with Eusope remaining as registered owner. Eusope was approached by the company, with a view to purchasing all of his land, including that portion occupied by Loke Yew. The company's agent, Glass, assured Eusope that Loke Yew's interest would be protected and he executed a document to this effect. This document was required by Eusope before he would proceed.]

LORD MOULTON. Their Lordships have no doubt that the true conclusion to be drawn from the evidence is that the above statement by Mr Glass to Haji Mohamed Eusope was intended to be and was a statement as to present intention as well as an undertaking with regard to the future, and that that statement was false and fraudulently made for the purpose of inducing Haji Mohamed Eusope to execute a conveyance which in form comprised the whole of the original grant, and that but for such fraudulent statement that conveyance would not have been executed. At that time it is evident that Mr Glass intended to eject Loke Yew if he did not accept whatever sum he chose to offer, and that therefore he did not intend to purchase Loke Yew's rights. It is also clear that it was understood, and intended by Mr Glass that it should be understood, that the document above set out was written (to use the words of one of the witnesses) "for the security of the vendor to shew that he was not selling Loke Yew's land", and their Lordships are of opinion that the document carries out that intention. The purchase price there mentioned of $336,000 makes allowance for the $14,000 to be paid for the land of Sz Woh Kongsi which is the last of the parcels noted in the margin and called therein "lease", the other 15 being the numbers of the sub-grants held by Loke Yew. It is important in this connection to note that the purchase price inserted in the conveyance is $417,000, shewing a difference of $67,000 when compared with the sum actually paid after allowing for the $14,000 for the land of Sz Woh Kongsi. This corresponds closely with the plaintiff company's own estimate of $70,000 as the value of Loke Yew's land which appears elsewhere in the suit. It is clear, therefore, from the amount actually paid that Loke Yew's lands were not included in the sale.

Having thus possessed himself of a formal transfer of the original grant to himself as trustee for the Port Swettenham Rubber Co. Ltd, Mr Glass procured its registration, and thereupon the solicitors for the plaintiffs wrote to Loke Yew the following letter:

> "Kuala Lumpur, Selangor,
> Federated Malay States,
> 22nd June 1910.
>
> Dear Sir,
> On behalf of the Port Swettenham Rubber Company Ltd, we are instructed to inform you that our clients have bought the land comprised in Grant 675, and we are further instructed to ask you to give directions to your coolies to cease from entering on this land and tapping the trees thereon. We are informed that you have an agreement of some nature with the former owner of this land, and that though our clients do not admit, and in fact deny, that you have any right against any person whatsoever under this agreement, yet to prevent any unpleasantness our clients are willing to pay you the sum of $20,000 if you will surrender to them any rights you claim under the said agreement.
>
> Yours faithfully,
> Hewgill and Day.
>
> Towkay Loke Yew."

and on the defendants refusing to vacate the land the plaintiffs brought the present action for ejectment.

Their Lordships therefore find that the formal transfer of all the rights under the original grant was obtained by the deliberate fraud of Mr Glass. He was aware that he could not obtain the execution of a transfer in that form otherwise than by fraudulently representing that there was no intention to use it until the plaintiff company were able to do so honestly by having acquired Loke Yew's sub-grants by purchase, and he therefore fraudulently made such representation, and thereby obtained the execution of the transfer. It is an important fact to be borne in mind that although this fraud was clearly charged in the defence, Mr Glass was not called at the trial, nor was his absence accounted for. The inference to be drawn from this is obvious and is entitled to great weight.

Appeal allowed.

NOTES

1. In *James A. Munro v. Stuart* (1924) 41 S.R. (N.S.W.) 203(n) Munro owned certain blocks of land subject to written leases. The leases were not registered. Munro sold to the defendant, who had actual notice of the tenancies. The defendant, after registering his transfer, proceeded to evict the tenants. The question for determination was whether Stuart had acted fraudulently in proceeding to evict the lessees. Harvey J. said:

> The clear language, that although you have knowledge that there is in existence an unregistered interest at the time you contract to purchase you may still go on and complete your transfer, seems to me to indicate that the legislature meant that a purchaser may shut his eyes to the fact of there being an unregistered interest, and need not take any consideration of the persons who claim under the unregistered interest. On both grounds, therefore, it seems to me that the ground of fraud is not one on which the plaintiff can succeed in this case. First, because if there is a fraud, it is not fraud against him which entitles him to ask for the assistance of the court of equity. Secondly, even if the lessees themselves were here as plaintiffs in the court in my opinion there is not a case of fraud within the meaning of s. 43.

2. In *Oertel v. Hordern* (1902) 2 S.R. (N.S.W.) 37 the plaintiff was in occupation, as lessee, of certain premises in Pitt Street, Sydney. The defendant, S. Hordern, entered a contract to purchase the property. He was aware of the existence of the lease. The transfer was registered. A. H. Simpson C.J. in Eq. held that mere notice of the lease did not amount to fraud on the part of Hordern. In fact, in the absence of a caveat to warn a purchaser it was held that Hordern, having heard of the lease, had done the only thing which he could in proceeding to register his transfer. It was the intention of the Act that parties should protect their rights by the lodgment of a caveat and/or registration; and omission to do so was at their own peril. The plaintiff tenant's claim to possession under the lease was dismissed by the court. Reference should be made now to the protection advanced by s. 42(1)(d). This result should be compared with the cases referred to in notes 3 and 4 following, which appear to take a far more liberal view of the conduct which may amount to fraud.

3. The defendant purchased a property and it was registered in his name. He went on a trip and returned home to find his wife in occupation with another man. The wife had made contributions to the development of the property. The defendant took matters into his own hands and decided to sell the property. The sale was completed with "bewildering" speed. The agent, but not the purchaser, was aware of the true facts throughout. The evidence was that purchases of property were not usually completed so expeditiously, and on this ground the purchaser was found guilty of fraud: *Efstratiou, H. Glantschnig and Petrovic v. Christine Glantschnig* [1972] N.Z.L.R. 594.

4. S entered into a contract for the purchase of land from a company, of which B was secretary-treasurer. The agreement was destroyed in a fire and the company asked S to make a statement of the land purchased. S described the relevant parcel as lot 15 block 15, instead of block 5 which was the correct block. The company then sold lot 15 block 5 to B. At all times B and the company were held to have full knowledge of S's error. It was held that this knowledge amounted to fraud on the part of the company and B: *Sydie v. Saskatchewan and Battle River Land and Development Co.* (1913) 14 D.L.R. 51.

5. The approach adopted in *Oertel v. Hordern* has been followed in two South Australian cases, despite the more liberal attitude of the courts to fraud in other jurisdictions: see *R. M. Hosking Properties Pty Ltd v. Barnes* [1971] S.A.S.R. 100; *Achatz v. De Reuver* [1971] S.A.S.R. 240.

6. Both *Loke Yew* and *Oertel* were rationalised in a decision of the New South Wales Court of Appeal: *Mock v. Thomson and Mel Studios Pty Ltd* (1982) C.C.H. N.S.W. Conv. R. 55-092. *Loke Yew* was explained as turning upon a lulling to sleep of the defrauded party through the conscious act of the defrauder. Otherwise, dealing with notice of an unregistered interest, would not amount to fraud: per Hutley J.A., with whom Moffitt P. and Hope J.A. concurred.

7. *Loke Yew's* case was applied in *Australian Guarantee Co. Ltd v. De Jager* [1984] V.R. 483.

BAHR v. NICOLAY (NO. 2)

High Court of Australia (1988) 62 A.L.J.R. 268

[The appellants, the Bahrs, sold their property to the first respondent, Nicolay. Under cl. 6 of the contract for sale, the sale was subject to a lease back in the Bahrs' favour together with a right to repurchase the property at a specified price at the end of the lease. On registration of the transfer, Nicolay became registered proprietor of the land. Nicolay then entered into a contract to sell the property to the Thompsons, the second respondents, on the basis that there was little likelihood that the Bahrs would be able to raise the necessary finance to repurchase the property. The contract for sale between the Thompsons and Nicolay contained the following further condition: "4. That the Purchaser acknowledges that an agreement exists between Walter Bahr and Joanna Maria Bahr and Marcus Grenville Nicolay as stamped and signed on 5 March 1980." The Thompsons became registered proprietors of the land. After registration, the Thompsons in a letter to the Bahrs' solicitors dated 6 January 1982 acknowledged the Bahrs' rights and on 8 January made two offers to the Bahrs relating to the sale of the property and relinquishment by the Bahrs of their rights over the property. The Thompsons subsequently refused to sell the land to the Bahrs. The Bahrs brought proceedings for an order vesting the property in them on payment of the agreed price or for specific performance. The Bahrs appealed to the High Court against a decision of the Full Court of Western Australia.]

MASON C.J., DAWSON J. [Their Honours first dealt with the nature of the Bahrs' rights under the first contract for sale and concluded that the rights granted gave rise to an equitable estate in the land. Their Honours continued:]

The outcome of the present case does not turn on the precise nature of the appellants' equitable interest. The outcome turns initially on the question whether ss 68 and 134 of the *Transfer of Land Act* 1893 (W.A.) (the Act) defeat that interest by reason of the second respondents having become registered proprietors of the land. And if this question be answered in the negative, there is the question whether the courts below were correct in holding that the appellants were not entitled to an order for specific performance against the second respondents, specific performance being unobtainable as against the first respondent.

By cl. 4 of the agreement between the first respondent and the second respondents, the second respondents "acknowledge[ ] that an agreement exists" between the appellants and the first respondent, that agreement being the undated 1980 agreement. The clause does not purport to create in favour of the appellants new rights over and above those previously existing. In terms it acknowledges the existence of the earlier agreement. Although the precise effect of the clause must be left for later consideration, it necessarily involves an acknowledgment of such rights as the appellants may have had under the earlier agreement.

This characterisation of cl. 4 lies at the heart of the second respondents' case: namely that mere notice of a prior unregistered interest does not amount to fraud within the meaning of s. 68. That section provides that, except in the case of fraud, the registered proprietor holds the land subject only to encumbrances notified on the Certificate of Title, save for exceptions not material to this case. Section 134 provides that, except in the case of fraud, no person taking a transfer of land shall be affected by actual or constructive notice of any trust or unregistered interest and that knowledge of any trust or unregistered interest "shall not of itself be imputed as fraud".

Sections 68 and 134 give expression to, and at the same time qualify, the principle of indefeasibility of title which is the foundation of the Torrens system of title. As the Judicial Committee observed in *Gibbs v. Messer* [1891] A.C. 248 at 254: "The object is to save persons dealing with registered proprietors from the trouble and expense of going behind the Register, in order to investigate the history of their author's title, and to satisfy themselves of its validity." Neither the two sections nor the principle of indefeasibility preclude a claim to an estate or interest in land against a registered proprietor arising out of the acts of the registered proprietor himself: *Breskvar v. Wall* (1971) 126 C.L.R. 376 at 384-385. Thus, an equity against a registered proprietor arising out of a transaction taking place after he became registered as proprietor may be enforced against him: *Barry v. Heider* (1914) 19 C.L.R. 197. So also with an equity arising from conduct of the registered proprietor before registration (*Logue v. Shoalhaven Shire Council* [1979] 1 N.S.W.L.R. 537 at 563), so long as the recognition and enforcement of that equity involves no conflict with ss 68 and 134. Provided that this qualification is observed, the recognition and enforcement of such an equity is consistent with the principle of indefeasibility and the protection which it gives to those who deal with the registered proprietor on the faith of the Register.

There is no fraud on the part of a registered proprietor in merely acquiring title with notice of an existing unregistered interest or in taking a transfer with knowledge that its registration will defeat such an interest: *Mills v. Stokman* (1967) 116 C.L.R. 61 at 78; *Waimiha Sawmilling Co. v. Waione Timber Co.* [1926] A.C. 101. The decision in *Waimiha Sawmilling* merely gives effect to s. 134 by excluding from the statutory concept of fraud an acquisition of title with notice of any trust or unregistered interest. However, Lord Buckmaster, in expressing the reasons for the decision, went rather further when he reproduced (at 106) the following passage of the remarks of Lord Lindley in the earlier decision (*Assets Co. v. Mere Roihi* [1905] A.C. 176 at 210): "Fraud . . . means actual fraud, dishonesty of some sort, not what is called constructive or equitable fraud." Lord Buckmaster went on (at 106-107) to instance, as examples of fraud, the transfer whose object is to cheat a man of a known existing right and a deliberate and dishonest trick causing an interest not to be registered.

These comments do not mean all species of equitable fraud stand outside the statutory concept of fraud. Far from it. In *Latec Investments Ltd v. Hotel Terrigal Pty Ltd (In liq.)* (1965) 113 C.L.R. 265, Kitto J. (at 273-274) held that a collusive and colourable sale by a mortgagee company to its subsidiary was a plain case of fraud. According to his Honour (at 274), "[t]here was pretence and collusion in the conscious misuse of a power", this being a "dishonest course". Likewise, in *Loke Yew v. Port Swettenham Rubber Co. Ltd* [1913] A.C. 491, Lord Moulton (at 504) instanced the case of an agent who has purchased land on behalf of his principal but has taken the conveyance in his own name, and in virtue thereof claims to be the owner of the land, though he is in law a trustee for his principal. It seems that his Lordship did not intend to make this illustration as an example of the statutory concept of fraud. His Lordship had earlier dealt with the issue of fraud and indefeasibility and was, when instancing the acquisition of title by an agent, propounding another answer based on the power and duty of the court to rectify the Register. See the analysis of *Loke Yew* by Starke J. in *Stuart v. Kingston* (1923) 32 C.L.R. 309 at 360-361. Despite this, the example given by Lord Moulton is in our view an instance of fraud within the meaning of s. 68.

According to the decisions of this court actual fraud, personal dishonesty or moral turpitude lie at the heart of the two sections and their counterparts: see *Butler v. Fairclough* (1917) 23 C.L.R. 78 at 90, 97: *Stuart v. Kingston* (1924) 19 C.L.R. 325 at 329, 356. However, from the appellants' point of view the examples may not travel quite far enough because the dishonesty which they exhibit is dishonesty on the part of the registered proprietor in securing his registration as proprietor.

This point, on which the second respondents heavily relied, emerges from the comments made by Lord Moulton for the Judicial Committee in *Loke Yew*. The appellant was the equitable owner of 58 acres of a parcel of 322 acres of land, his interest being unregistered. The registered proprietor of the entire parcel, who was the beneficial owner of 264 acres, transferred the entire parcel to the respondents who became registered as proprietors on their undertaking that they would purchase the appellant's interest. Their Lordships described (at 502) a contemporaneous document, which was designed to record the undertaking, as "false and fraudulently made for the purpose of inducing" the transferor to execute a conveyance of the entire parcel. Lord Moulton expressed the Judicial Committee's conclusion on the fraud issue by saying (at 504) that, as the transfer had been obtained by fraud, the case fell within the statutory exception to the principle of indefeasibility.

For our part we do not see the illustrations given and the statements made in the cases as amounting to definitive pronouncements that fraud is confined to fraud in the obtaining of a transfer or in securing registration. The statements, viewed in their context, merely express the reasons why particular circumstances fall within the statutory exception. Nor do we see anything in the language or the purpose of s. 68 which warrants such a restrictive interpretation. Indeed, we agree with Higgins J. in *Stuart v. Kingston* when his Honour said (at 345) that there was much to be said for the view, expressed by Stawell C.J. on the equivalent Victorian provision, that the section should be "construed strictly" and the exception "liberally". The section restricts, in the interests of indefeasibility of title, rights which would exist otherwise at law or in equity. And granted that an exception is to be made for fraud why should the exception not embrace fraudulent conduct arising from the dishonest repudiation of a prior interest which the registered proprietor has acknowledged or has agreed to recognise as a basis for obtaining title, as well as fraudulent conduct which enables him to obtain title or registration. In the context of s. 68 there is no difference between the false undertaking which induced the execution of the transfer in *Loke Yew* and an undertaking honestly given which induces the execution of a transfer and is subsequently repudiated for the purpose of defeating the prior interest. The repudiation is fraudulent because it has as its object the destruction of the unregistered interest notwithstanding that the preservation of the unregistered interest was the foundation or assumption underlying the execution of the transfer. For the same reason the subsequent repudiation by a transferee of property of a limited beneficial interest in that property is fraudulent, when the transferee took the property on terms that the limited beneficial interest would be retained by the transferor. It is immaterial that the transferee "may have been innocent of any fraudulent intent in taking the conveyance in absolute form": *Bannister v. Bannister* [1948] 2 All E.R. 133 at 136.

What then was the purpose and effect of cl. 4 of the agreement between the first and the second respondents? The matrix of circumstances in which the agreement was made throws up three significant factors. First, the making of an agreement between the first and second respondents which would result in the destruction of the appellants' existing rights, or allow the destruction of those rights, by registration of a transfer in favour of the second respondents in circumstances whereby the rights became unenforceable would expose the first respondent to liability for breach of contract: see the discussion by Jordan C.J. in *Queensland Insurance v. A.M.F. Insurance* (1941) 41 S.R. (N.S.W.) 195 at 200-201. Secondly, as we have seen, upon registration of such a transfer, the combined effect of ss 68 and 134 would, in the absence of fraud, bring about the destruction of the appellants' rights. Thirdly, at least until registration of such a transfer, the appellants' equitable interest under the 1980 agreement, being first in time, had priority over the interest of the second respondents as purchasers under their agreement with the first respondent.

Viewed in this setting, cl. 4 of the later agreement was designed to do more than merely evidence the fact that the second respondents had notice of the appellants' rights. If that were the only purpose to be served by the acknowledgment it would achieve nothing. It would enable the second respondents to destroy the appellants' interest and would leave the first respondent exposed to potential liability for breach of contract at the suit of the appellants. In the circumstances outlined it is evident that the purpose of cl. 4 was to provide that the transfer of title to lot 340 was to be subject to the appellants' rights under cl. 6 of the 1980 agreement in the sense that those rights were to be enforceable against the second respondents.

At first glance it might seem that the words of cl. 4 are inadequate to achieve this purpose. But an acknowledgment of an antecedent agreement in an appropriate context may amount to an agreement or undertaking to recognise rights arising under that antecedent agreement. And here the inferences to be drawn from the matrix of circumstances are so strong that they necessarily influence the interpretation of cl. 4. These inferences provide a secure foundation for imputing an intention to the parties and reading cl. 4 as a reflection of that intention: see *Hope v. R.C.A. Photophone of Australia Pty Ltd* (1937) 59 C.L.R. 348 at 362;

Thomas National Transport (Melbourne) Pty Ltd v. May and Baker (Aust.) Pty Ltd (1966) 115 C.L.R. 353 at 376; *Reardon Smith Line v. Hansen-Tangen* [1976] 3 All E.R. 570 at 574-575; *Khoury v. G.I.O. (N.S.W.)* (1984) 58 A.L.J.R. 502 at 507; 54 A.L.R. 639 at 648.

In *Munro v. Stuart* (1924) 41 S.R. (N.S.W.) 203 at 204, Harvey J. declined to interpret a clause in a contract in the way in which we have interpreted cl. 4. The clause was in these terms: "The Property is sold subject to existing tenancies or occupancies and to the conditions and reservations contained in every relative Crown Grant under which it is held." Harvey J., having asked whether the clause could be treated as an agreement between vendor and purchaser that the purchaser would give effect to the existing tenancies and that he would comply with the existing conditions and reservations in the Crown Grant, said (at 204) "that is not the most natural construction of the clause". His Honour read the clause as providing that the purchaser was to take the property subject to any existing tenancies for what they may be worth. His Honour seems to have thought that the result would have been otherwise if the purchaser had undertaken "to recognise" the leases, this being the construction we place on cl. 4. In *Munro v. Stuart* no account was taken of the matrix of circumstances, perhaps because the influence which it may have on the construction of a contract was not fully recognised at the time.

Brennan J. in his reasons for judgment has reviewed the evidence in detail in the course of reaching the conclusion that the parties, including the second respondents, made a collateral contract having an effect similar to the purpose that we have attributed to cl. 4. Although we agree that this is the effect of the evidence, it is impermissible to have regard to the negotiations leading up to the agreement for the purpose of interpreting it: see *Codelfa Construction Pty Ltd v. State Rail Authority of N.S.W.* (1982) 149 C.L.R. 337 at 352-353. The evidence was admissible on the issue of fraud and on the issue of rectification, matters no longer in issue in this appeal. Whether the oral evidence was admissible to set up a contract collateral to a written agreement for the sale of an interest in land is a question which we do not need to consider. We prefer to base our conclusion on the construction of cl. 4 ascertained in the light of inferences drawn from the matrix of circumstances.

Granted that the purpose of cl. 4 is as we have explained it, what is its legal effect? Is it simply an undertaking to perform the 1980 agreement if called upon so to do by the appellants? Contract scarcely seems to give sufficient effect to what the parties had in mind. A trust relationship is a more accurate and appropriate reflection of the parties' intention.

The appellants submitted that cl. 6 creates a trust in favour of them as third parties, in accordance with the principles enunciated in cases such as *Re Schebsman; Official Receiver v. Cargo Superintendents (London), Ltd and Schebsman* [1944] Ch. 83 and *Green v. Russell; McCarthy (Third Party)* [1959] 2 Q.B. 226. However, in the absence of the manifestation of a clear intention to create a trust, the courts have been reluctant to hold that a trust exists. Du Parcq L.J. elegantly expressed the traditional attitude when he said: "It is true that, by the use possibly of unguarded language, a person may create a trust, as Monsieur Jourdain talked prose, without knowing it, but unless an intention to create a trust is clearly to be collected from the language used and the circumstances of the case, I think that the court ought not to be astute to discover indications of such an intention.": *Re Schebsman* [1944] Ch. 83 at 104. This reluctance to accept that the parties have created an express trust has induced the English courts to impose what has been described as a constructive trust in order to protect a prior interest from destruction on the registration of a later interest: see *Bannister; Binions v. Evans* [1972] Ch. 359; *Lyus v. Prowsa Ltd* [1982] 1 W.L.R. 1044. *Bannister* itself was not a third party trust. It was simply a case in which a transferee, who took transfer as trustee, repudiated his trust and asserted a beneficial title in himself.

On the other hand, Fullagar J. stated a contrary view in *Wilson v. Darling Island Stevedoring & Lighterage Co. Ltd* (1956) 95 C.L.R. 43 at 67: "It is difficult to understand the reluctance which courts have sometimes shown to infer a trust in such cases." His Honour was referring to contracts whereby a benefit is promised to a third party. We agree with his Honour's comment. If the inference to be drawn is that the parties intended to create or protect an interest in a third party and the trust relationship is the appropriate means of creating or protecting that interest or of giving effect to the intention, then there is no reason why in a given case an intention to create a trust should not be inferred. The present is just such a case. The trust is an express, not a constructive, trust. The effect of the trust is that the second respondents hold lot 340 subject to such rights as were created in favour of the appellants by the 1980 agreement.

Even if we had not reached this conclusion, we would not have regarded the registration of the transfer in favour of the second respondents as destroying the appellants' rights. Having regard to the intention of the parties expressed in cl. 4 of the later agreement, the subsequent repudiation of cl. 6 of the 1980 agreement constituted fraud. The case therefore fell within the statutory exception with the result that the appellants' prior equitable interest prevails over the second respondents' title, the second respondents taking with notice of that interest.

[Their Honours then considered whether the plaintiffs (appellants) were required to prove that they were ready and willing to perform the contract, and concluded:]

With respect to the appellants' ability to provide the purchase price, the critical fact was that, on the evidence, the purchase price was significantly less than the true value of lot 340. In this situation there can be little reason for doubting the appellants' capacity to borrow the money needed to complete the purchase. Although we are reluctant to disturb concurrent findings of fact, the circumstances of this case justify the court in taking that course. Accordingly, we are of opinion that the court should order specific performance.

For these reasons we would allow the appeal.

WILSON AND TOOHEY JJ. On the proper construction of the agreement, cl. 6 constituted an executory contract for the sale of lot 340 by the first respondent to the appellants on the terms contained in that clause. In the words of the court in *Masters v. Cameron* (1954) 91 C.L.R. 353 at 360, there was "a contract binding the parties to join in bringing the formal contract into existence and then to carry it into execution". Implications of the Torrens system aside, on execution of the original contract the first respondent held the legal estate in lot 340 and the appellants held an equitable estate or interest, "measured by what a court of equity would decree in an action for specific performance": *Commissioner of Taxes (Qld) v. Camphin* (1937) 57 C.L.R. 127 at 134. As the holder of the legal estate in the land, the first respondent was free to dispose of his interests. But he could not relieve himself of his obligation to transfer the land to the appellants in accordance with cl. 6 and (the Torrens system and questions of priorities aside) the equitable estate held by the appellants was not affected by a disposition by the first respondent of his legal estate.

The agreement between the appellants and the first respondent in no way sought to restrain the latter from disposing of or dealing with the interest which he had acquired. He did not require the consent of the appellants to do such a thing. There was in truth no "bond or covenant or contract purporting to impose a total contractual restraint upon alienation", to use the language of Dixon C.J. in *Hall v. Busst* (1960) 104 C.L.R. 206 at 217. As Pidgeon J. pointed out in the Full Court, the first respondent was free to assign his interest in the land but "he could not discharge himself from liability on the covenant to enter into the contract with the appellants". "If, however", his Honour continued, "he assigned the land in a manner where he could compel the assignees to give title then I would consider he would have performed his obligations". Equally, if the first respondent failed to ensure that he could compel the second respondents to give title, he was in breach of his contract with the appellants.

Although the second respondents take their stand on the provisions of the *Transfer of Land Act* 1893 (W.A.) (the T.L.A.), it is useful to note the position of the parties divorced from those provisions. The second respondents were certainly purchasers with notice of the appellants' equitable interest in the land and, as such, they took their legal estate subject to that interest. The authorities relating to unregistered estates are noted in P. N. Wikrama-Nayake, *Voumard The Sale of Land in Victoria*, (4th ed., 1986), pp. 423-424, (n.) 44. However, the real question is — having registered their interest under the provisions of the T.L.A., did the second respondents acquire a title which was indefeasible in the sense that it was no longer open to attack by the appellants? The question may be further refined by asking — having regard to ss 68 and 134 of the T.L.A., was there in any relevant sense fraud on the part of the second respondents? Unless there was such fraud, the second respondents hold their title free of any interest the appellants have by reason of cl. 6, subject to any claim in personam that may lie against the second respondents. That is a matter to which we shall turn later in these reasons.

Section 68 of the T.L.A. asserts the principle that, except in the case of fraud, the registered proprietor of land holds the land subject only to such encumbrances as may be notified on the Certificate of Title save for certain exceptions, none of which is relevant here. Section 134 spells out the notion of fraud to some extent by providing that (again except in the case of fraud) no person taking a transfer of land "shall be affected by notice actual or constructive of any trust or unregistered interest any rule of law or equity to the contrary notwithstanding; and the knowledge that any such trust or unregistered interest is in existence shall not of itself be imputed as fraud".

The cases on ss 68 and 134 and their counterparts are legion. They are noted in the standard texts on the Torrens system and in periodical literature. There has been a divergence of approach by the Australian courts on the one hand and the New Zealand courts on the other: see Butt, "Notice and Fraud in the Torrens System: A Comparative Analysis" (1977-1978) 13 U.W.A.L. Rev. 354; also Whalan, "The Meaning of Fraud under the Torrens System" (1975) 6 N.Z.U.L. Rev. 207. Nevertheless, the basic elements are clear enough. The fraud referred to in ss 68 and 134 is actual fraud, involving some act of dishonesty on the part of the person whose title is sought to be impeached: *Assets Co. Ltd v. Mere Roihi* [1905] A.C. 176; *Waimiha Sawmilling Co. v. Waione Timber Co.* [1926] A.C. 101; *Butler v. Fairclough* (1917) 23 C.L.R. 78; *Wicks v. Bennett* (1921) 30 C.L.R. 80; *Stuart v. Kingston* (1923) 32 C.L.R. 309, decision reversed by the Privy Council on another point — see (1924) 34 C.L.R. 394.

It is equally clear that to acquire land with notice of an unregistered interest such as a lease, to become the registered proprietor and then to refuse to acknowledge the existence of the interest is not of itself fraud: *Oertel v. Hordern* (1902) 2 S.R. (N.S.W.) (Eq.) 37; *Wicks v. Bennett; Friedman v. Barrett; Ex parte Friedman* [1962] Qd R. 498; *R. M. Hosking Properties v. Barnes* [1971] S.A.S.R. 100; *Achatz v. De Reuver* [1971] S.A.S.R. 240. The point is made by Kitto J. in *Mills v. Stokman* (1967) 116 C.L.R. 61 at 78, where his Honour said: "but merely to take a transfer with notice or even actual knowledge that its registration will defeat an existing unregistered interest is not fraud."

What then constitutes fraud for the purposes of ss 68 and 134? A convenient starting point is a passage in the judgment of the Privy Council in *Waimiha Sawmilling Co. v. Waione Timber Co.* (at 106-107): "If the designed object of a transfer be to cheat a man of a known existing right, that is fraudulent, and so also fraud may be established by a deliberate and dishonest trick causing an interest not to be registered and thus fraudulently keeping the Register clear. It is not, however, necessary or wise to give abstract illustrations of what may constitute fraud in hypothetical conditions, for each case must depend upon its own circumstances. The act must be dishonest, and dishonesty must not be assumed solely by reason of knowledge of an unregistered interest."

The most often cited case in which fraud was held to have occurred is *Loke Yew v. Port Swettenham Rubber Co. Ltd* [1913] A.C. 491. There a purchaser, with knowledge of the existence of an unregistered interest, represented to the transferor that it would make its own arrangements with the holder of the unregistered interest. It failed to do so, in circumstances where it was held to have been the purchaser's intention to destroy the outstanding interest by registration of its own title. It was the purchaser's fraudulent misrepresentation that persuaded the previous registered proprietor to transfer the land to it.

With this decision may be contrasted *Waimiha Sawmilling Co. v. Waione Timber Co.* The registered proprietor of land, Howe, granted timber rights to the appellant which protected its agreement by caveat. Howe purported to determine the appellant's interest for breach of covenant. The appellant appealed against a judgment upholding Howe's re-entry. While the appeal was pending, Howe sold the land to Wilson who was acting as agent for a company to be formed, the respondent. Howe obtained an order for removal of the caveat (against which the appellant did not appeal) and transferred the land to Wilson. Wilson later transferred the land to the respondent. The appellant's appeal against the judgment upholding Howe's re-entry was itself upheld. Notwithstanding that Wilson knew of the appellant's claim and of the litigation between it and Howe, the Privy Council held that there had been no fraud on the part of the respondent.

Consistently with these authorities, evidence going no further than to show that when the second respondents took a transfer of lot 340 from the first respondent and became the registered proprietors of the land they were aware of the contents of cl. 6, cannot amount to fraud within the meaning of ss 68 and 134. More is needed before the appellants can disturb the second respondents' registered title on that ground.

The emphasis in the authorities is on actual fraud on the part of the registered proprietor. Such fraud may be found even though the registered proprietor has not himself made any representation. In *Latec Investments Ltd v. Hotel Terrigal Pty Ltd (in liq.)* (1965) 113 C.L.R. 265, Kitto J. commented (at 273-274): "we were invited to hold that nothing is fraud in the sense which is relevant under the *Real Property Act* unless it includes a fraudulent misrepresentation. The whole course of authority on this branch of the law is to the contrary. Moral turpitude there must be; but a designed cheating of a registered proprietor out of his rights by means of a collusive and colourable sale by a mortgagee company to a subsidiary is as clearly a fraud, as clearly a defrauding of the mortgagor, as a cheating by any other means.''

Had the second respondents acquired their interest in lot 340 without knowledge of the existence of the appellants' interest under cl. 6 of the earlier agreement, they would, as a matter of priorities, have taken free of that interest. Section 134 would protect them if thereafter they acquired knowledge of the appellants' interest. The position is that they took with knowledge of the contents of cl. 6. Again s. 134 operates to protect them if they did no more than take with notice. Did they do more?

The second respondents did do more by writing their letter of 6 January 1982. Of course by then they were the registered proprietors of lot 340; the fraud to which ss 68 and 134 refer is fraud committed in the act of acquiring a registered title: see *Loke Yew v. Port Swettenham Rubber Co. Ltd* [1913] A.C. 491 at 503-504; *Stuart v. Kingston* (1923) 32 C.L.R. 309 at 329; *Breskvar v. Wall* (1971) 126 C.L.R. 376 at 384; and note s. 199 of the T.L.A. which protects a registered proprietor against ejectment except in certain cases, one of which is:

> (iv) The case of a person deprived of any land by fraud as against the person registered as proprietor of such land through fraud or as against a person deriving otherwise than as a transferee bona fide for value from or through a person so registered through fraud.

Nevertheless, the trial judge found the letter of 6 January 1982 to have been written ''in recognition of the second defendants' acceptance of the right of the plaintiff [sic] to repurchase lot 340 for the price of $45,000 at the expiration of the term of the lease from the first defendant, but on the advice of Callard, in terms calculated to vary that right''. Certainly the letter was written within a week or so of the second respondents becoming the registered proprietors of lot 340. It is a recognition of an obligation to sell lot 340 to the appellants though, as his Honour pointed out and as mentioned earlier in these reasons, there was an attempt to alter the terms of sale in cl. 6.

And, importantly, on 8 January 1982 the second respondents made two offers to the appellants. The first was an offer to buy lot 221: ''Subject to vendors relinquishing all rights of repurchase of the land and buildings known as lot 340.'' The second was an offer to buy the businesses conducted on lots 221 and 340: ''Subject to the vendors relinquishing all rights to repurchase the freehold of lot 340.'' There can be only one explanation for each of the conditions attached to the offers, namely, that the second respondents accepted an obligation to the appellants in terms of cl. 6 and were seeking to extinguish it. . . .

Counsel for the second respondents submitted that the finding by the trial judge that his clients' purchase was ''subject to the plaintiff's right to repurchase lot 340 from them'' meant no more than that the first respondent had fulfilled his obligation to make proper disclosure to the second respondents. He referred to *Lyus v. Prowsa Developments Ltd* [1982] 1 W.L.R. 1044 where Dillon J. said (at 1051): ''By contrast, there are many cases in which land is expressly conveyed subject to possible incumbrances when there is no thought at all of conferring any fresh rights on third parties who may be entitled to the benefit of the incumbrances. The land is expressed to be sold subject to incumbrances to satisfy the vendor's duty to disclose all possible incumbrances known to him, and to protect the vendor against any possible claim by the purchaser if a third party establishes an overriding right to the benefit of the incumbrances against the purchaser.''

However, the trial judge's findings went further than the situation contemplated by Dillon J., for he said in a passage which we have already cited but which bears repetition: "I am satisfied that the second defendants purchased lot 340 with the knowledge that they were bound by the terms of the Agreement Ex 11 and with the belief that the plaintiffs had a right pursuant to the terms of the Agreement Ex 11 to repurchase the land for $45,000, and that their purchase was subject to the plaintiff's [sic] right to repurchase lot 340 from them."

It is in the conduct of the second respondents that fraud must be found. The evidence is far from precise. In cross-examination the second respondent, David George Thompson, said that when he offered $40,000 for lot 340 he believed from Mr Callard that the appellants were in financial trouble: "In other words, they weren't going to survive." The tenor of his evidence was that he knew of the "buy-back" arrangement between the appellants and the first respondent but thought that the appellants' financial position made it unlikely that they would be able to repurchase lot 340. There is no doubt that the second respondents took a calculated risk that the appellants would be unable to find the $45,000 required by cl. 6.

As early as February 1982 differences had arisen between the appellants and the second respondents, though it was in relation to the purchase by the latter of the business being conducted by Mr and Mrs Hesford on lot 340. On 17 February 1982 the appellants' solicitors wrote to the second respondents regarding occupancy of lot 340. That letter concluded in terms that are set out earlier in these reasons.

On 3 March 1982 the second respondents' solicitors replied: "our clients have no intention of entering into a contract with your clients to sell the property for $45,000 and maintain that they are not bound by any terms of the agreement between your clients and Mr Nicolay. We refer you to s. 68 of the *Transfer of Land Act* 1893 as amended and the authorities on this subject."

Can it be said, using the language of *Waimiha Sawmilling Co. v. Waione Timber Co.* [1926] A.C. 101 at 106, that the designed object of the transfer to the second respondents was to cheat the appellants of a known existing right? Notwithstanding the various matters to which we have referred, we think the evidence falls short of establishing that case. The second respondents agreed to buy lot 340 in the hope, even the expectation, that the appellants would not be able to buy back lot 340. But the evidence does not justify a finding that it was their intention to ensure that the appellants did not do so. However, it does establish that the second respondents took a transfer of lot 340, knowing of cl. 6, accepting an obligation to resell to the appellants and communicating that acceptance to Callard, but banking on the appellants' inability to find the $45,000 necessary to implement the clause. What are the consequences of that finding?

It is nearly a century since, in *Gibbs v. Messer* [1891] A.C. 248 at 254, the Privy Council described the Torrens system in these terms: "The object is to save persons dealing with registered proprietors from the trouble and expense of going behind the register, in order to investigate the history of their author's title, and to satisfy themselves of its validity. That end is accomplished by providing that every one who purchases, in bona fide and for value, from a registered proprietor, and enters his deed of transfer or mortgage on the register, shall thereby acquire an indefeasible right, notwithstanding the infirmity of his author's title."

That statement still stands as an exposition of the nature and purpose of the Torrens system, though "bona fide" must be equated with "in the absence of fraud", and "indefeasibility" is a word that does not appear in all the Torrens statutes of this country.

Nevertheless, in accepting the general principle of indefeasibility of title, the Privy Council in *Frazer v. Walker* [1967] 1 A.C. 569 at 585 made it clear that: "this principle in no way denies the right of a plaintiff to bring against a registered proprietor a claim in personam, founded in law or in equity, for such relief as a court acting in personam may grant."

Sir Garfield Barwick, who was a member of the Privy Council in *Frazer v. Walker*, commented in *Breskvar v. Wall* (1971) 126 C.L.R. 376 at 384-385: "Proceedings may of course be brought against the registered proprietor by the persons and for the causes described in the quoted sections of the Act or by persons setting up matters depending upon the acts of the registered proprietor himself. These may have as their terminal point orders binding the registered proprietor to divest himself wholly or partly of the estate or interest vested in him by registration and endorsement of the Certificate of Title."

This vulnerability on the part of the registered proprietor is not inconsistent with the concept of indefeasibility. The Certificate of Title is conclusive. If amended by order of a court it is, as Barwick C.J. pointed out (at 385), "conclusive of the new particulars it contains".

Returning to *Frazer v. Walker*, the Privy Council said (at 585) of claims in personam: "The principle must always remain paramount that those actions which fall within the prohibition of ss 62 and 63 may not be maintained." The reference to ss 62 and 63 is a reference to the *Land Transfer Act* 1952 (N.Z.), roughly corresponding with ss 68 and 199 of the T.L.A. The point being made by the Privy Council is that the indefeasibility provisions of the Act may not be circumvented. But, equally, they do not protect a registered proprietor from the consequences of his own actions where those actions give rise to a personal equity in another. Such an equity may arise from conduct of the registered proprietor after registration: *Barry v. Heider* (1914) 19 C.L.R. 197. And we agree with Mahoney J.A. in *Logue v. Shoalhaven Shire Council* [1979] 1 N.S.W.L.R. 537 at 563, that it may arise from conduct of the registered proprietor before registration.

The evidence leads irresistibly to the following conclusions. The second respondents understood through their agent, Callard, that the first respondent would not sell lot 340 unless they agreed to be bound by the obligation in cl. 6 which required the first respondent to resell to the appellants. The second respondents bought lot 340 on the understanding common to vendor and purchasers that they were so bound and cl. 4 was included to give effect to that understanding. Clause 4 may have been, of itself, insufficient for that purpose but the second respondents' letter of 6 January 1982 and their two offers of 8 January 1982 put beyond doubt their acknowledgment of their obligation to the appellants.

By taking a transfer of lot 340 on that basis, and the appellants' interest under cl. 6 constituting an equitable interest in the land, the second respondents became subject to a constructive trust in favour of the appellants: *Lyus v. Prowsa Developments Ltd*; *Binions v. Evans* [1972] Ch. 359 at 368. If it be the position that the appellants' interest under cl. 6 fell short of an equitable estate, they none the less had a personal equity enforceable against the second respondents. In either case, ss 68 and 134 of the T.L.A. would not preclude the enforcement of the estate or equity because both arise, not by virtue of notice of them by the second respondents, but because of their acceptance of a transfer on terms that they would be bound by the interest the appellants had in the land by reason of their contract with the first respondent.

In light of the conclusion that the appellants had, by reason of their contract with the first respondent, an equitable estate in lot 340 and that, as against the second respondents, they have such an estate or in any event a personal equity, the question arises whether the appellants may now enforce their rights in regard to lot 340. . . .

[Their Honours then considered whether the appellants were required to prove readiness and willingness to perform as a condition precedent to the grant of an order for specific performance and concluded that the appellants were entitled to a decree and that the appeal should be allowed.]

BRENNAN J. It is clear that the parties to the Thompsons' contract intended that the title to lot 340 which the Thompsons acquired pursuant to their contract should be subject to the Bahrs' interest under cl. 6 of the Bahrs' contract. In other words, their intention was not only that the Thompsons should have notice of the Bahrs' interest, but that the Thompsons, upon acquiring lot 340, should be bound by cl. 6 of the Bahrs' contract. Robertson would not have signed the contract of sale on Nicolay's behalf if the Thompsons had not agreed to be so bound. In *Munro v. Stuart* (1924) 41 S.R. (N.S.W.) 203, a contract of sale contained a provision that the property was sold subject to existing tenancies or occupancies. Harvey J. construed the provision (at 204) simply as a condition "that the purchaser is to take the property over subject to any existing tenancies for what they may be worth and cannot repudiate the contract because of their existence". However, his Honour thought that such a provision might "have to be given a wider construction than this had there been during negotiations for the contract any agreement between the parties . . . that the purchaser would recognise those leases, and that this clause had by mutual agreement been put into the contract for the purpose of giving effect to such an agreement". Though his Honour's tentative approach would lead to the conclusion that cl. 4 should be construed to accord with the parties' actual intention, that approach seems to me to involve an impermissible reference to evidence of intention as an aid to interpretation. Although it is permissible to refer to the factual matrix in which the parties were at the time of the contract in order to construe the terms of a contract (see *Codelfa Construction Pty Ltd v. State Rail Authority (N.S.W.)* (1982) 149 C.L.R. 337 at 401), it is not permissible to expand the meaning of the terms of the contract so construed so as to accord with the actual intention of the parties. I am unable therefore to embrace the tentative approach suggested by Harvey J. However, the extrinsic evidence is admissible to show that there is an independent and collateral unwritten contract which, together with the written contract, constitute the arrangements made by the parties: *De Lassalle v. Guildford* [1901] 2 K.B. 215, and see *J.J. Savage & Sons Pty Ltd v. Blakney* (1970) 119 C.L.R. 435 at 441-442. A collateral agreement that, in consideration of the vendor agreeing to sell, the purchaser will hold the land upon completion subject to the interest of a third party does not add to, vary or contradict the language of the contract of sale unless that contract contains a stipulation as to the terms on which the land should be held. As we shall see, such a collateral agreement though unwritten is effective to subject the title acquired by the purchaser on completion to the interest of the third party. It follows that I would hold the Thompsons to have given Nicolay an undertaking to hold their title subject to the Bahrs' interest. In my opinion such an undertaking is to be found in cl. 4 on its true construction but, if not in cl. 4, the undertaking was given by a collateral agreement.

The Thompsons, having acquired a registered title to lot 340 pursuant to their contract, shortly afterwards rejected any obligation to the Bahrs. The Bahrs' solicitors wrote to the Thompsons on 17 February 1982 insisting on their clients' right to repurchase, but the Thompsons' solicitors replied on 3 March 1982: "As to the last paragraph of your letter, our clients have no intention of entering into a contract with your clients to sell the property for $45,000 and maintain that they are not bound by any terms of the agreement between your clients and Mr Nicolay. We refer you to s. 68 of the *Transfer of Land Act* 1893 as amended and the authorities on this subject.''

The attitude of each party has been persisted in since that time. The Thompsons take their stand on the provisions of ss 68 and 134 of the *Transfer of Land Act* 1893 (W.A.) (the T.L.A.). Section 68 of the T.L.A. provides that, except in case of fraud, the registered proprietor of land holds the land subject only to such encumbrances as may be notified on the Certificate of Title save for certain exceptions, none of which is relevant here. Section 134 provides, inter alia, that, except in the case of fraud, no person taking a transfer of land "shall be affected by notice actual or constructive of any trust or unregistered interest any rule of law or equity to the contrary notwithstanding; and the knowledge that any such trust or unregistered interest is in existence shall not of itself be imputed as fraud''. These provisions are designed to achieve the main object of the Torrens system of registration of interests in land which the Privy Council in *Gibbs v. Messer* [1891] A.C. 248 at 254, perceived to be ''to save persons dealing with registered proprietors from the trouble and expense of going behind the register, in order to investigate the history of their author's title, and to satisfy themselves of its validity. That end is accomplished by providing that every one who purchases, in bona fide and for value, from a registered proprietor, and enters his deed of transfer or mortgage on the register, shall thereby acquire an indefeasible right, notwithstanding the infirmity of his author's title''. The consequence is that, whereas equity would subject the interest of a purchaser of land to an antecedent unregistered interest of which the purchaser has notice, a purchaser who takes with notice of an antecedent interest but who becomes registered under the T.L.A. without fraud takes free of that interest: *Oertel v. Hordern* (1902) 2 S.R. (N.S.W.) (Eq.) 37; *Munro v. Stuart*; *Friedman v. Barrett; Ex parte Friedman* [1962] Qd R. 498 at 511-512. Registration of the transfer is not fraudulent merely because the transferee knows that an antecedent interest of which he has notice will be defeated thereby. As Kitto J. said in *Mills v. Stokman* (1967) 116 C.L.R. 61 at 78: ''merely to take a transfer with notice or even actual knowledge that its registration will defeat an existing unregistered interest is not fraud.''

However, the title of a purchaser who not only has notice of an antecedent unregistered interest but who purchases on terms that he will be bound by the unregistered interest is subject to that interest. Equity will compel him to perform his obligation. In *Barry v. Heider* (1914) 19 C.L.R. 197, Isaacs J. said of the *Land Transfer Acts* (at 213): ''They have long, and in every State, been regarded as in the main conveyancing enactments, and as giving greater certainty to titles of registered proprietors, but not in any way destroying the fundamental doctrines by which Courts of Equity have enforced, as against registered proprietors, conscientious obligations entered into by them.'' In *Frazer v. Walker* [1967] 1 A.C. 569 at 585, the Privy Council said that the principle of indefeasibility ''in no way denies the right of a plaintiff to bring against a registered proprietor a claim in personam, founded in law or in equity, for such relief as a court acting in personam may grant''.

Barwick C.J., who was a member of the Judicial Committee in *Frazer v. Walker*, commented in *Breskvar v. Wall* (1971) 126 C.L.R. 376 at 384-385: ''Proceedings may of course be brought against the registered proprietor by the persons and for the causes described in the quoted sections of the Act or by persons setting up matters depending upon the acts of the registered proprietor himself. These may have as their terminal point orders binding the registered proprietor to divest himself wholly or partly of the estate or interest vested in him by registration and indorsement of the Certificate of Title.''

Orders of that kind do not infringe the indefeasibility provisions of the T.L.A. Those provisions are designed to protect a transferee from defects in the title of the transferor, not to free him from interests with which he has burdened his own title. In *Loke Yew v. Port Swettenham Rubber Co. Ltd* [1913] A.C. 491 Lord Moulton gave an example of a case where equity would enforce the terms on which a transfer was taken. He said (at 504-505): "Take for example the simple case of an agent who has purchased land on behalf of his principal but has taken the conveyance in his own name, and in virtue thereof claims to be the owner of the land whereas in truth he is a bare trustee for his principal. The court can order him to do his duty just as much in a country where registration is compulsory as in any other country, and if that duty includes fresh entries in the register or the correction of existing entries it can order the necessary acts to be done accordingly." By contrast, *Waimiha Sawmilling Co. v. Waione Timber Co.* [1926] A.C. 101 was a case where the purchaser had notice of a claim to an unregistered interest but had given no undertaking to be bound by it. That case illustrates the proposition that where a transferee has purchased with mere notice of an unregistered interest, registration of the transfer to him does defeat the unregistered interest, but *Waimiha Sawmilling Co. v. Waione Timber Co.* does not suggest that a registered proprietor who has purchased on terms that his title will be subject to an unregistered interest is able to defeat that interest upon the registration of his transfer.

A registered proprietor who has undertaken that his transfer should be subject to an unregistered interest and who repudiates the unregistered interest when his transfer is registered is, in equity's eye, acting fraudulently and he may be compelled to honour the unregistered interest. A means by which equity prevents the fraud is by imposing a constructive trust on the purchaser when he repudiates the unregistered interest. That is not to say that the registration of the transfer to such a proprietor is affected by such fraud as may defeat the registered title: the fraud which attracts the intervention of equity consists in the unconscionable attempt by the registered proprietor to deny the unregistered interest to which he has undertaken to subject his registered title. The principles are stated in *Bannister v. Bannister* [1948] 2 All E.R. 133 and *Lyus v. Prowsa Ltd* [1982] 1 W.L.R. 1044. In *Bannister*, Scott L.J. said (at 136): "It is, we think, clearly a mistake to suppose that the equitable principle on which a constructive trust is raised against a person who insists on the absolute character of a conveyance to himself for the purpose of defeating a beneficial interest, which, according to the true bargain, was to belong to another, is confined to cases in which the conveyance itself was fraudulently obtained. The fraud which brings the principle into play arises as soon as the absolute character of the conveyance is set up for the purpose of defeating the beneficial interest, and that is the fraud to cover which the *Statute of Frauds* or the corresponding provisions of the *Law of Property Act* 1925, cannot be called in aid in cases in which no written evidence of the real bargain is available. Nor is it, in our opinion, necessary that the bargain on which the absolute conveyance is made should include any express stipulation that the grantee is in so many words to hold as trustee. It is enough that the bargain should have included a stipulation under which some sufficiently defined beneficial interest in the property was to be taken by another.''

In *Lyus v. Prowsa Ltd* land was sold by a bank, as mortgagee exercising a power of sale, subject to, but with the benefit of, a prior agreement to sell made between the mortgagor and the plaintiffs. The bank had consented to but was not bound by the plaintiffs' contract. The purchaser from the bank (and a sub-purchaser who was subject to the same obligation) was held to take its interest subject to a constructive trust for the plaintiffs. Though a statutory provision similar to s. 68 of the T.L.A. was relied on, Dillon J. found (at 1054) that although there is no fraud merely in relying on legal rights conferred by statute, there was fraud in a purchaser's "reneging on a positive stipulation in favour of the plaintiffs in the bargain under which the [purchaser] acquired the land".

Therefore, although a purchaser who secures registration of a transfer of the fee simple merely with notice of a third party's right to purchase acquires on registration of his transfer a title freed of any obligation to the third party which equity would otherwise impose, a purchaser who has undertaken—whether by contract or by collateral undertaking—to hold his title subject to a third party's right to purchase remains bound by his undertaking after registration of his transfer. If he should repudiate the third party's right to purchase, equity imposes a constructive trust so that the registered proprietor holds his title on trust for the third party to the extent of the third party's interest. . . .

Appeal allowed.

SCHULTZ v. CORWILL PROPERTIES PTY LTD

Supreme Court of New South Wales (1969) 90 W.N. (Pt 1) (N.S.W.) 529

[Galea, a solicitor, forged a mortgage by Corwill Properties in favour of Schultz, and misappropriated the money. He acted as solicitor for both Schultz and Corwill Properties. The mortgage was registered. Galea later persuaded Schultz to sign a discharge of mortgage, on the false representation that the mortgage moneys would be re-invested on her behalf. The discharge of mortgage was registered.]

STREET J. Mr Smith, who appears for the plaintiff, submits, in reliance upon *Frazer v. Walker* [1967] 1 A.C. 569, that, the mortgage having been registered on the title, the plaintiff is entitled to the estate thereby conferred upon him. He contends, however, that whilst the plaintiff's mortgage is rendered unimpeachable by the principle of immediate indefeasibility for which *Frazer v. Walker* is authority, nevertheless that doctrine does not extend to the registration of a discharge of a mortgage. The argument is that the "indefeasibility" sections, namely ss 40, 42 and 124 of the *Real Property Act*, do not give to the registration of a discharge of a mortgage the same indefeasible characteristics that flow, for example, from the registration of a transfer of an estate or a grant of a mortgage by one person to another.

I have already in other suits stated my view of the effect of *Frazer v. Walker* (*Mayer v. Coe* [1968] 2 N.S.W.R. 747 at 754 and *Ratcliffe v. Watters* [1969] 2 N.S.W.R. 146 at 151), namely: "The Privy Council's decision is direct and binding authority laying down that a registered proprietor who acquires his interest under an instrument void for any reason whatever obtains on registration an indefeasible title. This will avail himself against all comers unless: (a) there is a specific basis under the statute rendering him open to challenge; an example of such a specific basis of challenge is actual fraud on his part or on the part of his agent (ss 42 and 124; *Frazer v. Walker* [1967] 1 A.C. at 580-581); or (b) he is subject to a *personal* obligation by which he may be bound in personam to deal with his registered title in some particular manner."

Neither counsel has referred me to any authority touching the argument that the indefeasibility sections operate differently upon the registration of a discharge of a mortgage from the manner in which they operate upon the registration of other dealings. In my view there is no warrant, either in principle or by way of reasoning based on the authorities, for recognising any such difference in the effect of registration. The Privy Council has laid down in *Frazer v. Walker* that the register is to be regarded as accurately disclosing the state of the title. An inroad may be made upon the state of the title disclosed by the register only upon one of the grounds recognised by the Privy Council in *Frazer v. Walker*. The differing approaches taken by those who propound the doctrine of deferred indefeasibility (exemplified in the judgment of Dixon J., as the learned Chief Justice then was, in *Clements v. Ellis* (1934) 51 C.L.R. 217) on the one hand, and on the other hand by those who propound the doctrine of immediate indefeasibility (exemplified in *Frazer v. Walker*) might conveniently be stated as follows: the deferred indefeasibility approach is based upon an inquiry into how the proprietor became registered (cf. s. 43)—this is the approach that treats the register as establishing an indefeasible *root of title*; the immediate indefeasibility approach is based upon an inquiry into how far the Act authorises correction of or interference with the register—this is the approach that treats the register as establishing *title*. On the deferred indefeasibility approach, unless the estate in question can be demonstrated to have got on to the register in a manner protected by the Act registration has no efficacy. The Privy Council has declined to uphold this approach and has expressed a clear preference for immediate indefeasibility: unless there is statutory authority for removal of a registered interest, or unless there is some personal equity outstanding against the proprietor of that registered interest, then the register is conclusive evidence establishing the title as disclosed by it on its face.

Once it is recognised that *Frazer v. Walker* substantiates immediate indefeasibility as the proper effect of the *Real Property Act*, then I see no valid basis for denying to the registration of a discharge of a mortgage the same effect in point of indefeasibility as the grant of a mortgage. The state of the register, as affected by the registration of the discharge, can only be altered in a manner permitted by the Act. It is immaterial whether that state of the register is a result of a mortgage or of a discharge having been registered. I accordingly do not assent to the submission that the doctrine of indefeasibility should be applied in the present case differently as between the registration of the mortgage on the one hand and, on the other hand, the registration of its discharge.

I turn, then, to a consideration of whether or not it is open to the parties to go behind the prima facie indefeasible title disclosed on the face of the register. The plaintiff, for his part, claims that the mortgage, having been registered, is indefeasible; the defendant, for its part, claims that the discharge having been registered, the consequent clearing of its title is indefeasible. Both parties seek to go behind the face of the register in challenging the dealing purporting to give rise to an interest adverse to their respective interests. The relevant basis upon which the parties seek in turn to do this is that the dealing in question was tainted by fraud. . . .

The essential question which must be determined in respect of the grant of the mortgage and its discharge respectively is whether the fraud associated therewith can be "brought home to the person whose registered title is impeached or to its agents. Fraud by persons from whom he claims does not affect him unless knowledge of it is brought home to him or his agents." . . . The mere fact that the existence of a fraud is known to an individual who is, in the transaction under consideration, the agent for some purposes of the person whose title is impeached will not of itself affect the indefeasibility of the title when registered. It is not enough simply to have a principal, a man who is acting as his agent, and knowledge in that man of the presence of a fraud. There must be the additional circumstance that the agent's knowledge of the fraud is to be imputed to his principal. . . . On ordinary principles of principal and agent Mrs Schultz does not thereby become answerable to the defendant for Clive Galea's forgery. It was not within the scope of his actual or apparent authority to do this. The forged execution of the mortgage was in furtherance of a felonious abuse by him of his custody of the defendant's certificate of title. It was an independent activity entirely in furtherance of his own interests and in no way done for or on behalf of Mrs Schultz. I hold that Mrs Schultz was not vicariously tainted by Clive Galea's forgery.

Before leaving this particular aspect I should state that there is no room, when assailing the title of a registered proprietor, for applying the rule that a man is considered to be vicariously responsible for a fraud committed in his name if he later deliberately asserts the validity of and seeks to take benefits under the fraudulently tainted transaction. In certain circumstances adoption by a principal of a fraud committed by his agent, being a fraud for which he, the principal, would otherwise not be liable, will render the principal answerable to the other party to the transaction: see *Bowstead on Agency* (13th ed, 1968), pp. 34-35. But where the efficacy of a registered title is in issue, it is the state of the register which is all-important. It cannot be said of a registered proprietor who relies simply upon the face of the register that he is thereby adopting a fraud for which he would not otherwise be liable on the part of his agent tainting the transaction leading to his becoming registered: this would travel far beyond the limits marked out by the Privy Council in *Assets Co. Ltd v. Mere Roihi* [1905] A.C. 106 as the type of fraud which will permit a successful challenge to the title shown on the register. A registered proprietor relies simply upon the state of the register and not upon the validity or otherwise of the transaction which led to the register being in that state. If, in that transaction, fraud or knowledge of it is brought home to him or his agents, the state of the register will not avail him; otherwise it will.

I pass to the second question of whether or not there is to be imputed to Mrs Schultz notice that the mortgage was a forgery. Clearly enough Clive Galea knew at the time he was acting for Mrs Schultz in the taking of the mortgage that the memorandum was a forgery. Did he, however, know this in such circumstances as to impute his knowledge to Mrs Schultz? In my view this question must be answered in the negative. The cases cited in *Williams on Vendor and Purchaser* amply substantiate both the existence and the scope of the exception that the learned author describes to the principle of imputed notice or knowledge. The fraud committed by Clive Galea was a fraud for his own independent benefit. In one sense it was a fraud committed by him at a time when he was acting as Mrs Schultz's solicitor; in another sense it was a felonious act so far as concerned the defendant, committed by him at a time when he was the secretary of the defendant. But, in the words of *Williams*, "the supposition that the agent [Clive Galea] communicated his own fraud to the principal [Mrs Schultz] is too improbable to be entertained even by a court of equity". Within ordinary principles governing vendor and purchaser I do not consider that the knowledge which Clive Galea had that the mortgage was a forgery is to be imputed to Mrs Schultz.

I therefore hold that so far as concerns the mortgage, although it was a forgery, and hence for the purposes of s 42 a fraud, that fraud was not "brought home to the person whose registered title is impeached or to his agents". Nor was "knowledge of it brought home to him or his agents". The exception of fraud recognised under s. 42 is not made out so as to invalidate the mortgage.

The discharge of the mortgage involves considerations in some respects similar to the considerations I have discussed in connection with the procuring of the mortgage. Here again the party whose title is sought to be impeached, in this instance the defendant, was innocent of participation in or knowledge of Clive Galea's fraudulent activities. That Clive Galea defrauded the mortgagee, the plaintiff, into signing the discharge is not open to dispute. But I do not see that any step taken by Clive Galea in this connection was such as to involve the defendant in vicarious responsibility. Clive Galea had no authority whatever from the defendant to approach the plaintiff for a discharge of the mortgage. It may be conceded that Clive Galea represented that he had such authority, but there was no basis, actual or ostensible, which would implicate the defendant in responsibility for his representation in this regard.

The only ground for suggesting that the defendant is in some way responsible for Clive Galea's fraud on the plaintiff is that, by asserting the validity of the discharge to clear its title, the defendant is now adopting the fraud Clive Galea practised on the plaintiff. I have already stated, in connection with the obtaining of the mortgage, my view that a registered proprietor who simply asserts the indefeasibility of his title as disclosed on the register does not thereby become subject to the operation of this principle of ex post facto adoption. I accordingly discard this as a ground for holding that the defendant is vicariously tainted by Clive Galea's fraud in procuring the discharge. There being no other basis for making out vicarious responsibility on the defendant in connection with the discharge, I hold that the fraud was not "brought home to" it or to its agent.

Suit dismissed.

ARTICLES

Butt, P. J., "Notice and Fraud in the Torrens System" (1978) 13 U.W.A.L.R. 354; Stein, R. T. J., "Some Aspects of Title by Registration in the Maritime Provinces of Canada" (1976) 2 Dal. L.J. 633.

2. Estates, interests and entries recorded in the folio of the Register

The Act indicates in s. 42 that the title of the registered proprietor is subject to estates interests and such entries as may be recorded in the folio of the Register for the land. The extent of the operation of an earlier version of the provision was considered in the following decision.

BURSILL ENTERPRISES PTY LTD v. BERGER BROS TRADING CO. PTY LTD

High Court of Australia (1971) 124 C.L.R. 73

[The facts are stated in the extract from the judgment of Windeyer J.]

BARWICK C.J. It seems to me that it was not intended that the certificate of title alone should provide a purchaser dealing with the registered proprietor with all the information necessary to be known to comprehend the extent or state of that proprietor's title to the land. The dealings once registered became themselves part of the register book. It was therefore sufficient that their registration should be by statement of their nature recorded on the certificate of title. Section 42 of the Act of 1862 provided for a memorandum of transfer as the appropriate instrument for the transfer of an estate or interest in land, or for the creation or transfer of any right of way or other easement. Section 49 provided for a memorandum of lease where land is intended to be leased for a life or lives or for any term exceeding those years. Section 54 provided for a memorandum of mortgage when land is to be charged or made security and for a memorandum of encumbrance where an annuity, rent charge or sum of money is to be charged on land.

These descriptions in this list indicate, in my opinion, the nature of the various principal instruments which can be registered under the Act. In my opinion, the nature of the instrument to which s. 37 refers is its description as a transfer, lease, mortgage, encumbrance, etc. What it achieves in particular is not part of its nature for relevant purposes. It is not necessary, in my opinion, to make a memorial effective as the registration of a dealing that the indorsement should particularise to any extent what the instrument does. It is sufficient to state, whether it is a transfer or a mortgage etc. Thus, in my opinion, the indorsement on a certificate of title of a statement, "Memorandum of Transfer No. 7922 dated 15 May 1872 produced and entered the 15th day of June 1872 at 12 o'clock noon", would be a sufficient memorial and upon its indorsement on the certificate of title, the memorandum of transfer would be duly registered and form part of the register book. There would be no need to state the subject matter of the transfer though the convenient practice is to state on a memorial of memorandum of transfer etc. the fact that the whole or part of the land comprised in the certificate of title is the subject of the memorandum. But, in my opinion, the absence of such information will not render the memorial ineffective. Once the memorial is sufficient to effect registration of the instrument then the interest of the registered proprietor becomes subject to the registered instrument because of the words in the body of the grant or certificate of title describing the proprietor's interest.

However, the indorsement in this case was not confined to the words I have set out. Both in the indorsement in 1862 and in the indorsement on the present certificate of title a description of what the memorandum of transfer achieved appears. In practical terms this inadequate description cannot be of moment because even to ascertain the nature and extent of the right or rights of way which it is said to have created or extended the memorandum of transfer must be searched and examined. Potent however as such a practical consideration must be, it cannot itself resolve the question whether or not the inadequate, or if you will, misleading, description of the effect of the memorandum of transfer vitiated the memorial as a registration of the memorandum of transfer or prevented an indorsement which otherwise would qualify as such being a memorial.

Although accompanied by a statement purporting to notify its effect, the indorsement did, in my opinion, state that a memorandum of transfer had been produced and numbered. That was a statement of the nature of the instrument. The relevant purpose of the indorsement was not to describe the effect of an unregistered instrument. It was evidently intended as a step in the registration of the memorandum of transfer. Consequently the addition of a statement of the operative effect as distinct from the nature of the instrument ought not to be regarded as of the essence of the indorsement but rather as surplusage so far as the process of registration is concerned. That statement, in my opinion, was not effective either to prevent the statement of the nature of the instrument and of the other relevant particulars being a memorial sufficient to effect the registration of the memorandum of transfer: nor would the addition of a statement of the operative effect of the instrument vitiate the indorsement as an effective memorial. Consequently, in my opinion, the memorandum of transfer was duly registered under the Act of 1862.

WINDEYER J. The memorandum of transfer of 1872, No. 7922, did two things: one in relation to an easement of way; the other in relation to buildings above the way.

As to the first aspect, the right of way: as a then existing easement, this was recognised, elaborated and extended in favour of William Long, his heirs and assigns. It was defined as a right of way for him, his and their workmen and persons authorised by him or them. It was declared to be exercisable at all reasonable times over the existing roadway and a prolongation thereof westward of 50 feet. This prolongation of the way was thereafter called an "extension of the right of way". And by that term the transfer of 15 May 1872 came to be compendiously described. That description is apt for it in one respect, because by it the right of way was extended, in the sense that further land was made servient to the same right: and the description would, no doubt, be meaningful too for those who are accustomed to the colloquial misuse of the term, right of way, as meaning the land, the passage or way over which a right of way exists.

In its second aspect, what the transfer did was to grant to the transferee the building over the passage way. That was not a grant of something necessarily incidental to or involved in the creation of the further easement of way. It was a quite separate matter, a disposition by the transferor of a specified part of his hereditament, to the intent that the transferee should become its owner and be entitled thereafter to exclusive possession of it. It is true that there is no express habendum. But I do not think that this is fatal, or that the "grant and transfer" of the right of way "Together with the buildings at present erected . . . and the right to pull down such buildings and to rebuild others . . ." was intended as anything other than a complete conveyance of the building then erected. The transferee entered into possession; and his successors in title of the land that is now Berger's have continued in possession as if the building formed part of their land. . . .

The critical question, as I see the matter, is then whether the interest in respect of buildings that Guy conveyed to Long can be said to have been "notified on the folium of the register book constituted by . . . the Certificate of Title" within the meaning of s. 42 of the Act. If it was, then Bursill holds its land subject to it; and that involves no inroad upon an indefeasible title.

The argument that the interest in the buildings is not notified on the Certificate of Title proceeded on the assumption that Bursill, when purchasing the land, could safely neglect to search transfer No. 7922, which was expressly referred to on the Certificate of Title. It is contended that this reference to the memorandum of transfer did not amount to constructive notice of its full operation, because it was described as creating an "Extension of the Right of Way". Doubtless this description would have been better if it had read "extension of right of way and rights in buildings above the way". But it seems to me that what is "notified" to a prospective purchaser by his vendor's Certificate of Title is everything that would have come to his knowledge if he had made such searches as ought reasonably to have been made by him as a result of what there appears. I here use the words of s. 164 of the *Conveyancing Act* 1919 (N.S.W.). We are not concerned in this case with s. 43, which gives a protection against unregistered instruments, for transfer No. 7922 was registered, and is noted on the Certificate of Title.

It seems to me that, at any time from 1872 till today, a prudent conveyancer acting for a purchaser of the land that is now Bursill's would have ascertained what it was that transfer 7922 referred to on the vendor's certificate of title in law effected. True he might have been surprised to discover all that his search revealed. But surely no prudent person, seeing the reference to a right of way, would neglect to ascertain what exactly was the nature of the right of way, the land subject to it, the persons who could avail themselves of it, for what purposes in what manner and at what times. The need to make such a search seems the more obvious if, by an inspection or survey of the land, the intending purchaser had become aware that there was a building over part of the land which was in the occupation of his neighbour. And it seems unlikely that a purchaser of this land in a built-up area of the City of Sydney would not be aware of the existence of the passage way and of the building above it. Whether he was so or not the reference on the certificate of title to transfer 7922 was I think constructive notice of what it provided, that is that the land was subject not only to a right of way but also to an interest of the adjoining landowner in the building above the way. I think that the registered proprietor of the land that is now Bursill's held his title subject to that interest. Therefore I consider that the owner of the land that is now Berger's has, and has had, in law a right to the exclusive use and occupation of this building. This Berger's predecessors in title have enjoyed for nearly a century. But no question of a right from adverse possession arises. The owners of Berger's land have held the building as of right by documentary title.

[The dissenting judgment of Menzies J. has been omitted.]

NOTES AND QUESTIONS

1. See *Mercantile Credits Ltd v. Shell Co. (Australia) Ltd* (1976) 136 C.L.R. 326, above, p. 133.

2. Blackacre is a parcel of land registered under the provisions of the *Real Property Act* (N.S.W.). The certificate of title states that it is encumbered with a lease. The registered proprietor, John Smith, enters into a contract to sell Blackacre to Peter Brown. The sale is completed and the certificate of title and transfer, properly executed and stamped, are lodged at the Office of the Registrar-General for registration. The transfer is registered and a new certificate of title is issued in favour of Brown. The lease is noted as an encumbrance on the new certificate of title. Jones, the registered proprietor of the lease, approaches Brown and seeks to exercise an option to purchase Blackacre. This option is contained in the lease. The option is not referred to on the face of the certificate of title but at all material times Brown was aware of the option. Can Jones enforce the option against Brown?

3. The principal case was followed in *Hutchinson v. Lemon* [1983] Qd R. 369.

3. Omission or misdescription of easements and profits

This subject is considered in the chapter on Easements, below, p. 280.

ARTICLE

Stein, R. T. J., "Profits à prendre and Torrens title in New South Wales" (1982) 56 A.L.J. 426.

4. Short term tenancies

In New South Wales s. 42(1)(d), extracted above, makes express provision for safeguarding of certain tenancies, where the tenant is in possession or entitled to immediate possession and where the term of the tenancy (together with any option to renew) does not exceed three years.

UNITED STARR-BOWKETT CO-OP. BUILDING SOCIETY (No. 11) LTD v. CLYNE

Supreme Court of New South Wales (Court of Appeal) (1967) 68 S.R. (N.S.W.) 331

[Clyne was the registered proprietor of premises subject to a weekly tenancy under the provisions of the *Landlord and Tenant (Amendment) Act* 1948. The property was subject to a mortgage in favour of United Starr-Bowkett ("the society"). Clyne defaulted under the mortgage and the society took proceedings in ejectment to gain possession. The tenant was given notice to vacate and he sought to be joined as a party to the proceedings. At all material times before completion the society had notice of the protected tenancy.]

HERRON C.J. In my opinion, since 1930 a tenancy for a term not exceeding three years is excluded from the operation of the *Real Property Act* whereby a registered proprietor holds the land, or his estate or interest in it, subject to estates, interests, encumbrances or liens as are notified but free of all others. Notice of the tenancy is a prerequisite to the operation of para. (d) of s. 42. If the registered proprietor had no notice of it, his title is not subject to the tenancy. The proper construction of s. 42(d) by reason of the added words "the registered proprietor before he became registered proprietor had notice against which he was not protected" is that the exception of the tenancy to which para. (d) relates does not apply if the registered proprietor had no notice of it at the moment he obtained the registrable instrument. This, I think, results from the decision in *I.A.C. (Finance) Pty Ltd v. Courtenay* (1963) 110 C.L.R. 550. . . .

SUGERMAN J.A. A tenancy of land under the *Real Property Act* which is not for a term of years exceeding three years may be created without the necessity for registration of a memorandum of lease, and this includes the creation of a periodical tenancy such as one from week to week: *Josephson v. Mason* (1912) 12 S.R. (N.S.W.) 249. But a tenancy so created was liable to be defeated by registration of a memorandum of transfer of the subject land though the transferee took with notice of the existence of the tenancy, and the tenant could be ejected by the transferee: *Munro v. Stuart* (1924) 41 S.R. (N.S.W.) 203. The same may be said of a registered memorandum of mortgage. The question which arises is whether this result has been affected, at least as regards a tenant in possession or entitled to immediate possession, by s. 42(d) read in conjunction with s. 43A, as seems to have been the intention underlying the enactment of those provisions. Their effect, and in particular the effect of s. 43A, has been the subject of much discussion by learned writers in periodicals and text books, but does not seem to have come up for consideration in any reported case until *Courtenay v. Austin* (1961) 78 W.N. (N.S.W.) 1082; in the High Court sub nom. *I.A.C. (Finance) Pty Ltd v. Courtenay* (1963) 110 C.L.R. 550. In that case, Taylor J. said, with respect to s. 43A: "It is, however, not unreasonable to assume that the section was intended to achieve some object. And that object, it seems, was to make some appropriate provision for 'filling' what has been called the 'gap' left in s. 43 by the 'settled law' concerning that section (Baalman, *A Commentary on The Torrens System in New South Wales* (1951), p. 177). Does the section, then go further than merely to afford a so-called protection against notice and operate to give to the holder of a registrable memorandum of transfer priority over an earlier equitable interest where he has, without notice thereof, paid his purchase money and obtained his registrable instrument? The suggestion that it does is based upon the contention that the holder of a registrable instrument in such circumstances is enabled to assert, as against the prior equitable interest, that he has by virtue of the section a legal estate in the land acquired without notice of the earlier interest and that he is, therefore, entitled to perfect his title by registration. Such a construction, it is said, does some violence to the terms of the section but it is, it seems to me, the result, which notwithstanding its 'ungainly approach' to the subject (see Baalman, above, p. 177), the section was intended to produce." Hardie J. had spoken to the same effect in this court, although in the end no expression of opinion on this question was necessary to the decision of the case. Although for the reason just stated they are not binding upon us, and indeed Kitto J. approached the question rather differently, I would wish, with respect, to adopt these expressions of opinion as agreeing with my own opinion on this question after consideration of the different points of view which have been expressed upon it. Then Taylor J. went on to say: "Some light is, I think, thrown on this particular problem by the provisions of s. 42(d) of the Act which, itself, was introduced into the Act at the same time as s. 43A. That subsection contains an exception from the conclusiveness of a registered proprietor's title in respect of any tenancy 'whereunder the tenant is in possession or entitled to immediate possession . . . of which . . . the registered proprietor before he became registered as proprietor had *notice against which he was not protected*'. The italicised expression, it seems to me, is intended as a reference to the measure of protection afforded by s. 43A." With this also I respectfully agree. The result, in combination, of ss 42(d) and 43A in my opinion is that, notwithstanding registration, the purchaser holds subject to a tenancy for a term not exceeding three years created by a previous registered proprietor (whereunder the tenant is in possession or entitled to immediate possession) if he had notice of that tenancy before he obtained a registrable instrument, or one which when appropriately signed by him or on his behalf would be registrable, that is, before completion of his purchase.

That is the situation in these present cases. It follows, to revert to the illustration which I have taken, that the Starr-Bowkett Society took its mortgage subject to the outstanding weekly tenancy of the tenant.

JAMES A. MUNRO v. STUART

(1924) 41 S.R. (N.S.W.) 203(n)

[See above p. 169.]

CLYNE v. LOWE

Supreme Court of New South Wales (Court of Appeal) (1968) 69 S.R. (N.S.W.) 433

[Clyne purchased land registered under the provisions of the *Real Property Act*. At the time of purchase Lowe was in occupation as a tenant. The premises were "prescribed premises" under the *Landlord and Tenant (Amendment) Act* 1948 (N.S.W.). That Act places restrictions upon a landlord's rights to evict tenants. Clyne knew that somebody other than the vendor was in possession of the property but did not know that Lowe was that person. Lowe contended that at all relevant times Clyne had notice of her interest against which he was not protected and that, consequently, he could not terminate her possession, except under the provisions of the *Landlord and Tenant (Amendment) Act*.]

SUGERMAN J.A. It is correct that there was no evidence that the respondent had actual notice that the appellant was in possession of the subject premises as tenant or at all, that is, of the identity of the person in possession thereof. It is equally correct that the terms of his contract of purchase and of the answers to his requisitions were calculated to convey to him that the vendor to him was not in possession thereof, but that some other person was. The question is whether these last-mentioned circumstances were in themselves sufficient to put the respondent on inquiry as to the title of the appellant and, if they were, whether that amounted to "notice against which he was not protected" within the meaning of s. 42(d) of the *Real Property Act*.

As to land under the old system of common law title, it is well established that if a purchaser has notice that the vendor is not in possession of the property sold, he must make inquiries of the person in possession—of the tenant who is in possession—and find out from him what his rights are, and, if he does not choose to do that, then whatever title he acquires as purchaser will be subject to the title of the tenant in possession. The leading case is *Hunt v. Luck* [1902] 1 Ch. 428. . . .

The remaining question is whether this doctrine applies to land under the *Real Property Act* for the purpose of affixing with notice of a tenancy within the meaning of s. 42(d) a purchaser who is aware that his vendor is not in possession, but does not seek out the person actually and visibly in possession and inquire of him what his title or rights are. If such title or rights happen to be a tenancy for a term not exceeding three years, or an agreement or option for a further term within the scope of s. 42(d), has the purchaser "notice" thereof within the meaning of that paragraph? Is the "notice" therein referred to confined to actual notice or does it include such constructive notice as flows from failure to make due inquiry of the person in possession?

This point is free from any authority. Having considered it, I have reached the conclusion that "notice" in s. 42(d) includes such constructive notice as I have mentioned. This, in my opinion, is the result of reading the word in its context, including not only s. 42 but also ss 43 and 43A. . . .

It seems clear that "notice" in s. 43A(1) has the same meaning as notice in s. 43, that is, notice "direct or constructive". Sections 42(d) and 43A(1) have to be read together: *United Starr-Bowkett Co-op. Building Society (No. 11) Ltd v. Clyne* [1968] 1 N.S.W.R. 134. The reference in the former to "notice against which he was not protected" is a reference to the expression "For the purpose only of protection against notice" in the latter. The natural conclusion is that "notice" in both sections means the same thing, that is, notice "direct or constructive" as in s. 43. The conclusion is reinforced by the circumstances that s. 42(d) deals, not only with the legal estates of tenants, but also with the equitable interests of those who have an agreement or option for the acquisition of a further term.

For these reasons I am of opinion that the respondent did have "notice", against which he was not protected, because he had it before he paid his purchase money and obtained a registrable interest, of the appellant's tenancy (if she had one) within the meaning of s. 42(d). He had such notice, that is, constructive notice, because of his failure to inquire from the person in fact in possession as to her title or rights.

JACOBS J.A. I am of the opinion that under the general law a purchaser cannot be satisfied merely with answers to requisitions or with the terms of the contract of sale, so far as they contain disclosures by the vendor. The duty of the purchaser extends beyond this. Once he is informed that there is a tenancy or a possession in someone other than the vendor, then the duty of the purchaser is to seek out the person in actual possession of the premises and to inquire from that person what tenant or other rights he or she claims. It is true that a purchaser who makes such inquiries may be misled into believing that rights do not exist, but the point, particularly in the present case, is that the duty of inquiry which, if it is not fulfilled, will lead to the purchaser being constructively taken to have notice, is to inquire from the person in occupation or possession of the premises.

I think that this is borne out by the cases and by the text writers. The leading case generally referred to by the text writers is *Hunt v. Luck* [1902] 1 Ch. 428.

So far I have assumed that the doctrine of constructive notice is applicable and appropriate to the "notice" which is referred to in s. 42(d) of the *Real Property Act* 1900. I turn now to this second question. In my view the assumption which I have so far made is a correct assumption. The doctrine of notice is in its origin an equitable one, and notice under the equitable doctrine includes not only actual notice but also imputed notice and constructive notice. . . .

It should be pointed out that in s. 43 of the *Real Property Act*, the following section, it is provided that a registered proprietor shall not be affected by notice, direct or constructive, of any trust or unregistered interest, and it is proper to bear in mind the difference in language adopted by the legislature. However, it seems to me that there is a single doctrine of notice which was developed in the courts of equity, and that a person has notice when he comes within any aspect of the doctrine. In other words, direct or actual notice and constructive notice are not different things but are different aspects of the same thing. Therefore when the legislature uses the general word "notice" it should prima facie be taken to intend thereby to comprehend the whole of the equitable concept, and not one particular part of it. There are of course cases at law which are not concerned with notice in conveyancing transactions where actual notice may be necessary (see *Vallee v. Dumergue* (1849) 4 Exch. 290; *Burgh v. Legge* (1839) 8 L.J. Ex. 258), but I do not think that these cases throw any light on the meaning to be given to the word "notice" in a conveyancing context.

I am therefore of the opinion that the word "notice" in s. 42(d) comprehends notice actual and constructive. I have expressed my conclusion that a purchaser has constructive notice of the rights of persons actually in possession of the land when he is informed by the vendor that the vendor himself is not in possession of the land, and even though the vendor may inform him that some person other than the person actually in possession is thus in possession. The duty of inquiry is not satisfied by taking the word of the vendor. The purchaser must seek the person actually in possession and inquire of that person concerning his title. If he does not do so then he has constructive notice of that title. When I apply this principle to the facts of the present case, I find therefore that the respondent had constructive notice of the title of the person in possession, if it is proved that that person is in possession. This may or may not in the long run be a question to be determined upon the trial of the ejectment action, but it leads to the conclusion that this would not be an appropriate case in which there should be summary judgment in ejectment. I have read the order proposed by Sugerman J.A. and I agree with that order.

[The concurring judgment of Holmes J.A. has been omitted.]

Appeal allowed.

HUNT v. LUCK

Court of Appeal [1902] 1 Ch. 428

[Mrs Hunt was the legal personal representative of her husband, Dr Hunt, and she was the tenant for life under his will. She sought to upset certain conveyances by her husband to Gilbert. Miss Luck was the legal personal representative and beneficiary under Gilbert's will. It was alleged that the signatures of Dr Hunt were either forgeries (because at the date of the purported conveyances he was totally incapable of transacting business) or that he had been tricked into transferring the property and that he believed Gilbert required the deeds to act as his agent for the purpose of the collection of rent from the property. Gilbert raised mortgages on the property and the mortgagees were the real parties to the action. It was argued that proper inquiry had not been made of the tenants and that such an inquiry would have revealed that Dr Hunt was the true owner of the property. The mortgagees did inquire as to the payment of the rent and they were told that it was paid to one Woodrow, but they did not pursue the inquiry to see on whose behalf Woodrow had collected the rent. Farwell J. (at first instance) held that even if the fraud was proven the mortgagees had neither actual nor constructive notice of the fraud or of the title of Dr Hunt. As they were purchasers for value their title prevailed against that of the plaintiff. As against the mortgagees, the action was dismissed. On Appeal.]

VAUGHAN WILLIAMS L.J. In my opinion, the judgment of Farwell J. was quite right. He has, so far as I can see, dealt with the case without reference to the provisions of the *Conveyancing Act* 1882. He stated what he considered to be the law as established by decisions, including those prior to the *Conveyancing Act*.

Speaking for myself, if we are to determine the question now raised with reference to the old law, I think that the conclusion of Farwell J. was right. In his judgment he, after quoting the older authorities, said: "The rule established by these two cases may be stated thus: (1) A tenant's occupation is notice of all the tenant's rights, but not his lessor's title or rights; (2) actual knowledge that the rents are paid by the tenants to some person whose receipt is inconsistent with the title of the vendor is notice of the person's rights." In the present case I do not understand that anyone suggests, and, if it suggested, in my opinion the suggestion is ill-founded, that there was actual knowledge that the rents were paid by the tenants to some person whose receipt would be inconsistent with the title of the mortgagor, Gilbert. We have, therefore, to apply the first of the rules stated by the learned judge. Now, what does that mean? It means that, if a purchaser or a mortgagee has notice that the vendor or mortgagor is not in possession of the property, he must make inquiries of the person in possession—of the tenant who is in possession—and find out from him what his rights are, and, if he does not choose to do that, then whatever title he acquires as purchaser or mortgagee will be subject to the title or right of the tenant in possession.

That, I believe, is a true statement of the law. . . .

In my judgment, the only inquiry which ought reasonably to have been made here by the intending mortgagees was an inquiry to protect themselves against any right which the tenant might have in the subject matter of the mortgage. I do not think that there is, for the purpose of ascertaining the title of the vendor, any obligation on the purchaser to make inquiries of the tenant in reference to anything but protection against the rights of the tenant. And I only desire to add that, in my judgment, on the facts of this case, as I take them from the statement in the report, if inquiry had been made of the tenants, the equitable title of Dr Hunt and Mrs Hunt would not have come to the knowledge of the intending mortgagees. All that they would probably have learned, if they had made inquiries of the tenants, would have been that the tenants paid the rent to Mr Woodrow, a local agent. In my judgment, it is not true to say that the facts as to the equitable title of Dr Hunt and Mrs Hunt would have come to the knowledge of the mortgagees if they had made those inquiries. And, even if they had been told that the rents were collected by Woodrow on account of Gilbert, I do not see that that would have carried the matter any further.

[The judgments of Stirling and Cozens-Hardy L.JJ. have been omitted.]

Appeal dismissed.

NOTES AND QUESTIONS

1. A purchaser agrees to buy a property which is located at a considerable distance from his normal place of residence. The property is subject to a lease not exceeding three years. Does the purchaser take subject to the tenancy? Would your answer be any different if the purchaser lived close to the property but had chosen not to inspect it?

2. A purchaser will take subject only to those rights of the tenant stated in the tenancy agreement. He is not obliged to inquire into any equities of rectification which may exist between the tenant and the vendor-landlord: *Smith v. Jones* [1954] 1 W.L.R. 1089.

3. *Hunt v. Luck* is an old system decision. However, the rule it advances applies to Torrens land (as is shown by the *Clyne* case (1968) 69 S.R. (N.S.W.) 433, extracted above p. 192).

5. Personal equities

The topic of personal equities and that of fraud might be considered together for those rights which amount to personal equities are, most likely, those rights which would amount to "equitable" fraud and hence not strict fraud within the interpretation of the Acts: see *Logue v. Shoalhaven Shire Council* [1979] 1 N.S.W.L.R. 537 per Mahoney J.A. A registered proprietor cannot set up the indefeasibility of his title against an interest which he has created.

FRAZER v. WALKER

Judicial Committee of the Privy Council [1967] 1 A.C. 569

LORD WILBERFORCE. [I]n following and approving in this respect the two decisions in *Assets Co. Ltd v. Mere Roihi* [1905] A.C. 176 and *Boyd v. Mayor etc. of Wellington* [1924] N.Z.L.R. 1174 their Lordships have accepted the general principle that registration under the *Land Transfer Act* 1952 confers upon a registered proprietor a title to the interest in respect of which he is registered which is (under ss 62 and 63) immune from adverse claims, other than those specially excepted. In doing so they wish to make clear that this principle in no way denies the right of a plaintiff to bring against a registered proprietor a claim in personam, founded in law or in equity, for such relief as a court acting in personam may grant. That this is so has frequently, and rightly, been recognised in the courts of New Zealand and Australia: see, for example, *Boyd v. Mayor, etc. of Wellington* [1924] N.Z.L.R. 1174 at 1223 and *Tataurangi Tairuakena v. Mua Carr* [1927] N.Z.L.R. 688 at 702.

Their Lordships refer to these cases by way of illustration only without intending to limit or define the various situations in which actions of a personal character against registered proprietors may be admitted. The principle must always remain paramount that those actions which fall within the prohibition of ss 62 and 63 may not be maintained.

LOGUE v. SHOALHAVEN SHIRE COUNCIL

Supreme Court of New South Wales (Court of Appeal) [1979] 1 N.S.W.L.R. 537

[The title to the subject land was registered under the provisions of the *Real Property Act* 1900. The council, under the provisions of the *Local Government Act* 1919, s. 602(1), purported to sell part of the land for overdue rates. The sales were held and the council, under s. 602(5A) purchased and became the registered proprietor. The executor of the now-deceased former registered proprietor sought a declaration that the sale was invalid, owing to the form of the pre-sale notices together with other deficiencies in the council's procedures. It was argued that the council (the respondent) held the land in trust for the executor (the appellant). At first instance Powell J. found in favour of the executor. The defendant appealed.

The question of whether or not there were personal equities arising out of the respondent's conduct and enforceable against it, was considered.]

HUTLEY J.A. I am unable to accept the argument that an inaccuracy in the statement of rates overdue means that the council has not complied with the terms of s. 602(2)(b). I cannot imagine that it was the intention of the legislature, or of those responsible for prescribing the forms, to invalidate the transaction for any error in the amount shown for rates overdue. Whether or not gross errors, for example, the insertion of $1 million where $100 was the correct amount, would invalidate the form, it is not necessary to decide. Some errors may mean that the notice itself was not really a notice at all. However, the discrepancy here is not such as to invalidate the form and, in my opinion, the notice which was given in this case was a compliance with s. 602(2)(b). In my opinion *Merten v. Shoalhaven Shire Council* [1975] 1 N.S.W.L.R. 720(n.) was wrongly decided and should be formally overruled. This really concludes the appeal; but, because a number of other issues of importance to councils were debated, I propose to deal with the further grounds of appeal which were argued. . . .

The appellant further relied upon the protection given to it as a registered proprietor by virtue of s. 42 of the *Real Property Act*. The decision of the Privy Council in *Frazer v. Walker* [1967] 1 A.C. 569 approving the decision of the majority of the Supreme Court of New Zealand in *Boyd v. Mayor etc. of Wellington* [1924] N.Z.L.R. 1174 and of the High Court in *Breskvar v. Wall* (1971) 126 C.L.R. 376 are, in my opinion, conclusive in favour of the council. It is true that indefeasibility of the registered proprietor does not defeat a personal equity between himself and a transferor to him; and reliance was placed on a passage from the judgment of Barwick C.J. in *Breskvar v. Wall* (1971) 126 C.L.R. 376 at 384, 385 in support of this exception. However, in my opinion, there is no personal equity existing here. The highest point at which the respondent's case can be put is that, because of want of care by the council in the exercise of its statutory powers, he has been improperly deprived of his land, which is vested in the council. It does not necessarily follow from this that he has a personal equity to have his land back. He may be merely entitled to take proceedings against the council for damages for deprivation of his land, because of the way it has exercised its statutory powers; or, indeed, he may have no remedy at all.

Even if it is correct that there is a distinction between this case and the decision in *Boyd v. Mayor etc. of Wellington* [1924] N.Z.L.R. 1174 in that, as Mahoney J.A. points out in his judgment, which I have read, the Mayor was in no relevant way involved in those matters which rendered the transaction void, it cannot avail the respondent, as the appellant has a dual protection based on s. 42 of the *Real Property Act* and s. 604 of the *Local Government Act*. The personal equity which might exist, if the appellant could rely on s. 42, is barred by the fact that the council is protected, in its capacity as purchaser, against equities; and because, as vendor, it is purporting to act under the *Local Government Act*. The central passage in the judgment under appeal ([1978] 1 N.S.W.L.R. 710 at 719): "It is my view that where, as in a case such as the present, a person or body, purporting, but failing, to act in accordance with the provisions of a statute enabling it to do so, procures its registration as the proprietor of land under the *Real Property Act*, he or it holds that land upon trust for, and thus, is subject to a personal equity in favour of, the prior registered proprietor of the land" is not applicable to this case, as complete protection against equities is given to transactions which purport to comply with the Act, even in the event that they do fail to do so.

However, I would not elevate the administrative blunders with which this sale was associated into a source of a personal equity binding the council, or regard the determination of the council after so many years to insist on retaining the land as a sign that at the time of the purchase there was any bad faith. That is the relevant time. If this is correct, the distinction between this case and *Boyd v. Mayor etc. of Wellington* is without substance and s. 42 of the *Real Property Act*, on its own, provides a complete answer to the plaintiff's claim.

Despite the courageous and frank argument of Mr McDougall, in my opinion, the appeal should be allowed, the declarations and orders set aside and the summons dismissed. The respondent should be ordered to pay the costs of the hearing before Powell J. and of this appeal, and have a certificate in respect of the appeal under the *Suitors' Fund Act* 1951.

MAHONEY J.A. Apart from fraud, the section, in terms, purports to free the registered proprietor from (in the sense here relevant) "all other . . . interests whatsoever". But it does not operate to protect him against what have been described as the "personal equities": *Breskvar v. Wall* (1971) 126 C.L.R. 376 at 385 per Barwick C.J.; see *Frazer v. Walker* [1967] 1 A.C. 569 at 585. These personal equities include, of course, equities created by the registered proprietor after he has become registered: see, for example, *Barry v. Heider* (1914) 19 C.L.R. 197. But, in my opinion, they are not limited to these. They include equities which have arisen from things which have happened before he became registered. Thus, if the registered proprietor had, before acquiring the land, agreed that, if he did acquire the land, he would hold it on trust or for a stated purpose, or had agreed that the land should be charged for a particular purpose, that agreement would be enforced against him. And this does not depend upon fraud: it follows even where, for example, the fact of the prior agreement had been forgotten by the registered proprietor, and there was no fraud involved.

The kind of interest which can, in this way, be enforced against a registered proprietor is not limited. In *Frazer v. Walker* [1967] 1 A.C. 569, 585, Lord Wilberforce was careful not to limit the "actions of a personal character" which could be brought. His Lordship referred to two decisions by way of illustration. In *Boyd v. Mayor, etc. of Wellington* [1924] N.Z.L.R. 1174 at 1223, Adams J. had said that the equivalent section left unrestricted obligations arising in relation to trusts, express or implied, the performance of contracts, and the rectification of transactions for mistake. In *Tataurangi Tairuakena v. Mua Carr* [1927] N.Z.L.R. 688, the court set aside registration of a transfer where the transferee had occupied a fiduciary position qua the transferor. But it is settled that the registered proprietor is protected against the effect of mere notice of the existence of another interest. Under the general law, a person who, when he took his interest, had notice of the existence of another interest, would normally take subject to that interest. It may be that originally this was based on the view that the contrary would be fraud: *Le Neve v. Le Neve* (1747) Amb. 436 at 446, 447; 27 E.R. 291 at 295. But the effect of notice was adopted as part of the ordinary rules applying in equity for the determination of priorities: see generally Snell's *Principles of Equity* (27th ed.), pp. 45-55. Section 42 protects the registered proprietor against the effect of such notice: *Stuart v. Kingston* (1923) 32 C.L.R. 309.

But there were, under the general law, reasons other than mere notice upon the basis of which a legal or equitable interest might be postponed to or qualified by another interest. The various kinds of equitable fraud are examples of this. It is necessary to determine whether these, or some of them, and the equities that flow from them, fall within the "personal equities" now in question. Counsel have not been able to refer the court to any cases in which this question has been considered. In the *Friedman* case [1962] Qd R. 498 at 512 Gibbs J. said that fraud, for the purpose of the Queensland equivalent of s. 42, did not include equitable fraud, but his Honour was there considering a case of mere notice of a pre-existing option and the effect of it, and was not concerned to consider the present question.

There are, in my opinion, kinds of equitable fraud in which the interests arising from what has happened may be enforced against a registered proprietor, notwithstanding that there has been no fraud within the meaning of that term in s. 42. I think that, in the kind of situation illustrated by *Nocton v. Lord Ashburton* [1914] A.C. 932, if the land had been transferred to the solicitor, the court would have interfered to enforce equitable rights against him. Such equity would not depend upon any intention to defraud ([1914] A.C. 932 at 945); and may arise merely because the defendant has, however innocently, misunderstood the obligation which equity imposes upon him ([1914] A.C. 932 at 954). Similarly, the kind of equitable fraud arising from negligence in advising a client: see *Bulkey v. Wilford* (1834) 2 Cl. & Fin. 102; 6 E.R. 1094, will, if the solicitor acquires the land, result in his holding it subject to the kinds of rights illustrated in that case.

In my opinion, the present is also such a case. Here, the fact that the sale and transfer were a nullity arose because of the breach of the duty which the statute imposed upon the council. The council knew of the matters from which the consequence of nullity flowed; and, in addition, it owed to the person in the position of the plaintiff a duty to observe, in dealings with him, a high standard. These facts, I think, give rise to a personal equity of the relevant kind.

Two things may be said in support of this conclusion. First, the present case differs from cases such as *Caldwell v. Rural Bank of New South Wales* (1951) 53 S.R. (N.S.W.) 415; 69 W.N. 246 and *Boyd v. Mayor, etc. of Wellington* [1924] N.Z.L.R. 1174. In those cases, the only right which, under the general law, the plaintiff had against the defendant arose from the fact that the resumption on which the defendant's registration was based was a nullity: that right would have allowed the plaintiff, under the general law, to have the purported vesting set aside upon the basis to which I referred earlier in this judgment, viz., that the plaintiff had not been divested of the land. The plaintiff's claim in such a case rested on the fact that he remained the owner. But, as was pointed out in *Frazer v. Walker* [1967] 1 A.C. 569 at 584, sections such as s. 42 operate to divest land from a person in the position of the plaintiff and, if his claim is based on nothing but his previous ownership the basis for that claim is destroyed by the section. In the *Caldwell* (1951) 53 S.R. (N.S.W.) 415; 69 W.N. 246 and the *Boyd* [1924] N.Z.L.R. 1174 cases, the defendants had not been involved in any relevant way with those matters which resulted in the resumption being void. There was, on the part of the defendants, nothing which was unconscionable other than their taking the benefit of the void resumptions. Nor were the defendants in breach of any duty imposed upon them in relation to the procedure whereby the land was taken from the plaintiff. In the present case, it is what the council did in this regard (and not merely the fact of the plaintiff's previous rights to ownership of the land) which is the basis of the plaintiff's claim.

Second, the enforcement of such rights in equity against the claimant is in accordance with the general purpose of s. 42. The Act in the main is a conveyancing statute: *Barry v. Heider* (1914) 19 C.L.R. 197 at 213. Its purpose is to remove the kinds of problems which traditionally have affected the process of conveyance, to ensure that, upon registration, those problems will no longer affect the transferee; and to enable a person dealing with the transferee to look merely to the register. But its purpose is not to put aside "the fundamental doctrines by which the courts of equity have enforced, as against registered proprietors, conscientious obligations entered into by them": *Barry v. Heider* (1914) 19 C.L.R. 197 at 213. In deciding whether a right in equity which would be enforceable against a transferee under the general law shall be enforced against him notwithstanding s. 42, it is of assistance to consider whether it is, to put the matter compendiously, a conveyancing matter, or whether it is based upon unconscionable conduct. To state the matter in that way is, in a sense, only to restate the problem; but it does, in my opinion, provide some assistance in determining an instant case.

I, therefore, think that the plaintiff is entitled to succeed. In reaching this conclusion, it has not been necessary to consider the effect of s. 135 of the Act.

[Reynolds J.A. concurred with Hutley J.A.]

Appeal allowed.

NOTE

As to whether a registered proprietor who has created an interest in land is able to rely on indefeasibility to escape his obligations, see *Bahr v. Nicolay (No. 2)* (1988) 62 A.L.J.R. 268, extracted above p. 170.

6. Correction of errors

In New South Wales the general power of the Registrar-General to correct errors in the Register is found set out in s. 12 which is supplemented by s. 136 and s. 137. Section 136 enables the Registrar-General to acquire the certificate of title for the purpose of making the correction. The power of correction must be limited, otherwise the principles of indefeasibility might be overcome through the Registrar-General exercising an unfettered power. Further, as a general rule the power to correct errors must be exercised before the acquisition of a right which is entitled to the indefeasibility conferred by the Act (but in this regard special reference should be made to s. 12(3)).

FRAZER v. WALKER

Judicial Committee of the Privy Council [1967] 1 A.C. 569

LORD WILBERFORCE. The second observation relates to the power of the registrar to correct entries under ss 80 and 81 [of the New Zealand Torrens Statute]. It has already been pointed out (as was made clear in the *Assets* case [1905] A.C. 176 at 194-195) by this Board that this power is quite distinct from the power of the court to order cancellation of entries under s. 85, and moreover while the latter is invoked here, the former is not. The powers of the registrar under s. 81 are significant and extensive: *Assets* case. They are not coincident with the cases excepted in ss 62 and 63. As well as in the case of fraud, where any grant, certificate, instrument, entry or indorsement has been wrongfully obtained or is wrongfully retained, the registrar has power of cancellation and correction. From the argument before their Lordships it appears that there is room for some difference of opinion as to what precisely may be comprehended in the word "wrongfully". It is clear, in any event, that s. 81 must be read with and subject to s. 183 with the consequence that the exercise of the registrar's powers must be limited to the period before a bona fide purchaser, or mortgagee, acquires a title under the latter section.

NOTES AND QUESTIONS

1. In *James v. Registrar-General* (1967) 69 S.R. (N.S.W.) 361 an easement had been noted upon the title in accordance with the provisions of the New South Wales Act. On transfer of the property the easement was omitted from the title and the Registrar-General sought to re-annotate the certificate of title after the purchase was registered. It was held that the renotation was valid as the easement came within the exception of indefeasibility of title stated in s. 42(1)(b): see below p. 280.

2. In *Pirie v. Registrar-General* (1963) 109 C.L.R. 619 at 623, 644 (a case on restrictive covenants) the following observations were made upon the powers of the Registrar-General to correct errors:

   > KITTO J. The situation in which the appellants made their application to the court was as follows. The appellants, being the registered proprietors as tenants in common in equal shares of an estate in fee simple in certain land under the Act, namely lot 181 on a certain deposited plan, No. 5275, had applied in writing to the Registrar-General for the cancellation of a notification, appearing on their certificate of title, of the terms of a restrictive covenant. The covenant was contained in a memorandum of transfer of the lots, which had been made in 1919 by one Halloran in favour of two persons named Maclure and Horton. The notification was entered in 1919 on the two certificates of title of lot 181 issued to Maclure and Horton respectively in that year. A new certificate of title was issued in respect of the lot in 1946 in consequence of transfers that had taken place, and the notification was carried onto the new certificate. It is under that certificate that the appellants are now the registered proprietors.

   > The Registrar-General refused to cancel the notification, and he stated in the following terms the ground of his refusal: "The notification relates to restrictions arising under covenant as to the user of the land comprised in the said certificate of title within the meaning of s. 88(3) of the *Conveyancing Act* 1919, as amended, and I am not satisfied that such restrictions have ceased to affect the said land."

   > From the nature of the Torrens system of registration of titles, and in particular from such provisions of the *Real Property Act* as ss 4, 12(1)(d) and (1)(f), 32, 40, 42 and 43, it is, I think, a necessary conclusion that the Registrar-General, as head of the department authorised to carry the provisions of the Act into execution (s. 4), is under the general duty to keep the register book clear of all notifications save those which are authorised by law: see *Wolfson v. Registrar-General (N.S.W.)* (1934) 51 C.L.R. 300. The removal of an unauthorised notification is therefore, in my opinion, an act or duty which by the Act is prescribed to be done or performed by the Registrar-General, within the meaning of s. 121.

   > WINDEYER J. The Torrens system of registered estates and interests, as it exists in New South Wales, has as its main foundation s. 42 of the *Real Property Act*. Once a grant or certificate of title has been issued the Registrar-General is, I think, under a duty to permit no entries or notifications to appear on the folium of the register book except such as the law authorises. Persons claiming equitable interests, or having other claims the notification of which on certificates of title the law does not authorise, may up to a point protect their interests by caveats. But that does not cut across the fundamental principle of the system. It follows, I think, that the Registrar-General whose duty it is to put no unauthorised entries in the register book is under a corresponding duty to remove any that ought not to be there.

3. What is the effect of s. 12(3) of the *Real Property Act* 1900 (N.S.W.) upon the observations in *Pirie v. Registrar-General* and is there any difficulty in reconciling paras (b) and (c) of that subsection? What is the effect of the provision on the principles of indefeasibility of title secured by s. 42?

7. Statutory charges

Later special statutes override earlier general statutes and earlier special statutes; later general statutes override earlier general statutes but not earlier special statutes (see *Pratten's* case, below). It is clear from the Torrens Acts that the original intention was that no interest should affect Torrens title properties unless that interest was recorded on the Register. However, this principle has been lost sight of by legislation passed since the introduction of the Torrens system. It has set up interests which do not need to be registered under the Torrens system and which ride over the Register according to the principles of statutory interpretation mentioned previously.

PRATTEN v. WARRINGAH SHIRE COUNCIL

Supreme Court of New South Wales (1969) 90 W.N. (Pt 1) (N.S.W.) 134

[The title to the subject land was registered under the provisions of the New South Wales *Real Property Act* 1900. Pursuant to the provisions of the *Local Government Act* 1919, s. 398, part of the plaintiff's land was vested in the local council for the purposes of drainage. There was no reference on the certificate of title to the fact that the relevant portion of the land had vested in the council.]

STREET J. It has long been accepted that in the case of *Real Property Act* land there can exist proprietary rights which do not depend upon registration for their efficacy. *Hogg on Australian Torrens System* discusses the existence of these rights at p. 804 et seq. Amongst the categories listed by *Hogg* are:

4. Charges in respect of rates, taxes, and other public burdens, and estates created on sale or lease by way of realising the amount of these charges.

5. Estates created on expropriation of the land for public purposes under powers conferred by the general statutes.

Earlier the learned author of *Hogg* said: "What are known as Resumption Acts constitute a class of the general statutes which must be considered as overriding, and pro tanto repealing, even the Torrens statutes. Provision, however, is often made, sometimes in the Torrens statutes, and sometimes in the general statutes, for having proper notice of the compulsory change of ownership entered on the register. But, in view of the scope and object of statutes under which land is expropriated for public purposes, it can hardly be doubted that the maxim, Generalia specialibus, etc., would not be held applicable so far as to exempt land under the Torrens system in the slightest degree from the operation of this class of general statutes."

The inefficacy of a clean certificate of title to override land which was in law a public highway was upheld by Rich A.J. in *Vickery v. Municipality of Strathfield* (1911) 11 S.R. (N.S.W.) 354 at 361-364. In *South-Eastern Drainage Board (South Australia) v. Savings Bank of South Australia* (1939) 62 C.L.R. 603, it fell to the High Court to consider whether charges on land purported to be created by the *South-Eastern Drainage Act* 1931 (No. 2062), of the State of South Australia took priority over a mortgage affecting land registered under the South Australian *Real Property Act* 1886 (No. 380). The decision of the court upheld the priority of the statutory charge as against a registered charge. Their Honours took the view that the problem involved a consideration of the interaction between the *Real Property Act* and the *Drainage Act*. At 627-628, Dixon J. (as he then was) said: "It follows, therefore, that the question upon which our decision must turn is whether in the enactments creating the statutory charges such a clear intention is expressed to include land under the *Real Property Act* and to give to the charges an absolute and indefeasible priority over all other interests that, notwithstanding s. 6 of that Act, no course is open but to allow the intention so expressed in the later enactments to be paramount over the earlier *Real Property Act*. In my opinion this question ought to be answered that such an intention so plainly appears that no other course is open."

Starke J. said (at 621-622): "The claim of the respondent that its mortgage had priority over the statutory charges was based, however, upon the well-known provisions of the *Real Property Act* 1886, which embodies the Torrens system of registration of title to land. One of the objects of the Act, declared in s. 10, was to secure indefeasibility of title to all registered proprietors except in certain specified cases. So it is enacted that the title of every registered proprietor of land, which includes a mortgage security, shall be absolute and indefeasible subject to certain qualifications, that no instrument shall be effectual to pass any land or to render any land liable as security for the payment of money unless registered as prescribed by the Act, that no unregistered estate, interest, right, power, contract or trust shall prevail against the title of a registered proprietor taking bona fide for valuable consideration or of any person bona fide claiming through or under him: see ss 3, 69, 67, 70, 71. *But the charges in the present case are created by and take their force and effect from the statutes creating them.''* (The italics are my own.) Lower down (at 622), Starke J. said: "The charges do not depend upon registration nor upon the execution or entry of any instrument. They are complete and effective by reason of the provisions of the Acts creating them. No room so far is left for the operation of the *Real Property Act* 1886, and the explicit and express provisions of the Drainage Acts must prevail. The charges are made first charges over the land and all interest therein and have priority over all other charges.''

A similar point of apparent statutory conflict came before the Privy Council in *Miller v. Minister of Mines* [1963] A.C. 484. . . . In the present case, if the question be asked in the terms in which Dixon C.J. stated it in the *South-Eastern Drainage Board* case, in the passage which I have quoted, the answer must clearly be that s. 398 overrode the provisions of the *Real Property Act*. The vesting under that section became immediately operative regardless of the fact that the land was registered under the *Real Property Act* in the name of some other party. *Ex parte Registrar-General; Re Council of Municipality of Randwick* (1951) 51 S.R. (N.S.W.) 220, is direct and binding authority establishing the operation of the section and the content of the estate so vested.

Guided by these authorities, it must in my view follow that the estate which became vested in the council in September 1920 vacated any further interest in the land in question on the part of the then registered proprietor. Thereafter it did not in law have the fee simple in the land. Nor was it able by transfer to call back, so to speak, that fee simple and vest it in a transferee. The absolute indefeasibility ordinarily flowing from registration (*Frazer v. Walker* [1967] 1 A.C. 569) will not avail where the fee simple has, by an overriding statute, been in effect removed from the registration system. Moreover, not only was the then registered proprietor incapable of calling back his fee simple, but no act of the Registrar-General otherwise than consequent upon the written request of the council pursuant to s. 14 of the *Real Property (Amendment) Act* 1921, could be recognised as effective to trench in any way upon the council's fee simple.

Decretal order accordingly.

NOTES

1. In *Hugh Thomas Miller v. Minister of Mines and the Attorney-General (New Zealand)* [1963] N.Z.L.R. 561, an owner of "old" system land had it registered under the New Zealand *Torrens Act* free from reservation of mines and minerals to the Crown. The whole of such rights were later transferred to the Glenorchy Scheelite Mining Co., which subsequently assigned its rights to the Crown. The plaintiff became the registered proprietor of the land and sought a declaration that the Crown was not entitled to mine scheelite on his land. Mining licences were granted under the *Mining Act* 1926.

    LORD GUEST. The *Mining Act* 1926, provides its own separate and independent code for the registration of mining licences. They are granted by the warden under s. 58 and registered under s. 180. A transfer of a mining privilege must be registered under s. 179 and the effect of registration is provided for under s. 185. If the licence is not registrable under the *Land Transfer Act* and the indefeasibility provisions of that Act are to override the grant, the licence would be of no value to the licensee except as against the original owner of the lands. Upon a transfer of the land the successor would be entitled in virtue of the provisions of the *Land Transfer Act* to determine the mining privilege. Their Lordships do not consider that this can have been the intention of the legislature in enacting the compendious code for mining privileges in the *Mining Act* which are to exist for at least 42 years.

> Their Lordships were referred to cases in New Zealand where statutory rights over land were held to exist despite the fact that they did not appear on the register. It is not necessary in their Lordships' opinion that there should be a direct provision overriding the provisions of the *Land Transfer Act*. It is sufficient if this is [a] proper implication from the terms of the relative statute.

2. The principal case was applied in *Christopoulos v. Kells* (1988) 13 N.S.W.L.R. 541.

H. VOLUNTEERS

It may be questioned whether the Torrens Acts confer an indefeasible title upon a volunteer (although clearly any transfer by that volunteer to a purchaser for value will confer an indefeasible title, upon registration).

KING v. SMAIL

Supreme Court of Victoria [1958] V.R. 273

[A and B (the applicants) were registered as proprietors as joint tenants. A executed a memorandum of transfer in favour of B, purporting to transfer to B his interest as a joint tenant, by way of gift. A then executed a deed of arrangement in favour of C, as trustee for his creditors. The memorandum of transfer to B was subsequently lodged for registration and registered. The question arose whether C's interest, as trustee for the creditors, took priority over the now registered interest which A had given to B.]

ADAM J. A search of behalf of the respondent on 28 September 1956 disclosed that the land in question was registered in the joint names of the applicant and her husband. Subsequently on the same day—28 September 1956—the transfer dated 24 July 1956 referred to above was lodged for registration.

On 11 October 1956 the respondent lodged a caveat claiming an equitable estate in fee simple under the deed of arrangement in the land in question then standing in the name of the applicant and the husband, and forbidding the registration of any person as transferee or proprietor of any instrument affecting the said estate. This caveat having been lodged subsequently to the said instrument of transfer did not prevent registration of the applicant as transferee of the husband's interest in the land and she is now the registered proprietor of the entirety. On 8 March 1957 the caveat was amended so as to apply to the said land standing in the register book in the name of the applicant alone.

It is this caveat, as amended, which by these proceedings the applicant seeks to have removed.

The question for determination is whether in the foregoing circumstances there is now vested in the respondent an estate or interest in the land which has priority over the registered title of the applicant so as to be entitled to the protection of this caveat.

Two subsidiary questions arise. The first is whether in the circumstances the respondent acquired any beneficial estate or interest in the land under and by virtue of the deed of arrangement and if so, the second question is whether such estate or interest prevails against the registered title subsequently acquired by the applicant. I deal with those questions in that order.

As to the first question, it was urged on behalf of the applicant that for a variety of reasons the respondent at no time acquired an estate or interest in the land under the deed of arrangement. One contention was that the deed of arrangement properly construed did not purport to assign to the respondent the husband's interest in the land in question. In my opinion, this contention fails.

True is that contrary to s. 192 of the *Bankruptcy Act* the deed did not specify in the first schedule thereto the estate and interest of the husband in the land as it should have if he had at the time a beneficial estate or interest therein, but the operative words of the deed are expressed to extend beyond property specified in the first schedule to "all other property of which the debtor is possessed or to which he is entitled legally or equitably" with exceptions immaterial for present purposes. I see no reason to doubt that these extending words operate to cover any property of a debtor not otherwise excepted which he may have innocently or wilfully concealed from the trustee, with the result that it was omitted from the First Schedule.

A further contention raised was that registration under the *Transfer of Land Act* of the assignment of the estate or interest which the deed purported to assign to the trustee thereunder was an indispensable condition to his acquiring such estate or interest in the land and that failure to procure registration of the assignment was fatal to his claim now sought to be protected by caveat. This contention was founded on s. 103(4) of the *Bankruptcy Act* which in effect provides that where a State Act requires registration for the effectual transfer of property from a debtor to a trustee for the benefit of his creditors "the vesting of the property . . . in the . . . trustee" under a deed of arrangement under Part XII "shall be subject to compliance with the requirements of the . . . State Act". A similar question was mooted before Clark J., in relation to the title of a trustee in bankruptcy in *Re Williams* (1931) 3 A.B.C. 157, and for the reasons given by him in that case I consider it clear that s. 103(4), while denying to the respondent the legal title to the husband's estate or interest in the land unless and until he obtained registration of a transfer thereof to himself, does not prevent the vesting in him of the husband's beneficial interest in so far as the same would pass by the terms of the deed of arrangement.

If at the time of the execution of the deed on 17 August 1956 the husband was possessed of a beneficial interest in the undivided moiety of the land in respect of which the applicant and himself were then registered as joint proprietors, I see no reason to doubt that such beneficial interest passed on execution of the deed subject only to avoidance should the deed in the result become void through failure to obtain the necessary assents of creditors or non-registration thereof under s. 193 of the *Bankruptcy Act*: see *Armstrong v. Wilkins* (1940) 63 C.L.R. 489.

In relation to the first question—whether the respondent acquired a beneficial estate or interest in the land under the deed—it remains to consider whether the husband at the material time, whether that be the date of the deed or the date of its registration, was competent to confer upon the respondent an estate or interest unaffected by any claims by the applicant. It appears that at the material date the husband had already executed an instrument of transfer of his estate or interest by way of gift to the applicant. It does not appear, however, from the material before me, whether or not the husband had prior to the material date delivered to the applicant or to any person on her behalf the said instrument of transfer. In these circumstances, as appears from the decision in *Brunker v. Perpetual Trustee Co. Ltd* (1937) 57 C.L.R. 555, the foundation for an argument that the applicant might at the material date and notwithstanding non-registration of her transfer have possibly acquired some right in or in relation to the land which might have prevailed over the respondent's subsequent assignment is lacking. Accordingly, I have resisted the temptation aroused by the judgment in *Brunker's* case to consider the effect upon the rights of an unregistered transferee to whom the instrument of transfer has been delivered by way of gift, of a subsequent disposition for value by the registered proprietor in favour of another party.

The conclusion I reach then, on the evidence before me, is that under and by virtue of the deed of arrangement the respondent acquired, as trustee for the creditors of the husband, the beneficial estate in the moiety of the land in question of which the husband was the registered proprietor, unaffected by any claim by the applicant.

The further question remains whether by virtue of the applicant on 18 September 1956, obtaining registration of the voluntary transfer of the husband's undivided half share in the land, the unregistered estate or interest of the respondent in the land has not been over-reached.

This, as fraud on the part of the applicant is not suggested, raises the far-reaching question whether by virtue of the *Transfer of Land Act* 1954 a volunteer who takes a transfer from a registered proprietor acquires, like a purchaser for value, a title free from equities which affected his transferor. It was, of course, not disputed that in relation to land under the general law a volunteer whether with or without notice took the legal estate subject to equities which affected his predecessor in title. In this respect a volunteer stood in the shoes of his predecessor in title.

The contention of the applicant was that the provisions of the *Transfer of Land Act* 1954, which by s. 3(1) prevail over rules of general law, were inconsistent with this conclusion and in the present case operated to confer on the applicant, although a volunteer, upon registration of the transfer a title which prevailed over the prior beneficial interest conferred on the respondent. . . .

Had it been intended by s. 43 to relieve a mere volunteer from equities which affected his transferor, the section would have been differently worded as, for example, by providing that persons dealing, etc., with registered proprietors would not be affected by any trust or unregistered interest any rule of law or equity to the contrary notwithstanding. . . .

In conclusion I should add that the view that Torrens legislation expressed in language not materially differing from the Victorian Acts does not confer a title, free from prior equities, on a registered proprietor being a mere volunteer finds confirmation in decisions in other jurisdictions. Suffice it for me to refer in particular to the persuasive judgment of Boucaut J., in *Biggs v. McEllister* (1880) 14 S.A.L.R. 86, a judgment concurred in by Way C.J. Apart from the statement by P. Moerlin Fox in his textbook referred to earlier in this judgment, the textbooks without exception appear to support this conclusion. Reference may be made to Hogg, *Australian Torrens System*, pp. 832-833; Hogg, *Registration of Title*, pp. 106-109; Wiseman's *The Transfer of Land* (2nd ed.), p. 316; Baalman's *Commentary on the Torrens System in New South Wales*, pp. 149-150; Kerr's *The Australian Lands Titles (Torrens) System*, p. 195.

Application dismissed.

BOGDANOVIC v. KOTEFF

Supreme Court of New South Wales (Court of Appeal)
(1988) 12 N.S.W.L.R. 472

[The respondent had become registered as proprietor by transmission. The appellant claimed a life interest in the property after the death of the registered proprietor and it was found, on the facts, that a promise of an interest had been made by the proprietor to the appellant. The respondent had become registered proprietor without notice of this promise.]

PRIESTLEY J.A. The argument for the appellant recognised that on the face of ss 42 and 43 [of the *Real Property Act* 1900 (N.S.W.)] the respondent would hold his registered interest in fee simple free of any equitable rights of the appellant. It was submitted however that it appeared from other sections in the Act, and from various decisions, that ss 42 and 43 cannot be given the absolute force that in their isolation they appear to have. For this proposition *Frazer v. Walker* [1967] A.C. 569 and *King v. Smail* [1958] V.R. 273 were particularly relied on. It was then submitted that it had for many years been accepted by text writers of authority that although s 42 (and its equivalents in other jurisdictions which have Torrens system statutes) makes no express distinction between the measure of indefeasibility afforded to a volunteer and to a purchaser for value, the section was not intended (this being arrived at as a matter of construction) to give indefeasibility to the volunteer. A number of text writers, including Baalman in his *Commentary on the Torrens System in New South Wales* (1951), pp. 149-150, have expressed that view, which is retained in the current descendant of Baalman, *The Torrens System in New South Wales* by Woodman and Nettle (1985) (loose-leaf), pp. 347-348. Woodman and Nettle also retains (at those pages) Baalman's comment: "The general result is that, on registration of a voluntary transfer, the transferee (as is the case of a volunteer under the general law) occupies no better position than did his transferor. But once registered, he occupies a position quite as good: his title is indefeasible against all claims except such as would have prevailed against his immediate predecessor."

There are certainly authorities to support the appellant's assertion. *King* decided in terms that the Victorian Torrens System Act, the *Transfer of Land Act* 1958, did not confer upon a registered proprietor, being a mere volunteer, a title free from prior equities. *Frazer* also supports the appellant's submission that there is some limitation upon the absoluteness of ss 42 and 43, but only in the sense that a person having rights in equity against a registered proprietor may procure orders against that registered proprietor which will bring about the result that the proprietor's registered interest may be altered, as a result of equity, in acting upon his conscience, forcing him to submit to what in practical terms amounts to a correction of the register in favour of the person having the rights in equity against him.

If, however, *King* represented the law in New South Wales at the times relevant to the present case, the appellant would be entitled to succeed. The reasoning in *King*, in summary, was that when the Victorian counterparts of ss 42, 43, 96, 124 and 135 were read together, the references in them to a purchaser for value (taking the New South Wales sections as examples, in s. 42(1)(c), s. 124(d) and (e) and s. 135) showed a general intention not to confer the benefit of indefeasibility upon volunteers. *King* is the latest of the cases cited by Woodman and Nettle, pp. 347-348 in support of the view stated in the text. *Frazer*, however, took the more limited view that the sections from which the general proposition was derived by those who said volunteers were not within the meaning of s. 42, did not support such a general proposition, but created only such exceptions to the general operative part of s. 42 as were specifically stated in the sections themselves. Speaking for the Privy Council, Lord Wilberforce (at 580-581) said that the indefeasibility of title concept: "is central in the system of registration. It does not involve that the registered proprietor is protected against any claim whatsoever; . . . there are provisions by which the entry on which he relies may be cancelled or corrected, or he may be exposed to claims in personam. These are matters not to be overlooked when a total description of his rights is required. But as registered proprietor, and while he remains such, no adverse claim (except as specifically admitted) may be brought against him.'' In New South Wales, at least two decisions at first instance have held the reasoning in *Frazer* applicable to the *Real Property Act*; see *Mayer v. Coe* (1968) 88 W.N. (Pt 1) (N.S.W.) 549; and *Ratcliffe v. Watters* (1969) 89 W.N. (Pt 1) (N.S.W.) 497.

In *Breskvar v. Wall* (1971) 126 C.L.R. 376 the High Court accepted *Frazer* as applicable to the Queensland Torrens system statute, the *Real Property Act* of 1877. Further, Barwick C.J., with whom Windeyer and Owen JJ. both agreed, said that both *Mayer* and *Ratcliffe* correctly applied *Frazer*. None of the four other judges expressly mentioned the two New South Wales decisions, but it seems implicit in their discussion of the authorities that they were proceeding on the footing that the principles in *Frazer* would be likewise applicable to Torrens system statutes in other Australian States unless a particular statute happened to contain some special provision requiring a different conclusion. So far as I have been able to see there is no such significantly distinguishing provision in the *Real Property Act*. Thus, it seems to me, the central ideas of *Frazer* are required by the High Court's decision in *Breskvar* to be applied by this court in dealing with the present case. The broad proposition arrived at by Adam J. in *King*, that a registered proprietor, being a mere volunteer does not obtain a title free from prior equities, must, following *Breskvar*, be replaced by a formulation based on what the High Court said in that case. There is such a formulation in Windeyer J.'s reasons. After referring to what Torrens himself said in his 1862 handbook on the *Real Property Act* of South Australia to the effect that his system left each freeholder in the same position as a grantee direct from the Crown, Windeyer J. went on (at 400): "This is an assertion that the title of each registered proprietor comes from the fact of registration, that it is made the source of the title, rather than a retrospective approbation of it as a derivative right. I say that only to emphasise that the doctrine of an indefeasible title arising by registration was seen as the very essence of the Torrens system from its beginning. In the present case, the decision of the Privy Council in *Frazer v. Walker* [1967] 1 A.C. 569 recognises that the registered proprietor has the legal property in the land, subject only to equities and such interests as the Act expressly preserves.'' Similar statements were made by other members of the court: see Barwick C.J. at 385, Menzies J. at 397, Walsh J. at 405 and Gibbs J. (indirectly) at 413.

In the present appeal the appellant has not been able to point to anything in the New South Wales Act preserving the rights she had in regard to the land against the registered proprietor. She could have enforced those rights against Mr S. Koteff and, I would assume, against his executor. But if knowledge of the appellant's interest by Mr N. Koteff before he became registered proprietor would enable her to assert her rights against him (a matter upon which it is unnecessary in this case to express any opinion) the materials earlier referred to show there is no basis for holding Mr N. Koteff knew anything which would put him on notice of those rights. Thus there was no material upon which the appellant could attempt to found an argument of any personal right against Mr N. Koteff, nor was there any provision in the *Real Property Act* on which she could rely to prevent s. 42 so operating that Mr N. Koteff held his interest in the land as registered proprietor of an estate in fee simple "absolutely free" from any estate or interest in her.

It seems to me that the provisions of the *Real Property Act* and the interpretations put on equivalent legislation by decisions which this court should follow, lead to the result that the appellant's appeal must be dismissed with costs.

[Hope and Samuels JJ.A. concurred with Priestley J.A.]

Appeal dismissed.

I. ADVERSE POSSESSION

Part VIA of the *Real Property Act* 1900 (N.S.W.) permits a person in adverse possession to make application to the Registrar-General for the issue of title with the supposed effect that the issue of the title extinguishes the interest of the previous registered proprietor: a person who has been in possession of land under circumstances which, had the statutes of limitation been in force in respect of the land, the interest of the registered proprietor would have been extinguished, may apply by way of possessory application to the Registrar-General to be recorded in the Register as the proprietor: s. 45D(1). The application must be in respect of a "whole parcel of land" (defined to mean, in effect, land which accords with minimum town planning standards: see s. 45B(1)), the intent being to prevent the acquisition of title to insignificant areas of land; where, however, the claimant has possession up to an "occupational boundary" (such as a fence, wall or river: see s. 45D(6)) which represents, but is not on, the true boundary, he may claim title to the area beyond the occupational boundary up to the true boundary, even though he does not occupy that area: s. 45D(2). The Registrar-General may grant the application if he is satisfied that certain of the requirements of Part VIA have been met (s. 45E(1)) by recording, in the Register, the applicant as proprietor: s. 45E(3).

By s. 45D(3), a possessory application may not be made in respect of land of which the Crown or any public or local authority is the registered proprietor; this would not prevent the extinction by adverse possession of the title of the Crown to land which it "owns" but of which it is not formally registered as proprietor. By s. 45D(4), a possessory application may not be made where a person has become registered as proprietor without fraud and for value and the whole of the limitation period has not run against him since his registration. The purpose of this provision is to protect purchasers of land in adverse possession by stipulating, in effect, that once a purchaser has intervened and become registered, time starts to run afresh and the adverse possessor receives no credit for prior periods of possession, unless the purchaser has been guilty of fraud; "fraud" presumably has the same meaning as it has in other sections of the Act, namely, "actual" fraud, so that merely to purchase with notice of the interest of an adverse possessor will not, of itself, be fraud: s. 43. Section 45E(4) preserves against extinction easements registered and covenants recorded in respect of the land. By s. 45H(1), a person claiming an estate or interest in the land may lodge a caveat against a possessory application; the caveator then has three months to institute court proceedings to resolve the question of title, in default of which the caveat lapses: ss 45I(2) and 45K.

There are two principal difficulties with these provisions: (1) It is unclear whether it is the grant of the application by the Registrar-General, or the expiration of the period of adverse possession which establishes title in a squatter: it seems that the approach taken to s. 41 of the Act might be applied to these provisions by treating his interest as "equitable" once the relevant period for the establishment of title by possession has passed, with the result that, before registration, any competition between a purchaser and the squatter will fall to be determined under the general rules of priorities concerning unregistered interests (which have been examined previously in this chapter), subject, of course, to the possibility that the transaction between the registered proprietor and the purchaser may have been collusive (which will then be determined by s. 45D(4)). (2) Since applications may only be made in respect of "whole" parcels (s. 45D(2)) no application will be able to be made by a person who has encroached over a substantial portion of a parcel but not the whole of the parcel.

J. THE ASSURANCE FUND

The purpose of the assurance fund is to provide a financial remedy where a person suffers loss through the operation of the Torrens Acts. In some jurisdictions an application may be made to the Registrar-General for such compensation and in others the right to recover necessitates suit in court. Even in the case of payments by the Registrar-General the matter may result finally in a court hearing if there is a disagreement as to the amount of compensation. A suit is required in New South Wales: ss 126-127, 130-133, 135.

PARKER v. REGISTRAR-GENERAL

Supreme Court of New South Wales (Court of Appeal) [1977] 1 N.S.W.L.R. 22

[The plaintiffs were the registered proprietors of land under the provisions of the *Real Property Act* 1900 (N.S.W.). They signed a transfer, induced by the fraud of one Gray, in favour of a company controlled by him for a net return of £642. The transfer was registered, as was a mortgage of the property in favour of an insurance company to secure the sum of £6,300. Subsequently the plaintiffs lodged a caveat forbidding any dealing with the property and, as a result of proceedings in equity, they were able to have the property retransferred to them subject to the mortgage. They borrowed money and paid out the mortgage. In an action against the Registrar-General to recover damages under s. 126, judgment was entered in their favour in the sum of $16,948.87. The Registrar-General sought to have the judgment set aside on appeal.]

GLASS J.A. The first ground argued was that s. 126 upon its proper construction does not authorise any recovery by the plaintiffs. The relevant parts of the section read as follows:

"(1) Any person deprived of land or of any estate, or interest in land—

  (a) in consequence of fraud; or

  (b) through the bringing of such land under the provisions of this Act; or

  (c) by the registration of any other person as proprietor of such land, estate or interest; or

  (d) in consequence of any error, omission or misdescription in the Register,

  may bring and prosecute in any court of competent jurisdiction an action for the recovery of damages.

(2) An action under subsection (1) shall, . . . subject to subsections (3), (4) and (5) be brought and prosecuted against the person— . . .

  (c) who acquired title to the land, or the estate or interest therein, through the fraud, error, omission or misdescription.

(5) In any of the following cases, that is to say—

  (a) where such person ceases to be liable for the payment of damages as aforesaid; or

  (b) when the person liable for damages under this section is dead, bankrupt, or insolvent, or cannot be found within the jurisdiction, such damages with costs of action may be recovered out of the assurance fund by action against the Registrar-General as nominal defendant."

It was submitted that, in two independent respects, the plaintiff's proofs failed to establish a statutory cause of action, viz. (i) there was no fraud, and (ii) they were not deprived of land or any estate in land. The construction advanced was that fraud in the section was limited to dishonest conduct which produced a failure of the system to achieve a true registration, for example, forged instruments, instruments signed in consequence of misrepresentations as to their nature and genuine instruments stolen and misapplied. This narrowing of the scope of the section was necessary, it was submitted, to avoid exposure of the assurance fund to claims based upon fraud unconnected with the registration system. The limited ambit of s. 126(1)(b), (c) and (d) were said to support this construction. For the plaintiffs it was argued that the principle of the indefeasibility of the title of the registered proprietor: *Frazer v. Walker* [1967] 1 A.C. 569 furnished a valid reason why all persons who suffer a loss of title caused by fraud of any kind should have a remedy. Mr Horton Q.C., in seeking to deny the plaintiff's statutory remedy, further submitted that the section excluded every instance where the registered proprietor voluntarily executed a memorandum of transfer, notwithstanding that he was acting under the influence of fraud duress or undue influence. But upon this construction his own example of the transfer signed in blank and later stolen would be outside the section. This illustrates the difficulty which faces any attempt to draw a line which separates fraud within the section from fraud outside it. In my opinion, the section should be construed so as to embrace all frauds within the ordinary legal meaning of that term. I can see every reason why some might think it undesirable that, whenever the fraudulent party absconds, dies or becomes bankrupt, the assurance fund should bear the brunt of the many varieties of moral turpitude normally encompassed by the word fraud. But I can see no warrant for reading down the language of the section so as to restrict it to forgery or quasi-forgery.

The second submission under this head was that the plaintiffs had not been deprived of their land because deprivation connotes an involuntary disposition. Although they had parted with it under the influence of fraud, they had not been deprived of it. The submission was based upon *Fawkes v. Attorney-General (Ontario)* (1903) 6 O.L.R. 490 at 494, which does contrast disposition which is voluntary and deprivation which is deemed to be involuntary. It says: "According to the *Oxford English Dictionary* 'To deprive a person of a thing, is to take it away from him.' Sub voce. It imports wrongful action, or action in invitum, and in the statute, I think, it intends some transaction ex parte, or behind the back of the true owner, or wherein his existence is concealed, whereby he being in ignorance of what is going on, is deprived of his property."

I must say, with respect, that I find this explication of the meaning of deprivation unconvincing, and its alleged lexicographic support nugatory. It seems to me that property is taken away from its owner, and he is just as surely deprived of it, whether it is done by a trick or by a theft.

It follows that, on the findings made by the trial judge, the plaintiffs are able to establish the following ingredients of the statutory cause of action: (a) the registration of the transfer in favour of the company deprived them of the land; (b) this happened in consequence of the fraud of Gray; (c) the company was responsible for the fraud of its agent: *Registrar of Titles (W.A.) v. Franzon* (1975) 132 C.L.R. 611; (d) accordingly the company was liable in damages to the plaintiff under s. 126(2)(c): ibid.; (e) as the company was insolvent, the damages could be recovered by action against the Registrar-General: s. 126(5) . . . [As to the second ground] . . . it was submitted that his Honour was wrong not to conclude that the plaintiffs, after discovery of the fraud, had elected to affirm the contract, and to rest upon their rights as unpaid vendors. So it was the contract and not the fraud which divested the plaintiffs of their land. I have stated the submission in a way which implies that a fraudulent party who alleges affirmation by a victim still being subjected to a continuing of fraudulent representations is bound to face problems at the trial of the issue, and still greater problems on appeal when he has lost. But there is a legal answer to the submission which intercepts the factual inquiry. In equity proceedings between the plaintiffs and the company it was decreed that the land be retransferred. This involved a solemn finding that the contract of sale had been rescinded. The company could not have defended its liability in an action under s. 126(2) by contending, to the contrary of that finding, that the contract had been affirmed. That issue estoppel does not bind the Registrar-General who was in no way privy to the proceedings. But, in my view, s. 126(5), on its proper construction, requires proof only that the company would, if sued, have been liable in damages, and that it was insolvent when action was brought against the Registrar-General. The damages for which the company is liable may then be recovered out of the fund in an action against the Registrar-General, sued as nominal defendant. There is no question of the Registrar-General being sued subject to an auxiliary liability of his own, as the Act fails to specify the conditions of such a statutory liability. Accordingly, affirmation is not available as a defence in determining the liability of the company, either in an action against it under s. 126(2), or in an action against the Registrar-General under s. 126(5).

The third ground upon which the appellant seeks to subvert the judgment enlists the exemption contained in s. 133 which provides as follows: "The assurance fund shall not, under any circumstances, be liable for compensation for any loss, damage, or deprivation occasioned—

(a) by the breach by a registered proprietor or any trust whether express, implied, or constructive".

It was argued that, upon the rescission of the contract, the company became a constructive trustee of the land in favour of the plaintiffs. Accordingly, the plaintiffs' loss, damage or deprivation was occasioned by the breach of a constructive trust and is not recoverable from the fund . . . I consider that s. 133(a) protects the fund from claims where the original default is that of the registered proprietor. It is not, in my view, concerned with loss or damage which is suffered because of a deprivation in consequence of a fraud practised upon the proprietor within the meaning of s. 126. To give the two sections any concurrent operation would largely defeat s. 126(5). They may be given a mutually exclusive operation by treating s. 133 as if the words "occasioned by" meant "solely occasioned by". Upon this construction the section has no application.

In conclusion, I would commend the ingenuity and resourcefulness of the arguments put on behalf of the defendant. But none of them, in my view, can succeed in wresting judgment out of the hands of the plaintiffs. I would propose that the appeal be dismissed with costs.

MAHONEY J.A. It is submitted that the s. 126(1)(a) should apply only to those consequences of fraud which have resulted from the operation of the system of title registration.

Mr Horton, in his argument, submitted that a distinction should be seen between a case where the plaintiff has been deprived of land because the fraud has resulted in the Registrar-General registering a dealing which he should not have registered, for example where the fraud lies in the lodgment for registration of a forged memorandum of transfer, and a case where the plaintiff has been induced to sign the relevant memorandum of transfer by a fraudulent misrepresentation. He submitted, in effect, that it is anomalous that the Registrar-General should be liable for cases of the second kind, because the fraud had no relevant connection with him or the operation of the Act.

I do not think that the context of the paragraph requires that the phrase be so limited. As I have said, the section provides a remedy primarily against the person who acquired title to the land through the fraud: s. 126(2)(c). There is, in my opinion, no reason either in the terms or the purpose of the section which would require that a right of recovery against such a person should be so limited. The categories of fraud are not closed; frauds may take on many different forms. There is no reason why a right of recovery should be limited as against the person responsible for the fraudulent deprivation of land according to whether, for example, the fraud involves the voluntary signing of a transfer induced by fraud, the signing of it by mistake, or the forgery of a document. Where as I have said, the particular fraud was directed to achieving the deprivation of land which occurred, I see no reason why the remedy against the person responsible for that fraud should be limited by reference to the accident of the means chosen to give effect to that fraud.

The liability of the Registrar-General is created by s. 126(5). It is imposed, not by reference to what the Registrar-General has or has not done; his liability is imposed merely in terms of the liability of the person primarily responsible for the fraud. It was not argued, nor could it be, that there was anything in the terms of s. 126(5) which would warrant limiting the liability of the Registrar-General under that subsection to anything less than the liability of the defrauder. Once it be accepted that the defrauder's liability is not limited in the manner suggested, the liability of the Registrar-General must be seen as similarly not limited.

[The concurring judgment of Street C.J. has been omitted.]

Appeal dismissed.

NOTES

1. For a similar interpretation of the right of access to the fund (in New South Wales) see *Armour v. Penrith Project Pty Ltd* [1979] 1 N.S.W.L.R. 98 per Needham J.

2. The principal case was approved in *Registrar-General v. Behn* (1981) 55 A.L.J.R. 541.

FIVE

EASEMENTS AND PROFITS À PRENDRE

A. INTRODUCTION

In this chapter we examine the nature of easements and profits à prendre, the requirements for their creation, and their operation within the Torrens system. Easements and profits are the more important, although not the only, forms of incorporeal hereditaments which can affect land; see Megarry and Wade, *The Law of Real Property* (5th ed.), pp. 851-853. Although the distinction between corporeal and incorporeal rights is fraught with theoretical difficulties (see Megarry and Wade, *The Law of Real Property* (5th ed.), pp. 814) the now accepted distinction is between the land the subject of rights (a corporeal hereditament) and the right itself (an incorporeal hereditament). These rights qualify as hereditaments, as at common law they were capable of passing to the heirs ("heres") on death.

An easement is "a right annexed to land to utilise other land of different ownership in a particular manner (not involving the taking of any part of the natural produce of that land or any part of its soil) or to prevent the owner of the other land from utilising his land in a particular manner": *Halsbury's Laws of England* (4th ed.), Vol. 14, p. 4. In contrast a profit à prendre is "a right to take something off another's land" (*Duke of Sutherland v. Heathcote* [1892] 1 Ch. 475 at 484), such as timber (*Reid v. Moreland Timber Co. Pty. Ltd* (1946) 73 C.L.R. 1 at 9, 11, 14; *McCauley v. Federal Commissioner of Taxation* (1944) 69 C.L.R. 235), cocos palms (*Silovi Pty Ltd v. Barbaro* (1988) 13 N.S.W.L.R. 466), nuts (*Commissioner for Corporate Affairs (W.A.) v. Nut Farms (Aust.) Pty Ltd* (1980) A.C.L.C. 34, 260), pasturage and crops (*Hindmarsh v. Quinn* (1914) 17 C.L.R. 623), rabbits (*Mason v. Clarke* [1955] A.C. 778), slate in dross (*Mills v. Stokman* (1966) 116 C.L.R. 61), salt (*Nicholls v. Lovell* (1923) S.A.S.R. 542), minerals (*Ex parte Henry; Re Commissioner of Stamp Duties* [1963] S.R. (N.S.W.) 298 and on appeal (1964) 114 C.L.R. 322; *Bayview Properties Pty Ltd v. A.-G. (Vic.)* [1960] V.R. 314), sand (*Unimin Pty Ltd v. Commonwealth (Aust.)* (1974) 2 A.C.T.R. 1) and sandstone: *Vukicevic v. Alliance Acceptance Co. Ltd* (1987) 9 N.S.W.L.R. 13. Other rights, such as the right to take wild animals (*Mason v. Clarke* [1955] A.C. 778) on the land, may also be the subject of a profit, provided that the subject of the right is capable of ownership: *Alfred F. Beckett Ltd v. Lyons* [1967] Ch. 449 at 482. In short "[A]n easement . . . confers a right to utilise the servient tenement in a particular manner, or to prevent the commission of some act on that tenement, whereas a profit à prendre confers a right to take from the servient tenement some part of the soil of that tenement or minerals under it or some of its natural produce, or the animals ferae naturae existing upon it": *Alfred F. Beckett Ltd v. Lyons* [1967] Ch. 449 at

water rights = east
∴ can't own water

482 per Winn L.J. Since water cannot generally be made the subject of ownership, the right to take water cannot exist as a profit but may be the subject of an easement: *Race v. Ward* (1855) 4 E. & B. 702; 119 E.R. 259; *Manning v. Wasdale* (1836) 5 Ad. & El. 758; 111 E.R. 1353.

An easement can only exist as a right appurtenant to other land; if the grantee has no land that can benefit from the right, a purported grant of an easement will operate merely as a personal right enforceable only between the contracting parties: *Concord Municipal Council v. Coles* (1905) 3 C.L.R. 96; *Hill v. Tupper* (1863) 2 H. & C. 121, extracted above p. 222. In contrast, a profit can exist either as a right appurtenant to particular land or as a right in gross; that is, a profit can be granted without the necessity of having land which is entitled to the benefit of the right: *Chesterfield v. Harris* [1908] 2 Ch. 397 at 421 per Buckley L.J.; *Lowe (Inspector of Taxes) v. J.W. Ashmore Ltd* [1971] Ch. 545 at 557. Where the profit is appurtenant, the right claimed must relate to the needs of the land entitled to the benefit in much the same way as an easement must benefit the dominant tenement: see p. 222. Thus, a right to catch salmon as a profit appurtenant to particular land must be related to the needs of the land entitled to the benefit of the profit; such a right would not allow commercial fishing (*Lord Chesterfield v. Harris* [1908] 2 Ch. 397 at 421, 424, 429; [1911] A.C. 623), or unlimited grazing: *Anderson v. Bostock* [1976] 1 All E.R. 560 referred to p. 223. These restrictions do not apply to profits in gross.

Profits à prendre can be granted as exclusive rights ("several" profits) or to be enjoyed in common with others (profits in common). The latter, which includes "rights of common", although very important in England, are of little significance in Australia: see Butt, *Land Law* (2nd ed.), p. 327.

In 1987 the New South Wales legislature specially recognised and provided for the enforcement of forestry rights under the *Conveyancing (Forestry Rights) Amendment Act* 1987 and the cognate *Real Property (Forestry Rights) Amendment Act* 1987. A forestry right under the *Conveyancing Act* is defined in s. 87A as "an interest in land pursuant to which a person having the benefit of the interest is entitled (a) to enter the land; (b) to establish, maintain and harvest a crop of trees on the land; and (c) to construct and use such buildings, works and facilities as may be necessary or convenient to enable the person to establish, maintain and harvest the crop". The right is deemed to be a profit à prendre: s. 88AB. The legislation also provides for the imposition of forestry covenants as obligations incidental to forestry rights: s. 88EA. These covenants may impose positive duties, such as construction and maintenance of roads, fencing and water supplies on the land the subject of the right: s. 87A. These rights run with the land and bind successors in title to the original covenanting party during the currency of the forestry right: s. 88EA (4), (8). For further details see Butt, *Land Law* (2nd ed.), pp. 328-329, 358. Amendments to the *Real Property Act* 1900, ss 46, 47, allow the creation of profits (and incidental covenants) by registered instrument, usually by transfer.

In this chapter, the major emphasis will be upon easements, with only brief mention of profits. For further discussion concerning the nature of profits, see Butt, *Land Law* (2nd ed.), Ch. 16.

B. THE ESSENTIAL REQUIREMENTS OF AN EASEMENT

RE ELLENBOROUGH PARK

Court of Appeal [1956] 1 Ch. 131

[In 1855 the original owners of Ellenborough Park owned an area of vacant land surrounding the park. Plots around the park were sold for building purposes. The conveyances of the plots were similar in form and granted to each purchaser "the full enjoyment . . . at all times hereafter in common with other persons to whom such easements may be granted of the pleasure ground (Ellenborough Park) but subject to the payment of a fair and just proportion of the costs charges and expenses of keeping in good order and condition the said pleasure ground". The vendors covenanted with each purchaser, his heirs, executors, administrators or assigns and with all others granted rights of usage in the park to keep Ellenborough Park as an ornamental pleasure ground. The park was requisitioned by the War Office from 1941-1946. Compensation was payable to those having a proprietary interest in the park. The issue before the Court of Appeal was whether surrounding owners, by their right to use the park, had a proprietary interest; the only relevant interest they could have here was an easement. On the question whether the surrounding owners had an easement:]

EVERSHED M.R. (delivering the judgment of the court). For the purposes of the argument before us (counsel) were content to adopt, as correct, the four characteristics formulated in Dr Cheshire's *Modern Real Property* (7th ed.), pp. 456 et seq. They are (1) there must be a dominant and a servient tenement; (2) an easement must "accommodate" the dominant tenement; (3) dominant and servient owners must be different persons; and (4) a right over land cannot amount to an easement, unless it is capable of forming the subject matter of a grant.

. . . The argument in the case is found, accordingly, to turn upon the meaning and application to the circumstances of the present case of the second and fourth conditions; that is, first, whether the alleged easement can be said in truth to "accommodate" the dominant tenement—in other words, whether there exists the required "connection" between the one and the other; and, secondly, whether the right alleged is "capable of forming the subject matter of a grant". The exact significance of this fourth and last condition is, at first sight perhaps, not entirely clear. As between the original parties to the "grant", it is not in doubt that rights of this kind would be capable of taking effect by way of contract or licence. But for the purposes of the present case, as the arguments made clear, the cognate questions involved under this condition are: whether the rights purported to be given are expressed in terms of too wide and vague a character; whether, if and so far as effective, such rights would amount to rights of joint occupation or would substantially deprive the park owners of proprietorship or legal possession; whether, if and so far as effective, such rights constitute mere rights of recreation, possessing no quality of utility or benefit; and on such grounds cannot qualify as easements.

. . . [I]t is clear from the deed . . . that the original common vendors were engaged upon a scheme of development . . . designed to produce a result of common experience; namely, a row of uniform houses facing inwards upon a park or garden which was intended to form, and formed in fact, an essential characteristic belonging, and properly speaking "appurtenant", to all and each of them. In substance, instead of each house being confined to its own small or moderate garden, each was to enjoy in common, but in common exclusively with the other houses in the crescent, a single large "private" garden. In our judgment the substance of the matter is not in this respect affected by the fact that some few houses in the immediate proximity of, but not actually fronting upon, the park were also entitled to share the privilege . . . [T]he language of the deed of 1864 is clearly to the effect that the right of enjoyment of the garden was intended to be annexed to the premises sold, rather than given as a privilege personal to their purchaser. The enjoyment was not exclusive to those premises alone; it was to be held in common with the like rights annexed to the other houses in (and in some few cases in close proximity to) the square or crescent. But it was not contemplated that like rights should be otherwise extended so as to belong in any sense to premises not forming part of (or at least closely connected with) the square or their owners. . . . It was conceded that the rights, if effectual and enforceable, were conditional; that is, upon the house owners making their appropriate contributions to the cost of upkeep. . . .

It remains to interpret the actual terms of the grant itself—"the full enjoyment of the pleasure ground set out and made", etc. (counsel) fastened upon the presence of the word "full", and the absence of any indication of the way in which the pleasure ground was to be used—or of any limitations upon its use—and contended that the right or privilege given was a jus spatiandi in its strict sense, that is, a right to go or wander upon the park and every part of it and enjoy its amenities (and even its produce) without stint. We do not so construe the words in their context. Although we are now anticipating to some extent the question which arises under the fourth of Dr Cheshire's conditions, it seems to us, as a matter of construction, that the use contemplated and granted was the use of the park as a garden, the proprietorship of which (and of the produce of which) remained vested in the vendors and their successors. The enjoyment contemplated was the enjoyment of the vendors' ornamental garden in its physical state as such—the right, that is to say, of walking on or over those parts provided for such purposes that is, pathways and (subject to restrictions in the ordinary course in the interest of the grass) the lawns; to rest in or upon the seats or other places provided; and, if certain parts were set apart for particular recreations such as tennis or bowls, to use those parts for those purposes, subject again, in the ordinary course, to the provisions made for their regulation; but not to trample at will all over the park, to cut or pluck the flowers or shrubs, or to interfere in the laying out or upkeep of the park. Such use or enjoyment is, we think, a common and clearly understood conception, analogous to the use and enjoyment conferred upon members of the public, when they are open to the public, of parks or gardens such as St James's Park, Kew Gardens or the Gardens of Lincoln's Inn Fields. In our judgment, the use of the word "full" does not import some wider, less well understood or less definable privilege. The adjective does not in fact again appear when the enjoyment of the garden is later referred to. It means no more than that to each plot was annexed the right of enjoyment of the park as a whole. . . . Nor does any difficulty arise out of the condition as to contribution. . . . The obligation being a condition of the enjoyment, each house would be bound to contribute its due (that is, proportionate) share of the reasonable cost of upkeep. . . .

We pass, accordingly, to a consideration of the first of Dr Cheshire's conditions—that of the accommodation of the alleged dominant tenements by the rights as we have interpreted them. . . .

[I]t is not sufficient to show that the right increased the value of the property conveyed, unless it is also shown that it was connected with the normal enjoyment of that property. It appears to us that the question whether or not this connection exists is primarily one of fact, and depends largely on the nature of the alleged dominant tenement and the nature of the right granted. As to the former, it was in the contemplation of the parties to the conveyance of 1864 that the property conveyed should be used for residential and not commercial purposes. That appears from the conveyance itself. . . .

[Their Lordships thought the rights granted were not in the nature of a personal licence which might be given to a householder to go to the zoo or Lord's Cricket Ground free of charge. They continued:]

A much closer analogy, as it seems to us, is the case of a man selling the freehold of part of his house and granting to the purchaser, his heirs and assigns, the right, appurtenant to such part, to use the garden in common with the vendor and his assigns. In such a case, the test of connection, or accommodation, would be amply satisfied; for just as the use of a garden undoubtedly enhances, and is connected with, the normal enjoyment of the house to which it belongs, so also would the right granted, in the case supposed, be closely connected with the use and enjoyment of the part of the premises sold. Such, we think, is in substance the position in the present case. The park became a communal garden for the benefit and enjoyment of those whose houses adjoined it or were in its close proximity. Its flower beds, lawns and walks were calculated to afford all the amenities which it is the purpose of the garden of a house to provide; and, apart from the fact that these amenities extended to a number of householders, instead of being confined to one (which on this aspect of the case is immaterial), we can see no difference in principle between Ellenborough Park and a garden in the ordinary signification of that word. It is the collective garden of the neighbouring houses, to whose use it was dedicated by the owners of the estate and as such amply satisfied, in our judgment, the requirement of connection with the dominant tenements to which it is appurtenant. The result is not affected by the circumstances that the right to the park is in this case enjoyed by some few houses which are not immediately fronting on the park. The test for present purposes, no doubt, is that the park should constitute in a real and intelligible sense the garden (albeit the communal garden) of the houses to which its enjoyment is annexed. But we think that the test is satisfied as regards these few neighbouring, though not adjacent, houses. We think that the extension of the right of enjoyment to these few houses does not negative the presence of the necessary "nexus" between the subject matter enjoyed and the premises to which the enjoyment is expressed to belong. . . .

For the reasons which we have stated, we are unable to accept the contention that the right to the full enjoyment of Ellenborough Park fails in limine to qualify as a legal easement for want of the necessary connection between its enjoyment and the use of the properties comprised in the conveyance of 1864, and in the other relevant conveyances.

We turn next to Dr Cheshire's fourth condition for an easement—that the right must be capable of forming the subject matter of a grant. As we have earlier stated, satisfaction of the condition in the present case depends on a consideration of the questions whether the right conferred is too wide and vague, whether it is inconsistent with the proprietorship or possession of the alleged servient owners, and whether it is a mere right of recreation without utility or benefit.

To the first of these questions the interpretation which we have given to the typical deed provides, in our judgment, the answer; for we have construed the right conferred as being both well-defined and commonly understood. In these essential respects the right may be said to be distinct from the indefinite and unregulated privilege which, we think, would ordinarily be understood by the Latin term "jus spatiandi", a privilege of wandering at will over all and every part of another's field or park, and which, though easily intelligible as the subject matter of a personal licence, is something substantially different from the subject matter of the grant in question, namely, the provision for a limited number of houses in a uniform crescent of one single large but private garden.

Our interpretation of the deed also provides, we think, the answer to the second question; for the right conferred no more amounts to a joint occupation of the park with its owners, no more excludes the proprietorship or possession of the latter, than a right of way granted through a passage . . . . We see nothing repugnant to a man's proprietorship or possession of a piece of land that he should decide to make it and maintain it as an ornamental garden, and should grant rights to a limited number of other persons to come into it for the enjoyment of its amenities.

The third of the questions embraced in Dr Cheshire's fourth condition rests primarily on a proposition stated in Theobald's *The Law of Land,* (2nd ed.), p. 263, where it is said that an easement "must be a right of utility and benefit and not one of mere recreation and amusement".

[Their Lordships, after examining the authorities concluded that the proposition was of doubtful validity and continued:]

In any case, if the proposition be well-founded, we do not think that the right to use a garden of the character with which we are concerned in this case can be called one of mere recreation and amusement . . . . No doubt a garden is a pleasure—on high authority, it is the purest of pleasures—but, in our judgment, it is not a right having no quality either of utility or benefit as those words should be understood. The right here in suit is, for reasons already given, one appurtenant to the surrounding houses as such, and constitutes a beneficial attribute of residence in a house as ordinarily understood. Its use for the purposes, not only of exercise and rest but also for such domestic purposes as were suggested in argument—for example, for taking out small children in perambulators or otherwise—is not fairly to be described as one of mere recreation or amusement, and is clearly beneficial to the premises to which it is attached. . . .

As appears from what has been stated earlier, the right to the full enjoyment of Ellenborough Park, which was granted by the 1864 and other relevant conveyances, was, in substance, no more that a right to use the park as a garden in the way in which gardens are commonly used. In a sense, no doubt, such a right includes something of a jus spatiandi, inasmuch as it involves the principle of wandering at will round each part of the garden, except of course, such parts as comprise flowerbeds, or are laid out for some other purpose, which renders walking impossible or unsuitable. We doubt, nevertheless, whether the right to use and enjoy a garden in this manner can with accuracy be said to constitute a mere jus spatiandi. Wandering at large is of the essence of such a right and constitutes the main purpose for which it exists. A private garden, on the other hand, is an attribute of the ordinary enjoyment of the residence to which it is attached, and the right of wandering in it is but one method of enjoying it. On the assumption, however, that the right now in question does constitute a jus spatiandi, or that it is analogous thereto, it becomes necessary to consider whether the right, which is in question in these proceedings, is, for that reason, incapable of ranking in law as an easement.

Farwell J. twice indicated that in his opinion the jus spatiandi is an interest which is not known to our law. . . .

[Their Lordships then referred to decisions of Farwell J. in *International Tea Stores Co. v. Hobbs* [1903] 2 Ch. 165 and *A.-G. v. Antrobus* [1905] 2 Ch. 188. In the latter case a claim of right by the public for access to Stonehenge was rejected. Their Lordships continued:]

It will be noted that in both of these cases the judge said that a jus spatiandi is "not known to our law" and the question arises as to what precisely he meant by using that phrase. . . . If, however, one attributes to the phrase "not known to the law" its ordinary signification, namely, that it was a right which our law had refused to recognise, it is clear, we think, that he would at least have expressed himself in less general terms had his attention been drawn to *Duncan v. Louch* (1845) 6 Q.B. 604. That case was not, however, cited to him in either the *International Tea Stores* case [1903] 2 Ch. 165 or in *A.-G. v. Antrobus* [1905] 2 Ch. 188 for the sufficient reason that it was not relevant to any issue that was before the judge upon the questions which arose for decision. There is no doubt, in our judgment, but that *A.-G. v. Antrobus* was rightly decided; for no right can be granted (otherwise than by statute) to the public at large to wander at will over an undefined open space, nor can the public acquire such a right by prescription. We doubt very much whether Farwell J. had in mind, notwithstanding the apparent generality of his language, a so-called jus spatiandi granted as properly appurtenant to an estate; for the whole of his judgment was devoted to a consideration of public rights; and, although this cannot be said of his observations as to the gardens and park in the *International Tea Stores* case, the view which he there expressed was entirely obiter upon a point which was irrelevant to the case and had not been argued. Inasmuch, therefore, as this observation is unsupported by any principle or any authority that are binding upon us, and is in conflict with the decision in *Duncan v. Louch,* we are unable to accept its accuracy as an exhaustive statement of the law and, in reference, at least, to a case such as that now before the court, it cannot, in our judgment, be regarded hereafter as authoritiative.

Duncan v. Louch, on the other hand, decided more than 100 years ago but not, as we have observed, quoted to Farwell J. in either of the two cases which we have cited, is authoritative in favour of the recognition by our law as an easement of a right closely comparable to that now in question which, if it involves in some sense a jus spatiandi, is nevertheless properly annexed and appurtenant to a defined hereditament.

Duncan v. Louch was an action brought by the plaintiff . . . on account of obstruction by the defendant of what the plaintiff . . . had in fact proved under his documents of title was a right to use Terrace Walk for the purposes of pleasure, that is, to pass and repass over every part of the close . . . Lord Denman C.J. in his judgment, . . . said (at 913), "there is no doubt in this case. Taking the right, as Mr Peacock suggests, to be like the right of the inhabitants of a square to walk in the square for their pleasure . . . I cannot doubt that, if a stranger were to put a padlock on the gate and exclude one of the inhabitants, he might complain of the obstruction." Similarly, Patteson J. [said]: "I do not understand the distinction that has been contended for between a right to walk, pass and repass forwards and backwards over every part of a close, and a right of way from one part of the close to another. What is a right of way but a right to go forwards and backwards from one place to another?" And Coleridge J., in his judgment, described the right as an "easement".

The reasoning of the decision and the circumstances of the case, no less than the language used, particularly by Lord Denman C.J., involve acceptance as an easement of a right such as that with which, according to our interpretation of the effect of the relevant deeds, we are here concerned.

. . . [W]e agree with Danckwerts J. in regarding *Duncan v. Louch* (1845) 6 Q.B. 904 as being a direct authority in the defendants' favour. It has never, so far as we are aware, been since questioned, and we think it should, in the present case, be followed.

For the reasons which we have stated, Danckwerts J. came, in our judgment, to a right conclusion in this case and, accordingly, the appeal must be dismissed.

Appeal dismissed.

NOTES

1. See also *Riley v. Pentilla* [1974] V.R. 547 where the facts were similar to those in the principal case, and *Dukart v. District of Surrey* (1978) 86 D.L.R. (3d) 609.

2. If there is no expressed or implied intention that the benefit of a right of way should extend to the successors and assigns of the purchaser, or that the benefit be annexed to particular land, the grant will be construed as a grant of a personal right to the purchaser: see *A. Victor Leggo & Co. Pty Ltd v. Aerosols (Aust.) Pty Ltd* (1986) C.C.H. N.S.W. Conv. R. 55-293.

1. Requirement of dominant and servient tenements

The first of Cheshire's requirements for the existence of a valid easement is that there be dominant and servient tenements. This requires that there be land capable of benefiting from the right (*Concord Municipal Council v. Coles* (1905) 3 C.L.R. 96) and land that is burdened and also that the dominant tenement be capable of identification. Thus, a right to occupy a burial site cannot exist as an easement, since there is no dominant tenement to which the right can attach: *Beard v. Baulkham Hills Shire Council* (1986) 7 N.S.W.L.R. 273. Attempts to attach rights to land unrelated to user of the dominant tenement have been held to constitute personal licences only, since (statutory exceptions apart, see below) an easement cannot exist in gross: see *Ackroyd v. Smith* (1850) 10 C.B. 164; 138 E.R. 68, below p. 223 and *Hill v. Tupper* (1863) 2 H. & C. 121; 159 E.R. 51, below p. 222. The benefit of an easement may be annexed to other incorporeal rights: see *Conveyancing Act* 1919, s. 88A (1)(b) and *Harada v. Registrar of Titles* [1981] V.R. 743 at 753.

Under the general law extrinsic evidence may be admitted to identify the dominant tenement: *Johnstone v. Holdway* [1963] 1 Q.B. 601; *Shannon Ltd v. Venner Ltd* [1965] 1 Ch. 682; *Gas & Fuel Corp. (Vic.) v. Barba* [1976] V.R. 743 at 750.

The first requirement that an easement can only exist if there is both a dominant and servient tenement has generally been accepted without debate. Sturley ("Easements in Gross" (1980) 96 L.Q.R. 557) argues, however, that neither the authorities nor the arguments in favour of this view are particularly strong. He points out that virtually every other right in land can be held without the requirement of land entitled to the benefit; examples are profits à prendre (see above p. 215), mortgages, and leases. There are many situations where easements in gross would be useful. Sturley lists the following as examples, the right to land helicopters, the right to run telephone, telegraph and power cables, and the right to maintain advertising signs. The risk of excessive user could always be obviated by the terms of the grant or the nature of the right granted: see, for example, *Todrick's* case p. 274. Note the criticism of these views by Young, "Easements in Gross" [1981] A.C.L.A.T. 13. Is there any special reason why leases should not be regarded as appropriate for creating such rights? Would an easement offer any special advantages or disadvantages over a lease?

Easements in gross may, however, be created in favour of the Crown and local or public authorities under s. 88A of the *Conveyancing Act* 1919 (N.S.W.) which provides:

(1) It shall be, and shall be deemed always to have been possible—
    (a) to create in favour of the Crown or any public or local authority constituted by Act of Parliament an easement without a dominant tenement; . . .

(3) This section applies and shall be deemed always to have applied to land under the provisions of the *Real Property Act* 1900, as amended by subsequent Acts.

We have seen that profits may exist either as rights appurtenant (annexed) to land or in gross: *Chesterfield v. Harris* [1908] 2 Ch. 397; [1911] A.C. 851. A profit appurtenant generally must comply with the same four requirements as an easement: *Harris v. Earl of Chesterfield* [1911] A.C. 851; Megarry and Wade, *The Law of Real Property* (5th ed.), p. 851.

In New South Wales easements created by instruments executed after 1 January 1931 must comply with the requirements of the *Conveyancing Act* 1919, s. 88, which requires, inter alia, that the instrument clearly indicate the land to be benefited: see below p. 240. A similar requirement exists in relation to profits appurtenant: *Conveyancing Act* 1919 (N.S.W.), s. 88AA, below pp. 240-241.

2. Accommodation of the dominant tenement

The second of Dr Cheshire's requirements is that the easement must accommodate the dominant tenement. The essential requirement of accommodation is that the easement must confer a benefit on the dominant tenement as such. The benefit conferred must not be a mere advantage, it must relate to user of the dominant tenement and the servient tenement must be sufficiently proximate to enable a practical benefit to be conferred on the dominant tenement.

Where the dominant tenement has been subdivided, it is a question of construction of the instrument creating the easement whether the benefit of the easement passes to the severed parts of the dominant tenement: *Jennison v. Traficante* (1980) 1 B.P.R. 9657. In the case of rights of way created after 31 December 1930 and coming within s. 181A of the *Conveyancing Act* 1919 (N.S.W.), the rights are declared under Sched. VIII to be for the benefit of the dominant tenement or any part thereof.

NOTES

1. See *Re Ellenborough Park* [1956] 1 Ch. 131, above p. 216; *Copeland v. Greenhalf* [1952] 1 Ch. 488, below p. 238.

2. In *Hill v. Tupper* (1863) 2 H. & C. 121; 159 E.R. 51, the plaintiff was lessee of land abutting onto a canal. The terms of the lease purported to grant to the plaintiff the sole and exclusive right or liberty to put or use boats on the canal. The defendant, who owned premises abutting on the canal, also put out pleasure boats on the canal. The plaintiff claimed that the defendant's conduct interfered with his exclusive rights and claimed damages. It was held that the exclusive rights claimed had no connection with the usage and enjoyment of the plaintiff's land and was not a right recognised at law. Pollock C.B. said:

> [I]t is not competent to create rights unconnected with the use and enjoyment of land, and annex them to it so as to constitute a property in the grantee. This grant merely operates as a licence or covenant on the part of the grantors and is binding on them as between themselves and the grantee, but gives no right of action in his own name for any infringement of the supposed exclusive right. . . . A new species of incorporeal hereditament cannot be created at the will and pleasure of the owner of property.

Martin B. said:

> To admit the right would lead to the creation of an infinite variety of interests in land, and an indefinite increase of possible estates.

Bramwell B. concurred.

Evershed M.R. in *Re Ellenborough Park* [1956] 1 Ch. 131 at 175 remarked that in *Hill v. Tupper* it was "clear that what the plaintiff was trying to do was set up, under the guise of an easement, a monopoly which had no normal connection with the ordinary use of his land, but which was merely an independent business enterprise. So far from the right claimed sub-serving or accommodating the land, the land was but a convenient incident to the exercise of the right."

3. In *Ackroyd v. Smith* (1850) 10 C.B. 164; 138 E.R. 68 a right was granted to owners and occupiers of premises conveyed "of passing and repassing, for all purposes, in, over, along, and through a certain road". Creswell J. said:

> Now, the privilege or right in question does not inhere in the land, does not concern the premises conveyed, or the mode of occupying them; it is not appurtenant to them. A covenant, therefore, that such a right should be enjoyed, would not run with the land. Upon the same principle, it appears to us that such a right, unconnected with the enjoyment or occupation of the land, cannot be annexed as an incident to it: nor can a way appendant to a house or land be granted away, or made in gross; for, no one can have such a way but he who has the land to which it is appendant. . . . If a way be granted in gross, it is personal only, and cannot be assigned. . . . . It is not in the power of a vendor to create any rights not connected with the use or enjoyment of the land, and annex them to it: nor can the owner of land render it subject to a new species of burthen, so as to bind it in the hands of an assignee. "Incidents of a novel kind cannot be devised, and attached to property, at the fancy or caprice of any owner": per Lord Brougham L.C. in *Keppel v. Bailey* (1834) 2 Myl. & K. 517; 39 E.R. 1042.
>
> This principle is sufficient to dispose of the present case. It would be a novel incident annexed to land, that the owner and occupier should, for purposes wholly unconnected with that land, and merely because he is owner and occupier, have a right of road over other land. And it seems to us that a grant of such a privilege or easement can no more be annexed, so as to pass with the land, than a covenant for any collateral matter.

Contrast *Thorpe v. Brumfitt* (1873) 8 Ch. App. 650 at 655-657 where a right of way was granted "at all times and for all purposes along a passage intended to run between the piece of land hereinbefore conveyed and a street called the Tyrrels". It was held that a valid easement was created, the grant being construed as a grant for the purposes of the land previously conveyed. See also *Guth v. Robinson* (1977) 1 B.P.R. 97017.

4. As is the requirement of proximity, see *Todrick v. Western National Omnibus* [1934] Ch. 54, extracted below p. 274; see also *Dewhirst v. Edwards* [1983] 1 N.S.W.L.R. 34 at 51.

5. The same requirement of accommodation applies to a profit appurtenant: see *Anderson v. Bostock* [1976] 3 W.L.R. 590 (grant of exclusive grazing rights over a moor). In the case of a profit in gross, the right exists without limit: *Chesterfield v. Harris* [1908] 2 Ch. 397; [1911] A.C. 851; *Staffordshire & Worcestershire Canal Navigation v. Bradley* [1912] 1 Ch. 91.

6. In the principal case, *Re Ellenborough Park*, the Court of Appeal held that it was no objection to the validity of the easement that the owners of the dominant tenement were bound to contribute to the upkeep of the park. The duty of the owner of the dominant tenement to contribute towards repairs of equipment on the servient tenement was in issue in *Frater v. Finlay* (1968) 91 W.N. (N.S.W.) 730, below.

FRATER v. FINLAY

District Court (1968) 91 W.N. (N.S.W.) 730

[The plaintiff and defendant were adjoining owners of land. Upon the plaintiff's land were several bores from which water was conveyed by pipes to the defendant's adjoining property. The right to water from these bores was created by documents executed by the plaintiff's and defendant's predecessors in title. Part of the land was under the *Real Property Act* 1900 (N.S.W.) and part under the Crown Lands legislation. The relevant part of the grant over the land under the Crown Lands legislation provided: "It is hereby agreed that the said well and the water therefrom shall be used and enjoyed by the said grantee his executors, administrators and assigns in common with the said grantors their respective executors, administrators and assigns and the expenses of keeping the said well and all pipes tanks and equipment used therewith in good order and condition shall be borne by the said grantors their respective executors administrators and assigns in equal moieties.'' In respect of land under the *Real Property Act* 1900, the grant was contained in a memorandum of transfer and was indorsed on the relevant Certificate of Title. Following the grant of the right to take water through the pipeline as marked on an annexed plan, the document continued "and it is hereby agreed and declared that the cost of keeping the said two wells and all mills pipes tanks and equipment used therewith in good order and condition shall be borne by the transferors as to one half and by the transferee as to the remaining one half thereof''.

The plaintiff sought to recover from the defendant one half of the costs of maintaining the pipes and equipment in good order.]

NEWTON D.C.J. It was contended on behalf of the defendant that there was no contractual relationship between the parties, and the provision in the document creating the easement was a personal one and was not one which ran with the land. Counsel were unable to refer me to any authority dealing directly with this matter other than a passage in *Halsbury's Laws of England* (3rd ed.), Vol. 12, para. 1257, under the heading "Obligation to repair", which is in the following terms: "The grantor and the grantee may respectively expressly bind themselves personally by agreements to repair the way. The question whether an obligation, as opposed to a right, to repair the site of an easement of way can be effectively imposed so as to run with the easement and the dominant tenement or with the servient tenement as the case may be, has never been conclusively decided. If the matter rests solely on a covenant, the benefit of it runs both at law and in equity with the interests of the covenantee; the burden is confined to the covenantor and his personal representatives and does not run at law or in equity so as to bind his successors in title except in certain cases between lessor and lessee. The obligation may, however, perhaps be framed or construed so as to constitute a continuing condition and to render the easement itself conditional on the dominant owner for the time being complying with an obligation to repair or contribute to repair, and so be determinable or defeasible on non-compliance. Where thus framed or construed the obligation would appear to be capable of being imposed as an incident of an easement itself, and not merely as a liability resting solely upon the covenant purporting to run with the land and the easement. Since the owner of the dominant tenement may, under the doctrine of prescription, claim to have the way repaired by the servient owner there appears to be no reason why a like obligation should not be cast upon the dominant owner. The fact that the doctrine of prescription is applicable at all to such a case shows that the right or obligation need not rest on a mere covenant purporting to run with the land, inasmuch as prescription always presumes an absolute grant, and notice is immaterial." It is to be noted that in the grant of the easements set out above the grant is not made subject to payment by the owner of the dominant tenement of one half of the cost of keeping the wells and mills and pipes and tanks and equipment in good order and condition. It is expressed as a covenant in the form of "It is hereby agreed and declared".

Where a grant is made subject to the payment by the grantee of the cost of keeping the easement granted in good order and condition there is some doubt as to whether the right to determine on default once occurring merely suspends the easement until the default is made good, or whether it brings to an end the easement itself.

Speaking generally an easement imposes no active obligation upon the owner of the servient tenement. His duty is to suffer something to be done upon his property or not do anything. Consequently he is under no liability to repair; such a condition is not a condition incident by law to the grant: *Taylor v. Whitehead* (1781) 2 Doug.

745 at 749; 99 E.R. 475 at 477; *Pomfret v. Ricroft* (1669) 1 Wms. Saund. 321 at 322, (n.) 3; 85 E.R. 454 at 455. But it is clear that the grantor may bind himself to repair. . . .

Although not directly in point, there is a very interesting decision of Herdman J. of the Supreme Court of New Zealand, in *Cameron v. Dalgety* [1920] N.Z.L.R. 155 in which the law is examined in some detail on the aspect of whether or not the grantor of an easement, who in the grant executed by him covenants to repair, binds his assigns to perform the obligations, and whether or not the assignee of the grantee has a remedy against the grantor or his assigns if the covenant be not performed . . . [H]is Honour says (at 162): "When endeavouring to determine the effect of a covenant contained in a grant of an easement, by which the grantor and his assigns undertake with the grantee and his assigns to repair, one remembers that it is clear that the owner of the dominant tenement may under the doctrine of prescription claim to have the way repaired by the servient owner: *Halsbury's Laws of England* (1st ed.), Vol. 11, p. 295, para. 576; *Rider v. Smith* (1790) 3 Term. 766; 100 E.R. 848; *Pomfret v. Ricroft* (1669) 1 Wms. Saund. 321; 85 E.R. 454. If the liability to repair can be created by prescription it would affect not the grantor only but his assigns likewise. The liability becomes in a sense part of the easement. If the obligation to repair can be cast upon the servient owner by prescription I cannot see why an obligation cannot be cast upon him by the terms of the grant. If such a covenant becomes part of the grant or is an incident to the grant, or if, to quote the words used in *Brewster v. Kidgill* (1698) 12 Mod. Rep. 166 at 171; 88 E.R. 1239 at 1241, it becomes 'a declaration going along with the grant' then the right or obligation does not rest upon a mere covenant running with the land." His Honour then goes on to say that he is by no means certain that it could not be argued with success that the covenant runs with the land, but he preferred to rest his decision upon the ground either that the covenant to repair is part of the grant or that it is an incident to the easement. His Honour (at 163) says that the problem he is concerned with is the grant of an incorporeal hereditament, the grant of an easement, and, according to Lindley L.J., if the burden amounts to an easement it will run with the land. His Honour thought that the covenant to repair was part of the grant. He said it is part of the benefit conferred upon the grantee, for, after all, what benefit did the grantor undertake to give, and what benefit did the grantee stipulate for? Surely a right to water which might run in a race in a state of repair. Whether the covenant does or does not run with the land does not seem to me to matter. If the covenant is an easement or part of an easement, or is an incident to an easement, that, I think, is sufficient to bind the assigns of the grantor and to confer a benefit upon the assigns of the grantee.

It seems to me, with great respect to Herdman J., that his reasoning is sound, and if the grantor of an easement can bind himself and his assigns to repair by the grant then, a fortiori, the owner of the dominant tenement can bind himself and his assigns to repair or to contribute to the cost of repairs if the repairs are carried out by the owner of the servient tenement.

[His Honour then referred to *Re Ellenborough Park* [1956] 1 Ch. 131, above p. 216, in support of the view that an easement could be granted subject to a duty to contribute to the upkeep of the park and continued:]

It also seems clear to me that the obligation of the owner of the dominant tenement to pay half the cost of keeping the well and pipes and tanks and equipment in good order and condition cannot, in itself, amount to an easement independent and separate from the easement to receive water. Viewed on its own, the obligation to contribute could not comply with the second essential of an easement, namely that it must accommodate the dominant tenement. This means that what is required is that the right "accommodates and serves the dominant tenement and is reasonably necessary for the enjoyment of that tenement; for if it has no necessary connection therewith, for although it confers an advantage upon the owner and renders his ownership of the land more valuable, it is not an easement at all but a mere contractual right personal to and enforceable between the two contracting parties". See *Gale on Easements* (13th ed.), p. 13. The obligation to contribute to the costs of repairs in itself does nothing for the owner of a dominant tenement, but failure to make the stated contribution may bring the easement to an end. I express no concluded view as to whether or not this would have this result, but the defendant's success in this action could extinguish the easement and may affect the value of his property in the future.

It will be noted that in the *Ellenborough Park* case [1956] 1 Ch. 131 the question was whether or not the owners of the dominant tenement were bound to contribute to the costs of keeping the park in good order and condition and it will also be noted that in the grant of the easement it was expressed to be subject to the payment of a fair and just proportion of the cost of upkeep; whereas in the incident case the grant is not made subject to the payment of a moiety of the costs of repairs but is expressed as an agreement between the parties as far as the land under the *Real Property Act* is concerned, and as far as the other land is concerned, as an agreement between the parties and their respective executors, administrators and assigns.

It will be noted that in *Cameron v. Dalgety* [1920] N.Z.L.R. 155 the covenant to repair was attached to the servient tenement. The reasoning of Herdman J. in coming to the conclusion that the covenant to repair was part of the grant and formed part of the benefit conferred, and bound the assigns of the grantors and benefited the assigns of the grantee, was in my opinion sound, and by analogy it seems to me that the grantor can attach to and make it part of the grant that the grantee shall contribute to the cost of repairs. I think it clear that this was the intention of the parties when the easement was created. . . .

In my opinion the obligation of the grantee of the easement to contribute half the cost of repairs formed part of the easement and therefore binds the successors in title, and therefore the plaintiff is entitled to recover one half of such moneys as he is able to prove were expended by him within the terms of the grants.

This is sufficient to dispose of the preliminary point, but it leaves unresolved many questions, such as, for instance, whether or not failure to pay the contribution has or will extinguish the easement, and whether or not the plaintiff by his conduct committed breaches of his obligation and thereby the defendant was entitled to treat his obligations under the easement as at an end, and whether or not the easement had become obsolete—these being defences which have been foreshadowed. . . .

Preliminary point decided in favour of plaintiff.

NOTES AND QUESTIONS

1. Contrast *Halsall v. Brizell* [1957] 1 Ch. 169 referred to below p. 313. Are these two cases compatible? Can any reason be advanced for the differences in approach adopted? Are the differences of any practical importance? In *Rufa Pty Ltd v. Cross* [1981] Qd R. 365 the owners of adjoining properties granted cross easements for the use of a party wall. It was provided that either party was at liberty on notice given to extend the wall longitudinally at his own expense and that if the other party desired to use any part of the extension he was to pay rateably therefor. The wall was later extended by the plaintiff's predecessor in title. The defendants, successors in title to the original grantor, used part of the extension but refused to contribute to the cost. The Full Court of Queensland held that the defendants were bound to contribute on the ground that the duty to contribute was part of the "essential fabric" of the easement, alternatively, it came within the principle enunciated in *Halsall v. Brizell*.

2. It has been suggested that cases such as *Frater v. Finlay* (1968) 91 W.N. (N.S.W.) 730 will allow the creation of new types of legal interest by allowing novel incidents to be attached to an easement. Do you agree?

3. As to the position where the easement requires expenditure of money on the part of the servient owner, see *Crow v. Wood* [1971] 1 Q.B. 77, below p. 231.

3. The dominant and servient tenements must not be owned and occupied by the same person

The third of Cheshire's requirements is that there must not be unity of possession and ownership of both dominant and servient tenements. This concerns the very essence of an easement, namely, that it is "some right which a person has over land which is not his own, but if the land is his own, if he has an interest in it, then his right is not an easement. You cannot have an easement over your own land": *Metropolitan Railway Co. v. Fowler* [1892] 1 Q.B. 165 at 171 per Lord Esher M.R. The rule requires unity of possession and ownership, and will not therefore prevent the creation of an easement in favour of a tenant against his own landlord occupying other land or against another tenant of the landlord: *Borman v. Griffith* [1930] 1 Ch. 493; *Maurice Toltz Pty Ltd v. Macy's Emporium Pty Ltd* (1969) 91 W.N. (N.S.W.) 591. (In respect of prescriptive easements user must be by and against the owner of the fee simple: see below p. 271.) An easement will not be extinguished where the owner of the fee simple absolute of one of the tenements acquires a limited interest in the other; this is discussed in the context of extinguishment of easements, below p. 295. A similar rule applies to profits appurtenant: see *White v. Taylor (No. 2)* [1969] 1 Ch. 160.

It is to be noted also that although there may be unity of possession and ownership of dominant and servient tenements the "rights" exercised over the servient tenement may, upon grant of the "quasi-dominant" or "quasi-servient" tenement, ripen into easements: see below p. 242.

There are two statutory exceptions to the rule in New South Wales. The first is contained in the *Real Property Act* 1900 (N.S.W.), s. 47(7) and the second statutory exception is contained in s. 88B (3)(c) of the *Conveyancing Act* 1919 (N.S.W.), which deals with registered plans. These provisions apply also to profits appurtenant.

s47(7) RPA
s88(3)(c) CA

4. The easement or profit must be capable of forming the subject matter of a grant *(ie) right must be capable of being granted by a deed*

The right claimed can constitute an easement or profit only if it is capable of being granted by deed; all easements and profits "lie in grant": *Halsbury's Laws of England* (4th ed.), Vol. 14, pp. 8, 121. Megarry and Wade, *The Law of Real Property* (5th ed.), pp. 838–842 state that this requirement gives rise to four rules *4 subrules* (1) the right must be within the general nature of rights capable of being created as easements; (2) the right must be sufficiently definite; (3) there must be a capable grantor; (4) there must be a capable grantee. The material following is directed to the general issue rather than the four subrules.

It is now trite law that the list of easements is not closed, but "it must not therefore be supposed that incidents of a novel kind can be devised and attached to property, at the fancy or caprice of any owner": per Lord Brougham L.C. in *Keppell v. Bailey* (1834) 2 My. & K. 517 at 535; 39 E.R. 1042 at 1048. See also *Re Ellenborough Park* [1956] 1 Ch. 131, above p. 216; *Hill v. Tupper* (1863) 2 H. & C. 121 above p. 222; *Copeland v. Greenhalf* [1952] 1 Ch. 488, below p. 238.

what can't be an eas't

It is commonly accepted that certain kinds of rights cannot exist as easements, for example, a right to a view: *Aldred's Case* (1610) 9 Co. Rep. 57b at 58b; 77 E.R. 816 at 820; an easement for privacy: *Browne v. Flower* [1911] 1 Ch. 219 at 225; an easement for the passage of air otherwise than through a defined channel: *Chastey v. Ackland* [1895] 2 Ch. 389; *Webb v. Bird* (1862) 13 C.B. (N.S.) 841; *Harris v. Da Pinna* (1886) 33 Ch. D. 238 at 262; *Bryant v. Lefever* (1879) 4 C.P.D. 172; *Bass v. Gregory* (1890) 25 Q.B.D. 481; *Cable v. Bryant* [1908] 1 Ch. 259. Contrast *Commonwealth v. Registrar of Titles (Vic.)* (1918) 24 C.L.R. 348: see below, note 3. It has long been accepted that easements of light can exist in respect of defined apertures such as windows and skylights: *Colls v. Home & Colonial Store Ltd* [1904] A.C. 179; *Levet v. Gas Light & Coke Co.* [1919] 1 Ch. 24; *Easton v. Isted* [1903] 1 Ch. 405. Solar energy requirements may provide an important application of this principle. Note especially in this context *Allen v. Greenwood* [1979] 2 W.L.R. 187 and Bradbrook, "The Development of an Easement of Solar Access" (1982) 5 U.N.S.W.L.J. 299.

As all easements "lie in grant", the right alleged to be an easement must be capable of sufficiently precise definition in order to be expressed in the grant at all. Megarry and Wade, *The Law of Real Property* (4th ed.), p. 812 suggest that the reason why certain rights have been held not to constitute easements is because the rights are not capable of reasonably precise definition. If this is so, ought the converse apply? That is, if all other prerequisites of an easement are satisfied, and the right is capable of sufficient definition, ought it be accepted as an easement? For example, noise and smoke can now be accurately measured. Does this mean that noise and smoke (pollution) easements could be granted? See *Scott-Whitehead v. National Coal Board* (1985) 53 P. & C.R. 263.

Contrast Lord Denning M.R.'s views in *Phipps v. Pears* [1965] 1 Q.B. 76 that the reason why some rights cannot exist as easements is that the rights would unduly restrict a neighbour in the enjoyment of his land. Do you agree with this view?

PHIPPS v. PEARS

Court of Appeal [1965] 1 Q.B. 76

[The plaintiff, the owner of No. 16 Market Street, claimed, inter alia, an easement for protection against the weather, against the owners of the adjoining property (No. 14). The building on the adjoining property had been demolished; it left the plaintiff's house exposed to the weather and resulted in substantial water damage. The plaintiff claimed damages for the harm sustained.]

LORD DENNING M.R. [T]he plaintiff said—or rather it was said on his behalf—that at any rate his house No. 16 was entitled to protection from the weather. So long as No. 14 was there, it afforded excellent protection for No. 16 from rain and frost. By pulling down No. 14, the defendant, he said, had infringed his right of protection from the weather. This right, he said, was analogous to the right of support. It is settled law, of course, that a man who has his house next to another for many years, so that it is dependent on it for support, is entitled to have that support maintained. His neighbour is not entitled to pull down his house without providing substitute support in the form of buttresses or something of the kind: see *Dalton v. Angus* (1881) 6 App. Cas. 740. Similarly, it was said, with a right to protection from the weather. If the man next door pulls down his own house and exposes his neighbour's wall naked to the weather whereby damage is done to him, he is, it is said, liable in damages.

The case, so put, raises the question whether there is a right known to the law to be protected—by your neighbour's house— from the weather. Is there an easement of protection?

There are two kinds of easements known to the law: positive easements, such as a right of way, which give the owner of land a *right himself to do something* on or to his neighbour's land: and negative easements, such as a right of light, which gives him a *right to stop his neighbour doing something* on his (the neighbour's) own land. The right of support does not fall neatly into either category. It seems in some way to partake of the nature of a positive easement rather than a negative easement. The one building, by its weight, exerts a thrust, not only downwards, but also sideways on to the adjoining building or the adjoining land, and is thus doing something to the neighbour's land, exerting a thrust on it: see *Dalton v. Angus* (1881) 6 App. Cas. 740 at 793 per Lord Selborne L.C. But a right to protection from the weather (if it exists) is entirely negative. It is a right to stop your neighbour pulling down his own house. Seeing that it is a negative easement, it must be looked at with caution. Because the law has been very chary of creating any new negative easements.

Take this simple instance: Suppose you have a fine view from your house. You have enjoyed the view for many years. It adds greatly to the value of your house. But if your neighbour chooses to despoil it, by building up and blocking it, you have no redress. There is no such right known to the law as a right to a prospect or view, see *Bland v. Moseley* (1587) Hut. 18; 123 E.R. 1070 cited in 9 Co. Rep. 58a cited by Lord Coke in *Aldred's Case* (1610) 9 Co. Rep. 57b; 77 E.R. 816. The only way in which you can keep the view from your house is to get your neighbour to make a covenant with you that he will not build so as to block your view. Such a covenant is binding on him by virtue of the contract. It is also binding in equity on anyone who buys the land from him with notice of the covenant. But it is not binding on a purchaser who has no notice of it: see *Leech v. Schweder* (1874) 9 Ch. App. 463.

Take next this instance from the last century. A man built a windmill. The winds blew freely on the sails for 30 years working the mill. Then his neighbour built a schoolhouse only 25 yards away which cut off the winds. It was held that the miller had no remedy: for the right to wind and air, coming in an undefined channel, is not a right known to the law: see *Webb v. Bird* (1861) 10 C.B.N.S. 268; (1862) 13 C.B.N.S. 841. The only way in which the miller could protect himself was by getting his neighbour to enter into a covenant.

The reason underlying these instances is that if such an easement were to be permitted, it would unduly restrict your neighbour in his enjoyment of his own land. It would hamper legitimate development: see *Dalton v. Angus* (1881) 6 App. Cas. 740 at 824 per Lord Blackburn. Likewise here, if we were to stop a man pulling down his house, we would put a brake on desirable improvement. Every man is entitled to pull down his house if he likes. If it exposes your house to the weather, that is your misfortune. It is no wrong on his part. Likewise every man is entitled to cut down his trees if he likes, even if it leaves you without shelter from the wind or shade from the sun: see the decision of the Master of the Rolls in Ireland in *Cochrane v. Verner* (1895) 29 I.L.T. 571. There is no such easement known to the law as an easement to be protected from the weather. The only way for an owner to protect himself is by getting a covenant from his neighbour that he will not pull down his house or cut down his trees. Such a covenant would be binding on him in contract: and it would be enforceable on any successor who took with notice of it. But it would not be binding on one who took without notice.

[His Lordship then went on to hold that the right claimed was not a right or advantage known to the law and therefore could not pass with the land by virtue of s. 62 of the *Law of Property Act* 1925 (U.K.).]

In my opinion, therefore, the plaintiff has not made out any right to the protection he seeks. I find myself in agreement with the county court judge: and I would dismiss the appeal.

[Pearson and Salmon L.JJ. concurred.]

NOTES AND QUESTIONS

1. Is Lord Denning M.R.'s distinction between negative and positive easements valid? See the critical comment by Megarry in (1964) 80 L.Q.R. 318 for the view that the alleged easement failed because it could not be defined with sufficient certainty. Note, however, that rights incapable of subsisting as easements may, under the general law, bind successors in title to the servient tenement by virtue of the duty not to derogate from grant: see discussion below p. 257.

2. Statutory right to shelter is extended to property held under the provisions of the *Strata Titles Act* 1973 (N.S.W.), s. 80 of which provides:

    A proprietor, mortgagee in possession (whether by himself or by other person), lessee or occupier of a lot shall not—(a) do anything or permit anything to be done on or in relation to that lot so that—

    (i) any support or shelter provided by that lot for another lot or common property is interfered with.

    See also *Ford v. Heathwood* [1949] Q.W.N. 11 where it was held that a right to a windbreak is capable of constituting an easement.

3. In *Commonwealth v. Registrar of Titles (Vic.)* (1918) 24 C.L.R. 348, the Commonwealth by notification in the Government *Gazette* pursuant to the *Lands Acquisition Act* 1906 (Cth) acquired a parcel of land and a right of way over an adjoining strip of land together with a right expressed in the following words: "together with full and free right to and for the Commonwealth of Australia and to and for the registered proprietor or proprietors for the time being of the land firstly above described, or any part thereof . . . to the uninterrupted access and enjoyment of light and air to the doors and windows of the building or buildings erected or to be erected on the land . . . above described". The Registrar of Titles for Victoria refused to register the right granted on the ground that it did not constitute an existing easement. The High Court held that the right granted was capable of constituting an easement under the general law. Griffith C.J. in the course of his judgment said:

    It is contended that the right is not an easement because it is not enjoyed in respect of any existing building. This argument seems to me to confuse the existence of a legal right with the present physical enjoyment or exercise of it, and also to treat the easement as appurtenant not to the land but to the building. Again, it is said that the easement of light can only exist in respect of existing defined apertures. Here, again, there is a confusion—between a right and the mode of its acquisition. It has always been held that an easement, which is an incorporeal hereditament, lies in grant. An easement of light has generally been rested on prescription, that is, on long and uninterrupted enjoyment, from which, it is said, a grant should be presumed. The presumption, of course, assumes the possibility of a valid grant. But, since the enjoyment could only have been of definite apertures, no such prescription could arise except in the case of their existence. The foundation of every implied or presumed agreement or grant is that it *must* have been intended by the parties, and in the case of vacant land adjoining other vacant land no one could suppose that the owners must have intended that neither should ever interfere with the other's light. But these difficulties do not arise in the case of an express grant, which may in general be formulated in any way the parties please.

    His Honour concluded by saying that on principle such a right as claimed was an easement at common law. Gavan-Duffy and Rich JJ. concurred. Griffith C.J. continued, however, that in any event the matter would be concluded by the *Lands Acquisition Act* 1906 (Cth), for "it is not disputed that the number of existing kinds of easements may be increased by statute". Their Honours did not refer to the English decisions limiting the extent to which rights to light and air might be capable of existing as easements under the general law.

    Do you think that the High Court would decide the common law question in the same way today?

4. In the United Kingdom, an easement requiring the owner of the servient tenement to maintain fences has been regarded as anomalous and an exception to the commonly held view that an easement cannot require expenditure of money on the part of the owner of the servient tenement: see *Gale on Easements* (14th ed.), p. 37; *Jones v. Price* [1965] 2 Q.B. 618; *Crow v. Wood* [1971] 1 Q.B. 77; Bradbrook, "Fencing Easements in Australia" (1979) 53 A.L.J. 306. For a contrary view see Waite, "Easements: Positive Duties on the Servient Owner?" [1985] Camb. L.J. 458.

5. Would a covenant to supply hot water to the dominant tenement constitute an easement? See *Regis Property Co. Ltd v. Redman* [1956] 2 Q.B. 612. If not could the costs of supplying water be recoverable in quasi-contract? See *Rance v. Elvin* (1985) 50 P. & C.R. 9. Note also Jackson, "Leases, Easements and Positive Obligations" [1985] Conv. 66.

6. A right claimed which amounts to a right to joint possession or entire user of the servient tenement cannot exist as an easement: see *Re Ellenborough Park* [1956] 1 Ch. 131 and the following extract.

MERCANTILE GENERAL LIFE REASSURANCE CO. (AUST.) LTD v. PERMANENT TRUSTEE AUSTRALIA LTD

Supreme Court (1989) C.C.H. N.S.W. Conv. R. 55-441

[The plaintiff and defendant were owners of adjoining buildings. In 1929 the plaintiff's predecessors in title (McArthur Shipping Co. Ltd) by registered transfer granted a number of easements in favour of the adjoining land, of which the defendant's predecessor in title (Rudders Ltd) was the then registered proprietor. The relevant easements were in the following terms:

An easement of full right and liberty for the transferee, its and their tenants and servants and all persons who shall hereafter be expressly or impliedly authorised by it or them in the ordinary course of business in that behalf from time to time and at all times hereafter at its and their will and pleasure to pass and re-pass with or without horses and other animals, carts, carriages, traction engines, motor cars and other vehicles, laden or unladen, upon, over and along all that part of the servient tenement delineated in the plan hereunto annexed marked "A" and therein edged (black) and upon and within the same part of the servient tenement to load and unload any such animals, carts, carriages, engines, cars or vehicles and generally to use the same part of the servient tenement in any manner and to any extent which shall be consistent with the rights hereby granted and shall not be inconsistent with the rights reserved by the transferror in, to, upon and over the same provided that nothing hereinbefore contained shall be deemed a license or authority for the transferee to build over or upon any part of the servient tenement *and also* an easement of full right and liberty for the transferee to maintain during the life of the existing south eastern wall of the building upon the dominant tenement the said wall and all existing lavatories, lifts and other encroachments projecting therefrom over, upon or above the servient tenement but this last mentioned easement shall cease and determine upon the said south eastern wall of the said building or that portion thereof where such encroachments exist being pulled down or rebuilt *and also* an easement of full right and liberty for the transferee its and their tenants and servants and all other persons who shall hereafter be expressly or impliedly authorised by it or them in the ordinary course of business in that behalf from time to time and at all times hereafter at its and their will and pleasure to pass and re-pass to and from Pitt Street from and to the land delineated in the plan hereto annexed marked "A" and therein edged (black) with or without horses and other animals, carts, carriages, traction engines, motor cars and other vehicles laden or unladen over and along all that part of the said servient tenement delineated in the said Certificate of Title thereof and therein tinted (pink) *and also* an easement of full, free and uninterrupted access of light and air at all times hereafter over and across all that part of the servient tenement which is tinted green upon the plan hereunto annexed marked "A" to the windows and other apertures now existing or which shall hereafter exist in the south eastern wall or walls of the present or any future building or buildings of the transferee upon the said dominant tenement but reserving unto the transferor full right and liberty nevertheless to build upon that part of the servient tenement so tinted green . . . *and also* an easement of full and free right and liberty for the transferee at all times hereafter to enclose and lock up and keep so enclosed and locked up the whole or any part or parts of the land delineated in the plan hereto annexed marked "A" and therein edged (black) and of the land shown by (orange) colour in the plan upon the said Certificate of Title *but reserving* nevertheless unto the transferror its tenants and servants and all persons who shall be expressly or impliedly authorised by it or them in the ordinary course of business in their behalf access at all reasonable times to pass and repass with or without horses and other animals, carts, carriages, traction engines, motor cars and other vehicles in, to, from and upon any part of the said lands which shall be so enclosed and locked up for the purpose only of access to the goods lift for the purpose of receipt and delivery of goods at all reasonable times otherwise the transferee is to have the sole and unrestricted right to the use of the said yard and passage *and* the transferror *doth hereby* for itself its successors and assigns *covenant* with the transferee (a) that the transferror will not park or permit to be parked any vehicles nor house or store or permit to be housed or stored any goods or chattels of any kind whatsoever therein *provided however* that notwithstanding anything herein contained the transferror *doth hereby reserve* unto itself the transferror full right and liberty at all times and from time to time to build extend or enlarge the present or any future building of the transferror over that part of the said servient tenement delineated in the plan hereunto annexed marked "A".

The defendant, owner of the dominant tenement, decided to add additional floors to its building. The plaintiff brought proceedings seeking to restrain the defendant from carrying out building work or erecting or storing building materials or equipment on the plaintiff's land.]

POWELL J. [His Honour after setting out the facts continued]: It is necessary, first, to determine what is the true legal effect of the grant of the "easement"—particularly the first and the fifth of such "easements"—contained in memorandum of transfer registered No. C21764, for, if, as was submitted by Mr Farmer, it operated, not as a grant of "easements", but as a transfer of rights of ownership to the surface of "the light area", and to some at least, of the airspace above "the light area", the initial question to be determined, so it seems to me, would be not whether the acts complained of were acts authorised by the "easements", but whether the acts complained of were being carried out upon and within that part of "the light area" and the airspace above it the ownership of which was in the trustee.

It is convenient, at this point, to record what I believe to be the principles by which I should be guided in seeking to determine that question. They are as follows:

1. although, prior to the coming into force of the provisions of the *Conveyancing (Strata Titles) Act* 1961, it was not possible to have a separate certificate of title to a stratum of land above the surface of the earth, by no later than the time of Lord Coke the common law had come to accept that a freeholder could dispose

of his holding by horizontal, as well as by vertical, subdivision (see, for example, *Reilly v. Booth* (1890) 44 Ch. D. 12; *Metropolitan Railway Co. v. Fowler* [1892] 1 Q.B. 165; [1893] A.C. 416; *Resumed Properties Department v. Sydney Municipal Council* (1937) 13 L.G.R. (N.S.W.) 170; *Bursill Enterprises Pty Ltd v. Berger Bros Trading Co. Pty Ltd* (1971) 124 C.L.R. 73;

2. it would seem that no particular form of words needed to be used in order that such limited rights of ownership be conveyed, or transferred; thus in *Reilly v. Booth* the words "together with the exclusive use of the gateway into Oxford Street, being 10 ft 11 ins in the clear on the north side, 11 ft 7 ins on the south side, in depth, 41 ft 6 ins, and in height 15 ft" appear to have been regarded by the Court of Appeal (Cotton L.J., Lindley L.J. (as he then was) and Lopes L.J. (as he then was)) as conveying the ownership of the space within "the gateway" (or covered passage in question); so too, in *Bursill Enterprises Pty Ltd v. Berger Bros Trading Co. Pty Ltd*, the words, "together with all buildings erected on the said road or gateway and the right to pull down such buildings and to rebuild others at the height of not less than 12 ft from the ground over such road or gateway to the extent and no further than the existing building goes" appear—despite the fact that Menzies J. dissented in the final result—to have been held by all the judges (Barwick C.J., Menzies and Windeyer JJ.) in the High Court as apt to convey to the then grantee title to the space then occupied by the building then erected over the site of "the said road or gateway";

3. an easement may be defined as: "a privilege without profit which the owner of one . . . tenement (has) of another, existing in respect of their several tenements, by which the servient owner is obliged 'to suffer or not to do' something on his own land for the advantage of the dominant owner" (*Gale on Easements* (7th ed.), p. 6 quoted with approval by Barton J. in *Municipal District of Concord v. Coles* (1906) 3 C.L.R. 96 at 110);

4. although there may be found, both in the authorities (see, for example, *Copeland v. Greenhalf* [1952] 1 Ch. 488; *Grigsby v. Melville* [1972] 1 W.L.R. 1355) and in textbooks (see, for example, Bradbrook and Neave *Easements and Restrictive Covenants in Australia*, p. 3; *Gale on Easements* (15th ed.), p. 31) that a right to the exclusive or unrestricted use of a piece of land, or a right, in effect, to share the proprietary rights of the so-called servient owner, cannot constitute an easement, such statements must be scrutinised with care because of the varying contexts in which they have originated. Thus:

(a) as I have recorded above, the express grant of exclusive use of land, or a portion of it, may, in an appropriate case, be held to convey, or transfer, not an easement to use, but rights of property in, the subject land (see, for example, *Reilly v. Booth* (1890) 44 Ch. D. 12; *Bursill Enterprises Pty Ltd v. Berger Bros Trading Co. Pty Ltd* (1971) 124 C.L.R. 73;

(b) there will be found in the authorities cases in which an express grant, albeit, at times, informal, apparently to use portion of the servient tenement to the exclusion of the servient owner (see, for example, *Wright v. McAdam* [1949] 2 K.B. 744), or to use the whole of the servient tenement in common with the servient owner, *or* with another deriving title from him (see, for example, *Miller v. Emcer Products Ltd* [1956] Ch. 304), or in common with the servient owner *and* with another deriving title from him (*Re Ellenborough Park* [1956] Ch. 131; *Riley and Real Property Act v. Pentilla* [1974] V.R. 547) has been upheld as validly creating an easement; to which cases may be added a reference to *Attorney-General of Southern Nigeria v. John Holt & Co. (Liverpool) Ltd* [1915] A.C. 599 in which case Lord Shaw of

Dumfermline, when delivering the opinion of the Judicial Committee, appears (at 667) to express the view that the rights to erect buildings, and to store goods, on the servient tenement can be the subject of an easement;

5. for the most part, those cases in which the existence of an easement involving the exclusive use of part of the servient tenement (as, for example, *Copeland v. Greenhalf* [1952] 1 Ch. 488; *Grigsby v. Melville* [1972] 1 W.L.R. 1355) or the use, in common with the servient owner, of the whole, or substantially the whole, of the servient tenement (see, for example, *Copeland v. Greenhalf*) has been denied, appear to be cases involving a claim to a prescriptive easement (*Copeland v. Greenhalf*), or an implied easement (*Grigsby v. Melville*), in which cases, so Upjohn J. (as he then was) seemed to suggest in *Copeland v. Greenhalf*, the relevant claim, in reality, amounts to a claim to the title to the land by reason of long adverse possession—it should, however, be noted that this view has not been universally accepted (see, for example, Bradbrook and Neave, *Easements and Restrictive Covenants in Australia*, p. 5);

6. since the grant of the several "easements" is made subject to "reservations", it should be noted that, strictly, there is a distinction between an "exception"— which is something excepted out of that which is granted, and which, *being in esse* would otherwise pass under the general words in a conveyance, and which, not being the subject matter of the conveyance, operated even though the grantee did not execute the deed—and a "reservation", which is some benefit, *not in esse* at the time of the grant, to be newly created. Originally, the term "reservation" referred to something "issuing out of the grant", as, for example, rent (see, for example, *Durham and Sunderland Railway Co. v. Walker* [1842] 2 Q.B. 940 at 967 per Tindal C.J.) but it has since acquired an extended meaning, and is now applied, as well, to some incorporeal right, such as a right of way, which the grantor desires regranted: see, for example, *Durham and Sunderland Railway Co. v. Walker; Mason v. Clarke* [1954] 1 Q.B. 460 at 466 per Denning L.J. (as he then was). As the subject of an intended re-grant, a "reservation" contained in a deed executed prior to the coming into operation of 45A of the *Conveyancing Act* 1919 did not operate *in law* unless the deed were executed by the grantee (see *Doe d. Douglas v. Lock* (1835) 2 A. & E. 705; 111 E.R. 271; *Wickham v. Hawker* (1840) 7 M. & W. 63 at 76 per Parke B; 151 E.R. 679 at 685)—the position *in equity* however varied (see, for example, *May v. Belleville* [1905] 2 Ch. 605);

7. however, while the technical meaning of the words "exception" and "reservation" was as I have set out, that meaning is not so strictly applied as to govern the construction of the instrument in which it appears; thus, in *Attorney-General (N.S.W.) v. Dickson* [1904] A.C. 273, the word "reserving" was held to operate as an exception, while, in *British Railways Board v. Glass* [1965] Ch. 538, the words "save and except" were construed as a reservation or a re-grant rather than as a true exception;

8. although the position is not entirely free from doubt, it seems clear enough that any ambiguity in an exception is to be construed against the grantor (see, *Savill Bros Ltd v. Bethell* [1902] 2 Ch. 523) and it is probable that, since the coming into operation of s. 45A of the *Conveyancing Act* 1919, a like approach is to be taken to ambiguities in a reservation (see *Cordell v. Second Clanfield Properties Ltd* [1969] 2 Ch. 9; cf. *Mason v. Clarke* [1954] 1 Q.B. 460; *Bulstrode v. Lambert* [1953] 1 W.L.R. 1064); however, a reservation in a conveyance executed prior to that time is probably to be construed against the conveyee: see *Mason v. Clarke*.

The question then is, whether, in the light of the various principles which I have recorded above, memorandum of transfer registered No. C21764 is, despite the form which it takes, to be regarded as having had the effect, in law, of transferring to Rudders title to "the light area" or to some part, and, if so which, of "the light area".

Having given that question such consideration as I have been able, I have concluded that, despite the apparent width of the rights intended to be conferred upon Rudders by memorandum of transfer registered No. C21764, those rights fell short of the transfer, or grant, to Rudders of the use, to the total exclusion of Macarthur, of any defined, or definable, portion of the surface of "the light area", or of any defined, or definable, stratum of the space above the surface of "the light area"; and since, as I understand it, the *ratio decidendi* of such cases as *Reilly v. Booth* (1890) 44 Ch. D. 12; The Metropolitan Railway Co. v. Fowler [1892] 1 Q.B. 165, and *Bursill Enterprises Pty Ltd v. Berger Bros Trading Co. Ltd* (1971) 124 C.L.R. 73, was that the conveyance, grant, or transfer, of *the exclusive use* of "the gateway", tunnel, or building in question, amounted to a conveyance, grant or transfer of the proprietary right to possession, it must follow that as memorandum of transfer registered No. C21764 did not have the effect of transferring to Rudders title to "the light area", or to some portion of the surface of "the light area", or to a stratum of the space over "the light area", or some portion of it—the title to "the light area" remained in Macarthur, albeit that, by reason of its grant of the various "easements", and of its entering into the various covenants, contained in memorandum of transfer registered No. C21764, its ability to exercise what would otherwise have been the rights of an owner was substantially reduced.

It is thus necessary to determine what was the true nature and extent of the various "easements" granted by memorandum of transfer registered No. C21764.

In construing the memorandum of transfer, it is legitimate to have regard to the circumstances existing at the time of its execution for the purpose of determining what was the intention of the parties: see *Bulstrode v. Lambert* [1953] 1 W.L.R. 1064. In particular, when one is concerned with a right of way, one must "consider (1) the locus in quo over which the way is granted; (2) the nature of the terminus ad quem; and (3) the purpose for which the way is to be used": *Gale on Easements* (12th ed.), p. 316 cited by Upjohn J. (as he then was) in *Bulstrode v. Lambert*.

Although the evidence is, in some respects, rather sparse, one can, I believe, proceed upon the basis of the following facts:

Rudders (now TNT Rudders Ltd) was, at the time of the execution of memorandum of transfer registered No. C21764, and, so far as I am aware, still is, a well-known customs and forwarding agent. One might reasonably assume that the business of a customs and forwarding agent then necessarily involved taking into its possession, or custody, whether from bond store, wharf, or railway terminal, goods for transport, or forwarding to its clients, and, as well, taking into its possession, or custody, from its clients, goods for transport by ship or train to its clients' customers. Further, one might reasonably assume that the business of a customs and forwarding agent then necessarily required that the agent occupied premises at, and from, which it could receive, and, if need be, unload, temporarily store, load, and despatch, such goods to their ultimate destination. Finally, one might reasonably assume that the business of a customs and forwarding agent would be made far easier if it had, immediately adjacent to the premises which it occupied, a yard, or parking area, to which its, or its clients' vehicles might come for the purpose of loading and unloading the goods with which it had to deal, and which yard, or parking area, although having ready access, could be locked, and made secure.

At the time of the execution of memorandum of transfer registered No. C21764 Rudders occupied the two buildings—joined above the level of the area marked pink on the plan which I have set out above—now known as 42-44 Pitt Street, Sydney, for the purposes of its business. Those buildings, which, so it seems, were no less than 30, and probably closer to 50, years old, were built to the western boundary and to some extent, at least, encroached upon, "the light area", and the eastern wall of the building was fitted with windows which opened on to "the light area".

Finally, at the time of the execution of memorandum of transfer registered No. C21764, "Kyle House" was in the course of being constructed.

These facts, so it seems to me, provide a good guide to the objects sought to be achieved by the grant of the several "easements", and the entry into the various covenants, contained in memorandum of transfer registered No. C21764. Those objects, so it seems to me were:

1. to permit the two buildings, Nos 42-44 Pitt Street, to be preserved on the land on which they were then erected, and to be kept in repair until the time for rebuilding arrived (the second easement);

2. to permit the two buildings to continue to enjoy the existing amenities, such as light to the windows fitted into the eastern wall of the building, and the right to maintain any existing encroachments on to, or above "the light area" (the second and fourth easements);

3. to permit the existing buildings to have the benefit of a yard, or parking area, such as I have earlier described, for use by the dominant owner or persons dealing with it in the ordinary course of its business, which yard, or parking area, although having a ready access to Pitt Street, could none the less be made secure (the first, third and fifth easements).

If these objects be kept in mind, then so it seems to me, the difficulties, to which the language of the several grants seemed to give rise, are seen to be more apparent than real. Thus:

1. as Macarthur retained the title to the right of way and "the light area" it was free to exercise all the rights of an owner upon or over the right of way and "the light area" unless:

    (a) the exercise of those rights would substantially and materially interfere with any easement granted by it in respect of the right of way and/or "the light area";

    (b) it had, by covenant, accepted some limitation upon those rights;

2. one of the rights of a servient owner is to restrain any excessive user of the servient tenement by the dominant owner, for an excessive user, not being authorised by the grant, is a trespass;

3. in the absence of any context indicating the contrary intention, the grant of an easement is to be construed as carrying with it such ancillary rights as are reasonably necessary to the effective and reasonable exercise and enjoyment of the rights expressly granted;

4. in the absence of any context indicating the contrary intention, the rights expressly granted, and the ancillary rights, are to be exercised in a manner which does not interfere to an extent greater than is reasonably necessary, with the rights of the servient owner;

5. the right to maintain the wall and encroachments (the second easement) would, of necessity, carry with it the right to repair, which latter right, in its turn, would necessarily carry with it the right to enter upon "the light area" and erect such

temporary scaffolding as may be necessary for the purpose (see, for example, *Ward v. Kirkland* [1967] Ch. 194; *Auerbach v. Beck* (1985) C.C.H. N.S.W. Conv. R 55-246; (1985) 6 N.S.W.L.R. 424); however, entry upon "the light area" for the purpose of erecting, and maintaining, scaffolding, and other structures, such as "a two-barrow hoist" intended to facilitate, not the repair of the existing wall, but the enlarging of the existing buildings by the adding of further storeys, cannot, in my view, be considered as reasonably ancillary to the right to repair;

6. while, in a particular case, the right to stop for the purpose of loading or unloading, and even the right to park, may be considered to be reasonably necessary for the proper enjoyment of a right of way (see, for example, *Bulstrode v. Lambert* [1953] 1 W.L.R. 1064; *McIlraith v. Grady* [1968] 1 Q.B. 468) this does not seem to be such a case, for such rights were expressly given by the first easement in respect of "the light area" (see, for example, *Zenere v. Leate* (1980) 1 B.P.R. 9300); still less, so it seems to me, could it be said to be reasonably necessary for the proper enjoyment of the right of way that the servient owner have the right to use the right of way as a site for storing building materials, or other goods, under cover (see, for example, Exhibit "B (xi)"");

7. although the introductory words of the first easement suggest that all that was intended to be granted was a right of way over "the light area", the latter parts of that easement, coupled with the latter parts of the fifth easement make it clear that the subject of the grants was far greater—clearly, it encompassed the rights to pass and re-pass over the whole of the surface of "the light area", to stop, to park, at least for the purposes of loading and unloading, and, as well, generally to use "the light area" in a manner "consistent with the rights hereby granted". These words, so it seems to me, would be apt to include such activities as leaving goods standing temporarily on the surface of "the light area" prior to their being loaded, or after their being unloaded and prior to their being moved into the building. As well, so it seems to me, those words would be apt to permit builder's materials and plant brought on to "the light area" in connection with the repair or maintenance of the eastern wall to be left temporarily on the surface of "the light area". So too, so it seems to me, those words, coupled with the words of the fifth easement, would be apt to permit the dominant owner's vehicles, in effect, to be "garaged" in "the light area", at least so long as their being so "garaged" did not interfere with the servient owner's use of "the light area" for access to the rear of "Kyle House";

8. despite the apparent breadth of the rights conferred by the grant of the fifth easement, its purpose is, I think, clear enough—as I have earlier indicated, it was, in my opinion, to permit Rudders to have a secure yard, or parking area, into which it could receive, upon which it could temporarily hold, and from which it could despatch, its clients' goods, and upon which it could garage its own vehicles when they were not in use;

9. if the purposes for which the various easements were granted were as I have set out above, and if the various easements are to be construed in the manner which I have set out above, then the words "the transferee is to have the sole and unrestricted right to use the said yard and passage" are seen to mean no more than that, except for so organising its activities in a manner that does not substantially and materially interfere with access by the servient owner, and those dealing with it, to the rear of "Kyle House", the dominant owner was to be free to use the right of way and "the light area" for the purposes of its receiving, unloading, loading and despatching goods, and for "garaging" its vehicles in such a manner as, being reasonably appropriate to such purposes, it might from

time to time think fit—contrary to what has been put, those words did not, in my view, mean that the dominant owner was, except for being required to permit access to the rear of "Kyle House", free to act in "the light area" as if it were the owner of the freehold. If any futher support for my view be thought necessary it is, in my view, readily to be found in the fact that the words "and generally to use . . . in any manner and to any extent" which appear in the first easement are immediately followed by the words: "which shall be consistent with the rights hereby granted and shall not be inconsistent with the rights reserved by the transferror in, to, upon and over ('the light area') provided that nothing hereinbefore contained shall be deemed a license or authority for the transferree to build over or upon any part of ('the light area')".

For these reasons, I conclude that, although there may be circumstances, associated with the maintenance of the eastern wall of Nos 42-44 Pitt Street, Sydney, in which activities of the type now in question might lawfully be carried out by the dominant owner or its contractors in "the light area", the activities now being carried out, are not, nor are the various structures now erected thereon, or the goods materials and plant now standing thereon, authorised by any of the easements in question.

[His Honour then went on to hold that unauthorised entry constituted a continuing trespass and ordered the removal of scaffolding and building materials from the yard.]

NOTES AND QUESTIONS

1. In *Copeland v. Greenhalf* [1952] 1 Ch. 488 referred to in the case extracted the defendant and his predecessor had deposited and repaired vehicles on a narrow strip of land belonging to the plaintiff. The strip of land, 150 ft in length and of variable width from 15 ft to 35 ft, formed an access road to the plaintiff's house and orchard. The plaintiff brought proceedings to restrain the defendant from so using the land. The defendant claimed a prescriptive right to leave vehicles in the course of his business on the land. Upjohn J. accepted that an easement could exist for the benefit of a business carried on on the land, but rejected the defendant's claim that an easement existed. His Lordship said:

> this claim . . . really amounts to a claim to a joint user of the land by the defendant. Practically the defendant is claiming the whole beneficial user of the strip of land . . . he can leave as many or as few lorries there as he likes for as long as he likes; he may enter on it by himself, his servants and agents to do repair work thereon. In my judgment, that is not a claim which can be established as an easement. It is virtually a claim to possession of the servient tenement, if necessary to the exclusion of the owner; or, at any rate, to a joint user, and no authority has been cited to me which would justify the conclusion that a right of this wide and undefined nature can be the proper subject of an easement. It seems to me that to succeed, this claim must amount to a successful claim of possession by reason of long adverse possession. I say nothing, of course, as to the creation of such rights by deeds or by covenant; I am dealing solely with the question of a right arising by prescription.

Could the right to store vehicles on the plaintiff's land have been granted expressly as an easement in a deed? Consider in this regard the cases mentioned in note 4 below.

2. In *Miller v. Emcer Products Ltd* [1956] 1 Ch. 304 there was a grant of an office to a lessee with a right to use toilet facilites in common with the landlords and third parties. It was held that the right granted was an easement. Romer L.J. in the course of his judgment observed (at 316):

> It is true that during the times when the dominant owner exercised the right, the owner of the servient tenement would be excluded, but this is greater or less degree is a common feature of many easements (for example, rights of way) and does not amount to such an ouster of the servient owner's rights as was held by Upjohn J. to be incompatible with a legal easement in *Copeland v. Greenhalf*.

3. See *Bursill Enterprises Pty Ltd v. Berger Bros Trading Co. Pty Ltd* (1971) 124 C.L.R. 73, above p. 238.

4. Whether a right claimed amounts to an easement or a right of exclusive possession or joint user is largely a matter of degree. For example, in *Taff Vale Railway Co. v. Cardiff Railway Co.* [1917] 1 Ch. 299, the Court of Appeal had to consider incidentally whether the right to construct and use a solid railway enbankment on a very narrow strip of land could constitute an easement. Scrutton L.J., in the course of his judgment, said (at 316-317):

> It is said that this Act gives an easement, and that an embankment which appropriates the whole of the land and excludes beneficial ownership by the landowner could not be an easement. An easement of appropriating the whole land was not known to the law. If the exercise of any easement did appropriate the whole land, it was because the part appropriated was so small and so incidental to the use of a wider easement that the law overlooked it. Thus in *Escott v. Newport Corp.* [1904] 2 K.B. 369 the space occupied in land by tramway standards was held not to be land taken within the *Land Clauses Act* and in *Chelsea Waterworks Co. v. Bowley* (1851) 17 Q.B. 358 the space occupied in land by water pipes was held not to be land, or an interest in land, but an easement. And it was said that a solid embankment was far beyond a negligible quantity of space.

See also *Harada v. Registrar of Titles* [1981] V.R. 743 at 753.

In *A.-G. (Southern Nigeria) v. John Holt & Co. (Liverpool) Ltd* [1915] A.C. 599 (discussed below p. 272) the Privy Council expressed the view that a right to store goods on the land of another could be an easement. By contrast, Brightman J., in *Grigsby v. Melville* [1972] 1 W.L.R. 1355, rejected a claim to an easement of storage. His Lordship said (at 1363):

> There are, I think, two issues here: first, whether an easement of unlimited storage within a confined or defined space is capable of existing as a member of law. Secondly, if so, whether such an easement was reserved in the present case.

[His Lordship then referred to the judgment of Upjohn J. in *Copeland v. Greenhalf*, and continued:]

> Mr Ainger countered by observing that *Copeland v. Greenhalf* was inconsistent with *Wright v. Macadam* [1949] 2 K.B. 744, an earlier decision of the Court of Appeal in which it was held that the right of a tenant to store domestic coal in a shed on the landlord's land could exist as an easement for the benefit of the demised premises. I am not convinced that there is any real inconsistency between the two cases. The point of the decision in *Copeland v. Greenhalf* [1952] Ch. 488, was that the right asserted amounted in effect to a claim to the whole beneficial user of the servient tenement and for that reason could not exist as a mere easement. The precise facts in *Wright v. Macadam* [1949] 2 K.B. 744 [see extract below p. 253] in this respect are not wholly clear from the report and it is a little difficult to know whether the tenant had exclusive use of the coal shed or of any defined portion of it. To some extent a problem of this sort may be one of degree.
>
> In the case before me, it is, I think, clear that the defendant's claim to an easement would give, to all practical intents and purposes, and exclusive right of user over the whole of the confined space representing the servient tenement. I think I would be at liberty, if necessary, to follow *Copeland v. Greenhalf* [1952] Ch. 488.

The court of Appeal affirmed the judgment of Brightman J. on another ground and without reference to this issue: see [1974] 1 W.L.R. 80.

Can it be argued that the distinction between the *Southern Nigeria* case [1915] A.C. 599 and *Grigsby v. Melville* is that there was in the first case a claim to a large area of foreshore where materials might be stored, and in the latter case a claim to unlimited storage in a confined space?

5. Is the right to park a car in a particular defined space a claim to the whole beneficial user incapable of existing as an easement? Is the result different if there is a right to park anywhere in a larger defined area? See Hayton Notes of Recent Cases, "*Grigsby v. Melville*" (1973) 37 Conv. (N.S.) 60 at 62.

C. CREATION OF EASEMENTS AND PROFITS

1. By express grant

An easement or profit à prendre may be created by express grant. With respect to old system title land, the express grant in order to be valid at law must be contained in a deed: *Conveyancing Act* 1919 (N.S.W.), s. 23(B)(1). The easement or profit may be enforceable in equity if it is in writing (*Conveyancing Act* 1919 (N.S.W.), s. 23C) or if there are sufficient acts of part performance: see *Talga Investments Pty Ltd v. Tweed Canal Estates Pty Ltd* (1974) 1 B.P.R. 8575 (easement); *Ellison v. Vukicevic* (1986) 7 N.S.W.L.R. 104; (1987) 9 N.S.W.L.R. 13; *Silovi Pty Ltd v. Barbaro* (1988) 13 N.S.W.L.R. 466 (profits); cf. *Elibank-Murray v. Dunne* (1982) C.C.H. N.S.W. Conv. R. 55-048; (1982) C.C.H. N.S.W. Conv. R. 55-057.

Easements and profits may be created over Torrens title land by an appropriate instrument (usually by transfer) and registration: (N.S.W.), *Real Property Act* 1900 (N.S.W.), ss 46, 47, see below p. 280. Following amendments to ss 46 and 47 in 1987 (*Real Property (Forestry Rights) Amendment Act* 1987 (N.S.W.)), specific provision was made for the creation and registration of gross and appurtenant profits over Torrens title land. Although it was accepted that profits over Torrens title land could be created by registered transfer prior to 1970 (see Baalman, "The Neglected Profit à Prendre" (1948) 22 A.L.J. 302), there had been some debate whether amendments to the *Real Property Act* 1900 in 1970 prevented the registration of profits. The 1970 amendments deleted reference in s. 47 to the recording of "any incorporeal right" in the register, leading to the argument that there no longer existed any authority to register such interests: see Stein, "Profits à prendre and Torrens title in New South Wales" (1982) 56 A.L.J. 426. In *Ellison v. Vukicevic* (1986) 7 N.S.W.L.R. 104 at 112, 119, 120 (appeal to the Court of Appeal was dismissed on other grounds (1987) 9 N.S.W.L.R. 13), Young J. thought that despite the 1970 amendments profits could still be created by registered transfer and would be properly recorded in the Register. The Land Titles Office practice supported this view (at 120). Even if profits were not capable of registration by reason of the 1970 amendments, Young J. (at 119) held that unregistered profits could be protected by caveat.

The effect of, and recording of, forestry covenants as rights incidental to a forestry right is referred to above p. 215.

After 1964, easements over both old system and Torrens title land may be created by a registered plan: see *Conveyancing Act* 1919, s. 88B, below p. 241. Under s. 88B(2)(c) and (3)(c), profits appurtenant may be similarly created, following amendments to s. 88B in 1987: *Conveyancing (Forestry Rights) Amendment Act* 1987 (N.S.W.).

In New South Wales easements expressly granted over old system title land and Torrens title land in order to be enforceable against a person not a party to their creation, must comply in form with the provisions of s. 88(1) of the *Conveyancing Act* 1919 (N.S.W.) which provides that an easement or covenant intended to be annexed to land shall not be enforceable against a person not a party to its creation unless the instrument creating the easement or covenant clearly indicates (1) the land to be benefited; (2) the land subject to the burden; (3) persons having the right to release, vary or modify the easement or restriction other than those entitled at law; (4) persons whose consent to a release, variation or modification is required. Section 88(1) does not apply to an easement acquired by or for the Crown, or by or for any public or local authority constituted by Act of Parliament, or to any restriction affecting the user of land in relation to any such easement: s. 88(4). The formal requirements of s. 88(1) are discussed when dealing with restrictive covenants: see below p. 361.

Formal requirements similar to, but not identical with, those contained in the *Conveyancing Act* 1919 (N.S.W.), s. 88(1) also apply to profits, whether over old system title land or Torrens title land, contained in instruments coming into operation after the commencement of the *Conveyancing (Forestry Rights) Amendment Act* 1987 (N.S.W.). The *Conveyancing Act* 1919 (N.S.W.), s. 88AA now provides that a profit is not enforceable against a person interested in the land other than a person who is a party to the instrument creating the profit, unless the instrument indicates (1) the land which is subject to the burden of the profit; and (2) in the case of a profit appurtenant, the land to which the benefit of the profit is appurtenant. As s. 88AA and s. 88(1) have much in common the case law concerning the operation of s. 88(1) should be referred to in the construction of s. 88AA: see below p. 361.

2. By express reservation   *- comply w. S 88(1) CA*

On a conveyance of land, the owner may reserve an easement to himself over land or part of land conveyed and make it appurtenant to other land retained by him. Under the common law, a reservation of an easement could only take effect where the conveyee regranted the right to the conveyor; this required execution of the conveyance by the conveyee: *Mercantile General Life Reassurance Co. (Aust.) Ltd v. Permanent Trustee Australia Ltd* (1989) C.C.H. N.S.W. Conv. R. 55-441 at 58-208, above p. 234. The reason for this was that an easement lay only in grant and a person could not at common law make a grant to the themselves: Megarry and Wade, *The Law of Real Property* (5th ed.), p. 857. In New South Wales, a regrant is no longer necessary by virtue of s. 45A of the *Conveyancing Act* 1919 which came into effect 1 January 1931 and see *St Edmundsbury v. Clarke (No. 2)* [1975] 1 W.L.R. 468.

An alternative method used by conveyancers which had the effect of reserving an easement to the grantor was a conveyance to uses. The grantor conveyed the land to a third party and his heirs to the use that the grantor should have a legal easement, and subject thereto, to the use of the grantee and his heirs. The use was executed by statute: *Conveyancing Act* 1919 (N.S.W.), s. 45(1). This method of reserving an easement is no longer available in New South Wales by virtue of the repeal of the *Statute of Uses* by the *Imperial Acts Application Act* 1969 (N.S.W.), s. 8.

In respect of Torrens title land in New South Wales, a reservation of an easement may be made in memorandum of transfer whereby the land is transferred: *Real Property Act* 1900 (N.S.W.), s. 46. The instrument containing the reservation must, both in respect of old system title and Torrens title, comply with the requirements of s. 88(1) of the *Conveyancing Act* 1919, as to which see above p. 240.

Similar rules will apply to the reservation of a profit.

3. By statute

The Crown and its various instrumentalities may compulsorily acquire easements over the land of a private citizen: see for example, *Public Works Act* 1912 (N.S.W.), s. 4A. Of general importance in New South Wales is the statutory creation of easements or profits on the registration of plans. Under the *Conveyancing Act* 1919, s. 88B, a plan (usually a plan of subdivision) lodged for registration or recording under Division 3 of Part 23 of the *Conveyancing Act* must set out any easements, restrictions as to user or profits appurtenant intended to be created which benefit or burden land comprised in the plan: s. 88B(2) (c). On registration or recording, the easements, restrictions as to user or profits so indicated are deemed to be created without any further assurance and by virtue of the registration: s. 88B(3)(c).

Section 88B applies to land under old system title and Torrens title. In respect of the latter, s. 88B(3A) provides:

When creating a folio of the Register kept under the *Real Property Act* 1900 for land benefited by any easement, or for land burdened by any easement, restriction on the use of land or positive covenant created by this section, the Registrar General shall record in that folio in such manner as he considers appropriate, the easement, restriction on the use of land or positive covenant, as the case may be.

The effect of failure to so record is discussed below pp. 280-294.

4. By implied grant or reservation

Although an easement may not be held over parcels owned by the same person where there is unity of ownership and possession, an owner may exercise rights which might be classified as easements if the parcels were held or occupied by different people. Such rights are known as "quasi-easements"; the land benefited is termed the "quasi-dominant tenement" and the land burdened as the "quasi-servient tenement". Upon the grant of the quasi-dominant tenement the grantee will be entitled to the benefit of all those "continuous and apparent" easements necessary for the reasonable enjoyment of the land granted and so used at the time of the grant: *Wheeldon v. Burrows* (1879) 12 Ch. D. 31, extracted below. The rights implied in favour of a purchaser on grant of the quasi-dominant tenement are much wider than the rights implied in favour of the vendor where she or he retains the quasi-dominant tenement without expressly reserving rights in the grant of the quasi-servient tenement. A vendor retaining the quasi-dominant tenement is entitled by implication of law only to easements of necessity and common intention. The reason is that a vendor who retains part of her or his land is in a position to expressly reserve such rights as he or she thinks fit. Where there is a simultaneous disposition of both the quasi dominant and quasi-servient tenements by the common vendor, the rule is that each parcel acquires, by way of implied grant, the same easements over the other parcel as would occur if the common vendor had in each case retained the other parcel: *Swansborough v. Coventry* (1832) 9 Bing. 305; 131 E.R. 629. The rule applies also to testamentary or voluntary dispositions of property: *Sunset Properties Pty Ltd v. Johnston* (1975) 3 B.P.R. 9185.

The principles enunciated in *Wheeldon v. Burrows* have been regarded as one aspect of the wider rule of property law that the grantor must not derogate from her or his grant. One very important result of the general rule that a grantor must not derogate from her or his grant has been that rights not capable at law of existing as easements may nevertheless be annexed to and run with the land: see below p. 257. It has also been argued that the effect of general words implied in conveyances of land by statute may be that mere personal rights, not amounting to easement at law, may pass with the land. The principal authorities are extracted below.

An implied grant or reservation can be expressly or impliedly excluded: see *Squarey v. Harris-Smith* (1981) 42 P. & C.R. 118. Compare *Lyme Valley Squash Club v. Newcastle under Lyme Borough Council* [1985] 2 All E.R. 405.

The Victorian Law Reform Commission has recommended that easements should no longer be created by implied grant or implied reservation. It is proposed that the Registrar should have power to grant an easement that is necessary for the reasonable enjoyment of land on payment of adequate compensation: Law Reform Commission of Victoria, *Easements and Covenants*, DP 15, 1989, para. 13.

The extent to which implied easements and profits are recognised by the Torrens system is discussed separately: see "Easements, Profits and the Torrens System", below p. 280.

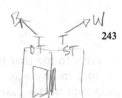

WHEELDON v. BURROWS

Court of Appeal (1879) 12 Ch. D. 31

[Tetley owned a workshop and an adjacent vacant lot of land. The workshop had windows overlooking and receiving light from the adjacent lot. Both the workshop and the vacant land were put up for auction, but only the vacant lot was sold and subsequently conveyed to Wheeldon. After a short period of time Tetley sold the workshop to Burrows. Wheeldon erected hoardings near the edge of the land for the purpose of preventing light to the windows of the workshop. The defendant Burrows knocked down the hoardings asserting that he had an easement of light over the adjoining land. Wheeldon brought proceedings for trespass claiming an injunction to restrain further trespassory acts by Burrows.]

THESIGER L.J. [His Lordship after stating the facts continued:] We have had a considerable number of cases cited to us, and out of them I think that two propositions may be stated as what I may call the general rules governing cases of this kind. The first of these rules is, that on the grant by the owner of a tenement of part of that tenement as it is then used and enjoyed, there will pass to the grantee all those continuous and apparent easements (by which, of course, I mean quasi-easements), or, in other words, all those easements which are necessary to the reasonable enjoyment of the property granted, and which have been and are at the time of the grant used by the owners of the entirety for the benefit of the part granted. The second propostion is that, if the grantor intends to reserve any right over the tenement granted, it is his duty to reserve it expressly in the grant. Those are the general rules governing cases of this kind, but the second of those rules is subject to certain exceptions. One of those exceptions is the well-known exception which attaches to cases of what are called ways of necessity; and I do not dispute for a moment that there may be, and probably are, certain other exceptions, to which I shall refer before I close my observations upon this case.

Both of the general rules which I have mentioned are founded upon a maxim which is as well established by authority as it is consonant to reason and common sense, viz., that a grantor shall not derogate from his grant. It has been argued before us that there is no distinction between what has been called an implied grant and what is attempted to be established under the name of an implied reservation; and that such a distinction between the implied grant and the implied reservation is a mere modern invention, and one which runs contrary, not only to the general practice upon which land has been bought and sold for a considerable time, but also to authorities which are said to be clear and distinct upon the matter.

[His Lordship, after reviewing the authorities, continued:]

These cases in no way support the proposition for which the appellant in this case contends; but, on the contrary, support the proposition that in the case of a grant you may imply a grant of such continuous and apparent easements or such easements as are necessary to the reasonable enjoyment of the property conveyed, and have in fact been enjoyed during the unity of ownership, but that, with the exception which I have referred to of easements of necessity, you cannot imply a similar reservation in favour of the grantor of land.

Upon the question whether there is any other exception, I must refer both to *Pyer v. Carter* (1857) 1 H. & N. 916; 156 E.R. 1472 and to *Richards v. Rose* (1853) 9 Ex. 218; 156 E.R. 93; and, although is it quite unnecessary for us to decide the point, it seems to me that there is a possible way in which these cases can be supported without in any way departing from the general maxims upon which we base our judgment in this case. I have already pointed to the special circumstances in *Pyer v. Carter*, and I cannot see that there is anything unreasonable in supposing that in such a case, where the defendant under his grant is to take this easement, which had been enjoyed during the unity of ownership, of pouring his water upon the grantor's land, he should also be held to take it subject to the reciprocal and mutual easement by which that very same water was carried into the drain on that land and then back through the land of the person from whose land the water came. It seems to me to be consistent with reason and common sense that these reciprocal easements should be implied; and, although it is not necessary to decide the point, it seems to me worthy of consideration in any after case, if the question whether *Pyer v. Carter* is right or wrong comes for discussion, to consider that point. *Richards v. Rose*, although not identically open to exactly the same reasoning as would apply to *Pyer v. Carter*, still appears to me to be open to analogous reasoning. Two houses had existed for some time, each supporting the other. Is there anything unreasonable—is there not, on the contrary, something very reasonable—to suppose in that case that the man who takes a grant of the house first and takes it with the right of support from that adjoining house, should also give to that adjoining house a reciprocal right of support from his own?

One other point remains, and that I shall dispose of in a very few words. It is said that, even supposing the maxims which I have stated to be correct, this case is an exception which comes within the rule laid down in *Swansborough v. Coventry* (1832) 9 Bing. 305; 131 E.R. 629 and *Compton v. Richards* (1814) 1 Price 27; 145 E.R. 1320, namely, that, although the land and houses were not in fact conveyed at the same time, they were conveyances made as part and parcel of one intended sale by auction. It seems to me that that proposition cannot be supported for one moment. We start here with an absolute conveyance in January 1876. What right have we to look back to any previous contract or to any previous arrangement between the parties? If it had been the case of an ordinary contract, and there had been parol negotiations, it is well-established law that you cannot look to those parol negotiations in order to put any construction upon the document which the parties entered into for the purpose of avoiding any dispute as to what might be their intentions in the bargain made between them. The same rule of law applies, and even more strongly in the case of a conveyance, which alone must regulate the rights of the parties. In the cases which have been cited the conveyances were founded upon transactions which in equity were equivalent to conveyances between the parties at the time when the transactions were entered into, and those transactions were entered into at the same moment of time and as part and parcel of one transaction. There may be, and there is, according to *Swansborough v. Coventry*, another exception to the rule which I have mentioned; but here the sale by auction was abortive as regards the defendant's property. There was a conveyance in January of the plaintiff's property without any reservation, and there was no contract of purchase on the part of the defendant until more than a month after that conveyance had been completed. I believe I am expressing the view of the other members of the court when I say that it appears to the court that under such circumstances there is no exception to the general rule. For these reasons, therefore, the appeal should be dismissed.

[The concurring judgments of James and Baggallay L.JJ. have been omitted.]

NOTES AND QUESTIONS

1. In *Ward v. Kirkland* [1967] Ch. 194, Ungoed-Thomas J. was called upon to decide whether, inter alia, there was an implied grant of a right to enter adjoining property to maintain the wall of a cottage. His Lordship referred to the judgment of Thesiger L.J. in the principal case and continued:

> Reading that passage on its own, on first impression, it would appear that the "easements which are necessary to the reasonable enjoyment of the property conveyed" might be a separate class from "continuous and apparent easements". It has been recognised that there is some difficulty in these descriptions, to which I have referred, of the easements which come within the ambit of the doctrine of *Wheeldon v. Burrows* (1879) 12 Ch. D. 31. It has been suggested that perhaps the "easement necessary to the reasonable enjoyment of the property conveyed" might refer to negative easements, whereas what we are concerned with here is positive easements. However that may be, I understand that there is no case in which positive easements which are not "continuous and apparent" have been held to come within the doctrine of *Wheeldon v. Burrows*. Here, there has certainly been continuous user, in the sense that the right has been in fact used whenever the need arose. But the words "continuous and apparent" seem to be directed to there being on the servient tenement a feature which would be seen on inspection and which is neither transitory nor intermittent; for example, drains, paths, as contrasted with the bowsprits of ships overhanging a piece of land.
>
> Here, it is conceded that it was only possible or practicable for the occupiers of the cottage to maintain the boundary wall by going onto the defendant's property as claimed in this case. That would be obvious on an inspection of the properties. But here there was no feature on the defendant's property designed or appropriate for such maintenance. The question is whether that requirement is necessary. If it is not necessary, then there are no clearly defined limits to the area of user; and if the easement extends to maintain the whole wall, as it must, then there could be no interference with that easement and therefore no building in the yard along that wall.
>
> Professor Cheshire, in his book on Real Property, says (*Modern Real Property* (9th ed.), p. 468) that:
>
>> The two words "continuous" and "apparent" must be read together and understood as pointing to an easement which is accompanied by some obvious and permanent mark on the land itself, or at least by some mark which will be disclosed by a careful inspection of the premises.
>
> Then he gives instances, and says (p. 469):
>
>> A right of way is not necessarily such a quasi-easement as will pass under the rule in *Wheeldon v. Burrows* (1879) 12 Ch. D. 31. To do so it must be apparent. There is no difficulty where there is a definite made road over the quasi-servient tenement to and for the apparent use of the quasi-dominant tenement. Such will clearly pass upon a severance of the common tenement. But the existence of a formed road is not essential and if there are other indicia which show that the road was being used at the time of the grant for the benefit of the quasi-dominant tenement and that it is necessary for the reasonable enjoyment of that tenement, it will pass to a purchaser of the latter.
>
> It seems to me that in the absence of a continuous and apparent feature designed or appropriate for the exercise of the easement on the servient tenement, there is not a continuous and apparent easement within the requirements of *Wheeldon v. Burrows* in the case of alleged positive easements, I, therefore come to the conclusion that the easement claimed was not created by implication of law.

   Ungoed-Thomas J. held, however, that there was a right to enter and maintain the wall, either by reason of the operation of the principle that a grantor must not derogate from her or his grant, or by virtue of the operation of "general words" implied by statute under *Law of Property Act 1925* (U.K.), s. 62 as to which see below p. 252.

2. In *Auerbach v. Beck* (1985) 6 N.S.W.L.R. 424 Powell J. considered the limitations of the *Wheeldon v. Burrows* principle. Briefly, the rather complicated facts of the case were as follows. In 1911 Onslow was the owner of old system title property on which houses known as "Tintern" (lot 42) and "Gareloch" (lot 43) were erected. On 11 December 1911, Onslow sold lot 42 (Tintern) to Docker. At the time of sale a substantial portion of the south eastern wall of Tintern stood on the common boundary with lot 43. Water, sewerage, exhaust and electrical pipes and conduits and parts of the Tintern protruded or encroached over the airspace of lot 43. The conveyance of the property together with the residence Tintern was expressed to be "Together with all buildings fixtures rights easements advantages and appurtenances whatsoever to the said hereditaments and premises appurtaining or with the same held or enjoyed or reputed as part thereof or appurtenant thereto". On 16 December 1911, Onslow sold lot 43 (Gareloch) to Stoddart. Subsequently both properties, lots 42 and 43, were brought under Torrens title, but no reference was made on the Register or on either certificate of title

to the existence of the alleged easements. The plaintiffs, owners of lot 42 (Tintern), sought permission from the defendant, the owner of lot 43, to enter for purposes of carrying out urgent repairs to the exterior wall, pipes and other fixtures thereon. The defendant refused. The plaintiffs sought a declaration, inter alia, that as owners of lot 42 they were entitled to the benefit of an easement allowing entry to lot 43 to carry out repairs and maintenance of the wall and other appurtenances.

POWELL J. [T]he first basis upon which Mr Rayment sought to support the plaintiffs' claims was that they constituted an "apparent accommodation", or quasi-easement, at the time of the conveyance of "Tintern" to Ernest Brougham Docker. With respect, it seems to me that this submission is ill-conceived, if only because there is no evidence to support it.

The fons et origo of the law on this subject is the well-known decision of the Court of Appeal in *Wheeldon v. Burrows*, in which case Thesiger L.J., with whom James and Baggallay L.JJ. concurred, said (at 49):

> We have had a considerable number of cases cited to us, and out of them I think that two propositions may be stated as what I may call the general rules governing cases of this kind. The first of these rules is, that on the grant by the owner of a tenement of part of that tenement as it is then used and enjoyed, there will pass to the grantee all those continuous and apparent easements (by which, of course, I mean quasi-easements), or, in other words, all those easements which are necessary to the reasonable enjoyment of the property granted, and which have been and are at the time of the grant used by the owners of the entirety for the benefit of the part granted.

Although, later (at 58-59), his Lordship said:

> [I]n the case of a grant you may imply a grant of such continuous and apparent easements or such easements as are necessary to the reasonable enjoyment of the property conveyed, and have in fact been enjoyed during the unity of ownership

which language, suggests that, for the purpose of the doctrine in *Wheeldon v. Burrows*, "continuous and apparent easements" and "easements which are necessary to the reasonable enjoyment of the property conveyed" form discrete classes of case, the better view seems to be that, at least in respect of claims for positive easements—as is the case here—the claim will fail unless it can be linked to some continuous and apparent feature upon the alleged servient tenement designed, or appropriate, for the exercise of the easement claimed on the servient tenement: see, for example, *Ward v. Kirkland* (at 225-226); *Cheshire's Modern Law of Real Property* (12th ed.), pp. 535-536; cf. Megarry and Wade, *The Law of Real Property* (3rd ed.), pp. 829-831.

In the present case, Mr Rayment has sought to submit that the existence of a pathway running along the common boundary between "Tintern" and "Gareloch" was a feature of the land on which "Gareloch" was erected to which the rights now claimed by the plaintiffs could attach. It seems to me, however, that there are two answers to this submission:

1. There is no evidence to suggest that such a path existed at the time of the conveyance of "Tintern" to Ernest Brougham Docker. . . .

2. Even if it had been otherwise, it seems to me that the mere existence of a footpath would not support the rights claimed, for it could hardly be said that a footpath was designed, or appropriate, for the exercise of such rights.

However, while the plaintiffs' claims may not be capable of being supported by recourse to the doctrine of *Wheeldon v. Burrows*, it does not follow that the court is precluded from implying into the conveyance of "Tintern" to Ernest Brougham Docker a grant of such rights—or some of them— as the plaintiffs now claim. In saying this I have not overlooked the fact that, as Mr Bennett rightly pointed out, the doctrine of *Wheeldon v. Burrows* involves the court in implying a grant of the quasi-easements in question—it following, so Mr Bennett submits, that if the doctrine of *Wheeldon v. Burrows* is not available, it is not open to the court, by some other means, to imply a grant of the rights claimed—for it seems to me that the authorites: see, for example, *Pinnington v. Galland* (1853) 9 Ex. 1; 156 E.R. 1; *Richards v. Rose* (1853) 9 Exch. 218; 156 E.R. 93; *Lyttleton Times Co. Ltd v. Warners Ltd* [1907] A.C. 476; *Jones v. Pritchard* [1908] 1 Ch. 630; *Pwllbach Colliery Co. Ltd v. Woodman* [1915] A.C. 634; *Keewatin Power Co. Ltd v. Lake of the Woods Milling Co. Ltd* [1930] A.C. 640; *Wong v. Beaumont Property Trust Ltd* [1965] 1 Q.B. 173; *Ward v. Kirkland* [1967] Ch. 194; *White v. Taylor (No. 2)* [1969] 1 Ch. 160; *North Sydney Printing Pty Ltd v. Sabemo Investment Corp. Pty Ltd* [1971] 2 N.S.W.L.R. 150; *Nickerson v. Barraclough* [1981] Ch. 426; see also *Cheshire's Modern Law of Real Property* (12 ed.), p. 532 et seq.; *Megarry and Wade* (3rd ed.), p. 828 et seq. establish that it is open to the court to imply into a conveyance or demise the grant of such rights as are absolutely necessary to the enjoyment of the subject matter of the conveyance or demise, or of such rights as are reasonably necessary for the use and enjoyment, in the way contemplated by the parties to the conveyance or demise, of the subject matter of the conveyance or demise.

The question thus is: can it be said that the rights now claimed by the plaintiffs were, in 1911, absolutely necessary for the enjoyment of "Tintern" or, alternatively, reasonably necessary for the use and enjoyment of "Tintern" in the way contemplated by James William Macarthur Onslow and Ernest Brougham Docker?

Although, as I have earlier pointed out, the resolution of this question is rendered difficult by the dearth of evidence, it seems to me that, at least to the extent of the right claimed to go onto "Gareloch" for the purpose of maintaining the southern half of the south-eastern wall, the answer must be in the affirmative. That this should be so in my view follows from the facts, first, that the subject of the conveyance from James William Macarthur Onslow to Ernest Brougham Docker was:

> All that piece or parcel of land comprised and described in the first Schedule hereto *upon which piece or parcel of land is erected the residence known as "Tintern"*. (My emphasis.)

Secondly, that it could not have been but known to the parties that the wall in question stood on the common boundary between "Tintern" and "Gareloch"; thirdly, that "Tintern" could not be enjoyed as a residence without the means of maintaining it as such; fourthly, since the only possible, or practicable, means of maintaining the wall then was by going upon "Gareloch" for the purpose; and, finally, since as Cotton L.J. put it in *Birmingham, Dudley and District Banking Co. v. Ross* ((1888) 38 Ch. D. 295 at 306): "when a man grants a house, he grants that which is necessary for the existence of that house."

Whether or not one is justified in implying into the conveyance of "Tintern" an easement or easements extending to the continuance and maintenance of the encroaching pipes, vents, conduits and the like depends upon whether one is justified in holding, first, that, more probably than not, in 1911 "Tintern" was serviced with a water supply, sewerage, gas and electricity; and, secondly, that such service pipes as then existed encroached into the airspace above "Gareloch".

Although there is no direct evidence upon the matter, I have, after much consideration, concluded that it is legitimate to hold that, in 1911, "Tintern" was serviced by such facilities. . . .

Even if I had been of a different view from that which I have recorded above, I would, nonetheless, have concluded that such rights as are now claimed by the plaintiffs passed under the words "*Together* with all buildings fixtures rights easements advantages and appurtenances whatsoever to the said hereditaments and premises appertaining or with the same held or enjoyed or reputed as part thereof or appurtenant thereto" contained in the conveyance of "Tintern" to Ernest Brougham Docker.

His Honour went on to hold that the easement had been "omitted" within the meaning of *Real Property Act* 1900 (N.S.W.), s. 42 (1) (b). His decision was affirmed by the Court of Appeal, (1986) 6 N.S.W.L.R. 454. That section of the decision dealing with the effect of general words in a conveyance is referred to below p. 252.

3. In *Kebewar Pty Ltd v. Harkin* (1987) 9 N.S.W.L.R. 738 the New South Wales Court of Appeal considered whether the plaintiff was entitled to an easement for support for any structure to be built upon the land. McHugh J.A. (Samuels and Priestley JJ.A. agreeing) said (at 741):

> Upon the sale by the owner of a part of his land as it is then used and enjoyed, the purchaser obtains all "those easements which are necessary to the reasonable enjoyment of the property granted and which have been and are at the time of the grant used by the owners of the entirety for the benefit of the part granted": *Wheeldon v. Burrows* (1879) 12 Ch. D. 31 at 49 per Thesiger L.J. and *Nelson v. Walker* (1910) 10 C.L.R. 560 at 582, 584. If an owner intends to reserve any right over the land sold, he must reserve it expressly. These rules are applications of the maxim that a grantor cannot derogate from his grant. . . .
>
> The right of support for a building for which the plaintiff contends is not a *Wheeldon v. Burrows* type of easement. It was not one of those "things enjoyed de facto during unity of possession as would, had that unity not existed, have been" an easement: *Nelson v. Walker* (1910) 10 C.L.R. 560 at 583 per Isaacs J. When the defendant's parents sold lot 11, no building stood on it. . . . There was, therefore, no apparent easement of support for a building.

Their Honours went on to hold that even if the plaintiff could rely on a duty not to derogate from grant (see below p. 257), any rights thereby created would be defeated by the operation of *Real Property Act* 1900 (N.S.W.), s. 42 since the claimed easement would not come within the s. 42 (1) (b) exception: see below p. 280.

Does the passage extracted suggest that the Court of Appeal implicitly accepts that there are two separate categories of easements that pass under an implied grant?

4. In *Schwann v. Cotton* [1916] 2 Ch. 120, Astbury J. accepted the view put in *Pyer v. Carter* (1857) 1 H. & N. 916 at 922; 156 E.R. 1472 that " 'by apparent signs must be understood not only those which must necessarily be seen, but those which may be seen or known on a careful inspection by a person ordinarily conversant with the subject,' that is, seen or known on the premises granted".

For further examples, see *Pyer v. Carter* (1857) 1 H. & N. 916; 156 E.R. 1472 (drain); *Watts v. Kelson* (1871) 6 Ch. App. 166; *Schwann v. Cotton* [1916] 2 Ch. 120 (underground drains or pipes with visible connections); *Brown v. Alabaster* (1887) 37 Ch. D. 490; *Tarrant v. Zandstra* (1973) 1 B.P.R. 97039 (made road); *Hansford v. Jago* [1921] 1 Ch. 322; *Margil Pty Ltd v. Stegul Pastoral Pty Ltd* [1984] 2 N.S.W.L.R. 1 (worn track).

5. The requirement of continuous user has not always been strictly insisted upon. In *Borman v. Griffith* [1930] 1 Ch. 493, Maugham J., in the course of his judgment, said: "It is true that the easement, or rather, quasi-easement is not continuous. But the authorities are sufficient to show that a grantor of property in circumstances where an obvious, that is, visible and made road is necessary for the reasonable enjoyment of the property by the grantee must be taken prima facie to have intended to grant a right to use it."

6. Where there is a simultaneous disposition of separate parcels of land by a common vendor, the rule is that each parcel acquires, by way of implied grant, the same easements over the other parcel such as would occur if the common vendor had in each case retained the other parcel: *Swansborough v. Coventry* (1832) 9 Bing. 305; 131 E.R. 629. The rule applies where there is a simultaneous disposition of parcels by a common vendor. Where conveyance is preceded by contract, the date of contract is the relevant point of time in determining whether there are simultaneous dispositions of parcels: *Sunset Properties Pty Ltd v. Johnston* (1975) 3 B.P.R. 9185; *White v. Taylor (No. 2)* [1969] 1 Ch. 160 at 181-181 (profits).

CORPORATION OF LONDON v. RIGGS

Chancery Division (1880) 13 Ch. D. 798

[On the conveyance of land to the Corporation of London, the defendant retained a parcel of land which was entirely surrounded by the land conveyed. No reservation of a right of way was made in the conveyance. The land retained was at the time of conveyance used exclusively for agricultural purposes. The defendant Riggs commenced to build tea rooms for the use of the public. The corporation brought proceedings alleging that the defendant had unlawfully drawn building materials across their land causing damage, and that he proposed to attract the public in carriages and on foot to his tea room by crossing the plaintiff's property to the damage of the plaintiff. The plaintiff claimed, inter alia, a declaration that the defendant was entitled to a way of necessity sufficient for the use of the land retained for agricultural purposes only and appropriate injunctive relief.]

JESSEL M.R. The real question I have to decide is this—whether, on a grant of land wholly surrounding a close, the implied grant, or regrant, of a right of way by the grantee to the grantor to enable him to get to the reserved, or excepted, or inclosed close, is a grant of a general right of way for all purposes, or only a grant of a right of way for the purpose of the enjoyment of the reserved or excepted close in its then state.

There is, as I have said, no distinct authority on the question. It seems to me to have been laid down in very early times . . . that the right of way to a way of necessity is an exception to the ordinary rule that a man shall not derogate from his own grant, and that the man who grants the surrounding land is in very much the same position as regards the right of way to the reserved close as if he had granted the close, retaining the surrounding land. In both cases there is what is called a way of necessity; and the way of necessity, according to the old rules of pleading, must have been pleaded as a grant, or, where the close is reserved, as it is here, as a regrant.

[His Lordship then referred to the judgment of Lord Cairns in *Gayford v. Moffatt* (1868) L.R. 4 Ch. 133, 135 and continued:]

It is therefore obvious to me that Lord Cairns thought a way of necessity meant a way suitable for the user of the premises at the time when the way of necessity was created; and that is all I can find in the shape of authority on the subject.

Well, now, if we try the case on principle—treating this right of way as an exception to the rule—ought it to be treated as larger exception than the necessity of the case warrants? That of course brings us back to the question, What does the necessity of the case require? The object of implying the regrant, as stated by the older judges, was that if you did not give the owner of the reserved close some right of way or other, he could neither use nor occupy the reserved close, nor derive benefit from it. But what is the extent of the benefit he is to have? Is he entitled to say, I have reserved to myself more than that which enables me to enjoy it as it is at the time of the grant? And if that is the true rule, that he is not to have more than necessity requires, as distinguished from what convenience may require, it appears to me that the right of way must be limited to that which is necessary at the time of the grant; that is, he is supposed to take a regrant to himself of such a right of way as will enable him to enjoy the reserved thing as it is.

That appears to me to be the meaning of a right of way of necessity. If you imply more, you reserve to him not only that which enables him to enjoy the thing he has reserved as it is, but that which enables him to enjoy it in the same way and to the same extent as if he reserved a general right of way for all purposes: that is—as in the case I have before me—a man who reserves two acres of arable land in the middle of a large piece of land is to be entitled to cover the reserved land with houses, and call on his grantee to allow him to make a wide metalled road up to it. I do not think that is a fair meaning of a way of necessity: I think it must be limited by the necessity at the time of the grant; and that the man who does not take the pains to secure an actual grant of a right of way for all purposes is not entitled to be put in a better position than to be able to enjoy that which he had at the time the grant was made. I am not aware of any other principle on which this case can be decided.

I may be met by the objection that a way of necessity must mean something more than what I have stated, because, where the grant is of the inclosed piece, the grantee is entitled to use the land for all purposes, and should therefore be entitled to a right of way commensurate with his right of enjoyment. But there again the grantee has not taken from the grantor any express grant of a right of way: and all he can be entitled to ask is a right to enable him to enjoy the property granted to him as it was granted to him. It does not appear to me that the grant of the property gives any greater right. But even if it did, the principle applicable to the grantee is not quite the same as the principle applicable to the grantor: and it might be that the grantee obtains a larger way of necessity—though I do not think he does—than the grantor does under the implied regrant.

I am afraid that I am laying down the law for the first time—that I am for the first time declaring the law; but it is a matter of necessity from which I cannot escape.

The demurrer must, therefore, be overruled, with costs.

NOTES AND QUESTIONS

1. Before an easement of necessity will arise it must be shown that the property cannot otherwise be used at all; this is not made out by showing that the right claimed is necessary for the reasonable enjoyment of the property: *Union Lighterage Co. v. London Graving Dock Co.* [1902] 2 Ch. 557 at 573 per Stirling L.J. The existence of an alternative way, even if inconvenient, will negate the existence of an easement of necessity: *Titchmarsh v. Royston Water Co. Ltd* (1899) 81 L.T. 673; *Bolton v. Clutterbuck* [1955] S.A.S.R. 253. Inconvenience is not sufficient; thus access by foot but not by car does not give rise to an easement of necessity: *MRA Engineering Ltd v. Timster Co. Ltd* (1987) 56

P. & C.R. 1. In *Tarrant v. Zandstra* (1973) 1 B.P.R. 9381 at 9386, Mahoney J. stated that it was not necessary to establish physical impossibility of any other access to the land, but at least there must be a substantial degree of practical difficulty before an easement of necessity can arise. Rath J. in *Parish v. Kelly* (1980) 1 B.P.R. 9394 at 9401 suggested the following test: "Would reasonable men in the position of the parties consider it unreasonable that the legal but untrafficable means of access be made trafficable in the circumstances of the case." A more liberal view was also taken in *Margil Pty Ltd v. Stegul Pastoral Pty Ltd* [1984] 2 N.S.W.L.R. 1 at 9. If the use of the alternative way is permissive only, that is, subject to the continuing consent of a third party (*Barry v. Hasseldine* [1952] Ch. 835) or would constitute unlawful user, trespass (*Hansford v. Jago* [1921] 1 Ch. 322 at 342, 343), an easement of necessity may arise; see also Bradbrook, "Access to Landlocked Land" (1983) 10 Syd. U.L.R. 39.

See also *Pryce and Irving v. McGuiness* [1966] Qd R. 591, rejecting claims for easements of necessity in respect of electricity and drainage, and *Gale on Easements* (14th ed.), p. 107 for the view that it is questionable whether any easement, other than access and support, can be of necessity (but contrast *Hansford v. Jago* above).

2. In *Wong v. Beaumont Property Trust Ltd* [1965] 1 Q.B. 173 the plaintiff and defendant were respectively assignees of a lease and the reversion. The lease contained covenants by the lessee to keep the premises open as a popular restaurant, to eliminate all smells and odours and to comply with health regulations. Compliance was not possible without the installation of a ventilation system with a duct on the exterior of the landlord's premises. The parties, at the time of the grant of the lease, were not aware of this necessity. But, subsequently, the health inspector required the installation of a proper ventilation system. The defendant refused the plaintiff's request to install the air duct. The plaintiff claimed damages for derogation from the grant and a declaration that he was entitled to enter the landlord's premises in order to install the ventilation system.

LORD DENNING M.R. [A] right of this kind, if it exists at all, must be by way of an easement. In particular, an easement of necessity. The law on the matter was stated by Lord Parker of Waddington in *Pwllbach Colliery Co. Ltd v. Woodman* [1915] A.C. 634 where he said (at 646) omitting immaterial words, "The law will readily imply the grant or reservation of such easements as may be necessary to give effect to the common intention of the parties to a grant of real property, with reference to the manner or purposes in and for which the land granted . . . is to be used. But it is essential for this purpose that the parties should intend that the subject of the grant . . . should be used in some definite and particular manner. It is not enough that the subject of the grant . . . should be intended to be used in a manner which may or may not involve this definite and particular use." That is the principle which underlies all easements of necessity. If you go back to Rolle's Abridgment you will find it stated in this way (2 Rol. Abr. 60, pl. 17, 18; 1 Saund. (1871 ed.) 570; see *Gale on Easements* (13th ed.), p. 98): "If I have a field inclosed by my own land on all sides, and I alienate this close to another, he shall have a way to this close over my land, as incident to the grant; for otherwise he cannot have any benefit by the grant."

I would apply those principles here. Here was the grant of a lease to the lessee for the very purpose of carrying on a restaurant business. It was to be a popular restaurant, and it was to be developed and extended. There was a covenant not to cause any nuisance; and to control and eliminate all smells; and to comply with the Food Hygiene Regulations. That was "a definite and particular manner" in which the business had to be conducted. It could not be carried on in that manner at all unless a ventilation system was installed by a duct of this kind. In these circumstances it seems to me that, if the business is to be carried on at all—if, in the words of Rolle's Abridgment (2 Rol. Abr. 60, pl. 17, 18), the lessee is to "have any benefit by the grant" at all—he must of necessity be able to put a ventilation duct up the wall. It may be that in Blackaby's time it would not have needed such a large duct as is now needed in the plaintiff's time. But nevertheless a duct of some kind would have had to be put up the wall. The plaintiff may need a bigger one. But that does not matter. A man who has a right to an easement can use it in any proper way, so long as he does not substantially increase the burden on the servient tenement. In this case a bigger duct will not substantially increase the burden.

There is one point in which this case goes further than the earlier cases which have been cited. It is this. It was not realised by the parties, at the time of the lease, that this duct would be necessary. But it was in fact necessary from the very beginning. That seems to me sufficient to bring the principle into play. In order to use this place as a restaurant, there must be implied an easement, by the necessity of the case, to carry a duct up this wall. The county court judge so held. He granted a declaration. I agree with him.

PEARSON L.J. There is, therefore, this choice for the court: either to say the provisions of the lease cannot be carried out and must remain inoperative or to imply an easement of necessity into the lease. The court should read this lease in such a way that res magis valeat quam pereat, and therefore the right course is to imply an easement of necessity in this case.

SALMON L.J. It seems to me to be plain on the authorities, as my Lord has said, that if a lease is granted which imposes a particular use on the tenant and it is impossible for the tenant so to use the premises legally unless an easement is granted, the law does imply such an easement as of necessity.

3. In *North Sydney Printing Pty Ltd v. Sabemo Investment Corp. Pty Ltd* [1971] 2 N.S.W.L.R. 150 the plaintiff subdivided land in respect of which it was registered proprietor and sold part of it. The land retained had no access to a public street and was zoned in the local planning scheme ordinance as reserved for "special purposes—parking". It was intended by the plaintiff that the land would be sold to the local council as an addition to the existing contiguous municipal car park. This did not eventuate. The plaintiff then sought a declaration that it was entitled to a right of way of necessity over the land sold.

HOPE J. It seems to me that the balance of authority establishes that a way of necessity arises in order to give effect to an actual or presumed intention. No doubt difficulties could arise in some cases because of differing actual intentions on the part of the parties, but it seems to me that at the least one must be able to presume an intention on the part of the grantor, in a case such as the present, that he intended to have access to the land retained by him over the land conveyed by him before one can imply the grant or reservation of a way of necessity over the land conveyed. In the present case, there was no such intention, and indeed the actual intention of the grantor was to the contrary. Its intention was that there should be no access over any part of lot 5, and that access should be had by joining lot 4 to the land of the council, which fronted Ward Street. If this consolidation had occurred, then lot 4 would have had access to a public way. As I have said, the plaintiff had in November 1969, and has now, a right to compel that consolidation, that is, the owner of lot 4 has a legal power to compel the joining of his lot with the land owned by the council, which will produce an access from a public way into lot 4, and so allow lot 4 to be used and not left useless. In these circumstances, I do not see how an intention to have access to lot 4 over any part of lot 5 can be presumed, or imputed to the parties or either of them. Indeed, I do not think it can be contended that if the principle upon which the doctrine of ways of necessity is based is related to giving effect to the intention of the parties in relation to the severance, any right of way of necessity could have arisen in the present case. The only basis for holding that such a right was created in the present case would be that the law inevitably makes provision for access over the land conveyed by the person in the position of the present plaintiff, regardless of that persons's intention and regardless of the other circumstances of the case.

Accordingly, in my opinion, the plaintiff has not established that, quite apart from the provisions of the *Real Property Act* 1900 (N.S.W.), it was entitled, upon the transfer of lot 5 to the first defendant in November 1969, to any way of necessity over any part of lot 5.

The Court of Appeal in *Nickerson v. Barraclough* [1981] Ch. 426 agreed with this view. Brightman L.J. (at 440-441), with whom Buckley L.J. concurred, rejected the view that public policy can play any part in construction of an instrument, "in construing a document the court is endeavouring to ascertain the expressed intention of the parties . . . public policy cannot help the court to ascertain what that intention was". This is to be contrasted with the view that the basis of easements of necessity is not the intention of the parties but public policy allowing the full utilisation of land: see Bodkin, "Easements of Necessity and Public Policy" (1973) 89 L.Q.R. 87. Note also Bradbrook "Access to Landlocked Land" (1983) 10 Syd. U.L.R. 39 and *M.R.A. Engineering Ltd v. Trimster Co. Ltd* (1987) 56 P. & C.R. 1 which applied the older test of whether the land was useless without the right of access.

Can an easement of necessity survive if alternative means of access subsequently become available? Would the answer in any way depend upon whether easements of necessity arise as a result of a common intention of the parties or as a result of a public policy against landlocked land?

4. Although there has been a tendency to regard easements of common intention and easements of necessity as one and the same (see above, notes 2 and 3), there are a number of authorities which clearly regard easements of common intention as an independent category of easement. For example, in *Re Webb's Lease* [1951] 1 Ch. 808, the landlord had, prior to the grant of the lease, painted advertisements on the exterior of the demised premises. The landlord claimed that there had been an implied reservation of rights to use the exterior of the premises for the purpose of advertisement.

JENKINS L.J. [The] question must be approached with the following principles in mind: (i) If the landlord intended to reserve any such rights over the demised premises it was his duty to reserve them expressly in the lease of 11 August 1949 (*Wheeldon v. Burrows* (1879) 12 Ch. D. 31); (ii) The landlord having failed in his duty, the onus was upon him to establish the facts to prove clearly, that his case was an exception to the rule (*Aldridge v. Wright* [1929] 2 K.B. 117); (iii) The mere fact that the tenant knew at the date of the lease of 11 August 1949, that the landlord was using the outer walls of the demised premises for the display of the advertisements in question did not suffice to absolve the landlord from his duty of expressly reserving any rights in respect of them he intended to claim, or to take the case out of the general rule: see *Suffield v. Brown* (1864) 4 De G.J. & S. 185; *Crossley & Sons Ltd v. Lightowler* (1867) 2 Ch. App. 478.

[His Lordship, after reviewing the evidence, continued:]

In short, I can hold nothing more established by the facts proved than permissive user of the outer walls by the landlord for the display of the advertisements during the original tenancy and thereafter from the granting of the lease until the tenant's objection in January 1950; with nothing approaching grounds for inferring, as a matter of necessary inference, an intention common to both parties and such permissive user should be converted by the lease into a reservation to the landlord of equivalent rights throughout the 21 years' term thereby granted.

If the hypothetical officious stranger sometimes used as a test of implied terms had intervened in the course of the negotiation of the lease and said: "What about Mr Webb's advertisements?" Would both parties have exclaimed with one voice? "Of course they are to stay!" I see no justification at all for this assumption. The landlord might well have said: "Of course I want them to stay", but as likely as not the tenant would have said: "At present I have no objection to your advertisements, but I cannot bind myself to allow them for 21 years. For all I know, I may at any time during that period for one reason or another want them removed. If you insist on reserving rights in matter you must reduce the rent or find some other tenant."

By contrast *Jones v. Pritchard* [1908] 1 Ch. 630 is a good illustration of a case where it has been held that an easement of common intention had been reserved to the vendor. The plaintiff's predecessor in title constructed a house which had fire-places and flues in the exterior wall. Some of these serviced the house but others were intended for the benefit of the adjoining lot, then vacant land, belonging to the defendant. The plaintiff's predecessor in title later granted to the defendant half his rights in the party wall, the chimneys and flues. Parker J. held on the basis of the cases *Richards v. Rose* (1853) 9 Ex. 218; 156 E.R. 93 and *Lyttleton Times Co. Ltd v. Warners Ltd* [1907] A.C. 476 that the law would imply the grant and reservation in favour of the grantor and grantee respectively of such easements as were necessary to carry out the common intention of the parties with regard to user of the wall. In this case the reservation and grant of such easements as necessary for use by the plaintiff and defendant of flues connected to their fireplaces.

(a) Easements implied by statute

The *Conveyancing Act* 1919 (N.S.W.), s. 67 provides:

67. (1) A conveyance of land shall be deemed to include and shall by virtue of this Act operate to convey with the land all buildings, erections, fixtures, commons, hedges, ditches, fences, ways, waters, watercourses, liberties, privileges, easements, rights, and advantages whatsoever appertaining to the land or any part thereof, at the time of conveyance.

(2) A conveyance of land having houses or other buildings thereon shall be deemed to include and shall by virtue of this Act operate to convey with the land, houses, or other buildings, all outhouses, erections, fixtures, cellars, areas, courts, courtyards, cisterns, sewers, gutters, drains, ways, passages, lights, watercourses, liberties, privileges, easements, rights, and advantages whatsoever appertaining to the land, houses, or other buildings conveyed, or any of them, or any part thereof, at the time of conveyance.

(3) This section applies only if and as far as a contrary intention is not expressed in the conveyance, and shall have effect subject to the terms of the conveyance and to the provisions therein contained.

(4) This section shall not be construed as giving to any person a better title to any property, right, or thing in this section mentioned than the title which the conveyance gives to him to the land expressed to be conveyed, or as conveying to him any property, right, or thing in this section mentioned further or otherwise than as the same could have been conveyed to him by the conveying parties.

(5) This section applies only to conveyances made after the commencement of this Act of land other than land under the provisions of the *Real Property Act* 1900.

Other State and English legislation, although similar, has very important additions in subss (1) and (2); subs. (1) of the English section, *Law of Property Act* 1925 (U.K.), s. 62, and legislation in other States extends to "liberties, privileges, easements, rights and advantages whatsoever, appertaining *or reputed to appertain* to the land, or any part thereof, or, at the time of the conveyance . . . enjoyed with, or reputed or known as part or parcel of or appurtenant to the land". Similar additions are read into the statutory equivalent of s. 67(2). These provisions apply to the acquisition of easements and profits: *White v. Williams* [1922] 1 K.B. 727; *White v. Taylor (No. 2)* [1969] 1 Ch. 160.

WRIGHT v. MACADAM

Court of Appeal [1949] 2 K.B. 744

[In 1940, the defendant landlord let a top floor flat to Mrs Wright for one week. At the expiration of the week Mrs Wright remained in occupation by virtue of the Rent Restriction Acts. In 1941, the defendant gave Mrs Wright permission to use a garden shed for the storage of coal; Mrs Wright thereafter used the shed for coal storage. In 1943, the defendant granted a new tenancy of the premises to Mrs Wright and her daughter; the tenancy agreement, an unsealed document, made no reference to the shed. The Wrights continued to use the shed until 1947 when the defendant suggested that an extra fee should be paid for its use. The plaintiffs objected, and were denied the use of the shed. The plaintiffs brought proceedings claiming a declaration as to their right to use the shed, and claimed damages.]

JENKINS L.J. The question in the present case, therefore, is whether the right to use the coal shed was at the date of the letting 28 August 1943, a liberty, privilege, easement, right or advantage appertaining or reputed to appertain, to the land, or any part thereof, or, at the time of the conveyance, demised, occupied or enjoyed with the land—that is the flat—or any part thereof. It is enough for the plaintiffs' purposes if they can bring the right claimed within the widest part of the subsection—that is to say, if they can show that the right was at the time of the material letting demised, occupied or enjoyed with the flat or any part thereof.

The predecessor of s. 62 of the Act of 1925 [*Law of Property Act* 1925 (U.K.)], in the shape of s. 6 of the Act of 1881 has been the subject of a good deal of judicial discussion, and I think the effect of the cases can be thus summarised. First, the section is not confined to rights which, as a matter of law, were so annexed or appurtenant to the property conveyed at the time of the conveyance as to make them actual legally enforceable rights. Thus, on the severance of a piece of land in common ownership, the quasi-easements de facto enjoyed in respect of it by one part of the land over another will pass although, of course, as a matter of law, no man can have a right appendant or appurtenant to one part of his property exerciseable by him over the other part of his property. Secondly, the right, in order to pass, need not be one to which the owner or occupier for the time being of the land has had what may be described as a permanent title. A right enjoyed merely by permission is enough. The leading authority for that proposition is the case of *International Tea Stores Co. v. Hobbs* [1903] 2 Ch. 165. . . .

There is, therefore, ample authority for the proposition that a right in fact enjoyed with property will pass on a conveyance of the property by virtue of the grant to be read into it under s. 62, even although down to the date of the conveyance the right was exercised by permission only, and therefore was in that sense precarious.

The next proposition deducible from the cases is the one laid down in *Burrows v. Lang* [1901] 2 Ch. 502 . . . It is that the right in question must be a right known to the law. In *Burrows v. Lang* it was held that a so-called right to take, for the purposes of watering cattle, so much water, if any, as might happen to be left in an artificial watercourse after the owner of the watercourse had taken what he required for his own purposes, was not such a right. . . . For the purposes of s. 62, it is only necessary that the right should be one capable of being granted at law, or, in other words, a right known to the law. If it is a right of that description it matters not, as the *International Tea Stores* case shows, that it has been in fact enjoyed by permission only. The reason for that is clear, for, on the assumption that the right is included or imported into the parcels of the conveyance by virtue of s. 62, the grant under the conveyance supplies what one may call the defect in title, and substitutes a new title based on the grant.

There is one other point to be mentioned. A further exception has been recognised in cases in which there could in the circumstances of the case have been no expectation that the enjoyment of the right could be other than temporary. That exception was recognised by Cotton L.J. in *Birmingham and Dudley District Banking Co. v. Ross* (1889) 38 Ch. D. 295 at 307. The learned Lord Justice was dealing with a situation of this kind. There had been a building scheme under which an area of land was to be developed and built up. Somebody took a lease of one of the houses at a time when an adjoining plot only had built upon it old buildings of less height than those contemplated by the scheme; but it was well known to everybody that the intention was, and the building scheme demanded, that this plot should be built upon to a greater height. The question for the court was whether the lessor of the houses would be committing a derogation from grant in building on the adjoining plot inasmuch as the effect of that would be to obscure to some extent the light enjoyed by the lessee of the building already erected next door. It was held in those circumstances, as one might expect, that there was no derogation from grant and there was no such enjoyment of the light over the vacant plot as would bring s. 6 of the Act of 1881 into operation. The learned Lord Justice said this: "Therefore, I think it could not be said that the light coming over that low building to those windows could be considered as enjoyed with it within the meaning of this section. The light did in fact at the time come over that building; but it came over it under such circumstances as to show that there could be no expectation of its continuance. It had not been enjoyed in fact for any long period; and in my opinion it was enjoyed under such circumstances, known to both parties, as could not make it light enjoyed within the meaning of that section." The learned Lord Justice, I think, meant no more than this, that it was knowledge common to both parties that the existing low building was going to be replaced by a higher one and, that being so, the fortuitous access of extra light to the lessee's building while the scheme was being carried to completion could not be regarded as an enjoyment of light which would pass to the lessee a right to have it continued in the same degree.

I think those are all the cases to which I can usefully refer, and applying the principles deducible from them to the present case one finds, I think, this. First of all, on the evidence the coal shed was used by Mrs Wright by the permission of Mr Macadam, but *International Tea Stores Co. v. Hobbs* [1903] 2 Ch. 165 shows that that does not prevent s. 62 from applying, because permissive as the right may have been it was in fact enjoyed.

Next, the right was, as I understand it, a right to use the coal shed in question for the purpose of storing such coal as might be required for the domestic purposes of the flat. In my judgment that is a right or easement which the law will clearly recognise, and it is a right or easement of a kind which could readily be included in a lease or conveyance by the insertion of appropriate words in the parcels. This, therefore, is not a case in which a title to a right unknown to the law is claimed by virtue of s. 62. Nor is it a case in which it can be said to have been in the contemplation of the parties that the enjoyment of the right should be purely temporary. No limit was set as to the time during which the coal shed could continue to be used. Mr Macadam simply gave his permission; that permission was acted on; and the use of the coal shed in fact went on down to 28 August 1943, and thereafter down to 1947. Therefore, applying to the facts of the present case the principles which seem to be deducible from the authorities, the conclusion to which I have come is that the right to use the coal shed was at the date of the letting of 28 August 1943, a right enjoyed with the top floor flat within the meaning of s. 62 of the *Law of Property Act* 1925 (U.K.), with the result that (as no contrary intention was expressed in the document) the right in question must be regarded as having passed by virtue of that letting, just as it would have passed if it had been mentioned in express terms in cl. 1, which sets out the subject matter of the lease. . . .

For these reasons I am of opinion that the learned judge came to a wrong conclusion when he held that s. 62 of the *Law of Property Act* had no application. He said that the right to use the coal shed was merely a temporary right. That, as I have said, is no sufficient ground for excluding the operation of s. 62, having regard to the principle laid down in *International Tea Stores Co. v. Hobbs* [1903] 2 Ch. 165. Further, he said that this was never a right or advantage appurtenant to the flat. But it is not only rights or advantages that are appurtenant to given premises that pass under s. 62. It is enough, as I have already said, that the right or advantage should in fact be enjoyed with the premises. Accordingly, it seems to me that the learned judge was wrong in excluding the operation of s. 62. It is plain, however, that he did not have the assistance of nearly so full an argument as has been presented to us in this court and, that being so, it is not suprising that in this rather difficult case he came to a conclusion different from mine.

For these reasons I would allow the appeal and direct that, inasmuch as the coal shed is now no longer in existence, judgment should be entered for the plaintiffs for the sum of damages claimed.

[The judgments of Tucker and Singleton L.JJ. agreeing with Jenkins L.J. have been omitted.]

NOTES AND QUESTIONS

1. The *Conveyancing Act* 1919 (N.S.W.), s. 67 (which does not apply to land under the provisions of the *Real Property Act* 1900 (N.S.W.)) applies only to "liberties, privileges, easements" etc. "appertaining to the land". This is to be contrasted with s. 62 of the *Law of Property Act* 1925 (U.K.) which extends to "liberties, privileges, easements, rights and advantages . . . appertaining or *reputed to appertain* to the land" (italics inserted). There are two lines of authority on the effect of a grant of rights "appertaining" to land. On the strict interpretation of the word "appertaining", s. 67 conveys only those rights existing at common law and appurtenant to the land. As these rights, of course, would pass without general words, on this view the section is superfluous: see *Barlow v. Rhodes* (1833) 1 C. & M. 439; 149 E.R. 471; *Worthington v. Gimson* (1860) 2 El. & El. 618; 121 E.R. 232. On the second line of authority, the word "appurtenant" includes those rights in fact enjoyed at the time of the conveyance. The effect of the two views is summed up by Fry L.J. in *Thomas v. Owen* (1887) 20 Q.B.D. 225 at 231:

It was contended before us that the absence in the lease of 1878 of any other general words than the word "appurtenances" made an important difference and distinguished this case from the earlier authorities. . . . No doubt the word "appurtenances" is not apt for the creation of a new right, and the word "appurtenant" is not apt to describe a right which had never previously existed; and therefore the mere grant of all appurtenances or of all ways appurtenant to the principal subject of the grant has been held in many cases not to create a new right of way where the right was not pre-existing at the date of the grant. But . . . the word "appurtenances" has easily admitted of a secondary meaning, and as equivalent in the case [*Hill v. Grange* (1556) Pld. 164 at 170; 75 E.R. 253] to "usually occupied". . . . I hold therefore that the word "appurtenances" in these conveyances was apt to include and did include this privilege or right which was being enjoyed by the existing tenants at the date of the sale.

In support of this view, see *Hansford v. Jago* [1921] 1 Ch. 322 at 331. It should be remembered, however, that the second view was espoused in cases where the courts were dealing with express grants, and in such cases the rights of the parties necessarily depend on the construction of the grant in its entirety in the light of surrounding circumstances. In contrast, the statutory meaning of "appertain" cannot depend on surrounding circumstances; it must, it is submitted, have a consistent meaning and semble on the strict meaning of the term "appurtenant" the effect of the section does no more than endorse the common law position. (Section 67 is subject to any contrary intention expressed in the instrument: s. 67(3).)

Compare the much more restrictive *Real Property Act* 1900, s. 51 which provides that upon registration of any transfer "the estate or interest of the transferor as set forth in such instrument, with all rights, powers and privileges thereto belonging or appertaining, shall pass to the transferee". Note also the definition of "land" in s. 3 and discussion by Starke J. in *Dabbs v. Seaman* (1925) 36 C.L.R. 538 at 574, above p. 293.

2. In *M.R.A. Engineering Ltd v. Trimster Co. Ltd* (1987) 56 P. & C.R. 1 at 7 per Nourse L.J. (Bingham L.J. concurring) said in relation to the *Law of Property Act* 1925 (U.K.):

It is essential to the application of s. 62 to quasi-easements, as it was to the application of the rule in *Wheeldon v. Burrows* before it, that the conveyancing (sic) party should be the owner of the quasi-servient tenement at the time he conveys away the quasi-dominant tenement. It is his ability to make the right the subject of an express grant which, by an application of the doctrine of non-derogation from grant, prevents him from denying that it has passed under an implied grant. If he does not have that ability, no implication is to be made against him.

3. In *Auerbach v. Beck* (1985) 6 N.S.W.L.R. 424 at 445 (the facts of which are set out above p. 245) Powell J. referred to the effect of general words in a conveyance which conveyed the land "Together with all buildings fixtures rights easements advantages and appurtenances whatsoever to the said hereditaments and premises appertaining or with the same held or enjoyed or reputed as part thereof or appurtenant thereto". His Honour said:

I accept that, in order that any such right to pass under such general words, it must appear, first, that the right existed at the date of the relevant conveyance or demise (see, for example, *Broomfield v. Williams* [1897] 1 Ch. 602; *Wright v. Macadam* [1949] 2 K.B. 744; *Goldberg v. Edwards* [1950] Ch. 247; *Ward v. Kirkland* [1967] Ch. 194), and, secondly, that if the right or privilege is imperceptible or non-apparent, corresponding with intermittent and non-apparent user over one of two tenements held in common ownership, the right or privilege will not pass unless there has been de facto enjoyment of it by an occupier not the owner or occupier of the other tenement: see *Long v. Gowlett* [1923] 2 Ch. 177; *Ward v. Kirkland.*

[His Honour found that this requirement had been satisfied and continued:]

This notwithstanding, Mr Bennett submits that any such rights as may have passed under the general words in the conveyance of "Tintern" to Ernest Brougham Docker were extinguished on the conveyance of "Gareloch" to Frederick William Stoddart, or, at the very least, expired by effluxion of time in 1981. With respect, it seems to me that these submissions stem from a misapprehension of the effect of the use of general words in a conveyance—such words, when used—or imported by statute—have the effect of creating new easements and profits *by way of express grant* out of all kinds of quasi-easements and quasi-profits so long only as it lies within the power of the grantor to do so: see, for example, *Broomfield v. Williams; Quicke v. Chapman* [1903] 1 Ch. 659; *Wright v. Macadam; Goldberg v. Edwards; Ward v. Kirkland; Cheshire's Modern Law of Real Property* (12th ed.), pp. 530-531; Megarry and Wade, *The Law of Real Property* (3rd ed.), pp. 832-833. Since, at the time of the conveyance of "Tintern" to Ernest Brougham Docker, James William Macarthur Onslow still owned the fee in "Gareloch", he retained the right to grant, as he purported to do, such rights as the plaintiffs claim passed under the general words in the conveyance—it would have been otherwise if he had earlier conveyed "Gareloch" to a purchaser without an express reservation of such rights in favour of "Tintern": *Dynevor (Lord) v. Tennant* (1886) 32 Ch. D. 375; *Quicke v. Chapman* [1903] 1 Ch. 659; *Re Young* (1924) 6 N.S.W.L.R. 449 (n.), Cheshire op cit., p. 533 et seq.; Megarry and Wade op. cit., p. 826 et seq.

4. Assuming that a more expansive view of s. 67 of the *Conveyancing Act* 1919 is accepted, consider whether the following "rights, privileges or advantages" pass with a conveyance of the land under s. 67:

   (1) the supply of hot water by a landlord (see *Regis Property Ltd v. Redman* [1956] 2 Q.B. 612);

   (2) the common owner of two adjoining terraces uses the garden of the adjoining terrace, there is a contemporaneous sale by the common owner to two separate purchasers, will a "right" to use the garden pass to the purchaser under s. 67? (see *Long v. Gowlett* [1923] 2 Ch. 177 at 200-201, 203 and *Ward v. Kirkland* [1967] 1 Ch. 194 at 228);

   (3) a "right" to protection from the weather afforded by an adjoining house (see *Phipps v. Pears* [1965] 1 Q.B. 76).

   For further authorities on the effect of the English section, *Law of Property Act* 1925, s. 62, see *Ward v. Kirkland* [1967] 1 Ch. 194; *Green v. Ashco Horticulturist Ltd* [1966] 1 W.L.R. 889; *Crow v. Wood* [1971] 1 Q.B. 77; *Graham v. Philcox* [1984] 3 W.L.R. 150.

(b) Non-derogation from grant

The principle enunciated in *Wheeldon v. Burrows* (1879) 12 Ch. D. 31 is but one facet of the rule of non-derogation from grant. The effect of the rule in some circumstances, it may be argued, will be to grant rights, binding on successors in title without notice, which are not capable at law of amounting to an easement. Parker J. in *Browne v. Flower* [1911] 1 Ch. 219 stated the principle as follows:

> Under certain circumstances there will be implied on the part of the grantor or lessor obligations which restrict the user of the land retained by him further than can be explained by the implication of any easement known to the law. Thus, if the grant or demise be made for a particular purpose, the grantor or lessor comes under an obligation not to use the land retained by him in such a way as to render the land granted or demised unfit or materially less fit for the particular purpose for which the grant or demise was made. In *Aldin v. Latimer Clark, Muirhead & Co.* [1894] 2 Ch. 437, land having been demised for the purpose of carrying on the business of a timber merchant, the lessor came under an obligation not to build on land retained by him so as to interrupt the access of air to sheds on the demised property used for drying timber, although the law does not recognise any easement of air unless it comes through or to some defined passage or aperture. Similarly in the case of *Grosvenor Hotel Co. v. Hamilton* [1894] 2 Q.B. 836 the lessee was held entitled to prevent the lessor from using property retained by him in such a way as to cause on the demised property vibrations which did not amount to a legal nuisance, though there is no such easement known to the law as an easement of freedom from vibration any more than there is an easement of freedom from noise. Once again, though possibly there may not be known to the law any easement of light for special purposes, still the lease of a building to be used for a special purpose requiring an extraordinary amount of light might well be held to preclude the grantor from diminishing the light passing to the grantee's windows, even in cases where the diminution would not be such as to create a nuisance within the meaning of the recent decisions: see *Herz v. Union Bank of London* (1854) 2 Giff. 686; 66 E.R. 287. In none of these cases would any easement be created, but the obligation implied on the part of the lessor or grantor would be analogous to that which arises from a restrictive covenant. It is to be observed that in the several cases to which I have referred the lessor had done or proposed to do something which rendered or would render the demised premises unfit or materially less fit to be used for the particular purpose for which the demise was made. I can find no case which extends the implied obligations of a grantor or lessor beyond this. Indeed, if the implied obligations

of a grantor or lessor with regard to land retained by him were extended beyond this, it is difficult to see how they could be limited at all. A landowner may sell a piece of land for the purpose of building a house which when built may derive a great part of its value from advantages of prospect or privacy. It would, I think, be impossible to hold that because of this the vendor was precluded from laying out the land retained by him as a building estate, though in so doing he might destroy the views from the purchaser's house, interfere with his privacy, render the premises noisy, and to a great extent interfere with the comfortable enjoyment and diminish the value of the property sold by him. It is quite reasonable for a purchaser to assume that a vendor who sells land for a particular purpose will not do anything to prevent its being used for that purpose, but it would be utterly unreasonable to assume that the vendor was undertaking restrictive obligations which would prevent his using land retained by him for any lawful purpose whatsoever merely because his so doing might affect the amenities of the property he had sold. After all, a purchaser can always bargain for those rights which he deems indispensable to his comfort.

Similarly if a vendor sells part of the land, knowing that the purchaser intends to build on that land, the vendor impliedly undertakes not to use the adjoining land so as to injure or interfere with the building, thus giving rise to an implied right of support for buildings: *Kebewar Pty Ltd v. Harkin* (1987) 9 N.S.W.L.R. 738 at 741.

For applications of the principle, see *Cable v. Bryant* [1908] 1 Ch. 259; *Harmer v. Jumbil (Nigeria) Tin Areas Ltd* [1921] 1 Ch. 200, extracted below p. 579; *Ward v. Kirkland* [1967] Ch. 194; *Woodhouse & Co. Ltd v. Kirkland (Derby) Ltd* [1970] 1 W.L.R. 1185; *Miller v. Jackson* [1977] 3 W.L.R. 20. For opposing views on the effect of the principle of non-derogation from grant, see Elliott, "Non-Derogation from Grant" (1964) 80 L.Q.R. 244 and Peel, "The Nature of Rights Arising Under the Doctrine of Non-Derogation from Grant" (1965) 81 L.Q.R. 28.

5. By prescription

At common law a grant of an easement would be presumed where there had been user as of right from time immemorial. The right claimed must have been capable of forming the subject matter of a grant. The right so acquired was founded "not on the ground that possession over a given period gave an indefeasible right, but on the assumption that where possession or enjoyment had been carried back as far as living memory would go that a grant had once existed which had since been lost": *Bryant v. Foot* (1867) L.R. 2 Q.B. 161 at 179 per Cockburn J. User as of right must have existed from time immemorial. In Littleton's words there must have been user as of right "from time whereof the memory of men runneth not to the contrary": Lyttleton *Treatise on Tenures* 170. The extent of legal memory was fixed by statute at 1189; *Statute of Westminster* 1 1275, c. 39. This rule originated in the practice of making the period of limitation for recovery of property run from particular dates or events, 1189 being the date of accession of Richard I. The limitation period for recovery of real property in the ensuing period became a fixed period of 60 years and was progressively shortened. These statutory modifications did not affect the acquisition of easements by prescription and the requirements of user from time immemorial. In this context it must be remembered that there is an essential distinction between the effect of extinguishment of rights by statutes of limitation and acquisition of rights by prescription. The difference is neatly expressed by Megarry and Wade, *The Law of Real Property* (4th ed.), pp. 846-847:

> By *limitation* one person may acquire the land of another by adverse possession for a period which is now generally 12 years. By *prescription* one person may acquire rights such as easements . . . over the land of another. One important

difference is that limitation is extinctive but prescription in acquisitive: that is to say, adverse possession of land for 12 years extinguishes the previous owner's title, leaving the adverse possessor with a title based on his own actual possession; but prescription creates a new right, an incorporeal hereditament, which no one possessed previously. Prescription therefore must have positive operation, so as to create a new title. This is brought about by presuming a grant.

As to other points of distinction, see Goodman, "Adverse Possession or Prescription? Problems of Conflict" (1968) 32 Conv. N.S. 270. The presumption of grant by virtue of long user could be rebutted by evidence showing that user as of right had not existed since time immemorial or that the right, if any, had ceased to exist, for example, by subsequent unity of ownership and possession. Proof of user from time immemorial presented enormous difficulties. These were substantially overcome by two devices. (1) Where user was claimed from 1189, the courts would, prima facie, presume that user had continued from time immemorial where user as of right for a period of 20 years or more could be shown: *Darling v. Clue* (1864) 4 F. & F. 326 at 344. (2) Where a prescriptive right based on user from time immemorial (1189) could not be made out (for example, where use could not have existed since 1189 as in *Dalton v. Angus* (1881) 6 App. Cas. 740, extracted below where a factory had been in existence only for 27 years) the doctrine of lost modern grant was evolved. The doctrine of lost modern grant required judges and juries, as a matter of law, to presume from 20 years' user as of right the existence of a lost modern grant of the easement. The case *Dalton v. Angus*, extracted below, is the principal authority establishing the principle of lost modern grant.

The impossibility of proving user from time immemorial in Australia is self-evident. It has, however, been accepted that the doctrine of lost modern grant is law in Australia: *Delohery v. Permanent Trustees Co. (N.S.W.)* (1904) 1 C.L.R. 283; *Hamilton v. Joyce* [1984] 3 N.S.W.L.R. 279. In *Delohery's* case the plaintiff there alleged that the building on his land had enjoyed free and uninterrupted access of light for 45 years over the defendants' adjoining land. The defendants had begun to erect buildings which would substantially reduce the amount of light to the plaintiff's windows. The plaintiff argued that he had an easement of light over the defendants' land and relied on the doctrine of lost modern grant. Griffith C.J. (delivering the judgment of the court) reviewed the English authorities and said:

> [I]t appears to have been settled in England long ago that the right to the uninterrupted access of light over the land of another may be acquired by a "long" and continual possession, without any formal instrument, and that the interpretation of the word "long" has by degrees been altered by judicial decisions, and had come by the year 1786 to mean unexplained enjoyment for a period of 20 years or upwards.

His Honour concluded:

> [W]e are of opinion that the law of prescription as to ancient lights was a law which could be applied in New South Wales within the meaning of the *Australian Courts Act* 1828 (Imp.) (Statute 9 Geo. IV c. 83) and therefore became part of the law of the colony at that time, even if it had not been brought with them by the first colonists.

Following *Delohery's* case easements of light and air cannot be acquired by prescription: *Conveyancing Act* 1919 (N.S.W.), s. 179.

The acquisition of easements by prescription has recently come under attack. By a small majority the Law Reform Committee (U.K.) in this *Report on Easements and Profits by Prescription* 1966 Cmnd 3100, recommended that the prescriptive acquisition of easements should be abolished and except for easements of support should not be replaced by any other method of acquisition. The committee said:

> 32. . . . The main considerations . . . are briefly, that there is little, if any, moral justification for the acquisition of easements by prescription, a process which either involves an intention to get something for nothing or, where there is no intention to acquire any right, is purely accidental. Moreover, the user which eventually develops into a full-blown legal right, enjoyable not only by the dominant owner himself but also by his successors in title for ever, may well have originated in the servient owner's neighbourly wish to give a facility to some particular individual, or (perhaps even more commonly) to give a facility on the understanding, unfortunately unexpressed in words or at least unprovable, that it may be withdrawn if a major change of circumstances ever comes about.

The Committee unanimously recommended the abolition of prescription as a basis for acquisition of profits à prendre. The Commission said that "broadly speaking, it can be said that it is less harsh and unfair to deprive a man of a profit which he has been enjoying, but to which he cannot adduce a documentary title, than is the case where an easement is concerned. The acquisition of a profit is normally a transaction of a more commercial character than is the acquisition of an easement and it is not unreasonable that the purchaser should be required to prove the bargain upon which he relies." These recommendations have not yet been implemented. Similar recommendations in relation to easements have been made by the Law Reform Commission of Victoria, *Easements and Covenants* DP 15, 1989, paras 10-11.

In New South Wales, prescriptive easements are of limited significance as they generally cannot be enforced over Torrens title land: see "Easements and the Torrens system" below p. 286.

Although profits may also be acquired by prescription on the principles extracted in the cases following (*White v. Taylor* [1969] 1 Ch. 150 at 158), our major concern in this section is with the general law relating to prescriptive easements.

DALTON v. ANGUS

House of Lords (1881) 6 App. Cas. 740

[The plaintiffs' factory was so built that it depended for lateral support on the adjoining land, and had done so for a period of 27 years. The defendant, owner of the adjoining house, employed a contractor to pull down the house and excavate, the contractor being bound to shore up adjoining buildings and make good the damage. The house was pulled down and land excavated for several feet. This had the effect of depriving the plaintiffs' factory of lateral support and caused a collapse of most of the factory.]

LORD SELBOURNE L.C. The questions upon these appeals may be reduced, shortly, to two: The first, whether a right to lateral support from adjoining land can be acquired by 27 years' uninterrupted enjoyment for a building proved to have been newly erected at the commencement of that time; the second, whether (if so) there was anything in the circumstances of this case, as appearing in the evidence, sufficient either to disprove the acquisition of such a right, or to make it dependent upon some question of fact, which ought to have been submitted to the jury. . . .

I proceed to consider the principal questions in the case.

In the natural state of land, one part of it receives support from another, upper from lower strata, and soil from adjacent soil. This support is natural, and is necessary, as long as the status quo of the land is maintained; and, therefore, if one parcel of land be conveyed, so as to be divided in point of title from another contiguous to it, or (as in the case of mines) below it, the status quo of support passes with the property in the land, not as an easement held by a distinct title, but as an incident to the land itself, sine quo res ipsa haberi non debet. All existing divisions of property in land must have been attended with this incident, when not excluded by contract; and it is for that reason often spoken of as a right by law; a right of the owner to the enjoyment of his own property, as distinguished from an easement supposed to be granted by grant; a right for injury to which an adjoining proprietor is responsible, upon the principle, sic utere tuo, ut alienum non laedas. . . .

In these cases, or in some of them, there were buildings upon the land; but no separate question was raised as to the support necessary for the buildings, as distinguished from that necessary for the land; and the doctrine laid down must, in my opinion, be understood of land without reference to buildings. Support to that which is artificially imposed upon land cannot exist ex jure naturae, because one thing supported does not itself so exist; it must in each particular case be acquired by grant, or by some means equivalent in law to grant, in order to make it a burden upon the neighbour's land, which (naturally) would be free from it. This distinction (and, at the same time, its proper limit) was pointed out by Willes J. in *Bonomi v. Backhouse* (1859) 1 E.B. & E. 655; 120 E.R. 643, where he said, "The right to support of land and the right of support of buildings stand upon different footings, *as to the mode of acquiring them*, the former being prima facie a right of property analogous to the flow of a natural river, or of air, though there may be cases in which it would be sustained as matter of grant (see *Caledonian Railway Co. v. Sprot* (1856) 2 Macq. 449): whilst the latter must be founded upon prescription or grant, express or implied; *but the character of the rights, when acquired, is in each case the same.*" Land which affords support to land is affected by the superincumbent or lateral weight, as by an easement or servitude; the owner is restricted in the use of his own property, in precisely the same way as when he has granted a right of support to buildings. The right, therefore, in my opinion, is properly called an easement, as it was by Lord Campbell in *Humphries v. Brogden* (1850) 12 Q.B. 742; 116 E.R. 1048; though when the land is in its natural state the easement is natural and not conventional. The same distinction exists as to rights in respect of running water, the easement of the riparian landowner is natural; that of the mill owner on the stream, so far as it exceeds that of an ordinary riparian proprietor, is conventional, that is, it must be established by prescription or grant.

If at the time of the severance of the land from that of the adjoining proprietor it was not in its original state, but had buildings standing on it up to the dividing line, or if it were conveyed expressly with a view to the erection of such buildings, or to any other use of it which might render increased support necessary, there would then be an implied grant of such support as the actual state or the contemplated use of the land would require, and the artificial would be inseparable from, and (as between the parties to the contract) would be a mere enlargement of, the natural. If a building is divided into floors or "flats", separately owned (an illustration which occurs in many of the authorities), the owner of each upper floor or "flat" is entitled, upon the same principle, to vertical support from the lower part of the building, and to the benefit of such lateral support as may be of right enjoyed by the building itself: *Caledonian Railway Co. v. Sprot* (1856) 2 Macq. 449.

I think it clear that any such right of support to a building, or part of a building, is an easement; and I agree with Lindley J. and Bowen J. that it is both scientifically and practically inaccurate to describe it as one of a merely negative kind. What is support? The force of gravity causes the superincumbent land, or building, to press downward upon what is below it, whether artificial or natural; and it has also a tendency to thrust outwards, laterally, any loose or yielding substance, such as earth or clay, until it meets with adequate resistance. Using the language of the law of easements, I say that, in the case alike of vertical and of lateral support, both to land and to buildings, the dominant tenement imposes upon the servient a positive and a constant burden, the sustenance of which, by the servient tenement, is necessary for the safety and stability of the dominant. It is true that the benefit to the dominant tenement arises, not from its own pressure upon the servient tenement, but from the power of the servient tenement to resist that pressure, and from its actual sustenance of the burden so imposed. But the burden and its sustenance are reciprocal, and inseparable from each other, and it can make no difference whether the dominant tenement is said to impose, or the servient to sustain, the weight. . . .

These principles go far, in my opinion, to establish, as a necessary consequence, that such a right of support may be gained by prescription. Some of the learned judges appear to think otherwise, and to doubt whether it could be the subject of grant. For that doubt I am unable to perceive any sufficient foundation. . . . Be the theory what it may, its true foundation, in point of fact, is that which the Romans called "usucapio", under the conditions defined by Sir Edward Coke. "Both to customs and prescriptions, these two things are incidents inseparable, viz., possession or usage, and time. Possession must have three qualities, it must be long, continual, and peaceable . . ." ((1628) 1 Co. Lit. 113b, 114a). All these conditions are capable, in my judgment, of being fulfilled as to the right of support to buildings, and, when they are fulfilled, I am unable to understand why the right should not be held to be prescriptively established.

The policy and purpose of the law on which both prescription and the presumptions which have supplied its place, when length of possession has been less than immemorial, rest, would be defeated, or rendered very insecure, if exceptions to it were admitted on such grounds as that a particular servitude (capable of a lawful origin) is negative rather than positive; or that the inchoate enjoyment of it before it has matured into a right is not an actionable wrong; or that resistance to or interruption of it may not be *conveniently* practicable. I assume, for the present purpose, that a man who places on his own land, where it adjoins that of his neighbour, a weight which increases its pressure upon his neighbour's land, is not thereby guilty of an actionable wrong. If this be so, the reason probably is, that the act is lawfully done upon his own land, and that the owner of the adjoining land suffers no actual or appreciable damage from the increased amount of pressure which it has to bear, except so far as the continuance of that pressure, if uninterrupted, may tend to ripen into a right, and so to enlarge the servitude to which this land was previously subject. But against this he has his own remedy, if he chooses to prevent and interrupt it. That power of resistance by interruption does and must in all such cases exist, otherwise no question like the present could arise. It is true that in some cases (of which the present is an example) a man acting with a reasonable regard to his own interest would never exercise it for the mere purpose of preventing his neighbour from enlarging or extending such a servitude. But, on the other hand, it would not be reasonably consistent with the policy of law in favour of possessory titles, that they should depend, in each particular case, upon the greater or less facility or difficulty, convenience or inconvenience, of practically interrupting them. They can always be interrupted (and that without difficulty or inconvenience), when a man wishes, and finds it for his interest, to make such a use of his own land as will have that effect. So long as it does not suit his purpose or his interest to do this, the law which allows a servitude to be established or enlarged by long and open enjoyment, against one whose preponderating interest it has been to be passive during the whole time necessary for its acquisition, seems more reasonable, and more consistent with public convenience and natural equity, than one which would enable him, at any distance of time (whenever his views of his own interest may have undergone a change), to destroy the fruits of his neighbour's diligence, industry, and expenditure. . . .

From the view which I take of the nature of the right of support, that it is an easement, not purely negative, capable of being granted, and also capable of being interrupted, it seems to me to follow that it must be within s. 2 of the *Prescription Act* 1832 (U.K.) (2 & 3 Will. 4 c. 71), unless that section is confined . . . to rights of way and rights of water.

[His Lordship then decided that the right claimed came within s. 2 of the *Prescription Act* and continued:]

But 20 years' user, under s. 2, may be defeated "in any other way by which" it was previously (that is, before 1 August 1832) "liable to be defeated", except that it can no longer be defeated or destroyed "by shewing only that it was first enjoyed at any time prior to such period of twenty years". The effect of this, as I understand it, is to apply the law of prescription, properly so called, to an easement enjoyed as of right for 20 years, subject to all defences to which a claim by prescription would previously have been open, except that of shewing a commencement within time of legal memory. To allege that there was no evidence from which a grant could be presumed, or that there was evidence from which it ought to be inferred that there was, in fact, no grant, would not (as I understand the law) have been, before the 1 August 1832, a competent mode of defeating or destroying any claim to an easement *by prescription*, and no jury would have been directed to find a grant in any such case, when there was no proof of a commencement within time of legal memory. The section, therefore (assuming it to apply), would in the present case be sufficient to establish a title by prescription to the right claimed by the plaintiffs, unless it had been enjoyed vi, or clam, or precario. Of vi, or precario, there is here no question.

Supposing, however, that s. 2 of the *Prescription Act* ought not to be held to apply to the easement of support, the same result would practically be reached by the doctrine, that a grant or some lawful title equivalent to it, ought to be presumed after 20 years' user. As to this, I think it unnecessary to say more than that I agree with the view of the authorities taken by Lush J., by the majority of the judges in the Court of Appeal, and by all the learned judges who attended this House (unless Bowen J., who preferred to rely upon the equitable doctrine or acquiescence, is an exception) in their answer to the first two questions proposed to them by your Lordships.

Upon the other three questions proposed to the learned judges, which involve the doctrine of clam, as applied to the easement of support, there has been much difference of opinion; four of the learned judges being in the plaintiff's favour, and the other three thinking that the jury were not properly directed on that point.

The inquiry on this part of the case is, as to the nature and extent of the knowledge or means of knowledge which a man ought to be shewn to possess, against whom a right of support for another man's building is claimed. He cannot resist or interrupt that of which he is wholly ignorant. But there are some things of which all men ought to be presumed to have knowledge, and among them (I think) is the fact, that, according to the laws of nature, a building cannot stand without vertical or (ordinarily) without lateral support. When a new building is openly erected on one side of the dividing line between two properties, its general nature and character, its exterior and much of its interior structure, must be visible and ascertainable by the adjoining proprietor during the course of its erection. When (as in the present case) a private dwelling-house is pulled down, and a building of an entirely difference character, such as a coach or carriage factory, with a large and massive brick pillar and chimneystack, is erected instead of it, the adjoining proprietor must have imputed to him knowledge that a new and enlarged easement of support (whatever may be its extent) is going to be acquired against him, unless he interrupts or prevents it. The case is, in my opinion, substantially the same as if a new factory had been erected, where no building stood before. Having this knowledge, it is, in my judgment, by no means necessary that he should have particular information as to those details of the internal structure of the building on which the amount or incidence of its weight may more or less depend. If he thought it material, he might inquire into those particulars, and then if information were improperly withheld from him, or if he received false or misleading information, or if anything could be shewn to have been done secretly or surreptitiously, in order to keep material facts from his knowledge, the case would be different. But here there was no evidence from which a jury could have been entitled to infer any of these things. Everything was honestly and (as far as it could be) openly done, without any deception or concealment. The interior construction of the building was, indeed, such as to require lateral support, beyond what might have been necessary if it had been otherwise constructed. But this must always be liable to happen, whenever a building has to be adapted to a particular use. The knowledge that it may or may not happen is in my opinion enough, if the adjoining proprietor makes no inquiry. I think, therefore, that in this case the kind and degree of knowledge which the adjoining proprietor must necessarily have had was sufficient; that nothing was done clam, and that the evidence did not raise any question on this point which ought to have been submitted to the jury.

My opinion, therefore, upon the whole case is in favour of the respondents, the plaintiffs in the action, and against the appellants; and the motion which I have to make to your Lordship is, that the judgment of the court below be affirmed, and the appeal dismissed with costs. . . .

LORD PENZANCE. My Lords, in dealing with the questions of law to which the present case gives rise, it is material to bear in mind that the exact proposition which the appellants call upon your Lordships to repudiate, or affirm, is to be found in the ruling at the trial given by the learned judge. It is in these words: "The authorities oblige me to hold, that when a building has stood for 20 years it has acquired a right to the support of the adjacent land, and I do not think that it all depends upon whether the opposite or adjacent neighbour had notice, or not, of what was done, or what weight was put upon it, nor does it rest on the fact of there being an implied grant. I think it has become absolute law, that when a building has stood for 20 years, supported by the adjacent soil, it has acquired a right to the support of the soil; and no one has a right to take all that soil without putting an equivalent to sustain the building. That is the ruling which I must lay down here, because that is upheld by many authorities" (Printed Papers, Appendix, p. 69). Your Lordships have now to say whether this view of the authorities is a correct one; and, with some reluctance, I feel constrained to say that in my opinion it is so, I say with some reluctance, not because I think that the support which the plaintiff claims for his house is unreasonable, or inequitable, but because the circumstances under which the claim is held to arise, are, so far as I am able to discover, incapable of giving rise to it in accordance with any known principle of law.

It must be borne in mind both what the claim is, and what it is not. It is not a claim asserted for the support of a house by the adjacent soil as soon as that house is built; but a claim that when the house has stood "for twenty years supported by the adjacent soil it has by absolute law acquired a right to the support of the soil"; and this not by reason of any implied grant, and quite independently of whether "the opposite or adjacent neighbour had notice or not of what was done or what weight was put upon" the ground to which the lateral support was required.

It is this sudden starting into existence of a right which did not exist the day before the 20 years expired, without reference to any presumption of acquiescence by the neighbour (to which the lapse of that period of time without interruption on his part might naturally give rise) which I find it impossible to reconcile with legal principles. I find myself therefore in entire accord with the opinion which Fry J. has offered to the House; and he has so fully and ably illustrated his views on the subject, which are also mine, that I have little to add.

If this matter were res integra, I think it would not be inconsistent with legal principles to hold, that where an owner of land has used his land for an ordinary and reasonable purpose, such as placing a house upon it, the owner of the adjacent soil could not be allowed so to deal with his own soil by excavation as to bring his neighbour's house to the ground. It would be, I think, no unreasonable application of the principle "sic utere tuo ut alienum non laedas" to hold, that the owner of the adjacent soil, if desirous of excavating it, should take reasonable precautions by way of shoring, or otherwise, to prevent the excavation from disastrously affecting his neighbour. A burden would no doubt be thus cast on one man by the act of another done without his consent. But the advantages of such a rule would be reciprocal, and regard being had to the practicability of shoring up during excavation, the restriction thus placed on excavation would not seriously impair the rights of ownership.

But the matter is not res integra. It has been the subject of legal decisions, and those decisions leave it beyond doubt that such is not the law of England. On the contrary it is the law, I believe I may say without question, that at any time within 20 years after the house is built the owner of the adjacent soil may with perfect legality dig that soil away, and allow his neighbour's house, if supported by it, to fall in ruins to the ground. This being so, and these being his legal rights (the rights incident to his ownership), it seems to me that these rights must remain to him, or those who come after him, for all time, unless he, or they, have done something by which these rights have been divested, restricted, or impaired. I find it impossible to conceive, within the application of any legal principles, that mere lapse of time can divest him or them of the rights they once had. Legal rights do not perish by lapse of time, but rather grow confirmed. What I mean to express is this, that the right to excavate the neighbouring soil not being impaired or restricted by the house being built, anything which afterwards impairs or restricts it must proceed from those who possess that right, and cannot come about, all things remaining unchanged, by the mere efflux of time.

In all the cases in which lapse of time is held to stand in the way of the assertion of rights attaching to the ownership of property, it is not the lapse of time itself which so operates but the inferences which are reasonably drawn from the continuous existence of a given state of things during that period of time. These inferences are inferences of acquiescence or consent, and they are drawn from the fact that the person against whom the right is claimed has for a length of time failed to interrupt or prevent an enjoyment by his neighbour which he might have interrupted had he so pleased. In *Chasemore v. Richards* (1859) 7 H.L.C. 349; 11 E.R. 140 the language held puts this beyond doubt. . . . In the more modern case of *Sturges v. Bridgman* (1859) 11 Ch. D. 852 it was distinctly determined that no easement could be created by lapse of time unless the defendant might have interrupted it. . . .

The question therefore in each particular case must be, could the defendant have interrupted the enjoyment in question? Now if these words are taken literally all cases are alike, and the question is no question at all. For an action for the disturbance of the enjoyment claimed involves the possibility of its being disturbed, and the fact that the defendant has at least interrupted the plaintiff's enjoyment (say of support to his house) which constitutes his cause of action, is a very simple proof, except under special circumstances, that the enjoyment was capable of interruption at an earlier period. The defendant's power of interruption therefore, in my opinion, means something very different from the mere physical possibility of interrupting. It involves knowledge that the necessity for support existed, and the possibility of withdrawing that support without the expenditure of so much labour or money, or the incurring of so much loss or damage, as a man could not reasonably be expected to incur.

There is direct authority for this proposition to be found in the case of *Webb v. Bird* (1861) 10 C.B. (N.S.) 285 in which Willes J. states the principle which is to be extracted from the previous cases, in the following language: "In general a man cannot establish a right by lapse of time and acquiescence against his neighbour, unless he shews that the party against whom the right is acquired might have brought an action, or done some act, to put a stop to the claim, *without an unreasonable waste of labour and expense.*" Nor is any other view of this matter, as it seems to me, consistent with the terms in which a right to be gained by prescription or lapse of time is defined. A claim by prescription to a right of this character is said only to arise when a right, or benefit, enjoyed over a length of time has been enjoyed "nec vi", "nec clam". What is the meaning and bearing of these qualifications? Or what place could they have in such a definition, unless they point to the fact that the benefit claimed after a lapse of years as a right is one, the existence of which the person against whom it is claimed had the means of knowing, and the enjoyment of which he had the power to stop? And of what importance are these matters, except that they lay the foundation, where the right or benefit has not been interfered with, for presuming that he who might have interfered with them, has granted or consented that they should be undisturbed in future?

Continuous enjoyment without interruption is surely insisted upon as the basis of the right for some reason, and for what reason except that it is the evidence of assent? The physical power to interrupt, if accompanied, as I have above suggested, by a knowledge that the enjoyment of support existed, and by the means of exercising that power of interruption without extravagant and unreasonable loss or expense, may well give ground for an implied assent if it be not exercised for so long a period as 20 years. But if unaccompanied by these qualifications, the fact of non-interruption appears to lead to no conclusion whatever, and the restrictions insisted upon, that the enjoyment must be "open" and not sustained by "force", cease to have an intelligent place in the definition. In the present case it is obvious that a power to interrupt is one which, although it has existed, and been physically possible ever since the plaintiff's house was built, could only be exercised by measures which no man in his senses would take. It would indeed be an unreasonable state of the law which should enforce upon the defendant, if he wished to retain his original right to excavate his own soil at such time as his interests might require him to do so, that he should pull his own house down, and drag his neighbour's to the ground with it at a time when his interest did not require it, and when it could be nothing but a grievous loss and injury to all parties concerned.

For these reasons I am unable to support the conclusion that a right such as that here in question could be gained by the plaintiff by anything in the shape of prescription or lost grant; but if I am mistaken in this, I think it is clear that in the present case the question should have been submitted to the jury whether the enjoyment of the support to the house was an "open" enjoyment at all. The house was built in an exceptional manner, and that, which seen from the outside, would appear to be nothing more than an ordinary chimney stack carrying nothing but its own weight, was in truth a pier of brickwork, intended to carry, and in fact carrying, one end of an iron girder, upon which girder the whole upper floor of the house rested. If the plaintiff's right, therefore, was to be established by prescription, I think it inevitable that the matter should have been dealt with by the learned judge in the manner clearly described by Lindley J. in his answer to your Lordship's fifth question. And I daresay it would have been so dealt with, if the learned judge had not considered the plaintiff's right to stand on a different ground altogether, and asserted it to be an absolute right acquired by 20 years' enjoyment, quite independent of grant, acquiescence, or consent. In so doing he relied, he said, upon the existing authorities. I will not recapitulate them or criticise them individually, as they have been carefully reviewed by others. They constitute the existing law on the subject; and I think the learned judge has drawn what is upon the whole the correct inference from them, though they are by no means uniform, and although, for the reasons I have given, and for those more fully expanded in the opinion of Fry J., I am unable to find a satisfactory legal ground upon which these authorities may be justified. I feel the less difficulty in acquiescing in them, inasmuch as they affirm a right to exist after 20 years, which in my opinion should have been held to exist as soon as the plaintiff's house was built. The learned judge's direction at the trial was therefore, in my opinion, correct, and this appeal should be dismissed with costs; and if I have ventured to question the legal principles upon which the authorities which guided him are founded, I have only done so lest this case should be thought an authority for the establishment of other rights more or less similar to the right here in question.

So far as my opinion goes this right, to the lateral support of the soil for an ancient house, stands upon the positive authority of a series of cases and a long acceptance in the courts of law, and the ratification of it by your Lordships ought not to be considered as the adoption of principles which might have a wide application in analogous cases.

LORD BLACKBURN. [His Lordship agreed that an easement of support could be acquired by prescription under the doctrine of lost modern grant. His Lordship, however, differed as to the basis upon which these prescriptive rights were granted:] No question here arises as to the effect of any disability on the part of the owner of the land, nor as to the effect of any restrictions arising from the state of the title.

But a question does arise as to whether there was not, or at least might have been, evidence of something which would prevent the enjoyment here being of that nature which would give rise to prescription on the ground that the possession was not open. The edict of the Prætor that possession must not be vi vel clam, as I think, is so far adopted in English law that no prescriptive right can be acquired where there is any concealment, and probably none where the enjoyment has not been open. And in cases where the enjoyment was in the beginning wrongful, and the owner of the adjoining land may be said to have lost the full benefit of his rights though his laches, it may be a fair test of whether the enjoyment was open or not to ask whether it was such that the owner of the adjoining land, but for his laches, must have known what the enjoyment was, and how far it went. But in a case of support where there is no laches, and the rights of the owner of the adjoining land are curtailed for the public benefit, on the assumption that, in general, rights not exercised during a long time are not of much value, and that it is for the public good that such rights (generally trifling) should be curtailed in favour of quieting title; where that is the principle, I do not see that more can be requisite than to let the enjoyment be so open that it is known that some support is being enjoyed by the building. That is enough to put the owner of the land on exercising his full rights, unless he is content to suffer a curtailment, not in general of any consequence. And in the present case all that is suggested is that the plaintiffs' building was not an ordinary house, but a building used as a factory, which concentrated a great part of its weight on a pillar. It had stood for 27 years, and, as far as appears, would, but for the defendants' operations, have stood for many more years; and there was nothing in the nature of concealment. Any one who entered the factory must have seen that it was supported in a great degree by the pillar. And there is not the slightest suggestion that those who made the excavation were not perfectly aware that the factory did rest on the pillar, or that they took such precautions as would have been sufficient if the building had been supported in a more usual way, but that the mischief happened from its unusual construction. That being so, I am at a loss to see what question the learned judge could, at the trial, on this evidence have left to the jury, beyond the question whether the building had for than 20 years openly, and without concealment, stood as it was and enjoyed without interruption the support of the neighbouring soil.

[Lord Coleridge concurred with the judgments of Lord Selbourne L.C. and Lord Blackburn. Lord Watson agreed with the judgment of Lord Selbourne L.C.]

Appeals dismissed.

NOTES

1. For a discussion of the differing views of the operation of the doctrine of lost modern grant evidenced in *Angus v. Dalton* in the courts of Queen's Bench Division, the Court of Appeal and the House of Lords in the principal case, see *Gale on Easements* (14th ed.), pp. 138-141.

The judgment of Fry J. in the Queen's Bench Division in *Dalton v. Angus* (1881) 6 App. Cas. 740 has often been cited as the basis of the doctrine of prescription. His Lordship said (at 773-774):

[I]n my opinion, the whole law of prescription and the whole law which governs the presumption of inference of a grant or covenant rest upon acquiescence. The courts and the judges have had recourse to various expedients for quieting the possession of persons in the exercise of rights which have not been resisted by the persons against whom they are exercised, but in all cases it appears to me that acquiescence and nothing else is the principle upon which these expedients rest. It becomes then of the highest importance to consider of what ingredients acquiescence consists. In many cases, as, for instance, in the case of that acquiescence which creates a right of way, it will be found to involve, first, the doing of some act by one man upon the land of another; secondly, the absence of right to do that act in the person doing it; thirdly, the knowledge of the person affected by it that the act is done; fourthly, the power of the persons affected by the act to prevent such act either by act on his part or by action in the courts; and lastly, the abstinence by him from any such interferences for such a length of time as renders it reasonable for the courts to say that he shall not afterwards interfere to stop the act being done. In some other cases, as, for example, in the case of lights, some of these ingredients are wanting; but I cannot imagine any case of acquiescence in which there is not shewn to be in the servient owner: (1) a knowledge of the acts done; (2) a power in him to stop the acts or to sue in respect of them; and (3) an abstinence on his part from the exercise of such power. That such is the nature of acquiescence and that such is the ground upon which presumptions or inferences of grant or covenant may be made appears to me to be plain, both from reason, from maxim, and from the cases.

As regards the reason of the case, it is plain good sense to hold that a man who can stop an asserted right, or a continued user, and does not do so for a long time, may be told that he has lost his right by his delay and his negligence, and every presumption should therefore be made to quiet a possession thus acquired and enjoyed by the tacit consent of the sufferer. But there is no sense in binding a man by an enjoyment he cannot prevent, or quieting a possession which he could never disturb.

In accord with this view, in what has become an accepted statement of principle, Thesiger L.J. in *Sturges v. Bridgman* (1878) 11 Ch. D. 852 said:

Consent or acquiescence of the owner of the servient tenement lies at the root of prescription, and of the fiction of a lost grant, and hence the acts or user, which go to the proof of either the one or the other, must be, in the language of the civil law, nec vi nec clam nec precario; for a man cannot, as a general rule, be said consent to or acquiesce in the acquisition by his neighbour of an easement through an enjoyment of which he has no knowledge, actual or constructive, or which he contests and endeavours to interrupt, or which he temporarily licenses. It is a mere extension of the same notion, or rather it is a principle into which by strict analysis it may be resolved, to hold, that an enjoyment which a man cannot prevent raises no presumption of consent or acquiescence.

2. Acquiescence in the acquisition of the right is essential. In *Hamilton v. Joyce* [1984] 3 N.S.W.L.R. 279, Powell J. held (at 291) that "where there are serious doubts as to the true state of the title of the owner of 'the servient tenement', the failure of the owner to assert a claim can hardly be regarded as acquiesence so as to permit a presumption of a lost grant. Since [the servient owner] . . . believed the 'right of way' to be a public thoroughfare, and since, even now, the exact location and extent of 'the right of way' remains a question of doubt . . . the facts necessary to permit the presumption of a lost grant . . . have not been proved".

User must be of right. User by force or under a licence cannot give rise to an easement. Thus, where use is only possible by constant removal of obstructions put there by the servient owner to prevent user, user will not be as of right: see *Newnham v. Willison* (1987) 56 P. & C.R. 8. Similarly, no easement will arise where there is user by permission (*Hamilton v. Joyce* [1984] 3 N.S.W.L.R. 279 at 291) or an annual fee is paid: *Gardner v. Hodgson's Kingston Brewery Co. Ltd* [1903] A.C. 339. As to the effect of permission before the commencement of the prescriptive period, see *Wilkinson v. Spooner* [1957] Tas S.R. 121 at 126; *Healey v. Hawkins* [1968] 1 W.L.R. 1967.

Where there is unity of possession of the dominant and servient tenements, there is no user of right; in *Outram v. Maude* (1881) 17 Ch. D. 391, Bacon V. C. commented "the law is clear that the tenant can in no case, and under no circumstances, establish such a right as acquired during his tenancy against his landlord, and that no easement can be acquired while unity of possession exists in the land demised and in the easement claimed".

3. User or enjoyment must be to the knowledge of the owner of the servient tenement. Proof of actual knowledge is not required; it is sufficient that the servient owner has constructive knowledge or the means of knowledge of user.

In *Lloyd's Bank v. Dalton* [1942] Ch. 466 the defendant was the owner of a factory and dye works which had for a period exceeding 20 years supported the adjoining land upon which outhouses were erected. The defendant demolished parts of his property with the result that part of the adjoining land was deprived of support and collapsed. In an action by the owners of the adjoining land for damages the defendant claimed that there was secrecy of enjoyment. There was evidence that before demolition it was not possible to see any part of the adjoining land or the outhouses built thereon from the defendant's property or the roadway. Bennett J. in holding for the plaintiffs said:

It is notorious that the owners of land and buildings are interested in their boundaries, and, in my judgment, the facts proved at the trial of this case lead irresistibly to the conclusion that the successive owners of the dye works, assuming them to have been reasonable persons, diligent in the protection of their interests, either must have known or must be taken to have had reasonable opportunity of becoming aware of the fact that the dye works were supporting the north-east part of the plaintiffs' yard and of the outbuilding standing thereon. For these reasons, the plea of clam, in my judgment, fails.

The case may be contrasted with *Union Lighterage Co. v. London Graving Dock Co.* [1902] 2 Ch 557. There the defendant's predecessor in title owned a dock and an adjacent wharf. The dock was secured by underground supports attached to piles on the wharf. The supports were not visible except for two nuts attaching them to the wharf piles. Subsequently the wharf was sold to the plaintiffs who, upon discovery of the underground supports, brought proceedings for their removal. It was held that the secrecy of enjoyment prevented an easement by prescription arising; see also *Milne v. James* (1910) 13 C.L.R. 168 at 178 per Griffiths C.J.

The requirement that the owner of the servient tenement have knowledge of user is not synonymous with the requirement that enjoyment be open and not secretive. In *Diment v. Foot* [1974] 1 W.L.R. 1427 the defendant claimed a right of way arising by prescription over the plaintiff's property, which was a large farm. The defendant claimed that the existence of a gate on a remote part of the plaintiff's property connecting the properties fixed the plaintiff with notice of user. During the period of user the plaintiff had employed an agent to manage the property (the servient tenement). The plaintiff had no personal knowledge, nor, as the court found, even with diligent inspection the means of knowledge, of user over the prescriptive period. The plaintiff upon becoming aware of user brought proceedings claiming an injunction restraining the defendant from exercising a right of way over her property. Pennycuick V.-C. held that no easement by prescription had been acquired. The existence of the gate the court found, did not necessarily point to user by the adjoining owner. In the absence of information as to the knowledge and duties of the managing agent, there was no ground for finding that the plaintiff's agent had knowledge or means of knowledge of user which should be imputed to the plaintiff.

See also *Anthony v. Commonwealth* (1973) 47 A.L.J.R. 83 at 91 per Walsh J. See also *Davies v. Du Paver* [1953] 1 Q.B. 184 where it was held that although there was common local knowledge of user, this was not sufficient to attribute knowledge to the owner of the servient tenement.

4. Enjoyment or user which the owner of the servient tenement cannot prevent raises no presumption of consent to user, and will not give rise to an easement by prescription. In *Sturges v. Bridgman* (1878) 11 Ch. D. 852 the defendant, a confectioner, had for a period exceeding 20 years, used a mortar and pestle for pounding ingredients. The accompanying noise and vibration caused no nuisance to the adjoining occupier, the plaintiff, a physician, until he set up a consulting room in his back garden. The plaintiff brought proceedings to restrain the nuisance. The defendant argued he had acquired an easement by prescription.

> THESIGER L.J. (delivering the judgment of the court). Here then arises the objection to the acquisition by the defendant of any easement. That which was done by him was in its nature such that it could not be physically interrupted; it could not at the same time be put a stop to by action. Can user which is neither preventible nor actionable found an easement? We think not. The question, so far as regards this particular easement claimed, is the same question whether the defendent endeavours to assert his right by common law or under the *Prescription Act*. That Act fixes periods for the acquisition of easements, but, except in regard to the particular easement of light, or in regard to certain matters which are immaterial to the present inquiry, it does not alter the character of easements, or of the user or enjoyment by which they are acquired. This being so, the laws governing the acquisition of easements by user stands thus. . . .

[His Lordship then stated, in a now famous passage, that acquisition depended on acquiescence and that enjoyment which a man cannot prevent raises no presumption of consent or acquiescence (the passage is extracted above, note 1) and continued:]

> Upon this principle it was decided in *Webb v. Bird* (1862) 13 C.B. (N.S.) 841; 143 E.R. 332 that currents of air blowing from a particular quarter of the compass, and in *Chasemore v. Richards* (1859) 7 H.L.C. 349 that subterranean water prelocating through the strata in no known channels, could not be acquired as an easement by user; and in *Angus v. Dalton* (1878) 4 Q.B.D. 162 a case of lateral support of buildings by adjacent soil, which came on appeal to this court, the principle was in no way impugned, although it was held by the majority of the court not to be applicable so as to prevent the acquisition of that particular easement. It is a principle which must be equally appropriate to the case of affirmative as of negative easements; in other words, it is equally unreasonable to imply your consent to your neighbour enjoying something which passes from your tenement to his, as to his subjecting your tenement to something which comes from his, when in both cases you have no power of prevention. But the affirmative easement differs from the negative easement in this, that the latter can under no circumstances be interrupted except by acts done upon the servient tenement, but the former, constituting, as it does, a direct interference with the enjoyment by the servient owner of his tenement, may be the subject of legal proceedings as well as of physical interruption. To put concrete cases—the passage of light and air to your neighbour's windows may be physically interrupted by you, but gives you no legal grounds of complaint against him. The passage of water from his land on to yours may be physically interrupted, or may be treated as a trespass and made the ground of action for damages, or for an injunction, or both. Noise is similar to currents of air and the flow of subterranean and uncertain streams in its practical incapability of physical interruption, but it differs from them in its capability of grounding an action. *Webb v. Bird* (1862) 13 C.B.

(N.S.) 841; 143 E.R. 332 and *Chasemore v. Richards* (1859) 7 H.C.L. 349 are not, therefore, direct authorities governing the present case. They are, however, illustrations of the principle which ought to govern it; for until the noise, to take this case, became an actionable nuisance, which it did not at any time before the consulting-room was built, the basis of the presumption of the consent, viz., the power of prevention physically or by action was never present.

Judgment for the plaintiff.

As a further illustration see *Scott-Whitehead v. National Coal Board* (1985) 53 P. & C.R. 263 at 275.

Difficulty or inconvenience in interrupting user is not a relevant consideration: see the judgment of Lord Selbourne L.C. in the principal case.

Inability to prevent user is also relevant in a different context. Where the servient tenement has been tenanted throughout the prescriptive period, the servient owner may have been unable to prevent user. In *Pugh v. Savage* [1970] 2 Q.B. 373 at 383 Cross L.J. said:

> [A] distinction can properly be drawn between cases where the tenancy was in existence at the beginning of the period of user and cases where the tenancy came into existence in the course of the period of user. . .
>
> If a tenancy is in existence at the beginning of a period of user, it may well be unreasonable to imply a lost grant by the owner at the beginning of the user. He might not have been able to stop the user, even if he knew about it. If, on the other hand, you get a period of user against an owner or owners without any evidence that they did not know about it when they were in possession, and then afterwards the grant of a tenancy, though undoubtedly such a tenancy during the period of user is a matter to be considered, it would be quite wrong to hold that it is a fatal objection to presuming a grant, or to a claim under the *Prescription Act* 1832 (U.K.).

See also *Diment v. Foot* [1974] 1 W.L.R. 1427; *Piromalli v. Di Masi* [1980] W.A.R. 173; *Connellan Nominees Pty Ltd v. Cameron* [1988] 2 Qd R. 248.

5. User must be by and against the owner of the fee simple. Two separate questions are relevant here:

   (1) What is the position where user is claimed against a tenant of the servient tenement?

   (2) Can a tenant of the dominant tenement acquire an easement by prescription in her or his own right? As to the first question, see above note 4. Note, however, the persuasive critical analysis of authorities by V. T. H. Delany, "Lessees and the Doctrine of Lost Grant" (1958) 74 L.Q.R. 82 and his conclusion that the authorities do not support the principle that user by or against the owner of the freehold is an essential feature of prescriptive easements. This conclusion is supported by dicta by the New South Wales Court of Appeal in *Rodwell v. Evans & Co. Pty Ltd* [1978] 1 N.S.W.L.R. 448 but rejected by Powell J. in *Hamilton v. Joyce* [1984] 3 N.S.W.L.R. 279 at 289-290. Is there any substantial reason why an easement by prescription can be acquired against an owner of the fee simple but not against a lessee under a lease for say 999 years? On the second question (whether an easement can be acquired by prescription where user was by a lessee of the dominant tenement), the position has been restated by Cross L.J. in *Pugh v. Savage* [1970] 2 Q.B. 373 at 380. His Lordship said: "Of course, a tenant cannot by user gain a prescriptive right of way for himself as tenant; but by user over land of a stranger he can gain a prescriptive right of way in fee for his landlord which he can use while he is a tenant and which his landlord can grant to a subsequent tenant. Of course, a tenant cannot gain a prescriptive right for anyone by user over land which itself belongs to his own landlord." See also *Wheaton v. Maple & Co.* [1893] 3 Ch. 48; *Kilgour v. Gaddes* [1904] 1 K.B. 457.

6. There must be continuity of user during the prescriptive period. This requirement is illustrated by *Hollins v. Verney* (1884) 13 Q.B.D. 304. (Although the case concerns the interpretation of the *Prescription Act* 1832 (U.K.), the principle there enunciated has similar application to the presumption of lost modern grant.) There a right of way had been claimed by the defendant over a roadway which he had used for the purpose of carting timber in the periods 1851-1853, 1866-1868 and again in the year before commencement of action.

> LINDLEY L.J. Common sense . . . is enough to shew that in order to establish a right of way under s. 2, it cannot be necessary to prove an actual continuous user of the way by day and by night for 20 years without any cessation whatever. Whatever fairly amounts to an actual enjoyment as of right of way claimed for the full period of 20 years mentioned in s. 2, is sufficient. But it is obvious, and it has often been pointed out, that in the case of a discontinuous easement like a right of way, it is extremely difficult, if not impossible, to say exactly what cessations of actual user are, and what are not, consistent with such an actual enjoyment for the full period of 20 years as the statute requires to establish the right.
>
> . . . No user can be sufficient which does not raise a reasonable inference of such a continuous enjoyment. Moreover, as the enjoyment which is pointed out by the statute is an enjoyment which is open as well as of right, it seems to follow that no actual user can be sufficient to satisfy

the statute, unless during the whole of the statutory term (whether acts of user be proved in each year or not) the user is enough at any rate to carry to the mind of a reasonable person who is in possession of the servient tenement, the fact that a continuous right to enjoyment is being asserted, and ought to be resisted if such right is not recognised, and if resistance to it is intended. Can a user which is confined to the rare occasions in which the alleged right is supposed in this instance to have been exercised, satisfy even this test? It seems to us that it cannot: that it is not, and could not reasonably be treated as the assertion of a continuous right to enjoy; and when there is no assertion by conduct of a continuous right to enjoy, it appears to us that there cannot be an actual enjoyment within the meaning of the statute. Without therefore professing to be able to draw the line sharply between long and short periods of non-user, without holding that non-user for a year or even more is necessarily fatal in all cases, without attempting to define that which the statute has left indefinite, we are of opinion that no jury can properly find that the right claimed by the defendant in this case has been established.

See also *Scott-Whitehead v. National Coal Board* (1985) 53 P. & C.R. 263. In *White v. Taylor (No. 2)* [1969] 1 Ch. 160 at 192 Buckley J., referring to the acquisition of a profit by prescription said: "[T]he user must be shown to have been of such a character, degree and frequency as to indicate an assertion by the claimant of a continuous right, and of a right of the measure of the right claimed."

7. A prescriptive right of way cannot be acquired against the Crown: *Conveyancing Act* 1919 (N.S.W.), s. 178.

8. In *Cargill v. Gotts* [1981] 1 W.L.R. 441 the plaintiff claimed a prescriptive right to take water for the purposes of his farm. On the question of the effect of increase in user over the prescriptive period, Templeman L.J. (Brandon L.J. agreeing) said (at 447):

Grove Farm was and at all times remained a farm. The right to take water from the mill pond was and at all times remained a right to take water for farm purposes. If bullocks were replaced by sheep, if pasture became arable, if beetroot was substituted for barley, the right was asserted for the benefit of Grove Farm, provided that the right asserted over the requisite period of 20 years was a right to take water for farm purposes and that right did not cease to be asserted by fluctuations for time to time in the amount and application of the water, fluctuations which were attributable to changes in the type and method of farming currently pursued at Grove Farm. Water used for crop spraying is just as much used for agricultural purposes as water used for bullocks and the fact that more water may be required for crop spraying than for watering bullocks is not sufficient to destroy or alter the nature of the right asserted or the easement acquired.

Where the prescriptive right claimed was a right to pollute a river or stream, Templeman L.J. recognised some modification to the rule:

If a plaintiff claims a prescriptive right to pollute a stream he must show that he has, for a 20 year period, asserted the right to introduce polluting material of a kind and quantity which produces the effect on the stream which he claims to be entitled to continue.

See also *Scott-Whitehead v. National Coal Board* (1985) 53 P. & C.R. 263 at 272, stating that a right to pollute is restricted to the extent of the pollution when the period of prescription commenced; and *White v. Taylor (No. 2)* [1969] 1 Ch. 160 at 195, holding that enjoyment of a grazing right not in excess of 300 sheep could not support a prescriptive claim to 448 "sheep rights" appertaining to the land.

9. The presumption of lost modern grant cannot be rebutted by showing that no grant has in fact been made (*Angus v. Dalton* (1878) 4 Q.B.D. 162 at 172, 187 per Thesiger and Cotton L.JJ.; *Dalton v. Angus* (1881) 6 App. Cas. 740 at 765, 767, 813, 814 per Lindley and Lopes JJ.; *Tehidy Minerals Ltd v. Norman* [1971] 2 Q.B. 528 at 552 [but see *White v. Taylor (No. 2)* [1969] 1 Ch. 160 at 195]), but it is a good defence that during the prescriptive period no grant could lawfully have been made, for example, because the owner of the servient tenement was a corporation with no power to grant an easement. See as examples, *Neaverson v. Peterborough R.D.C.* [1902] 1 Ch. 557; *Hulley v. Silverspring Bleaching & Dyeing Co. Ltd* [1922] 2 Ch. 268; see also *Thwaites v. Brahe* (1895) 21 V.L.R. 192; cf. *Tuckett v. Brice* [1917] V.L.R. 36.

User pursuant to a mistaken belief that a grant had been made will not prevent the acquisition of an easement by lost modern grant: *Bridle v. Ruby* [1988] 3 W.L.R. 279. Compare *Hamilton v. Joyce* [1984] 3 N.S.W.L.R. 279 referred to above p. 269.

10. The right claimed must be by way of easement not adverse possession. In principle, the distinction between prescriptive easements and rights obtained by adverse possession may be reasonably clear: see above p. 258. In practice the distinction is not easily applied. The Privy Council decision in *Attorney-General (Southern Nigeria) v. John Holt & Co. Ltd* [1915] A.C. 599 is illustrative.

The respondents there for 50 years had used a strip of reclaimed crown land for the storage of goods. The respondents' land was bounded by the sea and over a period of time preventive work was carried out to prevent erosion. This eventually led to reclamation of land which had originally been below high water mark. Stores and sheds were built on the reclaimed land. As the respondents were unable to prove 60 years adverse possession of the reclaimed land they relied on their conduct as giving rise to a prescriptive easement. The Privy Council, although finding for the respondents on different grounds, accepted the Crown's contention that (at 617-618):

> [T]he use to which the land was put by the respondents . . . could not be the foundation of any easement, as it was not a right assumed to be taken or asserted over the land of another; the possession founded upon was possession founded upon as owner thereof . . . It seems to be undoubtedly true that what was done by the respondents was done by them as in their opinion upon their own lands . . . An easement, however, is constituted over a servient tenement in favour of a dominant tenement. In substance the owner of the dominant tenement throughout admits that the property is in another, and that the right being built up or asserted is the right over the property of that other. In the present case this was not so.

This should be contrasted with the cases concerning joint or exclusive user, where the appropriate test relates to quantum of user: see above p. 238. For further discussion, see Goodman, "Adverse Possession or Prescription? Problems of Conflict" (1968) 32 Conv. 270; *Riley v. Pentilla* [1974] V.R. 547.

11. The absence of an easement for support may not preclude action in tort, for example, for negligence: *Stoneman v. Lyons* (1975) 133 C.L.R. 550 at 567; *Bognuda v. Upton and Shearer Ltd* [1973] N.Z.L.R. 741. This was doubted in *Kebewar Pty Ltd v. Harkin* (1987) 9 N.S.W.L.R. 738 at 743 which canvasses the various bases upon which a right of support might be argued, such as *Wheeldon v. Burrows* (1979) 12 Ch. D. 31, see above p. 258, duty not to derogate from grant and prescription.

6. By estoppel

See *Dabbs v. Seaman* (1925) 36 C.L.R. 538, extracted below; *Crabb v. Arun District Council* [1976] 1 Ch. 179; *Dewhirst v. Edwards* [1983] 1 N.S.W.L.R. 34 below p. 287.

D. EXTENT AND DURATION OF USER

The extent of user permitted by the easement will vary depending upon the mode of acquisition of the easement. In the case of an express grant or reservation, the extent of rights granted or reserved will depend upon the construction of the deed. If the grant is in wide terms general development will be allowed to accommodate changing usage of the dominant tenement: see *White v. Grand Hotel, Eastbourne, Ltd* [1913] 1 Ch. 113 below p. 277. Where the extent of user is not indicated in the deed, the physical layout of the premises may indicate that the mode and extent of user is to be limited: *Todrick v. Western National Omnibus Co. Ltd* [1934] Ch. 561 below p. 274. In respect of easements by prescription and easements arising under an implied grant or reservation, no development is allowed; user is restricted to those purposes necessary at the time of acquisition of the easement: *Corporation of London v. Riggs* (1880) 13 Ch. D. 798 above p. 248; *R.P.C. Holdings Ltd v. Rogers* [1953] 1 All E.R. 1029 below p. 279. Even authorised user, must not be excessive: *Todrick's* case; see also *Jelbert v. Davis* [1968] 1 W.L.R. 589 below p. 277. As to the effect of enlargement of the dominant tenement see *Graham v. Philcox* [1984] 3 W.L.R. 150 and comment [1985] Conv. 60.

Whatever the method of acquisition of an easement, whether by express grant, by implication or by prescription, development is allowed in the type of vehicle used so that a carriageway used for horsedrawn vehicles can be used by cars: *Lock v. Abercester* [1939] 1 Ch. 861; *Sunset Properties Pty Ltd v. Johnson* (1975) 3 B.P.R. 9185 per Holland J.

An easement or profit may be created by grant for the period of any freehold estate or for a term of years. Holders of limited interests can create easements for periods not exceeding their interest. As to acquisition of prescriptive easements by and against holders of limited interests, see above p. 271.

1. Express grant or reservation

TODRICK v. WESTERN NATIONAL OMNIBUS CO.

Court of Appeal [1934] Ch. 561

[In 1921, a house and land were conveyed to the plaintiff. The property included a garage built at the eastern end, and a private roadway leading from it to a highway on the west. By the conveyance, the vendor reserved to himself and his successors a perpetual right of way along the road, with power to extend it to certain land, east of the property conveyed, retained by him and coloured blue on the plan annexed. The vendor, having subsequently bought other land north of the blue land a deed was executed in 1926, substituting a right to extend the road to this land for the right to extend it to the blue land, and having the result that extension to the blue land could only be effected across an intervening strip of the newly bought land. The defendants, having purchased all the land belonging to the owner of the dominant tenement, built on the blue land a motor omnibus garage and extended the roadway to it. The ground on which this garage was built, being higher than the plaintiff's property, a gradual slope was obtained by building a concrete ramp which continued the roadway on to the plaintiff's land. In this action, the plaintiff contended that no right of way existed, as the alleged right pertained only to the blue land, to which there was no direct access from the roadway. He also contended that the user of the alleged right had been excessive by reason of the building of the ramp and the use by motor buses. Farwell J. at first instance held in favour of the plaintiff. On appeal:]

LORD HANWORTH M.R. [His Lordship after setting out the facts continued:] It is not suggested that there is any authority which lays down the proposition that in order that there should be a right of way the dominant land which is to enjoy the right of way must be contiguous to the land over which the right of way is to be enjoyed. I do not find that this proposition is established by *Ackroyd v. Smith* (1850) 10 C.B. 164; 138 E.R. 68, a case which is not easy to understand but which, I think, is properly and full explained by Mellish L.J. in *Thorpe v. Brumfitt* (1873) 8 Ch. App. 650 when he said that the words "for all purposes" were interpreted in the judgment of the court then delivered by Cresswell J. as being so wide as to include purposes that had no connection with the occupation of the piece of ground to which the right of way purported to be attached. Cresswell J. had said (*Ackroyd v. Smith* (1850) 10 C.B. 188; 138 E.R. 68): "It is not in the power of a vendor to create any rights not connected with the use or enjoyment of the land, and annex them to it, nor can the owner of land render it subject to a new series of burthen, so as to bind it in the hands of an assignee." I do not think it is necessary to examine that case further, because it does not really assist us in the question we have to determine.

Dealing with the point upon which Farwell J. founded himself, namely, that there must be contiguity between the dominant and the servient tenements for the purpose of a right of way, I find no such principle established in any of the cases. I think it would be unfortunate if I endeavoured to lay down a rule which might cause much difficulty having regard to the multifarious rights of way to be found in the country.

I think the true test which we have to apply is that which is broadly stated in *Gale on Easements* (11th ed.), p. 19: "So in English law an easement must be connected with the enjoyment of the dominant tenement and must be for its benefit."

. . . Hamilton L.J., as he then was, in *Attorney-General v. Horner (No. 2)* [1913] 2 Ch. 140 . . . said (at 196): "Now it is well settled that an easement appurtenant must be for the benefit of the inheritance to which it is appurtenant. It must be 'beneficial to the land and beneficial in respect of the ownership of the land, and not beneficial to any other person': *Bailey v. Stephens* 12 C.B. (N.S.) 112 per Willes J.: 'It must have some natural connection with the estate as being for its benefit': per Byles J." That seems to give the real test, which does not require physical contiguity. Applying that test to the present case the only consideration is whether or not there can be a better enjoyment of the blue land by virtue of this right of way, whether the right of way is beneficial in respect of the ownership of the land.

Now, as Romer L.J. has pointed out, supposing there is not physical contiguity, yet if the owner of the blue land can exercise the right of way that he has secured by this reservation why should he not be entitled to exercise it? The fact that he may have some difficulty in obtaining access to some intervening portion ought not to militate against his enjoyment of a right which is of such a nature that it is beneficial to the blue land which he occupies, and has a natural connection with the property as being for its benefit in the sense that it provides a speedier and easier access to the highway called Skidden Hill, to which he may wish to pass. Upon those authorities, therefore, I come to the conclusion that Farwell J. has not advised himself correctly in holding that by reason of the absence of physical contiguity there cannot be a valid grant of the right of way. . . .

Now comes the next question: Are the defendants entitled to do what they have done with this right of way? It is suggested that they ought not to be tied down to the original user of the right of way, such as walking along the road over which they exercise the right, or passing along it with horse or carriage, but that a development should be allowed, such as was given effect to with limitations in *Dand v. Kingscote* (1840) 6 M. & W. 174; 151 E.R. 370, I desire, however, to point out with regard to that case that while it was held that there could be what is called a railway—I should prefer to call it a tramway—on which tubs could pass, there was also given a right of compensation to the plaintiff in respect of the excessive user of the land such as, for instance, putting ditches and fences to the railway which do not appear to have been found necessary. Therefore *Dand v. Kingscote* does not justify any and every user of the right of way. Nor is that justification to be found in *Abson v. Fenton* (1823) 1 B. & C. 195 at 203; 107 E.R. 73 at 76. As was pointed out by Lord Tenterden, as he afterwards was, the question will be: "Whether the mode adopted has been such as a prudent and rational person would have adopted if he had been making the road over his own land, and not over the land of another." The test he applies is: "to exclude all wanton, capricious, and causeless injury to the owners of the allotments; and, on the other hand, to admit of an exercise of the right reserved by the statute in such a manner as may make the right beneficial to the lord."

In the present case, having to balance the rights of both parties, the owner of the dominant and the owner of the servient tenements, I find that the owner of the servient tenement has had a ramp put up on the surface of the land which belongs to him and that it circumscribes the area available to him for the purpose of washing his car or of getting his car out of the garage to the extent that it has so shortened the area in front of the garage as to make it difficult for him to use the garage freely and to take his car in and out of it with any freedom. In that sense there has been a distinct limitation imposed upon the plaintiff of his rights in respect of the garage and land which he owns. The defendants have for their own purposes put up upon the land belonging to the plaintiff this ramp in order to use the gradient which leads up to the garage upon their own ground. If the gradient had been steeper it would have been possible to commence the ramp at the point where the wall intersects the two properties of the plaintiff and the defendants, but rather than do that they have put upon this structure without bearing in mind the rights of the plaintiff over the land. It is an exercise of the right of way which is not merely a development such as occurred in the case of *Dand v. Kingscote*, but an intrusion on the rights and property of the plaintiff. In those circumstances there ought to be a mandatory injunction to restrain the defendants from doing what they have done and to compel them to remove the ramp which they have superimposed upon the plaintiff's land to their own advantage and to the disadvantage of the plaintiff.

Then comes the last question that Mr Spens does not press—namely, whether the right of way included a right to take the omnibuses through the gateway and along the right of way. Having regard to the fact that the omnibuses when they pass through the gateway would only have a margin of one and a half inches on either side, it is quite plain that the right of way was never intended for such vehicles, and I think Mr Spens was quite right in not pressing for his clients a claim to a right to use the right of way in such a matter as to introduce these heavy motor vehicles on to it for the purpose of the defendant's transport services.

The result is that the appeal fails.

[The judgments of Romer and Maugham L.JJ. who substantially agreed with Lord Hanworth M.R. have been omitted.]

NOTES

1. In *St Edmundsbury and Ipswich Diocesan Board of Finance v. Clark (No. 2)* [1975] 1 W.L.R. 468 the Court of Appeal considered the proper approach upon the construction of a conveyance containing a reservation of a right of way. Sir John Pennycuick, delivering the judgment of the Court of Appeal said:

> [T]he proper approach is that upon which the court construes all documents; that is to say, one must construe the document according to the natural meaning of the words contained in the document as a whole, read in the light of surrounding circumstances. In *Cannon v. Villars* (1878) 8 Ch. D. 415 this principle was applied by Sir George Jessel M.R., to rights of way in a passage which has often been quoted and never, so far as we are aware, questioned. He said (at 420):
>
>> [T]he grant of a right of way per se and nothing else may be a right of footway, or it may be a general right of way, that is a right of way not only for people on foot but for people on horseback, for carts, carriages, and other vehicles. Which it is, is a question of construction of the grant, and that construction will of course depend on the circumstances surrounding, so to speak, the execution of the instrument. Now one of those circumstances, and a very material circumstance, is the nature of the locus in quo over which the right of way is granted."
>
> Then, after certain illustrations, he goes on:
>
>> Prima facie the grant of a right of way is the grant of a right of way having regard to the nature of the road over which it is granted and the purpose for which it is intended to be used; and both those circumstances may be legitimately called in aid in determining whether it is a general right of way, or a right of way restricted to footpassengers, or restricted to footpassengers and horsemen or cattle, which is generally called a drift way, or a general right of way for carts, horses, carriages, and everything else.
>
> Mr Vinelott contended that the proper method of construction is first to construe the words of the instrument in isolation and then look at the surrounding circumstances in order to see whether they cut down the prima facie meaning of the words. It seems to us that this approach is contrary to well-established principle. It is no doubt true that in order to construe an instrument one looks first at the instrument and no doubt one may form a preliminary impression upon such inspection. But it is not until one has considered the instrument and the surrounding circumstances in conjunction that one concludes the process of construction. Of course, one may have words so unambiguous that no surrounding circumstances could affect their construction.

But that is emphatically not the position here, where the reservation is in the loosest terms, that is, simply "right of way". Indeed, those words call aloud for an examination of the surrounding circumstances and, with all respect, Mr Vinelott's contention, even if well founded, seems to us to lead nowhere in the present case.

2. In *White v. Grand Hotel, Eastbourne, Ltd* [1913] 1 Ch. 113 the defendants' predecessor in title was granted a right of way over the plaintiffs' property. At the time of the grant the premises were used as a private dwelling house and garden but had recently been converted into a garage and premises used in conjunction with the defendants' hotel business. The plaintiffs objected to the use of the right of way by hotel visitors and also objected to the defendants' conduct in altering the gateway to facilitate the passage of vehicles. The plaintiffs sought an injunction restraining the defendants from using the private road as a carriageway for the passage of motor cars and other vehicles and for an order that the defendants should rebuild part of a wall which had been pulled down.

COZENS-HARDY M.R. The plaintiffs' main point was this: they said that the right of way, which was granted under circumstances which I shall state hereafter, was limited in its nature; that it was only a right of way for what I may call domestic purposes as distinct from trade purposes; and that it was only for such use as could reasonably be expected to be in the contemplation of the parties at the time when the defendants' house, St Vincent Lodge, was a private residence, and ought not to be altered now that St Vincent Lodge is turned into a garage. We . . . have come to the conclusion that there is no ground for limiting the right of way in the manner suggested. It is not a right of way claimed by prescription. It is a right of way claimed under a grant, and, that being so, the only thing that the court has to do it to construe the grant; and unless there is some limitation to be found in the grant, in the nature of the width of the road or something of that kind, full effect must be given to the grant, and we cannot consider the subsequent user as in any way sufficient to cut down the generality of the grant.

His Lordship then considered the facts of the case and held that the defendants had no right to any access except through a gate in the position of the 9 ft gate which formerly stood there, and that the plaintiffs were entitled to an injunction to restrain them from exercising a right of way through a new and wider gate recently erected.

3. In *Jelbert v. Davis* [1968] 1 W.L.R. 589, the plaintiff, under a conveyance of land, was granted the land "together with the right of way at all times and for all purposes over the driveway retained by the vendor leading to the main road in common with all other persons having the like right subject to the purchaser or his successors in title paying a proper proportion of the cost of repairing and maintaining it in repair". At the time of the grant the plaintiff used his land for agricultural purposes; he later obtained planning approval to establish a camping area of up to 200 sites. The owners of the servient tenements (the defendants in the action) over which the right of way existed, objected to the use of the land by cars and caravans and put up notices saying "Private drive. No entry to campers or caravans". The plaintiff brought proceedings for nuisance and slander of title. The owners of the servient tenement counterclaimed for an injunction restraining the plaintiff from using the right of way in connection with the tourist, caravan and camping site.

LORD DENNING M.R. The issue has been exceptionally well argued before us by counsel on both sides. It turns eventually on the true construction of the grant contained in the conveyance of 5 October 1961. In particular, of the words "the right of way at all times and for all purposes over the driveway leading to the main road". What is the extent of that right when the land is changed from agricultural use to a caravan and camping site? The change will mean no doubt that a *different* kind of vehicle will be used for different purposes. But that change is, by itself, quite permissible.

It is covered by the words of the grant "at all times and for all purposes". That is shown in *White v. Grand Hotel, Eastbourne, Ltd* [1913] 1 Ch. 113. In that case a private dwelling-house was turned into a hotel. That meant a different user. But it was held to be within the grant. That case was applied in *Robinson v. Bailey* [1948] 2 All E.R. 791. In that case a plot of land, which was expected to be used as a dwelling-house, was turned into a place for storing building materials. The different user was held to be within the right of way. In view of those cases [counsel for the defendants] conceded that he could not complain that the way to be used for caravans instead of agricultural vehicles, such as carts or tractors. He could not object, for instance, to a user in connection with ten caravans. But he did object, he said, to excessive user.

In my opinion a grant in these terms does not authorise an unlimited use of the way. Although the right is granted "at all times and for all purposes", nevertheless it is not a sole right. It is a right "in common with all other persons having the like right". It must not be used so as to interfere unreasonably with the use by those other persons, that is, with their use of it as they do now, or as they may do lawfully in the future. The only way in which the rights of all can be reconciled is by holding that none of them must use the way excessively.

More generally, the true proposition is that no one of those entitled to the right of way must use it to an extent which is beyond anything which was contemplated at the time of the grant. The law on this subject was stated by Farwell J. in *Todrick v. Western Omnibus Co. Ltd* [1934] 1 Ch. 190 which was approved by the Court of Appeal [1934] 1 Ch. 561. Farwell J. said (at 206-207): "In considering whether a particular use of a right of this kind is a proper use or not, I am entitled to take into consideration the circumstances of the case, the situation of the parties and the situation of the land at the time when the grant was made . . . a grant of this kind must be construed as a grant for all purposes within the reasonable contemplation of the parties at the time of the grant." In that case Farwell J. held (and the Court of Appeal approved it) that a way, which was only 7 ft 9 ins wide, could not be used for omnibuses which were 7 ft 6 ins wide, leaving only 1½ ins clearance on each side between the gateposts. That was obviously not within the contemplation of the parties. We were also referred to a Canadian case, *Malden Farms Ltd v. Nicholson* (1956) 3 D.L.R. (2d) 236. There was a right of way alongside a lake which was at the time unspoilt land. The lake-shore was transformed into a camping site and a beach resort. The judges in Canada applied *Todrick's* case and granted an injunction against the way being used for the public bathing beach and picnic ground or otherwise using the way so as to substantially interfere with the other users' use of it.

The question thus turns on the facts and circumstances of the particular case. Is the proposed use so extensive as to be outside the reasonable contemplation of the parties at the time the grant was made? This way is 180 yds long. As you enter from the road there are stone gateposts. They are only 10 ft apart. Once you are through the gateposts and come into the drive, there is a hard metalled way. It has guttering on its outer fringes which is really part of the metalled way. It widens out from 10 ft at the gateposts up to 14 ft 6 ins and 15 ft inside. . . . It is bordered by trees for the whole of the 180 yds of its length. If 200 units, such as caravans, dormobiles or cars, used this caravan site, there would be 600 people there. All those people may go out in a car two or three times a day. In the morning to the beach. In the afternoon for an outing; and such like. All of them would be using this driveway.

It seems to me that user on that scale would interfere greatly with the rights of [the defendants]. [The second defendant] lives at the lodge at the end of the driveway. He has his grandchildren there in the summer. He farms land further up the lane. If [he] wishes to bring a combine harvester up the lane or a cattle lorry, or any other vehicle, he would find it very difficult indeed when there are 600 people in the camp. His life in the lodge would be far from peaceful. [The first defendant] has a cottage close to the lane and is interested in the hotel nearby. He has to go up and down the lane to get to his cottage. He could not fail to be much inconvenienced. I must say that, on the evidence, I think that if this caravan site is used to its full intensity for 200 units, there would be such congestion that it would interfere with the reasonable use by [the defendants] of their own right of way: and it would be a nuisance to them.

In my opinion, therefore, the proposed user for 200 units would be excessive. It would be far beyond anything contemplated at the time of the grant. I would point out, however, that there is a possible way in which the parties may resolve the difficulty. They are both very reasonable people. It appears that under this deed there is, some distance away, a special 10 ft right of way given to [the plaintiff] whereby he can get access to the main road by another route, not using this lane. [Counsel for the defendants] acknowledges that the [plaintiff] can use the alternative route for motor vehicles. . . . That would reduce considerably any nuisance or interference to the defendants. No planning permission has yet been given for this access; but it might be. So far as this lane is concerned, however, the parties must abide by the law as we declare it to be. I am quite clear that 200 units is excessive. We were asked to state what number is permissible. I am afraid that we cannot give any guidance on this point. It is a matter of fact and degree depending on what happens. Beyond saying that 200 units are too many, I am afraid we must leave it to the parties themselves to work out what is a reasonable user.

I think, therefore, that the appeal should be allowed. We will not grant an injunction but make a declaration. . . .

The judgments of Danckwerts and Edmund Davis L.JJ., which agree substantially with that of Lord Denning M.R. have been omitted.

4. See also *Rosling v. Pinnegar* (1986) 54 P. & C.R. 124; cf. *National Trust for Places of Historic Interest or Natural Beauty* [1987] 1 W.L.R. 907.

MERCANTILE GENERAL LIFE REASSURANCE CO. (AUST.) LTD v. PERMANENT TRUSTEE AUSTRALIA LTD

Supreme Court (1989) C.C.H. N.S.W. Conv. R. 55-441

See above p. 231

NOTE

In *Cannon v. Villars* (1878) 8 Ch. D. 415 at 421 Sir George Jessel said:

[I]f the road is not to a dwelling-house but to a factory, or a place used for business purposes which would require heavy weights to be brought to it, or to a wool warehouse which would require bags or packages of wool to be brought to it, then a grant of right of way would include a right to use it for reasonable purposes, sufficient for the purposes of the business, which would include the right of bringing up carts and wagons at reasonable times for the purpose of the business.

This principle was applied in *Bulstrode v. Lambert* [1953] 1 W.L.R. 245, which involved an express grant of a right of way to auction rooms. Upjohn J. said:

When I look at this reservation I see that the whole object of it is for the purpose of the vendor, his workmen, and others obtaining access to the auction mart. What is the object of that? It is to get access to business premises, and in particular to a place where goods are going to be auctioned and sold. The plaintiff can do it with or without vehicles. Therefore, as I have already held, he can, in my judgment, bring goods in the vehicles to his auction mart. If he is entitled to do that, then he must of necessity . . . be entitled to unload them. And if he is entitled to unload them he must, per contra, be entitled to load them.

In my judgment, therefore, the vehicles must be entitled to remain in the yard for such time as is necessary to enable the plaintiff to enjoy his easement of bringing vehicles into the yard; that is, for such time as it takes to load or unload the vehicles. It is only an incident of the right of way expressly granted and may be described as ancillary to that easement, because without that right he cannot substantially enjoy that which has been reserved to him.

For other illustrations of incidental rights, see *Deanshaw and Deanshaw v. Marshall* (1978) 20 S.A.S.R. 146; *National Trust for Places of Historic Interest or National Beauty* [1987] 1 W.L.R. 907.

2. Implied grant or reservation

NOTES

1. See *Corporation of London v. Riggs* (1880) 13 Ch. D. 798, above p. 248.

2. In respect of implied grants, although the purchaser of the dominant tenement is entitled to the benefit of all continuous and apparent easements reasonably necessary to the enjoyment of the dominant tenement, his rights of user are restricted to those purposes reasonably necessary at the time of the grant. No development is allowed: *Milner's Safe Co. Ltd v. Great Northern and City Railway* [1907] 1 Ch. 208. See also *Stevens v. Allan* (1955) 58 W.A.L.R. 1 at 19-20; *Sunset Properties Pty Ltd v. Johnston* (1975) 3 B.P.R. 9185.

3. Prescription

NOTES AND QUESTIONS

1. Where an easement is created by prescription, user is restricted to that which was necessary for the purposes of the dominant tenement at the time of acqusition. In *R.P.C. Holdings v. Rogers* [1953] 1 All E.R. 1029 a prescriptive easement appurtenant to land used during the prescribed period for agricultural purposes was held not to allow user for the purposes of a camping site.

2. In *Woodhouse & Co. Ltd v. Kirkland (Derby) Ltd* [1970] 1 W.L.R. 1185, Plowman J. had to consider a prescriptive right of access. His Lordship held that increase in user of the prescriptive easement was permissible. His Lordship said (at 1190):

Distinction has to be drawn between a mere increase in user and a user of a different kind or for a different purpose. The former is not, in my judgment, within the principle, the latter is.

His Lordship (at 1192) refrained from considering whether an increase in user, if very great, can ever amount to excessive user. In the earlier case of *British Railways Board v. Glass* [1965] 1 Ch. 538 Harman L.J. at (562-563) and Davies L.J. (at 567-568) held that an increase in user was permissible provided that it did not reflect a change in the character of the dominant tenement. Lord Denning M.R. dissenting, suggested much greater limitations on the rights of the dominant owner. His Lordship said (at 551):

> [W]hen you acquire a right of way by prescription, you are not entitled to change the character of your land so as substantially to increase or alter the burden upon the servient tenement. If you have a right of way for your pasture land, you cannot turn it into a manufactory and claim a right of way for the purposes of the factory. If you have a right of way by prescription for one house, you cannot build two more houses on the land and claim a right of way for the purposes of these houses also. I think this rule is not confined to the character of the property. It extends also to the intensity of user. If you use your land for years as a caravan site for six caravans and thereby gain a prescriptive right over a legal crossing, you are not thereby entitled to put 30 caravans on the site and claim a right for those 30.

Could it be argued that a very substantial increase in user may reflect a change in the character of the dominant tenement? See *Rugby Joint Water Board v. Walters* [1967] Ch. 397.

In the case of a claimed prescriptive right to pollute water, the right would be restricted to the limits of the pollution when the period of prescription commenced: see *Cargill v. Gotts* [1981] 1 W.L.R. 441 referred to above p. 272.

E. EASEMENTS, PROFITS AND THE TORRENS SYSTEM

Sections 46 and 47 of the *Real Property Act* 1900 (N.S.W.) make provision for registration of easements and profits and their notification on the Register. Section 46 provides that where an easement or profit à prendre affecting land under the Act is intended to be created, the proprietor shall execute a transfer in the approved form. Section 47(1), applying to easements and profits appurtenant, requires the Registrar-General "in addition to any other recording by this Act required, [to] record particulars of the dealing creating the easement or profit à prendre in the folio of the Register evidencing title to the land to which the easement or profit à prendre is annexed or with which it is used and enjoyed". Although the section does not expressly require notation on the title of the servient tenement, it is the clear duty of the Registrar-General to do so: *Papadopoulos v. Goodwin* [1983] 2 N.S.W.L.R. 113. With respect to profits in gross, s. 47(5) provides that: "The Registrar-General may record a dealing effecting a registered easement or profit à prendre in gross by making such records in the Register as he considers appropriate." One may suppose that a recording on folio of the Register for the land the subject of the right would be essential.

Difficulties arise in determining the extent to which the registered proprietor of an estate takes subject to unregistered easements (including easements arising by prescription and implication). In New South Wales the *Real Property Act* 1900 s. 42(1)(b) provides that a registered proprietor shall, except in the case of fraud, hold her or his estate subject to such encumbrances, liens, estates, or interests as may be recorded in the Register, but absolutely free from all other encumbrances, liens, estates, or interests whatever except: "42(1)(b) in the case of the omission or misdescription of any easement or profit à prendre created in or existing upon any land."

The interpretation of s. 42(1)(b) is dealt with in the following case extracts.

AUSTRALIAN HI-FI PUBLICATIONS PTY LTD v. GEHL

Court of Appeal [1979] 2 N.S.W.L.R. 618

MAHONEY J.A. (with whom Reynolds and Samuels JJ.A. concurred). The only question argued on this appeal was whether an easement (conveniently described as a *Wheeldon v. Burrows* (1879) 12 Ch. D. 31 easement) not noted on the relevant certificate of title can be enforced against a person who, after creation of that easement, becomes registered as proprietor of the servient tenement under the *Real Property Act* 1900 (N.S.W.).

There is no relevant dispute as to the facts. They are set forth in detail in the judgment of Helsham C.J. in Eq., and it will be sufficient, for the purposes of this appeal, to summarise them briefly.

The land comprising the suggested dominant and servient tenements ("the relevant land") has been registered under the Torrens system since about 1900. In about 1928, it passed into the ownership of persons described as "the Savage family". Two sets of buildings were erected on the relevant land: a block of shops was erected in earlier years and, in about 1966-1977, an office block was erected. In 1969, the relevant land was divided into two lots: lot 1 comprised the shops and some of the land at the rear of them; and lot 2 comprised the office block and the land adjoining it. In 1971, the Savage family sold lot 1 to the defendant and his wife. In 1978, they sold lot 2 to the plaintiff. The transfers consequent upon those sales were, in due course, registered. No reference was made in respect of contracts or transfers, or in the certificates of title for lots 1 and 2, to any matter relating to the relevant easement.

Helsham C.J. in Eq. held (and it is not now contested) that, prior to 1971 and thereafter until the events which precipitated the present proceedings, the persons who, as owners or lessees of the land comprised in lot 1, used portion of lot 2, and had used it in such a way that, had the relevant land been under the old system title, the basis would have been laid for the implication of an easement in accordance with the principles discussed in *Wheeldon v. Burrows* (1879) 12 Ch. D. 31. His Honour was of opinion that on that basis, there would have come into existence an easement appurtenant to lot 1 over the relevant portion of lot 2.

The present proceedings was commenced because the plaintiff sought an injunction restraining the defendant from trespassing upon lot 2, the trespass arising from the attempt by the defendant to exercise the easement claimed by him to exist over the relevant portion of that lot. His Honour held that, because of the effect of the *Real Property Act* 1900 (N.S.W.), s. 42(b), the defendant had no such easement; and made orders in favour of the plaintiff accordingly. The defendant has appealed against those orders.

In my opinion, the matter is determined in the plaintiff's favour by s. 42. . . . The opening words of s. 42 would, according to their terms, operate in the present case so that the plaintiff would hold its land free from the easement claimed by the defendant. Therefore, the defendant can avoid the effect of the section only if the present is a "case of the omission . . . of" the relevant easement within para. (b); or if, for some other reason, s. 42 is to be seen as inapplicable.

The meaning of "omission": According to what is, I think, its primary meaning, "omission" involves two things: that something is "not there", and that it is so because something which should have been done was not done: see, for example, the discussion of "omission" in *R. v. Phillips* (1971) 45 A.L.J.R. 467 at 470, 471, 477. It is, in a particular context, possible to see the term as meaning only that the relevant thing is "not there"; this may be the meaning adopted by Ferguson J. in the dissenting judgment in *Triest Investments Pty Ltd v. Watson* (1963) 64 S.R. (N.S.W.) 98 at 106, 107; see also *Wilkinson v. Spooner* [1957] Tas. S.R. 121 at 134. But I do not think that that is the meaning intended in s. 42.

. . . Each of the three paragraphs has, from its original enactment, looked to some defect in the operation of the system of registration of title. Section 42(a) envisages that there will have been two certificates issued in respect of the same estate or interests; s. 42(c) refers to a "wrong description" of land in documents under the Act; and s. 42(b) refers to "misdescription" of an easement. These paragraphs, in my opinion, look to the operation of the Act and, at least primarily, its operation by the Registrar-General, and they take effect if what ought to have been done under the Act, or by the Registrar-General, has not been done. I think "omission" in s. 42(b) should be given a corresponding meaning. . . .

It is arguable that s. 42(b) is not confined to what is "not there" because of the failure to discharge some form of obligation, and that it may also extend to a case where a thing is "not there" merely because a person did not do something which he was entitled to do: see, for example, *Eastwood v. Ashton* [1915] A.C. 900 at 908, 913, 917, 921. It is undesirable to attempt to delimit exhaustively the particular circumstances which may constitute "omission" within s. 42(b). Even were the terms to have this wider meaning, it would not avail the defendant in the present case. There was, in this case, no opportunity for the Act, or the Registrar-General, to operate on the relevant easement. The easement was not brought before the Registrar-General or otherwise brought forward for operation of the Act at any time prior to the plaintiff becoming registered as the proprietor. As Jordan C.J. said in *R. v. Earsman* (1936) 53 W.N. (N.S.W.) 118: "A person cannot, in any ordinary sense, be said to omit to do something which he had no opportunity of doing."

This construction of s. 42 accords, in my opinion, with the legislative intention to be derived from the terms of that section and from the Act generally. The intention of the Torrens legislation is, as has been authoritatively determined, that title be conferred by registration and that the registered proprietor hold, subject to the Register, free from competing interests of the kind referred to in, for example, s. 42: *Fraser v. Walker* [1967] A.C. 569; *Breskvar v. Wall* (1971) 126 C.L.R. 376. This does not mean that a party may not enforce any unregistered interests against a registered proprietor. The right to enforce, for example, equitable rights existing personally against the registered proprietor is well established: *Barry v. Heider* (1914) 19 C.L.R. 197 at 213. But the right here in question is not argued to be within this category. Whether a *Wheeldon v. Burrows* (1879) 12 Ch. D. 31 easement creates a legal or an equitable interest, it is not an easement which is, in the relevant sense, personal against the subsequent owner of the servient tenement.

Apart from matters such as these, the intention of the Act is that, in general, the registered proprietor shall hold subject only to the Register. Section 42 is an essential part of the statutory machinery by which that intention is carried into effect. The section, not unnaturally, provides for exceptions to what otherwise would be its operation, and s. 42(b) is one of these. If those exceptions be confined to cases where the Act has not functioned properly, there is an understandable qualification of the section. But if "omission" be given the wider meaning suggested by the defendant, the rationale of the paragraph is not so easily seen.

The argument that such an exception should be created has been put, in substance, upon the following basis: that interests such as *Wheeldon v. Burrows* easements are interests well recognised by the law; that, as they are incapable of being registered or noted on the Register, they will, unless protected by s. 42(b), be incapable of existing; and that it could not have been the intention of the Act to destroy such interest. But, in my opinion, such an argument involves at least two difficulties.

First, the proposition that a *Wheeldon v. Burrows* easement cannot be registered or noted is true only in a qualified sense. I shall (without entering on a full examination of the power of the Registrar-General in respect of the Register) assume that the interest arising from *Wheeldon v. Burrows* circumstances cannot, as such and without more, be noted on the Register. But in this it is in no different position from other interests, which, in respect of land under the old system title, could be validly created. It is in the same position in this regard as, for example, the interest which would be created by the express grant by deed of an easement in the same terms as that arising by implications from *Wheeldon v. Burrows* circumstances: such an interest cannot, as such and without more, be noted on the Register. But that does not mean that, in the ordinary case, the notation of such interest cannot be achieved. If, for consideration, there was an express grant of such an easement, the court would normally direct that the grantor do all things necessary (including execution of appropriate documents) to secure to the grantee the benefit of such a right under the Act. *Wheeldon v. Burrows* (1879) 12 Ch. D. 31 is based on the principle that the grantor may not derogate from its grant: see the cases collected in an article entitled "Non-Derogation from Grant" by Elliott: (1964) 80 L.Q.R. 244. I do not doubt (and the defendant has accepted) that such orders could have been made against the Savage family in the present case.

Secondly, in considering the effect of s. 42 upon unregistered interests, there must be borne in mind the distinction between the persons by whom those interests were created and subsequent registered proprietors. As between the parties actually involved in the *Wheeldon v. Burrows* circumstances, rights will be created. Rights, such as those which arose upon the sale of the land by the Savage family to the defendant and his wife, would normally be within the class of rights existing personally against the Savage family as proprietors and so enforceable against them notwithstanding s. 42. Those rights would not be enforceable against the subsequent registered proprietor taking without fraud; the existence of such rights is proscribed by s. 42 to that extent. There is, in my opinion, nothing special in this, such as would warrant the creation of an exception to the ordinary effect of s. 42 or the extension of the term "omission" to make such rights enforceable against the subsequent registered proprietor. I see no reason why, for example, a *Wheeldon v. Burrows* interest should be in a better position than the interest which would have arisen had the Savage family, by deed, purported to grant to the defendant exactly a right in similar terms. The right created by that deed would not be enforceable against a subsequent registered proprietor.

I, therefore, do not think that the term "omission" should be given the meaning contended for by the defendant.

Are such easements outside s. 42?: The defendant's argument was, in essence, that s. 42 should be held not to apply to *Wheeldon v. Burrows* easements, that is, that such interests should be seen as implied exceptions to the operation of that and other relevant sections. In support of this argument, the defendant submitted that the easements were not able to be registered or noted and that, this being so, it would be anomolous for s. 42 (which operates against unregistered interests) to affect such interests because they are not registered. He submitted that there are other interests which, though not registered or capable of registration, are accepted as exceptions to s. 42, and that the present interest should be so treated.

Several things may be said as to this argument. First, the fact that there are interests which, though not registered, have been held to be outside s. 42, does not assist the defendant unless, at least, the reason why those interests have been held to be outside s. 42 can be called in aid in relation to *Wheeldon v. Burrows* easements. Some of such interests owe their operation to the provisions of other statutes, for example, the *Local Government Act* 1919 (N.S.W.), as amended, s. 152 (municipal rates); s. 42 must be accommodated to the terms of any other relevant statute: see *Miller v. Minister of Mines* [1963] A.C. 484 at 498. The defendant referred also to public rights . . . But considerations which are sufficient to take public rights outside s. 42 are not available in respect of interests of the present kind.

Secondly, as far as counsel have been able to ascertain, the course of decision in this State, with one possible exception, has been that private rights, not created by statute, have not been held to be outside the operations of s. 42. The enforcement of rights existing personally against a registered proprietor is, as Barwick C.J. pointed out, "no impairment of the conclusiveness of the Register": *Breskvar v. Wall* (1971) 126 C.L.R. 376 at 385; what is in question is the enforcement of rights against a subsequent registered proprietor. I think that, as the headnote to the report says, it was the view of Nicholas C.J. in Eq. in *Jobson v. Nankervis* (1943) 44 S.R. (N.S.W.) 277 that, in respect of land under the *Real Property Act*, easements (with exceptions not here relevant) cannot arise otherwise than by instruments executed under the Act: cf. *James v. Registrar-General* (1967) 69 S.R. (N.S.W.) 277, so as to be enforceable against a subsequent registered proprietor. The judges of this court at first instance have from time to time felt it proper to apply the views of Nicholas C.J. in Eq. It was applied by me in *Tarrant v. Zandstra* (unreported, Mahoney J., 8 June 1973) and by Helsham C.J. in Eq. in the present case: see also *Kostis v. Devitt* (unreported, Powell J., 4 July 1979); *Baalman on the Torrens System in New South Wales* (2nd ed.), p. 240. Thirdly, I do not think that the construction of s. 42(b) is governed by the decisions upon this kind of point in other jurisdictions.

. . . *Wilkinson v. Spooner* [1957] Tas. S.R. 121 is, in my opinion, not a case relevant to the present argument. Burbury C.J. held at 135 that an easement could arise by prescription in respect of land under the Tasmanian Torrens legislation and held that the Tasmanian equivalent of s. 42 did not protect a subsequent registered proprietor against such an easement. His Honour said at 135: "The question simply is one of statutory construction. If s. 40 excepts prescriptive easements arising at any time then that is the end of it. I think *James v. Stevenson* [1893] A.C. 162 is a clear authority against the view that the issue of a Certificate of Title can operate to extinguish an easement which falls within the exceptions of s. 40."

His Honour had previously held at 134 that the word in s. 40 "omission" meant merely " 'left out' in a colourless sense". His conclusion, therefore, was not based upon the view that such easement constituted the kind of implied exception to the indefeasibility section for which this argument of the defendant contends. It may be observed that *James v. Stevenson* [1893] A.C. 162 involved an easement in existence before the land was brought under the Torrens legislation there relevant, and that failure to note it on the Certificate of Title which issued would be an "omission" upon any construction of that term.

[His Honour then referred to the decision in *Pryce v. McGuiness* [1966] Qd. R. 591 and commented:]

I do not think that the fact that an interest cannot, as such, be registered or noted on the Register, warrants the creation by implication of an exception to the indefeasibility provisions of the New South Wales Act. . . .

In *Stevens v. Allan* (1955) 58 W.A.L.R. 1 Wolff J., as he then was, considered the indefeasibility provisions of the Western Australian legislation. Armanasco had sold the suggested dominant tenement to Stevens, who was registered as proprietor of it and then contracted to sell it to Evans. Stevens and Evans claimed an easement by implication of law over a so-called right of way. His Honour found that, at the time when Armanasco sold the dominant tenement to Stevens, he was registered as proprietor of an undivided half interest in the suggested servient tenement, and that he had the right in equity to compel the registered proprietor of the other undivided interest to transfer it to him. His Honour held that the plaintiffs were entitled to a right of way over a servient tenement. On his Honour's findings, this was, in my respectful opinion, clearly correct: the plaintiffs had against Armanasco the kind of personal right against the registered proprietor which is enforceable against him.

However, his Honour, in the course of his judgment, said at 18, 19: "The question here is whether the Act precludes the recognition of an incorporeal right which comes into existence by implication of law—a right which comes into existence without the necessity of any express words in an instrument. So far as I have been able to ascertain the point has never squarely arisen for decision, and I make that statement after examination of the authorities just mentioned. In my opinion there is nothing in the Act inconsistent with the principle of quasi easements arising on severance by reason of continuous and apparent user. In fact there is the positive language of ss 4 and 82 of the Act in support of the view that the common law principles have not been abrogated."

I do not see his Honour's decision, or the observations made by him, as supporting the present submission. In considering the effect of the indefeasibility and other provisions of Torrens legislation, three questions have been referred to: Do those provisions have the result that (except by a registrable and registered instrument) no interest can be created in respect of Torrens land?; Do they admit of the creation, (by unregistered or unregistrable instruments) of equitable interests in the land, enforceable against the registered proprietor personally bound by those equities?; and, Do they admit of the creation (by unregistered or unregistrable instruments) of interests in the land which are enforceable not merely against such a registered proprietor but against any registered proprietor? In some of the cases (of which *Jobson v. Nankervis* (1943) 44 S.R. (N.S.W.) 277 may be one) language has, I think, been used which could support the view that, unless an interest can be enforced against any registered proprietor; it cannot exist at all in respect of Torrens land. *Frazer v. Walker* [1967] A.C. 569 and the cases stemming from it have emphasised that rights may arise in respect of Torrens land, notwithstanding that they arise from circumstances not involving an instrument or a registrable instrument. These, of their nature, are interests in the land but, not being registered interests, are in general not enforceable against registered proprietors other than those personally bound by them.

Finally, the defendant referred to the decisions of McClelland C.J. in Eq. in *Re Standard and the Conveyancing Act* 1919 (1967) 92 W.N. (N.S.W.) 953. I do not think that that decision assists the defendant. The relevant easement appears to have been noted on the certificate of the servient tenement and the applicant's argument was that the easements had been extinguished by merger. The reply was twofold: by s. 42, land was held subject to interests noted on it, and presumably, the doctrine of merger did not operate to the contrary. The second argument was, that if there had been merger, the easement had been "revived". His Honour accepted at 956 the first argument. Alternatively, his Honour thought that *Wheeldon v. Burrows* (1879) 12 Ch. D. 31 circumstances existed to support the drainage easement, one of those noted on the title. The decision was, as I would understand it, that, whatever happened to the other easements as the result of the suggested merger, there was at relevant times in existence a user of the drainage easement as noted on the title, the sale of the dominant tenement had been "with" that easement, and that, therefore, the easement (which at all times remained noted on the title) was enforceable against the servient tenement. I do not see the decisions as dealing with a *Wheeldon v. Burrows* easement, where no relevant notation existed upon the title.

In my opinion, the appeal should be dismissed with costs.

Appeal dismissed with costs.

NOTES

1. The principal case refers to several classes of easement as coming within the provisions of s. 42(1)(b), to which a registered proprietor of land will take subject even though they have been omitted from or misdescribed in the Register. Similar rules will apply to profits.

   (a) Easements in existence *before* the land was brought under the Act, whether these easements arise by prescription or under the principles of *Wheeldon v. Burrows* or otherwise: see *Beck v. Auerbach* (1985) 6 N.S.W.L.R. 424 (Powell J.) and on appeal (1986) 6 N.S.W.L.R. 454.

   (b) Easements created by provisions of other statutes: see, for example, *Pratten v. Warringah Shire Council* (1969) 90 W.N. (Pt 1) (N.S.W.) 134, extracted above p. 202. Consider also the *Conveyancing Act* 1919 (N.S.W.), s. 88B which by subs. (3)(c)(i) provides that on registration of a plan of subdivision, easements notifed on the plan as intended to be created as thereby created: see Woodman, "Some Nuts for Cracking under the Torrens System" (1977) 51 A.L.J. 100.

   (c) Easments which have been validly created in accordance with the provisions of the *Real Property Act* 1900 (N.S.W.) and which have been omitted from or misdescribed in the Register. Where an easement has been created by a registered transfer and recorded in the Register but the Registrar-General fails to note the easement on the folio of the Register for the servient tenement on a subsequent transfer of the servient tenement, the easement will come within s. 42 (1)(b): *James v. Registrar-General* (1967) 69 S.R. (N.S.W.) 361; *Papadopoulos v. Goodwin* [1983] 2 N.S.W.L.R. 113, reversed on other grounds on appeal (1985) C.C.H. (N.S.W.) Conv. R. 55-256; *Christopoulos v. Kells* (1988) 13 N.S.W.L.R. 541. In *James v. Registrar-General* an easement was created and duly registered under the provisions of the Act. On the re-issue of a Certificate of Title of the servient tenement, the easement was omitted apparently due to an oversight in the Registrar-General's office. The servient tenement was then transferred to James' predecessor in title. When James purchased the servient tenement there was no reference to the easement on the Certificate of Title. The Court of Appeal held that James took subject to the easement.

   The section will extend to cover easements which, although lodged for registration in the approved form, have never been formally recorded on the folio of the Register for the servient tenement. In *Christopoulos v. Kells* (1988) 13 N.S.W.L.R. 541 at 548 the New South Wales Court of Appeal said that it is sufficient that "the person creating the easement had executed a registrable instrument, that instrument had been lodged with the Registrar-General for registration, the Registrar-General had registered the instrument in so far as it affected a transfer but had erroneously omitted to indorse on the Certificate of Title of the servient tenement a notation of the creation of the easement."

   (As to the power of the Registrar-General to correct errors see above p. 200.)

   The notation of intended easements on a registered plan in existence prior to the enactment in 1964 of *Conveyancing Act* 1919, s. 88B (see above p. 241) will not of itself be effective to create these easements. This is the position even if the intended dominant tenements are indicated on the plan: *Torrisi v. Magame Pty Ltd* [1984] 1 N.S.W.L.R. 14. A notation on a registered deposited plan prior to 1964 of "site of proposed right of way" does not amount to registration of the right, and even if it could be regarded as being registered it would not create any interest: *Lamos Pty Ltd v. Hutchinson* (1984) C.C.H. N.S.W. Conv. R. 55-183. Contrast *Rock v. Todeschino* [1983] Qd R. 356.

2. *Australian Hi-Fi Publications Pty Ltd v. Gehl* (extracted above p. 280) also makes it clear that certain classes of unregistered easements coming into existence after the land is brought under the Act, will not bind a subsequent registered proprietor of the servient tenement. Thus, easements arising under the principles of *Wheeldon v. Burrows* (above p. 243) will not bind a subsequent registered proprietor. On similar reasoning to the principal case it has been held that personal rights enforceable against the vendor pursuant to the doctrine of non-derogation from grant (see above p. 257) will not bind a subsequent registered proprietor (*Kebewar Pty Ltd v. Harkin* (1987) 9 N.S.W.L.R. 738) nor will easements of necessity: *Parish v. Kelly* (1980) 1 B.P.R. 939; *Torrisi v. Magame Pty Ltd* [1984] 1 N.S.W.L.R. 14. Similarly, easements which under the general law would arise by prescription will not bind a subsequent registered proprietor of the servient tenement: *Dewhirst v. Edwards* [1983] 1 N.S.W.L.R. 34. Any other result would be inconsistent with the underlying philosophy of the Act, namely the conclusiveness of the Register (at 48). Prescriptive easements are unaffected by the *Real Property Act* 1900 (N.S.W.), Pt VIA and s. 45C (discussed above p. 209), as those provisions deal only with adverse possession. As to the distinction between rights obtained by prescription and title claimed by adverse possession, see above p. 258.

As to the position where easements over old system title arise after the dominant tenement is brought under Torrens title, see *Margil Pty Ltd v. Stegul Pastoral Pty Ltd* [1984] 2 N.S.W.L.R. 1 at 11.

3. An unregistered agreement to create an easement may be enforceable between the parties to the agreement, but will not be enforceable against a subsequent registered proprietor. The agreement has no greater status than any other unregistered instrument under the Torrens system: *Tarrant v. Zandstra* (1973) 1 B.P.R. 9381; *Stuy v. B. C. Ronalds Pty Ltd* [1984] 2 Qd R. 578. A similar rule applies to profits: *Connolly v. Noone and Cairns Timber Ltd* [1912] Qd R. S.R. 70.

Whilst it is clear that an unregistered agreement can create rights in personam between the parties to the agreement, how far can rights in personam be created between the parties by the operation of the *Wheeldon v. Burrows* principles or usage that under the general law would give rise to a prescriptive easement? In the *Hi-Fi* case, Mahoney J.A. made it clear that the principles of *Wheeldon v. Burrows* could give rise to rights in personam against the current registered proprietor. With respect to prescriptive easements, Powell J. in *Dewhirst v. Edwards* [1983] 1 N.S.W.L.R. 34 at 48 said:

> [I]t seems to me . . . that the mere use of an alleged easement for 20 years or more would not, without more, give rise to any personal rights against the registered proprietor even if he remained unchanged throughout the whole period; and . . . that, in those cases in which such rights are enforced, it is only as a consequence of the enforcement of rights in personam, by requiring the execution, delivery and registration of appropriate instruments that estates or interests in, or over the land are brought into being or transferred.

Powell J., however, recognised that if the plaintiffs were entitled to rely on the doctrine of proprietary estoppel, this would give rise to an equity, a right in personam (rather than an equitable estate or interest) against the registered proprietor. In the later cases of *Torrisi v. Magame Pty Ltd* [1984] 1 N.S.W.L.R. 14 at 22-23, Powell J., commenting upon the effect of proprietary estoppel, said that in the case before him such a claim would not take the plaintiffs any further, adding:

> Despite the fact that, as I have recently pointed out (*Dewhirst v. Edwards*) it does not follow that, when the facts necessary to establish "proprietary estoppel" are shown to have occurred, an estate in, or interest in respect of, land will be held to have been created, nonetheless, in the context of non-Torrens title land, the equity has been held to be enforceable against successors in title of the person whose "fraud" first gave rise to the equity: see, for example, *Ward v. Kirkland* [1967] Ch. 194; *E. R. Ives Investment Ltd v. High* [1967] 2 Q.B. 379.

His Honour declined to decide whether these cases were correctly decided adding that it was unnecessary to do so unless the current registered proprietor's conduct amounted to fraud for the purposes of s. 42(1). On this question, see *Bahr v. Nicolay* (1988) 62 A.L.J.R. 268, above p. 170 and *Silovi Pty Ltd v. Barbaro* (1988) 13 N.S.W.L.R. 466 (equitable profit).

DABBS v. SEAMAN

High Court of Australia (1925) 36 C.L.R. 538

[The plaintiff, Seaman, sold property to the defendant's predecessor in title (Smith). The land sold was described in the transfer (from Jenkins to Smith at the direction of Seaman) and subsequent Certificate of Title with reference to a plan which showed the defendant's land to be bounded by a strip marked "20 feet lane". The plaintiff was registered proprietor of the laneway together with other land adjacent and to the rear of the defendant's land. The laneway was originally intended to provide access to the land at the rear. The transfer to the defendant Dabbs made no mention of any easement, but the land transferred was shown on the plan on the Certificate of Title as abutting onto the lane. The plaintiff applied for consolidation of title of two pieces of land of which he was registered proprietor and for the deletion from the Certificate of Title the word "20 feet lane". The Registrar-General refused to delete the notation "20 feet lane" without the consent of Dabbs. Upon her refusal to consent the plaintiff, Seaman, commenced proceedings in equity claiming, inter alia, a declaration that the defendant was not entitled to any right of way over the laneway and other relief. At first instance the plaintiff was granted the declaration and relief claimed. The defendant then appealed to the High Court.]

ISAACS J. This appeal vitally concerns the safety of titles to land in New South Wales and, indeed, in Australia. The first step, and a very necessary one, is to clear the issues. When the mists of irrelevancy disappear, the question resolves itself into the following proposition, which I hold to be good law and to be absolutely necessary if titles under the *Real Property Act* 1900 (N.S.W.) are to be indefeasible: Where A, a registered proprietor of land under the *Real Property Act* 1900, (N.S.W.), transfers to B a part of his land described by a plan indicating that the transferred land is bounded on one side by a 20 ft lane situated on the other part of the transferor's land and the transfer is duly registered, then, in the absence of either a provision to the contrary on B's Certificate of Title or some subsequent personal legal or equitable relation to the contrary between B and the owner of the adjoining land, B, as long as he remains registered proprietor of the land so transferred and described, is entitled (1) to have the land marked "twenty feet lane" preserved as such, and (2) to a right of way over the lane . . .

Indefeasibility. To the facts so stated, there must be applied the broad principle of indefeasibility of title under the Act, subject only to such qualifications as the Act itself declares. This is entirely consonant with the existence of special personal obligations: see *Barry v. Heider* (1914) 19 C.L.R. 197 at 213-214. But the position I am so far dealing with is clear of personal obligations. Indefeasibility is universally acknowledged in Australia as the effect of a certificate unaltered and unchallenged; and this is confirmed by the decision of the Privy Council in *Assets Co. v. Mere Roihi* [1905] A.C. 176. . . . The Act itself says (s. 40(1)): "Every certificate of title . . . shall be *conclusive evidence* that the person named on such certificate of title or in any entry *thereon*, as seised of or as taking estate or interest in *the land therein described*, is seised or possessed of or entitled to such land for the estate or interest therein specified." The appellant being named in the relevant "entry" on the certificate entered 16 May 1922 as the transferee of Smith's estate, the certificate is "conclusive evidence" that she is seised or possessed of an estate in fee simple in the "land therein described". . . .

Construction. What, then, is the "land therein described". It was argued that that could only mean the physical substance contained within the metes and bounds marked red without reference to anything beyond those limits. I do not agree with that argument. The "land therein described" means the parcel delimited with all the inherent characteristics with which the terms of delimitation invest it. I say "inherent" in order to distinguish them from characteristics that are mere additions distinct in themselves but attached by some act quite independent of the original quality of the subject land. For instance, an easement to pass through a neighbour's garden is a superadded right of way and not an inherent characteristic of the subject land. Such an easement would properly fall within the terms of s. 47 of the *Real Property Act* 1900 (N.S.W.). But a right of access to the sea or a navigable river is an inherent quality of a riparian tenement. In the present case the "land therein described" is the parcel edged red bounded on the south by Shirley Road—a public road—and bounded on the east by a "20 feet lane". Its contiguity to a lane 20 ft wide is an inherent characteristic of the land described. The parcel, if Shirley Road or the lane were eliminated, would possess a quite different character. It would cease to be a parcel of which the owner is a frontager to a public road or private lane: see Stirling L.J. in *Mellor v. Walmesley* [1905] 2 Ch. at 180. The accessorial right is included in the grant itself, and is evidenced by the certificate without a special memorial or specification: *James v. Stevenson* [1893] A.C. 162 at 169. The principle recognising the right in such circumstances has been settled in many cases, of which *Roberts v. Karr* (1809) 1 Taunt. 495; 127 E.R. 926 is the root and *Furness Railway Co. v. Cumberland Co-op. Building Society* (1884) 52 L.T. 144 is the most authoritative. In *Roberts v. Karr* Lawrence J. (at 501; 929) says: "If a man buys a piece of ground described as abutting upon a road, does he not contemplate the right of coming out into the road through any part of the premises?" Mansfield C.J. (at 503; 929) says: "If then he afterwards prohibits the defendant from coming there, it is not a sufficient answer to say, you have told me in your lease, 'this land abuts on the road': you cannot now be allowed to say that the land on which it abuts is not the road." Those passages were quoted with approval by Kelly C.B. for himself and Cleasby B. in *Espley v. Wilkes* (1872) L.R. 7 Ex. at 303-304. There a lease described the land as "bounded on the east and north by newly made streets", and added "a plan whereof is indorsed on these presents". The Chief Baron thought the plan so important as to incorporate it pictorially in his judgment. There, as here, the "street" on the east was a piece of rough waste ground, and it so remained for the most part impassable as a road down to the time of the trial, that is, about 20 years. The Chief Baron said that the lessor was estopped from denying that there were streets which were in fact ways along the north and east fronts, and adds: "We should have thought this point clear upon the obvious and necessary *construction* of the lease and plan"; and then adds that *Roberts v. Karr* was a direct authority to that effect. It is important to observe that the "estoppel" arises on the "construction" of the deed. It is not unimportant to observe that Kelly C.B. ((1872) L.R. 7 Ex. at 304) says: "Here the land is *described* as abutting upon 'newly made streets'." Unless land shown on a certificate by a plan only is thereby "described", it is not described at all, and s. 40 would have no operation upon it. And if it is thereby described, as it must necessarily be, the plan showing the contiguity of the land to the subject land brings the case precisely within the authorities cited. . . . The principle has been acted upon in New South Wales in *Little v. Dardier* (1891) 12 N.S.W.L.R. (Eq.) 319 and *Bradley v. McBride* (1886) 2 W.N. (N.S.W.) 56, and doubtless, property rights in many cases rest upon those decisions. . . .

Estoppel. In view of the argument as to the estoppel established by the doctrine of *Roberts v. Karr*, it is necessary to say a few words respecting its nature. Estoppel in that case simply means that the conveyance or lease or other instrument is based upon a conventional state of facts, and therefore to dispute that conventional state of facts in order to set up another state of facts is an attempt to destroy the very basis of the transaction. . . . The governing principle is stated in *Blackburn's Contract of Sale* (3rd ed.), p. 204, that "when parties have agreed to act upon an assumed state of facts, their rights between themselves are justly made to depend on the conventional state of facts, and not on the truth." . . . But a question may always arise whether there has been adopted, for the purposes of an instrument and is its conventional basis, any given state of facts. That must be determined upon its construction. Brett L.J. expresses this truth in *Simm v. Anglo-American Telegraph Co.* (1879) 5 Q.B.D. 188 at 206, where, after speaking of other kinds of estoppels in business and daily life, he says: "I speak not of that estoppel, which is said to arise upon a deed of conveyance or other deed of a similar nature. I incline to think that when the word 'estoppel' is used with reference to deeds of that kind, it is merely a phrase indicating that they must be truly interpreted." If on the true construction of a conveyance it is found that a recorded state of facts is part of the very thing effected by the instrument, then the party so effecting it cannot dispute the state of facts without disrupting the transaction itself. If he succeeded, he would be leaving something other than was originally done. In the process of construction a court may be required to examine the document to determine whether that state of facts is clearly enough adopted. . . .

The result, so far, is that the estoppel relevant to this case is the estoppel which as a rule of law arises, not, it is true, upon the *operative* words of the transfer or certificate, but upon the *true construction as to the land transferred* of the appellant's certificate founded on the transfer by Jenkins by direction of the respondent. The construction being established that, as an essential part of the transaction and the certificate, the land is described as fronting a 20 ft lane on land belonging then to Jenkins or Seaman and now to Seaman, it is not permissible to Seaman to contradict or impugn that conventional state of facts. In order to test the position of the present appellant, suppose immediately after Smith became the registered proprietor Seaman had set up his present claim, basing it as here on the alleged facts that the lane had been intended solely for the residual part of lot 1, is it not plain he would have failed? Even if he had proved Smith's knowledge of that fact, he would have failed. The answer would have been that he had nevertheless accepted for the purpose of that transaction the conventional fact that the land transferred was to have the 20 ft lane abutting upon it. The words of Mansfield C.J. in *Roberts v. Karr* (1809) 1 Taunt 495 at 502; 127 E.R. 926 at 929 would have applied, namely: "But supposing that Pratt, which I do not believe, had in his mind the intent to reserve this land, he could not consistently with what appears *upon the face of these deeds*, prevent the defendant from opening his door into the street; because he has *described* the defendant's land in his lease at 36 ft 9 ins in breadth, and abutting on the street." Unless by reason of some recognised head of equity jurisprudence, such, for instance, as mutual mistake, the instruments were rectified, the claim must have been disallowed: *Creelman's Case* [1920] A.C. 194 at 197. The appellant stands in the same position now as Smith did then: *Little v. Dardier* (1891) 12 N.S.W.L.R. (Eq.) 319 at 324; *Phillips v. McLachan* (1884) 5 N.S.W.L.R. (L.) 168; *Assets Co. v. Mere Roihi* [1905] A.C. 176 at 202. . . .

Right of Way. The next question is, has the appellant also a right of way over the 20 ft lane? The answer depends on the natural import of the word "lane" used in the collocation and in such a document as we have before us. No direct definition of "lane" appears in any Act and therefore, as was said by Simpson C.J. in Eq., in *Rich v. Miles* (1909) 10 S.R. (N.S.W.) 84 at 90, its ordinary meaning must be found. The ordinary meaning of "lane" is a passage or way. It is a species of the same genus as street and road, their common characteristics being a place along which persons pass from one place to another. A "lane" imports a narrower passage than "street" or "road". In New South Wales it is found in many Acts of Parliament without special definition, showing that the legislature has recognised that it has a well-known acceptation. . . . In the present case the restrictive building covenant adds to the certainty that in the present case "lane" must be understood in its ordinary and popular sense of a place in the nature of a way or passage. That is the primary meaning ascribed to it in the *Oxford Dictionary*, namely: "A narrow way between hedges or banks; a narrow road or street between houses or walls; a bye-way." The illustrations show how deeply rooted in the word "lane" is the sense of a way or passage from Chaucer to the present day. Drury Lane in London, Flinders Lane in Melbourne, are notable instances of the use of the word in its primary sense. There are numerous instances in every capital city of a similar use. There can be no doubt that was the essential meaning attributed to it by Seaman and by Jenkins in August 1913. . . .

Other Circumstances. There has been a great body of oral evidence in order to establish (1) the original intention in fact of the respondent to restrict the lane to his residual land; (2) that the appellant was before purchasing made aware of that original intention; (3) that she was not induced to purchase by any belief that Seaman intended to attach a right of way over the lane to Smith's land. From those

circumstances it was argued that there could be no estoppel against Seaman, and
that consequently Dabbs took nothing but the bare land edged red fronting Shirley
Road. For the reasons already stated the facts referred to, even if established, are
utterly immaterial. They do not, and, so long as the principle definitely established
in *Assets Co. v. Mere Roihi* [1905] A.C. 176 remains unaltered by legislation, they
cannot, affect the conclusive force of a registered title. Nor do they as between the
parties create any subsequent relation referable to any known head of equity which
calls for the interposition of a court of equity. . . . I am clearly of opinion the appeal
should be allowed.

STARKE J. All the difficulties in this case have been created by loose and careless
conveyancing.

Maria Jenkins, the registered proprietor of certain lands under the *Real Property
Act* of New South Wales, subdivided it, and lodged a plan of the subdivision in the
office of the Registrar-General. The subdivision was clearly for building purposes.
In August 1913, she, by the direction of Seaman, who had purchased portion of the
subdivided lands from her, transferred to Sidney Louis Smith all her estate and
interest as such registered proprietor in a piece of land containing one acre, and
described as part of lot 1 on the plan of subdivision and shown on the plan attached.
The plan attached is, so far as material, as follows:

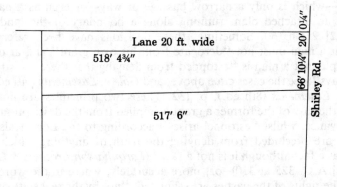

And by transfer the purchaser, for himself, his heirs, executors, administrators or
assigns, covenanted with the vendor, her heirs, executors, administrators or assigns,
that the purchaser, his heirs, executors, administrators or assigns would not erect
or permit to be erected upon the said land any main building of less value than £300.
This confirms the view that the subdivision was for building purposes. Maria
Jenkins was the registered proprietor of the land marked "Lane", and Seaman was
entitled to the lane in fee simple in equity as the purchaser from Maria Jenkins. The
lane, as a matter of fact, also gave entrance from Shirley Road to other portions
of the land purchased by Seaman from Maria Jenkins which lay at the back of the
one acre transferred to Smith. It will be noticed that the lane was not transferred
to Smith. There is no express reference in the transfer to any easement, though s. 46
of the *Real Property Act* 1900 (N.S.W.) provides that "where land under the
provisions of this Act or any estate or interest in such land is intended to be
transferred or any right of way or other easement is intended to be created or
transferred the registered proprietor may execute a memorandum of transfer" in
one of the forms in the Schedule to the Act, "which memorandum shall, for
description of the land intended to be dealt with, refer to the grant of Certificate
of Title of such land, or shall give such description as may be sufficient to identify

the same, and shall contain an accurate statement of the estate, interest, or easement intended to be transferred or created". The Certificate of Title issued to Smith followed the description in the plan of the land attached to the transfer, but made no express reference to any easement over the lane.

Under the general law, the cases decide that if land—particularly building land—is conveyed described as abutting on streets or ways and the land granted is separated from the streets or ways by a strip of land belonging to the grantor, the effect is that the grantee has a right of way over the strip to the road: see Theobald, *Law of Land*, p. 102. Lord Selborne says he is "bound to this effect, that the purchaser, his heirs and assigns", shall have the "use of those streets" or ways. "How is it possible to regard the description" of the land "as bounded by streets as otherwise than most material to the subject of the contract and to the bargain between the vendor and purchaser? Building land abutting upon a street means having access to and fro by that street": *Furness Railway Co. v. Cumberland Co-op. Building Society* (1884) 52 L.T. at 145; *Roberts v. Karr* (1809) 1 Taunt. 495; 127 E.R. 926; *Espley v. Wilkes* (1872) L.R. 7 Ex. 298; *Mellor v. Walmesley* [1905] 2 Ch. 164; *Donnelly v. Adams* [1905] 1 I.R. 154. It makes no difference that the land in the conveyance is described by reference to a plan attached to it: *Furness Railway Co. v. Cumberland Co-op. Building Society; Rudd v. Bowles* [1912] 2 Ch. 60. Nor does it make any difference that the abutting land is described as a street or way or as a lane—which is only a narrow passage or way—or even as a narrow strip coloured on an attached plan, running along a boundary of the land: *Rudd v. Bowles* [1912] 2 Ch. 60. Sometimes these decisions have been referred to the principle that a man must not "derogate from his own grant" and at other times to the principle that a man is "estopped from denying that there are streets which are in fact ways": see the cases cited above, and *Gale v. Easements* (9th ed.), p. 110; *Goddard on Easements* (8th ed.), p. 132. These two principles are not quite the same, for in the case of the former a grant is implied from the description contained in the conveyance, whilst "estoppel arises" according to the Lord Halsbury L.C. "where you are precluded from denying the truth of anything which you have represented as a fact although it is not a fact" (*Farquharson Brothers & Co. v. King & Co.* [1902] A.C. 325 at 330), or, more accurately, where in the words of Lord Blackburn, the rights of the parties are regulated, "not by the real state of the facts, but by that conventional state of facts which the . . . parties agree to make the basis of their action": *Burkinshaw v. Nicholls* (1878) 3 App. Cas. at 1026; cf. *Gale on Easements* (9th ed.), pp. 152, 153. But the distinction in theory is unimportant, if the benefit of the estoppel enures, as clearly it does, for the benefit of the grantee, and his transferees or assigns: *Taylor v. Needham* (1810) 2 Taunt. 278 at 283; 127 E.R. 1084 at 1086 (a case of estoppel by deed); *Wood v. Seely* (1865) 32 N.Y. 105 (a case of estoppel in pais); *Furness Railway Co. v. Cumberland Co-op. Building Society* (1884) 52 L.T. at 145 (the case of an assignee); *Mellor v. Walmesley* [1905] 2 Ch. at 176 (the case of an assignee); *Rudd v. Bowles* [1912] 2 Ch. 60 (the case of a mortgagee); *Sarat Chunder Dey v. Gopal Chunder Laha* (1892) L.R. Ind. App. 19 at 215, 220 (to which my brother Isaacs has referred me): see also Spencer Bower, *Estoppel by Representation*, s. 173, p. 149. Consequently, if this were a case of a conveyance under the general law, Smith would have been entitled to a right of way along the 20 ft lane abutting on the land transferred to him by Jenkins at the direction of Seaman. And in *Little v. Dardier* (1891) 12 N.S.W.L.R. (Eq.) 319, decided in the year 1891, these principles were applied to land under the *Real Property Act*. That decision was, in my opinion, right, either because the grant of a right of way was implied from the words and description used in the transfer, or because an equitable claim or right to the way arose by reason of estoppel: *Barry v. Heider* (1914) 19 C.L.R. 197. And in any case it would be difficult to depart from a decision which has been acted on for so long a time and upon which possibly many titles depend.

The remaining question is whether Smith's rights over the lane in question were transferred to the appellant Emily Dabbs. Smith died, and the Public Trustee became his legal personal representative. By transfer in the month of April 1922 the Public Trustee transferred all his estate and interest in all the land mentioned in Smith's Certificate of Title to Emily Dabbs, and she was, by indorsement on that certificate, registered as proprietor of the land. But the lane was not expressly mentioned in the transfer, not was any right of way over it expressly given. What is the effect of that transfer? It purports to transfer a parcel of land described in a Certificate of Title, which discloses, upon examination, that the land abuts on one of its sides on the lane. Under the general law a grant of land passed all that was "legally appendant or appurtenant thereto" without the words "with the appurtenances": see *Norton on Deeds*, p. 249. In practice "general words" were usually added so as to pass all appurtences enjoyed with the land. But in New South Wales, as in England, legislation has rendered this addition unnecessary: *Conveyancing Act* 1919 (N.S.W.), s. 67. It may be that the same result has been achieved under the *Real Property Act* 1900 (N.S.W.) by the definition of land in s. 3: "In the construction and for the purposes of this Act," the section provides "*and in all instruments* purporting to be made or executed thereunder (if not inconsistent with the context and subject matter) . . . the following terms shall bear the respective meanings set against them: . . . 'Land'—messuages, tenements, and hereditaments corporeal and incorporeal of every kind and description or any estate or interest therein, *together with* all paths, passages, ways, water-courses, liberties, privileges, easements, plantations, gardens, mines, minerals, quarries, and all trees and timber thereon or thereunder lying or being unless any such are specially excepted": cf. *Ex parte Cuningham; Re M'Carthy* (1877) 3 V.L.R. (L.) 199 at 204-205. And the title of the servient tenement is subject to any easement existing over the land although the same has not been registered: *Real Property Act* 1900 (N.S.W.), ss 42, 47. But it is unnecessary to decide the point because Smith's representative has transferred to Emily Dabbs a piece of land described in his Certificate of Title by means of a plan, as abutting on the lane. Now, if Smith's representative had owned the lane he could not, as we have seen, have denied the right of Emily Dabbs to use it. On similar principles, if Smith's representative has the right of way over the lane, incident to the land which he sold to Emily Dabbs, then, if he has not expressly or impliedly granted that right to her, he is estopped from denying, and must be taken to have granted to her the right of way he had in or over the land: cf. *Cooke v. Ingram* (1893) 68 L.T. 671 at 674.

Emily Dabbs thus succeeds in establishing her right by the application of legal principles to the forms of transfers executed in this case, but somewhat, I am afraid, at the expense of justice. She never bargained for a right of way over the lane at the time of the purchase, and the learned judge who tried the action was satisfied that she had been informed that she was buying the one acre of land and not any right to or over the lane. But a right of way over the lane was in point of law, in my opinion, granted or transferred to her, or must be assumed to have been so granted or transferred, and consequently her appeal must be allowed.

[Higgins J. dissented holding, inter alia, (1) that Mrs Dabbs did not acquire an easement by estoppel as Seaman made no misrepresentations and Mrs Dabbs was informed that she would have no right of way over the lane; (2) the reference to the lane was not sufficient to grant a right of way over the lane.]

Appeal allowed.

NOTES AND QUESTIONS

1. In *Jobson v. Nankervis* (1943) 44 S.R. (N.S.W.) 277, Nicholas C.J. in Eq. said:

> *Dabbs v. Seaman* decides that a right of way may exist over land described in a Certificate of Title, although not shown on the certificate, and not in existence before the land was brought under the Act, but the circumstances in which it may come into existence are exceptional and are limited to easements which arise by implication from the description appearing on the certificate or from estoppel.

Do the judgments of the High Court necessarily support the view that an easement can arise by estoppel? For the view that *Dabbs v. Seaman* is not authority for allowing easements by estoppel under the Torrens system, and that, on strict analysis, Dabbs obtained a mere personal licence to use the right of way: see Baalman, "The Dangers of Dabbs v. Seaman" (1950) 1 U.Q.L.J. 28.

2. Would the result be the same in the principal case if there were no notification of a laneway on Seaman's title?

F. EXTINGUISHMENT OF EASEMENTS AND PROFITS

An easement may be extinguished by express or implied release, by operation of law, or by order of the court.

1. Express release

In respect of old system title land, an express release must be effected by deed: *Conveyancing Act* 1919 (N.S.W.), s. 23B(1). The release of easements over Torrens title land in New South Wales is governed by *Real Property Act* 1900 s. 47(6), which provides that an easement recorded in the Register may be released by a registered transfer altered as the circumstances require: see also s. 47(6A).

Where an easement is informally created, but is such as would be enforceable in equity within the principle of *Walsh v. Lonsdale* (1882) 21 Ch. D. 9 (see below p. 560) the easement may be released in writing for value: *Conveyancing Act* 1919 (N.S.W.), s. 23C(1). Equity may intervene where a person has relied on an informal release: see *Davies v. Marshall* (1816) 10 C.B. (N.S.) 697 at 710; *Waterlow v. Bacon* (1866) L.R. 2 Eq. 514.

Similar rules apply to the release of profits.

2. Implied release

The owner of the dominant tenement will have impliedly released her or his rights over the servient tenement where it can be shown that he or she intended to abandon those rights. Non-user of itself does not amount to abandonment. It must be shown that the dominant owner intended to release the servient tenement; non-user is evidence of such intention: *Wolfe v. Freijah's Holdings Pty Ltd* [1988] V.R. 1017; *McIntyre v. Porter* [1983] 2 V.R. 439. In *Ward v. Ward* (1852) 7 Exch. 838; 155 E.R. 1189 non-user for over 20 years was held not to amount to abandonment, non-user being attributable to the existence of a more convenient means of access. In *James v. Stevenson* [1893] A.C. 162 despite non-user over a long period, the court held that there had been no abandonment; the owner of the dominant tenement had no occasion to use the right of way. Contrast *Swan v. Sinclair* [1924] 1 Ch. 254; [1925] A.C. 227 where it was held that the right had been abandoned by reason of non-user coupled with surrounding circumstances. The position is summed up in *Tehidy Minerals Ltd v. Norman* [1971] 2 Q.B. 528 at 533 where the Court of Appeal said:

Abandonment of an easement or of a profit à prendre can only, we think, be treated as having taken place where the person entitled to it has demonstrated a fixed intention never at any time thereafter to assert the right himself or to attempt to transmit it to anyone else.

See also *Treweeke v. 36 Wolseley Road Pty Ltd* (1973) 128 C.L.R. 274, extracted below.

Alteration of the dominant tenement, thereby preventing user, may be evidence of abandonment. In *Moore v. Rawson* (1824) 3 B. & C. 332; 107 E.R. 756 the plaintiff had bricked up windows in a wall for a period of 17 years. During this period a neighbour had erected a building which would have blocked out the light to the windows. It was held that the plaintiff had abandoned any easement to receive light through the windows. Contrast *Cook v. Mayor & Corp. of Bath* (1868) L.R. 6 Eq. 177 where the bricking up of a doorway for 30 years was held not to constitute abandonment. Similar rules apply to profits appurtenant: *Moore v. Rawson* (1824) 3 B. & C. 332 at 338; 107 E.R. 756 at 759.

Where the grant of an easement creates a parcel of rights, the grantee may, by reason of her or his acts or omissions, be held to have abandoned one or more of such rights: *Proprietors of Strata Plan No. 9968 v. Proprietors of Strata Plan No. 11173* [1979] 2 N.S.W.L.R. 605.

In New South Wales, there is no provision in the Torrens legislation empowering the Registrar-General to remove from the Register an easement which has been impliedly released. (As to current Titles Office practice in New South Wales, see Baalman and Wells, *Land Titles Office Practice* (3rd ed.), pp. 122-214).

As an illustration of the special difficulties involved with respect to Torrens title land, consider the following problem:

A Certificate of Title to Torrens title land states that the registered proprietor is entitled to a right of carriageway over the adjacent property. The predecessor in title to the registered proprietor has acted in such a way that under the general law he would be taken to have abandoned the easement. Is the current registered proprietor entitled to the benefit of the easement? See the judgment of Walsh J. in the principal case and *Webster v. Strong* [1926] V.L.R. 509; *Riley v. Pentilla* [1974] V.R. 547; *Proprietors Strata Plan No. 9968 v. Proprietors Strata Plan No. 11173* [1979] 2 N.S.W.L.R. 605, noted Butt (1979) 53 A.L.J. 661. See also *Pieper v. Edwards* [1982] 1 N.S.W.L.R. 336, discussed below p. 301.

3. Operation of law

Where there is unity of possession and ownership of both dominant and servient tenements, the easement is extinguished by operation of law: *Metropolitan Railway Co. v. Fowler* [1892] 1 Q.B. 165. Easements of necessity may, however, be an exception to this rule, *Margil Pty Ltd v. Stegul Pastoral Pty Ltd* [1984] 2 N.S.W.L.R. 1 at 10. The rule requires unity of both possession and ownership. Thus, if there is unity of ownership but not possession (for example, where dominant and servient tenements are in common ownership but either the dominant or servient tenement or both are leased to others), the easement survives: *Richardson v. Graham* [1908] 1 K.B. 39. Conversely, if there is unity of possession but not of ownership, there is no extinguishment; rather the easement is suspended during the continuance of the unity of possession: *Canham v. Fisk* (1831) 2 Cr. & J. 126; 149 E.R. 53. Ownership of the fee simple estate is requisite before an easement will be extinguished by operation of law. Thus, if the fee simple owner of the servient tenement acquires a limited interest in the dominant tenement (for example, a life estate), the easement is suspended during the period of unity of ownership and possession and revives on the termination of the limited interest: *Thomas v. Thomas* (1835) 2 Cr. M. & R. 34; 150 E.R. 15. Similarly, a profit will be extinguished if the owner of the profit becomes owner of the land the subject of the profit: *White v. Taylor* [1969] 1 Ch. 150. Purchase of even part of the servient tenement brings to an end the rights in respect of the whole of the land affected: at 158-159.

In New South Wales, there are two statutory exceptions to the rule that unity of ownership and possession extinguish the easement; first s. 47(7) of the *Real Property Act* 1900 abrogates the rule in relation to Torrens title land in respect of easements recorded in the register after the commencement of the *Real Property (Amendment) Act* 1970, s. 47(8).

Section 47(7) of the *Real Property Act* 1900 (N.S.W.) also applies to easements subsisting at the commencement of the 1970 amendments to the Act. Quaere the position where prior to 1970 there had been unity of ownership and possession of dominant and servient tenements but the notification of the existence of the easement had not been cancelled during the merged ownership: is a subsequent registered proprietor entitled to the benefit of the easement noted on title? See McLelland C.J. in *Re Standard and the Conveyancing Act 1919* (1967) 92 W.N. (N.S.W.) 953 and *Margil Pty Ltd v. Stegul Pastoral Pty Ltd* [1984] 2 N.S.W.L.R. 1 at 11 for the view that extinguishment on that basis is effective only if the notification is cancelled during the merged ownership. See also *Rock v. Todeschino* [1983] Qd R. 356 at 362-363.

Secondly, s. 88B(3)(c) of the *Conveyancing Act* 1919 (N.S.W.) abrogates the rule where the easement has been created by registration of a plan of subdivision after 15 June 1964.

Both the *Conveyancing Act* 1919 (N.S.W.), s. 88B(3)(c) and the *Real Property Act* 1900 (N.S.W.), s. 47(7) apply to profits appurtenant.

Rights may also be extinguished through the operation of the doctrine of merger: see *Re Young* (1924) 6 N.S.W.L.R. 449(n.) applied in *Auerbach v. Beck* (1985) 6 N.S.W.L.R. 424 at 429 (affirmed on appeal (1986) 6 N.S.W.L.R. 454).

4. Order of the court

Easements may be varied or extinguished by court order: *Conveyancing Act* 1919, s. 89. As these provisions also apply to the modification or extinguishment of covenants, they will be discussed in Chapter 6.

The case next extracted, *Treweeke v. 36 Wolseley Road Pty Ltd* (1973) 128 C.L.R. 274, is a good illustration of the application of the provisions in relation to easements. In addition, it demonstrates the difficulty of making out a case that an easement has been abandoned by reason of non-user.

TREWEEKE v. 36 WOLSELEY ROAD PTY LTD

High Court of Australia (1973) 128 C.L.R. 274

[The appellant was the registered proprietor of a battleaxe allotment, No. 34 Wolseley Road. The block had a water frontage and a narrow frontage onto Wolseley Road. The land was subject to a right of way to the waterfront in favour of the respondent's land, No. 36 Wolseley Road. The easement was notified on both the appellant's and the respondent's Certificates of Title. The appellant sought an order under s. 89 of the *Conveyancing Act* 1919 (N.S.W.) that her land was not affected by the easement, in the alternative that the easement was not enforceable by any person or that the easement had been extinguished. At first instance evidence was accepted that it was impossible to pass along the full length of the right of way because of natural and artificial obstructions. At several points there were vertical rock faces varying in height from 4 ft to 7 ft. There was also a swimming pool erected across part of the right of way, an impenetrable plantation of bamboo and a fence erected jointly by the appellant and respondent's predecessors in title. All of these obstructions had been there for a considerable period. There was no user of the entire right of way by the respondent or its predecessors in title, although there was some evidence of use of part of the way in using alternative routes to the beach across the appellant's land and adjoining property No. 38 Wolseley Road. At first instance, the trial judge refused to make the orders requested by the plaintiff. On appeal:]

MASON J. [His Honour after reviewing the facts continued.] The learned judge declined to infer from the non-user of the right of way by the respondent and its predecessors in title that it or any of them intended to abandon the right of way over the appellant's land or that there had been any such abandonment. In expressing his reasons for that conclusion his Honour stated that mere evidence of non-user is not of itself sufficient to justify an inference of intention to abandon and that the reason why the right of way had not been used was that it could not be used without the making of expensive improvements and that more convenient means of access to the waterfront from No. 36 was to be found through No. 38 or through No. 34 otherwise than by means of the right of way, except in so far as use was made of the path constructed by the appellant alongside her flats.

The learned judge then considered the artificial obstructions which had been placed upon the site of the right of way. He held that the respondent's acquiescence in the placing or maintenance of these obstructions was not enough to justify the inference of abandonment. Except as to the swimming pool, the obstructions involved insignificant expense. As to the pool his Honour said that it was constructed for the most part, as indeed it was, on land leased from the Maritime Services Board and that it occupied a small part only of the right of way.

It is necessary to refer in the first instance to s. 89 of the *Conveyancing Act* 1919 (N.S.W.) and the manner in which the appellant seeks to take advantage of it. Because s. 89(8) contains an express statement that the section applies to land under the *Real Property Act* 1900 (N.S.W.). The application of the section to *Real Property Act* land gives rise to some difficulty. At common law an easement may be lost by abandonment, but does this doctrine apply to land which is under the *Real Property Act* and, if it does, what is the consequence when the easement remains on the Register and a purchaser acquires the dominant tenement relying on the state of the Register? In so far as the appellant seeks an order under s. 89(3) that the land is not affected by the easement or that the easement is not enforceable by any person, the appellant's case proceeds on the footing that although there was at one time an enforceable easement it came to an end at some undefined point of time as a consequence of abandonment, notwithstanding that it is noted on the Certificates of Title of the dominant and servient tenements. The jurisdiction to make an order under subs. (3) is discretionary as it is declaratory in character.

The case for an order under [s. 89] subs. (1)(b) proceeds differently. Here the appellant seeks to show "that the persons of full age and capacity for the time being or from time to time entitled to the easement . . . by their acts or omissions may reasonably be considered to have abandoned the easement wholly" and that the court should therefore make an order extinguishing the easement. It is acknowledged that under subs. (1), considered alone, the easement is valid unless and until it is extinguished by the making of an order. However, the appellant submits that once she succeeds in establishing the existence of the condition or circumstances mentioned in subs. (1)(b) of the court is bound to make an order in her favour and has no discretion to do otherwise. This is the view which was taken of the subsection in *Re Rose Bay Bowling and Recreation Club Ltd* (1935) 52 W.N. (N.S.W.) 77. It is a view which would preclude the court from having regard to the interests of a respondent who has acquired the dominant tenement by purchase, relying on the existence of an easement as shown by the Register under the *Real Property Act*. Moreover, it is a view which differs from that taken by the Court of Appeal of the similar provisions contained in s. 84(1) of the *Law of Property Act* 1925 (Eng.). There it has been held that even if any of the conditions mentioned in s. 84(1) are made out the Lands Tribunal has a discretion to refuse to make an order: see *Driscoll v. Church Commissioners for England* [1957] 1 Q.B. 330; *Re Ghey and Galton's Application* [1957] 2 Q.B. 650 at 659-660 per Lord Evershed M.R.

It is, I think, unnecessary to resolve these questions in this appeal because in the circumstances of this case it is for the appellant to show on any view that the learned judge was incorrect in refusing to draw the inference that the respondent or its predecessors in title intended to abandon the easement. If the appellant fails to show that his Honour was incorrect in this respect, she has no ground for relief under subs. (1) or subs. (3). Conversely, if she is held to be successful on this issue and it is held that the respondent or its predecessors intended to abandon the easement then she is entitled to an order, either under subs. (1) or subs. (3). The fundamental question for this court is therefore whether his Honour was incorrect in declining to draw an inference of abandonment.

In argument there has been much discussion of the authorities. For my part I do not consider that they provide decisive assistance in resolving the present case. They are decisions upon their own facts and the question here is essentially one of fact. They contain statements of general application, which nevertheless require an evaluation of the particular facts. It has been said, for instance, that mere non-user of a right of way the subject of a grant, even for a long period of time, does not necessarily indicate an intention to abandon: *Ward v. Ward* (1852) 7 Ex. 838; 115 E.R. 1189. Non-user may be referable to the absence of a need to use the right of way and the use of an alternative and more attractive means of access; then it may be thought that the non-user indicates, not so much an intention to abandon the right of way, as a preference for the alternative means of access so long as it remains available. This, so it seems to me, but for the evidence of acquiescence or standing by, is the conclusion which should be reached here where the persons having the benefit of the easement had no right to use the alternative means of access which was therefore liable to be terminated at any time. A further circumstance which affords some slight support for this conclusion is that there has been a limited use of that part of the right of way on which is the path which the appellant constructed adjacent to her block of flats along her north-western boundary.

However, the failure of the persons having the benefit of the easement to take any action concerning, and their participation in, the construction of obstructions placed along the site of the right of way raise a different and more difficult problem. Acquiescence in, and failure to object to, the placing by the owner of the servient tenement of obstructions on the site of a right of way which are inconsistent with the exercise of rights by persons having the benefit of the right of way may lead to an inference that they intended to abandon it. The question here is whether that inference should be drawn. It is of some importance that the right of way over No. 34 Wolseley Road could not be effectively used until it was made suitable for pedestrian use by appropriate expenditure. To my mind the inference that should be drawn is that the persons having the benefit of the easement preferred to resort to the alternative means of access to the waterfront so long as it remained available that, during that time, they had no objection to the use by the appellant of the site of the easement for her own purposes.

The participation by the respondent's predecessor in the erection and renewal of the fence near the common boundary is again consistent with an intention not to use the right of way until occasion for that use should arise as a result of the loss of the means of access through No. 38. The fence seems, according to the evidence, initially to have been constructed as a safety precaution, there being a slope down which the husband of the respondent's predecessor in title had fallen in 1933. The construction of the swimming pool athwart the end of the right of way stands in a somewhat different position in that it involved greater expenditure on the part of the appellant. However, it occupies only a small section of the right of way and for the most part it is the subject of land leased from the Maritime Services Board. The respondent did object to the swimming pool once it ascertained the precise location of the easement.

Although the evidence leaves me with the general impression that the respondent and its predecessors did little or nothing over a long period to exercise the rights conferred by the easement I am in agreement with Hope J. that, when the evidence is considered in its entirety, an inference of abandonment should not be drawn. In my view the non-user and other acts and omissions of the respondent and its predecessors were equally consistent with the existence of an intention not to use the right of way whilst an alternative means of access remained available.

In my opinion the appeal should be dismissed.

WALSH J. (dissenting). The facts with which this appeal is concerned are set out in the judgment of Mason J. I shall discuss the questions raised by the appeal upon the basis of an acceptance of his Honour's statement of the facts, making such further reference to matters of fact as seems necessary in order to explain the reasons for my conclusions.

It is natural, I think, to feel some reluctance in accepting and applying two propositions upon which the appellant must rely in order to maintain that she was entitled to an order under s. 89 of the *Conveyancing Act* 1919 (N.S.W.), as amended. The first is that an easement formally created by express grant may be lost by the grantee or his successors in title, without any express release or surrender and without any written declaration of an intention to abandon it or to give up the benefit of it. The second is that even where the dominant land and the servient land are registered under the *Real Property Act* 1900 (N.S.W.) and notifications of the existence of the easement appear on the Certificates of Title relating to both parcels of land, the easement may become liable to be extinguished and may cease to be enforceable by the person for the time being registered as proprietor of the dominant tenement. But the first of those propositions is firmly established and is not in dispute. The second of them must be accepted because of the express provision contained in s. 89(8) of the *Conveyancing Act*. That subsection is applicable in the form in which it stood before the amendment made by the *Conveyancing (Amendment) Act* 1972 (N.S.W.), but the changes then made are not material for present purposes. It makes s. 89 applicable to land under the provisions of the *Real Property Act* and authority is conferred upon the Registrar-General to make such amendments and entries in the Register book as are necessary to give effect to an order made thereunder. The provision clearly contemplates that orders will be made which affect rights which were vested in the registered proprietor, according to the state of the Register, at and after the time when he acquired his title to the dominant tenement. It is, of course, the function of the court to give effect to the intention which it finds to be expressed in the provision, notwithstanding that it may operate as a limitation upon the conclusiveness of the Register, which is conferred, as to matters of title, subject to specified exemptions, by the provisions of the *Real Property Act*.

In his judgment Mason J. raises the question whether the court, when the circumstances specified in s. 89(1) are established, has a duty to make an order or has a discretion to make or to refuse an order. His Honour mentions as a fact which, if the court has a discretion, might be taken into account, the reliance by a purchaser of the dominant tenement on the existence of an easement as shown by the Register. However I am in agreement with his Honour in thinking that in this appeal it is not necessary to resolve this question. As his Honour states, if the ground upon which the application in the Supreme Court of New South Wales was decided is not shown to have been erroneous, the question of discretion does not arise. On the other hand, if this court holds that it ought to have been found that the respondent or its predecessors in title by their acts or omissions might reasonably be considered to have abandoned the easement, I am of opinion that upon the assumption that the Supreme Court retained a discretion to make or to refuse to make an order, there was in this case no ground upon which that discretion could properly have been exercised against the making of an order. It has been submitted on behalf of the respondent that it came late upon the scene and that the evidence does not support a view that the respondent itself by its own acts or omissions exhibited any intention to abandon the easement and it has been put that the requirements of para. (b) of s. 89(1) are not satisfied, unless *all* the persons of full age and capacity from time to time entitled to the easement have shown by their acts or omissions such an intention. If those arguments were accepted, the appellant would fail, not because the court's discretion ought to be exercised in favour of the respondent, but because of a lack of proof of the necessary requirements for the making of an order. However, they should not be accepted. My reason for not accepting them will appear later in this judgment. But at this point it is appropriate to say that, in my opinion, the mere circumstances that the existence of an easement was noted on the Register at the time when the title passed to a new owner would not furnish a reason for refusing, as a matter of discretion, to make an order under s. 89(1) or s. 89(3). If the new owner could show, also, that he took steps promptly to make use of the easement, or to claim the right to use it, it may be that the court could take that into account, together with any evidence which might be provided as to the conduct and attitude of the owner of the servient tenement at the time of the change of the ownership of the dominant tenement, in determining whether or not an order should be made. But this is a question which does not arise in this case, in which no such claim was made for several years after the acquisition by the respondent of its title.

The primary facts are not in dispute. The critical matter is the ultimate conclusion which should have been reached, by way of inference from those facts, upon the question of abandonment. In considering that question it is no doubt convenient to discuss separately different aspects of the facts, such as, (1) the length of time during which a failure to use the right of way and to make a claim to use it continued; (2) the effect of obstacles to its convenient use already existing at the time of its grant; (3) the effect of the creation by the appellant of further obstacles to its use and of the acquiescence therein by the respondent or its predecessors in title; (4) the failure of the respondent or its predecessors in title to take any action to render the right of way available for use; (5) the effect of the contribution by the respondent and by one of its predecessors in title towards the cost of a fence which cut off ready access to the right of way; and (6) the effect of the availability of another path from the dominant land to the waterfront. But in the end a decision has to be taken as to the inferences to be drawn from the whole of the relevant evidence, taking into account all the matters of fact which may tend towards or against a conclusion that the easement may reasonably be considered to have been abandoned. Each of the circumstances upon which an applicant seeks to rely may be insufficient in itself to support that conclusion, yet in their cumulative effect the circumstances may show that it is the right conclusion. . . .

In my opinion, it was not necessary for the appellant to establish that the abandonment of the easement had become complete at a particular date which could be specified as the definite date of its extinguishment. Section 89(1) of the *Conveyancing Act* is in a form which provides for an order extinguishing an easement and not, as does s. 89(3), for a declaration as to the existence or the enforceability of an easement. It may be said, therefore, that in form s. 89(1) contemplates that the easement continues to bind the land until an order is made. But the terms of para. (b) are such that the making of such an order is dependent upon a conclusion by the court concerning acts or omissions which have already occurred in the past. The paragraph indicates, in my opinion, that the court will be able to decide that, at some point of time before the application was made, there have been acts or omissions from which the inference should be drawn that the easement has already been abandoned. This does not mean, in my opinion, that it is essential to be able to fix upon a particular date at which it can be found that that has taken place. . . .

[His Honour then found that there was ample evidence of abandonment and held in favour of the plaintiff.]

[The judgment of McTiernan J. agreeing that there had been no abandonment has been omitted.]

Appeal dismissed.

NOTE

In *Pieper v. Edwards* [1982] 1 N.S.W.L.R. 336 there was a registered easement, a right of carriageway, appurtenant to the defendant's land. Before the defendant became registered proprietor of the land, all persons then entitled to the benefit of the easement agreed to the extinguishment of the easement and a transfer releasing the easement was executed. The release was, however, never registered and when the defendant became registered proprietor of the land, the easement was still noted in the register as benefiting his land and burdening the plaintiff's land. The plaintiff relying on s. 89(1) of the *Conveyancing Act* 1919 (N.S.W.) sought an order that the easement be extinguished. It was held by the New South Wales Court of Appeal (1) that the agreement releasing the easement by predecessors in title to the defendant gave the court jurisdiction to make an order extinguishing the easement under s. 89(1)(b) of the *Conveyancing Act* 1919; (2) that s. 89 operated as an exception to the principle of indefeasibility of the register, but (3) purchase on the faith of the register was a factor to be taken into consideration in the exercise of the court's discretion under s. 89. On the particular facts, the court, by majority, upheld the trial judge's order for extinguishing the easement. See also *Proprietors Strata Plan No. 9968 v. Proprietors Strata Plan No. 11173* [1979] 2 N.S.W.L.R. 605.

G. REMEDIES

The person entitled in law to the benefit of a profit has sufficient possession in the subject matter of the profit to maintain an action for trespass against a third party interferring with that possession: *Hindson v. Ashby* [1896] 2 Ch. 1 at 10 per Lindley L.J. Thus, the grantee of fishing rights has property in the fish and may bring a possessory action for interference with that right without making title to the land: *Smith v. Kemp* (1963) 2 Salk. 637; 91 E.R. 537. Equitable title, supported by actual possession in the exercise of the right, will be sufficient to support an action for trespass: *Mason v. Clarke* [1955] A.C. 778 at 794, 798, 806. The rights granted will not operate to give exclusive possession to the profit holder as against the owner of the land, unless exclusive rights are expressly granted or are a necessary implication from the terms of the grant: *Duke of Sutherland v. Heathcote* [1892] 1 Ch. 475 at 484-485; *Reid v. Moreland Timber Co. Pty Ltd* (1946) 73 C.L.R. 1; *Hindmarsh v. Quinn* (1914) 17 C.L.R. 623; cf. *Dudgeon v. Chie* (1955) 92 C.L.R. 342.

Where there is no direct interference with possession of the subject matter of the profit, the profit holder may nevertheless sue in nuisance or act to abate any nuisance which interferes with the enjoyment of the profit: Megarry and Wade, *The Law of Real Property* (5th ed.), pp. 893-894.

An easement, unlike a profit à prendre, does not give possessory rights in the servient tenement. The only action available for interference is an action for nuisance. In an action against the servient owner or occupier for interference with an easement, the plaintiff must prove that he or she is entitled to the benefit of the easement as the owner or occupier of the dominant tenement: *Aldred's Case* (1610) 9 Co. Rep. 57b; 77 E.R. 816; *Higgins v. Betts* [1905] 2 Ch. 210 at 215; *Paine & Co. v. St Neots Gas & Coke Co.* [1938] 4 All E.R. 592 at 598. In contrast where the action is brought against a person who is neither the lawful owner nor occupier of the servient tenement, there is authority that the plaintiff need only prove actual possession as distinct from legal or equitable title to the dominant tenement: *Jeffries v. Williams* (1850) 5 Exch. 792; 155 E.R. 347; *Bibby v. Carter* (1859) 4 H. & N. 153; 157 E.R. 795; *Keegan v. Young* [1963] N.Z.L.R. 720.

SIX

COVENANTS CONSTITUTING AN INTEREST IN LAND

A. INTRODUCTION

This chapter is concerned with covenants constituting an interest in land. A covenant is an agreement creating an obligation, contained in a deed. As between the parties to the covenant, the promises are enforceable under the law of contract. (Persons not party to the instrument containing the covenant may be able to take the benefit of the covenant as assignees, see below p. 322 or as persons entitled to benefit under *Conveyancing Act* 1919 (N.S.W.), s. 36C, see below p. 321.) In addition, where the covenants relate to land, in certain circumstances the enforcement of the covenant may extend beyond the immediate parties. The covenant may be enforceable by not only the person receiving the benefit of the covenant (the covenantee), but also the successors in title to the land to which the benefit of the covenant relates. Similarly, the covenant may be binding not only on the person originally assuming obligations under the deed (the covenantor), but also the successors in title to the land to which the burden of the covenant relates.

At *law*, the extent to which covenants affecting land could be enforced by successors in title to the original covenantee was restricted. A successor in title to land to which the *benefit* of the covenant related, at law, could enforce the covenant only against the original covenantor and then only where the covenant was annexed to the land: see below p. 322. By contrast, *equity* provided a more complicated set of rules whereby a successor in title to land to which the covenant related could enforce the covenant not only against the original covenantor but also against the successors in title: *Tulk v. Moxhay* (1848) 2 Ph. 774; 41 E.R. 1143, extracted below p. 340. The most important restriction in equity on enforceability of the covenant against successors in title to the covenantor of the land burdened by the covenant, was that the covenants would only be enforced if they were restrictive of user of the land—hence the term restrictive covenants: see below p. 340. It is now accepted that restrictive covenants enforceable under the principle enunciated in *Tulk v. Moxhay* are equitable interests in land: Hayton, "Restrictive Covenants as Property Interests" (1971) 87 L.Q.R. 539; Gardner, "The Proprietary Effect of Contractual Obligations under Tulk v. Moxhay and De Mattos v. Gibson" (1982) 98 L.Q.R. 279.

It has been commonplace to seek to draw analogies between restrictive covenants and easements. Some similarities are indeed evident. In both instances, the rights are "annexed" to the land, and require that there be a "dominant tenement" benefiting from the easement or covenant and a "servient tenement" subject to the burden of the easement or covenant. The right must benefit the land as such and not merely

303

collaterally; thus in the law of easements, the easement must "accommodate" the dominant tenement; in restrictive covenants, the covenant must "touch and concern" the land of the covenantee. But whereas an easement cannot be granted to protect a view, privacy or a general right to light or air (see above p. 228), a covenant can be used negatively to protect these amenities. Thus a vendor of land may protect a view by requiring a purchaser to enter into a covenant in the vendor's favour not to erect or construct a building of more than a defined height.

There are, however, also a number of important differences, other than historical ones. (As to the historical basis of covenants affecting land, see Simpson, *Introduction to History of Land Law*, pp. 109-111.) A restrictive covenant must be negative in effect (see below p. 342) but an easement may involve positive rights over another's land, and in the case of a fencing easement, require the expenditure of money: see *Crow v. Wood* [1971] 1 Q.B. 77, above p. 231; *Frater v. Finlay* (1968) 91 W.N. (N.S.W.) 730; cf. *Halsall v. Brizell* [1957] 1 Ch. 168, see above pp. 223, 313. A covenant not to allow fences to fall into disrepair would be a positive covenant, not enforceable in equity against a successor in title to the covenantor: see below p. 342. It is often sought to accommodate this difference by describing restrictive covenants as negative easements: *London and South Western Railway Co. v. Gomm* (1882) 20 Ch. D. 562 at 583; *Re Nisbet and Pott's Contract* [1905] 1 Ch. 391 at 397; cf. *Norton v. Kilduff* [1974] Qd R. 47. But even this description fails to explain perhaps the most important distinction to be drawn between the two interests. Restrictive covenants, as creatures of equity, suffer from the same vulnerability as all equitable interests. A restrictive covenant will not bind a bona fide purchaser of the legal estate for value without notice (below p. 343) but an easement validly created at law will bind a purchaser without notice of it.

The advent of the restrictive covenant has provided private land owners with a means of controlling the usage of large areas of land; indeed, the restrictive covenant has provided the basis for private planning schemes. Covenants were, and still are, imposed for the benefit of private land owners to protect their financial interests (for example by preventing competition), to protect the amenities of their land (for example by preventing building or other activities), or to further moral objectives (for example by preventing the sale of intoxicating liquor): Mellows, "Planning and Restrictive Covenants" (1964) 28 Conv. (N.S.) 190. Until recent times, these private planning schemes were largely unchecked. Limited controls now exist in three areas: first, public planning schemes may restrict the operation of inconsistent restrictive covenants; secondly, in most States there are statutory powers to modify, vary or extinguish the operation of restrictive covenants; thirdly, the *Trade Practices Act* 1974 (Cth) may render unenforceable covenants substantially lessening competition in the market place: ss 45B, 45C of the *Trade Practices Act* 1974. These controls in a limited way strike a balance between private rights and the public interest.

The introduction of planning schemes in the public sector generally has not reduced the operation of restrictive covenants. Planning schemes do not automatically render invalid inconsistent restrictive covenants, nor does the existence of planning permission to utilise land for particular purposes provide a good defence to proceedings for breach of covenant: *Re Chamberlain and the Conveyancing Act* (1969) 90 W.N. (Pt 1) (N.S.W.) 585. In most States planning restrictions and existing covenants binding the land have a cumulative effect: see as illustrations *Re Chamberlain and the Conveyancing Act* (1969) 90 W.N. (Pt 1) (N.S.W.) 585, extracted below p. 385. There is, however, provision in New South Wales enabling planning schemes to restrict or modify the operation of covenants. Section 28 of the *Environmental Planning and Assessment Act* 1979 provides:

28. (1) In this section, "regulatory instrument" means any Act (other than this Act), rule, regulation, by-law, ordinance, proclamation, agreement, covenant or instrument by or under whatever authority made.

(2) For the purpose of enabling development to be carried out in accordance with an environmental planning instrument or in accordance with a consent granted under this Act, an environmental planning instrument may provide that, to the extent necessary to serve that purpose, a regulatory instrument specified in that environmental planning instrument shall not apply to any such development or shall apply subject to the modifications specified in that environmental planning instrument.

(3) A provision referred to in subsection (2) shall have effect according to its tenor, but only if the Governor has, before the making of the environmental planning instrument, approved the provision.

A second limitation on the operation of private planning schemes through the medium of restrictive covenants, is the existence of legislation allowing modification or discharge of covenants in certain circumstances: *Conveyancing Act* 1919 (N.S.W.), s. 89. The effect of this legislation is discussed in detail below p. 378. In general terms, the section recognises obsolescence as a ground for modifying or extinguishing covenants, and introduces the concept of reasonable user; if the covenant prevents reasonable user without securing practical benefit, the court may modify or discharge the covenant. This brings to bear the community interest in maintaining the proper utilisation of land: Mellows, "Planning and Restrictive Covenants" (1964) 28 Conv. (N.S.) 190 at 193. This may not, however, go far enough in maintaining the community interest in effective utilisation of land: see below p. 379.

The third limitation on the operation of restrictive covenants is contained in ss 45B, 45C of the *Trade Practices Act* 1974 (Cth). (As to restrictive covenants contained in leases, see below p. 604.) These sections, along with other amendments, were introduced following the decision in *Quadramain Pty Ltd v. Sevastapol Investments Pty Ltd* (1976) 133 C.L.R. 390. The High Court there held the then current s. 45 of the *Trade Practices Act* 1974 (Cth), which dealt with contracts in "restraint of trade", did not apply to restrictive covenants under the *Tulk v. Moxhay* doctrine: see below. Section 45 of the Act as it then stood rendered unenforceable contracts in restraint of trade or commerce. The term "restraint of trade" was construed by the High Court in the light of the common law doctrine of restraint of trade. The House of Lords in *Esso Petroleum Co. Ltd v. Harper's Garage (Stourport) Ltd* [1968] A.C. 269 stated that the common law doctrine against restraints of trade generally did not apply to covenants entered into by purchasers or lessees restricting the usage of the land, because that doctrine required that a person contract to give up some freedom which otherwise he or she would have had; a person buying or leasing land has no previous right to be there at all and when he or she takes possession of the land subject to a restrictive covenant that person gives up no right or freedom which he previously had. Applying this reasoning, a majority of the High Court in *Quadramain Pty Ltd v. Sevastapol Investments Pty Ltd* held that there was no contract in restraint of trade within the meaning of s. 45. In addition, s. 45 regulated contractual relationships. In this case, both plaintiff and defendant were successors in title to the original covenantor and covenantee; there was no contractual relationship between them to which s. 45 could apply. For detailed discussion of the *Quadramain* case see Heydon, "Restraint of Trade in the High Court" (1976) 50 A.L.J. 290; Taperell, Vermeesch and Harland, *Trade Practices and Consumer Protection* (3rd ed.), pp. 190 et seq.

The *Trade Practices Act* 1974 was subsequently amended to overcome the limitations displayed by the *Quadramain* decision; s. 45B was enacted to render unenforceable covenants which have the effect of substantially lessening competition, and s. 45C to outlaw price fixing covenants. Section 45B does not apply to residential covenants or covenants required in accordance with the purposes or objects of a religious, charitable or public benevolent institution: s. 45B(9).

The operation of the *Trade Practices Act* 1974, s. 45B must be looked at in the light of the requirements for the enforceability of covenants at law and equity. There is conflicting authority on the question whether covenants restricting competition touch and concern the land of the covenantee, a prerequisite for the passing of the benefit of a covenant at law and in equity. More recent authorities support the view that a covenant to protect a business may touch and concern the land: see *Newton Abbot Co-op. Society Ltd v. Williamson and Treadgold Ltd* [1962] 1 Ch. 286 at 292-294, 297; *Allen v. Lawson* [1926] V.L.R. 1. See also *Quadramain Pty Ltd v. Sevastapol Investments Pty Ltd* (1976) 133 C.L.R. 390 at 411-413 per Jacobs J. In addition the land intended to benefit from the covenant must be sufficiently proximate to gain a practical benefit from the covenant: *Clem Smith Nominees Pty Ltd v. Farrelly* (1978) 20 S.A.S.R. 227; *McGuigan Investments Pty Ltd v. Dalwood Vineyards Pty Ltd* [1970] 1 N.S.W.R. 686. For detailed discussion of the operation of s. 45B and s. 45C, see Taperell, Vermeesch and Harland, op. cit., Chapter V, paras 580-592.

These limitations have not had a substantial impact on a vendor's power to impose restrictive covenants binding the land. How far should the law recognise and enforce such covenants? Is it in the public interest to do so? Although there are no available figures in this jurisdiction, in the United Kingdom the Law Commission reported that in the ten year period 1955-1965 there were 600,000 sets of new restrictive covenants entered in the Land Charges Registry with respect to unregistered land alone; figures were not available for registered land: The Law Commission, *Transfer of Land, Report on Restrictive Covenants No.* 11 (1967). This rate of new covenants applying to unregistered land continued in the period 1977-1982: The Law Commission, *Transfer of Land, The Law of Positive and Restrictive Covenants No.* 127 (1984), p. 7. Given that the number of restrictive covenants in Australia is likely to be substantially less than in England, it is nevertheless clear that covenants can have a very substantial impact on the utilisation and development of land in this country.

The New South Wales Land Titles Office, in a discussion paper reviewing restrictive covenants (Land Titles Office of New South Wales, *Review of Restrictive Covenants—Discussion Paper* (1988)), set out (p. 3) the most common covenants as follows: (1) that not more than one residential dwelling shall be erected on each lot; (2) not to erect a building in excess of a certain height (in order to protect a view); (3) not to erect a building using certain specified building materials, such as asbestos cement; (4) not to use land for certain purposes, such as a factory or business; (5) not to build a front fence; and (6) not to build a fence, except of certain height or of certain materials. Covenants such as not to build more than one residential building on a parcel of land, while no doubt providing amenity to those who enjoy the benefit, may be a contributing factor to growing urban sprawl, costs of providing public utilities to new areas of development, increasing use of prime agricultural land and the vast increase in land prices resulting from limited availability of land within the major capital cities. It is arguable that such covenants should give way to the public interest in the proper development of land and that there exist other mechanisms to protect the rights of the landowner such as statutory and common law controls on nuisance and extensive controls exercised through town planning legislation. One proposal for reform might be to prohibit the creation of new restrictive covenants on the basis that planning schemes should cover the field, with the further possibility of legislating to render all existing covenants ineffective: Land Titles Office of New South Wales, *Review of Restrictive Covenants—Discussion Paper* (1988), p. 5. This view is not universally shared. The English Law Commission rejected the view that planning laws can adequately deal with the needs of the community, particularly with reference to residential property developments. Planning laws apply only minimal general standards, whereas restrictive covenants allow detailed regulation of matters which planning laws could not do adequately, such as, preservation of the character and standard of the development as a whole: The Law Commission, *Transfer of Land, The Law of Positive and Restrictive Covenants* 127 (1984), pp. 5-6. However, a fairly simple measure can at least bring about conformity with planning schemes. Under the *Environmental Planning and Assessment Act* 1979 (N.S.W.), s. 28 (see above p. 305) an environmental planning instrument can suspend inconsistent covenants. The New South Wales Department of Planning has advised that from 1988 onwards all Local Environmental Plans will be required to contain provisions suspending inconsistent covenants: Land Titles Office of New South Wales, *Review of Restrictive Covenants—Discussion Paper* (1988), p. 10.

It is implicit in the preceding paragraphs that the law relating to restrictive covenants has not been sensitive to public needs and priorities, particularly needs and priorities reflected in planning laws. In another area, restrictive covenants by their very nature have failed to accommodate changing community requirements. A covenant will only bind a successor in title to the covenantor if it is negative in nature. And so covenants requiring expenditure will not be enforceable against successors in title to the land subject to the covenant: see below p. 342. Although a number of devices have been employed to avoid this result (see below p. 308), they have not been very satisfactory. The reader will appreciate that the restrictive covenant has not been able to pass on to successors in title to the covenantor the continuing costs involved in such areas as housing estates or strata title development (*Halsall v. Brizell* [1957] 1 Ch. 168 below p. 313), fencing (*Crow v. Wood* [1971] 1 Q.B. 77, above p. 231) or contributions to maintenance and repairs (*Frater v. Finlay* (1968) 91 W.N. (N.S.W.) 730, above p. 223). This has required legislative solutions in the form of Fencing Acts, Strata Titles Acts and, more recently, the permitting of the imposition of positive covenants on land in certain circumstances. With regard to the last of these, the *Conveyancing Act* 1919 (N.S.W.), ss 88D, 88E, 88EA, 88F allow the imposition and enforcement of a "public positive covenant" by prescribed authorities against "persons from time to time having any estate or interest in the land in the same way as if it were a covenant imposing a restriction on the use of the land": s. 88F. A prescribed authority is defined to mean the Crown, a public or local authority constituted by an Act, or a corporation prescribed for the purposes of s. 88D: s. 88D(1). A "public positive covenant" includes a covenant imposing obligations to develop land, to provide services on land or land in the vicinity, or to maintain repair or insure any structure or work on land: s. 87A. The covenant has also been pressed into service as a means of enforcing "forestry covenants" as rights incidental to the grant of "forestry rights" against successors in title to the covenantor: *Conveyancing Act* 1919 (N.S.W.), ss 88EA, 88F. Section 87A of the Act defines a "forestry covenant" to include any covenant that imposes obligations requiring "(a) the construction and maintenance of access roads within the land; (b) the erection and maintenance of fencing on the land; or (c) the provision and maintenance of water supplies within the land—or imposing any term or condition with respect to the performance or failure to perform any such obligation". These developments suggest that the legislature at least perceives no difficulties in the enforcement of positive obligations against both an original covenantor and the covenantor's successors in title.

As noted in the opening paragraphs of this chapter, the position at law and in equity differed on the question whether a covenant could be enforced against a successor in title to the covenantor in respect of land burdened by the covenant. The different approaches of law and equity on this issue will be dealt with separately.

B.   ENFORCING COVENANTS AT COMMON LAW

1. The burden of a covenant

The burden of a covenant will not run with the land at common law, *Austerberry v. Corporation of Oldham* (1885) 29 Ch. D. 750, extracted below p. 309. A number of devices may, however, indirectly achieve this result. These devices are unnecessary where the burden of the covenant would run with the land in equity according to the principles enunciated in *Tulk v. Moxhay* (1848) 2 Ph. 774; 41 E.R. 1143, see below p. 340. Where the burden of the covenant will not run with the land in equity (for example, where there is a positive covenant), the covenant may be enforced indirectly against successors in title to the covenantor by a number of methods. These devices have largely been utilised to ensure that a successor in title to the covenantor will be bound by positive covenants, that is, covenants which may require expenditure of money:

(1) As a condition of taking benefits: *Halsall v. Brizell* [1957] Ch. 169, referred to below p. 313; *Tito v. Waddell (No. 2)* [1977] Ch. 106, extracted below p. 311.

(2) By a chain of covenants. The original vendor requires the purchaser to enter into a positive covenant, for example, to maintain fencing. The purchaser remains liable on the covenant even after he or she has disposed of the property. Because of this continuing liability, the purchaser and subsequent purchasers in turn, as vendors require purchasers to enter into a covenant indemnifying against breach of the covenant. This device is effective so long as there is a chain of covenants which can be enforced; if there is a break in the chain, it ceases to be effective— for example, if there is a failure to insert a covenant in a transfer, or the original covenantor becomes bankrupt. As to the possible use of a mutual deed of covenant executed by each purchaser on acquisition: see Prichard, "Making Positive Covenants Run" (1973) 37 Conv. (N.S.) 194.

(3) By enlargement of a long lease into a freehold. Where there is a lease of freehold land for a period of not less than 300 years with at least 200 years yet to run, then a lease which complies with the relevant statutory provisions may be enlarged into a fee simple. The fee simple estate so acquired is subject to all the covenants relating to user and enjoyment and to all the obligations which it would have been subject had it not been enlarged. This, in theory, allows a positive covenant to be annexed to the freehold. The relevant statutory provisions in New South Wales are contained in *Conveyancing Act* 1919 (N.S.W.), s. 134. This method of imposing positive covenants has not yet received judicial sanction. See the critical discussion of the substantially similar English section by Taylor, "The Enlargement of Leasehold to Freehold" (1958) 2 Conv. (N.S.) 101. Leases can also be utilised to enforce positive burdens: see Chapter 8.

(4) By reserving a right of re-entry for breach of condition, the right of re-entry to be exercised within the perpetuity period. See *Shiloh Spinners Ltd v. Harding* [1973] A.C. 691 where it was held that a right of entry could be validly reserved on an assignment of leasehold property even though the assignor retained no interest. It was further held that the right of entry could subsist in law in respect of non-compliance with covenants, even if those covenants, as such, were not enforceable.

(5) By rent charge: See *Austerberry v. Corp. of Oldham*, below; *Morland v. Cook* (1868) L.R. 6 Eq. 252.

AUSTERBERRY v. CORP. OF OLDHAM

Court of Appeal (1885) 29 Ch. D. 750

[Austerberry was successor in title to one John Elliott who was the owner of property over which it was desired to construct a road. Elliott, for value, transferred part of the land to trustees for use as a road with a right of user by the public on payment of a toll. The trustees covenanted with Elliott, his heirs and assigns, that they would construct the road and thereafter keep and maintain the said road and every part thereof in good repair, order and condition. The corporation was successor in title to the trustees by virtue of statute. It was argued that the covenant bound the corporation as successors in title to the trustees.]

LINDLEY L.J. Plaintiff says: "You, the corporation, have bought or acquired this road under an Act of Parliament which places you in the position of, and in no better position than, those from whom you got it; you acquired it from certain trustees, and those trustees covenanted with my predecessors in title to keep this road open for the public, and to repair it: You are bound by that covenant to repair, and I am in a position to enforce against you that covenant." . . .

The first question which I will consider is whether that covenant runs with the land, as it is called—whether the benefit of it runs with the land held by the plaintiff, and whether the burden of it runs with the land held by the defendants; because, if the covenant does run at law, then the plaintiff, so far as I can see, would be right as to this portion of his claim. Now, as regards the benefit running with the plaintiff's land, the covenant is, so far as the road goes, a covenant to repair the road; what I mean by that is, there is nothing in the deed which points particularly to the portion of the road which abuts upon or fronts the plaintiff's land—it is a covenant to repair the whole of the road, no distinction being made between the portion of that road which joins or abuts upon his land and the rest of the road; in other words, it is a covenant simply to make and maintain this road as a public highway; there is no covenant to do anything whatever on the plaintiff's land, and there is nothing pointing to the plaintiff's land, in particular. Now it appears to me to be going a long way to say that the benefit of that covenant runs with the plaintiff's land. I do not overlook the fact that the plaintiff as a frontager has certain rights of getting on to the road; and if this covenant had been so worded as to shew that there had been an intention to grant him some particular benefit in respect of that particular part of his land, possibly we might have said that the benefit of the covenant did run with this land; but when you look at the covenant it is a mere covenant with him, as with all adjoining owners, to make this road, a small portion of which only abuts on his land, and there is nothing specially relating to his land at all. I cannot see myself how any benefit of this covenant runs with his land.

But it strikes me, I confess, that there is a still more formidable objection as regards the burden. Does the burden of this covenant run with the land so as to bind the defendants? The defendants have acquired the road under the trustees, and they are bound by such covenant as runs with the land. Now we come to face the difficulty; does a covenant to repair all this road run with the land—that is, does the burden of it descend upon those to whom the road may be assigned in future? We are not dealing here with a case of landlord and tenant. The authorities which refer to that class of cases have little, if any, bearing upon the case which we have to consider, and I am not prepared to say that any covenant which imposes a burden upon land does run with the land, unless the covenant does, upon the true construction of one deed containing the covenant, amount to either a grant of an easement, or a rent-charge, or some estate or interest in the land. A mere covenant to repair, or to do something of that kind, does not seem to me, I confess, to run with the land in such a way as to bind those who may acquire it.

. . . [I]n the absence of authority it appears to me that we shall be perfectly warranted in saying that the burden of this covenant does not run with the land. After all it is a mere personal covenant. If the parties had intended to charge this land for ever, into whosoever hands it came, with the burden of repairing the road, there are ways and means known to conveyancers by which it could be done with comparative ease; all that would have been necessary would have been to create a rent-charge and charge it on the tolls, and the thing would have been done. They have not done anything of the sort, and, therefore, it seems to me to show that they did not intend to have a covenant which should run with the land. That disposes of the part of the case which is perhaps the most difficult.

The last point was this—that even if it did not run with the land at law, still, upon the authority of *Tulk v. Moxhay* (1848) 2 Ph. 774; 41 E.R. 1143, the defendants, having bought the land with notice of this covenant, take the land subject to it. Mr Collins very properly did not press that upon us, because after the two recent decisions in the Court of Appeal in *Haywood v. Brunswick Permanent Benefit Building Society* (1881) 8 Q.B.D. 403 and *London and South Western Railway Co. v. Gomm* (1880) 20 Ch. D. 562 that argument is untenable. *Tulk v. Moxhay* (1848) 2 Ph. 774; 41 E.R. 1143 cannot be extended to covenants of this description. It appears to me, therefore, that upon all points the plaintiff has failed, and that the appeal ought to be dismissed with costs.

[The judgments of Cotton and Fry L.JJ. have been omitted.]

NOTES

The *Conveyancing Act* 1919 (N.S.W.), s. 70A provides:

70A.—(1) A covenant relating to any land of a covenantor or capable of being bound by him by covenant shall, unless a contrary intention is expressed, be deemed to be made by the covenantor on behalf of himself and his successors in title, and the persons deriving title under him or them, and, subject as aforesaid, shall have effect as if such successors and other persons were expressed.

This subsection extends to a covenant to do some act relating to the land, notwithstanding that the subject-matter may not be in existence when the covenant is made.

(2) For the purposes of this section in connection with covenants restrictive of the user of land "successors in title" shall be deemed to include the owners and occupiers for the time being of such land.

(3) This section applies only to covenants made or implied after the commencement of the *Conveyancing (Amendment) Act 1930.*

Despite the apparent width of the section, it does not alter the common law rule enunciated in the principal case. If the words implied by the section were expressed in a deed, this would not have had the effect of making the burden run at law: *Tophams Ltd v. Earl of Sefton* [1967] 1 A.C. 50 at 73, 81. Compare the position with regard to restrictive covenants in equity.

TITO v. WADDELL (No. 2)

Chancery Division [1977] Ch. 106

[In 1902 the British Crown granted a 99 year licence to a British company to mine phosphate on Ocean Island. In 1913 an agreement was entered into between the landowners and the company. The agreement provided for acquisition of certain areas for mining and, inter alia, required the company to return all worked out lands to the original owners and replant areas already mined or to be mined with coconut and other food bearing trees. Pursuant to the 1913 agreement, landowners entered into agreements with the company to allow phosphate mining. Of these the "A type" agreements replaced earlier agreements and the "C type" agreements related to new acquisitions by the company. Each agreement required the company on ceasing to mine the land, to carry out replanting. In 1920 pursuant to a purchase of the company's undertakings by the United Kingdom, Australian and New Zealand governments, the company's rights were vested in British Phosphate Commissioners. One of the many issues which came before the court was whether the British Phosphate Commissioners as successors in title to the original covenantor were bound by the obligation to replant mined areas.]

MEGARRY V.C.

BENEFIT AND BURDEN . . .

The basic principle has plainly been expanding. Its origin appears in at least two forms: see Megarry and Wade, *The Law of Real Property* (4th ed.), p. 750. One form of the principle is as a technical rule relating to deeds. If a person is named as a party to a deed, but does not execute it, the deed will nevertheless be held to bind him if he knowingly takes the benefit of it. In that form, it is not much more than part of a rule for determining who are to be treated as being parties to a deed. In another form, the rule is that if by an indenture to which A and B were the only parties A granted land to B for life with remainder to C, on terms that the land was to be held subject to certain conditions, then if C entered after B's death and took the land by virtue of the indenture, he thereupon became bound by the conditions, even though he was no party to the indenture. This is the instance given in a passage in Litt. 374 (and in Co. Litt. 230b) to which reference is made in the cases. In each form, it will be observed, the principle applied only to a specified person, either named as a party to the deed, or named (or perhaps ascertainable) as the grantee of an estate. . . . Before I turn to the cases, it is convenient to consider certain aspects of the doctrine that have been settled or are emerging. By no means all of them are clear.

(A) CONDITIONAL BENEFITS AND INDEPENDENT OBLIGATIONS. One of the most important distinctions is between what for brevity may be called conditional benefits, on the one hand, and on the other hand independent obligations. An instrument may be framed so that it confers only a conditional or qualified right, the condition or qualification being that certain restrictions shall be observed or certain burdens assumed, such as an obligation to make certain payments. Such restrictions or qualifications are an intrinsic part of the right: you take the right as it stands, and you cannot pick out the good and reject the bad. In such cases it is not only the original grantee who is bound by the burden: his successors in title are unable to take the right without also assuming the burden. The benefit and the burden have been annexed to each other ab initio, and so the benefit is only a conditional benefit. In the other class of case the right and the burden, although arising under the same instrument, are independent of each other: X grants a right to Y and by the same instrument Y independently covenants with X to do some act. In such cases, although Y is of course bound by his covenant, questions may arise whether successors in title to Y's right can take it free from the obligations of Y's covenant, or whether they are bound by them under what for want of a better name I shall call the pure principle of benefit and burden.

(B) QUI SENTIT COMMODUM SENTIRE DEBET ET ONUS. This ancient maxim, to be found in 2 Co. Inst. 489, bears an uncertain relationship to the principle under discussion. In spirit it is the same: yet the instances of its operation given in the books are curiously restricted and haphazard: see *Broom's Legal Maxims* (10th ed.), pp. 482-486. Cases of burdens annexed to property binding those who take it are given as instances of the maxim, and so are cases of election. I shall not attempt to explore these thickets. In the case of burdens attached to land, such as mortgages or easements, it hardly seems necessary to resort to any doctrine about benefit and burden: if you take something that has a burden annexed to it, you have to take it as it is, burden and all. Again, you cannot pick out the good and leave the bad. If more Latin is required, transit terra cum onere will do. The parallel between this head and conditional benefits under the previous head is obvious. The only essential difference seems to be that where there is a burden which in its nature is annexed to property there will be no initial question of determining whether or not the burden is a condition of the benefit. In neither case is there any question of applying any pure principle of benefit and burden: each in essence consists merely of having to take a thing as it stands. Perhaps I should add that there may be some ambiguity about the word "burden". Sometimes it is used in the sense of burdens annexed to property, such as mortgages, and sometimes it is used in the sense of some onerous but independent obligation which under the pure benefit and burden principle may or may not bind successors in title. In most cases the context will make the sense clear. I do no more than indicate a possible source of misunderstanding of what has been said in some of the cases and elsewhere.

(C) OBLIGATORY AND OPTIONAL. In some cases the principle of benefit and burden appears to operate in an obligatory form. In the two technical instances that I have given, once the benefit has been taken under the deed, or once the estate has been claimed under the indenture, the burdens are as binding as if the taker of the benefit or estate had executed the instrument. In the case of conditional benefits, the result seems to be the same: take the benefit, and at once the burdens bind you. But in the case of independent obligations, the pure principle of benefit and burden (if it applies at all) seems at least in some cases to operate in an optional manner. Thus if the benefit is a licence to cross a neighbour's land and the burden is the making of an annual payment, an assignee of the licence appears to be able to resist claims for future payments if he ceases to enjoy the licence. In such a case, he can say that he has never become contractually bound to make the payments, and that he is taking no benefit for the period to which the payments relate. Plainly there is a great difference between saying "As soon as you accept any benefit you become subject to the whole of the burdens, past, present and future", and saying "As long as you continue to accept the benefit you must continue to bear the burden". Whether in the latter case there would be any right to resume enjoying the benefit and bearing the burden after there has once been a discontinuance I do not know.

(D) CONTINUING AND UNITARY BURDENS. The previous head leads to the present head. In some cases the burden may be a continuing burden, such as an obligation to pay an annual sum. In other cases the burden may be a future unitary burden, such as an obligation to pay compensation for damage, or to restore land after opencast working; and of course there may be many variants and mixtures of burdens. In the case of continuing burdens, the pure principle of benefit and burden seems to apply in the optional form discussed under the previous head. But in the case of unitary burdens, how does that principle apply? Does every successor in title to the benefit become liable for the whole of the burden when it accrues, however brief his enjoyment of the benefit? If not, how is the burden to be borne?

(E) RELATIONSHIP TO ASSIGNMENT OF BENEFIT. It was, of course, accepted on all hands that the burden of positive covenants will not run with the land; and if matters such as novation are left on one side, it is clear that in general contractual burdens are not assignable, though contractual benefits are. How, then, does the principle that he who takes the benefit must bear the burden fit in with cases where benefits such as the right to receive certain payments under a contract have been assigned but the assignee of those benefits has been held or assumed to take free of the burdens under the contract?

(F) ACTIVE AND PASSIVE. The principle in its pure form may operate in two different ways; and during the argument these became known as the "active" and the "passive" forms. The active form looks to the future. X is seeking to exercise some right which has been assigned to him. If the doctrine applies, he can exercise the right only if he accepts the burdens; he has no choice. The passive form looks to the past. X has done some act, such as entering on Y's land and damaging it, and he is being sued by Y. X may then have a choice. He may claim to be an assignee under a grant of the right to do the act, in which case, if the doctrine applies, he must bear the burdens imposed by the instrument creating the right, for example, an obligation to pay compensation. Alternatively, he may refrain from relying on the instrument, and instead accept liability on the footing that his act was unauthorised. If the rate of compensation and the measure of damages at common law differ, the active and passive forms may thus operate differently, though I do not know that there is any great difference in principle between them.

(G) LEGAL AND EQUITABLE. It seems clear that the doctrine may operate not only at law, as in the two technical instances that I have given, but also in equity, as appears from the cases.

I think that I have said enough about some of the categories and problems of this branch of the law to make it desirable to turn to the authorities. They fall into three groups. In the first, the issue was on the pure principle of benefit and burden. The burden was held to have passed not because the right granted was held to be conditional upon assuming the burden, or to be qualified by it, but because of the principle that he who takes the benefit must bear the burden. In the second group of cases the issue has been whether or not the right granted was a conditional or qualified right; in all the cases save one the right has been held to be conditional, and the claimant has succeeded. The third group of cases consists of cases cited on the relationship that I have mentioned between the principle of benefit and burden, and the assignment of benefits. However, it will be seen on examination that there are cases in this category which really belong to the second group.

The leading case in the first group is the well-known decision of Upjohn J. in *Halsall v. Brizell* [1957] Ch. 169. In that case the owners of an estate laid it out in 174 building plots, and formed roads and sewers, a sea wall and a promenade and so on; and in disposing of the building plots the developers, as I shall call them, retained the roads, sewers, sea wall and promenade. A deed of covenant made between the developers, as trustees for the parties to the deed, and the owners of plots made a number of provisions for the regulation of the estate. All this was done in 1851, in the spacious conveyancing language of the day; I shall try to put matters briefly. One of the provisions was that each party to the deed, and his successors, should contribute and pay a due and just proportion, in respect of his plot of land, of the expenses of maintaining the roads, sewers, promenade and sea wall; and this was supported by a power of distress for the developers and their successors. The deed also provided machinery for the proprietors of plots to determine the expenses in general meeting, with provisions for voting and so on.

The litigation arose in respect of a house on one plot which, without being structurally divided, was let to five separate tenants; and much turned on a resolution passed at a general meeting of plot-holders in 1950. That resolution empowered the trustees to make additional annual calls for every house divided into two or more separate flats or dwellings, with a limit of three calls per plot. The defendants, who were executors of the plot owner who had divided the house, duly paid single calls in respect of the house. But they refused to pay the two additional calls each year which the plaintiffs (who were the present trustees of the deed) had demanded in accordance with the resolution. The plaintiffs did not sue for payment, but instead took out an originating summons which raised two main questions: first, whether the deed was valid and effectual at all in so far as it purported to make the successors of the original contracting parties liable to pay calls; and secondly, if it was, whether the 1950 resolution imposing additional calls was a valid resolution.

Upjohn J. answered the second question by holding, for reasons that I need not discuss, that the resolution was ultra vires and void. That by itself sufficed to dispose of the case: and a declaration that the resolution was ultra vires and void was accordingly made. The trustees therefore failed in their claim, for the single calls had been paid, and only the liability for the additional calls was in issue. But before reaching this conclusion, the judge had considered the first question that was before the court; and of course it is this question that is important in the present case. On this, the judge said (at 182) that it was plain that the defendants "could not be sued on the covenants contained in the deed for at least three reasons". These were that a positive covenant such as that in question did not run with the land; that the provisions for the payment of calls plainly infringed the rule against perpetuities; and that it was conceded that the provision for distress, not being annexed to a rentcharge, was invalid.

On these last two points I may mention, first, that the case seems to have escaped notice in books on perpetuities. Secondly, on rentcharges, there is an interesting contrast with *Morland v. Cook* (1868) L.R. 6 Eq. 252. In that case, a covenant by various landowners to share the expenses of maintaining a sea wall was held to be enforceable at law against successors in title of the covenantors. The reason subsequently given by the Court of Appeal was that, although framed as a covenant, the obligation was really a rentcharge; and this conclusion was reached because the covenant was to pay the money "out of the said lands": see *Austerberry v. Oldham Corp.* (1885) 29 Ch. D. 750 at 774, 775, 782.

Having held that the defendants could not be sued on the covenants of the deed, Upjohn J. continued [1957] Ch. 169 at 182:

> But it is conceded that it is ancient law that a man cannot take benefit under a deed without subscribing to the obligations thereunder. If authority is required for that proposition, I need but refer to one sentence during the argument in *Elliston v. Reacher* [1908] 2 Ch. 665 at 669, where Lord Cozens-Hardy M.R. observed: "It is laid down in Co. Litt. 230b, that a man who takes the benefit of a deed is bound by a condition contained in it, though he does not execute it." If the defendants did not desire to take the benefit of this deed, for the reasons I have given, they could not be under any liability to pay the obligations thereunder. But, of course, they do desire to take the benefit of this

deed. They have no right to use the sewers which are vested in the plaintiffs, and I cannot see that they have any right, apart from the deed, to use the roads of the park which lead to their particular house, No. 22, Salisbury Road. The defendants cannot rely on any way of necessity or on any right by prescription, for the simple reason that when the house was originally sold in 1931 to their predecessor in title he took the house on the terms of the deed of 1851 which contractually bound him to contribute a proper proportion of the expenses of maintaining the roads and sewers, and so forth, as a condition of being entitled to make use of those roads and sewers. Therefore, it seems to me that the defendants here cannot, if they desire to use this house, as they do, take advantage of the trusts concerning the user of the roads contained in the deed and the other benefits created by it without undertaking the obligations thereunder. Upon that principle it seems to me that they are bound by this deed, if they desire to take its benefits.

It will be seen that this passage is founded on a concession by counsel. Upjohn J. asked (at 180): "Is there not a rule that a person who accepts the benefit of a deed must also accept the burden of it?" Counsel for the defendants replied: "Yes, that is conceded"; and he cited *Norton on Deeds* (2nd ed.), p. 26, and the observation in *Elliston v. Reacher* which was cited in the passage of the judgment that I have just read. Before I go any further, I think I should say something about this observation and its sequel.

It is obvious that there is a considerable difference between a rule which applies only to a specified person who is named as party to a deed or as grantee of an estate, and who takes a benefit under the deed or takes the estate, and a rule which applies to "a man" or "a person" who takes the benefit of a deed. In the former case, the rule applies only to a persona designata who is within the contemplation of the other parties to the deed as being intended to take the benefits or the estate under it and bear the burdens of it: the doctrine simply cures the defect of that person not having bound himself by executing the deed. (It is old law that a person who is not a party to a deed may nevertheless bind himself by a covenant in the deed if he executes it: *Salter v. Kidgly* (1689) Carth. 76; 90 E.R. 648.) In the latter case "a man" or "a person" may, if taken literally, be anyone in the world, and outside the contemplation of the parties to the deed, though some limitation must no doubt be implied.

With that in mind, it seems plain that the interlocutory observation of Sir Herbert Cozens-Hardy M.R. in *Elliston v. Reacher* [1908] 2 Ch. 665 at 669, the concession by counsel in *Halsall v. Brizell* [1957] Ch. 169, and what Upjohn J. said in that case, all involve a substantial expansion of the principle. The proposition laid down in Co. Litt. 230b (and Litt. 374, which must be read with it), was not in terms of "a man" or "a person", but merely in terms of the grantee of an estate. Similarly, the passage in *Norton on Deeds* (2nd ed.), p. 26, cited in counsel's concession was merely in terms of a party to a deed who does not execute it. Cozens-Hardy M.R.'s observation was, indeed, an interlocutory observation not repeated in his judgment; and one must bear in mind the warning of Viscount Simon L.C. that such observations are not judicial pronouncements, and decide nothing, even provisionally, but are merely made in order to elucidate the argument or point the question or indicate what needs investigation: *Practice Note* [1942] W.N. 89. Furthermore, the judgment in *Halsall v. Brizell* was not a reserved judgment; indeed, I observe, a little wistfully, that the case was argued and decided in a single day.

Let it be accepted that a degree of historical frailty can be detected in the forensic process in this sphere, and let it also be accepted that, at any rate on one view, what Upjohn J. said on the point was not necessary for his decision and forms no part of his ratio decidendi. Accept all that, and there still remains the fact that, quite apart from other authorities, the propositions enunciated by Cozens-Hardy M.R. and Upjohn J. seemed right to them. Couple that with the simple principles of fairness and consistency that I have mentioned, and it will be seen that there is good reason why I should be ready to adopt and apply the broader proposition that has emerged from the technicalities of past ages. At the same time, in considering the application of the expanded doctrine to the case before me, it will be necessary to consider what are the true limits of that doctrine. With that, I turn to the only other case in this first group.

In *E. R. Ives Investment Ltd v. High* [1967] 2 Q.B. 379, the owner of Blackacre erected a building with foundations which trespassed to a small extent on Whiteacre. The owners of Blackacre and Whiteacre then orally agreed that the trespassing foundations of Blackacre could remain but that Whiteacre should have a right of way over Blackacre. The agreement was never registered as a land charge, and Blackacre passed to purchasers. Difficult questions of registration arose, as well as questions of estoppel. But the point with which I am concerned was that which appears at 394. There, Lord Denning M.R. applied the principle that he who takes the benefit must also take the burden, referring with approval to *Halsall v. Brizell* [1957] Ch. 169. "So long as" the owners of Blackacre took the benefit of having foundations which reached into Whiteacre, he said, they must shoulder the burden of the right of way over Blackacre: "so long as" the owner of Whiteacre took the benefit of the right of way, he must allow the trespassing foundations of Blackacre to remain. Danckwerts L.J. took a similar view (at 399, 400) whereas Winn L.J. put the emphasis on estoppel.

The words "so long as" plainly appear to indicate that with continuing benefits and burdens on both sides the burdens could be escaped at the price of ceasing to enjoy the benefits. A similar view appeared in *Hopgood v. Brown* [1955] 1 W.L.R. 213 at 226; but that was a case of reciprocal licences, and I think that Sir Raymond Evershed M.R. was putting matters more on the basis of estoppel than on a basis of benefit and burden. However, the point seems to have been explicitly decided by the Supreme Court of Canada in *Parkinson v. Reid* (1966) 56 D.L.R. (2d) 315. There, in the absence of privity either of contract or of estate, it was held that defendants who derive title under an instrument which conveyed land with the right to use the plaintiff's wall but subject to certain repairing obligations were not liable on those obligations after they had ceased to use the wall. Before I leave *E. R. Ives Investment Ltd v. High* [1967] 2 Q.B. 379 I should add that it makes it clear that the principle applies in the case of parol agreements as well as for deeds, and that in that case the principle was operating in equity, rather than at law.

I have now considered the only cases cited which seem to me to depend on the pure principle of benefit and burden. I must next turn to the second group of cases that were cited on this topic, being those which depended on whether or not the benefit was a qualified or conditional benefit. . . .

[His Lordship then referred to *Aspen v. Seddon* (1875) 10 Ch. App. 394; *Aspen v. Seddon (No. 2)* (1876) 1 Ex. D. 496; *Westhoughton Urban District Council v. Wigan Coal & Iron Co. Ltd* [1919] 1 Ch. 159 as illustrations. In these cases the right to mine was conditional or qualified by the duty to pay compensation for damage done. His Lordship continued:]

I pause to emphasise that in these cases there is plainly an initial question of construction. If an instrument grants rights and also imposes obligations, the court must ascertain whether upon the true construction of the instrument it has granted merely qualified or conditional rights, the qualification or condition being the due observance of the obligations, or whether it has granted unqualified rights and imposed independent obligations. In construing the instrument, the more closely the obligations are linked to the rights, the easier it will be to construe the instrument as granting merely qualified rights. The question always must be one of the intention of the parties as gathered from the instrument as a whole. It is familiar law that in leases the tendency is to construe the covenants of the lessor and the covenants of the lessee as being independent of each other, so that the observance of the one is not conditional upon the observance of the other. Such covenants, of course, usually appear separately and distinctly in the lease.

[His Lordship after referring to a number of other authorities continued:]

I now come to the third group of cases, those cited on the relationship of the pure principle of benefit and burden to the assignment of benefits. As I have already indicated, the point is that if the benefit and burden doctrine is to be given the full width claimed for it, questions must arise on the many instances of assignees of the benefit of a contract not being bound by the burdens of that contract. . . .

I emerge from a consideration of the authorities put before me with a number of conclusions and a number of uncertainties. First, for the reasons I have given, I think that there is ample authority for holding that there has become established in the law what I have called the pure principle of benefit and burden. Secondly, I also think that this principle is distinct from the conditional benefit cases, and cases of burdens annexed to property. Although language speaking of benefit and burden is sometimes used in the latter classes of case, I do not think it is really apt, and it is liable to confuse. In such cases the rule is really a rule of "all or none", an inelegant but convenient expression that may be used for brevity. A burden that has been made a condition of the benefit, or is annexed to property, simply passes with it: if you take the benefit or the property you must take it as it stands, with all its appendages, good or bad. It is only where the benefit and the burden are independent that the pure principle of benefit and burden can apply.

Thirdly, it is a question of construction of the instrument or transaction, depending on the intention that has been manifested in it, whether or not it has created a conditional benefit or a burden annexed to property. If it has, that is an end of the matter: if it has not, and the benefit and burden are independent, questions of the pure principle of benefit and burden may arise. On the question of construction, there is a possible parallel in the case of two or more things given by a will to the same person, for example a leasehold house and its contents: if the will is construed as making a single gift of the two things, as distinct from two separate gifts, the legatee cannot take one and reject the other, as he might wish to do if the lease is onerous.

Fourthly, the application of the benefit and burden principle will normally come later than the question of construction. If the initial transaction has created benefits and burdens which, on its true construction, are distinct, the question whether a person who is not an original party can take one without the other will prima facie depend upon the circumstances in which he comes into the transaction. If, for instance, all that is assigned to him is the benefit of a contract, and the assignor, who is a party to the contract, undertakes to continue to discharge the burdens of it, it would be remarkable if it were to be held that the assignee could not take the benefit without assuming the burden. The circumstances show that the assignee was intended to take only the benefit, and that the burden was intended to be borne in the same way as it had been borne previously.

On the other hand, if the assignee takes as a purported assignee of the whole contract from a company which is on the point of going into liquidation, he undertaking to discharge all the burdens and to indemnify the company, then, unless the benefit and burden principle is to be rejected in its entirety, I would have thought that the circumstances showed that he was not intended to take the benefit without also assuming the burdens, and that the result would accord with the intention, vis-à-vis not only the company but also the persons entitled to enforce those burdens. No doubt the terms of any relevant document would be of major importance: but I would regard the matter as one which has to be determined from the surrounding circumstances as a whole. One possible way of looking at it is to regard the subsequent transaction as doing what the initial transaction did not, namely, annex the burden to the benefit so that the one could not be taken free from the other: but there are difficulties in this.

Fifthly, a problem that is unsolved (and, it seems, unconsidered) is that of who falls within the benefit and burden principle. In the old forms of the rule there was no difficulty; a person named as a party to a deed, or a person granted an estate by a deed, could be identified without difficulty. But when the rule came to be stated in the form of "a person" or "a man" who takes the benefit of a deed, the answer is not so obvious. Plainly this is wider than merely those named in the original instrument, but equally plainly it cannot sensibly mean anyone in the world. In *Halsall v. Brizell* [1957] Ch. 169 and in *E. R. Ives Investment Ltd v. High* [1967] 2 Q.B. 379 the doctrine was applied to successors in title to land which one of the original parties had taken; and plainly such persons should be within the principle. But is it to be confined to those who are shown to be successors in title to land or other property? Should someone who has such a title be bound, while someone else, who may on investigation be found to have no proper title, take free? I do not see why there should be any such distinction. It seems to me that the principle ought to embrace anybody whose connection with the transaction creating the benefit and burden is sufficient to show that he has some claim to the benefit, whether or not he has a valid title to it. Mere strangers seem to me to be another matter: I would exclude them from the meaning of "a man" or "a person" for the purposes of the principle. I shall not attempt to explore the obvious difficulties in determining just where the dividing line lies or ought to lie.

I shall next consider whether the defendant British Phosphate Commissioners are liable under any form of the benefit and burden rule, whether pure or "all or none". First, there is the question of the construction of the 1913 agreement and the A and C deeds. In the former I can see nothing which gives any real support to the view that the benefits to the company under the agreement have been made conditional on accepting its burdens; and in particular that applies to cl. 12(a), relating to replanting. The mere fact that the same instrument creates both the benefit and the burden, or that they both relate to the same subject matter, cannot possibly, in my view, make the one conditional on the other. I can see no words in the instrument, or for that matter anything else, that manifest any intention to bring about this result. The contrast between this document and the documents in cases where there has been held to be a conditional benefit are obvious.

The A and C deeds are in like case. Of course, they have fewer clauses than the 1913 agreement, and they concentrate on mining, without extraneous matters such as cl. 12(d) and (e) of the 1913 agreement, which provide for uniform prices for goods and the supply of fresh water at 3/4d. a gallon. But I am quite unable to see anything which makes the grant of the rights to the company conditional on, or qualified by, the obligation to replant. In the result I hold that neither the 1913 agreement nor the A or C deeds confer benefits which are qualified by or conditional upon the replanting obligations. Accordingly, for the plaintiffs to succeed under this head the case must be brought within the pure principle of benefit and burden.

I propose first to consider whether the two defendant British Phosphate Commissioners fall within that principle. There are two questions. First, do the circumstances in which they became connected with the 1913 agreement and the A and C deeds show that they ought not to be able to take the benefit without accepting the burden; and, secondly, have they a sufficient title to the benefit? I can consider these together. . . .

When the first commissioners took over from the company, the contemporary documents and circumstances made it plain that the British Phosphate Commissioners were to take over not only the rights but also the liabilities: I have already read cl. 1(c) of the 1920 indenture. When thereafter a new commissioner was appointed there were no documents to make this plain, but the circumstances seem to me to be to the same effect. The thought that a new commissioner was intended to take over the assets, but not the liabilities, which the outgoing commissioner, stripped of the assets, was to bear for the rest of his life, and his estate after his death, seems to me to be absurd. I shall not pursue the matter in detail, since it seems to me overwhelmingly clear that at every stage of change the whole basis was that of there being no right to enjoy the benefits without undertaking the burdens. There is no question of any British Phosphate Commissioner having intended not to accept the benefits but to commit wholesale trespasses instead. Furthermore, the connection of the defendant commissioners with the instruments creating the benefits and the burdens seems to me to be ample for them to be held liable for the burdens if they took any benefits.

That brings me to the question of taking the benefits; and here there is a diversity between the 1913 agreement and the A and C deeds.

[His Lordship went on to find that insufficient benefit was obtained under the 1913 agreement and continued:]

As it has developed, I do not think that the pure benefit and burden principle is a technical doctrine, to be satisfied by what is technical and minimal. I regard it as being a broad principle of justice, to be satisfied by what is real and substantial. . . .

The A and C deeds are another matter. They produce a substantial stock of mining rights which successive British Phosphate Commissioners exploited over the years; and these cannot be brushed aside as being irrelevant or trivial. . . .

Where a right to mine has been exercised by predecessors, and successors who acquire that right remain able to exercise it in circumstances which give reality to the right, I think that the successors take a sufficient benefit to invoke the principle. I do not consider that it is, or should be, open to a successor Commissioner to say of a plot: "That was worked in the time of my predecessors. True, under the A or C deed I now have the right to work it further if I wish; but not unless I actually do so am I to be treated as taking a benefit under the deed. If instead of returning the plot to its owner I do nothing with it for years, thus keeping open any decision whether to work it further, and in the end I decide to work the plot no more, I have taken no benefit under the deed." . . .

The next question is: "What burden?" This case squarely raises the questions of the application of the pure principle of benefit and burden to unitary burdens, a question which does not seem to have appeared in any previous case. In the case of continuing benefits and burdens, *E. R. Ives Investment Ltd. v. High* [1967] 2 Q.B. 379 supports the proposition that if the benefit is given up, the burden ceases; and of course if that applied to unitary burdens, questions might arise in each case whether the benefit was still being taken. But in the case of a unitary burden such as this, I do not think that it can be the case that a person taking the benefit can, when challenged, cease to take it, and then say that he is no longer subject to the burden of restoring the land, or paying compensation for the damage done, or doing whatever else there is to be done. . . .

When the full features of the principle have been worked out, it may well be that if, as I think, any person who takes a sufficient benefit, for however short a period, is held liable for the whole burden, including future unitary burdens, it will also be held that there are implied rights of indemnity which will ensure that, whoever is held initially liable, the liability will ultimately be borne by the right persons. Where there is a terminal liability, such as the obligation of replanting in this case, it seems right that the burden should ultimately be borne by the latest in the chain of persons liable at the time when the burden accrues. Certainly this should be so in the case of an undertaking such as that of the British Phosphate Commissioners, where normal commercial methods contemplate some sinking fund or other provision for meeting future liabilities of this kind. On that footing, the two defendant British Phosphate Commissioners, being now in office, are in my judgment properly subject to the whole of the liability. . . .

I can deal quite shortly with one last matter, namely, whether the plaintiffs are entitled to enforce the obligations. This arises because they are not, of course, original contracting parties. Subject to one point, I can see no difficulty. There is no reason why the benefit of the replanting obligations should not run with the land both at law and in equity. The obligations could hardly more clearly touch and concern the land, and the benefit of them must have been intended to run with the land and be enforceable by the owner for the time being. The present owners of the land are therefore the persons entitled to enforce the obligations.

NOTE

See also *Rufa Pty Ltd v. Cross* [1981] Qd R. 365, above p. 226 and comment on *Tito's* case by Aughtersan, "Enforcement of Positive Burdens—A New Viability" (1985) Conv. (N.S.) 12. Would any advantage be gained by incorporating a covenant to pay or contribute as part of the grant of an easement? See *Frater v. Finlay* (1968) 91 W.N. (N.S.W.) 730, above p. 223.

2. The benefit of a covenant

In determining whether the benefit of a covenant can run at law, a distinction is drawn between the original covenantee and successors in title. Original covenantees can enforce the covenant on contractual principles, irrespective of whether the benefit of the covenant is annexed to the land.

(a) The original covenantee

The original covenantee by virtue of the contract with the covenantor is entitled to enforce the covenant whether or not the covenantor owns land which can benefit from the covenant: *London County Council v. Allen* [1914] 3 K.B. 642 at 660, 673. Where the covenantee, at the time of the breach, no longer owns the land benefiting from the covenant, nominal damages only can be recovered: *Formby v. Barker* [1903] 2 Ch. 539. Compare Hayton, "Restrictive Covenants as Property Interests" (1971) 87 L.Q.R. 539 at 542-543.

At common law a person not a party to a deed inter partes could not sue on the deed. (This rule did not apply to deed polls: see *Chelsea and Walham Green v. Armstrong* [1951] Ch. 853.) The common law rule has been the subject of legislative intervention. The *Law of Property Act* 1925 (U.K.), s. 56 provides that a person may take an interest in land or other property although he or she may not be named as a party to a conveyance or other instrument. It should be noted, however, that the operation of the *Law of Property Act* 1925 (U.K.), s. 56 is restricted to real property by reason of its enactment in a consolidated statute: *Beswick v. Beswick* [1968] A.C. 58. This limitation may not apply to the Australian provisions. In New South Wales, the *Conveyancing Act* 1919, s. 36C provides:

> 36C.—(1) A person may take an immediate or other interest in land or other property, or the benefit of any condition, right of entry, covenant, or agreement over or respecting land or other property, although he may not be named as a party to the assurance or other instrument.
>
> (2) Such person may sue, and shall be entitled to all rights and remedies in respect thereof as if he had been named as a party to the assurance or other instrument.

Several comments must be made on the operation of the section:

(1) The section can be called in aid only by a person in whose favour the grant purports to be made or with whom the covenant or agreement purports to be made, *Re Ecclesiastical Commissioners for Englands Conveyance* [1936] Ch. 430; *White v. Bijou Mansions* [1937] Ch. 610; [1938] Ch. 351; *Stromdale and Ball Ltd v. Burden* [1952] Ch. 223; *Beswick v. Beswick* [1968] A.C. 58 per Lords Upjohn and Pearce. Compare *Drive Yourself Hire Co. (London) Ltd v. Strutt* [1954] 1 Q.B. 250; *Smith and Snipes Hall Farm Ltd v. River Douglas Catchment Board* [1949] 2 K.B. 500 at 514-517. In *Re Caroline Chisholm Village Pty Ltd* (Master Cohen Q.C. (1980) 1 B.P.R. 9507) it was held that if in a deed between A and B, B enters into certain covenants, the benefit of the covenants is declared to be in favour of land owned by C but there is no separate covenant with, or grant to, C then the covenants will not be enforceable by C or C's successors in title under *Conveyancing Act* 1919 (N.S.W.), s. 36C: see also *Lyus v. Prowsa Developments Ltd* [1982] 1 W.L.R. 1045.

In *Re Ecclesiastical Commissioners for Englands Conveyance* [1936] Ch. 430 on a conveyance by the commissioners, the purchaser, Gotto, covenanted with the commissioners to observe certain covenants for himself and assigns. He also entered into a separate covenant in the conveyance with the vendors' assigns, owners for the time being of the lands adjoining or adjacent to the land conveyed, to observe certain covenants. It was held (a) the covenants were enforceable by the owners of the adjoining land against successors in title to Gotto; and (b) since the covenant was one capable of running with the land and was annexed to the land, successors in title to the adjoining owners were also entitled to enforce the covenant.

(2) The section applies to both realty and personalty, it is not restricted to covenants which run with the land. Compare the position in England where the term "property" is restricted to land: *Beswick v. Beswick* [1968] A.C. 58.

(3) A person claiming the benefit of the section must be in existence and identifiable at the time when the covenant is made: *Forster v. Elvet Colliery Co. Ltd* [1908] 1 K.B. 629 at 637 per Fletcher Moulton L.J.; *Bird v. Trustees, Executors & Agency Co. Ltd* [1957] V.R. 619.

(b) Successors in title to the original covenantee

A successor in title to the original covenantee may be entitled to enforce the covenant in either of two ways: First, the successor in title may be an express assignee of the benefit of the covenant; secondly, he or she may be entitled to enforce the benefit as successor in title to land to which the benefit of the covenant is annexed.

(i) Express assignment of the benefit. The benefit of a covenant may be assigned both in law and equity. The benefit may be assigned at law under the provisions of the *Conveyancing Act* 1919 (N.S.W.), s. 12. Section 12 allows the assignment of covenants having no connection with land. The section does not preclude equitable assignments: *William Brandt's Sons & Co. v. Dunlop Rubber Co.* [1905] A.C. 454 at 461 and see *Union of London and Smith's Bank Ltd's Conveyance; Re Miles v. Easter* [1933] 1 Ch. 611, below p. 347. Section 12 is limited to absolute assignments; thus, if the assignor seeks to assign only part of the benefit of the covenant, the assignment can be effective only in equity. As to the rules applicable to equitable assignments, see below pp. 347-349.

(ii) Covenant annexed to the land. At law successors in title to an original covenantee can enforce covenants against the original covenantor if the benefit of the covenant is annexed to the land. Once annexed, the benefit of the covenant passes automatically to successors in title. At common law the benefit of a covenant will be annexed to the land and enforceable by the successor in title to the covenantee against the original covenantor (covenants cannot be enforced against successors in title to the covenantor except in equity, see below) if the following conditions are met:

(1) The covenant touches and concerns the land of the covenantee. (Note the exceptions in favour of the crown and public or local authorities, *Conveyancing Act* 1919 (N.S.W.), ss 88D, 88E).

(2) The covenantee has a legal interest in the land to which the benefit of the covenant is annexed. (If the interest of the covenantee is an equitable interest, the benefit must run in equity, see below.)

(3) The party seeking to enforce the covenant must have the same legal estate as the original covenantee. This has now been amended by statute. The common law rule now applies only to those covenants contained in instruments coming into effect before amending legislation, see *Conveyancing Act* 1919 (N.S.W.), s. 70.

(4) The benefit must be intended to run with the land. The requisite intention is now supplied by statute: see *Conveyancing Act* 1919 (N.S.W.), s. 70; *Federated Homes v. Mill Lodge* [1980] 1 All E.R. 371. See discussion below, p. 324.

(5) The land benefiting must either be expressly identified in the instrument or ascertainable by extrinsic evidence.

The requirement that the covenant touch and concern the land of the covenantee exists in both law and equity as a condition for the passing of the benefit to a successor in title to the covenantee. In this respect equity followed the law and therefore the relevant principles to be extracted from the cases apply whether the issue is one determined in the equitable jurisdiction or at law. For convenience the cases are grouped under the running of the benefit at law although it should be noted that many of the cases concerned the position in equity. The lack of reported cases on the passing of the benefit at law is explicable having regard to the convenience of the equitable remedy of injunction and that the burden of a covenant would pass only in equity; many of the cases concern enforcement of covenants against successors in title to the covenantor.

The benefit of a covenant may run at law irrespective of whether the covenant is positive or negative. *Smith and Snipes Hall Farm Ltd v. River Douglas Catchment Board* [1949] 2 K.B. 500 is a good illustration of how a positive covenant may be annexed to land so as to be enforceable by a successor in title to the original covenantee even though there is no land subject to the burden and the covenantor is not a landowner.

SMITH AND SNIPES HALL FARM LTD v. RIVER DOUGLAS CATCHMENT BOARD

Court of Appeal [1949] 2 K.B. 500

[The defendant Board, a Drainage Authority constituted under the *Land Drainage Act* 1930 (U.K.), covenanted under seal with the freehold owners of certain land, which was subject to flooding, that in consideration of the Board's undertaking remedial work when it was completed, the landowners would contribute to the cost. The location of the land was described as being situated between the Leeds and Liverpool Canal and the River Douglas and adjoining Eller Brook. Ellen Smith, one of the owners with whom the Board covenanted, sold her land with the benefit of the covenant to the first plaintiff, John Smith. The second plaintiff leased the property from Smith under a yearly tenancy. Subsequently the river flooded causing considerable damage to the plaintiffs. The plaintiffs sued the Board in both tort and contract alleging that the damage was caused by the defendant's faulty work.]

TUCKER L.J. [His Lordship first considered whether the covenant "touched and concerned" the land and held that it did so as the object of the deed was to improve the drainage of land liable to flooding and to prevent future flooding. His Lordship continued:]

It [the covenant] affects the value of the land per se and converts it from flooded meadows to land suitable for agriculture, and shows an intention that the benefit of the obligation to maintain shall attach thereto into whosoever hands the lands shall come.

With regard to the covenantor being a stranger the case of *The Prior* (1368) is referred to in *Spencer's Case* (1583) 1 Sm L.C. (10th ed), pp. 56, 73, (13th ed.), pp. 51, 65, 73, ... The notes to *Spencer's Case* above state: "When such a covenant (namely, covenants running with the land made with the owner of the land to which they relate) is made it seems to be of no consequence whether the covenantor be the person who conveyed the land to the covenantee or be a mere stranger." . . .

In this state of the authorities it seems clear, despite some dicta tending to the contrary view, that such a covenant if it runs with the land is binding on the covenantor though a mere stranger, and that this point will not avail the defendant board. As to the requirement that the deed containing the covenant must expressly identify the particular land to be benefited, no authority was cited to us and in the absence of such authority I can see no valid reason why the maxim Id certum est quod certum reddi potest should not apply, so as to make admissible extrinsic evidence to prove the extent and situation of the lands of the respective land owners adjoining the Eller Brook situate between the Leeds and Liverpool Canal and the River Douglas.

On this part of the case the learned judge said: "In my judgment the contractual obligations of the board are not to be regarded as covenants running with the land. They do not differ from obligations which by agreement a firm of contractors might agree to discharge in reference to some particular land. The catchment board do not own any land and there is no question of any obligation in relation to or connection with any land of theirs. The circumstances are different from those in the case of *Shayler v. Woolf* [1946] Ch. 320. Section 78 of the *Law of Property Act* 1925 (U.K.) does not affect the question as to what are covenants relating to the land of a covenantee. Furthermore, much of the reasoning of Lindley L.J. in *Austerberry v. Corp. of Oldham* (1885) 29 Ch. D. 750 at 781, is applicable. Although work might have to be done on the land which formerly belonged to Mrs Ellen Smith, and now belongs to the first plaintiff, equally it might be that for the effectual preventing of flooding of low meadows work on the banks of Eller Brook at some place considerably higher up the brook might have to be undertaken." I do not find anything in the judgments in *Austerberry v. Corp. of Oldham* which conflicts with the law as I have endeavoured to set it out above, and I have accordingly arrived at the conclusion that the covenant by the board in the agreement of 25 April 1938, is one which runs with the land referred to therein, which land is capable of identification, and that it is binding on the defendant board; and, further, that by virtue of s. 78 of the *Law of Property Act* 1925 (U.K.), it can be enforced at the suit of the covenantee and her successors in title and the persons deriving title under her or them, so that both the plaintiff Smith and the plaintiff company can sue in respect of the damage resulting to their respective interests therein by reason of the defendants' breach of covenant.

[The judgments of Somervell and Denning L.JJ. finding for the plaintiffs have been omitted.]

NOTES

1. Provisions similar to *Law of Property Act* 1925 (U.K.), s. 78 have been enacted in New South Wales, the *Conveyancing Act* 1919 (N.S.W.), s. 70(1) provides:

> 70.—(1) A covenant relating to any land of the covenantee shall be deemed to be made with the covenantee and his successors in title and the persons deriving title under him or them, and shall have effect as if such successors and other persons were expressed.
>
> For the purposes of this subsection in connection with covenants restrictive of the user of land "successors in title" shall be deemed to include the owners and occupiers for the time being of the land of the covenantee intended to be benefited.

The section is important in several respects. First, it abrogates the common law rule (there is no similar rule in equity) that the person seeking to enforce the covenant must have the same legal estate as the original covenantee: see Megarry and Wade, *The Law of Real Property* (4th ed.), p. 748. At common law, if the covenant was made with the owner of the fee simple estate and annexed to the land so as to run with it, the covenant could not, for example, be enforced by a lessee of the land, *Westhoughton U.D.C. v. Wigan Coal Co.* [1919] 1 Ch. 159 at 170, 171. Under the *Law of Property Act* 1925 (U.K.), s. 78 and its Australian equivalents, the benefit of the covenant is extended to persons deriving title under the covenantee or the covenantee's successors in title. In the principal case a lessee of the land benefited was held entitled under s. 78 to enforce the covenant.

Where the covenant is restrictive of user, the covenant may be enforced not only by a successor in title and persons deriving title through him or her but also owners and occupiers for the time being of the land of the covenantee intended to be benefited. The benefit of the covenant would be extended to persons obtaining title by adverse possession, statutory tenants and perhaps even squatters, although in respect of the latter it might be said ex turpi causa non oritur actio: Preston and Newson, *Restrictive Covenants Affecting Freehold Land* (6th ed.), p. 61.

Secondly, there is a continuing dispute whether the section can give rise to an implied annexation of covenants. The differing views on the effect of the section are canvassed in the decision of the Court of Appeal in *Federated Homes Ltd v. Mill Lodge* [1980] 1 W.L.R. 594. The Court of Appeal considered, inter alia, whether covenants contained in a conveyance were enforceable by a successor in title to the covenantee against the original covenantor, Mill Lodge. Clause 5(iv) of the conveyance provided: "The purchaser hereby covenants with the vendor that . . . (iv) in carrying out the development of the 'blue' land the purchaser shall not build at a greater density than a total of 300 dwellings so as not to reduce the number of units which the vendor might eventually erect on the retained land under the existing planning consent." There was no express definition of the retained land but in clause 2 of the conveyance reference was made to "any adjoining or adjacent property retained by the vendor". Brightman L.J. (with whom Megaw and Browne L.JJ concurred) said, in reference to *Law of Property Act* 1925 (U.K.), s. 78:

[T]here were three possible views about s. 78. One view . . . "the orthodox view" hitherto held, is that it is merely a statutory shorthand for reducing the length of legal documents. A second view . . . is that the section only applies, or at any rate only achieves annexation, when the land intended to be benefited is signified in the document by express words or necessary implication as the intended beneficiary of the covenant. A third view is that the section applies if the covenant in fact touches and concerns the land of the covenantee, whether that be gleaned from the document itself or from evidence outside the document.

For myself, I reject the narrowest interpretation of s. 78, the supposed orthodox view, which seems to me to fly in the face of the wording of the section. Before I express my reasons I will say that I do not find it necessary to choose between the second and third views because, in my opinion, this covenant relates to land of the covenantee on either interpretation of s. 78. [The conveyance] shows clearly that the covenant is for the protection of the retained land and that land is described in cl. 2 as "any adjoining or adjacent property retained by the vendor". This formulation is sufficient for annexation purposes: see *Rogers v. Hosegood* [1900] 2 Ch. 388.

There is in my judgment no doubt that this covenant "related to the land of the covenantee", or, to use the old-fashioned expression, that it touched and concerned the land, even if Mr Price is correct in his submission that the document must show an intention to benefit identified land. The result of such application is that one must read cl. 5(iv) as if it were written: "The purchaser hereby covenants with the vendor and its successors in title and the persons deriving title under it or them, including the owners and occupiers for the time being of the retained land, that in carrying out the development of the blue land the purchaser shall not build at a greater density than a total 300 dwellings so as not to reduce, etc." I leave out of consideration s. 79 as unnecessary to be considered in this context, since Mill Lodge is the original covenantor.

The first point to notice about s. 78(1) is that the wording is significantly different from the wording of its predecessor s. 58(1) of the Conveyancing Act 1881. The distinction is underlined by s. 78(2), which applies s. 78(1) only to covenants made after the commencement of the Act. Section 58(1) of the Act of 1881 did not include the covenantee's successors in title or persons deriving title under him or them, or the owner or occupiers for the time being of the land of the covenantee intended to be benefited. The section was confined, in relation to realty, to the covenantee, his heirs and assigns, words which suggest a more limited scope of operation than is found in s. 78.

If, as the language of s. 78 implies, a covenant relating to land which is restrictive of the user thereof is enforceable at the suit of (1) a successor in title of the covenantee, (2) a person deriving title under the covenantee or under his successors in title, and (3) the owner or occupier of the land intended to be benefited by the covenant, it must, in my view, follow that the covenant runs with the land, because ex hypothesi every successor in title to the land, every derivative proprietor of the land and every other owner and occupier has a right by statute to the covenant. In other words, if the condition precedent of s. 78 is satisfied—that is to say, there exists a covenant which touches and concerns the land of the covenantee—that covenant runs with the land for the benefit of his successors in title, persons deriving title under him or them and other owners and occupiers.

This approach to s. 78 has been advocated by distinguished textbook writers; see Dr Radcliffe's article "Some Problems of the Law Relating to Restrictive Covenants" (1941) 57 L.Q.R. 203, Professor Wade's article, "Covenants—A Broad and Reasonable View" and the apt cross-heading "What is wrong with section 78?" [1972B] C.L.J. 151 at 171, and Megarry and Wade, *The Law of Real Property* (4th ed.), p. 764. Counsel pointed out to us that the fourth edition of Megarry and Wade indicates a change of mind on this topic since the third edition.

Although the section does not seem to have been extensively used in the course or argument in this type of case, the construction of s. 78 which appeals to me appears to be consistent with at least two cases decided in this court. The first is *Smith and Snipes Hall Farm Ltd v. River Douglas Catchment Board* [1949] 2 K.B. 500.

[His Lordship then referred to the facts and decision in that case and continued:]

The two important points are that the agreement was not expressed to be for the benefit of the landowner's successors in title; and there was no assignment of the benefit of the agreement in favour of the second plaintiff, the tenant. In reliance, as I understand the case, upon s. 78 of the Act of 1925, it was held that the second plaintiff was entitled to sue the catchment board for damages for breach of the agreement. It seems to me that that conclusion can only have been reached on the basis that s. 78 had the effect of causing the benefit of the agreement to run with the land so as to be capable of being sued upon by the tenant. . . .

[His Lordship then referred to further unreported authority in support of his view and continued:]

We were referred to observations in the speeches of Lord Upjohn and Lord Wilberforce in *Sefton v. Tophams Ltd* [1967] 1 A.C. 50 at 73 and 81, to the effect that s. 79 of the Act of 1925, relating to the burden of covenants, achieved no more than the introduction of statutory shorthand into the drafting of covenants. Section 79, in my view, involves quite different considerations and I do not think that it provides a helpful analogy.

The effect of s. 78 was further considered in *Roake v. Chadha* [1983] 3 All E.R. 503 where in a transfer of land the purchaser covenanted with the vendor to observe certain covenants and it was provided, inter alia, that "the covenant shall not enure for the benefit of any owner or subsequent purchasers of [the vendor's land] unless the benefit of the covenant shall be expressly assigned". It was argued that, *Law of Property Act* 1925 (U.K.), s. 78 effected an automatic annexation of the covenant and therefore a successor in title to the vendor could enforce the covenant against a successor in title to the covenantor even though the benefit of the covenant had not been expressly assigned. Judge Paul Baker Q.C. in rejecting this argument said:

> Counsel for the defendants made a frontal attack on this use of s. 78, [in the *Federated Homes Case*] which he reinforced by reference to an article by Newsom Q.C., "Universal Annexation?" (1981) 97 L.Q.R. 32 which is critical of the decision. The main lines of attack are: (1) the conclusion overlooks the legislative history of s. 78 which it is said shows that it has a narrower purpose than is claimed and does not in itself bring about annexation; (2) this narrower purpose has been accepted in relation to the corresponding s. 79 (relating to burden), which I have already read, by Lord Upjohn and Lord Wilberforce in *Tophams Ltd v. Earl of Sefton* [1967] 1 A.C. 50 at 73, 81. Further, it is said by way of argument sub silentio that in a number of cases, notably *Marquess of Zetland v. Driver* [1939] Ch. 1 and *Re Jeff's Transfer, Rogers v. Astley (No. 2)* [1966] 1 W.L.R. 841, the argument could have been used to good effect but was not deployed . . . I do not consider it to be my place either to criticise or to defend the decisions of the Court of Appeal. I conceive it my clear duty to accept the decision of the Court of Appeal as binding on me and apply it as best I can to the facts I find here.
>
> Counsel for the plaintiffs' method of applying it is simplicity itself. The *Federated Homes* case shows that s. 78 brings about annexation, and that the operation of the section cannot be excluded by a contrary intention. As I have indicated, he supports this last point by reference to s. 79, which is expressed to operate "unless a contrary intention is expressed", a qualification which, as we have already noticed, is absent from s. 78. Counsel for the plaintiffs could not suggest any reason of policy why s. 78 should be mandatory, unlike, for example, s. 146 of the 1925 Act, which deals with restrictions on the right to forfeiture of leases and which, by an express provision, "has effect notwithstanding any stipulation to the contrary".
>
> I am thus far from satisfied that s. 78 has the mandatory operation which counsel for the plaintiffs claimed for it. But, even if one accepts that it is not subject to a contrary intention, I do not consider that it has the effect of annexing the benefit of the covenant in each and every case irrespective of the other express terms of the covenant. I notice that Brightman L.J. did not go so far as that, for he said in the *Federated Homes* case [1980] 1 W.L.R. 594 at 606:
>
>> I find the idea of the annexation of a covenant to the whole of the land but not to a part of it a difficult conception fully to grasp. I can understand that a covenantee may expressly or by necessary implication retain the benefit of a covenant wholly under his own control, so that the benefit will not pass unless the covenantee chooses to assign; but I would have thought, if the benefit of a covenant is, on a proper construction of a document, annexed to the land, prima facie it is annexed to every part thereof, unless the contrary clearly appears.
>
> So at least in some circumstances Brightman L.J. is considering that despite s. 78 the benefit may be retained and not pass or be annexed to and run with land. In this connection, I was also referred by counsel for the defendants to Sir Lancelot Elphinstone's, *Covenants Affecting Land*, p. 17, where the author says, with reference to this point (and I quote from a footnote on that page):
>
>> but it is thought that, as a covenant must be construed as a whole, the court would give due effect to words excluding or modifying the operation of the section.

The true position as I see it is that, even where a covenant is deemed to be made with successors in title as s. 78 requires, one still has to construe the covenant as a whole to see whether the benefit of the covenant is annexed. Where one finds, as in the *Federated Homes* case, the covenant is not qualified in any way, annexation may be readily inferred; but, where, as in the present case, it is expressly provided that "this covenant shall not enure for the benefit of any owner or subsequent purchaser of any part of the Vendor's Sudbury Court Estate at Wembley unless the benefit of this covenant shall be expressly assigned", one cannot just ignore these words. One may not be able to exclude the operation of the section in extending the range of covenantees, but one has to consider the covenant as a whole to determine its true effect. When one does that, then it seems to me that the answer is plain and in my judgment the benefit was not annexed. That is giving full weight to both the statute in force and also what is already there in a covenant.

Whilst the proper scope of *Law of Property Act* 1925 (U.K.), s. 78(1) (*Conveyancing Act* 1919 (N.S.W.), s. 70(1)) may be of some importance where a covenant is sought to be enforced against the original covenantor (as was the position in the *Federated Homes* case), it will be of little consequence where it is sought to enforce the covenant against a successor in title to the covenantor. Section 88(1) of the *Conveyancing Act* 1919 in this situation requires the land benefited to be clearly indicated in the instrument creating the covenant. Usually this will result in a formal annexation of benefit to the land where the section is otherwise complied with.

2. In *Smith and Snipes Hall Farm Ltd v. River Douglas Catchment Board* [1949] 2 K.B. 500 it was held that it was not necessary for the deed containing the covenant to identify expressly the particular land to be benefited; extrinsic evidence could be admitted for that purpose. More stringent rules may apply in equity: see below p. 350. In New South Wales, the *Conveyancing Act* 1919, s. 88(1) (extracted below p. 361) provides that a restriction as to user arising under a covenant shall not be enforceable *against* a successor in title to the covenantor unless the instrument clearly indicates, inter alia, the land to which the benefit of the restriction is appurtenant. Section 88(1) will be dealt with under formal requirements for creation of covenants: see below p. 361.

ROGERS v. HOSEGOOD

Court of Appeal [1900] 2 Ch. 388

[The plaintiffs were successors in title to land to which the benefit of a restrictive covenant was annexed. The covenant was entered into by the Duke of Bedford. It was contained in a conveyance of part of land owned by a partnership but subject to mortgages. The covenant was expressed to be for the benefit of the partnership, its heirs and assigns, and others claiming under it with respect to lands adjoining or near to the lots purchased and was to the effect that a single dwelling house only would be erected on the lots and it would be used as a private residence only and not for trade or business purposes.

The land burdened by the covenant passed under the Duke's will and was sold eventually to Hosegood who purchased with notice of the covenants. He wished to erect flats on the site. An injunction was sought by the plaintiffs. The plaintiff Rogers was a successor in title to part of the partnership land. Other plaintiffs were trustees of the will of a purchaser from the partnership, Millais, who purchased without notice of the benefit of the restrictive covenant.]

FARWELL J. (at first instance). The . . . question is . . . whether the benefit of the covenants . . . passed to Sir John Millais, and through him to his trustees, so as to enable them to maintain this action. It is not contended that the burden of those covenants has not passed to the defendant; he is obviously bound, by reason of notice, whether the covenant as regards him runs with the land or not: *Tulk v. Moxhay* (1848) 2 Ph. 774; 41 E.R. 1143. It has been argued that this is a covenant the benefit of which runs with the land at law, or if not at law at any rate in equity; and further, that even if this is not so, the benefit of the covenants passes by the express general words, "rights, easements, or appurtenances belonging or reputed to belong thereto''. In my opinion, the benefit of the covenants runs at law with the land now vested in the Millais trustees. I do not think it necessary to call in aid the analogy of easements, as suggested by Mr Haldane, on the authority of *London and South Western Railway Co. v. Gomm* (1882) 20 Ch. D. 562. The accurate expression appears to me to be that the covenants are annexed to the land, and pass with it in much the same way as title deeds, which have been quaintly called the sinews of the land: Co. Litt. 6a. . . . Covenants which run with the land must have the following characteristics: (1) They must be made with a covenantee who has an interest in the land to which they refer. (2) They must concern or touch the land. It is not contended that the covenants in question in this case have not the first characteristic, but it is said that they fail in the second. I am of opinion that they possess both. Adopting the definition of Bayley J. in *Congleton Corp. v. Pattison* (1808) 10 East 130 at 135; 103 E.R. 725, the covenant must either affect the land as regards mode of occupation, or it must be such as per se, and not merely from collateral circumstances, affects the value of the land. It is to my mind obvious that the value of Sir J. Millais's land is directly increased by the covenants in question. . . .

[His Lordship then referred to authorities in support and continued:]

I see no difficulty in holding that the benefit of a covenant runs with the land of the covenantee, while the burden of the same covenant does not run with the land of covenantor. This must always be the case with regard to grants in fee if it be the better opinion (as Cotton L.J. in *Austerberry v. Oldham Corp.* (1885) 29 Ch. D. 750 at 775 and the editors of *Smith's Leading Cases* thinks) that the burden of such covenants never runs with the land. At common law the lessee's covenants ran with the land, but the lessor's did not run with the reversion; the statute *Grantees of Reversions* 1540 (U.K.) (32 Hen. VIII, c. 34) was passed to give the reversioner the same benefit that the lessee had; and the definition of a covenant which runs with the land, stated by the learned editors of *Smith's Leading Cases*, p. 58, is "when either the liability to perform it, or the right to take advantage of it, passes to the assignee of that reversion". But a covenant may have the two characteristics above mentioned and yet not run with the land; it is in each case a question of intention to be determined by the court on the construction of the particular document, and with due regard to the nature of the covenant and the surrounding circumstances. No covenant can run with the land which has not the two characteristics above mentioned, but every covenant which has those two characteristics does not necessarily run with the land. That it is a question of intention in each case, to be determined on construction, is apparent from the judgment of Hall V.-C. in *Renals v. Cowlishaw* (1878) 9 Ch. D. 125, a judgment of the highest authority. . . . Treating it then as a question of construction, I find the express contract to be that these covenants were entered into with intent that they should bind the premises conveyed by the deeds of 1869 and every part thereof into whosoever hands the same might come, and should enure to the benefit of [the covenantees] their heirs and assigns, and others claiming under them all or any of their lands adjoining or near to the said premises. . . . Inasmuch as the covenantees at the date of the covenant owned the land now belonging to the Millais trustees, and such land is in fact "near to" the defendant's land, I see no uncertainty as to the land to be benefited. I should add that, in my opinion, there can be no difference between law and equity in construing such covenants with a view to seeing whether they do or do not run with the land. The same words in the same document must necessarily bear the same meaning in all the courts. It is true that in many of the cases decided by the Court of Chancery expressions are found to the effect that the defendants are bound in equity, whether the covenants in strictness run with the land at law or not. But I think that such expressions are due to the reluctance that the Vice-Chancellors felt to express any opinion on points of common law, and, for the reason that I have already stated, I cannot see how such a covenant could run in equity if it did not run at law. One other point was made . . . that Sir J. Millais knew nothing of the existence of these covenants at the time that he bought . . . in my opinion it is immaterial: such knowledge has never been held a necessary condition to success in an action on a covenant which runs with the land at law. The plaintiff's right in such an action does not depend upon what he believes himself to have bought, but upon what he has in fact bought, and he has bought the land with the covenants annexed. The defendant is not injured, for he bought the land with knowledge of the covenant, and he can claim no more than the land with that burden upon it. . . . The defendant must, therefore, be restrained from building as he proposed to do, and he must also pay half the general costs of the action.

[The defendant then appealed to the Court of Appeal. On appeal:]

COLLINS L.J. read the judgment of the court (Lord Alverstone M.R., and Rigby and Collins L.JJ.).

[Their Lordships upheld Farwell J.'s view that the defendant was bound by the covenants and that the covenants in question touched and concerned the land of the covenantee so as to run with the land at law. Collins L.J. continued:]

Therefore, but for a technical difficulty which was not raised before Farwell J., we should agree with him that the benefit of the covenants in question was annexed to and passed to Sir John Millais by the conveyance of the land which he brought in 1873. A difficulty, however, in giving effect to this view arises from the fact that the covenants in question in the deeds of May and July, 1869, were made with the mortgagors only [the partnership], and therefore in contemplation of law were made with strangers to the land: *Webb v. Russell* (1789) 3 T.R. 393; 100 E.R. 639, to which, therefore, the benefit did not become annexed. That a court of equity, however, would not regard such an objection as defeating the intention of the parties to the covenant is clear; and therefore, when the covenant was clearly made for the benefit of certain land with a person who in the contemplation of such a court was the true owner of it, it would be regarded as annexed to and running with that land, just as it would have been at law but for the technical difficulty. We think this is the plain result of the observations of Hall V.-C. in the well-known passage in *Renals v. Cowlishaw* (1878) 9 Ch. D. 125, of Jessel M.R. in *London and South Western Railway Co. v. Gomm* (1882) 20 Ch. D. 562, and of Wood V.-C. in *Child v. Douglas* (1854) Kay 560; 69 E.R. 237, which, we agree with Farwell J., are untouched on this point by anything decided in the subsequent proceedings in that case. . . . [I]n equity, just as at law, the first point to be determined is whether the covenant or contract in its inception binds the land. If it does, it is then capable of passing with the land to subsequent assignees; if it does not, it is incapable of passing by mere assignment of the land. The benefit may be annexed to one plot and the burden to another, and when this has been once clearly done the benefit and the burden pass to the respective assignees, subject, in the case of the burden, to proof that the legal estate, if acquired, has been acquired with notice of the covenant.

[His Lordship then referred to the judgments of Hall V.-C. in *Renals v. Cowlishaw* (at 130) and Wood V.-C. in *Child v. Douglas* (1854) Kay 560 at 571; 69 E.R. 237 and continued:]

These authorities establish the proposition that, when the benefit has been once clearly annexed to one piece of land, it passes by assignment of that land, and may be said to run with it, in contemplation as well of equity as of law, without proof of special bargain or representation on the assignment. In such a case it runs, not because the conscience of either party is affected, but because the purchaser has bought something which inhered in or was annexed to the land bought. This is the reason why, in dealing with the burden, the purchaser's conscience is not affected by notice of covenants which were part of the original bargain on the first sale, but were merely personal and collateral, while it is affected by notice of those which touch and concern the land. The covenant must be one that is capable of running with the land before the question of the purchaser's conscience and the equity affecting it can come into discussion. When, as in *Renals v. Cowlishaw*, there is no indication in the original conveyance, or in the circumstances attending it, that the burden of the restrictive covenant is imposed for the benefit of the land reserved, or any particular part of it, then it becomes necessary to examine the circumstances under which any part of the land reserved is sold, in order to see whether a benefit, not originally annexed to it, has become annexed to it on the sale, so that the purchaser is deemed to have bought it with the land, and this can hardly be the case when the purchaser did not know of the existence of the restrictive covenant. But when, as here, it has been once annexed to the land reserved, then it is not necessary to spell an intention out of surrounding facts, such as the existence of a building scheme, statements at auctions, and such like circumstances, and the presumption must be that it passes on a sale of that land, unless there is something to rebut it, and the purchaser's ignorance of the existence of the covenant does not defeat the presumption. We can find nothing in the conveyance to Sir John Millais in any degree inconsistent with the intention to pass to him the benefit already annexed to the land sold to him. We are of opinion therefore, that Sir John Millais's assigns are entitled to enforce the restrictive covenant against the defendant, and that his appeal must be dismissed.

[Their Lordships went on to hold (overruling Farwell J. on this point) that the plaintiff Rogers was similarly entitled to enforce the covenants.]

NOTE

It has been argued that covenants against competing with a business conducted on the covenantee's land are not covenants which touch and concern the land because they do not benefit the land per se: see discussion of authorities in Elphinstone. "Assignment of the Benefit of Covenants Affecting Land" (1952) 68 L.Q.R. 353 at 362; Preston and Newsom, *Restrictive Covenants Affecting Freehold Land* (7th ed.) p. 84 and *Clem Smith Nominees Pty Ltd v. Farelly* (1978) 20 S.A.S.R. 227 at 236. However, in *Newton Abbott Co-op. Society Ltd v. Williamson and Treadgold Ltd* [1952] 1 Ch. 286 at 292-294, 297 (a case concerning the equitable assignment of the benefit of a covenant) Upjohn J. held that a covenant not to compete with business carried on the covenantee's land did touch and concern the land: see also *McGuigan Investments Pty Ltd v. Dalwood Vineyards Pty Ltd* [1970] 1 N.S.W.L.R. 686; *Allen v. Lawson* [1926] V.L.R. 1; *Quadramain Pty Ltd v. Sevastapol Investments Pty Ltd* (1976) 133 C.L.R. 390 at 411-413. See also Hayton, "Restrictive Covenants as Property Interests" (1971) 87 L.Q.R. 539 at 545 arguing that by analogy the law of easements that covenants which benefit a business carried on the land benefited should be held to touch and concern the land.

KERRIDGE v. FOLEY

Supreme Court of New South Wales (1964) 82 W.N. (N.S.W.) (Pt 1) 293

[A parcel of land was subdivided by the Australian Agricultural Co. In 1934 the company sold lot 53 subject to a restrictive covenant which provided, inter alia, that "only one house shall be erected upon each 40 feet of frontage". The benefit of the covenant was expressed to be appurtenant to the whole of the land shown in an endorsed plan—the land so shown being lots 52, 53, 54 and 61. At that date lot 54 had already been conveyed. Subsequently lot 52 was sold subject to identical covenants; the land benefiting from the covenants imposed on lot 52 was lots 51, 52, 53 and 62. In 1953 lots 52 and 53 were conveyed to one Richardson. Subsequently lot 52 was conveyed to the plaintiffs and lot 53 to the defendants. The defendants proposed to make alterations to the existing dwelling which the plaintiffs, owners of lot 52, alleged were in breach of the covenant.]

JACOBS J. There are thus two questions to be determined, first whether the covenants in indenture No. 624, Book 1684, are enforceable against the defendants being persons interested in lot 53 and not being parties to the creation of the covenants, and, secondly, whether the threatened use of the land infringes the restriction imposed by the covenant and is in breach of the covenant. There is also a counter-claim and a motion for modification of the restrictions imposed, but this application depends upon the validity of the covenant and the enforceability thereof being established; at this stage, therefore, I limit my consideration of the two questions which I have set out.

It is to be noted that lot 54 was conveyed by the Australian Agricultural Co. to Harold Vincent Moore prior to the conveyance of lot 53 to Mabel Eleanor McAuley. The conveyance registered No. 102, Book 1566 is earlier in date than the conveyance No. 624, Book 1684. The conveyance of lots 52 and 61 are subsequent in date to the conveyance of lot 53. In these circumstances it is submitted that the covenant contained in the conveyance of lot 53 to the predecessor in title of the defendants did not clearly indicate the land to which the benefit of the restriction is appurtenant. Mr Hope submitted that the wording of the covenant which would include all the lots shown on the endorsed plan including lot 53 was bad because lot 53 itself was included as part of the land to which the benefit of the covenants was expressed to be appurtenant. I am inclined to think that as a matter of construction of the covenant, it would be necessary to exclude lot 53 from the words "the whole of the land shown in the said plan"; but there can be no doubt that lot 54 is included in this description of the land to which the benefit of the restrictive covenants is appurtenant. However, the benefit of the restriction in the covenant can only be appurtenant to land owned by the covenantee or, possibly, if a building scheme is proved, to land which had previously been owned by the covenantee. It is quite clear to me from the various conveyances that there was no building scheme; there was no intended mutuality of rights and obligations since different lots were delineated on each different plan. It therefore cannot be said that the instruments of conveyance clearly indicated the land to which the benefit of the restriction was appurtenant because it included land, namely lot 54, to which the benefit of the restriction was not so appurtenant; that being so, s. 88 of the Conveyancing Act 1919 (N.S.W.) provides that a restriction shall not be enforceable against the defendants who are persons interested in the land claimed to be subject to the restriction and not parties to its creation. It is probable that the same result follows at common law: see Re Ballard's Conveyance [1937] Ch. 473.

Upon this ground alone, I am of opinion that the plaintiffs are not entitled to succeed in this suit, but there are other grounds: First, I think that the fact that the plaintiff's land and the defendant's land after the making of the covenants came into the same ownership, namely the ownership of Francis Henry Richardson, prevents the enforceability of the restrictions by the owner for the time being of lot 52. In my view the benefit and burden of a restrictive covenant does not survive such a unity of ownership. Between 1953 and 1958 there were no longer separate persons between whom the covenant could be regarded as continuing in force. There was no longer anything which could be regarded at law or in equity as a relation of covenantor and covenantee. A person cannot be regarded as subject to the burden of a covenant of which he alone has the benefit.

[His Honour went on to hold that in any event the defendants' proposed use of the land was not a breach of the covenant.]

NOTES

1. At common law the benefit of a covenant cannot be attached to land which the covenantor no longer owns: *Kerridge v. Foley* (1964) 82 W.N. (N.S.W.) (Pt 1) 294; *Langdale Pty Ltd v. Sollas* [1959] V.R. 634. There are two exceptions to this rule: a covenant attached to land which the covenantor no longer owns may be enforceable in equity as a scheme of development (see below p. 352), or if the covenant purported to be made with owners for the time being of that land, the *Law of Property Act* 1925 (U.K.), s. 56, *Conveyancing Act* 1919 (N.S.W.), s. 36c would be brought into play: see discussion above p. 321.

2. One of the grounds for rejecting the plaintiff's claim in the principal case was that the instrument containing the covenant did not comply with the *Conveyancing Act* 1919 (N.S.W.), s. 88(1) (see below p. 361), because it did not clearly indicate the land which in law was entitled to the benefit of the covenant. As to the position with regard to schemes of development, see *Re Louis and the Conveyancing Act* [1971] 1 N.S.W.L.R. 164, extracted below p. 365. But see *Re Application of Fox* (1981) 2 B.P.R. 9310 where Wootten J. held that where a covenant was annexed to "the whole of the land in the deposited plan" this meant all the lots in the plan and the covenant was enforceable to the extent that the benefit was validly annexed to some of the lots. Wootten J. also held that the requirements of s. 88(1) were satisfied; see also *Re Magney* (1981) 2 B.P.R. 9358.

3. In the absence of a scheme of development unity of ownership of land benefited and land burdened will extinguish a restrictive covenant under the general law: see below p. 376, and the principal case.

RE BALLARD'S CONVEYANCE

Chancery [1937] 1 Ch. 473

[Mrs Ballard, as life-tenant exercising powers under the *Settled Land Act*, sold two lots of land comprising 18 acres to Wright. The conveyance was subject to a covenant and certain building restrictions. The covenant forbade erection of buildings other than private dwellings, and buildings were to be of red brick and in conformity with plans and specifications previously submitted to, and approved in writing by the vendor or her surveyor. The land to be benefited was an area of 1,700 acres known as the Childwickbury Estate. Wright applied to the court for a declaration that the property comprised in the conveyance was no longer affected by any of the restrictions contained in the conveyance and that those restrictions were not enforceable against him. The respondents to the summons were successors in title to the land intended to be benefited by the covenants.]

CLAUSON J. [after stating the facts as above set out continued:] In *Osborne v. Bradley* [1903] 2 Ch. 446 at 450. Farwell J. classified such covenants as that now in question as falling under three classes (1) where the covenant is entered into simply for the vendor's own benefit; (2) where the covenant is for the benefit of the vendor in his capacity as owner of a particular property; and (3) where the covenant is for the benefit of the vendor in so far as he reserves unsold property, and also for the benefit of other purchasers as part of what is called a building scheme.

[His Lordship held that the present covenant came within the second category. He also decided that an area of 1700 acres presently owned by the respondents to the summons was the land intended to be benefited by the covenant and continued:]

That brings me to the remaining question, namely: Is the covenant one which, in the circumstances of the case, comes within the category of a covenant the benefit of which is capable of running with the land for the benefit of which it was taken? A necessary qualification in order that the covenant may come within that category is that it concerns or touches the land with which it is to run: see per Farwell J. in *Rogers v. Hosegood* [1900] 2 Ch. 388 at 395. That land is an area of some 1700 acres. It appears to me quite obvious that while a breach of the stipulations might possibly affect a portion of that area in the vicinity of the applicant's land, far the largest part of this area of 1700 acres could not possibly be affected by any breach of any of the stipulations.

Counsel for the respondents asked for an adjournment in order to consider whether they would call evidence (as I was prepared to allow them to do) to prove that a breach of the stipulations or of some of them might affect the whole of this large area. However, ultimately no such evidence was called.

The result seems to me to be that I am bound to hold that, while the covenant may concern or touch some comparatively small portion of the land to which it has been sought to annex it, it fails to concern or touch far the largest part of the land. I asked in vain for any authority which would justify me in severing the covenant and treating it as annexed to or running with such part of the land as it touched by or concerned with it, though as regards the remainder of the land, namely, such part as is not touched by or concerned with the covenant, the covenant is not and cannot be annexed to it and accordingly does not and cannot run with it. Nor have I been able through my own researches to find anything in the books which seems to justify any such course. In *Rogers v. Hosegood* [1900] 2 Ch. 388 the benefit of the covenant was annexed to all or any of certain lands adjoining or near to the covenantor's land, and no such difficulty arose as faces me here; and there are many other reported cases in which, for similar reasons, no such difficulty arose. But the requirement that the covenant, in order that the benefit of it may run with certain lands, must concern or touch those lands, is categorically stated by Farwell J. in the passage I have cited, in terms which are unquestionably in accord with a long line of earlier authority.

I would observe that the construction of the document and the intention of the parties to be gathered therefrom is material on the question what is the area of land to which the covenantor and the covenantee intended to annex the benefit of the covenant, or, in technical language, what is the land with which the parties intended the covenant to run; but that on the question whether, in the circumstances of the case, this covenant is capable of being annexed to or of running with the land to which it is sought to annex it, it is necessary first to ascertain whether in fact the covenant touches or concerns that particular land. If on the facts it appears that the covenant does not touch or concern that particular land, the only question which remains is whether by the law in regard to annexation of a covenant to land as recognised as long ago as the year 42 Edw. III (A.D. 1368) in *The Prior's Case* (see *Spencer's Case* (1583) 5 Co. Rep. 17b; 77 E.R. 267) such annexation can take place unless it can be predicated of the covenant that it touches or concerns the land to which it is sought to annex it. That is a question of dry technical law on which it would not be right, at all events for a judge of First Instance, to go beyond settled authority, or at all events beyond that which can logically be deduced from settled authority, though in the result the intention of the parties to the original covenant may be frustrated. As I have not been referred to and I cannot find any authority for the proposition that a covenant which it has been sought to annex to a particular area of land can be enforced by the person seised of that land, not being the original covenantee, in a case where it cannot truly be said that the covenant touches or concerns the land to which it was sought to annex it, I must hold that the attempted annexation has failed and that the covenant has not been effectually annexed to the land and does not run with it. The consequence is that I am bound to hold that the respondents, Childwick Bury Stud Ltd, cannot sue the applicant on the covenant.

As it is not suggested, nor does it appear, that the covenant in question is now enforceable by any one if the respondents are not in a position to enforce it, I shall declare that the property mentioned in the title to the summons is no longer affected by any of the restrictions contained in the conveyance of 28 June 1906.

[The burdened land was apparently separated from the rest of the estate by the four track main line of the railway. This does not appear from the report, see Preston and Newsom, *Restrictive Covenants Affecting Freehold Land* (6th ed.), p. 29.]

NOTES AND QUESTIONS

1. The courts will not read down a covenant so as to apply to that part of the land which is capable of benefiting, but the parties themselves may provide for severance of the covenant: see *Marquess of Zetland v. Driver* [1939] Ch. 1, below p. 339.

2. In the principal case Clauson J. thought it obvious that most of the area sought to be benefited by the covenant, 1700 acres, could not be affected by any breach of the stipulations. Is the result necessarily so obvious? It has been pointed out (Preston and Newsom, *Restrictive Covenants Affecting Freehold Land* (7th ed.), p. 37) that evidence has been accepted that an agricultural property of 7000 acres may be affected by the observance or non-observance of covenants *Marten v. Flight Refuelling Ltd* [1962] Ch. 115 at 136 and in *Earl of Leicester v. Wells-in-the-Sea U.D.C.* [1973] Ch. 110, an area of 32,000 acres was held to be affected by covenants. Compare *Clem Smith Pty Ltd v. Farrelly* (1978) 20 S.A.S.R. 227 where a covenant not to carry on a certain business on land was held not to touch and concern land some 35 kilometres distant; see also *McGuigan Investments Pty Ltd v. Dalwood Vineyards Pty Ltd* [1970] 1 N.S.W.L.R. 686.

3. Recent authorities indicate that the test of whether the covenant "touches and concerns" the land of the covenantee is not a purely objective test. The authorities are gathered in the judgment of Brightman J. in *Wrotham Park Estate Co. v. Parkside Homes Ltd* [1974] 1 W.L.R. 798:

> [I]n *Lord Northbourne v. Johnston and Son* [1922] 2 Ch. 309, Sargent J. said:
>
>> Benefit or detriment is often a question of opinion on which there may be the greatest divergence of view, and the greatest difficulty in arriving at a clear conclusion. It is, in my judgment, sufficient for the vendor to say, at any rate in the first instance, that the bargain was that he should be protected against certain acts which were recognised as being likely to prove noxious or detrimental to his building estate treated as a whole. The covenantor, being then, in my judgment, bound at the very least to show that the estate remaining to the covenantee at the date of action was not intended to be protected by the covenants, or that the breach of the covenants could not possibly hurt such remaining estate, the question arises whether this onus has been discharged in the present case.
>
> Wilberforce J. in *Marten v. Flight Refuelling Ltd* [1962] Ch. 115 dealing with a covenant restricting land to agricultural user said (at 136):
>
>> If an owner of land, on selling part of it, thinks fit to impose a restriction on user, and the restriction was imposed for the purpose of benefiting the land retained, the court would normally assume that it is capable of doing so. There might, of course, be exceptional cases where the covenant was on the face of it taken capriciously or not bona fide, but a covenant taken by the owner of an agricultural estate not to use a sold-off portion for other than agricultural purposes could hardly fall within either of these categories.
>
> He then picked up Sargent J.'s observations about benefit or detriment being matters of opinion upon which views might greatly diverge and added (at 137): "Why, indeed, should the court seek to substitute its own standard for those of the parties—and on what basis can it do so?" . . .
>
> In these circumstances I commence my review of the evidence with an inclination towards concluding that at the time when the stipulation was imposed responsible persons believed or accepted that the stipulation was capable of performing a service which would benefit and continue to benefit the Wrotham Park Estate. [His Lordship then reviewed the evidence and continued:] There can be obvious cases where a restrictive covenant clearly is, or clearly is not, of benefit to an estate. Between these two extremes there is inevitably an area where the benefit

to the estate is a matter of personal opinion, where responsible and reasonable persons can have divergent views sincerely and reasonably held. In my judgment, in such cases, it is not for the court to pronounce which is the correct view. I think that the court can only decide whether a particular view is one which can reasonably be held.

If a restriction is bargained for at the time of sale with the intention of giving the vendor a protection which he desires for the land he retains, and the restriction is expressed to be imposed for the benefit of the estate so that both sides are apparently accepting that the restriction is of value to the retained land, I think that the validity of the restriction should be upheld so long as an estate owner may reasonably take the view that the restriction remains of value to his estate, and that the restriction should not be discarded merely because others may reasonably argue that the restriction is spent. I think that this accords with the judgment of Sargent J. in the *Northbourne* case [1922] 2 Ch. 309 and of Wilberforce J. in the *Marten* case [1962] Ch. 115.

ELLISON v. O'NEILL

Supreme Court of New South Wales (1968) 88 W.N. (Pt 1) (N.S.W.) 213

[Benjamin was the owner of Torrens title land which he subdivided into two lots. The second lot was granted a right of way to the street in consideration of which the purchasers, Ellisons, covenanted with Benjamin for themselves and successors in title not to erect a building of more than a single storey; the purpose of the covenant was to protect the existing harbour views from Benjamin's land. The whole of Benjamin's land contained in Volume 7521 Folio 55 was entitled under the terms of the covenant to the benefit. On Benjamin's death his executor further subdivided the remaining land into three lots. One of these lots, lot 3, was conveyed to the original purchasers, Ellisons. Ellisons consolidated their lots and then subdivided. They wished to sell one of the lots free of the covenants. They applied to the court for a declaration under s. 89(3) of the *Conveyancing Act* 1919 (N.S.W.) that the covenants were unenforceable. The purchasers of lots 1 and 2, Stabback and O'Neill respectively, appeared in defence. At an early stage O'Neill withdrew from the proceedings as lot 2 obtained no practical benefit from the covenant.]

WALLACE P. The question is not whether the legal personal representative of the covenantee can enforce the covenants against the appellants as covenantors. Nor is it claimed that the covenants arose out of a building scheme. The question is solely whether as a matter of construction the covenants can be enforced by the owner— Mrs Stabback—of part of the area of land to which the benefit of the covenant was duly annexed.

For a number of reasons I have formed the view that the covenants are not enforceable by Mrs Stabback.

In the first place, I find that I am unable fully to appreciate the meaning of the phrase "each and every part" of the land intended to be benefited, as used in such cases as *Drake v. Gray* [1936] Ch. 451 and *Re Selwyn's Conveyance* [1967] 2 W.L.R. 647, or the phrase "parts as well as the whole", as used by Sholl J. in his dissenting judgment in *Re Arcade Hotel Pty Ltd* [1962] V.R. 274 at 290. Such phrases can scarcely be taken literally. If they are to be taken as a compendious reference to such subdivided portions of the land benefited as the local authority may permit (in accordance with the wishes of the covenantee or his successor) it to be subdivided, then in my opinion there should be clear words in the covenant to express such an intention. Minimal subdivisional areas in Sydney vary from municipality to municipality and even in some cases amongst wards within a particular municipality, so that merely to say that a covenant applies to "each and every part" of the burdened land is to ignore the realities of the situation and this aspect seems important, when a question of construction is involved, involving the extraction of the covenantee's intention.

In the second place I am unable to construe the wording of the subject covenants "the benefit . . . shall be appurtenant to the land in Certificate of Title Volume 7521 Folio 55" as meaning "each and every part" of the land comprised within such folio. To my mind such a phrase simply means what it says, namely the two roods 20 and a half perches (or whatever the particular area may be) shewn in the plan (invariably outlined in red) on the relevant Certificate of Title. How can (by way of extreme yet relevant example) a square foot of such land answer the description of "the land in Certificate of Title Volume 7521 Folio 55"? It would have been so easy for the covenantee when drafting the covenant to extend the benefit to (for example) "each and every lot into which the land benefited may hereafter be lawfully subdivided"—but this he did not do. I do not, with respect to Hardie J., see any difficulty in attempting to contrast the construction of the description of the land burdened with that of the land benefited. If the covenant, for example, were that not more than one residence be erected on land "in" or "comprised within" a certain Certificate of Title the meaning is clear and the construction attracts no problem of whether the whole of the land or each and every part thereof is meant. Indeed one could not seriously construe such a phrase as meaning "each and every part". The same comment, I think, applies to the covenants in the instant case. Generally (though perhaps not always) the problem only arises in connection with the land benefited.

Thirdly I find it difficult to assign to the covenantee, in the light of relevant circumstances and the words selected to compose the covenant, an intention that each and every part of his land (whatever be the full meaning of that phrase) should have the benefit of the covenant, because it is almost beyond dispute that the important first clause of the covenant (and probably the second covenant also) did not touch and concern a substantial proportion of the land comprised within Certificate of Title Volume 7521 Folio 55: cf. *Re Ballard's Conveyance* [1937] Ch. 473. This is because of the topography of the area and in particular the situation of lot 2 presently owned by the O'Neills.

The evidence and circumstances indicate that the late Mr Benjamin desired to protect the view from his cottage and as he then owned the whole of the land in Certificate of Title Volume 7521 Folio 55 it was natural enough that he should desire the whole of such land to be the land benefited.

Fourthly, we know that the covenantee intended to give the area which became Lot 3 of DP511176 to the appellants (an intention implemented by Miss Benjamin [the executrix]) and such lot 3 was part of the land benefited and to which in no circumstances could the covenant ever apply. With respect to those who hold the contrary view, it seems to me quite impossible to assign to the covenantee in these circumstances an intention that "each and every part" of his land should be benefited. For, if Mrs Stabback can enforce the covenants, so can not only the O'Neills but also the appellants, and such an odd result was almost certainly not intended to be achieved by the covenantee.

Fifthly, the concluding sentence of the covenants provides (s. 88): "The said covenants may be released varied or modified by the transferor or his executors administrators or assigns"—and this wording does not seem to me at all consistent with the intention that "each and every part" of the covenantee's land was intended by him to be benefited.

Along more general lines I would add that the view which I have reached seems to be consistent with the reasoning and decisions in the majority of the cases to which we were referred, although one does not doubt that in an appropriate case a different result is necessary (for example, as in *Re Ecclesiastical Commissioners*

[1936] Ch. 430). But I prefer the reasoning of Smith J. in *Bohn v. Miller Bros Pty Ltd* [1953] V.L.R. 354; of Adam J. in *Langdale Pty Ltd v. Sollas* [1959] V.R. 634 and of Lowe J. (with whom Gavan Duffy J. agreed) to that of Sholl J. in *Re Arcade Hotel Pty Ltd* [1962] V.R. 274. The explanation of these cases given by McInerney A.J. in *Re Miscamble's Application* [1966] V.R. 596 (a case in which it was necessary to examine the effect of s. 79A of the *Property Law Act* 1958 (Vic.), a provision inserted after the decision in *Re Arcade Hotel Pty Ltd*) in no way suggests disagreement from the reasoning therein, as I read his Honour's judgment.

[His Honour then held that the covenant was unenforceable because of its uncertainty. The covenant provided that any building "shall in relation to the mean lateral level of the said common boundary line be of a single storey construction and the floor of any such building shall be constructed at a height not greater than three feet above the mean lateral level of the common boundary".]

WALSH J.A. It was stated in the instrument by which the covenants were given that "the benefit of the foregoing covenants shall be appurtenant to the land in Certificate of Title Volume 7521 Folio 55". I agree with the proposition that the question whether they are to be regarded as being for the benefit of that land, considered as an entirety, or as being also for the benefit of any portion of that land which is subsequently held in separate ownership, is a question of construction. But that proposition does not in itself provide an answer to the question raised by this case. If the language of the instrument which contains the covenants, considered in the light of any surrounding circumstances which may legitimately be regarded as an aid to construction, contains a sufficient indication, either that the benefit of the covenants is attached only to the designated land as an entirety, or that it is attached also to portions of the land, then the problem is solved by construing the covenants in accordance with that indication.

But, if there is not any definite pointer towards one construction rather than the other, to be found in other provisions in the instrument or in the circumstances to which it relates, it has to be determined what meaning should be given, without such aid, to a provision that the benefit is to be appurtenant to the land in a specified Certificate of Title. In that situation, it is necessary to consider whether it is proper to attach to the words the meaning which, to one's own mind, seems preferable or whether there is a body of authority which suggests the answer which, in the absence of any sufficient contrary indications, ought to be given. The line of inquiry which I have just suggested is the same, I think, as that expressed herein by Jacobs J.A., by his reference to the submission for the appellants that such words have, according to the authorities, the prima facie meaning of the land in its entirety, and by his statement that it is consistent with authority to determine that the words are "neutral".

In the statement made in *Re Selwyn's Conveyance* [1967] 2 W.L.R. 647 at 656 . . . Goff J. referred to a submission that "the modern tendency is to regard a covenant for the benefit of adjoining or neighbouring land, especially if it be part of a specified estate, as for the whole and not the part". But, in my opinion, the authorities in England and in this country go further than showing a "modern tendency" towards that construction. The preference for treating the benefit as attaching to the whole has been indicated fairly consistently over quite a long period. I think it is shown by the Court of Appeal in *Drake v. Gray* [1936] Ch. 451, although in that case, for the particular reasons given, the opposite construction was adopted. In that case it was said, as it has been in many others, that the question is one of construction. But, nevertheless, the view was accepted that "it must be shown" that the benefit was intended to enure to each portion of the land, as had been stated in the earlier authorities to which the court referred. This was stated by Slesser L.J. (at 458 and 461) and the reasons of the other members of the court were not inconsistent with it. It is true that it was there asserted (see at 468) that it is not essential, in order that this may be shown, that some particular form of words such as "the land and every part of it" be used, and I am respectfully of opinion that that assertion could not be disputed. Nevertheless, although there may be a variety of ways in which that intention may be indicated, no particular form of words being necessary, the reasoning in the case supports the view that, unless there is some indication to the contrary, where there are words attaching to the benefit to land described simply as the land in a specified Certificate of Title, those words will be taken to refer to the land as a whole. . . .

I do not intend to discuss all the other authorities dealing with this question. I agree with the opinion expressed by Lowe J., with whom Gavan Duffy J. agreed, in *Re Arcade Hotel Pty Ltd* [1962] V.R. 274 that there was a course of authority which, if followed, required the view to be taken that, prima facie, the benefit of a covenant of the kind which the court was there concerned enured to the land as an entirety. I think the same view is consistent with *Re Roche* (1960) 77 W.N. (N.S.W.) 431 and with the recent English cases of *Russell v. Archdale* [1964] Ch. 38 and *Re Jeff's Transfer* [1966] 1 W.L.R. 841, as well as with the earlier Victorian cases discussed in *Re Arcade Hotel Pty Ltd.*

In that case, Sholl J. delivered a vigorous dissenting judgment. But, whatever criticism may be made in relation to the logic of the rule or in relation to its historical development in the case law, my opinion is that a rule of construction applicable to this problem has become established. The rule is not a hard and fast rule. It is a rule that, prima facie, one construction is to be adopted rather than the other. It may, of course, be displaced. . . .

Some would say that, if there is to be a rule, it should be the opposite of that which I regard as having become established. That would, no doubt, have been the view of Sholl J., and it has been adopted by the legislature in Victoria which enacted the amendment to the Real Property Act of that State, which was considered in *Re Miscamble's Application* [1966] V.R. 596.

However, I am of opinion that it is desirable to recognise and to make use of the rule which, in my opinion, has become established by the course of authority. In *Re Arcade Hotel Pty Ltd* [1962] V.R. 274 at 278 Lowe J. added to his reasons the following statement: "Since I wrote the above opinion I have had the opportunity of reading and considering the judgment of my brother Sholl J. I do not fail to appreciate the weight of the argument he submits on the question which I have considered and on which my own judgment rests. Nor can I say that I would have come to the same conclusion as I have if the matter had been free of authority, but it seems to me that where the decision rests on the meaning of language commonly used in the same context not only here but in England, it is undesirable that it should be construed differently here from the construction given to it in England . . .".

In my opinion, the substance of what Lowe J. said remains valid. It is still desirable that there should be uniformity upon such a subject as the law of property (cf. *Sexton v. Horton* (1926) 38 C.L.R. 240 at 244), although this is not to be purchased at too high a price, and this court is free to depart from it if it seems right to do so. But, in the present case, a departure from the prima facie rule to which I have referred would appear to be a reversal of what has been generally accepted, not only in England but in Victoria and in this State, and may be supposed to have been known to solicitors and conveyancers and, therefore, to have affected instruments executed on their advice. . . .

With respect, I do not dispute the correctness of the statement of Hardie J. that it is reasonable to suppose that the parties "contemplated that at some time or other the benefited land would probably be subdivided", if by this is meant that, assuming they had thought about the matter before the covenants were executed, they would have considered it likely that, at some time in the future, there would be some subdivision. But, in my opinion, that is not a sufficient indication that the words attaching the benefit of the covenants were meant to make it enure (to use the words of the learned judge) "for the benefit of any residential allotments into which it might subsequently be subdivided".

If the evidence had shown that, when the covenants were executed, Mr Benjamin, the covenantee, had already decided that there was to be a subdivision in the near future and that the appellants knew this, probably I should have regarded that a sufficient ground for construing the covenants in favour of the respondents.

[The dissenting judgment of Jacobs J.A. has been omitted.]

NOTES AND QUESTIONS

1. For similar applications of principle, see *Langdale Pty Ltd v. Sollas* [1959] V.R. 634; *Re Roche* (1960) 77 W.N. 431; *Re Gemmell Holdings* [1970] 1 N.S.W.L.R. 370 at 374; *Re Arcade Hotel* [1962] V.R. 274. Note in the latter case Sholl J.'s dissenting judgment in which he criticises the majority approach. In *Federated Homes Ltd v. Mill Lodge Ltd* [1980] 1 W.L.R. 594, Brightman L.J. (Browne L.J. agreeing) said (at 606):

   It was suggested by Mr Price that, if this covenant ought to be read as enuring for the benefit of the retained land, it should be read as enuring only for the benefit of the retained land as a whole and not for the benefit of every part of it; with the apparent result that there is no annexation of the benefit to a part of the retained land when any severance takes place. He referred us to a passage in *Re Union of London and Smith's Bank Ltd's Conveyance* [1933] Ch. 611 at 628, which I do not think it is necessary for me to read.

   The problem is alluded to in Megarry and Wade, *The Law of Real Property* (4th ed.), p. 763.

   > In drafting restrictive covenants it is therefore desirable to annex them to the covenantee's land "or any part of parts thereof". An additional reason for using this form of words is that, if there is no indication to the contrary, the benefit may be held to be annexed only to the whole of the covenantee's land, so that it will not pass with portions of it disposed of separately. But even without such words the court may find that the covenant is intended to benefit any part of the retained land; and small indications may suffice, since the rule that presumes annexation to the whole only is arbitrary and inconvenient. In principle it conflicts with the rule for assignments, which allows a benefit annexed to the whole to be assigned with part, and it also conflicts with the corresponding rule for easements.

   I find the idea of the annexation of a covenant to the whole of the land but not to a part of it a difficult conception fully to grasp. I can understand that a covenantee may expressly or by necessary implication retain the benefit of a covenant wholly under his own control, so that the benefit will not pass unless the covenantee chooses to assign; but I would have thought, if the benefit of a covenant is, on a proper construction of a document, annexed to the land, prima facie it is annexed to every part thereof, unless the contrary clearly appears. . . .

   Megaw L.J.:

   I would regard the observations made in the passage which Brightman L.J. read from Megarry and Wade, *The Law of Real Property* (4th ed.), p. 763, as being powerful reasons, and I find great difficulty in understanding how, either as a matter of principle, or as a matter of practical good sense in relation to a legal relationship of this sort, it can be said that a covenant, which ex hypothesi has been annexed to the land as a whole, is somehow or other not annexed to the individual parts of that land.

2. Could the problem in *Ellison v. O'Neill* (1968) 88 W.N. (Pt 1) (N.S.W.) 213 have been overcome by an express assignment of part of the benefit to the purchasers of lots in the plan of subdivision? See equitable assignment below p. 347.

3. The parties themselves may provide for severance. In *Marquess of Zetland v. Driver* [1939] 1 Ch. 1 a covenant was declared to be for the benefit and protection of "such part or parts of the lands . . . as shall for the time being remain unsold . . .". Farwell J. delivering the judgment of the Court of Appeal distinguished *Re Ballard* [1937] 1 Ch. 473 on the ground that in *Re Ballard* the covenant was

expressed to run with the whole estate whereas the covenants in the present case were expressed to be for the benefit of the whole or any part or parts of the unsold property. This allowed severance of the covenant.

4. No similar rule to that stated in *Ellison v. O'Neill* applies to easements where the dominant tenement is subdivided: Megarry, Note (1962) 78 L.Q.R. 334. Nor does the rule apply to a sale of part of the land, or subdivision of the land, burdened. Were it so the covenantor could defeat the covenant by selling part of the land or subdividing. Nor does the rule apply to schemes of development; see *Brunner v. Greenslade* [1971] Ch. 993 and discussion below pp. 352, 369.

5. Would the result in the principal case have been the same if instead of the dominant tenement being subdivided part of the land was compulsorily acquired for road widening purposes? If a purchaser of part of benefited land could not enforce the covenant, then presumably the vendor who retains part of the land cannot enforce: Hanbury, *Modern Equity* (9th ed.), p. 611.

6. Whether the benefit attaches to the whole of the land or to each and every part is a matter of construction of the relevant instrument. In *Re Gemmell Holdings* [1970] 1 N.S.W.L.R. 370 at 374 Helsham J. said:

> [T]he matter falls to be determined by finding the true meaning intended to be expressed by the parties in the words used in the covenant. . . . Relevant surrounding circumstances may be looked at as an aid in this search if the language is not clear.

Thus, where the land intended to benefit from a covenant is described as "the land in Certificate of Title Volume 1234 Folio 567" this may annex the benefit to each and every lot comprised in that Certificate of Title where there is evidence that this was the parties' intention: see *Re Application of Fox* (1981) 2 B.P.R. 9310; *Re Magney* (1981) 2 B.P.R. 9358. Note that these two cases involved situations where the land was either recently subdivided or where it was undergoing subdivision.

C.   ENFORCING COVENANTS IN EQUITY

1. The burden of a covenant

Although the burden of a covenant will not run at law so as to bind successors in title to the covenantor, it may, however, be enforceable against a successor in title to the original covenantor in equity: *Tulk v. Moxhay* (1848) 2 Ph. 774; 41 E.R. 1143, extracted below. There are four conditions for the passing of the burden of the covenant in equity:

(1) The covenant must be restrictive or negative in nature.

(2) The covenant must be for the benefit of land retained by the covenantee, (an exception exists in relation to schemes of development as to which see below p. 352.

(3) The burden of the covenant must have been intended to run with the covenantor's land.

(4) The person against whom it is sought to enforce the covenant is not a bona fide purchaser for value of the legal estate without notice of the covenant.

The basic principles were established in the first of the cases extracted.

TULK v. MOXHAY

Chancery (1848) 2 Ph. 774; 41 E.R. 1143

[In 1808 the plaintiff, Tulk, the fee simple owner of a vacant piece of land in Leicester Square, as well as several houses forming the square sold the fee simple estate in the vacant land to Elms. The deed of conveyance contained a covenant by Elms, for himself, his heirs, and assigns, with the plaintiff, his heirs, executors and administrators, that Elms, his heirs, and assigns "should, and would from time to time, and at all times thereafter at his and their own costs and charges, keep and maintain the said piece of ground and square garden . . . in sufficient and proper repair as a square garden and pleasure ground, in an open state, uncovered by any buildings, in a neat and ornamental order''. The defendant, Moxhay, was successor in title to Elms. Although the conveyance to Moxhay did not contain a similar covenant, Moxhay had notice of the original covenant. The defendant, Moxhay, asserted that he had a right to build on the garden area. Tulk, who still owned some houses in the square, sought an injunction restraining Moxhay from breaching the covenant. At first instance the injunction was granted. On a motion to discharge the order.]

LORD COTTENHAM L.C. That this court has jurisdiction to enforce a contract between the owner of land and his neighbour purchasing a part of it, that the latter shall either use or abstain from using the land purchased in a particular way, is what I never knew disputed. Here there is no question about the contract: the owner of certain houses in the square sells the land adjoining, with a covenant from the purchaser not to use it for any other purpose than as a square garden. And it is now contended, not that the vendee could violate that contract, but that he might sell the piece of land, and that the purchaser from him may violate it without this court having any power to interfere. If that were so, it would be impossible for an owner of land to sell part of it without incurring the risk of rendering what he retains worthless. It is said that, the covenant being one which does not run with the land, this court cannot enforce it; but the question is, not whether the covenant runs with the land, but whether a party shall be permitted to use the land in a manner inconsistent with the contract entered into by his vendor, and with notice of which he purchased. Of course, the price would be affected by the covenant, and nothing could be more inequitable than that the original purchaser should be able to sell the property the next day for a greater price, in consideration of the assignee being allowed to escape from the liability which he had himself undertaken.

That the question does not depend upon whether the covenant runs with the land is evident from this, that if there was a mere agreement and no covenant, this court would enforce it against a party purchasing with notice of it; for if an equity is attached to the property by the owner, no one purchasing with notice of that equity can stand in a different situation from the party from whom he purchased. There are not only cases before the Vice-Chancellor of England, in which he considered that doctrine as not in dispute; but looking at the ground on which Lord Eldon disposed of the case of *Duke of Bedford v. Trustees of the British Museum* (1822) 2 My. & K. 552; 39 E.R. 1055 it is impossible to suppose that he entertained any doubt of it . . .

With respect to the observations of Lord Brougham in *Keppell v. Bailey* (1834) 2 My. & K. 517; 39 E.R. 1042 he never could have meant to lay down that this court would not enforce an equity attached to land by the owner, unless under such circumstances as would maintain an action at law. If that be the result of his observations, I can only say that I cannot coincide with it. . . .

[T]his motion must be refused, with costs.

NOTES

1. In the principal case the plaintiff was held entitled to an injunction restraining the defendant as successor in title to the covenantor on the general equitable principle that it was contrary to equity and good conscience that the defendant who purchased with notice should be allowed to act inconsistently with the covenant. As stated, this principle was capable of application to both positive and negative covenants: *Cooke v. Chilcott* [1896] 3 Ch. D. 694. No point was taken in *Tulk v. Moxhay* (1848) 2 Ph. 774; 41 E.R. 1143 that the covenant was in part positive. Later cases, however, held that the *Tulk v. Moxhay* principle applied only to negative covenants: *Haywood v. Brunswick Permanent Building Society* (1881) 8 Q.B.D. 403.

2. A covenant will be positive if it requires affirmative conduct or expenditure of money. A negative covenant can be complied with simply by inaction and in determining whether the covenant is negative equity looks to the substance of the covenant not its form. Consider whether the following covenants are negative covenants: a covenant to keep a garden in an uncovered state, free of buildings (*Tulk v. Moxhay*); a covenant not to allow premises to fall into disrepair; a covenant that the covenantor will, before the commencement of any building submit building plans to the vendor for approval: *Powel v. Hemsley* [1909] 1 Ch. 680; [1909] 2 Ch. 252.

3. A number of reasons have been advanced for equity's insistence that the covenant be negative in substance. First, it is said that the covenant is annexed to the land not to the individual, "for the land cannot spend money on improving itself": *Re Nisbet and Pott's Contract* [1905] 1 Ch. 391 at 397 per Farwell J. Secondly, equity would act to restrain the commission or continuance of specified acts, but generally would not make orders to perform a series of acts requiring supervision: Megarry and Wade, *The Law of Real Property* (4th ed.), p. 754. Thirdly, policy reasons based on the fear that a purchaser of property may be rendered bankrupt through enforcement of an obligation he or she never intended to assume, coupled with the view that a negative restriction on land utilisation was, if not desirable, at least comparatively harmless since it could only lessen or destroy the owner's value in such property: Clark, "The American Law Institute's Law of Real Covenants" (1943) 52 Yale L.J. 699 at 702.

The rule has given rise to serious difficulties in several areas—first, covenants between neighbours as to such matters as fencing, boundary walls and the repair of roads; secondly, in relation to modern developments in building and construction, particularly the provision of flats and housing estates with common facilities and amenities. These difficulties have been in part overcome by legislation: see *Dividing Fences Act* 1951 (N.S.W.); *Strata Titles Act* 1973 (N.S.W.) and in part by the decisions in *Frater v. Finlay* (1968) 91 W.N. (N.S.W.) 730, above p. 223 and *Halsall v. Brizell* [1957] 1 Ch. 169, above p. 313. In United Kingdom, it has been recommended that the benefit and burden of positive covenants should run with the land: Report of the Committee on Positive Covenants Affecting Land (1965) Cmnd 2719 (U.K.).

The Law Commission in its report, *Transfer of Land, The Law of Positive and Restrictive Covenants* Law Com 127 (1984) thought that the existing law of restrictive covenants was not a suitable vehicle for the enforcement of positive obligations. Two main reasons were advanced for this view (at 32):

(a) . . . [T]he owner of any interest, however small, in the burdened land is bound to observe a restrictive covenant. This is as it should be, because a restrictive covenant requires people merely to refrain from doing something. But positive covenants require them actually to do something, and that something may be a burdensome and expensive thing. It would be quite wrong, for example, if a weekly tenant of the burdened land automatically became personally liable to perform a positive covenant to erect and maintain a costly sea wall. Liability to perform a positive covenant therefore cannot rest on all those interested in the burdened land.

(b) The burden of a restrictive covenant runs only in equity, so that equitable remedies alone are available for its enforcement. . . . The idea of enforcing a simple covenant to pay money by means of equitable remedies is wholly artificial. And the normal remedy for breach of a covenant to carry out works must be legal damages. . . . This point goes to the heart of the conceptual nature of the covenant: legal remedies cannot be available unless the burden runs at law and it cannot do that unless it amounts to a legal . . . interest in land. . . .

The Committee recommended (at 33) the creation of a new legal interest in land somewhat analogous to rights created by easements but without the complicated rules relating to annexation. The Committee proposed that the obligation imposed could be positive or negative and would run with the land where the parties expressly deemed it to be a "land obligation". Note also the proposal by the Law Reform Commission of Victoria that positive covenants should be allowed to run with the land and be governed by the same rules as restrictive covenants: *Easements and Covenants* DP 115, February 1989, para. 29.

4. A covenant will not bind a successor in title to the covenantor under the principle of *Tulk v. Moxhay* unless the burden of the covenant was intended to run with the covenantor's land. Under the *Conveyancing Act* 1919 (N.S.W.), s. 70A, above p. 310 covenants are deemed to be made on behalf of the covenantor and her or his successors in title and those deriving under them, unless a contrary intention is expressed in the instrument. The section has been regarded as essentially a word saving device and of itself has little or no weight in considering the liability of successors in title to the covenantor: *Tophams Ltd v. Earl of Sefton* [1967] 1 A.C. 50 at 73 per Lord Upjohn. In *Re Royal Victoria Pavilion Ramsgate* [1961] Ch. 681, Pennyquick J. (at 589) said the phrase "unless a contrary intention is expressed" meant:

[U]nless an indication to the contrary is to be found in the instrument, and that such an indication may be sufficiently contained in the wording and context of the instrument even though the instrument contains no provision expressly excluding successors in title from its operation. It can hardly be the intention of the section that a covenant which on its natural construction, is manifestly intended to be personal only, must be construed as running with the land merely because the contrary is not expressly provided.

This view was implicitly accepted by Needham J. in *Palm Beach Lands Pty Ltd v. Marshall* (1988) C.C.H. N.S.W. Conv. R. 55-411 where his Honour found that a covenant that "no buildings . . . shall be built . . . on the said land . . . until the design and location . . . have been approved in writing by the transferor", was a personal covenant not binding on a successor in title to the covenantor. The reasons for this finding were, to a large extent, practical matters. If the benefit of the right flowed through to a number of purchasers from the original covenantee, differing building and design requirements might be imposed on the defendant. No reference was made in the decision to *Conveyancing Act* 1919 (N.S.W.), ss 70 or 70A. To ensure that the burden of the covenant will run with the land, it should be expressly stated that it is intended that the burden of the covenant run with and bind the land conveyed and every part thereof: Preston and Newsom, *Restrictive Covenants Affecting Freehold Land* (7th ed.), p. 99.

5. The principle enunciated in *Tulk v. Moxhay* applies only where the person seeking to enforce the covenant retains land intended to be benefited by the covenant as the next case extract, *London County Council v. Allen*, illustrates. Schemes of development are an exception in this rule: see below p. 352.

6. It is a defence to an action based on the *Tulk v. Moxhay* principle, that the defendant is a purchaser of the legal estate for value without notice (actual or constructive) of the covenant. This rule does not derive from any special rule concerning notice, but from general rules of priorities whereby an equitable interest may be defeated by a purchaser of the legal estate for value without notice. Thus if the purchaser took only an equitable estate he would take subject to the burden whether the purchaser had notice or not: *London and South West Railway v. Gomm* (1882) 2 Ch. D. 562 at 583 per Jessel M.R. On these principles a restrictive covenant would be enforceable against a squatter, who is not a purchaser for value: *Re Nisbet and Pott's Contract* [1906] 1 Ch. 386. See also *Mander v. Falcke* [1891] 2 Ch. 554; *John v. Holmes* [1900] 1 Ch. 188. The defence of bona fide purchaser protects those who claim through a bona fide purchaser even if they have notice: see *Wilkes v. Spooner* [1911] 2 K.B. 473, above p. 164.

LONDON COUNTY COUNCIL v. ALLEN

Court of Appeal [1914] 3 K.B. 642

[M. J. Allen applied to the London County Council, the plaintiff, for permission to lay out a new road. The council agreed on condition that Allen enter into a covenant not to build on a plot of land which lay across the end of the proposed street; the purpose of the covenant was to allow a continuation of the proposed street. The council did not own, nor had any interest, in land which could benefit from the proposed covenant. An indenture was entered into by the council and M. J. Allen, pursuant to which, Allen covenanted, on behalf of himself, his heirs and assigns and other persons claiming through him, that he would not erect or place any building or structure on the land without the council's consent and that in any dealing with the land notice of the covenant would be given. M. J. Allen covenanted as owner, although at the time he held only an option to purchase the land. Subsequently he purchased the land and later sold one of the two lots to his wife, Emily Allen. Emily Allen erected houses on the land; the land was later mortgaged to Norris. M. J. Allen retained the second lot. On this lot he erected a wall which the council alleged to be in breach of the covenant. The London County Council then brought proceedings against M. J. Allen (as original covenantor) and against Emily Allen and Norris (as successors in title) to restrain breaches of the covenant. At first instance the trial judge found that Emily Allen and Norris had taken with notice of the covenant and that the council was entitled to enforce the covenants. On appeal:]

BUCKLEY L.J. The short proposition is that as matter of law a derivative owner of land, deriving title under a person who has entered into a restrictive covenant concerning the land, is not bound by the covenant even if he took with notice of its existence if the covenantee has no land adjoining or affected by the observance or non-observance of the covenant. I proceed to examine how the law upon this point stands upon the authorities.

The respondents do not contend that the covenant here in question runs with the land. It is the better opinion, and in *Austerberry v. Oldham Corp.* (1885) 29 Ch. D. 750 the Court of Appeal by way of opinion and not of decision held, that the burden of a covenant, not involving a grant, never runs with the land at law except as between landlord and tenant. . . . But it does not follow that the covenantee is without remedy where the covenant does not run with the land. *Tulk v. Moxhay* (1848) 2 Ph. 774; 41 E.R. 1143 established that as between the grantor of a restrictive covenant affecting certain land and the owner of adjoining land the covenantee may in equity enforce the covenant against the derivative owner taking with notice. . . . The reason given is that, if that were not so, it would be impossible for an owner of land to sell part of it without incurring the risk of rendering what he retains worthless. If the vendor has retained no land which can be protected by the restrictive covenant, the basis of the reasoning of the judgment is swept away. In *Haywood v. Brunswick Permanent Benefit Building Society* (1881) 8 Q.B.D 403 the Court of Appeal declined to extend the doctrine of *Tulk v. Moxhay* to covenants other than restrictive covenants. They rejected the doctrine that, inasmuch as the defendants took the land with notice of the covenants, they were bound in equity to perform them. That therefore is not the principle upon which the equitable doctrine rests. In the present case we are asked to extend the doctrine of *Tulk v. Moxhay* so as to affirm that a restrictive covenant can be enforced against a derivative owner taking with notice by a person who never has had or who does not retain any land to be protected by the restrictive covenant in question. In my opinion the doctrine does not extend to that case. The doctrine is that a covenant not running with the land, but being a negative covenant entered into by an owner of land with an adjoining owner, binds the land in equity and is enforceable against a derivative owner taking with notice. The doctrine ceases to be applicable when the person seeking to enforce the covenant against the derivative owner has no land to be protected by the negative covenant. The fact of notice is in that case irrelevant. . . . Upon the authorities, therefore, as a whole I am of opinion that the doctrine in *Tulk v. Moxhay* (1848) 2 Ph. 774; 41 E.R. 1143 does not extend to the case in which the covenantee has no land capable of enjoying, as against the land of the covenantor, the benefit of the restrictive covenant. The doctrine is either an extension in equity of the doctrine in *Spencer's Case* (1583) 5 Co. Rep. 16a; 1 Sm L.C. (11th ed.), p. 55 (in which ownership of land by both covenantor and covenantee is essential) or an extension in equity of the doctrine of negative easements, a doctrine applicable not to the case of easements in gross, but to an easement enjoyed by one land upon another land. Where the covenantee has no land, the derivative owner claiming under the covenantee has no land, the derivative owner claiming under the covenantor is bound neither in contract nor by the equitable doctrine which attaches in the case where there is land capable of enjoying the restrictive covenant.

The appeal of Emily Allen and Norris upon the point of law in my opinion succeeds. . . .

As regards the defendant M. J. Allen, he is not within the considerations above dealt with. He was the covenanting party. The erection of the three houses was a breach of covenant. The learned judge has refused any injunction but has given nominal damages for the technical breach. . . .

[His Lordship went on to hold that, in respect of lot 2, the building of the wall constituted a breach of the covenant and that the order to pull down the wall was properly made.]

SCRUTTON J. I think the result of this long chain of authorities is that, whereas in my view, at the time of *Tulk v. Moxhay* and for at least 20 years afterwards, the plaintiffs in this case would have succeeded against an assign on the ground that the assign had notice of the covenant, since *Formby v. Barker* [1903] 2 Ch. 539; *Re Nisbet and Potts' Contract* [1905] 1 Ch. 391; [1906] 1 Ch. 386, and *Millbourn v. Lyons* [1914] 1 Ch. 34; 2 Ch. 231, three decisions of the Court of Appeal, the plaintiffs must fail on the ground that they have never had any land for the benefit of which this "equitable interest analogous to a negative easement" could be created, and therefore cannot sue a person who brought the land with knowledge that there was a restrictive covenant as to its use, which he proceeds to disregard, because he is not privy to the contract. I think the learned editors of Dart on *Vendors and Purchasers* (7th ed.), Vol. II, p. 769, are justified by the present state of the authorities in saying that "the question of notice to the purchaser has nothing whatever to do with the question whether the covenant binds him, except in so far as the absence of notice may enable him to raise the plea of purchaser for valuable consideration without notice". If the covenant does not run with the land in law, its benefit can only be asserted against an assign of the land burdened, if the covenant was made for the benefit of certain land, all or some of which remains in the possession of the covenantee or his assign, suing to enforce the covenant. It may be, if the matter is considered by a higher tribunal, that tribunal may see its way to revert to what I think was the earlier doctrine of notice, or at any rate to treat it as co-existing with the later refinement of "an equitable interest analogous to a negative easement" binding on persons who are ignorant of it. The remarks of Lord Selborne in *Earl of Zetland v. Hislop* (1882) 7 App. Cas. 427 at 446, 447 are not favourable to the too rigid development or enforcement of the latter alternative; and the observations of Lord Macnaughten (at 32), Lord Davey (at 35), and Lord Lindley (at 36) in *Noakes & Co. v. Rice* [1902] A.C. 24 seem to suggest that the doctrine of *Tulk v. Moxhay* (1848) 2 Ph. 774; 41 E.R. 1143 may well be reconsidered and put on a proper footing. For I regard it as very regrettable that a public body should be prevented from enforcing a restriction on the use of property imposed for the public benefit against persons who bought the property knowing of the restriction, by the apparently immaterial circumstance that the public body does not own any land in the immediate neighbourhood. But, after a careful consideration of the authorities, I am forced to the view that the later decisions of this court compel me so to hold. . . .

[The judgment of Kennedy L.J. agreeing with Buckley L.J. and Scrutton J. has been omitted.]

NOTES

1. For applications of the principal case in the Australian jurisdiction, see *Lane Cove Municipal Council v. Hurdis* (1955) 55 S.R. (N.S.W.) 434; *Commissioner for Main Roads v. B.P. Australia* (1964) 82 W.N. (Pt 2) 27.

2. Legislation now exists in New South Wales to enable local authorities to enforce restrictions on user and public positive covenants (see above p. 307) even though there is no land to which the benefit of the covenant is annexed, see *Conveyancing Act* 1919 (N.S.W.), ss 88D, 88E.

3. The requirement that the covenantee retain land which benefits from the covenant is common both to the passing of the burden and the benefit of the covenant in equity.

4. In *Formby v. Barker* [1903] 2 Ch. 539, Vaughan Williams L.J. commented (at 550):

It becomes necessary therefore to ascertain whether the principle of *Tulk v. Moxhay* applies to a case in which the vendor sells his whole estate. I have not been able to find any case in which, after the sale of the whole of an estate in land, the benefit of a restrictive covenant has been enforced by injunction against an assignee of the purchaser at the instance of a plaintiff having no land retained by the vendor, although there are cases in which restrictive covenants seem to have been enforced at the instance of plaintiffs, other than the vendor, for the benefit of whose land it appears from the terms of the covenant, or can be inferred from surrounding circumstances, that the covenant was intended to operate. In all other cases the restrictive covenant would seem to be a mere personal covenant collateral to the conveyance. It is a covenant which cannot run with the land either at law or in equity, and therefore the burden of the covenant cannot be enforced against an assignee of the purchaser.

Similarly a developer who no longer owns any land in a subdivision cannot enforce a covenant against a successor in title to the covenantor: *Palm Beach Lands Pty Ltd v. Marshall* (1988) C.C.H. N.S.W. Conv. R. 55-411.

Although a plaintiff may not be able to enforce a covenant in equity because he or she retains no land benefiting from it, other areas of liability may allow enforcement of restrictions as to user, for example, the torts of conspiracy and inducing breach of contract: *Esso Petroleum v. Kingswood Motors* [1974] 1 Q.B. 142 at 156.

2. The benefit of a covenant

The benefit of a covenant may run, not only at law, but also in equity. The question whether the benefit will run in equity arises in the following situations: (1) where the covenant is sought to be enforced against a successor in title to the covenantor under the *Tulk v. Moxhay* doctrine; (2) where the covenantee or the party seeking to enforce the covenant holds an equitable interest in the land; (3) where before the *Conveyancing Act* 1919 (N.S.W.), s. 70 came into force, the party seeking to enforce the covenant did not hold the same legal estate as the original covenantee (see above p. 324, for discussion; (4) where the party seeking to enforce the covenant relies on an equitable assignment of the benefit; (5) where the plaintiff seeks to enforce the covenant as part of a scheme of development.

In determining whether the benefit of a covenant is enforceable in equity, it is necessary to distinguish between the position of the original covenantee and the covenantee's successors in title.

(a) Original covenantee

The original covenantee is entitled to enforce the covenant against the original covenantor in an action at law for damages: *Formby v. Barker* [1903] 2 Ch. 539, above p. 345. In addition, the court may in its discretion, issue an injunction restraining a breach of covenant by the original covenantor; damage need not be shown as a prerequisite to the issue of an injunction: *Doherty v. Allman* (1873) 3 App. Cas. 709 at 729.

Where the original covenantee seeks to enforce the covenant against a successor in title to the covenantor, it must be shown that the burden of the covenant has passed with the land: see above p. 340. The original covenantee, in order to enforce the covenant against a successor in title to the covenantor, must have an interest in the land intended to be benefited and capable of benefiting from the enforcement of the restrictive covenant: *Formby v. Barker* [1903] 2 Ch. 539, above p. 345. Thus, an original covenantee who no longer retains any land benefiting from the covenant cannot enforce the covenant against a successor in title to the covenantor.

A person entitled to enforce a covenant under s. 36C of the *Conveyancing Act* 1919 (N.S.W.) is in the same position as an original covenantee. For discussion of that section, see above p. 321.

(b) Successors in title to the covenantee

The benefit of a covenant may be enforced in equity by a successor in title to the covenantee in any of three ways: (1) the benefit of the covenant has passed by assignment to the plaintiff in accordance with the equitable rules for assignment; (2) the benefit of the covenant is annexed to land to which the person seeking to enforce the covenant is entitled; or (3) the plaintiff is entitled to enforce the covenant under a scheme of development.

These three methods by which a plaintiff may be entitled to enforce a covenant are not mutually exclusive. Thus, a covenant may be annexed to the entirety of land the owner of which may be entitled to assign the benefit of the covenant to a purchaser of part of that land: *Stillwell v. Blackman* [1968] 1 Ch. 508 discussed below p. 349, or a covenant may be annexed to land and yet form part of a scheme of development: *Texaco Antilles Ltd v. Kernochan* [1973] A.C. 609.

(c) Express assignment

The *Conveyancing Act* 1919 (N.S.W.), s. 12 enables the assignment of legal choses in action at law. This does not prevent the assignment of the benefit of a covenant in equity: *William Brandt's Sons & Co. v. Dunlop Rubber Co.* [1905] A.C. 454 at 461. Assignment of the benefit of a covenant must comply with the equitable rules (set out in *Re Union of London and Smith's Bank Ltd's Conveyance, Miles v. Easter* [1933] 1 Ch. 611, extracted below) in the following situations: (1) where the assignment does not comply with statutory requirements: for example, where the requisite notice has not been given; (2) where the benefit of a covenant is annexed to the whole of an estate and the vendor wishes to sell part of the land and assign the benefit of the covenant, as far as it relates to that part, to the purchaser. This issue remains controversial: see below p. 349.

UNION OF LONDON AND SMITH'S BANK LTD's CONVEYANCE, RE MILES v. EASTER

Court of Appeal [1933] 1 Ch. 611

ROMER L.J. (delivering the judgment of the Court of Appeal). It is plain . . . that if the restrictive covenant be taken not merely for some personal purpose or object of the vendor, but for the benefit of some other land of his in the sense that it would enable him to dispose of that land to greater advantage, the covenant, though not annexed to such land so as to run with any part of it, may be enforced against an assignee of the covenantor taking with notice, both by the covenantee and by persons to whom the benefit of such covenant has been assigned, subject however to certain conditions. In the first place, the "other land" must be land that is capable of being benefited by the covenant—otherwise it would be impossible to infer that the object of the covenant was to enable the vendor to dispose of his land to greater advantage. In the next place, this land must be "ascertainable" or "certain". . . . For, although the court will readily infer the intention to benefit the other land of the vendor where the existence and situation of such land are indicated in the conveyance or have been otherwise shown with reasonable certainty, it is impossible to do so from vague references in the conveyance or in other documents laid before the court as to the existence of other lands of the vendor, the extent and situation of which are undefined. In the third place, the covenant cannot be enforced by the covenantee against an assign of the purchaser after the covenantee has parted with the whole of his land.

This last point was decided, and in our opinion rightly decided, by Sargent J. in *Chambers v. Randall* [1923] 1 Ch. 149. As pointed out by that learned judge, the covenant having been entered into to enable the covenantee to dispose of his property to advantage, that result will in fact have been obtained when all that property has been disposed of. There is therefore no longer any reason why the court should extend to him the benefit of the equitable doctrine of *Tulk v. Moxhay* (1848) 2 Ph. 774; 41 E.R. 1143. That is only done when it is sought to enforce the covenant in connection with the enjoyment of land that the covenant was intended to protect. But it was also held by Sargent J. in the same case [1923] 1 Ch. 149, and in our opinion rightly held, that although on a sale of the whole or part of the property intended to be protected by the covenant the right to enforce the covenant may be expressly assigned to the purchaser, such an assignment will be ineffective if made at a later date when the covenantee has parted with the whole of his land. The covenantee must, indeed, be at liberty to include in any sale of the retained property the right to enforce the covenants. He might not otherwise be able to dispose of such property to the best advantage, and the intention with which he obtained the covenant would be defeated. But if he has been able to sell any particular part of his property without assigning to the purchaser the benefit of the covenant, there seems no reason why he should at a later date and as an independent transaction be at liberty to confer upon the purchaser such benefit. To hold that he could do so would be to treat the covenant as having been obtained, not only for the purpose of enabling the covenantee to dispose of his land to the best advantage, but also for the purpose of enabling him to dispose of the benefit of the covenant to the best advantage. Where, at the date of the assignment of the benefit of the covenant, the covenantee has disposed of the whole of his land, there is an additional reason by the assignee should be unable to enforce it. For at the date of the assignment the covenant had ceased to be enforceable at the instance of the covenantee himself, and he cannot confer any greater rights upon the assignee than he possessed himself.

NOTES

1. See also *Re Barry and the Conveyancing Act* (1962) 79 W.N. (N.S.W.) 759, holding that the benefit of a personal covenant cannot be assigned in equity.

2. In the principal case Romer L.J. stated that the land to be benefited must be "indicated in the conveyance or have been otherwise shown with reasonable certainty". More recent authority, however, suggests that it is not necessary that the land intended to benefit from the covenant should be described in the conveyance creating the covenant; it is sufficient if it can be ascertained with reasonable certainty by extrinsic evidence: *Newton Abbott Co-op. Society Ltd v. Williamson and Treadgold Ltd* [1952] 1 Ch. 286; *Marten v. Flight Refuelling Ltd* [1962] 1 Ch. 115 at 131.

3. Issues of special difficulty arise in the New South Wales jurisdiction by virtue of s. 88(1) of the *Conveyancing Act* 1919, extracted below p. 361. Several points need to be made in this context:

   (1) The section applies only where it is sought to enforce the covenant *against* a successor in title to the covenantor. Thus the section would not apply where an express assignee sought to enforce the covenant against the original covenantor; in this instance the equitable rules set out in *Union of London and Smith's Bank Ltd's Conveyance, Re Miles v. Easter* would apply. On the authority of the *Newton Abbott* case, the benefit of the covenant could pass by express assignment even if the instrument creating the covenant did not identify the land to be benefited.

   (2) Where an express assignee seeks to enforce the covenant against a successor in title to the covenantor, the operation of s. 88(1) is uncertain. Section 88(1) requires, inter alia, that the instrument creating the restriction as to user clearly indicate the land to which the benefit of the restriction is appurtenant. The effect of this requirement may leave very little scope for equitable assignments in New South Wales. The reason is that if the instrument creating the restriction as to user clearly indicates the land benefiting from the restriction, this in combination with s. 70 of the *Conveyancing Act* 1919 (N.S.W.) (covenants deemed to be made with successors in title to the covenantee) would almost invariably amount to annexation of the covenant to the land. See *Rogers v. Hosegood* [1900] 2 Ch. 388, above p. 327, for an example of an effective annexation of the benefit to the land. In the present context, it will be an extremely rare case where an express assignee could enforce a covenant against a successor in title to the covenantor, see *Stillwell v. Blackman* [1968] 1 Ch. 508, below, as a possible example.

(3) It may, however, be argued that s. 88(1) does not apply to an express assignment of the benefit of a covenant because the section applies only to covenants the benefit of which is "intended to be annexed to other land". It is arguable that covenants capable of assignment are not "intended to be annexed to other land".

4. There is some authority (although the point cannot be regarded as settled) that an express assignment of the benefit of a covenant in accordance with the equitable rules, annexes the covenant to the land so that it thereafter passes to future owners without express assignment. On this view express assignment is regarded as delayed annexation. For a summary and discussion of authorities see Baker, "The Benefit of Restrictive Covenants" (1968) 84 L.Q.R. 22; Megarry and Wade, *The Law of Real Property* (4th ed.), pp. 766-767.

5. If the benefit of a covenant is annexed to the entirety of land, can the benefit of the covenant be expressly assigned to the purchaser of part of that land? This was answered in the affirmative by Ungoed-Thomas J. in *Stillwell v. Blackman* [1968] 1 Ch. 508. In addition, an express assignee can still enforce the covenant when he has conveyed part of the benefited land; see also *Russell v. Archdale* [1964] Ch. 38; *Re Jeff's Transfer* [1966] 1 W.L.R. 841.

Contrast the view of Sholl J. (dissenting) in *Re Arcade Hotel Pty Ltd* [1962] V.R. 274 at 293 that "[t]here would indeed seem to be some logical contradiction involved in saying that one can assign in parts, and thereby attach by severance to different parcels of the benefited land, the benefit of a covenant which *ex hypothesi* is so expressed as to confine that benefit to the land while it is enjoyed by one owner and as a whole, and no longer, nor otherwise. But apart altogether from that, and even if it could be done, why should one attribute to the parties—especially to the covenantee—an intention to effect an annexation of benefit to land, which he is proposing to dispose of in portions in such a way that, once he transfers any part of the benefited land, however small, annexation will at once be defeated and recourse must be had instead to the different mechanism of express assignment? I can see little sense in that." See also the critical comment in Preston and Newsom, *Restrictive Covenants Affecting Freehold Land* (7th ed.), pp. 24-29; Moot Point (1970) 44 A.L.J. 40; *Federated Homes Ltd v. Mill Lodge Ltd* [1980] 1 All E.R. 371, above p. 339.

(d) Benefit annexed to the land

A covenant may be enforced by a successor in title to land to which the benefit of the covenant is annexed. The successor in title under the *Conveyancing Act* 1919 (N.S.W.), s. 70 is deemed to include an occupier for the time being of the land of the covenantee. The section is set out above p. 324.

The party seeking to enforce the covenant must show that the benefit of the covenant is annexed to that part of the land to which he or she is entitled: see *Ellison v. O'Neill* (1968) 88 W.N. (Pt 1) (N.S.W.) 213, above p. 335; *Re Ballard's Conveyance*; *Marquess of Zetland v. Driver* [1939] Ch. 1, above p. 332. If the benefit of the covenant is effectively annexed to the land to which the plaintiff is entitled, it passes automatically on conveyance of the land without special bargain: *Rogers v. Hosegood* [1900] 2 Ch. 388, above p. 327.

Prior to the decision in *Federated Homes* [1980] 1 All E.R. 371, see above p. 324 the formal requirements for annexation of a covenant to land so as to run with the land in equity could be quite easily stated as the following: (1) the covenant must touch and concern the land of the covenantee; (2) there must be an intention to annex the benefit of the covenant to the land; (3) the land benefiting from the covenant must be sufficiently identified in the instrument creating the covenant; this would have been required independently by the *Conveyancing Act* 1919 (N.S.W.), s. 88(1).

The effect of these three requirements was as follows:

(1) The covenant must touch and concern the land of the covenantee.

This requirement is the same in law and equity although most of the authorities concern the passing of the benefit in equity: see *Rogers v. Hosegood* [1900] 2 Ch. 388, above p. 327; *Kerridge v. Foley* (1964) 82 W.N. (N.S.W.) (Pt 1) 294, above p. 330; *Re Ballard's Conveyance* [1937] 1 Ch. 473, p. 332; *Ellison v. O'Neill* (1968) 88 W.N. (Pt 1) (N.S.W.) 213, above p. 335; *Marquess of Zetland v. Driver* [1939] Ch. 1, above p. 339.

(2) *There must be an intention to annex the benefit of the covenant to the land.*

(3) *The land to be benefited must be sufficiently identified in the instrument creating the covenant.*

Prior to the *Federated Homes* case, a distinction was drawn between the position at law and the position in equity. At law, it was sufficient that the parties intend the benefit to run with the land. At law, there was no requirement of formal words of annexation, nor that the property entitled to the benefit be identified in the instrument creating the covenant: *Smith and Snipes Hall Farm Ltd v. River Douglas Catchment Board* [1949] 2 K.B. 500, above p. 323. The intention that the covenant run with the land was supplied by the *Conveyancing Act* 1919 (N.S.W.), s. 70(1).

In contrast, in equity, it had to be shown that there was an intention to annex the benefit of the covenants to the land. Appropriate words of annexation would demonstrate the requisite intention. A covenant with a named person as owner for the time being of particular land sufficed, as did a declaration that the covenant was taken "for the benefit of" particular lands: *Drake v. Gray* [1936] Ch. 451 at 466 per Greene L.J.; *Osborne v. Bradley* [1903] 2 Ch. 466 at 450 and see *Rogers v. Hosegood*, above p. 327. Prior to the *Federated Homes* case equity also required that the benefited land be sufficiently identified in the instrument creating the covenant: *Renals v. Cowlishaw* (1879) 11 Ch. D. 866; *Miles v. Easter* [1933] Ch. 611 at 625, above p. 347; *Newton Abbott Co-op. Society Ltd v. Williamson and Treadgold Ltd* [1952] Ch. 286. Thus, in *Renals v. Cowlishaw* there was a covenant not to build on part of the land conveyed, expressed to be in favour of the covenantees "their heirs executors administrators and assigns". The conveyance did not state that the covenant was for the protection of residential property or in reference to other adjoining parcels of land or in any way identify any land to benefit from the covenant. It was held that the conveyance did not demonstrate an intention to annex the benefit of the covenant to the land. Similarly, in *Sutton v. Shoppee* (1963) 63 S.R. (N.S.W.) 853 a covenant with the Rose Bay Land Co. "its successors and assigns" was held by Sugerman J., in the absence of formal words of annexation, not to indicate an intention to annex the benefit of the covenant to land retained by the company. Sugerman J. said (at 859):

> It is, no doubt true . . . that surrounding circumstances may be looked at as an aid to construction. But what [counsel] has asked us to do . . . is really not to confine our attention to surrounding circumstances within the legitimate bounds of their use for that purpose but to eke out, by the inference of an intention from them, the absence of any express indication of intention in the conveyance itself. Express annexation is in this respect a different matter from the spelling out of an intention to annex from the surrounding circumstances where there is a building scheme.

A similarly restrictive view was taken in the earlier case of *Newton Abbott Co-op. Society Ltd v. Williamson and Treadgold Ltd* [1952] Ch. 286. There a covenant by a purchaser not to carry on the business of ironmonger, entered into in favour of a vendor, was held not to be annexed to the land. The vendor was described in the conveyance as "Mrs Mardon of Devonia" but otherwise no reference was made to the land intended to be benefited by the covenant. (The benefit of the covenant was, however, held to pass by express assignment: see above p. 348.) Subsequent authority also affirms that a more generous rule applies to express assignments of the benefit of a covenant: see *Marten v. Flight Refuelling Ltd* [1962] Ch. 115 and Ryder, "Restrictive Covenants: The Problems of Implied Annexation" (1972) 36 Conv. (N.S.) 20. Some writers in England have contested the view that equity required express annexation. The argument is best put by Megarry and Wade, *The Law of Real Property* (5th ed.), pp. 784-785 (footnotes omitted):

Although it has often been stated that annexation must appear from the covenant itself, this may not be an invariable rule where the facts make the connection with the benefited land so obvious that to ignore it would be not only an injustice but a departure from common sense. In the past, some decisions have overstated and overformalised the requirement of annexation, whereas the present tendency is to relax it. In a suitable case, therefore, the court may find that there has been an implied annexation without any express words to that effect.

This is merely to recognise that virtually all restrictive covenants are in fact taken for the benefit of the covenantee's other land in circumstances which are often clear. Where the facts admit no real doubt about the intention of the parties there is no merit on insisting on formalities which are not demanded by the rules governing other similar interests. No formal annexation is required in order that the benefit run at law, even when negative: it need only touch and concern the benefited land, and it is out of character for equity to be more formalistic than common law. . . . An express annexation of the benefit is not required in order that the burden may run or for the purposes of assignment or by the doctrine of *Spencer's Case* [(1583) 5 Co. Rep. 16a, see below p. 625] or the rules for easements, the two closest analogies at common law.

There is, however, only scant English authority supporting this view, and no direct authority in New South Wales which would support such an approach. The argument is beside the point if the *Conveyancing Act* 1919 (N.S.W.), s. 70(1) is interpreted in line with the *Federated Homes* case [1980] 1 All E.R. 371, above p. 324. The effect would be that where the covenantee owned some land in fact capable of benefiting from the covenant even if not referred to in the instrument creating the covenant, s. 70 automatically annexes the benefit of the covenant to that land unless the instrument expressly states otherwise: see *Roake v. Chadha* [1983] 3 All E.R. 503, above p. 326. The earlier equitable requirements of intention to annex the benefit to identifiable land would no longer be required. The *Federated Homes* case concerned an action to enforce the covenant against an original covenantor but there is no suggestion in the decision that the principles there stated could not equally apply to the passing of the benefit in equity. Even if accepted as good law, the *Federated Homes* case will have little impact on restrictive covenants in New South Wales. This is because of the *Conveyancing Act* 1919 (N.S.W.), s. 88(1) (see below p. 361) requires, inter alia, that the land entitled to the benefit of the covenant be clearly indicated in the instrument creating the covenant. If the land is not so indicated, the covenant will not be enforceable against a successor in title to the covenantor. Section 88(1) will almost invariably result in a formal annexation of the covenant to the land without the necessity of any argument concerning implied annexation under *Conveyancing Act* 1919 (N.S.W.), s. 70(1). Of course, the only situation where *Federated Homes* will be significant is where a successor in title to the original covenantee seeks to enforce the covenant against the original covenantor (the situation in *Federated Homes* case itself).

There has been some suggestion in England that the statutory form of general words (see above p. 252) may allow an implied annexation of covenants to land: see Megarry and Wade, *The Law of Real Property*, (5th ed.), p. 787; Hayton, "Restrictive Covenants as Property Interests" (1971) 87 L.Q.R. 470.

(e) Schemes of development

As we have seen already, a person may be entitled to enforce a covenant in equity, as successor in title to the original covenantee, in three situations: (1) as the person entitled to land to which the benefit of the covenant is annexed; or (2) as an express assignee of the benefit of the covenant in accordance with the equitable rules; or (3) as the person entitled to land comprised in a scheme of development. These three methods by which the benefit of a covenant may pass with the land in equity may not be mutually exclusive: see p. 347. We turn now to consider the law relating to schemes of development.

A scheme of development exists where there is a "local law" relating to a defined area of land, pursuant to which restrictions as to user are intended by vendor and purchasers to be mutually enforceable by all purchasers of lots within that defined area. Schemes of development most commonly involve controlled building development (building schemes). There may, however, be a general scheme of development not involving building development; the term scheme of development is the genus and "building scheme" a species: *Brunner v. Greenslade* [1971] 1 Ch. 993 at 999 per Megarry J.

Apart from a scheme of development, under the general law, the benefit of a covenant cannot be annexed to land not owned by the covenantee: *Kerridge v. Foley* (1964) 82 W.N. (N.S.W.) (Pt 1) 294, above p. 330. This has the effect that in the sale of lots in an estate or plan of subdivision subject to restrictive covenants, earlier purchasers cannot enforce the covenant against later purchasers. A simple illustration will demonstrate the point. A owns an area of land divided into three lots. A sells lot 1 to B taking from B a covenant the benefit of which is annexed to the remaining unsold lots, lots 2 and 3. A then sells lot 2 to C taking a similar covenant the benefit of which is annexed to lot 3; the benefit could not be annexed to lot 1 as A is no longer owner of that land. The effect is that a later purchaser of lot 3, D, can, as successor in title to land to which the benefit of covenants are annexed, enforce the covenant against the owners of lots 1 and 2. The converse does not apply; the owner of lot 1 cannot enforce the covenant against the owners of lot 2 or lot 3.

In contrast, the most important feature of the scheme of development is that it allows all purchasers of lots within the scheme to enforce restrictions imposed by the scheme, one against the other, irrespective of the dates of purchase. If a scheme of development exists, it is no objection that the benefit of covenants is sought to be annexed to land no longer owned by the vendor.

The second important attribute of the scheme of development is that the covenants are enforceable, not only by and between all purchasers, but also against the vendor. Where there is a scheme of development, in the absence of a reservation by the vendor, the vendor is obliged to observe the covenants in respect of the remaining unsold land within the scheme and is also obliged to insert like covenants in conveyances of the remaining unsold land with the scheme: *MacKenzie v. Childers* (1889) 43 Ch. D. 265. In the absence of a reservation by the vendor a purchaser of land within the scheme is entitled to insist that in her or his conveyance the vendor expressly covenant to observe the restrictions imposed by the scheme in respect of the remaining unsold land within the scheme: *Re Birmingham and District Land Co. and Allday* [1893] 1 Ch. 342.

In the first of the cases extracted, *Elliston v. Reacher* [1908] 2 Ch. 374, Parker J. formulated four prerequisites for a scheme of development. These rules, however, are not to be treated as an exclusive statutory definition of what will constitute a valid scheme of development: *Re Dolphin's Conveyance* [1970] Ch. 654, extracted below. The presence of these four prerequisites may, however, help prove that the vendor sold the land, and the purchasers bought the land, on the basis that all purchasers would be able to enforce the covenants one against the other, and in the absence of reserved right, to enforce the covenant against the vendor.

The essence of a scheme of development is the common intention of vendor and purchasers that the scheme be mutually enforceable; it is this community of interest and common intention which provides the "local law" governing the estate: *Re Dolphin's Conveyance*. The scheme of development is "an independent equity which is created by circumstances and is independent of contractual obligation": *Brunner v. Greenslade* [1971] 1 Ch. 993 at 1005 per Megarry J. It is therefore unnecessary to show that the purchaser expressly covenanted in favour of all other purchasers to observe the covenants, nor is it necessary that the vendor covenanted expressly with each purchaser to observe the restrictions with respect to the unsold lots and to insert like covenants in future conveyances of land within the scheme. What is critical is not the formal requirements for annexation of covenants to land but the local law of the estate: *Re Dolphin's Conveyance* [1970] Ch. 654, extracted below p. 355. In *Re Fox* (1981) 2 B.P.R. 9310 at 9317 Wootten J. said:

> The point of a building scheme lies . . . not in the "one to one" relationship between particular blocks of land, and their effect on each other, but in the impact of the various restrictions on the area as a whole, creating a "local law" which may impinge differently on different parts of the area, but overall works to give a particular character and amenity to the area. To endeavour to pick it to pieces and examine the relationship between a lot in one corner and a lot in another corner is to miss the point of a building scheme.

The existence of a scheme of development is to be determined as a matter of fact from all the circumstances; inferences may be drawn from the terms of the conveyances, contracts for sale, sale brochures, and oral evidence may be adduced by the vendor, the purchasers, and their representatives.

It is because the scheme of development does not rely on express covenants between all purchasers and express covenants by the vendor, that it presents difficulties in respect of Torrens title land. A separate section will be devoted to covenants under the Torrens system. In New South Wales, there is the added difficulty of s. 88(1) of the *Conveyancing Act* 1919 (N.S.W.), as to which see below p. 361.

Before turning to the cases on this topic, it should be noted that mutual enforcement of covenants between all purchasers and against the vendor can be achieved largely by a series of express covenants without reference to a scheme of development. This is achieved by requiring each purchaser to enter into covenants the benefit of which are annexed to the remaining unsold lots of the estate and to separately covenant with each purchaser of land already sold. This brings into play the provisions of, *Conveyancing Act* 1919 (N.S.W.), s. 36C: see above p. 321. The purchasers of lots already sold are then in the position of original covenantees and can enforce the covenants against later purchasers. The second step is for the vendor to covenant with each purchaser to observe the covenants in respect of the remaining unsold lots and to insert like restrictions in subsequent sales of lots remaining in the estate: cf. *Re Caroline Chisholm Village* (1980) 1 B.P.R. 9507 at 9512 per Master Cohen Q.C.

The modern law relating to schemes of development begins with the case *Elliston v. Reacher*.

ELLISTON v. REACHER

Chancery [1908] 2 Ch. 374

[A building society owned an area of land which it divided up into lots for the purpose of sale. Purchasers were shown a plan of lots together with printed conditions of sale which contained, inter alia, a covenant against the use of land for the purpose of an hotel. The restrictions were also contained in an unexecuted deed between the trustees of the building estate and the purchasers. The deed, with the plan of the lots annexed, provided that each of the purchasers was to covenant with the other of them and separately with the trustees to observe the restrictions on the use of the land. The deed was never executed either by the purchasers or the trustees. A printed form of conveyance was prepared for the society. The conveyance contained a covenant by the purchaser to observe the restrictions and covenants contained in the unexecuted deed. The covenants were expressed to be made between the persons whose names were subscribed in the second schedule (where the purchasers' names were to be set out here) of the first part and the vendors of the second part. This printed form of conveyance was used for all conveyances of the society's land. The defendants were owners of two lots conveyed to their predecessors in title by conveyance in the printed form on 27 December 1861 and 18 April 1866. The defendants erected an hotel on the land. The plaintiffs were the owners of three lots conveyed to their predecessor in title on 27 December 1861. The plaintiffs sought an injunction restraining the defendants from carrying on the business of an hotel.]

PARKER J. I pass, therefore, to the consideration of the question whether the plaintiffs can enforce these restrictive covenants. In my judgment, in order to bring the principles of *Renals v. Cowlishaw* (1879) 9 Ch. D. 125; 11 Ch. D. 866 and *Spicer v. Martin* (1888) 14 App. Cas. 12 into operation it must be proved (1) that both the plaintiffs and defendants derive title under a common vendor; (2) that previously to selling the lands to which the plaintiffs and defendants are respectively entitled the vendor laid out his estate, or a defined portion thereof (including the lands purchased by the plaintiffs and defendants respectively), for sale in lots subject to restrictions intended to be imposed on all the lots, and which, though varying in details as to particular lots, are consistent and consistent only with some general scheme of development; (3) that these restrictions were intended by the common vendor to be and were for the benefit of all the lots intended to be sold, whether or not they were also intended to be and were for the benefit of other land retained by the vendor; and (4) that both the plaintiffs and the defendants, or their predecessors in title, purchased their lots from the common vendor upon the footing that the restrictions subject to which the purchasers were made were to enure for the benefit of the other lots included in the general scheme whether or not they were also to enure for the benefit of other lands retained by the vendors. If these four points be established, I think that the plaintiffs would in equity be entitled to enforce the restrictive covenants entered into by the defendants or their predecessors with the common vendor irrespective of the dates of the respective purchases. I may observe, with reference to the third point, that the vendor's object in imposing the restrictions must in general be gathered from all the circumstances of the case, including in particular the nature of the restrictions. If a general observance of the restrictions is in fact calculated to enhance the values of the several lots offered for sale, it is an easy inference that the vendor intended the restrictions to be for the benefit of all the lots, even though he might retain other land the value of which might be similarly enhanced, for a vendor may naturally be expected to aim at obtaining the highest possible price for his land. Further, if the first three points be established, the fourth point may readily be inferred, provided the purchasers have notice of the facts involved in the three first points; but if the purchaser purchases in ignorance of any material part of those facts, it would be difficult, if not impossible, to establish the fourth point. It is also observable that the equity arising out of the establishment of the four points I have mentioned has been sometimes explained by the implication of mutual contracts between the various purchasers, and sometimes by the implication of a contract between each purchaser and the common vendor, that each purchaser is to have the benefit of all the covenants by the other purchasers, so that each purchase is in equity an assign of the benefit of these covenants. In my opinion the implication of mutual contract is not always a perfectly satisfactory explanation. It may be satisfactory where all the lots are sold by auction at the same time, but when, as in cases such as *Spicer v. Martin*, there is no sale by auction, but all the various sales are by private treaty and at various intervals of time, the circumstances may, at the date of one or more of the sales, be such as to preclude the possibility of any actual contract. For example, a prior purchaser may be dead or incapable of contracting at the point of a subsequent purchase, and in any event it is unlikely that the prior and subsequent purchasers are ever brought into personal relationship, and yet the equity may exist between them. It is, I think, enough to say, using Lord Macnoughten's words in *Spicer v. Martin*, that where the four points I have mentioned are established, the community of interest imports in equity the reciprocity of obligation which is in fact contemplated by each at the time of his own purchase.

[The decision was upheld on appeal to the Court of Appeal [1908] 2 Ch. 665 and Parker J.'s statement of the requisites for enforcing restrictive covenants between different purchasers approved.]

RE DOLPHIN'S CONVEYANCE

Chancery [1970] Ch. 654

[Ann and Valerie Dolphin were owners of the fee simple estate as tenants in common of property known as the Selly Hill Estate, an area of about 30 acres. In 1871 the Dolphin sisters sold four lots. In each conveyance the purchaser, for himself, his heirs and assigns covenanted with the vendors, their heirs, executors, administrators and assigns to observe certain restrictive covenants including a covenant that only detached dwelling-houses, each on at least one quarter acre of land, should be built on the land. The vendors, on their part, covenanted for themselves, their heirs and assigns, with the purchaser, his heirs and assigns, that on sale or lease of any other part of the Selly Hill Estate like covenants would be included in the conveyance. In 1877 five more parcels of land were sold and conveyed by Watts who was entitled to the fee simple estate by way of gift from the Dolphin sisters. These conveyances were in identical terms with the earlier conveyances. On the sale of the last parcel of land by Watts, the conveyance, although otherwise identical in terms to the previous conveyances, did not include a covenant by the vendor to subject the remaining part of the estate to like covenants as all the Selly Hill Estate had been sold. The plaintiff, the Birmingham Corporation, was successor in title to part of land conveyed by the Dolphin sisters to Coleman and another lot of land conveyed by Watts to Coleman. The corporation, who purchased with notice of the covenants, wished to erect buildings on the land in contravention of the covenants. The corporation sought a declaration that the land was no longer subject to, or affected by, any of the restrictive covenants, and, alternatively, a declaration whether the restrictive covenants were enforceable and if so, by whom. Successors in title to other lots were represented by the defendant.]

STAMP J. I must make it clear that the defendants do not assert, nor could they, that the benefit of the covenants by the several purchasers from the Dolphins was in terms expressed to be attached to the vendors' land, and to each and every part of it, so as to pass without express assignment to a purchaser of the land to be benefited. Nor was there any express assignment of that benefit in the conveyances under which the defendants to this summons claim title. Nor is there any personal representative of any of the vendors in a position to enforce the covenants. But, to quote a passage in the judgment of Cross J. in *Baxter v. Four Oaks Properties Ltd* [1965] Ch. 816 at 825: "for well over 100 years past where the owner of land deals with it on the footing of imposing restrictive obligations on the use of various parts of it as and when he sells them off for the common benefit of himself (in so far as he retains any land) and of the various purchasers inter se a court of equity has been prepared to give effect to this common intention notwithstanding any technical difficulties involved." It is the submission of the defendants that that was done by the vendors in the present case.

That it was the intention of the two Miss Dolphins, on the sale of the parcel comprised in Coleman's conveyance, that there should be imposed upon each and every part of the Selly Hill Estate the restrictions set out in the conveyance—precluding the erection of buildings other than dwelling houses having the characteristics specified in the restrictions—cannot be doubted. And each conveyance evidenced the same intention. Nor can it be doubted that each purchaser, when he executed his conveyance, was aware of that intention. The covenant by the vendor in each conveyance, to the effect that the same restrictions would be placed on all future purchasers and lessees, makes this clear. Furthermore, I would, unless constrained by authority to the contrary, conclude as a matter of construction of Coleman's conveyance, and of all the others, that the vendor was dealing with the Selly Hill Estate on the footing of imposing obligations for the common benefit, as well of himself, as of the several purchasers of that estate. It is trite law that if you find conveyances of the several parts of an estate all containing the same or similar restrictive covenants with the vendor, that is not enough to impute an intention on the part of that vendor that the restrictions should be for the common benefit of the vendor and of the several purchasers inter se: for it is at least as likely that he imposed them for the benefit of himself and of the unsold part of the estate alone. That is not this case. Here there is the covenant by the vendors that on a sale or lease of any other part of Selly Hill Estate "it shall be sold or leased subject to the stipulations above mentioned numbered 1, 2, 3, 4, 5, 6, 7 and that the vendors their heirs or assigns will procure a covenant from each purchaser or lessee upon Selly Hill Estate to the effect of those seven stipulations". What was the point of it? For what possible reason does a vendor of part of an estate who has extracted restrictive covenants from a purchaser, covenant with that purchaser that the other parts of the estate, when sold, shall contain the same restrictions, unless it be with the intention that the purchaser with whom he covenants, as well as he himself, shall have the benefits of the restrictions when imposed? In view of these covenants by the vendor in the several conveyances, I cannot do otherwise than find that the covenants were imposed, not only for the benefit of the vendors or of the unsold part of their estate, but as well for the benefit of the several purchasers. As a matter of construction of the conveyances, I find that what was intended, as well by the vendors as the several purchasers, was to lay down what has been referred to as a local law for the estate for the common benefit of all the several purchasers of it. The purpose of the covenant by the vendors was to enable each purchaser to have, as against the other purchasers, in one way or another, the benefit of the restrictions to which he had made himself subject.

Holding, as I do, that these covenants were imposed for the common benefits of the vendors and the several purchasers, and that they had a common interest in their enforcement, I must, in a moment, turn to consider what is, in my judgment, the separate and distinct question whether there is an equity in the owner of each parcel to enforce the covenants against the owners of the other parcels. . . .

As Cross J. pointed out in the course of the judgment in *Baxter v. Four Oaks Properties Ltd* [1965] Ch. 816, to which I have already referred, the intention that the several purchasers from a common vendor shall have the benefit of the restrictive covenants imposed on each of them, may be evidenced by the existence of a deed of mutual covenant to which all the several purchasers are to be parties. That common intention may also be evidenced by, or inferred from, the circumstances attending the sales: the existence of what has often been referred to in the authorities as a building scheme. I have referred to a considerable number of authorities where the court has had to consider whether there were, or were not, present in the particular case those facts from which a building scheme—and, therefore, the common intention to lay down a local law involving reciprocal rights and obligations between the several purchasers—could properly be inferred. In *Elliston v. Reacher* [1908] 2 Ch. 374 at 384, Parker J. laid down the necessary concomitants of such a scheme.

What has been argued before me is that here there is neither a deed of mutual covenant nor a building scheme. In the latter connection, it is pointed out that there was not a common vendor, for the parcels were sold off, first by the Dolphins and then by Watts. Nor, prior to the sales, had the vendors laid out the estate, or a defined portion of it, for sale in lots. Therefore, so it is urged, there were not present the factors which, on the authority of *Elliston v. Reacher* [1908] 2 Ch. 374, are necessary before one can find the existence of a building scheme.

In my judgment, these submissions are not well founded. To hold that only where you find the necessary concomitants of a building scheme or a deed of mutual covenant can you give effect to the common intention found in the conveyances themselves, would, in my judgment, be to ignore the wider principle on which the building scheme cases are founded and to fly in the face of other authority of which the clearest and most recent is *Baxter v. Four Oaks Properties Ltd* [1965] Ch. 816. The building scheme cases stem, as I understand the law, from the wider rule that if there be found the common intention and the common interest referred to by Cross J. at 825 in *Baxter v. Four Oaks Properties Ltd* the court will give effect to it, and are but an extension and example of that rule. Hall V.-C. remarked in his judgment in *Renals v. Cowlishaw* (1878) 9 Ch. D. 125 at 129: "This right exists not only where the several parties execute a mutual deed of covenant, but wherever a mutual contract can be sufficiently established. A purchaser may also be entitled to the benefit of a restrictive covenant entered into with his vendor by another or others where his vendor has contracted with him that he shall be the assign of it, that is, have the benefit of the covenant. And such contract need not be express, but may be collected from the transaction of sale and purchase."

That passage was quoted, with approval, by Lord Macnaghten in *Spicer v. Martin* (1889) 14 App. Cas. 12 at 24. (I ought perhaps to mention that the word "contract" in the last sentence I have quoted was substituted for the word "covenant" in the errata in the volume of the reports in which *Renals v. Cowlishaw* is reported.) Moreover, where deeds of mutual covenant have fallen to be considered, effect has been given not to the deed of mutual covenant itself as such but to the intention evidenced by its existence. *Baxter v. Four Oaks Properties Ltd* [1965] Ch. 816 is such a case. As Parker J. in *Elliston v. Reacher* [1908] 2 Ch. 374 at 384, pointed out in a passage quoted by Cross J. in *Baxter v. Four Oaks Properties Ltd* [1965] Ch. 816 at 826, the equity arising out of the establishment of the four points which he mentioned as the necessary concomitants of a building scheme has been sometimes explained by the implication of mutual contracts between the various purchasers and sometimes by the implication of a contract between each purchaser and the common vendor, that each purchaser is to have the benefit of all the covenants by the other purchasers, so that each purchaser is in equity an assign of the benefit of those covenants; but the implication of mutual contracts is not always a satisfactory explanation.

[His Lordship then referred to the judgment of Parker J. in *Elliston v. Reacher* [1908] 2 Ch. 374, above p. 355, on this point and continued:]

There is not, therefore, in my judgment, a dichotomy between the cases where effect has been given to the common intention inferred from the existence of the concomitants of a building scheme and those where effect has been given to the intention evidenced by the existence of a deed of covenant. Each class of case, in my judgment, depends upon a wider principle. Here the equity, in my judgment, arises not by the effect of an implication derived from the existence of the four points specified by Parker J. in *Elliston v. Reacher* [1908] 2 Ch. 374 at 384, or by the implication derived from the existence of a deed of mutual covenant, but by the existence of the common interest and the common intention actually expressed in the conveyances themselves.

In *Nottingham Patent Brick and Tile Co. v. Butler* (1885) 15 Q.B.D. 261 at 268, Wills J., in a passage which I find illuminating and which was referred to with approval in the Court of Appeal (1886) 16 Q.B.D. 778, put the matter thus: "The principle which appears to me to be deducible from the cases is that where the same vendor selling to several persons plots of land, parts of a larger property, exacts from each of them covenants imposing restrictions on the use of the plots sold without putting himself under any corresponding obligation, it is a question of fact whether the restrictions are merely matters of agreement between the vendor himself and his vendees, imposed for his own benefit and protection, or are meant by him and understood by the buyers to be for the common advantage of the several purchasers. If the restrictive covenants are simply for the benefit of the vendor, purchasers of other plots of land from the vendor cannot claim to take advantage of them. If they are meant for the common advantage of a set of purchasers, such purchasers and their assigns may enforce them inter se for their own benefit. Where, for instance, the purchasers from the common vendor have not known of the existence of the covenants, that is a strong, if not a conclusive, circumstance to shew that there was no intention that they should enure to their benefit. Such was the case in *Keates v. Lyon* (1869) L.R. 4 Ch. 218; *Master v. Hansard* (1876) 4 Ch. D. 718; and *Renals v. Cowlishaw* (1879) 11 Ch. D. 866. But it is in all cases a question of intention at the time when the partition of the land took place, to be gathered, as every other question of fact, from any circumstances which can throw light upon what the intention was: *Renals v. Cowlishaw*. One circumstance which has always been held to be cogent evidence of an intention that the covenants shall be for the common benefit of the purchasers is that the several lots have been laid out for sale as building lots, as in *Mann v. Stephens* (1846) 15 Sim. 377 60 E.R. 665; *Western v. Macdermott* (1866) L.R. 2 Ch. 72; *Coles v. Sims* (1853) Kay 56; 69 E.R. 25; (1854) 5 D.M. & G. 1; 43 E.R. 768; or, as it has been sometimes said, that there has been "a building scheme": *Renals v. Cowlishaw* (1879) 11 Ch. D. 866 at 867."

I can approach the matter in another way. The conveyances of the several parts of the estate taking the form they do, and evidencing the same intention as is found in a deed of mutual covenant. I equate those conveyances with the deed of mutual covenant considered by Cross J. in *Baxter v. Four Oaks Properties Ltd* [1965] Ch.

816 the deed which he did not treat for the purposes of his judgment as itself bringing all the successive purchasers and persons claiming through them into contractual relations one with the other, but as showing the common intention. So equating them, I follow what I conceive to be the ratio decidendi of *Baxter v. Four Oaks Properties Ltd* [1965] Ch. 816 and give effect to that intention by holding that the restrictive covenants are enforceable by the successors in title of each of the original covenantors against any of them who purchased with notice of those restrictions.

Order accordingly.

NOTES AND QUESTIONS

1. *Re Dolphin's Conveyance* [1970] Ch. 654 indicates that the four requirements for a scheme of development set out by Parker J. in *Elliston v. Reacher* are not mandatory, and that the essence of the scheme of development is the common intention of vendor and purchasers that the covenants be mutually enforceable. Thus, a scheme of development will not be negatived simply because the land subject to the scheme has not been laid out in lots prior to the sale. In *Baxter v. Four Oaks Properties Ltd* [1965] 1 Ch. 816 at 828. Cross J. said:

> [T]he fact that the common vendor did not divide his estate into lots before beginning to sell it is an argument against there having been intention on his part and on the part of the various purchasers that there should be a building scheme, because it is, perhaps, prima facie unlikely that a purchaser of a plot intends to enter into obligations to an unknown number of subsequent purchasers. But I cannot believe that Parker J. [in *Elliston v. Reacher* [1908] 2 Ch. 374] was intending to lay down that the fact that the common vendor did not bind himself to sell off the defined area to which the common law was to apply in lots of any particular size but proposed to sell off parcels of various sizes according to the requirement of the various purchasers must, as a matter of law, preclude the court from giving effect to a clearly proved intention that the purchasers were to have rights inter se to enforce the provisions of the common law.

It is necessary, however, that there be a defined area within which the scheme is operative. Cozens-Hardy M.R. in *Reid v. Bickerstaff* [1909] 2 Ch. 305 at 326 explained the rule in the following way:

> Reciprocity is the foundation of the idea of a scheme. A purchaser of one parcel cannot be subject to an implied obligation to purchasers of an undefined and unknown area. He must know both the extent of his burden and the extent of his benefit. Not only must the area be defined, but the obligations to be imposed within that area must be defined. Those obligations need not be identical. For example, there may be houses of a certain value in one part and houses of a different value in another part. A building scheme is not created by the mere fact that the owner of an estate sells it in lots and takes varying covenants from various purchasers. There must be notice to the various purchasers of what I may venture to call the local law imposed by the vendors upon a definite area.

Buckley L.J. in the same case (at 323) said that the requirement that there be a defined area which the scheme is operative served to identify the class or persons as between whom reciprocity of obligations is to exist.

In *Re Dolphin's Conveyance* it was argued that since there was no plan showing the extent of the Selly Hill Estate there could be no building scheme. Stamp J. held (at 659) that the references to Selly Hill Estate in the several conveyances by the Dolphins and Watts, were references to identified land: "identified not in the sense that by looking at the conveyances you could, today, without researches, identify it, because the conveyances contained no plan or description of it, but identified in the sense that a reference in a document to Richmond Park would be a reference to an identified piece of land, notwithstanding the absence of a plan on the document delineating Richmond Park."

2. There is also no necessity that there be a common vendor. In *Re Mack and the Conveyancing Act* [1975] 2 N.S.W.L.R. 623 Wootten J. said (at 630):

> It is now accepted that this is the nature of the equity which makes the covenants in a building scheme reciprocally enforceable as between the owners for the time being of the lots in the scheme—"an equity which is created by circumstances and is independent of contractual obligation": per Simonds J. in *Lawrence v. South County Freeholds Ltd* [1939] Ch. 656 at 682. Compare *New South Wales Aged Pensioners' Hostel and Conveyancing Act* [1967] 1 N.S.W.L.R. 332 at 334; *Ridley v. Lee* [1935] Ch. 591 at 604; *Re Martyn* (1965) 65 S.R. (N.S.W.) 387. The result has been described as the creation of a common law or local law for the area: *Baxter v. Four Oaks Properties Ltd* [1965] Ch. 816 at 826; *Texaco Antilles Ltd v. Kernochan* [1973] A.C. 609 at 624.

This being the basis of the equity, there is no ground of reason or justice for requiring that there be a common vendor, unless indeed that term be understood in an artificial sense to include several vendors sharing a common intention. The "community of interest" between the purchasers is as real in the one case as the other. No doubt in cases where there is only one vendor it may be easier to infer the intention to take the covenants for the benefit of all of the land in a scheme, but that is no reason for refusing to give effect to the common intention of several vendors to establish reciprocal benefits and obligations throughout an estate where such intention is established. In the present case the laying out of a single estate on the lands of two owners who joined in the subdivision provides a foundation on which it would not be surprising to find a common building scheme established.

Contrast *Re Pinewood Estate, Farnborough* [1958] Ch. 280 coming to the opposite conclusion; but see Preston and Newsom, *Restrictive Covenants Affecting Freehold Land* (7th ed.), p. 58 for the view that the case would now be decided differently.

3. In *Elliston v. Reacher* [1908] 2 Ch. 374, it was argued that no scheme of development could exist because the vendor had reserved a power to sell lots without the imposition of covenants. On appeal to the Court of Appeal, Cozens-Hardy M.R. rejected the argument, but added that the insertion of such a power is an element to be considered. His Lordship noted that it would be altogether exceptional not to see some power reserved to the vendor to abstract certain property from the scheme and that in the present case the power to release unsold property from the covenants was of no real importance. Thus the existence of a scheme of development will not be rebutted if some few of the lots are not subject to the restrictive covenants: *Re Mack and the Conveyancing Act* [1975] 2 N.S.W.L.R. 623 at 635 (nine lots out of a total of 115 lots were sold without restrictions); *Re Louis* [1971] 1 N.S.W.L.R. 164, below p. 365; *Re Application of Amory Pty Ltd* (1984) C.C.H. N.S.W. Conv. R. 55-180. If, however, the restrictions are unenforceable in respect of a large proportion of lots, this will destroy the required mutuality and the whole scheme will fail. This was held in *New South Wales Aged Pensioners' Hostel and the Conveyancing Act* [1967] 1 N.S.W.R. 332 where restrictive covenants were validly annexed to five lots only out of a total of 185 lots. The five lots were not in a defined area but were scattered throughout the subdivision. It was argued in that case that a subsidiary scheme of development may exist between the five lots bound by the covenant. Street J. rejected this argument as the five lots were scattered throughout the subdivision; there was such a marked divergence between the concept of a scheme binding five lots compared with a scheme binding 185 lots that a subscheme should not be held to exist. Compare *Texaco Antilles Ltd v. Kernochan* [1973] A.C. 609 where a scheme of development was upheld despite the fact that 300 lots out of a total of 500 lots were sold in a single conveyance without being subject to the covenants.

There is no requirement that all covenants be identical: *Reid v. Bickerstaff* [1909] 2 Ch. 305, above note 1.; nor is it an objection that a third party who no longer retains any interest in the land is given the power to release, vary or modify the covenants applying to the land: *Jones v. Sherwood Hills Pty Ltd* (unreported, Supreme Court of New South Wales, Equity Division, Waddell J. 8 July 1975) noted in (1978) 52 A.L.J. 223. The power to release, vary or modify covenants may be unrestricted, in which case there is no duty to exercise the power bona fide and in accordance with the principles of natural justice: *Jones v. Sherwood Hills Pty Ltd* (above).

4. In the principal case the common intention of the vendor and purchasers that the covenants were to be mutually enforceable was to be found in the terms of the conveyances themselves. This is not necessarily so in all cases. A scheme of development may exist even though there is nothing on the face of the conveyances to indicate that the vendor and purchasers intend that covenants be mutually enforceable: *Re Louis and the Conveyancing Act* [1971] 1 N.S.W.L.R. 164, below p. 365, and it may be that a scheme of development can exist even where the purchaser has not covenanted expressly with the vendor to observe any restrictions, provided that all concomitants of a scheme of development are present: Preston and Newsom, *Restrictive Covenants Affecting Freehold Land* (6th ed.), p. 51. In such cases extrinsic evidence assumes the greatest importance. Evidence may include the terms of any advertisements soliciting purchasers for the land, the contracts for sale signed by the several purchasers, as well as negotiations and conversations between the vendor and his agents, and the purchasers or their representatives. See, for example, *Elliston v. Reacher*. This poses special problems in respect of Torrens title land and gives rise to difficulties of enforcement because of the provisions of s. 88(1), *Conveyancing Act* 1919 (N.S.W.) which imposes certain formal requirements where a covenant is sought to be enforced against a successor in title to the covenantor: see below p. 361.

5. Assume that a scheme of development is found to exist over a defined area of land, then one of the lots subject to the scheme is subdivided and sold off to purchasers; each purchaser has notice of the covenants but does not expressly covenant to observe the restrictions imposed by the scheme. Can the purchasers of the subdivided lot enforce the covenants in the scheme one against the other? Further, if new covenants varying the original scheme are entered into by purchasers of the subdivided lot, can these covenants be enforced as a separate scheme of development—a subscheme? See *Brunner v. Greenslade* [1971] Ch. 993; *Texaco v. Kernochan* [1973] A.C. 609 at 624.

D. RESTRICTIVE COVENANTS—CREATION—CONVEYANCING ACT 1919 (N.S.W.) REQUIREMENTS

In New South Wales, the *Conveyancing Act* 1919 contains a number of important provisions relating to restrictive covenants. Section 88(1) imposes formal requirements on easements and restrictive covenants contained in instruments and s. 88B provides a statutory method for creating easements, profits and restrictive covenants. These sections apply to both old system title land and to Torrens title land.

1. Section 88(1)

88. (1) An easement expressed to be created by an instrument coming into operation after the commencement of the Conveyancing (Amendment) Act 1930, and a restriction arising under covenant or otherwise as to the user of any land the benefit of which is intended to be annexed to other land, contained in an instrument coming into operation after such commencement, shall not be enforceable against a person interested in the land claimed to be subject to the easement or restriction, and not being a party to its creation unless the instrument clearly indicates

(a) the land to which the benefit of the easement or restriction is appurtenant;

(b) the land which is subject to the burden of the easement or restriction:

Provided that it shall not be necessary to indicate the sites of easements intended to be created in respect of existing tunnels, pipes, conduits, wires, or other similar objects which are underground or which are within or beneath an existing building otherwise than by indicating on a plan of the land traversed by the easement the approximate position of such easement;

(c) the persons (if any) having the right to release, vary, or modify the easement or restriction, other than the persons having, in the absence of agreement to the contrary, the right by law to release, vary, or modify the easement or restriction; and

(d) the persons (if any) whose consent to a release, variation, or modification of the easement or restriction is stipulated for.

[Subsections 2 and 3 have been omitted.]

(4) Subsection one of this section shall not apply to an easement acquired by or for the Crown, or by or for any public or local authority constituted by Act of Parliament, nor to any restriction affecting the user of land in relation to any such easement.

The substance of s. 88(1), so far as it relates to restrictive covenants, was enacted originally as s. 89(1) of the *Conveyancing Act* 1919 (N.S.W.). In its original form, the section did not apply to easements. The section in its present form came into force 1 January 1931.

Section 88(1) does not itself give validity to the easement or restriction as to user but imposes a number of formal requirements necessary for validity. If the easement or restrictive covenant does not comply with general law requirements compliance with s. 88(1) will not validate it.

It should be noted at the outset, that s. 88(1) will apply only where it is sought to enforce the covenant or easements against a person not a party to its creation. Thus if the question in issue is whether a covenant or easement can be enforced against the original covenantor or against the original owner of the servient tenement, s. 88(1) does not apply. In addition the section imposes formal requirements on "instruments" only; an easement arising by prescription would be unaffected by s. 88(1).

(a) Clear indication of land benefitted and land burdened

The section requires that the land to be benefited and the land burdened be clearly indicated. Wootten J. in *Papadopoulos v. Goodwin* [1982] 1 N.S.W.L.R. 413 at 417 held that an instrument clearly indicated the prescribed matters if that instrument referred to another document in which those matters were clearly stated: "The section does not in terms require the matters to be stated in the instrument itself, nor does the fulfilment of the purpose of the section, viz, clear notice of those matters, so require . . . 'indicate' carries the meaning 'point to' rather than 'state'." His Honour said "the words 'clearly indicate' suggest an intention to impose a higher standard than that the dominant tenement is capable of being ascertained by ordinary processes of construction, which processes include the use of extrinsic evidence to identify the dominant tenement when its identity does not clearly appear from the instrument". The phrase "clearly indicate" also admitted the meaning "in a clear manner, without entanglement or confusion; without uncertainty". (This interpretation was adopted in *Kerridge v. Foley* (1964) 82 W.N. (N.S.W.) (Pt 1) 294, above p. 330.) The decision was reversed on appeal on grounds not affecting these statements of principle: *Goodwin v. Papadopoulos* (1985) C.C.H. N.S.W. Conv. R. 55-256 per Mahoney J.A. at 56,417 specifically approving Wootten J.'s interpretation of s. 88(1).

A more generous interpretation of s. 88(1) was adopted by Needham J. in *Margil Pty Ltd v. Stegul Pastoral* [1984] 2 N.S.W.L.R. 1 at 8. The conveyance creating the easement did not expressly identify the dominant tenement. Needham J. said:

> I do not understand Wootten J. to be saying that nothing but the instrument can be looked at to see whether it "clearly indicates" the dominant tenement; indeed, he looked at another document in order to identify the servient tenement. There does not seem to be any reason why one should be restricted to extrinsic evidence of a written nature but the subsection requires the instrument clearly to indicate the prescribed information. In this respect it may be necessary to depart in some degree from the English decisions, as they have no statutory requirement. The subsection does not require that the instrument "specify" or "set forth" the prescribed information.

His Honour turned to the facts indicating that in the conveyance before him, the conveyance creating the easement described the easement on the servient tenement by reference to metes and bounds and traced it to the northern boundary of the lot owned by the vendor, lot 2. His Honour continued:

> That, it seems to me is some indication that lot 2 may be the dominant tenement, and when one looks at the surrounding circumstances, one finds that the conveyor is the owner of lot 2 and that lot 2, without the right of way, would be landlocked. I cannot see any valid reason why the requirement of the statute should be held to deny the person construing the conveyance the ordinary aids to construction which the general law allows. The conveyance, construed according to those principles, "clearly indicates" that lot 2 is the dominant tenement.

Do you think that this approach negates the very benefits that s. 88(1) was intended to confer, viz. certainty of land benefited and burdened without the need to rely on extrinsic evidence?

The major authorities dealing with the interpretation s. 88(1) are *Kerridge v. Foley* (above p. 330) and *Re Louis and the Conveyancing Act* [1971] 1 N.S.W.L.R. 164, below p. 365. Consider whether the views of Jacobs J. in these two decisions are entirely consistent. Note in this context the suggestion by Helmore, *The Law of Real Property in New South Wales* (2nd supp. to 2nd ed.), p. 102 that the cases can be distinguished on the basis that where a scheme of development exists, as in *Re Louis*, it is no objection that covenants entered into by the respective purchasers are expressed to be for the benefit of land no longer owned by the vendor covenantee, and that this represents an exception to the interpretation of s. 88(1) laid down in *Kerridge v. Foley*. For a detailed discussion of s. 88(1) and its impact on the enforceability of restrictive covenants, particularly in relation to schemes of development, see below p. 372.

(b) Rights to release, vary or modify covenants

Paragraphs (c) and (d) of s. 88(1) require the instrument to stipulate those persons, other than those so entitled at law, who are entitled to release, vary or modify the covenants or whose consent is required for such release, variation or modification of covenants. The Registrar-General takes the view that these paragraphs are primarily concerned with restrictive covenants and not with easements: Baalman, *The Torrens System in New South Wales* (2nd ed.), p. 439. The section assumes that a third party not retaining any interest in the land may be vested with the right to release, vary or modify the restrictions: see the decision of Waddell J. in *Jones v. Sherwood Hills Pty Ltd* (unreported, Supreme Court of New South Wales, Equity Division, Waddell J., 8 July 1975); see also *Whitehouse v. Hugh* [1906] 1 Ch. 253; [1906] 2 Ch. 283; *Mayner v. Payne* [1914] 2 Ch. 555. *Jones v. Sherwood Hills Pty Ltd* is the subject of critical comment in a note in (1978) 52 A.L.J. 223. It has been argued that to give rights to release, vary or modify restrictive covenants to third parties who hold no interest in the land, conflicts with the fundamental principle that a covenantee must retain some land which can be protected by the restrictive covenant in order to enforce the covenant against a successor in title to the convenantor: Baalman, op. cit., p. 439, and see Baalman, "Variation of Restrictive Covenants" (1948) 21 A.L.J. 427 at 461.

It has been suggested that the provision that the covenant may be released, varied or modified by the "transferor or his successors" refers to the transferor whilst he or she remains the owner of the land benefited, and, on disposal of that land, her or his successors in title. But this does no more than set out those persons entitled at law to release, vary or modify the covenants, such information is unnecessary for the purposes of s. 88(1): *Goodwin v. Papadopoulos* (1985) C.C.H. N.S.W. Conv. R. 55-256. Wherever the word "transferor" is used, either alone or in conjunction with other words, it would seem that all persons holding land benefited by the covenant are necessary parties to its release, variation or modification: Helmore, op. cit., p. 94.

For the purposes of para. (c), there must have been an agreement between the parties to the transfer that there be persons having the right to release, vary or modify the easement or covenant other than the persons who would in the absence of such agreement have the right by law to release, vary or modify the right granted. The court must be able to decide who it was that the parties agreed were to be para. (c) persons: *Goodwin v. Papadopoulos* (1985) C.C.H. N.S.W. Conv. R. 55-256 at 56-419 per Priestley J.A., Samuels J.A. agreeing.

2. Section 88B

Section 88B was inserted in the *Conveyancing Act* in 1964 by the *Local Government and Conveyancing (Amendment) Act* 1964 (N.S.W.). It provides a convenient and simple method for creating restrictive covenants, easements and profits over land. In addition, it greatly simplifies the creation of schemes of development over both old system and Torrens title land.

Easements and restrictive covenants created under s. 88B must comply with s. 88(1) of the *Conveyancing Act* and also satisfy the general law requirements for validity as easements or covenants. It should also be observed that in s. 88B(3), unity of ownership will not extinguish the covenant.

As to the effect of an omission by the Registrar-General to record the easement or restriction as to user on the folio of the Register, see Chapter 5.

E.   RESTRICTIVE COVENANTS AND TORRENS TITLE

In New South Wales the Registrar-General has recorded covenants as encumbrances on the title of the land burdened, although before 1930 there was no express statutory authority to do so. There was considerable doubt whether this practice was valid: *Re Pirie* [1962] N.S.W.R. 1004 at 1006 per Jacobs J. on appeal: *Pirie v. Registrar-General* (1962) 109 C.L.R. 619, where Kitto J. (Owen J. concurring) indorsed the views of Jacobs J.; *Re Martyn* (1965) 65 S.R. (N.S.W.) 387 at 390 per Walsh J. (Asprey J. concurring). In 1930 the *Conveyancing Act* 1919 (N.S.W.) was amended to give the Registrar-General retrospective authority to record covenants as encumbrances in the folio of the burdened land. Section 88(3) of the *Conveyancing Act* now provides:

> (3) This section applies to land under the provisions of the Real Property Act, 1900, and in respect thereof—
>
> (a) the Registrar-General shall have, and shall be deemed always to have had, power to record a restriction referred to in subsection one of this section upon the folio of the Register kept under that Act that relates to the land subject to the burden of the restriction, to record in like manner any dealing purporting to affect the operation of a restriction so recorded and to record in like manner any release, variation or modification of the restriction;
>
> (b) a recording in the Register kept under that Act of any such restriction shall not give the restriction any greater operation than it has under the dealing creating it; and
>
> (c) a restriction so recorded is an interest within the meaning of section forty-two of that Act.

The Registrar-General's authority to record restrictive covenants in the Register under s. 88(3), is restricted to covenants contained in instruments complying with s. 88(1). As s. 88(3) is retrospective in operation, it has the effect that covenants contained in registered transfers executed before the *Conveyancing Act* 1919 (N.S.W.) came into force (1 July 1920) must also comply with s. 88(1): *Re Pirie* [1962] N.S.W.R. 1004 per Jacobs J. (indorsed on appeal sub nom. *Pirie v. Registrar-General* (1962) 109 C.L.R. 619 by Kitto and Owen JJ. concurring); *Re Martyn* (1965) 65 S.R. (N.S.W.) 387 per Walsh J., noted below; *Re Louis* [1971] 1 N.S.W.L.R. 164, extracted below. It also follows that where land is brought under

Torrens title by conversion from old system title restrictive covenants in old system conveyances not complying with s. 88(1) cannot be recorded in the Register: see (1965) 39 A.L.J. at 63.

Despite the express authorisation given to the Registrar-General to record restrictions as to user in the Register, there remained considerable uncertainty whether schemes of development, particularly building schemes, could validly subsist over Torrens title land in New South Wales. The first of the cases extracted in this section, *Re Louis and the Conveyancing Act*, now states the settled view that schemes of development can bind Torrens title land.

RE LOUIS AND THE CONVEYANCING ACT

Court of Appeal [1971] 1 N.S.W.L.R. 164

[The facts appear in the judgment of Jacobs J.A.]

JACOBS J.A. Mr James Stanley Louis is the registered proprietor of certain land at Vaucluse being the whole of the land comprised in Certificate of Title Volume 3402 Folio 16. This land is lot 68 of section 1 in Deposited Plan No. 9328. Some time not long before 1 July 1920, a large area of land at Vaucluse was subdivided by the owners, William Charles Wentworth and Francis William Hixson, and the court is asked to assume for the purpose of the present application that these owners laid out the lands in lots subject to restrictions intended to be imposed on all lots in accordance with a general scheme of development, with the intention that the restrictions under this scheme would be for the protection of all the lots intended to be sold. We are thus asked to assume that there was a building scheme intended and that the necessary conditions for the existence of such a scheme in respect of land other than land under the *Real Property Act* 1900 (N.S.W.) were met. However, it is desirable to state that the court is asked to make that assumption, not because all parties are agreed that there is a building scheme, but rather so that certain questions of law can be determined in a preliminary way. If the court determines that there is nothing in law which would prevent restrictions being enforceable, then it is proposed that in other proceedings the actual existence or otherwise of the building scheme be, if necessary, determined.

Deposited Plan No. 9328 contained a large number of lots. Of this number 10 were transferred to purchasers prior to the coming into operation of the *Conveyancing Act* 1919 (N.S.W.). In respect of these lots the form of covenant did not indicate the land to which the benefit of the restriction was appurtenant. In respect of the 37 lots transferred after 1 July 1920, the covenants on transfer contained these indications.

The original transfer of lot 68, the lot of the present applicant, contained a covenant in the later form and described the land intended to be benefited as the whole of the land in the deposited plan together with other language which made it clear that the land intended to be benefited was the whole of the land and each part thereof. It bore date 15 September 1922, and prior to this date there had been registered not only the ten first transfers to which I have referred but also 20 more. However, of the objectors in the present application at least six, namely the proprietors of lots 39, 52, 61, 69, 70 and 71, take title from a transferee whose transfer was executed on the same day as or subsequently to the transfer of the applicant's land. Since all these transfers are subsequent to and comply with the requirements of what was then s. 89 of the *Conveyancing Act* 1919 (N.S.W.), then certainly they come within s. 88(3) of the present Act and, subject to any special matter which may be raised because of any lack of reciprocity, may be enforced by the proprietors of those lands against Mr Louis, whether or not a building scheme either existed or was effective. These objectors do not need the assistance of the equitable doctrine of the building scheme; they have the benefit of restrictions arising from covenants which run with the land at law. All they need is the application in equity of the rule in *Tulk v. Moxhay* (1848) 1 H. & Tw. 105 so that Mr Louis' land will be burdened even though Mr Louis was not the original covenantor.

To this extent it may be said that the present preliminary question cannot in any event resolve all the matters arising under the summons, which also seeks orders for extinguishment or modification of the restrictions. However, it is desirable that it be known by whom the restrictions are enforceable (s. 89(3)) and therefore it is desirable that the particular questions asked on this application be dealt with as far as it is necessary and convenient so to do. These questions are as follows:

3. (a) Whether, assuming that the necessary conditions for the existence of a common building scheme under the general law exist in respect of the lands comprised in Deposited Plan 9328, the fact that at the time when the scheme came into existence the said lands were under the provisions of the *Real Property Act* 1900 prevents the covenants noted on the titles in that deposited plan being enforceable.

   (b) Whether, assuming 3(a) is answered in the negative:

(1) The fact that there are two types of covenants, as stated in the schedule hereto, indorsed on the titles to the land in the said deposited plan prevents there being a common building scheme in respect of: (i) All lots in the deposited plan. (ii) Lots 20, 21, 23, 25, 38, 42, 48, 50, 52, 53, 54, 60, 61, 62, 65, 67, 68, 69, 70, 71, 72, 73, 74, 75, 76, 77 and 78 of section 1 and lots 39, 43, 45, 47, 48, 52, 53, 54 and 55 of section 2. [Covenants contained in the transfers were expressed as intended to bind the land transferred and appurtenant to the whole of the land comprised in the Deposited Plan—new covenant.] (iii) Lots 19, 43, 44, 45, 47, 59 and 66 of section 1 and lots 49, 50 and 57 of section 2. [Covenants contained in the transfers were not expressed to be for the benefit of any particular land—old covenants.] (2) Whether the second covenant . . . is an enforceable covenant. [The covenant was not expressed to be for the benefit of any particular land.] (3) Whether a finding that the answer to 3(b)(2) is in the negative prevents there being a common building scheme in respect of: (i) All lots to the deposited plan. (ii) Lots 20, 21, 23, 25, 38, 42, 50, 52, 53, 54, 60, 61, 62, 65, 67, 68, 69, 70, 71, 72, 73, 74, 75, 76, 77 and 78 of section 1 and lots 39, 42, 45, 47, 48, 52, 53, 54 and 55 of section 2. (iii) Lots 19, 43, 44, 45, 47, 59 and 66 of section 1 and lots 49, 50 and 57 of section 2.

The questions, generally speaking, are concerned with the meaning and application, particularly to land under the provisions of the *Real Property Act* of s. 88 of the *Conveyancing Act* 1919. The original 1919 section which dealt with restrictive covenants affecting land was s. 89. This section was as follows:

   (1) No purchaser of any land shall be affected by any covenant restrictive of the use of the land contained in any instrument coming into operation after the commencement of this Act unless the instrument containing such covenant clearly defines—

      (a) the land to which the benefit of the covenant is intended to be appurtenant; and

      (b) the land which is to be subject to the burden of such covenant; and

      (c) the persons (if any) by whom or with whose consent the covenant may be released, varied, or modified.

(2) This section applies to land under the provisions of the Real Property Act, 1900.

In 1930 this section was repealed and a new s. 88 was introduced. . . . [Section 88 is extracted above p. 361.]

The objectors, other than those to whom I have already specifically referred, depend upon the existence of a building scheme to give them the benefit of the covenant, and the question is whether the doctrine of the common building scheme can apply to land under the provisions of the *Real Property Act*.

The subject is a difficult one but I state my conclusion at the outset—Yes, provided the restriction purports to be created by an instrument and that instrument, upon which the notification of the restriction in the Register is based, indicates the land to which the benefit of the restriction is intended to be appurtenant and all the other terms of the restriction, including the persons (if any) intended to have the right to release, vary or modify the restriction and the persons (if any) whose consent to a release, variation or modification of the restriction is intended to be stipulated for.

I have previously expressed the view that subs. (3) of s. 88 can only apply in order to subject land under the *Real Property Act* to the burden of a restriction when the instrument purporting to create the restriction describes the land to which the benefit of the restriction is appurtenant. I adhere to that view. I do not regard subs. (3) as intended to permit the notification upon the Register of restrictions which were wholly ineffectual at common law except between the immediate parties thereto, and which do not satisfy the terms of s. 88(1). If at common law the land intended to be benefited was not described, it could not be said that the essential conditions of annexure at common law were complied with. The instrument must show an intention that the benefit of the covenant was intended to pass to the holders of certain land and if the land was not described this condition could not be fulfilled. Thus Elphinstone, at p. 49 of his book, *Covenants Affecting Land*, could state as the fourth essential condition for the benefit of a restrictive covenant to be capable of passing by conveyance that the land intended to be protected should be described by the instrument creating the covenant so as to be ascertainable with reasonable certainty. Therefore, in the present case the covenants which were entered into without describing the land intended to be benefited could not be construed at law as intended to be for the benefit of any land and this was as true in the years preceding July 1920 as it was true after 1920 when the original section was enacted.

There was, however, always the equitable doctrine of the common building scheme. That doctrine was concerned with notice of a vendor's intention and not with the existence of a covenant in actual fact. It is possible to envisage a case where there was never one covenant contained in a conveyance and yet there might be a common building scheme, because purchasers purchased on the basis that there would be such covenants. If they did so then the obligations of the proposed covenants would be enforceable between all the parties concerned, including the common vendor. No such case, so far as I know, has ever existed. The usual and the significant case of the common building scheme is where equity permits an owner of land to have the benefit of a covenant of which he was intended to have the benefit, but of which under the principles of the common law he could not have the benefit. Under the common law the benefit could only enure for subsequent purchasers and an earlier purchaser would be bound by the burden of a covenant which he had entered into with the vendor and the various purchasers from the vendor but could not obtain a reciprocal benefit. Therefore, by the doctrine of the common building scheme, by way of extension of the rule in *Tulk v. Moxhay* (1848) 1 H. & Tw. 105, equity intervened in order to declare that, provided the intention existed at the time of the original sales from the common vendor, the earlier purchasers should not only be bound by the covenants of the common scheme vis-à-vis the later purchasers but should have the benefit of the covenants which the later purchasers would in the ordinary case or should in the rare case have entered into with the common vendor.

The doctrine of the common building scheme could also be applied where the form of the covenants was ineffectual to annex the benefit at common law. It is to this part of the doctrine that recourse would be had in respect of a covenant such as is found in the earlier transfers in the present application. These covenants would be ineffectual to create restrictions appurtenant to the land because the land to be benefited was not described. However, covenants to the like effect could create restrictions under a common building scheme provided that they were supplemented extrinsically by the additional matters necessary in order to constitute a good scheme. The land is then burdened with the restriction in favour of all the other land in the scheme, provided the original purchaser took with the requisite knowledge of the scheme and provided all subsequent purchasers took with the notice of the scheme. The validity of any particular restriction would cease when the lot was acquired by the purchaser of a legal estate for value without notice of the scheme.

It therefore appears that there are two different ways in which it may be necessary to invoke the doctrine of the common building scheme. One of these is when there were the requisite intention and the necessary steps taken and the necessary notice in the relevant parties but the documentation was either non-existent or inadequate. The second is where there were the necessary intention and the necessary steps taken and the necessary knowledge and where the documentation was quite adequate to give those entitled at law to the benefit of a restriction the right to enforce it, but where the benefit at law could not be enjoyed by the earlier purchasers in respect of land subsequently sold by the vendor. It was to meet the latter type of case that the doctrine of the building scheme in equity was primarily developed. Therefore, the ordinary case of a building scheme would involve covenants the benefit of which enured in favour of subsequent purchasers by operation of law but enured in favour of earlier purchasers by operation of the doctrine in equity of the common building scheme. Therefore, in any particular case it could not be said that a particular restriction was a restriction which took its validity only from a common building scheme or only by operation of law. Generally any particular restriction would be annexed to some of the land at law because the latter land was subsequently transferred by the vendor who had taken the original covenant and by operation of the common building scheme doctrine in equity in respect of the earlier transferees or conveyees from the vendor.

It is against this background that I approach the question whether s. 88 is appropriate in all or any circumstances to enable a registered proprietor who has not and cannot have the benefit of the covenant at law to enforce that covenant in equity by reliance on the doctrine of the common building scheme.

It is necessary in order to amplify this conclusion to consider the scope and intent of s. 88(1) generally and then to consider its application by s. 88(3) to land under the *Real Property Act*. Section 88 deals only with the benefit and burden of restrictions under equitable doctrine in that it deals, so far as burden is concerned, only with the burden or enforceability of the restriction against a person who is not a party to the creation of the restriction. There could be no such burden at law.

In respect of restrictions expressed in instruments, s. 88 imposes conditions of validity, but it does not otherwise deal with validity. It takes the instrument as it is drawn with the intention revealed by the instrument, but without regard to the effectiveness in law or equity of that intention. It is concerned with form, not with substance. The words "intended to be annexed" in my opinion refer to the expression of the intention, not to the effectiveness of that intention. The substantial effectiveness remains a matter of the general principles of law and equity. That is why the words "intended to be annexed" are so important and I regret that in my judgment in *Re Pirie and the Real Property Act* (1961) 79 W.N. (N.S.W.) 701 at 704 I did not italicise there words and the words "intention to annex" there appearing or otherwise indicate the importance which I attached to them. If I had, a number of misunderstandings of my words would have been avoided. See the commentary of Helmore in "The Common Building Scheme and Statutory Provisions" (1963) 37 A.L.J. 81 et seq.; (1963-1964) 6 U.W.A.L. Rev. 283 at 317: see also *Pirie v. Registrar-General* (1962) 109 C.L.R. 619 at 647 per Windeyer J.

Since s. 88(1) deals with intention disclosed by indication in the instrument, the words "is appurtenant" in s. 88(1)(a) do not in my opinion refer to intrinsic validity of the annexation or appurtenance but to the intention disclosed by the instrument. Of course in many situations if the intention to annex fails to any extent, so that the benefit of the restriction is not appurtenant to the whole of the land described, then the restriction will have no effect. In such cases the language of s. 88(1)(a) is precisely appropriate. But there are other cases where the land is described by reference to its several parts. Even if the intention fails as to some parts the intention may be effectual as to other parts the restriction touches and concerns those parts. This is a question of construction of the instrument in the light of the surrounding circumstances.

Where the situation is that of a building scheme, of necessity the restrictions are intended to bind the whole of the land and its several parts. The intention will be disclosed to give the benefit of the covenant to the whole of the land and to each and every part. If this intention were not disclosed then any extrinsic intention to create a building scheme would be of no avail so far as the application of s. 88 is concerned, because the requirements of s. 88(1) would not be complied with. In the case of old system land this defect might not be fatal because a building scheme might have validity quite apart from s. 88(1). But in the case of land under the *Real Property Act* the deficiency in form would be fatal because the restriction can only be effective by virtue of s. 88(3).

I adhere to the view that "restriction" in s. 88(3) is limited to its meaning in s. 88(1): *Re Pirie and the Real Property Act* (1961) 79 W.N. (N.S.W.) at 704. In this whole context a resort to general principles of registered title under the *Real Property Act* is of little value. This is so for two main reasons. First, the whole subject matter of restrictions dealt with by s. 88 is an equitable subject matter in which validity never comes from mere form but from the substantive equitable principle. Secondly, in case it should otherwise have been asserted that as in other situations registration conferred validity, s. 88(3)(b) provided expressly to the contrary. In effectuating an intention to apply s. 88 to land under the *Real Property Act* (and it is most important to note that these are the opening words of subs. (3)) the legislature was providing that an equitable interest and an equitable obligation should be enforceable in respect of land under the Act. There was something of a dilemma. Unless the restriction was made an interest within the meaning of the Act, a purchaser would not take subject to it, because of the terms of s. 42. However, if it was made an interest, there was a likelihood that mere registration would give validity and that was not intended. The restriction, especially as it was an equitable interest, was not intended to gain validity from registration.

These intentions are reflected in s. 88(3)(b) and (c). The latter paragraph provides that the restriction will on registration be an interest. The former paragraph provided that registration shall not give the restriction any greater operation than it has under the instrument creating it. It is necessary, in the light of these factors, to consider what was meant by the words "under the instrument creating it". The actual restriction in the instrument creating it has strictly no operation in respect of any situation with which s. 88 deals, that is, enforceability against a person not being a party to its creation. The actual operation of the instrument is limited to binding the party thereto by the covenant. A purchaser from that party is only bound by the rule in *Tulk v. Moxhay* (1848) 1 H. & Tw. 105. Section 88(3)(b) of necessity therefore must be referring to something more than legal operation by virtue of the words of the instrument which creates the legal rights and obligations. I think that the paragraph looks only to neutralising the effect of registration, and that it does not codify the extent of the operation of a restriction. It may be that it assumes wrongly that the instrument creates the restriction which is referred to in s. 88(1). It may be that in the particular circumstances no more is meant by "creating" than "containing the expression of". In any case s. 88(3)(b) does not say positively that the operative effect of the restriction must be found in the instrument and the instrument alone. If it did in the context of s. 88 it would be nonsense. It says negatively that registration shall not extend the operable effect of the restriction. The operation of the restriction will continue to depend upon the relevant legal and equitable principles. Thus the rule in *Tulk v. Moxhay* is applicable, a rule of equity which extends beyond the effect at law of the instrument creating the restriction. I see no reason why the language of s. 88(3) should not also extend to the equitable rights and duties which arise from the extension of the rule in *Tulk v. Moxhay* to give the benefit to prior purchasers.

I reach the position, therefore, that in most circumstances a restriction, the intrinsic validity of which depends upon the existence of a building scheme, will in its actual form of expression come within the terms of s. 88(1). I also conclude that such a restriction may also come within the terms of s. 88(3) where the circumstances are that the restriction has its origin in an instrument and the instrument complies in its form with the terms of s. 88(1). I conclude, therefore, that in the limited class of case where not only can a building scheme be provided in order to give intrinsic validity to the restriction, but also the formal requirements of s. 88(1) are observed, a restriction the validity of which depends on a building scheme may come within the terms of s. 88(1), and consequently may, in respect of land under the *Real Property Act*, come within s. 88(3).

If, therefore, all the covenants in the present case were in the later form I would be of the opinion that those covenants could be enforced, not only by subsequent purchasers from the common vendor, but also by prior purchasers who were bound to depend upon the proof of the common building scheme. I would be of the same opinion if the earlier covenants had sufficiently described the land intended to be benefited, so that they were effective at common law to annex the benefit of the covenant to the land in the hands of subsequent purchasers. However, the form of the earlier covenants makes it necessary to consider first whether the lands purported to be burdened with those covenants can in fact be so burdened in the hands of a transferee under the *Real Property Act*; and, secondly, if the answer to this question be "no", whether the result is to vitiate the whole building scheme which was intended because that scheme fails in respect to these lots.

Upon the first of these questions I think that my answer follows from what I have said earlier. Section 88(3), in respect of land under the *Real Property Act*, deals only with notifications of restrictions where the notification can be seen to express the land which is intended to have the benefit of the restriction. This is not only because in my opinion the word "restriction" in s. 88(3) refers to a restriction created by an instrument which complies on its face with s. 88, but because the restrictions dealt with by the whole of s. 88, including subs. (3), are restrictions the benefit of which were capable of being annexed to land at law. Both before and after the enactment of s. 88 and its predecessor section in 1919 it was necessary that the land intended to be benefited be described.

Section 88(3) is not a subsection independent of the rest of s. 88, although it deals with a different form of land title, land under the provisions of the *Real Property Act*. The opening words of the subsection are: "This section applies to land under the provisions of the *Real Property Act*, 1900, and in respect thereof. . . .". It does not provide a separate code upon the subject matter in respect of land under the provisions of the *Real Property Act*. It takes the provisions of the section, that is to say subss (1), (2) and (4), and applies these provisions to land under the *Real Property Act*, and then, incidentally to that application, makes the special provisions necessary for such land. With those and the reasons therefore I have already dealt. I recognise a difficulty in the provision that the Registrar-General shall have and be deemed always to have had power to enter in the register book a notification of the restriction. It is true that the use of the word "always" means that the Registrar-General had the power prior to the enactment of s. 88 and the predecessor s. 89. That, however, does not in my opinion lead to the result that the Registrar-General's power prior to the enactment of those sections extended beyond the power to enter a notification where the substance of the now existing statutory requirements had been complied with. It must be borne in mind that these statutory requirements do little, if anything, more than express the previously existing law. Equity, it is true, extended that law to comprehend building schemes where legal requirements as to the form of instrument had not been complied with. I see nothing in s. 88(3) which enables the notification upon the Register, of anything other than an instrument which complies with the law, even though the intrinsic validity of the instrument depends upon an equitable doctrine. To say more would be to repeat views which I have expressed earlier in this judgment. I conclude that neither before nor after 1919 was a covenant in the earlier form valid to annex the benefit thereof to land so that it ran with the land either at common law, or by the retrospective effect of s. 88(3), in respect of land under the provisions of the *Real Property Act*. The deficiency might have been supplied in respect of old system land by the operation of the equitable doctrine of the common building scheme, but the formal deficiency precludes the application of this doctrine in respect of the land being laid under the *Real Property Act*.

There remains then the question whether, the scheme failing in respect of these ten blocks first transferred, the lack of reciprocity with these lots makes it inequitable to apply the rule in *Tulk v. Moxhay* (1848) 1 H. & Tw. 105 in respect of any lots within the scheme. That a deficiency in the reciprocity or mutuality of obligation may lead to the court of equity declining to interfere is well recognised in *Re New South Wales Aged Pensioners' Hostel and the Conveyancing Act* [1967] 1 N.S.W.R. 332. However, that was a very different case. As was submitted to us, it is a question of fact and degree whether or not the breaches of the scheme are so great as to prevent on equitable grounds the scheme continuing to operate between those bound by it. In the case referred to very few of a great number of lots were effectively bound by the scheme. In the present case a comparatively few lots escape from the operation of the scheme. There is in my opinion no good reason why the rule in *Tulk v. Moxhay* should not apply so that land is burdened with a covenant in favour of subsequent purchasers who take the benefit of the covenant at law and in favour of prior purchasers who take the benefit of the covenant in equity by virtue of the application of the doctrine of the common building scheme, provided always that in the case of the prior purchaser from the common vendor his own land is effectively bound. In other words, I do not think that the covenants of subsequent purchasers from the common vendor can be enforced by those prior purchasers whose land is not effectively bound with the reciprocal burden.

For these reasons I would answer the questions which have been propounded as follows:

3. (a) No.

3. (b)(1)(i) Yes; (ii) No; (iii) Yes.

3. (b)(2) No.

3. (b)(3)(i) Yes; (ii) No; (iii) Yes.

I would make an order declaring that the restriction arising under the covenant notified on the Certificate of Title registered Volume 3402 Folio 16 is enforceable by some, but not all, of the registered proprietors of lots in the subdivision. The objectors who thus have the benefit of the restriction should have their costs of the summons paid by the applicant.

[Helsham J. concurred with the judgment of Jacobs J. The dissenting judgment of McLelland C.J. (in Eq.) has been omitted.]

NOTES

1. In the principal case, it is made clear that s. 88(1) applies only to restrictions the benefit of which is intended to be annexed to other land. Jacob J.'s views are more fully explained in the earlier decision in *Re Pirie and the Real Property Act* [1962] N.S.W.R 1004 at 1007:

   Section 88(1) is limited in its operation to restrictions the benefit of which is intended to be annexed to other land; that is to say, it does not purport to deal with restrictions which might be valid because the benefit of them is capable of express assignment or simply because they arise under a common building scheme. . . .

   Once it is realised that s. 88(1) is dealing with one only of a number of types of restrictive covenants, it may properly be said, in my view, that the subsection, except in one respect with which I shall deal presently, goes little if at all beyond the general law. Under the general law the benefit of a covenant would only be annexed to land so that it ran with the land and passed upon a conveyance of that land without express assignment if the land to be benefited was stated in the instrument of covenant either by being expressed to be for the benefit of the land or by being expressed to be made with the covenantee as owner for the time being of such land and others claiming such land under him: *Rogers v. Hosegood* [1900] 2 Ch. 388. In these cases any difficulty in identification of the land intended to be benefited must be solved by construction of the instrument in the light of any extrinsic evidence which is admissible to explain the meaning of words used in the instrument. If the land cannot be so ascertained then the benefit of the covenant is not annexed to the land.

   This requirement that the land be ascertainable from the instrument in which the covenant is contained is not necessary in the case of a building scheme, and, it has recently been held, in the case of a covenant the benefit of which may be expressly assigned: *Newton Abbot Co-op. Society Ltd v. Williamson and Treadgold Ltd* [1952] Ch. 286. This decision has been criticised; see *Preston and Newsom on Restrictive Covenants* (3rd ed.), p. 27.

   It does not follow that s. 88 can never apply to a building scheme. A restrictive covenant will be good in respect of land under the provisions of the *Real Property Act* if it complies with the requirements of s. 88, because, if it does so comply, it will show an intention to annex the benefit of the covenant to the other land. The fact that extrinsic evidence may show that a building scheme was intended will not exclude the intention to annex the covenant to the other land and the benefit of the covenant will pass at least to transferees from the common vendor subsequent to the making of the covenant sought to be enforced. In regard to transferees prior to the making of the covenant sought to be enforced, the position is less clear but I can see no substantial reason why, if an intention is shown to annex the benefit of the covenant to land previously transferred, in the course of creating a building scheme, the covenant should not be enforceable by a transferee from the common owner prior to the transfer of the land sought to be burdened.

As I have said, s. 88(1) does not deal with covenants which are not intended to be annexed to other land. The covenant in the present case cannot be taken to have been intended to be annexed to other land because it contains no description of the land intended to be benefited from which that land may be ascertained. At the most, therefore, it would under the general law be a covenant the benefit of which would be capable of express assignment or a covenant the benefit of which could be enjoyed by owners of other land in a common building scheme.

On appeal to the High Court, the judgment of Jacobs J. was reversed on a procedural point: *Pirie v. Registrar-General* (1962) 109 C.L.R. 619. The High Court also addressed itself to the substantive issue. Kitto J., with whom Owen J. concurred, adopted the views of Jacobs J., including the view that the authority of the Registrar-General to record covenants in the Register was restricted to the notification of covenants contained in instruments which complied with s. 88(1). Kitto J. said (at 630):

The expression "is intended to be annexed to other land", as here used [in s. 88(1)], is not satisfied . . . unless the instrument creating the restriction discloses an intention that by force of its own language the benefit of the restriction shall be annexed to other land. This excludes the case where annexation is not express but is the result of a building scheme. It excludes also the case where the benefit of a restriction is not annexed to other land and is merely made assignable with other land—excludes it even if the law is, as Mr H. W. R. Wade maintains (1957) Camb. L. J. 146, not withstanding the case of *Re Pinewood Estate, Farnborough* [1958] Ch. 280 that an assignment of the benefit together with the other land brings about an annexation.

Windeyer J., generally agreed with the views of Jacobs J. in *Re Pirie* subject to the following qualification. His Honour said (at 647):

I agree that since 1931, and in some cases since 1920, the doctrine of common building scheme will not, of itself, suffice to sustain in New South Wales a restrictive covenant, whether of land under the *Real Property Act* or under common law title. The statutory conditions must be complied with. But, these express statutory provisions aside, I do not agree that the benefit of a restriction on the user of one lot in a building scheme cannot be said to be intended to be annexed to other land. Whether or not the covenant be with the common vendor alone, and whatever form it takes, its benefit may have been intended to be annexed either to other land of the vendor or to all the other lots in the subdivision. Therefore, in my view, it does not follow that because in this case the instrument in which the restrictive covenant appears does not expressly state to what land its benefit is intended to be annexed, that the land in question could not, at the date when the note was made in the register book, have been "subject to the burden of the restriction" within the meaning of s. 88(3), para. (a) . . . there is no evidence that that was so, for there is no evidence that there was in the relevant sense a building scheme.

For a detailed and useful summary, see Bradbrook and Neave, *Easements and Restrictive Covenants in Australia*, pp. 310-321.

2. The reasoning in *Re Louis* [1971] 1 N.S.W.L.R. 164 suggests that the effect of s. 88(1) on schemes of development over *old system title land* is as follows:

(1) Since s. 88(1) applies only to restrictions as to user contained in "instruments", a scheme of development may exist over old system title land even though there are no express covenants restricting user contained in the conveyances.

(2) If a valid scheme of development was in existence *before* the *Conveyancing Act* 1919 (N.S.W.) came into operation (1 July 1920) it does not have to comply with s. 88(1). The predecessor to s. 88 (s. 89) applied only to covenants contained in instruments coming into operation *after* the commencement of the Act.

(3) Schemes of development coming into existence *after* the enactment of the *Conveyancing Act* 1919 (N.S.W.) (1 July 1920) until the enactment of the present s. 88 (inserted by the *Conveyancing Amendment Act* 1930 (N.S.W.)) are governed by the old s. 89 which was in more general terms than the present section. The section, which is set out in the judgment of Jacobs J. in *Re Louis* (p. 366) was not limited to covenants "intended to be annexed to other land". The section, on one view, could extend to schemes of development although, it is not clear from the authorities what is necessary for compliance; see *Pirie v. Registrar-General* (1963) 109 C.L.R. 619 at 634 per Taylor J.; cf. (1948) 22 A.L.J. at 72.

(4) The present s. 88(1) introduced in 1930 applies only to covenants contained in instruments coming into operation after the commencement of the amending act. In respect of building schemes in existence after the enactment of s. 88(1) a scheme of development may exist where restrictions as to user are contained in an "instrument" which complies with s. 88(1). According to *Re Louis*, there will be compliance with the terms of s. 88(1) if the instrument itself, without reference to extraneous evidence, reveals an intention to annex the benefit of covenants to all lots within the scheme of development, in addition to setting out the land burdened. This can now be achieved simply by noting restrictions as to user intended to be created on a plan of subdivision within s. 88B of the *Conveyancing Act* 1919 (N.S.W.): see below p. 376.

A scheme of development will not be invalidated by s. 88(1) merely because all obligations arising out of the "local law" of the estate and which are enforced in equity are not expressed in the conveyance. Equity will, consistently with s. 88(1), enforce the "local law" by requiring the vendor (in the absence of a reserved right) to insert like covenants in all future conveyances of land subject to the scheme despite the fact that the vendor has not expressly covenanted to observe the restrictions; similarly earlier purchasers are entitled to enforce covenants against later purchasers despite the fact that no express covenants are entered into by later purchasers in favour of earlier purchasers.

Helmore, *The Law of Real Property in New South Wales* (2nd ed.), p. 215 sums up the position by saying that as between later purchasers and earlier purchasers there is no "instrument"; the obligations are implied, and s. 88(1) does not apply to such implied covenants. The section, however, does apply to *instruments* containing restrictions as to user. Therefore, covenants restrictive of user entered into by a purchaser in the conveyance must comply with s. 88(1). Dr Helmore submitted that the term "instrument" referred to in s. 88(1) means the instrument containing the restriction; it is that instrument which must comply with s. 88(1).

The position might not be quite as broad as Dr Helmore suggests. In *Re Louis* [1971] 1 N.S.W.L.R. 164, Jacobs J. suggests that in order to comply with s. 88(1) the restrictions as to user must be expressed to be for the benefit of all the area within the proposed scheme of development. In short, the instrument must demonstrate an intention to annex the benefit of the covenants to all lots within the scheme. On this view, it would not be sufficient simply to express the covenant to be for the benefit of the vendor's remaining unsold land.

3. (1) The operation of building schemes over *Torrens title* land is circumscribed by s. 88(3) *Conveyancing Act* 1919 (N.S.W.). Subsequent to the decision in *Re Louis*, s. 88(3) was amended. The *Conveyancing (Amendment) Act* 1972 (N.S.W.) inserted the words "a restriction referred to in subs. 1 of this section" thus confirming the established view that the power of the Registrar-General to notify restrictions as to user on title is limited to instruments complying with s. 88(1). Thus it is clear that the Registrar-General's authority to notify restrictions on title is limited to restrictions contained in instruments "the benefit of which is intended to be annexed to other land". The critical issue is whether this necessarily excludes building schemes. *Re Louis* clearly supports the view that building schemes can exist over Torrens title land. This is to be contrasted with the much more restrictive view of the Court of Appeal in *Re Martyn* (1965) 65 S.R. (N.S.W.) 387. That case concerned covenants contained in a registered transfer of Torrens title land executed in 1913. There was no express annexation of the benefit of the covenant to any specified land, nor was the covenant expressed to be for the benefit of the covenantee as owner of any particular land. Although there was no reference to land intended to be benefited by the covenants, it was accepted that a scheme of development existed over the land which would have been enforceable under the general law. It was held that the scheme was not enforceable. Walsh J. said (Asprey J. concurring):

> It is to be noticed that in s. 88(1), there is reference to a restriction arising "under covenant or otherwise". Perhaps the words "or otherwise" are meant to refer to some other document such as the conditions of a sale by auction, or the like. Perhaps they have a wider ambit. But when subs. (3)(a) refers to "a notification of the restriction", it must refer to some written statement and this, in my opinion must contain the information necessary to enable a person who subsequently searches the title to become aware of the nature and extent of the restriction which is notified. As applied to a restriction sought to be enforced as one not simply "arising under covenant", but as dependent upon and enforceable because of the existence of a building scheme and of the equitable obligations flowing from the scheme, I think it must be requisite, in order that para. (c) of s. 88(3) can have any effect, that the notification should refer in some way to the circumstances upon which the enforceability of the restriction depends. The notification in the present case does not fulfil this requirement. It takes one to the transfer, with its covenant in the form which I have set out. It does incorporate a reference to a specified deposited plan, but it contains no statement, express or implied, of any circumstances showing that there was a building scheme or that there was any connection between the sale of the lot to which this transfer related and the sale of any other lots.
>
> I do not think that in this situation, one can reach the conclusion that s. 88(3) operates so that the restriction thus notified becomes an "interest" in the land within the meaning of s. 42 of the *Real Property Act* 1900 (N.S.W.), of such a kind that the land is held subject not only to the rights which can be enforced by relying solely upon the covenant and attaching to it the relevant rules as to the passing of its burden and of its benefits to successors, but subject also to additional rights supportable not in that manner but by reference to the equitable principles relating to building schemes.

The problem to which I have just referred would be avoided if one limited the whole operation of s. 88(3) in the manner in which Kitto J. and Owen J. [*Pirie's Case* (1963) 109 C.L.R. 619, above p. 373] thought it should be limited. Perhaps it would be avoided also if one took the view that para. (b) of that subsection shows that the subsection does not operate at all except upon a restriction which is, in the strict sense, "created" by an instrument. The application of the subsection [sic] to restrictions which, although defined and evidenced by an instrument, are not created by it but are created out of the community of interest of the participants in a building scheme, requires that one should treat the term "creating" in para. (b) as used in an imprecise sense. But without deciding whether or not it is a necessary corollary of the view which I have stated above that one or both of the constructions just mentioned should be adopted, I am of opinion that it is not possible to treat a restriction of the kind which the appellants here assert to be enforceable as part of a building scheme, as one to which the notification must be deemed to have given the character of an "interest" within s. 42 of the *Real Property Act* 1900 (N.S.W.).

Another difficulty in the way of the appellants seems to me to be involved in para. (b) of the subsection. If it be supposed that the subsection covers restrictions other than those which are actually dependent upon the instrument, and that the term "creating" in para. (b) is not used in any strict sense, it still appears to be true that para. (b) is intended to ensure that the effect of the notification is to be a limited one. If a covenant is given and taken as part of and in the course of carrying into effect a building scheme, then restrictions which are defined in an instrument may operate, so far as the general law is concerned, in part "under the instrument" and in part in a wider field, because of the building scheme. But the notification is not to give the restriction "any greater operation" than it has "under the instrument", which defines and evidences its terms. Thus, it would seem that the notification cannot be called in aid in a case which is concerned with the wider field of the operation of the restriction, going beyond the operation which it has under the instrument.

(2) *Re Louis* [1971] 1 N.S.W.L.R. 164 has been followed in preference to *Re Martyn* (1965) 65 S.R. (N.S.W.) 387 in *Re Mack and the Conveyancing Act* [1975] 2 N.S.W.L.R. 623; *Jones v. Sherwood Hills Pty Ltd* (unreported, Supreme Court of New South Wales, Waddell J., 8 July 1975), noted (1978) 52 A.L.J. 223; *Application of Fox* (1981) 2 B.P.R. 9310; *Re Application of Poltava Pty Ltd* [1982] 2 N.S.W.L.R. 161; *Application of Amory Pty Ltd* (1984) C.C.H. N.S.W. Conv. R. 55-180; *Pike v. Venables* (1984) C.C.H. N.S.W. Conv. R. 55-170 at 57, 216.

(3) In *Re Dennerstein* [1963] V.R. 688, Hudson J. referred to the difficulties engendered by schemes of development over Torrens title land in the following terms:

In my view, a purchaser of land under the *Transfer of Land Act* 1915 (Vic.) is not bound to prosecute inquires and searches and make deductions such as would be involved if Mr Searby's contentions were accepted. Even when all the materials and evidence in relation to the circumstances under which an estate has been subdivided and sold are available it is not by any means easy to determine whether the sale of allotments in the estate has been made under or pursuant to a common building scheme. To require a person interested in purchasing one of those allotments to make this determination after obtaining the necessary evidence perhaps years after the original sale if it is available would render conveyancing a hazardous and cumbersome operation, and, in the case of dealings in land under the operation of the *Transfer of Land Act*, would defeat the object of the Act and destroy in large measure the efficacy of the system sought to be established thereby.

I have reached the conclusion that, even assuming there is power under the Act to notify as encumbrances on a Certificate of Title restrictions arising under a building scheme, such notification will not be effective to bind transferees of the land unless not only the existence of the scheme and the nature of the restrictions imposed thereunder, but the lands affected by the scheme (both as to the benefit and the burden of the restrictions) are indicated in the notification, either directly or by reference to some instrument or other document to which a person searching the register has access. In the present case these requirements are not satisfied. The covenants contained in the instrument of transfer notified as an encumbrance, though they certainly set out the restrictions, give no indication that they arose under a building scheme, nor of the land to which the benefit thereof was intended to be annexed, under such a scheme. The applicant, therefore, had no notice of the existence of the scheme or of the restrictions imposed thereby. She did have notice that the covenants contained in the instrument of transfer had been entered into by her predecessor in title but those covenants as she had no doubt been advised are no longer enforceable by any person and, therefore, she took her transfer free of the restrictions contained therein and is entitled to a declaration accordingly.

Although the case concerned Victorian legislation which has no equivalent to s. 88(1) *Conveyancing Act* 1919 (N.S.W.), semble the views of Hudson J. achieve a similar result to that required by s. 88(1) and (3) of the *Conveyancing Act* 1919.

4. Since 1964 in New South Wales schemes of development may be created by registration of an approved plan of subdivision: see s. 88B *Conveyancing Act* 1919. The restrictions as to user referred to on the plan of subdivision must comply with s. 88(1).

5. An express covenant the benefit of which is not annexed to land, but which is capable of assignment in accordance with the equitable rules (see above p. 347) cannot be recorded in the Register in New South Wales; s. 88(3) set outs, exhaustively the authority of the Registrar-General to record restrictive covenants in the Register, and such authority is restricted to those covenants contained in instruments complying with s. 88(1) of the *Conveyancing Act* 1919 (N.S.W.). An assignable covenant is likely to breach s. 88(1) because there may be no intention to annex the benefit of the covenant to other land, a prerequisite for the operation of s. 88(1) (*Re Louis* [1971] 1 N.S.W.L.R. 164; *Pirie v. Registrar-General* (1962) 109 C.L.R. 619, see Kitto J. above p. 373) in any case, in such a situation the instrument would almost never indicate the details required by s. 88(1) particularly details of the land intended to benefit from the covenant.

F.   MODIFICATION AND EXTINGUISHMENT OF COVENANTS

1. Express release

In respect of land under old system title, at law, covenants must be released by deed: *Conveyancing Act* 1919 (N.S.W.), s. 23B(1). The principle in *Walsh v. Lonsdale* (1882) 21 Ch. D. 9 (see below Chapter 8) may be applied in equity to give effect to a release for value not contained in a deed.

In respect of Torrens title land, in New South Wales a deed of release with a request to the Register-General to have the purport of the deed recorded in the Register is necessary.

2. Operation of law

Restrictive covenants are extinguished where the land burdened and the land benefited are in common ownership: *Kerridge v. Foley* (1964) 82 W.N. (Pt 1) (N.S.W.) 293, above p. 330; *Re Tiltwood, Sussex; Barrett v. Bond* [1978] 3 W.L.R. 474. See also Preece, "The Effect of Unity of Ownership of Benefited and Burdened Land on Easements and Restrictive Covenants" (1982) 56 A.L.J. 587 and critical note (1980) 54 A.L.J. 156. Where a scheme of development subsists over land, covenants may be suspended during the unity of ownership of part of the land within the scheme: *Brunner v. Greenslade* [1971] Ch. 993. In *Texaco Ltd v. Kernochan* [1973] A.C. 609 the Privy Council approved the decision in *Brunner v. Greenslade*. Lord Cross of Chelsea, delivering the advice of the Privy Council said (at 624):

At this point it is convenient to clarify a point upon which there seems to have been some misunderstanding in the Court of Appeal. A passage in the judgment of Bourke J.A. suggests that he understood the contention of the appellants to be that the fact that two or more lots came into the same hands would cause the whole scheme to collapse so that the owners of other lots would no longer be able to enforce the covenants. The appellants' argument as presented to the Board did not involve any such far-reaching conclusion. According to it the covenant would continue to be enforceable by the owners of other lots against the owner of the lots in unity of seisin but if and when those lots came once more into different hands their respective owners—while remaining subject to and entitled to the benefit of the covenants as regards other owners—would not be entitled to enforce the covenants inter se. Another point which should be mentioned at this stage is that it was common ground between counsel that even if the covenants would prima facie become once more enforceable inter se by the owners of lots which had previously been in unity in seisin it was competent to the parties to the transaction which put an end to the unity of seisin to provide that the restrictions should no longer apply as between themselves. That this is so is shown by *Knight v. Simmonds* [1896] 1 Ch. 653 at 660-661 and also by the part of the judgment in *Elliston v. Reacher* which deals with the claim of the plaintiffs other than Elliston: see [1908] 2 Ch. 374 at 393-395. Their Lordships would add that the same consequence may well flow from the surrounding circumstances even if there is nothing said in the conveyance which puts an end to the unity of seisin to indicate that the restrictions are no longer to apply as between the parties to it. Suppose, for example, that the owner of two adjoining houses subject to a scheme of development which forbad [sic] user for professional purposes started to use one of the houses for professional purposes and shortly afterwards sold it to someone who to his knowledge proposed to continue such user. In such circumstances the purchaser would run the risk of actions by other owners but any claim by the vendor as owner of the adjoining house to enforce the covenant would be a derogation from his grant even though the conveyance contained no express release of the purchaser from the restrictions in the scheme so far as concerned the vendor as owner of the adjoining house. The point of law which arises for consideration is therefore whether in a case where there is nothing in the conveyance putting an end to the unity of seisin or in the surrounding circumstances to indicate that the restrictions in the scheme are no longer to apply as between the owners of the lots previously in common ownership the fact that they have been in common ownership puts an end to the restrictions so far as concerns the relations of subsequent owners for the time being of that part of the estate inter se so that if the common owner of those lots wished them to apply after the severance he would have to reimpose them as fresh restrictions under a subscheme relating to them. It would, their Lordships think, be somewhat unfortunate if this was the law. In the last century at all events it cannot have been unusual when an estate was laid out for development in lots subject to restrictions intended to apply to all the owners of lots for the time being inter se for several adjoining lots to be brought by one builder who built houses on them which he sold to separate purchasers subject to the provisions of the scheme. It is most unlikely in such a case that the builder and the purchasers of his houses would have wished that the restrictions while enforceable by and against the owners of more distant properties should not be enforceable by the adjoining purchasers from the builder inter se, yet, if the appellants' contention is right, they would not be so enforceable unless the builder as well as selling subject to the restrictions in the head scheme created a subscheme on similar terms in relation to his houses. Nor can their Lordships see any compelling considerations of principle leading to the conclusion for which the appellants contend. It is no doubt true that if the restrictions in question exist simply for the mutual benefit of two adjoining properties and both those properties are bought by one man the restrictions will automatically come to an end and will not revive on a subsequent severance unless the common owner then recreates them. But their Lordships cannot see that it follows from this that if a number of people agree that the area covered by all their properties shall be subject to a "local law" the provisions of which shall be enforceable by any owner for the time being of any part against any other owner and the whole area has never at any time come into common ownership an action by one owner of a part against another owner of a part must fail if it can be shown that both parts were either at the inception of the scheme or at any time subsequently in common ownership. The view which their Lordships favour is supported by dicta of Sir H. H. Cozens-Hardy M.R. in *Elliston v. Reacher* [1908] 2 Ch. 665 at 673 and of Simonds J. in *Lawrence v. South County Freeholds Ltd* [1939] Ch. 656 at 677-683, but at the time when this case was heard by the Court of Appeal there was no decision on the point. Subsequently, however, in *Brunner v. Greenslade* [1971] Ch. 993 which raised the point, Megarry J. followed those dicta. The appellants submitted that his decision was wrong but in their Lordships' view it was right.

In New South Wales, the *Conveyancing Act* 1919, s. 88B provides a statutory exception to extinguishment by common ownership in respect of easements, appurtenant profits and covenants created under a plan of subdivision registered pursuant to the section. Note *Real Property Act* 1900 (N.S.W.), s. 47(7) abrogates the rule in respect of easements and appurtenant profits only.

3. Implied release

Equity would refuse to enforce a restrictive covenant, thereby giving rise to an implied release of the covenant, in two situations. The first was where an estoppel operated against the plaintiff, as, for example, where past breaches of the covenant were disregarded and the defendant was led to believe that future breaches would be similarly disregarded: *Chatsworth Estate Co. v. Fewell* [1931] 1 Ch. 224. Farwell J. in that case (at 229-230) set out a second ground upon which equity may refuse to enforce a restrictive covenant:

> The defendant's first ground of defence is that there has been such a complete change in the character of the neighbourhood, apart from the plaintiffs' acts or omissions, that the covenants are now unenforceable. But to succeed on that ground the defendant must show that there has been so complete a change in the character of the neighbourhood that there is no longer any value left in the covenants at all. A man who covenants for the protection of his property cannot be deprived of his rights thereunder merely by the acts or omissions of other persons unless those acts or omissions bring about such a state of affairs as to render the covenants valueless, so that an action to enforce them would be unmeritorious, not bona fide at all, and merely brought for some ulterior purposes.

In New South Wales, the Registrar-General has no statutory authority to remove from the Register restrictive covenants impliedly released. The proper course is an application to the court for an order extinguishing the covenant under s. 89 of the *Conveyancing Act* 1919 (below); the Registrar-General is required to give effect to this order.

4. Order of court

The equitable rules outlined above form the basis of the present statutory provisions for modification or extinguishment of covenants.

Section 89 of the *Conveyancing Act* 1919 (N.S.W.) provides:

> 89. (1) Where land is subject to an easement or to a restriction or obligation arising under covenant or otherwise as to the user thereof, the court may from time to time, on the application of any person interested in the land, by order modify or wholly or partially extinguish the easement, restriction or obligation upon being satisfied—

(a) that by reason of change in the user of any land having the benefit of the easement, restriction or obligation, or in the character of the neighbourhood or other circumstances of the case which the court may deem material, the easement, restriction or obligation ought to be deemed obsolete, or that the continued existence thereof would impede the reasonable user of the land subject to the easement, restriction or obligation without securing practical benefit to the person entitled to the easement or to the benefit of the restriction or an obligation, or would, unless modified, so impede such user; or

(b) that the persons of the age of eighteen years or upwards and of full capacity for the time being or from time to time entitled to the easement or to the benefit of the restriction, whether in respect of estates in fee simple or any lesser estates or interests in the land to which the easement or the benefit of the restriction is annexed, have agreed to the easement or restriction being modified or wholly or partially extinguished, or by their acts or omissions may reasonably be considered to have abandoned the easement wholly or in part or waived the benefit of the restriction wholly or in part;

(b1) in the case of an obligation—

(i) that the prescribed authority entitled to the benefit of the obligation has agreed to the obligation's being modified or wholly or partially extinguished or by its acts or omissions may reasonably be considered to have waived the benefit of the obligation wholly or in part; or

(ii) that the obligation has become unreasonably expensive or unreasonably onerous to perform when compared with the benefit of its performance to the authority; or

(c) that the proposed modification or extinguishment will not substantially injure the persons entitled to the easement, or to the benefit of the restriction.

(2) Where any proceedings are instituted to enforce an easement, restriction or obligation, or to enforce any rights arising out of a breach of any restriction or obligation, any person against whom the proceedings are instituted may in such proceedings apply to the court for an order under this section.

(3) The court may on the application of any person interested make an order declaring whether or not in any particular case any land is affected by an easement, restriction or obligation, and the nature and extent thereof, and whether the same is enforceable, and if so by whom.

These provisions are to be contrasted with the much more extensive powers given to the Lands Tribunal in Britain under the *Law of Property Act* 1925 (U.K.), s. 84. Section 84, in addition to provisions similar to those contained in s. 89 of the *Conveyancing Act* 1919 (N.S.W.), provides that a covenant may be modified or discharged if its continued existence would impede *some* reasonable user of the land for public or private purposes where the covenant either confers no practical benefit of substantial value or is contrary to the public interest and (in either case) any loss can be adequately compensated in money. In addition, the Lands Tribunal is directed to take into account the development plan and any declared or ascertainable pattern for the grant or refusal of planning permissions in the relevant areas: s. 84(1B). The power to modify a restriction includes power to add such further provisions restricting the user of land as appear to be reasonable in view of the relaxation of the covenant: s. 84(1C). Note also the more extensive provisions in

Queensland (*Property Law Act* 1974 (Qld), s. 18(2)) and Tasmania: *Conveyancing and Law of Property Act* 1884 (Tas.), s. 84C. The Tasmanian provision, the *Conveyancing and Law of Property Act* 1884 (Tas.), s. 84C(1)(b) goes further in providing that a covenant may be extinguished or modified if "(b) . . . the continued existence of the interest would impede a user of the land in accordance with an interim order or planning scheme or, as the case may be, would, unless modified, so impede such a user". The New South Wales Land Titles Office in a Discussion Paper reviewing Restrictive Covenants (*Review of Restrictive Covenants—Discussion Paper* (1988), p. 14) recommends the adoption of a similar provision in New South Wales.

The Victorian case *Re Robinson* [1972] V.R. 278 provides an excellent illustration of the restricted operation of the Victorian legislation which is substantially similar to that in New South Wales. The applicant was the registered proprietor of four lots which were subject to a restrictive covenant whereby no building other than a private dwelling house was to be erected on any lot. Under the relevant planning scheme, the use of the land for residential buildings was forbidden. An application was made for modification of the covenant to allow seven shops to be built on the land. The application was refused by Adam J. who held that the covenant was not obsolete. The land entitled to benefit was still a purely residential area semi-rural in aspect, and the covenant therefore was of value in maintaining the character of the area. In addition, although the covenant viewed in light of planning restrictions did impede reasonable user, practical benefits nevertheless accrued to the land entitled to the benefit of the covenant, namely the benefits of living in a residential area as distinct from living next to a shopping centre. On similar grounds his Honour held that substantial injury would result to the persons entitled to the benefit.

(a) General considerations

The power of the court under the *Conveyancing Act* 1919 (N.S.W.), s. 89 and similar interstate provisions, is discretionary; the court is not bound to make an order even if the applicant has satisfied the conditions set out in the section: *Treweeke v. 36 Wolseley Road Pty Ltd* (1976) 128 C.L.R. 274, above p. 296.

Persons entitled to the benefit of the restrictions may object to the granting of the application. If objectors rely on a scheme of development as the basis for their right to enforce the covenant, they bear the onus of proving the existence of the scheme: *Re Application of Poltava Pty Ltd* [1982] 2 N.S.W.L.R. 161.

Under the relevant English legislation (*Law of Property Act* 1925 (U.K.), s. 84, outlined above) planning considerations are relevant in considering whether a covenant should be varied or discharged. In New South Wales, however, planning considerations are relevant in a very limited context only.

Planning schemes would appear to be relevant in a practical sense in at least two situations:

(1) They may, when considered in conjunction with covenants affecting the land, considerably restrict the permissible use of the land.

(2) They may be relevant in the wider context of determining what kind of development is consistent with the public interest.

In the absence of legislation directing the court to take planning considerations into account, it has been accepted that planning restrictions are relevant in determining whether the covenants prevent reasonable user of the land: *Re Chamberlain and the Conveyancing Act* (1969) 90 W.N. (N.S.W.) (Pt 1) 585, extracted below; *Re Robinson* [1972] V.R. 278 at 282. But they are not relevant in any wider context:

Re Mason and the Conveyancing Act (1960) 78 W.N. (N.S.W.) 925, extracted below; *Re Ghey and Galton's Application* [1957] 2 Q.B. 650 at 662. Although an environmental planning instrument can suspend existing restrictive covenants binding the land (*Environmental Planning and Assessment Act* 1979 (N.S.W.), s. 28, see above p. 305.) this provision has not been greatly utilised. The New South Wales Department of Planning advised that from 1988 onwards all Local Environmental Plans in accordance with s. 28 will be required to contain provisions suspending inconsistent covenants, Land Titles Office of New South Wales, *Review of Restrictive Covenants—Discussion Paper* (1988), p. 10.

In interpreting the provisions of s. 89 of the *Conveyancing Act* 1919 (N.S.W.), and comparable interstate legislation, the words of Farwell J. in *Re Henderson's Conveyance* [1940] Ch. 835 at 846 are relevant. His Lordship said:

> Speaking for myself, I do not view this section of the Act as designed to enable a person to expropriate the private rights of another purely for his own profit. I am not suggesting that there may not be cases where it would be right to remove or modify a restriction against the will of the person who has the benefit of that restriction, either with or without compensation, in a case where it seems necessary to do so because it prevents in some way the proper development of the neighbouring property, or for some such reason of that kind; but in my judgment this section of the Act was not designed, at any rate prima facie, to enable one owner to get a benefit by being freed from the restrictions imposed upon his property in favour of a neighbouring owner, merely because, in view of the person who desires the restriction to go, it would make his property more enjoyable or more convenient for his own private purposes. I do not think the section was designed with a view to benefiting one private individual at the expense of another private individual. At any rate, primarily, that was not, in my judgment, the object of this section. If a case is to be made out under this section, there must be some proper evidence that the restriction is no longer necessary for any reasonable purpose of the person who is enjoying the benefit of it, or that by reason of a change in the character of the property or the neighbourhood, the restriction is one which is no longer to be enforceable or has become of no value.

See also *Re Mason* (1960) 78 W.N. (N.S.W.) 925, extracted below; *Smith v. Australian Real Estate and Investment Co. Ltd* [1964] W.A.R. 163.

In an application for variation or extinguishment of a covenant under the various statutory provisions, the applicant has the onus of proving one of the alternative bases for modification or extinguishment set out in the section. The first of the grounds set out in the legislation is obsolescence.

(b) Obsolescence

In *Re Truman, Hanbury, Buxton & Co. Ltd's Application* [1956] 1 Q.B. 261, Romer L.J., with whom Lord Evershed M.R. and Birkett L.J. concurred, gave the following definition of "obsolete" (at 272):

> It seems to me that if, as sometimes happens, the character of an estate as a whole or of a particular part of it gradually changes, a time may come when the purpose to which I have referred can no longer be achieved, for what was intended at first to be a residential area has become, either through express or tacit waiver of the covenants, substantially a commercial area. When that time does come, it may be said that the covenants have become obsolete, because their original purpose can no longer be served and, in my opinion, it is in that sense that the word "obsolete" is used in s. 84(1)(a). . . . If serious injury

would result to the opponents and others if the covenant was discharged . . . I cannot see how, on any view, the covenant can be described as obsolete, because the object of the covenant is still capable of fulfilment, and the covenant still affords a real protection to those who are entitled to enforce it.

On the facts before the court, a covenant not to carry on the business of hotel keeper within a residential estate had not become obsolete simply because some of the houses within the estate had been converted to shops: see also *Re Mason and the Conveyancing Act* (1960) 78 W.N. (N.S.W.) 925, extracted below; *Perth Construction Pty Ltd v. Mount Lawley Pty Ltd* (1955) 57 W.A.L.R. 41.

As to what constitutes "neighbourhood" for the purposes of these provisions, see, *Re Miscamble's Application* [1966] V.R. 596 at 602; *Re A. R. Wilson and Conveyancing Act* (1949) 49 S.R. (N.S.W.) 276; *Wall v. Australian Real Estate Investment Co. Ltd* [1978] W.A.R. 187; *Re Application of Poltava Pty Ltd* [1982] 2 N.S.W.L.R. 161.

(c) Impedes reasonable user without securing practical benefit

In *Re Ghey and Galton's Application* [1957] 2 Q.B. 650 at 663 Lord Evershed M.R., with whom Morris and Pearce L.JJ. concurred, said that in order to show that a covenant impeded reasonable user without securing practical benefits, it must be shown "that the continuance of the unmodified covenants hinders, to a real, sensible degree, the land being reasonably used, having regard to the situation it occupies, to the surrounding property, and to the purpose of the covenants" (at 663). His Lordship indorsed the view of Farwell J. in *Re Henderson's Conveyance* [1940] Ch. 835 at 846 that there must be evidence that the restriction is no longer necessary for any reasonable purpose of the person who is enjoying the benefit of it.

It is not sufficient to show that what the applicant proposes to do is a reasonable user of the land. It must appear that no reasonable user of the land is possible unless the restriction is modified: *Stannard v. Issa* [1987] 2 W.L.R. 188 (P.C.). The paragraph does not relate to the use which can be made of the land by the *present* owner, but the use which can be made of it in the lands of *any* owner: *Heaton v. Loblay* (1960) 77 W.N. (N.S.W.) 140 at 142; *P. M. Williams and the Conveyancing Act* (1959) 32 A.L.J. 382; *Re Miscamble's Application* [1966] V.R. 596; *Pike v. Venables* (1984) C.C.H. (N.S.W.) Conv. R. 55-170 at 57-216; see also *Re Alexandra* [1980] V.R. 55. It must be shown also that the covenant does not secure any practical benefit to the person entitled to enforce it. The restriction must be no longer necessary for any reasonable purpose of the persons entitled to the benefit of it: *Re Henderson's Conveyance* [1940] Ch. 835 at 846; *Re Alexandra* [1980] V.R. 55. In *Gilbert v. Spoor* [1982] 3 W.L.R. 183 the English Court of Appeal held that a view from the vicinity of the objector's land but not from the land itself was a practical benefit entitled to protection. Eveleigh L.J. (at 187), referring to a similar but not identical English subsection, said: "The subsection does not speak of a restriction for the benefit or protection of land . . . but rather of a restriction which secures any practical benefits." In any event his Lordship thought that the preservation of the view was a benefit which added to the amenity of the land and the general character of the area and therefore the benefit was one which touched and concerned the land. See generally *Re Chamberlain* (1969) 90 W.N. (Pt 1) (N.S.W.) 585, extracted below.

(d) Express or implied release

Where there is agreement by all interested parties to vary or extinguish the covenant, there are no difficulties presented by the section. As to the effect of a prior unregistered agreement to release the covenant or easement by predecessors in title to the parties to the action, see *Pieper v. Edwards* [1982] 1 N.S.W.L.R. 336, above p. 301. Implied release is discussed above. For an illustration of the application of this provision to easements, see *Treweeke v. 36 Wolseley Road Pty Ltd* (1973) 128 C.L.R. 117, extracted above p. 296.

(e) No substantial injury

The court may modify or extinguish the covenant if the proposed modification or extinguishment will not substantially injure the persons entitled to the benefit of the restriction. This is an independent ground for modification or extinguishment of covenants, and is not limited by s. 89(1)(a) or (b), although it is suggested that the test of whether substantial injury will result from the proposed modification or extinguishment is similar to the test of whether the covenant secures any practical benefit under s. 89(1): *Re Alexandra* [1980] V.R. 55. In *Ridley v. Taylor* [1965] 1 W.L.R. 611, the subsection was described as "a long stop against vexatious objections to extended user and is to deal with frivolous objections". In order to succeed under s. 89(1)(c), it is not necessary to prove a depreciation in the value of property; it is sufficient if there is a substantial interference with the amenities of the property. Indeed, if the purpose of the covenant is to preserve not the value of the covenantee's land, but the amenities of the land, proof of value becomes irrelevant: *Heaton v. Loblay* (1960) 77 W.N. (N.S.W.) 140; *Re Cook* [1964] V.R. 808. There is authority that the court has jurisdiction under this limb to order extinguishment of an easement if it were replaced by another easement subject to suitable conditions: *Manly Properties Pty Ltd v. Castrisos* [1973] 2 N.S.W.L.R. 420; *Ex parte Proprietors of "Averil Court" Building Units Plan No. 2001* [1983] Qd R. 66 at 70. The two principal New South Wales cases, *Re Mason* (1960) 78 W.N. (N.S.W.) 925 and *Re Chamberlain* (1969) 90 W.N. (N.S.W.) (Pt 1) 585 have been extracted.

RE MASON AND THE CONVEYANCING ACT

Supreme Court of New South Wales (1960) 78 W.N. (N.S.W.) 925

[A restrictive covenant provided, inter alia, that no building of more than one storey and basement should be erected on the land. The applicant wished to erect home units in contravention of the covenant, and applied to the court for an order under s. 89 of the *Conveyancing Act* 1919 (N.S.W.) modifying the covenant. The land benefited by the covenants was higher adjoining land on which, at the time the covenant was entered into, was a single storey residence. By the time of the application, the residence had been replaced by a three storey block of home units owned by the plaintiff company; shareholders in the company were given rights to occupy the units. At the time the covenant was entered into, buildings on the surrounding land were predominantly single units of residence, but by the time of the application they were large three storey home unit blocks. Evidence was accepted that the erection of the proposed home units would decrease the value of the plaintiff company's land by £1,500 and further that some of the occupants of the company units would lose both their privacy and views.]

JACOBS J. [His Honour after stating the facts continued:] I therefore proceed, as I say, to the questions whether the covenant is obsolete or whether no practical benefit is secured to the persons entitled to the benefit of the restriction. . . .

First, upon the question whether this covenant is obsolete, I consider that the word "obsolete" can be taken to mean that the object of the covenant is now incapable of fulfilment or perhaps that it serves no present useful purpose. That brings me to the question: What is the object of this covenant? The immediate object of it was, of course, to preserve the privacy of and the views from the cottage residence erected upon No. 36 Pacific Highway. That cottage is now gone. However, I do not think that the covenant can be so narrowly limited in object. It must have a present usefulness if it preserves benefits to those entitled to No. 36 Pacific Highway or persons claiming under the owner of the fee simple, the company.

In the evidence, in which there is little real differences of opinion when it is finally analysed, the various experts have stated their views in regard particularly to the loss of view which would or would not occur by the erection of the home units on the subject land . . . I consider that the applicant is entitled to approach the matter by taking, as it were, the worst that could be done under the restrictions imposed by the covenant and to compare that with the effect that the proposed block of home units would have, and I have approached the matter in that way.

[His Honour then pointed out that the erection of a unit block would deprive some units of the plaintiff company of their view, and continued:]

. . . the substantive amenity of the view would be gone. Now, that being so, I do not consider that the covenant can be said to be obsolete. As I have said, and it seems to be vital in this case, it does not become obsolete because there are now home units instead of a residence. The land No. 36 when purchased by the present owners had the benefit of this covenant and it is not disputed that the effect of the erection of the block of home units would be to decrease the value of the premises No. 36 Pacific Highway by some £1,500. I cannot consider that, when there is that value in the covenant, it can be said that it is obsolete or that it serves no useful purpose or that it is out of date and incapable of fulfilment. That very fact seems to me to show that it is capable of fulfilment.

The same reasoning applies when one considers the question of practical benefit. For the reasons I have stated I consider that there is this practical benefit of securing the view across to the west and I can only conclude that the western balconies would have been built with the thought that there was a covenant in existence which would make them useful. . . . I consider that the loss of view and the loss of privacy to the first floor by the erection of the block of home units would be a substantial loss. To use the words without referring to the cases to which I have been carefully referred in the argument, I would find that this covenant does afford a real protection to those who are entitled to enforce it, that is to say, to the company No. 36 Pacific Highway Pty Ltd and to those claiming under the company.

Now, what I have said by my use of the word "substantial" deals also with the last matter to be considered, namely, whether the covenant could be modified without causing substantial injury. As I have said, I consider that there would be a substantial loss, a substantial injury. It has been submitted to me that the word "substantial" is a word which introduces a comparison between the disadvantage to the subject land and the disadvantage by modification of the covenant to the land having the benefit of the covenant I do not take this view of the meaning of the word "substantial". I consider in its context it does not mean large or considerable but it means an injury which has present substance; that is to say, not a theoretical injury but something which is real and which has a present substance. Mr Officer has pointed out that that view of the word means that very little is attained by para. (c) of s. 89(1). It would really cover the whole field of para. (a) without having to find change in user in land having the benefit or change in the character of the neighbourhood or other circumstance the court may deem material. I realise this fact, but I do not consider that the introduction of the word "substantial" at the end of a section which goes into very considerable detail on what must be found before relief can be granted can, as it were, open the field for the modification of covenants not on the ground that they serve no purpose or that they are obsolete, but on a ground whereby the court can compare the disadvantage to the land subject to the burden of the covenant with the disadvantage to the land benefited if the restriction were modified. This would change the whole nature of s. 89 as it has been applied in the cases, particularly the recent English cases to which I have been referred: *Re Ghey and Galton* [1957] 2 Q.B. 650; *Driscoll v. Church Commissioners for England* [1957] 1 Q.B. 330; *Re Truman, Hanbury, Buxton & Co. Ltd* [1956] 1 Q.B. 261. It is made clear in these cases that there is no general power given to the court to extinguish presently valuable rights of property. The purpose of the section is to enable covenants which have no practical utility to the land intended to be benefited to be removed and thus to clear the title. In other words, it is not a section which includes in any part of it any element of town planning. In the present case, if it were a question of town planning, I would feel that the degree of disadvantage to No. 36 Pacific Highway would be outweighed by the advantage accruing from a proper use of the subject land in accordance with the character of the neighbourhood, but I feel I cannot take that view and therefore, as I have said, I have no alternative but to dismiss the application.

It would seem to me that the factors which particularly have caused me to reach the conclusion which I have reached would not be present if it were proposed to limit the height of the intended building to a two storey block of home units. I have founded my conclusion to such a large extent upon the effect of this proposal on the first floor of No. 36 Pacific Highway that I doubt whether there is a sufficient distate left in the disadvantage from a loss of privacy to flats on the ground floor if there were erected a two storey building.

I order that the application be dismissed with costs.

RE CHAMBERLAIN AND THE CONVEYANCING ACT

Supreme Court of New South Wales (1969) 90 W.N. (Pt 1) (N.S.W.) 585

[Application was made under s. 89 of the *Conveyancing Act* 1919 (N.S.W.) for modification of a covenant affecting land owned by the applicants. The land burdened comprised two lots on which a boarding house stood; the home was at least 100 years old. The covenant provided that no more than one main building should be erected on each of the lots, that no main building or any other building so erected should be more than two storeys high, and that any main building so erected should not be used otherwise than as a dwelling house, duplex flats or a block of flats containing not more than four flats. The applicants wished to erect an eight storey home unit block and accordingly sought modification of the covenant. The owners of the land benefited opposed the application on the ground, inter alia, that the erection of a home unit block would deprive the occupants of flats erected on the land benefited of advantages and amenities presently enjoyed, namely, sunlight, privacy and absence of noise. In addition, it was argued that the proposed home unit block would make the flats erected on the land benefited less attractive for letting or sale. Evidence was accepted that there had been no change in the neighbourhood, nor had there been a change in user of the lands to which the benefit of the covenant was appurtenant. Evidence was also accepted that the only kind of development which could comply with both the existing covenants and current planning requirements would be a residential home using the whole land, two residential homes each using one block, or a duplex flat building on the whole land with one flat above the other.]

HELSHAM J. [His Honour after setting out the facts and the evidence of an owner of one of the two blocks of flats erected on the land benefited, continued:] She has given evidence of the practical benefits which she claims, as a person entitled to the benefit of the restrictions imposed by the covenant, are secured to her whilst those restrictions continue in existence, including privacy, absence of noise, absence of high buildings, and the absence of traffic. She says that she bought with knowledge of the covenant and desirous of retaining the advantages which she believes flow from it. I do not think that I should be too critical of her claims if they are genuine, as I believe they are, and provided they are not unreasonable. The proposed high-rise development as contrasted with development permitted by the covenant (to which I shall refer shortly) could result in deprivation to a greater or less extent of some or all of the advantages which she claims are practical benefits secured to her by the restrictions; probably the degree of deprivation, if any, would not be known until the building is erected. Providing the advantages which she claims to exist could be said to be practical benefits, and I think they could, I do not believe that I would be justified in preferring any conclusions of my own formed from a view of the area and the plans and the evidence for the somewhat subjective views which a person entitled to the benefit of the restrictions genuinely holds as to those advantages, providing those views are not unreasonable. The fact that I may have formed contrary views as to the degree to which the proposed development might interfere with privacy, noise, traffic and so on, which must involve subjective evaluation does not entitle me to substitute my views for those of a person who has for fifteen years enjoyed those aspects and who is entitled to retain them so far as the restrictions permit. In this respect I believe that my views are not dissonant with some expressed by Myers J. in *Re Parimax (S.A.) Pty Ltd* [1956] S.R. (N.S.W.) 130.

It is not necessary to rest my decision in this case solely upon the interference with the sensual aspects of the advantages enjoyed by an occupier of a flat entitled to the benefit of the restriction.

[His Honour then referred to the evidence that the erection of the building proposed would diminish the attractiveness of the flats for letting and sale and continued:]

[I]f the extinguishment of the restriction as to height would lessen the value to the owners of the business carried on on the land of the owners entitled to the benefit of it, or possible sale price of portions of the building erected thereon, then the retention of the restrictions seems to me to secure a practical benefit to the persons entitled to the benefit of the restriction. The fact that this benefit is not quantified does not mean that it can be given no consideration. Coupled with the sensual aspects enjoyed by one of such persons this seems to me to be enough to establish that the continued existence of the restriction does secure practical benefit to such persons.

It follows, I think, turning to the wording of s. 89(1)(c) and ignoring other difficulties that might lie in the path of an appellant seeking to rely upon this avenue of modification or extinguishment, that it cannot be said in this case that such modification as is sought would not substantially injure the persons entitled to the benefit of the restriction. Upon either count it is unnecessary in this case to be concerned with the relevance of interference to the enjoyment of their flats as the result of the proposal in the case of other tenants. There is evidence that some of them value their present amenities and fear their loss. Whether this is a matter that is of direct relevance or only through its effect upon the persons proved in this case to be entitled to the benefit of the restriction need not be decided here.

These conclusions, if they be right, are sufficient to defeat the application here. But for the sake of completeness I think I should express my views upon the evidence called with reference to the reasonable user of the land and one matter of law arising out of it. For the applicants must establish, in order to succeed under s. 89(1)(a), that the continued existence of the restriction would impede the reasonable user of their land.

[His Honour then referred to the permissible new development of the land in conformity with the covenant and planning restrictions and continued:]

It is said that the narrowing of possible use of the subject land can be used to the advantage of the applicants as a step in proving impediment to reasonable user; I agree. It is also said that it cannot be used to the advantage of the respondents in considering the practical benefit to them of the continued existence of the restriction; I disagree. It is claimed that it must be assumed that possible development by way of two storey four-flat buildings (of necessity close to the boundaries) not infringing the restriction is still available, that such development could bring in train all the disadvantages of the proposed high-rise development—or more—and that therefore the continued existence of the restriction secures no practical benefit. This argument follows the wording of Jacobs J., as he then was, in *Re Mason and the Conveyancing Act* (1960) 78 W.N. (N.S.W.) 925 at 927, where his Honour said: "I consider that the applicant is entitled to approach the matter by taking, as it were, the worst that could be done under the restrictions imposed by the covenant and to compare that with the effect that the proposed block of home units would have, and I have approached the matter in that way." In my view the court must look at the matter at the time of the application; if, for whatever reason possible, lawful conforming use of the subject land has dwindled, this may increase the impediment to reasonable user; but if the dwindling has enhanced the practical benefit of the restriction this may be relied upon by those seeking to retain its existence.

Leaving aside for the moment a continuation of the present user, there is again a conflict of evidence of the experts as to whether reasonable user of the subject land is open to an owner thereof in one of the three ways already mentioned. I accept Mr Ashwell on this aspect. He says there would be a demand for the land for use as a home site for one or two houses; for a duplex perhaps not so much as a house site. He bases his views on a price of the subject land of $65,000 (or $32,500 for each block) subject to the covenant. This figure is the improved capital value according to a Valuer-General's valuation as at February 1968 (U.C.V. $45,000); it is the only valuation which has been put before me in the case. While I can imagine cases in which the fact that land might be saleable for a very small price would be no evidence that the buyer's proposed use was a reasonable user, that is not the case here. In a wholly industrial area, to take an example, persons might be prepared to use land subject to a residential covenant for the purpose of a residence if the land could be acquired for a very small sum; this would not necessarily establish use for residential purposes as reasonable user. But there is nothing to suggest here that the valuation of $65,000 is wrong or false in any respect, and it is at this price that there would be a demand for the subject land as home sites. In my view that is sufficient to establish use for residential purposes subject to the covenant as reasonable user. In that case the continued existence of the restrictions does not impede the reasonable user of the subject land. It is nothing to the point to assert, as I think is established in this case, that freed from the covenant the value of the land would be such as to make high density residential development as home units essential in the hands of a purchaser.

Assuming that permissible user at the date of the application is the proper basis for the comparison which may be made between the effect of conforming user and the effect that the proposed block of home units or flats would have, there is nothing to suggest that new development in conformity with the restrictions in one of the three ways mentioned would deprive the persons having their benefit of any of the advantages which it is claimed are preserved thereby. Indeed I think it is tacitly assumed, and common sense would so indicate, that those practical benefits would be improved. So far as continuation of the present use of "Galway" is concerned, the retention of the house itself is as it were the fons et origo of the restrictions; its use is not said to have any adverse effect upon the benefits. Reasonable user of the subject land with the continued existence of the restrictions arising under the covenant will not therefore lessen the practical benefits; they are in fact secured by such continued existence.

For all these reasons I propose to dismiss the applications with costs.

Order accordingly.

SEVEN

MORTGAGES

I. THE NATURE OF A MORTGAGE

Traditionally, the mortgage has taken the form of an absolute conveyance of the property to the mortgagee (the lender) together with an agreement by which the mortgagor (the borrower) is entitled to "redeem", or obtain a reconveyance of, the property upon payment of the amount outstanding (the so-called "proviso for redemption"). Mortgages of old system land in Australia still take this form. Upon failure by the mortgagor to pay on the date specified for payment, the common law, in accordance with its policy of requiring strict adherence to time stipulations, regarded the rights of the mortgagor as at an end and the mortgagee's interest in the property as absolute and indefeasible.

A mortgage may be defined as follows:

> According to the modern concept, a "mortgage" is a conveyance, assurance, transfer, or assignment of real or personal property either operative at law or enforceable in equity, for the purpose of securing the payment of money or the performance of a monetary or pecuniary obligation in respect of which it is given. Its essential elements are two: first, the personal contract for the payment of the money or the performance of the obligation, and, secondly, the alienation, or at least the right of the mortgagee to procure the alienation, of the property: Francis, *Mortgages and Securities* (3rd ed.), p. 1.

A number of judicial definitions of "mortgage" will be found discussed in *Wilcox Mofflin Ltd v. Commissioner of Stamp Duties* [1978] 1 N.S.W.L.R. 341 at 346, 349.

Of course, despite its outward form, the intention with which the conveyance was executed was that it should be by way of security only. In time, equity intervened to give effect to the security nature of the transaction, and allowed the mortgagor to redeem after the due date for payment had passed. This was the so-called "equitable right to redeem", which was given effect to on the ground that once the mortgagee had been paid all principal and interest and any loss suffered by reason of late payment, he had received all that he had bargained for and it would be against good conscience for him to retain the property. Equity also developed the concept that the mortgagor retained an estate in the land (the so-called "equity of redemption"), which could be dealt with in the same way as any other estate in land. However, "[t]he equitable right to redeem, which arises on failure to exercise the contractual right of redemption, must be carefully distinguished from the equitable estate which, from the first, remains in the mortgagor": *Kreglinger v. New Patagonia Meat & Cold Storage Co. Ltd* [1914] A.C. 25 at 48. The history of the intervention of equity is traced in Sykes, *The Law of Securities* (4th ed.), pp. 50-52.

Equity looks to the substance of the transaction, rather than to its form, to determine whether it is intended to be a mortgage or an absolute conveyance. If it is in substance a mortgage, the mortgagor is entitled to redeem on repayment.

GURFINKEL v. BENTLEY PTY LTD
GURFINKEL v. PANIZZA

High Court of Australia (1966) 116 C.L.R. 98

[The plaintiff was the registered proprietor of land which was subject to two mortgages. He was in default under both, and the mortgagees were taking steps to sell the land by public auction. The plaintiff had for some time been endeavouring to persuade the defendant to lend him money to meet his obligations under the mortgages. Just prior to the auction an agreement in writing was entered into for the transfer of the land by the plaintiff to the defendant for £3,760 which was the approximate amount required to pay out the mortgages and to meet all expenses in connection therewith. By the agreement, the defendant undertook to carry on with the construction of a partly completed building on the land, and to expend not less than £1,240 in completing the building. It was further agreed that, in consideration of £10 paid by him to the defendant, the plaintiff should have an option of repurchasing the land for £5,500 exercisable within 12 months on giving one month's written notice. The agreement was signed by the plaintiff after he had consulted his solicitor. Out of the moneys so raised the plaintiff discharged the mortgages. He did not exercise the option but after the expiration of 12 months he brought an action against the defendant alleging that the transaction was one of loan and that the transfer was made merely to secure repayment of the loan. He alleged that the sum of £5,500 was made up of the amount of £3,760 plus the amount to be expended on the building, together with £500 by way of interest calculated at the rate of ten per cent per annum for one year, and claimed a declaration that he was entitled to redeem notwithstanding that the 12 month period had expired. The trial judge held that the transfer was intended to be by way of security only. The Full Court of the Supreme Court of Western Australia reversed the decision of the trial judge. On appeal.]

BARWICK C.J. (dissenting). The case, therefore, in its essentials is simple and the principles currently valid to be applied in its resolution are well documented in the law. The lands having been found to have been conveyed so as to form a security for money lent, the transfers, though absolute in form and though expressed to be executed for a price paid as distinct from money lent, will be regarded in equity as but mortgages of the land. Thus, though there be no contractual right to redeem at all, the borrower will have in equity a right of redemption. If in such a case there be a contractual right of repurchase, equity will none the less decree redemption, though the borrower has not met the contractual terms for repurchase. On the other hand, if no more is known than that land is conveyed with a right of repurchase, the conveyance will not be regarded as a mortgage nor the party with the right of repurchase accorded redemption. He will be confined to the exercise of his option to repurchase according to its precise terms. Here, . . . there was, in my opinion, in substance, an express finding [by the trial judge], not derived merely from the circumstances that the conveyance was accompanied by an option to repurchase, that the conveyances were intended by both parties to be by way of security only. The existence of the option to repurchase does not militate against that conclusion nor is it inconsistent with it. Indeed, it may quite consistently be regarded as the contractual right of redemption mutually agreed by the parties. . . .

It is beyond question that oral evidence will be admitted to determine with what intention the parties entered into a writing which is a sale or a conveyance of land. This is not an exception to the rule that oral evidence will not be admitted to contradict or vary a writing into which the parties have reduced their entire agreement for the very question at issue is whether the parties have made the writing the expression of their whole agreement or of their mutual intention. Also, a sale or conveyance is a common means of providing security. Thus, the intention with which parties enter into the sale or conveyance becomes an issue to be resolved by evidence, whether oral or documentary. It cannot be resolved merely by resort to the conveyance for the mutual intention to use the document as security, if it exists, by hypothesis lies dehors that instrument. . . .

The critical question in the case was "with what mutual intention did the parties execute the transfer" bearing in mind in deciding that question that the transferee will not be allowed to hold the transfer as absolute, if at the time of taking it he knows that the transferor intends it to be by way of security only and he allows him to execute with that understanding on his part: see, for example, *Douglas v. Culverwell* (1862) 4 De G.F. & J. 20 at 23; 45 E.R. 1089 at 1091. Of course, proof of an antecedent agreement of loan upon security followed by execution of the transfers without any change in circumstances meantime would be enough to establish the mutual intention. But absence of such an agreement does not mean that at the time of execution the parties did not have the mutual intention that the execution of the transfer was by way of security or that at that time the transferor to the knowledge of the transferee intended the execution by way of security only and was allowed to sign it with that intention.

The Full Court spoke of an "agreement to lend money . . . on the security of a mortgage". If by this the Full Court meant that it was necessary that an agreement binding the respondent Panizza to lend money should be proved to exist before the execution of the transfer, I would respectfully disagree that such an agreement was necessary. It would be sufficient that the parties at the time of execution mutually contemplated a lending transaction, though there be no antecedent enforceable obligation to lend. . . .

In my opinion, there was ample evidence to support the finding of the learned trial judge. . . .

WINDEYER J. In my opinion these appeals should be dismissed . . . I appreciate that certain incidents of the transaction between Gurfinkel and Panizza are incidents which ordinarily are more likely to be accompaniments of a conveyance by way of mortgage than of a conveyance on a sale. But none of them precludes the present transaction being in fact and in law what the document the parties executed states it to be, a sale with a right of repurchase. They do not, it seems to me, in the circumstances of this case of themselves shew that both parties intended the transaction to be not what they expressed it to be but something different.

"As regards their legal incidents, there is all the difference in the world between a mortgage and a sale with a right of repurchase. But if the transaction is completed by redemption or repurchase as the case may require there is no difference in the actual result." Lord Macnaghten said that in *Manchester, Sheffield and Lincolnshire Railway Co. v. North Central Wagon Co.* (1888) 13 App. Cas. 554 at 567, 568. He went on to say (1888) 13 App. Cas. 554 at 568: "In all these cases the question is what was the real intention of the parties? As Lord Cranworth observed in a case where the documents were of a more formal character, 'The rule of law on this subject is one dictated by common sense; that prima facie an absolute conveyance, containing nothing to shew that the relation of debtor and creditor is to exist between the parties, does not cease to be an absolute conveyance and become a mortgage merely because the vendor stipulates that he shall have a right to repurchase' ": *Alderson v. White* (1858) 2 De G. & J. 97 at 105; 44 E.R. 924 at 928.

It is not enough that Gurfinkel approached Panizza for financial assistance to get him out of his difficulties and that Panizza came to his rescue. "A conditional sale is not a mortgage simply because both parties enter into the transaction in the confident expectation that the purchaser will take advantage of the condition, and that the final result will be the same as if they had agreed to reach that end by the road of mortgage": per Cave J. in *Beckett v. Tower Assets Co.* [1891] 1 Q.B. 1 at 25. Gurfinkel did not exercise his option to repurchase in accordance with the condition stipulated in the agreement. Panizza has thus been able to obtain the property at much less than its true value, Gurfinkel (or his creditors, he being bankrupt) being the loser. But that does not mean that the transaction was not what the parties expressed it to be.

It has of course long been the law that parol evidence is admissible to shew that a conveyance, absolute in its terms, was intended by both parties to be by way of security only. That was perhaps more easily shewn in earlier times when, as Maitland has said, a mortgage deed was "one long suppressio veri and suggestio falsi" than it is today, especially in the case of land held under the Torrens system. In 1750 Lord Hardwicke could say: "There is indeed a distinction in the nature of the transaction, between a power of redeeming and of repurchasing, obtained by usage, which governs the sense of words. But it is well known that the court leans extremely against contracts of this kind, where the liberty of repurchasing is made at the same time, concomitant with the grant, as it must be considered in this case; being part of the same transaction; the court going very unwillingly into that distinction, and endeavouring if possible to bring them to be cases of redemption": *Longuet v. Scawen* (1750) 1 Ves. Sen. 402 at 405, 406; 27 E.R. 1106 at 1108.

But the law has moved on since then. The attitude of the Court of Chancery in the mid 18th century does not I think justify a court in the mid 20th century endeavouring to find that a bargain is not as the parties expressed it. A court will now ordinarily take at their word persons who execute agreements for sale at a price with an option of repurchase within a stipulated time: *Rowe v. Oades* (1905) 3 C.L.R. 73.

Of course if it can be shewn by parol evidence that both parties to a document adopted the form they did as a disguise, then their true intent and not the form will prevail. Thus agreements that were in form sales have sometimes been held to be mortgages when the form of a sale had been adopted as a disguise: for example, in *Douglas v. Culverwell* (1862) 4 De G.F. & J. 20; 45 E.R. 1089, the purported sale at a price which preceded the conveyance was—Turner L.J. said (at 28; 1093)— "contemplated merely as a device for securing to the defendant usurious interest" (that is, a rate of interest more than the law then allowed). Similarly in *Williams v. Owen* (1840) 5 Myl. & Cr. 303; 41 E.R. 386, Lord Cottenham, holding that what had occurred was a sale with a proviso for repurchase and not a mortgage, distinguished the case of *Baker v. Wind* (1748) 1 Ves. Sen. 160; 27 E.R. 956, which had been relied upon because there, he said, "it was proved that the parties had throughout treated the transaction as a mortgage and had made it assume the appearance of a purchase to deceive the creditors of the mortgagor" (1840) 5 Myl. & Cr. at 308; 41 E.R. at 388. In the present case the transaction between the parties was put into writing. The writing was approved by the legal advisers of each. After the action had been commenced on the basis that the writing meant what it said the plaintiff changed his ground and said that the parties always intended a different transaction. But the evidence does not, in my view, enable this to be said. They are,

I consider, bound by the terms of their document. I do not think it necessary to discuss all the cases that were referred to in the course of the argument. I add to them *Rees v. Guardian Trust & Executors Co. of New Zealand Ltd* [1956] N.Z.L.R. 340 at 344, 345. The conclusion of the Full Court was in my opinion correct. I would dismiss the appeals.

[Menzies and Owen JJ. in separate judgments came to the same conclusions as Windeyer J. on the facts; McTiernan J. agreed with Barwick C.J.]

Appeal dismissed.

NOTES

1. For other examples of the considerations to be taken into account in determining whether the transaction is a mortgage or an absolute conveyance or transfer, see *Danby v. Read* (1675) Rep. Temp. Finch 226; 23 E.R. 124; *Croft v. Powell* (1738) 2 Comyns 603; 92 E.R. 1230; *Williams v. Owen* (1840) 5 My. & Cr. 303; 41 E.R. 386; *Muttyloll Seal v. Annundochunder Sandle* (1849) 5 Moo. Ind. App. 72; 18 E.R. 822; *Waters v. Mynn* (1850) 15 L.T.O.S. 157; *Lincoln v. Wright* (1859) 4 De G. & J. 16; 45 E.R. 6; *Re Watson* (1890) 25 Q.B.D. 27; *Marquess of Northampton v. Salt* [1892] A.C. 1; *Mason v. Island Air Pty Ltd* (1983) A.N.Z. Conv. R. 136; *Road Chalets Pty Ltd v. Thornton Motors Pty Ltd* (1986) 47 S.A.S.R. 532: see also *Kreglinger v. New Patagonia Meat and Cold Storage Co. Ltd* [1914] A.C. 25 at 35-36, 46, 47, extracted below p. 412.

2. It will be important to distinguish between mortgages and other forms of security over land or chattels. The remedies available to the lender will vary depending upon the form of security chosen. In this chapter mortgages only are dealt with. For a comparison between mortgages and other forms of securities, such as charges, pledges and liens, see Francis, op. cit., pp. 3-8; Sykes, op. cit., Chs 6 and 8.

II. CREATION OF MORTGAGES

A. LEGAL MORTGAGE OF FREEHOLD LAND UNDER OLD SYSTEM TITLE

The form of the mortgage of freehold land under old system title has been outlined in the previous section: above p. 389.

To be effective at law, a mortgage of land under old system title must be by deed: see *Conveyancing Act* 1919 (N.S.W.), s. 23B.

In New South Wales (unlike some other States) there is no statutory short form of mortgage, but there is a statutory short form of conveyance which it may be possible to adapt to the form of conveyance by way of mortgage, by the insertion of a proviso for reconveyance and any special covenants desired: see Sykes, op. cit., pp. 43-44; *Conveyancing Act* 1919 (N.S.W.), s. 43 and Second Schedule.

Under s. 78(1)(C) of the *Conveyancing Act*, there are implied into conveyances by way of mortgage, where the mortgagor conveys "as beneficial owner", the so-called covenants for title. By these, the mortgagor covenants that he has full power to convey the property; that upon default under the mortgage, the mortgagee may take possession and this possession will not be disturbed lawfully by the mortgagor or any other person; that the property is free from encumbrances and claims; and that he will do whatever may be reasonably required to perfect the mortgagee's title to the property.

B. LEGAL MORTGAGE OF LEASEHOLDS UNDER OLD SYSTEM TITLE

1. By assignment

A mortgage of a leasehold interest in old system land may be effected by an assignment of the term with a proviso for re-assignment upon repayment on the due date. As with the mortgage of a freehold interest, equity recognises the mortgagor's equity of redemption, and also permits redemption after expiry of the contractual date for repayment.

The disadvantage of a mortgage of a leasehold by assignment is that the mortgagee, as assignee of the lease, becomes liable on the covenants in the lease: see below p. 618 et seq.

2. By sub-lease

As an alternative to mortgage by assignment, a leasehold interest may be mortgaged by way of sub-lease with a proviso for the mortgagee to surrender the sub-lease upon repayment of the debt. This has the advantage that the mortgagee, as sub-lessee, is not liable on the covenants in the head-lease. It is, however, subject to two disadvantages: (1) should the head-lease be forfeited for breach of covenant by the mortgagor or lessee, the sublease would fall with it; (2) the mortgagor still holds the reversion expectant on the sub-lease, with the result that the mortgagee, should he wish to exercise his power of sale, cannot vest the whole leasehold interest in a purchaser.

The first disadvantage is alleviated to some extent by statutory provisions empowering the court to grant relief to a sub-lessee upon forfeiture of the head-lease: see below p. 655. The second disadvantage is overcome by s. 112(2) of the *Conveyancing Act* 1919 (N.S.W.), under which a mortgagee by demise in exercise of his power of sale (as to which, see below) has power to convey the reversion held by the mortgagor. Were it not for such a provision, the mortgagee would have to adopt the device of having the mortgagor declare himself trustee of the reversion for the mortgagee (see *London and County Banking Co. v. Goddard* [1897] 1 Ch. 642 at 650), and enabling the mortgagee to obtain a vesting order under ss 70 and 71 of the *Trustee Act* 1925 (N.S.W.) in the event of default by the mortgagor: see further, Sykes, op. cit., pp. 334-339.

C. EQUITABLE MORTGAGES

1. Mortgage of the equity of redemption in old system land

Once a legal mortgage has been given over old system land, any further mortgage must be of the equity of redemption, and is, therefore, equitable. As each mortgage is given, a new equity of redemption arises which, in turn, can be mortgaged. There is no limit to the number of mortgages which can be given in this fashion, although, because later mortgages generally are subject to earlier mortgages, they become decreasingly attractive to investors.

A mortgage of the equity of redemption is in the same form as a legal mortgage (that is, a conveyance of the equitable interest, with a proviso for reconveyance upon due payment). It must be in writing, but need not be by deed: *Conveyancing Act* 1919 (N.S.W.), s. 23C(1)(a), (c).

2. Executory agreement to grant a legal mortgage

Under the maxim, "equity regards as done that which ought to be done", an agreement for consideration to grant a legal mortgage creates a mortgage in equity. For example, there may be an attempt to create a legal mortgage, but it is ineffective because the requisite formalities for a deed have not been observed; provided that the money has been advanced, an equitable mortgage is created: *Taylor v. Wheeler* (1707) 2 Salk. 449; 91 E.R. 388. Again, the documentation may not take the form of a legal mortgage at all, but an equitable mortgage will be created where the powers conferred on the lender are consistent with an intention to give a mortgage, as where a creditor is given a power of attorney to receive the rents and profits from the debtor's land until repayment of the debt: *Spooner v. Sandilands* (1842) 1 Y. & C. Ch. 390; 62 E.R. 939. For further examples, see *Re Cook* (1821) 1 Gl. & J. 12; *Craddock v. Scottish Provident Institution* (1893) 69 L.T. 380; *Eyre v. McDowall* (1861) 9 H.L.C. 619; 11 E.R. 871.

ROGERS v. CHALLIS

High Court of Chancery (1859) 27 Beav. 175; 54 E.R. 68

[By an agreement in writing, the plaintiff had agreed to lend to the defendant, and the defendant had agreed to borrow, the sum of £1,000 with interest at 10 per cent per annum on the security of certain property. Later, the defendant refused to perform the agreement, having obtained money elsewhere on better terms. The plaintiff sought specific performance of the agreement.]

SIR JOHN ROMILLY M.R. The case cannot be put higher than this: that the defendant applies to the plaintiff for the loan of £1,000 upon a security which he specifies, and the plaintiff assents to the proposal, but on the next day the defendant says: "I have changed my mind, I do not require your £1,000, I can get it upon better terms elsewhere." Is that a case in which a person can come to this court for a specific performance, and say: "You, the defendant, are bound to let me advance the £1,000 to you—it is true your circumstances may be altered, but you are bound to let me advance the money to you?" It is very justly said that the *Statute of Frauds* does not apply to such a case; therefore, if the court has jurisdiction in such a case, any conversation may be made the subject of a suit for specific performance: thus, if two friends are walking together, and one says, "Will you lend me £100, at 5 per cent for a year upon good security", and the other says, "I will", that conversation might be made the subject of a suit for specific performance in this court, if on the next day one friend should say, "I do not want the money", or the other should say, "I will not lend it". Nothing would be more difficult and more dangerous than the task which this court would have to perform, if it were to investigate cases of that description. This is not an agreement to purchase or sell anything, it is not the case of a contract to buy a particular debt upon certain terms, or a contract for the purchase of a certain quantity of goods, to be paid for by instalments and in a particular manner, in which case the court has held that these were circumstances which took the transaction out of the rule of this court, that an ordinary contract for the sale or purchase of goods is not the proper subject of a suit for specific performance in this court. It is nothing more than this: a proposal to borrow a certain sum of money, upon certain terms, for a certain time, which is accepted, and the borrower says two or three days afterwards, I do not want the money, and I have got it elsewhere, upon better terms. It certainly is new to me, that this court has ever entertained jurisdiction in a case where the only personal obligation created is, that one person says, if you will lend me the money I will repay it and give you good security, and the terms are settled between them. The court has said that the reason for compelling a specific performance of a contract is because the remedy at law is inadequate or defective. But by what possibility can it be said that the remedy here is inadequate or defective? It is a simple money demand; the plaintiff says, I have sustained a pecuniary loss by my money remaining idle, and by my not getting so good an investment for it as you contracted to give me. This is a mere matter of calculation, and a jury would easily assess the amount of the damage which the plaintiff has sustained.

Suit dismissed.

NOTE

In *Durkowyak v. Durkowyak* (1981) 7 Fam. L.R. 1002 at 1008, Powell J. said:

> While, if, in pursuance of an agreement to lend money on a security to be given, the contemplated loan is then made, equity would treat the lender as being, in fact, secured (see, for example, *Re Strand Music Hall Co.* (1865) 3 De G.J. & Sm. 147; 46 E.R. 594; *Re Queensland Land & Coal Co.*; *Davis v. Martin* [1894] 3 Ch. 181; *Pegge v. Neath and District Tramways Co. Ltd* [1898] 1 Ch. 183; *Simultaneous Colour Printing Syndicate v. Foweraker* [1901] 1 K.B. 771; *Re Mount Tomah Blue Metals Ltd* (*in liq.*) [1963] A.L.R. 346) and, if its aid is invoked, the court will order the execution and delivery of the appropriate instrument of security (*Ashton v. Corrigan* (1871) L.R. 13 Eq. 76; *Hermann v. Hodges* (1873) L.R. 16 Eq. 18) the court would not, I think, enforce an agreement to borrow, even on security, if the intending borrower declined to accept the preferred loan; at best, so it seems to me, the intending lender's remedy would be an action for damages.

WIGHT v. HABERDAN PTY LTD

Supreme Court of New South Wales [1984] 2 N.S.W.L.R. 280

[The plaintiff, Wight, had entered into a contract to purchase land (the Haberdan land) from the first defendant, Haberdan Pty Ltd (Haberdan). The land adjoined other land (the Bowd Farm land) being purchased by Wight, who intended to subdivide the two parcels into seven smaller lots for sale. Wight approached the second defendant, Beneficial Finance (Beneficial), for mortgage finance to enable him to complete the purchase of the two parcels of land. Beneficial advanced a sum of money to enable Wight to complete the purchase of the Bowd Farm land, but refused to advance the further funds required to enable him to complete the purchase of the Haberdan land. Wight had received a notice to complete from the vendor of the Haberdan land, calling upon him to complete the contract upon pain of termination of the contract.

Kearney J. held that there existed a contract between Beneficial and Haberdan by which Beneficial had agreed to advance a sum of money to enable Wight to complete the purchase of the Haberdan land. A second question then arose for decision, namely, whether Wight could obtain an order for specific performance of that contract.]

KEARNEY J.: As to question (2), there is no doubt that the general rule is that a contract to lend money cannot be specifically enforced either by the proposed borrower or the proposed lender, and that it is immaterial whether the loan is to be with or without security: see *Ashburner on Equity* (2nd ed.), p. 390; Meagher, Gummow and Lehane, *Equity Doctrines and Remedies* (2nd ed.), para. 2010, p. 478. This rule stands upon the authority, inter alia, of the decision of the House of Lords in *South African Territories Ltd v. Wallington* [1898] A.C. 309, and the authorities referred to in the more recent decision of the Privy Council in *Loan Investment Corp. (Aust.) Ltd v. Bonner* [1970] N.Z.L.R. 724.

The rule is generally accepted to be founded upon the proposition that in the case of such an agreement damages are an adequate remedy, that is, that the complaining party's proper remedy lies at law. It is in relation to this rule generally rather than to the limited technical aspect of it mentioned by me in my decision of 6 April that I determine the matter.

The circumstances emerging from the evidence show that the agreement has been fully performed by the plaintiff, who furthermore has spent some $25,000 on the project. It is clear that a subdivision approval has been granted to a seven lot subdivision embracing the combined areas. It further appears that the plaintiff has mortgaged to Beneficial for the purposes of the agreement all assets available to him. It further appears that the subject lands are the only lands in the immediate vicinity above the flood level and therefore suitable for building purposes. It is further apparent that the plaintiff from the outset on his approach to Beneficial intended that the development should be of the combined area and this was known to Beneficial, not only from what the plaintiff said but also from documents provided to it. . . . .

It further seems that the plaintiff had pre-existing approval from his bank but was persuaded to deal with Beneficial on the footing that the matter would proceed in the stages as outlined to him by [officers of Beneficial] so that any further application for finance to complete the Haberdan purchase would be a formality, the initial application being structured so as to meet the guidelines of Beneficial at that stage of the transaction. It is further to be noted that when the time came for the Haberdan purchase to be completed Beneficial treated the provision of the additional funds as "[a]n increase in your existing advance", and did so without the necessity for any fresh application to be made.

Now, it may be noted that the general rule against the granting of specific performance on a contract to lend money is not founded upon any philosophical objection to such an order being made where it entails a mere payment of money. This is illustrated in the decision in *Turner v. Bladin* (1951) 82 C.L.R. 463 where the equitable doctrine of mutuality was invoked to found an order for specific performance at the suit of a vendor seeking merely the payment of the purchase price under a contract for sale of land. A further illustration emerges from the following passage in the speech of Lord Wilberforce in *Miliangos v. George Frank (Textiles) Ltd* [1976] A.C. 443 at 467: "In *Beswick v. Beswick* [1968] A.C. 58 this House laid down that in a suitable case specific performance may be ordered of an agreement to pay a sum of money of the United Kingdom. Lord Pearce (at 89) quoted from *Hart v. Hart* (1881) 18 Ch. D. 670, 685, the words: 'when an agreement for valuable consideration . . . has been partially performed, the court ought to do its utmost to carry out that agreement by a decree for specific performance.' "

Again, the High Court in *Coulls v. Bagot's Executor & Trustee Co. Ltd* (1967) 119 C.L.R. 460 invoked the fact that damages would not be an adequate remedy in considering the question of whether an agreement for payment could be specifically enforced.

In relation to the question of whether damages are an adequate remedy the true rule requires in my view consideration of the circumstances of the particular case in hand. The test is, in my view, whether by leaving a plaintiff to a remedy in damages justice is done. In other words, the question to be determined is whether such a remedy in damages is adequate to satisfy the demands of justice. In the present instance it is obvious that if the plaintiff is left to pursue common law claims for damages the most complex questions will arise. There will be necessarily difficult questions as to the measure of damages and the remoteness of damage. There will be obviously great delay and expense and at the end of the day the question of what damages could be awarded would, in my view, be extremely difficult, if not virtually impossible, to assess with reasonable accuracy. After all, the rule under which a plaintiff is left to his remedy in damages is founded on an assumption of fact, as was pointed out by Barwick C.J. in *Bonner's* case where his Honour says (at 742): "No doubt the general assumption is that damages for breach of a mere promise to lend money adequately compensates the would be borrower. But, in my opinion, that assumption of fact is not necessarily of universal validity and, again in my opinion, must yield in any case when in fact in the particular circumstances damages would not do justice between the parties. So it seems to me that equity in the more complicated situations of the modern world may well yet find an occasion when justice can only be done in relation to a contract merely to lend money by ordering its specific performance."

Following his Honour's train of thought, the complications involved in the plaintiff being left to pursue a claim for damages in this instance are so monumental and the prospects of an adequate recovery are so remote as to render such a course an unjust imposition upon the plaintiff: see *Vandeventer v. Dale Construction Co.* 534 P. 2d 183 (1975).

Again, in the circumstances such as exist, in the present instance there is not only the factor of damages being on the face of the matter inadequate, but also such circumstances are apt to render Beneficial's primary obligation an obligation to perform the agreement. I consider that the following statement of Windeyer J. in *Coulls'* case (at 504) fits the present case: "The primary obligation of a party to a contract is to perform it, to keep his promise. That is what the law requires of him. If he fails to do so, he incurs a liability to pay damages. That however is the ancillary remedy for his violation of the other party's primary right to have him carry out his promise. It is, I think, a faulty analysis of legal obligations to say that the law treats a promisor as having a right to elect either to perform his promise or to pay damages. Rather, using one sentence from the passage of Lord Erskine's judgment which I have quoted above, the promisee has 'a legal right to the performance of the contract'."

See also Heydon, Gummow and Austin, *Equity and Trusts* (2nd ed.), para. 3817 at 806, 807, where the learned authors point to the watershed effect of the decision in *Beswick v. Beswick* [1968] A.C. 58 and the dicta in *Coulls'* case in treating specific performance of a contract as being a remedial entitlement unless displaced by the particular circumstances of the case. Finally on this point, there is the well-known statement of Kay J. in *Hart v. Hart* (1881) 18 Ch. D. 670 at 685: "when an agreement for valuable consideration . . . has been partially performed, the court ought to do its utmost to carry out that agreement by a decree for specific performance", which was quoted with approval in *Beswick v. Beswick*.

These circumstances clearly indicate that the subject agreement formed part of a larger transaction between the parties which was intended to avoid the necessity for a separate and independent transaction relating to the further advance. The blended transaction was clearly intended to turn to account as part of a single enterprise both parcels of land.

The plaintiff was persuaded by the initial representations by Beneficial's officers to embark upon his venture with the assurance of Beneficial's backing. Beneficial has performed the first limb of the transaction, and by performing the second limb up to within a few days of the time of the essence deadline for completion of this Haberdan contract, has led the plaintiff to commit himself irreversibly to complete performance of this whole transaction between them. Beneficial's last minute repudiation of its contract with the plaintiff leaves him exposed to the threatened rescission of the Haberdan contract without any realistic chance to prevent it. This in turn spells the collapse of the plaintiff's enterprise.

Even assuming that the plaintiff can avert rescission of the Haberdan contract, the position in which the plaintiff would be left if specific performance were denied him, is that he is locked into the mortgages granted to Beneficial securing the Bowd Farm advance, and left obviously, unless at ruinous expense he can refinance the whole transaction, without the resources which would be necessary to enable him to obtain finance elsewhere. . . .

In short, the circumstances create an exception to the general rule, and warrant the conclusion that specific performance ought to be ordered.

Orders accordingly.

3. Mortgage by deposit of title deeds

Equity regards the deposit of the title deeds to a property by way of security for an advance as evidence of an agreement to grant a mortgage over the property; therefore, an equitable mortgage arises. The principle applies to both old system and Torrens title land (for an example of the latter, see *J. & H. Just (Holdings) Pty Ltd v. Bank of New South Wales* (1971) 125 C.L.R. 546, extracted above p. 147). The mortgage can by discharged only by repayment of the debt (*Bank of New South Wales v. O'Connor* (1889) 14 App. Cas. 273 at 282), and the mortgagee is entitled to keep the title deeds until repayment or other extinguishment of the debt: *Re Molton Finance Ltd* [1968] Ch. 325 at 333. Writing is not necessary, as the act of deposit of the deeds with the lender is regarded as a sufficient act of part performance to take the transaction out of the *Statute of Frauds* and its latter-day equivalents.

However, title deeds are, in themselves, merely chattels, and it is open to the borrower to show that what was intended to be given was a security over the deeds as chattels and not an interest in the land which they represent.

SWANLEY COAL CO. v. DENTON

Court of Appeal [1906] 2 K.B. 873

[By a bill of sale, the defendant as mortgagor assigned to the mortgagee "all and singular the several chattels and things specifically described in the schedule hereto annexed and now being in and about the dwelling-house and premises known as the Lion Hotel Farningham in the county of Kent". The bill of sale gave the mortgagee the power, upon default by the mortgagor, to seize and sell by auction the "chattels and things" assigned.

The schedule to the bill of sale contained a long list of articles in and about the hotel, and concluded with the following: "Assignment dated 24 January 1902 . . . of lease . . . of the said Lion Hotel Farningham Kent aforesaid and all the muniments of title referred to in the said assignment." However, it had been held that a bill of sale which purported to confer a security over "chattels real" was void: *Cochrane v. Entwhistle* (1890) 25 Q.B.D. 116.

The question before the court was whether the inclusion in the schedule to the bill of sale of the assignment of the lease of the hotel and the title deeds thereto rendered the bill of sale void. The county court judge held that the bill of sale did not create any charge on the property the subject matter of the deeds. The Divisional Court reversed his decision, holding that the bill of sale, by including in the schedule the deeds in question, created an equitable charge on the land and was void. On appeal.]

ROMER L.J. The whole question really turns on the true construction of this bill of sale so far as concerns the title deeds mentioned in the schedule. If the effect of the bill of sale was to create a charge on the land the subject matter of the title deeds, then the appellant is clearly wrong. If, on the other hand, the effect of the bill of sale was not to create a charge on the land but only to pledge the title deeds as documents, then the appellant is right. For although title deeds savour of realty and are the symbols, if I may so describe it, of the land to which they relate in the hands of the owner, yet it is quite possible for the owner to sever the title deeds from the land and to deal with them as so many pieces of paper and pledge them accordingly; and in that case they come within the description in the *Bills of Sale Act* 1878 (U.K.), s. 4, of "articles capable of complete transfer by delivery". I am far from saying that the documents themselves would be valueless in the hands of the pledgee, for though the mere documents may have little or no intrinsic value, they might have a value to the pledgee inasmuch as the owner of the land might wish to recover them, and would be forced to pay the pledgee to get them back. Therefore the question is, was it intended to create a charge on the land or was it only intended to give a charge on the documents not as charging the land but as conferring by virtue of the assignment under the bill of sale the right to hold the documents for what they were worth. Now seeing that the title deeds savour of realty and are the symbols of the land to which they relate, I quite agree that in an ordinary case you might well infer an intention to give a charge on the land, though the instrument itself might only refer to the title deeds and not to the land, or though there might be no instrument at all. Take first the case where no instrument is used at all, the case of an owner merely pledging the title deeds to secure an advance, and nothing more. I should infer that the object and interest of that transaction was to charge the land; and further, I have no doubt that if the owner of the land possessing the deeds were to retain them and were to sign an instrument declaring in that instrument that he held the deeds as security for the sum advanced, I should again infer that the object was to charge the land; and similar cases might be given. But after all it is a question of what is to be inferred from a consideration of the instrument and the surrounding circumstances. Now, having made these preliminary observations, I will shortly deal with the bill of sale itself. In the first place it is something to be borne in mind that it is a bill of sale. I do not think that is a circumstance to be overlooked. It is a document purporting to be a bill of sale securing money advanced upon chattels and things. And if you look at the assignment you find that what is assigned is nothing but what is described as "chattels and things". Then if you turn to the schedule all the items except the last are undoubtedly chattels of the ordinary kind. Then you come to this last item, and how is that item described? It is described as an assignment by certain persons to certain others there enumerated of the lease of a certain house and the title deeds referred to in that assignment. In my opinion what is there referred to is a document. The assignment must be a document. It is a document which follows a whole series of chattels in a bill of sale, which one would expect to deal only with chattels, and which in the assignment describes the subject matter of the bill of sale as chattels and things. The matter does not stop there because there is a power of sale, and when one reads that power of sale it is difficult to suppose that it was intended to cover the land itself. It would clearly be departing from the words of that power of sale if you were to attempt to include in it anything except the chattels properly so called, that is to say, if you were to attempt to include in it the land itself. Taking the instrument as a whole, I ask myself this: Suppose the bill of sale holder had immediately after its execution come to a court of equity and claimed a charge on the land itself, would he have succeeded? In my opinion he would not. I think the court would have come to the conclusion on the instrument as a whole, having regard to what I have already said, that it was not the intention of the parties as appearing from this instrument that any charge should be created on the land itself, and that the mortgagee was not justified in asserting that he had a charge on the land. Therefore the appeal succeeds, with the usual consequences.

[Vaughan Williams L.J. came to the same conclusion as Romer L.J. Cozens-Hardy L.J. dissented, agreeing with the view taken by the Divisional Court.]

Appeal allowed.

NOTES AND QUESTIONS

1. The presumption of the creation of an equitable mortgage over the property represented by the title deeds may be rebutted by proving that the deposit was not for the purpose of giving a security: see *Norris v. Wilkinson* (1805) 12 Ves. 192; 33 E.R. 73, where the evidence established that the debtor's title deeds had been deposited with the creditor's solicitor not for the purpose of conferring an immediate security over the land, but to enable the solicitor to prepare a mortgage to be signed at a later date.

2. It is no bar to the creation of a mortgage by deposit of title deeds that the debt they secure is owed not by the owner of the deeds but by a third party: *Re Wallis and Simmonds (Builders) Ltd* [1974] 1 W.L.R. 391.

3. Equity implies into an equitable mortgage an obligation to pay interest, unless there is evidence of an agreement to the contrary: *Mendl v. Smith* (1943) 112 L.J. Ch. 279.

4. As to the duty of a mortgagor under an equitable mortgage by deposit of title deeds, consider the following remarks of Dean J. in *Ryan v. O'Sullivan* [1956] V.L.R. 99 at 100:

   I do not think it is true to say that an equitable mortgage by deposit of title deeds carries an implied obligation on the part of the mortgagor to execute a legal mortgage, notwithstanding what was said by Sir Charles Pepys M.R. in *Parker v. Housefield* (1834) 2 My. & K. 419; 39 E.R. 1004, and by other judges whom he quotes: see *Ashburner on Equity* (2nd ed.), pp. 194-195; *Fisher and Lightwood's Law of Mortgage* (7th ed.), p. 18; *Ashburner on Mortgages* (2nd ed.), pp. 23-24; *Coote on Mortgages* (9th ed.), p. 88. In *Sporle v. Whayman* (1855) 20 Beav. 607; 52 E.R. 738, Sir John Romilly M.R. refused to decree the execution of a legal mortgage in the absence of proof that this was intended by the parties. I think the obligation on the mortgagor is to do all that is necessary to vest the legal title in the mortgagee in case of default and to give the mortgagee all the rights he would have if the mortgage were legal: see *Pryce v. Bury* (1853) 2 Drew. 41; 130 E.R. 968. The remedy of the mortgagee should correspond as nearly as possible with those of legal mortgagees.

5. Can one only of a number of joint tenants create a mortgage by deposit of title deeds? Does it matter that the mortgage purports to affect only her or his own interest in the property rather than the whole of the property? See *Thames Guaranty Ltd v. Campbell* [1984] 3 W.L.R. 109.

6. Where the land is under old system title, there may be many "title deeds" to the property, extending back over many years. Some may have been lost or destroyed. What title deeds must be deposited to create a mortgage by deposit of title deeds? See *Goodwin v. Waghorn* (1835) 4 L.J. (N.S.) Ch. 172.

D. MORTGAGES OF LAND UNDER TORRENS TITLE

A mortgage of land under Torrens title takes effect as a statutory charge or security only, and not as a transfer of the land mortgaged: see *Real Property Act* 1900 (N.S.W.), s. 57(1). "It confers an *interest* but no *estate*": *Robert Reid & Co. v. Minister for Public Works* (1902) 2 S.R. (N.S.W.) 405 at 416; *Partridge v. McIntosh & Sons Ltd* (1933) 49 C.L.R. 453 at 466. The mortgagee's charge is created upon registration of the mortgage: *Real Property Act* 1900 (N.S.W.), s. 41.

In accordance with settled principles in the interpretation of the Torrens legislation, an unregistered mortgage will be operative as an equitable mortgage: *Barry v. Heider* (1914) 19 C.L.R. 197 at 208, 213, 216; *J. & H. Just (Holdings) Pty Ltd v. Bank of New South Wales* (1971) 125 C.L.R. 546.

AUSTRALIAN AND NEW ZEALAND BANKING
GROUP LTD v. GREIG

Supreme Court of New South Wales [1980] 1 N.S.W.L.R. 112

[Greig was the registered proprietor of a parcel of Torrens title land, subject to a registered mortgage. A third party (the bank) obtained a judgment against Greig for a substantial amount of money. Section 27(1) (b) of the *Judgment Creditors' Remedies Act* 1901 (N.S.W.) permitted a judgment creditor to approach the court for an order charging the amount of a judgment upon "any equity of redemption or other equitable interest" of the debtor. The bank made an application for an order under s. 27(1) (b), and one of the questions which arose for decision was whether Greig had an "equity of redemption" in the mortgaged land.]

MASTER ALLEN.

EQUITY OF REDEMPTION

If the land were under old system title, there is no doubt that the defendant's [Greig's] estate in the land would be described correctly as the equity of redemption under the mortgage. The form of mortgage under old system title is a conveyance by the mortgagor to the mortgagee of the whole of his estate. All that remains in law under such a mortgage to the mortgagor is the contractual right of being given a reconveyance upon the paying out of the mortgage in accordance with its terms. But, in equity, the mortgagor under such a mortgage has much more. Equity has regard to the real substance of the transaction—namely, that the conveyance is simply by way of security for the mortgage debt. In the eyes of equity, the mortgagor remains the owner, and the mortgagee has a mere charge. Such being the nature of the transaction, equity permits the mortgagor to redeem the mortgage and to obtain a reconveyance of the legal title, even where he has made default under the mortgage, so that he cannot avail himself of his contractual right to redeem. This equitable right to redeem may be exercised at any time before the mortgagor's interest is foreclosed by an order made in equity. In a real sense, the equity of redemption, this right of redemption given by equity, is the estate and interest of the mortgagor. For it is implicit that, in the eyes of equity, the mortgagor has, until a foreclosure, the equitable estate in the land.

But what is the equity of redemption, if any, of the mortgagor of land under the *Real Property Act* 1900 (N.S.W.)? A mortgage of land under the Act is not a conveyance of the legal estate to the mortgagee. The Act is specific. It provides that the mortgage "shall have effect as a security but shall not operate as a transfer of the land thereby charged": s. 57. The mortgagor remains the registered proprietor. He retains, not only the legal estate, but also the equitable estate. Nonetheless, the mortgagor of land under the *Real Property Act*, like the mortgagor of land under old system title, is not confined to his contractual right to receive a discharge of the mortgage. Despite default under the mortgage, he has the right to pay out the mortgagee, and to receive from him a duly executed discharge document in registrable form.

Is it correct to refer to this right as the "equity of redemption"? Technically, there is some doubt as to this. There is judicial support for the view that the right is not one conferred in equity, but one given by statute, in that the right is implicit in the provisions of the *Real Property Act*: *Browne v. Cranfield* (1925) 25 S.R. (N.S.W.) 443; *Greig v. Watson* (1881) 7 V.L.R. 79; *Perry v. Rolfe* [1948] V.L.R. 297. But there is a contrary view. It is that, as in the case of the old system mortgage, the right to redeem notwithstanding default is the creature of equity. The *Real Property Act*, on this view, does not create the right. The Act merely assumes that the right exists—that is, it recognises that the principles of equity which confer the right in respect of the old system mortgages likewise confer that right in respect of mortgages of land under the Torrens system: *Re Forrest Trust* [1953] V.L.R. 246. There is, indeed, much to be said in favour of the approach that the principles developed in equity in relation to mortgages apply equally to land under the Torrens system, save in so far as they are inconsistent with provisions of the Act: see generally, Sykes, *The Law of Securities* (3rd ed.) p. 194 et seq.; *Simpson v. Forrester* (1973) 132 C.L.R. 499 at 514 per Gibbs J. If the source of the right of a mortgagor to receive, after default, a discharge of the mortgage is equity, then it is not inappropriate to refer to that right as the "equity of redemption". But, even if it be technically incorrect so to describe that right, it is undoubtedly a common usage of the expression "equity of redemption" in legal parlance. Indeed, that usage is reflected in s. 62(2) of the *Real Property Act* itself. That subsection provides that an order for foreclosure, "shall have the effect of vesting in the mortgagee of [sic] the estate and interest of the mortgagor . . . free from all right and equity of redemption on the part of the mortgagor . . .".

Whilst it is arguable whether it is technically correct to refer to the mortgagor's right to obtain a discharge of a *Real Property Act* mortgage as the equity of redemption, it is clear, beyond argument, that it is not technically correct to use the expression as a reference to the estate of the mortgagor in the land. His estate is not a mere equity of redemption, which in the eyes of equity gives him the estate in equity. Notwithstanding the security given to the mortgagee by the mortgage, the mortgagor remains the registered proprietor of the land—the owner, not only in equity, but also in law itself. There is a clear distinction, in the case of land under the *Real Property Act*, between the estate enjoyed by the registered proprietor, the mortgagor, on the one hand and his right to pay out the mortgage and receive a duly executed document of discharge in registrable form: Sykes, op. cit., p. 195. Nonetheless, although it is a technically incorrect usage, it is not uncommon in legal parlance to use the expression "equity of redemption" as a convenient reference to the estate of the mortgagor of land under the *Real Property Act*, or like legislation, under which the mortgagee receives a mere statutory charge, both the legal and equitable estate remaining in the mortgagor. The judgment of Barwick C.J. in *Simpson v. Forrester* (1973) 132 C.L.R. 499 illustrates this usage. Throughout his judgment in that case the Chief Justice (at 502 et seq.) refers to the estate of the mortgagor as the "equity of redemption". On the other hand, in his judgment in that case, Gibbs J. (at 511 et seq.) avoids using the expression in that sense, and cites (at 514) with approval a dictum of Kitto J. in *Anderson v. Liddell* (1968) 117 C.L.R. 36 at 48 that the interest of the mortgagee [sic] is "a legal interest subject to a charge and therefore . . . not, in a strict sense, an equity of redemption or any other form of equitable interest". The remaining judgment in that case was given by Stephen J. (at 519 et seq.). His Honour was precise in using language which stated with technical accuracy the difference between the estate of a mortgagor under old system title and the estate of a mortgagor under Torrens or like statutory title. His Honour said (at 521), of a particular doctrine there being considered, that it "applies equally to the purchase of an equity of redemption in the case of a mortgage at general law and to the purchase of the mortgagor's interest in property subject to a mortgage which takes the form of a hypothecation as does the familiar Torrens system mortgage". It would be wholly wrong, of course, to infer that there was any difference of opinion between the judges in that case as to the nature of the estate of a mortgagor of land under Torrens or like statutory title. The difference is one only of the use of language.

Indeed, use of the expression "equity of redemption" as a description of the very estate of a mortgagor under a Torrens mortgage has a long usage. The judgment of Martin C.J. in 1886, in *Re Elliott* (1886) 7 L.R. (N.S.W.) 271, illustrates this. His Honour there described the "right, title and interest" of a mortgagor of land under the *Real Property Act*. His Honour said (at 276): "He had only an equity of redemption."

[Master Allen went on to hold that the earlier New South Wales case of *Coleman v. De Lissa* (1885) 6 L.R. (N.S.W.) (E.) 104 required him to hold that a mortgagor of Torrens title land has an "equity of redemption" in the land for the purposes of s. 27(1) (b) of the *Judgment Creditors' Remedies Act* 1901 (N.S.W.).

In a later case, *Quint v. Robertson* (1985) 3 N.S.W.L.R. 398, Young J. declined to follow *Coleman v. De Lissa* and *Australian and New Zealand Banking Group Ltd v. Greig*, and held that the interest of a mortgagor of Torrens title land was not an "equity of redemption" for the purposes of s. 27 (1)(b).]

III. CLOGS ON THE EQUITY OF REDEMPTION

The right of the mortgagor to redeem upon repayment is regarded as a "fundamental characteristic of a mortgage": Hinde, McMorland and Sim, *Land Law*, Vol. 1, p. 780. "Redemption is of the very nature and essence of a mortgage, as mortgages are regarded in equity. It is inherent in the thing itself": *Noakes & Co. Ltd v. Rice* [1902] A.C. 24 at 30 per Lord Macnaghten. Equity guards jealously the right of the mortgagor to redeem, and "will not permit any device or contrivance designed or calculated to prevent or impede redemption": Hinde, McMorland and Sim, op. cit., Vol. 1, p. 780.

There is a time honoured maxim in the law of mortgages: "Once a mortgage, always a mortgage": *Seton v. Slade* (1802) 7 Ves. Jun. 265 at 273; 32 E.R. 108 at 111. What this means is, first, that whether a transaction is a mortgage is to be determined as a matter of substance and not form; secondly, that the equity of redemption is not to be "clogged" or fettered. The first meaning has already been considered: above pp. 389-393. We turn now to examine the second aspect. The reported cases in which clogs or fetters on the equity of redemption have been alleged are legion, and it will be convenient to consider them under three headings: (A) Where the mortgagee has the power to extinguish the equity of redemption; (B) Where time limitations are imposed on the right to redeem; (C) Where the mortgagee is given collateral advantages over and above the right to receive payment under the mortgage. Several miscellaneous matters (D) relating to clogging the equity of redemption will also be considered, as will a number of modern statutory provisions (E).

A. POWER TO EXTINGUISH EQUITY OF REDEMPTION

SAMUEL v. JARRAH TIMBER AND WOOD PAVING CORP. LTD

House of Lords [1904] A.C. 323

[Samuel advanced money to the respondent company upon the security of its debenture stock. The advance was to become due and payable upon 30 days' notice by either party. The mortgage also conferred on Samuel an option to purchase the whole or any part of the debenture stock within 12 months.

Within the 12 months, and before the company gave notice of intention to repay the advance, Samuel purported to exercise the option. Thereupon the company brought proceedings for redemption and a declaration that the option was illegal and void. Kekewich J. gave judgment for the company, and his decision was affirmed by the Court of Appeal. On appeal.]

EARL OF HALSBURY L.C. My Lords, I regret that the state of the authorities leaves me no alternative other than to affirm the judgment of Kekewich J. and the Court of Appeal. A perfectly fair bargain made between two parties to it, each of whom was quite sensible of what they were doing, is not to be performed because at the same time a mortgage arrangement was made between them. If a day had intervened between the two parts of the arrangement, the part of the bargain which the appellant claims to be performed would have been perfectly good and capable of being enforced; but a line of authorities going back for more than a century has decided that such an arrangement as that which was here arrived at is contrary to a principle of equity, the sense or reason of which I am not able to appreciate, and very reluctantly I am compelled to acquiesce in the judgments appealed from.

LORD MACNAGHTEN. My Lords, both Kekewich J. and the Court of Appeal decided in favour of the company. Having regard to the state of the authorities binding on the Court of Appeal if not on this House, it seems to me that they could not have come to any other conclusion, although the transaction was a fair bargain between men of business without any trace or suspicion of oppression, surprise, or circumvention.

It is, I think, unnecessary to consider what the true construction of the agreement between Mr Samuel and the company may be. The result would have been precisely the same if the agreement had in terms declared that the option was not to continue after repayment. The law undoubtedly is that a condition such as that in question, if legal and binding at all, must come to an end on repayment of the loan.

In the Court of Appeal the question was treated as governed by the principle, of which *Noakes v. Rice* [1902] A.C. 24 is a recent example, that on redemption the mortgagor is entitled to have the thing mortgaged restored to him unaffected by any condition or stipulation which formed part of the mortgage transaction.

That principle, I think, is perfectly sound. But, in my opinion, the question here depends rather upon the rule that a mortgagee is not allowed at the time of the loan to enter into a contract for the purchase of the mortgaged property.

This latter rule, I think, is founded on sentiment rather than on principle. It seems to have had its origin in the desire of the Court of Chancery to protect embarrassed landowners from imposition and oppression. And it was invented, I should suppose, in order to obviate the necessity of inquiry and investigation in cases where suspicion may be probable and proof difficult. I gather from some general observations made by Lord Hardwicke in *Mellor v. Lees* (1742) 2 Atk. 494; 26 E.R. 698 that he would have been disposed to confine the rule to cases in which the court finds or suspects "a design to wrest the estate fraudulently out of the hands of the mortgagor", and to cases of "common mortgage"—that is, as I understand it, mortgage of land by deed. It will be observed that in the later case of *Toomes v. Conset* (1745) 3 Atk. 261; 26 E.R. 952, which is often referred to for a statement of the rule, his Lordship speaks only of "a deed of mortgage"; an instrument which perhaps rather lends itself to imposition—for no one, I am sure, by the light of nature ever understood an English mortgage of real estate.

In *Vernon v. Bethell* (1761) 2 Eden 113; 28 E.R. 838, however, Northington L.C. (then Lord Henley) laid down the law broadly in the following terms: "This court, as a court of conscience, is very jealous of persons taking securities for a loan and converting such securities into purchases. And therefore I take it to be an established rule that a mortgagee can never provide at the time of making the loan for any event or condition on which the equity of redemption shall be discharged and the conveyance absolute. And there is great reason and justice in this rule, for necessitous men are not, truly speaking, free men, but to answer a present exigency will submit to any terms that the crafty may impose upon them."

This doctrine, described by Lord Henley as an established rule nearly 150 years ago, has never, so far as I can discover, been departed from since or questioned in any reported case. It is, I believe, universally accepted by textwriters of authority. Speaking for myself, I should not be sorry if your Lordships could see your way to modify it so as to prevent its being used as a means of evading a fair bargain come to between persons dealing at arms' length and negotiating on equal terms. The directors of a trading company in search of financial assistance are certainly in a very different position from that of an impecunious landowner in the toils of a crafty money-lender. At the same time I quite feel the difficulty of interfering with any rule that has prevailed so long, and I am not prepared to differ from the conclusion at which the Court of Appeal has arrived.

[Lord Lindley delivered a separate concurring judgment.]

Appeal dismissed.

NOTES

1. There is nothing to prevent mortgagor and mortgagee, by a separate and independent transaction, giving the mortgagee an option to purchase the property, even though, if the option is exercised, the effect will be to deprive the mortgagor of the right to redeem. The rule in the principal case only strikes down the option where it is part and parcel of the mortgage transaction: see *Reeve v. Lisle* [1902] A.C. 461. In *Kreglinger v. New Patagonia Meat and Cold Storage Co. Ltd* [1914] A.C. 25 at 52-53 Lord Parker of Waddington said that there could be no objection to the following transaction: A agrees to give B an option for one year to purchase property for £10,000; in consideration of such option B agrees to lend, and does lend, A £1,000 to be charged on the property without interest, repayable at the expiration or earlier exercise of the option; however, "it would have been very different if A had conveyed the property to B with a proviso that on payment of the £1,000 there should be a reconveyance, and the deed had then provided for the year's option".

   Further, despite the statement of the Earl of Halsbury L.C. in the principal case that the option would have been valid "if a day had intervened between the two parts of the arrangement", it seems clear that as it is the substance of the transaction, rather than its form, which governs the application of the rule, "the mere separation of documents will not, of itself, affect the existence of a clog on the equity of redemption. The transactions must be independent" (*Re Supreme Court Registrar to Alexander Dawson Inc.* [1976] 1 N.Z.L.R. 615 at 627); "it is immaterial in how many documents a transaction, if it is really one transaction, is expressed": *Onehunga Sawmilling Co. Ltd v. Official Assignee of King* (1914) 34 N.Z.L.R 257 at 283.

2. Although the rule in the principal case is well-established, the New Zealand Court of Appeal has held that a solicitor who failed to advise his client of the effect of the rule was not liable for professional negligence: "I do not take the view that the average solicitor in New Zealand can be expected to carry in his mind the full implications of the rule in question": *Bannerman Brydone Folster & Co. v. Murray* [1972] N.Z.L.R. 411 at 423.

3. It has been suggested that a right of *pre-emption* conferred on the mortgagee as part and parcel of the mortgage transaction would not be invalid, as it does not oblige the mortgagor to sell to the mortgagee, but is merely an agreement that if the mortgagor sells he or she will give the mortgagee first right of refusal: see Sykes, op. cit., p. 61.

B. TIME LIMITS ON RIGHT TO REDEEM

KNIGHTSBRIDGE ESTATES TRUST LTD v. BYRNE

Court of Appeal [1939] Ch. 441

[In 1931, the respondents executed a mortgage over their freehold property in favour of the appellants, to secure an advance of £310,000. The respondents covenanted to repay the advance by 80 half-yearly instalments of principal and interest, with a provision that the whole of the amount outstanding should become payable immediately upon default in any payment.

Between 1931 and 1937, the ruling rate of interest on mortgages fell and the respondents, no doubt hoping to obtain better terms elsewhere, issued a writ claiming to be entitled to redeem on payment of the balance outstanding notwithstanding the provision in the mortgage for payment by 80 half-yearly instalments. The respondents claimed that the provision "if and so far as it prevents the [respondents] from redeeming the said mortgage at any time upon proper payment of principal and interest is illegal and void as a clog on their right to redeem the said mortgage".

Luxmoore J. held that the postponement of the contractual right to redeem until repayment of the instalments had been effected, was void. On appeal.]

THE COURT (SIR WILFRED GREENE M.R., SCOTT AND FARWELL L.JJ.). [The court referred to the respondents' argument that postponement of a contractual right to redeem is void unless it is for a reasonable period, and continued:]

But in our opinion the proposition that a postponement of the contractual right of redemption is only permissible for a "reasonable" time is not well founded. Such a postponement is not properly described as a clog on the equity of redemption, since it is concerned with the contractual right to redeem. It is indisputable that any provision which hampers redemption after the contractual date for redemption has passed will not be permitted. Further, it is undoubtedly true to say that a right of redemption is a necessary element in a mortgage transaction, and consequently that, where the contractual right of redemption is illusory, equity will grant relief by allowing redemption. This was the point in the case of *Fairclough v. Swan Brewery Co.* [1912] A.C. 565 decided in the Privy Council, where in a mortgage of a lease of 20 years the contractual right to redeem was postponed until six weeks before the expiration of the lease. The following passage from the judgment explains the reason for that decision (at 570): "The learned counsel on behalf of the respondents admitted, as he was bound to admit, that a mortgage cannot be made irredeemable. That is plainly forbidden. Is there any difference between forbidding redemption and permitting it, if the permission be a mere pretence? Here the provision for redemption is nugatory."

Moreover, equity may give relief against contractual terms in a mortgage transaction if they are oppressive or unconscionable, and in deciding whether or not a particular transaction falls within this category the length of time for which the contractual right to redeem is postponed may well be an important consideration. In the present case no question of this kind was or could have been raised.

But equity does not reform mortgage transactions because they are unreasonable. It is concerned to see two things—one that the essential requirements of a mortgage transaction are observed, and the other that oppressive or unconscionable terms are not enforced. Subject to this, it does not, in our opinion, interfere. The question therefore arises whether in a case where the right of redemption is real and not illusory and there is nothing oppressive or unconscionable in the transaction, there is something in a postponement of the contractual right to redeem, such as we have in the present case, that is inconsistent with the essential requirements of a mortgage transaction? Apart from authority the answer to this question would, in our opinion, be clearly in the negative. Any other answer would place an unfortunate restriction on the liberty of contract of competent parties who are at arm's length—in the present case it would have operated to prevent the respondents obtaining financial terms which for obvious reasons they themselves considered to be most desirable. It would, moreover, lead to highly inequitable results. The remedy sought by the respondents and the only remedy which is said to be open to them is the establishment of a right to redeem at any time on the ground that the postponement of the contractual right to redeem is void. They do not and could not suggest that the contract as a contract is affected, and the result would accordingly be that whereas the respondents would have had from the first the right to redeem at any time, the appellants would have had no right to require payment otherwise than by the specified instalments. Such an outcome to a bargain entered into by business people negotiating at arm's length would indeed be unfortunate, and we should require clear authority before coming to such a conclusion.

We will now turn to the relevant authorities cited in argument by counsel for the parties. . . .

The respondents' sheet-anchor was a dictum of Sir George Jessel M.R. in *Teevan v. Smith*: (1882) 20 Ch. D. 724 at 729. He said: "although the law will not allow a mortgagor to be precluded from redeeming altogether, yet he may be precluded from redeeming for a fixed period, such as five or seven years." We cannot treat this dictum as representing a considered opinion to the effect that the contractual right of redemption may only be postponed for a period of the order mentioned where the right of redemption is a real and not an illusory one. Sir George Jessel was merely giving an example to illustrate a point in his reasoning, and he naturally chose one with regard to which no possible controversy could arise. He was not, in our opinion, asserting any such doctrine as that for which the respondents contend.

This dictum was referred to by Romer J. in *Biggs v. Hoddinott* [1898] 2 Ch. 307 at 311. In that case a mortgage to brewers was for five years certain with a "tie" during the continuance of the mortgage. Two questions arose in the case, one as to the right of the mortgagor to redeem before the expiration of the five years, the other as to the validity of the tie. Romer J. held that there was no objection to the five year period, either in itself or when taken in conjunction with the tie. He said: "I am of opinion that it is obviously to the advantage of both the mortgagor and the mortgagee that such a provision should be enforced. Of course, that does not prevent the court in a proper case from preventing the application of the clause if it is too large, or there are circumstances connected with the proviso which renders it, in the opinion of the court unreasonable or oppressive." Here again we cannot read these observations as meaning that, in a case where there is no circumstance of oppression, a real contractual right of redemption is to be displaced merely because it is postponed for a substantial period. We do not think that the word "unreasonable" should be interpreted as meaning that the court is to disregard the bargain made by the parties merely because it comes to the conclusion that it is an unreasonable one. A postponement of the right of redemption may be the badge of oppression, or it may be unreasonable in the sense that it renders the right of redemption illusory. We doubt whether Romer J. meant more than this. . . .

In *Williams v. Morgan* [1906] 1 Ch. 804 the period of the mortgage was 14 years, but it does not appear to have been suggested that there was any objection to it.

Morgan v. Jeffreys [1910] 1 Ch. 620 was a case in which, as appears from a copy of the mortgage with which we were furnished, the covenant was to repay the mortgage money on a date six months after the date of the mortgage with a proviso for reconveyance on such payment. This circumstance is not stated in the report, but it is for present purposes very important. The mortgage then contained a provision by which the mortgagor was precluded from paying off the debt for a period of 28 years unless the mortgagee was willing to receive it earlier. The mortgage also contained a "tie"—it was a public-house mortgage and the mortgagee was a brewer—and this tie was to last during the 31 years. [This period of 31 years was calculated to commence three years prior to the mortgage and expire at the same time as the 28 year period referred to in the mortgage.] The mortgagor (who was a working miner) claimed to be entitled to redeem before the 31 years had elapsed, and Joyce J. held that he was entitled to do so. He relied on the length of the period, the absence of mutuality, the position of the mortgagor, the character of the stipulation in the agreement and the severity of the provisions for the benefit of the mortgagee, and held that in all the circumstances the period of 28 years "exceeded all reasonable limit". In fact the provision precluding the right of the mortgagor to redeem for 28 years unless the mortgagee agreed was a device intended to make the contractual right to redeem in six months inoperative, the object clearly being to enable the mortgagee to enjoy the benefit of the tie during that period. This case does not, in our opinion, assist the respondents.

The last case is *Davis v. Symons* [1934] Ch. 442, decided by Eve J. As appears from copies of the documents supplied to us, the covenant in that case was to pay the principal moneys on February 25 then next with a corresponding proviso for redemption with regard to an endowment life policy which was included in the mortgage. There was no express proviso for redemption in the case of the land which formed part of the security, since no such proviso was required in view of s. 115 of the *Law of Property Act* 1925. The deed contained a covenant by the mortgagee to allow the mortgage to remain on foot for 20 years—namely, until 25 November 1946, or until the earlier death of the mortgagor, and a covenant by the mortgagor that the whole of the principal money should remain on the security for the like period. In this respect the case resembled that of *Morgan v. Jeffreys* [1910] 1 Ch. 620. The policy was due to mature eight days before the expiration of the 20 years. There was a further charge upon the same terms which included also another policy which matured in 1942, and it was provided that, if the mortgagor survived that date, the policy moneys were to be paid to the mortgagee. The mortgage contained a covenant by the mortgagor not to sell the equity of redemption except to a responsible person. The mortgagor was held entitled to redeem before the expiration of the 20 years. Eve J. pointed to the distinction between cases where there was and those where there was not mutuality in the matter of the postponement of redemption, and expressed the view that in cases of mutuality, even if the postponement was a long one, there was no reason why the court should allow the mortgagor to escape from his contract. The test which he applied for the purpose of this observation was whether or not the postponement was "extravagant and oppressive"—a test with which we do not quarrel. But he also introduced the word "reasonable", and, if that means something less than oppressive, we cannot agree with its use in this connection for reasons which already sufficiently appear. He then went on to point out that the policies were in substance irredeemable, a circumstance of doubtful materiality in view of Lord Parker's observations in *G. & C. Kreglinger v. New Patagonia Meat and Cold Storage Co.* [1914] A.C. 25 at 53. He also placed some reliance on the covenant by the mortgagor with regard to a sale of the equity of redemption, which he thought must "hamper the mortgagor to an unreasonable extent". With regard to this suggested test of reasonableness it is worth pointing out that even in the case of collateral advantages extending beyond redemption which do not amount to a clog on the equity of redemption there is no rule of equity which prohibits them if they are not either (1) unfair and unconscionable, (2) in the nature of a penalty clogging the equity of redemption, or (3) inconsistent with or repugnant to the contractual and equitable right to redeem: *G. & C. Kreglinger v. New Patagonia Meat and Cold Storage Co.* [1914] A.C. 25 at 61. In our judgment the decision in *Davis v. Symons* [1934] Ch. 442 can be supported on the ground that the provision for postponement of redemption was a device to fetter the right to redeem on performance of the covenant for payment on 25 February following the date of the mortgage. In so far as it is based upon the view that the court is concerned with questions of reasonableness in such a case we respectfully dissent from it.

Luxmoore J. does not express the opinion that the postponement in the present case is to be regarded as void by reason merely of its length. He holds that the period is "having regard to all the provisions of the deed, unreasonable". The provisions to which he refers are set out in his judgment and we need not repeat them. We find ourselves unable to take the view that the court is entitled in such a case as the present to treat as unreasonable provisions in a mortgage deed entered into by two parties such as we have here with the assistance of competent advisers. For all the court can know, provisions which may appear to it to be disadvantageous to the mortgagor may have been regarded by him, and correctly regarded, as of no practical consequence from a business point of view.

Appeal allowed.

NOTES

1. The Court of Appeal also held (affirming the decision of Luxmoore J. on this point) that postponement of the contractual right to redeem is not subject to the rule against perpetuities.

2. The decision of the Court of Appeal in the principal case was upheld by the House of Lords ([1940] A.C. 613), but on a different ground. The House of Lords held that the mortgage was a "debenture" within the meaning of s. 74 of the *Companies Act* 1929 (U.K.), which provided:

   A condition contained in any debentures . . . shall not be invalid by reason only that the debentures are thereby made irredeemable or redeemable only . . . on the expiration of a period, however long, any rule of equity to the contrary notwithstanding.

   In New South Wales, s. 150 of the *Companies (N.S.W.) Code* 1981 provides:

   A condition contained in any debenture or in any deed for securing any debentures . . . is not invalid by reason only that the debentures are thereby made irredeemable or redeemable only on the happening of a contingency however remote or on the expiration of a period however long, any rule of law or equity to the contrary notwithstanding.

   By s. 5(1), "debenture" includes "debenture stock, bonds, notes and any other document evidencing or acknowledging indebtedness of a corporation in respect of money that is or may be deposited with or lent to the corporation, whether constituting a charge on the property of the corporation or not" (then follow certain exclusions). By the same subsection, "charge" means "a charge created in any way and includes a mortgage and an agreement to give or execute a charge or mortgage, whether upon demand or otherwise".

3. In *Fairclough v. Swan Brewery Co. Ltd.* [1912] A.C. 565, referred to in the principal case, the mortgagor of a leasehold interest in property which had some 17 years to run covenanted to repay the loan by monthly instalments for the ensuing 17 years, the last instalment being payable six weeks before the expiration of the lease. The mortgage further provided that the mortgage could not be repaid except by the stipulated instalments. In holding the provision for redemption to be nugatory, the Privy Council said (at 570):

The incumbrance on the lease the subject of the mortgage according to the letter of the mortgage falls to be discharged before the lease terminates, but at a time when it is on the very point of expiring, when redemption can be of no advantage to the mortgagor even if he should be so fortunate as to get his deeds back before the actual termination of the lease. For all practical purposes this mortgage is irredeemable.

The mortgagor was therefore entitled to redeem in advance of the 17 years.

The advice of the Privy Council, however, would appear to conflict with the earlier Court of Appeal decision in *Santley v. Wilde* [1899] 2 Ch. 474. There, under a mortgage of a leasehold interest, the advance was to be repaid by quarterly instalments, the last of which would fall due more than four years before the end of the lease. By the mortgage, the mortgagor covenanted to pay to the mortgagee, in addition, one third of the net profits from sub-leases granted by the mortgagor for the *whole* of the term of the lease, including the period after the advance should have been repaid. The property was redeemable only on repayment of the advance and all other moneys covenanted to be paid. The Court of Appeal held that the additional covenant was not a clog on the equity of redemption. The result of the decision, however, was that the mortgagor could never redeem his leasehold interest in its pre-mortgage condition; it would always remain subject to the mortgagee's right to receive a percentage of profits.

Santley v. Wilde does not appear to have been cited to the court in the *Swan Brewery* case or in the principal case, and has been criticised in the House of Lords: *Noakes & Co. Ltd v. Rice* [1902] A.C. 24 at 31-32, 34.

4. A provision which attempts to restrict the right to redeem to a particular person is inoperative as a clog on the equity of redemption: see *Salt v. Marquess of Northampton* [1892] A.C. 1 at 15, where a stipulation that in the event of the debtor dying without having paid off the debt, the mortgaged property should not be redeemable but would become the absolute property of the mortgagee, was held void.

5. The principal case must be read in the light of modern business and consumer protection legislation which impinges upon its area of operation. Important examples are the *Trade Practices Act* 1974 (Cth), *Industrial Arbitration Act* 1940 (N.S.W.) and the *Contracts Review Act* 1980 (N.S.W.). This legislation is discussed below pp. 434 et seq.

6. The principal case should also be read in the light of s. 93 of the *Conveyancing Act* 1919 (N.S.W.), discussed below p. 427, by which a mortgagor is given a statutory right to redeem before the contractual date for redemption, but only upon payment of outstanding principal and interest for the unexpired portion of the term of the mortgage. Can it be argued that, where the mortgage is for a long term (say, 50 years) with no express right for early repayment, it is "oppressive and unconscionable" to require the mortgagor exercising the statutory right to repay early to pay interest for the full unexpired term of the mortgage? See Hinde, McMorland and Sim, op. cit., pp. 783-784:

There appears to be nothing in [s. 93] which necessarily ousts the doctrines of equity concerning the postponement of the right to redeem.

C. COLLATERAL ADVANTAGES

Sometimes, mortgages attempt to secure to the mortgagee some advantage over and above repayment of the loan with interest. Such advantages are termed "collateral advantages".

At one time, all collateral advantages were regarded as void: "A man shall not have interest for his money, and a collateral advantage besides for the loan of it, or clog the equity of redemption with any by-agreement": *Jennings v. Ward* (1705) 2 Vern. 520 at 521; 23 E.R. 935. Such a view was taken because collateral advantages were seen as a means of avoiding the restrictions imposed on interest rates by the old usury laws. Since the repeal of the usury laws by the *Usury Laws Repeal Act* 1854 (U.K.), however, the approach of the courts to collateral advantages has been modified.

KREGLINGER v. NEW PATAGONIA MEAT AND COLD STORAGE CO. LTD

House of Lords [1914] A.C. 25

[The appellants, G. & C. Kreglinger, a firm of woolbrokers, agreed to lend a sum of money to the respondents, who, in the course of their business, had at their disposal a large number of sheepskins. If the interest was punctually paid, the loan was not to be called in for five years, although the respondents could pay off at any time beforehand on giving one month's notice. The loan was secured by a floating charge on the respondents' assets. By the terms of the agreement, the respondents agreed that for the next five years they would not sell sheepskins to anybody except the appellants (so long as the appellants were willing to pay the best price offered by any other person), and that should the appellants decline to purchase any sheepskins the respondents would pay to the appellants a commission on all sheepskins sold to any other person.

The respondents paid off the loan within two and a half years, but the appellants claimed that the right of pre-emption in respect of the sheepskins continued. Swinfen Eady J. held that the right of pre-emption was a clog on the equity of redemption and void. His decision was affirmed by the Court of Appeal. On appeal.]

VISCOUNT HALDANE L.C. What the respondents say is that the stipulation is one that restricts their freedom in conducting the undertaking or business which is the subject of the floating charge; that it was consequently of the nature of a clog on their right to redeem and invalid; and that, whether it clogged the right to redeem or was in the nature of a collateral advantage, it was not intended and could not be made to endure after redemption. The appellants, on the other hand, say that the stipulation in question was one of a kind usual in business, and that it was in the nature not of a clog but of a collateral bargain outside the actual loan, which they only agreed to make in order to obtain the option itself. . . .

My Lords, before I refer to the decisions of this House which the courts below have considered to cover the case, I will state what I conceive to be the broad principles which must govern it.

The reason for which a court of equity will set aside the legal title of a mortgagee and compel him to reconvey the land on being paid principal, interest, and costs is a very old one. It appears to owe its origin to the influence of the Church in the courts of the early Chancellors. As early as the Council of Lateran in 1179, we find, according to Matthew Paris, *Historia Major* (1684 ed.), pp. 114-115, that famous assembly of ecclesiastics condemning usurers and laying down that when a creditor had been paid his debt he should restore his pledge [footnote omitted]. It was therefore not surprising that the Court of Chancery should at an early date have begun to exercise jurisdiction in personam over mortgagees. This jurisdiction was merely a special application of a more general power to relieve against penalties and to mould them into mere securities. The case of the common law mortgage of land was indeed a gross one. The land was conveyed to the creditor upon the condition that if the money he had advanced to the feoffor was repaid on a date and at a place named, the fee simple should revest in the latter, but that if the condition was not strictly and literally fulfilled he should lose the land for ever. What made the hardship on the debtor a glaring one was that the debt still remained unpaid and could be recovered from the feoffor notwithstanding that he had actually forfeited the land to his mortgagee. Equity, therefore, at an early date began to relieve against what was virtually a penalty by compelling the creditor to use his legal title as a mere security.

My Lords, this was the origin of the jurisdiction which we are now considering, and it is important to bear that origin in mind. For the end to accomplish which the jurisdiction has been evolved ought to govern and limit its exercise by equity judges. That end has always been to ascertain, by parol evidence if need be, the real nature and substance of the transaction, and if it turned out to be in truth one of mortgage simply, to place it on that footing. It was, in ordinary cases, only where there was conduct which the Court of Chancery regarded as unconscientious that it interfered with freedom of contract. The lending of money, on mortgage or otherwise, was looked on with suspicion, and the court was on the alert to discover want of conscience in the terms imposed by lenders. But whatever else may have been the intention of those judges who laid the foundations of the modern doctrines with which we are concerned in this appeal, they certainly do not appear to have contemplated that their principle should develop consequences which would go far beyond the necessities of the case with which they were dealing and interfere with transactions which were not really of the nature of a mortgage, and which were free from objection on moral grounds. Moreover, the principle on which the Court of Chancery interfered with contracts of the class under consideration was not a rigid one. The equity judges looked, not at what was technically the form, but at what was really the substance of transactions, and confined the application of their rules to cases in which they thought that in its substance the transaction was oppressive. Thus in *Howard v. Harris* (1683) 1 Vern. 33; 2 Ch. Cas. 147 Lord Keeper North in 1683 set aside an agreement that a mortgage should be irredeemable after the death of the mortgagor and failure of the heirs of his body, on the ground that such a restriction on the right to redeem was void in equity. But he went on to intimate that if the money had been borrowed by the mortgagor from his brother, and the former had agreed that if he had no issue the land should become irredeemable, equity would not have interfered with what would really have been a family arrangement. The exception thus made to the rule, in cases where the transaction includes a family arrangement as well as a mortgage, has been recognised in later authorities.

The principle was thus in early days limited in its application to the accomplishment of the end which was held to justify interference of equity with freedom of contract. It did not go further. As established it was expressed in three ways. The most general of these was that if the transaction was once found to be a mortgage, it must be treated as always remaining a mortgage and nothing but a mortgage. That the substance of the transaction must be looked to in applying this doctrine and that it did not apply to cases which were only apparently or technically within it but were in reality something more than cases of mortgage, *Howard v. Harris* (1683) 1 Vern. 33; 2 Ch. Cas. 147 and other authorities shew. It was only a different application of the paramount doctrine to lay it down in the form of a second rule that a mortgagee should not stipulate for a collateral advantage which would make his remuneration for the loan exceed a proper rate of interest. The legislature during a long period placed restrictions on the rate of interest which could legally be exacted. But equity went beyond the limits of the statutes which limited the interest, and was ready to interfere with any usurious stipulation in a mortgage. In so doing it was influenced by the public policy of the time. That policy has now changed, and the Acts which limited the rate of interest have been repealed. The result is that a collateral advantage may now be stipulated for by the mortgagee provided that he has not acted unfairly or oppressively, and provided that the bargain does not conflict with the third form of the principle. This is that a mortgage (subject to the apparent exception in the case of family arrangements to which I have already alluded) cannot be made irredeemable, and that any stipulation which restricts or clogs the equity of redemption is void. It is obvious that the reason for the doctrine in this form is the same as that which gave rise to the other forms. It is simply an assertion in a different way of the principle that once a mortgage always a mortgage and nothing else.

My Lords, the rules I have stated have now been applied by Courts of Equity for nearly three centuries, and the books are full of illustrations of their application. But what I have pointed out shews that it is inconsistent with the objects for which they were established that these rules should crystallise into technical language so rigid that the letter can defeat the underlying spirit and purpose. Their application must correspond with the practical necessities of the time. The rule as to collateral advantages, for example, has been much modified by the repeal of the usury laws and by the recognition of modern varieties of commercial bargaining. In *Biggs v. Hoddinott* [1898] 2 Ch. 307 it was held that a brewer might stipulate in a mortgage made to him of an hotel that during the five years for which the loan was to continue the mortgagors would deal with him exclusively for malt liquor. In the 17th and 18th centuries a Court of Equity could hardly have so decided, and the judgment illustrates the elastic character of equity jurisdiction and the power of equity judges to mould the rules which they apply in accordance with the exigencies of the time. The decision proceeded on the ground that a mortgagee may stipulate for a collateral advantage at the time and as a term of the advance, provided, first, that no unfairness is shewn, and, secondly, that the right to redeem is not thereby clogged. It is no longer true that, as was said in *Jennings v. Ward* (1705) 2 Vern. 520; 23 E.R. 935, "a man shall not have interest for his money and a collateral advantage besides for the loan of it". Unless such a bargain is unconscionable it is now good. But none the less the other and wider principle remains unshaken, that it is the essence of a mortgage that in the eye of a Court of Equity it should be a mere security for money, and that no bargain can be validly made which will prevent the mortgagor from redeeming on payment of what is due, including principal, interest, and costs. He may stipulate that he will not pay off his debt, and so redeem the mortgage, for a fixed period. But whenever a right to redeem arises out of the doctrine of equity, he is precluded from fettering it. This principle has become an integral part of our system of jurisprudence and must be faithfully adhered to.

My Lords, the question in the present case is whether the right to redeem has been interferred with. And this must, for the reasons to which I have adverted in considering the history of the doctrine of equity, depend on the answer to a question which is primarily one of fact. What was the true character of the transaction? Did the appellants make a bargain such that the right to redeem was cut down, or did they simply stipulate for a collateral undertaking, outside and clear of the mortgage, which would give them an exclusive option of purchase of the sheepskins of the respondents? The question is in my opinion not whether the two contracts were made at the same moment and evidenced by the same instrument, but whether they were in substance a single and undivided contract or two distinct contracts. Putting aside for the moment considerations turning on the character of the floating charge, such an option no doubt affects the freedom of the respondents in carrying on their business even after the mortgage has been paid off. But so might other arrangements which would be plainly collateral, an agreement, for example, to take permanently into the firm a new partner as a condition of obtaining fresh capital in the form of a loan. The question is one not of form but of substance, and it can be answered in each case only by looking at all the circumstances, and not by mere reliance on some abstract principle, or upon the dicta which have fallen obiter from judges in other and different cases. Some, at least, of the authorities on the subject disclose an embarrassment which has, in my opinion, arisen from neglect to bear this in mind. In applying a principle the ambit and validity of which depend on confining it steadily to the end for which it was established, the analogies of previous instances where it has been applied are apt to be misleading. For each case forms a real precedent only in so far as it affirms a principle, the relevancy of which in other cases turns on the true character of the particular transaction, and to that extent on circumstances. . . . .

My Lords, it is not in my opinion necessary for your Lordships to form an opinion as to whether you would have given the same decisions as were recently given by this House in certain cases which were cited to us. These cases, which related to circumstances differing widely from those before us, have been disposed of finally, and we are not concerned with them excepting in so far as they may have thrown fresh light on questions of principle. What is vital in the appeal now under consideration is to classify accurately the transaction between the parties. What we have to do is to ascertain from scrutiny of the circumstances whether there has really been an attempt to effect a mortgage with a provision preventing redemption of what was pledged merely as security for payment of the amount of the debt and any charges besides that may legitimately be added. It is not, in my opinion, conclusive in favour of the appellants that the security assumed the form of a floating charge. A floating charge is not the less a pledge because of its floating character, and a contract which fetters the right to redeem on which equity insists as regards all contracts of loan and security ought on principle to be set aside as readily in the case of a floating security as in any other case. But it is material that such a floating charge, in the absence of bargain to the contrary effect, permits the assets to be dealt with freely by the mortgagor until the charge becomes enforceable. If it be said that the undertaking of the respondents which was charged extended to their entire business, including the right to dispose of the skins of which they might from time to time become possessed, the comment is that at least they were to be free, so long as the security remained a floating one, to make contracts in the ordinary course of business in regard to these skins. If there had been no mortgage such a contract as the one in question would have been an ordinary incident in such a business. We are considering the simple question of what is the effect on the right to redeem of having inserted into the formal instrument signed when the money was borrowed an ordinary commercial contract for the sale of skins extending over a period. It appears that it was the intention of the parties that the grant of the security should not affect the power to enter into such a contract, either with strangers or with the appellants, and if so I am unable to see how the equity of redemption is affected. No doubt it is the fact that on redemption the respondents will not get back their business as free from obligation as it was before the date of the security. But that may well be because outside the security and consistently with its terms there was a contemporaneous but collateral contract, contained in the same document as constituted the security, but in substance independent of it. If it was the intention of the parties, as I think it was, to enter into this contract as a condition of the respondents getting their advance, I know no reason either in morals or in equity which ought to prevent this intention from being left to have its effect. What was to be capable of redemption was an undertaking which was deliberately left to be freely changed in its details by ordinary business transactions with which the mortgage was not to interfere. Had the charge not been a floating one it might have been more difficult to give effect to this intention. [His Lordship then referred to *Noakes & Co. Ltd v. Rice* [1902] A.C. 24 and *Bradley v. Carritt* [1903] A.C. 253, and continued:] To render it invalid the bargain must, when its substance is examined, turn out to have formed part of the terms of the mortgage and to have really cut down a true right of redemption. I think that the tendency of recent decisions has been to lay undue stress on the letter of the principle which limits the jurisdiction of equity in setting aside contracts. The origin and reason of the principle ought, as I have already said, to be kept steadily in view in applying it to fresh cases. There appears to me to have grown up a tendency to look to the letter rather than to the spirit of the doctrine. The true view is, I think, that judges ought in this kind of jurisdiction to proceed cautiously, and to bear in mind the real reasons which have led courts of equity to insist on the free right to redeem and the limits within which the purpose of the rule ought to confine its scope. I cannot but think that the validity of the bargain in such cases as *Bradley v. Carritt* [1903] A.C. 253 and *Santley v. Wilde* [1899] 2 Ch. 474 might have been made free from serious question if the parties had chosen to seek what would have been substantially the same result in a different form. For form may be very important when the question is one of the construction of ambiguous words in which people have expressed their intentions. I will add that, if I am right in the view which I take of the authorities, there is no reason for thinking that they establish another rule suggested by the learned counsel for the respondents, that even a mere collateral advantage stipulated for in the same instrument as constitutes the mortgage cannot endure after redemption. The dicta on which he relied are really illustrations of the other principles to which I have referred.

LORD PARKER OF WADDINGTON. My Lords, the defendants in this case are appealing to the equitable jurisdiction of the court for relief from a contract which they admit to be fair and reasonable and of which they have already enjoyed the full advantage. Their title to relief is based on some equity which they say is inherent in all transactions in the nature of a mortgage. They can state no intelligible principle underlying this alleged equity, but contend that your Lordships are bound by authority. That the court should be asked in the exercise of its equitable jurisdiction to assist in so inequitable a proceeding as the repudiation of a fair and reasonable bargain is somewhat startling, and makes it necessary to examine the point of view from which courts of equity have always regarded mortgage transactions. . . .

[His Lordship considered at some length the history of the rule against clogging the equity of redemption, and a number of the leading cases. He concluded:]

My Lords, after the most careful consideration of the authorities I think it is open to this House to hold, and I invite your Lordships to hold, that there is now no rule in equity which precludes a mortgagee, whether the mortgage be made upon the occasion of a loan or otherwise, from stipulating for any collateral advantage, provided such collateral advantage is not either (1) unfair and unconscionable, or (2) in the nature of a penalty clogging the equity of redemption, or (3) inconsistent with or repugnant to the contractual and equitable right to redeem. . . .

I doubt whether, even before the repeal of the usury laws, this perfectly fair and businesslike transaction would have been considered a mortgage within any equitable rule or maxim relating to mortgages. The only possible way of deciding whether a transaction is a mortgage within any such rule or maxim is by reference to the intention of the parties. It never was intended by the parties that if the defendant company exercised their right to pay off the loan they should get rid of the option. The option was not in the nature of a penalty, nor was it nor could it ever become inconsistent with or repugnant to any other part of the real bargain within any such rule or maxim. The same is true of the commission payable on the sale of skins as to which the option was not exercised. Under these circumstances it seems to me that the bargain must stand and that the plaintiffs are entitled to the relief they claim.

[The Earl of Halsbury and Lord Atkinson concurred in both judgments extracted. Lord Mersey, in a short concurring judgment, commented: "I have nothing to say about the doctrine [prohibiting clogs on the equity of redemption] itself. It seems to me to be like an unruly dog, which, if not securely chained to its own kennel, is prone to wander into places where it ought not to be. Its introduction into the present case would give effect to no equity and would defeat justice."]

Appeal allowed.

NOTES AND QUESTIONS

1. The following are brief notes on some of the leading cases in this area:

   (1) *Noakes & Co. Ltd v. Rice* [1902] A.C. 24. The purchaser of a leasehold interest in a public house mortgaged it to a brewery. The lease had 26 years to run. The mortgagor covenanted in the mortgage that he would not, at any time during the continuance of the term, whether or not money was still owing under the mortgage, sell any malt liquors except those purchased from the mortgagee. The House of Lords held that the collateral advantage was void as a clog on the equity of redemption, and that the mortgagor was entitled to get back a "free" public house upon repayment of the mortgage: the equity of redemption was "clogged and fettered here by the continuance of an obligation which would render this house less available in the hands of its owner during the whole period . . . of the term . . .": *Noakes & Co. Ltd v. Rice* [1902] A.C. 24 at 29 per Earl of Halsbury L.C.

   (2) *Biggs v. Hoddinott* [1898] 2 Ch. 307. The owner in fee simple of a hotel mortgaged it to a brewery. The loan was not to be repaid in less than five years, and the mortgagor covenanted that during the continuance of the mortgage he would deal exclusively with the mortgagee for all beer sold on the mortgaged premises. The Court of Appeal held that the collateral advantage did not fetter the equity of redemption, and was valid. The distinction between this case and *Noakes & Co. Ltd v. Rice* seems to be that here the collateral advantage was not to endure beyond the repayment of the loan: on repayment the mortgagor would get back a property free from all claims of the mortgagee.

   (3) *Bradley v. Carritt* [1903] A.C. 253. A holder of shares in a tea company mortgaged the shares to a tea broker. In consideration of the advance, the mortgagor agreed to use his best endeavours as a shareholder to ensure that the mortgagee should always thereafter be employed as broker for the sale of the company's teas, and that should any of the company's teas be sold through other brokers, the mortgagor would pay to the mortgagee an amount equal to the commission he would have earned had the teas been sold through him. The mortgagor was the major shareholder in the tea company. The House of Lords held by majority that the collateral advantage was a clog on the equity of redemption, and could not be enforced once the mortgage had been repaid. It was true that the mortgagor's obligation to use his best endeavours was a purely personal one, and that there was nothing to make the shares any less valuable to a purchaser, but the mortgagor's rights over the shares were affected in the sense that in order to prevent the company changing its broker (thereby rendering the mortgagor liable on the covenant), he would have to maintain his interest as majority shareholder; in a practical sense, his previous right of free alienation of the shares was restricted. Sykes, op. cit., p. 64, regards *Bradley v. Carritt* [1903] A.C. 253 as the "high-water mark of the doctrine of the clog", and as an unsatisfactory decision in so far as it involved "too much of a dependence on the possible motives of the mortgagor. The covenant did not bind the mortgagor qua his ownership of the shares though it might have influenced the question as to whether or not he should sell them. The view of the majority appears almost to involve the proposition that no collateral stipulation can survive."

2. In Hinde, McMorland and Sim, op. cit., Vol. 2, pp. 788-792 it is said that four propositions are justified by the cases:

   (a) If the collateral advantage ceases to affect both the security and the mortgagor as soon as the contractual or equitable right to repay is exercised, it is not a clog on the equity of redemption and is valid: *Biggs v. Hoddinott* [1898] 2 Ch. 307.

(b) If the covenant creating the collateral advantage is so framed that the collateral advantage is actually charged on the security in the same way as the principal and interest itself, so that the mortgagor, by the contract, is not entitled to a discharge of his mortgage until the end of the period during which the collateral advantage is intended to operate, the collateral advantage may be enforceable notwithstanding the repayment of the loan and interest thereon. *Santley v. Wilde* [1899] 2 Ch. 474 is cited as authority, although the criticisms of that case are noted, as is its apparent inconsistency with *Fairclough v. Swan Brewery Co. Ltd* [1912] A.C. 565.

(c) If the collateral advantage is not made a charge on the security then, even though it is expressed to be binding for a specified period, it will, after payment of the principal, interest, and costs, be regarded as a clog on the equity of redemption and will not be enforceable: *Noakes & Co. Ltd v. Rice* [1902] A.C. 24 and *Bradley v. Carritt* [1903] A.C. 253.

(d) If the mortgage document can be construed as containing two independent transactions, one a mortgage transaction, and the other a separate transaction relating to the collateral advantage which is in substance independent of the mortgage, the collateral advantage may not be regarded as a clog and may be held to be binding even after the loan has been repaid: *Kreglinger v. New Patagonia Meat and Cold Storage Co. Ltd* [1914] A.C. 25.

Do you agree with this explanation of the cases?

3. Professor Sykes, op cit., p. 65, rationalises the cases under this test: "the courts insist that redemption must be a blotting out of everything which can be considered a part of the mortgage transaction. If a so-called collateral covenant is really part of the mortgage transaction, then it too must be framed so as to cease on redemption." But where there are really two transactions, one a contract for loan and mortgage, and the other a contract embodying the collateral stipulation, "then the separate transaction involving the collateral stipulation will stand even though it contemplates existence during the period after redemption and affects the mortgaged property before and after redemption".

Do you agree? Are there problems in applying this test?

4. In *Toohey v. Gunther* (1928) 41 C.L.R. 181, the owner of a hotel mortgaged it in 1921 to a brewery company to secure an advance, and in addition entered into a bond tying the trade of the hotel to the brewery company until 1935. The conditions attached to the bond were incorporated in a separate document, expressed to be a contract "independent of and collateral to" the contract to repay the mortgage. The brewery company was entitled to hold and retain possession of the Certificate of Title as security for performance of the conditions of the bond. Knox C.J. and Isaacs J. held that the bond was void as a clog on the equity of redemption.

Isaacs J. said (at 194-196):

The bond on its own individual construction unquestionably contains an obligation which would prevent and impede the redemption of the property mortgaged by means of the instrument of mortgage of even date, although full payment were made of principal, interest and costs, that is to say, redemption in as free and unfettered a condition as before the mortgage was given. Not only does it bind the obligor to trade for a fixed term not necessarily ending with the payment of the debt, but it stipulates that for a fixed period or until the bond is discharged the obligee (who was the mortgagee) should hold and retain the Certificate of Title to the land, the subject of the mortgage and of the purchase. . . . The central principle governing the determination of [the] question is stated by Lord Macnaghten for the Privy Council, in *Fairclough v. Swan Brewery Co.* [1912] A.C. 565 at 570, in these words: "It is now firmly established by the House of Lords that . . . equity will not permit any device or contrivance being part of the mortgage transaction or contemporaneous with it to prevent or impede redemption." . . . To this statement of the law, Lord Parker of Waddington gave his assent in *Kreglinger's* case [1914] A.C. at 60. It thus appears that, if the bond was given either (a) as part of the mortgage transaction or (b) contemporaneously with that transaction, the obligation and stipulation referred to would be inoperative. The appellant contends that the bond, though given contemporaneously, was not part of the mortgage transaction but was a separate and independent instrument. One answer is that, even so, the bond on construction comes within the principle stated by the two supreme judicial tribunals of the Empire, and within the mischief which that principle is intended to guard against. The other answer is that the contention is true only if the expression "mortgage transaction" is limited to the narrow sense of the mortgage instrument creating the formal legal relation of mortgagee and mortgagor under the [*Real Property Act* 1900 (N.S.W.)]. That by force of the statute is necessarily a separate instrument, a circumstance which plays an important part later, but in no way alters the broad character of the transaction from which it flows and of which it forms part. "The mortgage transaction" in this connection must be understood in the wider sense as the general comprehensive arrangement or agreement made between [the mortgagor] and the brewery company whereby the company was to advance £4,500 and [the mortgagor] was to execute the mortgage, . . . and the bond: see per Lord Parker in *Kreglinger's* case [1914] A.C. 25 at 48. Had the bond been executed on a later date, the fact that in truth it was part of the mortgage transaction would bring it within the principle quoted.

See also per Knox C.J. at 191-192.

For other Australian cases, see *Tooth & Co. v. Parkes* (1900) 21 L.R.(N.S.W.) (Eq.) 173; *Perth Brewery Co. Ltd v. Simms* (1903) 5 W.A.L.R. 24; *Queensland Brewery Ltd v. Baker* [1936] St. R. Qd 98.

5. Covenants securing collateral advantages must also be considered in the light of modern business and consumer protection legislation, such as the *Trade Practices Act* 1974 (Cth), the *Industrial Arbitration Act* 1940 (N.S.W.) and the *Contracts Review Act* 1980 (N.S.W.). This legislation is discussed below p. 434 et seq.

D. MISCELLANEOUS MATTERS

1. Covenant to repay a greater amount than that advanced

A covenant in a mortgage by which the mortgagor agrees, upon default occurring under the mortgage, to pay a larger amount than would otherwise be payable, is not enforceable. The true rationale for this rule probably is that such a covenant is in the nature of a penalty, but it has been explained also as constituting a clog on the equity of redemption: see *Booth v. Salvation Army Building Association Ltd* (1897) 14 T.L.R. 3.

There is no rule, however, preventing the mortgage requiring the mortgagor to pay a bonus, or premium, over and above the sum advanced (such as an advance of £700 on the security of a mortgage for £1,000 plus interest: *Potter v. Edwards* (1857) 26 L.J. Ch. 468), provided the agreement is not unconscionable or oppressive.

MULTISERVICE BOOKBINDING LTD v. MARDEN

Chancery Division [1979] Ch. 84

[The plaintiff company borrowed £36,000 from the defendant on the security of a mortgage over its business premises. Both parties were represented by solicitors at the time the mortgage was agreed to. The defendant wanted to preserve the purchasing power of the sum advanced, and, to that end, the mortgage provided: (1) that the plaintiff throughout the term of the mortgage would pay interest at 2 per cent above the ruling bank rate, quarterly in advance, on the whole of the £36,000 (notwithstanding that capital repayments were to be made); (2) that the mortgage could not be redeemed within ten years; and (3) (clause 6) that repayments of principal and interest were to be linked to the Swiss franc (this being intended as a guard against depreciation of the pound sterling).

At the end of the ten year period the plaintiff sought to redeem the mortgage. During that period, the pound sterling had depreciated greatly in value against the Swiss franc, such that the original capital of £36,000 had increased to over £87,500 and the original interest liability of £31,000 had increased to £45,000. The plaintiff sought orders that: (1) the clause linking repayments to the Swiss franc (the "Swiss franc uplift" clause) was void or unenforceable as against public policy; and (2) the Swiss franc uplift clause and the terms of the mortgage, taken together, were unenforceable on the ground of unreasonableness.]

BROWNE-WILKINSON J. [His Lordship held that an index-linked money obligation, such as the Swiss franc uplift clause, was not contrary to public policy. He proceeded:] I turn then to the question whether the mortgage is unconscionable or unreasonable. The plaintiffs' starting point on this aspect of the case is a submission that a lender on mortgage is only entitled to repayment of principal, interest and costs. If the lender additionally stipulates for a premium or other collateral advantage the court will not enforce such additional stipulation unless it is reasonable. Then it is submitted that clause 6, providing for the payment of the Swiss franc uplift in addition to the nominal amount of capital and interest, is a premium which in all the circumstances is unreasonable. Alternatively it is said that the terms of the mortgage taken together are unreasonable. In my judgment the argument so advanced is based on a false premise. Since the repeal of the usury laws there has been no general principle that collateral advantages in mortgages have to be "reasonable". The law is fully explained by the House of Lords in *Kreglinger v. New Patagonia Meat and Cold Storage Co. Ltd* [1914] A.C. 25 and in particular in the speech of Lord Parker of Waddington.

[His Lordship quoted extensively from the judgment of Lord Parker in *Kreglinger's* case, concluding with that portion in which Lord Parker had said, "there is now no rule in equity which precludes a mortgagee, whether the mortgage be made upon the occasion of a loan or otherwise, from stipulating for any collateral advantage, provided such collateral advantage is not either (1) unfair and unconscionable, or (2) in the nature of a penalty clogging the equity of redemption, or (3) inconsistent with or repugnant to the contractual and equitable right to redeem". His Lordship continued:]

It is not suggested in this case that any of the terms of the mortgage clog the equity of redemption or are inconsistent with the right to redeem. Therefore on Lord Parker's test, if the plaintiffs are to be excused from complying with any of the terms of the mortgage they must show that the term is, "unfair and unconscionable": the test is not one of reasonableness.

Lord Parker's reasoning is entirely consistent with that of Viscount Haldane L.C. [1914] A.C. 25 who stated (at 37) that since the repeal of the usury laws "a collateral advantage may now be stipulated for by the mortgagee provided that he has not acted unfairly or oppressively".

In the *Kreglinger* case the exact question whether the true test was "unconscionableness" or "unreasonableness" did not arise for decision because it was conceded that the bargain was a reasonable one in that case. But in my judgment the exact point was decided by the Court of Appeal in *Knightsbridge Estates Trust Ltd v. Byrne* [1939] Ch. 441. . . .

In my judgment the Court of Appeal in overruling the decision of Luxmoore J. based on the unreasonableness of the term made a decision, first that if a postponement of the right to redeem is not objectionable on the grounds that it is a clog on the right to redeem, it is enforceable like any other stipulation unless it falls into Lord Parker's first category as being oppressive or unconscionable; and secondly that mere unreasonableness does not make a term oppressive or unconscionable.

Knightsbridge Estates Trust Ltd v. Bryne [1939] Ch. 441 went to the House of Lords ([1940] A.C. 613) where the decision of the Court of Appeal was upheld on other grounds, but so far as I can see no doubt was thrown on the reasoning of the Court of Appeal.

I have dealt with these authorities at some length because the sheet anchor of Mr Nugee's [counsel for the plaintiff] argument, that mere unreasonableness is sufficient to invalidate a stipulation, is the use of the word "unreasonable" by Goff J. in *Cityland and Property (Holdings) Ltd v. Dabrah* [1968] Ch. 166. In that case the plaintiff company was the freehold owner of a house of which the defendant had been the tenant for 11 years. His lease expired and the plaintiff company sold the freehold to him for £3,500, of which the defendant paid £600 in cash and the balance of £2,900 was left by the plaintiff company on mortgage. The mortgage was in unusual terms in that it contained simply a covenant to pay, by instalments, the sum of £4,553, that is to say, a premium of 57 per cent over the sum advanced. No explanation was given as to what this premium represented. The defendant defaulted in paying his instalments after only one year, and the plaintiff was seeking to enforce his security for the full sum of £4,553 less payments actually made. Not surprisingly Goff J. refused to permit this on the grounds that the excess over £2,900 was an unlawful premium. Bearing in mind the relative strength of lender and borrower, the size of the premium and the lack of any explanation or justification for it, the premium in that case was unconscionable and oppressive. The difficulty arises from a passage in the judgment, where after reviewing the authorities, including citations at length from Lord Parker's speech in the *Kreglinger* case [1914] A.C. 25, Goff J. quoted (at 180) this passage from *Halsbury's Laws of England* (3rd ed.), Vol. 27, p. 238: "but a contract for payment to the mortgagee of a bonus in addition to the sum advanced is valid if the bonus is reasonable and the contract was freely entered into by the mortgagor." Having quoted that passage Goff J. continued (at 180): "It follows from those authorities that the defendant cannot succeed merely because this is a collateral advantage, but he can succeed if—and only if—on the evidence, the bonus in this case was, to use the language of Lord Parker, 'unfair and unconscionable', or, to use the language used in *Halsbury's Laws of England*, 'unreasonable'; and I therefore have to determine whether it was or was not." There are other passages in the judgment where Goff J. seems to treat the words "unreasonable" and "unconscionable" as being interchangeable. But in that case it was unnecessary for him to distinguish between the two concepts, since on either test the premium was unenforceable. I do not think that Goff J. intended to cut down the obvious effect of the *Kreglinger* case [1914] A.C. 25 in any way. Moreover, the decision of the Court of Appeal in *Knightsbridge Estates Trust Ltd v. Byrne* [1939] Ch. 441 was not cited to him.

I therefore approach the second point on the basis that, in order to be freed from the necessity to comply with all the terms of the mortgage, the plaintiffs must show that the bargain, or some of its terms, was unfair and unconscionable: it is not enough to show that, in the eyes of the court, it was unreasonable. In my judgment a bargain cannot be unfair and unconscionable unless one of the parties to it has imposed the objectionable terms in a morally reprehensible manner, that is to say, in a way which affects his conscience.

The classic example of an unconscionable bargain is where advantage has been taken of a young, inexperienced or ignorant person to introduce a term which no sensible well-advised person or party would have accepted. But I do not think the categories of unconscionable bargains are limited: the court can and should intervene where a bargain has been procured by unfair means.

Mr Nugee submitted that a borrower was, in the normal case, in an unequal bargaining position vis-á-vis the lender and that the care taken by the courts of equity to protect borrowers—to which Lord Parker referred in the passage I have quoted—was reflected in a general rule that, except in the case of two large equally powerful institutions, any unreasonable term would be "unconscionable" within Lord Parker's test. I cannot accept this. In my judgment there is no such special rule applicable to contracts of loan which requires one to treat a bargain as having been unfairly made even where it is demonstrated that no unfair advantage has been taken of the borrower. No decision illustrating Mr Nugee's principle was cited.

However, if, as in the *Cityland* case [1968] Ch. 166, there is an unusual or unreasonable stipulation the reason for which is not explained, it may well be that in the absence of any explanation, the court will assume that unfair advantage has been taken of the borrower. In considering all the facts, it will often be the case that the borrower's need for the money was far more pressing than the lenders [sic] need to lend: if this proves to be the case, then circumstances exist in which an unfair advantage could have been taken. It does not necessarily follow that what could have been done has been done: whether or not an unfair advantage has in fact been taken depends on the facts of each case.

Applying those principles to this case, first I do not think it is right to treat the "Swiss franc uplift" element in the capital-repayments as being in any sense a premium or collateral advantage. In my judgment a lender of money is entitled to insure that he is repaid the real value of his loan and if he introduces a term which so provides, he is not stipulating for anything beyond the repayment of principal. I do not think equity would have struck down clause 6 as a collateral advantage even before the repeal of the usury laws. The decision in *Booth v. Salvation Army Building Assoc. Ltd* (1897) 14 T.L.R. 3, turned on quite different considerations. It is in my opinion correctly explained by Professor Waldock in his *Law of Mortgages* (2nd ed.), p. 182 as a decision that any additional sum expressed to be payable on redemption or default is not recoverable since it is a clog on the equity of redemption. . . .

[His Lordship went on to hold that there was no substantial inequality of bargaining power between the parties; that no unfair advantage had been taken of the plaintiff; and that, had it been relevant, he would have found the terms of the mortgage to be unreasonable.]

NOTES

1. In *Stanwell Park Hotel Co. Ltd v. Leslie* (1952) 85 C.L.R. 189 at 201, the High Court of Australia said:

   There is no principle of law preventing parties adopting a fixed figure as the primary monetary expression of a liability and then proceeding to effect a substantive variation of the liability by providing that more or less money must be actually paid according as index numbers evidence a variation of price levels. That is only a method of measuring the actual liability contracted for.

2. The principal case was applied by the New South Wales Court of Appeal in *Charmelyn Enterprises Pty Ltd v. Klonis* (1982) A.N.Z. Conv. R. 356. The Court of Appeal held that a stipulation in a mortgage tying the principal sum to the consumer price index was not void. See also *Nationwide Building Society v. Registry of Friendly Societies* [1983] 3 All E.R. 296.

3. The principal case is noted in (1979) 42 M.L.R. 338-342; (1981) 55 A.L.J. 820.

2. Covenant to pay a higher rate of interest upon default

Equity regards as a penalty, and so unenforceable, a clause which provides that upon default in payment the mortgagor must pay a higher rate of interest than that otherwise reserved by the mortgage. It has long been assumed, however, that a clause which provides for a lower rate of interest upon prompt payment is in order: *Strode v. Parker* (1694) 2 Vern. 316; 23 E.R. 804. This latter rule, if correct, provides a convenient method for avoiding the former rule: a mortgagee who wishes to charge interest at the rate of 9 per cent but also to impose a penalty rate of 10 per cent as an incentive for prompt payment, simply charges interest at 10 per cent with a proviso that 9 per cent will be accepted on prompt payment of each instalment.

QUESTION

Is there a penalty in the following situation: A mortgage provides that the mortgagor will repay the sum of $ (X + Y), being the principal sum ($X) plus the total of the interest payable over the term of the mortgage ($Y), by 119 equal monthly instalments, but that in the event of default in any payment the mortgagee may charge simple interest on the amount unpaid from the date of default to the date of payment at the rate of 12 per cent per annum, and also that upon default the unpaid balance of the principal sum (not included in any overdue instalment) should at the mortgagee's election become payable on demand and liable to simple interest at the rate of 12 per cent per annum from the date of demand to the date of payment: see *C.J. Belmont Pty Ltd v. A.G.C. (General Finance) Ltd* [1976] 1 N.S.W.L.R. 507.

3. Covenant to pay whole of principal and interest immediately upon default

Mortgages often contain provisions whereby on default in any payment the whole of the principal and interest becomes immediately due and payable.

WANNER v. CARUANA

Supreme Court of New South Wales [1974] 2 N.S.W.L.R. 301

[The vendor of a farm advanced part of the purchase price to the purchasers, secured by a mortgage and bill of sale over the farm and certain chattels. By the mortgage (the bill of sale was in identical terms), interest was payable at the rate of 10 per cent, reducible to 9 per cent on prompt payment, and the whole amount advanced plus interest was to be repaid within six years, namely by 23 August 1978. By a proviso to clause 18, in the event of default in any payment for 14 days, "the whole of the balance of the principal sum . . . with interest thereon at the rate of ten dollars ($10.00) per centum per annum shall in the case of such default immediately become due and payable for the balance of the term up to and including the 23rd day of August 1978". The mortgagors/purchasers defaulted under the mortgage, and the mortgagee claimed to be entitled to repayment of the principal then outstanding together with interest at the rate of 10 per cent per annum for the remainder of the term of the mortgage (which still had about five years to run). The mortgagee sought a declaration that the proviso to clause 18 was not void as a penalty. The purchasers/mortgagors argued that it was void as a penalty.]

STREET C.J. IN EQ. In determining whether or not this provision for the payment of future and as yet unaccrued interest throughout the next five years upon default in payment of stipulated instalments is void, it is relevant to bear in mind that the mortgage and bill of sale were given simply and solely to secure the outstanding balance of the purchase price of this farm. It is also relevant to note that neither the mortgage nor the bill of sale purported to quantify in an aggregate sum the amount of interest which would accrue during the agreed term of the loan.

The point is a relatively short one, but is apparently not directly covered by authority. The matter has accordingly been argued from first principles, and I should make reference to some of the cases. In *Protector Endowment Loan and Annunity Co. v. Grice* (1880) 5 Q.B.D. 592 the facts disclosed a present debt, acknowledged by the parties at the time of the transaction, but agreed between them to be paid by a series of instalments. There was provision for the whole amount to become immediately due and payable in the event of default in the payment of any instalment. The Court of Appeal took the view that this agreement was not void as a penalty. Cockburn L.J. said (1880) 5 Q.B.D. 592 at 594, 595: "The clauses in question in the present case were essential parts of the contract; it is an agreement for a discharge by quarterly instalments of the whole debt, but if there is a failure to perform the agreement, a condition is inserted that the whole amount shall become payable at once; it is not merely a mode of securing payment of the instalments." . . .

Bramwell and Brett L.JJ. took a similar view. Brett L.J. said ((1880) 5 Q.B.D. 592 at 596): "The contract is that the borrower shall repay £70, there is no other debt, and no other sum is mentioned. It is an agreement to repay by quarterly instalments; but if default should be made, then the whole sum of £70 was to become payable at once. In my opinion the stipulation to pay immediately is not to be treated as a penalty; but a stipulation to pay a larger sum upon default would be a penalty, and could not be recovered: *Sterne v. Beck* (1863) 1 De G.J. & Sm. 595; 46 E.R. 236 and *Thompson v. Hudson* (1869) L.R. 4 H.L. 1 shew what the true rule is; if a larger sum is to be paid upon default, it is a penalty; a stipulation to pay upon default a sum not larger than the total amount is not a penalty."

Grice's case (1880) 5 Q.B.D. 592 was considered by the High Court in *Lamson Store Service Co. Ltd v. Russell Wilkins & Sons Ltd* (1906) 4 C.L.R. 672. In that case the court was concerned with an agreement for the hire of certain plant. The agreement made provision, in the event of default, for rent for the balance of the term to become immediately due and payable. There was a division of opinion in the High Court. Griffith C.J. and Barton J. held that the stipulation did not amount to a penalty; O'Connor J. considered that it did. The point of departure between the opposing conclusions turned to no small extent upon the construction that the learned judges respectively put upon the document before the court. O'Connor J., in his dissenting judgment (1906) 4 C.L.R. 672 at 692, took the view that "the principle of acceleration of payments" as recognised in *Grice's* case (1880) 5 Q.B.D. 592 was not called into play by the nature of the agreement before the High Court. The majority regarded the provision for the acceleration of rent as a genuine pre-estimate of the creditor's probable or possible interest in the due performance of the principal obligation. They held that in those circumstances there was a present debt payable in the future. This appears clearly in the judgment of Griffith C.J. [His Honour quoted from the judgment of Griffith C.J. (1906) 4 C.L.R. 672 at 683, and continued:]

Upon the facts before the High Court in the *Lamson Store* case (1906) 4 C.L.R. 672, as is apparent from the passage I have just read from the judgment of Griffith C.J., the equipment which was the subject of the hiring agreement was of such a nature that it was reasonable to attribute to the lessor a commercial desire to have the advantage of his equipment actually being in use during the agreed term. It was this that led the majority, in construing the document, to hold that the provision for the advancement of the future rent was a provision which in substance amounted to a single quantification of the damage which would be suffered by the lessor, in the event of a default on the part of the lessee so that the term did not run its full contractual period. As I have already said, O'Connor J. took a different view of the construction of the bargain made by the parties.

The decision of the High Court in *I.A.C. (Leasing) Ltd v. Humphrey* (1972) 126 C.L.R. 131 provides a recent instance of the case [sic] with which a court will examine the details of a bargain providing for acceleration of payments in the event of default in order to ascertain whether the acceleration can be regarded as a genuine pre-estimate of damage. The analysis capable of being made, and actually made, of the factual situation in that case is in sharp contrast with the limited scope of the facts in the present case. Here there is simply a mortgage back at interest to protect the unpaid balance of purchase price on an ordinary contract of sale and purchase.

The provision here is for acceleration of unaccrued, indeed unearned, interest referable to a period when the vendors will have, in consequence of the default, recovered the full amount of the balance of the purchase price.

In the present case there was no commercial advantage to the mortgagees from the mortgage running a full six year term as distinct from terminating, as it did, within one year of its inception. This mortgage was simply a document which provided for payment of the principal debt by instalments, and provided for future interest to accrue periodically throughout the six year term. The falling in of the mortgage debt prior to the expiration of the six year term might have occurred within a month, a year or five years of the initial date. The lumping together of unaccrued interest, and the imposition upon the mortgagors of the burden of making that payment, appears to me to bear no relationship whatever to the loss which the mortgagees might suffer by reason of the mortgage falling in and the mortgage debt being repaid to them prior to the expiration of the six year term. There is a significant difference between the facts of this case and the facts in the two High Court cases I have referred to; the approach taken by the High Court in each of those cases shows the consequence in point of invalidity of that significant factual difference. The present mortgage has, in this respect, the hallmarks of a stipulation in terrorem designed to force the mortgagors to adhere to their bargain, and I do not see that this provision has any of the ingredients of a genuine pre-estimate.

Nor do I regard the present agreement as falling within the type of provision which permits acceleration of future instalments of an agreed present debt, as was the case in *Protector Endowment Loan and Annuity Co. v. Grice* (1880) 5 Q.B.D. 592. If the mortgagees had stipulated for a single lump sum premium or an aggregation of interest at the outset to be paid by instalments throughout the term, then it might be that the mere form of such a document would render a challenge on the ground of penalty difficult. But that is not this case.

The provisions of s. 93 of the *Conveyancing Act* 1919 (N.S.W.)—a statutory enactment which I note has no parallel in England—have of necessity led me to hesitate before stating this view. Under that section, a mortgagor has a statutory right at any time during the term of the mortgage to pay off the principal, together with interest for the whole of the originally agreed term, and then to receive a discharge of the mortgage. That section is not directly in issue in the present proceedings. But whilst its precise scope may be left for due determination if and when the point arises, one cannot fail to observe that it apparently proceeds upon the basis that the obligation on a mortgagor to pay presently unaccrued interest was regarded as acceptable by the legislature. Whatever may be the rationalisation of s. 93, it does not apply in the present case, and I do not consider that it should stand in the way of reaching, and giving effect to, the conclusion I have stated, namely that the provision in this mortgage for the advancement of the as yet unaccrued instalments of interest is a penalty, against which relief should be granted to the mortgagors. If the legislature intended to fetter the court's wholesome power to recognise and invalidate penalties, it would have expressed this intention in clear and unmistakable terms. An inference based upon presumed tacit assumption by the legislature is far too weak a basis for treating as valid a bargain which, in the absence of s. 93, would be void as a penalty.

For the foregoing reasons I shall refuse the declaration sought by the plaintiffs, and in lieu declare that the proviso to clause 18 of the memorandum of mortgage is a penalty against which the defendants are entitled to relief.

Declaration granted.

NOTES

1. Section 93 of the *Conveyancing Act* 1919 (N.S.W.), referred to by Street C.J. in Eq., is discussed below.

2. How might the proviso to clause 18 of the mortgage have been drafted to avoid being characterised as a penalty?

3. The two decisions discussed by Street C.J. in Eq. in the principal case (namely, *Protector Endowment Loan and Annuity Co. v. Grice* and *Lamson Store Service Co. Ltd v. Russell Wilkins & Sons Ltd*) were themselves discussed by the High Court in *O'Dea v. Allstates Leasing System (W.A.) Pty Ltd* (1983) 57 A.L.J.R. 172. There were some reservations expressed as to the decision in *Lamson's* case. Gibbs C.J. (at 178) thought that unless *Lamson's* case was confined to its own particular facts he would decline to follow it; Murphy J. (at 178) thought it should be overruled; both Wilson J. (at 181) and Brennan J. (at 183) were able to distinguish it on its facts so that it was unnecessary to re-examine its correctness; and Deane J. (at 190-191) thought that both it and *Grice's* case accorded "neither with the principle that the question whether a sum is a penalty is a question of substance and not of mere form nor with the approach adopted in the subsequent cases . . . and should not be followed."

   See generally Ong, "Chattel Leasing: Indulgences, Liquidated Damages and Penalties" (1986) 60 A.L.J. 272.

4. The fact that a provision for acceleration of payments in the event of default is unenforceable as a penalty, does not prevent a claim for damages for actual loss suffered as a result of the default. In *AMEV-UDC Finance Ltd v. Austin* (1986) 60 A.L.J.R. 741, the High Court considered the extent of damages due to a lessor of goods under a leasing agreement which provided, inter alia, that the whole amount payable over the term of the agreement should become immediately due and payable upon default by the lessee. In the light of *O'Dea's* case, the acceleration provision was conceded to be a penalty, but its unenforceability was held to be no bar to the recovery of damages, although substantial differences of opinion were expressed as to the extent of the damages recoverable. However, it does at least now seem clear from dicta in *Austin's* case and from the subsequent decision of the High Court in *Esanda Finance Corp. Ltd v. Plessing* (1989) 63 A.L.J.R. 238, that no penalty will exist where the mortgage provides that upon default by the mortgagor all future payments under the mortgage shall become immediately due and payable, but *discounted* by an appropriate formula so as to ensure that the mortgagee receives no more than the present value of the amounts outstanding; such a provision is no more than a genuine pre-estimate of the mortgagee's loss in the event of default—namely, the loss of the right to receive the future payments.

4. Unconscionable dealing

Mortgages, like other transactions affecting property, may be set aside on the general equitable ground of unconscionable dealing. The principle of unconscionable dealing has been said to apply:

> whenever one party to transaction is at a special disadvantage in dealing with the other party because illness, ignorance, inexperience, impaired faculties, financial need or other circumstances affect his ability to conserve his own interests, and the other party unconscientiously takes advantage of the opportunity thus placed in his hands: *Blomley v. Ryan* (1956) 99 C.L.R. 362 at 415 per Kitto J.

In *Commercial Bank of Australia v. Amadio* (1983) 57 A.L.J.R. 358, the High Court of Australia set aside a mortgage given by elderly parents to guarantee the indebtedness of their son's business to a bank. The parents were not aware of the serious financial difficulties being experienced by the business; nor were they aware that the bank stood to gain from the guarantee a significant improvement on its previously inadequate security whilst they faced the prospect of immediate loss of their property. The parents had little command of written English, and it appeared that had they received independent advice they would not have entered into the mortgage. Deane J. expressed the relevant principles in these words ((1983) 57 A.L.J.R. 358 at 369):

The jurisdiction of courts of equity to relieve against unconscionable dealing developed from the jurisdiction which the Court of Chancery assumed, at a very early period, to set aside transactions in which expectant heirs had dealt with their expectations without being adequately protected against the pressure put upon them by their poverty: see *O'Rorke v. Bolingbroke* (1877) 2 App. Cas. 814 at 822. The jurisdiction is long established as extending generally to circumstances in which (i) a party to a transaction was under a special disability in dealing with the other party with the consequence that there was an absence of any reasonable degree of equality between them; and (ii) the disability was sufficiently evident to the stronger party to make it prima facie unfair or "unconscientious" that he procure, or accept, the weaker party's assent to the impugned transaction in the circumstances in which he procured or accepted it. Where such circumstances are shown to have existed, an onus is cast upon the stronger party to show that the transaction was fair, just and reasonable: "the burthen of shewing the fairness of the transaction is thrown on the person who seeks to obtain the benefit of the contract": see *O'Rorke v. Bolingbroke* (1877) 2 App. Cas. 814 at 823 per Lord Hatherley; *Fry v. Lane* (1888) 40 Ch. D. 312 at 322; *Blomley v. Ryan* (1956) 99 C.L.R. 362 at 428-429.

5. Early redemption of mortgages

A mortgagor is entitled on the contractual date for repayment to redeem the mortgage and have the legal estate reconveyed to her or him: *Crickmore v. Freestone* (1870) 40 L.J. Ch. 137. He or she is also entitled in equity to redeem after the contractual date for redemption has passed. But he or she is not entitled to redeem before the contractual date for repayment, in the absence of agreement or statutory right to that effect (*Brown v. Cole* (1845) 14 Sim. 427; 60 E.R. 424); and the fact that the mortgage requires repayment on a certain date of the advance "or so much as shall then remain outstanding" does not, of itself, amount to an agreement that the mortgagor may redeem before the due date: *Hyde Management Services Pty Ltd v. F.A.I. Insurances Ltd* (1979) 144 C.L.R. 541.

In New South Wales, s. 93(1) of the *Conveyancing Act* 1919 provides:

> (1) A mortgagor is entitled to redeem the mortgaged property although the time appointed for redemption has not arrived; but in such case he shall pay to the mortgagee, in addition to any other moneys then owing under the mortgage, interest on the principal sum secured thereby for the unexpired portion of the term of the mortgage: Provided that redemption under this subsection shall not prejudice the right of the mortgagee to any collateral benefit, or to enforce any burden or restriction to the extent to which he would be entitled under the mortgage or otherwise if the mortgage were paid off at the due date.

This provision applies notwithstanding any stipulation to the contrary: s. 93(3).

STOCKS AND ENTERPRISES PTY LTD v. McBURNEY

New South Wales Court of Appeal (1977) 1 B.P.R. 9521

[Pursuant to a mortgage dated 16 April 1975, the mortgagor covenanted to repay the principal sum advanced, or so much as should remain unpaid, on 16 April 1978, and, by clause 2, to pay interest each quarter "until the said principal sum shall be fully paid and satisfied". The mortgage did not specify an aggregate gross sum of principal plus interest payable over the three years. By clause 7, upon default in payment of principal or interest, "the principal money hereby secured shall immediately fall due, and the mortgagor will thereupon pay the same on demand and it shall be lawful for the mortgagee to sue for [the interest and principal] although the time for payment . . . shall not have arrived".

The mortgagor defaulted in payment of interest, and on 15 April 1976 the solicitors for the mortgagee wrote stating that they had been instructed to institute proceedings to recover the mortgage advance and arrears of interest.

By late 1976 the mortgagor had sold the property and was in a position to pay out the mortgage. Whilst conceding that there had been default under the mortgage, the mortgagor claimed that it was obliged to pay interest to the date of payment only. The mortgagee claimed that it was entitled to receive interest for the unexpired term of the mortgage.

Waddell J. upheld the mortgagee's claim. On appeal.]

STREET C.J. The seventh clause, in the facts of the present case, operated to make the $30,000 principal sum fall *due* upon the date of the first default, that is to say, on 13 September 1975. But, whilst due at all times thereafter, the principal sum did not become *payable* by the mortgag[or] until the mortgag[ee], in the due exercise of its rights under the seventh clause, made demand for it. Although the principal sum had fallen due, it was not yet payable. Prior to the making of a demand the mortgagor could not be heard to assert any right on its part to pay the sum to the mortgagees until the expiration of the agreed three year term. There is no substance in the proposition, courageously advanced on behalf of the mortgagor, that by committing a default it could unilaterally foreshorten the three year term and acquire a right to effect immediate repayment. The debt secured by the mortgage was for a three year term. The mortgagor was obliged to keep the principal sum and to pay interest on it as required by the second clause through until the expiration of the three year term. The seventh clause went on to contain the promise by the mortgagor that it "will thereupon pay the sum on demand". This is of critical significance. The making of the demand by the mortgagees rendered the principal sum due and payable. The debt ceased to be one for a three year term. This change in its objective character, arising as it did on the making of the demand, resulted in the debtor-creditor relationship, existing between the parties and constituting the basis of the mortgage, becoming one in which the mortgagor, as debtor, was entitled to make, equally as the mortgagee, as creditor, was entitled to enforce, immediate repayment of the debt together with such interest as was required by the terms of the mortgage document. . . .

The seventh clause itself in express terms provides for the consequence of a default in the payment of interest: the principal sum immediately falls due and is payable on demand. The mortgagees may choose to refrain from making a demand in which case the originally agreed term will run on. The mortgagees may lose their right to make a demand by conduct on their part rendering it inequitable to permit them to assert this right. The present case does not involve any investigation in that area. On the other hand, the mortgagees may, as they have done here, exercise their express contractual right to make a demand. Once they have done so, that is an end of the originally agreed term—the principal sum becomes and remains presently due and payable.

I should add that, although I regard the form of the relevant portion of the seventh clause as involving a distinction between the debt falling due and the debt becoming payable, this distinction is not critical to the approach I make to the construction of this clause. The significant element is that wrapped up in the words "on demand". It is immaterial for present purposes whether the clause involves the demand as rendering the debt both due and payable, or whether the demand operates to render payable a debt that has already fallen due.

It is upon the foregoing rights and obligations affecting the respective parties that the liability of the mortgagor to pay interest is to be determined. The second clause does not, as I have previously emphasised, expressly require the payment of interest throughout the three year term. The clause is specifically drawn so as to impose upon the mortgagor a liability to pay interest at the stated rate "until the said principal sum shall be fully paid and satisfied". I see no satisfactory alternative to construing this clause in such a way as to impose upon the mortgagor, in a case where the principal sum has become due and payable as it has here, an obligation to pay interest up to and not beyond the date when the principal sum is fully paid and satisfied. The mortgage document does not in its terms purport to impose any greater obligation upon the mortgagor. There is no justification for importing such an obligation from some source extraneous to the terms of the mortgage document itself.

Not only is this the construction that follows from the ordinary meaning of the seventh clause, but it is the only construction consistent with the concluding portion of that clause. This concluding portion after requiring that the mortgagor shall pay the principal sum on demand, prescribes that it shall be lawful for the mortgagor [sic] to sue for, recover and receive not only such interest as may already have fallen due but also the principal sum although the time for payment shall not have arrived. This concluding portion is wholly silent as to any continuing obligation on the mortgagor to pay interest for the balance of the three year term at a point of time after the mortgagees have received the principal sum and "such interest as may be due as aforesaid"—that is to say, interest already accrued. It is difficult to find within the terms of the mortgage document any contractual obligation on the mortgagor to pay interest at a point of time after the principal sum has been received in full by the mortgagees. The second clause does not, on its face, give rise to any such obligation and there is no other source from which it could readily be said to arise.

The appellant, having, as Waddell J. held, made a demand for payment, the obligation of the respondents in the matter of interest was to make payment of interest accrued up until the principal sum was fully paid and satisfied in response to the demand. I do not consider that there was any obligation on the respondents to pay interest beyond that point.

SAMUELS J.A. Waddell J. found that the letter of 15 April constituted a demand "for payment of all moneys then due under the mortgage including, of course, the principal sum, the time for payment of which had been accelerated by the plaintiff's default"; and that this demand "was still on foot when these proceedings were commenced". These conclusions were only faintly challenged. They are, if I may say so, clearly right. It is equally clear, I think, that the mortgagor did not at any time seek to redeem. It sought to satisfy the mortgagees' lawful demand by selling the property, and paying the moneys due out of the proceeds of sale.

I find it difficult therefore to understand how the mortgagees can make good their argument, based as it is upon the provisions of s. 93 of the *Conveyancing Act* 1919 (N.S.W.) (as amended). Section 93(1) commences "A mortgagor is entitled to redeem the mortgaged property although the time appointed for redemption has not arrived"; and then provides that in such case he shall pay to the mortgagee, in addition to any other moneys then owing under the mortgage, interest on the principal sum secured thereby for the unexpired portion of the term. The subsection therefore applies in the case of a mortgagor who seeks a premature redemption. But that was never the case here. One of [counsel for the mortgagees'] opening submissions was: "The situation with which one here is confronted is a situation in which a mortgagor is seeking to redeem a mortgage prior to the contractual date fixed by the mortgage document." But that was not the situation. The evidence establishes not that the mortgagor sought to redeem, but that it sought to answer the mortgagees' demand. And that situation is not the one to which s. 93(1) is directed.

Let me see if I can test the matter in this way. Suppose that immediately following the letter of 15 April the mortgagor had tendered to the mortgagees the principal sum and all other moneys due under the mortgage, including arrears of interest; and, for completeness, any costs to which the mortgagees were entitled. Would the mortgagees have been entitled to reject the tender made and require the mortgagor to add to it a sum for interest to the end of the term? I would have thought not. The mortgagor's answer to such a demand would no doubt have been that, while ready to satisfy the mortgagees' demand under clause 7, it had no wish to redeem the mortgage, and had never sought to do so. Suppose that the mortgagees, dissatisfied with this answer, sued to recover the whole of their further demand. How would the action be framed? The claim for principal and interest overdue would be well founded upon the mortgage. But the mortgage contains no footing for the demand for prospective interest. So this claim would have to depend upon s. 93(1), and would be successfully met by the mortgagor's previous answer. In short, the subsection would have no application, because its factual basis—that is, the mortgagor's claim or request to redeem before the contractual date for redemption—was lacking.

Suppose that the mortgagees did not sue, but exercised their power of sale. Or suppose that they sold in the absence of any tender by the mortgagor of the amount due. If the sale realised more than was necessary to satisfy the amount of principal and overdue interest, could the mortgagees then pay themselves interest to the end of the term out of the surplus? Clearly not, as the authorities establish.

So, in the present case, if the mortgagees had carried out their threat and exercised their power of sale, they could not have applied the proceeds to meet their claim for prospective interest. I can see no rational basis for concluding that they were entitled to get more from their demand than they could have got from a sale; or that the mortgagor could satisfy the mortgagees' demand only by tendering more than their entitlement from the proceeds of any sale.

It seems to me that the error made by the learned judge lay in treating compliance with a demand for payment as the exercise of a right to redeem. But in truth, as I have endeavoured to point out, no questions arose of premature redemption or of the application of s. 93(1).

[Reynolds J.A. dissented, on the ground that the mortgagee had a contractual right to receive interest for the whole of the term of the mortgage and had done nothing to disentitle him to that interest.]

Appeal allowed.

NOTES

1. In *Branwood Park Pastoral Co. Pty Ltd v. Willing & Sons Pty Ltd* (1977) 1 B.P.R. 9534, the mortgage was in similar terms to that in the principal case, but the New South Wales Court of Appeal distinguished the principal case on the ground that although the mortgagor was in default, the mortgagee had made no demand for payment of principal. In the course of his judgment, Street C.J. made the following comments about s. 93 of the *Conveyancing Act* 1919 (N.S.W.):

I wish to add, however, that [this] case exposes a harsh contractual situation as between mortgagees and mortgagors in general—a situation indeed which could well fetter fair and reasonable dealings with real property. Take the case, for example, of a married couple buying a home and obtaining finance by way of a ten year mortgage. After five years their family may have grown to the point where the house is too small and they wish to sell it to buy something larger; their mortgagee would have the right, under the ordinary form of mortgage in common use, to refuse to discharge the mortgage so as to enable an unencumbered sale of the house unless it, the mortgagee, received, pursuant to s. 93, as well as immediate payment of the principal, interest for the remaining five years of the ten year term. This is an affront to ordinary notions of fairness. It was possible, in the light of the particular form of the document before the court in *Wanner v. Caruana* [1974] 2 N.S.W.L.R. 301 to deny to the mortgagees in that case a right to future and unearned interest after receipt by them of the principal sum in full, such denial proceeding on the basis that the right to future interest was void as a penalty. That decision, however, turned essentially upon the documents there in issue and it cannot avail mortgagors in ordinary cases.

The legislature may well take the view that this particular area of conveyancing practice should be freed from the otherwise harsh price demanded by s. 93 of the *Conveyancing Act*. There is much to be said for conferring upon a mortgagor a right to early discharge on the payment of some far more modest price, perhaps the payment of six months interest, or, perhaps even at six months notice. The precise manner in which s. 93 should be brought up-to-date in the interests of mortgagors is no doubt a matter which will require careful evaluation. I am clear in my opinion, however, that the section itself needs to be brought up-to-date by some means or other.

2. In *Van Kempen v. Finance & Investments Pty Ltd* (1984) 6 N.S.W.L.R. 293, the mortgage provided in a "repayment schedule" for repayment of the amount advanced plus interest by 208 equal weekly payments. In the event of default, the principal sum was to become immediately due and payable by the mortgagor upon demand by the mortgagee. The mortgagor defaulted under the mortgage and the mortgagee took steps to enforce its security. As a result of these steps, the mortgagee recovered a substantial part of the amount repayable under the terms of the repayment schedule, but refused to discharge the mortgage unless it received the amount it would have received had the mortgage run its course and all of the 208 payments been made. The mortgagor claimed to be entitled to a discharge of the mortgage upon repayment of the principal plus arrears of interest to the date of repayment, with no liability for interest after the date of repayment. In the course of deciding in favour of the mortgagor, Holland J. said (at 300-301):

The decision of the majority in *Stocks & Enterprises* was basically placed upon the terms of the mortgage rather than on general principles. The same terms do not appear in the mortgage in the present case. In my opinion, the terms here provide no solution to the problem except in the fact that they do not express a right to future interest on recovery of principal after default. The objections made by Reynolds J.A. to reliance on the English cases seem to me, if I may respectfully say so, to be well founded in so far as he pointed out that they do not support the existence of any equitable right to redeem without payment of future interest before the due date of the mortgage. However, there is, in my opinion, an equitable basis in a case like the present for denying the mortgagee future interest. Whatever the position where the mortgagee after default has made a mere demand, here the mortgagee has made the choice of not leaving the balance of the principal out at interest on the security of the mortgaged property but getting it in by realising the security. The mortgagee's action, justified though it was, has accelerated recovery by the mortgagee of the principal. Instead of remaining available to the use of the mortgagor to the end of the four years as contemplated by the mortgage, the money is already back with the mortgagee and available for his own use and, as a consequence, the operation of the repayment schedule has ceased to be applicable. As the mortgage can no longer continue as intended by its terms but does not define the rights of the parties in relation to its present discharge, the situation would seem to me to entitle either party to seek from the court an accounting on equitable principles to enable the mortgage to be discharged.

In my opinion, the principle upon which Kay J. resolved an analogous situation in *Banner v. Berridge* (1881) 18 Ch. D. 254 is applicable. The relevant facts were that after default the mortgagee had entered into possession, sold the mortgaged property and was awaiting receipt of the proceeds of sale. These were to be paid to him two days after a date specified in the mortgage as the date on which six months interest in advance was to become due and payable. The mortgagee claimed to be entitled to payment of that interest notwithstanding the fact that he would be recovering his principal two days after the period of six months had commenced to run. Of this claim Kay J. said (at 279):

I conceive that this not being a case in which the mortgagor was paying off a mortgage, or in which the mortgagor had requested anything in the matter to be done, but where the mortgagee was acting of his own mere motion in realising the subject of the mortgage, it would be in the last degree inequitable to allow him to have six months' interest for a period, during the whole of which, except two days, he would have the mortgage money in his own pocket. I, therefore, upon the ground of its being an inequitable claim—one of those inequitable claims which the court always watches with jealousy in a case between mortgagor and mortgagee—disallow that six months' interest, and allow him interest down to the 3rd of January 1874, on the moneys from time to time due and owing on the mortgages.

The jurisdiction of the English court to intervene between mortgagor and mortgagee in circumstances similar to the present case, as it was described by the English Court of Appeal in *Ex parte Wickens* [1898] 1 Q.B. 543, also provides, I think, by analogy, a source of principle for dealing with cases like the present one even though the English mortgage conveyancing system was so different from our own. In that case it was found that the mortgagee had taken possession not to protect the mortgaged property but to realise his security. A. L. Smith L.J. said (at 548):

It has been pointed out that where a mortgagee has entered into possession or taken other steps for the purpose of realising his security, the court has jurisdiction, upon payment of the debt, the interest then due, and the costs, to order the security to be given up.

Chitty L.J. and Collins L.J. both (at 550) described the jurisdiction in similar terms.

Finally, it would seem to me that, although the terms of the present mortgage differ from those of the mortgage in the *Stocks & Enterprises* case, part of the reasoning of Samuels J.A. in that case would be against the mortgagee having a right to future interest here. In the report of the case Samuels J.A. said (at 9531-9532):

[His Honour then quoted from the third, fourth and fifth paragraphs of the extract from the judgment of Samuels J.A. above, and continued:]

In my opinion, as a matter of equity in the circumstances of cases like the present, the mortgagee is not entitled to require the mortgagor to pay interest for any period after recovery by the mortgagee of the principal sum; and the mortgagor is entitled to have the mortgage discharged when the whole of the principal sum and accrued interest has been received by or paid to the mortgagee.

It is unnecessary to decide whether the mortgagee's claim to future interest would in any event be void as a penalty. As Street C.J. himself observed, in his judgment on the appeal in the *Branwood Park* case, his decision in *Wanner v. Caruana* turned essentially upon the particular form of the documents there in question and could not avail mortgagors in ordinary cases. The form of the provision here is not a parallel to that case although the construction for which the defendant contends would produce a similar result. I prefer to leave the question open and base my decision on the grounds earlier stated.

The decision of Holland J. was varied on different grounds on appeal to the Court of Appeal, (1986) 6 N.S.W.L.R. 305.

6. Late redemption—"the six months rule"

A mortgagor who seeks to redeem after the contractual date for repayment must give six months' notice of intention to redeem or pay six months' interest in lieu of notice: *Smith v. Smith* [1891] 3 Ch. 550. The reason for this rule is said to be that such a mortgagor is relying upon the assistance of equity (the contractual date for repayment having passed), and that on the basis of the maxim, "He who seeks equity must do equity" the mortgagee is entitled to a reasonable opportunity to find a new security for the investment: *Centrax Trustees Ltd v. Ross* [1979] 2 All E.R. 952 at 955-956. However, the six months rule does not apply where the mortgagee has demanded repayment or taken steps to enforce her or his security: *Re Alcock* (1883) 23 Ch. D. 372. Nor does it apply where the mortgage is of a "temporary" nature.

FITZGERALD'S TRUSTEE v. MELLERSH

Chancery Division [1892] 1 Ch. 385

[In taking an account of moneys due to a bank under a mortgage by deposit of title deeds, the question arose whether the bank was entitled to six months' notice of repayment or six months' interest in lieu of notice.]

CHITTY J. The question is whether an equitable mortgagee, by deposit of title deeds of land accompanied by a memorandum of deposit, is entitled to six months' notice before he is bound to accept a tender of the amount due or to six months' interest in lieu of notice. The memorandum in this case contains an undertaking by the mortgagor to execute a legal mortgage on request; but no request has been made, nor can any now be made, as the land has been sold pursuant to an arrangement between the mortgagor and the mortgagee. The undertaking, therefore, may be disregarded. The memorandum limits no time for repayment. The mortgagee has not called in the money, nor taken any steps to enforce his security. The mortgagee is willing to accept three months' interest only; but this is by way of concession. His claim is founded on his supposed right to six months' notice. There are two authorities on the question of the right of a mortgagee to six months' notice or interest in lieu of notice.

[His Lordship discussed *Browne v. Lockhart* (1840) 10 Sim. 420 at 424; 59 E.R. 678 and *Smith v. Smith* [1891] 3 Ch. 550, and continued:]

There is no express authority, so far as I am aware, that the rule as to six months' notice or interest applies to the simple case of a mortgage by deposit of deeds. This form of security is now in very common use between bankers and their customers and among commercial men and others where a temporary loan is required. It was admitted by counsel for the mortgagee that it is not the practice amongst bankers or commercial men to require six months' notice or interest; and, so far as my experience goes, this admission is in accordance with the fact. It was argued, however, for the mortgagee, that the rule existed although it was not insisted upon. There was no evidence one way or the other as to the practice. The textwriters state the rule, but not one of them intimates that it applies to a mortgagee by deposit. . . .

Where no time is limited for the repayment of the debt, as is almost universally the case where the mortgage is by deposit, there is nothing to prevent the mortgagee from calling in his money at once, and it is inappropriate language, to say the least of it, to speak of the mortgagor being in default because he does not pay on the next day after the loan is made. There being, then, no authority on the point, I must decide this question on principle; and, on principle, I think that an equitable mortgagee by deposit is not entitled to six months' notice. The true ground for the rule, where it applies, appears to me to be that it is equitable or, what is the same thing, reasonable to apply it. If I applied the rule to the case before me I should be inflicting great hardship on persons who give such securities. Money is generally borrowed on them for a short time only, and often at a higher rate of interest, because it is expected that the loan will shortly be paid off. Having regard to what has been and what has not been decided, I venture to express the rule thus: Where the just inference from the transaction is that the loan on mortgage is intended to be of a permanent character, it is reasonable to infer that the parties intended that after default the mortgagee should be entitled to a six months' notice. That appears to be the just inference whenever there is a regular mortgage deed with a proviso for redemption. This point is covered by the authorities. But where the just inference from the transaction is that the mortgage is merely temporary, as I think is the case where the mortgage is in the usual form by deposit merely, then it is not reasonable to infer that the parties intended that so long a notice should be given. I do not say that the mortgagor may suddenly pounce down on the mortgagee without any notice at all with the money and demand back his deeds. He must not act unreasonably or vexatiously; he must at least give the mortgagee a reasonable time, though it may be short, to look up the deeds. Even the mortgagee, when the loan is payable on demand, must give a reasonable notice to the mortgagor to enable him to find the money: *Toms v. Wilson* (1862) 4 B. & S. 442, and *Brighty v. Norton* (1862) 3 B. & S. 305. . . .

The debt will carry interest up to the date of actual payment; but no further interest in lieu of notice is payable.

Order accordingly.

NOTE

The six months rule has been criticised both because of the inflexibility of the period of six months (in modern times, suitable alternative securities normally can be arranged in less than six months) and because of its alleged inappropriateness in the context of Torrens title: see *Cromwell Property Investment Co. Ltd v. Western and Toovey* [1934] Ch. 322 at 331-332; Fox, "The Redemption of Torrens System Mortgages After Default" (1950) 24 A.L.J. 311. Nevertheless, the rule appears to remain good law: *Hyde Management Services Pty Ltd v. F.A.I. Insurances Ltd* (1979) 144 C.L.R. 541 at 548. In *Friend v. Mayer* [1982] V.R. 941 at 946, Young C.J. said:

> The so-called six months' rule is too firmly established in the law for the court to disregard it. Whether it should be abrogated is a matter that would require very careful consideration, but if the conclusion were reached that a change was necessary or desirable, it seems to me, as at present advised, that the change could not be made by the court.
>
> [Counsel] said that the rule was in essence a rule that reasonable notice should be given of an intention to redeem, and that although six months might have been reasonable when the rule was developed, it was not reasonable at the present time, and that the court should fix a reasonable time in its place. There is, however, in my view, no justification whatever for the court to legislate in that way and I do not think that we should do so.

E. MODERN STATUTORY PROVISIONS

Before leaving the general topic of clogs on the equity of redemption, reference should be made to a number of statutory provisions which a mortgagor may be able to invoke in order to avoid onerous obligations under a mortgage. In some situations, the mortgagor may have a choice between proceeding either under the equitable principles considered above or under the statutory provisions, and often it may be advantageous for him to resort to the statute. In other situations, the statute may afford a remedy where none is available in equity.

Chief amongst the statutory provisions are the following:

1. Trade Practices Act 1974 (Cth)

A number of provisions of the *Trade Practices Act* 1974 (Cth) may be applicable to mortgages. One section of the Act increasingly being resorted to is s. 52, which provides that a corporation shall not, in trade or commerce, engage in conduct that is misleading or deceptive or is likely to mislead or deceive. A mortgage entered into in breach of this provision may give rise to an action in damages (s. 82), or may even be set aside (s. 87): see, for example, *National Australia Bank Ltd v. Nobile* (1988) A.T.P.R. 40-856.

In appropriate circumstances, mortgages may also be struck down as being in restraint of trade. Mortgages are subject to the common law doctrine of restraint of trade; also, they may be in breach of the restraint of trade provisions of the *Trade Practices Act*, such as ss 45 and 45B. For example, even though in the particular circumstances a postponement of the contractual right to redeem may not infringe the rules discussed earlier concerning undue postponement of the right to redeem (see above p. 407), the postponement may nevertheless be unenforceable if coupled with other conditions which amount to an unreasonable restraint of trade, or if in breach of the *Trade Practices Act*, thus allowing the mortgagor to redeem: see *Esso Petroleum Co. Ltd v. Harper's Garage (Stourport) Ltd* [1968] A.C. 269 at 320-321, 341-343; Donald and Heydon, *Trade Practices Law*, Vol. 1, p. 195.

2. Contracts Review Act 1980 (N.S.W.)

The *Contracts Review Act* 1980 (N.S.W.) provides that where the court finds a contract or a provision of a contract to have been "unjust in the circumstances relating to the contract at the time it was made", it may, inter alia, refuse to enforce any or all of the provisions of the contract, or make an order declaring the contract void in whole or in part: s. 7(1). For the purposes of the Act, "unjust" includes "unconscionable, harsh or oppressive": s. 4(1). By s. 9 (1), the court is required, when deciding whether a contract is unjust at the time it was entered into, to have regard to the public interest and all the circumstances of the case, including the foreseeable consequences of carrying out the contract and of defaulting under the contract; and s. 9(2) lists some of the matters to which the court shall have regard, including bargaining inequality, opportunity for negotiations, the ability of a party to protect his interest, the language of the contract, the use of unfair tactics, similar dealings, subsequent conduct of the parties, and the commercial setting of the contract. Relief under the Act is not available to the Crown, a public or local authority or a corporation (s. 6(1)), nor can relief be sought in relation to a contract entered into for the purpose of a trade, business or profession, other than farming: s. 6(2).

Clearly, the potential for operation of the *Contracts Review Act* in areas traditionally occupied by equitable doctrines, such as those concerning clogs on the equity of redemption and penalties, is considerable. Further, in so far as it confers jurisdiction over contracts and provisions of contracts that are "unjust" (especially having regard to the inclusive definition of "unjust"), it appears to confer a jurisdiction wider than that traditionally available in equity, although it is to be noted that it does not go so far as to confer jurisdiction where the contract or a provision of the contract is merely "unfair". (On the meaning of "unjust" in the Act, see Peden, *The Law of Unjust Contracts*, pp. 107-109.) The New South Wales Court of Appeal in *West v. A.G.C. (Advances) Ltd* (1986) 5 N.S.W.L.R. 610 at 611-612, 621, 631 described the Act as "beneficial legislation", to be interpreted liberally, intended by Parliament to counter the inability of the courts to develop a general doctrine of relief against unconscionable or unjust contracts. Kirby P. expressed the view that the court's discretion under the Act is not to be limited by reference to the relief available under the pre-existing law, and that in proceedings under the Act the courts should not first identify what relief would be available under the pre-existing law, as that might defeat the beneficial purposes of the Act.

In a subsequent Court of Appeal decision involving the Act, *Antonovic v. Volker* (1986) 7 N.S.W.L.R. 15, Mahoney J.A. (dissenting in the result) made the point that the term "unjust" as used in the Act requires that the objectionable features of the contract be such as to have "substantial weight", and that, notwithstanding that "unjust" is defined in the Act to *include* "unconscionable, harsh or oppressive" and so is not limited by those words, "unjust" was not intended to provide a basis for intervention by the court "in every case in which there is abrasion in negotiation or inequality in result" (at 168).

In the context of mortgages, it is especially important to note that the Act regulates contracts, not investments. So, relief will not be granted under the Act merely because a mortgagor has overstretched herself or himself by borrowing on mortgage more than she or he is able to repay, there being no undue influence, unfair pressure or similar conduct by the mortgagee in granting the mortgage: *Hogan v. Howard Finance Ltd* (1987) A.S.C. 55-594.

Also, it is clear that the relief which the court is empowered to grant under s. 7 of the Act is "for the purpose of avoiding as far as practicable an unjust consequence or result", and so no remedy can be given, even where the contract or a provision of the contract is found to be unjust, unless an unjust consequence or result flows: *S. H. Lock (Aust.) Ltd v. Kennedy* (1988) 12 N.S.W.L.R. 482; *Edward Keller (Australia) Pty Ltd v. Hennelly* (1987) C.C.H. N.S.W. Conv. R. 55-357; *Westpac Banking Corp. v. Sugden* (1988) C.C.H. N.S.W. Conv. R. 55-377.

The number of reported cases where the application of the *Contracts Review Act* to mortgages has been considered is growing rapidly. Depending upon the circumstances, the whole of the mortgage and the obligations under it could be declared void or unenforceable, or certain of its terms could be varied, or a party could be relieved of specific obligations under it, or (of course) the court might decline to interfere at all. For examples of cases under the Act involving mortgages, see *West v. A.G.C. (Advances) Ltd* (1986) 5 N.S.W.L.R. 610; *Toscano v. Holland Securities Pty Ltd* (1985) 1 N.S.W.L.R. 145; *Cook v. Bank of New South Wales* (1982) 2 B.P.R. 9580; *Hogan v. Howard Finance Ltd* (1987) A.S.C. 55-594; *Edward Keller (Aust.) Pty Ltd v. Hennelly* (1987) C.C.H. N.S.W. Conv. R. 55-357; *Commonwealth Bank of Australia v. Cohen* (1988) A.S.C. 55-681; *Farnham v. Orrell* (1989) C.C.H. N.S.W. Conv. R. 55-443.

3. Credit Act 1984 (N.S.W.)

Certain mortgages over land come within the ambit of the *Credit Act* 1984. Where this is so, various sections of the Act impose restrictions upon the conduct of the mortgagee and the permissible terms of the mortgage, and allow for subsequent variation of the mortgage.

As to what mortgages are subject to the provisions of the *Credit Act* 1984: in general terms the Act applies to mortgages (including mortgages over land) given by mortgagors (not being corporations) involving a principal sum of not more than $20,000 at an interest rate exceeding 14 per cent: see ss 5(1) (definitions of "regulated contract", "regulated loan contract", "loan contract"), 30(2), 89. However, the Act does not apply where the mortgagee is a registered building society, co-operative society, or credit union (s. 18(1)), nor does it apply to overdraft mortgages where the mortgagee is a bank or pastoral finance company: s. 18(2). In addition, there is a general power for the Governor by order published in the Gazette to exempt specified transactions (including mortgages) from the operation of the Act (s. 19); under this provision, exemptions have been granted for such transactions as housing loans (*Government Gazette* No. 38, 8 February 1985), loans by pawnbrokers (*Government Gazette* No. 38, 8 February 1985), staff loans (*Government Gazette* No. 131, 15 August 1986), and loans for the payment of educational expenses (*Government Gazette* No. 136, 29 August 1986).

Under s. 146 of the Act, the Commercial Tribunal of New South Wales (the Tribunal) may upon application by the mortgagor under a mortgage to which the Act applies (called in the section a "regulated mortgage") re-open the transaction that gave rise to the mortgage if it appears to the Tribunal that the mortgage was "unjust" in the circumstances relating to the mortgage at the time it was entered into. A mortgage is "unjust" for these purposes if it is "unconscionable, harsh or oppressive", or if the interest rate is "excessive" having regard to the risk, the value of any security, the amount of the consideration, the time for repayment, the amount financed, and "any other relevant circumstances": s. 145. Section 147 sets out, in terms similar to s. 9 of the *Contracts Review Act* 1980 (N.S.W.) (referred to above), criteria for consideration by the Tribunal in determining whether the mortgage is "unjust" in the circumstances relating to it at the time it was made. Where the Tribunal re-opens a transaction under these provisions, it may, inter alia, relieve the mortgagor from payment of any amount in excess of the amount which the Tribunal considers "reasonably payable" in the circumstances or even (it seems) the whole amount financed, set aside or modify the mortgage, and give judgment for whatever amount it thinks is justly due to a party under the mortgage: s. 146(2).

Section 171 preserves the operation of the *Contracts Review Act*, so that mortgages remain liable to review under the *Contracts Review Act* whether or not they are caught by the *Credit Act* provisions.

There is also a more general provision in the *Credit Act*, not confined to "unjust" contracts, permitting the variation of contracts (including mortgages) which are subject to the Act. Under s. 74, a debtor who, by reason of illness, unemployment, or other reasonable cause is unable reasonably to discharge her or his obligations under the contract, may apply to the lender for a variation of the contract, provided that the debtor reasonably expects to be able to discharge her or his obligations if (a) the period of the contract were extended and the amount of each payment due under it correspondingly reduced (without a change being made in the interest rate), or (b) the dates for payments under the contract for a specified period were postponed (without a change in the interest rate), or (c) both (a) and (b). If the lender refuses the request, the debtor may apply to the Commissioner for Consumer Affairs for assistance in negotiating a variation of the contract. If the Commissioner, having decided to negotiate a variation, fails to persuade the lender to agree, the Commissioner must refer the matter to the Tribunal, which may order a variation of the contract.

Reference should also be made to a cognate Act, the *Credit (Home Finance Contracts) Act* 1984 (N.S.W.). That Act is concerned with "home finance contracts", a term defined in s. 4 of the same Act to mean, in general terms, a contract (which will include a mortgage) for the provision of credit not exceeding $67,500 for (a) the acquisition or erection of the debtor's home, (b) the provision of additional accommodation in, or the carrying out of structural alterations to, the debtor's home, or (c) the acquisition of land on which to erect the debtor's home. There are no provisions in the Act conferring jurisdiction to deal with "unjust" home finance contracts, but the provisions of the *Contracts Review Act* will apply to such contracts. Section 5 of the *Credit (Home Finance Contracts) Act* does, however, permit variation of home finance contracts in terms similar to those of s. 74 of the *Credit Act*, discussed above.

4. Industrial Arbitration Act 1940 (N.S.W.)

By s. 88F of the *Industrial Arbitration Act* 1940, the Industrial Commission may declare void in whole or in part, or vary in whole or in part, any contract or arrangement whereby a person performs work in an industry, on the ground that the contract or arrangement is unfair, or harsh or unconscionable, or against the public interest. In *Morgan v. Coulson* [1981] 2 N.S.W.L.R. 801, an employer advanced money by way of registered mortgage to an employee to assist the employee in purchasing a home. The mortgage was to be interest free so long as the mortgagor remained in the employ of the mortgagee for 20 years, but in the event of the mortgagor ceasing to be so employed within the 20 years, the mortgagor was to be liable (retrospectively) to pay interest at current bank rates for the full amount of the advance and was obliged to offer the property to the mortgagee at its original purchase price. Macken J. held that the arrangement was unfair, and against the public interest. The mortgagee was ordered to execute a registrable discharge of mortgage, subject to the mortgagor paying the balance of principal outstanding.

IV. REMEDIES OF THE MORTGAGEE

A. RIGHT TO SUE ON THE PERSONAL COVENANT

At the beginning of this chapter it was stated that one of the elements in a mortgage was the personal contract (or covenant) by the mortgagor for the repayment of the money advanced or the performance of the obligation undertaken. The mortgagee has a contractual right to sue upon and to enforce this personal covenant.

The mortgagor's obligation to repay is conditional upon the mortgagee's ability to reconvey the mortgaged property. Thus, if the mortgagee deals with the mortgaged property without the consent of the mortgagor in such a way as to render it impossible for him to restore it on full payment, he cannot sue on the personal covenant: *Palmer v. Hendrie* (1859) 27 Beav. 349; 54 E.R. 136. There is one important exception to this rule: a mortgagee who has disposed of the property in the exercise of a power of sale (as to which, see below) can sue on the personal covenant to recover any balance outstanding under the mortgage after deduction of the proceeds of sale.

In New South Wales, foreclosure (as to which, see below) extinguishes the mortgagee's right to sue on the personal covenant: see *Conveyancing Act* 1919 (N.S.W.), s. 100.

A mortgagee who has obtained judgment against the mortgagor on the personal covenant may buy the property at a sale by the sheriff: *Union Bank of Australia v. Atkins* (1900) 10 Q.L.J. 11. What the sheriff is selling, however, is the equity of redemption (that is, the property subject to the mortgage), and under the rule in *Waring v. Ward* (1802) 7 Ves. Jun. 332; 32 E.R. 136 a purchaser of the equity of redemption is obliged to indemnify the mortgagor against his liability under the personal covenant. The result is that where the mortgagee buys from the sheriff the mortgage debt is extinguished (*Simpson v. Forrester* (1973) 132 C.L.R. 499), although it appears that as the sheriff is obliged to pay the proceeds of sale towards reduction of the mortgage debt, the mortgagee is entitled to receive back from the sheriff the purchase price he or she has paid: *Simpson v. Forrester* (1973) 132 C.L.R. 499; see also (1973) 47 A.L.J. 544 at 557. This result is not possible, however, in New South Wales, where legislation provides that the interest of a mortgagor in the mortgaged land cannot be taken in execution under a judgment for a debt secured by the mortgage: *Conveyancing Act* 1919 (N.S.W.), s. 102.

When a mortgage is discharged, the mortgagee executes a formal discharge of mortgage, which operates to free the land from the charge or interest of the mortgagee. Whether the discharge is effective also to extinguish the personal covenant to repay is a matter of construction of the terms of the discharge: *Groongal Pastoral Co. Ltd (in liq.) v. Falkiner* (1924) 35 C.L.R. 157 at 164-165. For example, the form of discharge of mortgage approved by the New South Wales Registrar-General contains an acknowledgment by the mortgagee of receipt of all moneys due and payable under the mortgage "in full satisfaction and discharge of the . . . mortgage so far as it affects the land". The concluding words, "so far as it affects the land", restrict the effect of the discharge to releasing the *land* from the charge and do not discharge the mortgagor from liability under the personal covenant to repay, leaving the mortgagee free to sue on the personal covenant if he has not in fact been paid the full amount owing: *Grundy v. Ley* [1984] 2 N.S.W.L.R. 467; cf. Hinde "Effect of a Release of Mortgage — is the Mortgagee Estopped from Denying the Release?" [1981] N.Z.L.J. 23.

Credit Act 1984 (N.S.W.)

Where the mortgage is a "regulated mortgage" under the *Credit Act* 1984 (see above p. 436), the mortgagee is not entitled to exercise a right under the mortgage (which would encompass a right to sue on the personal covenant) unless the mortgagor is in default, the mortgagee has given at least one month's notice of intention to exercise the right unless the default is remedied, and the mortgagor fails to comply with the notice: s. 107(2), (3). By s. 168, a notice under s. 107 may be combined with any notice required to be given before exercising mortgagees' powers, such as notices required by the *Conveyancing Act* 1919 (N.S.W.) or the *Real Property Act* 1900 (N.S.W.) as a pre-condition to the exercise of a power of sale: see below p. 452.

Further, where the mortgage is a "home finance contract" (as to which, see above p. 437), the mortgagee cannot exercise a right as a consequence of default by the mortgagor unless he or she has first served one month's notice in the prescribed form of intention to exercise the right: *Credit (Home Finance Contracts) Act* 1984 (N.S.W.) s. 7(1), (2). Here also, the notice may be combined with a notice under any other Act required to be given by the mortgagee before exercising a right under the mortgage: s. 7(4).

B. RIGHT TO POSSESSION

1. Old system title

(a) Right to possession

Because the first mortgagee of old system land has the legal estate, he is entitled, at common law (but subject to any statutory restraints), to possession of the mortgaged property. This right to possession is not dependant upon prior default by the mortgagor: "The mortgagee may go into possession before the ink is dry on the mortgage unless there is something in the contract, express or by implication, whereby he has contracted himself out of that right": *Four Maids Ltd v. Dudley Marshall (Properties) Ltd* [1957] Ch. 317 at 320. An equitable mortgagee, however, has no such right to possession: *Barclay's Bank Ltd v. Bird* [1954] Ch. 274 at 280, in the absence of agreement between the parties: *Mills v. Lewis* (1986) C.C.H. N.S.W. Conv. R. 55-273.

However, the Court of Appeal in England has held that a legal mortgagee can be restrained in equity from exercising his right to possession where he is not acting "bona fide and reasonably for the purpose of enforcing the security" (*Quennell v. Maltby* [1979] 1 W.L.R. 318 at 322); he will not be entitled to possession when actuated by ulterior motives, as where, at the behest of the mortgagor, he moves to evict a tenant of the mortgagor under a tenancy which binds the mortgagor but not the mortgagee: *Quennell v. Maltby* [1979] 1 W.L.R. 318 at 322. But this decision has been strongly criticised as an unjustified departure from the previous law: see, for example, Pearce, "Keeping a Mortgagee out of Possession" [1979] C.L.J. 257; Smith, "The Mortgagee's Right to Possession—The Modern Law" [1979] Conv. 266.

(b) Attornment clauses

Old system first mortgages often overcome the rule as to the mortgagee's right to possession by providing that the mortgagor may remain in possession, at least until default. Sometimes the mortgage merely provides that the mortgagee is empowered to take possession upon default, which would appear to give the mortgagor an implied contractual right to remain in possession until default: see *Birmingham Citizens Permanent Building Society v. Caunt* [1962] Ch. 883 at 890. The most common provision, however, is an "attornment clause", whereby the mortgagor attorns tenant to the mortgagee for the duration of the mortgage at a rent equivalent to the instalments of interest payable under the mortgage. This is designed to give the mortgagor some security of tenure while at the same time enabling the mortgagee to take advantage of the summary procedures available to landlords for recovering possession of land; and because the relationship of landlord and tenant is created, it also enables the mortgagee to enforce against assigns of the mortgagor those covenants by the mortgagor which touch and concern the land: *Regent Oil Co. Ltd v. J. A. Gregory (Hatch End) Ltd* [1966] Ch. 402. (As to covenants which touch and concern the land in the context of the law of landlord and tenant, see below p. 620 et seq.)

There are two principal disadvantages with attornment provisions. The first is that proceedings under such clauses may amount to distress for rent, a remedy now forbidden in New South Wales: see below p. 628; Sykes, op. cit., p. 86. The second is that the "rent", by being linked to the instalments of interest payable under the mortgage, may bring the matter within the jurisdictional limit of the Supreme Court and the mortgagee unwittingly may find herself or himself deprived of the very remedy the clause was designed to provide: see *Australian Express Pty Ltd v. Pejovic* [1963] N.S.W.R. 954.

2. Torrens title

Unlike her or his old system title counterpart, the mortgagee of land under Torrens title has no automatic right to possession. But statute gives her or him the right to take possession upon default by the mortgagor in payment of principal or interest: *Real Property Act* 1900 (N.S.W.), s. 60. As to the effect of attornment clauses in mortgages of Torrens title land, see Sykes, op. cit., pp. 246-248.

3. Credit Act 1984

As in the case of a mortgagee suing on the personal covenant, so where a mortgagee exercises a right to go into possession of the mortgaged property the notices required under s. 107 of the *Credit Act* 1984 and s. 7 of the *Credit (Home Finance Contracts) Act* 1984 must be given in respect of mortgages caught by those provisions. The provisions are discussed above pp. 436-437.

4. Liability of mortgagee in possession

A mortgagee who takes possession of the mortgaged property will be liable to account to the mortgagor not only for all rents and profits received but also for all he or she would have received but for her or his wilful default: *Parkinson v. Hanbury* (1867) L.R. 2 H.L. 1 at 15; *National Bank of Australasia v. The United Hand-in-Hand and Band of Hope Co.* (1879) 4 App. Cas. 391 at 409; *Chaplin v. Young* (1864) 33 Beav. 330; 55 E.R. 395. By "wilful default" in this context is meant "some gross lack of diligence" in the mortgagee's acts or omissions: *Kennedy v. General Credits Ltd* (unreported, Court of Appeal (N.S.W), 14 May 1982). The reason for this rule is that a mortgagee who takes possession does so for the purpose of recovering his principal and interest, but as in equity his estate is a security only for the money, "the court requires him to be diligent in realising the amount which is due, in order that he may restore the estate to the mortgagor, who, in the view of this court, is entitled to it": *Lord Kensington v. Bouverie* (1855) 7 De G.M. & G. 134 at 157; 44 E.R. 53 at 62.

The mortgagee in possession is bound to effect all necessary repairs (*Sandon v. Hooper* (1843) 6 Beav. 246; 49 E.R. 820), but only to the extent which the income of the property, after deduction of her or his interest under the mortgage, permits: *Richards v. Morgan* (1753) 4 Y. & C. Ex. 570; 160 E.R. 1136. Where the property is a building in the course of construction, the mortgagee in possession who chooses to complete the building (usually as a prelude to its sale) must act as a "provident owner" in so doing, and will be liable on the basis of wilful default if he or she omits to take adequate precautions to ensure the building is completed in a workmanlike manner: at the very least, the mortgagee must act bona fide, and the construction must be a genuine effort to complete the building in a proper and economical way: *Midland Credit Ltd v. Hallad* (1977) 1 B.P.R. 9570 at 9577-9578.

The account against a mortgagee in possession is not directed with "rests". That is, the account of rents and profits runs on from beginning to end without reference to the question whether at any particular time the mortgagee had in her or his hands more than sufficient to pay the interest then outstanding, there being no requirement for any surplus income to be set off from time to time against the principal outstanding. The reason is that the mortgagee is not bound to accept payment in a piecemeal fashion, but is entitled to have her or his account taken as a whole: *Wrigley v. Gill* [1905] 1 Ch. 241 at 253-254.

In taking accounts, the mortgagee in possession will be charged an occupation rent, unless the property has no rental value.

FYFE v. SMITH

Supreme Court of New South Wales [1975] 2 N.S.W.L.R. 408

[The plaintiffs owned a hotel in a small country town. The defendants were mortgagees of the hotel. Upon default under the mortgage, the mortgagees took possession and, in order to run the hotel business, occupied one room in the premises. On a taking of accounts, the plaintiffs claimed that the mortgagees should give credit for board and lodging at the rate of $5 per day.]

HELSHAM J. There is a proposition in Coote on *Mortgages* (9th ed.), p. 1226 and in Fisher and Lightwood's *Law of Mortgages* (8th ed.), pp. 294 and 555, which is said to govern the position in this case. At p. 294 of the latter work it is put in this way: "Amount of rent to be accounted for. Where a mortgagee enters into receipt of rents he accounts at the rate of the rent reserved. Where he enters into actual possession, it has been said that he will be charged with the utmost value the lands are proved to be worth. But this liability is limited by the circumstances of the case, and he will not usually be required to account for more than he has received, unless it is proved that, but for his gross default, mismanagement or fraud, he might have received more."

At p. 555, under the heading of "Occupation Rent", the following is stated: "The mortgagee, if he has been in actual occupation of the whole or some part of the property, may be charged an occupation rent."

It is said, relying on these propositions, that as a general rule a mortgagee in possession will be charged an occupation rent, and it is further said that the cases support this proposition. Thus in *Trimleston (Lord) v. Hamill* (1810) 1 Ball & B. 377 at 385 Lord Manners, Lord Chief Justice of Ireland, said: "If a mortgagee enters into possession of the lands, he is always charged with the utmost value they are proved to be worth; but if he only enter [sic] into receipt of the rents, he accounts at the rate of the rent reserved.", and in *Metcalf v. Campion* (1828) 1 Mol. 238 at 239 Sir Anthony Hart, Lord Chancellor of Ireland, in dealing with the matter of onus in relation to the taking of accounts by a mortgagee in possession, said: "If the mortgagee occupied a fair occupation rent should be charged to him."

The basic principle upon which the court approaches the matter of accounts between a mortgagor and a mortgagee in possession is that the mortgagee will be charged with an account for the rents and profits. If a complaint is made that a mortgagee has not properly accounted for the rents and profits received by him during the period that he was in possession under the mortgage, the onus is on the party making the surcharge to show that he has received rents and profits in excess of those which are stated in his accounts, or that he would, except for his wilful neglect and default, have received rents and profits for which he must account. That is what a mortgagee in possession must account for. But it assumes that premises have yielded rents and profits during the period of possession or that they could, with proper management, have yielded rents and profits. In a circumstance such as this, where one is dealing with a case of rents, and not profits, the principle assumes that the property is producing, or can produce, a return from the fact of it being occupied. That is a proper basis for the taking of an account in the form in which accounts are ordered to be taken in such cases. It stems from the possession of a mortgagee who, although clothed in the legal title, is regarded, once he has taken possession, either before or after default, as a mortgagee, as being under a duty to account. He is regarded as exercising a special right over somebody else's property in which he has merely a limited interest. The basis of the approach to the taking of accounts will not be different in the case of land held under statutory title. The mortgagee must give a mortgagor, of whose property he has taken possession, the full benefit of what the mortgagor was getting before possession was taken, or could have got from his continued possession of the land. But I do not believe that the converse of this position is true, namely that the mortgagee must pay for his occupation merely because he occupies premises. Counsel seeks to support the proposition put by him upon the basis that a mortgagee may be saved the expense of providing other accommodation for himself by virtue of his occupation of the mortgaged premises. But that is not the basis upon which an account of rents and profits must be taken. A mortgagee is not obliged to account to a mortgagor upon the same basis that a trustee must account to his cestui que trust. A mortgagee in possession is obliged to account for rents and profits received by him or which, but for his wilful neglect and default, would have been received. Where there is no rental value of the property then there is no obligation upon a mortgagee taking possession to pay an occupation rent. That is the case here. There is no evidence that the property was let to or was occupied by anybody paying rent or fee for such occupation. And there is no evidence that the property could have been let or so occupied to anyone who would pay for the fact of occupation, whether in order to run the business or otherwise. Therefore the claim put forward by the plaintiffs for an account by the mortgagee on the basis that he must pay an occupation rent fails.

Summons dismissed.

NOTES

1. In the light of the way in which a mortgagee in possession of the property is strictly controlled and accountable, why should a mortgagee ever bother to go into possession? Some reasons are given by Buckley L.J. in *Western Bank Ltd v. Schindler* [1977] Ch. 1 at 9-10.

2. As to the position of a mortgagee in possession of leasehold property under Torrens title, see ss 63 and 64 of the *Real Property Act* 1900 (N.S.W.).

5. Right to improve the property

The mortgagee is entitled to take all necessary steps to perfect, protect and maintain her or his security. This includes a right to be reimbursed for expenditure required to put the mortgaged property into a saleable condition. There are, however, limits on the extent of permissible expenditure.

MATZNER v. CLYDE SECURITIES LTD

Supreme Court of New South Wales [1975] 2 N.S.W.L.R. 293

[The mortgagee agreed to advance up to $273,600 on the security of a block of home units in the course of construction. When $258,000 had been advanced, the mortgagor defaulted in his repayments. After an unsuccessful attempt to sell the building in its uncompleted state, the mortgagee expended $76,000 in completing the building and claimed to be entitled to include that amount in the principal sum charged on the security.]

HOLLAND J. The expenditure effected permanent improvements to the land but only by way of completing partially completed buildings in order to make the mortgaged property saleable at its full value. It is clear that, as between mortgagor and mortgagee in possession, the right of the mortgagee to charge the mortgagor with the cost of permanent improvements depends on the application of equitable principles where there is no contractual right to charge: *Southwell v. Roberts* (1940) 63 C.L.R. 581 at 599, 600 per McTiernan J. where there is quoted from *Quarrell v. Beckford* (1816) 1 Madd. 269 at 281; 56 E.R. 100 at 104: "a court of equity considers itself competent in this relation between mortgagor and mortgagee to go beyond the contract—to consider what is just and equitable between parties, standing in that relation;". . . . I think that the relevant equitable principles which would apply are as follows:

(1) Each case is to be considered on its own merits.

(2) The mortgagee in possession is not to be considered as a potential owner entitled to spend what he likes, but as a creditor looking to the security as a means of repayment.

(3) He ought not to be allowed, under the colour of protecting and effectuating his security, to burden the property with a debt out of all relation to the principal sum borrowed or the mortgage moneys owing at the time. Therefore, the proportion which the expenditure bears to the amount of the debt is to be taken into consideration.

(4) He ought not to be allowed expenditure so disproportionate to the mortgage debt and the value of the security and the equity of redemption that the mortgagor would be hampered in redeeming.

(5) The character of the mortgaged premises must be considered, as, on redemption, the mortgagor is entitled to have restored to him the substance of the thing he mortgaged; so expenditure incurred in making changes to buildings or otherwise which radically alter the nature or useful purpose of the property may not be allowed.

(6) Expenditure made, not to alter the nature of the property, but reasonably to improve its actual state for the purpose of realising it by sale, and in fact increasing its saleable value ought to be allowed: *Shepard v. Jones* (1882) 21 Ch. D. 469 at 482, 483 per Cotton L.J.

(7) The mortgagor cannot load the security with expenditure which is not represented in the enhanced value which it has given the premises.

(8) If the mortgagor is seeking, not be redeem, but to obtain the surplus proceeds of sale, the mortgagor is not entitled to recover the increase in saleable value brought about by the mortgagee's expenditure. "If it should turn out that the mortgagee has done something to the property at his own expense which increased its saleable value, I think it is plain on ordinary principles of justice, that that increase should not go into the pocket of the mortgagor without his paying the sum of money which caused the increase.": *Shepard v. Jones* (1882) 21 Ch. D. 469 at 477, 478 per Jessel M.R.; approved by the Privy Council in *Henderson v. Astwood* [1894] A.C. 150 at 163. The foregoing principles are derived from the judgments in *Southwell v. Roberts* (1940) 63 C.L.R. 581 at 597, 598 especially per Dixon J. In that case Starke J. said (1940) 63 C.L.R. 581 at 586 that a mortgagee had been allowed to complete buildings which were uncompleted and charge the security. The cases to which he referred in his judgment were not such cases, but the principles would clearly include such a case.

On the evidence so far, the expenditure of the . . . mortgagee would, prima facie, fall within the above principles, and the . . . mortgagee would be entitled to an inquiry and account on the basis of a claim by the mortgagor for surplus proceeds of sale and on the basis that the mortgagor was chargeable with the expenditure to the extent that it did not offend those principles.

[Other aspects of this case are discussed below p. 486 et seq.]

NOTE

In *Southwell v. Roberts* (1940) 63 C.L.R. 581, referred to in the principal case, the mortgaged property consisted partly of vacant land and partly of land on which stood two old and dilapidated semi-detached houses. The mortgagee demolished the existing buildings and built (partly on the land where they had stood and partly on the vacant land) two new semi-detached houses and a new cottage. The new buildings more than trebled the value of the security, and were suitable to the character of the neighbourhood. The High Court rejected the mortgagee's claim for reimbursement, on the ground that the amount was excessive having regard to the nature of the mortgaged property. Dixon J. summarised the relevant considerations in these terms:

The first consideration is the amount of the mortgage debt and the proportion which the expenditure bears to it. A mortgagee is a creditor who enjoys rights in the mortgaged premises only for the purpose of securing repayment. He ought not to be allowed under colour of protecting and effectuating his security to burden the property with debt out of all relation to the principal sum borrowed or the mortgage moneys owing at the time. Closely related to this consideration is the effect produced upon the mortgagor's ability to redeem. The mortgagee ought not to be allowed against the mortgagor expenditure so disproportionate to the mortgage moneys and so out of keeping with the value of the security and of the equity of redemption that the mortgagor may be hampered in redeeming the property.

Then the character of the mortgaged premises must be considered. Changes are not to be made in buildings or otherwise which radically alter the nature or useful purpose of the property. However much the value is increased, the mortgagor is entitled, on redemption, to have restored to him the substance of the thing he has mortgaged.

A further consideration is the permanence of the improvement. A mortgagee cannot charge expenditure on things, other than maintenance and repairs, which do not or may not outlast his own possession or enure for the actual benefit of the mortgagor and those claiming under him. Then the effect of the expenditure upon the value of the property is important. The mortgagee in possession cannot load the security with expenditure which is not represented in the enhanced value which it has given the premises.

These, however, are matters not in themselves affording decisive tests but providing the considerations upon which the reasonableness of the conduct of the mortgagee in effecting the improvements is to be judged. His own position is, of course, not to be left out of account. But he is to be considered, not as a potential owner, but as a creditor looking to a security as a means of repayment.

Upon the facts in the present case there can, I think, be only one conclusion when these matters are regarded. The disproportionate amount of the expenditure and the alteration in the nature of the premises produced by demolishing the old buildings and erecting new semi-detached cottages on the vacant portion of land and a single cottage on the site of the former building combine to make it impossible to allow the mortgagee to add the cost to the mortgage moneys.

It is no doubt very unfortunate for the mortgagee, and at the same time there can be almost as little doubt that the result to the mortgagor is a windfall. But the loss to the mortgagee arises altogether from her ignoring the mortgagor's position and proceeding to build upon the tacit assumption that she was an absolute owner and not simply a mortgagee in possession of a security for a debt.

C. RIGHT TO LEASE

1. Old system title

Being the owner of the legal estate, at common law the mortgagee could grant leases, but equity did not consider the leases as binding on the mortgagor after redemption, for otherwise they would constitute a clog on the equity of redemption. It became common practice, therefore, for mortgages to contain express provisions whereby leases by the mortgagee would continue to bind the mortgagor after redemption.

Legislation now empowers a mortgagee in possession (subject to any agreement to the contrary) to grant leases upon certain terms and conditions: *Conveyancing Act* 1919 (N.S.W.), s. 106.

Where a lease has been granted by the mortgagor prior to the granting of the mortgage, the mortgagee will take subject to it: the mortgagee's only security is over the reversion. Conversely, a lease granted by the mortgagor after the date of the mortgage could not bind the mortgagee: the mortgagee could regard the tenant as a trespasser (*Dudley and District Benefit Building Society v. Emerson* [1949] Ch. 707 at 714), unless the mortgagee did some act which recognised the existence of a tenancy between herself or himself and the mortgagor's tenant (as in *Chatsworth Properties Ltd v. Effiom* [1971] 1 W.L.R. 144). To overcome this, it became common for mortgages expressly to permit mortgagors to lease the mortgaged premises, but usually only with the mortgagee's prior consent and subject to stringent conditions designed to protect the mortgagee.

The legislation referred to above also permits the mortgagor to grant leases after the date of the mortgage binding against the mortgagee, but only upon certain terms and conditions.

2. Torrens title

It might appear at first sight that a mortgagee of land under Torrens title has no power to grant a lease until there has been default by the mortgagor, that is, until the mortgagee has become entitled to enter into possession (*Finn v. London Bank of Australia* (1898) 19 N.S.W.L.R. 364): until then, the mortgagee is a mere chargee. Further, by analogy with the position at general law, such a lease would not bind the mortgagor once the mortgage had been discharged. However, the leasing powers of an old system mortgagee now have been conferred by statute upon her or his Torrens title counterpart: *Conveyancing Act* 1919 (N.S.W.), s. 106(17).

If the lease has been granted before the mortgage, and has been registered, it will bind the mortgagee. Even if unregistered, it may still bind the mortgagee if it comes within the "short term lease" exception to indefeasibility of title: see above p. 190 et seq.

Section 107 of the *Conveyancing Act* 1919 (N.S.W.) also enables a mortgagor of Torrens title land to grant leases binding upon the mortgagee, provided they comply with the terms of the section. A lease which does not comply with the terms of the section is not binding upon the mortgagee unless he or she has consented to it prior to its registration: *Real Property Act* 1900 (N.S.W.), s. 53(4).

D. RIGHT TO APPOINT A RECEIVER

It is common for mortgages of income producing properties to contain provisions empowering the mortgagee to appoint a receiver in the event of actual or threatened default by the mortgagor. The receiver then manages and administers the property in the interests of the mortgagee, in order to preserve the mortgagee's security, and sets off the income from the property against payments due under the mortgage.

In the absence of an express power, a power to appoint a receiver is implied under s. 109(1)(c) of the *Conveyancing Act*, subject to any contrary provision in the mortgage: s. 109(3). This provision applies also to land under the provisions of the *Real Property Act*: s. 109(5). The rights and obligations of a receiver appointed under this implied power are set out in s. 115 of the *Conveyancing Act*. They include the right to demand and recover all income from the property and exercise any powers which may have been delegated to the receiver by the mortgagee pursuant to the Act: s. 115(3). The advantage to the mortgagee of appointing a receiver under this implied power rather than going into possession personally is that the receiver is deemed the agent of the mortgagor and the mortgagor is solely responsible for the receiver's acts or defaults unless the mortgage instrument otherwise provides (s. 115(2)) or unless the mortgagee directs or interferes with the receiver's activity, in which case by the mortgagee's conduct the receiver becomes the mortgagee's agent: *Standard Chartered Bank Ltd v. Walker* [1982] 1 W.L.R. 1410 at 1417, 1418; *American Express International Banking Corp. v. Hurley* [1985] 3 All E.R. 564 at 568. In like vein, under an express power in the mortgage instrument authorising the appointment of a receiver, it is the invariable practice for the receiver specifically to be deemed the agent of the mortgagor, so as to relieve the mortgagee from liability for the receiver's activities; here also, the clause is effective according to its terms, unless by subsequent conduct the mortgagee constitutes the receiver as her or his agent.

Whether the right to appoint a receiver is conferred by an express or implied power, no appointment can be made by the mortgagee unless there has been default under the mortgage: *Conveyancing Act* 1919 (N.S.W.), s. 115A(2)(a). Where the receiver is appointed pursuant to an express power in the mortgage instrument, the appointment must of course also comply with any other conditions imposed upon the appointment by the terms of the instrument. Sometimes, receivers are appointed as part of the security arrangements themselves and not pursuant to a provision in the mortgage instrument whereby the mortgagee may appoint a receiver upon default; in such a case, the receiver cannot exercise any powers unless there has been default under the mortgage *and* the instrument which appoints the receiver has been registered (s. 115A(2)(c), as interpreted in *Isherwood v. Butler Pollnow Pty Ltd* (1986) 6 N.S.W.L.R. 363 at 386-389; it is thought that amendments made to s. 115A(2) in 1986 do not affect the authority of *Isherwood's* case).

In addition, in the case of mortgages subject to the provisions of the *Credit Act* 1984 (N.S.W.) or the *Credit (Home Finance Contracts) Act* 1984 (N.S.W.), the notice requirements of s. 107 and s. 7 respectively of those Acts must be complied with. These requirements have been discussed above p. 439.

There is also a power in the Supreme Court to appoint a receiver whenever it is "just and convenient" to do so: *Supreme Court Act* 1970 (N.S.W.), s. 67.

A receiver owes certain duties to the mortgagor which are enforceable by the latter directly against the receiver. These duties include the duty to exercise her or his powers in good faith (including the duty not to sacrifice the mortgagor's interests recklessly), to act strictly within the conditions of her or his appointment, to account to the mortgagor after the mortgagee's security has been discharged not only for any surplus assets but also for her or his conduct of the receivership; and, if he or she chooses to exercise a power of sale, he or she is under a duty similar to that of a mortgagee exercising a power of sale: see *Expo International Pty Ltd v. Chant* [1979] 2 N.S.W.L.R. 820 at 834; *Standard Chartered Bank Ltd v. Walker* [1982] 1 W.L.R. 1410. The duty of a mortgagee exercising a power of sale is discussed below.

The English courts have held that a receiver also owes a duty to guarantors of the mortgage: *Standard Chartered Bank Ltd v. Walker* [1982] 1 W.L.R. 1410; *American Express International Banking Co. v. Hurley* [1985] 3 All E.R. 564. This principle is based upon the premise that a receiver, like a mortgagee, may be liable in negligence for the conduct of the receivership. Whether this principle applies in Australia may turn upon the precise nature of the mortgagee's duty, a matter open to debate in Australia and discussed further below. To date, such authority as exists in New South Wales suggests that in this State a receiver's liability is not based in negligence: *Expo International Pty Ltd v. Chant* [1979] 2 N.S.W.L.R. 820 at 834.

E. FORECLOSURE

1. General

It has been seen (above p. 432) that equity permits the mortgagor to redeem even though the contractual date for redemption has passed. Clearly, there must be some limit to this equitable right to redeem, otherwise a mortgagee would never be able to enforce his security. One limit is supplied by the mortgagee's power of sale, to be considered below; the other limit is supplied by the remedy of foreclosure, by which the mortgagee can extinguish the mortgagor's right, title and interest in the property, and put an end to the equitable right to redeem:

> [T]he effect of the order for foreclosure absolute [this term is discussed below] is to vest the ownership of, and the beneficial title to, the land, for the first time, in the person who previously was a mere encumbrancer. The equitable estate of the mortgagor is then forfeited and transferred to the mortgagee: *Heath v. Pugh* (1881) 6 Q.B.D. 345 at 360.

The right to foreclose cannot arise until the equitable right to redeem has arisen, that is, until the contractual date for redemption has passed. Where the mortgage contains a proviso for redemption on repayment of principal, the equitable right to redeem, and thus the right to foreclose, cannot arise until there has been default in the payment of principal: see *Williams v. Morgan* [1906] 1 Ch. 804. Where, however, the mortgage makes the proviso for redemption conditional upon due payment of interest, the equitable right to redeem, and thus the right to foreclose, will arise upon default in payment of interest: *Twentieth Century Banking Corp. Ltd v. Wilkinson* [1977] Ch. 99.

Where the mortgagee seeks to foreclose a mortgage which is subject to the *Credit Act* 1984 (N.S.W.) or the *Credit (Home Finance Contracts) Act* 1984 (N.S.W.), he must first give the notices required by s. 107 and s. 7 respectively of those Acts. These notices are discussed above p. 439.

2. Old system title

Where the land is under old system title, foreclosure is effected by order of court. There are two steps in the foreclosure process. First, the court makes a decree nisi, by which an account is directed of the amount outstanding under the mortgage, and the mortgagor is given a certain time to make payment; then, if payment is not made within that time, the order is made absolute, and the mortgagor's right title and interest in the premises is extinguished. For a detailed discussion of the procedure, see Sykes, op. cit., pp. 126-127; Francis, op. cit., pp. 155-160.

The right to foreclose attaches not only to legal mortgages but also to equitable mortgages, including mortgages by deposit of title deeds. A second or subsequent mortgagee is entitled to foreclose as against mortgagees subsequent to himself and the mortgagor, but he cannot defeat the rights of prior mortgagees.

The court has a discretion to order a sale of the property in lieu of foreclosure: *Conveyancing Act* 1919 (N.S.W.), s. 103(2).

In New South Wales, foreclosure extinguishes the mortgagee's right to sue on the personal covenant and the mortgagor's right to redeem the property: see *Conveyancing Act* 1919 (N.S.W.), s. 100.

A foreclosure will be re-opened where the order has been obtained through fraud, and may be re-opened where the mortgagor's failure to pay on time has been due to such factors as mistake or accident: see generally, *National Mutual Life Assoc. v. Benjamin* (1900) 21 L.R. (N.S.W.) Eq. 96; Sykes, op. cit., pp. 126-127.

In some circumstances, a foreclosure may be re-opened against a purchaser from the mortgagee.

CAMPBELL v. HOLYLAND

Chancery Division (1877) 7 Ch. D. 166

[B was entitled to a reversionary interest in a fund of approximately £7,000. B mortgaged his interest in the fund to Campbell to secure an advance of £1,000. On B's death, administration of his estate was granted to Holyland.

In May 1876 a decree nisi for foreclosure was made, and later it was certified that the decree would be made absolute on 4 January 1877 unless the sum of £1,523 was paid by that date.

In October 1876 the equity of redemption was sold to M and G, who then negotiated with Campbell for the purchase of the mortgagee's interest. M and G mistakenly (but apparently honestly) believed that they had entered into a binding contract with Campbell to purchase his interest for £800, so that on 4 January 1877 they stated that they were willing to complete the purchase, but they did not pay the amount of £1,523 due under the mortgage.

It later transpired that on 3 January 1877, Campbell had sold his interest as mortgagee to Ford, a solicitor, who was aware of the negotiations between M and G and Campbell. On 11 January, the decree nisi was made absolute upon an ex parte application made by Campbell at Ford's instance. The assignments of the equity of redemption and the mortgagee's interest were not disclosed to the Court.

In November 1877 M and the executors of G (G having died) applied to have the foreclosure re-opened.]

JESSEL M.R. I have no doubt that I ought to make the order asked for.

The question in dispute is really whether a mortgagor can be allowed to redeem after an order of foreclosure absolute, and I think, on looking at the authorities, that no Chancellor or Vice-Chancellor has ever laid down that any special circumstances are essential to enable a mortgagor to redeem in such a case.

Now what is the principle? The principle in a court of equity has always been that, though a mortgage is in form an absolute conveyance when the condition is broken, in equity it is always security; and it must be remembered that the doctrine arose at the time when mortgages were made in the form of conditional conveyance, the condition being that if the money was not paid at the day, the estate should become the estate of the mortgagee; that was the contract between the parties; yet courts of equity interfered with the actual contract to this extent, by saying there was a paramount intention that the estate should be security, and that the mortgage money should be debt; and they gave relief in the shape of redemption on that principle. Of course that would lend, and did lend, to this inconvenience, that even when the mortgagor was not willing to redeem, the mortgagee could not sell or deal with the estate as his own, and to remedy that inconvenience the practice of bringing a foreclosure suit was adopted, by which a mortgagee was entitled to call on the mortgagor to redeem within a certain time, under penalty of losing the right of redemption. In that foreclosure suit the court made various orders—interim orders fixing a time for payment of the money—and at last there came the final order which was called foreclosure absolute, that is, in form, that the mortgagor should not be allowed to redeem at all; but it was form only, just as the original deed was form only; for the courts of equity soon decided that, notwithstanding the form of that order, they would after that order allow the mortgagor to redeem. That is, although the order of foreclosure absolute appeared to be a final order of the court, it was not so, but the mortgagee still remained liable to be treated as mortgagee and the mortgagor still retained a claim to be treated as mortgagor, subject to the discretion of the court. Therefore everybody who took an order for foreclosure absolute knew that there was still a discretion in the court to allow the mortgagor to redeem.

Under what circumstances that discretion should be exercised is quite another matter. The mortgagee had a right to deal with an estate acquired under foreclosure absolute the day after he acquired it; but he knew perfectly well that there might be circumstances to entitle the mortgagor to redeem, and everybody buying the estate from a mortgagee who merely acquired a title under such an order was considered to have the same knowledge, namely, that the estate might be taken away from him by the exercise, not of a capricious discretion, but of a judicial discretion by the court of equity which had made the order.

That being so, on what terms is that judicial discretion to be exercised? It has been said by the highest authority that it is impossible to say á priori what are the terms. They must depend upon the circumstances of each case. For instance, in *Thornhill v. Manning* (1851) 1 Sim. (N.S.) 451 at 454; 61 E.R. 174 Lord Cranworth said you cannot lay down a general rule. There are certain things laid down which are intelligible to everybody. In the first place the mortgagor must come, as it is said, promptly; that is, within a reasonable time. He is not to let the mortgagee deal with the estate as his own—if it is a landed estate, the mortgagee being in possession of it and using it—and then without any special reason come and say: "Now I will redeem." He cannot do that; he must come within a reasonable time. What is a reasonable time? You must have regard to the nature of the property. As has been stated in more than one of the cases, where the estate is an estate in land in possession—where the mortgagee takes it in possession and deals with it and alters the property, and so on—the mortgagor must come much more quickly than where it is an estate in reversion, as to which the mortgagee can do nothing except sell it. So that you must have regard to the nature of the estate in ascertaining what is to be considered reasonable time.

Then, again, was the mortgagee [sic] entitled to redeem, but by some accident unable to redeem? Did he expect to get the money from a quarter from which he might reasonably hope to obtain it, and was he disappointed at the last moment? Was it a very large sum, and did he require a considerable time to raise it elsewhere? All those things must be considered in determining what is a reasonable time.

Then an element for consideration has always been the nature of the property as regards value. For instance, if an estate were worth £50,000, and had been foreclosed for a mortgage debt of £5,000, the man who came to redeem that estate would have a longer time than where the estate was worth £5,100, and he was foreclosed for £5,000. But not only is there money value, but there may be other considerations. It may be an old family estate or a chattel, or picture, which possesses a special value for the mortgagor, but which possesses not the same value for other people; or it may be, as has happened in this instance, that the property, though a reversionary interest in the funds, is of special value to both the litigants: it may possess not merely a positive money value, but a peculiar value having regard to the nature of the title and other incidents, so that you cannot set an actual money value upon it. In fact, that is the real history of this contest, for the property does not appear to be of much more money value—though it is of some more—than the original amount of the mortgage. All this must be taken into consideration.

Then it is said you must not interfere against purchasers. As I have already explained, there are purchasers and purchasers. If the purchaser buys a freehold estate in possession after the lapse of a considerable time from the order of foreclosure absolute, with no notice of any extraneous circumstances which would induce the court to interfere, I for one should decline to interfere with such a title as that; but if the purchaser bought the estate within 24 hours after the foreclosure absolute, and with notice of the fact that it was of much greater value than the amount of the mortgage debt, is it to be supposed that a court of equity would listen to the contention of such a purchaser that he ought not to be interfered with? He must be taken to know the general law that an order for foreclosure may be opened under proper circumstances and under a proper exercise of discretion by the court; and if the mortgagor in that case came the week after, is it to be supposed a court of equity would so stultify itself as to say that a title so acquired would stand in the way? I am of opinion it would not.

Now I come to the circumstances of this case, and I must say they are very strong in favour of opening the foreclosure. As I said before, it is a sum of money in reversion, the title to which, no doubt, is to some extent in dispute, but which both parties are very desirous to possess for special reasons of their own. It appears to have a special value as well for the purchaser as the mortgagor. The intrinsic money value was thought by the parties at the time of the negotiations I am about to mention, to be really less than the mortgage debt; the mortgage money was carrying 7 per cent interest, and negotiations were entered into by the mortgagor—or the persons standing in the position of mortgagor—with the mortgagee not to redeem in terms, but to buy up the mortgage for a less sum. Those negotiations were supposed by the mortgagor to have resulted in an agreement to purchase, and acting under that belief he did not attend at the day with the money to pay off the mortgage, but he came and told the mortgagee he was willing to pay the purchase-money for the mortgage and keep the property.

Now, what happened in the meantime? The present purchaser, Mr Ford, being very desirous to acquire the property for a collateral object—I am not saying a wrong object, but a collateral object—had, before the time for foreclosure absolute had arrived, entered into a contract with the mortgagee to buy it. He was not a purchaser coming in even the day after foreclosure, but a purchaser coming in before foreclosure, and at that time of course he knew the property was redeemable. He brought a property certainly redeemable, for the day of redemption had not even arrived. That is the kind of purchase I am dealing with. He was aware on the day of redemption that it was not from unwillingness to redeem that the mortgagor failed to pay the money, but because the mortgagor was under the belief that he had acquired a right to take the property on paying less than the mortgage money, by reason of a contract of purchase with the mortgagee . . . .

I think, under these circumstances, that the mortgagor has been sufficiently prompt. I entirely agree with the various authorities which have been quoted, that reasonable promptness ought always to be shewn. I say reasonable promptness, because what is promptness is, as I have said, not an abstract proposition, but must depend on the circumstances of the case. I think the mortgagor has been sufficiently prompt. I think the purchaser is not in a position to terrorise the court as to the evils that would happen by opening a foreclosure after sale. As I said before, I by no means say that the fact of a sale would not be an important fact; it ought to weigh with the court in opening foreclosure.

I am of opinion, however, that such a sale as this ought to have no weight whatever, and that under the circumstances the mortgagor is entitled to open the foreclosure on the usual terms, that is, on payment of principal, interest, and costs.

Order accordingly.

3. Torrens title

Sections 61 and 62 of the *Real Property Act* 1900 (N.S.W.) outline the procedure to be followed in the foreclosure of mortgages over Torrens title land. By their own terms, the provisions apply only to *registered* mortgages. In brief, the procedure is as follows. Where default has been made in the payment of principal or interest for six months, the mortgagee may apply to the Registrar-General for an order for foreclosure. The application must state that the required default has been made, that the land has been offered for sale by auction (after the appropriate notices had been given under s. 57 of the Act: see below p. 452) but without the highest bid reaching the amount outstanding under the mortgage plus the expenses of the sale, and that notice of the application has been served upon, inter alios, the mortgagor, all registered mortgagees under mortgages having less priority than that of the applicant, and each caveator claiming an interest in the land as an unregistered mortgagee. The Registrar-General may thereupon issue the foreclosure order, or may require the applicant first to offer the land for sale and issue the order only after the land fails to be sold or is sold for an amount insufficient to satisfy the debt and the expenses of the sale. An order for foreclosure when issued by the Registrar-General and recorded in the Register vests in the applicant mortgagee all the estate and interest of the mortgagor in the land, free from the mortgagor's equity of redemption and free from the rights of mortgagees under registered mortgages having less priority than the applicant's mortgage.

It will be observed from the above that the order for foreclosure is made by the Registrar-General and not by court order. Further, as already noted, the procedure is available only to registered mortgagees: an unregistered mortgagee seeking foreclosure must apply to the court.

Where the security is partly old system title land and partly Torrens title land, the procedures for old system title are followed for both: *Conveyancing Act* 1919 (N.S.W.), s. 101.

As in the case of old system title land, so in the case of Torrens title land foreclosure deprives the mortgagee of the right thereafter to sue on the personal covenant: *Conveyancing Act* 1919, s. 100(2).

It would seem from the provisions of s. 100(2) of the *Conveyancing Act* and s. 62 of the *Real Property Act* that foreclosure of a Torrens title mortgage cannot be re-opened: see Sykes, op. cit., pp. 291-292; *Campbell v. Bank of New South Wales* (1883) 16 L.R. (N.S.W.) Eq. 285; *Fink v. Robertson* (1907) 4 C.L.R. 864 at 876.

F. POWER OF SALE

The need to obtain a court order to foreclose an old system mortgage, and to follow the complex procedures under the Torrens legislation to foreclose a Torrens title mortgage, has made foreclosure a remedy availed of rarely in Australia. A more convenient and less expensive remedy upon default by the mortgagor is the exercise by the mortgagee of a power to sell the mortgaged property.

Mortgages invariably contain provisions empowering the mortgagee to sell the mortgaged property upon default by the mortgagor. Even in the absence of express provision, however, a power of sale is implied into every mortgage, pursuant to s. 109(1)(a) of the *Conveyancing Act* 1919 (N.S.W.), although subject to any contrary intention expressed in the mortgage deed: s. 109(3). Section 109 applies also to mortgages under the *Real Property Act* 1900 (N.S.W.): see s. 109(5). The power of sale implied under s. 109 is amplified by the provisions of s. 110.

Before the power of sale can be exercised upon default by the mortgagor, certain notice requirements must be complied with. These are set out in the *Conveyancing Act* 1919 (N.S.W.), s. 111 and the *Real Property Act* 1900 (N.S.W.), ss 57 and 58A. In addition, where the mortgage comes within the definition of a "home finance contract" under the *Credit (Home Finance Contracts) Act* 1984 (N.S.W.), or of a "regulated mortgage" under the *Credit Act* 1984 (N.S.W.), the mortgagee cannot exercise a power of sale unless the notice requirements of those Acts are complied with. As to those Acts and notices under them, see above pp. 436-437 and 439.

The exercise of a power of sale does not preclude the mortgagee from suing on the personal covenant to recover any deficiency where the sale does not realise sufficient to satisfy the mortgage debt.

1. Manner of exercise of power

(a) A mortgagee cannot sell to herself or himself

FARRAR v. FARRARS LTD

Chancery Division and Court of Appeal (1888) 40 Ch. D. 395

[A solicitor, one of three mortgagees of land used as a quarry, acted as solicitor for the promoters of a company formed for the purpose of acquiring the mortgaged property from the mortgagees in exercise of their power of sale. He became the solicitor for the company and acquired shares in it. The company subsequently purchased the property from the mortgagees. The mortgagees had earlier tried unsuccessfully to sell the property by auction. Chitty J. found that the sale to the company was not at an undervalue, that the price was the best that could reasonably be obtained in the circumstances, and refused an application by the mortgagors to have the sale set aside.]

CHITTY J. A mortgagee exercising a power of sale is not a trustee of the power. The power arises by contract with the mortgagor, and forms part of the mortgagee's security. He is bound to sell fairly, and to take reasonable steps to obtain a proper price; but he may proceed to a forced sale for the purpose of paying the mortgage debt. In most cases (as in that before me) he is required by the terms of the power to give notice to the mortgagor, and to allow a certain time to elapse before he can duly proceed to a sale. . . . The mortgagor has no right after the power has arisen to insist that the mortgagee shall wait for better times before selling. This observation applies in full force where the mortgaged property is of a speculative character, and is not producing any income. The mortgagee has a right to obtain payment of his debt through the exercise of his power when it has arisen, without regard to the then existing condition of the market. He cannot be required to run any risk in postponing the sale, or to speculate for the mortgagor's benefit. . . .

A mortgagee cannot sell to himself, nor can two mortgagees sell to one of themselves, nor to one of themselves and another. The reasons for this are obvious, and are not merely formal but substantial. A man cannot contract with himself, and in the cases supposed there cannot be any independent bargaining as between opposite parties. For similar reasons a mortgagee cannot sell to a trustee for himself; he cannot buy in the name of another. But when mortgagees sell to a corporation there are, prima facie, two independent contracting parties and a valid contract, and if the bargaining is real and honest, and conducted independently by the mortgagees on the one hand, and by the directors or officers of the corporation on the other, and it is satisfactorily shewn that in concluding the terms of the sale the parties were in no way affected by the circumstance that one of the mortgagees had some interest as a shareholder in the corporation, I see no sufficient reason that the sale ought not to stand. By way of illustration, I put the case of an honest transaction of sale between the mortgagees and one of the great railway companies, such as the London and North Western Railway Co. It is urged that, as a matter of principle and on the ground on which a court of equity acts where there is a conflict between interest and duty, the sale to Farrars Ltd, must be avoided, simply because the defendant John Riley Farrar held shares. But the proposition is contrary to the decision of Bacon V.-C. in *Hickley v. Hickley* (1876) 2 Ch. D. 190 . . . .

It appears to me, then, that this sale ought not necessarily to be set aside simply because the defendant John Riley Farrar had an interest in the thing purchased as a member of the company which bought. Holding, as I do, that the material terms of the bargain were honestly and independently settled, and that the terms were not in any degree affected by the circumstance that the defendant John Riley Farrar subsequently agreed to become a member of and to act as solicitor for the company, I am of opinion that the sale ought not to be set aside merely because he was a member and acting as solicitor for the company when the formal contract was signed. As to the argument that a decision in favour of the defendants will open the door to fraud, the answer is, that every transaction of the nature disclosed by the facts of this case must be carefully inquired into and jealously watched, and that each case as it arises must be decided on its own merits.

[The mortgagors appealed to the Court of Appeal.]

THE COURT (delivered by LINDLEY L.J.). The plaintiffs on appeal did not question the view of the judge that there was no fraudulent sale at an undervalue, but they contended that fraud or no fraud, undervalue or no undervalue, the sale could not stand, inasmuch as it was in substance a sale by a mortgagee to himself and others under the guise of a sale to a limited company.

If this proposition were true the sale could not stand as against the mortgagor. It is perfectly well settled that a mortgagee with a power of sale cannot sell to himself either alone or with others, nor to a trustee for himself: *Downes v. Grazebrook* (1817) 3 Mer. 200; 65 E.R. 983; *Robertson v. Norris* (1848) 1 Giff. 421; 36 E.R. 77; nor to any one employed by him to conduct the sale: *Whitcomb v. Minchin* (1820) 5 Madd. 91; 56 E.R. 830; *Martinson v. Clowes* (1880) 21 Ch. D. 857. A sale by a person to himself is no sale at all, and a power of sale does not authorise the donee of the power to take the property subject to it at a price fixed by himself, even although such price be the full value of the property. Such a transaction is not an exercise of the power, and the interposition of a trustee, although it gets over the difficulty so far as form is concerned, does not affect the substance of the transaction.

A sale by a person to a corporation of which he is a member is not, either in form or in substance, a sale by a person to himself. To hold that it is, would be to ignore the principle which lies at the root of the legal idea of a corporate body, and that idea is that the corporate body is distinct from the persons composing it. A sale by a member of a corporation to the corporation itself is in every sense a sale valid in equity as well as at law. There is no authority for saying that such a sale is not waranted by an ordinary power of sale, and in our opinion, such a sale is warranted by such a power, and does not fall within the rule to which we have at present referred. But although this is true, it is obvious that a sale by a person to an incorporated company of which he is a member may be invalid upon various grounds, although it may not be reached by the rule which prevents a man from selling to himself or to a trustee for himself. Such a sale may, for example, be fraudulent and at an undervalue or it may be made under circumstances which throw upon the purchasing company the burden of proving the validity of the transaction, and the company may be unable to prove it. Fraud in the present case is not now alleged; it was alleged in court below, and was clearly disproved. But, for reasons which will appear presently, the circumstances attending the sale were such as, in our opinion, throw upon the company the burden of sustaining the transaction. . . .

A mortgagee with a power of sale, though often called a trustee, is in a very different position from a trustee for sale. A mortgagee is under obligations to the mortgagor, but he has rights of his own which he is entitled to exercise adversely to the mortgagor. A trustee for sale has no business to place himself in such a position as to give rise to a conflict of interest and duty. But every mortgage confers upon the mortgagee the right to realise his security and to find a purchaser if he can, and if in exercise of his power he acts bona fide and takes reasonable precautions to obtain a proper price, the mortgagor has no redress, even although more might have been obtained for the property if the sale had been postponed: *Cholmondeley v. Clinton* (1815) 2 Jac. & W. 1 at 182; 35 E.R. 527; *Warner v. Jacob* (1882) 20 Ch. D. 220. . . .

The evidence shews that the transaction was thoroughly honest and fair, and, notwithstanding its suspicious appearance, the company has proved its validity. . . .

Mr Farrar was not a trustee selling to himself, or to others for him, nor was he buying directly or indirectly for himself, and although a sale by a mortgagee to a company promoted by himself, of which he is the solicitor, and in which he has shares, is one which the company must prove to have been bona fide, and at a price at which the mortgagees could properly sell, yet, if such proves to be the fact, there is no rule of law which compels the court to set aside the sale.

Appeal dismissed.

NOTES

1. The principal case was applied by the High Court in *Australian and New Zealand Banking Group Ltd v. Bangadilly Pastoral Co. Pty Ltd* (1978) 52 A.L.J.R. 529, discussed by Butt, "The Mortgagee's Duty on Sale" (1979) 53 A.L.J. 172; cf. Note (1979) 53 A.L.J. 842 (Stone). The mortgagee, a company, exercised its power of sale and sold the property to another company. The same persons effectively controlled each company. The High Court held that although not a sale by a company to itself, there was no "truly independent bargain": see (1978) 52 A.L.J.R. 529 at 541. Although the sale had been by public auction, it had been poorly advertised and had been held on a day when purchaser interest was likely to be low (for another example, see *Latec Investments Ltd v. Hotel Terrigal Pty Ltd* (1965) 113 C.L.R. 265); the persons who controlled the companies had been the only bidders at the auction, and had set the reserve price, well below the market value; they had purchased for exactly the reserve price, although they knew that the purchaser company was in a position to pay a substantially higher price; and there had been unexplained delays in, and unsatisfactory handling of other aspects of, the sale.

   The principal case was also applied by the Privy Council in *Tse Kwong Lam v. Wong Chit Sen* [1983] 3 All E.R. 54. The mortgagee in purported exercise of the power of sale had sold the mortgaged property at auction to a company of which he was a director and in which he held approximately one quarter of the issued shares. The auction sale had not been widely advertised, no action had been taken to canvass potential buyers before the auction, and the purchaser had made the only bid at the auction. The property was knocked down to the purchaser at the reserve price set by the mortgagee. The Privy Council held that there was "no hard and fast rule that a mortgagee may not sell to a company in which he is interested", but that a "heavy onus lies on the mortgagee to show that in all respects he acted fairly to the borrower and used his best endeavours to obtain the best price reasonably obtainable for the mortgaged property": at 59. On the facts, that onus had not been discharged, but because of the delay taken by the mortgagor in prosecuting the case their Lordships declined to order the sale to be set aside; instead, the mortgagor was held entitled to damages for the loss sustained as a result of the improper exercise of the power of sale.

2. The *Conveyancing Act* 1919 (N.S.W.), s. 109(1)(a), authorises the mortgagee exercising power of sale to "buy in" at auction. (This provision applies to Torrens title mortgages (s. 109(5)); but cf. s. 58(1) of the *Real Property Act* 1900 (N.S.W.) which also empowers a mortgagee to "buy in" but with no qualification concerning "at auction".) The provision appears designed to enable the mortgagee to bid and buy at auction to prevent the property being sacrificed at an undervalue, but not to retain the property for himself beneficially; he may sell again at a later date: *Wynne v. Moore* (1870) 1 A.J.R. 156; *Henderson v. Astwood* [1894] A.C. 150.

3. It has been said that a mortgagee cannot sell to any officer, solicitor or agent acting for him in the sale: *Martinson v. Clowes* (1882) 21 Ch. D. 857 at 860. The Australian courts have refused to condone a sale by auction to a clerk employed by the mortgagee's solicitors and who had himself conducted the auction sale (*Re White*; *Ex parte Goggs* (1866) 1 Q.S.C.R. 149), and a sale to a person employed by the mortgagee to find a buyer (*Conroy v. Knox* (1901) 11 Q.L.J. 112 at 121). These are not, however, universal principles: the High Court has refused to set aside a sale by a mortgagee bank to an employee where the sale had been made in good faith, at a realistic price, and after genuine but unsuccessful attempts to sell to the public: *Sewell v. Agricultural Bank of Western Australia* (1930) 44 C.L.R. 104.

4. A mortgagee may sell to a subsequent mortgagee: *Shaw v. Bunny* (1865) 2 De G.J. & Sm. 468; 46 E.R. 456.

5. A mortgagee may sell to the mortgagor, but the mortgagor cannot thereby claim to have extinguished the rights of any subsequent mortgagee: *Otter v. Lord Vaux* (1856) 6 De G.M. & G. 638; 43 E.R. 1381; *Edwards v. McDowell* (1933) 50 W.N. (N.S.W.) 244; *R. v. Registrar of Titles; Ex parte Watson* [1952] V.L.R. 470.

(b) Must be a genuine sale

BELTON v. BASS, RATCLIFFE AND GRETTON LTD

Chancery Division [1922] 2 Ch. 449

[The plaintiff Belton mortgaged certain shares in a brewery to the defendant company. On default by the plaintiff, the defendant proposed to exercise its power of sale by granting to one of its directors, Garrard, an option to purchase the shares. On being advised by its solicitors that the granting of an option would not be a proper exercise of its power of sale, the defendant company instead sold the shares to Garrard at a fair market price, advanced to him the whole of the purchase money for three years interest free and gave him the right to call on the defendant company to repurchase the shares at the same price at any time within the next three years. Garrard later sold the shares to a third party at a considerable profit.

The plaintiff claimed that the sale of the shares to Garrard was not a valid sale and sought a declaration that they or their proceeds were still subject to redemption.]

RUSSELL J. [N]o one, I think, can deny that the transaction . . . had for one of its objects a benefit to Garrard, that its terms were shaped so as to put Garrard (as he himself admitted) as far as possible on the same footing as if he had been granted the option which the solicitors had advised could not or should not be granted. . . .

In form the transaction was a sale by a mortgagee, the whole of the purchase money being allowed to remain for a fixed period as a loan secured on the property sold, and the purchaser during that period having the right to put the property back on to his vendor at a price which was the amount of the original purchase money.

A mortgagee is entitled to sell at a proper price upon the terms of allowing a considerable portion of the purchase money to remain on mortgage. In the case of *Davey v. Durrant* (1857) 1 De G. & J. 535 at 553; 44 E.R. 830 Knight Bruce L.J. uses the following language: "It was said that the arrangement by which part of the purchase money was suffered to remain on a mortgage of the property sold was such as to reduce the price, and was otherwise unjustifiable. But that arrangement appears to me to have increased rather than diminished the price, if the price was at all affected by it. Nor can I say that it is beyond the right or authority of a mortgagee with a power of sale to effect a sale, of which one of the terms shall be that even a considerable portion of the purchase money shall be allowed to remain on mortgage of the property, that mortgage being as between the seller and those entitled to the equity of redemption at the seller's risk; that is, he charging himself with the whole amount of the purchase money in account with them, as has been done in the present instance.''

If this is correct I see no reason why the whole purchase money should not be allowed to remain on security: see *Bettyes v. Maynard* (1883) 31 W.R. 461; *Thurlow v. Mackeson* (1868) L.R. 4 Q.B. 97, and *Farrar v. Farrars Ltd* (1888) 40 Ch. D. 395.

But as is pointed out by the authorities, the mortgagee must in account give the mortgagor full credit for the price. From the moment of the sale, however, the purchase money and security, if any, for it, stand at the risk of the mortgagee. As between him and his mortgagor he is treated as having in fact received the full amount.

The fact that the mortgagee chooses to give to the purchaser the additional right of reselling the property to him can, in my opinion, make no difference. Such a right would certainly not tend to diminish the price which the purchaser would be prepared to give. If such right were exercised the property would not come back to the mortgagee in the capacity of mortgagee. The sale to the purchaser frees it from all right of redemption under the mortgage. It would come back to the mortgagee as a purchaser from an absolute owner, in whose hands the property was, subject to no right in third parties of redemption or otherwise. . . .

That in law there was a sale cannot be doubted. Garrard became the legal owner and the registered holder of the shares. Subject to the security on them in favour of the defendants Bass, he was free to exercise the voting power in respect thereof, to receive any dividends which might be paid, and to dispose of the shares. The defendants Bass became his creditors for the purchase money, and except for their interest therein as security for that debt they had no right or title to the shares. So too as between themselves and the plaintiff £750 [being the purchase price] of his debt was wiped out, and they could never have asserted any claim in respect thereof. In law the transaction was a sale by the mortgagee, the purchaser becoming owner of the property sold, freed from all right of redemption by the mortgagor, the mortgagor ceasing to be indebted to the mortgagee to the amount of the purchase price of the property sold.

Thus the transaction was a sale by a mortgagee in exercise of his power of sale at a price admitted to be fair.

But then it is said that the mortgagee exercised his power of sale with an indirect motive, not with the view of realising his security, but with the object of conferring a benefit upon the defendant Garrard by giving him an option masquerading as a sale.

No doubt the net result flowing from the transaction must be the same as the net result flowing from the grant of an option.

Notwithstanding this identity in the ultimate positions of the parties, their respective legal rights and liabilities are throughout the period in question, wholly different according as the transaction is an option or a sale.

At one time there was colour for the suggestion that the motive of the mortgagee in selling might be weighed as an element in considering whether a mortgagee's power of sale had been or not validly exercised.

In *Robertson v. Norris* (1848) 1 Giff. 421 at 424; 116 E.R. 716 Stuart V.-C. cited Lord Eldon as an authority in favour of the principle that the mortgagee is a trustee for the benefit of the mortgagor in the exercise of his power of sale, and added that if he used the power for any purpose other than to secure repayment of the mortgage, to effect other purposes of his own or to serve the purpose of other individuals, that would be a fraud on the exercise of his power, and the sale would be vitiated against the purchaser.

Sir George Jessel in the Court of Appeal would have none of this. The case is that of *Nash v. Eads* (1880) 25 Sol. J. 95. The court consisted of Sir George Jessel, and Cotton and Lush L.JJ., and held that there was no foundation for this proposition. Sir George Jessel said: "The mortgagee was not a trustee of the power of sale for the mortgagor, and if he was entitled to exercise the power, the court could not look into his motives for so doing. If he had a right to sell on 1 June and he then said, 'The mortgagor is a member of an old county family, and I don't wish to turn him out of his property, and will not sell it at present', and then on 1 July he said, 'I have had a quarrel with the mortgagor, and he has insulted me; I will show him no more mercy, but will sell him up at once'—if all this was proved, the court could not restrain the mortgagee from exercising his power of sale, except on the terms of payment of the mortgage debt. The court could not look at the mortgagee's motives for exercising his power. Lord Eldon had never said anything of the kind which Vice-Chancellor Stuart supposed him to have said. The Vice-Chancellor was entirely mistaken, and must have been citing the judgments to which he referred from his recollection, without looking at the reports. Of course there were some limits to the powers of the mortgagee. He, like a pledgee, must conduct the sale properly, and must sell at a fair value, and he could not sell to himself. But he was not bound to abstain from selling because he was not in urgent want of his money, or because he had a spite against the mortgagor."

I am unable accordingly to inquire into the motives of the defendants Bass, or to hold that the sale is vitiated because they desired to confer a benefit on the purchaser by selling to him upon terms, which included a fair price.

In the result, I must come to the conclusion on this part of the case that in September 1914 the defendants Bass validly exercised their power of sale as mortgagees by selling the 750 shares to the defendant Garrard at a fair and proper price, and that the plaintiff has no cause of action in respect thereof.

Suit dismissed.

NOTES AND QUESTIONS

1. In *Davey v. Durrant* (1857) 1 De G. & J. 535; 44 E.R. 830, referred to in the principal case, a mortgagee wished to make a gift of the mortgaged property to a charity, the mortgagor having defaulted under the mortgage. On being advised that the making of such a gift would not be a proper exercise of the power of sale (it would not have been a "sale" at all), the mortgagee sold the property to the charity at a fair value; by agreement with the charity, however, the consideration was not paid, but was to be considered as a gift from him to the charity. The transaction was held to be an improper exercise of the power of sale, and the mortgagor was entitled to redeem the property.

   Would the result have been different if the charity had paid the consideration but, by prearrangement, the mortgagee had then made a gift of an equivalent amount to the charity?

2. Where the mortgage authorises a sale for cash or on terms, and the mortgagee sells on terms by which the payment of the purchase price is spread over a number of years, the mortgagee is not bound to account to the mortgagor for the whole of the purchase money on the day of the sale, but only for the instalments as they are received: *Irving v. Commercial Banking Co. (Syd.)* (1898) 19 L.R. (N.S.W.) Eq. 54 at 61; approved in *Wright v. New Zealand Farmers Co-op. Assoc. of Canterbury Ltd* [1939] A.C. 439 at 446.

(c) Duty to mortgagor

There have long been two contrasting lines of authority as to the mortgagee's duty to the mortgagor in exercising a power of sale. One, as re-stated by the English Court of Appeal in *Cuckmere Brick Co. Ltd v. Mutual Finance Ltd* [1971] Ch. 949, says that the mortgagee is under an obligation to take reasonable care to obtain "the true market value" or "a proper price". The other, which is said to find its locus classicus in *Kennedy v. de Trafford* [1897] A.C. 180, states that the mortgagee's only duty is to act bona fide in the conduct of the sale, and, provided he or she acts in that fashion, the mortgagor cannot complain if the property is sold for less than its market value. There is common ground in both tests—a person who acts mala fide cannot fulfil either test—but the former line of authority insists that it is not sufficient simply to act in good faith, but that there is, in addition, a positive duty not to act negligently in the conduct of the sale.

KENNEDY v. DE TRAFFORD

House of Lords [1897] A.C. 180

[Mortgagees, under a mortgage by two tenants in common, exercised their power of sale by selling the mortgaged property to one of the mortgagors, Dodson, for a sum equal to the amount owing under the mortgage plus costs. A substantial part of the purchase price was then advanced to Dodson by way of mortgage, to enable him to complete the purchase. The other mortgagor (through his trustee in bankruptcy, Dr Kennedy) sought to have the sale set aside as an invalid exercise of the power of sale.

The mortgagees had given notice to each of the mortgagors of their intention to exercise their power of sale, and had further advised Dr Kennedy that they proposed to sell for the amount outstanding under the mortgage plus costs, but they had not advised Dr Kennedy that the purchaser was the other mortgagor, Dodson.

The Vice-Chancellor of the Duchy of Lancaster held that Dodson stood in a fiduciary relationship to Dr Kennedy and ordered that the sale be set aside. The Court of Appeal reversed this decision. On appeal.]

LORD HERSCHELL L.C. My Lords, the appellant seeks to set aside the [sale], on the ground that the mortgagees have been guilty of a breach of duty in relation to this sale. First of all it is said that they have sold at an undervalue, and that that sale at an undervalue had arisen from their not discharging the duties incumbent upon them as mortgagees. Now, it is not disputed that they sold in good faith. They did not intend to do anything else but properly exercise the power of sale vested in them under their mortgage. But it is alleged that they did not put up the premises for sale by auction, that they only inserted two advertisements inviting a sale by tender, and that they ultimately sold for the amount of principal, interest and costs to Mr Dodson.

My Lords, I am myself disposed to think that if a mortgagee in exercising his power of sale exercises it in good faith, without any intention of dealing unfairly by his mortgagor, it would be very difficult indeed, if not impossible, to establish that he had been guilty of any breach of duty towards the mortgagor. Lindley L.J., in the court below, says that "it is not right or proper or legal for him either fraudulently or wilfully or recklessly to sacrifice the property of the mortgagor". Well, I think that is all covered really by his exercising the power committed to him in good faith. It is very difficult to define exhaustively all that would be included in the words "good faith", but I think it would be unreasonable to require the mortgagee to do more than exercise his power of sale in that fashion. Of course, if he wilfully and recklessly deals with the property in such a manner that the interests of the mortgagor are sacrificed, I should say that he had not been exercising his power of sale in good faith.

My Lords, it is not necessary in this case to give an exhaustive definition of the duties of a mortgagee to a mortgagor, because it appears to me that, if you were to accept the definition of them for which the appellant contends, namely, that the mortgagee is bound to take reasonable precautions in the exercise of his power of sale, as well as to act in good faith, still in this case he did take reasonable precautions. Of course, all the circumstances of the case must be looked at. To sell in the manner in which the sale here took place might, let us assume for the moment, be under some circumstances improper. What we have to deal with are the existing circumstances. Now here there are the two co-owners, who are not acting in all respects harmoniously together. The mortgagee communicates what he is about to do to each of these co-owners. He tells each of them that he is preparing to sell, and that he is willing to take principal, interest and costs. To that he has received from the present appellant no remonstrance, no answer. Why is he to suppose for a moment that he would receive no answer or remonstrance if Dr Kennedy thought that selling on such terms would be an improper sale as being at an undervalue, because it must be certain that more than that sum could easily be obtained? It is obvious that where such a communication is made, and no answer is received and no objection put forward, the mortgagee may very reasonably suppose that no objection can be taken, and that nobody considers that he will be selling at an undervalue if he sells for principal, interest and costs. My Lords, having regard to the notice given under those circumstances to Dr Kennedy, and to the fact that he had heard in February 1889 that the property was being sold for principal, interest and costs, and then took no objection to it, it seems to me preposterous for him to come forward at this time of day and allege that he has a right on that ground to insist that the sale is invalid on the ground that the mortgagee did not take proper precautions in making the sale.

[Lord Herschell also held that Dodson did not stand in any fiduciary relationship to Dr Kennedy.]

LORD MACNAGHTEN. I think they did everything that could reasonably be expected of them; but I agree with what has fallen from my noble and learned Friend on the Woolsack: if a mortgagee selling under a power of sale in his mortgage takes pains to comply with the provisions of that power and acts in good faith, I do not think his conduct in regard to the sale can be impeached.

[Lords Morris and Shand concurred.]

Appeal dismissed.

QUESTIONS

What is the ratio of Lord Herschell's judgment? The headnote to the report of the principal case reads (in part):

> The only obligation incumbent on a mortgagee selling under and in pursuance of a power of sale in his mortgage is that he should act in good faith. In determining whether the mortgagee's conduct in that respect comes up to the required standard regard must be had to the circumstances of the particular case.

Does the first sentence of the headnote reflect accurately the substance of Lord Herschell's opinion as to the nature of the mortgagee's duty?

CUCKMERE BRICK CO. LTD v. MUTUAL FINANCE LTD

Court of Appeal [1971] Ch. 949

[The plaintiffs owned land in respect of which there had been granted planning permission to erect 100 flats. They mortgaged the land to the defendants. Later, the plaintiffs obtained planning permission to erect 35 houses on the land. Several years later, no development yet having been undertaken, the defendants became entitled to exercise their power of sale. They instructed auctioneers to sell the land, but the advertisements prepared by the auctioneers referred only to the planning permission for 35 houses. As a result, the only persons who took part in the auction were those interested in the land for the building of houses. The land was sold at auction for £44,000, but the evidence was that as a site for flats it was worth between £65,000 and £75,000, and that had the auction been attended by flat developers a figure in excess of £44,000 would, in all probability, have been attained.

Plowman J. held that the defendants had been negligent in not taking into account the planning permission for flats, and considered that £65,000 was a fair and conservative value to put on the land. Accordingly, he ordered accounts to be taken between the plaintiffs and the defendants on the basis of a sale price of £65,000. The defendants appealed.]

SALMON L.J. It is well settled that a mortgagee is not a trustee of the power of sale for the mortgagor. Once the power has accrued, the mortgagee is entitled to exercise it for his own purposes whenever he chooses to do so. It matters not that the moment may be unpropitious and that by waiting a higher price could be obtained. He has the right to realise his security by turning it into money when he likes. Nor, in my view, is there anything to prevent a mortgagee from accepting the best bid he can get at an auction, even though the auction is badly attended and the bidding exceptionally low. Providing none of those adverse factors is due to any fault of the mortgagee, he can do as he likes. If the mortgagee's interests, as he sees them, conflict with those of the mortgagor, the mortgagee can give preference to his own interests, which of course he could not do were he a trustee of the power of sale for the mortgagor.

Mr Vinelott contends that the mortgagee's sole obligation to the mortgagor in relation to a sale is to act in good faith; there is no duty of care, and accordingly no question of negligence by the mortgagee in the conduct of the sale can arise. If this contention is correct it follows that, even on the facts found by the judge, the defendants should have succeeded.

It is impossible to pretend that the state of the authorities on this branch of the law is entirely satisfactory. There are some dicta which suggest that unless a mortgagee acts in bad faith he is safe. His only obligation to the mortgagor is not to cheat him. There are other dicta which suggest that in addition to the duty of acting in good faith, the mortgagee is under a duty to take reasonable care to obtain whatever is the true market value of the mortgaged property at the moment he chooses to sell it: compare, for example, *Kennedy v. de Trafford* [1896] 1 Ch. 762; [1897] A.C. 180 with *Tomlin v. Luce* (1889) 43 Ch. D. 191 at 194.

The proposition that the mortgagee owes both duties, in my judgment, represents the true view of the law. Approaching the matter first of all on principle, it is to be observed that if the sale yields a surplus over the amount owed under the mortgage, the mortgagee holds this surplus in trust for the mortgagor. If the sale shows a deficiency, the mortgagor has to make it good out of his own pocket. The mortgagor is vitally affected by the result of the sale but its preparation and conduct is left entirely in the hands of the mortgagee. The proximity between them could scarcely be closer. Surely they are "neighbours". Given that the power of sale is for the benefit of the mortgagee and that he is entitled to choose the moment to sell which suits him, it would be strange indeed if he were under no legal obligation to take reasonable care to obtain what I call the true market value at the date of the sale. Some of the textbooks refer to the "proper price", others to the "best price". Vaisey J. in *Reliance Permanent Building Society v. Harwood-Stamper* [1944] Ch. 362 at 364, 365, seems to have attached great importance to the difference between these two descriptions of "price". My difficulty is that I cannot see any real difference between them. "Proper price" is perhaps a little nebulous, and "the best price" may suggest an exceptionally high price. That is why I prefer to call it "the true market value".

In *Tomlin v. Luce* (1889) 41 Ch. D. 573; (1889) 43 Ch. D. 191, the first mortgagees by mistake misdescribed the property being offered for sale. It was knocked down for £20,000. When the buyers discovered the mistake they refused to complete unless they were allowed £895 off the purchase price. This allowance was made and the price accordingly reduced to £19,105. The second mortgagees, who can be treated as in the same position as mortgagors, brought an action against the first mortgagees claiming that those mortgagees were responsible for the mistake of their auctioneer, that as a result of this mistake £895 had been deducted from the purchase price, and that this deduction ought not to be allowed in taking the account between the first and second mortgagees. The trial judge found in favour of the plaintiff and disallowed the whole of the £895. This was obviously wrong because the first mortgagees could only be answerable for any loss occasioned by the misdescription. The question should have been: but for the misdescription, would the land have sold for anything and if so how much more than £19,105? The judge's order was accordingly varied in the Court of Appeal. Cotton L.J., after pointing out the judge's mistake, said (at 194): "The defence seems really to have been . . . directed to this, that the first mortgagees, selling under their power, employed a competent auctioneer, and were not answerable for any blunder which the auctioneer committed. There they were wrong, and that point was not, I think, argued before us. . . . What we think is this—that the first mortgagees are answerable for any loss which was occasioned by the blunder made by their auctioneer at the sale." Bowen and Fry L.JJ. concurred. Although the point was not argued in the Court of Appeal, the passage in Cotton L.J.'s judgment which I have read must be treated with the greatest respect. He was a master in this branch of the law, and he and the other members of the court as well as counsel treated the point as too plain for argument. Indeed it had long been so regarded by the courts: see *Wolff v. Vanderzee* (1869) 20 L.T. 353 and *National Bank of Australasia v. United Hand-in-Hand and Band of Hope Co.* (1879) 4 App. Cas. 391 in which the Privy Council expressed the clear view that a mortgagee is chargeable with the full value of the mortgaged property sold if, from want of due care and diligence, it has been sold at an undervalue. It would seem, therefore, that many years before the modern development of the law of negligence, the courts of equity had laid down a doctrine in relation to mortgages which is entirely consonant with the general principles later evolved by the common law.

Then came *Kennedy v. de Trafford* [1897] A.C. 180 (with which I will presently deal) in which none of the authorities to which I have referred were cited. After that case came *McHugh v. Union Bank of Canada* [1913] A.C. 299, in which *Kennedy v. de Trafford* was not cited. In the *McHugh* case, Lord Moulton, in giving the opinion of an exceptionally strong Board, said (at 311): "It is well settled law that it is the duty of a mortgagee when realising the mortgaged property by sale to behave in conducting such realisation as a reasonable man would behave in the realisation of his own property, so that the mortgagor may receive credit for the fair value of the property sold.'' In that case the plaintiffs recovered damages because of a depreciated price having been realised for mortgaged horses on account of the negligent manner in which the mortgagees had had them driven to market. Mr Vinelott argues that this case was concerned only with the duty of a mortgagee to take care to preserve the mortgaged property when he goes into possession so as not to preclude the equity of redemption and has nothing to do with the mortgagee's duty upon a sale. I am afraid that I cannot accept that the case is susceptible of being explained away in the manner which Mr Vinelott suggests.

I now come to *Kennedy v. de Trafford* [1897] A.C. 180 which is the linch-pin of the defendants' case on the law. [His Lordship referred to the facts of that case, and continued:] There was no allegation of bad faith against the mortgagees and the Court of Appeal and the House of Lords concluded that there was no evidence of negligence, nor that any better price could have been obtained than the price paid by Dodson. Mr Vinelott strongly relies, however, upon certain observations made in that case by Lindley L.J. in the Court of Appeal [1896] 1 Ch. 762 at 772 and by Lord Herschell in the House of Lords [1897] A.C. 180 at 183. The passage in Lindley L.J.'s judgment appears to me to be rather equivocal. In that passage he seems perhaps to be resiling from what he had said in *Farrar v. Farrars Ltd* (1888) 40 Ch. D. 395 at 411, namely, that the duty of a mortgagee is to take reasonable precautions to obtain a proper price. I agree with Mr Vinelott that the word ''recklessly'' in the context of those passages connotes something akin to bad faith and more than gross carelessness. It means not caring whether or not the interests of the mortgagors are sacrificed. I do not regard these passages, however, as overruling *Tomlin v. Luce* (1889) 43 Ch. D. 191 and the earlier authorities to which I have referred. Indeed they were never cited in *Kennedy v. de Trafford*. Lord Herschell, in the first part of the passage relied on by Mr Vinelott, certainly expresses grave doubt as to whether a mortgagee in exercising a power of sale is under any duty except to act in good faith. I think, however, that in the second part of that passage he expressly refrains from deciding whether or not in such circumstances a mortgagee owes a duty to take reasonable precautions as well as a duty to act in good faith. It was certainly unnecessary for him to decide that question for the purpose of the case he was considering because, as he points out, the mortgagees in that case had taken all reasonable precautions in exercising their powers of sale and no allegation of bad faith was made. In my view, therefore, *Kennedy v. de Trafford* does not weaken the effect of the other cases to which I have referred. I accordingly conclude, both on principle and authority, that a mortgagee in exercising his power of sale does owe a duty to take reasonable precautions to obtain the true market value of the mortgaged property at the date on which he decides to sell it. No doubt in deciding whether he has fallen short of that duty the facts must be looked at broadly, and he will not be adjudged to be in default unless he is plainly on the wrong side of the line.

CROSS L.J. A mortgagee exercising a power of sale is in an ambiguous position. He is not a trustee of the power for the mortgagor for it was given him for his own benefit to enable him to obtain repayment of his loan. On the other hand, he is not in the position of an absolute owner selling his own property but must undoubtedly pay some regard to the interests of the mortgagor when he comes to exercise the power.

Some points are clear. On the one hand, the mortgagee, when the power has arisen, can sell when he likes, even though the market is likely to improve if he holds his hand and the result of an immediate sale may be that instead of yielding a surplus for the mortgagor the purchase price is only sufficient to discharge the mortgage debt and the interest owing on it. On the other hand, the sale must be a genuine sale by the mortgagee to an independent purchaser at a price honestly arrived at.

Suppose, however, that the mortgagee acts in good faith but that through the negligence either of the mortgagee himself or of an agent employed by him a smaller purchase price is obtained than would otherwise have been the case? In 1869, in *Wolff v. Vanderzee* (1869) 20 L.T. 353, Stuart V.-C. held that a mortgagee was accountable to the mortgagor for the loss in purchase price occasioned by the negligence of the auctioneer employed by him in stating that the property was let at a rent lower than the rent in fact being paid by the tenant. It is to be observed that in deciding that case the Vice-Chancellor relied on *Marriott v. Anchor Reversionary Co. Ltd* (1861) 3 De G. F. & J. 177, where a mortgagee who had taken possession of a mortgaged ship with a view to its sale was held accountable for a loss incurred by the improvident working of the vessel in the period between the taking of possession and the sale.

In 1888 in *Farrar v. Farrars Ltd* (1888) 40 Ch. D. 395 (which was not a claim for damages for negligence but an unsuccessful attempt by the mortgagor to set aside the sale on the ground that one of the mortgagees was a shareholder in the company which was the purchaser) Lindley L.J. said, at 411, that if in the exercise of his power the mortgagee "acts bona fide and takes reasonable precautions to obtain a proper price" the mortgagor has no redress even though more might have been obtained if the sale had been postponed. That formulation of the mortgagee's duty is not on the face of it inconsistent with the decision in *Wolff v. Vanderzee* (1869) 20 L.T. 353.

In 1889, in *Tomlin v. Luce* (1889) 41 Ch. D. 573 Kekewich J., applying the same principle as that applied by Stuart V.-C. 20 years earlier, held that a mortgagee was liable to account to those interested in the equity of redemption for loss occasioned by a negligent misdescription of the property by their auctioneers. The Court of Appeal (Cotton, Bowen and Fry L.JJ. (1889) 43 Ch. D. 191) varied the order made below on the ground that the method of calculating the loss adopted by the judge was wrong. The mortgagees seem not to have argued in the Court of Appeal that they were not liable to account at all for an innocent mistake made by their auctioneers, and the Court of Appeal plainly thought that the judge was right on this point.

In 1896 came *Kennedy v. de Trafford* [1897] A.C. 180, which is the sheet anchor of the defendants' submissions of law and which, accordingly, it is necessary to consider in some detail. The mortgage there was by two tenants in common (one of whom subsequently became bankrupt) and the sale was by the mortgagee to the other tenant in common for a purchase price equal to what was owing under the mortgage, the greater part of the purchase price being left on a fresh mortgage. The trustee of the bankrupt mortgagor took proceedings against the mortgagee and the purchasing mortgagor, claiming to have the sale set aside or, alternatively, for damages against the mortgagee for negligence.

The judge of first instance held that the mortgagee acted in good faith and that the sale was not at such an undervalue as to be evidence of fraud; but he also held (a) that the mortgagee had not made reasonable efforts to get a better price before selling to the other mortgagor; and (b) that the relationship between the purchasing mortgagor and the mortgagee on the one hand and the other mortgagor on the other was such as to put the purchasing mortgagor in the position of a trustee and to justify the setting aside of the sale.

The second ground was rejected both by the Court of Appeal and the House of Lords and need not be further considered here.

In deciding against the mortgagee on the first ground as well, the judge relied on the words used by Lindley L.J. in *Farrar's* case (1888) 40 Ch. D. 395, which I have cited above. In his judgment in *Kennedy v. de Trafford* [1896] 1 Ch. 762, as I read it, Lindley L.J. explained that when he had spoken of the mortgagee taking "reasonable precautions to obtain a proper price" he did not mean to imply that the mortgagee would be liable for mere negligence on his own part or on that of his agent, but simply that he must not "fraudulently or wilfully or recklessly" sacrifice the interests of the mortgagor. He went on, however, to say (at 773) that on the facts of the case before him the mortgagee had not failed to take any step which it was reasonable and proper for him to have taken.

In the House of Lords, Lords Herschell and Macnaghten both expressed the view that a mortgagee who acts in good faith is not liable for mere negligence in the exercise of his power of sale. But they both added (as had Lindley L.J.) that if the mortgagee as well as acting in good faith was under a duty to take reasonable precautions in the exercise of the power, the mortgagees in the case before them had taken reasonable precautions.

There are several points to be observed about this decision. The first concerns the use by Lindley L.J. and Lord Herschell of the word "recklessly". Plowman J., as I read his judgment in this case, thought that they meant by the word no more than "with gross negligence". With all respect to him, I cannot agree. They indicated that a man who acted "recklessly" in their sense of the word would not be acting in good faith. This shows, to my mind, that they were using the word in the sense of simply not caring whether what he did injured the mortgagor or not. Secondly, it is not, as I see it, possible to treat the views expressed by Lindley L.J. and Lords Herschell and Macnaghten to the effect that the only duty of the mortgagee is to act in good faith as limited to cases where the mortgagor is seeking to have the sale set aside and as not covering cases where he is simply asking that the mortgagee should be charged in his accounts with any loss attributable to his negligence. There was in fact an alternative claim for damages in *Kennedy v. de Trafford*, but in any case the language used is quite general. Whether the mortgagor can or cannot have the sale set aside will depend on whether the purchaser had notice of the breach of duty, but the standard of duty cannot vary with the nature of the remedy available for the breach of it. Thirdly, it is to be observed that though the view that the mortgagee's duty is simply to act in good faith is inconsistent with *Wolff v. Vanderzee* (1869) 20 L.T. 353 and *Tomlin v. Luce* (1889) 43 Ch. D. 191, those cases were not referred to either in the argument or the judgment. It is a curious fact that the textbooks do not comment on the inconsistency, but, while stating Lindley L.J.'s view of the law—namely, that the mortgagee need only act in good faith—continue to refer to *Tomlin v. Luce* as an authority for making him liable for mere negligence.

The only other case to which it is necessary to refer is the Privy Council decision of *McHugh v. Union Bank of Canada* [1913] A.C. 299, where the mortgage security was a number of horses. The mortgagor did not allege that the mortgagee had been guilty of any breach of duty in connection with the actual sale of the horses. The points at issue were, first, whether he was liable in damages for the manner in which he had dealt with the horses between the time when he took possession of them and the date of the sale and, secondly, as to the amounts with which he was entitled to charge the mortgagor in respect of expenses. The opinion of the Board, delivered by Lord Moulton, does, however, contain the following general statement which is inconsistent with the views expressed by Lindley L.J. and Lords Herschell and Macnaghten in *Kennedy v. de Trafford*. He said (at 311): "It is well settled law that it is the duty of a mortgagee when realising the mortgaged property by sale to behave in conducting such realisation as a reasonable man would behave in the realisation of his own property, so that the mortgagor may receive credit for the fair value of the property sold." Lord Macnaghten was a member of the Board which heard the case but, as Cairns L.J. pointed out in the course of the argument in this case, he died on the very day (17 February 1913) on which the opinion of the Board was delivered, and it would be wrong to assume that he gave his approval to the manner in which the mortgagee's duty is stated in the passage quoted above.

[Counsel for the defendants] submitted—rightly, as I think—that even if [the agents] were guilty of professional negligence they did not act "recklessly" within the meaning of that word as used by Lindley L.J. and Lord Herschell in *Kennedy v. de Trafford* [1897] A.C. 180. They may have been hopelessly wrong, but they directed their minds to the question at issue and tried their best to answer it.

[Counsel for the defendants] next submitted that we should accept the views expressed by Lindley L.J. and Lords Herschell and Macnaghten as an authoritative definition of the duty of a mortgagee exercising his power of sale and allow the appeal on that ground. I am not prepared to accede to this second submission. In the confused state of the authorities we are, I think, entitled—indeed, I think that we ought—to treat the views in question, though deserving of the greatest respect, as not essential to the decision in *Kennedy v. de Trafford* [1897] A.C. 180, and to consider for ourselves whether we prefer them to the views expressed in *Wolff v. Vanderzee* (1869) 20 L.T. 353 and *Tomlin v. Luce* (1889) 43 Ch. D. 191.

Approaching the problem in that way, I have no hesitation in saying that I prefer the latter. There is no doubt that a mortgagee who takes possession of the security with a view to selling it has to account to the mortgagor for any loss occurring through his negligence or the negligence of his agent in dealing with the property between the date of his taking possession of it and the date of the sale, including, as in the *McHugh* case [1913] A.C. 299, steps taken to bring the property to the place of sale. It seems quite illogical that the mortgagee's duty should suddenly change when one comes to the sale itself and that at that stage if only he acts in good faith he is under no liability, however negligent he or his agent may be.

[Counsel for the defendants] further submitted that even if we should be of opinion that a mortgagee was liable to account to the mortgagor for loss occasioned by his own negligence in the exercise of his power of sale, it was not right that he should be liable for the negligence of an agent reasonably employed by him. It may well be that this point is not open to him in view of the way the argument proceeded below—but in any case I do not accept the submission. In support of it, counsel pointed out that a trustee is not liable for the default of an agent whom it is reasonable for him to employ. But the position of a mortgagee is quite different from that of a trustee. A trustee has not, qua trustee, any interest in the trust property, and if an agent employed by him is negligent his right of action against the agent is an asset of the trust. A mortgagee, on the other hand, is not a trustee and if he sues the agent for negligence any damages which he can recover belong to him. Of course, in many cases the mortgagee may suffer no damage himself by reason of the agent's negligence because the purchase price, though less than it should have been, exceeds what is owing to the mortgagee. In such circumstances it may be that nowadays the law would allow the mortgagor to recover damages directly from the agent although not in contractual relations with him; but that was certainly not so a hundred years ago when *Wolff v. Vanderzee* (1869) 20 L.T. 353 was decided. In those days the only way to achieve justice between the parties was to say that the mortgagee was liable to the mortgagor for any damage which the latter suffered by the agent's negligence and to leave the mortgagee to recover such damages, and also any damage which he had suffered himself, from the agent. I do not think that we can say that the mortgagee used to be liable to the mortgagor for the negligence of his agent but that that liability disappeared at some unspecified moment of time when the law had developed enough to allow the mortgagor to sue the agent himself.

In my judgment, therefore, if either the defendants or [the agents] were guilty of negligence in connection with the sale, the defendants are liable to compensate the plaintiffs for any damage which they have suffered by reason of that negligence.

CAIRNS L.J. The issues in this appeal are: (1) Does the duty of a mortgagee to a mortgagor on the sale of the mortgaged property include a duty to take reasonable care to obtain a proper price or is it sufficient for the mortgagee to act honestly and without a reckless disregard of the interests of the mortgagor? . . .

(1) I find it impossible satisfactorily to reconcile the authorities, but I think the balance of authority is in favour of a duty of care. That there is such a duty was certainly the view of Kekewich J. and of the Court of Appeal in *Tomlin v. Luce* (1889) 41 Ch. D. 573; (1889) 43 Ch. D. 191; also of the Judicial Committee in *McHugh v. Union Bank of Canada* [1913] A.C. 299. It also appears to have been the view of Lindley L.J. at the time of his judgment in *Farrar v. Farrars Ltd* (1888) 40 Ch. D. 395. That judgment was so interpreted by the judge of first instance in *Kennedy v. de Trafford*, but on the appeal in that case Lindley L.J. said ([1896] 1 Ch. 762 at 772) that when he had referred in *Farrar's* case to a mortgagee's duty to take reasonable precautions he had meant merely that the mortgagee must not act fraudulently or wilfully or recklessly; and in the House of Lords [1897] A.C. 180 at 185, Lord Herschell said that he thought it would be unreasonable to require the mortgagee to do more than act in good faith, that is, not wilfully or recklessly to sacrifice the interests of the mortgagor. These expressions of opinion in the Court of Appeal and in the House of Lords were, however, not necessary to the decision. Lindley L.J. said ([1896] 1 Ch. 762 at 772), that the mortgagees "acted from first to last in an honourable and businesslike manner, without in the least sacrificing the interests of the mortgagor". Lord Herschell said ([1897] A.C. 180 at 185): "My Lords, it is not necessary in this case to give an exhaustive definition of the duties of a mortgagee to a mortgagor, because it appears to me that, if you were to accept the definition of them for which the appellant contends, namely, that the mortgagee is bound to take reasonable precautions in the exercise of his power of sale, as well as to act in good faith, still in this case he did take reasonable precautions." I therefore consider that *Tomlin v. Luce* (1889) 43 Ch. D. 191 is the stronger authority and I would hold that the present defendants had a duty to take reasonable care to obtain a proper price for the land in the interest of the mortgagors.

[The court then held (1) (Cross L.J. dissenting) that there had been a breach of the relevant duty by the defendants; and (2) (Salmon L.J. dissenting) that Plowman J. ought not to have accepted the evidence offered to him that the land could have been sold for £65,000, but that an inquiry should be directed as to the price the property would have fetched had it been advertised in accordance with the relevant duty and that the plaintiffs' loss should be compensated accordingly.]

Appeal allowed in part.

NOTES AND QUESTIONS

1. The "neighbour" approach taken by the Court of Appeal in the principal case has been condemned as a "fusion fallacy", on the ground that, as the interest sold by the mortgagee includes the equity of redemption, any complaint by the mortgagor regarding the manner of exercise of the power of sale ought to be made in equity, not at law, and that the approach of the court here was inappropriate in so far as it "strove to reassess the obligations of the mortgagee in terms drawn from the tort of negligence and treated the remedy as lying in damages": Meagher, Gummow and Lehane, *Equity, Doctrines and Remedies* (2nd ed.), para. 230. Do you agree? Does anything turn on the criticism?

2. In the principal case, the following passage was quoted from the judgment of the Privy Council in *McHugh v. Union Bank of Canada* [1913] A.C. 299 at 311:

   It is well settled law that it is the duty of a mortgagee when realising the mortgaged property by sale to behave in conducting such realisation as a reasonable man would behave in the realisation of his own property, so that the mortgagor may receive credit for the fair value of the property sold.

   Does this impose the same standard of care as the decision in the principal case?

3. The principal case has since been followed in England: *Duke v. Robson* [1973] 1 All E.R. 481; *Bank of Cyprus (London) Ltd v. Gill* [1980] 2 Lloyd's Rep. 51 (noted (1982) 56 A.L.J. 39); *Standard Chartered Bank Ltd v. Walker* [1982] 1 W.L.R. 1410 (noted (1983) 57 A.L.J. 238); *American Express International Banking Corp. v. Hurley* [1985] 3 All E.R. 564. It has also been applied by the Privy Council: *Tse Kwong Lam v. Wong Chit Sen* [1983] 3 All E.R. 54.

4. In *Standard Chartered Bank Ltd v. Walker* [1982] 1 W.L.R. 1410, the English Court of Appeal held that a mortgagee owes a duty not only to the mortgagor, but also to guarantors of the mortgage, to use reasonable care to obtain the best possible price which the circumstances of the case permit. Lord Denning M.R. said (at 1415) that the mortgagee's duty was "only a particular application of the general duty of care to your neighbour which was stated by Lord Atkin in *Donoghue v. Stevenson* [1932] A.C. 562 and applied in many cases since. . . . The mortgagor and the guarantor are clearly in very close 'proximity' to those who conduct the sale." The Court of Appeal also held that a receiver appointed by the mortgagee owes a similar duty to guarantors of the mortgage. On this matter, Lord Denning said (at 1415-1416):

   The receiver is the agent of the [mortgagor], not of the [mortgagee]. He owes a duty to use reasonable care to obtain the best possible price which the circumstances of the case permit [his Lordship is here applying the *Cuckmere Brick Co.* principle]. He owes the duty not only to the [mortgagor], of which he is the agent, to clear off as much of its indebtedness to the [mortgagee] as possible, but he also owes a duty to the guarantor, because the guarantor is liable only to the same extent as the [mortgagor]. The more the [debt] is reduced, the better for the guarantor.

   The guarantor and receiver were "well within the test of 'proximity' ".

   By contrast, such authority as exists to date in Australia suggests that a receiver's liability is not based in negligence: *Expo International Pty Ltd v. Chant* [1979] 2 N.S.W.L.R. 820 at 834.

5. In the principal case, the agents engaged by the mortgagee to conduct the sale had been negligent. Are there any circumstances in which a mortgagee may discharge his duty towards the mortgagor by carefully selecting reputable and competent estate agents and entrusting the entire conduct of the sale to them? See *Commercial and General Acceptance Ltd v. Nixon* (1981) 56 A.L.J.R. 130, noted further below p. 477.

6. In the principal case, mention is made of a rule that the mortgagee may exercise his power of sale immediately upon default (subject to the terms of the mortgage instrument and any relevant statutory provisions), no matter what the state of the market happens to be at that time. Many other cases contain dicta to the same effect. The mortgagee is not obliged to wait until the market improves: *Davey v. Durrant* (1857) 1 De G. & J. 535 at 553; 44 E.R. 830 at 838; *Nutt v. Easton* [1899] 1 Ch. 873 at 877; *Hartley v. Humphris* [1928] St. R. Qd 83 at 91. He does not have to "nurse" the property through difficult times: *Reliance Permanent Building Society v. Harwood-Stamper* [1944] Ch. 362 at 372. As Barton J. expressed it in *Pendlebury's* case (1912) 13 C.L.R. at 659: "the mortgagee is entitled to force a sale even when the market is not favourable".

   However, in *Standard Chartered Bank Ltd v. Walker* [1982] 1 W.L.R. 1410 at 1415, Lord Denning M.R. cast doubt upon the universality of this principle. In that case, the mortgagor's business stock had been sold at a substantial undervalue by the mortgagee in exercise of its power of sale. The mortgagor alleged that the low sale price was due to the fact, inter alia, that the sale had been conducted at the wrong time of the year. Lord Denning M.R., after affirming the *Cuckmere Brick Co.* principle, said: "There are several dicta to the effect that the mortgagee can choose his own time for the sale, but I do not think this means that he can sell at the worst possible time. It is at least arguable that, in choosing the time, he must exercise a reasonable degree of care."

PENDLEBURY v. COLONIAL MUTUAL LIFE ASSURANCE SOCIETY LTD

High Court of Australia (1912) 13 C.L.R. 676

[The mortgaged land was an area of 640 acres used for farming and grazing, situated in the "Mallee Country", some 235 miles from Melbourne. Upon default by the plaintiff/mortgagor, the defendant/mortgagee proposed to exercise its power of sale. The proposed sale was advertised by the mortgagee's agent in two Melbourne newspapers (which also circulated throughout Victoria), but not in any local newspapers; the text of the advertisement gave only the barest description of the location of the land, and no indication of the quality of the soil or the extent of its cultivation and development.

At the auction, the defendant's agent disclosed the reserve price, which was fixed at the amount outstanding under the mortgage plus the costs of sale. The property was sold for £720 (slightly above the reserve price); its true value was about £2,000.

The plaintiff sought damages in respect of the sale, and, in the alternative, an account of the sum which but for the wilful default or neglect of the defendant would have been realised on the sale. The plaintiff alleged that the sale had been made "wrongfully, recklessly, and/or in bad faith, and/or without due regard to the interests of the plaintiff, and/or collusively with the purchaser".

Hood J. in the Supreme Court of Victoria gave judgment for the defendant, holding that the sale was honestly carried out in due exercise of the power, and that there was no absence of bona fides and no want of reasonable care. On appeal.]

GRIFFITH C.J. The obligations of a mortgagee who sells the mortgaged property were considered by this court in the case of *Barns v. Queensland National Bank* (1906) 3 C.L.R. 925, in which the rule laid down by Lord Herschell L.C., in the case of *Kennedy v. de Trafford* [1897] A.C. 180 was stated and applied. The learned Lord Chancellor said, in the course of his speech ([1897] A.C. 180 at 185): "My Lords, I am myself disposed to think that if a mortgagee in exercising his power of sale exercises it in good faith, without any intention of dealing unfairly by his mortgagor, it would be very difficult indeed, if not impossible, to establish that he had been guilty of any breach of duty towards the mortgagor. Lindley L.J., in the court below, says that 'it is not right or proper or legal for him either fraudulently or wilfully or recklessly to sacrifice the property of the mortgagor'. Well, I think that is all covered really by his exercising the power committed to him in good faith. It is very difficult to define exhaustively all that would be included in the words 'good faith', but I think it would be unreasonable to require the mortgagee to do more than exercise his power of sale in that fashion. Of course, if he wilfully and recklessly deals with the property in such a manner that the interests of the mortgagor are sacrificed, I should say that he had not been exercising his power of sale in good faith."

I understand Lord Herschell to mean that the mortgagee must not recklessly or wilfully sacrifice the interests of the mortgagor, and that if he does he is to be regarded as not having acted in good faith. A good deal of discussion took place as to the meaning in which the terms "recklessly" and "good faith" were used by the learned Lord Chancellor. [Counsel for the defendant] suggested that the word "reckless" is used in a sense analogous to that in which it is used in *Derry v. Peek* (1889) 14 App. Cas. 337. If a man makes a material statement which is false in fact, careless whether it be true or false, he is as much guilty of fraud as if he knew it to be false. That is a case of an act of commission. So, he suggested, in the case of a sale by a mortgagee, if he omits to take obvious precautions to ensure a fair price, and the facts show that he was absolutely careless whether a fair price was obtained or not, his conduct is reckless, and he does not act in good faith. I am disposed to accept this analogy as sound. In the case of *Kennedy v. de Trafford* [1896] 1 Ch. 762 at 772 Lindley L.J., had said in the Court of Appeal, immediately before the words quoted by Lord Herschell L.C.: "A mortgagee . . . is not at liberty to look after his own interests alone, and it is not right, or proper, or legal, for him, either fraudulently, or wilfully, or recklessly, to sacrifice the property of the mortgagor: that is all."

The question therefore to be determined in this case is, in my judgment, whether the facts establish that on the sale complained of the defendants by their agent, Gill, "looked after their own interests alone", and absolutely disregarded the interests of the mortgagor.

BARTON J. I proceed then to consider the manner in which the respondents exercised their power, first pointing out that though their assistant secretary was not authorised to proceed to a sale, yet his acts on behalf of the respondents were adopted by them. In *Farrar v. Farrars Ltd* (1888) 40 Ch. D. 395 at 398, Chitty J., whose judgment was affirmed by the Court of Appeal, said: "The power arises by contract with the mortgagor, and forms part of the mortgagee's security. He is bound to sell fairly, and to take reasonable steps to obtain a proper price; but he may proceed to a forced sale for the purpose of paying the mortgage debt." On the appeal Lindley L.J. said, in delivering the judgment of Cotton and Bowen L.JJ. as well as himself (1888) 40 Ch. D. 395 at 411: "Every mortgage confers upon the mortgagee the right to realise his security and to find a purchaser if he can, and if in exercise of his power he acts bona fide and takes reasonable precautions to obtain a proper price, the mortgagor has no redress, even although more might have been obtained for the property if the sale had been postponed." It is the mortgagee's duty to sell fairly, says one of these distinguished judges. It is his duty to act bona fide, says the other—for what is good faith but fairness?

I add these passages to those cited by the Chief Justice, because they are clear and pointed, though I think the statements of the law which they contain are involved in his quotation from the speech of Lord Herschell in the case of *Kennedy v. de Trafford* [1897] A.C. 180. As Lindley L.J. said in the same case in the Court of Appeal ([1896] 1 Ch. 762 at 772) a mortgagee's "right is to look after himself first. But he is not at liberty to look after his own interests alone"; and these words immediately precede those quoted by Lord Herschell. If he confines his attention to his own interests, and sacrifices the mortgagor's property by doing so, he certainly acts unfairly, that is, in bad faith. Can it not be said truly that this unfairness, this disregard of the mortgagee's obvious duty, is fraudulent, or wilful, or merely reckless, according as the surrounding facts show—in addition to a sale at a gross undervalue—deceit or collusion, or deliberate exclusion of the interest of the mortgagor, or utter lack of care for that interest—another way of saying that the only interests he considers are his own? And he considers nothing else if he cares no jot whether a fair price be obtained, so only that the price pays his debt.

. . . I think we have to consider in this case whether the mortgagees so used their power as to sacrifice the mortgagor's property by conducting the sale in complete disregard of the mortgagor's interest. It is said that this disregard was shown by evidence that they took no pains to secure a fair price, the facts showing that such a price would have very largely exceeded that which they accepted.

ISAACS J. A mortgagee of land is always in equity, and under the *Transfer of Land Act* 1890, s. 114 [*Real Property Act* 1900 (N.S.W.), s. 57], at law also, merely the holder of a security. The power of sale is given to him entirely for his own benefit, and its purpose is to enable him to realise enough to satisfy his claim, if the property will produce it, and to return whatever balance may remain to the mortgagor. It is undoubted law that so long as he observes specified formalities and acts in good faith his conduct cannot be challenged. But what is included in "good faith"? Lindley L.J. in *Kennedy v. de Trafford* [1896] 1 Ch. 762 at 772, said: "It is not right, or proper, or legal, for him, either fraudulently, or wilfully, or recklessly, to sacrifice the property of the mortgagor." Lord Herschell in the House of Lords ([1897] A.C. 180 at 185) said that was all included in good faith. In the same case Lord Macnaghten ([1897] A.C. 180 at 192) said: "If a mortgagee selling under a power of sale in his mortgage takes pains to comply with the provisions of that power and acts in good faith, I do not think his conduct in regard to the sale can be impeached."

There are some words of Lord Herschell which to some extent leave undetermined the question how far the mortgagee is bound to take reasonable precautions in the exercise of his power of sale, but the inclination of his mind seems to be against it.

Regarding the matter from the standpoint of principle it seems to me clear that the word "recklessly" cannot include mere negligence or carelessness in carrying out the sale.

If the right to sell is a power which, as laid down in *Warner v. Jacob* (1882) 20 Ch. D. 220 at 224 is given to him not as a trustee for the mortgagor but for his own benefit, it must carry with it the consequence that with respect to the way he carries out the sale, not merely is he not liable as for breach of trust, but also that he owes no duty of care to the mortgagor, so long as he is bona fide acting within the limits of his power. His rights under the power are adverse to the mortgagor. He cannot, therefore, on any principle known to the law be liable for mere negligence, because that assumes a standard of care owed to another. The mortgagee is however confined by the expressed and implied limits of his power and by nothing else. Lord Lindley said in *Free Church of Scotland (General Assembly of) v. Overtoun (Lord)* [1904] A.C. 515 at 695: "There is a condition implied in this as well as in other instruments which create powers, namely, that the powers shall be used bona fide for the purpose for which they are conferred." And in a later case, *British Equitable Assurance Co. Ltd v. Baily* [1906] A.C. 35 at 42, the same learned Lord observed regarding the power of a company to alter its bylaws: "Of course, the powers of altering bylaws, like other powers, must be exercised bona fide, and having regard to the purposes for which they are created, and the rights of persons affected by them."

If he bona fide endeavours to do so, if he takes the best steps to that end, which he honestly believes will secure it, and the circumstances warrant, then he has acted in good faith and cannot be called to account however disastrous to the mortgagor the outcome may be.

Two extreme views may be mentioned to be put aside. To say that so long as he exercises his power with the real object of getting his debt paid he is absolved, is too low a standard of responsibility, because that loses sight of his obligation to deal fairly with the mortgagor's residual property. On the other hand, to make him answerable for mere carelessness in realisation, however anxious to act fairly by the mortgagor, is placing the standard too high, and would not only be cutting across principles, but would become a serious impediment to, and, by recoil, impose a heavy burden upon, needy borrowers. The mortgagee, when the permitted time arrives, is not bound to wait for his money, merely because the mortgagor might profit by delay. And as ex hypothesi he is engaged in a lawful endeavour to get back money which is overdue, he cannot be expected to further increase the advances of the mortgagor by expending further sums for his sole possible benefit, in the shape of a higher surplus price. A prudent owner might well risk considerable outlay in order to secure a possibly enhanced return. But the mortgagee is not called upon to do this, without express stipulation to that effect. He would get no advantage from the outlay beyond the amount of his debt, and he might end in increasing that.

But if a further outlay is in the circumstances reasonable, and apparently necessary and prudent to conserve the mortgagor's interest, and to prevent his residual property being sacrificed, and if, having regard to what a cautious man would consider the total selling value of the property, it is manifestly safe, the mortgagee is, in my opinion, not justified in refusing to make or incur it merely because he can get enough for himself without it. It must, however, be safe; if it is not, the mortgagee would be taking risks for the benefit of the mortgagor which he is not called upon to do; if it is, he is merely using part of the mortgagor's own property to preserve the rest. Neglect in such circumstances would be manifestly improvident and would afford cogent evidence upon which a tribunal would be at liberty to think, and probably would think, the neglect reckless or wilful. It would be so grossly unfair to the mortgagor who is unable to protect himself that the court would find it difficult to resist the conclusion that the mortgagee had no intention of observing Lord Lindley's rule in the *British Equitable* case already quoted. By "recklessness" then, I understand a disregard of the mortgagor's interest, ignoring his property in the possible surplus, in short, not caring whether its fair and proper value was obtained or not, as distinguished from the mere want of care or prudence in the course of honestly trying to conserve it.

The first is not compatible with good faith in enforcing the power of sale; the second is entirely consistent with good faith in carrying out its purpose, though lacking in skill or attention.

The question in the present case is whether the evidence shows a reckless disregard by the respondents of the appellant's interest as mortgagor.

[All three justices held, on the facts, that the mortgagee had not acted bona fide, and had entirely disregarded the interests of the mortgagor. The court directed that an account be taken of the amount which would have been realised but for the mortgagee's wilful default, and gave judgment for the plaintiff for a sum equal to the difference between the amount so ascertained and the amount outstanding under the mortgage at the date of the sale.]

Appeal allowed.

FORSYTH v. BLUNDELL

High Court of Australia (1973) 129 C.L.R. 477

[Blundell mortgaged his petrol station to A.S.L. Upon default under the mortgage, A.S.L. arranged for the land to be sold by public auction. The amount outstanding under the mortgage was approximately $120,000.

Before the date fixed for the auction, discussions took place between A.S.L. and XL (an oil company), in the course of which XL expressed interest in either paying out the mortgage or bidding up to $150,000 at the auction. Despite these discussions,

A.S.L. sold the garage privately to Forsyth (as agent for Shell Oil Company of Australia Ltd) for $120,000. A.S.L. did not inform Shell of the interest expressed in the property by XL, nor did it inform XL of Shell's offer to purchase for $120,000.

Blundell commenced proceedings in the Supreme Court of the Australian Capital Territory against Forsyth, Shell and A.S.L. for a declaration that the sale to Shell had not been a bona fide exercise of the mortgagee's power of sale and for an injunction restraining completion of the sale. Fox J. made a declaration that the mortgagor was entitled to redeem the mortgage and granted an injunction restraining A.S.L. (the mortgagee) from completing the sale to Shell. A.S.L., Forsyth and Shell appealed to the High Court. Fox J. also found that not only did the mortgagee fail "to take reasonable steps to obtain the best price available in all the circumstances", but also that it had acted with "calculated indifference" to the position of the mortgagor, and had been "reckless" and had "sacrificed" the interests of the mortgagor. He was satisfied on the evidence, however, that at the time of entering into the contract, Shell had no notice of any breach of duty by A.S.L. in the manner of exercise of its power of sale.

In the High Court, Walsh and Mason JJ. agreed with Fox J.'s view of the facts. Menzies J., however, thought that A.S.L. had been entitled to treat with scepticism the representations of XL and that A.S.L. had been justified in selling to Shell privately.]

MENZIES J. The rule to be applied here is not in doubt; it was stated authoritatively by Lord Herschell in the last century. In *Kennedy v. de Trafford* [1897] A.C. 180, which has been followed by this court in *Barns v. Queensland National Bank Ltd* (1906) 3 C.L.R. 945 and *Pendlebury v. Colonial Mutual Life Assurance Society Ltd* (1912) 13 C.L.R. 676, the Lord Chancellor said [1897] A.C. at 185: "if a mortgagee in exercising his power of sale exercises it in good faith, without any intention of dealing unfairly by his mortgagor, it would be very difficult indeed, if not impossible, to establish that he had been guilty of any breach of duty towards the mortgagor. Lindley L.J. in the court below, says that 'it is not right or proper or legal for him either fraudulently or wilfully or recklessly to sacrifice the property of the mortgagor.' Well, I think that is all covered really by his exercising the power committed to him in good faith. It is very difficult to define exhaustively all that would be included in the words 'good faith', but I think it would be unreasonable to require the mortgagee to do more than exercise his power of sale in that fashion. Of course, if he wilfully and recklessly deals with the property in such a manner that the interests of the mortgagor are sacrificed, I should say that he had not been exercising his power of sale in good faith."

I do not think that statements in some cases, such as *McHugh v. Union Bank of Canada* [1913] A.C. 299 or *Cuckmere Brick Co. Ltd v. Mutual Finance Ltd* [1971] Ch. 949, that the mortgagee is under a duty to take reasonable precautions to obtain a proper price, are at odds with the rule stated by Lord Herschell. To take reasonable precautions to obtain a proper price is but a part of the duty to act in good faith. This duty to act in good faith falls far short of the Golden Rule and permits a mortgagee to sell mortgaged property on terms which, as a shrewd property owner, he would be likely to refuse if the property were his own.

WALSH J. In the authorities there are to be found conflicting views on the question whether the obligation cast upon the mortgagee is simply that he should act "in good faith" (which means, in my opinion, in the language used in most of the authorities, that he should act without fraud and without wilfully or recklessly sacrificing the interests of the mortgagor) or is an obligation which is broken also if there is negligence in carrying out the sale. Support for the former view may be found in the statements in *Kennedy v. de Trafford* [1896] 1 Ch. 762 at 772 by Lindley L.J. and in the same case on appeal [1897] A.C. 180 at 184-185, by Lord Herschell, in the adoption of those statements by this court in *Barns v. Queensland National Bank Ltd* (1906) 3 C.L.R. 925 at 942, 943 and in *Pendlebury v. Colonial Mutual Life Assurance Society Ltd* (1912) 13 C.L.R. 676 at 680, 694, 700 and in the definite opinion expressed by Isaacs J. in the latter case (1912) 13 C.L.R. 676 at 700, that the mortgagee is not answerable for "mere negligence or carelesness". On the other hand, it appears that the view that negligence is enough to make the mortgagee liable to account to the mortgagor for loss arising from a sale is supported, not only by the recent cases of *Holohan v. Friends Provident and Century Life Office* [1966] I.R. 1 and *Cuckmere Brick Co. Ltd v. Mutual Finance Ltd* [1971] Ch. 949, but also by the decision of the Privy Council in *McHugh v. Union Bank of Canada* [1913] A.C. 299. But I do not think it necessary to resolve this question in this appeal. The breach of duty which has been found to have been committed by A.S.L. did not consist merely of a careless failure to carry out the sale in a manner which reasonable care required. . . . [I]t appears that in proceeding with the sale to Shell without referring to Blundell or Sykes, A.S.L. acted in a way which would produce enough money to satisfy its own interests, and it was those interests alone that were really considered. While A.S.L. as mortgagee was entitled to have regard primarily to its own interests, it was not entitled, if those interests were not at risk, to act in a manner which sacrificed the interests of the mortgagor. What the mortgagee did in this case was done deliberately and not through carelessness.

In my opinion, the decision that there was a breach of duty on the part of A.S.L. should not be set aside by this court.

I proceed to consider whether the plaintiffs were entitled, having regard to the findings made at the trial, to injunctive relief. I stated earlier that I did not think it was necessary to decide whether or not a breach of duty for which a mortgagee can be held liable is made out if all that is found is that he has acted negligently, although in good faith, in carrying out a sale. That statement needs some elaboration. If a mortgagee has acted in breach of his duty, it may become necessary to decide whether the available relief is limited to make him liable to make good to the mortgagor such loss as has been caused by that breach of duty or includes the obtaining of an order to set aside a conveyance or transfer by which a sale had been carried into effect or, in cases in which the contract of sale has not been completed, an injunction to restrain the mortgagee from completing it. On behalf of Shell it was argued that if a mortgagor has any remedy in respect of negligence in carrying out a sale, this must be limited in all cases to holding the mortgagee liable to account for the loss suffered. In this case there is a question whether or not in the circumstances it was proper for the Supreme Court to grant an injunction to restrain A.S.L. from completing the agreement made with Shell. But, in my opinion, the answer to that question does not depend upon the acceptance or rejection of the distinction made in the submissions to which I have just referred. This is not a case in which the only relevant finding against A.S.L. was a finding of negligence. In effect, there was also a finding that in making the contract there was a reckless disregard of the interests of the mortgagor. I am of opinion that in such circumstances the completion of the contract may be restrained.

It has been argued that a passage in the judgment of Kay J. in *Warner v. Jacob* (1882) 20 Ch. D. 220 at 224, which has often been quoted in subsequent cases, is an exhaustive and correct statement of the circumstances in which a sale will be set aside or an injunction granted and it is said, therefore, that if a mortgagor has any remedy in respect of a sale not shown to have been affected by "corruption or collusion with the purchaser" or to have been at a price so low as in itself to be evidence of fraud, his only remedy can be in damages. In my opinion, this submission should not be accepted. There may be an improper exercise of a power of sale (that is one which constitutes a breach of the duty owed to the mortgagor) where although there is not any actual fraud (in the ordinary sense of that term) or any collusion between the mortgagee and the purchaser, there is improper conduct which goes beyond mere negligence in carrying out the sale. There may be impropriety of various kinds. What has sometimes been described as a fraud on the power and sometimes as a wilful or reckless disregard of the interests of the mortgagor and sometimes as a sacrificing of the interests of the mortgagor does not necessarily involve, in my opinion, the commission of actual fraud. It has been said that the word "recklessly" as used by Lord Herschell in *Kennedy v. de Trafford* [1897] A.C. at 185 and in other judgments, was used in a sense analogous to that in which it was used in *Derry v. Peek* (1889) 14 App. Cas. 337: see *Pendlebury v. Colonial Mutual Life Assurance Society Ltd* (1912) 13 C.L.R. at 680. Whether or not that view is accepted, I think it is in accordance with authority and that it should be affirmed that there may be conduct which amounts to a reckless sacrificing of the interests of a mortgagor, although it is not shown that there is an actual intention to defaud him or that there is corruption or collusion with the purchaser. It is concerning conduct of that kind that inquiry must be made in this case whether or not it warranted the granting of an injunction.

I do not doubt that as between himself and his mortgagee who has conducted himself in that way in entering into a contract of sale, a mortgagor is entitled to invoke the aid of the court to prevent the completion of the contract. As between those parties, the proprietary right of the mortgagor will be protected against such a wrongful alienation by the mortgagee. But the critical question is whether the purchaser under the contract acquires a right which entitles him to have the contract completed and therefore precludes the grant of any injunction to restrain its completion . . . .

It has been submitted that a person who has entered into a contract as purchaser cannot be affected in any case by impropriety on the part of the mortgagee, not involving collusion with the purchaser. It has been put as an alternative argument that, if a purchaser may be affected by notice of the facts which constitute the impropriety (not involving collusion), he can be affected only if he has such notice at the time when he enters into the contract. In my opinion, if the mortgagee does not exercise the power of sale "in good faith" (in the sense explained above) and the purchaser has knowledge of the facts which show the lack of good faith, the purchaser cannot obtain a right superior to the right of the mortgagor. Even when a contract made in such circumstances is carried to completion, in many cases the transaction may be set aside, or, alternatively, the conveyance or transfer treated as operating only as a transfer of the mortgage and of the debt secured by it, and not as a transfer of the mortgagor's interest: see *Latec Investments Ltd v. Hotel Terrigal Pty Ltd (in liq.)* (1965) 113 C.L.R. 265 at 274-275. But if the person who agrees to purchase has no notice of any impropriety at the date of contract and continues to have no notice at the time when it is completed, he will obtain a title which cannot be challenged by the mortgagor. (It is here assumed that all statutory and contractual conditions essential to the exercise of the power of sale have been fulfilled.)

If the purchaser is without notice of the relevant facts at the date of the contract, but the mortgagor takes action to challenge its propriety before completion and proves that on the part of the mortgagee it was improper, the question is whether the purchaser has a right which prevails over the right which the mortgagor would have, as between himself and the mortgagee, to restrain the completion of the contract. That is the question in this case.

The mortgagor's interest was, of course, prior in time to any interest acquired by the purchaser. The right of the mortgagor was not merely an equity of redemption. The mortgages did not operate as transfers of his title to the land: see the Ordinance, s. 99(1). [*Real Property Act* 1900 (N.S.W.), s. 57.] His title could be divested by a transfer in pursuance of a contract of sale made by the mortgagee in the exercise of the power of sale. But until that occurred, he retained a legal interest in the land.

Even if the contest between these parties should be resolved on the basis that there is a competition between equitable interests, in my opinion the position of the purchaser, so far as the applicable general principles are concerned, would not be any better. In my opinion, the situation was not one in which it was open to the purchaser to claim that, although it had not acquired a legal estate, it could maintain, against a claim by the mortgagor to prevent the completion of the sale, a defence that it was a purchaser for value without notice. After a consideration of the decision and of the judgments in *Latec Investments Ltd v. Hotel Terrigal Pty Ltd (in liq.)* (1965) 113 C.L.R. 265, I am of opinion that the circumstances in which the interest of the trustee for the debenture holders in that case was held to prevail over the claim of the mortgagor were so different from those upon which the contest here depends that the case is not an authority upon which Shell can rely.

I am of opinion, also, that the contest cannot be resolved in favour of Shell by the application of the principles upon which in *Abigail v. Lapin* [1934] A.C. 491 and in *Breskvar v. Wall* (1971) 126 C.L.R. 376 the claims of the parties whose interests were first in time were postponed to the claims of the other parties. This is not merely for the reason that in the present case Blundell had more than an equitable interest. If his interest is considered as being for present purposes no more than an equitable interest, his conduct did not contribute in my opinion, to any false assumption or belief upon which Shell acted in entering into the transaction (see *Breskvar v. Wall* (1971) 126 C.L.R. 376), nor did it affect Shell in any other way which would make it inequitable to assert against Shell the interest of Blundell.

By executing the mortgages and defaulting in payments under them, Blundell did bring about a situation in which A.S.L. was empowered to sell the property. But if the mortgagee did not act bona fide in the exercise of the power of sale, and the purchaser, being unaware of this, assumed that the mortgagee was acting bona fide, that assumption was not one which any conduct of Blundell caused the purchaser to make.

If a contract of sale had been made which was not affected by any impropriety, it would not have been open to the mortgagor to claim that until the contract had been completed his right to redeem the mortgage continued notwithstanding the contract and was superior to the right of the purchaser. Although he retained his title to the land this was subject to the power of sale as defined in the Ordinance and as incorporated into the mortgage instruments. In my opinion, a contract of sale properly made in the course of the exercise of that power is binding upon the mortgagor, not because the mortgagee contracts as agent for the mortgagor, but because by entering into a mortgage to which the Ordinance applies the mortgagor makes his own rights subject to its provisions, including those which confer and regulate the power of sale, and, therefore, subject to any action which is properly taken in good faith by the mortgagee. On this question, I regard as applicable and as correct the decision in *Waring (Lord) v. London and Manchester Assurance Co. Ltd* [1935] 1 Ch. 310, approved in *Property & Bloodstock Ltd v. Emerton* [1968]

1 Ch. 94 that a contract by the mortgagee to sell the property is binding, before completion, upon the mortgagor unless it be proved that the mortgagee exercised his power of sale in bad faith. But here it is contended that as a matter of general principle and independently of the meaning and effect of the provisions of s. 94(2), 94(3) and 94(5) of the Ordinance, such a contract is binding *before completion* upon the mortgagor, even if the mortgagee acted in bad faith, unless he acted in collusion with the purchaser, or alternatively, unless the purchaser had knowledge *at the date of the contract* of the facts which affected the propriety of the sale. In my opinion, this proposition should not be accepted. If the matter is to be determined in accordance with the general principles by which disputes as to priority between competing claims are resolved, there is no principle which operates to postpone the right of the mortgagor to that of the purchaser. In my opinion, the authorities to which we were referred do not support the foregoing submission. . . .

It was argued that the position of a purchaser from a mortgagee is analogous to that of a purchaser who makes a contract with an agent acting within his ostensible authority but in breach (unknown to the purchaser) of his duty to his principal. In my opinion, the analogy is not acceptable. The mortgagee in making a sale is acting on his own behalf and primarily in his own interests. The sale is not one by which the mortgagor, through the medium of an agent, is disposing of his own property. It is one by which his property is being divested from him. If the power vested in the mortgagee is properly exercised the mortgagor is bound. But if it is not exercised in good faith there is, in my opinion, no reason that can be derived from any general principle for holding that before completion the purchaser gets a good title as against the mortgagor.

MASON J. It will be seen that the conclusion which I reach is that A.S.L. was in breach of its duty to the mortgagors in that it exercised its power of sale without taking reasonable steps to obtain a proper price and in so doing acted otherwise than bona fide, that is, recklessly, not caring whether the price obtained was in the circumstances a proper price or not. Accordingly, I need not consider the vexed question whether the mortgagee's duty is merely to act bona fide or whether, in addition, he is bound to take reasonable precautions to obtain a proper price. The conflicting authorities have recently been reviewed by the Court of Appeal in *Cuckmere Brick Co. v. Mutual Finance Ltd* [1971] Ch. 949: see also *Holohan v. Friends Provident and Century Life Office* [1966] I.R. 1. It was held in these cases that the mortgagee is bound to act bona fide and take reasonable precautions to obtain a proper price, or, as Salmon L.J. would prefer to express it, "the true market value". In any resolution of the question in this court account must be taken of what was said in *Barns v. Queensland National Bank Ltd* (1906) 3 C.L.R. at 942-943, and *Pendlebury v. Colonial Mutual Life Assurance Society Ltd* (1912) 13 C.L.R. at 692, 693-695, 699-702. However, as I have said, on the view which I take of the facts this problem does not arise for decision . . . .

With respect to the questions which arise in consequence of the conclusion that A.S.L. was in breach of its duty I agree with what Walsh J. has written, save only that I express no opinion as to the correctness of the proposition stated in *Waring (Lord) v. London and Manchester Assurance Co. Ltd* [1935] Ch. 310 and *Property & Bloodstock Ltd v. Emerton* [1968] Ch. 94, that an exercise by the mortgagee of his power of sale is binding on the mortgagor, before completion, unless the power of sale was not exercised bona fide.

Appeal dismissed.

NOTES AND QUESTIONS

1. In two cases decided since *Forsyth v. Blundell* (1973) 129 C.L.R. 477 the High Court has discussed the nature of the mortgagee's duty on sale, but without finding it necessary to decide which of the two apparently conflicting lines of authority should be followed. In the first, *Australian and New Zealand Banking Group Ltd v. Bangadilly Pastoral Co. Pty Ltd* (1978) 52 A.L.J.R. 529 (discussed above p. 455, note 1), it was not necessary to resolve the conflict, because there was on the facts no "truly independent bargain" between purchaser and mortgagee. In the leading judgment, Aickin J. referred to the discussion of the nature of the mortgagee's duty by the High Court in *Forsyth v. Blundell*, saying that the earlier decisions of the court in *Barns's* case (1906) 3 C.L.R. 925 and *Pendlebury's* case were "of importance on this aspect of the matter": (1978) 52 A.L.J.R. 529 at 540. The only other judgment to cast light on the nature of the mortgagee's duty was that of Jacobs J., who said, speaking of the concept of bona fides:

> It is true that bona fides in this connection is not concerned with the motive for exercising the power of sale but, once the decision to sell has been made, it is concerned with a *genuine primary desire* to obtain for the mortgaged property the *best price obtainable* consistently with the right of a mortgagee to realise his security: (1978) 52 A.L.J.R. 529 at 531 (emphasis added).

Does Jacobs J. support the *Cuckmere* test?

The second case, *Commercial and General Acceptance Ltd v. Nixon* (1981) 56 A.L.J.R. 130 was an appeal from Queensland. In that State, the nature of the mortgagee's duty on sale is defined by statute. Section 85(1) of the *Property Law Act* 1974 (Qld) provides: "It is the duty of a mortgagee, in the exercise . . . of a power of sale . . . to take reasonable care to ensure that the property is sold at the market value." These words make it clear that in Queensland the "reasonable care" test is the yardstick by which mortgagees' sales are to be measured. There is in that State no need to decide whether mere bona fides in the conduct of the sale is sufficient. There was, therefore, no need for the High Court to decide whether, in States where there is no counterpart to s. 85(1), the proper test is "reasonable care" or "bona fides". Nevertheless, three of the justices commented on the matter.

Gibbs C.J. said (at 130) that the question whether, apart from statute, a mortgagee exercising a power of sale is under an obligation to act in good faith, was one on which "the authorities are conflicting, and indeed in my opinion irreconcilable": cf. Stone (1979) 53 A.L.J. 842. Mason J. said (at 134) that it was "not unreasonable to require mortgagees . . . to bear the responsibility of seeing that adequate steps are taken to ensure that property is sold at the market level". (Although stated in general terms, his Honour probably intended this dictum to be read strictly subjectam materiam— that is, in the light of s. 85(1)—and not as a statement that mortgagees' sales ought to be governed by the "reasonable care" test.)

Aickin J., after discussing *Kennedy v. de Trafford* [1987] A.C. 180 and *Cuckmere Brick Co. Ltd v. Mutual Finance Ltd* [1971] Ch. 949, expressed the opinion (at 138) that there was no sound reason in principle for confining the mortgagee's responsibility to the mortgagor (in respect of the sale) to fraud alone, and (at 139) that the power of sale is not to be exercised "exclusively in [the mortgagee's] interest without regard to the interests of the mortgagor by directing attention exclusively to the recovery of the mortgage debt, interest and expenses rather than obtaining the market value of the property as at the date of the sale." Can these words be taken as an indication that Aickin J. regarded the "reasonable care" test to be the proper test at general law of the mortgagee's duty on sale?

The High Court has discussed the mortgagee's duty on sale in the following additional cases: *Barns v. Queensland National Bank Ltd* (1906) 3 C.L.R. 925 at 942; *Latec Investments Ltd v. Hotel Terrigal Pty Ltd* (1965) 113 C.L.R. 265 at 273, 280, 288. These cases, along with those extracted, are discussed in Butt, "The Mortgagee's Duty on Sale" (1979) 53 A.L.J. 172.

2. On the assumption that there is a conflict between the authorities on the nature of the mortgagee's duty, and that the conflict remains unresolved in the High Court, what approach should be taken by inferior courts: pending a determinative decision in the High Court, should inferior courts apply the "reasonable care" test or the "bona fides" test? Of course, where on the facts of a particular case the mortgagee has both acted bona fide and taken reasonable care to obtain a proper price the question will not arise: both tests will be satisfied (as occurred in *Porter v. Associated Securities Ltd* (1976) 1 B.P.R. 9279 and in *Dimmick v. Pearce Investments Pty Ltd* (1980) 43 F.L.R. 235). But such findings of fact are not always appropriate, and in a number of cases trial judges have taken that view that, pending clarification by the High Court and notwithstanding the *Cuckmere Brick Co.* case, they should follow the approach of Griffith C.J. in *Pendlebury's* case, namely, that the mortgagee must not "recklessly or wilfully sacrifice the interests of the mortgagor": see, e.g., *Expo International Pty Ltd v. Chant* [1979] 2 N.S.W.L.R. 820 at 835-836; *Brutan Investments Pty Ltd v Underwriting and Insurance Ltd* (1980) 39 A.C.T.R. 47 at 55; *Citicorp Australia Ltd v. McLoughney* (1984) 35 S.A.S.R. 375; *Cachalot Nominees Pty Ltd v. Prime Nominees Pty Ltd* [1984] W.A.R. 380.

3. The *Cuckmere Brick Co.* case has been applied in New Zealand and Ireland: *Alexandre v. New Zealand Breweries Ltd* [1974] 1 N.Z.L.R. 497; *Holohan v. Friends Provident and Century Life Office* [1966] I.R. 1.

4. In Victoria also, statute defines the nature of the mortgagee's duty on sale. The *Transfer of Land Act* 1958 (Vic.), s. 77(1), provides that, after compliance with certain prescribed formalities as to notice, a mortgagee may sell the mortgaged property "in good faith and having regard to the interests of the mortgagor . . .". It has been held in the Victorian Supreme Court that this section removes the doubt about the extent of the mortgagee's duty, at least so far as concerns land under the provisions of the *Transfer of Land Act*. The effect of the section is to *combine* both the "bona fides" test and the "reasonable precautions" test. In the words of Lush J.:

> The effect of its words is to bring together the concept of an obligation to act in good faith and an obligation akin to an obligation to exercise care in much the same way as they are blended in the dissenting judgment of Menzies J. in *Forsyth v. Blundell* (1973) 129 C.L.R. 477 at 481, and that of Salmon L.J. in the *Cuckmere Brick Co.'s* case [1971] Ch. 949 at 966: *Henry Roach (Petroleum) Pty Ltd v. Credit House (Vic.) Pty Ltd* [1976] V.R. 309 at 312. See also *Goldcel Nominees Pty Ltd v. Network Finance Ltd* [1983] 2 V.R. 257.

No similar section exists in New South Wales. The only provision in New South Wales possibly relevant to the mortgagee's duty on sale is s. 112(7) of the *Conveyancing Act* 1919 (N.S.W.), which provides that a mortgagee is not "answerable for any involuntary loss happening in or about the exercise or execution of the power of sale". But it is generally accepted that this provision adds nothing to the existing general law relating to the mortgagee's liability for loss on sale, and does not resolve the question as to which of the two tests is to be preferred: see Stuckey, *The Conveyancing Act 1919-1969* (2nd ed.), pp. 238-239; *Wolstenholme and Cherry's Conveyancing Statutes* (10th ed.), Vol. 1, p. 215.

2. Injunction to restrain sale

Where the power of sale has arisen, and the amount of the mortgage debt is not in dispute, the general rule is that the court will not restrain the exercise of the power of sale unless the amount of the mortgage debt is paid into court: *Inglis v. Commonwealth Trading Bank of Australia* (1972) 126 C.L.R. 161 at 164; *Cunningham v. National Australia Bank Ltd* (1987) A.T.P.R. 40-826. Where there is no dispute that the power of sale is exercisable but there is dispute about the amount of the mortgage debt, the amount claimed by the mortgagee must be paid in, although the court may go behind the mortgagee's claim and require a lesser amount where it appears from the terms of the mortgage instrument that a lesser amount is due: *Harvey v. McWatters* (1948) 49 S.R. (N.S.W.) 173 at 176.

Where, however, the mortgagor is challenging the very existence of the power to sell or the propriety of the exercise of the power, there is no such general rule. To insist on payment in every such case could lead to hardship and injustice on the mortgagor: *Harvey v. McWatters* (1948) 49 S.R. (N.S.W.) 173 at 174. The rule rather applied, therefore, is that the court may decree that there be paid in by the mortgagor such amount as will ensure "that justice between the parties" is achieved: *Harvey v. McWatters* (1948) 49 S.R. (N.S.W.) 173 at 177; *Henry Roach (Petroleum) Pty Ltd v. Credit House (Vic.) Pty Ltd* [1976] V.R. 309 at 320), or, more particularly, will ensure that the mortgagee is afforded "adequate protection": *Harvey v. McWatters* (1948) 49 S.R. (N.S.W.) 173 at 177-178.

Special difficulties arise where the mortgagee has already entered into a binding contract with a purchaser.

FORSYTH v. BLUNDELL

High Court of Australia (1973) 129 C.L.R. 477

[See above, p. 472.]

NOTES AND QUESTIONS

1. In *George v. Commercial Union Assurance Co. of Australia Ltd* (1977) 1 B.P.R. 9649, Powell J. expressed the following views about the position of a mortgagor seeking redress against a mortgagee for alleged impropriety in the exercise of a power of sale:

> The remedies available to a mortgagor who is clearly in default under his mortgage, but who, nonetheless, seeks to attack the propriety of a sale or purported sale by his mortgagee, seem to be three, or, perhaps, four:
>
> 1. if there has been a contract, alleged to have been entered into in fraud of the power of sale, which contract has not been completed, to seek to obtain an injunction to restrain the completion of that contract;
>
> 2. if there has been a contract alleged to have been entered into in fraud of the power of sale, which contract has been completed, to seek to obtain an order of the court setting aside that contract and any conveyance or transfer made pursuant to it;
>
> 3. if there has been a contract alleged to have been entered into in fraud of the power of sale, which contract has been completed, to seek to obtain a declaration to that effect and an order that the mortgagee account to the mortgagor as on the basis of wilful neglect and default; and, possibly,
>
> 4. if there has been a contract not alleged to have been entered into in fraud of the power of sale, but, nonetheless, alleged to have been entered into negligently, in the sense that the mortgagee did not obtain the best possible price, and which contract has been completed, to seek to obtain a declaration to that effect and an order for damages.
>
> What are the essential facts to be established by the mortgagor in such case, and what, if any, are the conditions to which the court will or might subject him, in order that he might obtain the relief he seeks, will vary not only with the circumstances but also with the nature of the relief sought.
>
> As to the first, it seems to me now to be well established that, when the relief sought is an injunction, the courts will require payment into court of an appropriate amount, the amount being determined in part by the fact that the plaintiff either disputes or does not dispute the amount claimed by the mortgagee: *Harvey v. McWatters* (1948) 49 S.R. (N.S.W.) 173. Further, the plaintiff will be required to demonstrate, so it seems to me, a wilful or reckless disregard of the mortgagor's interest in the matter of the auction or other sale. However, it would seem not to be necessary to demonstrate that the purchaser (who must, of course, be joined in any such proceedings) had any knowledge of the alleged impropriety: see, e.g., *Inglis v. Commonwealth Trading Bank of Australia* (1972) 126 C.L.R. 161; *Blundell v. Associated Securities Ltd* (1971) 19 F.L.R. 17 and sub nom. *Forsyth v. Blundell* (1973) 129 C.L.R. 477.
>
> In the second of the cases to which I have referred, again it seems to me to be well established that it will be a condition of ultimate relief that the plaintiff discharge the mortgage debt of its mortgagee: see, e.g., *Latec Investments Ltd v. Hotel Terrigal Pty Ltd (in liq.)* (1965) 113 C.L.R. 265 at 274-275 per Kitto J., and at 292 for the form of decree made in that case. As well, that the plaintiff will be required again to show a wilful or reckless disregard of his interests by his mortgagee in the matter of the auction or other sale, but, in addition, it will be necessary in such case for the plaintiff to establish that the purchaser (who again will need to be joined in such a proceeding) either knew or ought to have known of the circumstances giving rise to the impropriety alleged against the mortgagee: see, e.g., *Latec Investments Ltd v. Hotel Terrigal Pty Ltd (in liq.);* see also *Lukass Investments Pty Ltd v. Makaroff* (1964) 82 W.N. (N.S.W.) (Pt 1) 226; *Blundell v. Associated Securities Ltd* (1971) 19 F.L.R. 17 at 39.
>
> In the third of the cases to which I have referred, it is not necessary, since the aid of the court is not sought either to restrain the completion of the impugned sale or to have any conveyance or transfer made pursuant to it set aside, for a plaintiff to bring into court or to offer to bring into court, as in a redemption suit, or to submit to any condition as to payment of, any amount owing in respect of the mortgage. It is, however, necessary for the plaintiff again to show that there has been a wilful or reckless disregard by his mortgagee of his interests in the matter of the auction or other sale: see, e.g., *Pendlebury v. Colonial Mutual Life Assurance Society Ltd* (1912) 13 C.L.R. 676.
>
> Whether or not the fourth possible remedy to which I have referred above will ultimately be recognised in Australia may be open to doubt: cf. and cp. *Cuckmere Brick Co. Ltd v. Mutual Finance Ltd* [1971] Ch. 949; 2 All E.R. 633; *Forsyth v. Blundell*, above. However, having regard to the views expressed by Barwick C.J. in *Public Transport Commission of New South Wales v. J. Murray-More (N.S.W.) Pty Ltd* (1975) 132 C.L.R. 336 at 341 as to the way in which the court, at first instance, should proceed, I propose to proceed upon the basis that such a remedy might in an appropriate case, be granted to a mortgagor. In such case, so it seems to me, it is not necessary, since the plaintiff is not seeking the aid of the court either to restrain completion of the contract or to have set aside any conveyance or transfer made pursuant to it, for him to bring into court or to offer to bring into court,

as in a redemption suit, or to submit to any condition as to payment of, the amount owing under the mortgage. All that is necessary in such a case, if the principle in *Cuckmere Brick Co. Ltd v. Mutual Finance Ltd* [1971] Ch. 949 is to be applied in Australia, is that the plaintiff demonstrate that the mortgagee, when exercising his power of sale, failed to take reasonable care to obtain a proper price, or, perhaps the true market value. I have put the matter in this way since there appears to be a distinction drawn by the Lords Justices who constituted the bench in *Cuckmere Brick Co. Ltd v. Mutual Finance Ltd* between "a proper price" and "the true market value".

2. Must a mortgagor offer to redeem where he or she seeks to restrain the sale on the ground that the statutory notice procedures (above p. 452) have not been followed? See *Mediservices International Pty Ltd v. Stocks & Realty (Security Finance) Pty Ltd* [1982] 1 N.S.W.L.R. 516.

3. A registered proprietor of Torrens title land may lodge a caveat to prevent registration of a dealing pursuant to an improper exercise of a power of sale. See *Real Property Act* 1900 (N.S.W.), s. 74F(2); *Sinclair v. Hope Investments Pty Ltd* [1982] 2 N.S.W.L.R. 870.

3. Protection of purchaser

(a) Old system title.

Section 112(3) of the *Conveyancing Act* 1919 (N.S.W.) contains provisions designed to protect a purchaser buying from a mortgagee in purported exercise of a power of sale:

(3) Where a conveyance is made in professed exercise of the power of sale conferred by this Act—

(a) a purchaser shall not, either before or on conveyance, be concerned to see or inquire whether a case has arisen to authorise the sale, or due notice has been given, or the power is otherwise properly and regularly exercised;

(b) the title of the purchaser shall not be impeachable on the ground that no case had arisen to authorise the sale, or that due notice was not given, or that the power was otherwise improperly or irregularly exercised, but any person damnified by an unauthorised or improper or irregular exercise of the power shall have his remedy in damages against the person exercising the power.

This provision will not protect a purchaser who has notice of impropriety in the exercise of the power of sale.

JENKINS v. JONES

High Court of Chancery (1860) 2 Giff. 99; 66 E.R. 43

[Mortgagees of a leasehold property refused to allow the plaintiff mortgagor to redeem the mortgage by tendering the amount owing (£261), alleging wrongfully (as they knew) that the amount owing was substantially in excess of the amount tendered. The mortgagees, in spite of the plaintiff's protests, insisted on exercising their power of sale by selling at auction. The plaintiff attended the auction, placed the sum of £261 in bank notes and gold on the table in the auction room, stating the amount, and offered it to the auctioneer. He also "gave notice of his title to the property and asserted his right to redeem", but the auctioneer and the clerk of the mortgagees' solicitor refused to accept the amount. The property was knocked down to the defendant.

The mortgage contained a clause which provided that no purchaser should be bound to enquire as to the propriety or regularity of any sale purported to be made in pursuance of a power of sale, and that "notwithstanding any impropriety or irregularity of such sale, the same should, as regards the purchaser or purchasers, be deemed to be within the aforesaid power, and be valid accordingly".

The plaintiff filed a bill to redeem.]

STUART V.-C. The whole object [of the mortgagees' conduct] seems to have been to have a sale at all hazards, and to pay the surplus moneys, if any, into court . . . . As regards the mortgagee[s], therefore, I must hold that the sale was oppressive, and must be set aside, if it can be done, without injustice to the purchaser.

The purchaser contends that, as a bona fide purchaser for value under a power of sale so framed as to relieve him from the duty of making any inquiry, he is entitled, according to the rules of this court, to hold the property against all claimants. But, although a power of sale so framed relieves the purchaser from all obligation to make inquiries, yet the terms in which this clause is expressed would seem to shew that, though a purchaser under a power of sale need make no inquiries, yet if circumstances which put in question the propriety of the sale are brought to his knowledge, and he purchases with that knowledge, he becomes a party to the transaction which is impeached. In this case the purchaser was present, and saw the struggle to redeem, and he must have known that the effect of his act would be to destroy that right to redeem which the plaintiff was endeavouring to establish while the sale was pending. This knowledge on the part of the purchaser puts him in exactly the same situation as the persons from whom he was about to purchase. There seems nothing to relieve the purchaser from the consequences of this proceeding to complete his purchase in the face of what ought to have put him on inquiry. It is said, and truly said, that had he seen nothing he need not have made any inquiry; but, having been a witness to what was going on, he became in one sense a party to the transaction, and cannot now rely on the immunity given by the deed in favour of an indifferent purchaser. In other words the purchaser, having seen the struggle to redeem, and heard the plaintiff's claim, proceeded at his peril . . . .

On the whole case, I must consider the sale oppressive and invalid as against the mortgagor, and it must be set aside.

The decree must be as follows: "Declare that, having regard to the circumstances, the sale is invalid, and that the same ought to be set aside. Ordered, that an account be taken of what is due to the defendants . . . for principal, interest and costs, as mortgagees on their mortgage debt of £250, and order that such amount be paid by the plaintiff within three calender months from the date of the chief clerk's certificate to the defendant, Arthur Jones. Thereon, ordered that Jones do convey and assign the mortgaged premises to the plaintiff."

NOTES

1. For other cases where the purchaser's notice deprived the purchaser of the benefit of the statutory protection, see *Selwyn v. Garfitt* (1888) 38 Ch. D. 273; *Bailey v. Barnes* [1894] 1 Ch. 25; *Lukass Investments Pty Ltd v. Makaroff* (1964) 82 W.N. (N.S.W.) (Pt 1) 226. See also *Forsyth v. Blundell* (1973) 129 C.L.R. 477 at 499-503; cf. *Brigers v. Orr* (1932) 32 S.R. (N.S.W.) 634 at 638.

2. The reference in the legislation to the mortgagor's remedy in "damages" does not give a right to a common law action for damages. Rather, it is a reference to the mortgagor's right in equitable proceedings to hold the mortgagee liable to account on the basis of wilful default: *McGinnis v. Union Bank of Australia Ltd* [1935] V.L.R. 161 at 164-165. The New South Wales Court of Appeal has held that a claim for damages for wrongful exercise of a power of sale is misconceived and that there is "no such proceeding, known to New South Wales law": *Colin D. Young Pty Ltd v. Commercial and General Acceptance Ltd* (1982) C.C.H. N.S.W. Conv. R. 55-097.

(b) Torrens title

It might be thought that where the mortgage is over Torrens title land, a purchaser from a mortgagee, upon registration, would obtain an indefeasible title, even if he (the purchaser) had notice of some irregularity in the exercise of the power of sale, unless he had been guilty of "fraud", as that term is understood in the context of the Torrens system, or was subject to the "rights in personam" exception to indefeasibility of title. Nevertheless, the *Real Property Act* 1900 (N.S.W.) also contains a provision designed to absolve a purchaser from the need to inquire into the circumstances surrounding the exercise of the power of sale: see *Real Property Act* 1900 (N.S.W.), s. 58(2), and discussion in Sykes, op. cit., pp. 277-281.

4. Application of proceeds of sale

Although the mortgagee is not a trustee of the power of sale for the mortgagor, he or she is a trustee of the proceeds of sale; that is to say, if the sale yields a surplus over and above the amount due under the mortgage, the mortgagee holds the surplus upon trust for the various persons interested in the surplus. This had been established by general law (see *Prosser v. Rice* (1859) 28 Beav. 68 at 74; 54 E.R. 291 at 294; *Banner v. Berridge* (1881) 18 Ch. D. 254 at 269; *Hodson v. Deans* [1903] 2 Ch. 647 at 652), and is now enshrined in s. 112(4) of the *Conveyancing Act* 1919 (N.S.W.):

> (4) The money which is received by the mortgagee, arising from the sale, after discharge of prior incumbrances to which the sale is not made subject (if any), or after payment into court under this Act of a sum to meet any prior incumbrance, shall in the absence of an express contract to the contrary be held by him in trust to be applied by him, first in payment of all costs, charges, and expenses properly incurred by him as incident to the sale or any attempted sale or otherwise; and, secondly, in discharge of the mortgage money, interest, and costs, and other money (if any) due under the mortgage; and the residue of the money so received shall be paid to the person entitled to the mortgaged property or authorised to give receipts for the proceeds of the sale thereof.

The "person entitled to the mortgaged property or authorised to give receipts for the proceeds of the sale thereof" is the mortgagee next in priority after the mortgagee who is selling. A mortgagee who sells with notice of a subsequent mortgage, but pays the surplus to the mortgagor, will be liable to that subsequent mortgagee: *West London Commercial Bank v. Reliance Permanent Building Society* (1885) 29 Ch. D. 954. As to the liability of the solicitor for the mortgagee concerning application of the proceeds of sale, see *Adams v. Bank of New South Wales* [1982] 2 N.S.W.L.R. 659; on appeal [1984] 1 N.S.W.L.R. 285.

Section 58(3) of the *Real Property Act* 1900 (N.S.W.), although differently worded to s. 112(4) of the *Conveyancing Act* 1919 (N.S.W.), directs substantially similar application of the proceeds of sale. A Torrens title mortgagee must account for any surplus proceeds of sale not only to subsequent mortgagees who are registered but also to those who are not registered (provided he or she has notice of them): *Re Murrell* (1984) 57 A.L.R. 85.

V. PRIORITIES

A. GENERAL

Where there are two or more mortgages over the same property, questions of priorities arise. Generally, priority between mortgages will be decided according to the general rules considered in the chapter on old system title and the registration of instruments (above Chapter 3) and the chapter on the Torrens system (above Chapter 4). By way of summary, the following are the relevant principles:

1. Old system title

(1) Where there is a prior legal mortgage followed by a later equitable mortgage, the legal mortgage will prevail, unless the holder of the prior legal mortgage is postponed by such conduct as fraud or gross negligence in controlling the title deeds: see *Northern Counties Fire Insurance Co. v. Whipp* (1884) 26 Ch. D. 482, discussed above p. 109.

(2) Where there is a prior equitable mortgage (for example, a mortgage by deposit of title deeds) followed by a subsequent legal mortgage, the legal mortgage will prevail if the holder took bona fide for value and without notice of the prior equitable mortgage: see discussion above p. 110.

(3) Where there are two equitable mortgages, the first in time will prevail, unless there has been conduct on the part of the holder of the mortgage first in time making it inequitable for her or his interest to prevail.

These rules may be upset, however, by the provisions of the registration of instruments legislation, under which priority is determined according to the date of registration and not the date of execution of the respective instruments. The effect of this legislation has been discussed above pp. 110 et seq.

2. Torrens title

(1) Where there are two or more registered mortgages, priority is determined by order of registration, which, in turn, is determined by order of lodgment for registration: see *Real Property Act* 1900 (N.S.W.), s. 36(9). The priority of registered mortgages may be varied by agreement between the mortgagees: s. 56A.

(2) Where there is a registered mortgage and an unregistered mortgage, the registered mortgage will take priority under the indefeasibility provisions of the Torrens legislation: see discussion above pp. 127 et seq.

(3) Where there are two or more unregistered mortgages, priority will be determined by the general rules governing equitable priorities (discussed above pp. 106 et seq.), but subject to the special principles developed relating to competing unregistered interests in Torrens title land: see discussion and case extracts, above pp. 133 et seq.

B. TACKING

Over and above the general principles governing priorities between mortgages lies the doctrine of "tacking". There are two limbs to this doctrine: (1) tabula in naufragio; and (2) the rule against further advances.

1. Tabula in naufragio

(a) Old system title

Where land under old system title is mortgaged successively to A (legal mortgage), B (equitable mortgage) and C (equitable mortgage), priority generally will be determined according to the date of creation of the respective mortgages. C, however, can upset this: if C, at the time he made his advance, had no notice of the equitable mortgage to B, and if he (C) can acquire the legal estate by paying out A, he may "tack" his third equitable mortgage to the first legal mortgage. C will then be entitled to be repaid both amounts in priority to B; B is, in effect, "squeezed out". "The legal estate was regarded as tabula in naufragio, a plank in a shipwreck, to be scrambled for by drowning equitable mortgagees": Hanbury, *Modern Equity* (9th ed.) p. 583. C will be entitled to avail himself of the rule even though he in fact receives notice of B's interest before paying out A.

BAILEY v. BARNES

Court of Appeal [1894] 1 Ch. 25

[Johnson gave a first legal mortgage over his property to certain mortgagees, who subsequently transferred the mortgage to Barnes. Barnes exercised his power of sale improperly by selling the property to his nominee, M. Later, M granted a legal mortgage of £6,000 over the property, and then sold and conveyed the equity of redemption to Lilley.

The plaintiffs, who had become entitled under a court order to Johnson's interest in the property, obtained a declaration that the sale was invalid and that they were entitled to redeem the property. At the time when Lilley acquired the equity of redemption, he had no notice of the impropriety in the exercise of the power of sale, and therefore had no notice of Johnson's right to have the sale set aside. Lilley subsequently learned of the declaration, paid off the £6,000 legal mortgage, and took a conveyance of the legal estate from the mortgagee.

The present proceedings were brought to determine the rights of the plaintiffs and Lilley to the property. Stirling J. held that Lilley took free of any rights in the plaintiffs to redeem. On appeal.]

LINDLEY L.J. (Delivering the judgment of the court). The case, then, stands thus: The plaintiffs had a judgment affecting Johnson's equity of redemption. Lilley had acquired by purchase for value an equitable interest in the same property from a person whose title apparently displaced Johnson's, and also, consequently, the plaintiffs' judgment. Lilley had no notice of any defect in his own title, no notice that the plaintiffs' judgment affected him. Lilley afterwards discovers that the plaintiffs' judgment is not displaced, and in order to protect himself he pays off the £6,000 mortgage and gets in the legal estate. The question is whether he can now hold the property free from the plaintiffs' judgment.

We are of opinion that he can. The maxim qui prior est tempore potior est jure is in the plaintiffs' favour, and it seems strange that they should, without any default of their own, lose a security which they once possessed. But the above maxim is, in our law, subject to an important qualification, that, where equities are equal, the legal title prevails. Equality, here, does not mean or refer to priority in point of time, as is shewn by the cases on tacking. Equality means the non-existence of any circumstance which affects the conduct of one of the rival claimants, and makes it less meritorious than that of the other. Equitable owners who are upon an equality in this respect may struggle for the legal estate, and he who obtains it, having both law and equity on his side, is in a better situation than he who has equity only. The reasoning is technical and not satisfactory; but, as long ago as 1728, the law was judicially declared to be well settled and only alterable by Act of Parliament: see *Brace v. Duchess of Marlborough* (1728) 2 P. Wms. 491; 24 E.R. 829.

It was contended that this doctrine was confined to tacking mortgages. But this is not so. The doctrine applies in favour of all equitable owners or incumbrancers for value without notice of prior equitable interests, who get in the legal estate from persons who commit no breach of trust in parting with it to them: see *Saunders v. Dehew* (1692) 2 Vern. 271; 23 E.R. 775 and *Pilcher v. Rawlins* (1872) L.R. 7 Ch. 259. It is true that the doctrine does not apply to an equitable owner or incumbrancer who gets in the legal estate from a trustee who commits a breach of trust in conveying it to him—at all events, if such breach of trust is known to the person who gets in the estate, and, perhaps, even if he does not know of it: see *Carter v. Carter* (1857) 3 K. & J. 617; 69 E.R. 1256; *Mumford v. Stohwasser* (1874) L.R. 18 Eq. 556. But the present case does not fall within this exception to or qualification of the general principle; for Lilley obtained the legal estate from a mortgagee whom he paid off, and who committed no breach of trust in conveying the legal estate to him.

Appeal dismissed.

NOTES

1. There is some doubt whether the plea of tabula in naufragio will be defeated merely by the fact that the conveyor of the legal estate acted in breach of trust, or whether, in addition, the purchaser of the legal estate must know that the conveyance to him was in breach of trust. See further, *Mumford v. Stohwasser* (1874) L.R. 18 Eq. 556; *Taylor v. Russell* [1892] A.C. 244 at 253; Sykes, op. cit., pp. 391-392.

2. The doctrine of tabula in naufragio cannot apply where the second (equitable) mortgage to B is registered under the registration of deeds legislation; the third mortgagee, C, will be on notice of B's mortgage, as registration is notice to persons subsequently dealing with the title: *Mills v. Renwick* (1901) 1 S.R. (N.S.W.) (Eq.) 173.

(b) Torrens title

The doctrine of tabula in naufragio cannot apply to mortgages registered under the *Real Property Act* 1900 (N.S.W.). In such a case, the priority of the second mortgage is determined by the order of registration, and cannot be defeated by the registered proprietor of the third mortgage taking a transfer of the first mortgage: *Matzner v. Clyde Securities Ltd* [1975] 2 N.S.W.L.R. 293 at 305.

Professor Sykes, op. cit., p. 461 expresses the view that the doctrine does apply where there is a first registered mortgage to A followed by successive unregistered mortgages to B and C; C can "squeeze out" B by taking a transfer of the first mortgage to A. Do you think this is correct?

2. Further advances

(a) Old system title

Where the owner of land under old system title gives a first legal mortgage to A to secure advances already made, and then gives a second (equitable) mortgage to B, and thereafter A makes further advances over the same security without notice of the mortgage to B, A is permitted to "tack" his further advances to his existing legal mortgage and take priority over B in respect of them. A's right is based upon his possession of the legal estate (although this basis of the rule was doubted in *Matzner v. Clyde Securities Ltd* [1975] 2 N.S.W.L.R. 293, extracted below). Here, unlike in the tabula in naufragio situation, A has the legal estate from the outset and is not required to salvage it from the shipwreck. But A cannot so tack his further advances if, at the date of making them, he had notice of the mortgage to B.

There is also a form of tacking of further advances which is based on *contract*, rather than possession of the legal estate, and which therefore is available to equitable mortgagees as well. This operates in the following manner: where the mortgage provides either that the mortgagee *may* make further advances upon the same security, or that he *shall* make further advances upon the same security, he is permitted to tack such further advances to his existing mortgage, whether it be legal or equitable. Here also, the right to tack will be lost where, at the time of making the further advances, the mortgagee had notice of a subsequent mortgage; the fact that the mortgage permits (as in *Hopkinson v. Rolt* (1861) 9 H.L. Cas. 514; 11 E.R. 829) or requires (as in *West v. Williams* [1899] 1 Ch. 132) the making of the further advances cannot confer priority over subsequent mortgages of which there is notice. As to the kind of notice which precludes the right to tack further advances, see *Central Mortgage Registry of Australia Ltd v. Donemore Pty Ltd*, extracted below p. 494.

The general law rules may be affected also by the operation of the registration of instruments legislation. Two situations may be contrasted. First, where a mortgage to A secures the payment of further advances and is registered, and the mortgagor subsequently gives a mortgage to B which is also registered, A may tack any further advances provided he has no notice of the mortgage to B, and the mere act of registration of the mortgage to B does not put A on notice—he is not required to, nor should he, search the Register afresh before making each further advance: see *Re O'Byrne's Estate* (1885) L.R. 15. Ir. 189, 373, extracted above p. 122. Secondly, however, where the mortgage to A is not expressed to secure the payment of further advances, it seems that A must search the Register before making each further advance, otherwise the further advance will be postponed to B's registered mortgage: *Credland v. Potter* (1874) 10 L.R. Ch. App. 8. See further, note 1 to *Re O'Byrne's Estate* (1885) L.R. 15 Ir. 189, above p. 124; Hogg, *Deeds Registration* (1908), p. 98, n. 32.

(b) Torrens title

MATZNER v. CLYDE SECURITIES LTD

Supreme Court of New South Wales [1975] 2 N.S.W.L.R. 293

[The registered proprietor of land under the provisions of the *Real Property Act* 1900 (N.S.W.) gave a first mortgage for $273,600 over the land to finance the construction of home units on the land. By clause 22 of the mortgage, the mortgagor covenanted to complete the building in a proper and workmanlike manner. By clause 23, the principal sum was to be advanced by progress payments as the building proceeded, subject to a proviso that the accumulated progress payments from time to time were not to exceed 73.4 per cent of the aggregated value of the land and the building work at the time of any particular progress payment. By clause 24, the total amount advanced was not to exceed the amount required to complete the building work. Clause 25 provided that any further moneys advanced by the mortgagee in its absolute discretion in addition to the principal sum should be repayable on the same terms as the principal sum. Clause 26 provided that, in the event of default by the mortgagor in the completion of the building or the power of sale becoming exercisable, it should be lawful for the mortgagee to enter upon the land and complete the building, and "all moneys expended by the mortgagee in such . . . completion with interest . . . shall be payable by the mortgagor on demand and shall be a charge on the said land notwithstanding that the mortgagor shall have further encumbered the said land in favour of any person other than the mortgagee".

When $249,927 had been advanced under the first mortgage, a second mortgage for $10,000 was given with the knowledge and consent of the first mortgagee. Later, when $252,863 had been advanced under the first mortgage, a third mortgage for $30,000 was given with the knowledge and consent of the first and second mortgagees. The second and third mortgagees were fully aware of the terms of the first mortgage when they took their respective mortgages. After the date of the third mortgage, further sums were advanced under the first mortgage, bringing the total to $258,000. At this stage, the building was well advanced, but a substantial amount of work remained to be done.

The mortgagor then defaulted in the payment of interest under the first mortgage. The first mortgagee, in exercise of its power of sale, attempted to sell the property by auction, but was unsuccessful. The first mortgagee concluded that the property could be disposed of satisfactorily only if the building was completed, and thereupon outlayed $76,000 to complete the building, purporting to act under clause 26 of the mortgage.

The mortgagee subsequently sold the property, but the amount realised was not sufficient to repay all three mortgages in full. The present suit was brought to determine the priority between the mortgages.]

HOLLAND J. For the plaintiffs [the second and third mortgagees] it is submitted by Mr Bennett that the rules against the tacking of further advances to a prior mortgage apply to the present case, and preclude the defendant [the first mortgagee] from claiming priority over the plaintiffs for any advances made after notice of their mortgages. It is further submitted that all amounts outlayed by the defendant since notice were in the nature of further advances, whether they purported to be progressive instalments of the principal sum stated in the mortgage or to be payments made pursuant to the specific power to complete the buildings on default. As to the latter, it is submitted that the defendant elected to make the payments as further advances and was bound by its election, but, if they are found to be expenditure by a mortgagee in possession and not further advances, it is submitted that the rules governing the right of a mortgagee to charge the security with such expenditure would apply, and the defendant would have to justify, under those rules, any claim for priority for that expenditure.

The contentions of Mr Hely on behalf of the defendant are, firstly, that the rules against tacking do not apply to registered mortgages of land under the *Real Property Act* 1900 (N.S.W.), or, if they do, they do not apply to advances made under this particular type of first mortgage at all, or at least not up to the full amount of the principal sum stated in the mortgage; and, secondly, that the expenditure in excess of the principal sum was not to be regarded as a further advance, but as a reasonable outlay by a mortgagee in possession for the purpose of preserving and perfecting the security and was, therefore, to be added to the principal, at least in so far as it increased the value of the property. . . .

The rule on which the plaintiffs rely is that a mortgagee to whom the property is mortgaged for advances already made cannot, after receiving notice of a second mortgage, have priority over the second mortgagee for further advances upon the first mortgage, even if the first mortgage, to the knowledge of the second mortgagee, is expressed to be a security for further advances that may be made. It is unnecessary to trace the origin of the rule. It was declared to be the law by a majority of the House of Lords in *Hopkinson v. Rolt* (1861) 9 H.L. Cas. 514; 11 E.R. 829 and has been explained by the same court in *London and County Banking Co. Ltd v. Ratcliffe* (1881) 6 App. Cas. 722; *Bradford Banking Co. Ltd v. Henry Briggs Son & Co. Ltd* (1886) 12 App. Cas. 29; *Union Bank of Scotland v. National Bank of Scotland* (1886) 12 App. Cas. 53 and *Deeley v. Lloyds Bank Ltd* [1912] A.C. 756. The plaintiffs contend that it has further been established by the Court of Appeal in *West v. Williams* [1899] 1 Ch. 132 that the rule applies even where the first mortgagee has bound himself under the mortgage to make further advances. Therefore, it is submitted, it must be taken that the rule applies in the present case.

In order to deal with this submission, and with the defendant's submissions that the rule is inapplicable to the present mortgage or to mortgages registered under the *Real Property Act* 1900 (N.S.W.), I think it is necessary to examine the basis upon which the rule rests, particularly in view of the fact that counsel for the defendant, in support of his submission that the rule does not apply to mortgages registered under the *Real Property Act*, has submitted, inter alia, that the rule rests on the doctrine of estates in land under old system titles whereby a mortgagor, having conveyed to the second mortgagee the equity of redemption which remained with him when he conveyed the legal estate to the first mortgagee, was disabled from creating in favour of the first mortgagee a further charge upon it in priority to the second mortgagee's interest. Thus, it was submitted, there is no basis for applying it where the mortgagor does not part with the legal estate, but merely creates statutory charges upon it, as he does under the Torrens System of titles.

It is evident from the reasoning in the cases to which I have referred that an underlying object of the rule was to leave the mortgagor in a position to raise further moneys on his property, which he could be prevented from doing, if the first mortgagee was free to defeat a second mortgagee by diminishing the security by further advances. Lord Chelmsford in *Hopkinson v. Rolt* said (1861) 9 H.L. Cas. 514 at 553; 11 E.R. 829 at 845: ". . . if it is to be held that he is always to be secure of his priority (for further advances), a perpetual curb is imposed on the mortgagor's right to encumber his equity of redemption." But I think that the rule must be taken to rest primarily upon considerations of justice as between the competing mortgagees. In all of the House of Lords cases to which I have referred, the making of further advances was optional. In none of them did the first mortgage bind the mortgagee to make or the mortgagor to receive further advances. In *Hopkinson v. Rolt* both the Lord Chancellor, Lord Campbell (1861) 9 H.L. Cas. 514 at 534, 535; 11 E.R. 829 at 838, and Lord Chelmsford (1861) 9 H.L. Cas. 514 at 553; 11 E.R. 829 at 845 who formed the majority, made a point of this. So also did the Lord Chancellor, Lord Selborne, in *London and County Banking Co. Ltd v. Ratcliffe* (1881) 6 App. Cas. 722 at 727; Lord Blackburn in *Bradford Banking Co. Ltd v. Henry Briggs Son & Co. Ltd* (1886) 12 App. Cas. 29 at 36, 37 and Lord Halsbury in *Union Bank of Scotland v. National Bank of Scotland* (1886) 12 App. Cas. 53 at 94. In all of the House of Lords cases it was considered unjust as between the two mortgagees for the first, after notice of the second, to encroach upon the security given to the second by seeking to enlarge the burden of the first mortgage. It was also considered unjust on the part of the mortgagor, having granted two successive mortgages, to take a further advance on the first thereby to enlarge the scope of the first to the detriment of the second; per Lord Halsbury in *Union Bank of Scotland v. National Bank of Scotland* (1886) 12 App. Cas. 53 at 95 and Lord Shaw in *Deeley v. Lloyds Bank Ltd* [1912] A.C. 756 at 782. In speaking of the first mortgagee's position Lord Campbell said (1861) 9 H.L. Cas. 514 at 534, 535; 11 E.R. 829 at 838: "The first mortgagee is secure as to past advances, and he is not under any obligation to make any further advances. He has only to hold his hand when asked for a further loan", and (1861) 9 H.L. Cas. 514 at 535; 11 E.R. 829 at 838: "the first mortgagee will have no reason to complain (of preference to the second mortgagee against subsequent advances by the first mortgagee), knowing that this is his true position, if he chooses voluntarily to make further advances to the mortgagor". Lord Chelmsford said (1861) 9 H.L. Cas. 514 at 553; 11 E.R. 829 at 845: "And, as the first mortgagee is not bound to make the stipulated further advances, and with notice of a subsequent mortgage, he can always protect himself by inquiries as to the state of the accounts with the second mortgagee, if he chooses to run the risk of advancing his money with the knowledge, or the means of knowledge, of his position, what reason can there be for allowing him any priority?" Lord Blackburn said (1886) 12 App. Cas. 29 at 37: "It (the rule) seems to me to depend entirely on what I cannot but think a principle of justice, that a mortgagee who is entitled, but not bound, to give credit on the security of property belonging to the debtor, cannot give that credit after he has notice that the property has so far been parted with by the debtor."

Whilst reference is made in those of the above cases which dealt with mortgages of land to the respective legal and equitable estates of the mortgagors and mortgagees and to the mortgagor's right to further encumber his equity of redemption, all of the judgments emphasise, in one way or another, that the rule is founded on principles of justice and fair dealing as between mortgagor and the mortgagees, and as between the competing mortgagees. In *Bradford Banking Co. Ltd v. Henry Briggs Son & Co. Ltd* (1886) 12 App. Cas. 29 the rule was applied to defeat a claim of priority for a lien on the shares in a company for debts of a shareholder, a case where the application of the rule did not depend on the doctrine of estates in land. In *Union Bank of Scotland v. National Bank of Scotland* (1886) 12 App. Cas. 53 at 99 Lord Watson expressly said that the principle of *Hopkinson v. Rolt* (1861) 9 H.L. Cas. 514; 11 E.R. 829 did not "rest upon any rule or practice of English conveyancing, but upon principles of natural justice". Lord Blackburn agreed with Lord Watson (1886) 12 App. Cas. 53 at 100. In *West v. Williams* [1899] 1 Ch. 132 at 143 Lord Lindley M.R. said: "These three cases (*Hopkinson v. Rolt* (1861) 9 H.L. Cas. 514; 11 E.R. 829; *Bradford Banking Co. Ltd v. Henry Briggs Son & Co. Ltd* (1886) 12 App. Cas. 29 and *Union Bank of Scotland v. National Bank of Scotland* (1886) 12 App. Cas. 53) shew very clearly that the principle which underlies the rule established in *Hopkinson v. Rolt* (1861) 9 H.L. Cas. 514; 11 E.R. 829 is simply this, that an owner of property, dealing honestly with it, cannot confer on another a greater interest in that property than he himself has. The rule rests on no technicality of English law; it is based on the plainest good sense, and it is as much the law of Scotland as the law of England." In *Deeley v. Lloyds Bank Ltd* [1912] A.C. 756 at 781, 782 Lord Shaw quoted with approval the passage from Lord Lindley's judgment in which that statement was made. In view of the forthright statements as to the basis upon which the rule rests, I am unable to accept Mr Hely's submission that the rule here in question depended entirely upon the English doctrine of estates in land, which is applicable only to land held under old system title.

As I have already mentioned, none of the cases in the House of Lords had to deal with a mortgage under which the mortgagee was bound to make, and the mortgagor was bound to accept, the advances that were made after the date of the second mortgage or with a mortgage on terms like the present. The argument that the rule applies in such a case rests upon the decision of the Court of Appeal in *West v. Williams* [1899] 1 Ch. 132. In that case a spendthrift mortgaged his life interest in his father's estate to his uncles to secure the repayment of a sum advanced by them to assist him to pay his debts, and further sums of £200 per annum which they covenanted to pay him for five years for his personal maintenance. It was a condition of the mortgage that the life tenant should execute a settlement of his life interest, so that it would be determinable on alienation by him, with a trust, in that event, for the application of the income at the discretion of the settlement trustees for the maintenance of the settlor and his family. The settlement contained a covenant by the uncles to pay the life tenant £200 per annum if he should leave England, proceed to some country out of Europe and remain there for five years and comply with certain other conditions. This covenant was recited in the mortgage. A settlement to the effect recited in the mortgage was executed contemporaneously with the execution of the mortgage. Unknown to the uncles the life tenant had previously mortgaged his life interest to the plaintiff who had given no notice of the mortgage to the trustees of his father's will. The uncles became aware of the prior mortgage only after they had made several payments to the life tenant on account of the annuity which they had covenanted to pay him. They claimed against the plaintiff priority, not only for all advances made to the life tenant before receiving notice of the plaintiff's mortgage, but also for all further advances which they had bound themselves to make under their covenant. The Court of Appeal, Lindley M.R., Chitty and Vaughan Williams L.JJ., held that the uncles were not entitled to priority for advances made after receiving notice of the plaintiff's prior mortgage. The court overcame the objection that the uncles had, without notice, covenanted to make the further advances by holding that the obligation to make them was discharged by the life tenant having given the prior mortgage. Lord Lindley M.R. said [1899] 1 Ch. 132 at 143, 144: "When a man mortgages his property he is still free to deal with his equity of redemption in it, or, in other words, with the property itself subject to the mortgage. If he creates a second mortgage he cannot afterwards honestly suppress it, and create another mortgage subject only to the first. Nor can any one who knows of the second mortgage obtain from the mortgagor a greater right to override it than the mortgagor himself has. On the other hand, the first mortgagee has no right to restrain the mortgagor from borrowing money from some one else, and from giving him a second mortgage, subject to the first. Even if the first mortgagee has agreed to make further advances on the property mortgaged to him, the mortgagor is under no obligation to take further advances from him and from no one else, and if the mortgagor chooses to borrow money from some one else, and to give him a second mortgage, the mortgagor thereby releases the first mortgagee from his obligation to make further advances. Whatever prevents the mortgagor from giving to the first mortgagee the agreed security for his further advances releases the first mortgagee from his obligation to make them. A plea of exoneration and discharge before breach would be a good defence at law to an action by the mortgagor against the first mortgagee for not making further advances. If, notwithstanding his release, the first mortgagee makes further advances, with notice of a second mortgage, he is in no better position than any one else who does the like."

Chitty L.J. after referring to *Hopkinson v. Rolt* (1861) 9 H.L. Cas. 514; 11 E.R. 829; *Bradford Banking Co. Ltd v. Henry Briggs Son & Co. Ltd* (1886) 12 App. Cas.

29 and *Union Bank of Scotland v. National Bank of Scotland* (1886) 12 App. Cas.
53 said [1899] 1 Ch. 132 at 146: "The principle on which these decisions are founded
appears to me to be, that a mortgagee cannot obtain a charge on property which
is no longer the mortgagor's to charge, and which the mortgagee knows at the time
when he makes his further advance is no longer the property of the mortgagor. No
charge arises for a further advance until it is actually made. This principle is plain
and simple, and is based on natural justice and fair dealing. If this be the principle
(which I think it is), the covenant to make further advances creates no difficulty:
and for this reason; the covenant is to make the further advance on the security of
the property, and, inasmuch as the mortgagor has by his own act deprived himself
of the power to give the stipulated security, no action for damages would lie on the
covenant. It is hardly necessary to add that no action lies for specific performance
of any agreement to make a loan. The result, then, thus far is, that the uncles are
not entitled as against the plaintiff to tack any advance which they made to the
nephew after 15 February 1897."

Vaughan Williams L.J. concurred ([1899] 1 Ch. 132 at 150) in these judgments.

In my opinion, the case of *West v. Williams* [1899] 1 Ch. 132 differs from the
present case in a respect which is most material when considering the application of
the rule laid down by the House of Lords. The rule was consistently applied by the
House of Lords on the basis that the further advances would necessarily diminish
the security of the second mortgagee, if they could be tacked to the prior advances,
and the same consequence would have followed on the facts in *West v. Williams*
[1899] 1 Ch. 132, but in the present case the advances are intended and, indeed, are
expressly destined by the mortgage to be applied entirely in increasing the value of
the security. The features of the present mortgage which, in my opinion, distinguish
it radically from the mortgage considered in *West v. Williams* [1899] 1 Ch. 132 are
as follows:

(1) The mortgaged property was not land or land with established buildings
    thereon, but land with buildings about to be or in the course of erection.

(2) The total loan which the mortgagee contracted to make was not to be by way
    of one advance to be secured on the property as it stood. The security for the
    total loan was intended to be the land with the buildings completed, the total
    sum of the advances increasing as the value of the property increased.

(3) The mortgagor bound himself to complete the buildings as soon as possible in
    a proper and workmanlike manner: clause 22.

(4) The total amount of the advance stipulated by the mortgage was not to be
    available to the mortgagor at the outset, but only by progress payments as the
    project proceeded, and the amount of each progress payment was not to exceed
    a specified proportion of the aggregate value of the land and the work (at cost
    price and exclusive of all expenses other than those incurred for labour and
    material) carried out at the time of the payment of each progress payment:
    clause 23.

(5) Thus the whole of the sum to be advanced by the mortgagee was to be measured
    by additions to the value of the buildings; and the total amount advanced by
    the mortgagee was not to exceed the amount required for such completion:
    clause 24.

(6) The mortgagor covenanted to accept the whole of the stipulated principal sum
    from the mortgagee so that the same "shall be and remain a first charge upon
    the land hereby mortgaged". It seems to me that an important feature of the
    mortgage is its scheme that, under clause 23, progress payments are to be made
    only after the works have been done, and are to be less than the value of the

works at cost, so that the value of the mortgagor's equity cannot be diminished by each progress payment, but will have been increased at the time the progress payment is made. Under clauses 23 and 24 the final payment is not to be made until the project is completely finished and fit for use and occupation, and is not to exceed in amount the costs required to complete the project, so that the final payment also will not diminish the equity, although it may be that it would only equal the last increase in value.

If my analysis of the effect of this mortgage is correct, I see no grounds for denying to the mortgagee first priority for advances made pursuant to clauses 23 and 24 of the mortgage up to the total amount of the principal sum, or the amount required to complete the buildings, whichever was the less, on the basis of justice and fair dealing between the parties. Advances made under those clauses after notice of the subsequent mortgages were not designed or liable to diminish the value of the security given to the subsequent mortgagees. On the contrary, while the buildings are unfinished the security is incomplete. Completion of the buildings puts the mortgaged property into a saleable condition and serves the interests of all parties. To regard, in this case, the mortgagee's obligation to make advances under the terms of the mortgage as having been discharged by notice of the subsequent mortgages would not only violate the contract between the mortgagor and first mortgagee, but could produce an unfair result between the mortgagor and the first mortgagee and a result unsatisfactory to all parties. If the mortgagee could decline to make the promised progress advances for work already done the mortgagor could be thrust into insolvency with the mortgagor's building contractor or workmen and suppliers left lamenting, the building incomplete and all mortgagees with an unsaleable or not readily saleable security, and all this with the subsequent mortgagees having been fully aware of the terms of the first mortgage and of the restrictions upon the extent and purpose of the advances to be made under it. There would, in my opinion, be no reason, justice or fair dealing in a rule which produced such a result, and I question, therefore, whether a rule said to be founded on the principles of reason, justice and fair dealing was intended to apply to such a case.

Counsel have been unable to refer me to any authority that the rule applies to what may be called a building mortgage such as the present. . . . I find nothing in the judgments in the House of Lords cases which laid down and explained the rule to lead to a conclusion that it was to be applicable in a case like the present. I think that [in *West v. Williams*] Lord Lindley M.R. and Chitty L.J. [1899] 1 Ch. 132 at 143, 144, 146 went further in expounding what was to be derived from the judgments in the House of Lords than was necessary for a decision on the facts before the court, if they intended to lay down that the rule was applicable to all cases where a first mortgagee had covenanted to make advances and the mortgagor to accept them, irrespective of the purpose of the advances and the effect upon the value of the mortgagor's equity. Lord Lindley himself said [1899] 1 Ch. 132 at 143 that the rule was based on good sense and honest dealing, and I would find it difficult to accept that he would have regarded it as good sense and honest dealing to apply it to the facts before me. In my opinion, the rule does not apply in the present case, and the defendant is entitled to first priority for progress instalments of the principal made pursuant to clauses 23 and 24 of the mortgage after notice of the second and third mortgages. These include instalments between the dates of those mortgages and the two instalments made after the date of the third mortgage which brought the total advanced up to 3 September 1974, to $258,000. I defer for the moment the question of priority for expenditure by the first mortgagee to complete the buildings after the unsuccessful attempt to exercise the power of sale in order that I may deal first with Mr Hely's submission that the doctrine of tacking does not apply to mortgages registered under the *Real Property Act*.

As well as submitting that the doctrine rested on the theory of estates in land under old system title, Mr Hely submitted that the statutory scheme of titles under the Torrens system was inconsistent with the whole doctrine of tacking in relation to mortgages. The argument was that registered mortgages constituted only statutory charges upon the land, the priorities of which were governed by s. 36(9) of the *Real Property Act* which prescribed that dealings registered with respect to, or affecting, the same estate or interest should, notwithstanding any notice, be entitled in priority the one over the other according to the order of registration, and that s. 42 gave indefeasible title to each mortgagee as to his own mortgage, and the full ambit of the charge expressed to be given by it "[N]otwithstanding the existence in any other person of any estate or interest . . . which but for this Act might be held to be paramount or to have priority". He submitted that the priority given by the Act to a superior registered mortgagee can only be postponed by registration of a memorandum of postponement executed by him and registered under s. 56A of the Act. He pointed out that one of the rules under the doctrine of tacking rested on a basis which was excluded by the *Real Property Act*. This was the rule called tabula in naufragio whereby a third mortgagee, holding only a mortgage of the equity of redemption, could defeat or prejudice a second mortgagee, holding also only a mortgage of the equity of redemption, by acquiring the estate of the first mortgagee who held by his mortgage the legal title. The third mortgagee was allowed to tack his puisne mortgage to the first mortgage if, when he made his advance, he had no notice of the second mortgage, even if he knew of it at the time he acquired the first mortgage. This rule was based upon the superiority of the legal estate and was much criticised for the injustice it did to the second mortgagee: see Waldock, *The Law of Mortgages* (2nd ed.), pp. 388-389, 390-392. The rule undoubtedly depended upon the doctrine of estates, and I agree with Mr Hely's submission that it is excluded by the *Real Property Act*, because the priority of the second mortgagee is determined by the order of registration, and could not be defeated, against his will, by the registered proprietor of the third mortgage having taken a transfer of the first mortgage. Mr Hely submitted that, if that part of the doctrine of tacking has gone in relation to registered mortgages, the whole doctrine should be regarded as inapplicable. If the rule against tacking which is here in question had been based entirely upon the doctrine of estates I would be inclined to agree but, as I have said earlier, I do not find that to be the case. I find it to have been based finally on equitable principles and, although, because of its foundation in equitable principles, I do not think it applicable to the present mortgage, I do not, for the same reason, think that it has been excluded by the statutory scheme of the *Real Property Act*. In this I am supported by Baalman, *The Torrens System in New South Wales* (2nd ed.), p. 275 and by the cases on the application of equitable principles to dealings with land under the Act referred to in Baalman, p. 5. The rule here in question relates to the taking of accounts between the respective mortgagees and the priorities to be observed therein, and I do not think that the application of equitable rules in taking such accounts is inconsistent with the system of conveyancing established by the *Real Property Act*.

[Holland J. then dealt with the question whether an amount of $76,000 expended by the first mortgagee in completing the buildings could be added to the first mortgage as against the subsequent mortgagees. He held that the amount was not intended by the first mortgagee to be a further instalment of principal under clauses 23 and 24, but was intended to be, and was, expended pursuant to the first mortgagee's rights under clause 26. He continued:]

If this class of expenditure is properly to be regarded as further advances, I think that the rule against tacking would apply, because expenditure under clause 26 is optional; furthermore, it is not subject to the restrictions and limitations provided in clause 23. Clause 26 entitles the mortgagee to enter the land and erect and complete the project "in any manner or omitting any portion of the original design". The mortgagee is entitled under the clause to accept any tender, use any material on the land and employ any architect or other person "without liability to account as mortgagee in possession". The considerations which led me to hold that the rule against tacking did not apply to advances made pursuant to cll. 23 and 24 would not lead me to hold that the rule did not apply to expenditure under clause 26, if that expenditure is properly to be regarded as further advances for the purpose of the rule. However, the question is whether the expenditure should be so regarded.

[Holland J. then discussed the principles governing the right of a mortgagee to improve the mortgaged property as against the mortgagor—this part of the judgment is extracted above p. 443—and held that the same right existed as between a mortgagee and a subsequent encumbrancer. He found that the expenditure here came within the permissible limits. The existence of clause 26 and the fact that the first mortgagee had elected to exercise its powers under that clause did not change the character of the expenditure. The first mortgagee accordingly was entitled to add the amount to its security in priority to the second and third mortgagees.]

Order accordingly.

QUESTION

Consider the following situation: A registered mortgage over Torrens title land to secure a contemporaneous advance also contains a covenant by the mortgagee to advance a further sum of $10,000 in 12 months' time. There is no requirement for the further advance to be applied in developing the mortgaged property. Six months later, the registered proprietor gives a second mortgage over the property with the knowledge and consent of the first mortgagee. The second mortgagee takes with notice of the first mortgage, including the covenant for the further advance. In due course, the first mortgagee makes the further advance. Can it be argued that the further advance should be allowed to take priority over the second mortgage?

CENTRAL MORTGAGE REGISTRY OF AUSTRALIA LTD v. DONEMORE PTY LTD

Supreme Court of New South Wales [1984] 2 N.S.W.L.R. 128

[Warden was the registered proprietor of land at Beacon Hill under the provisions of the *Real Property Act* 1900 (N.S.W.). He gave a first registered mortgage over the land to the plaintiff. The mortgage secured an advance made at that time as well as any money which later might become owing by the mortgagor to the mortgagee (clause 17); it also forbade the granting of further mortgages over the land without the consent of the plaintiff (clause 16). Later, Warden gave a second mortgage over the land to the defendant. This mortgage was not registered, but a caveat was lodged in respect of it. The plaintiff was unaware of this mortgage and of the caveat. The plaintiff thereafter lent a further sum of money which Warden guaranteed to repay, and which for the purposes of the case was treated as though it were a further advance under the first mortgage. The plaintiff did not search against the title to the land before making the further advance, and still had no notice of the defendant's mortgage and caveat. Following default by Warden, the plaintiff exercised its power of sale. The sale proceeds were not sufficient to pay off both the defendant's mortgage and the plaintiff's further advance. The defendant claimed priority in respect of the sale proceeds under the rule against tacking.]

KEARNEY J. The defendant invokes the principle declared by the House of Lords in *Hopkinson v. Rolt* (1861) 9 H.L. Cas. 514; 11 E.R. 829, to the effect that a mortgagee to whom a property is mortgaged for advances already made cannot, after receiving notice of a second mortgage, have priority over the second mortgagee for further advances under his first mortgage even if the first mortgage, to the knowledge of the second mortgagee, is expressed to be a security for further allowances which may be made. This principle has since been adopted and applied universally as appears from the various authorities referred to in the judgment of Holland J. in *Matzner v. Clyde Securities Ltd* [1975] 2 N.S.W.L.R. 293 at 298, 299.

It emerges from these various authorities that the principle so enunciated and applied is, in the words of Holland J. (at 300), "founded on principles of justice and fair dealing as between the mortgagor and the mortgagees, and as between the competing mortgagees". It further follows from the decision of Holland J. that this principle is applicable in respect of land under the *Real Property Act* 1900 (N.S.W.).

The rationale of the principle is summarised in the speech of Lord Blackburn in *Bradford Banking Co. Ltd v. Henry Briggs Son & Co. Ltd* (1886) 12 App. Cas. 29 at 36, 37, where his Lordship said: "As I understand it, the principle of *Hopkinson v. Rolt* (1861) 9 H.L.C. 534-536; 11 E.R. 829 is explained by Lord Campbell then Lord Chancellor, and it is this:—The owner of property does not, by making a pledge or mortgage of it, cease to be owner of it any further than is necessary to give effect to the security which he has thus created. And if the security is, as that in *Hopkinson v. Rolt* 9 H.L.C. 514 was, a security for present and also for future advances, the pledgee or mortgagee, though not bound to make fresh advances, may, if he pleases, do so, and will, if the property at the time of the further advance remains that of the pledgor, have the security of that property.

But the mortgagor (unless there is something to make it against conscience in him to do so) may cease to take further advances from the first mortgagee, and borrow money from anyone else ready to lend it on the security of that property remaining in him not already pledged to the first, subject to the priority of the first pledgee for advances made or begun to be made. The first mortgagee is entitled to act on the supposition that the pledgor who was owner of the whole property when he executed the first mortgage continued so, and that there has been no such second mortgage or pledge until he has notice of something to shew him that there has been such a second mortgage, but as soon as he is aware that the property on which he is entitled to rely has ceased so far to belong to the debtor, he cannot make a new advance in priority to that of which he has notice. As Lord Campbell says, 'the hardship upon the bankers from this view of the subject at once vanishes, when we consider that the security of the first mortgage is not impaired without notice of a second'. It seems to me to depend entirely on what I cannot but think a principle of justice, that a mortgagee who is entitled, but not bound, to give credit on the security of the property belonging to the debtor, cannot give that credit after he has notice that the property has so far been parted with by the debtor."

There is no contest between the parties but that this principle applies in the present instance, the issue upon which the parties diverge being the question as to whether the plaintiff, before the further advance constituted by the taking of the guarantee, had received notice, within the meaning of the principle, of the defendant's second mortgage.

The plaintiff submits that actual notice is required in order to bring the principle into operation so as to deprive a first mortgagee of the benefit covenanted for under the mortgage. It is pointed out on behalf of the plaintiff that in this instance it is plain that the plaintiff had no actual notice of the defendant's mortgage or caveat until the time of its mortgagee's sale of the Beacon Hill property in January 1984. The plaintiff further submits that in paying regard to principles of justice and fair dealing as between the parties, it is to be borne in mind that the defendant was aware, when taking its second mortgage, of the first mortgage, which incorporated the provisions of clauses 16 and 17. It follows, according to the plaintiff, that the defendant took its mortgage without ensuring that the consent of the first mortgagee was obtained and, of course, with knowledge of the entitlement of the first mortgagee to have secured under its first mortgage further amounts becoming due by the mortgagor to the first mortgagee. The plaintiff further points to the fact that the defendant did not take any step to notify the plaintiff of the defendant's second mortgage, beyond merely lodging the above-mentioned caveat.

The plaintiff submits that in these circumstances where the plaintiff in effect made a further advance to the mortgagor through the medium of taking the guarantee from Warden, it did so without any knowledge of there having been any loan made by the defendant to the mortgagor in the meantime.

The underlying basis of the rule in *Hopkinson v. Rolt* deferring the entitlement of a first mortgagee is that it would be inequitable, that is, would constitute equitable fraud, on the part of a first mortgagee to claim priority in respect of further advances made with notice of an intervening equity. This is illustrated by the decision on appeal in the Chancery Division in *Re O'Byrne's Estate* (1885) L.R. 15 (Ir.) 373 where the headnote, so far as relevant reads: "A registered deed of mortgage, to secure moneys due and further advances, is, as regards a puisne mortgage, a valid security for such further advances if made bona fide and without notice of the subsequent mortgage, though after its registration. . . .

Registration of a petition for sale by the second mortgagee as a lis pendens has not the effect of notice to the first mortgagee, so as to affect the priority of further advances made by him in ignorance of such petition and registration."

Naish C., after stating that the case of *Hopkinson v. Rolt* proceeded on the ground of notice, contained [sic] (at 375, 376): "It was on the ground of notice, and of notice alone, that the priority of the first mortgage was interfered with; and, as the ground on which courts of equity interfere, where notice is proved, with what otherwise would be the rights of the party, is, that it is necessary to do so in order to prevent fraud, it follows that the ground on which the first mortgagee was postponed was that it was considered that his making, voluntarily and without any legal obligation on his part to do so, a further advance when he knew of the second mortgage, and so knowingly and deliberately ousting, or endeavouring to oust, the right acquired by the second mortgagee, would be, if it were allowed to prevail, a fraudulent act, and as such could not be allowed to stand."

The other two members of the Bench concurred in the necessity for actual notice, FitzGibbon L.J. expressing the point succinctly (at 379): "*Hopkinson v. Rolt* (1861) 9 H.L. Cas. 514; 11 E.R. 829, as it seems to me, rests entirely on the doctrine of equitable fraud, which arises only on *actual* notice, and the same principle appears to require actual notice, as distinguished from mere registration, of the lis pendens."

As indicated by the Lord Chancellor in *Re O'Byrne's Estate*, mortgages providing security for further advances are well recognised and serve a useful commercial and conveyancing purpose. His Lordship further remarked (at 378), that "so very obvious a precaution" assumed to be taken by a subsequent mortgagee as searching the title properly would have enabled notice to be served on the first mortgagee, whereas it would be an "unusual, and, as I consider it, unnecessary precaution" for the first mortgagee (a bank in that case) to make fresh searches "before each cheque drawn by Mr O'Byrne was honoured by them". Otherwise, as his Lordship says (at 379): "Where the party holding the security is a bank, as is the case here, and the security is given to cover the indebtedness resulting from the usual accommodation afforded by bankers to customers, which includes the overdrawing of a current account, it would follow that the bank would require to have a continual search kept up."

Likewise in *Pierce v. Canada Permanent Loan & Savings Co.* (1894) 25 O.R. 671, Boyd C. said (at 676): "The *onus* is not on the first mortgagee who has registered to do something more to complete his claim upon the land for all that is specified in the mortgage: the *onus* is on the one subsequently acquiring an interest in the land by conveyance from the mortgagor to give express notice of that to the first mortgagee in order to intercept payments or advances thereafter made pursuant to the first mortgage.

In the absence of notice (that is, notice which gives him real and actual knowledge, and so affects his conscience), the mortgagee is entitled to assume and act on the assumption that the state of the title has not changed."

The Chancellor continued: "That protection is given to him by virtue of the Registry Act, as well as by the doctrine enunciated in *Hopkinson v. Rolt* (1861) 9 H.L.C. 514; 11 E.R. 829 until he is made aware of a change, not by the hypothetical operation of an instrument registered subsequent to his, but by a reasonable communication of the fact by the one who comes in under the subsequent instrument", and made the further point (at 678): "The difference between statutable and actual notice is aptly expressed by Lord Redesdale in *Underwood v. Lord Courtown* (1804) 2 Sch. & Lef. 41: 'Actual notice might bind the conscience of the parties; the operation of the Registry Act may bind their title, but not their conscience.' Now, as to the case in hand, the title is not bound by the registration of the second mortgage, so as to detract from the operation of the first mortgage, and the conscience of the first mortgagee is not affected by the subsequent act of merely registering the second mortgage. So that the grounds of broad natural justice on which *Hopkinson v. Rolt* depends are non-existent."

I adopt these persuasive expressions of opinion. I conclude that in this instance, there being no notice in fact communicated to the plaintiff, the principle of *Hopkinson v. Rolt* does not operate to preclude the plaintiff from the priority claimed by it in respect of the balance of moneys remaining after discharge of the first mortgage and expenses of sale. I merely add that there is in this case no suggestion of dishonest or fraudulent conduct on the part of the plaintiff designed to prevent its receiving actual notice.

This conclusion renders strictly unnecessary consideration of the further point as to whether the lodgment and entry of the defendant's caveat would of itself constitute adequate constructive notice to affect the plaintiff's entitlement. However, in deference to the arguments of counsel, I will shortly mention my views on this matter. I do so with some diffidence, having regard to the present state of the law as to the effect of the lodgment of a caveat. An earlier statement of the position is to be found in the judgment of Real J. in *Queensland Trustees Ltd v. Reigstrar of Titles* (1893) 5 Q.L.J.R. 46 at 51 where his Honour said: "A caveat is one of the few things that can be registered without producing the Certificate of Title. I hold that a caveat is not notice. In my opinion the lodging of a caveat does not affect anything done outside the office. A man cannot be affected by anything done behind his back unless he has had notice. It protects any act within the Registrar's office but not outside, unless there is something in the Act. Otherwise, in the case of a mortgage with further advances, it would be necessary to go and search for a caveat before every further advance was made."

It is submitted on behalf of the defendant that the position as so stated has been overwhelmed by the subsequent decision of the High Court and the decision of the Privy Council in *Abigail v. Lapin* (1934) 51 C.L.R. 58. The defendant relies upon this decision which itself is submitted to uphold the earlier decision of the High Court in relevant respects in *Butler v. Fairclough* (1917) 23 C.L.R. 78 especially at 91 per Griffith C.J. The plaintiff points to another view as to the effect of lodgment of a caveat as emerging from the decision of the High Court in *J. & H. Just (Holdings) Pty Ltd v. Bank of New South Wales* (1971) 125 C.L.R. 546, epitomised in the words of Barwick C.J. (at 556): "the purpose of the caveat is protective: it is not to give notice." The defendant in turn points to the subsequent consideration of this subject in the Supreme Court of Queensland in the case of *Clark v. Raymor (Brisbane) Pty Ltd (No. 2)* in the first instance before Connolly J. ([1982] Qd R. 479) and on appeal before the Full Court ([1982] Qd R. 790).

The gravamen of the defendant's submission is that the earlier High Court decisions, as upheld in the Privy Council, establish that the lodgment of the caveat creates "notice to all the world" that the registered proprietor's title is subject to the equitable interest alleged in the caveat. In *J. & H. Just (Holdings) Pty Ltd v. Bank of New South Wales*, and also in the Queensland case, the precise question concerned not so much the effect of lodgment of a caveat, but rather the effect of non-lodgment of a caveat to protect an equitable interest in a contest as to priority between competing equitable interests. Nevertheless, the position appears in my view to be succinctly summarised in the judgment of Thomas J. in the Full Court of the Supreme Court of Queensland where his Honour says (at 798): "I do not propose to analyse the different fact situations which confronted the courts in those cases, which led to different emphases being placed upon that circumstance [that is, the failure to lodge a caveat]. Just as it is clear that there is no such thing as a legal duty upon a party to lodge a caveat, it is equally clear that the failure to do so may, in particular circumstances, contribute to a party losing priority with respect to his equitable interest."

Accordingly, this topic seems on analysis to resolve itself into a matter of ascertaining, by examination of the particular circumstances in each instance, what effect is to be attributed to the non-lodgment of a caveat to protect an equitable interest. It is evident that this was the approach also adopted by Connolly J. in the Queensland case (at 485, 486).

In so far as the cases make reference to "notice to all the world", it seems to me that the proposition adduced by counsel for the plaintiff in this case provides the answer to the defendant's claim based upon such statements in the above-mentioned cases. I agree with counsel for the plaintiff that such expressions as "notice to all the world" are to be treated as references to the world comprising such persons as are proposing to deal with the registered proprietor in respect of his land, and who accordingly should as a matter of prudence check upon the title which is to be offered to them by a registered proprietor.

The present case is far removed from such a circumstance. The terms of the plaintiff's first mortgage created immediate rights in respect of the kinds of indebtedness mentioned in clause 17, and all that was needed for the plaintiff's entitlement to security under its mortgage for the further advance was for such advance to be made. The mortgaged property was charged from the outset, not only in respect of the particular present advance but also in respect of further advances and other liabilities which may be incurred by the mortgagor to the plaintiff: see also *Re O'Byrne's Estate; Pierce v. Canada Permanent Loan & Savings Co.*

There was, accordingly, in my view no occasion for the plaintiff to be called upon to search the title of the mortgagor, more particularly when the plaintiff had no notice of any circumstances suggesting any impediment to the further advance being immediately and automatically secured under the plaintiff's first mortgage. In the absence of any such obligation on the plaintiff, it would be a perversion of the rule as to constructive notice to fix the plaintiff, in the circumstances of this case, with constructive notice of something which all the circumstances known to it indicated had not occurred.

Furthermore, in the contest as between the plaintiff and defendant based upon justice and fair dealing as between them, the defendant had it in his own hands to ensure that its position was protected vis-á-vis the first mortgage by the simple act of either seeking consent to the second mortgage or, upon the second mortgage being given, giving express notice to the first mortgage [sic] that its rights with respect to further advances were correspondingly affected. The mere lodgment of a caveat was in my view quite inadequate to render it unfair or inequitable on the part of the first mortgagee to proceed upon the well-based assumption that its further advance was automatically secured pursuant to the terms of its first mortgage.

Orders accordingly.

EIGHT

LEASEHOLDS

1. ESSENTIAL REQUIREMENTS OF A LEASEHOLD INTEREST

The relation of landlord and tenant arises whenever one person (called the landlord or lessor) confers upon another (called the tenant or lessee) the right to the exclusive possession of certain land for a period less than that for which the landlord holds the land, which period is either certain or capable of being rendered certain, with the intention of conferring upon that other person an interest in the land as opposed to a mere personal privilege: Hinde, McMorland and Sim, *Land Law*, Vol. 1, p. 416.

Two elements of this statement call for special attention: first, the requirement that the tenant should have the right to exclusive possession; secondly, the requirement that the term of the lease be certain or capable of being rendered certain.

1. The right to exclusive possession

A lease confers on the tenant the right to exclude all other persons (including the landlord) from the leased premises; by way of contrast, a licence, which is a permission to occupy premises, confers no such right. Thus, a tenant may sue in trespass to protect his right of occupancy, but a licensee may not. It used to be thought that where a person enjoyed exclusive possession of the property of another, the relationship of landlord and tenant necessarily was created between them, but it is now clear that this will not always be the case.

ERRINGTON v. ERRINGTON

Court of Appeal [1952] 1 K.B. 290

[A father wished to provide a home for his recently married son. He purchased a dwelling-house through a building society, paying a lump sum and leaving the balance on mortgage to be paid by weekly instalments; he retained the conveyance in his own name and paid the rates, but promised that if the son and daughter-in-law continued in occupation and duly paid all the instalments, he would transfer the property to them. Being on affectionate terms with the daughter-in-law, he handed her the building society's payment book and told her not to part with it. When he died, by his will he left all his property, including the house in question, to his widow. Up to that time the son and the daughter-in-law had occupied the house together and had paid the instalments, but the son then left and went to live with his widowed mother. The daughter-in-law continued to occupy the dwelling-house and to pay the instalments.

The mother brought an action for trespass against the daughter-in-law, but it was dismissed by the county court judge on the ground that the son and daughter-in-law were tenants at will and the claim was barred by the *Limitation Act* 1939 (U.K.). The mother appealed to the Court of Appeal.]

DENNING L.J. The relationship of the parties is open to three possible legal constructions:

(i) That the couple were tenants at will paying no rent. That is what the judge thought they were. He said that, in this case, just as in *Lynes v. Snaith* [1899] 1 Q.B. 486 the defendant "was in exclusive possession and was therefore not a mere licensee but in the position of a tenant at will". But in my opinion it is of the essence of a tenancy at will that it should be determinable by either party on demand, and it is quite clear that the relationship of these parties was not so determinable. The father could not eject the couple as long as they paid the instalments regularly to the building society. It was therefore not a tenancy at will. I confess that I am glad to reach this result: because it would appear that, if the couple were held to be tenants at will, the father's title would be defeated after the lapse of 13 years, long before the couple paid off the instalments, which would be quite contrary to the justice of the case.

(ii) That the couple were tenants at a rent of 15s. 0d. a week, that rent being for convenience paid direct to the building society instead of to the father, and the tenancy being either a weekly tenancy or a tenancy for the duration of the mortgage repayments. But I do not think that that 15s. 0d. can possibly be regarded as rent, for the simple reason that the couple were not bound to pay it. If they did not pay it, the father could not sue for it or distrain for it. He could only refuse to transfer the house to them. If the 15s. 0d. was not rent, then it affords no ground for inferring a tenancy.

(iii) That the couple were licensees, having a permissive occupation short of a tenancy, but with a contractual right, or at any rate, an equitable right to remain so long as they paid the instalments, which would grow into a good equitable title to the house itself as soon as the mortgage was paid. This is, I think, the right view of the relationship of the parties. I will explain how I arrive at it.

The classic definition of a licence was propounded by Vaughan C.J. in the 17th century in *Thomas v. Sorrell* (1673) Vaughan 351; 124 E.R. 1098: "A dispensation or licence properly passeth no interest nor alters or transfers property in any thing, but only makes an action lawful, which without it had been unlawful." The difference between a tenancy and a licence is, therefore, that in a tenancy, an interest passes in the land, whereas, in a licence, it does not. In distinguishing between them, a crucial test has sometimes been supposed to be whether the occupier has exclusive possession or not. If he was let into exclusive possession, he was said to be a tenant, albeit only a tenant at will (see *Doe v. Chamberlaine* (1839) 5 M. & W. 14 at 16; 151 E.R. 6 at 7 and *Lynes v. Snaith* [1899] 1 Q.B. 486), whereas if he had not exclusive possession he was only a licensee: *Peakin v. Peakin* [1895] 2 I.R. 359. This test has, however, often given rise to misgivings because it may not correspond to realities. A good instance is *Howard v. Shaw* (1841) 8 M. & W. 118; 51 E.R. 973, where a person was let into exclusive possession under a contract for purchase. Alderson B. said that he was a tenant at will; and Parke B., with some difficulty, agreed with him, but Lord Abinger said that "while the defendant occupied under a valid contract for the sale of the property to him, he could not be considered as a tenant''. Now, after the lapse of a hundred years, it has become clear that the view of Lord Abinger was right. The test of exclusive possession is by no means decisive.

The first case to show this was *Booker v. Palmer* [1942] 2 All E.R. 674 at 677, where an owner gave some evacuees permission to stay in a cottage for the duration of the war, rent free. This court held that the evacuees were not tenants, but only licensees. Lord Greene M.R. said: ''To suggest there is an intention there to create a relationship of landlord and tenant appears to me to be quite impossible. There is one golden rule which is of very general application, namely, that the law does not impute intention to enter into legal relationships where the circumstances and the conduct of the parties negative any intention of the kind.'' Those emphatic words have had their effect. We have had many instances lately of occupiers in exclusive possession who have been held to be not tenants, but only licensees. When a requisitioning authority allowed people into possession at a weekly rent (*Minister of Health v. Bellotti* [1944] K.B. 298; *Southgate Borough Council v. Watson* [1944] K.B. 541; *Ministry of Agriculture v. Matthews* [1950] 1 K.B. 148); when a landlord told a tenant on his retirement that he could live in a cottage rent free for the rest of his days (*Foster v. Robinson* [1951] 1 K.B. 149 at 156); when a landlord, on the death of a widow of a statutory tenant, allowed her daughter to remain in possession, paying rent for six months (*Marcroft Wagons Ltd v. Smith* [1951] 2 K.B. 496), when the owner of a shop allowed the manager to live in a flat above the shop, but did not require him to do so, and the value of the flat was taken into account at £1 a week in fixing his wages (*Webb Ltd v. Webb* (unreported, 24 October 1951)); in each of those cases the occupier was held to be a licensee and not a tenant. Likewise there are numerous cases where a wife, who has been deserted by her husband and left by him in the matrimonial home, has been held to be, not a tenant of the husband owner (*Bramwell v. Bramwell* [1942] 1 K.B. 370; *Pargeter v. Pargeter* [1946] 1 All E.R. 570), nor a bare licensee (*Old Gate Estates v. Alexander* [1950] 1 K.B. 311), but to be in a special position—a licensee with a special right— under which the husband cannot turn her out except by an order of the court: *Middleton v. Baldock* [1950] 1 K.B. 657.

The result of all these cases is that, although a person who is let into exclusive possession is prima facie to be considered to be a tenant, nevertheless he will not be held to be so if the circumstances negative any intention to create a tenancy. Words alone may not suffice. Parties cannot turn a tenancy into a licence merely by calling it one. But if the circumstances and the conduct of the parties show that all that was intended was that the occupier should be granted a personal privilege, with no interest in the land, he will be held to be a licensee only. In view of these recent cases I doubt whether *Lynes v. Snaith* [1899] 1 Q.B. 486, and the case of the gamekeeper referred to therein, would be decided the same way today.

Applying the foregoing principles to the present case, it seems to me that, although the couple had exclusive possession of the house, there was clearly no relationship of landlord and tenant. They were not tenants at will but licensees. They had a mere personal privilege to remain there, with no right to assign or sub-let. They were, however, not bare licensees. They were licensees with a contractual right to remain. As such they have no right at law to remain, but only in equity, and equitable rights now prevail. I confess, however, that it has taken the courts some time to reach this position. At common law a licence was always revocable at will, notwithstanding a contract to the contrary: *Wood v. Leadbitter* (1845) 13 M. & W. 838; 153 E.R. 351. The remedy for a breach of the contract was only in damages. That was the view generally held until a few years ago: see, for instance, what was said in *Booker v. Palmer* [1942] 2 All E.R. 674 at 677 and *Thompson v. Park* [1944] K.B. 408 at 410. The rule has, however, been altered owing to the interposition of equity. . . .

In the present case it is clear that the father expressly promised the couple that the property should belong to them as soon as the mortgage was paid, and impliedly promised that so long as they paid the instalments to the building society they should be allowed to remain in possession. They were not purchasers because they never bound themselves to pay the instalments, but nevertheless they were in a position analogous to purchasers. They have acted on the promise, and neither the father nor his widow, his successor in title, can eject them in disregard of it. The result is that in my opinion the appeal should be dismissed and no order for possession should be made.

[Somervell L.J. and Hodson L.J., in separate judgments, agreed that the son and daughter-in-law were licensees and not tenants. On the point of whether they would be entitled to a conveyance of the house on payment of all the instalments due under the mortgage, Somervell L.J. said that although the contract between them and the father was purely oral and so did not satisfy the requirements of the *Statute of Frauds* 1677 (U.K.) (29 Car. II c. 3), "it would seem to me that the doctrine of part performance would clearly apply" ([1952] 1 K.B. at 294); Hodson L.J. left the question open: at 301.]

Appeal dismissed.

NOTES

1. In *Cobb v. Lane* [1952] 1 All E.R. 1199, a mother allowed her son into possession of a newly purchased home. The son claimed that by entry into occupation he became a tenant at will (as to which, see below), and that having remained in possession in that capacity for at least 13 years, he had gained a possessory title to the premises. The Court of Appeal held, however, that the son was a mere licensee. Somervell L.J. said that recent cases, including *Errington v. Errington* [1952] 1 K.B. 290, showed that "exclusive possession is not a test negativing the possibility of the occupier's being a licensee. . . . [I]t must depend on the intention of the parties. . . . [T]hat is the guide which we have to apply": *Cobb v. Lane* [1952] 1 All E.R. 1199 at 1201. Denning L.J. said: "The question . . . is one of intention: Did the circumstances and conduct of the parties show that all that was intended was that the occupier should have a personal privilege with no interest in the land?": at 1202.

2. In *Isaac v. Hotel de Paris Ltd* [1960] 1 W.L.R. 239, the respondent hotel company had allowed Isaac to occupy premises of which the hotel company was a lessee, for the purpose of managing a bar on the hotel company's behalf. Isaac obtained a liquor licence in his own name and, at first, accounted to the hotel company for receipts and expenditure; later, by agreement with the hotel company, he paid all expenses, kept all profits, but undertook to pay as "rent" to the hotel company an amount of $250 per month, being the amount which the hotel company paid in respect of its lease of the premises. The hotel company served a notice on Isaac requiring him to remove his stock from the premises. Isaac thereupon claimed that he had a monthly tenancy; the hotel company claimed he was a licensee only. The notice would have been sufficient to terminate a licence, but not a tenancy. The Privy Council held that the arrangement was a licence only. Lord Denning, in delivering the advice of the Privy Council, said ([1960] 1 W.L.R. 239 at 245):

   It appears to their Lordships that the law on this matter was correctly interpreted and applied by Archer J. in the Federal Supreme Court when he said: "It is clear from the authorities that the intention of the parties is the paramount consideration and while the fact of exclusive possession together with the payment of rent is of the first importance, the circumstances in which exclusive possession has been given and the character in which money paid as rent has been received are also matters to be considered. The circumstances in which Isaac was allowed to occupy the Parisian Hotel show that Joseph never intended to accept him as a tenant and that that he was fully aware of it. The payments he made were only part of the disbursements for which he made himself responsible and the so-called rent was in the nature of a reimbursement of the rent payable by the plaintiff."

   Their Lordships are therefore of opinion that the relationship between the parties after 17 February 1956, was not that of landlord and tenant, but that of licensor and licensee. The circumstances and conduct of the parties show that all that was intended was that the defendant should have a personal privilege of running a night bar on the premises, with no interest in the land at all.

3. The comments of Lord Denning in the cases mentioned above should be read in the light of his Lordship's comments in *Facchini v. Bryson* [1952] 1 T.L.R. 1386, where an employer had let an employee into possession under a written agreement. The court held that the agreement had all the features of a tenancy agreement, and that therefore, despite a clause which read, "nothing in this agreement shall be construed to create a tenancy", the parties were in the relationship of landlord and tenant. In the course of his judgment, Lord Denning said (at 1389):

> We have had many cases lately where an occupier has been held to be a licensee and not a tenant. In addition to those which I mentioned in *Errington v. Errington* [1952] 1 K.B. 290 we have recently had three more. . . . In all the cases where an occupier has been held to be a licensee there has been something in the circumstances, such as a family arrangement, an act of friendship or generosity, or suchlike, to negative any intention to create a tenancy. In such circumstances it would be obviously unjust to saddle the owner with a tenancy, with all the momentous consequences that that entails nowadays, when there was no intention to create a tenancy at all. It is a simple case where the employer let a man into occupation of a house in consequence of his employment at a weekly sum payable by him. The occupation has all the features of a service tenancy, and the parties cannot by the mere words of their contract turn it into something else. Their relationship is determined by the law and not by the label which they choose to put on it.

This passage was quoted in *Addiscombe Garden Estates Ltd v. Crabbe* [1958] 1 Q.B. 513 by Jenkins L.J. (with whom Parker and Pearce L.JJ. agreed), who, after describing the facts in *Errington v. Errington* as "very unusual circumstances", and after referring to Lord Denning's opinion in *Errington v. Errington* that the test of exclusive possession "is by no means decisive", said ([1958] 1 Q.B. 513 at 528):

> I think that wide statement [in *Errington v. Errington*] must be treated as qualified by his observations in *Facchini v. Bryson*; and it seems to me that, save in exceptional cases of the kind mentioned by Denning L.J. in that case, the law remains that the fact of exclusive possession, if not decisive against the view that there is a mere licence, as distinct from a tenancy, is at all events a consideration of the first importance.

In *Addiscombe Garden Estates Ltd v. Crabbe* [1958] 1 Q.B. 513 at 524, 525, the Court of Appeal held that an agreement, whereby the owners of certain tennis courts and clubhouses purported to grant a "licence" to occupy, on its true construction created the relationship of landlord and tenant. One of the clauses in the agreement which the court regarded as important was that which permitted the "grantor" to enter and inspect the state of repair of the premises, because it showed that "the right to occupy the premises conferred on the grantees was intended as an exclusive right of occupation, in that it was thought necessary to give a special and express power to the grantors to enter. The exclusive character of the occupation granted by a document such as this has always been regarded, if not as a decisive indication, at all events as a very important indication to the effect that a tenancy, as distinct from a licence, is the real subject matter of a document such as this": see also *Hardwick v. Johnson* [1978] 1 W.L.R. 683 at 688. Compare the comments on *Errington v. Errington* by Lord Upjohn in *National Provincial Bank Ltd v. Ainsworth* [1965] A.C. 1175 at 1239.

4. Lord Denning also commented in the instant case ([1952] 1 K.B. 290 at 299) that where a licence of the kind held to exist had been created, "neither the licensor nor anyone who claims through him can disregard the contract except a purchaser for value without notice". This contradicted the traditional understanding that a contractual licence was not binding on a purchaser, even with notice, since it conferred no interest in the land. The English Court of Appeal in *Ashburn Anstalt v. Arnold* [1988] 2 W.L.R. 706, extracted on another point below p. 535, has now reaffirmed the traditional view, holding that this aspect of *Errington v. Errington* is inconsistent with a number of decisions of both the Court of Appeal (*Daly v. Edwardes* (1900) 83 L.T. 548; *Frank Warr & Co. v. London County Council* [1904] 1 K.B. 713; *Clore v. Theatrical Properties Ltd* [1936] 3 All E.R. 483; *National Provincial Bank Ltd v. Hastings Car Mart Ltd* [1964] Ch. 665 at 697 per Russell L.J.) and the House of Lords (*Edwardes v. Barrington* (1901) 85 L.T. 650; *King v. David Allen & Sons (Billposting) Ltd* [1916] 2 A.C. 54).

RADAICH v. SMITH

High Court of Australia (1959) 101 C.L.R. 209

[A deed made 29 May 1954, between George William Edward Smith and Ada Smith (therein called the licensors of the one part) and Maria Radaich (therein called the licensee) of the other part provided:

"that the Licensors hereby grant to the Licensee for a term of five years from the Twentyninth day of May One thousand nine hundred and fifty four (determinable as hereinafter mentioned) the sole and exclusive license and privilege to supply refreshments to the public admitted to premises situated at 81-83 Parriwi Road The Spit Mosman aforesaid and to carry on the business of a milk bar therein (hereinafter called the building) in such rooms as are shown in sketch contained in Schedule one annexed hereto and the right to use of toilet at rear and passage thereto PROVIDED ALWAYS that this License shall be revocable on the breach of any of the covenants and agreements on the part of the Licensee herein contained or in the event of the Special Lease from the Crown of which the building forms part being terminated by the Crown for any reason whatsoever but subject in the last mentioned event to the Licensee being compensated by the Licensor for any loss suffered AND IT IS HEREBY AGREED between the parties hereto as follows:—1. The Licensee shall during the continuance of this license pay to the Licensors the annual sum of Two hundred and eighty six pounds (£286) by equal weekly payments of Five Pounds Ten shillings (£5 10s. 0d.) in advance the first of such payment having been made on the Twentyninth day of May instant. 2. The Licensee shall pay for all gas and electricity consumed in connection with the Business carried on by her and also all telephone charges (if any) and shall pay one half of any excess water rates payable by the Licensors on the whole of the special lease. 3. The Licensee shall keep open her business at all times allowed by law and shall carry on the said business in a proper orderly manner and will not do or make or allow to be done or made any act or omission whereby any license granted or to be granted in respect of the said business shall become forfeited. 4. The Licensee shall not assign this license or any part thereof to any person or persons whomsoever without the written consent of the Licensors previously obtained but such consent shall not be unreasonably withheld. 5. Upon the expiration or sooner determination of this license the Licensee shall immediately give up possession of the said building occupied by her for the purpose of the said business and will execute and do all such assurances and things as may be requisite for transferring to or vesting in the Licensors or any person whom they may nominate any existing license or licenses in payment only of the proper proportion of the sum or sums paid for same. 6. The Licensors shall not be in any way responsible for any stock or other property of the Licensee which may be placed or left by them in the building of the Licensors pursuant to the license hereby given. 7. The Licensee shall in that part of the premises occupied by her be at liberty to carry on the business of providors of meals excluding cooked poultry fish oysters and cooked prawn with meals at table or bar and shall not sell prawn bait oysters in bottles fish and chips in bags raw fish lobsters or bait of any other variety or dressed poultry and also shall not sell cooking oils or dripping. 8. The Licensors shall not carry on any business which shall be the same as that carried on by the Licensee. 9. The Licensee shall have the option of continuing this license upon the same terms and conditions as are herein contained except this option provided the terms thereof have been duly carried out for a further term of five years upon giving notice in writing of their intention to exercise such option at least three months before the expiration of the term of years for which this License is hereby granted. 10. The License herein granted shall be deemed to be a lease as defined in the *Landlord and Tenant (Amendment) Act* 1948-1952".

Maria Radaich entered into possession of the premises pursuant to the deed and paid the weekly sums of £5 10s. In June 1956, she applied to the Fair Rents Board to have the fair rent determined under the *Landlord and Tenant (Amendment) Act*

1948 (N.S.W.). Before the Board, the Smiths argued that the deed created a licence, not a lease, so that the Board had no jurisdiction. The Board found that the deed created a lease, and determined the fair rent at £2 13s. per week. The Smiths appealed to the Supreme Court, where Brereton J. held that the Board had erred in law in holding that the deed created a lease and not merely a licence. Maria Radaich appealed to the High Court.]

McTIERNAN J. Neither party denies that all the terms of the agreement are embodied in their deed. The deed contains ten clauses. In form and matter, it resembles an ordinary lease; it contains, inter alia, a covenant that the "licensors" shall not unreasonably disallow an assignment of the "licence". Another clause, clause 9, confers an option of renewal. The words "lease", "lessor" and "lessee", however, are entirely excluded from the document, and the term "licence", and its appropriate mutations, are sedulously applied to the rights purported to be created. This fact is, of course, far from conclusive in favour of the respondents. It is the substance of the deed that matters. As Denning L.J. said in *Facchini v. Bryson* [1952] 1 T.L.R. 1386: "the parties cannot by the mere words of their contract turn it into something else. Their relationship is determined by the law and not by the label they choose to put on it": [1952] 1 T.L.R. 1386 at 1389, 1390. The true test of a supposed lease is whether exclusive possession is conferred upon the putative lessee. The validity of this test is confirmed by the judgment of the Court of Appeal in *Addiscombe Garden Estates Ltd v. Crabbe* [1958] 1 Q.B. 513 where Jenkins L.J. states: "We were also referred by Mr Blundell to *Errington v. Errington and Woods* [1952] 1 K.B. 290. In that case it was held that in very unusual circumstances a lady was a licensee, and entitled to remain in occupation of premises so long as she paid the instalments on a certain mortgage; and in the course of his judgment, Denning L.J. said: 'The test of exclusive possession is by no means decisive': [1952] 1 K.B. 290 at 297. I think that wide statement must be treated as qualified by his observations in *Facchini v. Bryson* [1952] 1 T.L.R. 1386 at 1389 and it seems to me that, save in exceptional cases of the kind mentioned by Denning L.J. in that case, the law remains that the fact of exclusive possession, if not decisive against the view that there is a mere licence, as distinct from a tenancy, is at all events a consideration of the first importance": [1958] 1 Q.B. 513 at 528.

It certainly appears that the "exclusive possession" test has survived intact the criticism it received in *Errington v. Errington and Woods* [1952] 1 K.B. 290. Parker and Pearce L.JJ. concurred in the judgment of Jenkins L.J., which is cited in part above.

What kind of possession did the present deed confer? Clause 5 is in these terms: "Upon the expiration or sooner determination of this licence the Licensee shall immediately give up possession of the said building occupied by her for the purpose of the said business and will execute and do all such assurances and things as may be requisite for transferring to or vesting in the Licensors or any person whom they may nominate any existing license or licenses in payment only of the proper proportion of the sum or sums paid for same."

The preamble recites that the respondents are "to carry on the business of a milk bar" in the subject premises. I think that such a business could only be carried on in reasonable convenience by persons having the exclusive possession of the premises. Nothing in the deed suggests that the parties did not recognise this as an implication of their agreement embodied therein. The premises, it appears, constituted what is often called a "lock-up shop". On several of the rent receipts given by the respondents, and which are in evidence, is the notation: "All window, door keys, locks, etc., lost or broken, shall be paid for by the tenant." The agreement contemplates that the so-called "licensee" is to have control of the premises, and of the persons entering them, during business hours and, indeed, at all other times.

I am satisfied that what was granted by this deed was an interest in the premises, therein described, which amounts in truth and in substance to a lease. Accordingly, these premises are subject to the determinations of the Fair Rents Board, under the provisions of the *Landlord and Tenant (Amendment) Act* 1948-1954 (N.S.W.). . . .

TAYLOR J. [His Honour considered some of the clauses in the deed, and continued:] So far I have not referred to the provisions of clause 10 of the deed and I do so now only for the purpose of dismissing them from consideration. That clause provided that "The licence herein granted shall be deemed to be a lease as defined in the *Landlord and Tenant (Amendment) Act* 1948-1952". Before the Supreme Court it was suggested that the word "not" had been omitted after the word "deemed" in this clause and there was some speculation as to whether this was so. But since the question whether a lease or a licence was granted must be determined having regard to the substance and effect of the instrument itself this is of no consequence and it is unnecessary to make any further reference to this problem.

I have no doubt that the substance and effect of the instrument in question here was to grant to the appellant a right to the exclusive possession of the subject premises upon the specified conditions for the prescribed term. The deed obviously contemplated that the appellant should have the right to occupy the premises for the purposes of her business and the business was to be carried on upon the premises at all times when they might lawfully be kept open. The character of the business was such that it could only be effectively carried on if the appellant had exclusive occupation and it seems clear that, even at times when they could not lawfully be kept open for the purposes of the business, the premises were to remain under her effective control. That being so it is inevitable that we should hold that the instrument created a leasehold interest and that at the material time the relationship of lessor and lessee existed between the parties.

It will be seen that I have treated the question in the case as concluded by the fact that the instrument conferred upon the appellant the right to exclusive possession for the specified term. And, it seems to me, that where, as in cases such as the present, it becomes necessary to identify a particular transaction as either a lease or a licence this factor must be decisive. The instrument either makes a grant of an interest in the land or it does not; if it does a leasehold interest is created and if it does not then nothing more than a licence is given. I do not, of course, overlook that an interest in land—for example, an easement or a profit à prendre—may be created without a grant of possession. Nor do I wish to assert that whenever a legal owner admits another to possession of his land a leasehold interest is necessarily created. For instance, possession given to a builder under the terms of a building contract does not create such an interest. What I have in mind is that where there is a grant of a right for a determinate period in respect of land and the question is posed whether the grant creates a lease or a licence the question may be resolved by considering whether the right in question is a right to exclusive possession.

In recent years, however, some doubt has been thrown upon the validity of this proposition and in *Errington v. Errington and Woods* [1952] 1 K.B. 290 Denning L.J. (as he then was) expressed the view that the test of exclusive possession is by no means decisive: at 297.

[Taylor J. referred to *Errington v. Errington, Facchini v. Bryson* and *Addiscombe Garden Estates Ltd v. Crabbe*, and continued:]

. . . [I]t must be taken as beyond doubt that in cases where there is a real contest between the issues of lease and licence the problem may be solved by considering whether the right which is conferred is a right to the exclusive possession of the property in question. This, however, does not deny that exceptional cases may arise in which it will be seen that a right to exclusive occupation or possession has been given without the grant of a leasehold interest. But if, as Denning L.J. himself agreed, the relationship created between the parties by a particular transaction is to be determined by its substance and not by its mere form, I am unable to see that the fact that a particular transaction may have been induced by ties of kinship, or by friendship or generosity could operate to bring it within this exceptional class. Such considerations cannot operate to transmute a lease into a licence or a licence into a lease. Indeed, one might venture to observe that until the effect of the transaction had been determined it would be impossible to appreciate the extent of the grantor's generosity or to know how far the ties of kinship or friendship had carried him. Upon examination it will, I think, be seen that this exceptional category is constituted by cases in which the facts do not give rise to a contest of the character abovementioned. The present case is clearly not such a case and the conclusion is inevitable that the relationship of landlord and tenant existed between the parties at the relevant time. Accordingly, the appeal should be allowed and the order of the Supreme Court set aside.

MENZIES J. The deed is called a "license" (sic) and the parties thereto "licensors" and "licensee", and it was argued that not only did these descriptions in a formal document show the intention of the parties but also that the substance of its provisions justified these descriptions. When looked at as a matter of both form and substance, the deed seems to me to speak with two voices, but what I regard as decisive in favour of its creating the relationship of landlord and tenant is that it gives the "licensee" the right of exclusive possession of the premises for the term granted thereby.

The conclusion that it does this flows from the provisions which require the appellant to conduct a cafe and milk bar in the shop and, upon the expiration or sooner determination of the "license", to "give up possession of the said building occupied by her for the purpose of the said business". . . . [The] obligations to occupy a shop, to carry on a business there that needs plant and stock, and to give up possession at the end of the term, taken together, seem to me to require the conclusion that the occupier has, during the term, the right of exclusive possession. Counsel for the respondents did press us with the differences between the deed before us and that under consideration in *Addiscombe Garden Estates Ltd v. Crabbe* [1958] 1 Q.B. 513 where the Court of Appeal decided that there was a lease rather than a licence because the grantees were entitled to exclusive occupation. The most significant difference relied upon was that there the grantees were to permit the owners to enter and inspect and it was pointed out that this was inconsistent with a general right to come upon the premises. This was, however, but one of the matters upon which the court relied and I do not think anything is to be gained by a point for point comparison of the deeds because the matters I have referred to satisfy me that it was intended that the appellant here should have the exclusive occupation of 83 Parriwi Road.

WINDEYER J. The distinction between a lease and a licence is clear. "A dispensation or licence properly passeth no interest, nor alters or transfers property in anything but only makes an action lawful which without it had been unlawful": *Thomas v. Sorrell* (1673) Vaughan 333; 124 E.R. 1098. Whether when one man is allowed to enter upon the land of another pursuant to a contract he does so as licensee or as tenant must, it has been said, "be in the last resort a question of intention", per Lord Greene M.R. in *Booker v. Palmer* [1942] 2 All E.R. 674 at 676. But intention to do what?—Not to give the transaction one label rather than another.—Not to escape the legal consequences of one relationship by professing that it is another. Whether the transaction creates a lease or a licence depends upon intention, only in the sense that it depends upon the nature of the right which the parties intend the person entering upon the land shall have in relation to the land. When they have put their transaction in writing this intention is to be ascertained by seeing what, in accordance with ordinary principles of interpretation, are the rights that the instrument creates. If those rights be the rights of a tenant, it does not avail either party to say that a tenancy was not intended. And conversely if a man be given only the rights of a licensee, it does not matter that he be called a tenant; he is a licensee. What then is the fundamental right which a tenant has that distinguishes his position from that of a licensee? It is an interest in land as distinct from a personal permission to enter the land and use it for some stipulated purpose or purposes. And how is it to be ascertained whether such an interest in land has been given? By seeing whether the grantee was given a *legal right of exclusive possession* of the land for a term or from year to year or for a life or lives. If he was, he is a tenant. And he cannot be other than a tenant, because a legal right of exclusive possession is a tenancy and the creation of such a right is a demise. To say that a man who has, by agreement with a landlord, a right of exclusive possession of land for a term is not a tenant is simply to contradict the first proposition by the second. A right of exclusive possession is secured by the right of a lessee to maintain ejectment and, after his entry, trespass. A reservation to the landlord, either by contract or statute, of a limited right of entry, as for example to view or repair, is, of course, not inconsistent with a grant of exclusive possession. Subject to such reservations, a tenant for a term or from year to year or for a life or lives can exclude his landlord as well as strangers from the demised premises. All this is long-established law: see Cole on *Ejectment* (1857), pp. 72, 73, 287, 458.

Recently some transactions from which in the past tenancies at will would have been inferred have been somewhat readily treated as creating only licences. And it has been said—especially in connection with family relationships, charity or hospitality—that allowing a person to have the exclusive possession of premises does not necessarily indicate a tenancy as distinct from a licence. These decisions are largely a by-product of rent restriction statutes and other legislation here and in England. They are all explicable if they mean, as I think they all do, that persons who are allowed to enjoy sole occupation in fact are not necessarily to be taken to have been given a right of exclusive possession in law. If there be any decision which goes further and states positively that a person legally entitled to exclusive possession for a term is a licensee and not a tenant, it should be disregarded, for it is self-contradictory and meaningless. We are not here concerned with the way in which a court of equity would control the parties in the exercise of legal rights, but with the simple question whether at law this document created a lease or a licence. And the proper touchstone still is: did it give the so-called licensee a legal right to the exclusive possession of the premises during the term? The question must of course, be resolved by considering the terms of the deed. But they are to be read in relation to the relevant surrounding circumstances, in particular the nature of the premises; for this deed, like any other instrument, is to be interpreted having regard to its subject matter. Here the subject premises are in fact a lock-up shop at The Spit, Mosman. . . . Turning then to its terms: its opening operative clause is expressed to be a grant for a five-year term of "the sole and exclusive license and privilege to supply refreshment to the public admitted to premises situate at 81-83 Parriwi Road, The Spit, Mosman, and to carry on the business of a milk bar therein in such rooms as are shown in the sketch contained in Schedule one annexed hereto and the right to use of toilet at rear and passage thereto". These words, standing by themselves, would create only an exclusive licence to supply refreshments, which is essentially different from an exclusive right to possession. But these opening words are not at all appropriate to the actual circumstances—and they do not stand by themselves. To describe the lock-up shop as "such rooms as are shown in sketch" is inapt, for one room, the shop, is what is shown by the sketch. And it is inapt to speak of a right to supply refreshments "to the public admitted to premises 81-83". And several of the later provisions are not only not appropriate to a mere licence to sell refreshments on the landlord's premises, but clearly suppose a grant of possession of specific premises to the appellant so that she can carry on a business there. It was argued that the deed follows an accepted precedent for the grant of a licence, having been taken from the form given in *Evatt and Beckenham's Conveyancing Precedents* (2nd ed., 1938), p. 542, which in turn is taken from a form in *The Conveyancer*, Vol. 10, p. 485. We have to decide what is the result of the words used by the parties, not what is the result which the draftsman of a form thought they would have. But what has happened is simply that the form has been used in circumstances for which it was never intended. In *The Conveyancer* it is described as a "Licence for the Exclusive Right of Supplying Refreshments within a Railway Station or Building"; and in *Evatt and Beckenham's Precedents* as "Licence for the Exclusive Right of Supplying Refreshments within a Building". Whether all its clauses are really appropriate to a licence to sell refreshments at a stall on a railway station or in the foyer of a theatre to persons admitted to such premises need not be considered. It is inapt to create a licence of a lock-up milk bar at The Spit. References in the deed to the licensee "giving up possession of the said building occupied by her", and to "that part of the premises occupied by her", are consistent with a tenancy, and in their setting are not really consistent with the supposed licence. The appellant is required to keep her business open during business hours. Clearly she could shut it at other times. I imagine all concerned would have been astounded if they had been told that the appellant had no right to exclude persons from her shop; that the respondent might, if he wished, licence other people to carry on any activity there other than the sale of refreshments, provided their presence did not prevent her selling refreshments or conducting the milk bar; and that, although she might lock the shop up at night and on holidays, the respondents could not only enter it themselves whenever they wished but could admit as many persons as they chose, provide them with keys and license them to use the premises in the absence of the appellant for any purpose of pleasure or business they liked, provided only that they did not sell refreshments. If the matter is to be tested by the apparent intention of the parties arising from the circumstances, that clearly was not their intention. If it is to be tested, as I consider it is, by their intention as reflected in the words of their deed with knowledge of the nature of the subject premises, then, in the words of Blackburn J. (as he then was) in *Roads v. Overseers of Trumpington* (1870) L.R. 6 Q.B. 56 "the whole nature of the agreement shews that the appellant was intended to have exclusive possession of the land": (1870) L.R. 6 Q.B., at 63. The use in what purports to be the principal provision of the deed of words taken from a precedent designed for another purpose cannot outweigh its total effect.

The final clause of the deed may, I think, be ignored. In the Supreme Court the learned judge thought that the word "not" must have been dropped out. But whether the clause be read with "not" in or out, makes, I think, no difference. Such a provision could not make the deed a lease if it were not one, and it cannot prevent it being a lease if it be one.

[The concurring judgment of Dixon C.J. has been omitted.]

Appeal allowed.

NOTES AND QUESTIONS

1. Is there any inconsistency between the approach taken by the High Court in this case and that taken by the Privy Council in *Isaac's* case? It has been assumed by the courts of the Australian States that there is an inconsistency, and that the High Court's approach is to be followed: see, for example *Joseph Abraham Pty Ltd v. Emelin* (1960) 77 W.N. (N.S.W.) 903; *Robert John Pty Ltd v. Fostar's Shoes Pty Ltd* (1963) 80 W.N. (N.S.W.) 408 at 411; *Danita Investments Pty Ltd v. Rockstrom* (1962) 80 W.N. (N.S.W.) 1287 at 1289; *Butcher v. Bowen* (1963) 80 W.N. (N.S.W.) 1520 at 1522-1523; *Commonwealth of Australia v. K. N. Harris Pty Ltd* [1965] N.S.W.R. 63 at 70; *Lapham v. Orange City Council (No. 2)* (1968) 88 W.N. (N.S.W.) 309 at 314; *Hayes v. Seymour-Johns* (1983) C.C.H. N.S.W. Conv. R. 55-124; cf. *Cornish v. Lloyd* (1961) 78 W.N. (N.S.W.) 639 at 641-642 and *Frieze v. Unger* [1960] V.R. 230 at 234-238.

In the few subsequent cases in the High Court in which the question of the distinction between a lease and licence has arisen, the Court has applied the approach adopted in *Radaich v. Smith* (1959) 101 C.L.R. 209. In *Chelsea Investments Pty Ltd v. Commissioner of Taxation* (1966) 115 C.L.R. 1 at 7, Windeyer J. expressed the view that the right to exclusive possession as against all others, including the landlord, "is the very essence of tenancy", citing *Radaich v. Smith* (although not referring to *Isaac's* case). Then, in *Claude Neon Ltd v. Melbourne and Metropolitan Board of Works* (1969) 43 A.L.J.R. 69 at 71 Kitto J. (with whom Windeyer J. agreed) said:

> The law as to the difference between a lease, which confers an interest in land, and a licence, which does not, was considered by the Court in *Radaich v. Smith* (1959) 101 C.L.R. 209, and I need do no more here than say that the enquiry must be whether the substance and effect of the documents in question was to grant a right of exclusive possession.

Kitto J. did not refer to *Isaac's* case [1960] 1 W.L.R. 239. In *Goldsworthy Mining Ltd v. Federal Commissioner of Taxation* (1972) 128 C.L.R. 199 at 212, Mason J. (sitting at first instance) said that whether a "lease" of an area of the sea-bed for dredging purposes was a lease rather than a licence was a question "to be answered initially by reference to the test: Does it confer on the appellant a right of exclusive possession?", citing *Radaich v. Smith*. His Honour also expressed the opinion that *Isaac's* case was "not inconsistent with" *Radaich v. Smith*. Mason J.'s decision was affirmed on other grounds, (1975) 132 C.L.R. 463; see also *Dampier Mining Co. Ltd v Commissioner of Taxation (Cth)* (1981) 55 A.L.J.R. 497 at 504-505.

2. In *Heslop v. Burns* [1974] 1 W.L.R. 1241, the defendants (a married couple) had become friends with, and offered companionship to, T. T allowed the defendants to reside in a succession of cottages owned by him, requiring no rent and paying the rates himself. T visited the defendants every day, was generous in offering them financial assistance from time to time, and had on more than one occasion said to the defendants that after his death the house they were then occupying would be theirs. On T's death, T's executors brought an action for possession of the house in which the defendants were then residing, claiming that the defendants' only right to occupy the premises was under a personal licence which had terminated on T's death. The defendants argued that they were tenants at will, and that the right to evict them had been defeated by the *Limitation Act* 1939 (U.K.). The Court of Appeal held that the defendants were licensees only, because there was no intention to enter legal relationships, let alone any intention to create in the defendants any interest in the land. Stamp L.J. said (at 1246-1247):

> In the course of the debate we were referred to a number of passages in judgments where the effect of exclusive possession in the determination of the question "tenancy or licence?" has been discussed. As Somervell L.J. indicated in *Cobb v. Lane* [1952] 1 All E.R. 1199 at 1200, the expression "exclusive possession" in relation to the occupier of a property may be used in more than one sense. It may, as I see it, be used to mean that, as a factual matter, the occupant, alone or together with his family, occupies the premises and does not share them with any other person. Such a situation is not inconsistent with the occupation being enjoyed under a mere licence. Or the expression may be used to mean that the occupant has a right to exclude the owner from the premises. I think it must have been in the former sense that Lord Denning M.R. used that

expression in *Shell-Mex and B.P. Ltd v. Manchester Garages Ltd* [1971] 1 W.L.R. 612 at 616 in dealing with the argument of Mr Dillon: for there the occupant had by the very terms of the contract no right to exclude the owner; and possibly he used it in that same sense in the earlier case of *Errington v. Errington and Woods* [1952] 1 K.B. 290. Where the expression is used in the latter sense as describing a situation where the occupier has the right to exclude the owner it is clearly more difficult to reconcile it with the existence of a mere licence to occupy. But rights do not arise in vacuo and before concluding that an occupant was intended to be in a position to exclude the owner from the premises, one must, as I see it, ask the question: did the parties intend that the occupant should have such a right? It may, I think, be that, coming to the conclusion that that indeed was the intention of the parties, the court may usually be constrained to hold that what was intended was a tenancy at will and not a mere licence to occupy. It is, however, not in my judgment necessary to express any concluded view on this aspect of the matter. The deceased here could, as Mrs Burns remarked, "come into the house any time he wanted"; and in a conversation to which I have not hitherto referred with the plaintiff's representative when he came to value the property for the purposes of probate after the death of the deceased, she told him that the deceased regarded the house as "his second home". The home was not to be the defendants' castle but the house in which he allowed them to live.

In the circumstances in which the deceased let the defendants into occupation, I find it impossible to infer that he intended them to have the right to exclude him; for in my judgment the circumstances and the relationship between the parties were wholly inconsistent with such a view of his intentions.

3. In construing whether an agreement creates a lease or a licence, the whole of the agreement must be looked at; no part can be read in isolation. Some clauses, however, may point clearly in one direction: see, for example, the discussion in *I.C.I. Alkali (Aust.) Pty Ltd (in liq.) v. Commissioner of Taxation* [1977] V.R. 393 at 396-400; affirmed (1979) 53 A.L.J.R. 220; noted (1977) 121 Sol. J. 804. For example, provisions in a document permitting the grantor to enter and inspect the premises, to enter and determine on non-payment of fees, or covenanting for quiet enjoyment, would point to the existence of a lease (*Addiscombe Garden Estates Ltd v. Crabbe* [1958] 1 Q.B. 513 at 522, 529), as would a clause imposing restrictions on the right to assign or sub-let: *Barnes v. Barratt* [1970] 2 Q.B. 657 at 669. On the other hand, a clause which requires the occupier not to impede the grantor's "rights of possession and control" of the premises would point to a licence (*Shell-Mex and B.P. Ltd v. Manchester Garages Ltd* [1971] 1 W.L.R. 612 at 616), as would a clause reserving to the grantor the right to use the premises "in common with" the grantee (*Somma v. Hazelhurst* [1978] 1 W.L.R. 1014 at 1027-1028; *Aldrington Garages Ltd v. Fielder* (1979) 37 P. & C.R. 461; cf. *Walsh v. Griffiths-Jones* [1978] 2 All E.R. 1002; *Varella v. Marsicovetere* [1954] V.L.R. 550), although previous decisions in this area must now be viewed with caution in the light of the decision of the House of Lords in *Street v. Mountford* [1985] A.C. 809, extracted below.

STREET v. MOUNTFORD

House of Lords [1985] A.C. 809

[By an agreement dated 7 March 1983, Mr Street granted to Mrs Mountford the right to occupy certain rooms. The terms of the agreement are set out in the judgment of Lord Templeman, extracted below. Mrs Mountford obtained an order in the County Court that the agreement created a tenancy (which was protected by the Rent Acts). On appeal, the Court of Appeal held that the agreement created only a licence (which was not protected by the Rent Acts). On appeal to the House of Lords:]

LORD TEMPLEMAN. A licence in connection with land while entitling the licensee to use the land for the purposes authorised by the licence does not create an estate in the land. If the agreement dated 7 March 1983 created a licence for Mrs Mountford to occupy the premises, she did not acquire any estate in the land. If the agreement is a licence then Mrs Mountford's right of occupation is not protected by the Rent Acts. Hence the practical importance of distinguishing between a tenancy and a licence.

In the course of argument, nearly every clause of the agreement dated 7 March 1983 was relied upon by the appellant as indicating a lease and by the respondent as indicating a licence. The agreement, in full, was in these terms: "I Mrs Wendy Mountford agree to take from the owner Roger Street the single furnished room number 5 and 6 at 5 St Clements Gardens, Boscombe, Bournemouth, commencing 7 March 1983 at a licence fee of £37 per week.

I understand that the right to occupy the above room is conditional on the strict observance of the following rules:

1. No paraffin stoves, or other than the supplied form of heating, is allowed in the room.

2. No-one but the above-named person may occupy or sleep in the room without prior permission, and this personal licence is not assignable.

3. The owner (or his agent) has the right at all times to enter the room to inspect its condition, read and collect money from meters, carry out maintenance works, install or replace furniture or for any other reasonable purpose.

4. All rooms must be kept in a clean and tidy condition.

5. All damage and breakages must be paid for or replaced at once. An initial deposit equivalent to 2 weeks' licence fee will be refunded on termination of the licence subject to deduction for all damage or other breakages or arrears of licence fee, or retention towards the cost of any necessary possession proceedings.

6. No nuisance or annoyance to be caused to the other occupiers. In particular, all music played after midnight to be kept low so as not to disturb occupiers of other rooms.

7. No children or pets allowed under any circumstances whatsoever.

8. Prompt payment of the licence fee must be made every Monday in advance without fail.

9. If the licence fee or any part of it shall be seven days in arrear or if the occupier shall be in breach of any of the other terms of this agreement or if (except by arrangement) the room is left vacant or unoccupied, the owner may re-enter the room and this licence shall then immediately be terminated (without prejudice to all other rights and remedies of the owner).

10. This licence may be terminated by 14 days' written notice given to the occupier at any time by the owner or his agent, or by the same notice by the occupier to the owner or his agent.

Occupier's signature

Owner/agent's signature

Date 7 March 1983

I understand and accept that a licence in the above form does not and is not intended to give me a tenancy protected under the Rent Acts.

Occupier's signature."

On behalf of Mrs Mountford her counsel, Mr Hicks Q.C., seeks to reaffirm and re-establish the traditional view that an occupier of land for a term at a rent is a tenant providing the occupier is granted exclusive possession. It is conceded on behalf of Mr Street that the agreement dated 7 March 1983 granted exclusive possession to Mrs Mountford. The traditional view that the grant of exclusive possession for a term at a rent creates a tenancy is consistent with the elevation of a tenancy into an estate in land. The tenant possessing exclusive possession is able to exercise the rights of an owner of land, which is in the real sense his land albeit temporarily and subject to certain restrictions. A tenant armed with exclusive possession can keep out strangers and keep out the landlord unless the landlord is exercising limited rights reserved to him by the tenancy agreement to enter and view and repair. A licensee lacking exclusive possession can in no sense call the land his own and cannot be said to own any estate in the land. The licence does not create an estate in the land to which it relates but only makes an act lawful which would otherwise be unlawful.

On behalf of Mr Street his counsel, Mr Goodhart Q.C., relies on recent authorities which, he submits, demonstrate that an occupier granted exclusive possession for a term at a rent may nevertheless be a licensee if, in the words of Slade L.J. in the present case [1985] 49 P. & C.R. 324 at 332: "there is manifested the clear intention of both parties that the rights granted are to be merely those of a personal right of occupation and not those of a tenant." In the present case, it is submitted, the provisions of the agreement dated 7 March 1983 and in particular clauses 2, 4, 7 and 9 and the express declaration at the foot of the agreement manifest the clear intention of both parties that the rights granted are to be those of a personal nature and not those of a tenant.

My Lords, there is no doubt that the traditional distinction between a tenancy and a licence of land lay in the grant of land for a term at a rent with exclusive possession. In some cases it was not clear at first sight whether exclusive possession was in fact granted. For example, an owner of land could grant a licence to cut and remove standing timber. Alternatively the owner could grant a tenancy of the land with the right to cut and remove standing timber during the term of tenancy. The grant of rights relating to standing timber therefore required careful consideration in order to decide whether the grant conferred exclusive possession of the land for a term at a rent and was therefore a tenancy or whether it merely conferred a bare licence to remove the timber.

In *Glenwood Lumber Co. Ltd v. Phillips* [1904] A.C. 405, the Crown in exercise of statutory powers "licensed" the respondents to hold an area of land for the purpose of cutting and removing timber for the term of 21 years at an annual rent. Delivering the advice of the Judicial Committee of the Privy Council, Lord Davey said (at 408-409): "The appellants contended that this instrument conferred only a licence to cut timber and carry it away, and did not give the respondent any right of occupation or interest in the land itself. Having regard to the provisions of the Act under the powers of which it was executed and to the language of the document itself, their Lordships cannot adopt this view of the construction or effect of it. In the so-called licence itself it is called indifferently a licence and a demise, but in the Act it is spoken of as a lease, and the holder of it is described as the lessee. It is not, however, a question of words but of substance. If the effect of the instrument is to give the holder an exclusive right of occupation of the land, though subject to certain reservations or to a restriction of the purposes for which it may be used, it is in law a demise of the land itself. By [the Act] it is enacted that the lease shall vest in the lessee the right to take and keep exclusive possession of the lands described therein subject to the conditions in the Act provided or referred to, and the lessee is empowered (amongst other things) to bring any actions or suits against any party unlawfully in possession of any land so leased, and to prosecute all trespassers thereon. The operative part and habendum in the licence is framed in apt language to carry out the intention so expressed in the Act. And their Lordships have no doubt that the effect of the so-called licence was to confer a title to the land itself on the respondent."

This was a case in which the court after careful consideration of the purposes of the grant, the terms of the grant and the surrounding circumstances, came to the conclusion that the grant conferred exclusive possession and was therefore a tenancy.

A contrary conclusion was reached in *Taylor v. Caldwell* (1863) 3 B. & S. 826; 122 E.R. 309 in which the defendant agreed to let the plaintiff have the use of the Surrey Gardens and Music Hall on four specified days giving a series of four concerts and day and night fetes at the gardens and hall on those days, and the plaintiff agreed to take the gardens and the hall and to pay £100 for each day. Blackburn J. said (at 832): "The parties inaccurately call this a 'letting', and the money to be paid a 'rent', but the whole agreement is such as to show that the defendants were to retain the possession of the hall and gardens so that there was to be no demise of them, and that the contract was merely to give the plaintiffs the use of them on those days."

That was a case where the court after considering the purpose of the grant, the terms of the grant and the surrounding circumstances came to the conclusion that the grantee was not entitled to exclusive possession but only to use the land for limited purposes and was therefore a licensee.

In the case of residential accommodation there is no difficulty in deciding whether the grant confers exclusive possession. An occupier of residential accommodation at a rent for a term is either a lodger or a tenant. The occupier is a lodger if the landlord provides attendance or services which require the landlord or his servants to exercise unrestricted access to and use of the premises. A lodger is entitled to live in the premises but cannot call the place his own. In *Allan v. Liverpool Overseers* (1874) L.R. 9 Q.B. 180 at 191-192 Blackburn J. said: "A lodger in a house, although he has the exclusive use of rooms in the house, in the sense that nobody else is to be there, and though his goods are stowed there, yet he is not in exclusive occupation in that sense, because the landlord is there for the purpose of being able, as landlords commonly do in the case of lodgings, to have his own servants to look after the house and the furniture, and has retained to himself the occupation, though he has agreed to give the exclusive enjoyment of the occupation to the lodger."

If on the other hand residential accommodation is granted for a term at a rent with exclusive possession, the landlord providing neither attendance nor services, the grant is a tenancy; any express reservation to the landlord of limited rights to enter and view the state of the premises and to repair and maintain the premises only serves to emphasise the fact that the grantee is entitled to exclusive possession and is a tenant. In the present case it is conceded that Mrs Mountford is entitled to exclusive possession and is not a lodger. Mr Street provided neither attendance nor services and only reserved the limited rights of inspection and maintenance and the like set forth in clause 3 of the agreement. On the traditional view of the matter, Mrs Mountford not being a lodger must be a tenant.

There can be no tenancy unless the occupier enjoys exclusive possession; but an occupier who enjoys exclusive possession is not necessarily a tenant. He may be owner in fee simple, a trespasser, a mortgagee in possession, an object of charity or a service occupier. To constitute a tenancy the occupier must be granted exclusive possession for a fixed or periodic term certain in consideration of a premium or periodical payments. The grant may be express, or may be inferred where the owner accepts weekly or other periodical payments from the occupier.

Occupation by service occupier may be eliminated. A service occupier is a servant who occupies his master's premises in order to perform his duties as a servant. In those circumstances the possession and occupation of the servant is treated as the possession and occupation of the master and the relationship of landlord and tenant is not created: see *Mayhew v. Suttle* (1854) 4 El. & Bl. 347; 119 E.R. 133. The test is whether the servant requires the premises he occupies in order the better to perform his duties as a servant. . . .

The cases on which Mr Goodhart relies begin with *Booker v. Palmer* [1942] 2 All E.R. 674. The owner of a cottage agreed to allow a friend to install an evacuee in the cottage rent free for the duration of the war. The Court of Appeal held that there was no intention on the part of the owner to enter into legal relationships with the evacuee. Lord Greene M.R. said (at 677): "To suggest there is an intention there to create a relationship of landlord and tenant appears to me to be quite impossible. There is one golden rule which is of very general application, namely, that the law does not impute intention to enter into legal relationships where the circumstances and the conduct of the parties negative any intention of the kind. It seems to me that this is a clear example of the application of that rule."

The observations of Lord Greene M.R. were not directed to the distinction between a contractual tenancy and a contractual licence. The conduct of the parties (not their professed intentions) indicated that they did not intend to contract at all.

In the present case, the agreement dated 7 March 1983 professed an intention by both parties to create a licence and their belief that they had in fact created a licence. It was submitted on behalf of Mr Street that the court cannot in these circumstances decide that the agreement created a tenancy without interfering with the freedom of contract enjoyed by both parties. My Lords, Mr Street enjoyed freedom to offer Mrs Mountford the right to occupy the rooms comprised in the agreement on such lawful terms as Mr Street pleased. Mrs Mountford enjoyed freedom to negotiate with Mr Street to obtain different terms. Both parties enjoyed freedom to contract or not to contract and both parties exercised that freedom by contracting on the terms set forth in the written agreement and on no other terms. But the consequences in law of the agreement, once concluded, can only be determined by consideration of the effect of the agreement. If the agreement satisfied all the requirements of a tenancy, then the agreement produced a tenancy and the parties cannot alter the effect of the agreement by insisting that they only created a licence. The manufacture of a five-pronged implement for manual digging results in a fork even if the manufacturer, unfamiliar with the English language, insists that he intended to make and has made a spade.

It was also submitted that in deciding whether the agreement created a tenancy or a licence, the court should ignore the Rent Acts. If Mr Street has succeeded, where owners have failed these past 70 years, in driving a coach and horses through the Rent Acts, he must be left to enjoy the benefit of his ingenuity unless and until Parliament intervenes. I accept that the Rent Acts are irrelevant to the problem of determining the legal effect of the rights granted by the agreement. Like the professed intention of the parties, the Rent Acts cannot alter the effect of the agreement.

In *Marcroft Wagons Ltd v. Smith* [1951] 2 K.B. 496 the daughter of a deceased tenant who lived with her mother claimed to be a statutory tenant by succession and the landlords asserted that the daughter had no rights under the Rent Acts and was a trespasser. The landlords expressly refused to accept the daughter's claim but accepted rent from her while they were considering the position. . . .

In that case, as in *Booker v. Palmer* [1942] 2 All E.R. 674 the court deduced from the conduct of the parties that they did not intend to contract at all.

[His Lordship then referred to *Errington v. Errington* [1952] 1 K.B. 290, extracted above p. 500, and continued:]

In *Errington v. Errington* [1952] 1 K.B. 290 and in the cases cited by Denning L.J. at 297 there were exceptional circumstances which negatived the prima facie intention to create a tenancy, notwithstanding that the occupier enjoyed exclusive occupation. The intention to create a tenancy was negatived if the parties did not intend to enter into legal relationships at all, or where the relationship between the parties was that of vendor and purchaser, master and service occupier, or where the owner, a requisitioning authority, had no power to grant a tenancy. These exceptional circumstances are not to be found in the present case where there has been the lawful, independent and voluntary grant of exclusive possession for a term at a rent.

If the observations of Denning L.J. are applied to the facts of the present case it may fairly be said that the circumstances negative any intention to create a mere licence. Words alone do not suffice. Parties cannot turn a tenancy into a licence merely by calling it one. The circumstances and the conduct of the parties show that what was intended was that the occupier should be granted exclusive possession at a rent for a term with a corresponding interest in the land which created a tenancy.

[His Lordship then discussed the following cases: *Cobb v. Lane* [1952] 1 All E.R. 1199, referred to above p. 503, note 1, which he characterised as an example of conduct negativing any intention to enter into a contract; *Facchini v. Bryson* [1952] 1 T.L.R. 1386, referred to above p. 504, note 3; *Murray Bull & Co. Ltd v. Murray* [1953] 1 Q.B. 211, which he regarded as wrongly decided; and *Addiscombe Garden Estates Ltd v. Crabbe* [1958] 1 Q.B. 513, referred to above p. 504, note 3. He continued:]

Exclusive possession is of first importance in considering whether an occupier is a tenant; exclusive possession is not decisive because an occupier who enjoys exclusive possession is not necessarily a tenant. The occupier may be a lodger or service occupier or fall within the other exceptional categories mentioned by Denning L.J. in *Errington v. Errington and Woods* [1952] 1 K.B. 290.

In *Isaac v. Hotel de Paris Ltd* [1960] 1 W.L.R. 239 an employee who managed a night bar in a hotel for his employer company which held a lease of the hotel negotiated "subject to contract" to complete the purchase of shares in the company and to be allowed to run the nightclub for his own benefit if he paid the head rent payable by the company for the hotel. In the expectation that the negotiations "subject to contract" would ripen into a binding agreement, the employee was allowed to run the nightclub and he paid the company's rent. When negotiations broke down the employee claimed unsuccessfully to be a tenant of the hotel company. The circumstances in which the employee was allowed to occupy the premises showed that the hotel company never intended to accept him as a tenant and that he was fully aware of that fact. This was a case, consistent with the authorities cited by Lord Denning in giving the advice of the Judicial Committee of the Privy Council, in which the parties did not intend to enter into contractual relationships unless and until the negotiations "subject to contract" were replaced by a binding contract.

In *Abbeyfield (Harpenden) Society Ltd v. Woods* [1968] 1 W.L.R. 374 the occupier of a room in an old people's home was held to be a licensee and not a tenant. Lord Denning M.R. said (at 376): "The modern cases show that a man may be a licensee even though he has exclusive possession, even though the word 'rent' is used, and even though the word 'tenancy' is used. The court must look at the agreement as a whole and see whether a tenancy really was intended. In this case there is, besides the room, the provision of services, meals, a resident housekeeper, and such like. The whole arrangement was so personal in nature that the proper inference is that he was a licensee."

As I understand the decision in the *Abbeyfield* case the court came to the conclusion that the occupier was a lodger and was therefore a licensee, not a tenant.

In *Shell-Mex and B.P. Ltd v. Manchester Garages Ltd* [1971] 1 W.L.R. 612 the Court of Appeal after carefully examining an agreement whereby the defendant was allowed to use a petrol company's filling station for the purposes of selling petrol, came to the conclusion that the agreement did not grant exclusive possession to the defendant who was therefore a licensee. At 615 Lord Denning M.R. in considering whether the transaction was a licence or a tenancy said: "Broadly speaking, we have to see whether it is a personal privilege given to a person (in which case it is a licence), or whether it grants an interest in land (in which case it is a tenancy). At one time it used to be thought that exclusive possession was a decisive factor. But that is not so. It depends on broader considerations altogether. Primarily on whether it is personal in its nature or not: see *Errington v. Errington and Woods* [1952] 1 K.B. 290."

In my opinion the agreement was only "personal in its nature" and created "a personal privilege" if the agreement did not confer the right to exclusive possession of the filling station. No other test for distinguishing between a contractual tenancy and a contractual licence apears to be understandable or workable.

[His Lordship then referred to *Heslop v. Burns* [1974] 1 W.L.R. 1241, discussed above p. 511, note 2, and continued:]

In *Marchant v. Charters* [1977] 1 W.L.R. 1181 a bedsitting room was occupied on terms that the landlord cleaned the rooms daily and provided clean linen each week. It was held by the Court of Appeal that the occupier was a licensee and not a tenant. The decision in the case is sustainable on the grounds that the occupier was a lodger and did not enjoy exclusive possession. But Lord Denning M.R. said (at 1185): "What is the test to see whether the occupier of one room in a house is a tenant or a licensee? It does not depend on whether he or she has exclusive possession or not. It does not depend on whether the room is furnished or not. It does not depend on whether the occupation is permanent or temporary. It does not depend on the label which the parties put upon it. All these are factors which may influence the decision but none of them is conclusive. All the circumstances have to be worked out. Eventually the answer depends on the nature and quality of the occupancy. Was it intended that the occupier should have a stake in the room or did he have only permission for himself personally to occupy the room, whether under a contract or not? In which case he is a licensee."

But in my opinion in order to ascertain the nature and quality of the occupancy and to see whether the occupier has or has not a stake in the room or only permission for himself personally to occupy, the court must decide whether upon its true construction the agreement confers on the occupier exclusive possession. If exclusive possession at a rent for a term does not constitute a tenancy then the distinction between a contractual tenancy and a contractual licence of land becomes wholly unidentifiable.

In *Somma v. Hazelhurst* [1978] 1 W.L.R. 1014, a young unmarried couple H and S occupied a double bedsitting room for which they paid a weekly rent. The landlord did not provide services or attendance and the couple were not lodgers but tenants enjoying exclusive possession. But the Court of Appeal did not ask themselves whether H and S were lodgers or tenants and did not draw the correct conclusion from the fact that H and S enjoyed exclusive possession. The Court of Appeal were diverted from the correct inquiries by the fact that the landlord obliged H and S to enter into separate agreements and reserved power to determine each agreement separately. The landlord also insisted that the room should not in form be let to either H or S or to both H and S but that each should sign an agreement to share the room in common with such other persons as the landlord might from time to time nominate. The sham nature of this obligation would have been only slightly more obvious if H and S had been married or if the room had been furnished with a double bed instead of two single beds. If the landlord had served notice on H to leave and had required S to share the room with a strange man, the notice would only have been a disguised notice to quit on both H and S. The room was let and taken as residential accommodation with exclusive possession in order that H and S might live together in undisturbed quasi-connubial bliss making weekly payments. The agreements signed by H and S constituted the grant to H and S jointly of exclusive possession at a rent for a term for the purposes for which the room was taken and the agreement therefore created a tenancy. Although the Rent Acts must not be allowed to alter or influence the construction of an agreement, the court should, in my opinion, be astute to detect and frustrate sham devices and artificial transactions whose only object is to disguise the grant of a tenancy and to evade the Rent Acts. I would disapprove of the decision in this case that H and S were only licensees and for the same reason would disapprove of the decision in *Aldrington Garages Ltd v. Fielder* (1978) 37 P. & C.R. 461 and *Sturolson & Co. v. Weniz* (1984) 272 E.G. 326.

In the present case the Court of Appeal (49 P. & C.R. 324) held that the agreement dated 7 March 1983 only created a licence. Slade L.J. (at 329) accepted that the agreement and in particular clause 3 of the agreement "shows that the right to occupy the premises conferred on the defendant was intended as an exclusive right of occupation, in that it was thought necessary to give a special and express power to the plaintiff to enter. . .". Before your Lordships it was conceded that the agreement conferred the right of exclusive possession on Mrs Mountford. Even without clause 3 the result would have been the same. By the agreement Mrs Mountford was granted the right to occupy residential accommodation. The landlord did not provide any services or attendance. It was plain that Mrs Mountford was not a lodger. Slade L.J. proceeded to analyse all the provisions of the agreement, not for the purpose of deciding whether his finding of exclusive possession was correct, but for the purpose of assigning some of the provisions of the agreement to the category of terms which he thought are usually to be found in a tenancy agreement and of assigning other provisions to the category of terms which he thought are usually to be found in a licence. Slade L.J. may or may not have been right that in a letting of a furnished room it was "most unusual to find a provision in a tenancy agreement obliging the tenant to keep his rooms in a 'tidy condition' ": at 329. If Slade L.J was right about this and other provisions there is still no logical method of evaluating the results of his survey. Slade L.J. reached the conclusion that "the agreement bears all the hallmarks of a licence rather than a tenancy save for the one important feature of exclusive occupation'': at 329. But in addition to the hallmark of exclusive occupation of residential accommodation there were the hallmarks of weekly payments for a periodical term. Unless these three hallmarks are decisive, it really becomes impossible to distinguish a contractual tenancy from a contractual licence save by reference to the professed intention of the parties or by the judge awarding marks for drafting. Slade L.J. was finally impressed by the statement at the foot of the agreement by Mrs Mountford: "I understand and accept that a licence in the above form does not and is not intended to give me a tenancy protected under the Rent Acts." Slade L.J. said (at 330): "it seems to me that, if the defendant is to displace the express statement of intention embodied in the declaration, she must show that the declaration was either a deliberate sham or at least an inaccurate statement of what was the true substance of the real transaction agreed between the parties". My Lords, the only intention which is relevant is the intention demonstrated by the agreement to grant exclusive possession for a term at a rent. Sometimes it may be difficult to discover whether, on the true construction of an agreement, exclusive possession is conferred. Sometimes it may appear from the surrounding circumstances that there was no intention to create legal relationships. Sometimes it may appear from the surrounding circumstances that the right to exclusive possession is referable to a legal relationship other than a tenancy. Legal relationships to which the grant of exclusive possession might be referable and which would or might negative the grant of an estate or interest in the land include occupancy under a contract for the sale of the land, occupancy pursuant to a contract of employment or occupancy referable to the holding of an office. But where as in the present case the only circumstances are that residential accommodation is offered and accepted with exclusive possession for a term at a rent, the result is a tenancy.

The position was well summarised by Windeyer J. sitting in the High Court of Australia in *Radaich v. Smith* (1959) 101 C.L.R. 209 at 222.

[His Lordship quoted from the portion of the judgment of Windeyer J., extracted above p. 509, beginning "What then is the fundamental right which a tenant has" and concluding with the reference to Cole on *Ejectment*. He concluded:]

My Lords, I gratefully adopt the logic and the language of Windeyer J. Henceforth the courts which deal with these problems will, save in exceptional circumstances, only be concerned to inquire whether as a result of an agreement relating to residential accommodation the occupier is a lodger or a tenant. In the present case I am satisfied that Mrs Mountford is a tenant, that the appeal should be allowed, that the order of the Court of Appeal should be set aside and that the respondent should be ordered to pay the costs of the appellant here and below.

[Lords Scarman, Keith of Kinkel, Bridge of Harwich and Brightman agreed.]

Appeal allowed.

NOTES AND QUESTIONS

1. Counsel for Mr Street conceded that Mrs Mountford had been granted exclusive possession of the premises. Was this concession necessary, and would the result have been different if it had not been made?

2. Mr Street was a solicitor and had deliberately drafted the agreement so as to take advantage of the law as it was then perceived to be. His views on the case will be found in Street, "Coach and Horse Trip Cancelled?: Rent Act Avoidance after Street v. Mountford" [1985] Conv. 328.

LEWIS v. BELL

New South Wales Court of Appeal (1985) 1 N.S.W.L.R. 731

[The Australian Jockey Club (A.J.C.), through the chairman of its committee, Mr Bell, granted to the defendant (the appellant in these proceedings Mr Lewis) certain rights in respect of a number of horse stables and staff living accommodation near Randwick Racecourse, Sydney. The rights were set out in a document made on 1 October 1983, the salient provisions of which are repeated in the judgment of Mahoney J.A., extracted below. In November 1984 the A.J.C. gave notice to the defendant terminating the rights he held under the document and took proceedings to recover possession of the premises. Miles J. held that the A.J.C. were entitled to recover possession. The defendant appealed to the Court of Appeal on two grounds: (1) that the document created a lease and the lease had not been effectively terminated by what the A.J.C. had done; and (2) that if the document created only a licence, the licence had not been effectively terminated by what the A.J.C. had done.]

MAHONEY J.A. The document in question commences with the words "This Licence Agreement". It recites that "the A.J.C. controls the premises described in the First Schedule hereto" and that "the A.J.C. has agreed to allow the trainer to use the said premises on the terms and conditions hereinafter contained". The following clauses of the document set forth those terms and conditions.

Clause 1 is in the following terms: "1. The A.J.C. and the trainer agree that this agreement shall operate for a term of one month from 1 October 1983, and thereafter from month to month providing however and it is hereby agreed that it may be determined at any time by either party giving to the other party one month's notice of such determination in writing save that it shall be automatically determined without the necessity for notice if the trainer is disqualified or suspended provided that the committee in its absolute discretion may permit the trainer the use of the premises on such terms and conditions as may be laid down by the committee."

Clause 2 provides that: "The monthly fee payable in advance by the trainer to the A.J.C. on the first working day of each month for the use of the premises shall be the amount specified in the Second Schedule hereto."

Clause 3 obliges the trainer "to pay interest on any unpaid rent" at the rate specified.

The agreement obliges the trainer to repair damage done to the premises and to keep them and surrounding areas in good and sanitary order and condition: clause 4; to control all horses kept on the premises: clause 5; and to give up the premises in good order and condition upon termination of the agreement: clause 6. Provision is also made in respect of the care of the horses on the premises: clause 7; acts apt to avoid any insurance policy of the A.J.C.: clause 10; payment of charges for services on the premises: clause 11; and the compliance by the trainer with certain statutory notices: clause 15.

It is stipulated that the trainer "shall only use the premises for the stabling of horses which are being prepared for racing under the rules of racing and shall not without the written consent of the A.J.C. first had and obtained stable any horse of which he is not the trainer": clause 12; and he must use the stables "solely for the purpose of training racehorses": clause 17.

Clause 14 provides: "The trainer shall permit the A.J.C. and its authorised officials to enter and inspect the premises provided twenty-four (24) hours notice is given except in special circumstances."

Clauses 8 and 9 are in the following terms:

"8. Nothing contained in this agreement shall be construed as granting or shall be deemed to grant to the trainer any estate or interest in the licensed premises and save as to the rights hereby conferred on the trainer the licensed premises remain in the possession and control of the A.J.C.

9. The rights given to the trainer by this agreement are personal to the trainer and are not assignable or transferable nor may they be held on trust for any person."

1. THE FIRST SUBMISSION: WHETHER A LEASE

As I have said, the document is described as a "licence agreement". However, Mr McQuillan has submitted that the rights granted are of a leasehold nature. He relies for this submission upon, in the main, two things: the claim that the terms of the document show that it was the parties' intention that the defendant be a lessee; and the claim that that which was granted to Mr Lewis could not have been effective without, and therefore must be held to include, the right to a leasehold interest in the premises. In these submissions reliance was placed upon the decision of the High Court of Australia in *Radaich v. Smith* (1959) 101 C.L.R. 209.

In determining whether the relationship created by a document is one of lessor and lessee, it is necessary to decide what is the test, or tests, of the existence of such a relationship. The conventional view was that there was one test and that it was whether the grantee was given the rights to exclusive possession of the premises: see *Glenwood Lumber Co. Ltd v. Phillips* [1904] A.C. 405 at 408; *McPherson v. Temiskaming Lumber Co. Ltd* [1913] A.C. 145 at 152-153; *Minister of State for the Army v. Dalziel* (1944) 68 C.L.R. 261 at 299 et seq. per Williams J. However, in England there was (at least in some of the decisions) a departure from this. Exclusive possession was seen as relevant but not decisive; or, alternatively, was seen as being one of the several tests of the existence of the relationship of lessor and lessee: see *Halsbury's Laws of England* (4th ed.), Vol. 27, paras 6-7 at 13-15, and the cases there referred to.

In the present case, it was accepted, or at least assumed, that the test is that of exclusive possession. That, in my opinion, is correct. It is the test which was adopted by at least the majority of their Honours in *Radaich v. Smith*: at 214, 217-220, 223. That that is, at least initially, the test, was affirmed by Mason J. in *Goldsworthy Mining Ltd v. Federal Commissioner of Taxation* (1973) 128 C.L.R. 199 at 212; affirmed (1975) 132 C.L.R. 463.

It is not necessary to analyse the precise nature of the right to exclusive possession which is here in question. It is, for present purposes, sufficient to say that it involves that the lessee have the general right to exclude others, including the lessor, from the premises, subject at least to such specific provisions for entry as may be particularly provided for in the document: cf. the rights reserved in the *Glenwood Lumber* case (at 408).

Whether a particular document grants such a right to the grantee depends, of course, upon the construction of the document. Regard is to be had, in the normal process of construction, to all of the terms of the document considered in their context. But, with this rule in mind, certain things may be said as to the process of determining whether the rights granted are those of a lessee.

First, if the right to exclusive possession is the test, then, in determining whether the grantee has been given the right of exclusive possession, the court must go initially to the terms of the grant: see *Radaich v. Smith* (at 223) per Windeyer J. The grant of a right to exclusive possession, in terms, is of course prima facie sufficient.

But the use, in the operative part of the document, of words such as "lease" or "devise" [scil. "demise"] will ordinarily be understood to involve the grant of such a right. Conversely, if what is granted is not in terms exclusive possession or if the words used in the grant are not words understood to convey the right of exclusive possession, then (subject to what I shall say) the transaction is prima facie not one of lease. Thus, if that which is granted is not of its nature the right to possession or exclusive possession but, for example, the right to use the premises only for a defined and particular purpose, there will prima facie be no lease.

But there are cases in which it is not clear from the terms of the grant, construed in the light of the whole agreement and its context, what it is that is being granted by them. In such cases, it is necessary to determine what is granted by looking at other aspects of the transaction. Thus, a grant may not be in terms of "possession" but of something else. It may be the grant of a right to occupy premises: cf. *O'Keefe v. Malone* [1903] A.C. 365 at 377; *Landale v. Menzies* (1909) 9 C.L.R. 89 at 91, 100, 101; the right to "carry on a business on" the premises: cf. *Radaich v. Smith* (1959) 101 C.L.R. 209 at 210; or, as in the present case, the right "to use" the premises either generally or in a particular way. In such cases, the court must, by the process of construction, determine whether what is granted is mere occupation or use, or is possession in the relevant sense. And where what is granted is possession, it still, in principle, may remain to be decided whether what is granted is exclusive possession. But it is not necessary to consider, in this case, whether there can be a distinction between possession and exclusive possession and (if there can) what distinctions there may be between possession and exclusive possession in this context.

In deciding, in such cases, whether what has been granted is the right to exclusive possession, the court, in the process of construction, has in practice looked, inter alia, to two things: the nature of the rights which, in terms, have been granted; and the intention of the parties.

The nature of the rights which have been granted has been seen of significance for this purpose because, as the argument is put, if the grantee has been granted such rights, it is to be inferred that he was (or was not) granted the right to exclusive possession. And that inference has been put on at least two bases. First, it has been held proper to infer that the rights granted do not carry by implication the grant of exclusive possession because the rights granted are inconsistent with the right to exclusive possession. Thus, a leasehold interest is an interest in land and, as such, is of its nature transferable: *Richardson v. Landecker* (1950) 50 S.R. (N.S.W.) 250 at 255; 67 W.N. 149 at 151. If the right granted is, of its nature, not transferable or is otherwise personal to the grantee it will, as such, not be a leasehold interest: cf. *Abbeyfield (Harpenden) Society Ltd v. Woods* [1968] 1 W.L.R. 374 at 376; [1968] 1 All E.R. 352(n.) at 353. In principle, where the rights are of their nature inconsistent with there being a lease, there will be no implication of a grant of exclusive possession.

Second, it has been held necessary to infer the grant of exclusive possession because the rights which have in terms been granted can be enjoyed only by one who has been granted exclusive possession. The grant of exclusive possession has been inferred from the nature of what has been expressly granted. This was the basis of the decision of their Honours in *Radaich v. Smith*: see at 215, 217, 221, 223-225.

Where the argument for the existence of a lease is of this kind, it is, I think, important to have in mind that the argument depends upon the process of implication. Such an implication is, in my opinion, of the same nature as that involved in, for example, the implication of a term in the construction of transactions generally: at least, the principles upon which the implication is to be made are the same. These principles have been discussed in, for example, *Liverpool City Council v. Irwin* [1977] A.C. 239 at 255; and were referred to in *Codelfa Construction Pty Ltd v. State Rail Authority of New South Wales* (1982) 149 C.L.R. 337: see, for example, (at 345 et seq.) per Mason J.; (at 400 et seq.) per Brennan J. As was there indicated, there are several and distinct bases upon which terms may be implied. In a case such as the present, the basis of implication is normally that it is necessary in order to give business efficacy to the rights which otherwise have been granted. Such being its basis, the implication will not be made merely because it is reasonable or convenient to do so; it must be necessary that the implication be made. And it will not be made if the parties have directed their attention to the subject matter of the suggested implication and have otherwise provided or have stipulated in terms that no such implication is to be made.

And that leads to the significance of intention in deciding whether the rights granted are of the nature of a lease. There is a difference between the Australian and the English cases as to the significance in this regard of the parties' intention: at least, there is a difference in the way in which that significance is stated. In the Australian cases, it is the nature of the rights which are granted which determines the matter (see *Radaich v. Smith*); in England, "the decisive consideration is the intention of the parties": *Halsbury's Laws of England* (4th ed.), Vol. 27, para. 6 at 13.

But, in my opinion, part at least of the difference lies in the different meanings given to "intention". It is necessary, I think, to consider the significance of the parties' intention at two stages in the court's reasoning: that in which it decides what is the nature of the rights which are granted by the transaction; and that in which, the nature of the rights having been determined, it decides whether the relationship is to be classified as one of lease or licence.

At the first stage, that of construction of the document, intention has the functions which ordinarily it has in accordance with the accepted rules of interpretation and construction. In the process of construction, the court's purpose is to determine, from the words used in their context, what was the intention of the parties as to what should be the rights granted. That intention is, of course, to be taken from the words used. But, once the intention has been ascertained, words which, for example, would in isolation convey a more limited right may be construed as granting exclusive possession, and vice versa. And, in the process of construction, an express statement of the parties' intentions as to, for example, the nature of the relationship to be created, will be of substantial, though not necessarily conclusive, importance: it will, in accordance with the rules of construction, yield to the intention to be derived from the document as a whole.

Similarly, intention will be relevant in the construction of the document for the purpose of deciding what terms are to be implied. Thus, if the grant of the right to exclusive possession depends, in the instant case, upon whether, for example, the business efficacy test requires its implication, an express statement by the parties of their intention may, in accordance with the established rules governing the implication of terms, operate to prevent such an implication.

At the second stage, that of classification, the significance of intention will, in Australia, be less. Once the nature of the rights granted is finally determined, the classification of the transaction, as lease or licence, will depend upon whether the rights are or are not those of exclusive possession. It is in this sense that, as it has been said, expressions of intention are irrelevant: the parties cannot "escape the legal consequences of one relationship by professing that it is another": *Radaich v. Smith* (1959) 101 C.L.R. 209 at 222 per Windeyer J.

One further thing may be said as to the significance of intention. It is, in my opinion, important in determining the nature of a transaction, to have in mind that, in the end, it is for the parties to determine what rights they will grant and accordingly what is the nature of their transaction. The parties (or the party who effectively determines the form of the transaction) may desire, for example, that the transaction does not produce the incidents of a lease and they may, to achieve that result, grant or reserve rights which are inconsistent with the grant of exclusive possession. For example, in circumstances in which it would ordinarily be expected that the rights granted would carry, by implication, the right to exclusive possession, the transaction may reserve to the grantor the right to possession or to do such things in relation to the premises as are inconsistent with the grantee having exclusive possession. And that may be done in order that the transaction be one of licence rather than of lease. If, upon its proper construction, that be the transaction into which the parties have entered, effect should, in my opinion, be given to it according to its terms.

There are, of course, cases in which rights purport to be granted or reserved which are intended never to be operative. Instances of this have been found in, for example, the context of legislative restrictions on eviction or control of rents. The court may treat such rights as not having operation and construe the transaction accordingly. But, if on its proper construction the relevant rights were intended to be granted then, in my opinion, the transaction is to be construed and classified accordingly.

I come now to apply these principles to the present case. In my opinion, Miles J. was correct in his construction and classification of the transaction. That which is the subject of the agreement is "the use of the premises": the document does not purport to grant possession or exclusive possession. I do not think that, as a matter of construction, that which is granted should be read as possession or exclusive possession or that, by implication, a right to exclusive possession is to be seen as granted.

The property over which the rights of user are granted is, in substance, a series of separate boxes or rooms, situated at different parts of the general stable complex. Areas adjacent are obviously to be used by or in common with others. The use which is granted is, in terms, for a limited purpose only, viz., for the stabling of horses "which are being prepared for racing under the rules of racing" and of which the grantee is trainer: clauses 12 and 17. The rights are in terms stated to be "personal to the trainer" and therefore not assignable: clause 9; and the stables may not be used for "any horse of which he is not the trainer": clause 12. And the intention of the parties, as expressed in the document, is that the transaction be one of licence rather than lease. It is so described; and clause 8 states, in terms, that that which is granted is not an estate or interest and that the property shall "remain in the possession and control of the A.J.C.".

The main submission of the defendant was, in my opinion, that, because what is granted is the right to use premises to stable racehorses, it is to be implied, as a matter of construction, that that right is exclusive and that, upon reasoning similar to that adopted in *Radaich v. Smith* (1959) 101 C.L.R. 209, there is by implication a grant of exclusive possession. And, it may be added, that argument was seen, in *Radaich v. Smith*, as being of such force that the implication was drawn notwithstanding that the parties had used a form which the established precedent books had put forward as creating a licence rather than a lease.

There is, of course, force in this argument: it follows from the rights granted to the defendant that some term must be implied. But the question is whether the implication is that the defendant have exclusive possession.

The grant of a right to use premises as stables for horses or as accommodation for employees will carry certain rights by implication. The grant of such a right, whether in the context of a lease or licence, will ordinarily require by implication that the grantor will not, for example, grant to a third party the right to stable horses or to accommodate employees in the same areas. But an exclusive licence to stable a horse in a horse box is not, as such, a right to exclusive possession of that box. A licensor may covenant not to grant a concurrent licence to another and yet not be held to have given the licensee a right to exclusive possession of the box. In the present context, I do not think that the implication is that what was intended to be granted was possession or exclusive possession.

Reference was made in argument to the provisions of clause 14. The argument was that, if possession was retained to the A.J.C. and the trainer had merely a licence exclusive of third parties, it would not have been necessary to provide specifically for entry and inspection by "the A.J.C. and its authorised officials". The force of this argument depends upon the assumption that the clauses of the document are self consistent and do not overlap. I do not think that the drafting of the document warrants such an assumption. Clause 8 stipulates for the retention of possession and control by the A.J.C. and it may be that clause 14 was added by way of preventing disputes or, perhaps, because of the obligations imposed upon a trainer as to the security of stables under the rules of racing.

There are in the document terms which, standing alone, would support an inference of exclusive possession: terms such as "rent" and "sub-let" are arguably such. However, such terms are not inconsistent with a relationship of licensor and licensee and, in the context of the document, I do not think that they warrant an inference that the rights intended to be created were those of possession or of exclusive possession. In my opinion, the defendant was not the lessee of the A.J.C.

[His Honour then held that the licence had been effectively terminated by the steps taken by the A.J.C. Kirby P. and Samuels J.A. agreed with Mahoney J.A.]

Appeal dismissed.

A.G. SECURITIES v. VAUGHAN

House of Lords [1988] 3 W.L.R. 1205

[This was an appeal from two Court of Appeal decisions, *A.G. Securities v. Vaughan* [1988] 2 W.L.R. 689 and *Antoniades v. Villiers* [1988] 3 W.L.R. 139.

In *A.G. Securities v. Vaughan*, four occupants of a flat had, on dates some three years apart, signed separate agreements conferring on each the right to share the premises in common with others who might from time to time be granted the like right. Each occupant had one of the four bedrooms in the flat; the sitting room and bathroom they shared. Each agreement was carefully cast in the form of a licence and not a lease, and provided that the occupant should not have "exclusive possession of any part of the said flat". The owner of the premises was in effect granting occupancy rights to a "floating population": as one occupant vacated, another was found to take his place, each signing a similar form of agreement. The Court of Appeal held by majority (Fox and Mustill L.JJ.; Sir George Waller dissenting) that the four occupants together had exclusive possession of the whole flat and that together they were tenants of the whole; the provision denying each of them exclusive possession of "any part" was held not inconsistent with a joint right to exclusive possession of the whole. This result followed, the majority held, notwithstanding that the periods of possession of each of the four commenced at different times, and notwithstanding that each paid a different amount of rent.

In *Antoniades v. Villiers*, the owner of the flat agreed to allow two prospective occupants to occupy the flat together. The occupants had been looking for some time for a flat in which they could live together as a quasi-matrimonial home. The flat was small, with a double bed in its only bedroom. Each occupant was required by the owner to sign a separate but identical "licence" agreement. Each agreement studiously used the terms "licensee" and "licensor" throughout and reiterated on a number of occasions that no right to exclusive possession was given to the licensee. Each agreement expressly provided that the licence was personal to the licensee (clause 17); and each agreement permitted the licensor to occupy the flat together with the licensee and to introduce additional occupants to the premises (clause 16). Each agreement began with the recital, "Whereas the licensor is not willing to grant the licensee exclusive possession of any part of" the premises, and concluded with an addendum by which the licensee acknowledged that "no person will have exclusive possession" of the premises. The trial judge held that, despite its terms, the agreement created a lease and not a licence. He appeared to base this decision upon two factors: (1) that the agreement was a "sham" and so to be ignored for the purpose of determining the true nature of the transaction between the parties; and (2) that although the agreement had been drafted on the basis of the agreement which the Court of Appeal in *Somma v. Hazelhurst* [1978] 1 W.L.R. 1014 had held to be a licence, the House of Lords in *Street v. Mountford* [1985] A.C. 809 had overruled that decision. The Court of Appeal reversed this decision, holding that although courts should be astute to detect and frustrate "sham" devices whose object was to avoid the restrictive provisions of the tenancy legislation, there was no ground of public policy prohibiting parties from casting their arrangements in the form of a licence rather than a lease, and that on the facts the true arrangement between these parties was that of licensee/licensor.]

LORD OLIVER OF AYLMERTON. My Lords, since lettings of residential property of an appropriate rateable value attract the consequences of controlled rent and security of tenure provided by the Rent Acts, it is not, perhaps, altogether surprising that those who derive their income from residential property are constantly seeking to attain the not always reconcilable objectives on the one hand of keeping their property gainfully occupied and, on the other, of framing their contractual arrangements with the occupants in such a way as to avoid, if they can, the application of the Acts. Since it is only a letting which attracts the operation of the Acts, such endeavours normally take the form of entering into contractual arrangements designed, on their face, to ensure that no estate is created in the occupant for the time being and that his occupation of the land derives merely from a personal and revocable permission granted by way of licence. The critical question, however, in every case is not simply how the arrangement is presented to the outside world in the relevant documentation, but what is the true nature of the arrangement. The decision of this House in *Street v. Mountford* [1985] A.C. 809 established quite clearly that if the true legal effect of the arrangement entered into is that the occupier of residential property has exclusive possession of the property for an ascertainable period in return for periodical money payments, a tenancy is created, whatever the label the parties may have chosen to attach to it. Where, as in that case, the circumstances show that the occupant is the only occupier realistically contemplated and the premises are inherently suitable only for single occupation, there is, generally, very little difficulty. Such an occupier normally has exclusive possession, as indeed she did in *Street v. Mountford*, where such possession was conceded, unless the owner retains control and unrestricted access for the purpose of providing attendance and services. As my noble and learned friend, Lord Templeman, observed in that case, the occupier in those circumstances is either a lodger or a tenant. Where, however, the premises are such as, by their nature, to lend themselves to multiple occupation and they are in fact occupied in common by a number of persons under different individual agreements with the owner, more difficult problems arise. These two appeals, at different ends of the scale, are illustrations of such problems.

The relevant facts have been fully set out in the speech of my noble and learned friend, Lord Templeman, which I have had the advantage of reading in draft, and I reiterate them only to the extent necessary to emphasise the points which appear to me to be of critical importance.

ANTONIADES *v.* VILLIERS

The appellants in this appeal are a young couple who at all material times were living together as man and wife. In about November 1984 they learned from a letting agency that a flat was available in a house at 6 Whiteley Road, London, S.E.19, owned by the respondent, Mr Antoniades. They inspected the flat together and were told that the rent would be £174 per month. They were given the choice of having the bedroom furnished with a double bed or two single beds and they chose a double bed. So, right from the inception, there was never any question but that the appellants were seeking to establish a joint home and they have, at all material times, been the sole occupants of the flat.

There is equally no question but that the premises are not suitable for occupation by more than one couple, save on a very temporary basis. The small living room contains a sofa capable of being converted into a double bed and also a bed-table capable of being opened out to form a narrow single bed. The appellants did in fact have a friend to stay with them for a time in what the trial judge found to be cramped conditions, but the size of the accommodation and the facilities available clearly do not make the flat suitable for multiple occupation. When it came to drawing up the contractual arrangements under which the appellants were to be let into possession, each was asked to and did sign a separate licence agreement in the terms set out in the speech of my noble and learned friend, Lord Templeman, under which each assumed an individual, but not a joint, responsibility for payment of one half of the sum of £174 previously quoted as the rent.

There is an air of total unreality about these documents read as separate and individual licences in the light of the circumstance that the appellants were together seeking a flat as a quasi-matrimonial home. A separate licensee does not realistically assume responsibility for all repairs and all outgoings. Nor in the circumstances can any realistic significance be given to clauses 16 and 17 of the document. It cannot realistically have been contemplated that the respondent would either himself use or occupy any part of the flat or put some other person in to share accommodation specifically adapted for the occupation by a couple living together. These clauses cannot be considered as seriously intended to have any practical operation or to serve any purpose apart from the purely technical one of seeking to avoid the ordinary legal consequences attendant upon letting the appellants into possession at a monthly rent. . . .

The conclusion seems to me irresistible that these two so-called licences, executed contemporaneously and entered into in the circumstances already outlined, have to be read together as constituting in reality one single transaction under which the appellants became joint occupiers. That of course does not conclude the case because the question still remains, what is the effect?

The document is clearly based upon the form of document which was upheld by the Court of Appeal as an effective licence in *Somma v. Hazelhurst* [1978] 1 W.L.R. 1014. That case, which rested on what was said to be the impossibility of the two licensees having between them exclusive possession, was overruled in *Street v. Mountford* [1985] A.C. 809. It was, however, a case which related to a single room and it is suggested that a similar agreement relating to premises containing space which could, albeit uncomfortably, accommodate another person is not necessarily governed by the same principle. On the other hand, the trial judge found that apart from the few visits by the respondent (who, on all but one occasion, sought admission by knocking on the door) no one shared with the appellants and that they had exclusive possession. He held that the licences were "artificial transactions designed to evade the Rent Acts", that a tenancy was created and that the appellants occupied as joint tenants.

His decision was reversed by the Court of Appeal [1988] 3 W.L.R. 139 on, broadly, the grounds that he had erred in treating the subsequent conduct of the parties as admissible as an aid to construction of the agreements and that in so far as the holding above referred to constituted a finding that the licences were a sham, that was unsupported by the evidence inasmuch as the appellants' intention that they should enjoy exclusive possession was not shared by the respondent. The licences could not, therefore, be said to mask the real intention of the parties and fell to be construed by reference to what they said in terms.

If the documents fall to be taken seriously at their face value and to be construed according to their terms, I see, for my part, no escape from the conclusion at which the Court of Appeal arrived. If it is once accepted that the respondent enjoyed the right—whether he exercised it or not—to share the accommodation with the appellants, either himself or by introducing one or more other persons to use the flat with them, it is, as it seems to me, incontestable that the appellants cannot claim to have had exclusive possession. The appellants' case therefore rests, as Mr Colyer [counsel for the occupants] frankly admits, upon upholding the judge's approach that the true transaction contemplated was that the appellants should jointly enjoy exclusive possession and that the licences were mere sham or window-dressing to indicate legal incidents which were never seriously intended in fact, but which would be inconsistent with the application to that transaction of the Rent Acts. Now to begin with, I do not, for my part, read the notes of the judge's judgment as showing that he construed the agreement in the light of what the parties subsequently did. I agree entirely with the Court of Appeal that if he did that he was in error. But though subsequent conduct is irrelevant as an aid to construction, it is certainly admissible as evidence on the question of whether the documents were or were not genuine documents giving effect to the parties' true intentions. Broadly what is said by Mr Colyer is that nobody acquainted with the circumstances in which the parties had come together and with the physical layout and size of the premises could seriously have imagined that the clauses in the licence which, on the face of them, contemplate the respondent and an apparently limitless number of other persons moving in to share the whole of the available accommodation, including the bedroom, with what, to all intents and purposes, was a married couple committed to paying £174 a month in advance, were anything other than a smoke-screen; and the fact the respondent, who might be assumed to want to make the maximum profit out of the premises, never sought to introduce anyone else is at least some indication that that is exactly what it was. Adopting the definition of a sham formulated by Purchas L.J. in *Hadjiloucas v. Crean* [1988] 1 W.L.R. 1006 at 1013, Mr Colyer submits that the licences clearly incorporate clauses by which neither party intended to be bound and which were obviously a smoke-screen to cover the real intentions of both contracting parties. In the Court of Appeal [1988] 3 W.L.R. 139 at 149, Bingham L.J. tested the matter by asking two questions, viz.: (1) on what grounds, if one party had left the premises, could the remaining party have been made liable for anything more than the £87 which he or she had agreed to pay; and (2) on what ground could they have resisted a demand by the respondent to introduce a further person into the premises? For my part, however, I do not see how this helps. The assumed negative answers prove nothing, for they rest upon the assumption that the licences are not sham documents, which is the very question in issue.

If the real transaction was, as the judge found, one under which the appellants became joint tenants with exclusive possession, on the footing that the two agreements are to be construed together, then it would follow that they were together jointly and severally responsible for the whole rent. It would equally follow that they could effectively exclude the respondent and his nominees.

Although the facts are not precisely on all fours with *Somma v. Hazelhurst* [1978] 1 W.L.R. 1014, they are strikingly similar and the judge was, in my judgment, entitled to conclude that the appellants had exclusive possession of the premises. I read his finding that, "the licences are artificial transactions designed to evade the Rent Acts" as a finding that they were sham documents designed to conceal the true nature of the transaction. There was, in my judgment, material on which he could properly reach this conclusion and I, too, would allow the appeal.

A.G. SECURITIES v. VAUGHAN

The facts in this appeal are startlingly different from those in the case of *Antoniades*. To begin with the appeal concerns a substantial flat in a mansion block consisting of four bedrooms, a lounge, a sitting room and usual offices. The trial judge found, as a fact, that the premises could without difficulty provide residential accommodation for four persons. There is no question but that the agreements with which the appeal is concerned reflect the true bargain between the parties. It is the purpose and intention of both parties to each agreement that it should confer an individual right on the licensee named, that he should be liable only for the payment which he had undertaken, and that his agreement should be capable of termination without reference to the agreements with other persons occupying the flat. The judge found that the agreements were not shams and that each of the four occupants had arrived independently of one another and not as a group. His finding was that there was never a group of persons coming to the flat altogether. That has been challenged because, it is said, the evidence established that initially in 1977 and 1978 there was one occupant who was joined by three others who, although they came independently and not as a trio, moved in at about the same [sic]. Central heating was then installed, so that the weekly payments fell to be increased and new agreements were signed by the four occupants contemporaneously. Speaking for myself, I cannot see how this can make any difference to the terms upon which the individuals were in occupation. If they were in as licensees in the first instance, the mere replacement of their agreements by new agreements in similar form cannot convert them into tenants, and the case has, in my judgment, to be approached on the footing that agreements with the occupiers were entered into separately and individually. The only questions are those of the effect of each agreement vis-à-vis the individual licensee and whether the agreements collectively had the effect of creating a joint tenancy among the occupants of the premises for the time being by virtue of their having between them exclusive possession of the premises.

Taking first, by way of example, the position of the first occupier to be let into the premises on the terms of one of these agreements, it is, in my judgment, quite unarguable, once any question of sham is out of the way, that he has an estate in the premises which entitles him to exclusive possession. His right, which is, by definition, a right to share use and occupation with such other persons not exceeding three in number as the licensor shall introduce from time to time, is clearly inconsistent with any exclusive possession in him alone even though he may be the only person in physical occupation at a particular time. He has no legal title which will permit him to exclude other persons to whom the licensor may choose to grant the privilege of entry. That must equally apply to the additional licensees who join him. None of them has individually nor have they collectively the right or power lawfully to exclude a further nominee of the licensor within the prescribed maximum.

I pause to note that it has never been contended that any individual occupier has a tenancy of a particular room in the flat with a right to use the remainder of the flat in common with the tenants of other rooms. I can envisage that as a possibility in cases of arrangements of this kind if the facts support the marking out with the landlord's concurrence of a particular room as the exclusive domain of a particular individual. But to support that there would, I think, have to be proved the grant of an identifiable part of the flat and that simply does not fit with the system described in the evidence of the instant case.

The real question—and it is this upon which the respondents rely—is what is the position when the flat is occupied concurrently by all four licensees? What is said then is that since the licensor has now exhausted, for the time being, his right of nomination, the four occupants collectively have exclusive possession of the premises because they can collectively exclude the licensor himself. Because, it is argued (1) they have thus exclusive possession; and (2) there is an ascertainable term during which all have the right to use and occupy; and (3) they are occupying in consideration of the payment of periodic sums of money, *Street v. Mountford* [1985] A.C. 809 shows that they are collectively tenants of the premises. They are not lodgers. Therefore they must be tenants. And because each is not individually a tenant, they must together be joint tenants.

My Lords, there appear to me to be a number of fallacies here. In the first place, the assertion of an exclusive possession rests, as it seems to me, upon assuming what it is sought to prove. If, of course, each licence agreement creates a tenancy, each tenant will be sharing with other persons whose rights to be there rest upon their own estates which, once they have been granted, they enjoy in their own right independently of the landlord. Collectively they have the right to exclude everyone other than those who have concurrent estates. But if the licence agreement is what it purports to be, that is to say, merely an agreement for permissive enjoyment as the invitee of the landlord, then each shares the use of the premises with other invitees of the same landlord. The landlord is not excluded for he continues to enjoy the premises through his invitees, even though he may for the time being have precluded himself by contract with each from withdrawing the invitation. Secondly, the fact that under each agreement an individual has the privilege of user and occupation for a term which overlaps the term of user and occupation of other persons In the premises, does not create a single indivisible term of occupation for all four consisting of an amalgam of the invidual [sic] overlapping periods. Thirdly, there is no single sum of money payable in respect of use and occupation. Each person is individually liable for the amount which he has agreed, which may differ in practice from the amounts paid by all or some of the others.

The respondents are compelled to support their claims by a strange and unnatural theory that, as each occupant terminates his agreement, there is an implied surrender by the other three and an implied grant of a new joint tenancy to them together with the new incumbent when he enters under his individual agreement. With great respect to the majority in the Court of Appeal, this appears to me to be entirely unreal. For my part, I agree with the dissenting judgment of Sir George Waller in finding no unity of interest, no unity of title, certainly no unity of time and, as I think, no unity of possession. I find it impossible to say that the agreements entered into with the respondents created either individually or collectively a single tenancy either of the entire flat or of any part of it. I agree that the appeal should be allowed.

[Lords Bridge of Harwich, Templeman, Ackner, and Jauncey of Tullichettle, in separate judgments, came to the same conclusion.]

Appeal dismissed.

2. Duration of the lease

The commencement and the maximum duration of a lease must be either certain or capable of being rendered certain before the lease takes effect.

LACE v. CHANTLER

Court of Appeal [1944] K.B. 368

[The plaintiff leased a dwelling-house to the defendant at a weekly rent. One of the terms of the leasing was that the premises were furnished "for the duration of the war". In the county court, the plaintiff obtained an order for possession on the ground of alleged breaches of the lease by the defendant. One of the defendant's defences was that she had a lease "for the duration of the war".]

LORD GREENE M.R. Normally there could be no question that this was an ordinary weekly tenancy, duly determinable by a week's notice, but the parties in the rent book agreed to a term which appears there expressed by the words "furnished for duration", which must mean the duration of the war. The question immediately arises whether a tenancy for the duration of the war creates a good leasehold interest. In my opinion, it does not. A term created by a leasehold tenancy agreement must be expressed either with certainty and specifically or by reference to something which can, at the time when the lease takes effect, be looked to as a certain ascertainment of what the term is meant to be. In the present case, when this tenancy agreement took effect, the term was completely uncertain. It was impossible to say how long the tenancy would last. Mr Sturge in his argument has maintained that such a lease would be valid, and that, even if the term is uncertain at its beginning when the lease takes effect, the fact that at some future time it will be rendered certain is sufficient to make it a good lease. In my opinion, that argument is not to be sustained

I do not propose to go into the authorities on the matter, but in Foa's *Landlord and Tenant* (6th ed.), p. 115, the law is stated in this way, and, in my view, correctly: "The habendum in a lease must point out the period during which the enjoyment of the premises is to be had; so that the duration, as well as the commencement of the term, must be stated. The certainty of a lease as to its continuance must be ascertainable either by the express limitation of the parties at the time the lease is made, or by reference to some collateral act which may, with equal certainty, measure the continuance of it, otherwise it is void. If the term be fixed by reference to some collateral matter, such matter must either be itself certain (for example, a demise to hold for 'as many years as A has in the manor of B') or capable before the lease takes effect of being rendered so (for example, for 'as many years as C shall name').'' The important words to observe in that last phrase are the words "before the lease takes effect". Then it goes on: "Consequently, a lease to endure for 'as many years as A shall live', or 'as the coverture between B and C shall continue', would not be good as a lease for years, although the same results may be achieved in another way by making the demise for a fixed number (99 for instance) of years determinable upon A's death, or the dissolution of the coverture between B and C." In the present case, in my opinion, this agreement cannot take effect as a good tenancy for the duration of the war.

The question then arises whether it can take effect in any other way. It was suggested that the difficulty would be got over by construing the tenancy as a lease for a long period, for example, 99 years, determinable on the cessation of the war. In my opinion, it is impossible to construe this tenancy in that way. It is true that, in *Great Northern Railway Co. v. Arnold* (1916) 33 T.L.R. 114, Rowlatt J. found it possible to treat a tenancy for the duration of the last war, the rent being payable weekly, as though a lease for 999 years terminable on the cessation of the war had been created. He had some assistance in arriving at that conclusion in the fact that there was a definite undertaking by the landlords not to serve a notice to quit during the period. The actual words, as stated in the headnote, were: "The landlords said that they did not intend that he should be subject to a week's notice." That case can, in my opinion, only be supported because of the presence of that term of the agreement.

Is there any other possible construction? It is not contended that this tenancy agreement can be construed as though it were a grant of a freehold interest. The only way in which one could convert this into a freehold interest would be by construing it as an agreement for a life tenancy terminable at the end of the war. It is impossible to construe this agreement as anything of the kind.

Lastly, Mr Sturge argued that the agreement could be construed as an agreement to grant a licence. In my opinion, it is impossible to construe it in that sense. The intention was to create a tenancy and nothing else. The law says that it is bad as a tenancy. The court is not then justified in treating the contract as something different from what the parties intended, and regarding it merely as a contract for the granting of a licence. That would be setting up a new bargain which neither of the parties ever intended to enter into. The relationship between the parties must be ascertained on the footing that the tenant was in occupation and was paying a weekly rent. Accordingly, it must be the relationship of weekly tenant and landlord and nothing else.

[Mackinnon L.J. delivered a concurring judgment; Luxmoore L.J. agreed.]

NOTES AND QUESTIONS

1. Leases for the duration of the war were subsequently saved from defeat by the *Validation of War Time Leases Act* 1944 (U.K.); by this Act, leases for the duration of the war were converted into leases for a term of ten years determinable at the end of the war by one month's notice on either side.

2. A lease for a fixed term to commence "from the completion of the building" is valid: *Pirie v. Saunders* (1961) 104 C.L.R. 149 at 154.

3. In *Bishop v. Taylor* (1968) 118 C.L.R. 518 at 523 McTiernan and Taylor JJ. expressed the opinion that a lease expressed to subsist "until the end of the peanut crop in 1968 or end of harvesting period or as otherwise agreed upon" was void, citing *Lace v. Chantler* [1944] K.B. 368. Is a lease "for the period during which the lessee shall hold shares in a company" void? See *Re Lehrer and the Real Property Act* [1961] S.R. (N.S.W.) 365 at 377.

4. Where the maximum duration of the lease is certain, the fact that it may be determined at an earlier uncertain time does not render the lease void. For example, a lease "for 21 years, determinable if the tenant ceases to live on the premises" (*Doe d. Lockwood v. Clarke* (1807) 8 East 185; 103 E.R. 313) is valid; other examples are given in the extract from *Lace v. Chantler*. Further, it is common practice

for leases for a fixed term to contain a clause enabling the lessor to re-enter and determine the lease should the tenant fail to observe the covenants in the lease; such clauses do not breach the rule in *Lace v. Chantler*.

5. The requirement that the maximum duration of a lease be certain does not apply to periodic tenancies, such as tenancies from week to week or from month to month (periodic tenancies are discussed below p. 557): see *Re Midland Railway Co.'s Agreement* [1971] Ch. 725, where the Court of Appeal upheld as valid a periodic lease from half-year to half-year which contained a proviso that the lease could be determined by either party on giving three months' written notice to the other. Similarly, in *Centaploy Ltd v. Matlodge Ltd* [1974] Ch. 1 a lease from week to week, subject to a proviso that it was determinable by the lessee only, did not fail for uncertainty, even though the maximum duration could never be known by the lessor, who had no power to determine it; it was further held, however, that the absolute bar on the lessor's power to terminate the lease was repugnant to the grant of a lease and thus void: "a tenancy in which the landlord is never going to have the right to determine it at all is . . . a complete contradiction in terms": [1974] Ch. at 15.

ASHBURN ANSTALT v. ARNOLD

Court of Appeal [1988] 2 W.L.R. 706

[By an agreement dated 28 February 1973, Arnold & Co. Ltd (Arnold), the holder of a leasehold interest, agreed to sell that interest to the lessor, Matlodge Ltd (Matlodge), who intended to redevelop the site. Clause 5 of the agreement provided that Arnold should be at liberty to remain in possession of the property rent-free. The agreement did not specify any period for which Arnold could remain in possession; but it did provide that Arnold could be required by Matlodge to give up possession "on not less than one quarter's notice" upon Matlodge certifying that it was ready to proceed with the redevelopment of the property.

A successor in title of Matlodge argued that it was not bound by any right of Arnold to remain in possession. It was clear that Arnold's possession would be protected if the agreement of 28 February had created a lease. The trial judge held that a licence only had been created. The Court of Appeal held that the agreement conferred exclusive possession upon Arnold. It then turned to consider the argument that no lease could have been created because the term was of uncertain duration.]

Fox L.J. (delivering the judgment of the court).

There remains the question of the existence of a term. It is the plaintiff's case that clause 5 created no term sufficiently identifiable to be capable of recognition by the law, and that accordingly no tenancy was created. For that, the plaintiff relies upon *Lance v. Chantler* [1944] K.B. 368. In that case a house was let "for the duration of the war". The Court of Appeal held that a leasehold interest was not created. The basis of that decision was stated by Lord Greene M.R. (at 370): "A term created by a leasehold tenancy agreement must be expressed either with certainty and specifically or by reference to something which can, at the time when the lease takes effect, be looked to as a certain ascertainment of what the term is meant to be. In the present case, when this tenancy agreement took effect, the term was completely uncertain. It was impossible to say how long the tenancy would last." The ambit of the decision in *Lace v. Chantler* was limited by the further decision of this court, *Re Midland Railway Co.'s Agreement* [1971] Ch. 725. Russell L.J., giving the judgment of the court in that case, said (at 732): "Now it appears to us that that decision is confined to a case in which that which was purported to be done was simply to create a leasehold interest for a single and uncertain period. The applicability of this matter of certainty to a periodic tenancy was not under consideration."

In the *Midland Railway* case the grant was for a period of six months from 10 June 1920, "and so on from half year to half year until the said tenancy shall be determined". Clause 2 of the agreement provided for the termination of the agreement by three months' written notice given by either party to the other, but subject to a proviso that the landlords should not exercise that right unless they required the premises for their undertaking. The court observed that, in the ordinary case of a periodic tenancy, for example, a yearly tenancy, it was plain that, in one sense at least, it was uncertain at the outset what would be the maximum length of the tenancy; the term would grow from year to year as a single term springing from the original grant. Accordingly, the simple statement of the law that the maximum duration of a term must be certainly known in advance of its taking effect could not have direct reference to periodic tenancies. It had been argued that the reason why the principle of avoidance through uncertainty was not applicable to a periodic tenancy was because either party could at any time define the maximum period of the term by giving notice of determination: neither party was left in a state of unknowing as to his maximum commitment. But it was said that where, by the terms of the agreement, either party was deprived of that power until some event the occurrence of which was uncertain, then that person was in such a state of unknowing. On that argument the conclusion of the court (at 733) was: "In the course of the argument we found this approach logically attractive. Here one term growing period by period and there is no knowing (on one side) its maximum length, if (on that side) there is no power to determine save in an event the occurrence of which is in point of time uncertain. Why logically should that differ from a lease directly for a term of which the maximum duration is uncertain? But in the end we are persuaded that, there being no authority to prevent us, it is preferable as a matter of justice to hold parties to their clearly expressed bargain rather than to introduce for the first time in 1971 an extension of a doctrine of land law so as to deny the efficacy of that bargain."

In the present case there was an initial term from the date of the agreement of 28 February [1973] until 29 September 1973, the Michaelmas Quarter Day. Thereafter, the term would continue until (a certificate of readiness to proceed having been given) Matlodge should give not less than one quarter's notice to give up possession. It may be that the notice has to take effect on a quarter day calculated from the date of the commencement of the term rather than on one of the usual quarter days: see *Kemp v. Derrett* (1814) 3 Camp. 510; 170 E.R. 1463 and *King v. Eversfield* [1897] 2 Q.B. 475; but, as Cotton L.J. said in *Re Threlfall* (1880) 16 Ch. D. 274 at 281: "I know of no law or principle to prevent two persons agreeing that a yearly tenancy may be determined on whatever notice they like." We see no reason to limit that approach to yearly tenancies.

So far as *Lace v. Chantler* [1944] K.B. 368 is concerned, the present case, it seems to us, is distinguishable. In *Lace v. Chantler* the duration of the war could not be predicted and there was no provision for either party to bring the tenancy to an end before the war ended, and that event might itself be very hard to pinpoint. In the present case the arrangement, so far as Matlodge was concerned, would continue until Matlodge determined it by giving not less than a quarter's notice, upon Matlodge giving the required certificate. The event entitling Matlodge to give the certificate might not, of course, occur. But the same applies to the qualifying event for the giving of the landlord's notice in the *Midland Railway Co.'s Agreement* [1971] Ch. 725. The plaintiff says, however, that in this case (unlike the *Midland Railway* case) there is no provision for determination by Arnold & Co. It was said, therefore, that in the absence of notice by Matlodge, the term was uncertain in duration. We do not agree with that. As a matter of construction of the document, the possibilities are as follows.

(i) Arnold & Co. was not entitled to determine the arrangement at all. We reject that entirely. Bearing in mind that Arnold & Co. was not required to pay any rent, such a construction is quite unreal in business terms; Arnold & Co. was not obliged to occupy the premises and, if it did not occupy, the outgoings would be nil or negligible, so there was no benefit to Matlodge in continuing the relationship.

(ii) Arnold & Co. was required to give more than a quarter's notice. That seems to us equally unreal.

(iii) Arnold & Co. was required to give a quarter's notice. If that is right, the case in substance is really indistinguishable from the *Midland Railway Co.'s Agreement*. The occupancy continues from quarter to quarter until determined.

(iv) Arnold & Co. was required to give notice of less than a quarter or no notice at all—it could simply walk out. Apart, possibly, from the need of some short notice to enable Matlodge to make the premises secure, the latter would do no harm to Matlodge since no rent was payable.

It is not necessary to determine which of the possibilities under heads (iii) and (iv) above is correct. The matter would be capable of resolution by the court. Whatever the correct answer, the position would be free from uncertainty.

The result, in our opinion, is that the arrangement could be brought to an end by both parties in circumstances which are free from uncertainty in the sense that there would be no doubt whether the determining event had occurred. The vice of uncertainty in relation to the duration of a term is that the parties do not know where they stand. Put another way, the court does not know what to enforce. That is not the position here. It seems to us therefore that, as in the *Midland Railway Co.'s Agreement*, there is no reason why the court should not hold the parties to their agreement. That is so even though the tenancy is not (or may not be) an ordinary periodic tenancy. The rights of the parties are no more subject to uncertainty than those in the *Midland Railway* case. We do not see why the mere absence of a formula referring to a periodic tenancy or occupancy should alter the position. The nearest one comes to uncertainty is the circumstance that Matlodge might not be able to give a certificate. A similar circumstance existed in the *Midland Railway* case, in that the lessor might not have been able to establish that it needed the premises for its undertakings. The Court of Appeal stated expressly that it did *not* decide the case on the basis that the grantor might have been able to tailor the requirements of its undertaking to satisfy the provisions. The result, in our opinion, is that, contrary to the view of the deputy judge, the agreement of 28 February 1973 conferred upon Arnold & Co. possession of the premises for a term which was not uncertain. Consistently with the statement of principle in *Radaich v. Smith* (1959) 101 C.L.R. 209 at 222, that creates a tenancy. We appreciate that, as pointed out by the deputy judge, clause 5 is drafted in terms of a licence. But the parties' description of their transaction cannot affect the substance of it: see *Street v. Mountford* [1985] A.C. 809 at 819 and *Radaich v. Smith* (1959) 101 C.L.R. 209 at 222.

II. TYPES OF TENANCIES

1. Tenancy at sufferance

A tenancy at sufferance arises where a lessee who initially entered under a valid tenancy holds over after the tenancy has come to an end, without either the assent or dissent of the lessor (*Remon v. City of London Real Property Co. Ltd* [1921]

1 K.B. 49 at 58; *Anderson v. Bowles* (1951) 84 C.L.R. 310 at 319; *March v. Neumann* [1945] S.A.S.R. 167); it also arises where a tenant pur autre vie holds over on the death of the cestui que vie: *Rouse's case* (1587) Tudor's L.C.R.P. 1; 76 E.R. 927.

A tenancy at sufferance is to be distinguished from a tenancy at will, which exists with the consent of the lessor: see *Wheeler v. Mercer* [1957] A.C. 416 at 427, and discussion of tenancies at will below.

Because it assumes a lack of agreement between lessor and lessee, a tenancy at sufferance can arise only by operation of law, and cannot give rise to any obligation to pay "rent"; but a tenant at sufferance is liable to claim for "use and occupation" of the premises: *Bayley v. Bradley* (1848) 5 C.B. 396 at 406; 136 E.R. 932 at 936; *Leigh v. Dickeson* (1884) 15 Q.B.D. 60 at 68; *Leonida v. Scotson Pty Ltd* (1984) C.C.H. N.S.W. Conv. R. 55-161; see also *Zegir v. Woop* [1955] V.L.R. 394.

A lessor may eject a tenant at sufferance at any time, without the need for a notice to quit: *Doe d. Bennett v. Turner* (1840) 7 M. & W. 226 at 235; 151 E.R. 749 at 752.

NATURAL GAS AND OIL CORP. LTD (IN LIQ.) v. BYRNE

Supreme Court of New South Wales (1951) 68 W.N. (N.S.W.) 207

[A lease of a wharf for a term of six months expired on 15 November 1950. The lessor (the plaintiff) and lessees (the defendants) had entered into negotiations for a further lease, but the negotiations proved fruitless and no extension or fresh lease was agreed upon. The lessor had written to the lessees on 31 October 1950 pointing out that the lease was due to expire on 15 November and said, "should you wish to continue in occupation we are prepared to give you a lease for a further period of six months" at an increased rental. Further inconclusive negotiations then took place, the lessees remaining in possession after 15 November in the hope that the lessor might regard them as satisfactory tenants and renew the lease at the old rent. On 27 November 1950, the lessees sent a cheque for rent at the old figure, but the cheque was returned by the lessor with the explanation that it was not in accordance with the lessor's letter of 31 October. In the words of Herron J., "It is quite clear that at that point of time the [lessees] must have understood that it was a case of paying [the increased rent] or no further lease". The lessees in December sent a further cheque for rent at the old figure; this also was returned. Following further negotiations between the parties for some attempt to settle the matter amicably, the lessor on 5 March 1951 formally requested vacant possession on 13 March, and on 30 March issued a writ of ejectment.]

HERRON J. What was the position in law of the defendants between 15 November and 30 March? That is a question which I have to decide.

In the first instance, I do not think it can be said that the defendants were trespassers. They were probably invitees with regard to the premises at common law in the sense that they were on the premises at least for the purpose of negotiating a matter of business between themselves and the liquidators. Prior to 5 March 1951, I do not think that it can be safely said that there had been any active dissent to the defendants' presence on the property. As I have said, I think that both parties hoped or anticipated that the negotiations would bear fruit and that the defendants eventually would stay on the premises at an agreed rental. Until it was clear to the liquidators that the proposed rental of £50 per week was not forthcoming, they did not wish to get rid of the defendants and, naturally, the defendants did not wish to bring the issue of the rental to a head sooner than was absolutely necessary as they were most anxious, I believe, to continue in occupation.

So that the position was between November and March there was no active dissent to the defendants remaining there nor was there any active assent to their being there, at least on any agreed terms and conditions.

What then is the position of a tenant who remains in occupation of the premises after the expiry by effluxion of time of a lease? I have examined with care the argument of Mr Pilcher relating to this matter and I find myself ultimately driven to the conclusion that the defendants were there on sufferance. This is said to be a form of tenancy but that is, perhaps, an attempt to put a label on to an occupant of premises when his position is far from clear.

In *Remon v. City of London Real Property Co. Ltd* [1921] 1 K.B. 49, Scrutton L.J. refers to this position. In that case the tenant had stayed on in possession after his tenancy had expired and had been asked by the landlords to leave, and had referred them to his solicitors. The question was strictly whether he was a tenant under the Rent Restrictions Acts in England. Dealing with this position, Scrutton L.J. (at 58) said: "Whom did they (the Legislature) mean to include in the term 'tenant'? If a tenant by agreement whose tenancy had expired was not within those terms, the whole purpose of the Act would have been defeated, for it was obviously intended to allow former tenants who were willing to carry out the terms of their old tenancy, as modified by any permissible statutory increases of rent, to stay on. If this was not so every weekly or monthly tenant, the small tenant for whose benefit the Acts were obviously framed, was outside the Act. Unless 'tenant' includes a former tenant by agreement holding over against the will of the landlord, and 'letting' includes the landlord's relation to such a tenant, the whole object of the Acts is defeated. It is true that some of these persons would never previously have been called 'tenants' by any lawyer. The nearest approach to them is 'tenant by sufferance' who as Lord Coke says (Co. Litt. 57b): 'Entreth by a lawful lease and holdeth over by wrong', whose tenure was probably invented to prevent their obtaining a title by adverse possession as disseisors. But tenants by sufferance seem to have been confined to persons who held over without the assent or dissent of their landlords, and not to have included persons who held over wrongfully in spite of the active objection of their landlords."

This passage was applied and adopted by Roper J. in *Simms v. Lee* (1945) 45 S.R. 352. His Honour was there dealing with the case where the plaintiff was a lessee of property for the term of two years, the lease had expired by effluxion of time and no agreement creating a new tenancy had been entered into. The plaintiff nonetheless depastured sheep and other stock on the property and the defendant lessor had threatened to enter upon the property and remove the stock and take possession. Dealing with this situation, his Honour examined the position of the plaintiff as at common law. He pointed out that the lease had expired by effluxion of time and there had been no agreement creating a new tenancy. Apart from the National Security Regulations which were then in force, his Honour thought that the plaintiff was not a tenant of the defendant at all. He said (at 354): "Even if he were what is called a tenant by sufferance that relationship is not strictly a tenancy at all but a holding over by wrong. I think, however, that he is not even a tenant by sufferance because 'tenants by sufferance' seem to have been confined to persons who hold over without the assent or dissent of their landlords, and not to have included persons who held over wrongfully in spite of the active objection of their landlord."

In Woodfall's *Law of Landlord and Tenant* (24th ed.), p. 285, it is said: "A tenant on sufferance is one who entered by a lawful demise or title, and, after that has ceased, wrongfully continues in possession without the assent or dissent of the person next entitled; as where a tenant for years holds over his term." The author cites the note from Coke on Littleton, above. He then continues: "Or where anyone continues in possession without agreement after a particular estate is ended." The author distinguishes between a tenant at will and a tenant on sufferance by pointing out that the former is in by right but the latter holds over by wrong after the expiration of the lawful title.

In my opinion these passages cited are appropriate to describe the position of the defendants. I hold as a fact that there never was any agreement to let the property to the defendants after 15 November 1950. At most, there were negotiations proceeding which ended in nothing.

Prior to 5 March, the defendants were holding over in the pious hope that some agreement might be reached with regard to their position; none in fact was, and, in my opinion they cannot be said to be tenants at will and at most are tenants by sufferance.

For the same reasons as I have advanced, I do not think that the position of the defendants can be said to be that of licensees, for in order to constitute a licence there must be some express or implied agreement to permit a person to remain in occupation of land for a specified purpose under circumstances not amounting to a demise. I do not find any such express or implied agreement and I am forced to hold that none exists.

It seems to me, therefore, that the position of the defendants as at the date of the writ was untenable in law. They had received a notice on 5 March 1950 saying that as from that date they were not entitled to continue in possession as from the 13th of that month. This being so, at any rate after 13 March, the defendants had no right in law whatever to remain in possession of the property.

A so-called tenancy by sufferance can be brought to an end at any time by the landlord. The position is accurately stated, in my opinion, in Woodfall (at 286): "A landlord may maintain ejectment against his tenant on sufferance without any previous demand of possession. A tenant on sufferance, who is turned out of possession by his landlord, without any demand of possession, cannot maintain ejectment." In all the circumstances, therefore, I hold that the claimant company had a right as at the date of the writ to possession as against the defendants, and there must be a verdict and judgment in ejectment for the claimant.

Order accordingly.

2. Tenancy at will

A tenancy at will has been defined as a tenancy which comes into being whenever a person occupies land as tenant (and not merely as servant or agent), with the consent of the owner, on the terms that either party may determine the tenancy at any time: Megarry and Wade, *Law of Real Property* (5th ed.), p. 654. The concluding words of that definition—the requirement that either party may determine *at any time*—is a matter discussed in *Landale v. Menzies* (1909) 9 C.L.R. 89, extracted below.

Tenancies at will are usually created by implication rather than expressly. They most commonly arise where a tenant "holds over" under an expired lease with the lessor's consent but without having yet paid rent on a periodic basis (for an example, see *Meye v. Electric Transmission Ltd* [1942] Ch. 290 at 292); once rent is paid on a periodic basis, the tenancy becomes a periodic tenancy (as to which, see below; see also *Landlord and Tenant Act* 1899 (N.S.W.), s. 22A(a), (b)). A tenancy at will also arises where a purchaser is let into possession after exchange of contracts for the sale of a property (*Wheeler v. Mercer* [1957] A.C. 416 at 425), or where a prospective tenant is let into possession of the premises during negotiations for the granting of a lease: *Coggan v. Warwicker* (1852) 3 Car. & K. 40 at 42; 175 E.R. 454 at 455; *Fox v. Hunter-Paterson* [1948] 2 All E.R. 813.

For an example of the creation of a tenancy at will by express agreement, see *Hagee (London) Ltd v. Erikson and Larson* [1976] 1 Q.B. 209, where the relevant clause in the agreement for lease was as follows:

> You shall occupy our premises as tenants at will only and shall pay us in respect of your occupation at the rate of £5,000 per annum, payment to be made by four quarterly payments in advance, the first of such payments to be made on 6 September 1971. Any payment made by you in advance of the date upon which this agreement is terminated shall subject to the terms hereof be refundable to you.

The clause was worded in this fashion so as to avoid creating any rights in favour of the tenant under the *Landlord and Tenant Act* 1954 (U.K.). Lord Denning M.R. clearly had this in mind when he warned (at 215) that "a tenancy at will of this kind is very rare. The court will look into it very closely to see whether or not it really is a tenancy at will, or whether it is a cloak for a periodic tenancy" (periodic tenancies were subject to the Act). See also *Turner v. York Motors Pty Ltd* (1951) 85 C.L.R. 55 at 67; Weidberg, "Case Note" (1976) 39 M.L.R. 337.

LANDALE v. MENZIES

High Court of Australia (1909) 9 C.L.R. 89

[The plaintiff and the defendants were the owners of adjoining pastoral properties. The common boundary was a winding creek bed, liable to become dry for long periods, but containing occasional waterholes. In about 1874, the predecessors in title of the plaintiff and defendants had erected a "give and take fence", which was considerably shorter in length than the creek bed itself and cut across the creek bed in several places. The result was that each owner, by occupying up to the fence, was in possession of some of the land of the other, and in particular gained the sole use of a waterhole on the other's land. There was no written record of the agreement.

In 1895 the then owners of the two properties agreed to make the existing fence rabbit-proof (because of requirements under the *Rabbit Act* 1890 (N.S.W.)) and to maintain the fence as the working boundary between them, each being responsible for the cost of repairing so much of the fence as was on his land.

In 1908 water was scarce, and the defendants, giving three days' written notice of their intention, cut the give and take fence near a waterhole, called "the Bridge waterhole", on their land but on the plaintiff's side of the fence, constructed a fenced laneway to the waterhole and watered their flocks at the waterhole. The existence of the laneway, when coupled with the natural configuration of the land, meant that the plaintiff's flocks could not gain access to the waterhole.

The plaintiff claimed an injunction to restrain the defendants from so destroying the fence, and damages. The defendants argued that there was a tenancy at will of the land concerned, and that it could be terminated at a moment's notice. The plaintiff argued that the tenancy lasted for the probable life of the fence, or, alternatively, that it was not terminable without reasonable notice.]

GRIFFITH C.J. If one has regard to the natural features and conditions of Australia it is obvious that the secure possession of permanent water is an essential condition to the profitable occupation of land for grazing purposes, especially where the flocks are large, and the enclosures in which they run are of great extent. It may be mentioned incidentally that one of the paddocks dependent on the Bridge waterhole for water contained an area of about three square miles.

The practice of adopting a "give and take fence" between two properties separated by a watercourse is well known. Even without the express testimony of the plaintiff I should take it to be notorious that the object of such an arrangement is two-fold, (1) to obtain a more convenient location for a dividing fence; and (2) to divide the permanent water in the watercourse between the parties.

It is manifest that the intention of the parties in entering into such an agreement cannot be carried out unless the agreement has such a degree of permanency as not to be terminable by either party without reasonable notice to the other. What is reasonable notice must, as in all cases where the question of reasonableness arises, depend upon the circumstances of the particular case. What might be a sufficient notice in the case of an area of land divided by a watercourse containing permanent water at frequent intervals might be wholly insufficient in the case of a large area bounded by a channel containing a scanty supply of water at long intervals of distance.

In my opinion, therefore, it is an implied term of such an agreement that it cannot be terminated without reasonable notice. This conclusion is strongly supported by a consideration of the permanency of the mutual obligations of adjoining owners under the Fencing Acts and Rabbit Acts.

Another incident of such an agreement is that each party has the exclusive use of the land and water lying on his own side of the fence. This result necessarily follows so long as the fence actually divides the land occupied. The parties may, of course, stipulate that it shall be a term of the agreement that they shall have common access to the water, but in the absence of such a stipulation I think that the right to exclusive occupation should be inferred. . . .

What, then, are the legal consequences of such an agreement followed by possession? A contract for the exclusive occupation of land for a determinate period, however short, constitutes a lease: *R. v. Morrish* (1863) 32 L.J.M.C. 245. A period determinable at the will of either party is such a period. In such a case the lease is called a lease at will. And, in one sense, and perhaps in strictness, every lease which is not for a term certain is a lease at will, although of late years the phrase is ordinarily used to describe a tenure under which the lessor may determine the lease instanter. But this was not the original idea of a lease at will. Thus, a tenant under the tenancy now called tenancy from year to year was originally spoken of as a tenant at will whose tenancy could not be determined by either party without due notice to quit: Woodfall, citing *Parker d. Walker v. Constable* (1769) 3 Wils. 25; 95 E.R. 913. But "the judges, seeing the inconvenience of so uncertain a holding, and that the tenant was usually entitled to emblements, very early adopted the inference that it was intended that the tenancy should be a tenancy to be put an end to by either party expressing such to be his will, but only at the end of the year; and they superadded to that, what is expressed in the *Year Book*, 13 H. 8, fo. 13 b., viz., that it must be a half-year's notice. Thus we have the general rule of law that no notice was necessary; and then we have the exception established for the sake of convenience, that, in the case of a tenancy from year to year, the notice to determine it shall be a six months' notice": *Jones v. Mills* (1861) 10 C.B. (N.S.) 788 at 799;

142 E.R. 664 at 668 per Willis J. The reason for adopting this rule was that six months was considered a reasonable length of notice: *Doe d. Martin v. Watts* (1797) 7 T.R. 85; 101 E.R. 866.

In 19 Car. II it was agreed by the Court of King's Bench that if land be leased at will and the rent is received half-yearly or quarterly the lessee cannot determine his will two or three days before the rent day, because that would be a fraudulent determination: *Kighly v. Bulkly* (1667) 1 Sid. 338; 82 E.R. 1143.

In *Jones v. Mills* (1861) 10 C.B.N.S. 788; 142 E.R. 664 the learned judges treated what is commonly called a weekly tenancy as a form of tenancy at will which could not be determined without some notice, that is, reasonable notice, but did not decide what length of notice was necessary. The same considerations apply to any other tenancy the termination of which is not definitely fixed. In my opinion there is no authority for saying that there cannot be a lease at will terminable upon reasonable notice. In some cases such a tenancy may also be described as a tenancy from year to year terminable upon reasonable notice. The rule that a tenancy from year to year is only terminable by a half-year's notice terminating at the end of the year is not a rule of law, but only a rebuttable presumption. Such a tenancy may be made terminable on the happening of any event which the parties think fit: *R. v. Herstmonceaux* (1827) 7 B. & C. 551; 108 E.R. 828.

A lease until either party shall give six months' notice to the other does not constitute a tenancy from year to year, but it is a good lease: *Doe d. King v. Grafton* (1852) 18 Q.B. 496. I suppose it is technically a lease at will, and it was so described by counsel arguendo in *Lewis v. Baker* [1906] 2 K.B. 599. Farwell L.J., however, described it as a term certain (at 603). *Jones v. Mills* (1861) 10 C.B.N.S. 788; 142 E.R. 664 shows that a reasonable notice may be stipulated for as well as a fixed notice.

The principles of the common law of England introduced into Australia on its first settlement are rules of common sense founded on general convenience, and are not in their application limited to cases of which an exact analogue can be found in some law book. That law allows parties to enter into any agreement they choose, provided that it is not forbidden by Statute or contrary to the public welfare, and endeavours to give effect to such agreements. If it is necessary to classify every contract for occupation of land as belonging to some recognised genus or species (which I do not admit) there is, as I have shown, no difficulty in classifying the contract now in question.

If regard is had to the annual obligations of owners of land under the *Pastures Protection Act* 1902 (N.S.W.) and Fencing Acts, there is some ground for saying that the respective tenancies were from year to year. But it is not necessary to decide the point.

For the reasons I have given I am of opinion that the plaintiff was, in point of law, lessee (whether at will or from year to year) of the land upon which the Bridge waterhole lay, the lease being terminable upon reasonable notice, and that the action of the defendants in cutting the fence and taking the water and excluding the plaintiff from the use of it was unlawful and actionable unless they had first determined the tenancy.

Even in the view (which I think is without support in principle or authority) that a tenancy at will is at law necessarily determinable instanter at the will of either party, notwithstanding that, as in this case, there is a valuable continuing consideration, which is in the nature of rent (see *Doe d. Edney v. Benham* (1845) 7 Q.B. 976), a court of equity would, in my opinion, enforce specific performance of an agreement to give exclusive occupation of land for purposes requiring permanency of tenure and containing a stipulation that the occupation should not be determined without reasonable notice.

If it were necessary that a formal instrument of demise should be executed, it might be in the form of a demise for one day certain, and thereafter until the expiration of a reasonable notice given by either party to the other. It is not disputed that in the present case the right of exclusive occupation was to endure for one day at least. It cannot be doubted that such a demise, although in form unusual, would be perfectly valid, and would not be an attempt to create a new kind of tenure unknown to the law. And, if effect could not be given to the intention of the parties without such a deed, a court of equity would compel its execution.

In either view, therefore, whether the case is regarded as a trespass by a lessor upon his lessee under claim of right, or as a breach of agreement for valuable consideration relating to permanent occupation of land, the plaintiff is entitled to relief, unless the notice given by the defendants of their intended action was reasonable. Having regard to the facts already stated, I think it impossible to take the view that it was reasonable. Under Australian pastoral conditions water cannot be provided for a flock of hundreds of sheep in dry country at a few days' notice.

In my opinion, then, the agreement has not been terminated but is still subsisting, and is a lawful and valid agreement.

I think that there should be a declaration that the plaintiff is entitled under the agreement of 1895 to the exclusive occupation of the land and natural water lying to the north of the fence as it stood on 9 April 1908 until the agreement shall have been terminated by a reasonable notice given by one party to the other, and to an injunction to restrain the defendants until such termination from interfering with such occupation or with the fence as it then stood. He is also entitled to an inquiry as to damages, which should be assessed as in an action for trespass.

[Barton and O'Connor JJ., in separate judgments, came to a similar result.]

ISAACS J. (Dissenting).

[His Honour stated the facts, and found that the agreement between the adjoining owners from time to time concerning the position of the give and take fence, "though indefinite was not perpetual but revocable or determinable"; on the other hand, "it could not be that either party was understood to be at liberty to abandon the line of fence at any moment and in any circumstances without warning. That would have been wholly unreasonable. . . ." He rejected arguments that there existed a tenancy for the expected life of the fence, or a tenancy from year to year, and concluded that the only tenancy which could be implied from the facts was a tenancy at will. He went on, however, to distinguish between a right to continue in possession until the expiration of a reasonable period of notice, and a right to possession terminable on notice, whether reasonable or not, but subject to liability for damages for an unreasonably short notice or an injunction restraining eviction until a reasonable time after notice. He continued:]

Well, if it be not a tenancy from year to year, it must in the circumstances be a tenancy at will. Then it was argued that even a tenancy of this nature may yet be impliedly non-determinable except at the expiration of a reasonable notice to quit. This appears to me to involve a contradiction. Merely because the lessor under an implied tenancy at will is bound contractually by a further implication to give reasonable notice so as not to prejudice the lessee, the contention is that, therefore, the tenancy itself must continue, that is the lessee's legal title to and tenure in the land itself continues, until the expiration of a reasonable notice to quit. This proposition likewise suffers from a dearth of supporting authority, and, if true, would afford a defence in ejectment in a court of law, and render equitable interposition unnecessary. That argument was addressed to a court once, and I think only once before, in 1830, in the case of *Doe d. Nicholl v. M'Kaeg* (1830) 10 B. & C. 721; 109 E.R. 618. It was urged that the tenant at will was entitled to some notice, that he was occupying the house as part of his reward for doing the duties of minister to a chapel, and could not at a moment's warning be called upon to go out with his family and furniture into the street at the peril of being dealt with as a trespasser. In all cases of continuing contract, it was urged, some reasonable notice must be given of putting an end to it. Now that is precisely what is urged here. But Lord Tenterden C.J., who spoke for himself and the whole Court of King's Bench, said what appears to me to equally answer the plaintiff's contention in this case. His words were: "It was contended, that a demand of possession was not sufficient in this case to determine the tenancy, but that a reasonable time ought to have been allowed the defendant for the purpose of removing his goods. We can find no authority in the law for such a position. The general rule is, that where an estate is held at the will of another, a demand by that other determines the will. If, in this case, we were to hold otherwise, we should introduce a new rule, not to be found in the books, which might be productive of great inconvenience; for then, in every case of tenancy at will, it might be made a question, what is a reasonable time for removing goods. If the tenant, after the determination of his tenancy in this case, by a demand of possession, had entered on the premises for the sole purpose of removing his goods, and continued there no longer than was necessary for that purpose, and did not exclude the landlord, perhaps he might not have been a trespasser; but, however that may be, we are of opinion, that he being a tenant at will, his estate was determined by a demand of possession, and, consequently, that the lessors of the plaintiff were entitled to recover."

What Lord Tenterden and his fellow judges refused to do, appears to me not distinguishable from what this court is now asked to do. Nor is it a valid answer that equity would take a different view from the standpoint of implied agreement. In *Spurgin v. White* (1860) 7 Jur. (N.S.) 15 at 18; 66 E.R. 198 at 199, Vice-Chancellor Stuart followed *Doe v. M'Kaeg* (1830) 10 B. & C. 721; 109 E.R. 618, in circumstances which strongly emphasise the view that I have expressed. White was engaged as manager of an association of which plaintiffs were trustees, upon the terms of receiving a certain salary, and while manager, of occupying part of the house, the legal estate of which was in the trustees, and also of using another part of the house, during his occupation as manager, for the purpose of carrying on his own trade as bookseller. It was part of the agreement that six months notice of separation should be given on either side.

The Committee terminated his engagement instanter, and the question arose what was the nature of his holding. The Vice-Chancellor said: "It seems to me that the true view of Mr White's rights of occupation and use of the shop for the purposes of trade or any other use is this, that it is the same precarious right which has been dealt with in many cases, but in particular such as was dealt with by the Court of Queen's Bench in the two cases of *Doe d. Jones v. Jones* (1829) 10 B. & C. 718; 109 E.R. 267, and *Doe v. M'Kaeg* (1830) 10 B. & C. 721; 109 E.R. 618."

The learned Vice-Chancellor after quoting Lord Tenterden said that in the case before him, however, there was a right to six months notice, but he was clearly of opinion that the only liability of the plaintiff at law for not giving that notice was in damages; and he left the question of equitable interposition of the court on grounds of *personal obligation* to be determined upon the facts as they should appear at the hearing of the cause. So far therefore as the plaintiff's case rests upon any tenure in the land beyond that of a strict tenancy at will it fails.

I do not agree with the view that because a tenancy from year to year can be created, with any period of termination: see *Re Threlfall* (1880) 16 Ch. D. 274, that the same can be done in the case of a tenancy at will. In the first case there is a term—a definite duration prima facie agreed upon—and that may be made defeasible upon any condition the parties choose. But you cannot defeat a term that does not exist, and when a letting is entirely indefinite as to its duration you cannot convert it into a definite term by a condition as to notice which is equally indefinite. Once concede it is a tenancy at will, there can be no condition inconsistent with it. . . .

The plaintiff contends that, even if the defendants could at their will determine the tenancy, they have not done so; and that what they have done amounts merely to a trespass, because the defendants had not evinced the intention to put an end to the entire arrangement. Here again, I am unable to agree to the view so presented. As I understand the law, the landlord of a tenant at will can never trespass on the property let. If the act complained of is with the consent of the tenant, or in pursuance of the agreement of tenancy, it is of course not a trespass, because lawful: see *Lynes v. Snaith* [1899] 1 Q.B. at 486. If it is opposed to or without the tenant's consent it is regarded by the law as ipso facto a determination of the tenancy, and equally free from liability to trespass. . . .

The act complained of in the case at bar was, on the authorities I have referred to, a clear determination of whatever tenancy at will existed and, as shown by *Spurgin v. White* (1860) 7 Jur. N.S. 15; 66 E.R. 198, equity would so regard it as well as law. Looking at the plaintiff's case therefore from the standpoint of actual title to or interest legal or equitable in the defendants' land, I am of opinion it cannot be sustained.

COMMONWEALTH LIFE (AMALGAMATED) ASSURANCE LTD v. ANDERSON

Supreme Court of New South Wales (1945) 46 S.R. 47

JORDAN C.J. A tenancy at will exists whenever, by virtue of an express or implied agreement between the landowner and another person, the other is in exclusive possession of the land, otherwise than as servant or agent of the owner, for an estate which is not of freehold or for a term. A tenancy at will is subject to many inconveniences. It is necessarily terminable at the will of either party by demand of possession, express or implied. It differs in this respect, as in others, from a licence: *Minister of Health v. Bellotti* [1944] K.B. 298, in that no period of notice is necessary for its termination; although, on termination by the owner, the tenant has a reasonable time to enter and remove his goods, but not a right to exclusive possession for the purpose: *Doe d. Nicholl v. M'Kaeg* (1830) 10 B. & C. 721; 109 E.R. 618. Indeed, it is at least doubtful whether (apart from statute, as in the *Conveyancing Act* 1919 (N.S.W.), s. 127) an express provision for notice prevents termination without notice by either party, although the other may have remedies for breach of contract: *Landale v. Menzies* (1909) 9 C.L.R. 89. Since the existence of the tenancy depends upon the will of the parties, the death of either terminates his will, and, therefore, the tenancy: *James v. Dean* (1805) 11 Ves. Jr 383 at 391; 32 E.R. 1135 at 1138. The estate created by the tenancy is unassignable, because a purported assignment terminates it as soon as it comes to the notice of the owner: *Pinhorn v. Souster* (1858) 8 Exch. 763 at 772-773.

NOTES AND QUESTIONS

1. In *Errington v. Errington* [1952] 1 K.B. 290, above p. 500, Denning L.J. said: "[I]n my opinion it is of the essence of a tenancy at will that it should be determinable by either party on demand": [1952] 1 K.B. 290 at 296. Does this conflict with the view of Griffith C.J., Barton and O'Connor JJ. in *Landale v. Menzies* (1909) 9 C.L.R. 89, above p. 540.

2. In *Heslop v. Burns* [1974] 1 W.L.R. 1241, noted above p. 511 Scarman L.J. referred to the recent emergence of the licence to occupy, which he saw as the result of changed social conditions, and said:

> In the books, and we were referred to a passage in Woodfall, *Landlord and Tenant* (27th ed.), Vol. 1, para. 669, one finds still the assertion that an exclusive occupation of indefinite duration can create a tenancy at will. The social changes to which I have alluded seem to show that less and less will the courts be inclined to infer a tenancy at will from an exclusive occupation of indefinite duration. It may be that the tenancy at will can now serve only one legal purpose, and that is to protect the interests of an occupier during a period of transition. If one looks to the classic cases in which tenancies at will continue to be inferred, namely, the case of someone who goes into possession prior to a contract of purchase, or of someone who, with the consent of the landlord, holds over after the expiry of his lease, one sees that in each there is a transitional period during which negotiations are being conducted touching the estate or interest in the land that has to be protected, and the tenancy at will is an apt legal mechanism to protect the occupier during such a period of transition: he is there and can keep out trespassers: he is there with the consent of the landlord and can keep out the landlord as long as that consent is maintained. It may be, therefore, that, not under any change in the law, but under the impact of changing social circumstances, the tenancy at will has suffered a certain change, at any rate in its purpose and function.

3. Tenancy from year to year

MOORE v. DIMOND

High Court of Australia (1929) 43 C.L.R. 105

[Moore had leased premises to Dimond for a term of five years and eight months expiring on 30 November 1927. In May 1927, the parties made an agreement in writing for a lease for a further term of five years at a weekly rent of £16 10s., but no formal lease was ever executed. Dimond remained in occupation, paying rent of £16 10s. weekly in advance.

Dimond vacated the premises on 17 November 1928, and Moore brought an action in the Local Court of Adelaide claiming £16 10s. as rent due for the week ending 24 November 1928. The judge of the Local Court held that Moore was entitled to succeed, on two grounds: (1) the agreement for the further lease was specifically enforceable in equity; and in the alternative, (2) that at common law the circumstances gave rise to a tenancy from year to year which had not been validly terminated by the tenant.

A case was then stated for the opinion of the Supreme Court, which held (1) that the Local Court had no jurisdiction to decree specific performance (the value of the premises being above the statutorily prescribed limit to the equitable jurisdiction of the Local Court); and (2) that the common law tenancy which arose was a tenancy from week to week. The basis of the Supreme Court's finding on the second point was that occupation and payment of a weekly rent were prima facie evidence of a weekly tenancy.

Moore then appealed to the High Court against the second finding of the Supreme Court. The High Court proceeded on the basis that the rights of the parties fell to be determined at law only, without reference to their position in equity.]

KNOX C.J., RICH AND DIXON JJ. Another conclusion which sufficiently appears is that the respondent remained, and the appellant permitted him to remain, in occupation of the premises after 30 November 1927 in intended performance of the agreement and that the appellant, as lessor, accepted, and the respondent, as lessee, paid the weekly sum of £16 10s. from 1 December 1927 to 17 November 1928, as the rent stipulated for in the agreement. An examination of the correspondence shows that it does support the conclusion that a complete agreement was made. As the agreement for a lease was not a demise, but an executory contract to grant a lease, it could not operate to create an interesse termini and, immediately upon the effluxion of the prior term, the respondent became at law (although of course not in equity) a tenant at will only. Upon the first payment of rent he became entitled at law to a term, but the question is whether the term was from week to week or from year to year. In *Hamerton v. Stead* (1824) 3 B. & C. 478 at 483; 107 E.R. 811 at 813 Littledale J. said: "Where parties enter under a mere agreement for a future lease they are tenants at will; and if rent is paid under the agreement, they become tenants from year to year, determinable on the execution of the lease contracted for, that being the primary contract." This statement was approved by Hill J. in *Anderson v. Midland Railway Co.* (1861) 3 E. & E. 614 at 622; 121 E.R. 573 at 576. It was well settled at law that the terms and conditions of the agreement, save in so far as they are inconsistent with a tenancy from year to year, apply to the tenancy. It was further settled that the tenancy from year to year continued only during the term contracted for, and expired at the end of that term by effluxion of time without notice to quit, being in the meantime liable to a sooner determination by notice to quit. In *Doe d. Davenish v. Moffatt* (1850) 15 Q.B. 257 at 265; 117 E.R. 455 at 458 Lord Campbell C.J. says: "According to *Doe d. Bromfield v. Smith* (1805) 6 East 530; 102 E.R. 1390, and other cases cited on the argument, this would be the effect of a holding under an agreement to grant a lease for a term certain. At the expiration of that term, no notice to quit is necessary; and it would be strange if the tenant had a more extended interest under an agreement to grant a lease than he would have had under the lease had it actually been granted. In *Doe d. Tilt v. Stratton* (1828) 4 Bing. 446; 130 E.R. 839 a reason is given for the judgment, which would not apply here, that the agreement for a term certain was a notice to quit at the end of the term. Here the lease, turned into an agreement, contemplated a probability of the tenancy continuing after the expiration of the three years. But, instead of considering the agreement a notice to quit, we think the better view of the subject is that possession under the agreement creates a tenancy from year to year, which may be determined by a notice to quit during the time specified in the agreement for the duration of the lease, but which expires at the end of that time without any notice to quit.": see *Doe d. Oldershaw v. Breach* (1807) 6 Esp. 106; 170 E.R. 844. These principles applied whenever the tenant held under an agreement for a lease whether the agreement was expressed as an executory contract or consisted of an intended demise for more than three years void, because not under seal. In such cases the contractual intention of the parties is completely expressed in a binding manner, but is formally inefficacious to create a legal interest of the intended duration.

There is little resemblance between such a case and the very many instances in which a person has been let into, or has retained, possession of land without any express contract, and the question is whether he is a tenant, and if so, for a term of what duration. Such cases occur when a tenant overholds; when a tenant for life has granted a lease in excess of his power and dies before its determination, and the remainderman allows the lessee to retain possession; when a mortgagor has granted a lease without statutory or other power; and when the terms of entry are too vague or uncertain to be ascertainable. In such cases payment or acknowledgment of rent constitutes evidence of the establishment of a tenancy, and the fact that the rent is paid by reference to a year, or aliquot part of a year, affords evidence of a tenancy from year to year. The existence and duration of the tenancy in such a case were, however, questions of fact. On the other hand, in *Doe d. Thomson v. Amey* (1840) 12 A. & E. 476; 113 E.R. 892, in deciding that a proviso for re-entry formed a condition of a tenancy from year to year, implied from entry and payment of rent pursuant to an agreement for a lease containing such a condition, Patteson J. said ((1840) 12 A. & E. 476 at 480; 113 E.R. 892 at 893-894): "The terms upon which the tenant holds are in truth a conclusion of law from the facts of the case, and the terms of the articles of agreement."

In the one case the question is what common intention should be attributed to the parties, in the other the question is what duration of tenancy replaces that upon which they have expressly agreed? In the latter case it is difficult to see why the period in respect of which rent is paid should afford a criterion of or determine the term. Nevertheless, in *Braythwayte v. Hitchcock* (1842) 10 M. & W. 494 at 497; 152 E.R. 565 at 567 Parke B. said: "Although the law is clearly settled, that where there has been an agreement for a lease, and an occupation without payment of rent, the occupier is a mere tenant at will; yet it has been held that if he subsequently pays rent under that agreement, he thereby becomes tenant from year to year. Payment of rent, indeed, must be understood to mean a payment with reference to a yearly holding; for in *Richardson v. Langridge* (1811) 4 Taunt. 128; 13 R.R. 570; 128 E.R. 277 a party who had paid rent under an agreement of this description, but had not paid it with reference to a year or any aliquot part of a year, was held nevertheless to be a tenant at will only." In point of fact Parke B. was mistaken in his reference to *Richardson v. Langridge*, because there the land was let to the carrier "without any reference to time" ((1811) 4 Taunt. 128 at 129; 13 R.R. 570 at 571; 128 E.R. 277), and Mansfield C.J. said ((1811) 4 Taunt. 128 at 131; 13 R.R. 570 at 573; 128 E.R. 277 at 278): "Here you speak, all along, of an indefinite agreement. If there were a general letting at a yearly rent; though payable half-yearly, or quarterly, and though nothing were said about the duration of the term, it is an implied letting from year to year. But if two parties agree that the one shall let, and the other shall hold, so long as both parties please, that is a holding at will." In the later case of *Lee v. Smith* (1854) 9 Ex. 662; 156 E.R. 284 Parke B. relied upon payment of a quarterly rent as proof of a tenancy from year to year, and Martin B. said his impression was that the party would have succeeded without the receipts (scilicet, for rent) and that he would have been entitled to refer to the instrument for the purpose of seeing what the terms of the tenancy were; whereupon Parke B. said ((1854) 9 Ex. 662 at 666; 156 E.R. 284 at 285): "I do not say that I dissent from that proposition, but here the proof of that fact appeared more strongly without it."

In the many cases at law in which it was decided that a tenant entering or holding under an agreement for a lease became on payment of rent a tenant from year to year, the rent or the render has been annual; and apparently no case has before come for decision in which the rent was not calculated by reference to a year or a part of a year. But, save for these observations of Parke B., no case of an agreement for a term of years has been found in which the character of the rent has been relied upon as determining the duration of the tenancy. At an early stage of the history of tenancies from year to year a presumption arose in favour of that tenure. In his

History of English Law, Vol. VII., p. 245, Sir W. S. Holdsworth says that the ruling of Holt C.J. that the tenancy could only be terminated at the end of each year "shows that opinion was beginning to lean in favour of construing a tenancy, when no certain term was mentioned, as a tenancy from year to year. In the latter part of the 18th century this leaning became so pronounced that, on one occasion, Lord Mansfield even went so far as to say that, 'in the country, leases at will . . . being found extremely inconvenient exist only notionally; and were succeeded by another species of contract which was less inconvenient'. This, of course, was an exaggeration. Tenancies at will still exist; and the presumption of the existence of a tenancy from year to year, arising from the payment of rent, can always be rebutted. But the presumption had undoubtedly come to be very strong in the 18th century—so strong that it was held that, though the *Statute of Frauds* had enacted that a parol lease should operate only as a lease at will, such a parol lease will operate as a lease from year to year if rent has been paid thereunder." This presumption has continued and still prevails. In *Doe d. Martin and Jones v. Watts* (1797) 7 T.R. 83 at 85, 86; 101 E.R. 866 at 868 Grose J. said: "The plaintiff received rent of the defendant; and from that moment he admitted that the defendant was a tenant to him of some kind; and no other tenancy appearing here, the defendant must be considered as tenant from year to year." In *Roe v. Prideaux* (1808) 10 East 158 at 187; 103 E.R. 735 at 746 Lord Ellenborough says: "The receipt of rent is evidence to be left to a jury that a tenancy was subsisting during the period for which that rent was paid; and if no other tenancy appear, the presumption is that that tenancy was from year to year." In Preston's edition of *Watkins' Principles of Conveyancing* (1820) he says: "All leases made generally and not for any particular period, are by construction of law, leases from year to year." This was recognised by Cozens-Hardy J. in *Low v. Adams* [1901] 2 Ch. 598 at 601: "A general occupation of land was, as long ago as the Year-Books, held to be an occupation from year to year." In principle there appears to be no reason why the circumstance that the rent paid under an agreement for a term of five years is weekly should displace this presumption in favour of the yearly tenancy. The doctrine which justifies reference to the period of the rent in order to ascertain the term no doubt is that the rent is a compensation for the land, and the parties have so understood it. A quarterly payment thus implies a yearly tenancy because it is part of the compensation for a year's holding. When the parties agree for a five years' holding with weekly payments of the compensatory rent, their intention is not that each week's rent shall represent a distinct and therefore terminable holding of a week. The weekly rent is part of the compensation for the entire period. Where the intention of the parties is to hold for a greater duration than a yearly tenancy would give them, and this intention fails because of its want of appropriate expression or of formal demise, the presumption or assumption that a general holding is from year to year supplies the term.

It should, perhaps, be added that the conclusion which has been thus reached appears to be supported by the views adopted in four of the Australian States in relation to the implication of tenancies from year to year: see *Ex parte Murphy* (1856) 2 Legge (N.S.W.) 976; *Bloomfield v. Bloomfield* (1893) 9 N.S.W.W.N. 188; *Bank of Victoria v. M'Hutchison* (1881) 7 V.L.R. (L.) 452; *Box v. Attfield* (1886) 12 V.L.R. 574; 8 A.L.T. 45; *Morison v. Edmiston* [1907] V.L.R. 191; 26 A.L.T. 148; *Beattie v. Fine* [1925] V.L.R. 363; 47 A.L.T. 19; *Marshall v. Coupon Furnishing Co.* [1916] S.R. (Q.) 120 at 125; *Styles & Co. v. Richardson* (1915) 17 W.A.L.R. 81.

It follows that at law, whatever may be the position in equity, the respondent would be considered a tenant from year to year.

The appeal is allowed with costs.

The second answer or statement of opinion of the Supreme Court is set aside, the opinion of this court being that at common law the defendant was a tenant from year to year.

Order that the case be remitted to the Supreme Court to do what is right in accordance with this opinion.

ISAACS J.

[His Honour, after stating the facts, referred to the appellant Moore's argument that occupation plus payment of any rent whatsoever raised a presumption, subject to rebuttal, that a tenancy from year to year exists. He said that he did not agree with this argument, and proceeded:]

In *Landale v. Menzies* (1909) 9 C.L.R. 89 at 129-130 I cited cases and textwriters from 1778 to 1907—which I need not now repeat—establishing as a firmly-rooted doctrine that in order to raise the implication of a tenancy from year to year the rent paid must be what is called an "annual" rent, that is, a rent referable to a year or some aliquot part of it, so as to give it, so to speak, a yearly character. Later authorities confirming this will be mentioned presently. There are to be found some judicial observations referring to tenancies from year to year which employ the word "rent" without the adjective "annual" or its equivalent. But those are always, so far as I have seen, alio intuitu, and in cases where the rent was in fact of a yearly character and "annual" was verbum inauditum. No judicial decision or even dictum has been brought under notice contrary to those included in *Landale v. Menzies* (1909) 9 C.L.R. 89. If we approach the matter from the standpoint of principle, the same conclusion is reached, and very naturally so. The implied tenancy from year to year does not rest on the actual intention of the parties to create such a tenancy. It is "a conclusion of law": per Patteson J. in *Doe d. Thomson v. Amey* (1840) 12 A. & E. at 480; 113 E.R., at 894. It rests on a presumption that the law makes from their acts, that they have contracted to create a tenancy from year to year. The presumption is the same for all persons, including corporations: *Doe d. Pennington v. Taniere* (1848) 12 Q.B. 998; 116 E.R. 1144. . . .

In my opinion, therefore, unless in view of all the circumstances the rent paid has a yearly character, the court cannot presume a tenancy from year to year, for the payment of rent would be repugnant to such tenancy. . . .

It follows from what I have already said that, if nothing more appeared, the payment of a weekly rent would not be sufficient to raise the presumption of a tenancy from year to year. In *Adams v. Cairns* (1901) 85 L.T. 10 at 11 Williams L.J. said: "If there were nothing more than the reservation of a weekly rent, the inference would be drawn that there was a weekly tenancy." But the matter does not end there. It is important to observe that the court examines all the relevant circumstances which taken as a whole may overcome the prima facie effect of the payment taken alone. That is to say, the fact of a rent being a weekly rent or a yearly rent is not conclusive that the tenancy is weekly or from year to year. As to the weekly rent, the cases of *Bank of Victoria v. M'Hutchison* (1881) 7 V.L.R. (L.) 452 and *Box v. Attfield* (1886) 12 V.L.R. 574; 8 A.L.T. 45 are cases in point, and, in my opinion, are correct. As to a yearly rent, the observations of Parke B. in *Doe d. Dixie v. Davies* (1851) 7 Ex. 89; 155 E.R. 868 are relevant. *Smith v. Widlake* (1877) 3 C.P.D. 10 is an authority on the point. The rent of sixpence was paid as yearly rent, but, having regard to its disproportion in relation to the annual value of the property, the court declined to regard it as sufficient to raise the presumption. Bramwell L.J. said ((1877) 3 C.P.D. 10 at 15): "the payment of rent is at most only evidence of a tenancy from year to year." Then on the facts he held that the money was not received as rent under such a tenancy, but under a mistaken notion of confirmation of a void lease.

Once the principle is granted that the court makes the presumption or implication *in law* from all the relevant facts evidencing the conduct of the parties, and in so doing adheres inexorably to the essentiality of the rent having an annual character, for the plain reason that, unless it is so, it cannot be rent for a lease from year to year, the matter here seems to present no difficulty on the facts. First of all, it is undeniable that the respondent did not hold over; that is, his occupation after 30 November was not an unauthorised occupation which apart from payment of rent would have made him a tenant at sufferance and would have referred prima facie the payment of rent to the terms of the expired tenancy. He held as tenant at will, at least until payment of rent, because he held under the terms of the agreement for a new lease. The rent of itself, which was not paid for a full year, though very nearly so, would, as already stated, have effected no change, because without more the court would have no evidence on which to base a legal conclusion from conduct that the rent was paid with reference to a yearly holding. But part of the relevant conduct may, in accordance with judicial authority already stated, include entry upon or retention of possession upon the faith of an agreement: see *Doe d. Rigge v. Bell* (1793) 5 T.R. 471 at 472; 101 E.R. 265 at 266 and per Williams J. in *Doe d. Thomson v. Amey* (1840) 12 A. & E. at 480; 113 E.R. at 894. *Tress v. Savage* (1854) 4 E. & B. 36 is an authority for this, and has been followed in *Martin v. Smith* (1874) L.R. 9 Ex. 50 at 52. So in *Bank of Victoria v. M'Hutchison* (1881) 7 V.L.R. (L.) 452. The agreement for this purpose is regarded not as a binding contract, but as evidence of the mutual understanding and intention of the terms on which the premises were held and the rent was paid, that is, of the conduct of the parties. Looking at the agreement in this case for that purpose, and all the attendant circumstances, I entertain no doubt there was abundant evidence of circumstances without repugnance on which to found the necessary presumption of a tenancy from year to year. That conclusion being a matter of law, I am of opinion it should be drawn, and this the court, in the words of Warrington L.J. ([1919] 2 Ch. 343 at 353), "is bound to do"; and the fourth question, namely, "Is the defendant liable for the rent claimed?" should be answered in the affirmative.

STARKE J. In this case we are dealing with technical aspects of the law rather than with the real rights of the parties.

[O]wing to the limited jurisdiction of the Local Court of Adelaide and the form of the plaintiff's claim, the question in this case is whether the defendant is at law a tenant from year to year. It is not a question of fact, but rather an implication of law from the proved facts and circumstances of the case. It would be idle, after the exhaustive examination by the Chief Justice and my learned brethren of the authorities, to traverse them again. The learned judges of the Supreme Court of South Australia held that the mode in which the rent was reserved—on the basis of £16 10s. per week—"affords a presumption that the tenancy is of a character corresponding to it": Foa on *Landlord and Tenant* (6th ed.), p. 3. But that presumption is not conclusive, and "other parts of the instrument" may rebut it. An agreement to grant "a further five years' lease", coupled with the payment and acceptance of rent, effectively destroys, in my opinion, any implication that the intention of the parties was to create a weekly tenancy, and raises an implication in point of law that the parties, as they could not by agreement lawfully create a term of five years, must have intended to create a yearly tenancy. I therefore agree that the appeal should be allowed.

One other observation is perhaps desirable: the plaintiff and his advisers should consider whether they can enforce specific performance of the agreement for a five years' lease if they take a judgment in the present proceedings on the footing of a tenancy from year to year subsisting at law between the parties. An estoppel by judgment may arise, but I have formed no opinion upon the question, and I express none.

Appeal allowed.

NOTES

1. The High Court in the instant case considered only the position of the parties *at law*. It is apparent that the position *in equity* would have been quite different. As to the position in equity, see below p. 559. For another instance where the court was considering only the position at law, see *I.C.I. Alkali (Aust). Pty Ltd (in liq.) v. Commissioner of Taxation (Cth)* (1979) 53 A.L.J.R. 220 at 224.

2. In *Bank of Victoria v. M'Hutchison* (1881) 7 V.L.R. (L.) 452 and *Box v. Attfield* (1886) 12 V.L.R. 574, approved in the above extracts from the principal case, the Victorian Full Court held that where a tenant, holding over at the expiration of a tenancy for a fixed term of one year under which rent was payable weekly, continues to pay rent weekly, a tenancy from year to year arises. These cases were not followed by the English Court of Appeal in *Adler v. Blackman* [1953] 1 Q.B. 146, where a distinction was drawn between a lease for a fixed term of one year with the rent stated as a rent per year, but payable by weekly instalments, and a lease for a fixed term of one year with the rent expressed simply as so much per week: in the former case, a tenancy from year to year may arise where the tenant holds over and pays rent weekly, because the weekly amounts can be viewed as instalments of a yearly sum; but in the latter case, all that can be presumed on a holding over is a tenancy for the period in respect of which rent is expressed, namely, a weekly tenancy.

3. The history of the development of the tenancy from year to year was traced by Jordan C.J. in *Dockrill v. Cavanagh* (1944) 45 S.R. (N.S.W.) 78 at 80-82, in these terms:

> At common law, no formalities were required for the making of a lease. It could be granted by word of mouth. In 1677, however, the following provisions were enacted by the *Statute of Frauds* 1677 (U.K.) (29 Charles II c. 3):

> > Section 1 . . . all leases, estates, interests of freehold, or terms of years, or any uncertain interest of, in, to or out of any messuages, manors, lands, tenements or hereditaments, made or created by livery and seisin only, or by parol, and not put in writing, and signed by the parties so making or creating the same, or their agents thereunto lawfully authorised by writing, shall have the force and effect of leases or estates at will only, and shall not either in law or equity be deemed or taken to have any other or greater force or effect; any consideration for making any such parol leases or estates, or any former law or usage, to the contrary notwithstanding.

> > Section 2 . . . Except nevertheless all leases not exceeding the term of three years from the making thereof, whereupon the rent reserved to the landlord, during such term, shall amount unto two third parts at the least of the full improved value of the thing demised.

> > Section 4 . . . no action shall be brought . . . upon any contract or sale of lands, tenements or hereditaments, or any interest in or concerning them . . . unless the agreement upon which such action shall be brought, or some memorandum or note thereof, shall be in writing, and signed by the party to be charged therewith, or some other person thereunto by him lawfully authorised.

> The Statute did not affect dispositions by deed, which stood outside it, and hence leases upon any terms could still be made by deed: *Cherry v. Heming* (1849) 4 Exch. 631; 154 E.R. 1367. But apart from this, the Statute provided that, as regards form, there should thenceforth be only two types of lease, (1) leases in writing and signed by the parties: such leases might be on any terms and for any period; and (2) leases not in writing signed by the parties: such leases were to operate only as leases at will, unless they were for a period not exceeding three years from their making, at a rack-rent, in which case they operated according to their terms.

> After the Statute, if a tenant entered under a lease for more than three years which was not in writing, he held prima facie as tenant at will only: *Goodtitle v. Herbert* (1792) 4 T.R. 680; 100 E.R. 1241. It was soon decided, however, that if such a tenant paid rent which could be referred to a yearly tenancy, as where it was for an aliquot part of a year, the lease at will prima facie

became changed to a lease from year to year: *Berrey v. Lindley* (1841) 3 Man. & Gr. 498 at 512
(n.); 133 E.R. 1240 at 1245; *Braythwayte v. Hitchcock* (1842) 10 M. & W. 494; 152 E.R. 565;
Tooker v. Smith (1857) 1 H. & N. 732 at 735-736. "The tenancy from year to year succeeded
to the old tenancy at will, which was attended with many inconveniences. In order to obviate
them, the courts very early raised an implied contract for a year, and added that the tenant could
not be removed at the end of the year without receiving six months previous notice": *Doe dem
Shore v. Porter* (1789) 3 T.R. 13 at 16-17; 100 E.R. 429 at 429. It was further held that if,
although there was no written lease, the tenant went into possession and paid rent referable to
a yearly tenancy under an agreement for a lease which would be specifically enforceable in equity,
not only did he become tenant from year to year, but he became entitled and subject to all the
provisions of the agreement which were applicable to a tenancy from year to year: *Coatsworth
v. Johnson* (1886) 54 L.T. 520. "It is argued, that the tenancy arises by operation of law upon
payment of rent, and that the law implies no particular mode of cropping, nor any condition of
re-entry. But the terms upon which the tenant holds are in truth a conclusion of law from the
facts of the case, and the terms of the articles of agreement": *Doe dem Thomson v. Amey* (1840)
12 A. & E. 476 at 480; 113 E.R. 892 at 893; *Moore v. Dimond* (1929) 43 C.L.R. 105 at 119-120;
12 Austn Digest 906. In this respect there was no difference between a person holding over and
a person who entered and paid rent on the faith of an executory agreement for a lease: *Moore
v. Dimond* (1929) 43 C.L.R. 105 at 114-115. And it has been held that where the agreement under
which the rent was paid provided for a term of years at a weekly rent, the fact that it was weekly
rent that was paid did not prevent the payment from creating a tenancy from year to year, it being
clear that something greater than a yearly tenancy had been intended: *Moore v. Dimond* (1929)
43 C.L.R. 105 at 116-117; 12 Austn Digest 906. The law imputed an intention to create a tenancy
from year to year unless an intention repugnant to this appeared: *Moore v. Dimond* (1929) 43
C.L.R. 105 at 119-123; 12 Austn Digest 906; *Re Weigall & Dawes' Lease* [1942] V.L.R. 49; Austn
Digest (1942) 269. On the other hand, if it appeared that no more than a quarterly or a weekly
tenancy was intended, payment of a quarterly or weekly rent would not bring into existence more
than a lease for a periodic quarterly or weekly tenancy: *Cole v. Kelly* [1920] 2 K.B. 106; *Ladies'
Hosiery and Underwear Ltd v. Parker* [1930] 1 Ch. 304 at 328-329. And if it appeared that only
a tenancy at will was intended, that only would be created: *Richardson v. Langridge* (1811) 4
Taunt. 128; 128 E.R. 277; *Meye v. Electric Transmission Ltd* [1942] Ch. 290. In *Doe dem Rigge
v. Bell* (1793) 5 T.R. 471; 101 E.R. 265 where a tenant had entered and paid rent under a parol
lease which was void because for seven years it was held that it was void only as to the duration
of the lease, and hence a special term that it was to be terminable at Candlemas was enforceable,
so that although notice to quit could be given within the seven years, it must be to quit at some
Candlemas. Further, it is well settled that the tenancy from year to year, although it could be
determined by six months' notice, yet if it were allowed to continue until the end of the term
provided for by the agreement between the parties, became then automatically terminated
without the necessity for any notice: *Doe dem Davenish v. Moffatt* (1850) 15 Q.B. 257; 117 E.R.
455; *Moore v. Dimond* (1929) 43 C.L.R. 105 at 112-113.

It will be seen, therefore, that by a process of judicial legislation, considerable encroachments
had been made upon the provisions of the *Statute of Frauds* 1677 (U.K.). Leases not in writing
signed by the parties were by the Statute to have the force and effect of leases at will only, and
were not either in law or equity to be deemed or taken to have any other or greater force or effect.
If, however, the lessee under such a lease entered into posession and paid rent, not only was the
lease treated as having the force and effect of a lease from year to year, but all the terms of any
agreement between the parties applicable to such a lease were treated as incorporated into it:
Moore v. Dimond (1929) 43 C.L.R. 105 at 116, 123.

Dockrill v. Cavanagh (1944) 45 S.R. (N.S.W.) 78 is extracted further below p. 554 and p. 570.

4. Tenancies under s. 127 of the Conveyancing Act

The common law position stated in *Moore v. Dimond* has to some extent been
altered by statute. Section 127(1) of the *Conveyancing Act* 1919 (N.S.W.) provides:

127. (1) No tenancy from year to year shall, after the commencement of this
Act, be implied by payment of rent; if there is a tenancy, and no agreement as
to its duration, then such tenancy shall be deemed to be a tenancy determinable
at the will of either of the parties by one month's notice in writing expiring at
any time.

The section is poorly drafted. As Dixon J. pointed out in *Turner v. York Motors Pty Ltd* (1951) 85 C.L.R. 55 at 70-71, the second part of the provision, if detached from the first and read literally, would govern every case where the character of the tenancy was implied from the payment of rent and where there was no agreement as to its duration; thus, payment of rent by the week, the month, the quarter or the year (assuming no agreement as to duration) would all alike result in a tenancy at will terminable by a month's notice expiring at any time. The section, however, has been held to apply only where, at common law, a tenancy from year to year would have been implied from the manner of payment of rent. Thus, in *Burnham v. Carroll Musgrove Theatres Ltd* (1927) 28 S.R. (N.S.W.) 169 at 180, Ferguson J. said of s. 127:

> That section was intended to prevent the implication of a tenancy from year to year from the payment of rent, and to substitute for such implied tenancy a tenancy determinable by a month's notice. It was never intended to apply to cases where before the Act no implication of a tenancy from year to year would have arisen.

This statement was approved by the High Court on appeal ((1928) 41 C.L.R. 540 at 548, 563) and has been followed ever since. Thus, s. 127 has been held inapplicable where on the facts there was inferred from the manner of payment of rent a tenancy from week to week (*Burnham v. Carroll Musgrove Theatres Ltd* (1928) 41 C.L.R. 540; *Rowston v. Sydney County Council* (1954) 92 C.L.R. 605 at 615-616) or from month to month (*Turner v. York Motors Pty Ltd* (1951) 85 C.L.R. 55). For a case where s. 127(1) was held applicable, see *Cram v. Bellambi Coal Co. Ltd* (1964) 82 W.N. (Pt 1) (N.S.W.) 18 at 23-24; see also *Harty v. Kolman* [1977] 1 N.S.W.L.R. 674 at 681-682.

DOCKRILL v. CAVANAGH

Supreme Court of New South Wales, Full Court (1944) 45 S.R. (N.S.W.) 78

[Dockrill granted Cavanagh a lease for four years over Torrens title land, together with an option for renewal for a further term of two years. Cavanagh exercised the option for the further term, to take effect upon the expiry of the four years' term, namely, 1 November 1941. No lease was executed for the further two year term, but Cavanagh remained in possession for the two years (that is, until 1 November 1943) and paid rent monthly. He also remained in possession after 1 November 1943, but his payments of rent due after that date were not accepted. In 1944, Dockrill's executors (Dockrill having died) sought to eject Cavanagh. Cavanagh claimed that he was a tenant at will under s. 127 of the *Conveyancing Act* 1919 (N.S.W.) and that he was entitled under that section to one month's notice (it being conceded that no such notice had been given). Dockrill's executors claimed that the tenancy created by the exercise of the option, retention of possession and payment of rent, came to an end on 1 November 1943 and that, having thus expired, no notice was necessary. There was no evidence that the rent was the best rent reasonably obtainable for the purposes of s. 23D(2) of the *Conveyancing Act*: as to which, see below p. 567. The Full Court held, for reasons which appear in the extract from the judgment of Jordan C.J. below, that possession and payment of rent pursuant to the agreement for a lease for two years constituted by the exercise of the option brought into existence a tenancy at will under s. 127, but on such of the terms of the agreement as were applicable to such a tenancy; so that the tenancy automatically expired at the end of the two years, without the need for any notice.]

JORDAN C.J. Prior to the introduction of s. 127, if there was a lease but no agreement between the parties operative at common law to incorporate as part of it a provision that it was to continue for a term of years, or to be at will or for a periodic tenancy, then, in the contemplation of a court with jurisdiction to enforce only common law rights, although upon entry by the lessee the lease became a lease at will, upon payment of rent it ceased to be a lease at will and became a lease for the periodic tenancy of from year to year. It was to this that s. 127 was addressed, and what it provides is that where this state of things exists, the conditions which would previously have brought into existence a lease from year to year shall instead bring into existence a lease at will terminable by a month's notice expiring at any time. The phrase "and no agreement as to its duration" means no agreement as to its duration which, at common law, is incorporated in the lease for all purposes: *Larke Hoskins & Co. Ltd v. Icher* (1929) 29 S.R. 142; *Burnham v. Carroll Musgrove Theatres Ltd* (1927) 28 S.R. 169 at 179-180. But there is nothing to indicate that it was intended to alter in any other respect the rules of the common law applicable in courts administering only that law. Hence, where the common law would previously have incorporated into the lease such of the terms of an agreement dehors the lease as were applicable to a lease from year to year, it will now incorporate such as are applicable to a lease at will terminable by a month's notice, and where the agreement dehors the lease provides for a term of years, then, if when the period of that term comes to an end, the lease at will has not already been terminated by a month's notice, it is now that lease which becomes automatically terminated without notice. I quite agree with Mr Saddington that it was illogical that the common law, being prevented by statute from giving effect to an agreement, should nevertheless not only give full force and effect to most of the details of the agreement, but also treat one of its provisions as operating to terminate an independent legal relationship which it had itself brought into existence; but this argument was addressed to the court in *Doe dem Tilt v. Stratton* (1828) 4 Bing. 446; 130 E.R. 839, and did not prevail.

LEITZ LEEHOLME STUD PTY LTD v. ROBINSON

Supreme Court of New South Wales, Court of Appeal [1977] 2 N.S.W.L.R. 544

[The plaintiff company, as lessor, sued the defendant, as lessee, for damages for breach of the lessee's obligations under a memorandum of lease. The trial judge found the issue of liability in favour of the plaintiff, and ordered judgment to be entered in its favour, with damages to be assessed. The defendant appealed. The facts appear sufficiently from the judgment of Glass J.A.]

GLASS J.A. The agreed facts which are relevant to the issues debated before us may be shortly set out. On 11 July 1973, the defendant executed the memorandum of lease and went into possession of the property. On 14 September 1973, the memorandum of lease was executed by the plaintiff company. On 16 December 1974, the plaintiff's solicitors lodged the memorandum with the Registrar-General, together with duplicate Certificates of Title. For various reasons which are not material, the memorandum was never registered. Between 11 July 1973, and 8 March 1976, the defendant remained in occupation of the property and paid the rent reserved by the lease. On that date the defendant wrote a letter in the following terms: "I would advise that in view of my selling of the horses presently on Leeholme Stud I will not be able to continue to pay the rental for such stud. Further in view of my being at present in arrears in relation to the payment of rent and in view of my not having the capability to pay additional rentals it is with regret that I will be vacating the property known as Leeholme Stud at St Marys leased from you and I shall be vacated from such property on the 9th day of April 1976.''

By letter of 12 March the plaintiff informed the defendant that it accepted his repudiation of the lease and expected to receive vacant possession on 9 April. It also informed him of its intention to proceed against him for damages for breach of contract. On 9 April the defendant gave up possession and the plaintiff entered into possession of the subject property. In its statement of claim filed on 23 March the plaintiff claimed rent due to it under the memorandum for the balance of the term together with interest. In an amended statement of claim filed on 30 September it claimed damages for breach of contract.

The first argument put to the court on behalf of the defendant involved a series of steps. Because the memorandum of lease was never registered it was ineffectual to pass any estate or interest in the land to the lessee: s. 41 of the *Real Property Act* 1900 (N.S.W.). However, by virtue of s. 127 of the *Conveyancing Act* 1919 (N.S.W.), the defendant's entry into possession and payment of rent gave rise to an implied tenancy at will determinable by one month's notice in writing. There was, prior to 8 March, an agreement to give and take a lease for six years which was capable of specific performance by order of an equity court. However, the notice given by the lessee on 8 March determined, not only the tenancy at will, but also the whole of the relationship between the parties, including the pre-existing agreement. When asked for authority in support of the final proposition counsel could only answer that there was no authority to the contrary of what was being put. It was argued on general principles that the notice given by the lessee did not involve a repudiation of the agreement, but a lawful termination of it, since it was entitled by notice to terminate the tenancy at will. It was put that you could not have a lawful termination of the right to remain in possession by a notice which took effect as a wrongful repudiation of the agreement, thus entitling the lessor to sue for damages. The two positions were entirely inconsistent. The lessee could not be sued for doing something which he was lawfully entitled to do.

In my view, the argument involves a misconception. The agreement and the tenancy at will are independent sources of rights. At no stage do they merge, so that the termination of the estate automatically extinguishes the agreement. The relevant principles are, in my view, as follows. A lease of land under the *Real Property Act* for a term exceeding three years creates no legal term unless it is both registrable and registered. But the informal instrument may be treated as evidencing an agreement for a formal lease: *Carberry v. Gardiner* (1936) 36 S.R. (N.S.W.) 559 at 569. The unregistered memorandum of lease operates merely as an agreement specifically enforceable in equity, but not itself creating a legal term in the land: *Australian Provincial Assurance Assoc. Ltd v. Rogers* (1943) 43 S.R. (N.S.W.) 202 at 205. Entry into possession and payment of rent bring into existence a common law tenancy upon such terms of the unregistered memorandum as are applicable to the tenancy at will: (1943) 43 S.R. (N.S.W.) 202 at 206. But, in so far as the memorandum operates as an agreement, it retains a separate identity as the repository of the substantial rights of the parties: (1943) 43 S.R. (N.S.W.) 202 at 206. The doctrine relevant for present purposes had been previously worked out in relation to demises which were void at law, not having been made by deed as required by the statute. The purported lease, nevertheless, took effect as an executory agreement for a lease enforceable in equity, and there entitling the lessee to a formal lease: *Hoyt's Pty Ltd v. Spencer* (1919) 27 C.L.R. 133 at 142, 143; *Butts v. O'Dwyer* (1952) 87 C.L.R. 267 at 285. The existence or otherwise of a contract is determined exclusively by common law principle: *Parkin v. Thorold* (1851) 2 Sim. N.S. 1 at 6; 61 E.R. 239 at 241. Accordingly, when these decisions allude to an informal lease operating as an agreement for a lease enforceable in equity, they affirm, not only the availability of equitable relief, but also the existence of a contract at law. If the innocent party deems damages to be adequate, there is no reason why the contract may not be enforced at law. But, in any event, the actionability at law of the executory agreement is supported by authority. Prior to the *Judicature Act* 1873 (Imp.) actions for damages were successfully brought on instruments which for want of a seal were void at law as demises: *Bond v. Rosling* (1861) 1 B. & S. 371; 121 E.R. 753; *Tidey v. Mollett* (1864) 16 C.B.N.S. 298; 143 E.R. 1143; *Rollason v. Leon* (1861) 7 H. & N. 73; 158 E.R. 398.

Given the availability of the legal remedy, the contractual position is entirely clear. The defendant, by executing the memorandum of lease, concluded an agreement to take a lease for six years. On 8 March, after being in occupation for under three years, he gave a notice which amounted to a wrongful repudiation of his obligations under that agreement. The plaintiff accepted the repudiation, and thereby elected no longer to be bound by the agreement. Upon such rescission, it became entitled to sue for damages for loss of its bargain: *Heyman v. Darwins Ltd* [1942] A.C. 356 at 361. The trial judge ruled that the plaintiff, though unable to sue for damages at common law, could enforce the agreement in equity and obtain damages in lieu of specific performance. The defendant advanced arguments why his Honour should have held, on discretionary grounds, that equitable relief was not available to the plaintiff. In view of the conclusion I have reached, I find it unnecessary to consider these submissions. The defendant also submitted that the effect of the agreement for a lease was in some undefined way circumscribed by the necessity to obtain the consent of the mortgagee to the lease, and referred to the period of delay before this was done. In as much, however, as all necessary consents had been obtained before the repudiation, I cannot see that any default in this respect on the plaintiff's part (assuming such occurred) provides any answer to the defendant.

I would propose that the appeal be dismissed with costs, and that the proceeding be remitted to the Common Law Division so that the plaintiff's damages for loss of its bargain may be assessed.

[Hope J.A. agreed with Glass J.A. Mahoney J.A., in a separate judgment, reached the same result as Glass J.A. for substantially similar reasons.]

Appeal dismissed.

5. Other periodical tenancies

Other periodical tenancies may be implied from the manner of payment of rent. For example, where rent is paid and accepted on a weekly basis then (in the absence of agreement to the contrary) a periodical tenancy from week to week will arise; where rent is paid and accepted on a monthly basis, a tenancy from month to month will arise; and, in the same way, tenancies for any other period (quarter to quarter, half year to half year, and so on) will arise. Periodic tenancies may also be created by express agreement: see *Land Settlement Association Ltd v. Carr* [1944] K.B. 657 (lease for successive periods of 364 days).

However, whether payment of rent on a periodic basis gives rise to a periodic tenancy is a question of *intention*; and so, for example, a tenant could pay rent on a monthly basis without a monthly tenancy arising, if the parties did not intend a monthly tenancy to arise (as in *Cardiothoracic Institute v. Shrewdcrest Ltd* [1986] 1 W.L.R. 368: payment of rent on a periodic basis during holding-over period held not to create periodic tenancy, since the parties did not intend to create a periodic tenancy but to keep on foot a tenancy at will only).

A lease for a periodic tenancy, such as a lease from year to year, quarter to quarter, month to month, or week to week, continues indefinitely until either party terminates it by giving notice equal to the length of the period and terminating at the end of a complete period: see *Dockrill v. Cavanagh* (1944) 45 S.R. (N.S.W.) 78 at 82; *Fink v. McIntosh* [1946] V.R. 290 at 292; *Re Belajev* (1979) 22 S.A.S.R. 1.

6. Tenancies for a fixed term of years

A tenancy for a fixed term of years, by way of contrast with other tenancies, is fixed to expire at a certain time. The term of the lease may be for any period, no matter how short (for example, one day, one week, or one month) or how long (one year, or 1,000 years). It may even be for discontinuous periods: see *Smallwood v. Sheppards* [1895] 2 Q.B. 627 (lease for three consecutive bank holidays); *Cottage Holiday Associates Ltd v. Customs and Excise Commissioners* [1983] 2 W.L.R. 861 (lease for one week per year for 80 years, in timeshare holiday premises). Both the commencement and the maximum duration of the term must be certain, or at least capable of being rendered certain, before the lease takes effect; this matter has been discussed above p. 532 et seq.

Under s. 134 of the *Conveyancing Act* 1919 (N.S.W.), in certain circumstances a lease for a term of not less than 300 years, with not less than 200 years still to run, may be enlarged into a fee simple.

7. Concurrent leases

A landlord who has granted a lease may subsequently grant another lease of the same land for all or some of the period of the existing lease. The second grant is, in reality, a lease of the reversion, and the two leases are known as concurrent leases. The second lease creates the relationship of lessor and lessee between the second and the first lessee respectively, and this supplants the relationship of landlord and tenant between the landlord and the first lessee (see Megarry and Wade, op. cit. pp. 664-665; *Richardson v. Landecker* (1950) 50 S.R. (N.S.W.) 250.

If, for example, L grants a lease of Blackacre to T_1 for a term of 20 years, and one year later grants a lease of Blackacre to T_2 for 30 years, T_2 becomes the reversioner expectant on the lease to T_1, and thus becomes lessor to T_1, entitled to the rent and to enforce the covenants under the lease. On the expiration of T_1's lease, T_2 becomes entitled to possession. Similarly, L may grant to T_2 a lease for a term less than the residue of the term vested in T_1, in other words a lease for a term to take effect in reversion expectant upon a longer term; this was always possible at common law, and has received statutory indorsement in s. 120A(5) of the *Conveyancing Act* 1919 (N.S.W.).

8. Reversionary leases

A reversionary lease (to be contrasted with a lease of the reversion) is a lease to begin at some time in the future. At common law, there was no limit to the period of time which might elapse before the term began; and there was no breach of the rule against perpetuities, as the lessee took an interest immediately vested (in interest), the vesting in possession only being postponed.

Section 120A(3) of the *Conveyancing Act* 1919 (N.S.W.) now renders void a lease limited to take effect more than 21 years from the date of the instrument purporting to create it.

9. Agreements for a lease: Walsh v. Lonsdale

There is a clear distinction between a lease and an agreement to grant a lease: the distinction is between "I hereby grant you a lease" and "I hereby agree that I will grant you a lease [at a future time]": Megarry and Wade, op. cit., p. 639. A lease contains words of present demise, either expressly (by the use of words such as "lease" or "demise") or by implication (by the use of words which otherwise indicate an intention that one party will part with and the other acquire possession for a fixed period: *Bicknell v. Hood* (1839) 5 M. & W. 104 at 108; 151 E.R. 45 at 47), whereas an agreement for a lease is but a promise to grant a lease in the future. See Lewis and Cassidy, *Tenancy Law of New South Wales* (1966), Vol. 1, p. 85.

Although at common law a lease which did not comply with the requisite formalities was not effective to pass the legal term agreed upon by the parties, a legal tenancy could nevertheless arise: for example, possession by the tenant and payment of rent under an agreement to lease would give rise to a tenancy from year to year upon such of the agreed terms as were consistent with a yearly tenancy: see *Moore v. Dimond* (1929) 43 C.L.R. 105, above p. 546. But both equity and common law regarded an imperfect lease as an agreement to grant a lease, and as long as it was made for value and evidenced in writing, or supported by sufficient acts of part performance, equity would order specific performance of the agreement. Once a formal lease had been granted pursuant to an order for specific performance, the position of the parties was the same as if a formal lease had been granted from the outset.

Before the Judicature Acts 1873-1875 (U.K.), a tenant holding under an agreement to lease had to enforce his or her rights in the Court of Chancery: he or she would obtain a decree for specific performance of the agreement to grant a lease and in the meantime seek an injunction restraining the landlord from interfering with his or her (the tenant's) equitable rights. See generally, Megarry and Wade, op. cit., pp. 639-641. Since the Judicature Acts in England, and now in all Australian States, in a court exercising concurrent jurisdiction, where the circumstances are such that the court would order specific performance of the agreement to grant a lease, the parties are treated *as if* a formal lease had been executed: see *Swain v. Ayres* (1888) 21 Q.B.D. 289 at 293. This is pursuant to the maxim that equity looks on that as done which ought to be done. The leading case is *Walsh v. Lonsdale*.

WALSH v. LONSDALE

Court of Appeal (1882) 21 Ch. D. 9

[By an agreement in writing in 1879, Lonsdale agreed to grant Walsh a lease of a mill for a term of seven years at a rental of £1 10s. for each loom worked by Walsh, the minimum number of looms to be 540. In the relevant year (1881), Walsh worked 560 looms. The agreement provided that the lease was to incorporate, inter alia, such of the covenants in the lease of another mill (the Newfield Mills) as could be made applicable to this particular lease. One of the terms of the Newfield Mills lease was that the lessor could demand payment of one year's rent in advance.

Walsh went into possession under the agreement in 1879 and duly paid rent quarterly in arrears. In 1882, Lonsdale served a demand for, inter alia, payment of one year's rent in advance. Upon Walsh's refusal to pay, Lonsdale levied distress for rent. (Distress for rent was a remedy available at law enabling a landlord to enter and seize and sell certain chattels on the demised premises to satisfy arrears of rent.) Walsh thereupon commenced the present action claiming damages for improper distraint, an injunction to restrain sale under the distress and from continuing in possession, and specific performance of the agreement for a lease.

On a motion for an injunction before trial, Fry J. held that the clause in the Newfield Mills lease concerning payment of rent in advance could be made applicable to the present lease and held Lonsdale entitled to the amount demanded. He made an order that on payment by Walsh into court of the amount claimed by Lonsdale, Lonsdale should withdraw from possession under the distress.

On appeal, Walsh argued that distress was a legal, not an equitable, remedy; that at law, as no deed of lease had been executed, he was a tenant from year to year, with no obligation to pay rent in advance; that the provision in the Newfield Mills lease about payment in advance could not be made applicable to the present tenancy, because being quantified by reference to the number of looms used, the rent could not be calculated until the end of the year; and that the manner of payment of rent to date was evidence of a tenancy under which rent was payable quarterly in arrears.]

JESSEL M.R. It is not necessary on the present occasion to decide finally what the rights of the parties are. If the court sees that there is a fair question to be decided it will take security so that the party who ultimately succeeds may be in the right position. The question is one of some nicety. There is an agreement for a lease under which possession has been given. Now since the *Judicature Act* the possession is held under the agreement. There are not two estates as there were formerly, one estate at common law by reason of the payment of the rent from year to year, and an estate in equity under the agreement. There is only one court, and the equity rules prevail in it. The tenant holds under an agreement for a lease. He holds, therefore, under the same terms in equity as if a lease had been granted, it being a case in which both parties admit that relief is capable of being given by specific performance. That being so, he cannot complain of the exercise by the landlord of the same rights as the landlord would have had if a lease had been granted. On the other hand, he is protected in the same way as if a lease had been granted; he cannot be turned out by six months' notice as a tenant from year to year. He has a right to say, "I have a lease in equity, and you can only re-enter if I have committed such a breach of covenant as would if a lease had been granted have entitled you to re-enter according to the terms of a proper proviso for re-entry". That being so, it appears to me that being a lessee in equity he cannot complain of the exercise of the right of distress merely because the actual parchment has not been signed and sealed.

The next question is, how ought the lease to be drawn? And that is a question of some nicety. I do not wish now finally to decide it, and on an application of this kind it is not necessary to do so, but I think the court is bound to say what its present opinion is, because that is material on the question of what ought to be done until the trial. The whole difficulty arises from a single clause. Instead of taking the trouble to state in detail what covenants the lease was to contain they have adopted this short form [of incorporation of terms by reference to the Newfield Mills lease].

When we look at the lease of the Newfield Mills we find that it is a lease at a rent certain payable beforehand, and the question is how far that provision can be made applicable to the present very peculiar agreement. [He referred to the terms of the Newfield Mills lease, and continued:]

Now the lessee agrees to run not less than 540 looms, and the next question is, whether in drawing the lease a dead or minimum rent ought to be reserved for 540 looms, or is it to be left on covenant. My present opinion is that there ought to be a dead rent . . . of £810, being at the rate of 30s. a loom for 540 looms. If that is so, the stipulation as to paying rent beforehand can apply to that £810 a year, and the covenants and provisions in the lease of the Newfield Mills, could be made applicable to this minimum rent. Therefore it is my present opinion, though I do not give it as a final opinion, that the rent is payable beforehand to the extent of £810.

The result, therefore, will be to vary the order of the court below by making the sum to be paid into court £810 instead of £1005 14s. The plaintiff will pay the costs of the appeal.

[Cotton and Lindley L.JJ. came to a similar conclusion.]

NOTES

1. It has been said that the result of *Walsh v. Lonsdale* (1882) 21 Ch. D. 9 is that "there is no distinction . . . between a lease and an agreement for a lease, because equity looks upon that as done which ought to be done": *Re Maughan* (1885) 14 Q.B.D. 956 at 958; see also *Lowther v. Heaver* (1889) 41 Ch. D. 248 at 264.

   There are, however, substantial differences between a lease and an agreement for a lease, stemming from the fact that the former creates a legal interest whilst the latter creates only an equitable interest. These differences are examined in the following notes.

2. The doctrine in *Walsh v. Lonsdale* can be invoked only in a court having equitable jurisdiction, because it depends upon the grant of a decree of specific performance: see *Manchester Brewery Co. v. Coombs* [1901] 2 Ch. 608 at 617.

3. Even where the court has jurisdiction to grant specific performance it may decline to do so, for specific performance is a discretionary remedy. Where specific performance is refused, the agreement for a lease cannot give rise to an equitable interest in the land, and the parties must be left to their rights at law. Specific performance has been refused where the tenant has already committed a breach of the agreement which would have amounted to breach of covenant had a formal lease been executed (*Coatsworth v. Johnson* (1886) 54 L.T. 520 at 523, 524: breach of requirement to cultivate properly; *Swain v. Ayres* (1888) 21 Q.B.D. 289: breach of requirement to repair); where the tenant has failed to perform some act which, by the terms of the agreement, was to be performed before the formal lease was granted and the performance of which has not been waived by the landlord (*Cornish v. Brook Green Laundry Ltd* [1959] 1 Q.B. 394 at 407); where to grant specific performance would involve the lessor in a breach of a pre-existing contractual obligation or would compel the lessor to do that which he or she is not lawfully competent to do (*Warmington v. Miller* [1973] Q.B. 877 at 886: order for specific performance of agreement to grant a sub-lease would have resulted in a breach of covenant against sub-letting contained in the head lease); and where the landlord has no title to grant the lease (*Clemow v. Cook* [1920] G.L.R. 70: agreement to grant a sub-lease for three years by tenant who held under a tenancy at will). Without detracting from the discretionary nature of the remedy, it has been said that once the tenant has been let into possession under the agreement, the court should not refuse to order specific performance unless there are compelling reasons to the contrary, such as gross or wilful breaches on the part of the tenant (see *Upper Hutt Arcade Ltd v. Burrell* [1973] 2 N.Z.L.R. 699 at 703, citing *Parker v. Taswell* (1859) 2 De G. & J. 559 at 571; 44 E.R. 1106 at 1111), a fortiori where the tenant's only breach is failure to pay rent and this breach has since been remedied by payment in full (see *Baxton v. Kara* [1982] 1 N.S.W.L.R. 604; *Kemp v. Lumeah Investments Pty Ltd* (1984) C.C.H. N.S.W. Conv. R. 55-162).

4. A tenant under an agreement to lease in respect of which a decree for specific performance has been made still has only an equitable interest in the land; not until a formal lease is executed can he or she obtain a legal leasehold interest. Until then, the tenant's equitable interest is liable to be defeated by a bona fide purchaser of the legal estate in the land without notice of that equitable interest, although if the tenant is in possession it will be difficult for the purchaser to prove lack of notice: *Hunt v. Luck* [1902] 1 Ch. 428.

5. In *Manchester Brewery Co. v. Coombs* [1901] 2 Ch. 608 at 617, Farwell J. said that the doctrine in *Walsh v. Lonsdale* (1882) 21 Ch. D. 9 is applicable "only in those cases where specific performance can be obtained between the same parties in the same court, and at the same time as the subsequent legal question falls to be determined. . . . It was clear that the agreement [in *Walsh v. Lonsdale*] would

be enforced in the same court and between the same parties: the act of distress was therefore held to be lawful." In the New Zealand case of *Geddes v. Fraser* (1898) 1 G.L.R. 66, the plaintiff, who was in possession under an agreement to lease, sought to enforce an agreement for a sub-lease of part of the premises; it was admitted that the plaintiff could not enforce the agreement for the sub-lease unless his own title was good. The plaintiff sought to invoke *Walsh v. Lonsdale*, to show that he stood in the same position as if a formal lease had been granted to him, but the court held that *Walsh v. Lonsdale* could not be invoked because the plaintiff's own landlord was not represented in the suit. But see *Industrial Properties (Barton Hill) Ltd v. Associated Electrical Industries Ltd* [1977] Q.B. 580, extracted below. See generally, Hinde, McMorland and Sim, *Land Law*, p. 458.

6. Subject to the law as to part performance, no agreement to grant a lease can be the subject of an order for specific performance under *Walsh v. Lonsdale* unless the agreement, or some note or memorandum thereof, is in writing and signed by the party to be charged or by some other person thereunto by him lawfully authorised. This requirement, derived initially from the *Statute of Frauds*, is now to be found in the *Conveyancing Act* 1919 (N.S.W.), s. 54A.

10. Leases by estoppel

(a) General

There is a well established principle that a tenant is estopped from denying the landlord's title, and, conversely, that a landlord is estopped from denying the tenant's title. So, for example, the landlord cannot allege her or his own want of title in making the lease, nor can the tenant set up the landlord's lack of title as a defence for non-performance of covenants contained in the lease. The estoppel binds successors in title to both landlord and tenant. It was thought at one time that the estoppel bound the tenant only so long as he or she remained in possession, and that once possession was given up, the tenant could dispute the landlord's title; by this means, the tenant might, for example, escape liability for breaches of covenant which had occurred during the term: *Harrison v. Wells* [1967] 1 Q.B. 263. This principle has now been discarded by the English Court of Appeal: see *Industrial Properties (Barton Hill) Ltd v. Associated Electrical Industries Ltd*, extracted below; the tenant is now estopped from denying the landlord's title even after he or she has gone out of possession.

The estoppel does not extend, however, to preventing the tenant from denying the landlord's title where the tenant has been evicted by title paramount.

INDUSTRIAL PROPERTIES (BARTON HILL) LTD v. ASSOCIATED ELECTRICAL INDUSTRIES LTD

Court of Appeal [1977] Q.B. 580

[Associated Electrical Industries Ltd (A.E.I.) had been the lessee for many years of premises owned by family trustees (the Parker trustees). In 1959 the Parker trustees, for tax purposes, agreed to transfer the premises to the plaintiff company, subject to the lease. The agreement to transfer was specifically enforceable, but no formal conveyance of the legal estate was ever executed. However, the trustees and the plaintiff company thereafter proceeded on the assumption that the plaintiff company held the legal estate. The former lease having expired, in 1966 the plaintiff company granted a new lease to A.E.I., determinable, inter alia, after seven years. The lease contained a covenant by the lessee to repair. The lease was determined after seven years, and A.E.I. gave up possession, leaving the premises in a dilapidated condition. When the plaintiff company sued A.E.I. for breach of the covenant to repair, they were met with the argument that as they were not the owners of the freehold they had no title to grant the lease and therefore could not sue on the covenants contained in the lease.]

LORD DENNING M.R.

THE CORRECT PROPOSITIONS

IV. In the course of the discussion we were referred to many authorities, old and new. I have considered them all—and others, too—but the result can be stated thus: If a landlord lets a tenant into possession under a lease, then, so long as the tenant remains in possession *undisturbed by any adverse claim*—then the tenant cannot dispute the landlord's title. Suppose the tenant (not having been disturbed) goes out of possession and the landlord sues the tenant on the covenant for rent or for breach of covenant to repair or to yield up in repair. The tenant cannot say to the landlord: "You are not the true owner of the property." Likewise, if the landlord, on the tenant's holding over, sues him for possession or for use and occupation or mesne profits, the tenant cannot defend himself by saying: "The property does not belong to you, but to another."

But if the tenant is disturbed *by being evicted by title paramount or the equivalent* of it, then he can dispute the landlord's title. Suppose the tenant is actually turned out by the third person—or if the tenant, without going out, acknowledges the title of the third person by attorning to him—or the tenant contests the landlord's claim on an indemnity from the third person—or there is anything else done which is equivalent to an eviction by title paramount—then the tenant is no longer estopped from denying the landlord's title: see *Wilson v. Anderton* (1830) 1 B. & Ad. 450 at 457; 109 E.R. 855, per Littledale J. The tenant, being thus disturbed in his possession, can say to the landlord: "You were not truly the owner at the time when you demanded and received the rent from me. I am liable to pay mesne profits to this other man. So you must repay me the rent which I overpaid you. Nor am I liable to you on the covenants during the time you were not the owner." See *Newsome v. Graham* (1829) 10 B. & C. 234; 109 E.R. 437; *Mountnoy v. Collier* (1853) 1 E. & B. 630; *Watson v. Lane* (1856) 11 Exch. 769. The tenant can also claim damages for the eviction if there is, as here, an express covenant for quiet enjoyment covering interruption by title paramount.

Short of eviction by title paramount, or its equivalent, however, the tenant is estopped from denying the title of the landlord. It is no good his saying: "The property does not belong to you but to a third person" unless that third person actually comes forward and successfully makes an adverse claim—by process in the courts or by the tenant's attornment; or acknowledgment of it as by the tenant defending on an indemnity. If the third person, for some reason or other, makes no adverse claim or is debarred from making it, the tenant remains estopped from denying the landlord's title. This is manifestly correct: for, without an adverse claim, it would mean that the tenant would be enabled to keep the property without paying any rent to anybody or performing any covenants. That cannot be right. That was the reasoning adopted by the Court of Queen's Bench in *Biddle v. Bond* (1865) 6 B. & S. 225; 122 E.R. 1179, a case of a bailor and bailee, but the court treated it as the same as landlord v. tenant.

EFFECT ON THE PRESENT CASE

VI. In the present case the tenants, A.E.I., are not subject to any adverse claim whatever. The lessor to A.E.I. was the plaintiff company which was the equitable owner. The legal owners were the Parker trustees. They were also the directors and shareholders of the plaintiff company. They acquiesced in the lease being made by the plaintiff company to A.E.I. They could not by any possibility make any adverse claim against A.E.I. on their own account. Not only that. They have actually come in as plaintiffs in these proceedings jointly with the plaintiff company—so as to make sure that the benefit of these proceedings goes to the plaintiff company only.

Seeing that A.E.I. are absolved from any adverse claim by the legal owners, it is a very proper case for the doctrine of tenancy by estoppel. A.E.I. have had the full benefit of the lease for the stipulated term of years. They should perform the covenants—or pay damages in lieu—to the only persons entitled to sue them, namely, the plaintiff company. Even though A.E.I. have gone out of possession, they cannot avoid their responsibilities by reliance on a technical rule of law—which on investigation is found to be groundless.

EQUITY

VIII. Thus far I have considered the position at common law. But in equity there is a much shorter way to a decision. It is quite plain that, if the lease to A.E.I. was defective in point of law, nevertheless it was good in equity, and for this simple reason. There were two agreements of which specific performance would be granted. One was the agreement by the Parker trustees to convey to the plaintiff company. The other was the agreement by the plaintiff company to grant a lease to A.E.I. In respect of each of these agreements, equity looks upon that as done which ought to be done. It follows that, by combining the two agreements, the tenants, A.E.I., hold upon the same terms as if a lease had actually been granted by the Parker trustees to A.E.I. This is, of course, an extension of the doctrine of *Walsh v. Lonsdale* (1882) 21 Ch. D. 9, where there was only one agreement. But I see no reason why the doctrine should not be extended to a case like the present, where there were two agreements, each of which was such that specfic performance would be granted.

ACTION ON THE COVENANT

IX. Even at law all the discussion about estoppel may be unnecessary. Throughout this case, I have seen no reason why the plaintiff company should not sue A.E.I. on the covenant to repair and to yield up in repair. It is plain that the plaintiff company had an interest in having the property kept in repair. They were the equitable owners of it. They could stipulate with anyone to repair it. It might be a builder, or a licensee, or anyone else. So why should they not stipulate with A.E.I. that they should keep it in repair? It makes no difference to A.E.I. what the title was. Not in the least whether the plaintiff company were the legal owners or the equitable owners. So why should not A.E.I. be liable on the covenant? It would be different, of course, if A.E.I. had been evicted by title paramount or anything equivalent to it, but nothing of that kind happened. Seeing that A.E.I. have had the whole of the consideration, they are liable in covenant: see *Hodson v. Sharp* (1808) 10 East 350 at 364; 103 E.R. 808 at 813 per Bayley J.; or, in the old phrase, on privity of contract: see *Baker v. Gostling* (1834) 1 Bing. N.C. 19 at 28; 131 E.R. 1024 at 1027, and the damages would not be nominal. They would be substantial.

CONCLUSION

In my opinion, therefore, *Harrison v. Wells* [1967] 1 Q.B. 263 was wrongly decided per incuriam: and we can, and should, overrule it.

The doctrine of tenancy by estoppel has proved of good service and should not be whittled down. It should apply in all cases as between landlord and tenant—no matter whether the tenant is still in possession or gone out of possession—so long as he is not confronted with an adverse claim by a third person to the property.

ROSKILL L.J. [T]he plaintiff company argued that that "lease" took effect in equity as an agreement for a lease and that since the plaintiff company were in a position to obtain the legal estate from the trustees and could without difficulty have done so had A.E.I. so required, and since equity assumes that to be done which ought to be done, the parties were to be treated as being in the same position as if a lease had been granted. Reliance was naturally placed by the respondents upon the well known doctrine enunciated by Jessel M.R. in *Walsh v. Lonsdale* (1882) 21 Ch. D. 9. . . . In that case . . . the defendant landlord was possessed of the legal estate and the plaintiff tenant was in direct contractual relationship with him. Thus, as Jessel M.R. held at 14 and 15 of the report, the defendant held under the same terms in equity (since he held under an agreement for a lease) as if a lease had been granted, it being, he added, "a case in which both parties admit that relief is capable of being given by specific performance".

Does it make any difference that A.E.I. as lessees had no contractual relationship with the persons in whom the legal estate was vested? [Counsel for A.E.I.] says that it does. He relied strongly upon the judgment of Farwell J. in *Manchester Brewery Co. v. Coombs* [1901] 2 Ch. 608 at 617, as showing that the *Walsh v. Lonsdale* doctrine has no application to a case where the alleged lessor had never had the legal estate, and also upon the judgment of the Divisional Court in *Schalit v. Joseph Nadler Ltd* [1933] 2 K.B. 79 at 82.

It appears to be the case that no decision has in terms yet so extended the *Walsh v. Lonsdale* doctrine. But facts such as those giving rise to the present dispute must be rare in the extreme and I find the argument based solely on lack of precedent unconvincing if, authority apart, principle appears to require the application of the doctrine so as to achieve an inherently just and to prevent an obviously unjust result.

[Roskill and Lawton L.JJ. otherwise delivered similar judgments to that of Lord Denning.]

NOTES

1. See further, Martin, "Tenancies by Estoppel, Equitable Leases and Priorities" [1978] Conv. 137.

2. In *National Westminster Bank Ltd v. Hart* [1983] Q.B. 773, the defendants, who had been sub-tenants of a house for many years, had paid rent to the head tenants of the house until 1978, when they discovered for the first time that the head tenants' lease had expired in 1967. Thereafter, they refused to pay rent until the executor of the head tenants (the head tenants having since died) proved its title. The trial judge held that the defendants were estopped from denying the executor's right to demand the rent. This decision was reversed by the Court of Appeal, which held that the principle of estoppel did not prevent the defendants from showing that the title of their landlord (formerly the head tenants, and now the executor of the head tenants) had expired, and this notwithstanding that there was no adverse claim by a third party to the property. The fact that the defendants had continued to pay rent between 1967 and 1978 could not work an estoppel, because the defendants were not aware until 1978 that the head tenants' title had determined.

(b) Tenancies by estoppel

Where a person with no legal estate in the land purports to grant a lease, no legal estate can pass to the tenant. Nevertheless, because the parties and their successors are estopped from denying the effectiveness of the grant, a tenancy by estoppel arises. If the purported landlord later acquires the legal estate (for example, by purchasing the fee simple), the estoppel is "fed", and the tenant acquires a legal leasehold estate in place of the tenancy by estoppel.

As an illustration of the operation of the doctrine, consider the following situation. A purchaser under a binding agreement for the sale of land under old system title goes into possession before completion and purports to grant a legal lease to a tenant. The purchaser, at that point in time, has no legal estate in the land (her or his only interest being equitable) so that no legal estate can pass to the tenant. Suppose further that the purchaser, on completion of the purchase, grants a legal mortgage of the land to a mortgagee. Will the mortgagee take priority over the tenant? The answer is, he or she will not; for, at the moment of completion of the purchase, the conveyance vests the legal estate in the purchaser, thereby feeding the estoppel and giving the tenant a legal leasehold interest in the land. The mortgage which, in theory at least, is given subsequently to the conveyance of the legal estate to the purchaser (in practice, the two transactions are simultaneous), is thus merely a mortgage of the reversion expectant on the determination of the lease: see *Church of England Building Society v. Piskor* [1954] Ch. 553.

III. FORMAL REQUIREMENTS FOR THE CREATION OF LEASES

1. Statutory requirements

Sections 23B-23E of the *Conveyancing Act* 1919 (N.S.W.) provide:

23B. (1) No assurance of land shall be valid to pass an interest at law unless made by deed.

(2) This section does not apply to—

(a) an acknowledgment under s. 83 of the Wills, Probate and Administration Act, 1898;

(b) a disclaimer made in accordance with any law relating to bankruptcy in force before or after the commencement of the Conveyancing (Amendment) Act, 1972, or not required to be evidenced in writing;

(c) a surrender by operation of law, and a surrender which may, by law, be effected without writing;

(d) a lease or tenancy or other assurance not required by law to be made in writing;

(e) a vesting order;

(f) any other assurance taking effect under any Act or Commonwealth Act.

(3) This section does not apply to land under the provisions of the Real Property Act, 1900.

23C. (1) Subject to the provisions of this Act with respect to the creation of interests in land by parol—

(a) no interest in land can be created or disposed of except by writing signed by the person creating or conveying the same, or by his agent thereunto lawfully authorised in writing, or by will, or by operation of law;

(b) a declaration of trust respecting any land or any interest therein must be manifested and proved by some writing signed by some person who is able to declare such trust or by his will;

(c) a disposition of an equitable interest or trust subsisting at the time of the disposition, must be in writing signed by the person disposing of the same or by his will, or by his agent thereunto lawfully authorised in writing.

(2) This section does not affect the creation or operation of resulting, implied, or constructive trusts.

23D. (1) All interests in land created by parol and not put in writing and signed by the person so creating the same, or by his agent thereunto lawfully authorised in writing, shall have, notwithstanding any consideration having been given for the same, the force and effect of interests at will only.

(2) Nothing in this section or in ss 23B or 23C shall affect the creation by parol of a lease at the best rent which can reasonably be obtained without taking a fine taking effect in possession for a term not exceeding three years, with or without a right for the lessee to extend the term at the best rent which can reasonably be obtained without taking a fine for any period which with the term would not exceed three years.

23E. Nothing in s. 23B, 23C, or 23D shall—

(a) invalidate any disposition by will; or

(b) affect any interest validly created before the commencement of the Conveyancing (Amendment) Act, 1930; or

(c) affect the right to acquire an interest in land by virtue of taking possession; or

(d) affect the operation of the law relating to part performance.

It will be seen that by s. 23B(3) of the *Conveyancing Act* 1919 (N.S.W.), the requirements of s. 23B do not apply to land under the provisions of the *Real Property Act* 1900 (N.S.W.). That Act contains certain provisions concerning the creation of leasehold interests. Section 53(1) of the *Real Property Act* provides:

53. (1) When any land under the provisions of this Act is intended to be leased or demised for a life or lives or for any term of years exceeding three years, the proprietor shall execute a lease in the approved form.

The Act does not in terms require leases exceeding three years to be registered, but registration will be necessary if it is desired to obtain for such leases the benefits of indefeasibility of title. Section 42(1)(d) of the same Act seeks to protect lessees under certain unregistered leases not exceeding three years from eviction at the hands of registered proprietors of the land. Section 42(1)(d) is discussed in the chapter on Torrens title above p. 190 et seq.

CARBERRY v. GARDINER

Supreme Court of New South Wales, Full Court (1936) 36 S.R. (N.S.W.) 559

[On 2 December 1926, Carberry by deed leased land to Richards for a term of two years with an option for a further term of five years. Part of the land was under Torrens title and part was under old system title. Richards exercised the option, but no further document was executed granting the further term. Richards remained in possession pursuant to the exercise of the option.]

JORDAN C.J. The case is one in which the parties sought to create leasehold interests in land which is partly under old system title and partly under the *Real Property Act* 1900 (N.S.W.), and did so without paying due regard to the proper forms. It is convenient, therefore, before tracing the course of events, to indicate the principles of law which are applicable. At common law a lease could be made for any length of term by parol, without the necessity for either writing or seal. At first, a grant of a term of years was treated as no more than an agreement; and as giving the tenant no interest in the land at common law, save to the extent that, if he were turned out by his landlord and the lease was by deed, he could recover possession against the landlord in an action on the covenant. By the end of the 15th century, however, writs had been devised which were held to enable the lessee to recover the land from anyone by whom he might be unlawfully ejected. The real actions were denied to him; but he was regarded as having an interest in the land at common law, although only a chattel interest and not a real interest: Holdsworth, *History of English Law* (3rd ed.), Vol. III, pp. 213-217; *Hoyt's Proprietary Ltd v. Spencer* (1919) 27 C.L.R. 133 at 142-143. In the 17th century, by the *Statute of Frauds* 1677 (U.K.), it was enacted by ss 1 and 2, by provisions which now find their counterpart in s. 23D of the *Conveyancing Act* 1919 (N.S.W.), as amended, that all interests in land created by parol and not put in writing and duly signed should take effect as interests at will only, except leases at a rack rent for not exceeding three years from the making thereof; and, by s. 3 of the *Statute of Frauds* (replaced by s. 23C of the *Conveyancing Act*) it was provided that no lease should be granted except by deed or note in writing duly signed. Finally, by s. 23B of the *Conveyancing Act* 1919 (N.S.W.), as amended, which adopts a provision introduced in England in 1845 by 8 and 9 Vict. c. 106, it was enacted that no assurance of land shall be valid to pass an interest at law, unless made by deed, except, inter alia, a lease or tenancy not required by law to be in writing. Agreements to grant a lease, as contrasted with documents by which leases are purported to be granted, come within the provisions of s. 4 of the *Statute of Frauds* (now replaced by s. 54A of the *Conveyancing Act* 1919 (N.S.W.)), which enacts that no action shall be brought to charge any person upon any contract or sale of land, or any interest therein, unless the agreement or some memorandum or note thereof is in writing and duly signed.

As regards land under common law title, these statutes have been held to operate at common law in the following way: Apart from the special cases of leases for not exceeding three years at a rack rent, it followed from the *Statute of Frauds* that a lease which was not in writing, could, of itself, create, at most, a tenancy at will at common law. If, however, the lessee entered into possession under an oral lease for a term, he became, at common law, a tenant at will by virtue of his entry, and if he then paid rent which, in all the circumstances, could be referred to a yearly holding (*Moore v. Dimond* (1929) 43 C.L.R. 105; 45 C.L.R. 159), this further fact was treated as presumably substituting for the tenancy at will a common law tenancy from year to year. Where the entry and payment were in fact referable to an informal lease, the constructive common law tenancies were treated as including all such terms of the lease as were consistent with such tenancies, and the landlord could treat any such tenancy as having come to an end at the expiry of the term of the informal lease without the necessity for any notice to quit. Further, although an oral agreement for a lease was unenforceable, entry under such an agreement created an implied common law tenancy at will; and payment of rent which could be referred to a yearly holding had the effect, as a matter of presumption, [of] replacing this tenancy at will by a common law tenancy from year to year. As regards s. 23B which provides that, with the exception stated, no lease shall be valid to pass an interest at law unless made by deed, this does not prevent a purported lease which is not by deed from evidencing an agreement for a lease. Hence, entry under such a document creates an implied tenancy at will, which may alter its incidents upon payment of rent: *Larke Hoskins & Co. Ltd v. Icher* (1929) 29 S.R. 142. By virtue of s. 127 of the *Conveyancing Act*, as amended, payment of rent under such an implied common law tenancy at will can no longer have the effect of substituting an implied tenancy from year to year, but can do no more than make the tenancy at will become terminable only by one month's notice.

A court of equity approached the matter somewhat differently. The doctrine of part performance enabled it, in certain cases, to decree the execution of a formal lease in cases where no lease had been made and where the agreement for a lease was oral only.

Again, after the enactment which provided that all leases should be by deed, the court treated a written lease which was not under seal as evidencing an agreement for a lease, and would decree specific performance of this agreement by the execution of a proper lease under seal. In the meantime, in equity, although not at common law, the relationship of landlord and tenant was regarded as existing between the parties by virtue of the specifically enforceable agreement.

As regards land under the provisions of the *Real Property Act* 1900 (N.S.W.), no instrument until registered in manner prescribed is effectual to pass any estate or interest therein (s. 41) and no instrument is registrable unless it is in accordance with the provisions of the Act: s. 39. When any such land is intended to be leased for any term of years exceeding three years, a memorandum of lease must be registered: s. 53. It follows that, subject to any exception introduced by s. 53, no common law term can be created in such land by an instrument unless it is both registrable and registered. An informal instrument may, however, be treated as evidencing an agreement for a formal lease, of which a court of equity may decree specific performance by the execution of a registrable instrument: *Wellington City Corp. v. Public Trustee* [1921] N.Z.L.R. 1086. And, although the informal instrument of itself creates no common law term in the land (*Davis v. McConochie* (1915) 15 S.R. 510), entry under it will constitute a common law tenancy at will inter partes, upon which payment of rent may produce the effect provided for by s. 127 of the *Conveyancing Act* 1919 (N.S.W.). There is nothing in the Act to prevent a common law tenancy at will from arising, inter partes, by implication, out of occupancy (*Josephson v. Mason* (1912) 12 S.R. 249 at 257-258), nor, irrespectively of any occupancy, to prevent the creation, inter partes, of a common law term by means of an oral lease at the best rent taking effect in possession for a term not exceeding three years: *Daniher v. Fitzgerald* (1919) 19 S.R. 260.

[His Honour then referred to certain of the facts, and to the terms of the document executed on 2 December 1926, and continued:] It is clear that in equity this document was a perfectly good and effectual document. So far, if at all, as it did not operate to create the term which it was intended to create, a court of equity, upon the principle of *Parker v. Taswell* (1858) 2 De G. & J. 559; 44 E.R. 1106, would treat it as an agreement to execute any necessary formal documents, and would decree specific performance of this agreement: *York House Proprietary Ltd v. Federal Commissioner of Taxation* (1930) 43 C.L.R. 427. It is not necessary, in this case, to consider whether s. 41 of the *Real Property Act*, has the effect of preventing an informal instrument of lease from creating a common law term in land which is under the provisions of that Act even if the term does not exceed three years, or whether s. 53 of the Act should be taken to imply that such an informal lease may still be good, inter partes, so long as it takes effect immediately in possession for a term not exceeding three years, and is proved to be at the best rent which can reasonably be obtained: *Conveyancing Act* 1919 (N.S.W.), s. 23D. In any case in which land under the Act and land not under the Act are included in a common law deed of lease, and the deed creates no term in the land which is under the Act, the question may arise whether, as between lessor and lessee, an action can be maintained on the covenant to pay rent, in view of the rule that, as between lessor and lessee, such a covenant is not apportionable: *Stevenson v. Lambard* (1802) 2 East 575; 102 E.R. 490; *Hughes v. Mockbell* (1909) 9 S.R. 343. However this may be, there can be no doubt that, in the present case, as soon as Richards entered into possession of the whole area, if he did not become lessee for a term, and therefore liable on the covenants as such: *Mouat v. Ross* (1935) 35 S.R. 566, he became, at common law, tenant at will of the whole 1,700 acres upon terms corresponding with such of the covenants of the deed as were applicable to such a tenancy (*Richardson v. Gifford* (1834) 1 A. & E. 52 at 55-6; 110 E.R. 1127 at 1128) and upon payment of rent by him, this being a yearly rent, although, having regard to s. 127 of the *Conveyancing Act*, as amended, he did not become a tenant from year to year, his tenancy at will became terminable only by a month's notice. But this was the position only at common law; and if Carberry had attempted to terminate the tenancy by a month's notice, his action would have been promptly countered by a suit in equity for specific performance, in which an injunction would have been granted to stay any ejectment proceedings by him.

DOCKRILL v. CAVANAGH

Supreme Court of New South Wales, Full Court (1944) 45 S.R. (N.S.W.) 78

[The facts of this case have been summarised above p. 554. After the passage extracted above at p. 555, Jordan C.J. continued:]

JORDAN C.J. The position at common law in New South Wales, as regards form, with respect to the creation of leases, is as follows:

In the case of land under old system title, a purported lease, to be operative at common law as such, must be by deed if it is for a period exceeding three years: *Conveyancing Act* 1919 (N.S.W.), s. 23B. If it is for a period not exceeding three years, it may be by deed: if it is not by deed but is at the best rent which can reasonably be obtained it is operative however made, whether it be written or oral: *Conveyancing Act* 1919 (N.S.W.), s. 23D. And whenever a lease is intended, whatever its period, and is not otherwise validly created at common law, a lease at will, terminable by a month's notice, may arise at common law by the combined operation of s. 127 of the *Conveyancing Act*, and the implication of law arising from possession and payment of rent: *Conveyancing Act* 1919 (N.S.W.), ss 23C(1)(a) and 23E(c).

In the case of land under the *Real Property Act* 1900 (N.S.W.), a purported lease, to be operative as such, must be both in the form of a memorandum of lease and duly registered if it is for a period exceeding three years: *Real Property Act* 1900 (N.S.W.), s. 53. If it is for a period not exceeding three years, it may be made by a duly registered memorandum of lease: if it is not so made, then, since ss 1 and 2 of the *Statute of Frauds* were repealed by s. 2 of the schedule to the *Conveyancing (Amendment) Act* 1930 (N.S.W.), it is operative inter partes if made in writing duly signed (*Conveyancing Act* 1919 (N.S.W.), s. 23C(1)(a)), whilst if it is for the best rent which can reasonably be obtained it is operative at common law inter partes however made, whether it be written or oral: *Conveyancing Act* 1919, s. 23D(2). And in this case, too, whenever a lease is intended, whatever its period, and is not otherwise validly created, a lease at will, terminable by a month's notice, may arise at common law inter partes by the combined operation of s. 127 and the implication of law arising from possession and payment of rent.

In the present case, the land is under the *Real Property Act* 1900 (N.S.W.). There was no registered memorandum of lease for the two-year period beginning on 1 November 1941; and it is obvious from the language of the special cl. 6 [this was the clause of the lease conferring the option to renew] that the notification by the lessee of his desire for a renewed lease did not bring into existence a lease in writing for two years signed by the lessor or his agent. There is no evidence that it was at the best rent reasonably obtainable, and hence the conduct of the parties cannot be regarded as evidencing an oral lease for two years: *Larke Hoskins & Co. Ltd v. Icher* ((1929) 29 S.R. 142). But the possession and payment of rent after 1 November 1941, pursuant to the agreement for a lease for two years constituted by the exercise of the option, brought into existence at common law a lease at will on such of the terms of the agreement as were applicable, which terminated at the end of the two years without notice since it had not been previously terminated by a month's notice.

Appeal dismissed.

2. Entry

At common law, the lessee acquired no leasehold estate in the land until he or she had taken possession; until then, the lessee had a mere interesse termini (an interest of a term), which was an assignable interest in the land, but, not being an estate, carried no reversion: see *Lewis v. Baker* [1905] 1 Ch. 46. The inconvenience of this doctrine could be avoided by a grant to uses (for example, "to A and his heirs to the use of T for 21 years"), because the *Statute of Uses* 1535 (U.K.) (27 Hen. 8 c. 10) deemed the tenant to be in legal possession without the need for actual entry.

The doctrine of interesse termini has now been abolished, the lease taking effect without the need for actual entry: see *Conveyancing Act* 1919 (N.S.W.), s. 120A(1), (2).

IV. RIGHTS AND OBLIGATIONS OF LESSOR AND LESSEE: COVENANTS IN LEASES

It is usual for the parties to a lease to set out in some detail in the written document their respective rights and obligations. But where the lease is not in writing, or although in writing does not exhaustively cover the parties' rights and obligations, the law may imply certain terms into their agreement to fill the gaps. Indeed, as we shall see, in some instances the law may even require that certain terms be read into the lease to vary or qualify terms expressly agreed upon by the parties.

The term "covenant" is used in the following discussion to mean simply a "term" or "condition" of the lease (although there is a distinction between "covenants" and "conditions" for other purposes: see below p. 630). Strictly speaking, a covenant is a promise contained in a deed, so that covenants cannot be implied by law into a lease unless it is in the form of a deed. It seems, however, that in the absence of a deed, corresponding contractual rights will be implied: *Baynes & Co. v. Lloyd & Sons* [1895] 1 Q.B. 820 at 826.

A. COVENANTS IMPLIED BY THE GENERAL LAW

At common law, there are six covenants implied in a lease, three on the part of the lessor and three on the part of the lessee. On the part of the lessor, they are: (1) for quiet enjoyment; (2) not to derogate from grant; (3) in the case of furnished dwellings, that they are reasonably fit for habitation at the commencement of the tenancy. On the part of the lessee, they are (1) to use the premises in a tenant-like manner; (2) to yield up possession to the lessor at the end of the tenancy; (3) in the case of agricultural lands, to cultivate in a husband-like manner.

Where there is an express covenant covering the same area as an implied covenant, there will be no room for operation of the implied covenant (*Malzy v. Eichholz* [1916] 2 K.B. 308 at 314; *Grosvenor Hotel Co. v. Hamilton* [1894] 2 K.B. 836 at 840), and the protection afforded by the covenant will be a matter of construction of its terms (as in *Celsteel Ltd v. Alton House Holdings Ltd (No. 2)* [1987] 2 All E.R. 240). However, subject to contrary provision in the terms of the express covenant, the principles in the cases examined below as to the ambit and operation of the implied covenants will be relevant in determining the ambit and operation of the express covenants.

1. For quiet enjoyment

KENNY v. PREEN

Court of Appeal [1963] 1 Q.B. 499

[The plaintiff was the tenant of a small flat owned by the defendant landlord. In late 1959, the landlord purported to serve a notice to quit on the tenant. The validity of the notice was disputed by the tenant's solicitors in a letter to the landlord. The landlord wrote a number of letters to the tenant, extending over the next two years, in which he threatened physically to evict her from the premises, and, ultimately, to have her belongings forcibly removed. He also knocked on her door on a number of occasions shouting such threats as "I must have these rooms", and "I am going to put your furniture in the street". The tenant sued the landlord in the County Court for breach of the implied covenant for quiet enjoyment. She was awarded damages of £100 for breach of the covenant, and an injunction restraining the landlord from interfering with her quiet enjoyment of the flat. The landlord appealed on the ground, inter alia, that his conduct could not amount to breach of the covenant for quiet enjoyment, arguing that, on the authorities, there must be a substantial physical interference with the possession of the demised premises.]

PEARSON L.J. Mr Lester has contended on behalf of the landlord that the evidence does not reveal any breach of the covenant, because the landlord only made communications to the tenant and did nothing amounting to physical interference with the tenant's possession and enjoyment of the premises. He relied on passages in the judgment in *Owen v. Gadd* [1956] 2 Q.B. 99, and in judgments in previous cases there cited, as showing that some direct physical interference is necessary to constitute a breach of the covenant.

Mr Sheridan has contended on behalf of the tenant, first, that a mere challenge by the landlord to the tenant's title, a denial by him of her title, would be sufficient to constitute a breach of the covenant; secondly, that in this case there was in fact some physical interference with the tenant's possession and enjoyment of the premises; and thirdly, more generally, that on the facts of this case, taken as a whole, there was a breach of the covenant. He cited *Edge v. Boileau* (1885) 16 Q.B.D. 117 at 119 as showing that physical interference is not necessarily required to constitute a breach of the covenant. That was a case in which the landlord was held to have committed a breach of the covenant by telling the subtenants to pay their rent to him instead of to the tenant. It is easy to see that that was an interference by the landlord with the tenant's enjoyment of his rights as tenant.

The judge accepted Mr Sheridan's first contention that a mere challenge by the landlord to the tenant's title, a denial by him of her title, would be sufficient to constitute a breach of the covenant. I am not able to adopt the judge's view on that point. We are not concerned in this case with a denial of the tenant's initial title by virtue of the letting, and I am not considering whether or not that could be a breach of the covenant. In this case the landlord was asserting that the tenant's title, her right to possession of the premises, although initially valid, had been wholly determined by a notice to quit. In my judgment, a landlord by merely making that assertion, however wrong he may be, does not commit a breach of covenant. He is entitled to make that assertion, at any rate if he believes it to be true, frequently, emphatically and even rudely. He is entitled also to threaten proceedings in the courts for possession and damages.

In the present case, however, there was much more than that. The landlord evaded answering the solicitors' letters raising the tenant's defences to his claim. He concentrated his attention on the tenant herself and tried, by a series of threatening communications, to drive her out of her possession of the premises. The threats were not merely of legal proceedings: there were threats of physical eviction of the tenant and removal of her belongings. Moreover, there was an element of direct physical interference by repeatedly knocking on the door and shouting the threats to her. That element of direct physical interference was not trivial but substantial in this case, because it was persisted in and because it has to be seen against the background of the threatening letters.

The implied covenant for quiet enjoyment is not an absolute covenant protecting a tenant against eviction or interference by anybody, but is a qualified covenant protecting the tenant against interference with the tenant's quiet and peaceful possession and enjoyment of the premises by the landlord or persons claiming through or under the landlord. The basis of it is that the landlord, by letting the premises, confers on the tenant the right of possession during the term and impliedly promises not to interfere with the tenant's exercise and use of the right of possession during the term. I think the word "enjoy" used in this connection is a translation of the Latin word "fruor" and refers to the exercise and use of the right and having the full benefit of it, rather than to deriving pleasure from it.

I would decide on two grounds in favour of the tenant's contention that there was, in this case, a breach of the covenant for quiet enjoyment. First, there was a deliberate and persistent attempt by the landlord to drive the tenant out of her possession of the premises by persecution and intimidation, and intimidation included threats of physical eviction of the tenant and removal of her belongings. In my view that course of conduct by the landlord seriously interfered with the tenant's proper freedom of action in exercising her right of possession, and tended to deprive her of the full benefit of it, and was an invasion of her rights as tenant to remain in possession undisturbed, and so would in itself constitute a breach of covenant, even if there were no direct physical interference with the tenant's possession and enjoyment. No case of this kind has ever been considered by the courts before, and I do not think the dicta in the previous cases should be read as excluding a case of this kind where a landlord seeks, by a course of intimidation, to "annul his own deed", to contradict his own demise, by ousting the tenant from the possession which the landlord has conferred upon her.

Secondly, if direct physical interference is a necessary element in the breach of covenant that element can be found in this case to a substantial extent, as I have already stated.

Next there is the question as to the amount of damages for the breach of the covenant. The sum adjudged was £100. There was, however, no allegation or evidence of any actual pecuniary or material damage suffered by the tenant. The only wrongful act alleged was a breach of covenant, that is, a breach of contract. No tort such as trespass or nuisance was alleged. An application at the trial for leave to amend by adding a claim in nuisance was refused. As the claim was only in contract and not in tort, punitive or exemplary damages could not properly be awarded: *Perera v. Vandiyar* [1953] 1 W.L.R. 672. Accordingly, there was no ground for awarding any damages other than nominal damages, which I would assess at 40s.

DONOVAN L.J. I do not think that the court here is making any alarming extension to the scope of an implied covenant for quiet enjoyment. We are not saying it is a covenant that the tenant shall enjoy peace throughout his tenancy, or be immune from even a temporary disturbance of his quiet. We are here dealing with a special—and, I hope, unusual—case. It is a case of a somewhat bullying landlord and an elderly and apparently timid woman who is his tenant. From November 1959, to March 1962, a period of some 17 months, he pursued a set campaign to get rid of her by means of abusive and defamatory letters, coupled with calls at her rooms, where he knocked on the outside door demanding to have the rooms and threatening to put the tenant's furniture in the street. When eventually the tenant took advice and her solicitors wrote to the landlord, he preferred to ignore the solicitors and to reply to her, repeating the threats and abuse. The effect of this campaign must have been, among other things, to make her afraid that if she left her accommodation for sufficient time she might return to find that the landlord had dispossessed her and put her belongings in the street. In this way her peaceable enjoyment of the occupation of the rooms was certainly diminished.

I have no difficulty in concluding that the landlord's conduct was direct physical interference with the enjoyment of the premises let, and more than the creation of a mere personal annoyance. If that view be justified then, on the authorities, there has been a breach of the covenant for quiet enjoyment.

It was argued for the landlord that there was no physical act done here; but short of a battery how more physical can you get than by knocking on the tenant's door and shouting threats through it?

It may be that modern conditions of life may call for a review of the requirement that some physical act is an essential element in a breach of the covenant for quiet enjoyment; but in the present case I think the physical element is present.

On the question of damages, I agree that nominal damages only should have been awarded, and that these should be the sum of £2.

[Ormerod L.J. agreed with Pearson L.J.]

Appeal allowed as to damages.

NOTES AND QUESTIONS

1. It was formerly said that the covenant for quiet enjoyment would only be implied if the word "demise" was used in the grant of the lease: *Baynes & Co. v. Lloyd & Sons* [1895] 2 Q.B. 610 at 615. It is now clear, however, that the covenant will be implied wherever the relationship of landlord and tenant exists (*Budd-Scott v. Daniell* [1902] 2 K.B. 351 at 356, 358, 361; *Markham v. Paget* [1908] 1 Ch. 697 at 715-716), even where the lease is quite informal.

2. The word "quiet" in this covenant is used in the sense of "free from interruption", or "peaceful", and not in the sense of "free from noise". For example, in *Hudson v. Cripps* [1896] 1 Ch. 265 at 268, North J. said:

> I do not understand the [covenant] for quiet enjoyment to be one which means that the plaintiff is to enjoy the premises without the nuisance of noise in the neighbourhood. A covenant for quiet enjoyment is a covenant for freedom from disturbance by adverse claimants to the property.

See also *Jenkins v. Jackson* (1888) 40 Ch. D. 71 at 74. But in appropriate circumstances, interference by noise may, by itself or in combination with other factors, constitute a breach of the covenant: as in *Sampson v. Hodson-Pressinger* [1981] 3 All E.R. 710.

3. In the principal case the interference was from the landlord himself. Other examples of breach by the landlord's acts will be found in *Lavender v. Betts* [1942] 2 All E.R. 72 (landlord removing windows and doors to cajole tenant into giving up possession); *Perera v. Vandiyar* [1953] 1 W.L.R. 672 (landlord disconnecting gas and electricity supply to the premises); *Dowse v. Wynyard Holdings Ltd* (1962) 79 W.N. (N.S.W.) 122 (landlord attempting to make structural repairs within an area properly occupied by tenant); *Martins Camera Corner Pty Ltd v. Hotel Mayfair Ltd* [1976] 2 N.S.W.L.R. 15 (landlord allowing rainwater to enter and damage demised premises). The covenant also extends to protecting the tenant from interference by third parties, but subject to two qualifications. First, the act of disturbance must have been committed by someone claiming through the landlord, and not by title paramount. Thus, in *Baynes & Co. v. Lloyd & Sons* [1895] 2 Q.B. 610, there was held to be no breach of this implied covenant where a sub-tenant who had been granted a sub-lease for ten and a half years by a tenant whose lease had only eight and a half years to run was evicted by the owner of the freehold; similarly, in *Jones v. Lavington* [1903] 1 K.B. 253, there was no breach of the implied covenant where the owner of the freehold obtained an injunction restraining the use of the premises by a sub-lessee in a manner contravening a term of the head lease, the sub-lessee having no knowledge of that term. The second qualification is that the protection extends only to the *lawful* acts of persons claiming through the lessor; the tenant has his remedy in tort for the wrongful acts of third parties: but cf. *Sampson v. Hodson-Pressinger* [1981] 3 All E.R. 710, discussed [1982] Conv. 155. For example, in *Malzy v. Eichholz* [1916] 2 K.B. 308 there was held to be no breach of a covenant (express, not implied) for quiet enjoyment where other tenants of the landlord created a nuisance on the premises; see also *Mantania v. National Provincial Bank Ltd* [1936] 2 All E.R. 633. This second qualification, however, does not apply where (contrary to the usual practice) the covenant is not against interference by persons generally, but is against interference by a specific person; in such a case, the covenant is taken to extend to *unlawful* acts of that person: *Queensway Marketing Ltd v. Associated Restaurants Ltd* (1984) 271 E.G. 1106.

4. In the principal case, the landlord succeeded in having the award of damages reduced to a nominal amount, on the ground that there was no evidence of actual damage suffered by the tenant, and that punitive or exemplary damages could not be awarded for breach of covenant. However, in *McCall v. Abelesz* [1976] Q.B. 585 at 594, Lord Denning M.R. said:

> It is now settled that the court can give damages for the mental upset and distress caused by the defendant's conduct in breach of contract. . . . So, if the facts in *Perera v. Vandiyar* [1953] 1 W.L.R. 672 were to occur again today, the plaintiff would recover, not only the £25 for his own inconvenience, but also the additional £25 for the injury and inconvenience which his wife and child suffered, and the mental distress which he and they suffered. Not as damages for tort, but as damages for breach of contract. Likewise, in *Kenny v. Preen* [1963] 1 Q.B. 499, the damages of £100 would stand.

In some circumstances, the conduct of the landlord may amount to trespass. Exemplary damages may be awarded against a tortfeasor to prevent the reaping of a profit from the wrongdoing—"whenever it is necessary to teach a wrongdoer that tort does not pay": *Rookes v. Barnard* [1964] A.C. 1129 at 1227 per Lord Devlin. For recent examples of a landlord being ordered to pay exemplary damages for his "monstrous behaviour" in wrongfully evicting his tenant, see *Drane v. Evangelou* [1978] 1 W.L.R. 455; *Guppys (Bridport) Ltd v. Brookling* (1984) 269 E.G. 846, 942, noted (1985) 129 Sol. J. 6; cf. *Vassiliou v. Criterion Holdings Ltd* [1979] C.C.H. Aust. & N.Z. Conv. Rep. 197. On exemplary damages in tort, see *Fleming on Torts* (7th ed.), pp. 566-568.

5. Can there be a breach of the implied covenant if there is no "direct physical interference"? Compare the remarks of Pearson L.J. and Donovan L.J. in the principal case. In *Browne v. Flower* [1911] 1 Ch. 219 at 228, Parker J. said:

> It appears to me that to constitute a breach of [a covenant for quiet enjoyment] there must be some physical interference with the enjoyment of the demised premises, and that a mere interference with the comfort of persons using the demised premises by the creation of a personal annoyance such as might arise from noise, invasion of privacy, or otherwise is not enough.

In that case, the erection of an external staircase which allowed persons using the stairs to see into some of the windows of the premises so as to interfere with the privacy of the tenant, was held not to be a breach of the covenant for quiet enjoyment. That passage was approved by Lord Evershed M.R. in *Owen v. Gadd* [1956] 2 Q.B. 99 at 107, where it was held on the facts, however, that the erection of scaffolding outside the demised premises (a shop) did amount to direct physical interference. In the same case, Romer L.J. said (at 107-108):

> It has become quite well established by the authorities that no act of a lessor will constitute an actionable breach of a covenant for quiet enjoyment unless it involves some physical or direct interference with the enjoyment of the demised premises.

But compare the statement of Lord Denning M.R. in *McCall v. Abelesz* [1976] Q.B. 585 at 594 (basing himself on the opinion of Pearson L.J. in the principal case) that the implied covenant for quiet enjoyment "is not confined to direct physical interference by the landlord. It extends to any conduct of the landlord or his agents which interferes with the tenant's freedom of action in exercising his rights as tenant. . . . It covers, therefore, any acts calculated to interfere with the peace or comfort of the tenant, or his family." Similarly, the New Zealand Court of Appeal has said that "breach of a covenant for quiet enjoyment can occur without actual physical interference": *Kalmac Property Consultants Ltd v. Delicious Foods Ltd* [1974] 2 N.Z.L.R. 631 at 637.

6. The *Residential Tenancies Act* 1987 (N.S.W.) provides by s. 22(1) that it is a term of every "residential tenancy agreement": (a) that the tenant shall have quiet enjoyment of the premises "without interruption by the landlord or any person claiming by, through or under the landlord or having superior title (for example, a head landlord) to that of the landlord"; and (b) that the landlord or the landlord's agent shall not "interfere, or cause or permit any interference, with the reasonable peace, comfort, or privacy" of the tenant in using the premises. In so far as para. (a) extends to acts of persons having "superior title", the covenant goes beyond that implied by law; and para. (b) would seem to overcome any argument that direct physical interference is necessary to establish breach of the covenant.

From the definitions of "residential tenancy agreement" and "residential premises" in s. 4, it is clear that the Act extends to any agreement granting for value a right of occupation of premises used or intended to be used as a place of residence, whether or not the right is one of exclusive occupation and whether the agreement is express or implied, oral or written.

J. C. BERNDT PTY LTD v. WALSH

Supreme Court of South Australia [1969] S.A.S.R. 34

[The plaintiff tenant carried on the business of a retail jeweller and watchmaker on the demised premises, a shop in a city building. The defendant landlord engaged a contractor to make extensive alterations to other parts of the building. This involved the erection, with the consent of the Corporation of the City of Adelaide, of a substantial hoarding along the street frontage of the building. The hoarding obscured the tenant's shop windows from pedestrians, with consequent loss of trade. The tenant sued the landlord for breach of his (express) covenant for quiet enjoyment. Walters J. found that there was no evidence to suggest that the building works were not executed with all reasonable care and skill; he also found that there was no evidence to suggest that reasonable precautions had not been taken to obviate and mitigate the annoyances resulting. He also accepted that in carrying out the alterations, the landlord was executing what would ordinarily be lawful works and was making a legitimate use of its land and building.]

WALTERS J. The essence of the plaintiff's complaint is that because of the erection of the hoarding, there was an obscuration of the shop windows from the view of persons passing along Gawler Place in the immediate locality of the shop; that the nature, extent and site of the hoarding left only a narrow tunnel between the hoarding and the shop frontage for the passage of persons along the footpath in front of the shop, and that in the result there was an interference with, or prejudice to, the custom of the business derived from members of the public who would, but for the existence of the hoarding, have been attracted from their passage along the footpath in Gawler Place or, indeed, from other convenient points in that street, to the display of goods in the windows. On the evidence I have no doubt that the hoarding was capable of creating a destructive influence on the plaintiff's business during the period for which it was erected and that any injury resulting to the business from the presence of the hoarding was produced by an interference with the ordinary use and enjoyment by the plaintiff of the demised premises. There can be no doubt that an unrestricted view of, and access to, the shop windows by passers-by were necessary for the enjoyment of the shop, and in my opinion any obscuring of the windows, or any impediment to access to them, was an interference with, or a restriction of, a convenience ordinarily enjoyed by the tenant of a lock-up shop and was consequently incompatible with the covenant for quiet enjoyment.

Interruption contemplated by a covenant for quiet enjoyment need not be an actual interference with the possession or occupancy of the premises demised, but embraces "every interruption to a beneficial enjoyment of the thing demised, whether accidental or wrongful, or in whatever way the interruption may be caused": *Harrison Ainslie & Co. v. Muncaster* [1891] 2 Q.B. 680 at 684. And thus it seems to me that a disruption of the access to, or of the view of, windows of a retail shop is sufficient to constitute an interference with the enjoyment of the premises themselves. In the instant case, a free and unrestricted passageway for members of the public along the eastern footpath of Gawler Place and an unobstructed view of the shop frontage were an implied accommodation of the demised premises, and any interference with that apparent accommodation was an interference with the ordinary use and enjoyment of the premises themselves: cf. *Dowse v. Wynyard Holdings Ltd* (1962) 79 W.N. (N.S.W.) 122 at 131.

In considering the question whether the plaintiff has established a breach of covenant for quiet enjoyment, I have been guided by the authority of the dictum of Fry L.J. in *Sanderson v. Mayor of Berwick-on-Tweed* (1884) 13 Q.B.D. 547 at 551, where the learned Lord Justice, in delivering the judgment of the court, said: "It appears to us to be in every case a question of fact whether the quiet enjoyment of the land has or has not been interrupted; and where the ordinary and lawful enjoyment of the demised land is substantially interfered with by the acts of the lessor, or those lawfully claiming under him, the covenant appears to us to be broken, although neither the title to the land nor the possession of the land may be otherwise affected." This proposition of law was considered in *Owen v. Gadd* [1956] 2 Q.B. 99 by Lord Evershed M.R. who had no hesitation in rejecting a submission that the language of Fry L.J. must be read with the qualification "that there could be no breach of covenant for quiet enjoyment unless there was . . . an actual physical irruption into or on the premises demised on the part of the landlords or some person authorised by them by their actually entering on or invading the premises". In *Owen v. Gadd* [1956] 2 Q.B. 99, the Court of Appeal held that the erection of scaffold poles immediately in front of the windows and doors of a retail shop, in order that necessary repairs should be carried out by the lessor in the upper floors of the premises, constituted an interference sufficiently physical and direct as to be a breach of a covenant for quiet enjoyment. Applying the reasoning of the Court of Appeal to the present case, I think that the erection of the hoarding in front of the plaintiff's shop constituted an act which prevented the plaintiff from the enjoyment of the premises leased to it for the very purpose for which they were in fact leased, namely, for the retail sale of articles falling within the general description of jewellery.

It seems to me that by the terms of the lease, the defendant agreed to become bound for any act of interruption of the quiet enjoyment of the premises and that the defendant is therefore liable for any act of interruption by any other person whom it expressly or impliedly authorised to do the act. In the present case, the defendant actively participated in, and authorised, the consequences complained of and, in my view, it must be held in law responsible for them. By its covenant, the defendant in effect guaranteed the plaintiff against any acts, or the consequences of any acts, done by it or with its authority which could disturb the plaintiff's enjoyment of the premises. And it is none the less a breach of covenant for quiet enjoyment that the interferences of which the plaintiff complains were caused by an independent contractor, however competent that contractor may have been, and however little may have been the defendant's control over the building works. The defendant cannot escape liability because it entrusted the execution of the works to a competent contractor over which it exercised no control: cf. *Bower v. Peate* (1876) 1 Q.B.D. 321; *Harrison Ainslie & Co. v. Muncaster* [1891] 2 Q.B. 680 at 685. Nor in my opinion does it avail the defendant to say that it is freed from any obligation to the plaintiff by reason of the erection of the hoarding under a licence granted by a statutory authority. The licence granted by the Corporation of the City of Adelaide merely authorised the erection of the hoarding, but it had nothing to do with the manner of execution of the building works carried out at the instance of the defendant; it certainly did not, and cannot, authorise consequences to the plaintiff which could follow from the erection of the hoarding.

[Walters J. gave judgment for the plaintiff, assessing damages for loss of profit resulting from the breach of covenant at $2,800.]

2. Not to derogate from grant

This implied covenant is an application to the area of landlord and tenant of the well established principle that "a grantor must not derogate from his grant": see *Palmer v. Fletcher* (1663) 1 Lev. 122; 83 E.R. 329. As expressed by Bowen L.J. in *Birmingham, Dudley and District Banking Co. v. Ross* (1888) 38 Ch. D. 295 at 312:

> the maxim that a grantor shall not derogate from his own grant . . . is as old,
> I will not say as the hills, but as old as the Year Books, and a great deal older.
> . . . [T]he principle will be applied in a proper case by the law that a grantor
> having given a thing with one hand is not to take away the means of enjoying
> it with the other.

In other words, in the context of the landlord and tenant relationship, the landlord is not permitted to do anything inconsistent with the purposes for which the premises are let. As expressed by Parker J. in *Browne v. Flower* [1911] 1 Ch. 219 at 226, "if the grant or demise be made for a particular purpose, the grantor or lessor comes under an obligation not to use the land retained by him in such a way as to render the land granted or demised unfit or materially less fit for the particular purpose for which the grant or demise was made".

In some cases—perhaps most—the covenant for quiet enjoyment will cover the acts which might amount to a derogation by the landlord from her or his grant (as in *Markham v. Paget* [1908] 1 Ch. 697), but the two covenants will not always overlap: see *O'Keefe v. Williams* (1910) 11 C.L.R. 171 at 217, 218; *Telex (Australasia) Pty Ltd v. Thomas Cook & Son (Australasia) Pty Ltd* [1970] 2 N.S.W.R. 257 at 266.

HARMER v. JUMBIL (NIGERIA) TIN AREAS LTD

Court of Appeal [1921] 1 Ch. 200

[In 1911, the life tenant of certain property granted the plaintiff a lease for 21 years, under which the plaintiff covenanted to use the land for the storage of explosives. The lease contained an express covenant for quiet enjoyment. The plaintiff obtained the necessary licence for the storage of explosives, a condition of which was that specified distances should be maintained between magazines in which explosives were stored and any buildings on adjoining land. Breach of this condition meant automatic cancellation of the licence. The lessor knew that the purpose for which the land was leased involved restrictions on the use to which adjoining land could be put. In 1919, the successor in title of the lessor granted to the defendants a licence to mine for minerals on adjoining land, provided that they were not to interfere in any way with the plaintiff's explosives magazines or the access thereto. The defendants re-timbered some existing mining shafts, and erected buildings, within the prohibited distances from the plaintiff's magazines. The plaintiff sought: (1) an injunction restraining the defendants from so building as to put the plaintiff's licence at risk; (2) an order removing the offending buildings; and (3) damages. The plaintiff's claim to relief was based upon the argument that the acts of the defendants were in derogation of the grant under which the plaintiff held. It was admitted that, in relation to derogation from grant, the defendants stood in the same position as the original lessor, and that if the acts would have amounted to a derogation from the grant of the original lessor the defendants also would be liable. At first instance, Eve J. held that the defendants were not in breach of the non-derogation from grant principle. The plaintiff appealed.]

YOUNGER L.J. The question here is how far the original lessor was, or how far the defendants as now claiming under him are, bound to restrict the user of their adjoining land so as not to render illegal the only enjoyment of the demised premises which the lessee under his lease is entitled to have. Or, putting the question in another way, was the lessor, or are the defendants, as now claiming under him, entitled to use their adjoining lands in such a way as that for the convenience of such user and for the protection of their own premises the only authorised user of the demised premises by the lessee will become a statutory offence.

 Now if these questions are to be answered in a sense favourable to the lessee, it must be on the principle that a grantor shall not derogate from his grant, a principle which merely embodies in a legal maxim a rule of common honesty. "A grantor having given a thing with one hand", as Bowen L.J. put it in *Birmingham, Dudley and District Banking Co. v. Ross* (1888) 38 Ch. D. 295 at 313, "is not to take away the means of enjoying it with the other". "If A lets a plot of land to B", as Lord Loreburn phrases it in *Lyttleton Times Co. v. Warners* [1907] A.C. 476 at 481, "he may not act so as to frustrate the purpose for which in the contemplation of both parties the land was hired". The rule is clear but the difficulty is, as always, in its application. For the obligation laid upon the grantor is not unqualified. If it were, that which was imposed in the interest of fair dealing might, in unscrupulous hands, become a justification for oppression, or an instrument of extortion. The obligation therefore must in every case be construed fairly, even strictly, if not narrowly. It must be such as, in view of the surrounding circumstances, was within the reasonable contemplation of the parties at the time when the transaction was entered into, and was at that time within the grantor's power to fulfil. But so limited, the obligation imposed may, I think, be infinitely varied in kind, regard being had to the paramount purpose to serve which it is imposed. If, for instance, the purpose of a grant would in a particular case be frustrated by some act of the lessor on his own land which, while involving no physical interference with the enjoyment of the demised property, would yet be completely effective to stop or render unlawful its continued user for the purpose for which alone it was let, I can see no reason at all in principle why "ut res magis valeat quam pereat" that act should not be prohibited, just as clearly as an act which, though less completely effective in its result, achieved it by some physical interference. There can, in my judgment, be no valid principle in the contention which was addressed to us in this case by [counsel for the defendants] that, while the lease of 1911 carried with it the obligation of doing or permitting nothing on the adjoining land which would make the explosive magazine less fit for use as a magazine, that is to say, more likely to blow up, it did leave the lessor perfectly free to use his land for his own convenience in any way he chose, even although the result of his doing so would ipso facto make the continued user of a powder magazine as such a statutory offence. If that contention were to be accepted it would enable this grantor, if so minded, in pure caprice, to defeat the whole purpose of the grant and completely sterilise the property in his tenant's hands, he himself remaining entitled to the rent reserved for the whole term.

In my judgment the principle here applicable is far too great to be in effect destroyed, in the case of such a property as this, by introducing this distinction which, so far as I can see, has no sound foundation on which to rest.

[The concurring judgments of Lord Sterndale M.R. and Warrington L.J. have been omitted.]

Appeal allowed.

NOTES AND QUESTIONS

1. Why was the plaintiff not able to sue on the covenant for quiet enjoyment? See *Harmer v. Jumbil (Nigeria) Tin Areas Ltd* [1921] 1 Ch. 200 at 213 per Eve J.

2. *Harmer's* case was really an extension of the non-derogation principle, because the landlord's act had no direct physical effect on the demised premises: see *Port v. Griffith* [1938] 1 All E.R. 295 at 298.

3. The precise limits of the non-derogation principle are not clear. As one writer has put it: "there is a borderland which is not reached by the ordinary law but is reached by the doctrine of non-derogation, provided and provided only that failure to restrain the lessor would be seriously to prejudice the essential purposes, known to both sides, of the lease": Elliott, "Non-Derogation from Grant" (1964) 80 L.Q.R. 244 at 276. Consider whether the obligation not to derogate is breached in the following situations:

    (1) The lessor, during the currency of the lease, had used large engines installed on land adjoining the demised premises for the purpose of pumping water from the adjoining property. Vibrations from the engines damaged the demised premises, which were used as a dwelling house. The demised premises were old and in poor structural condition, and the evidence was that houses of reasonably solid construction would not have been damaged by the vibrations: see *Grosvenor Hotel Co. v. Hamilton* [1894] 2 Q.B. 836.

    (2) M sold his timber merchant's business to the plaintiff and gave the plaintiff a lease of the premises on which the business was conducted. The lease contained a covenant that the lessee would use the land to carry on the trade of a timber merchant. On M's death, the demised land, together with adjoining land owned by M, was sold to the defendants, who proceeded to erect substantial buildings on the adjoining land. The plaintiff claimed that in so doing, the defendants had interfered with the flow of air to drying sheds on the demised premises used in connection with his timber merchant business: see *Aldin v. Latimer Clark, Muirhead & Co.* [1894] 2 Ch. 437.

    (3) A lease contained a covenant whereby the lessees were to use the demised premises as a shop for the sale of wool and general trimmings. The lessor subsequently let an adjoining shop to a business competitor of the lessee: see *Port v. Griffith* [1938] 1 All E.R. 295.

    (4) The trustee of a national park leased a portion of the park to a motel company for the purposes of the motel company's business. The lease was conditional upon the lessee being a holder of a licence to trade within the park. For the first four years of the lease, the trustee granted the required licence for a nominal amount, but it then proposed to change radically its method of fixing licence fees, with the result that the fee payable might be increased seventy-fold: see *Mount Cook National Park Board v. Mount Cook Motels Ltd* [1972] N.Z.L.R. 481.

    (5) A lease of factory premises provided that the plaintiff lessee would reimburse the defendant lessor for the cost of insuring the demised premises against fire, that the lessee would not do anything to increase the fire insurance premium payable, and that the lessor would keep the premises insured against fire. For the first three years of the lease, the lessee was required to reimburse the lessor for insurance premiums calculated at a maximum rate of 3.5 per cent of the value of the lessee's premises and stock. Thereafter, however, the lessor demised adjoining premises to a woodworker, which greatly increased the risk of damage by fire to the premises

occupied by the plaintiff. As a result of the extra risk, the insurance premium payable for the plaintiff's premises increased sharply to 18¾ per cent of their value: see *O'Cedar Ltd v. Slough Trading Co. Ltd* [1927] 2 K.B. 123.

(6) An area of the sixth floor of a city building was leased for the purposes of conducting a cafeteria. At the date of the grant of the lease, access to the sixth floor was provided by four lifts (two of which were operated by lift operators) and by two centrally placed escalators. The only other means of access was by fire escape stairs. Under the terms of the lease, the "common areas" of the building (which included the lifts and escalators) were subject to the control of the lessor, and the tenant was entitled to the use of the lifts and escalators, subject to the terms of the lease. After the lessee had been in occupation for one year, the lessor ceased operating the escalators and reduced the passenger-operated lift service. The lessor's reasons were that three of the intermediate floors had become unoccupied and to continue the full service would result in heavy financial loss and a risk of vandalism to the unoccupied floors: see *Karaggianis v. Malltown Pty Ltd* (1979) 21 S.A.S.R. 381.

(7) An area in a warehouse complex was leased for the purpose of storing goods. The lessor demolished other parts of the warehouse complex in such a way that thieves were able to break into the lessee's area and steal the goods: see *Lend Lease Development Pty Ltd v. Zemlicka* (1985) 3 N.S.W.L.R. 207.

4. On this covenant and the covenant for quiet enjoyment, see further, Russell, "Nuisance by Landlords" (1977) 40 M.L.R. 651.

3. That furnished premises are reasonably fit for human habitation at the commencement of the term

COLLINS v. HOPKINS

King's Bench Division [1923] 2 K.B. 617

[The previous tenant of the demised premises had died of tuberculosis. Upon discovering that fact, the plaintiff, the present tenant, vacated the premises and sued to recover rent paid from the date of commencement of the lease, plus damages.]

McCARDIE J. The result of the decisions as a whole seems to be that there is an absolute contractual warranty in the nature of a condition by the person who lets a furnished house or lodging to the effect that the premises and furniture are fit for habitation. What is the meaning of "fit for habitation"? The meaning of the phrase must vary with the circumstances to which it is applied. In the case of unclean furniture or defective drains or a nuisance by vermin the matter is not, as a rule, one of difficulty. The eye or the nostrils can detect the fault and measure its extent. But in the case of a house lately occupied by a person suffering from an infectious disease, the eye and other senses are of no avail. The bacilli of infection are not apparent to the eye. Yet a peril is none the less grave because it is hidden.

This case before me definitely raises the question as to the contractual duty of a person who lets a furnished house lately occupied by one suffering from an infectious disease. It is not, of course, enough for the landlord to say that he honestly believes that the house is fit and proper for safe habitation. It must in fact be fit and safe. The mere belief of the landlord is not the point. Nor, on the other hand, can a tenant renounce his contract because of mere apprehension of risk or through mere dislike to the premises through the fact, for example, that a person has died upon the premises of smallpox or scarlet fever. He must show more than mere apprehension or dislike. In my view the question in such a case as the present is this: Was there an actual and appreciable risk to the tenant, his family or household, by entering and occupying the house in which the infectious disorder had occurred? If the risk be serious, no one, I think, could doubt that the tenant may renounce. But in dealing with bacilli, which may mean illness and death, I think further that an appreciable measure of actual risk justifies the tenant in throwing up his contract. A man should not be called on to expose his wife and children, household or himself to peril.

Amongst the matters to be considered are the nature of the disease; the degree and persistence of its infectivity; the date when the sufferer resided in the house; the steps taken to prevent risk of infection and the like. Let me illustrate the matter further by taking a case where the landlord says to an incoming tenant of a furnished house: "I admit that my child died in the house but a short time ago of a contagious disease. I admit it to be doubtful whether the bacilli of the disease are still in the house or not, but I require you to fulfil your bargain." Surely, in such a case the tenant could rightly refuse to enter and could renounce his agreement of tenancy. I should so hold. The law would be in a regrettable state if it were otherwise. It would be gravely opposed to the elementary requirements of public health. I should respectfully but firmly dissent from any doctrine which suggested that in the case I put, the law would enable the landlord to enforce the bargain of tenancy.

Judgment for the plaintiff.

NOTES

1. There are strict limits upon this implied covenant. First, it applies only to furnished dwelling-houses; there is no equivalent covenant where the premises are let unfurnished: *Cruse v. Mount* [1933] Ch. 278; *Hart v. Windsor* (1843) 12 M. & W. 68; 152 E.R. 1114. Secondly, it applies only to the condition of the dwelling-house at the commencement of the term; there is no implied covenant that it shall continue to be fit for habitation: *Sarson v. Roberts* [1895] 2 Q.B. 395. Thirdly, the covenant applies only to the condition of the premises (including fixtures), not to furnishings or appliances within the premises: *Pampris v. Thanos* (1967) 69 S.R. (N.S.W.) 226 at 229.

2. There is no implied covenant that demised premises generally are suitable for the purposes for which they are let, or that they can be lawfully used for the purposes for which they are let: *Edler v. Auerbach* [1950] 1 K.B. 359 at 373, 374; *Hill v. Harris* [1965] 2 Q.B. 601 at 614, 615. For example, in *Balcairn Guest House Ltd v. Weir* [1963] N.Z.L.R. 301, the demised premises were leased for the express purpose of a guest house, and a provision in the lease forbade the lessee from using them for any other purpose without the lessor's consent. The lessor was aware that there was no current licence for their use as a guest house, a fact he carefully (but without fraud) kept from the lessee. Held, there was no implied covenant that the premises were fit for use as a guest house.

   By way of contrast, there is no rule preventing the implication into a contractual *licence* of a term that the premises are fit for the purposes of the licence, where such a term is necessary to give business efficacy to the agreement: *Wettern Electric Ltd v. Welsh Development Agency* [1983] 2 W.L.R. 897.

3. In *Gabolinscy v. Hamilton City Corp.* [1975] 1 N.Z.L.R. 150 at 163, Moller J. said:

   > although warranties as to the quality of any land which is the subject of a contract of sale or lease are not in general to be implied, the totality of the circumstances of any particular case may lead the court to a decision that such a warranty should be implied.

   In that case, the defendant corporation executed a long term lease to the plaintiff of land in a residential subdivision upon condition that the lessee build a house thereon within two years. The house the lessee built suffered substantial damage as a result of subsidence, caused by the corporation's negligence. Did the lessee have an action for breach of an implied warranty that the leased land was suitable for building purposes?

4. There are some statutory inroads into the common law principle in Australia: cf. the Housing Acts 1957 and 1961 (U.K.); *Campden Hill Towers Ltd v. Gardner* [1977] Q.B. 823; Reynolds, "Statutory Covenants of Fitness and Repair: Social Legislation and the Judges" (1974) 37 M.L.R. 377; Robinson, " 'Social Legislation' and the Judges: A Note by way of Rejoinder" (1976) 39 M.L.R. 43. An early provision in New South Wales is s. 39 of the *Landlord and Tenant (Amendment) Act* 1948, which provides: "A person shall not let a dwelling-house which to his knowledge is, at the date of the letting, not in fair and tenantable repair". The definition of "dwelling-house" in s. 8(1A) makes it clear, however, that s. 39 relates only to "prescribed premises", that is, premises subject to the restrictions of the Act, and the number of such premises is diminishing rapidly; and, in any case, the section would not appear to require the lessor to repair where the premises fall into disrepair during the currency of the term. More recently, s. 25 of the *Residential Tenancies Act* 1987 (N.S.W.) implies into every "residential tenancy agreement" (as to which, see above p. 576) a term that the landlord

shall provide the "residential premises" in a "reasonable state of cleanliness and fit for habitation by the tenant" and shall maintain them in a "reasonable state of repair", having regard to their age and prospective life and the rent payable. The section defines "residential premises" to include everything provided with the premises for use by the tenant.

In addition, ss 57 and 58 of the *Public Health Act* 1902 (N.S.W.) permit State or Local Government bodies to close premises unfit for human habitation (these provisions are not restricted to leased premises).

4. To use the premises in a tenant-like manner

WARREN v. KEEN

Court of Appeal [1954] 1 Q.B. 15

[The plaintiff lessor sued the defendant lessee to recover the cost of repairs which the lessor had effected to the demised premises. The defendant was on a weekly tenancy. Paragraph 2 of the plaintiff's particulars of claim said: "It was an implied term of the said tenancy that the defendant would use the said premises in a tenant-like manner, would keep the same wind and water tight and would make fair and tenantable repairs thereto. The tenant in breach of the said implied term, has failed to use the said premises in a tenant-like manner, has not kept the same wind and water tight and has not made fair and tenant-like repairs thereto." The particulars of disrepair were: "(a) First floor front room (large). Walls—plaster damp—stained below window opening. (b) First floor front room (small). Walls—plaster damp—stained and perished below window opening. (c) External. Front wall—rendering cracked and broken in parts. Front floor window opening—sills not weather proof, joints and paintwork decayed. (d) Leak in hot water boiler." The trial judge held for the landlord. On appeal.]

DENNING L.J. Apart from express contract, a tenant owes no duty to the landlord to keep the premises in repair. The only duty of the tenant is to use the premises in a husband-like, or what is the same thing, a tenant-like manner. This is how it was put by Sir Vicary Gibbs C.J. in *Horsefall v. Mather* (1815) Holt N.P. 7; 171 E.R. 141 and by Scrutton L.J. and Atkin L.J. in *Marsden v. Edward Heyes Ltd* [1927] 2 K.B. 7 at 8. But what does "to use the premises in a tenant-like manner" mean? It can, I think, best be shown by some illustrations. The tenant must take proper care of the place. He must, if he is going away for the winter, turn off the water and empty the boiler. He must clean the chimneys, when necessary, and also the windows. He must mend the electric light when it fuses. He must unstop the sink when it is blocked by his waste. In short, he must do the little jobs about the place which a reasonable tenant would do. In addition, he must, of course, not damage the house, wilfully or negligently; and he must see that his family and guests do not damage it: and if they do, he must repair it. But apart from such things if the house falls into disrepair through fair wear and tear or lapse of time, or for any reason not caused by him, then the tenant is not liable to repair it.

The landlord sought to put upon the tenant a higher obligation. She said that the duty of the tenant was to keep the premises wind and water tight and to make fair and tenantable repairs thereto. That seems to be based on Hill and Redman on *Landlord and Tenant* (11th ed.), p. 186. I do not think that is a correct statement of the obligation.

Take the first branch, "to keep the premises wind and water tight". Lord Tenterden, in one of two cases at nisi prius, used that expression and it was followed by the Court of Appeal in *Wedd v. Porter* [1916] 2 K.B. 100, but it is very difficult to know what "wind and water tight" means. I asked counsel whether there was any case to be found in the books where a tenant had been held liable for breach of that obligation. I wanted to see what sort of thing it had been held to cover. But there was no such case to be found. In the absence of it, I think that the expression "wind and water tight" is of doubtful value and should be avoided. It is better to keep to the simple obligation "to use the premises in a tenant-like manner".

Take the second branch, "to make fair and tenantable repairs". Lord Kenyon used the expression in *Ferguson v. Anon* (1798) 2 Esp. 500; 170 E.R. 465, which is only reported by Espinasse [footnote omitted], who was notoriously defective. It is said that he only heard half of what went on and reported the other half. If you read the whole sentence used by Lord Kenyon, however, it is clear that he was only referring to cases where a tenant does damage himself, such as breaking the windows or the doors. Then, of course, he must repair them. The sentence, used by Lord Kenyon, was explained by Bankes L.J. in *Marsden v. Heyes* [1927] 2 K.B. 1 by saying that if a tenant commits waste—that is, if he commits voluntary waste by doing damage himself—he must do such repairs to the premises as will enable them to exclude wind and water. So explained, it does not support the proposition stated in Redman.

It was suggested by Mr Willis that an action lies against a weekly tenant for permissive waste. I do not think that that is so. It has been held not to lie against a tenant at will, see the *Countess of Shrewsbury's case* (1600) 5 Co. Rep. 13b, and in my opinion it does not lie against a weekly tenant. In my judgment, the only obligation on a weekly tenant is to use the premises in a tenant-like manner. That does not cover the dampness and other defects alleged in the particulars of claim. The appeal should be allowed accordingly.

[The judgments of Somervell and Romer L.JJ. have been omitted.]

Appeal allowed.

NOTES AND QUESTIONS

1. The principle in *Warren v. Keen* must be read subject to the provisions of s. 84(1) of the *Conveyancing Act* 1919 (N.S.W.); see below p. 587.

2. The judgments in *Warren v. Keen* seem to require the conclusion that, as regards liability for waste, a weekly tenancy is on the same footing as any other periodic tenancy. Are there any reasons why, for example, a tenant from quarter to quarter might justifiably be made subject to a higher duty to repair than a tenant from week to week?

3. By the *Statute of Marlborough* 1267 (U.K.), a tenant for a term of years was made liable for both voluntary and permissive waste, in the absence of agreement to the contrary. Thus, unless the terms of the tenancy required the landlord to repair, the tenant was liable for repairs: cf. the remarks of Denning L.J. in the principal case.

   The *Statute of Marlborough* no longer applies in New South Wales, by virtue of the *Imperial Acts Application Act* 1969 (N.S.W.). Section 32(1) of the 1969 Act provides: "A tenant for life or lives or a leasehold tenant shall not commit voluntary waste". By subs. (3), "leasehold tenant" is defined to include a tenant for a term, a tenant under a periodical tenancy, a tenant holding under s. 127 of the *Conveyancing Act* 1919 (N.S.W.), and a tenant at will.

4. Although a tenant at will is not liable for permissive waste, if he or she commits voluntary waste the tenancy is thereby terminated and the tenant is liable to an action for damages. A tenant at sufferance is liable for voluntary waste, but probably not for permissive waste: see Megarry and Wade, op. cit., p. 703.

5. To yield up possession to the lessor at the end of the tenancy

HENDERSON v. SQUIRE

Court of Queen's Bench (1869) L.R. 4 Ex. 170

[The defendant tenant sub-leased the premises to T. At the expiration of the sub-lease, T refused to vacate, and remained in possession against the will of the defendant. The defendant's lease having expired, the plaintiff landlord sought to recover from the defendant damages for the time he was kept out of possession by the sub-lessee and for the costs of ejecting the sub-lessee.]

BLACKBURN J. The question is, where there is a tenancy, and nothing is expressed as to delivering up possession at its determination, whether there is an implied contract that the tenant shall not only go out of possession, but restore the possession to the landlord. Here the tenant had sublet the premises to a man who, under some fancied claim of right, held over without the consent and against the will of the tenant, his landlord. I think that there is such an implied contract; for as the landlord who is to put the tenant into possession could not fulfil his contract unless he put him into absolute possession, the obligation on the part of the tenant at the end of the term is correlative. Lord Kenyon in *Harding v. Crethorn* (1793) 1 Esp. 57; 170 E.R. 278 expressly rules that "the lessor is entitled to receive the absolute possession, at the end of the term", and he further lays down the artificial rule, that the lessee would be liable for rent not on an actual but constructive occupation by the under-tenant holding over. . . . It is true that there is very little authority on the question under discussion; but, independently of authority, on principle, seeing that the landlord gives the tenant absolute possession, it is the duty of the tenant to restore absolute possession.

Then comes the next question, what measure of damages the plaintiff is entitled to recover. He is entitled to what the rent would have amounted to for the time he was kept out of possession, and also to the sum of £13 10s., the costs of the action of ejectment; for we must take it that was the best mode of recovering possession: and these costs follow as a necessary consequence of letting to an under-tenant if he refuses to go out of possession: *Collen v. Wright* (1857) 7 E. & B. 301; 120 E.R. 241 proceeded precisely on this principle.

[Cockburn C.J., Mellor J. and Hayes J. delivered separate judgments agreeing with Blackburn J.]

Judgment for the plaintiff.

NOTE

See also *Henderson v. Van Cooten* [1922] W.N. 340.

6. To cultivate in a husband-like manner

WILLIAMS v. LEWIS

King's Bench Division [1915] 3 K.B. 493

BRAY J. The first question is: What is the extent of the implied obligations of the tenant of a farm to his landlord? I think the law is correctly stated in Volume 1 of Lord Halsbury's *Laws of England*, title *Agriculture*, s. 505 [see now *Halsbury's Laws of England* (4th ed.), Vol. 1 para. 1019] thus: "The law implies an undertaking or covenant on the part of an agricultural tenant to cultivate the land in a husband-like manner, unless there is a particular agreement dispensing with that engagement; and the bare relation of landlord and tenant is a sufficient consideration for the tenant's promise to cultivate the land in a good and husband-like manner according to the custom of the country." Farming in accordance with this obligation I will for short call "proper farming", and the condition of the land when it has been so farmed for a lengthened period I will call "proper conditions". Section 507 says the custom of the country does not imply an immemorial or universal usage, but only the prevalent usage of the neighbourhood where the land lies which has subsisted for a reasonable length of time; and s. 509 says evidence showing that a holding has been managed in accordance with the custom of the country is proof that it has been treated in a good and husband-like manner. It was not really disputed that the law was as so laid down, but it was contended for the plaintiff that there was a further obligation, namely, that the tenant should deliver up the land at the termination of the tenancy in a clean and proper condition, properly tilled and manured. In my opinion, so far as this imports some greater obligation than the first obligation, it does not exist. That the tenant must continue to farm properly down to the termination of the tenancy is, of course, true, but so long as he does this he has, in my opinion, performed the whole of his obligation. I will give an illustration to show what I mean. Suppose that at the beginning of the tenancy the land is in an impoverished condition, that is, below proper condition, and the tenant enters and farms properly, but yet the land at the end of the tenancy has not got into proper condition. This may well happen if the tenancy has been a short one, say only two or three years. In such a case there has been, in my opinion, no breach of the obligation. The contention of the plaintiff would impose it, but the contention is wrong. I ought to add that in this case I find there was no custom imposing this greater obligation.

NOTES AND QUESTIONS

1. See also *Powley v. Walker* (1793) 5 Term Rep. 373; 101 E.R. 208.

2. How might the *Agricultural Holdings Act* 1941 (N.S.W.) affect the rules in the principal case, in respect of lands to which that Act applies? Section 15(2) of the Act allows the landlord to claim compensation where the tenant farmer fails to cultivate "according to the rules of good husbandry". The term "rules of good husbandry" is defined in s. 4(1) in the following manner:

   "Rules of good husbandry" means (due regard being had to the character of the holding) so far as is practicable having regard to its character and position—

   (a) the maintenance of the land (whether arable or pasture) clean and in a good state of cultivation and fertility and in good condition; and

   (b) the adoption of farming methods to mitigate or prevent soil erosion;

   (c) the maintenance and clearing of drains, embankments and ditches; and

   (d) the maintenance and proper repair of fences and gates; and

   (e) the execution of repairs to buildings, being repairs which are necessary for the proper cultivation and working of the land on which they are to be executed; and

   (f) such rules of good husbandry as are generally recognised as applying to holdings of the same character and in the same neighbourhood as the holding in respect of which the expression is to be applied:

   Provided that the foregoing definition shall not imply an obligation on the part of any person to maintain or clear drains, embankments or ditches, if and so far as the execution of the works required is rendered impossible (except at prohibitive or unreasonable expense) by reason of subsidence of any land or the blocking of outfalls which are not under the control of that person or, in its application to land in the occupation of a tenant, imply an obligation on the part of the tenant—

   (i) to maintain or clear drains, embankments or ditches, or to maintain or properly repair fences or gates where such work is not required to be done by him under his contract of tenancy; or

   (ii) to execute repairs to buildings which are not required to be executed by him under his contract of tenancy.

B. COVENANTS IMPLIED BY STATUTE

Covenants may be implied into leases by statute. For example, the *Conveyancing Act* 1919 (N.S.W.), s. 84(1) implies covenants on the part of the lessee to pay rent (subject to abatement in the event that the premises or part of them become unfit for occupation through damage by fire, flood, lightning, storm, or tempest), and to keep and yield up the premises "in good and tenantable repair, having regard to their condition at the commencement of the . . . lease, accidents, war damage and damage from fire, flood, lightning, storm and tempest, and reasonable wear and tear excepted". The proviso for abatement is necessary to overcome the limited application of the doctrine of frustration to leases: *National Carriers Ltd v. Panalpina (Northern) Ltd* [1981] A.C. 675.

By s. 85(1) there are implied powers in the lessor to enter and view the state of repair (at a reasonable time of the day, and after giving two days' notice), to require the lessee to repair and in default thereof to enter and repair, to enter for the purpose of carrying out the requirements of competent authorities or to effect structural repairs, and to re-enter and determine the lease in the event of default in payment of rent or breach of some other covenant in the lease.

These covenants and powers may be expressly negatived, varied or modified: s. 74(2).

In practice, leases usually contain express provisions covering the same, or substantially the same, field as these statutory covenants. Sometimes, however, an express covenant is more favourable to the landlord than is its statutory counterpart. For example, the tenant's covenant to repair in s. 84(1)(b) of the *Conveyancing Act* 1919 (N.S.W.) is qualified by reference to the condition of the premises at the commencement of the lease; such a qualification is not always present in express covenants to repair: see *Payne v. Haine* (1847) 16 M. & W. 541; 153 E.R. 1304, extracted below p. 589. Further, s. 84(1)(b) excepts liability for, inter alia, "accidents" (as to which, see *Saviane v. Stauffer Chemical Co. (Aust.) Pty Ltd* [1974] 1 N.S.W.L.R. 665: an "accident" within s. 84(1)(b) is an event causing unintentional and unexpected damage to the premises, and damage is unexpected if it is such that a reasonable person in the position of the lessee would not have foreseen it as likely to result from the event and which could not reasonably have been guarded against); it is not usual for express covenants to repair to contain such an exception.

The *Residential Tenancies Act* 1987 (N.S.W.) also implies terms into leases to which that Act applies: as to which, see above p. 576. Notable amongst the implied terms are the following: the tenant must pay the rent on or before the day set out in the agreement (s. 18); if the premises are destroyed, rendered wholly or partly uninhabitable, cease to be lawfully useable for a residence, or resumed, the rent abates (s. 61); the landlord must maintain the premises (and everything provided with them) in a reasonable state of repair having regard to their age, prospective life, and the rent payable (s. 25); the tenant must keep the premises in a reasonable state of cleanliness and at the termination of the tenancy leave them as nearly as possible in the same condition (fair wear and tear excepted) as set out in any condition report forming part of the residential tenancy agreement (s. 26); the landlord must reimburse the tenant for the reasonable cost of urgent repairs effected by the tenant (s. 28); and the landlord may enter the premises in a number of situations (including the following: in an emergency; to inspect the premises; to carry out necessary repairs and maintenance; to show through prospective purchasers, mortgagees or tenants): s. 24.

1. Covenant to pay rent

"Rent" is "a sum issuing out of the land demised payable by the lessee to the lessor for the right to occupy that land and all that [goes] with it for the purpose for which it [is] demised": *Junghenn v. Wood* [1958] S.R. (N.S.W.) 327 at 330. See further Markson, "Rent: A Changing Concept" (1974) 118 Sol. J. 586.

The covenant to pay rent implied under s. 84 of the *Conveyancing Act* 1919 (N.S.W.) may be considered deficient in several ways. First, it does not provide for payment of rent in advance, whereas express covenants to pay rent invariably so provide. Secondly, although it contains a proviso for abatement of rent as outlined above (and the abatement proviso cannot be completely negatived: see *Conveyancing Act* 1919 (N.S.W.), s. 84A), that proviso is not necessarily suitable in all cases. For example, the landlord may want the right to determine the lease in the event of serious damage; the tenant may want a similar right, or the right to demand that the premises be repaired or rebuilt. The statutory covenant does not give such rights.

Payment of rent by a third party (such as a guarantor) is not payment by the tenant; the tenant remains liable for the rent, and the lease liable to forfeiture for non-payment, even though the amount has been paid by a third party: *London and County (A. & D.) Ltd v. Wilfred Sportsman Ltd* [1971] Ch. 764.

In accordance with normal contract law principles, where the tenant fails to pay rent and the landlord treats the failure as a repudiation and terminates the lease, the landlord's recovery of damages will be qualified by a duty to mitigate loss. But if the landlord elects, as he or she is entitled to do, not to terminate the lease but to treat it as still subsisting, he or she may sue for rent as it falls due and comes under no duty to mitigage the loss (by, for example, attempting to find a new tenant); in such a case, even where the tenant has abandoned possession, the landlord may simply let the lease run on and sue for rent as it accrues, although of course the premises must be kept available for the tenant: see *Boyer v. Warbey* [1953] 1 Q.B. 234; *Tall-Bennett & Co. Ltd v. Sadot Holdings Pty Ltd* (1988) C.C.H. N.S.W. Conv. R. 55-428.

Where, however, a "residential tenancy agreement" exists (as to which, see above p. 576), s. 15 of the *Residential Tenancies Act* 1987 provides that the "rules of law relating to mitigation of loss or damage on breach of a contract" apply to breach of the residential tenancy agreement; and s. 78 provides that a tenant who abandons the premises must pay compensation to the landlord for any loss (including loss of rent) caused by the abandonment, but the landlord must take "all reasonable steps to mitigage the loss and is not entitled to compensation for any loss that could have been avoided by taking those steps".

2. Covenant to repair

(a) Keeping in good repair

The covenant to repair implied by the *Conveyancing Act* 1919 (N.S.W.), s. 84, qualifies the duty to repair by reference to the condition of the premises at the commencement of the term. Without such a qualification, a tenant's covenant to "keep premises in good and tenantable repair" requires the tenant to put them in repair if they are in disrepair at the commencement of the lease.

PAYNE v. HAINE

(1847) 16 M. & W. 541; 153 E.R. 1304

PARKE B. If, at the time of the demise, the premises were old and in bad repair, the lessee was bound to put them in good repair as old premises; for he cannot "keep" them in good repair without putting them into it. He might have contracted to keep them in the state in which they were at the time of the demise. This is a contract to keep the premises in good repair, as old premises; but that cannot justify the keeping them in bad repair because they happened to be in that state when the defendant took them. The cases all shew that the age and class of the premises let, with their general condition as to repair, may be estimated, in order to measure the extent of the repairs to be done. Thus, a house in Spitalfields may be repaired with materials inferior to those requisite for repairing a mansion in Grosvenor Square; but this lessee cannot say he will do no repairs, or leave the premises in bad repair, because they were old and out of repair when he took them. He was to keep them in good repair, and in that state, with reference to their age and class, he was to deliver them up at the end of the term.

NOTES AND QUESTIONS

1. A tenant covenanted "at all times to keep in good and tenantable repair all fences, buildings and structures existing on the demised premises at the commencement of the term". The dwelling-house was in a completely ruinous state: it was infested with borers, full of dry rot, and bees had built hives between the outer walls and lining. The evidence was that there was no means of extirpating the borers, there was no remedy for dry rot once it had set in, and to put the house into a satisfactory condition "it would be necessary to pull half of it down and practically to make a new place of it". Is the tenant obliged to repair under the covenant? See *Puhi Maihi v. McLeod* [1920] N.Z.L.R. 372. Compare *Woodifield v. Bond* [1922] 2 Ch. 40 at 49-50.

2. Can a tenant, otherwise under a duty to repair under a covenant to repair, argue that he is absolved from responsibility because the state of disrepair is due to breach of a covenant to repair by a previous tenant? Consider the following comments of Isaacs J. in *Bailey v. John Paynter (Mayfield) Pty Ltd* [1966] 1 N.S.W.R. 596 at 605-606:

   One can well understand and comprehend situations in which a breach of a covenant to repair and deliver up in good repair by a former tenant necessarily leaves the premises in a physically dilapidated and deteriorated state in the ordinary accepted connotation of those terms. If a tenant takes a tenancy of premises where by reason of user, decay, dilapidation or deterioration, floors are unsafe or rotting, windows are broken, locks missing, walls and ceilings dirty or plaster thereon broken and enters into a covenant to repair, keep in repair and deliver up in repair, that is one thing, then there is no reason why he should not be held to his covenant in the terms described by Lord Esher and Lord Justice Lopes [in *Proudfoot v. Hart* (1890) 25 Q.B.D. 42, extracted below p. 590]. But although this condition of the premises may be due to or the result of the breach of some earlier tenant's covenant to repair, etc., the latter is irrelevant to the factual or physical state of the property at the time of the new lease. The nature of the repairs the new lessee is required to do to fulfil his covenant to repair is governed by the principles set out above relating to the condition and general state of the building and its location. It is not because some other lessee has allowed it to get into that condition in breach of that lessee's covenant that gives rise to the new tenant's obligation. His obligation to repair arises from the state of facts that actually existed at the time of the lease and the nature of the covenant that is entered into.

   Moreover it is obvious that it is not every breach of covenant to repair that results in the premises being out of repair or in disrepair or not in tenantable repair at the termination of a lease vis-à-vis some new tenant. It may very well be so regarded as between the lessor and the former tenant inter se and for which the former tenant may be answerable in damages. But qua the new tenant whether he is aware or not of structural alterations done by the former tenant, such do not put the premises in a state of disrepair or out of repair or not in tenantable repair unless they produce a factual or physical state of deterioration and dilapidation.

   One can well imagine structural alterations which produce the diametrically opposite result— for example, suppose a tenant breaks open a wall and puts in view windows which give a panoramic view of the harbour. This might well constitute a breach of covenant to repair and keep in repair and surrender in good repair by the tenant who did it.

But, if he leaves the premises at or before the expiration of the lease and the landlord then leases it in that condition to a new tenant the premises and the view window and its surrounds then being in a perfectly sound state of repair, and the lease contains a covenant to repair and deliver up in repair, it would be ludicrous to suppose that the landlord could the very next day demand that the new tenant take out the view window and block it up, and that if he fails to do it, himself enter and carry out that work on the footing of the new tenant being in default.

(b) The standard of repair required

PROUDFOOT v. HART

Court of Appeal (1890) 25 Q.B.D. 42

[The plaintiff landlord leased to the defendant tenant a house for a term of three years. The tenant agreed to "keep the said premises in good tenantable repair, and so leave the same at the expiration thereof". The question was whether the tenant was responsible for the cost of repapering the walls, repainting the internal woodwork, whitewashing and cleaning the staircases and ceilings, and replacing a kitchen floor.]

LORD ESHER M.R. Now, what is "tenantable repair"? Definitions have been given at different times by the courts. . . .

The result of the cases seems to be this: the question whether the house was, or was not, in tenantable repair when the tenancy began is immaterial; but the age of the house is very material with respect to the obligation both to keep and to leave it in tenantable repair. It is obvious that the obligation is very different when the house is fifty years older than it was when the tenancy began. Lopes L.J. has drawn up a definition of the term "tenantable repair" with which I entirely agree. It is this: " 'Good tenantable repair' is such repair as, having regard to the age, character, and locality of the house, would make it reasonably fit for the occupation of a reasonably-minded tenant of the class who would be likely to take it." The age of the house must be taken into account, because nobody could reasonably expect that a house 200 years old should be in the same condition of repair as a house lately built; the character of the house must be taken into account, because the same class of repairs as would be necessary to a palace would be wholly unnecessary to a cottage; and the locality of the house must be taken into account, because the state of repair necessary for a house in Grosvenor Square would be wholly different from the state of repair necessary for a house in Spitalfields. The house need not be put into the same condition as when the tenant took it; it need not be put into perfect repair; it need only be put into such a state of repair as renders it reasonably fit for the occupation of a reasonably-minded tenant of the class who would be likely to take it. I think our definition is an expansion of the definitions given in the earlier cases, or rather it is a collocation of all the different parts of the definition to be collected from those cases. . . .

I will add a few words as to the way in which the definition should be worked out in the present case. The official referee appears to have said that in his view "tenantable repair" included painting, papering, and decorating. If he meant, as I think he must have meant, that it included *all* papering, painting, and decorating, I have no hesitation in saying that his construction of the term "tenantable repair" was wrong. Again, he has said that the tenant's obligation is to "repaper with similar paper to that which was on the walls before, and repaint with similar paint to that which was on the painted portion of the premises before". I think that view was wrong also. With regard to the papering, Cave J., in the court below, said: "I cannot see how in any case a man can be bound to put new paper on the walls simply because the old paper which was on at the time when he took the house, or which he has subsequently put on the walls, has become worn out.'' I agree that he is not bound to repaper simply because the old paper has become worn out, but I do not agree with the view that under a covenant to keep a house in tenantable repair the tenant can never be required to put up new paper. Take a house in Grosvenor Square. If when the tenancy ends, the paper on the walls is merely in a worse condition than when the tenant went in, I think the mere fact of its being in a worse condition does not impose upon the tenant any obligation to repaper under the covenant, if it is in such a condition that a reasonably-minded tenant of the class who take houses in Grosvenor Square would not think the house unfit for his occupation. But suppose that the damp has caused the paper to peel off the walls, and it is lying upon the floor, so that such a tenant would think it a disgrace, I should say then that the tenant was bound, under his covenant to leave the premises in tenantable repair, to put up new paper. He need not put up paper of a similar kind—which I take to mean of equal value—to the paper which was on the walls when his tenancy began. He need not put up a paper of a richer character than would satisfy a reasonable man within the definition.

The same view applies as to painting. If the paint is in such a state that the woodwork will decay unless it is repainted, it is obvious that the tenant must repaint. But I think that his obligation goes further than that. A house in Spitalfields is never painted in the same way as one in Grosvenor Square. If the tenant leaves a house in Grosvenor Square with painting only good enough for a house in Spitalfields, he has not discharged his obligation. He must paint it in such a way as would satisfy a reasonable tenant taking a house in Grosvenor Square. As to whitewashing, one knows it is impossible to keep ceilings in the same condition as when they have just been whitewashed. But if, though the ceilings have become blacker, they are still in such a condition that a reasonable man would not say, ''I will not take this house because of the state of the ceilings'', then I think that the tenant is not bound, under his covenant to leave the house in tenantable repair, to whitewash them. Take, again, the case of a house in Grosvenor Square having an ornamental ceiling, which is a beautiful work of art. A tenant goes in and finds such a ceiling in the house, and in course of time the gilding becomes in such a bad condition, or so much worn off, that the ceiling is no longer ornamental. I should think that a reasonable tenant taking a house in Grosvenor Square would not require a gilded ceiling at all. If that be so, on the mere covenant to leave the premises in tenantable repair, I should think that the tenant who has entered into that covenant was not bound to regild the ceiling at all. As to the floor, it may have been rotten when the tenancy began. If it was in such a state when the tenancy began that no reasonable man would take the house with a floor in that state, then the tenant's obligation is to put the floor into tenantable repair. The question is, what is the state of the floor when the tenant is called upon to fulfil his covenant? If it has become perfectly rotten he must put down a new floor, but if he can make it good in the sense in which I have spoken of all the other things—the paper, the paint, the whitewashing—he is not bound to put down a new floor. He may satisfy his obligation under the covenant by repairing it. If he leaves the floor out of repair when the tenancy ends, and the landlord comes in, the landlord may do the repairs himself and charge the costs as damages against the tenant; but he is only entitled to charge him with the necessary cost of a floor which would satisfy a reasonable man taking the premises. If the landlord puts down a new floor of a different kind, he cannot charge the tenant with the cost of it. He is entitled to charge the cost of doing what the tenant had to do under his covenant; but he is not entitled to charge according to what he has himself in fact done.

LOPES L.J. What is the meaning of "good tenantable repair"? That expression appears to me to mean such repair as, having regard to the age, character, and locality of the house, would make it reasonably fit for the occupation of a reasonably-minded tenant of the class who would be likely to take it. I do not say that there is anything new in this definition; but it appears to me a good definition as the result of the authorities which have been referred to by the Master of the Rolls. What is the obligation of the tenant under such a contract? First, he must, if the premises are out of repair when he takes them, put them into good tenantable repair. *Payne v. Haine* (1847) 16 M. & W. 541; 153 E.R. 1304 is an authority for saying that this is his obligation. It is clear also that under such a contract as this he must commit no waste. Therefore, with respect to the kitchen floor, the tenant's obligation in the present case was either to repair the old floor, or to put down a new one. As to papering and painting, generally speaking the tenant would not be bound to repaper or repaint. Most clearly he is not bound to repaper with similar paper to that which was on the walls when the tenancy began, or to repaint with similar paint. Most clearly, also, he is not bound to do repairs which are merely decorative. But if at the end of the lease the paper and paint are in such a condition as to cause portions of the premises to go into decay, he is bound to repaper and repaint to such an extent as will satisfy the terms of the definition which I have stated. Again, if the paint through the lapse of time has worn off, or the paper has become worn out, so that their condition has become such as not to satisfy a reasonably-minded tenant of the class who would be likely to take the house, then he must repaper and repaint so as to make the premises reasonably fit, within the definition, for the occupation of such a tenant; and what I have said with respect to papering and painting applies also to all the other kinds of repair which have been mentioned.

NOTE

Lopes L.J.'s definition of "good tenantable repair" was applied in *Abrahams v. Shaw* (1969) 89 W.N. (N.S.W.) (Pt 2) 215, where the Court of Appeal upheld a magistrate's finding that there was no breach of a covenant to repair contained in a lease of a block of flats, where some of the sinks and draining boards needed replacing and some of the bathroom mirrors needed resilvering: the premises were held to be reasonably fit for the occupation of a reasonably-minded tenant of the class who would be likely to take them.

ANSTRUTHER-GOUGH-CALTHORPE v. McOSCAR

Court of Appeal [1924] 1 K.B. 716

[A lease of three newly erected country houses contained a covenant that the tenant would "well and sufficiently repair support uphold maintain . . . and keep the three several messuages and buildings . . . with all and all manner of needful and necessary reparations and amendments whatsoever" and yield them up at the end of the term well and sufficiently repaired, supported, etc., as aforesaid. The lease was for a term of 95 years. At the end of the term, the successor in title of the original lessor sought damages from the successor in title of the original lessee for breach of the covenant to repair. There was no dispute that the covenant had been breached, but the tenant argued, on the basis of *Proudfoot v. Hart* (1890) 25 Q.B.D. 42, that she was responsible only for such repairs as having regard to the age, character, and locality of the premises would make them reasonably fit to satisfy the requirements of reasonably minded tenants of the class that would be likely to occupy them. The evidence was that the character of the neighbourhood had deteriorated during the term of the lease, and that the class of tenant likely to occupy the premises at the end of the term would be content as long as they were rain-proof and not a health risk.]

BANKES L.J. [I]t appears that the class of tenant at the present time likely to occupy these houses is content so long as the rain does not penetrate the walls or the sanitary inspector does not interfere on the ground that a nuisance exists on the premises, and that in the lower figure arrived at by the arbitrator he has, acting upon the defendant's contention as to the rule laid down in *Proudfoot v. Hart* (1890) 25 Q.B.D. 42, allowed only such items of repair as will satisfy this class of tenant. It seems impossible that any court can have laid down a rule which requires so extraordinary a construction to be placed upon the covenant in the present case. If the rule contended for by the defendants exists it must apply to cases where the status of the house to be repaired has appreciated as well as to cases where it has depreciated, and it must descend to such depths of degradation as to meet the case where what had at the commencement of the tenancy been a high-class residence is at the end of the tenancy occupied in tenements by a class of tenants who look upon an outer door or an area gate as an unnecessary obstruction, and who therefore require neither the one or the other. If the rule in *Proudfoot v. Hart* is of universal application it would have to be applied in such a case as that just mentioned, and apparently also even although the condition of things at the end of the tenancy had been largely, if not entirely, brought about by a failure to perform the covenant to repair. In my opinion the case of *Proudfoot v. Hart* lays down no rule of general application. The language used by the Lords Justices is quite appropriate to the facts of that case and must, I think, be read as applicable to those facts and to similar facts only. To extend it, as was done by the learned judge in the court below and as has been done in many other cases, is not only, in my opinion, to misapply it, but to put the decision into conflict with a previous decision of the Court of Appeal to which Lord Esher himself was a party. The decision to which I refer is that of *Morgan v. Hardy* (1886) 17 Q.B.D. 770; (1887) 18 Q.B.D. 646. . . .

In construing the covenant in the present case, or any other covenant, it is material to see what the subject matter was which the parties had in their contemplation when the covenant was entered into: see per Willes J. in *Heffield v. Meadows* (1869) L.R. 4 C.P. 595 at 599. Here there is no doubt as to the subject matter. It was the three houses described in the lease, and the obligation undertaken was the repair of those houses. How can the extent of such an obligation be measured by the requirements of the class of tenants who happen to be occupying the premises 95 years afterwards? *Proudfoot v. Hart* did not, in my opinion, lay down any such rule. When the facts of that case are looked into it is manifest that the Lords Justices who decided the case had no such question in their minds. What they were dealing with, and all they were dealing with, was a three years' agreement for a tenancy, in which case the class of tenants at the end of the tenancy was, in their view, no doubt the same class as the class of tenants at the commencement.

Upon that assumption, and upon that assumption only, is the rule laid down by Lopes L.J. and accepted by the Master of the Rolls, in my opinion, explicable or intelligible.

SCRUTTON L.J. In my view this question has been decided, as far as this court is concerned, by the decision in *Morgan v. Hardy* (1886) 17 Q.B.D. 770. In that case the referee had to decide between the claim that the premises must be properly repaired and the contention that, as the premises and the neighbourhood had deteriorated, and in consequence of such deterioration a great portion of the repairs required "were not suited to the said premises and were unnecessary for their use and enjoyment" (1886) 17 Q.B.D. 777, they need not be considered in awarding damages. This court, affirming Denman J., said very summarily that it was a wholly untenable proposition to say that the depreciation of the neighbourhood ought to lower the amount of damages for breach of a covenant to repair. This can only mean that the fact that the class of persons who would use the house at the end of the term had deteriorated, so that their requirements in the way of repairs were less, was immaterial in ascertaining the repairs that the tenant was bound to execute. *Morgan v. Hardy* (1886) 17 Q.B.D. 770 was the case of a 50 years' lease.

In *Proudfoot v. Hart* the lease was for three years only, and the covenant was to keep in good tenantable repair. There was no suggestion of any change in character of the house or its probable tenants between the beginning and the end of the term. Lopes L.J. framed a definition which Lord Esher adopted as follows ((1890) 25 Q.B.D. 42 at 55): "Such repair, as having regard to the age, character, and locality of the house, would make it reasonably fit for the occupation of a reasonably-minded tenant of the class who would be likely to take it." I do not think there was any intention of suggesting that a deterioration in the class of tenants would lower the standard of repairs; the point was not before the court, and had been decided the other way by the court four years previously. Therefore in my view we are bound to look to the character of the house and its ordinary uses at the time of the demise. It must then be put in repair and kept in repair. An improvement of its tenants or its neighbourhood will not increase the standard of repair, nor will their deterioration lower that standard.

[Atkin L.J. delivered a separate concurring judgment.]

(c) The meaning of "repair"

LURCOTT v. WAKELY AND WHEELER

Court of Appeal [1911] 1 K.B. 905

[The lease of a dwelling-house contained a covenant that the lessee would "well and substantially repair, paint, glaze, cleanse and keep in thorough repair and good condition all the said premises thereby demised, with the appurtenances thereto belonging, and the said premises being repaired and kept would at the end or sooner determination of the term peaceably yield up to the lessors". The house was more than 200 years old. One outer wall had deteriorated through old age to such an extent that it had become dangerous. The local authority, shortly before the termination of the lease, served notice on the owner and the occupier to demolish the wall. The plaintiff landlord, in turn, required the defendant tenants to comply with the notice and then to deliver up the premises at the termination of the lease in a proper state of repair. At the expiration of the lease, however, the tenants gave up possession without having complied with the notice. The landlord thereafter demolished and rebuilt the wall, and claimed the cost from the tenants. The wall could not have been repaired without being completely rebuilt. The Divisional Court held in favour of the landlord, and the tenants appealed to the Court of Appeal.]

BUCKLEY L.J. "Repair" and "renew" are not words expressive of a clear contrast. Repair always involves renewal; renewal of a part; of a subordinate part. A skylight leaks; repair is effected by hacking out the putties, putting in new ones, and renewing the paint. A roof falls out of repair; the necessary work is to replace the decayed timbers by sound wood; to substitute sound tiles or slates for those which are cracked, broken, or missing; to make good the flashings, and the like. Part of a garden wall tumbles down; repair is effected by building it up again with new mortar, and, so far as necessary, new bricks or stone. Repair is restoration by renewal or replacement of subsidiary parts of a whole. Renewal, as distinguished from repair, is reconstruction of the entirety, meaning by the entirety not necessarily the whole but substantially the whole subject matter under discussion. I agree that if repair of the whole subject matter has become impossible a covenant to repair does not carry an obligation to renew or replace. That has been affirmed by *Lister v. Lane* [1893] 2 Q.B. 212 and *Wright v. Lawson* (1903) 19 T.L.R. 203, 510. But if that which I have said is accurate, it follows that the question of repair is in every case one of degree, and the test is whether the act to be done is one which in substance is the renewal or replacement of defective parts, or the renewal or replacement of substantially the whole. It is with such limitations as these that the language in the cases which have been cited to us must be read. For instance, in *Gutteridge v. Munyard* (1834) 1 Mod. & R. 334; 174 E.R. 114 Tindal C.J. says: "What the natural operation of time flowing on effects, and all that the elements bring about in diminishing the value, constitute a loss, which, so far as it results from time and nature, falls upon the landlord." Every decay which is the subject of repair is effected by the operation of the lapse of time and the elements diminishing the value. Decay always results from time and nature. Of course the Chief Justice did not mean his words to be understood as meaning that all decay is to be borne by the landlord. They are words which follow upon a sentence in which he was speaking of a building of a particular character, namely, a very old building, and was negativing the argument that the old building was, under the operation of a covenant to repair, to be converted into a new one. Lord Esher in *Lister v. Lane* [1893] 2 Q.B. 212 at 216 says: "If a tenant takes a house which is of such a kind that by its own inherent nature it will in the course of time fall into a particular condition, the effects of that result are not within the tenant's covenant to repair." Now every house is of such a kind that by its own inherent nature it will in the course of time fall into a particular condition. Lord Esher, of course, did not mean that decay is in every case not within the tenant's covenant to repair. The context shews that he did not mean that. He goes on to say this: "However large the words of the covenant may be, a covenant to repair a house is not a covenant to give a different thing from that which the tenant took when he entered into the covenant. He has to repair that thing which he took; he is not obliged to make a new and different thing." If "repair" be understood in the sense which I suggest, the authorities are not, I think, difficult. In *Gutteridge v. Munyard* (1834) 1 Mod. & R. 334 the building was a very old building, and the finding of the jury under the directions of Tindal C.J. only involved that the tenants had substantially kept the building such as it was in repair, although they had not improved it. *Lister v. Lane* [1893] 2 Q.B. 212 and *Wright v. Lawson* (1903) 19 T.L.R. 203, 510 were cases in which the buildings could not by any repair be brought into their original condition. In *Lister v. Lane* [1893] 2 Q.B. 212 the only thing that could be done was, not to replace the old timber platform, but to support the house entirely anew by walls carried down another 17 ft to the subjacent gravel. That would be not repairing such a house as was there in question, namely, a house whose foundations were timbers lying on oozy soil, but providing a new house in the sense that its foundations would be on the gravel. In *Wright v. Lawson* (1903) 19 T.L.R. 203, 510 the bay window could not be replaced, supported as it must have been before by cantilevers, but could be reproduced only by that which would be a new structure, namely, a bay window supported by vertical supports from the ground. *Proudfoot v. Hart* (1890) 25 Q.B.D. 42 contains, I think, no general principle. It was a question as to what was performance of a covenant to keep in good tenantable repair. All that Lord Esher says (at 54) is that if the floor became rotten the tenant must put in a new floor unless he can make the floor good by ordinary repair. The floor was a subsidiary part of the whole. The house could not be occupied if the floor were rotten, and the tenant, to comply with his covenant as to tenantable repair, must either make it good by repair or replace it, for otherwise the house would not be tenantable. *Torrens v. Walker* [1906] 2 Ch. 166 was a case in which the covenant was to keep the outside of the premises in repair. The house was triangular in form at the junction of two streets. The pulling down amounted to a demolition of substantially the whole subject matter of the covenant. In these circumstances the finding of the learned judge [1906] 2 Ch. at 171 was justified, that repairing the building, or, as I prefer to say, repairing the subject matter of the covenant, namely, the outside of the premises, was impossible, and that nothing could be done but rebuild. The learned judge found in that case that the act to be done was not only of renewal or replacement of a subsidiary part, but substantially a rebuilding of the whole subject matter of the covenant. All the cases, to my mind, come only to this, that the question is one of degree, and what we have to look to in the present case is to see whether the official referee in his findings of fact has treated the front wall of this house as being a subsidiary part of a larger structure, or has regarded the necessary operations as amounting to substantially re-erection of the house. His findings of fact are these. First, he finds that the decay of the front wall is not due to any vibration superinduced by the tenants; he thinks it is caused by old age. That of course is in the appellants' favour. He then finds that the wall could not have been repaired without rebuilding. That again is in the appellants' favour. But then, after discussing the authorities, *Proudfoot v. Hart, Lister v. Lane* [1893] 2 Q.B. 212, *Wright v. Lawson* (1903) 19 T.L.R. 203, 510, and *Torrens v. Walker* [1906] 2 Ch. 166, he goes on to say: "In this case it is clear that the whole house does not require rebuilding. The wall can be rebuilt, and has been rebuilt, and the old tie plates have been retained, and the case appears to me to be exactly like that of the new floor mentioned by Lord Esher." That is a material finding of fact on the part of the referee. He finds that this is not the erection of a new house; it is only repair in the sense that it is restoring to stability and safety a subordinate part of the whole. He likens it to the case where the house requires a new floor; here it requires a new wall. When it has got its new wall it will not be a new house; it will be the old house put into repair in the sense that there has been renewed or replaced a worn out subordinate part of the whole. On that finding of fact it appears to me that the appeal fails.

[The concurring judgments of Cozens-Hardy M.R. and Fletcher Moulton L.J. have been omitted.]

Appeal dismissed.

NOTES AND QUESTIONS

1. In *Lister v. Lane and Nesham* [1893] 2 Q.B. 212, referred to in the principal case, Lord Esher M.R. said (at 216-217):

   However large the words of the covenant [to repair] may be, a covenant to repair a house is not a covenant to give a different thing from that which the tenant took when he entered into the covenant. He has to repair that thing which he took; he is not obliged to make a new and different thing.

   Kay L.J. said that the tenant is not responsible for "damage which accrued from such a radical defect in the original condition".

2. In *Graham v. Markets Hotel Pty Ltd* (1942) 43 S.R. (N.S.W.) 98 at 103, Jordan C.J. said of the scope of the covenant to repair:

   The scope of an agreement to repair depends upon its language. If the agreement is to repair so as to maintain a special standard, all repairs must be effected which are necessary to maintain the prescribed standard. Under an ordinary agreement to repair, there is no obligation to replace the structure wholly or substantially if, without the fault of the party agreeing, replacement of this kind becomes necessary. But, as a general rule, the fact that the structure has fallen into such a state of disrepair that the necessary repairs can be effected only by the replacement of part—even a considerable part—of the structure, does not absolve a party from his liability to repair; because repair normally involves replacement from time to time of different parts of the structure: *Lurcott v. Wakely and Wheeler* [1911] 1 K.B. 905 at 918-919. The extent of the obligation may, however, be conditioned by the state of the structure at the date when the agreement was made. If it was then a first-class structure, it must be repaired so as to maintain it in first-class condition. If it was then old and out-moded, it is necessary only to effect such repairs as are required to maintain it in repair at the standard at which it was received: *Lurcott v. Wakely and Wheeler* [1911] 1 K.B. 905 at 916, 917; *Anstruther-Gough-Calthorpe v. McOscar* [1924] 1 K.B. 716 at 734. Further, if, when it was taken over, it was subject to some inherent defect of a substantial kind, an agreement merely to repair does not impose an obligation to remove the defect, but only to maintain the structure subject to the defect so far as this can be effected by repair. By inherent defect is meant some original or supervening defect of an abnormal kind, such as would not be found in a properly built structure, would not be produced in such a structure by the degenerative processes of user or decay, and cannot be remedied except by the replacement or remodelling of the structure or some substantial part of it: *Lister v. Lane and Nesham* [1893] 2 Q.B. 212 at 216-217; *Wright v. Lawson* (1903) 19 T.L.R. 203, 510; *Pembery v. Lamdin* [1940] 2 All E.R. 434. The question whether a particular defect is inherent or matter of repair is one of fact and degree: cf. *Lyon v. Greenhow* (1892) 8 T.L.R. 457; *Howe v. Botwood* [1913] 2 K.B. 387. If it is the latter it is nothing to the point that changed conditions have made the work unexpectedly and unpleasantly expensive: *Howe v. Botwood* [1913] 2 K.B. 387.

The decision of the Full Court was reversed on appeal: (1943) 67 C.L.R. 567. The High Court disagreed with Jordan C.J.'s finding of fact that there was an "inherent defect" in the premises, but did not take a different view of the applicable law. In the course of his judgment, Latham C.J. said (at 579):

> The learned trial judge and the Full Court examined the leading authorities upon the construction of covenants to repair. It is now well established that the repair of a structure may involve renewal or rebuilding of part of it, and that all repairs involve renewal to some extent: *Lurcott v. Wakely and Wheeler* [1911] 1 K.B. 914 at 923-926. There is a difference between repairing a house and building a new house in place of an old house. It is a question of degree whether rebuilding part of a house does or does not fall within the category of repairing a house. A covenant to repair does not involve the covenantee [scilicet: covenantor] in an obligation to make improvements, but if he cannot perform his covenant to repair without making improvements, then the expense of making the improvements falls upon him. This is the case whether the necessity arises from physical causes, or from legal causes. If, owing to the requirements of the law, repairs cannot be made without also making improvements, then he must perform his covenant to repair in the manner which the law requires: *Howe v. Botwood* [1913] 2 K.B. 387 at 392, where Lord Coleridge stated that he could draw no distinction between what was physically necessary and what was legally necessary to enable the party bound to perform his covenant.

3. In *Ravenseft Properties Ltd v. Davstone (Holdings) Ltd* [1979] 2 W.L.R. 897, the demised premises consisted of a 16 storey block of maisonettes. To the concrete frame of the building had been affixed decorative stone cladding. However, parts of the stone cladding were found to be in danger of falling off, because no expansion joints had been included when the building was being constructed (it had not been realised that the different co-efficients of expansion of stone and concrete made such joints necessary) and the stonework had not been tied in properly to the building.

The lease contained a covenant by the tenants to repair. The landlords required the tenants to carry out the necessary work but the tenants denied that they were liable under the covenant to repair. The landlords carried out the necessary work of taking down the cladding stones, retying the stones and inserting expansion joints, and claimed to recover the cost from the tenants.

The tenants' argument was that the lack of expansion joints was an "inherent defect", to which a covenant to repair could not extend. Forbes J., however, after a survey of some of the leading cases on repairing covenants, concluded that there was no doctrine of inherent defect by which a tenant has a complete defence to an action for breach of a covenant to repair. In his Lordship's opinion, whether a repairing covenant covers the work demanded is always a question of degree: does it require the tenant to give the landlord something different from that which was demised: "The true test is, as the cases show, that it is always a question of degree whether that which the tenant is being asked to do can properly be described as repair, or whether on the contrary it would involve giving back to the landlord a wholly different thing from that which he demised": [1979] 2 W.L.R. 897 at 905.

Is this approach inconsistent with *Graham v. Markets Hotel Pty Ltd* (1942) 43 S.R. (N.S.W.) 98?

4. Accepting that the doctrine of inherent defect is part of the law of New South Wales, it seems that a covenant to "repair" does not require the tenant to rectify inherent defects which have existed from the time of construction of the building in the absence of any actual damage to or deterioration in the building as a result of the inherent defect, since the building is in no worse condition than it was when first constructed and "repair" connotes putting back into good condition something which was formerly in a better condition than it now is: see *Quick v. Taff Ely Borough Council* [1986] Q.B. 809; *Post Office v. Aquarius Properties Ltd* [1987] 1 All E.R. 1055.

5. Is the tenant liable in the following situation? A lease contains a covenant by the tenant to "repair uphold support maintain" the premises "with all necessary reparations and amendments whatsoever". The walls of the premises (a dwelling-house) are "bulged, fractured and overhanging", and the premises have been condemned as a dangerous structure. The cause of the trouble is defective foundations, and the only way the problem can be overcome is by underpinning, that is, by shoring up the premises, removing the existing foundations, and substituting new and far more substantial foundations: see *Sotheby v. Grundy* [1947] 2 All E.R. 761. For similar examples, see *Collins v. Flynn* [1963] 2 All E.R. 1068 and *Brew Bros Ltd v. Snax (Ross) Ltd* [1970] 1 Q.B. 612.

(d) "Fair wear and tear"

HASKELL v. MARLOW

Divisional Court [1928] 2 K.B. 45

[A life tenant was bound, by the terms of the will creating his interest, to keep premises "in good repair and condition (reasonable wear and tear excepted)". The life tenant occupied the premises for over 40 years, and during that period did nothing actively to injure the premises, but also did little to counteract the natural process of decay, so that by the time the life tenant died, the premises were in very bad disrepair. The plaintiffs, the trustees of the will, claimed damages from the defendants, the executors of the life tenant, for breach of the duty to repair.]

TALBOT J. The plaintiffs said that, while the tenant for life was not liable for defects directly caused by wear and tear, the exception did not supersede the first part of the condition, and she was bound to do such repairs as were necessary to prevent damage, even if originally caused by wear and tear, from producing further damage; or (putting it somewhat differently) that damage caused by reasonable wear and tear meant damage so caused by a tenant who acted reasonably. The defendants said that as to any damage caused by reasonable wear and tear the tenant for life was entitled to do nothing, simply to be inactive, whatever may be the consequences to the property. It is scarcely too much to say that as to this class of damage the result is to leave the tenant for life liable for voluntary waste only, to which she would be liable without any express condition. On the other hand, it is true that the plaintiffs' surveyors admitted that for all practical purposes they had disregarded the exception altogether. It is obviously the duty of the court to give effect if possible to the whole of the condition and exception and, bearing this in mind, I will state what is, in my opinion, its true construction, which must, I think, be the same as of like words in a covenant in a lease.

The meaning is that the tenant (for life or years) is bound to keep the house in good repair and condition, but is not liable for what is due to reasonable wear and tear. That is to say, his obligation to keep in good repair is subject to that exception. If any want of repair is alleged and proved in fact, it lies on the tenant to show that it comes within the exception. Reasonable wear and tear means the reasonable use of the house by the tenant and the ordinary operation of natural forces. The exception of want of repair due to wear and tear must be construed as limited to what is directly due to wear and tear, reasonable conduct on the part of the tenant being assumed. It does not mean that if there is a defect originally proceeding from reasonable wear and tear the tenant is released from his obligation to keep in good repair and condition everything which it may be possible to trace ultimately to that defect. He is bound to do such repairs as may be required to prevent the consequences flowing originally from wear and tear from producing others which wear and tear would not directly produce.

For example, if a tile falls off the roof, the tenant is not liable for the immediate consequences; but, if he does nothing and in the result more and more water gets in, the roof and walls decay and ultimately the top floor, or the whole house, becomes uninhabitable, he cannot say that it is due to reasonable wear and tear, and that therefore he is not liable under his obligation to keep the house in good repair and condition. In such a case the want of repair is not in truth caused by wear and tear. Far the greater part of it is caused by the failure of the tenant to prevent what was originally caused by wear and tear from producing results altogether beyond what was so caused. On the other hand, take the gradual wearing away of a stone floor or staircase by ordinary use. This may in time produce a considerable defect in condition, but the whole of the defect is caused by reasonable wear and tear, and the tenant is not liable in respect of it.

NOTE

This case had a chequered history. It was overruled by the Court of Appeal in *Taylor v. Webb* [1937] 2 K.B. 283, where it was held that a "fair wear and tear" exception relieves a tenant from responsibility not only for disrepair arising initially, but also for damage which flows from the initial disrepair. In 1958, however, in *Regis Property Co. Ltd v. Dudley* [1959] A.C. 370, the House of Lords disapproved this aspect of *Taylor v. Webb* and reinstated *Haskell v. Marlow* as a correct statement of the law. *Regis Property Co. Ltd v. Dudley* is not extracted, as the meaning of the "fair wear and tear" exception was only an incidental aspect of that case. In the course of his judgment in *Dudley's* case, Lord Denning said (at 410):

> The next question is what is the effect of the exception of "fair wear and tear" in a repairing covenant. I find myself in full agreement with what Talbot J. said on this subject in *Haskell v. Marlow* [1928] 2 K.B. 45. I think the Court of Appeal in *Taylor v. Webb* [1937] 2 K.B. 283 were wrong in overruling *Haskell v. Marlow* [1928] 2 K.B. 45. I have never understood that in an ordinary house a "fair wear and tear" exception reduced the burden of repairs to practically nothing at all. It exempts a tenant from liability for repairs that are decorative and for remedying parts that wear out or come adrift in the course of reasonable use, but it does not exempt him from anything else. If further damage is likely to flow from the wear and tear, he must do such repairs as are necessary to stop that further damage. If a slate falls off through wear and tear and in consequence the roof is likely to let through the water, the tenant is not responsible for the slate coming off but he ought to put in another one to prevent further damage.

(e) Damages for breach of covenant to repair

At common law, the measure of damages for breach of a tenant's covenant to repair differed according to whether the action was brought before or after the termination of the lease. Where the action was brought during the currency of the lease, the measure of damages was the diminution in the value of the reversion by reason of the failure of the tenant to perform the covenant: *Conquest v. Ebbets* [1896] A.C. 490; but where the action was brought after the termination of the lease, the measure of damages was the sum required to put the premises into the state of repair in which the tenant ought to have kept them: *Joyner v. Weeks* [1891] 2 Q.B. 31. The latter situation could give the landlord a windfall in circumstances where the failure to repair had not affected the value of the reversion. This result has been overcome by legislation. The *Conveyancing Act* 1919 (N.S.W.), s. 133A(1) provides:

133A. (1) Damages for a breach of a covenant or agreement to keep or put premises in repair during the currency of a lease, or to leave or put premises in repair at the termination of a lease, whether such covenant or agreement is expressed or implied, and whether general or specific, shall in no case exceed the amount (if any) by which the value of the reversion (whether immediate or not) in the premises is diminished owing to the breach of such covenant or agreement as aforesaid; and in particular no damage shall be recovered for a breach of any such covenant or agreement to leave or put premises in repair at the termination of a lease, if it is shown that the premises, in whatever state of repair they might be, would at or shortly after the termination of the lease have been or be pulled down, or such structural alterations made therein as would render valueless the repairs covered by the covenant or agreement.

The operation of this provision is discussed in *Graham v. Markets Hotel Pty Ltd* (1943) 67 C.L.R. 567. The section applies only to breach of covenant by the *tenant* to repair; as to the measure of damages where the *landlord* breaches a covenant to repair, see *Calabar Properties Ltd v. Stitcher* [1983] 3 All E.R. 759.

C. USUAL COVENANTS

The term "usual covenants" has a technical meaning in the law of landlord and tenant. Many covenants which are to be found quite commonly in leases are not "usual" covenants within the legal meaning of that term. Questions of identifying "usual" covenants arise where the parties to an executory agreement to enter into a lease (or to enter into a sub-lease, or to assign a lease) agree that the "usual covenants" shall apply, or where their agreement is silent as to what covenants shall apply.

HAMPSHIRE v. WICKENS

Chancery Division (1878) 7 Ch. D. 555

[The plaintiff sought specific performance by the defendant of an agreement to grant a lease "on all the usual covenants and provisoes (sic)". The plaintiff insisted on inserting in the formal grant of the lease a covenant against assignment. The defendant claimed that this was not a "usual" covenant, and therefore not within the terms of the agreement.]

JESSEL M.R. Usual covenants may vary in different generations. The law declares what are usual covenants according to the then knowledge of mankind. Lord Eldon, in *Church v. Brown*, puts it thus (1808) 15 Ves. 258; 33 E.R. 752: "Before the case of *Henderson v. Hay* (1792) 3 Bro. C.C. 632; 29 E.R. 738, therefore, upon an agreement to grant a lease with nothing more than proper covenants, I should have said they were to be such covenants as were just as well known in such leases as the usual covenants under an agreement to convey an estate." Now what is well known at one time may not be well known at another time, so that you cannot say that usual covenants never change. I have therefore looked at the last edition of Davidson's *Precedents in Conveyancing*, to see whether the usage is said to have changed. He says ((3rd ed.), Vol V, pp. 48, 49): "The result of the authorities appears to be that in a case where the agreement is silent as to the particular covenants to be inserted in the lease, and provides merely for the lease containing 'usual covenants', or, which is the same thing, in an open agreement without any reference to the covenants, and there are no special circumstances justifying the introduction of other covenants, the following are the only ones which either party can insist upon, namely:

Covenants by the lessee
1. To pay rent;
2. To pay taxes, except such [as] are expressly payable by the landlord;
3. To keep and deliver up the premises in repair; and
4. To allow the lessor to enter and view the state of repair.

And the usual qualified covenant by the lessor for quiet enjoyment by the lessee.''

When he refers to "special circumstances" he means peculiar to a particular trade, as for example, in leases of public houses, where the brewers have their own forms of leases, the "usual covenants" would mean the covenants always inserted in the leases of certain brewers.

There is no mention of any other "usual covenants", and as nothing in this case has been lost for want of industry on the part of the counsel who have argued it, I am justified in saying that there is nothing in any textbook or book of precedents to shew that a covenant not to assign is a usual covenant.

I am therefore of opinion that it is not a usual covenant, and I dismiss the action with costs.

Suit dismissed.

NOTES AND QUESTIONS

1. In addition to the five "usual" covenants referred to in the principal case, there is also the covenant allowing the lessor to re-enter for breach of the covenant to pay rent (but not for breach of any other covenant). This additional covenant was discussed by his Lordship in an earlier part of the judgment: see also *Hodgkinson v. Crowe* (1875) 10 Ch. App. 622; *Re Anderton and Milner's Contract* (1890) 45 Ch. D. 476; *Re Lander and Bagley's Contract* [1892] 3 Ch. 41.

2. That the usual covenants may vary from time to time, and may depend upon the type of premises involved, may be seen also from *Flexman v. Corbett* [1930] 1 Ch. 672 at 677, and *Charalambous v. Ktori* [1972] 1 W.L.R. 951 at 953. In the former case, Maugham J. said:

   I think it right to express my opinion, after having heard and considered all the numerous authorities which have been cited to me, that the question whether particular covenants are usual covenants is a question of fact, and that the decision of the court on that point must depend upon the admissible evidence given before the court in relation to that question. I think that it is proper to take the evidence of conveyancers and others familiar with the practice in reference to leases and that it is also permissible to examine books of precedents. It is permissible to obtain evidence with regard to the practice in the particular district in which the premises in question are situated. I would add that in my view it is a complete mistake to suppose that the usual covenants in regard to a lease, for instance, of a country house are necessarily usual covenants in regard to the lease of a London residence, and I would add that it seems to me that it may very well be that what is usual in Mayfair or Bayswater is not usual at all in some other part of London such, for instance, as Whitechapel. Further, in my opinion, "usual" in this sense means no more than "occurring in ordinary use", and I think that it is an error to suppose that the court is entitled to hold that a particular covenant is not usual because it may be established that there are some few cases in which that covenant is not used. If it is established that (to put a strong case) in nine cases out of ten the covenant would be found in a lease of premises of that nature for that purpose and in that district, I think that the court is bound to hold that the covenant is usual.

3. Are the "usual" covenants in Australia the same as those in England? In *Bennett v. Excelsior Land, etc., Co. Ltd* (1893) 14 L.R. (N.S.W.) (Eq.) 179 at 183 Owen C.J. in Eq. said:

   I see no reason why what are the usual covenants [in England] should not also be the usual covenants here. There is not such a difference between the circumstances of such a lease in this colony and in England as to induce me to hold that "the usual covenants" in a lease in this colony are not the same as those which the English courts have held to be intended by that term.

It may be, however, that this no longer holds true. It can be argued that the "usual" covenants now include those implied by statute (that is, by *Conveyancing Act* 1919 (N.S.W.), ss 84 and 85, and its equivalents in other States): see the argument in Hinde, McMorland and Sim, op. cit., p. 488; " 'Usual' Covenants in Leases" (1931) 5 A.L.J. 15; Helmore, *The Law of Real Property in New South Wales* (2nd ed.), p. 121. If this argument is correct, then several of the general law usual covenants have been modified substantially. For example, a lessor would be entitled to re-enter for breach of any covenant, and not simply for non-payment of rent (s. 85(1)(d)), the payment of rent would be subject to abatement in the event of damage or destruction, the liability to repair would be qualified by reference to the state of the premises at the commencement of the term and subject to an exception for fair wear and tear, and the lessor's right to enter and view the state of repair would be modified.

4. In *Chester v. Buckinham Travel Ltd* [1981] 1 W.L.R. 96, the question arose as to the "usual" covenants to be included in a lease of certain garage workshops in London for a term of 14 years commencing in 1971. The premises were situated in a predominantly residential area and formed part of a complex which included the landlord's own property, a garage, a yard and four residential flats. Foster J. held that the following covenants would be included amongst those "usual" when regard was had to "the nature of the property, their situation, the purpose for which they are being let, the length of the term, the evidence of conveyancers and the books of precedents": (1) a covenant by the tenant not to alter the building without the landlord's consent, such consent not to be unreasonably withheld; (2) a covenant by the tenant not to obstruct windows or light coming to the demised premises, or to permit encroachments or the acquisition of easements over the demised premises; (3) a covenant by the tenant that (except with the landlord's consent, such consent not to be unreasonably withheld) the premises should be used only as a garage/workshop; (4) a covenant by the tenant not to permit on the premises any act which might grow to be a nuisance, annoyance or disturbance to the landlord or any tenant of the landlord; and (5) a covenant empowering the landlord to re-enter and determine the lease in the event of a breach by the tenant of any of the covenants in the lease. The following covenants were held not to be "usual": (1) a covenant by the tenant not to hold any sale or auction on the premises; (2) a qualified covenant against assigning, sub-letting or parting with possession without the landlord's consent (as to such "qualified" covenants, see below p. 605); (3) a covenant by the tenant to procure from any sub-lessee a covenant to perform the tenant's covenants; and (4) a covenant by the tenant to pay the landlord's costs of abiding by the statutory procedures necessary to forfeit the lease upon breach by the tenant, notwithstanding that the forfeiture might subsequently be avoided otherwise than by relief granted by the court (as to such statutory procedures and relief against forfeiture, see pp. 633 and 644 respectively).

D. COVENANTS IMPLIED BY CONSTRUCTION

Covenants may be implied into leases by construction. The rules to be applied are the same as those which govern the implication of terms into contracts generally, namely, that the court has no right to imply into a written contract any term "unless, on considering the terms of the contract in a responsible and business manner, an implication necessarily arises that the parties must have intended that the suggested stipulation should exist. It is not enough to say that it would be a reasonable thing to make such an implication. It must be a necessary implication in the sense that I have mentioned": *Hamlyn & Co. v. Wood & Co.* [1891] 2 Q.B. 488 at 491; see also *Cox v. Hoban* (1911) 12 C.L.R. 256 at 267. The court is entitled in making the implication to look not only at the express terms of the lease but also at the surrounding facts and the knowledge of the parties of those facts: *Krell v. Henry* [1903] 2 K.B. 740 at 752. The relevant principles are discussed in *Liverpool City Council v. Irwin* [1977] A.C. 239.

For instances of covenants implied by construction, see Lewis and Cassidy, op. cit., pp. 199-201; *Burfort Financial Investments v. Chotard* (1976) 239 Estates Gazette 891; *Karaggianis v. Malltown Pty Ltd* (1979) 21 S.A.S.R. 381.

E. SHORT FORM COVENANTS

Section 86 of the *Conveyancing Act* 1919 (N.S.W.), together with Pt II of Schedule IV of the Act, supplies a short form of certain covenants which may be used as a word saving device. Where the required short form is used, there is implied into the lease a long form of the particular covenant, setting out in detail the rights and obligations of the parties. The long form may be amended by making an appropriate amendment to the short form. These provisions are discussed in *Barina Properties Pty Ltd v. Bernard Hastie (Aust.) Pty Ltd* [1979] 1 N.S.W.L.R. 480 at 487-489, 490-491.

F. STATUTORY PROVISIONS AFFECTING COVENANTS

In the chapter on "Covenants" above pp. 305-306, reference was made to the way in which covenants affecting freehold land may be struck down either by the common law doctrine of restraint of trade or by certain provisions of the *Trade Practices Act* 1974 (Cth). The same comments apply to covenants in leases. A covenant in a lease may be unenforceable because it infringes the common law doctrine of restraint of trade (see *Esso Petroleum Co. Ltd v. Harper's Garage (Stourport) Ltd* [1968] A.C. 269; *Amoco Australia Pty Ltd v. Rocca Bros Motor Engineers Co. Pty Ltd* (1973) 47 A.L.J.R. 681), or because it infringes such provisions of the *Trade Practices Act* 1974 (Cth) as s. 45B (covenants substantially lessening competition) or s. 47 (exclusive dealing substantially lessening competition, noting especially s. 47(9) as discussed in *Trade Practices Commission (Cth) and A.-G. for the Commonwealth v. Tooth & Co. Ltd and Tooheys Ltd* (1979) 53 A.L.J.R. 696). See generally Donald and Heydon, op. cit., Vol 1, pp. 193-194.

Other legislation which may affect the operation of covenants in leases includes the *Restraints of Trade Act* 1976 (N.S.W.), *Industrial Arbitration Act* 1940 (N.S.W.) (especially s. 88F), and the *Contracts Review Act* 1980 (N.S.W.) (discussed in the chapter on mortgages, above p. 435 et seq).

V. ASSIGNMENTS AND SUB-LEASES

A. THE RIGHT TO ASSIGN OR SUB-LEASE

The right to assign or sub-lease a leasehold estate is a right incident to every leasehold estate: *Keeves v. Dean* [1924] 1 K.B. 685 at 695; *Allcock v. Moorhouse* (1882) 9 Q.B.D. 366. In *Doe d. Mitchinson v. Carter* (1798) 8 T.R. 57 at 60; 101 E.R. 1264 at 1266 Lord Kenyon C.J. said:

> Generally speaking, the grant of an estate carries with it all legal incidents, and therefore the grantee has a right to sell and convey it, unless he be controlled by the terms of his grant.

This right also attaches to periodic tenancies, including tenancies from week to week: *Commonwealth Life (Amalgamated) Assurance Ltd v. Anderson* (1945) 46 S.R. (N.S.W.) 47 at 51. If he or she so desires, a tenant may assign or sub-lease part only of the demised premises: *G. J. Coles & Co. Pty Ltd v. Commissioner of Taxation* (1975) 49 A.L.J.R. 188 at 193.

There are two exceptions to this common law right to assign or sub-lease. Neither a tenancy at sufferance nor a tenancy at will arising at common law may be assigned or sub-leased. Any attempt to do so will terminate the interest of the lessee and confer no interest on the purported assignee or sub-lessee: see *Anderson v. Toohey's Ltd* (1937) 37 S.R. (N.S.W.) 70 at 74; *Sangster v. Burns* [1960] N.Z.L.R. 910 at 915, 916; *Picone v. Grocery & General Merchants Ltd* [1964] N.S.W.R. 1018; cf. *Landlord and Tenant (Amendment) Act* 1948 (N.S.W.), s. 62B. A tenancy "at will" under s. 127 of the *Conveyancing Act* 1919 (N.S.W.), however, can support an assignment or sub-lease: it is not a tenancy at will as at common law, but is a periodic tenancy from month to month terminable by one month's notice in writing expiring at any time: see *Metropolitan Trade Finance Co. Pty Ltd v. Coumbis* (1973) 131 C.L.R. 396 at 398, and in the court below [1972] 1 N.S.W.L.R. 1 at 4, 10; *Kater v. Kater* (1961) 104 C.L.R. 497 at 506.

Where the lease is over land under old system title, an assignment or sub-lease must be by deed if it is to be effective at law, although to be effective in equity mere writing will suffice: see *Conveyancing Act* 1919 (N.S.W.), ss 23B and 23C, extracted above p. 566.

Where the lease is over land under Torrens title, and has been registered, there is an approved form of transfer of lease which itself should be registered. Where a lease over Torrens title land has not been registered, it seems that to be effective at law any assignment or sub-lease must be by deed: this follows from s. 23B(3) of the *Conveyancing Act* 1919 (N.S.W.), read with the definition in s. 7 of that Act of the phrase "land under the provisions of the *Real Property Act* 1900": see *Chronopoulos v. Caltex Oil (Aust.) Pty Ltd* (1983) 45 A.L.R. 481.

B. COVENANTS AGAINST ASSIGNING OR SUB-LEASING

Because of the common law right to assign or sub-lease, it has become common for leases to contain express covenants against assigning or sub-leasing. Such covenants are categorised as either "absolute" or "qualified". An absolute covenant is one which completely forbids assignment or sub-leasing; a qualified covenant is one which permits it, but subject to the lessor's consent.

1. Absolute covenants

Where the covenant is absolute, the lessor cannot be compelled to consent, no matter how unreasonable his refusal may seem. The landlord may, of course, waive the prohibition against assignment or require conditions for the granting of permission to assign. Reference should be made to *Conveyancing Act* 1919 (N.S.W.), ss 120 and 123, which allow a lessor to consent to an assignment, in the face of an absolute prohibition against assignment, without prejudicing his right to object to future assignments. These sections were designed to overcome the inconvenient rule in *Dumpor's Case* (1603) 4 Co. Rep. 119b; 76 E.R. 1110, which stated that once the lessor had given an express licence to do an act contrary to the terms of a covenant, his right of re-entry in respect of future breaches of that covenant was destroyed.

Covenants against assigning or sub-leasing are construed strictly against the lessor. Thus, a covenant against assigning simpliciter will not prohibit a sub-lease of the premises (*Church v. Brown* (1808) 15 Ves. Jun. 258 at 265; 33 E.R. 752 at 755; *Sweet and Maxwell Ltd v. Universal News Service Ltd* [1964] 2 Q.B. 699; *Russell v. Beecham* [1924] 1 K.B. 525; cf. *Serjeant v. Nash, Field & Co.* [1903] 2 K.B. 304), although it is not clear whether a covenant against sub-leasing prohibits an assignment: see *Marks v. Warren* [1979] 1 All E.R. 29 at 31. A covenant against both assigning and sub-leasing does not prevent the lessee from parting with possession under a revocable licence: *Stoyles v. Job* (1954) 73 W.N. (N.S.W.) 41. However, a covenant "not to underlet or part with possession" will be breached by an assignment, at least where the assignment involves a parting with possession: *Marks v. Warren* [1979] 1 All E.R. 29.

A covenant against assigning prohibits only voluntary acts of the lessee: involuntary assignments caused by bankruptcy (*Re Farrow's Bank Ltd* [1921] 2 Ch. 165 at 174, 175) or by devolution on death (*Bryen v. Reus* (1960) 61 S.R. (N.S.W.) 396 at 399) are not caught. See also *Conveyancing Act* 1919 (N.S.W.), s. 133.

NOTES AND QUESTIONS

1. A lessee covenanted that he would not "assign or underlet" the premises without the lessor's prior written consent. Without seeking consent, the lessee later executed a deed by which, inter alia, he declared himself trustee of the demised premises for K; K had earlier been appointed trustee for the benefit of the lessee's creditors. K took possession of the premises. No legal assignment of the premises was executed. Was there a breach of the covenant? See *Gentle v. Faulkner* [1900] 2 K.B. 267.

2. A lease of a dwelling house was subject to a condition, "no sub-letting allowed without the written consent of the landlord". Without the lessor's consent, the lessee sub-let part only of the premises, namely the basement and a room on the upper floor. Was there a breach of the condition? See *Esdaile v. Lewis* [1956] 1 W.L.R. 709, following *Cook v. Shoesmith* [1951] 1 K.B. 752; cf. *Rhodes v. Dalby* [1971] 1 W.L.R. 1325 at 1329.

2. Qualified covenants

Where the covenant against assigning or sub-letting is qualified, the lessor cannot unreasonably withhold his consent, notwithstanding any express stipulation to the contrary in the lease: see *Conveyancing Act* 1919 (N.S.W.), s. 133B(1). But this provision may be side-stepped by careful drafting. For example, in *Creer v. P. & O. Lines (Aust.) Pty Ltd* (1971) 125 C.L.R. 84 the lease provided that "the lessee shall not assign sublet . . . or part with possession of the premises . . . without the consent in writing of the lessor . . . PROVIDED that should the lessee desire to sublet lease or assign . . . the lessee shall before doing so offer in writing to the lessor to surrender this lease . . . without any consideration". The lessee sought to obtain the lessor's consent to a proposed assignment of the lease, but the lessor withheld its consent because the lessee had not offered to surrender the lease to the lessor (the lessor having intimated that it would accept any surrender offered). There was held to be no breach of s. 133B(1) of the *Conveyancing Act* 1919 (N.S.W.).

A qualified covenant against alienation in the usual form will be broken if the lessee alienates the lease without first seeking the lessor's consent; it is irrelevant that failure to seek consent is due to mere forgetfulness or oversight on the part of the lessee (or the lessee's solicitor), or that the lessor could not have reasonably refused consent had it been sought: *Barrow v. Isaacs & Son* [1891] 1 Q.B. 417; *Eastern Telegraph Co. Ltd v. Dent* [1899] 1 Q.B. 835. The lessor must be allowed a reasonable time to give his consent: *Wilson v. Fynn* [1948] 2 All E.R. 40.

A lessor is not obliged to give reasons for his refusal of consent, but failure to do so leads more readily to the inference that his refusal was unreasonable: *Frederick Berry Ltd v. Royal Bank of Scotland* [1949] 1 K.B. 619 at 623.

Where the lessor refuses to give consent, the lessee has two possible courses of action: first, he or she may go ahead and assign without consent, having been careful first to seek it (*Eastern Telegraph Co Ltd v. Dent* [1899] 1 Q.B. 835; *McMahon v. Docker* (1945) 62 W.N. (N.S.W.) 155), and take the risk that in any proceedings instituted by the lessor the court will find that the lessor's withholding of consent has been unreasonable (see *Treloar v. Bigge* (1874) L.R. 9 Ex. 151); secondly, and more prudently, the lessee may, before assigning, seek a declaration that the consent is being unreasonably withheld: see *Supreme Court Act* 1970 (N.S.W.), s. 75, overcoming *Harvey v. Walker* (1945) 46 S.R. (N.S.W.) 73.

The view has been expressed in the High Court that the lessor may, in any such proceedings, rely upon a ground which has come to her or his knowledge after the date of refusal, for example, the impending bankruptcy of the proposed assignee: *Secured Income Real Estate (Aust.) Ltd v. St Martin's Investments Pty Ltd* (1979) 53 A.L.J.R. 745 at 750. More recently, however, the English Court of Appeal has preferred the view that although the lessor is not restricted to relying upon the reasons (if any) actually communicated to the tenant at the time of refusing consent, he or she is restricted to relying upon reasons which did actually influence his or her mind at the time of refusal: see *Bromley Park Garden Estates Ltd v. Moss* [1982] 1 W.L.R. 1019 at 1034.

A landlord who fears that an assignment is about to occur in breach of the covenant is entitled to an unjunction to restrain the breach: *McEacharn v. Colton* [1902] A.C. 104. If the breach has already occurred, the lessor may bring an action against the assignor for damages, although actual damage may be hard to prove where all that has happened is that one tenant has taken the place of another (but see *Lepla v. Rogers* [1893] 1 Q.B. 31, where the premises were destroyed by a fire caused by the hazardous nature of the business carried on by the unauthorised assignee; the assignor, not having sought the lessor's prior consent, was held responsible for the loss caused by the fire, being a consequence of the breach of the covenant). The lessor may also re-enter and terminate the lease (assuming he has an express or implied power to that effect) subject to the provisions relating to relief against forfeiture: as to which, see below p. 644 et seq.

3. Unreasonably withholding consent

RE GIBBS AND HOULDER BROS & CO. LTD'S LEASE; HOULDER BROS & CO. LTD v. GIBBS

Chancery Division [1925] Ch. 198

[A lease for a term of 21 years contained a covenant by the lessees not to assign or sub-let without the lessor's consent, such consent "not to be withheld unreasonably in the case of a respectable and responsible person or corporation". The lessees proposed to assign the residue of their term to R Ltd, who were yearly tenants of adjoining premises from the same lessor. The lessor refused his consent to the proposed assignment, not because of the character or reputation of R Ltd, but because he feared that R Ltd would subsequently terminate its yearly tenancy and leave him (the lessor) with a vacant property which could be difficult to re-let.]

TOMLIN J. The facts of the case are not in dispute, and the question which I have to determine is one of construction upon the lease—namely, whether on the admitted facts and having regard to the reason given for the refusal of consent to the assignment, that refusal was, within the meaning of the lease, unreasonably withheld. . . .

It is said by Mr Simonds on behalf of the lessor that a clause such as this must be read in such a way that for the purpose of determining reason or unreason, the court is entitled to have regard to all the circumstances which may affect the interest of the lessor, however extrinsic they may be to the fact of the lease, or the user of the premises in the lease, or the personality of the lessee or assignee; in other words, that wherever a lessor finds that an assignment to a particular individual may result in something which will be detrimental to him wholly without regard to the character of the assignee, or the user which the assignee may make of the premises, the lessor may assert that as a reason for refusing his assent. On the other hand it is said: No, the considerations with reference to which reason or unreason is tested must necessarily be much narrower than that; they must be reasons which have some relation to, and arise in some way out of, the personality of the lessee or the proposed user or occupation of the premises, and the mere fact that some indirect detriment may follow to the lessor by reason of the assignment does not of itself afford the lessor a ground for refusing his assent to the assignment. . . .

. . . [I]t is by reference to the personality of the lessee or the nature of the user or occupation of the premises, that the court has to judge of the reasonableness of the lessor's refusal. It is quite true that the injury threatened or apprehended to the lessor may be in respect of something which has nothing to do with the lease of the demised premises; it may be in relation to other property of which he is the owner, but the danger must come from the nature of the user or occupation or from the personality of the assignee. In the present case what is the real reason of the refusal? The real reason is not one which had anything to do with the personality of the lessee, or with the user or occupation of the premises; the real reason is that the lessor wants to prevent the assignee from giving up other premises of which he is also lessor; in other words, his real purpose in refusing an assignment is not in relation to the demised premises at all, but in relation to other property, and to bring pressure to bear on the assignee not to give up a tenancy of different premises belonging to him.

In my view, therefore, the necessary conclusion is that the refusal in this case was unreasonable, and that being so the lessee is free to assign.

[The decision of Tomlin J. was later affirmed, and his reasoning approved, by the Court of Appeal [1925] Ch. 575.]

NOTE

The test proposed by Tomlin J. has been criticised by two members of the House of Lords as being too restrictive: see *Viscount Tredegar v. Harwood* [1929] A.C. 72 at 78 per Viscount Dunedin, at 81-82 per Lord Phillimore. But the English Court of Appeal has stated on subsequent occasions that it remains bound by the decision in the principal case: see *Lee v. K. Carter Ltd* [1949] 1 K.B. 85 at 96; *Swanson v. Forton* [1949] 1 Ch. 143 at 149; *International Drilling Fluids Ltd v. Louisville Investments (Uxbridge) Ltd* [1986] 2 W.L.R. 581 at 586, extracted below p. 615. (cf. the discussion in *Pimms Ltd v. Tallow Chandlers Co.* [1964] 2 Q.B. 547 at 567-573). The decision in *Re Gibbs and Houlder Bros & Co. Ltd's Lease* has been applied in Australia: see *Colvin v. Bowen* (1958) 75 W.N. (N.S.W.) 262 at 264; *Bambury v. Chapman* (1959) 77 W.N. (N.S.W.) 191 at 192; *Stack v. Cameron* [1941] St. R. Qd 284 at 287. It should be noted, however, that in all of the above cases, the qualification that the lessor's consent could not be unreasonably withheld was expressly contained in the lease; it has been doubted whether the lessor's reason for refusing consent must, as a matter of law, be connected with the assignee or the use and occupation of the premises where the qualification of reasonableness is imported into the lease by statutory provisions such as s. 133B of the *Conveyancing Act* 1919 (N.S.W.): see *McKenzie v. McAllum* [1956] V.L.R. 208 at 214. Is there any reason for such a distinction?

BICKEL v. DUKE OF WESTMINSTER

Court of Appeal [1977] Q.B. 517

[By the terms of a lease, the lessee was not permitted to assign without the lessor's written consent, "provided that such [consent] shall not be unreasonably withheld". The lessor, Grosvenor Estate, refused permission to the lessee, The Ancient Order of Foresters Friendly Society ("Foresters"), to assign the lease to a lady who was already in possession under an existing sub-lease, on the ground that to permit the assignment would give the lady the right to purchase the freehold under the provisions of the *Leasehold Reform Act* 1967 (U.K.) at substantially less than its market value. The County Court judge held that the lessor's consent had been unreasonably withheld and that the lessees were entitled to assign to the sub-lessee. The lessor appealed.]

LORD DENNING M.R. Two propositions have been canvassed in this case as if they were propositions of law. The first proposition is that, in order to be reasonable, the landlord's refusal must be based on (i) either the personality of the assignee or (ii) the user or occupation of the premises. If his reasons have nothing to do with either, then his refusal is unreasonable. Such is said to be the ground of the decision in *Re Gibbs and Houlder Bros & Co. Ltd's Lease* [1925] Ch. 198, 575, which was doubted in the House of Lords in *Viscount Tredegar v. Harwood* [1929] A.C. 72 at 82: but is said to be still binding in this court.

If such be the law, then it follows that Grosvenor Estate cannot reasonably refuse consent to the assignment by the Foresters to the lady. The personality of the assignee cannot be impeached on any score, and her user and occupation of the premises cannot be criticised in any respect.

The other proposition is that, where a house is subject to the Rent Acts, the landlord cannot reasonably refuse his consent to a *normal* assignment during the contractual term, even though it means that the assignee will be able to stay on afterwards as a statutory tenant. Such is the result of *Thomas Bookman Ltd v. Nathan* [1955] 1 W.L.R. 815. But he can reasonably refuse it in the case of an *abnormal* assignment of the "fag end" of the contractual term, made for the purpose of giving the assignee the benefit of the Acts. Such is said to be the result of *Lee v. K. Carter Ltd* [1949] 1 K.B. 85; *Swanson v. Forton* [1949] Ch. 143; *Dollar v. Winston* [1950] Ch. 236. Those decisions are said to be binding on this court. If they are good law, they bear a close analogy to the present case. This is an absolutely normal assignment of the lease for the last seven years of the term. It is not the "fag end" of the lease. There is nothing abnormal about it. The Grosvenor Estate cannot, therefore, reasonably refuse their consent, even though it means that the lady will be able afterwards to enfranchise the premises under the *Leasehold Reform Act* 1967 (U.K.).

If those cases can properly be regarded as laying down propositions of law, I would agree that we ought to hold the landlords' refusal to be unreasonable. But I do not think they do lay down any propositions of law, and for this reason. The words of the contract are perfectly clear English words: "such licence shall not be unreasonably withheld." When those words come to be applied in any particular case, I do not think the court can, or should, determine by strict rules the grounds on which a landlord may, or may not, reasonably refuse his consent. He is not limited by the contract to any particular grounds. Nor should the courts limit him. Not even under the guise of construing the words. The landlord has to exercise his judgment in all sorts of circumstances. It is impossible for him, or for the courts, to envisage them all. When this lease was granted in 1947 no one could have foreseen that 20 years later Parliament would give a tenant a right to buy up the freehold. Seeing that the circumstances are infinitely various, it is impossible to formulate strict rules as to how a landlord should exercise his power of refusal. The utmost that the courts can do is to give guidance to those who have to consider the problem. As one decision follows another, people will get to know the likely result in any given set of circumstances. But no one decision will be a binding precedent as a strict rule of law. The reasons given by the judges are to be treated as propositions of good sense—in relation to the particular case—rather than propositions of law applicable to all cases. It is rather like the cases where a statute gives the court a discretion. It has always been held that this discretion is not to be fettered by strict rules: and that all that can be properly done is to indicate the chief considerations which help to arrive at a just conclusion: see *Blunt v. Blunt* [1943] A.C. 517; *Ward v. James* [1966] 1 Q.B. 273.

I have studied all the previous cases and find little guidance in any of them to solve our present problems. The reason is simply because it is a new situation, consequent on the *Leasehold Reform Act* 1967 (U.K.), which was never envisaged before. I would test it by considering first the position of the landlords—the Grosvenor Estate. They hold a large estate which they desire to keep in their hands so as to develop it in the best possible way. This would be much impeded if one house after another is bought up by sitting tenants. Further, if they are compelled to sell under the *Leasehold Reform Act*, they will suffer much financial loss, because the price is much less than the value of the house. Test it next by considering the position of the tenants—the Foresters. They hold the premises as an investment and want to sell it. It matters not to them whether they sell to the landlord or to sub-tenants, so long as they receive a fair price for it. The landlords say they are willing to negotiate a fair price for it. They will give the Foresters a sum equivalent to that offered by the sub-tenant. Test it next by considering the position of the sub-tenant herself. When she took her sub-lease, she had no possible claim to enfranchisement. It was at a high rent, outside the Act of 1967. She is quite well protected by the Rent Acts so far as her own occupation is concerned. She will not be evicted at the end of her term. The only result on her of a refusal will be that she will not be able to buy up the freehold for a very low figure.

Taking all these circumstances into account, I do not think the Grosvenor Estate are withholding their consent unreasonably. At any rate, it is for the Foresters to prove that they are. And they have not proved it.

I would, therefore, allow the appeal.

ORR L.J. On these authorities, in my judgment, the withholding of consent in the present case was reasonable because it related to an attribute of the personality of the proposed assignee in that he [sic] would be eligible in due course to acquire the freehold by virtue of the *Leasehold Reform Act* 1967 (U.K.), and to the effect of the proposed assignment on the user and occupation of the premises, and to the relationship of landlord and tenant in regard to the subject matter of the demise, and because, on the evidence, the object of the refusal was based on views which a reasonable man could well entertain as to the proper management of the lessor's estate of which the premises in question form part.

For the reasons I have indicated, I also consider that the judge was in error in holding that the proposed assignment was, for the present purposes, a normal and not an abnormal one, and wrongly attached importance in this connection to the fact that the request for consent was not made at the tail-end of the tenancy, which would have been a relevant consideration as respects the rights conferred by the Rent Acts, but cannot, in my judgment, be a factor of any importance where the object of the assignment is that rights should be acquired under the *Leasehold Reform Act* 1967 (U.K.), which requires five years' occupancy for that purpose.

For these reasons, as well as those given by Lord Denning M.R., I would allow this appeal.

WALLER L.J. The appellants are, of course, landlords of a considerable area in the City of Westminster and wish to retain, so far as they can, control over the development of their estates. If premises are enfranchised they will, to some extent, lose their control. The question which this court has to decide is whether or not it is a good reason for refusing permission to assign that the assignee would be in a position to become an enfranchised tenant when the present lessee would not be in that position. We were referred to a number of cases in which the question arose as to whether or not consent had been unreasonably withheld. These cases had facts which were different from those in the present case and I only propose to consider three.

The first was *Re Gibbs and Houlder Bros & Co. Ltd's Lease* [1925] Ch. 198, 575 a decision which has been criticised in some dicta in the House of Lords but which in this court I am content to follow. In that case the landlord refused permission to assign because the proposed assignee happened to be another tenant of his and in the particular economic circumstances existing at the time it would probably be difficult to relet the premises which would be vacated by that tenant. Both at first instance and in the Court of Appeal the court came to the conclusion that that was an unreasonable refusal. The judgments of the three members of the court vary slightly in their reasoning and those variations were considered in a later case, *Lee v. K. Carter Ltd* [1949] 1 K.B. 85, so I shall not repeat them here. It is sufficient to say that Warrington L.J. was of the opinion that there must be something which connects it, that is to say, the objection, either with the personality of the intended assignee or with the user which the intended assignee is likely to make of the property, and Sir Ernest Pollock M.R., while agreeing with that, thought that the fact that the reason was extraneous to the relationship of landlord and tenant was another factor making refusal unreasonable.

In *Lee v. K. Carter Ltd*, the question before the Court of Appeal was whether, when a company was a lessee and wished to assign to a director, who would become a personal tenant, it was unreasonable to refuse permission. In that case the company could never have protection from the Rent Acts whereas the director, as a personal tenant, could. The Court of Appeal came to the conclusion that it was reasonable to refuse, and Tucker L.J. used a phrase which is helpful when he said (at 96): "it was a contractual relationship pregnant with future possibilities . . . which would not have resulted from the previous existing contractual relationship between the landlord and the company."

The third case to which I wish to refer is *Pimms Ltd v. Tallow Chandlers Co.* [1964] 2 Q.B. 547. In that case the landlord refused permission to assign some premises to a tenant who would be a developer of those premises because he, the landlord, had entered into an arrangement with the owners of adjoining properties to carry out a joint development scheme and that joint development scheme would have been interfered with if there was an extra developer concerned. The Court of Appeal, having considered the cases to which I have referred, came to the conclusion that this was an assignment pregnant with future possibilities, that they were matters which clearly related to the personality of the proposed assignees and affected the property the subject matter of the lease and affected the relationship of landlord and tenant in respect of the lease.

In my opinion, in the present case the proposed assignment would be pregnant with future possibilities because the present lessees are not in a position to enfranchise their leasehold interest. If, however, this assignment were permitted, then the assignee would be in a position to enfranchise his leasehold interest. In my opinion, this clearly affects the property which is the subject matter of the lease and the relationship between the landlord and the tenant, and accordingly, in my view, the landlord was entitled to refuse consent to an assignment and that refusal is wholly within the principles set out in *Re Gibbs and Houlder Bros & Co. Ltd's Lease* [1925] Ch. 198 and within the principles of the other two cases which I have cited.

I would allow this appeal.

Appeal allowed.

NOTES AND QUESTIONS

1. Does Lord Denning M.R., in the second paragraph of the above extract, correctly apply the principle in *Re Gibbs and Houlder Bros & Co. Ltd's Lease*? Compare *Norfolk Capital Group Ltd v. Kitway Ltd* [1977] Q.B. 506. See Clements, "Assignment of Tenancies and the Leasehold Reform Act" (1977) 127 New L.J. 1131.

2. Lord Denning M.R.'s approach in the principal case has been applied by a differently constituted Court of Appeal in *West Layton Ltd v. Ford* [1979] 3 W.L.R. 14. Roskill L.J. said that he "respectfully agreed" with that part of Lord Denning's judgment in the principal case, commencing with the words "But he can reasonably refuse it" and concluding with the words "rather than propositions of law applicable to all cases". Roskill L.J. continued:

> I think that the right approach, as Lord Denning M.R. suggested in the *Bickel* case [1977] Q.B. 517, is to look first of all at the covenant and construe that covenant in order to see what its purpose was when the parties entered into it; what each party, one the holder of the reversion, the other the assignee of the benefit of the relevant term, must be taken to have understood when they acquired the relevant interest on either side. . . . The landlord has not got to consider anybody else's interest except his own. He is the person who has in all the circumstances to decide whether or not he will grant consent. As Lord Denning M.R. said, circumstances may vary endlessly. In the present case one of the matters which has caused a change of circumstance is the passing of the *Rent Act 1974*": [1979] 3 W.L.R. 14 at 22.

Megaw and Lawton L.JJ. agreed. Lawton L.J. said:

> Whether anything is "unreasonable" depends upon all the circumstances of the case; and, in relation to lettings, unreasonableness must be considered against the background of the statutory provisions which are applicable. . . . The statutory provisions, however, are just one factor. There may be others. When during the period of the contractual tenancy a landlord is asked to consent to one tenant being replaced by another well able to pay the rent and likely to observe the covenants in the lease, in almost all cases it would be unreasonable for him to refuse his consent. . . . But cases tend to differ on their facts . . . : at 23.

3. Consider whether there has been an unreasonable refusal to consent to assignment in the following circumstances:

   (a) A shop and a kiosk, two separate premises in a large complex, had been leased to the one tenant, who carried on the business of a tobacconist in both places. The kiosk was better positioned than the shop, and was the more successful of the two sites. The lessor refused to consent to an assignment of the kiosk, because he feared that to introduce competition between the kiosk and the shop would place the shop at a considerable disadvantage, thereby rendering it less attractive to prospective tenants, with a consequent reduction in the rent which could be obtained: see *Premier Confectionary (London) Co. Ltd v. London Commercial Sale Rooms Ltd* [1933] Ch. 904.

   (b) The lessor refused his consent on the ground that the proposed sub-lessee was entitled to diplomatic immunity, and so could not be sued in the courts: see *Parker v. Boggon* [1947] K.B. 346.

   (c) The demised premises consisted of a shop together with facilities for baking bread. The lease contained a covenant whereby the lessee agreed to "keep the shop . . . open for the sale of bread", but contained no covenant requiring the lessee to bake bread on the premises. The lessee entered into partnership with another baker in the same town, and sought the lessor's consent to an assignment of the lease to himself and the other baker. The lessor refused to give his consent, because he feared that the baking of bread on the demised premises would cease (the other baker had baking facilities of his own), with consequent loss of the goodwill attached to the business conducted on the demised premises and a reduction in their rental value: see *Stack v. Cameron* [1941] St. R. Qd 284.

4. Reference should be made to the statutory provision which provides that qualified covenants against alienation shall be deemed to be subject to a proviso that no fine shall be taken in return for granting consent: *Conveyancing Act 1919* (N.S.W.), s. 132, discussed in *Barina Properties Pty Ltd v. Bernard Hastie (Aust.) Pty Ltd* [1979] 1 N.S.W.L.R. 480.

BROMLEY PARK GARDEN ESTATES LTD v. MOSS

Court of Appeal [1982] 1 W.L.R. 1019

[The plaintiff was the landlord of premises consisting of an upstairs flat and maisonette ("the flat") and a ground floor restaurant. The tenant of the flat (Miss Wynn-Higgins) sought the landlord's consent to the assignment of the lease to the defendant. Her lease contained a covenant against assigning without the lessor's consent, such consent not to be unreasonably withheld. When approached for consent, the landlord's agent replied that the landlord was not in the habit of permitting assignments of residential properties, but if the tenant were prepared to surrender her lease, consideration would be given to the grant of a new lease to the defendant. The tenant subsequently assigned the lease to the defendant, taking the view that the landlord's refusal to consent was unreasonable, whereupon the plaintiff landlord issued a plaint for possession of the flat for breach of the covenant against assignment.

At the hearing, the landlord gave as further reasons for refusing consent: that it was against the landlord's interests to have "multiple occupation lettings", and that it would be advantageous if the ground floor restauranteur took a lease of the whole building (including the flat) and that the restauranteur had expressed interest in such a lease, notwithstanding that it would be a requirement of any such lease that the restauranteur surrender his existing lease and accept a more onerous repairing obligation under the new lease; and that although there were no doubts that the defendant could meet the present rent, the landlord doubted whether the defendant would be able to meet any substantially increased rent which a rent tribunal might award if approached.

The trial judge held that the landlord's refusal of consent was not unreasonable, because the landlord was genuinely and reasonably of the view that such a refusal was "in the interests of the proper management of [its] estate", a test stated in Woodfall's *Landlord and Tenant* (28th ed., 1978), p. 485, para. 1181: the landlord had a positive opportunity to let the whole premises as a single building at an increased rent, with a full repairing covenant, and an enhanced capital value should it decide to sell at some future date. On appeal:]

CUMMING-BRUCE L.J. Mr Sedley [counsel for the defendant] submits that the statement in Woodfall, op. cit., p. 485, para. 1181, is too wide. The statement which he criticised was this: "A refusal of consent or licence will generally be considered unreasonable if it is on a ground having no reference either to the personality of the proposed assignee or to the effect of the proposed assignment (or under-letting) on the user and occupation of the demised premises or kindred matters arising either during or after the tenancy. This statement of principle should be regarded however rather as a guide than as a rigid doctrine; it is considered that a landlord may reasonably be influenced in his decision by considerations of the proper management of the estate of which the demised property forms part."

Mr Sedley accepts that the landlord has only to consider his own interests and in pursuing those interests he may withhold consent if, by giving his consent, he apprehends that he will cause detriment to the interests granted or reserved to him by the lease, whether by reference to the personal or financial characteristics of the intended assignee, or by reference to the anticipated adverse effect upon the landlords' interests of the user of the premises by the intended assignee. It is submitted that the landlord is unreasonable if he withholds consent in order to obtain a new advantage which he does not enjoy under the lease. The judge, Mr Sedley says, was wrong because the advantage that he found to have been proved was quite outside the interest granted or reserved by the lease.

Mr Belben [counsel for the plaintiff landlord] contested this proposition. . . .

A convenient starting point from which to consider the issue is *Lehmann v. McArthur* (1867) L.R. 3 Eq. 746. The landlord there withheld licence to assign to a person wholly unobjectionable, his object being to get a surrender of the lease for the purpose of rebuilding. Sir John Stuart V.-C. said (at 751): "This is a purpose not contemplated by the lease. The lease by Shakerley is a demise unto McArthur, his executors, administrators, and assigns, and this entitled him to assign to another person, if there should be no reasonable ground, within the terms of the covenant, on the part of Shakerley for refusing his licence. The question now is, whether or not there was any power in the lessor, who has contracted to allow his lessee to assign where he might reasonably assign, to refuse to allow the lessee to assign at all, because he wishes him to give up the lease, and himself make a new bargain with the lessee. In my opinion, no lessor has a right to use a stipulation in a covenant of this kind, so as to defeat the right of the lessee to assign, where the assignment or agreement for an assignment has been honestly made."

Then in *Bates v. Donaldson* [1896] 2 Q.B. 241, A. L. Smith L.J. in his judgment expressed his view in a passage which in this court was later preferred to the judgment of Kay L.J. A. L. Smith L.J. said (at 247): "Now, when the lessor granted the lease he parted with his interest in the premises for the entire term. The tenant during that term can assign to any respectable and responsible assignee—in which case the lessor is bound not to unreasonably withhold his permission. It is not, in my opinion, the true reading of this clause that the permission can be withheld in order to enable the lessor to regain possession of the premises before the termination of the term. It was in my judgment inserted alio intuitu altogether, and in order to protect the lessor from having his premises used or occupied in an undesirable way or by an undesirable tenant or assignee, and not in order to enable the lessor to, if possible, coerce a tenant to surrender the lease so that the lessor might obtain possession of the premises, which was the reason why in the present case the assent was withheld."

[His Lordship then quoted extensively from the judgments of the members of the Court of Appeal in *Houlder Bros & Co. Ltd v. Gibbs* [1925] Ch. 575 (which affirmed the decision and reasons of Tomlin J., extracted above) and quoted a short passage from the judgment of Roskill L.J. in *West Layton Ltd v. Ford* [1979] Q.B. 593 at 605, and continued:]

The cases on which Mr Belben relied on behalf of the defendant [scilicet, plaintiff] were, with one exception, cases which prove on analysis to be cases in which the reason of the landlord for withholding his consent was because he apprehended that the prospective user of the parcels after assignment would have the effect of injuring his interests, albeit they might be consequences suffered by him in neighbouring property. The landlord reasonably apprehended that the consequence of the assignment would damage his interest in neighbouring property; an example is the *Bridewell Hospital Case* (1887) 8 T.L.R. 637; 116 E.R. 323. The effect of the anticipated activities of the assignee upon the neighbouring property of the landlord caused reasonable apprehension to the landlord: so, too, in the case in which the expected activities of the assignee would produce adverse consequences upon the trade and rental of a shop which also was held from the same landlord.

One can distinguish the uncovenanted advantage sought to be gained by the landlord in this case by refusing to honour the right of the tenant to assign. . . .

Mr Belben submitted that the withholding of consent had as its object and consequence a return of the premises to unified possession which he described as the status quo, but he could not bring his suggested status quo within the contemplation of the parties to the grant to Miss Wynn-Higgins or [her predecessor as tenant], as the shop was then used as a restaurant . . . and there was no evidence of the date when the whole house had last been in single occupation. I would therefore hold that the statement in Woodfall, op. cit., p. 485, para. 1181 is misleading, and its reference to good estate management as a valid reason for withholding consent is altogether too wide; it does not represent the true effect of the judgments in the cases to which I have referred.

The reason described by [the landlord's agent] in evidence, and accepted by the judge as his ground for decision, was wholly extraneous to the intention of the parties to the contract when the covenant was granted and accepted. That reason cannot be relied upon merely because it would suit the landlords' investment plans, or their purpose in obtaining from Miss Wynn-Higgins the surrender of her lease. It may well enhance the financial interests of the landlord to obtain a single tenant holding the whole building on a full repairing covenant with long-term capital advantage when they put the building upon the market, but that intention and policy is entirely outside the intention to be imputed to the parties at the time of the granting of the lease to Brown or the assignment to Miss Wynn-Higgins.

DUNN L.J. I agree and I only add a few words of my own because we are differing from the view expressed by the judge.

I agree with Cumming-Bruce L.J. that the passage in Woodfall, op. cit., p. 485, para. 1181, on which the judge relied, states the law too widely. The cases cited in support of the proposition as stated by Woodfall show that, although the question of unreasonableness depends on all the circumstances of the case, including considerations of proper management of the estate of which the demised premises form a part, in no case has it been held reasonable for a landlord to refuse his consent for the purposes of destroying the lease in question or merging it on terms with another lease in the same building, even though that would probably be good estate management and would be a pecuniary advantage to the landlord.

In *West Layton Ltd v. Ford* [1979] Q.B. 593, the proposal of the tenant had the effect of altering the nature of the letting from a single letting of commercial property with residential property over to two separate tenancies—the commercial tenancy downstairs and a separate residential letting upstairs. This would have been detrimental to the landlord because the residential tenancy would, as a result of the *Rent Act* 1974 (U.K.), attract *Rent Act* protection.

Similarly, in *Premier Confectionery (London) Co. Ltd v. London Commercial Sale Rooms Ltd* [1933] Ch. 904, although there were separate tenancies of shop and kiosk, the lease of the kiosk had been granted to the same tenant as the lessee of the shop. The proposal of the tenant was to assign the tenancy of the kiosk so as to create two tenants instead of one. These would have been detrimental to the landlords because competition from the kiosk would have been likely to affect the rent they would be able to charge for the shop.

In both cases the withholding of consent to the assignments by the landlord were held not to have been unreasonable. In both cases the landlords were seeking to uphold the status quo and to preserve the existing contractual arrangements provided by the leases. In both cases the landlords reasonably believed that they would suffer detriment if the assignments were made. It is true that in deciding the question of unreasonableness the courts did not confine themselves to narrow considerations as to the personality of the proposed assignee or the subject matter of the lease, as had been done in some of the older cases—and it may be that the passage in Woodfall was intended to draw attention to that—but there is nothing in the cases to indicate that the landlord was entitled to refuse his consent in order to acquire a commercial benefit for himself by putting into effect proposals outside the contemplation of the lease under consideration, and to replace the contractual relations created by the lease by some alternative arrangements more advantageous to the landlord, even though this would have been in accordance with good estate management.

West Layton Ltd v. Ford [1979] Q.B. 593 shows that in considering whether the landlords' refusal of consent is unreasonable, the court should look first at the covenant in the context of the lease and ascertain the purpose of the covenant in that context. If the refusal of the landlord was designed to achieve that purpose then it may not be unreasonable, even in the case of a respectable and responsible assignee; but if the refusal is designed to achieve some collateral purpose wholly unconnected with the terms of the lease, as in *Houlder Bros & Co. Ltd v. Gibbs* [1925] Ch. 575, and as in the present case, then that would be unreasonable, even though the purpose was in accordance with good estate management.

For those reasons and for the reasons given by Cumming-Bruce L.J., I agree that this appeal should be allowed on that ground.

SLADE L.J. I agree with Cumming-Bruce and Dunn L.JJ. that the statement in Woodfall, op. cit., p. 485, para. 1181 to the effect that a landlord may properly be influenced in his decision by considerations of the proper management of the estate of which the demised property forms a part is too wide.

A landlord is not in my judgment entitled to rely on a clause, such as [the relevant clause] of the tenancy agreement in the present case, for the purpose of securing a collateral benefit such as the landlords have sought to secure for themselves in the present case. The reason which influenced the landlords in the present case is in my judgment in the words of Sargant L.J. in *Houlder Bros & Co. Ltd v. Gibbs* [1925] Ch. 575 at 588: "a reason wholly dissociated from, and unconnected with, the bargain made between the lessor and the lessees under the lease that we have to consider, and is, from that point of view, a purely arbitrary and irrelevant reason.

Appeal allowed.

INTERNATIONAL DRILLING FLUIDS LTD v. LOUISVILLE INVESTMENTS (UXBRIDGE) LTD

Court of Appeal [1986] 2 W.L.R. 581

[The lease of an office block provided that the premises should only be used for offices, and that the tenant could not assign without the landlord's consent, such consent not to be unreasonably withheld. The landlord refused the tenant's request for permission to assign the lease to a prospective tenant which intended to use the building for "serviced" office accommodation, that is, accommodation for businesses which required temporary accommodation with the services of receptionists and typists, and so on. This use would be permitted under the lease. The landlord purported to justify its refusal principally on the ground that, since the assignor-tenant had vacated the premises, they would be worth more for sale or mortgage purposes if they remained vacant than if they were occupied by the proposed assignee. There was no real likelihood of the premises being placed on the market or mortgaged, but there was evidence (which the trial judge felt obliged to accept, although not without expressing a personal view that he found it difficult to accept) that should they be, they would in fact be more valuable if vacant than if occupied by the proposed assignee. The trial judge found that the refusal of consent was nevertheless unreasonable. The landlord appealed.]

BALCOMBE L.J. During the course of argument many cases were cited to us, as they were to the judge. I do not propose to set them out in detail here; many of the older cases were considered in the full judgment of the Court of Appeal in *Pimms Ltd v. Tallow Chandlers Co.* [1964] 2 Q.B. 547. From the authorities I deduce the following propositions of law.

(1) The purpose of a covenant against assignment without the consent of the landlord, such consent not to be unreasonably withheld, is to protect the lessor from having his premises used or occupied in an undesirable way, or by an undesirable tenant or assignee: per Smith L.J. in *Bates v. Donaldson* [1896] 2 Q.B. 241 at 247, approved by all the members of the Court of Appeal in *Houlder Bros & Co. Ltd v. Gibbs* [1925] Ch. 575.

(2) As a corollary to the first proposition, a landlord is not entitled to refuse his consent to an assignment on grounds which have nothing whatever to do with the relationship of landlord and tenant in regard to the subject matter of the lease: see *Houlder Bros & Co. Ltd v. Gibbs*, a decision which (despite some criticism) is binding on this court: *Bickel v. Duke of Westminster* [1977] Q.B. 517. A recent example of a case where the landlord's consent was unreasonably withheld because the refusal was designed to achieve a collateral purpose unconnected with the terms of the lease is *Bromley Park Garden Estates Ltd v. Moss* [1982] 1 W.L.R. 1019.

(3) The onus of proving that consent has been unreasonably withheld is on the tenant: see *Shanly v. Ward* (1913) 29 T.L.R. 714 and *Pimms Ltd v. Tallow Chandlers Co.* [1964] 2 Q.B. 547 at 564.

(4) It is not necessary for the landlord to prove that the conclusions which led him to refuse consent were justified, if they were conclusions which might be reached by a reasonable man in the circumstances: *Pimms Ltd v. Tallow Chandlers Co.* [1964] 2 Q.B. 547 at 564.

(5) It may be reasonable for the landlord to refuse his consent to an assignment on the ground of the purpose for which the proposed assignee intends to use the premises, even though that purpose is not forbidden by the lease: see *Bates v. Donaldson* [1896] 2 Q.B. 241 at 244.

(6) There is a divergence of authority on the question, in considering whether the landlord's refusal of consent is reasonable, whether it is permissible to have regard to the consequences to the tenant if consent to the proposed assignment is withheld. In an early case at first instance, *Sheppard v. Hongkong and Shanghae Banking Corp.* (1872) 20 W.R. 459 at 460, Malins V.-C. said that by withholding their consent the lessors threw a very heavy burden on the lessees and they therefore ought to show good grounds for refusing it. In *Houlder Bros & Co. Ltd v. Gibbs* [1925] Ch. 575 at 584, Warrington L.J. said: "An act must be regarded as reasonable or unreasonable in reference to the circumstances under which it is committed, and when the question arises on the construction of a contract the outstanding circumstances to be considered are the nature of the contract to be construed, and the relations between the parties resulting from it."

In a recent decision of this court, *Leeward Securities Ltd v. Lilyheath Properties Ltd* (1983) 271 E.G. 279 concerning a sub-letting which would attract the protection of the *Rent Act* 1974 (U.K.), both Oliver L.J. and O'Connor L.J. made it clear in their judgments that they could envisage circumstances in which it might be unreasonable to refuse consent to an underletting, if the result would be that there was no way in which the tenant (the sub-landlord) could reasonably exploit the premises except by creating a tenancy to which the *Rent Act* 1974

(U.K.) protection would apply, and which inevitably would affect the value of the landlord's reversion. O'Connor L.J. said (at 283): "It must not be thought that, because the introduction of a *Rent Act* tenant inevitably has an adverse effect upon the value of the reversion, that that is a sufficient ground for the landlords to say that they can withhold consent and that the court will hold that that is reasonable."

To the opposite effect are the dicta, obiter but nevertheless weighty, of Viscount Dunedin and Lord Phillimore in *Viscount Tredegar v. Harwood* [1929] A.C. 72 at 78, 82. There are numerous other dicta to the effect that a landlord need consider only his own interests: see, for example, *West Layton Ltd v. Ford* [1979] Q.B. 593 at 605, and *Bromley Park Garden Estates Ltd v. Moss* [1982] 1 W.L.R. 1019 at 1027. Those dicta must be qualified, since a landlord's interests, collateral to the purposes of the lease, are in any event ineligible for consideration: see proposition (2) above. But in my judgment a proper reconciliation of those two streams of authority can be achieved by saying that while a landlord need usually only consider his own relevant interests, there may be cases where there is such a disproportion between the benefit to the landlord and the detriment to the tenant if the landlord withholds his consent to an assignment that it is unreasonable for the landlord to refuse consent.

(7) Subject to the propositions set out above, it is in each case a question of fact, depending upon all the circumstances, whether the landlord's consent to an assignment is being unreasonably withheld: see *Bickel v. Duke of Westminster* [1977] Q.B. 517 at 524, and *West Layton Ltd v. Ford* [1979] Q.B. 593 at 604, 606-607.

In the present case, the judge, having made the findings of specific fact set out above, carefully considered the relevant authorities. He then reached the conclusion that the views of the landlords' expert witnesses about the effect of the proposed assignment on the value of the reversion, although views which could be held by reasonable professional men, did not in the circumstances of this case, where there was no prospect of the landlords wishing to realise the reversion, constitute a ground for reasonable apprehension of damage to its interests. That was a decision on the facts to which the judge was entitled to come. He made no error of law in reaching his decision; he took into account nothing which he ought not to have considered, and he omitted nothing which he ought to have considered. In my judgment, this court ought not to interfere.

But in any event, in my judgment, the judge reached the right decision. Although he did not expressly mention the disproportionate harm to the tenants if the landlords were entitled to refuse consent to the assignment, compared with the minimum disadvantage which he clearly considered the landlords would suffer by the diminution in the paper value of the reversion—"paper value" because he was satisfied there was no prospect of the landlords wishing to realise the reversion—he clearly recognised the curious results to which the landlords' arguments, based solely upon a consideration of their own interests, could lead. As he said in his judgment: "It seems to me that, if Mr Lewison is right, the more substantial the lessee, the more easily the landlord would be able to justify a refusal of consent to an assignment, since unless the proposed assignee's covenant was as strong as the assignor's, a reasonable man might form the view that the market would consider the reversion less attractive if the lease were vested in the proposed assignee than if it were vested in the assignor. To take the matter to extremes, if a lease was made in favour of a government department it would be unassignable except to another government department; for as Mr Matthews [one of the expert witnesses] accepted in cross-examination, the market would prefer to have the government as the lessee, whether the premises were being used as serviced offices or not, even if they were standing empty, rather than a company, however strong its covenant."

In my judgment, the gross unfairness to the tenants of the example postulated by the judge strengthens the arguments in favour, in an appropriate case of which the instant case is one, of it being unreasonable for the landlord not to consider the detriment to the tenant if consent is refused, where the detriment is extreme and disproportionate to the benefit to the landlord.

I am also satisfied that the judge could, and should, have had regard to the fact that the proposed serviced office user was within the only form of user permitted by the lease. I have already stated the proposition of law, derived from the cases, that it may be reasonable for the landlord to refuse his consent to an assignment on the grounds of the proposed user, even though that proposed user is permitted by the lease. But it does not follow from that that, in all circumstances, it will be reasonable for the landlord to object to a proposed user which is not forbidden by the lease. In most of the cases cited to us in which it was held reasonable to object to the proposed user, even though not forbidden by the lease, the user clause was, in general terms, merely prohibiting the carrying on of any noxious or offensive trade or business: see, for example, *Governors of Bridewell Hospital v. Fawkner* (1892) 8 T.L.R. 637 and *Re Spark's Lease* [1905] 1 Ch. 456.

[Fox L.J. and Mustill L.J. agreed.]

Appeal dismissed.

4. Effect of breach of covenant against assigning

In *Property & Bloodstock Ltd v. Emerton* [1968] Ch. 94 at 119, Danckwerts L.J. said:

> A covenant against assignment of leasehold property does not make an assignment unlawful or ineffective in itself. A breach by the lessee assigning may involve him in an action for damages, but unless the lease contains a proviso for re-entry on breach of covenant, no more effect is produced. Of course, as in the present case, there is normally such a proviso for re-entry. But forfeiture of the term is not automatic. The landlord may elect not to enforce his right of re-entry, or he may waive it involuntarily by acceptance of rent with knowledge of the breach, and then the term will continue.

See also *Massart v. Blight* (1951) 82 C.L.R. 423 at 440; *Old Grovebury Manor Farm Ltd v. W. Seymour Plant Sales & Hire Ltd (No. 2)* [1979] 3 All E.R. 504; *Peabody Donation Fund v. Higgins* [1983] 3 All E.R. 122.

C. THE ENFORCEMENT OF COVENANTS AGAINST ASSIGNEES AND SUB-LESSEES

The relationship of landlord and tenant involves both privity of contract and privity of estate.

1. Privity of contract

The landlord and the tenant are in direct contractual relations. Thus, the covenants contained in the lease are enforceable by and between landlord and tenant as a matter of contract law, even after they have assigned their respective interests in the land: *Stuart v. Joy* [1904] 1 K.B. 362. But there is no privity of contract between the original landlord and an assignee or sub-lessee of the original tenant, nor between the original tenant and an assignee of the original landlord; in such circumstances, contractual remedies are not open to the parties.

2. Privity of estate

Wherever the relationship of landlord and tenant exists between parties there is present privity of estate. This is so not only as between the original landlord and the original tenant but also as between successors in title to the interests of the original parties. In this regard, however, it becomes essential to distinguish between an assignment of a lease and a sub-lease. An assignment is the transfer of the whole of the interest of the lessee remaining in the lease (that is, the whole unexpired portion of his leasehold estate); a sub-lease is a transfer of something less than the whole of the lessee's interest, the lessee retaining a reversion in the lease. There is privity of estate between a landlord and an assignee of the tenant, the assignee becoming tenant to the landlord. On the other hand, there is no privity of estate between a landlord and a sub-lessee of the original tenant, because the original tenant retains her or his own leasehold interest and creates out of it a new leasehold interest which is lesser in duration, and dependent for its existence upon the tenant's own.

The principles may be illustrated by the following diagram:

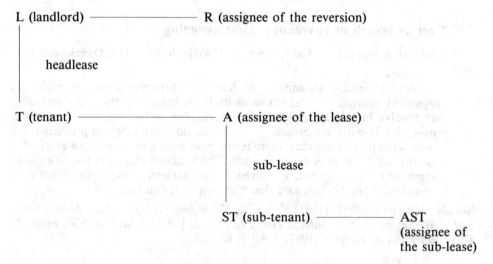

The landlord (L) has granted a lease for, say, five years, to the tenant (T). There is both privity of contract and privity of estate between L and T. The landlord has then assigned the reversion to R. There is privity of estate, but not privity of contract, between R and T. The tenant, T, has then assigned his leasehold interest to A. There is privity of estate, but not privity of contract, between R and A. A, the assignee of the lease, has sub-leased to ST for, say, the residue of the term less one day. There is both privity of contract and privity of estate between A and ST; but there is neither privity of contract nor of estate between R and ST, ST being the tenant of A, not of R. Finally, ST assigns his sub-lease to AST. There is privity of estate between A and AST, but not privity of contract; and there is neither privity of estate nor privity of contract between R and AST.

The importance of establishing the existence of privity of contract and privity of estate appears from the following well-established propositions. First, as discussed above, where privity of contract exists, the covenants in the lease are enforceable as a matter of contract law. Secondly, where privity of estate exists, the covenants are enforceable where they "touch and concern" the land (see below), and (unlike covenants affecting freehold land) this is so whether the covenants are positive or negative. Thirdly, where neither privity of contract nor privity of estate exists, the covenants are not enforceable, unless the benefit of the covenants has been effectively assigned or unless they fall within the principles governing covenants generally (as to which, see Chapter 6).

3. Covenants which "touch and concern" the land

HORSEY ESTATE LTD v. STEIGER AND PETRIFITE CO. LTD

Court of Appeal [1899] 2 Q.B. 79

[A lease contained a proviso entitling the lessor to re-enter and forfeit should the lessee enter into voluntary liquidation. The term "lessee" was defined to include assigns where the context so required. The reversion was subsequently assigned to the plaintiff and the lease was later assigned to the defendant. The defendant went into voluntary liquidation. One of the questions which arose was whether the covenant relating to voluntary liquidation ran with the land so as to be enforceable by the plaintiff against the defendant.]

LORD RUSSELL OF KILLOWEN C.J. Is, then, the condition in question one the burden of which runs with the land so that its obligation binds the assignee of the lease? The answer to this question depends, in this case, upon whether it is a condition touching the thing demised or is merely collateral. I say "in this case" because there are undoubtedly collateral covenants or conditions, which on equitable principles, but only in a restrictive sense, bind the assignee. But this principle is confined to covenants and conditions of a negative character, and depends upon notice. But apart from cases of this class the true principle is that no covenant or condition which affects merely the person, and which does not affect the nature, quality, or value of the thing demised or the mode of using or enjoying the thing demised, runs with the land: see *Mayor of Congleton v. Pattison* (1808) 10 East 130; 103 E.R. 725. Does, then, the condition or proviso in question "run with the land"? On the whole, and after much hesitation, I have arrived at the conclusion that it does. It must be taken as fully established that a covenant against assignment and also a proviso for re-entry in the case of bankruptcy run with the land: see *Roe v. Sales* (1813) 1 M. & S. 297; 105 E.R. 111; *Doe v. David* (1846) 1 C.M. & R. 405; 153 E.R. 933; *Doe v. Ingleby* (1846) 15 M. & W. 465; *Williams v. Earle* (1868) L.R. 3 Q.B. 739; *Varley v. Coppard* (1872) L.R. 7 C.P. 505; *Smith v. Gronow* [1891] 2 Q.B. 394. I think that a proviso for re-entry in case of liquidation by a company or an individual falls within the principle of these cases, and indeed that the proviso as to liquidation is cognate both to a covenant against assignment and to a proviso relating to bankruptcy. It partakes of the character of each of them. The proviso against bankruptcy was introduced into leases in consequence of the ordinary covenant against assignment being held not to apply to the involuntary assignment which is the consequence of bankruptcy: see *Doe v. Ingleby* (1846) 15 M. & W. 465 at 470; 153 E.R. 933 at 935; and, like the covenant against assignment, it touches the question who shall have and occupy the premises demised, and therefore touches and concerns the thing demised: see *Williams v. Earle* (1868) L.R. 3 Q.B. 739 at 749 per Blackburn J. I find myself unable to draw any distinction in principle between these cases and the case of a proviso for re-entry in case the assign of the lessee should enter into liquidation.

[A. L. Smith and Collins L.JJ. concurred.]

NOTES

1. The statement of principle in the principal case ("no covenant or condition . . . which does not affect the nature, quality, or value of the thing demised or the mode of using or enjoying the thing demised, runs with the land") is drawn from the judgment of Lord Ellenborough C.J. in *Mayor of Congleton v. Pattison* (1808) 10 East 130 at 135; 103 E.R. 725 at 726. In the same case, Bayley J. said:

   > in order to bind the assignee the covenant must either affect the land itself during the term, such as those which regard the mode of occupation; or it must be such as per se, and not merely from collateral circumstances, affects the value of the land at the end of the term.

   In *Breams Property Investment Co. Ltd v. Strougler* [1948] 2 K.B. 1 at 7 Scott L.J. (citing Cheshire's *Modern Real Property* (see now (12th ed.), p. 451) stated the test as to whether a covenant runs to be:

   > whether the covenant affects either the landlord qua landlord or the tenant qua tenant. A covenant may very well have reference to the land, but unless it is reasonably incidental to the relation of landlord and tenant, it cannot be said to touch and concern the land so as to be capable of running therewith or with the reversion.

2. A New Zealand case has pointed out that the test propounded in the *Horsey Estate* case is not exhaustive, and that a number of covenants universally accepted as binding assignees do not "affect the nature, quality, or value of the thing demised [that is, the land], or the mode of using or enjoying the thing demised"; for example, covenants for quiet enjoyment and for further assurance have been held to run with the land, but they support the *title* to the term rather than affect the "nature, quality, or value of the land or the mode of using or enjoying it": see *Bates v. Casey and Milne* (1915) 34 N.Z.L.R. 714 at 716-722.

3. A list of covenants which have been held to "touch and concern" the land will be found in Megarry and Wade, op. cit., pp. 744-745. Of the more significant covenants on the part of the lessee which have been held to "touch and concern" the land are covenants to pay rent, to repair, to insure against fire, and not to assign without the lessor's consent. Covenants on the part of the lessor which have been held to "touch and concern" the land include covenants to supply the premises with water, not to build on a certain part of adjoining land, and not to determine a periodic tenancy during its first three years.

4. A covenant by the lessor to sell the reversion to the tenant (in popular language, an option to purchase) does not run with the land: *Woodall v. Clifton* [1905] 2 Ch. 257 at 279 (although see the discussion of this case in (1955) 19 Conv. 255); *Davenport Central Service Station Ltd v. O'Connell* [1975] 1 N.Z.L.R. 755.

P. & A. SWIFT INVESTMENTS v. COMBINED ENGLISH STORES GROUP PLC

House of Lords [1988] 3 W.L.R. 313

[The holder of a leasehold interest in land (and therefore a lessee, but for the purposes of the following narrative called the landlord) granted a sub-lease to a company (the lessee). The appellant guaranteed performance of the lessee's obligations under the sub-lease. The landlord's interest was later conveyed to the respondent, but the conveyance contained no specific assignment of the benefit of the appellant's guarantee. The lessee defaulted in payment of rent under the lease, and the respondent successfully sued the appellant on its guarantee. On appeal:]

LORD OLIVER OF AYLMERTON. The relationship between the landlord and a surety in a case such as the present is, of course, contractual only. The surety has no interest in the land the subject matter of the demise and there is thus no privity of estate. In seeking, therefore, to enforce the surety's covenant, an assignee of the reversion cannot rely upon the *Grantees of Reversions Act* 1540 (U.K.) (Statute 32 Hen. 8 c. 34), the provisions of which were substantially re-enacted in s. 141 of the *Law of Property Act* 1925 [see *Conveyancing Act* 1919 (N.S.W.), s. 117] and which apply only to covenants between landlord and tenant. His claim to enforce rests upon the common law rule, under which the benefit of the covenant would run with the land if, but only if, the assignee had the legal estate in the land and the covenant was one which "touched and concerned" the land. There is no question but that the first of these conditions is complied with in the instant case, but it is said, first, that a reversion on a lease is not "land" for the purposes of the application of the common law rule and, secondly, and in any event, that the covenant of a surety is no more than a covenant to pay a sum of money which is entirely collateral and does not therefore touch and concern the land.

[His Lordship held that a reversion on a lease is properly "land", and continued:]

In my opinion the question of whether a surety's covenant in a lease touches and concerns the land falls to be determined by the same test as that applicable to the tenant's covenant. That test was formulated by Bayley J. in *Congleton Corp. v. Pattison* (1808) 10 East 130; 103 E.R. 725 and adopted by Farwell J. in *Rogers v. Hosegood* [1900] 2 Ch. 388 at 395: "the covenant must either affect the land as regards mode of occupation, or it must be such as per se, and not merely from collateral circumstances, affects the value of the land."

The meaning of those words "per se, and not merely from collateral circumstances" has been the subject matter of a certain amount of judicial consideration and the judgment of Sir Nicolas Browne-Wilkinson V.-C. in *Kumar v. Dunning* [1987] 3 W.L.R. 1167 (where the problem was identical to that in the instant case save that the covenant was given on an assignment and not on the grant of the lease), contains a careful and helpful review of the authorities. No useful purpose would be served by repeating this here and I am both grateful for and content to accept both his analysis and his conclusion that the correct principle was that pronounced by Best J. in *Vyvyan v. Arthur* (1823) 1 B. & C. 410 at 417; 107 E.R. 152 at 155 and approved by this House in *Dyson v. Forster* [1909] A.C. 98: "The general principle is, that if the performance of the covenant be beneficial to the reversioner, in respect of the lessor's demand, and to no other person, his assignee may sue upon it; but if it be beneficial to the lessor, without regard to his continuing owner [sic] of the estate, it is a mere collateral covenant, upon which the assignee cannot sue."

The Vice-Chancellor stated his conclusion (at 1177): "From these authorities I collect two things. First, that the acid test whether or not a benefit is collateral is that laid down by Best J., namely, is the covenant beneficial to the owner for the time being of the covenantee's land, and to no one else? Secondly, a covenant simply to pay a sum of money, whether by way of insurance premium, compensation or damages, is a covenant capable of touching and concerning the land provided that the existence of the covenant, and the right to payment thereunder, affects the value of the land in whomsoever it is vested for the time being."

It is objected that this states the matter too broadly because, for example, it is said that it would involve the conclusion that a simple covenant to pay an annuity of £x per annum to the owner for the time being of Blackacre would then be treated as a covenant touching and concerning the land because it would enhance the value of the land. This is, I think, to read the Vice-Chancellor's words too literally, for it is, as it seems to me, implicit in them that he is referring to a monetary obligation related to something which issues out of or is to be done on or to the land. His approach to the problem, (which, again, I respectfully adopt) emerges from the following passage from his judgment (at 1174): "The surety covenant is given as a support or buttress to covenants given by a tenant to a landlord. The covenants by the tenant relate not only to the payment of rent, but also to repair, insurance and user of the premises. All such covenants by a tenant in favour of the landlord touch and concern the land, that is, the reversion of the landlord. The performance of some covenants by tenants relates to things done on the land itself (for example, repair and user covenants). Other tenants' covenants (for example, payment of rent and insurance) require nothing to be done on the land itself. They are mere covenants for the payment of money. The covenant to pay rent is the major cause of the landlord's reversion having any value during the continuance of the term. Where there is privity of estate, the tenants' covenant to pay rent touches and concerns the land: *Parker v. Webb* (1822) 3 Salk. 4; 91 E.R. 656. As it seems to me, in principle a covenant by a third party guaranteeing the performance by the tenant of his obligations should touch and concern the reversion as much as do the tenants' covenants themselves. This view accords with what, to my mind, is the commercial common sense and justice of the case. When, as in the present case, the lease has been assigned on the terms that the sureties will guarantee performance by the assignee of the lease, justice and common sense ought to require the sureties, not the original tenant, to be primarily liable in the event of default by the assignee. So long as the reversion is not assigned, that will be the position. Why should the position between the original tenant and the sureties be rendered completely different just because the reversion has been assigned, a transaction wholly outside the control of the original tenant and the sureties?"

I entirely agree and would add only this. It has been said that the surety's obligation is simply that of paying money and, of course, in a sense that is true if one looks only at the remedy which the landlord has against him in the event of default by the tenant. But for my part I do not think that this is a complete analysis. The tenant covenants that he will do or refrain from doing certain things which undoubtedly touch and concern the land. A surety covenants that those things shall be done or not done as the case may be. Now it is true that the remedy for breach will sound in damages only, but the primary obligation is the same, namely that that which is covenanted to be done will be done. Take for instance the tenant's covenant to repair. There is nothing here requiring personal performance by the tenant. The effect of the covenant is that the tenant must procure the premises to be kept in repair. Equally, a guarantee by the surety of the repairing covenant is no more than a covenant or warranty that the guarantor will procure that the tenant, in turn, procures the premises to be kept in repair. The content of the primary obligation is, as it seems to me, exactly the same and if that of the tenant touches and concerns the land that of the surety must, as it seems to me, equally do so.

Formulations of definitive tests are always dangerous, but it seems to me that, without claiming to expound an exhaustive guide, the following provides a satisfactory working test for whether, in any given case, a covenant touches and concerns the land: (1) the covenant benefits only the reversioner for time being, and if separated from the reversion ceases to be of benefit to the covenantee; (2) the covenant affects the nature, quality, mode of user or value of the land of the reversioner; (3) the covenant is not expressed to be personal (that is to say neither being given only to a specific reversioner nor in respect of the obligations only of a specific tenant); (4) the fact that a covenant is to pay a sum of money will not prevent it from touching and concerning the land so long as the three foregoing conditions are satisfied and the covenant is connected with something to be done on, to or in relation to the land.

For my part, I am entirely satisfied that the decision of the Court of Appeal in *Kumar v. Dunning* [1987] 3 W.L.R. 1167 was correct and was reached for the correct reasons. The instant case is indistinguishable in any material respect. Nothing I think turns upon the precise terms of the covenant in either case. It follows that I would dismiss this appeal.

[Lords Keith of Kinkel, Roskill, Templeman, and Ackner agreed.]

Appeal dismissed.

4. Assignment of the lease

(a) Burden of covenants

(i) Running of burden. The rule of the common law, as stated in *Spencer's Case* (1583) 5 Co. Rep. 16a; 77 E.R. 72, was that where a covenant "touches and concerns" the land and relates to a thing already in existence (in esse), such as a covenant to repair an existing house, it will be binding on assignees of the lease. On the other hand, where the covenant "touches and concerns" the land but relates to something not in existence (in posse), such as a covenant to build a new house on the land, the covenant will bind assignees only if the original lessee covenanted for himself *and his assigns*. The distinction between covenants in esse and in posse has now been abolished, and it is no longer necessary for the lessee expressly to covenant for himself and his assigns: the covenant is "deemed to be made by the covenantor on behalf of himself and his successors in title and the persons deriving title under him or them . . . and shall have effect as if such successors and other persons were expressed . . . notwithstanding that the subject matter may not be in existence when the covenant is made": *Conveyancing Act* 1919 (N.S.W.), s. 70A.

(ii) Right of indemnity

MOULE v. GARRETT

Court of Exchequer Chamber (1872) L.R. 7 Ex. 101

[The plaintiff was the lessee of premises under a lease containing a covenant to repair. He assigned the lease to B, who assigned it to the defendants. The assignment from the plaintiff to B, and from B to the defendants, contained express covenants by each to indemnify their respective assignor against all subsequent breaches of the covenants in the lease. The defendants, while in possession, breached the covenant to repair, in respect of which the lessor recovered damages against the plaintiff. In the Court of Exchequer, the plaintiff succeeded in recovering from the defendants the damages he had paid. On appeal.]

COCKBURN C.J. I am of opinion that the judgment of the Court of Exchequer is right, and that it must be affirmed. The defendants are the ultimate assignees of a lease, and the plaintiff, who is suing them for indemnity against the consequence of a breach of a covenant contained in that lease, is the original lessee. There is no doubt that the breach of covenant is one in respect of which the defendants, as such assignees, are liable to the lessor, and that they have acquired by virtue of mesne assignments the same estate which the plaintiff originally took. And I think that taking this estate from the assignee of the plaintiff, their own immediate assignor, they must be taken to have acquired it, subject to the discharge of all the liabilities which the possession of that estate imposed on them under the terms of the original lease, not merely as regards the immediate assignor, but as regards the original lessee.

Another ground on which the judgment below may be upheld, and, as I think, a preferable one, is that, the premises which are the subject of the lease being in the possession of the defendants as ultimate assignees, they were the parties whose duty it was to perform the covenants which were to be performed upon and in respect of those premises. It was their immediate duty to keep in repair, and by their default the lessee, though he had parted with the estate, became liable to make good to the lessor the conditions of the lease. The damage therefore arises through their default, and the general proposition applicable to such a case as the present is, that where one person is compelled to pay damages by the legal default of another, he is entitled to recover from the person by whose default the damage was occasioned the sum so paid. This doctrine, as applicable to cases like the present, is well stated by Mr Leake in his work on *Contracts*, p. 41: "Where the plaintiff has been compelled by law to pay, or, being compellable by law, has paid money which the defendant was ultimately liable to pay, so that the latter obtains the benefit of the payment by the discharge of his liability; under such circumstances the defendant is held indebted to the plaintiff in the amount."

Whether the liability is put on the ground of an implied contract, or of an obligation imposed by law, is a matter of indifference: it is such a duty as the law will enforce. The lessee has been compelled to make good an omission to repair, which has arisen entirely from the default of the defendants, and the defendants are therefore liable to reimburse him.

WILLES J. I am of the same opinion, on the ground that where a party is liable at law by immediate privity of contract which contract also confers a benefit, and the obligation of the contract is common to him and to the defendant, but the whole benefit of the contract is taken by the defendant; the former is entitled to be indemnified by the latter in respect of the performance of the obligation.

[Blackburn, Mellor, Brett and Grove JJ. concurred.]

Judgment affirmed.

NOTE

This common law principle is given statutory force in the context of old system covenants for title, where the assignment of the lease is by way of mortgage: see *Conveyancing Act* 1919 (N.S.W.), s. 78(1)(D).

(b) Benefit of covenants

It is clear from *Spencer's Case* (1583) 5 Co. Rep. 16a; 77 E.R. 72, that an assignee of the lease may sue the lessor on such of the lessor's covenants as "touch and concern" the land.

(c) Informal leases

Privity of estate traditionally has been regarded as a legal relationship, not an equitable one. In accordance with this view, privity of estate can exist only where the lease confers a legal estate; it cannot exist between a lessor and an assignee of a lease enforceable only in equity, in which case the landlord's only remedy for breach of the covenant lies against the original lessee: *Camden v. Batterbury* (1860) 7 C.B. (N.S.) 864; 141 E.R. 1055; *Thornton v. Thompson* [1930] S.A.S.R. 310, discussed (1931) 4 A.L.J. 324. It may be, however, that the courts are now prepared to depart from that view. In *Boyer v. Warbey* [1953] 1 Q.B. 234 the Court of Appeal held that the burden of a covenant by the lessee to redecorate the premises, contained in a lease which was in writing but not in the form of a deed, bound the assignee of the lessee. Lord Denning said (at 245-246):

> I know that before the *Judicature Act* 1873 (U.K.), it was said that the doctrine of covenants running with the land only applied to covenants under seal and not to agreements under hand . . . But since the fusion of law and equity, the position is different. The distinction between agreements under hand and covenants under seal has been largely obliterated. There is no valid reason nowadays why the doctrine of covenants running with the land—or with the reversion—should not apply equally to agreements under hand as to covenants under seal.

The principle espoused by Lord Denning in this passage is convenient, but is it correct to base it upon the fusion of law and equity supposedly effected by the *Judicature Act*? Upon what other grounds might it be based? See further, Fenton, "The Assignment of Informal Leases" (1977) 7 N.Z.U.L. Rev. 342; Martin, "Tenancies by Estoppel, Equitable Leases and Priorities" [1978] Conv. 137; Smith, "The Running of Covenants in Equitable Leases and Equitable Assignments of Legal Leases" (1978) 37 Camb. L.J. 98.

5. Assignment of the reversion

The common law held that covenants which touched and concerned the land could not run with the reversion, as it was thought that a reversion was not a corporeal thing to which the covenants could be attached. The assignee of the reversion could only sue on *implied* covenants, that is, those inherent in the nature of the landlord and tenant relationship, such as the covenant to pay rent, and not on the express covenants in the lease.

To remedy this, the *Grantees of Reversion Act* 1540 (U.K.) (Statute 32 Hen. 8 c. 34) was passed, which provided that assignees of reversions should have the same right of enforcing forfeitures and the same right of suing for breach of any covenant as the original lessor, and further, that the lessee and his assigns should have the same remedies against the assignees of the lessor as the original lessee would have had against the lessor.

The modern counterpart is to be found in ss 117 and 118 of the *Conveyancing Act* 1919 (N.S.W.). Section 117(1) contains two quite separate elements. Its operation may be expressed thus: (1) rent reserved by the lease and the benefit of every lessee's covenant "having reference to the subject-matter" of the lease, is annexed to and passes with the reversion, and may be enforced by the person from time to time entitled to the income from the reversion; *and* (2) every condition of re-entry "and other condition" in the lease is annexed to and passes with the reversion, and may be enforced by the person from time to time entitled to the income from the reversion.

By subs. (2) of s. 117, the benefit of every condition of re-entry or forfeiture for breach of condition in the lease may be enforced by the person from time to time entitled to the income of the reversion, notwithstanding that he or she did not become entitled to that income until after the condition of re-entry or forfeiture became enforceable.

By s. 118, the burden of a covenant by the lessor "with reference to the subject-matter of the lease" is annexed to and runs with the reversion and may be enforced by the persons in whom the lease is vested from time to time.

The Act of 1540 applied only to leases by deed, but ss 117 and 118 extend to leases in writing not under seal, although not to oral leases: *Ex parte Anderson; Re Green* (1946) 46 S.R. (N.S.W.) 389 at 392. The words in s. 117, "having reference to the subject-matter" of the lease, and the similar expression in s. 118, are regarded as synonymous with "touching and concerning" the land: *Re Hunter's Lease; Giles v. Hutchings* [1942] Ch. 124. Further, ss 117 and 118 (like their 1540 forebear) apply only where there exists privity of estate: *Kumar v. Dunning* [1987] 2 All E.R. 801 at 806. And so, for example, s. 117 does not enable an assignee of the reversion to enforce obligations under a surety given by a third party to guarantee performance of the tenant's obligations under the lease, there being no privity of estate (or privity of contract) between the assignee of the reversion and the guarantor: *Kumar v. Dunning* [1987] 2 All E.R. 801 at 806; *Sacher Investments Pty Ltd v. Forma Stereo Consultants Pty Ltd* [1976] 1 N.S.W.L.R. 5 at 11-12. However, it will be observed that element (2) (as it is numbered above) of s. 117(1) goes considerably further than element (1), and has the effect of annexing to the reversion "every . . . other condition" in the lease, so as to cause to pass with the reversion the benefit of all covenants regardless of whether they touch and concern the land: *Dalegrove Pty Ltd v. Isles Parking Station Pty Ltd* (1988) 12 N.S.W.L.R. 546 at 555; Megarry and Wade, op. cit., pp. 758-759.

6. Land under the Real Property Act

Sections 117 and 118 of the *Conveyancing Act* 1919 (N.S.W.) extend to land under the provisions of the *Real Property Act* 1900 (N.S.W.). The *Real Property Act* itself has three provisions which are relevant to assignments of leases and reversions. By ss 51 and 52 of the *Real Property Act*, it appears that upon registration of every "transfer" (the term "transfer" is defined in s. 3(a) to mean "[t]he passing of any estate or interest in land under this Act"), the transferee becomes subject to and liable for the same requirements and liabilities to which he or she would have been subject and liable had he or she been the original lessee (s. 51), and the transferee may sue upon the lease to recover any damages thereunder, such as for breach of covenant (s. 52). These two sections appear by their terms to apply only to the transfer of the *lease*, not to transfer of the reversion. But the High Court has assumed that they apply also to transfer of the reversion, so as to vest in the transferee the rights of the original landlord to sue upon the tenant's covenants in the lease, although (so the court held), s. 52 does not go so far as to enable a transferee of the reversion to sue for breach of covenant by the tenant where the breach was complete before the transfer: *Measures v. McFadyen* (1910) 11 C.L.R. 723.

Section 40(3) provides that the person recorded in any folio of the Register as entitled to the land therein described shall be held in every court to be seised of the reversion expectant upon any lease recorded thereon, and to have "all powers, rights, and remedies to which a reversioner is by law entitled, and shall be subject to all covenants and conditions therein expressed to be performed on the part of the lessor". The reason for the subsection is obscure, as it is doubtful whether it adds anything to ss 117 and 118 of the *Conveyancing Act* 1919 (N.S.W.): see Baalman, *The Torrens System in New South Wales* (2nd ed.), pp. 168-169.

VI. REMEDIES

A. DISTRESS FOR RENT

The traditional remedy by which the landlord recovered arrears of rent was the right to levy distress for rent. At common law this right entitled the landlord to enter the premises and impound chattels found thereon. Only as much as was reasonably necessary to cover the outstanding rent and expenses could be taken. Much of the old learning on the remedy of distress will be found conveniently summarised in Megarry and Wade, op. cit., pp. 691-694.

Distress for rent has been abolished: see *Landlord and Tenant Amendment (Distress Abolition) Act* 1930 (N.S.W.), s. 2.

B. ACTION FOR COMPENSATION FOR THE USE OF THE LAND

Where there is an agreement to pay a defined amount for rent, the landlord is entitled to recover the rent accrued in the same way as he or she is entitled to recover any other debt. This is so whether the covenant to pay rent is express or implied.

Where the tenant has agreed to pay rent, but no precise amount has been agreed upon, the landlord is entitled to an action for use and occupation. The landlord will be awarded what is a reasonable sum for use and occupation of the land: *Mayor, etc., of Thetford v. Tyler* (1845) 8 Q.B. 95 at 100; 115 E.R. 810 at 812; *Gibson v. Kirk* (1841) 1 Q.B. 850; 113 E.R. 1357. But there must be an express or implied agreement to pay for the use of the land: see *A.-G. v. De Keyser's Royal Hotel Limited* [1920] A.C. 508 at 533; *Australian Provincial Assurance Ltd v. Rogers* (1943) 43 S.R. (N.S.W.) 202 at 204; *Sanders v. Cooper* [1974] W.A.R. 129.

It has been said that there are four elements necessary in an action for use and occupation: that the relationship of landlord and tenant exists between the parties; that the use was on terms that the tenant would pay; that the tenant in fact used or occupied the premises (constructive occupation is sufficient: *Woodhouse v. Ah Peck* (1900) 16 W.N. (N.S.W.) 166); and the quantum that the landlord should recover: see Lewis and Cassidy, *Tenancy Law of New South Wales*, Vol. 1, p. 339. What is a reasonable sum is a matter to be determined on all the evidence, but where the parties have entered into an agreement for a lease which is unenforceable for some reason (for example, for failure to comply with the *Statute of Frauds*) the amount agreed upon as rent will be an important, though not necessarily decisive, factor in determining what is a reasonable sum: *Murdock v. Kennedy* (1952) 69 W.N. (N.S.W.) 191 at 192-193.

Where the tenancy has been lawfully terminated, but the tenant refuses to vacate the premises, the landlord is entitled to "mesne profits", that is, to damages for the rent which might have been obtained but for the tenant's continued occupation. The landlord may claim for the period from the date of service on the lessee of the court process claiming possession to the date when physical possession is recovered, for service of the process constitutes a notional re-entry by the landlord: *Canas Property Co. Ltd v. K.L. Television Services Ltd* [1970] 2 Q.B. 433 at 442; *Lidsdale Nominees Pty Ltd v. Elkharadly* [1979] V.R. 84; *N.G.L. Properties Pty Ltd v. Harlington Pty Ltd* [1979] V.R. 92 at 98.

A tenant who wrongfully remains in possession after the determination of the tenancy by effluxion of time is a trespasser, and the landlord is entitled to receive as damages the ordinary letting value of the premises for the period of the trespass. It is not necessary for the landlord to prove that he or she could or would have let the premises to someone else in the absence of the trespasser: *Swordheath Properties Ltd v. Tabet* [1979] 1 W.L.R. 285 at 288.

C. DAMAGES AND INJUNCTION

The lessor is entitled to damages for breach of covenant (express or implied) by the lessee, and, in an appropriate case, to an injunction to restrain further breaches. For a discussion of the principles to be applied in assessing damages, see *Maori Trustee v. Bolton* [1971] N.Z.L.R. 226 at 236-239. Where the lessee breaches the covenant to yield up possession at the termination of the lease, the lessor's damages will include the cost of removing the lessee and the loss of profits from the premises for the period during which the lessee wrongfully remains in possession. The question of damages for breach of a covenant to repair is discussed above p. 599.

D. FORFEITURE BY RE-ENTRY

1. The right to forfeit

It is common for leases to contain a provision whereby the lessor is entitled to re-enter the premises and forfeit the lease for breach of covenant on the part of the lessee. In such a case, the lessor has the option of forfeiting the lease for the tenant's breach, either by commencing an action for possession or (in some situations) by "peaceable re-entry" upon the land. A lessor who chooses physically to re-enter should take care not to breach the modern equivalent of the Forcible Entry Acts of 1381, 1391 and 1429, to be found in ss 18-20 of the *Imperial Acts Application Act* 1969 (N.S.W.). Section 18 of that Act provides:

No person shall make any entry into any land except where such entry is given by law and, in such case, with no more force than is reasonably necessary.

Subject to these provisions, however, a landlord may use such force as is reasonably necessary to expel the tenant without becoming liable for an action for damages for trespass or assault: see *Hemmings v. Stoke Poges Golf Club* [1920] 1 K.B. 720; *Aglionby v. Cohen* [1955] 1 Q.B. 558; *Housing Commission (N.S.W.) v. Allen* (1967) 86 W.N. (N.S.W.) (Pt 2) 204 at 206-207.

Where a lessor has the right either to take curial proceedings to obtain possession of the premises from the lessee or peaceably to re-enter, and elects to adopt the former course of action, he may have lost the right peaceably to re-enter, because the institution of the proceedings involves the parties in an issue as to the lessor's right to possession: *Argyle Art Centre Pty Ltd v. Argyle Bond & Free Stores Co. Pty Ltd* [1976] 1 N.S.W.L.R. 377.

In New South Wales it is no longer lawful to terminate a lease of a "dwelling-house" by re-entry. Possession of a dwelling-house the subject of a tenancy may only be taken pursuant to a court order: *Landlord and Tenant (Amendment) Act* 1978 (N.S.W.), s. 2, inserting a new section, s. 2AA, into the *Landlord and Tenant Act* 1899 (N.S.W.). (A tenancy of a single room in a dwelling-house, the tenant sharing with others the use of kitchen, bathroom and toilet facilities, is not a tenancy of a "dwelling-house" for the purposes of s. 2AA of the *Landlord and Tenant Act* 1899 (N.S.W.): *Louinder v. Stuckey* [1984] 2 N.S.W.L.R. 354.) Further, where the premises are the subject of a "residential tenancy agreement" (as to which, see above p. 576), possession may only be taken pursuant to a notice of termination and, if the tenant fails to vacate in response to the notice, an order of the Residential Tenancies Tribunal: *Residential Tenancies Act* 1987 (N.S.W.), ss 53, 57, 72.

A lessor has no right to re-enter and forfeit unless the lease expressly or by implication gives the lessor that right or unless the lessor has some statutory or common law right to forfeit the lease (as, for example, where the tenant has repudiated her or his obligations under the lease—although repudiation is difficult to establish: see *Shevill v. Builders Licensing Board* (1982) 56 A.L.J.R. 793: cf. *Progressive Mailing House Pty Ltd v. Tabali Pty Ltd* (1985) 59 A.L.J.R. 373; *Wood Factory Pty Ltd v. Kiritos Pty Ltd* (1985) 2 N.S.W.L.R. 105. The mere fact that the lessee has breached a covenant does not, of itself, give a right to forfeit the lease. In this regard, however, reference should be made to s. 85(1)(d) of the *Conveyancing Act* 1919, which implies into a lease the power to re-enter and forfeit the lease in certain circumstances. Section 74 of the same Act enables this implied power to be varied by agreement, a course usually adopted in practice to impose terms more favourable to the lessor. Further, there is no forfeiture until the lessor exercises his right: breach by the lessee does not automatically terminate the lease (even, it seems, where the lease expressly provides that it shall determine upon breach: *Jones v. Carter* (1846) 15 M. & W. 718 at 725; 153 E.R. 1040 at 1043; *Quesnel Forks Gold Mining Co. Ltd v. Ward* [1920] A.C. 222 at 227).

A distinction should be drawn between a right to forfeit for breach of *covenant* and a right to forfeit for breach of *condition*. A condition is a fundamental term of the lease, breach of which, as in the general law of contract, entitles the lessor to treat the lease as at an end, and, unlike the position with regard to mere breach of covenant, entitles the lessor to re-enter without any express or implied power to that effect contained in the lease. It is quite open for the parties to stipulate that the lessee's obligations shall be conditions rather than covenants. Even here, however, the lease is voidable, not void, on beach of the condition: the lessor must choose to exercise the right of re-entry: see generally on conditions, Lewis and Cassidy, op. cit., Vol. 1, pp. 382-383; *Bashir v. Commissioner for Lands* [1960] A.C. 44; *Shevill v. Builders Licensing Board* (1982) 56 A.L.J.R. 793.

2. Exercise of the right

MOORE v. ULLCOATS MINING CO. LTD

Chancery Division [1908] 1 Ch. 575

[A lease of mines contained a covenant by the lessee to allow the lessor or his agents to inspect the mines from time to time. The lease also provided that in the event of default by the lessee in the performance or observance of any of the covenants in the lease, the lessor could re-enter, and that thereupon the lease would determine. On 26 April 1907, the lessee, in breach of his covenant refused to allow the lessor's agent to inspect the mines. On 29 April, the lessor gave notice that "the lease . . . [has] been determined by . . . breach of the covenant to permit inspection", and that "we intend to re-enter upon the premises demised by the said lease". On 3 May, a further notice was given demanding "possession of the mines". Then, on 4 May, the lessor (plaintiff) issued a writ against the lessee (defendant) claiming the following relief: (1) recovery of possession; (2) mesne profits; (3) an injunction restraining the defendants from further working the mines so as to damage them; (4) an order permitting inspection of the mines by the plaintiffs "as often as they shall think proper"; (5) a receiver; (6) damages; (7) costs. One of the issues raised was whether the lease had been effectively determined by the lessor by the issue of the writ or by the prior notices.]

WARRINGTON J. Now, two questions arise; the first is: Is the writ issued on 4 May a re-entry within the words of the proviso for re-entry or equivalent to a re-entry? I think that it is now settled that under a proviso for re-entry, such as the one in the present case, a writ claiming possession simpliciter, and any further relief which is incidental to a claim for possession, would be equivalent to a re-entry, and if this writ is to be regarded as a writ of that nature, then there has been a sufficient re-entry within the meaning of the covenant, and the lease is terminated. The question I have to determine on this part of the case is this: Is this writ an unequivocal claim for possession, a claim by which both parties are bound? It is argued on behalf of the plaintiffs that claims 3 and 4 of the writ must be read as claims for interlocutory relief only, and that not only is an opposite construction a wrong construction to put upon them, but it is so impossible a construction that it is quite absurd to suppose that those claims can have any such meaning. I think the real question that I have to consider is whether this writ is in such a form that it would not have been open to the plaintiffs thereafter, if they had considered that their most convenient course, to ask for relief on the footing of the lease being in existence, and to abandon their claim for possession. I think I am bound to come to the conclusion that this writ was equivocal, and that it is a writ to which the plaintiffs, had they been so minded, might have given a meaning contrary to that which they now contend is the only meaning which could be given to it.

[His Lordship then considered the effect of the inclusion in the writ of claims (3) and (4), and continued:]

. . . It seems to me, therefore, that the writ was not an uneqivocal demand for possession. I think the writ was so framed that it might have been possible for the plaintiffs, if they had been so minded, to say, "We will go for the other relief expressed in the writ; we will not go for possession": in other words, I think that the claim for possession and the claim for an injunction and for the order expressed in claim 4 are inconsistent, and therefore the plaintiffs cannot obtain possession in this present action.

It is enough for me to refer to *Evans v. Davis* (1878) 10 Ch. D. 747; 148 E.R. 1503, before Fry J. It is quite true that the facts there were different from those in the present case, and that there were some circumstances in that case which rendered it easier for Fry J. to come to the conclusion to which he did than it is for me to come to the same conclusion in this case, but the principle laid down by Fry J. applies as much to this case as it applied to that. That principle is this, that the writ, in order to be equivalent to re-entry under the proviso for re-entry, must be an unequivocal demand for possession and nothing else.

Then the plaintiffs contend that if the writ was not an unequivocal demand there was a previous expression of their election contained in the two notices of 29 April and 3 May, to which I have already referred. I am of opinion upon the authorities— and I refer particularly to *Jones v. Carter* (1845) 15 M. & W. 718 at 725; 153 E.R. 1040 at 1043 and to a dictum of Bayley J.'s in *Fenn v. Smart* (1810) 12 East 444 at 448; 104 E.R. 173—that where the condition in the lease is that the landlord may re-enter he must actually re-enter, or he must do that which is in law equivalent to re-entry, namely, commence an action for the purpose of obtaining possession. Parke B. in *Jones v. Carter* (1845) 15 M. & W. 718 at 725; 153 E.R. 1040 at 1043 puts that quite plainly. [Warrington J. discussed *Jones v. Carter*, and continued:] In *Fenn v. Smart* Bayley J.—although it is only a dictum in the course of the argument, but it shews the view he took—said: "Must not the necessity of an entry depend upon the wording of the condition? If the words be, that upon the doing of such an act, the reversioner may enter, there must be an entry to avoid the estate; but if the estate be granted upon condition that if the grantee do such an act, the estate shall thereupon immediately cease and determine, there no entry is necessary." He there draws a distinction between the two classes of cases. In my opinion the present case falls within the first class, and I do not see how it is possible, on any construction of this proviso for re-entry, to say that the lessors have re-entered, when all that they have done is to give a notice of their intention to re-enter, founded on a statement that the lease had determined, which had not in fact happened, or a demand for possession founded on that notice. I think the only thing here that could be relied upon as equivalent to actual re-entry was the issue of the writ. In my opinion the issue of that writ, for the reasons I have stated, was not unequivocal, and therefore the plaintiffs are not entitled to possession.

The result is, in my view, that the action fails altogether, and there must be judgment for the defendants with costs.

[The plaintiffs appealed; but ultimately, after the appeal had been argued for several days, the judgment below was discharged by consent and the case was settled.]

NOTES AND QUESTIONS

1. A lease contained a covenant restricting the use to which the premises could be put by the lessee. It also contained a provision permitting re-entry by the lessor for breach of covenant by the tenant. The lessor, alleging a breach of covenant by the lessee, issued a writ claiming, inter alia, (1) possession and (4) injunctions restraining breaches of the covenant as to user. When the lessor asked for certain injunctions pending trial, the lessee took the preliminary point that the lessor, having issued a writ claiming possession, had effected a re-entry and thereby determined the lease, and could not thereafter seek injunctions on the basis that the lease was still on foot. Was the objection well founded? See *Calabar Properties Ltd v. Seagull Autos Ltd* [1969] 1 Ch. 451.

2. Where the lessor exercises the right to forfeiture for breach of covenant, it is the *service* of the court process, and not merely its *issue*, which is equivalent to re-entry: *Canas Property Co. Ltd v. K. L. Television Services Ltd* [1970] 2 Q.B. 433 at 442. The proper procedure is for the lessor to claim *rent* up to the date of service of the process, and *mesne profits* from that date to the date of delivery of possession: at 442.

3. There are conflicts in the cases as to the physical extent of the re-entry necessary where the landlord chooses to terminate the lease by physically re-entering. In some Australian States, it appears to be sufficient for the lessor merely to do something amounting to an unequivocal "demand" for physical possession, without actually obtaining it, such as telling the tenant (by verbal or written notice) to vacate the premises: see, for example, *Fremantle Trades Hall Industrial Assoc. v. Victor Motor Co. Ltd* [1963] W.A.R. 201; *N.G.L. Properties Pty Ltd v. Harlington Pty Ltd* [1979] V.R. 92; *Price v. Mayman* [1948] S.A.S.R. 241; *Ex parte Whelan* [1986] 1 Qd R. 500. But in New South Wales (as in England), the lessor must obtain possession by the physical exclusion of the lessee or anyone properly claiming under the lessee: *Tatersall's Hotel Penrith Pty Ltd v. Permanent Trustee Co. of New South Wales Ltd* (1942) 42 S.R. (N.S.W.) 104; *Consolidated Development Pty Ltd v. Holt* (1986) 6 N.S.W.L.R. 607.

3. Formal requirements

(a) Breach of covenant to pay rent

At common law, before a landlord could exercise a right under the lease to re-enter and forfeit for breach of the covenant to pay rent, he or she had first to make a formal demand for payment, unless the lease expressly dispensed with the need for such formal demand: *Boroughe's* case (1596) 4 Co. Rep. 72b at 73a; 76 E.R. 1043 at 1044; as to the formalities required for such a demand, see Lewis and Cassidy, op. cit., Vol. 1, pp. 385, 386. The learning surrounding demands for payment of rent is now largely of historical interest only because of legislative provisions which, subject to agreement to the contrary, imply into leases a power on the part of the lessor to re-enter without formal demand for payment where rent is in arrear for a specified period: see *Conveyancing Act* 1919 (N.S.W.), s. 85(1)(d) (one month). It is most unusual for leases to express an intention or agreement contrary to this provision and to require the making of a formal demand for payment. But in any event, even where the lessor is not otherwise relieved of the duty to make a formal demand, there is legislation which provides that he or she is entitled to re-enter without prior demand where the rent is more than six months in arrears: *Landlord and Tenant Act* 1899 (N.S.W.), s. 8(1), (2). These provisions are discussed further below p. 644.

(b) Breach of covenant other than to pay rent

Where the lesser seeks to re-enter for breach of a covenant other than to pay rent, s. 129(1) of the *Conveyancing Act* 1919 (N.S.W.) requires the giving of certain prior notice:

> 129. (1) A right of re-entry or forfeiture under any proviso or stipulation in a lease, for a breach of any covenant, condition, or agreement (express or implied) in the lease, shall not be enforceable by action or otherwise unless and until the lessor serves on the lessee a notice—
>
> (a) specifying the particular breach complained of; and
>
> (b) if the breach is capable of remedy, requiring the lessee to remedy the breach; and
>
> (c) in case the lessor claims compensation in money for the breach, requiring ·the lessee to pay the same,
>
> and the lessee fails within a reasonable time thereafter to remedy the breach, if it is capable of remedy, and where compensation in money is required to pay reasonable compensation to the satisfaction of the lessor for the breach.

This provision applies notwithstanding any agreement to the contrary (s. 129(10)), and does not affect the rules relating to forfeiture for breach of the covenant to pay rent: s. 129(8).

FOX v. JOLLY

House of Lords [1916] 1 A.C. 1

[The respondent brought an action to recover possession of premises for breach of covenants to repair. The lease contained a proviso for re-entry for breach of covenant. The lessor served a notice upon the tenant alleging breach of the covenants to repair. The lessee challenged the validity of the notice.]

LORD BUCKMASTER L.C. The question that is raised is very simple, involving the consideration of only a few facts and but one section of an Act of Parliament; it is, however, of undoubted importance to landlords and tenants, and consequently it may be desirable to state their relative position in some detail. Before the passing of the *Conveyancing Act* of 1881, a right of re-entry reserved in a lease conditional upon breach of a covenant to repair could be enforced by the landlord at common law without the tenant having opportunity to meet the complaint, and often without his knowing that the breach had in fact occurred. It is true that the courts of equity attempted to mitigate the harshness of this procedure, and in several reported cases restrained the landlords from exercising their rights where the breach was one which, by accident or surprise, the tenant had been unable to rectify. There was, however, no general rule relating to such relief on which reliance could be placed. In these circumstances the *Conveyancing Act* of 1881 was passed, and it was to extend and render certain the rights of tenants in such cases that s. 14 of that statute was framed. Subsection 1 of that section is in the following terms: "A right of re-entry or forfeiture under any proviso or stipulation in a lease, for a breach of any covenant or condition in the lease, shall not be enforceable, by action or otherwise, unless and until the lessor serves on the lessee a notice specifying the particular breach complained of, and, if the breach is capable of remedy, requiring the lessee to remedy the breach, and, in any case, requiring the lessee to make compensation in money for the breach, and the lessee fails, within a reasonable time thereafter, to remedy the breach, if it is capable of remedy, and to make reasonable compensation in money, to the satisfaction of the lessor, for the breach."

The effect of this subsection is plain. The right of re-entry which the lessor enjoys on the breach of a covenant is not capable of being exercised against the lessee until the conditions in that subsection have been satisfied. If such condition were not satisfied and entry were attempted at common law, such entry would be a trespass; if proceedings were instituted to obtain possession they would be instantly demurrable. That is the meaning of the phrase, "shall not be enforceable by action or otherwise". Now the conditions precedent which the lessor must perform are these. He must serve a notice, and that notice must specify the breach of covenant which is the subject of complaint. That is, he must point out the covenant which he says is broken, and he must specify the breach of which he complains. He must also call upon the lessee to remedy the breach, and if he requires compensation in money he must ask for it. After this has been done a reasonable time must elapse in which the lessee has the opportunity of complying with the requirements of the notice. It is only when this has been done, when the time has expired, and the work is incomplete, that the landlord can proceed to the assertion of his rights.

All this is common and familiar ground, and I do not know that it is in any way disputed by the appellants in this case, whose real complaint is that in the particular circumstances in which they stand no sufficient notice specifying the breach of contract was served upon them within the meaning of the section. This leads me to examine the facts that have given rise to the present dispute. . . .

In March of 1912 the premises were out of repair, and on March 21 of that year a notice was served dated the 20th, the sufficiency or insufficiency of which is the sole matter in this appeal. The notice was framed in paragraphs. The first set out in full the repairing covenants, and also a covenant as to painting inside and out. The second paragraph was in these terms: "The abovementioned covenants have been broken, and the particular breaches which are complained of are the committing or allowing the dilapidations mentioned in the schedule hereto." And para. 4 stated that if the requirements of the notice were not complied with within a reasonable time power of re-entry would be enforced. This notice has unquestionably complied with the first condition referred to in s. 14 of the Act. It has plainly set out the covenants which it is alleged are broken, and the schedule contains what is alleged by the respondent to be a sufficient specification of the breach. The work mentioned in this schedule was not done within a reasonable time, and the present proceedings were accordingly instituted by the respondent against the people who were in actual occupation of the premises, claiming that he was entitled to enforce his right of re-entry. . . .

Now the schedule is attacked on several grounds. It is said that it does not tell the tenant what it is he ought to do in order to remedy the breach of which the complaint is made. I am not prepared to accede to that view of the schedule. But even if it did not, I can find nowhere in the section any words which cast upon the landlord the obligation of telling the tenant what it is that he must do. All that the landlord is bound to do is to state particulars of the breaches of covenants of which he complains and call upon the lessee to remedy them. The means by which the breach is to be remedied is a matter for the lessee and not for the lessor. In many cases specification of the breach will of itself suggest the only possible remedy. For example, complaint that a covenant to paint or to paper has been broken can only be met by painting and papering. But it does not follow that this is always so. A particular covenant to keep the roof watertight, if broken, would be sufficiently defined by a reference to the covenant, a statement that the roof had not been kept watertight, and that the tenant was required to remedy the omission; the means by which this could be accomplished would be for the tenant to determine.

It was further urged that the schedule called upon the tenant to make examination on his own account of certain parts of the premises, and that this was a request to survey rather than a request to repair. It is true that in two cases, that of the roof and the drains, the schedule contains the following directions: "Examine, repair, and reinstate all broken or loose tiles to main and w.c. roofs." "Examine and repair and put in good sanitary condition all sinks, cisterns, waterclosets, supply and waste pipes, ball valves and taps, and all drains and gullies, and flush out the same." Both these clauses would, in my opinion, have been perfectly good if the word "examine" were omitted; and I cannot see that its introduction vitiates the rest of the clause. It is true, also, that the schedule does not, except in two cases, refer to the numbers of the houses where particular work is to be done, and it is suggested that each house should have been particularised and the schedule separated so as to apply to each in turn. In certain cases this might be necessary, but each case must depend upon its own circumstances, and I can see no reason for such a course in the present instance. All these premises form one block of similar houses; they are held on one lease, are bound by one covenant, and it is alleged in general terms that the covenants have been broken throughout. It is indeed admitted that, in part at least, the breaches as specified in the schedule were sufficiently specified without the numbers. But then it is said that though this may be true the whole of the notice is rendered useless because other breaches are stated in general terms, and in particular because the schedule concludes with a general statement in the following words: "Well and substantially repair, uphold, maintain, and put the premises and appurtenances in thoroughly good repair and condition, and note that the completion of the items mentioned in this schedule does not excuse the execution of other repairs if found necessary."

I do not think the description in the schedule is too general in its nature, nor am I able to see that the addition of the general phrase at the foot can possibly destroy the efficacy of the schedule as a whole. No form whatever is provided by the statute as the form in which the notice is to be given. It might be associated with useless and irrelevant matter, and it would none the less be a notice under the section if it was clear from its terms that it was so intended and if in fact it contained in plain language the information the section requires.

My Lords, several authorities were referred to in the course of the arguments to which some reference is necessary. The first is *Lock v. Pearce* [1893] 2 Ch. 271. In that case no request was made for compensation in the notice. It was none the less held that it was good. The notice also demanded payment of the surveyor's fees, which the lessor had no right to require, and it was decided that this in no way vitiated the notice. So far, therefore, as this case affects the matter it affords authority for the views I have expressed.

The next case is *Fletcher v. Nokes* [1897] 1 Ch. 271. In that case a notice was served containing no further details than the statement that the covenants for repairing the inside and outside of certain houses had been broken. It was decided, and in my opinion quite rightly, that this notice did not comply with the terms of the statute.

The judgment of North J., however, contained statements which have, I think, been misunderstood in one of the subsequent cases; he said: "Suppose that s. 14 had not been passed, and the previous law had remained in operation, and the landlord had brought an action against the tenant for breach of covenant, the first thing which the landlord would have been compelled to do would be to give particulars of the breaches on which he relied, in order that the tenant might know what he had to meet. I think that s. 14 was intended to place the tenant in a better position than he was in before. He was to have the option of doing, before action brought, all those things the neglect of which would have been the ground of relief against him if s. 14 had not been passed. It is impossible to suppose that the tenant was intended to be before action in a worse position, with respect to alleged breaches, than he would formerly have been in after action. I think the notice which is to be given under s. 14 ought to be such a notice as will enable the tenant to understand with reasonable certainty what it is which he is required to do. I do not mean that the landlord need go through every room in a house and point out every defect. But the notice ought to be so distinct as to direct the attention of the tenant to the particular things of which the landlord complains, so that the tenant may have an opportunity of remedying them before an action to enforce forfeiture of the lease is brought against him."

I see no reason to differ from this statement, except so far as it seeks to establish the standard—often fluctuating and uncertain—of particulars in an action as a test of the sufficiency of the notice. Even, however, if this were accepted, it should be remembered that the particulars which would be required in an action that merely claimed possession for breach of a covenant to repair would not necessarily be as detailed and minute as the particulars that would be wanted where a claim was being made for damages for breach of the covenant, and it is rather in comparison with this latter class of particulars that the appellant seeks to have the notice tested.

The next case, of *Penton v. Barnett* [1898] 1 Q.B. 276, is a case which has no bearing upon the present dispute, excepting for the following statement in the judgment of Collins L.J. (at 281): "I think, however, that we ought to construe the words 'particular breach' in the section according to the obvious intention of the Legislature, which was that the tenant should be informed of the particular condition of the premises which he was required to remedy. The expression 'breach' means the neglect to deal with the condition of the premises so pointed out, and not merely failure to comply with the covenants of the lease. The common sense of the matter is, that the tenant is to have full notice of what he is required to do."

A statement to the similar effect was made by Lord Russell in the case of *Horsey Estate Ltd v. Steiger* [1899] 2 Q.B. 79 at 91. These cases add little to the former decision of North J., they only express the same view in different language.

Re Serle [1898] 1 Ch. 652 involved a different question. In that case the notice was sufficiently specific with regard to two of the covenants referred to, but was indefinite in relation to another. Kekewich J. held that it was bad altogether. The exact point decided in that case does not arise here for decision and it may be reserved for the future. So far as it assumed that the landlord would be at liberty to proceed to re-enter for breach of the covenant which had been the subject of the indefinite description, it was not, I think, warranted by the terms of the statute. The landlord could not re-enter for such a breach, since in respect of that covenant he had not satisfied the statutory requirements; but it does not necessarily follow that imperfect description of the breach of one covenant would take away from him the right to re-enter for breach of the other covenants which had been sufficiently described.

The last case is that of *Pannell v. City of London Brewery Co.* [1900] 1 Ch. 496, where it was decided that a notice which specified two breaches and something else which was not a breach was none the less good since the breach complained of had been specified together with the addition of something which was immaterial.

I regard this view as the correct interpretation of the section. The notice must state with sufficient particularity the breach of which the landlord complains, and that breach the tenant must satisfy within a reasonable time. If he does satisfy it, it would not be open to the landlord to allege that there was another breach of another covenant, which had been referred to in the notice, but had not been sufficiently specified, which had not been remedied.

In the present case I think the notice sufficiently specified the landlord's complaints. It gave the tenant adequate notice of what he was required to do, and it provided full and sufficient information upon which he could determine what course of action he should adopt. For these reasons I think this appeal should fail.

I have only to add that it would be very unfortunate if, in every case where a landlord was serving notice under s. 14, he should feel himself bound to obtain a surveyor's detailed specification of the work to be done. It would greatly increase the cost which, if the work were performed by the tenant before proceedings were instituted, would fall on the landlord, or, if the tenant were compelled to obtain relief, would, by the Act of 1892, fall upon the tenant.

I am glad to think that no such obligation is imposed by the statute.

[Lords Atkinson, Sumner and Parmoor came to a similar result.]

Appeal dismissed.

NOTES AND QUESTIONS

1. A landlord served a notice pursuant to an alleged breach of covenant to repair. The notice said, inter alia, "2. That you have failed and neglected to keep in good and tenantable repair the [premises] on the said land". The High Court held that the notice was invalid, as it did not specify with sufficient particularity the breach complained of: see *Gerraty v. McGavin* (1914) 18 C.L.R. 152 at 159-160, 164-165.

2. The *Conveyancing Act* 1919 (N.S.W.), s. 129 requires the notice to be given in a prescribed form. The scope of permissible departure from the exact terms of the prescribed form is discussed in *Ex parte Dally-Watkins; Re Wilson* (1955) 72 W.N. (N.S.W.) 454, and *Johnson v. Senes and Berger* (1961) 78 W.N. (N.S.W.) 861: see generally Lewis and Cassidy, op. cit., Vol. 1, pp. 403-407.

3. In *Holden v. Blaiklock* [1974] 2 N.S.W.L.R. 262, a lease for two years contained a proviso that upon non-performance of any covenant, the lease should become a tenancy from week to week, terminable upon one week's notice in writing. Lee J. held that the proviso was "a right of . . . forfeiture" arising under a "stipulation in a lease" within the meaning of s. 129(1), and that such right was not enforceable until after the lessor had given the lessee the notice required by s. 129(1) and had otherwise complied with the section. See also *Plymouth Corp. v. Harvey* [1971] 1 W.L.R. 549.

4. Section 129(1) applies even where the breach of covenant by the lessee is involuntary: see *Halliard Property Co. Ltd v. Jack Segal Ltd* [1978] 1 W.L.R. 377 (proviso for re-entry on bankruptcy of lessee's sureties).

5. Can the lessor himself remedy the tenant's breach of covenant and then serve a notice under s. 129 requiring the tenant to compensate the lessor for the cost of the remedial work on pain of forfeiture? See *SEDAC Investments Ltd v. Tanner* [1982] 1 W.L.R. 1342.

6. Where the lessor is proceeding for breach of a qualified covenant against assignment (the lessee having assigned without consent), the notice should be served upon the assignee, in whom the term has vested and who is the person concerned to avoid forfeiture, and not on the original lessee: *Old Grovebury Manor Farm Ltd v. W. Seymour Plant Sales & Hire Ltd* [1979] 3 All E.R. 504.

4. Waiver

The point has been made above that breach of a covenant or condition does not automatically make the lease void; it is voidable at the option of the lessor. It is, therefore, open to the lessor to waive the right to forfeit for breach. Waiver may be express or implied. It has been said that there will be waiver where the lessor "with knowledge of the facts upon which his right to re-enter arises, does some unequivocal act recognising the continued existence of the lease": *Matthews v. Smallwood* [1910] 1 Ch. 777 at 786 per Parker J. The usual situation where waiver occurs is where the lessor accepts rent after receiving notice of the breach of covenant.

SEGAL SECURITIES LTD v. THOSEBY

Queen's Bench Division [1963] 1 Q.B. 887

[A maisonette was demised to the tenant for a term of 21 years. Rent was payable quarterly in advance. The tenant covenanted in the lease "to use the demised premises for the purpose of a private residence in the occupation of one household only". In the period immediately before June 1962, the tenant had two other women sharing the premises with her: one was a personal friend who shared the accommodation, meals and expenses on terms yielding no profit to the tenant; the other was a paying guest who had come in answer to a newspaper advertisement and who did not share the meals or live as part of the family. On 8 June 1962, the landlord served a notice on the tenant under s. 146 of the *Law of Property Act* 1925 (the equivalent of s. 129 of the *Conveyancing Act* 1919 (N.S.W.)) alleging breach of the covenant as to user and giving 28 days to remedy the breach. The 28 days was due to expire on 6 July, but the quarter day for payment of rent fell on 24 June. On 25 June, the solicitors for the landlord wrote to the tenant in the following terms: "Without prejudice. On behalf of our clients . . . we should be glad if you would forward to us a remittance for £75 being the quarter's rent due on the 24th instant. . . . This demand and any receipt for rent is made or given without prejudice to the service of the [notice] . . . and to any breaches of covenant in respect of user." On 28 June, the tenant sent a cheque for the rent, but it was returned to her on 3 July; she sent it back, but it was again returned.

In August, the landlord issued a writ against the tenant for forfeiture for breach of covenant as to user, and claiming possession, damages and rent or mesne profits. The tenant denied breach of covenant, and in the alternative alleged waiver by the landlord, and counterclaimed for relief against forfeiture.]

SACHS J.

[His Lordship held that, although there was nothing in the terms of the covenant to preclude a true sharing between a tenant and a personal friend, the taking in of the paying guest as a result of the newspaper advertisement did amount to a breach of the covenant, and the breach had continued until the expiry of the 28 days in the notice. He continued:]

On behalf of the tenant counsel submitted that the landlord could not succeed in this action, and contended that there had been a waiver of the breaches and any right to forfeiture. By his submissions he relied, first of all, on a waiver of the pre-notice breaches—founding this on the acceptance by the landlord of the rent due on 25 March, and further on the demand made on 25 June. (The 25 March rent was, of course, rent which covered the period between that date and the issue of the notice under s. 146 of the *Law of Property Act* 1925 (U.K.), on 8 June.) Secondly, he relied on the demand for rent dated 25 June, coupled, if relevant, with the tender of that rent, as being a waiver not only in relation to past breaches, but also for the period 6 July to date of writ issued, being dates to which the rent in advance related. Thirdly, he relied on the acceptance of rent for all those quarter days which followed the receipt by the landlord's solicitor of a letter dated 27 January 1961, in which the tenant's position in regard to the taking in of paying guests was made fully known to the landlord—that being indeed the letter relied upon by the landlord in the opening of the case, and one which was followed by the s. 146 notice of 17 March 1961. (In parenthesis, it is to be noted that, without that letter, the landlord in practice would, having regard to the fact that there can be no discovery in forfeiture actions, have probably been unable to get a case on its feet.)

When one approaches the law relating to waiver of forfeiture, one comes upon a field—one might say a minefield—in which it is necessary to tread with diffidence and warily. That is to no small degree due to the number of points in that field that are of a highly technical nature, originating in the days before the court was able to give relief, if at all, with such freedom as it can nowadays.

My diffidence in this case is not diminished by finding so little authority dealing with cases where rent is payable in advance. But novel and, indeed, difficult as are some of the problems posed here, I do not think that their solution will be facilitated by reserving judgment, having regard to the careful nature of the arguments of counsel. The conflicting submissions in relation to the relevant law of waiver, made by counsel, were full and helpful, and I would express my indebtedness to both.

In this field of law, one point, however, is plain and was conceded by counsel for the landlord. The law as to the effect of the acceptance of rent "without prejudice" must be taken as that stated in a classic passage in the judgment of Parker J. in *Matthews v. Smallwood* [1910] 1 Ch. 777 at 786—a passage that already in 1923 (see *Fuller's Theatre & Vaudeville Co. v. Rofe* [1923] A.C. 435 at 443) was referred to as having been many times cited with approval. This well-known exposition of the common law rule that acceptance of rent without prejudice is in law a waiver, reads ([1910] 1 Ch. 777 at 786): "It is also, I think, reasonably clear upon the cases that whether the act, coupled with the knowledge, constitutes a waiver is a question which the law decides, and therefore it is not open to a lessor who has knowledge of the breach to say 'I will treat the tenancy as existing, and I will receive the rent, or I will take advantage of my power as landlord to distrain; but I tell you that all I shall do will be without prejudice to my right to re-enter, which I intend to reserve.' That is a position which he is not entitled to take up. If, knowing of the breach, he does distrain, or does receive the rent, then by law he waives the breach, and nothing which he can say by way of protest against the law will avail him anything."

That authority was again cited in the Court of Appeal with approval more recently in *Oak Property Co. Ltd v. Chapman* [1947] K.B. 886, where Somervell L.J., in reading the judgment of the court, said (at 898): "The acceptance of rent being, in the circumstances, an unequivocal act, waiver of the breach followed, according to Parker J. in *Matthews v. Smallwood* [1910] 1 Ch. 777 at 786 as a matter of law; and so unequivocal was the act of acceptance of rent that the landlord was held disentitled to get the best of both worlds by attempts to qualify his acceptance, for example, by stating that he accepted the rent without prejudice to his rights of forfeiture."

It is thus a matter of law that once rent is accepted a waiver results. The question of quo animo it is accepted in forfeiture cases is irrelevant in relation to such acceptance. (I would mention that of course that is not so where the acceptance of rent has to be considered after the expiry of a lease by effluxion of time or notice—a distinction which has been adverted to in more than one authority.) Where forfeiture is involved, in essence once the landlord has knowledge of a past breach, the law thus treats the rent as a piece of cake equivalent to the land out of which it derives: its nutritional qualities in the landlord's hands being unaffected by attaching to it the label "without prejudice", the law treats that attachment as having no effect.

Whether a demand for rent made without prejudice similarly operates as a waiver has, apparently, not been specifically decided. When one looks at the authorities, it is, however, clear that a demand can operate as a waiver in the same way as an acceptance: an instance of this view is to be found in the opinion of Bramwell B. in *Croft v. Lumley* (1856) 6 H.L.C. 672 at 705. That demand is often stated in textbooks and authorities to need to be "unqualified" or "unequivocal"—words that seem to have originated before Parker J.'s view of the law became fully accepted, and at a time when the position of a receipt of rent "without prejudice" was still in doubt. Nowadays, however, a word such as "unqualified" seems redundant where the demand itself speaks specifically of "rent".

As both demand and acceptance respectively are in law merely different forms of a notification by a landlord of election not to avoid or forfeit the lease, to my mind no distinction can nowadays be drawn between them in relation to a question whether the label "without prejudice" affects their quality as an election. I note, incidentally, that Bramwell B., in the passage already mentioned drew no such distinction. He stated: "When a lessee commits a breach of covenant on which the lessor has a right of re-entry, he may elect to avoid or not to avoid the lease, and he may do so by deed or by word. If in that notice he says, under circumstances which bind him that he will not avoid the lease, or he does an act inconsistent with his avoiding as distraining the rent or demanding subsequent rent, he elects to not avoid the lease."

Thus, whatever the origin and history of the use of the word "unqualified" it seems to be that since 1910 it should not be so construed as to cause a "without prejudice" demand to be a qualified demand. It follows that the letter of 25 June is, to my mind, a demand of a type that waives forfeiture.

[His Lordship then went on to hold, following *Doe d. Ambler v. Woodbridge* (1829) 9 B. & C. 376; 109 E.R. 140, that breach of a covenant against user was a continuing breach, not a once and for all breach. He continued:]

. . . I now turn to the important and decisive question as to the circumstances in which a demand for or acceptance of rent payable in advance constitutes a waiver of breaches during the period covered by the rent demanded. Clearly it cannot be a waiver of future breaches of which the landlord has no advance knowledge: *Ellis v. Rowbotham* [1900] 1 Q.B. 740, which relates to a default in payment of rent in advance, seems to illustrate this point, despite being an *Apportionment Act* case. Equally clearly, an acceptance of rent in advance does waive a once and for all—that is to say, a non-continuing—breach in the past: such a waiver applies both to the past and to the period covered by the rent.

As regards continuing breaches, it seems to me that, in the absence of express agreement, the acceptance of rent in advance can at highest only waive those breaches that are at the time of demand known to be continuing, and to waive them for such period as it is definitely known they will continue. When it is a question of estimating the chances as to whether the tenant's breach will continue, the position is, in my view, different, irrespective of whether those chances are high or low. The object of a covenant by which rent has to be paid in advance is to obtain a certain security for that payment: *Ellis v. Rowbotham* points to the nature and effect of that covenant. A landlord cannot, to my mind, lightly be deprived of the benefit of such rights: he cannot be put in the position of having to wait until the end of the period covered by the rent before demanding or accepting it merely because there are chances that the tenant may so break or continue in breach of covenant as to render himself liable to forfeiture.

Taking seriatim the breaches which are relevant and the submissions made by counsel for the tenant in relation to them, one turns first, of course, to the pre 8 June breaches. The payment of rent due on 24 March clearly waived all breaches before that date, and it may just be arguable that the landlord's knowledge, in the particular circumstances of this case, was such that the landlord knew definitely that the breach would continue throughout the ensuing quarter: if so, there would have been a waiver as regards also the breaches up to 8 June. But anyway those breaches were waived by the demand for rent made on 25 June. That demand of 25 June, as already indicated, waived all breaches up to the time that the 8 June notice under s. 146 of the *Law of Property Act* 1925 (U.K.), was issued and, therefore, the landlord cannot rely in this action on those breaches as constituting a foundation for bringing this action.

What, however, is the position as regards those breaches which occurred between 6 July and the date of the issue of the writ? Counsel for the tenant argued persuasively that at the time of the 25 June demand the landlord had such knowledge of the state of affairs that the landlord must have known definitely that the tenant would remain in breach after the notice had expired. Counsel also advanced other arguments as to why the knowledge of what he termed "the state of affairs generally" was such that the demand operated as a waiver. These arguments were attractive, even though not supported by any questions on the subject of such knowledge put to, or answers given by, Mrs Segal. I do not, however, think that the tenant, even in the present case, can say that the landlord must be taken to have had definite knowledge that the breaches would continue after the expiration of the notice. Incidentally, in that respect, one observes that the tenant has in fact now told the ladies in question to go, and they have gone.

Nor do I think that any argument favourable to the tenant's case can be founded on the breaches during the period of 25 June to 6 July.

It follows that in the upshot I feel bound to hold that the plea of waiver does not succeed.

In addition to submitting that there was waiver, counsel for the tenant argued that there was an implied licence given to the tenant to continue in breach of the covenant or, at any rate, to continue having the ladies there as before. In that behalf, he relied on the previous repeated waivers. For my part, I doubt whether a tenant who fails to establish a waiver in a case such as the present can then, on the same facts, say that he had a licence to commit those acts. But in any event, in the present case, even if the previous waivers might be some evidence of such a licence, the contemporaneous correspondence taken as a whole is such that it cannot be held that such a licence was given. So this submission must also fail.

[His Lordship then proceeded to grant the tenant relief against forfeiture. (Relief against forfeiture is discussed below.)]

NOTES

1. In the passage extracted, Sachs J. expressed the opinion that the question of quo animo [with what intention] rent is accepted in forfeiture cases is irrelevant, and that as a matter of law, once rent is accepted a waiver results. Such, however, is not necessarily the case where rent is demanded or accepted after a lease has expired by effluxion of time, and the tenant is trying to prove the existence of a *new* lease by such demand or acceptance: cf. *Landlord and Tenant (Amendment) Act* 1948 (N.S.W.), s. 80, discussed in Hope, Mackerras and Freeman, *Landlord and Tenant Practice and Procedure in New South Wales* (7th ed., 1971), pp. 205-207. Consider the following comments of Lord Denning M.R. in *Central Estates (Belgravia) Ltd v. Woolgar (No. 2)* [1972] 1 W.L.R. 1048 at 1051-1052:

> The cases on waiver are collected in the notes to *Dumpor's* case (1603) 4 Co. Re[p]. 119b in *Smith's Leading Cases* (13th ed., 1929), pp. 39-44. Those notes show that the demand and acceptance of rent has a very different effect according to how the question arises. If it is sought to say there is *a new tenancy* by acceptance of rent; for instance, after a notice to quit has expired, the question always is, as Lord Mansfield said: "Quo animo the rent was received and what the real intention of both parties was": see *Doe d. Cheny v. Batten* (1775) 1 Cowp. 243 at 245; and *Clarke v. Grant* [1950] 1 K.B. 104. But, if it is sought to say that an existing lease continues in existence by waiver of forfeiture, then the intention of the parties does not matter. It is sufficient if there is an unequivocal act done by the landlord which recognises the existence of the lease after having knowledge of the ground of forfeiture. The law was well stated by Parker J. in *Matthews v. Smallwood* [1910] 1 Ch. 777 at 786, which was accepted by this court in *Oak Property Co. Ltd v. Chapman* [1947] K.B. 886 at 898.
>
> I know that Harman J. in *Creery v. Summersell and Flowerdew & Co. Ltd* [1949] Ch. 751 at 761, said that in waiver of forfeiture "the question remains quo animo was the act done". But that statement was explained by Megaw J. in *Windmill Investment (London) Ltd v. Milano Restaurant Ltd* [1962] 2 Q.B. 373. He said (at 376) that it meant only that:
>
>> it is a question of fact whether the money tendered is tendered as, and accepted as, rent . . . Once it is decided as a fact that the money was tendered and accepted as rent, the question of its consequences as a waiver is a matter of law.
>
> Similarly, Sachs J. in *Segal Securities Ltd v. Thoseby* [1963] 1 Q.B. 887 said (at 898):
>
>> It is thus a matter of law that once rent is accepted a waiver results. The question of quo animo it is accepted in forfeiture cases is irrelevant in relation to such acceptance.

In the *Central Estates* case, the landlord's agent for the collection of rent demanded and accepted rent after knowledge of events which gave rise to the right of forfeiture. An internal office memorandum, ordering that no rent be demanded or accepted from the tenant, had been circulated by a partner in the firm of agents, but, by an oversight, the memorandum did not reach the particular clerk who issued demands and received rents for this property. The receipt issued to the tenant on payment by him was unqualified: "Received with thanks the sum of £10". The tenant, when he paid the rent, knew that the landlord intended to forfeit the lease, and neither the landlord nor the agent intended to waive the breach. Nevertheless, the Court of Appeal held that the right of forfeiture was waived by the demand and acceptance of rent. Lord Denning M.R. said (at 1052-1053):

> The position here is quite plain. The agents, who had full authority to manage these properties on behalf of the landlords, did demand and accept the rent with full knowledge. It may be that the instructions did not get down the chain of command from the partner to the subordinate clerk who issued the demands and gave the receipts for rent. That cannot affect, to my mind, the legal position. It comes within the general rule that the knowledge of the agent—and of his clerks—is the knowledge of the principal. A principal cannot escape the doctrine of waiver by saying that one clerk had the knowledge and the other received the rent. They must be regarded as one for this purpose. The landlords' agents knew the position and they accepted the rent with knowledge. That is a waiver.
>
> I know that the judge found that the agents had no intention to waive, and finds also that the tenant knew they had no intention to waive. That seems to me to make no difference. The law says that if the agents stated in terms: "We do not intend to waive", it would not have availed them. If an express statement does not avail a landlord, nor does an implied one. So it does not avail the landlords here.

See also *Argyle Art Centre Pty Ltd v. Argyle Bond & Free Stores Co. Pty Ltd* [1976] 1 N.S.W.L.R. 377; *Lidsdale Nominees Pty Ltd v. Elkharadly* [1979] V.R. 84.
See generally, Tyler, "Waiver of Notice" (1976) 40 Conv. 327.

2. For a further illustration of waiver by the act of an agent, see *David Blackstone Ltd v. Burnetts (West End) Ltd* [1973] 1 W.L.R. 1487.

3. It may be thought to be harsh on lessors that acceptance of rent should necessarily lead to waiver of the right to forfeit, especially where the practical consequence may be to require the lessor to refuse a payment which may prove difficult to recover later. There is, however, an important qualification to the principle that waiver results from acceptance of rent. That qualification is that, at least in the case of a once-and-for-all breach (as distinct from a continuing breach, such as a breach of a covenant to repair or a covenant to use the premises in a particular manner), acceptance of rent which has accrued due *prior* to the arising of the right to forfeit (even though, in the case of forfeiture for non-payment of rent, it be a right to forfeit for non-payment of that rent) does not constitute a waiver: see Woodfall, op. cit., Vol. 1, p. 852; *Rasheed v. Burns Philp Trustee Co. Ltd* (1982) C.C.H. N.S.W. Conv. R. 55-102.

4. A statement by a lessor as to the amount of rent he or she considers to be payable may not, in given circumstances, be a "demand" for rent such as to waive the right of forfeiture. Thus, in *Inner City Businessmen's Club Ltd v. James Kirkpatrick Ltd* [1975] 2 N.Z.L.R. 636, a lessor's "statement of accounts", which was prepared following a dispute as to how much was owing for rent and negotiations for consent to assignment of the lease, was held "not truly a demand for rent in the strict sense but only a statement of what the position would be relevant to the proposals discussed, if they could be settled": at 641. See also *Owendale Pty Ltd v. Anthony* (1967) 117 C.L.R. 539 at 557 where Windeyer J. expressed the opinion (which would appear to be contrary to the decision in *David Blackstone Ltd v. Burnetts (West End) Ltd* [1973] 1 W.L.R. 1487) that "a mere demand for rent . . . made as a matter of routine by the landlord's agent or clerk" would not necessarily amount to a waiver.

5. In *R. v. Paulson* [1921] 1 A.C. 271, the Privy Council held that a term of a lease, providing that "no waiver . . . of any breach shall take effect or be binding . . . unless the same be expressed in writing", was ineffective to prevent waiver by conduct where the lessor accepted rent with knowledge of the breach of covenant. Their Lordships said (at 282-283):

   The authorities appear to their Lordships to establish that the landlord, by the receipt of rent under such circumstances, shows a definite intention to treat the lease or contract as subsisting, has made an irrevocable election so to do, and can no longer avoid the lease or contract on account of the breach of which he had knowledge. They further think the presence in a lease or contract of a provision requiring a waiver to be expressed in writing, such as exists in the present case, does not render inapplicable the principle established, and does not enable the landlord at the same time to blow hot and cold, to approbate and reprobate the same transaction, to say to his tenant, "You were my tenant under a lease or contract of tenancy all the time during which the rent which you have paid me and which I hold, has been accruing", and at the same time say to him, "You were only my tenant for half that time, and were a mere trespasser during the other half, for I evicted you or cancelled your lease in the middle of the time for which you paid me. I had no right to more than half the rent you paid, but I'll keep the whole of it". It would be wrong and unjust on the part of the landlord so to treat the tenant; to hold in fact the price of what the latter paid for, the enjoyment of his holding for the entire time during which the rent actually paid was accruing, and yet to deprive him of half of that very property.

   Later in the judgment, however, their Lordships cast some doubt on the apparent absolute nature of this statement when, having found on the facts that an acceptance of rent did amount to waiver without writing, they said (at 286):

   It may well be that many cases may occur to which the clause as to waiver would be applicable; their Lordships think that it is not applicable in the present case under all its circumstances.

   By way of contrast, the High Court has held that the parties to a lease may agree that acceptance of rent (or, presumably any other act) shall not, as a matter of *law*, amount to waiver, although such a clause could not prevent the court from finding as a matter of *fact* (as distinct from being forced to the same conclusion as a question of *law*), that in the circumstances of the case the lessor had accepted rent with the intention of waiving the breach: see *Owendale Pty Ltd v. Anthony* (1967) 117 C.L.R. 539 at 560, 581, 590, 609. The same approach has been followed in New Zealand: see *Inner City Businessmen's Club Ltd v. James Kirkpatrick Ltd* [1975] 2 N.Z.L.R. 636 at 641-644.

6. Acceptance of rent (or, indeed, any other act which otherwise would constitute waiver) will not amount to a waiver if the landlord, in an unequivocal fashion, already has exercised his right to forfeit, for example, by issuing and serving on the tenant a writ claiming possession—the issue and service of a writ is such a final election by the landlord to determine the tenancy that a subsequent receipt of rent is no waiver of the forfeiture: *Civil Service Co-op. Society Ltd v. McGrigor's Trustees* [1923] 2 Ch. 347 at 358; *Grimwood v. Moss* (1872) L.R. 7 C.P. 360; *Hinton v. Fawcett* [1957] S.A.S.R. 213 at 221; cf. *Majala Pty Ltd v. Ellas* [1949] V.L.R. 104; *Lidsdale Nominees Pty Ltd v. Elkharadly* [1979] V.R. 84. On the other hand, service of a notice to quit is not an unequivocal

determination of the lease; indeed, it is a recognition by the lessor that the lease is still on foot for at least the period specified in the notice, and so a lessor, by serving a notice to quit, waives the right to re-enter and forfeit for a breach of which he was aware at the date of service of the notice: *Re Register (A Bankrupt); Ex parte Official Assignee* [1958] N.Z.L.R. 1050 at 1054-1056; *Lowenthal v. Vanhoute* [1947] K.B. 342 at 345.

7. Under the rule in *Dumpor's* case (1601) 4 Co. Rep. 119b; 76 E.R. 1110 covenants were regarded as indivisible, and waiver of one breach meant that the landlord could not object to future breaches of the same covenant. This rule has been abrogated by statute. Sections 120 and 123 of the *Conveyancing Act* 1919 (N.S.W.) now provide that any waiver or licence to do any act which otherwise would create a forfeiture extends only to the particular breach concerned and does not operate as a waiver or licence of any other breaches, unless an intention to that effect appears.

8. A waiver need not be in writing. An oral waiver may be enforceable, and relied upon, by the tenant and (it seems) his assigns: *Brikom Investments Ltd v. Carr* [1979] Q.B. 467.

5. Relief against forfeiture

Notwithstanding that the lessor has properly exercised her or his right to re-enter and forfeit the lease, in certain circumstances a court of equity may intervene on application by the lessee and grant relief against forfeiture. Where relief is granted, the effect is to restore the lease as if it had never been forfeited (*Howard v. Fanshawe* [1895] 2 Ch. 581), although it does not preclude the lessor from enforcing her or his rights in respect of breaches of other covenants in the lease: *Toleman v. Portbury* (1872) L.R. 7 Q.B. 344 at 352; *Mayor, etc., of Dunedin v. Searl* (1915) 34 N.Z.L.R. 861 at 867.

(a) Relief against forfeiture for non-payment of rent

Equity has traditionally regarded itself as having an inherent jurisdiction to relieve against forfeiture for breach of the covenant to pay rent; it looked upon a condition of re-entry for non-payment as being merely security for payment of the rent, and, provided the landlord was recouped for all arrears of rent and costs the landlord was receiving all that he or she was entitled to under the lease: *Chandless-Chandless v. Nicholson* [1942] 2 K.B. 321 at 323; *Richard Clarke & Co. Ltd v. Widnall* [1976] 1 W.L.R. 845 at 850; *Ezekiel v. Orakpo* [1976] 3 W.L.R. 693 at 699.

Sections 8-10 of the *Landlord and Tenant Act* 1899 (N.S.W.) now set a time limit on the exercise of the jurisdiction to relieve against forfeiture for non-payment of rent. In particular, under s. 8(3), where rent is in arrear for one half-year and the tenant suffers judgment for possession to be entered and executed against her or him without paying the arrears of rent and costs, and fails to seek relief against forfeiture within the following six months, the tenant is "barred and foreclosed from all relief or remedy in law or equity".

GILL v. LEWIS

Court of Appeal [1956] 2 Q.B. 1

[The plaintiffs granted a lease of two dwelling-houses to the defendants Lewis and Wright, who proved to be bad payers: on two occasions legal proceedings had to be instituted to enforce payment of arrears of rent; on each occasion, service was difficult because of the itinerant nature of their occupation. The present case arose out of a third writ, in which the lessors claimed possession of the premises, arrears of rent amounting to £412 10s., and costs. The writ was served on Wright, but Lewis could not be found; it later transpired that he was serving a prison sentence for indecent assault, the offence having taken place on the demised premises. The plaintiffs signed judgment against Wright in May, 1955, but before that time the defendants paid £400 by way of arrears of rent; the balance of the arrears was paid subsequently. In July 1955 the defendants applied for relief against forfeiture. The Master and, later, the trial judge, held that the defendants were entitled to relief, both on the ground of certain statutory provisions (not discussed in the extract below) and as a matter of the exercise of the court's discretion. The plaintiffs appealed.]

JENKINS L.J.

[His Lordship agreed with the opinion of the trial judge as to the operation of the particular statutory provisions, and continued:]

On the part of the plaintiff landlords it is urged that the court's jurisdiction in this matter is a discretionary jurisdiction; and, while it is conceded that in the ordinary way the court will make the order as a matter of course when satisfied that the landlord has received, or has been tendered, all that is due to him for rent and for costs, that is not a wholly inflexible rule, for the conduct of the tenant may be looked into, and if upon looking into his conduct it may appear that it would be inequitable or unfair to grant relief, the court ought, in the exercise of its discretion, to refuse relief.

As grounds on which, in his submission, relief should have been refused by the judge in the present case, Mr Grundy relied, in effect, on three matters. The first was the previous history of the difficulties which the landlords had experienced in extracting the rent from the defendants; the second was the elusive habits of the defendants, which led to difficulties of service; and the third was the defendant Lewis's conviction of the two acts of indecent assault, committed actually upon a part of the demised premises. Taking all those matters into consideration the judge (says Mr Grundy) ought to have come to the conclusion that the defendants here were so wholly unmeritorious that it would be inequitable to grant them relief so as to saddle the landlords for a further period with such undesirable tenants.

On the other hand, Mr Rochford, for the defendants, says that, although there may be exceptions, a case must be an exceptional one indeed for the court to refuse relief on other grounds when all the rent and costs have been paid up. He does not go so far, I think, as to say that the court would never refuse relief, but he says that the court would only do so in very exceptional circumstances, such as do not exist in this case. . . .

As to the conclusion of the whole matter, in my view, save in exceptional circumstances, the function of the court in exercising this equitable jurisdiction is to grant relief when all that is due for rent and costs has been paid up, and (in general) to disregard any other causes of complaint that the landlord may have against the tenant. The question is whether, provided all is paid up, the landlord will not have been fully compensated; and the view taken by the court is that if he gets the whole of his rent and costs, then he has got all he is entitled to so far as rent is concerned, and extraneous matters of breach of covenant, and so forth, are, generally speaking, irrelevant.

But there may be very exceptional cases in which the conduct of the tenants has been such as, in effect, to disqualify them from coming to the court and claiming any relief or assistance whatever. The kind of case I have in mind is that of a tenant falling into arrear with the rent of premises which he was notoriously using as a disorderly house: it seems to me that in a case of that sort if the landlord brought an action for possession for non-payment of rent and the tenant applied to the court for relief, the court, on being apprised that the premises were being consistently used for immoral purposes, would decline to give the tenant any relief or assistance which would in any way further his use or allow the continuance of his use of the house for those immoral purposes. In a case of that sort it seems to me that it might well be going too far to say that the court must disregard the immoral user of the premises and assist the guilty tenant by granting him relief.

I cannot, however, find any facts in the present case approaching the exceptional state of affairs I have in mind. Here we have the previous actions for rent, but, in my view, those are not material; and it will be remembered that Rigby L.J. said in *Newbolt v. Bingham* (1895) 72 L.T. 852 that he knew of no case where a court of equity had refused relief because actions had had to be brought on previous occasions to recover rent. Nor, in my view, can anything really be made of the difficulty experienced in finding the two defendants for the purpose of bringing proceedings against them to recover the rent. Other breaches of covenant are hinted at, but none of them is clearly dealt with in the evidence, and I do not think it can affect the result so far as the present case is concerned. If there are indeed other breaches of covenant, then a landlord objecting to them has his remedy in bringing an action for breach of the covenants in question after all proper notices have been given.

We are left as the sole reason for refusing relief the fact of the two acts of indecent assault committed by the defendant Lewis at No. 92, Ifield Road, against two boys. Mr Grundy urged that that matter was enough in itself to justify the court in refusing relief. This is the aspect of the case which has occasioned me most difficulty, but, in my view, that matter is not in itself enough to justify the court in refusing relief. So far as the evidence goes, although there are some rather vague hints in an affidavit filed on the plaintiffs' side, this was apparently one isolated instance. We have no evidence at all beyond the bare fact of the conviction; we know nothing of the circumstances. I should add that it is a charge made against one only of the two joint tenants, and the acts were done at one only of these two houses, which are comprised in two separate and distinct leases.

I am therefore of opinion that no such exceptional case is here made out as to justify the court in refusing relief on payment or tender of the whole of the amount due. Accordingly, if the matter depends on the equitable jurisdiction to give relief, I think that the defendants are entitled to succeed in this appeal.

[Hodson L.J. and Singleton L.J. agreed. In the course of his judgment, Hodson L.J. said:]

That being the case, it must, I think, necessarily follow that, as equity reserves to itself the right to refuse relief in an appropriate case, the only remaining question is whether this is an appropriate case. I am confirmed in the view I have formed by the observations of Sir James Wigram V.-C. in *Bowser v. Colby* (1841) 1 Hare 109 at 130; 66 E.R. 969 at 977 et seq. Although I respectfully agree with what has fallen from my brother Jenkins and with his reference to the fact that breaches of covenant have to be read in the light of the present requirements of notice since the Conveyancing Acts, Wigram V.-C. clearly had in mind that which I think the court must always keep in mind, that there may be cases where the court will refuse relief because the conduct of the applicant for relief is such as to make it inequitable that relief should be given to him. Particularly must that be so where his conduct is in relation to the premises in question—as in the instance which my brother gave, where a tenant is supposed to have been conducting the premises as a disorderly house; it could hardly be thought, I should suppose, in such a case, that the court would grant relief.

Appeal dismissed.

NOTES

1. For an illustration of the rule, adverted to by Jenkins L.J., that relief against forfeiture will not be granted where, at the time of the application, the position has altered in such a way that relief would cause injury to third parties, see *Stanhope v. Haworth* (1886) 3 T.L.R. 34, where the lessee delayed many months before making his application for relief, during which time the lessor had spent considerable money in the upkeep of the premises and had entered into an arrangement to lease the premises to another tenant. For a case with similar facts, see *Re Catholic Supplies Ltd and Jones* [1922] N.Z.L.R. 196 at 198.

2. Relief against forfeiture for non-payment of rent will generally be refused where the tenant is in a hopelessly insolvent financial position: see *Inner City Businessmen's Club Ltd v. James Kirkpatrick Ltd* [1975] 2 N.Z.L.R. 636 at 644-645. This is so even where the lessee is able to pay the arrears at the time of the proceedings, because the court is entitled to take into account the improbability that any future rent will be paid, or that, if it is, such payments may turn out to be a preference for creditors: *Direct Food Supplies (Victoria) Pty Ltd v. D.L.V. Pty Ltd* [1975] V.R. 358 at 360-361. Where, however, the lessee's financial position was not "hopeless", but the lessee had entered into a scheme of arrangement with its creditors in an attempt to trade out of its difficulties, relief against forfeiture was granted on payment of arrears to date: *Greenwood Village Pty Ltd v. Tom the Cheap (W.A.) Pty Ltd* [1976] W.A.R. 49 at 53.

3. A tenant is not required, as a condition of relief against forfeiture, to pay outstanding rent the recovery of which is barred by statutes of limitation: see, for example, *Limitation Act* 1969 (N.S.W.), s. 25.

STIEPER v. DEVIOT PTY LTD

New South Wales Court of Appeal (1977) 2 B.P.R. 9602

[The appellant Stieper was lessee of premises on which he conducted a business requiring the storage of inflammable liquids. The respondent lessor forfeited the lease for non-payment of rent and brought proceedings seeking possession of the premises; the lessee cross-claimed for relief against forfeiture. By the time of the trial the lessee had paid all arrears of rent, but the trial judge (Needham J.) refused to grant relief against forfeiture. It appeared that the lessee had been storing the inflammable liquids in a manner which was dangerous and illegal and which (as the lessee knew) caused the lessor's insurer (being an insurer nominated by the lessor's mortgagee, pursuant to a clause in the mortgage over the premises) to refuse to continue to cover the premises. The lease contained no covenant regulating the manner of storage of explosives and did not provide that breaches of law by the lessee entitled the lessor to terminate the lease, but the decision of the trial judge to refuse relief was based on the lessee's conduct in this regard. The lessee appealed against the refusal to grant relief, arguing that since all arrears of rent had been paid the judge was in error in refusing relief on the basis of conduct which did not constitute a breach of any covenant in the lease.]

HUTLEY J.A. The first submission by counsel for the appellant was that the appellant having paid all arrears of rent was entitled to have the lease reinstated. This is contradicted by all the authorities. The most favourable statement in the authorities for the appellant is the following passage from the judgment of Jenkins L.J. in *Gill v. Lewis* [1956] 2 Q.B. 1 at 13 and 14. [His Honour quoted the two paragraphs from the judgment of Jenkins L.J., beginning with the paragraph commencing "As to the conclusion of the whole matter", extracted above p. 645, and continued:]

A somewhat special meaning has to be given to "very exceptional". The standard illustration of facts which justify refusal is the use of premises as a brothel. Indeed, where this was a breach of covenant, the Court of Appeal held it was a breach incapable of remedy (*Rugby School v. Tannahill* [1935] 1 K.B. 87) but the use of premises as a brothel is the rule rather than the exception in parts of some cities. It must, in my opinion, refer to the very exceptional impact on the premises, not the frequency or infrequency of the occurrence.

In the same case Hodson L.J. said (at 17): "I think the court must always keep in mind that there may be cases where the court will refuse relief because the conduct of the applicant for relief is such to make it inequitable that relief should be given to him. Particularly must this be so where his conduct is in relation to the premises in question."

The judgment of Hodson L.J. has been referred to with approval by Gillard J. in *Platt v. Ong* [1972] V.R. 197 and in *Belgravia Insurance Co. v. Meah* [1964] 1 Q.B. 436 by Lord Denning M.R. In his judgment in *Shiloh Spinners Ltd v. Harding* [1973] A.C. 691 Lord Wilberforce with whom Viscount Dilhorne, Lord Pearson and Lord Kilbrandon agreed and with whom Lord Simon of Glaisdale expressed general agreement, adopted a similar position.

However, even accepting the formulation of Jenkins L.J. that very exceptional circumstances must be shown, in my opinion the judgment appealed from is correct. It was submitted by counsel for the appellant that the only facts which could be considered were those which traditionally amounted to valid equitable defences and that the "very exceptional circumstances" had to be confined in the way in which traditional equity would have confined them.

This submission seems to me to be quite unsupportable; no authority was cited which even approaches it. Assuming that the circumstances have to be very exceptional, it is for the court dealing with the matter to decide whether it comes within this category. By their very nature the whole gamut of very exceptional situations is not capable of being foreseen. It is the situation in the particular case which makes it very exceptional, except in certain cases traditionally accepted as such. I can find no connection between those cases where relief against forfeiture can be properly refused and any traditional category of equity. The existing authorities can give a weighty guide, but they can never close the class of very exceptional events.

The burden of establishing that a forfeiture should not be relieved against once all arrears of rent have been paid is a very heavy one. It lies upon the landlord who has effected the forfeiture but no further definition except by example can or should be undertaken. Nor do I think that any of the facts quoted above upon which his Honour held relief should be refused, should be excluded in determining whether an exceptional situation had occurred.

Looking at the matter in this way, it seems to me that his Honour was clearly right in regarding the situation of the landlord of a building in which considerable quantities of inflammable liquid were stored and used in the course of the business carried on, when by reason of the behaviour of the tenant he had lost the insurance on the building and no other insurer had been found who was prepared to insure it as very exceptional. It is not necessary to speculate what would have been the position if proper insurance, but one not approved by the mortgagee, was available.

If the less rigid test propounded by Hodson L.J., which would appear to have the support of the preponderance of authority is accepted, the position of the appellant is quite hopeless, for the unsatisfactory conduct of the tenant which was calculated to imperil the safety of the building, even if insured, would also have to be considered. He was guilty of accumulating rubbish and lack of care in stacking and storing inflammable liquids even within the legally permitted limits, despite warning by the respondents and others. If the court is entitled to consider the general conduct of the tenant as a tenant in relation to the property, even disregarding, as I think the court should, past irregularities in payment of rent, it would be quite inequitable to compel the respondents who have, in accordance with the law, terminated the lease, to take such a tenant back.

In my opinion the judgment of Needham J. is correct and the appeal should be dismissed with costs. The respondents should have the costs of the motion for security and of the application for a stay which was brought before the court on 5 May 1977.

[Moffitt P. and Glass J.A., in separate judgments, came to the same conclusion.]

Appeal dismissed.

(b) Relief against forfeiture for breach of covenant other than to pay rent

Relief against forfeiture for breach of covenant other than the covenant to pay rent is treated separately from relief against forfeiture for non-payment of rent, because in the former the court's power to grant relief is generally conceived to depend upon statutory provisions rather than upon inherent jurisdiction. Traditionally, the preferred view has been that the equitable jurisdiction to relieve against forfeiture applies only in the case of forfeiture for non-payment of rent; hence the need for statutory provision. (In modern times, however, the view has been expressed that the inherent jurisdiction is not circumscribed in this fashion: *Esther Investments Pty Ltd v. Cherrywood Park Pty Ltd* [1986] W.A.R. 279; *Abbey National Building Society v. Maybeech Ltd* [1985] Ch. 190; and see generally, *Shiloh Spinners Ltd v. Harding* [1973] A.C. 691 at 721-725.)

The relevant provision in New South Wales is s. 129(2) of the *Conveyancing Act 1919* (N.S.W.):

> (2) Where a lessor is proceeding by action or otherwise to enforce such a right of re-entry or forfeiture, or has re-entered without action the lessee may, in a suit brought by himself, apply to the Court for relief; and the Court, having regard to the proceedings and conduct of the parties under the foregoing provisions of this section, and to all the other circumstances, may grant or refuse relief, as it thinks fit; and in case of relief may grant the same on such terms (if any) as to costs, expenses, damages, compensation, penalty or otherwise, including the granting of an injunction to restrain any like breach in the future, as the Court in the circumstances of each case thinks fit.

See also *Conveyancing Act* 1919 (N.S.W.), s. 129(2A).

HYMAN v. ROSE

Court of Appeal [1911] 2 K.B. 234
House of Lords [1912] A.C. 623

[By a sub-lease executed in 1845, the predecessors of the present lessees covenanted with the predecessor of the present lessor to complete the building of a chapel on the demised land, and during the term of the lease (99 years) "from time to time and as often as occasion shall require . . . [to] well and substantially repair . . . the said demised chapel . . . and all other appurtenances thereto belonging in good substantial and tenantable repair''. The lease was later assigned to the present lessees (Hyman and another), who proceeded to make substantial alterations to the chapel so as to convert it into a picture theatre. In particular, the lessees removed a dwarf wall dividing the building's grounds from the street, cut a hole in the walls to make a new doorway, removed part of the gallery, replaced the stairs, removed the organ, erected a projection loft, and put in a sloping ceiling. The majority of the Court of Appeal (Cozens-Hardy M.R. and Fletcher Moulton L.J.) held that the lessees had breached the covenant to repair, and that as the lessees were not prepared to remedy the breaches immediately—but only to re-instate the premises at the end of the term—relief against forfeiture could not be granted. Buckley L.J. dissented, holding that there was nothing in the lease prohibiting change of user from a chapel to a picture theatre, and that the alterations to the building were permissible for the purposes of the new user. In the course of their judgments, the majority made the following comments on the power to grant relief against forfeiture:]

COZENS-HARDY M.R. When Parliament in 1881 empowered the courts to relieve against forfeiture for breach of the covenants in a lease a wide discretion was given to the court either to grant or refuse relief, having regard to the conduct of the parties and to all other circumstances, and in case of relief such terms, including the granting of an injunction to restrain a like breach in the future, may be imposed as the court in the circumstances thinks fit. I am aware of the danger of defining the mode in which discretionary powers of this nature ought to be exercised. Yet I think it expedient to attempt to lay down some general principles. In the first place the applicant must, so far as possible, remedy the breaches alleged in the notice and pay reasonable compensation for the breaches which cannot be remedied. In the second place, if the breach is of a negative covenant, such as not to carry on a particular business on the demised premises, the applicant must undertake to observe the covenant in future, or at least must not avow his intention to repeat the breach complained of. In the third place, if the act complained of, though not a breach of a negative covenant, is of such a nature that the court would have restrained it during the currency of the lease on the ground of waste, the applicant must undertake to make good the waste if it be possible to do so. In the fourth place, if the act complained of does not fall under either the second or the third head, but is one in respect of which damages, other than nominal, might be recovered in an action on the covenant, the applicant must undertake not to repeat the wrongful act or to be guilty of a continuing breach.

In short, subject only to the maxim de minimis, the applicant must come into court with clean hands, and ought not to be relieved if he avows an intention to continue or to repeat a breach of covenant.

FLETCHER MOULTON L.J. In my opinion it is not necessary to discuss exhaustively the terms on which the court will grant relief from forfeiture. One thing appears to me to be axiomatic, namely, that the court will not grant relief to a lessee who persists in a continuing breach and who informs the court that it is his intention so to persist. Whatever other terms the court feels justified in requiring as a condition for relief, the applicant must be willing to repair the breach so far as it has been committed and put himself in a position in which he can observe the covenants in the future. If, therefore, what the applicants have done and propose to continue is a breach of the covenants of the lease the matter is at an end. The court cannot vary the contract between the parties. It can only relieve from the penal consequences of a past breach. It cannot condone future breaches or free the contracting party from the obligations imposed upon him by his covenant. The ground on which jurisdiction to relieve from forfeiture has been asserted by the courts or granted to them by statute is obviously that penal provisions such as a clause for re-entry should be in truth regarded as solely intended to secure the due observance of the terms of the bargain. The court is therefore not changing the true bargain between the parties by granting relief from forfeiture if in so doing it takes care to secure the object of the penal clause, that is, the due performance of the covenants. But to use the powers as possessed by it to change the true contractual relations between the parties by sanctioning and protecting breaches of the covenants would be to depart from the principles which in the past had guided its action in granting relief and shut its eyes to that which is evidently the object of the statutory increase of its powers.

[The lessees appealed to the House of Lords, which unanimously reversed the decision of the Court of Appeal. The House of Lords held that the alterations to the chapel were permissible as consequent on a permitted change of user. Apparently, the lessees had conceded that some of their acts were in breach of covenant, but their Lordships held that as the lessees had undertaken to deposit a sufficient sum of money to secure restoration at the end of the lease, relief against forfeiture was granted. The case is extracted below only on the question of relief against forfeiture.]

EARL LOREBURN L.C. I desire in the first instance to point out that the discretion given by the section is very wide. The court is to consider all the circumstances and the conduct of the parties. Now it seems to me that when the Act is so express to provide a wide discretion, meaning, no doubt, to prevent one man from forfeiting what in fair dealing belongs to some one else, by taking advantage of a breach from which he is not commensurately and irreparably damaged, it is not advisable to lay down any rigid rules for guiding that discretion. I do not doubt that the rules enunciated by the Master of the Rolls in the present case are useful maxims in general, and that in general they reflect the point of view from which judges would regard an application for relief. But I think it ought to be distinctly understood that there may be cases in which any or all of them may be disregarded. If it were otherwise the free discretion given by the statute would be fettered by limitations which have nowhere been enacted. It is one thing to decide what is the true meaning of the language contained in an Act of Parliament. It is quite a different thing to place conditions upon a free discretion entrusted by statute to the court where the conditions are not based upon statutory enactment at all. It is not safe, I think, to say that the court must and will always insist upon certain things when the Act does not require them, and the facts of some unforeseen case may make the court wish it had kept a free hand.

[Lords Macnaghten, Atkinson and Shaw agreed.]

Appeal allowed.

CENTRAL ESTATES (BELGRAVIA) LTD v. WOOLGAR (No. 2)

Court of Appeal [1972] 1 W.L.R. 1048

LORD DENNING M.R. In 1930 the Duke of Westminster let No. 13 Denbigh Street, Pimlico, to a lessee on lease for 63 years. So it is due to end in the year 1993. The lease was at a ground rent which is now £40 a year, payable quarterly. The lessor's interest became vested in Central Estates (Belgravia) Ltd (the "landlords").

In the lease there was this covenant by the tenant: "nor shall any act deed or thing be done in or about the demised premises which shall or may be or become a nuisance (whether indictable or not) or which may be grow or lead to the damage annoyance inconvenience or disturbance of the landlord or the tenant or occupier of any adjacent or neighbouring hereditaments." There was the usual proviso for re-entry in case of breach of the covenant.

In October 1957, Mr Sidney Woolgar (the "tenant") took an assignment of that lease. He was then about 60. He is now 75. He is sick and aged. He is a pensioner from the 1914-1918 war. According to a doctor, he is a harmless and ineffectual old man who supports himself by letting furnished rooms in his house. The landlords now seek to forfeit the lease.

On 22 May 1970, the police found out that he was keeping a brothel in the house—not for people of opposite sexes, but for people of the same sex—homosexuals. He was summoned before the magistrate at Bow Street under the Acts which make keeping such a brothel—a homosexual brothel—a criminal offence, just as heterosexual brothels are. On 23 June 1970, at Bow Street, he was convicted. He pleaded not guilty, but he was found guilty. It was proved. But he was not punished. He was discharged conditionally for 12 months.

That conviction imperilled his possession of the premises. His solicitors applied quickly to the landlords' solicitors for permission to sell the premises. But the landlords did not agree to his selling his leasehold interest. Then the landlords' agents, not knowing of the conviction, notified him that they were going to inspect the premises for the purpose of a schedule of dilapidations. Before they had done it, they found out about the conviction.

Each side gave a notice which crossed in the post. On the one hand, on 22 July 1970, the tenant gave notice to the landlords that he wanted to buy the freehold. That was under the *Leasehold Reform Act* 1967 (U.K.). On the other hand, on 23 July 1970—the date is important—the landlords served notice on Mr Woolgar complaining that he had been unlawfully keeping a brothel at the premises and had been convicted of the offence. That notice was served under s. 146 of the *Law of Property Act* 1925 (U.K.) preliminary to a forfeiture.

Seeing that the tenant had applied to buy the freehold, the landlords could not seek to forfeit without the leave of the court. Leave was granted by the county court judge, and, on appeal to this court, we affirmed the decision ([1972] 1 Q.B. 48). So the landlords were entitled to bring an action for forfeiture. They issued proceedings in the county court which were served on 10 December 1970. The case was heard by the county court judge on the claim for possession. Two points arose for decision. First, had the landlords waived the forfeiture? Second, if they had not waived it, was the tenant entitled to relief? The county court judge held that there was no waiver, but he granted relief. Both sides appeal to this court.

[Lord Denning held that there was waiver by demand and acceptance of rent (this aspect of the case is dealt with above p. 642), and proceeded:]

In case I am wrong on this point, I go on to consider the next point about relief from forfeiture. It is settled law that, when a tenant keeps a brothel in breach of covenant, that breach is one which is not capable of remedy. So if a landlord gives a notice under s. 146, he need not require it to be remedied (see *Rugby Schools (Governors) v. Tannahill* [1935] 1 K.B. 87 and *Egerton v. Esplanade Hotels, London, Ltd* [1947] 2 All E.R. 88) and the same has been applied to a gaming case: *Hoffman v. Fineberg* [1949] Ch. 245. It has also been said that relief is not to be exercised in favour of persons who suffer premises to be used as a brothel: see *Borthwick-Norton v. Romney Warwick Estates Ltd* [1950] 1 All E.R. 362 per Hilbery J., affirmed by this court in [1950] 1 All E.R. 798. But I think that is going too far. In a somewhat parallel case under the Rent Acts, a county court judge allowed a tenant to remain in possession, and this court affirmed his decision: see *Yates v. Morris* [1951] 1 K.B. 77. It seems to me that in a proper case—I emphasise "in a proper case"—the court can grant relief from forfeiture even for a breach of covenant against immoral user. After all, the statute does give a discretion to the court. It would not be right for the court to take away that discretion by applying a fixed rule of law that relief could never be given where a tenant has been convicted of keeping a brothel. It is true, as I said when this case was previously before us: "forfeiture was the almost inevitable consequence: relief is rarely given for such a breach." But it may sometimes be given. Suppose there was a breach by a tenant four or five years ago—a conviction of immoral user—but never any breach since. The landlord did not know of it at the time. Then, after four or five years, he discovers it and he seeks to forfeit. I should say it was plain in such a case as that that it would be open to the court to grant relief. The present case is not nearly so strong a case, but the judge, who saw the witnesses and considered the whole case, thought it was a case for relief. It is to be noticed that the past user has not affected the value of the premises. The stigma has not diminished the value of the landlord's estate. And there are many mitigating factors in favour of the tenant. The judge put it this way: "The defendant is both sick and aged. There is no evidence suggesting that the immoral user to which he put these premises continued over a long period. There is no evidence that he persisted in such user after a preliminary warning, for example, from his landlord, as happened in the *Borthwick-Norton* case [1950] 1 All E.R. 798. There is no suggestion that his illegal user continued after 27 May 1970, which was the date offence proved against him. Indeed, all the evidence points to the opposite conclusion." He pointed out that "in terms of hard cash, the defendant stands to lose and the plaintiffs stand to gain a very substantial sum of money—it was £9,000 or thereabouts at that time, we are told much more now—which is as it seems to me wholly disproportionate to the harm actual or potential that the deplorable lapse that this otherwise respectable old man can be said to have occasioned to the plaintiffs." After considering all those matters, the judge came "to the conclusion that there are grounds upon which it would be proper for me to exercise my discretion and to give relief to the defendant from forfeiture." I have had some hesitation about this point, but on the whole I would not interfere with the judge's discretion. This old man has repented of his wrongdoing. He is doing all he can, and will do all he can, to keep the premises aright, and to see that they are properly used. There was material on which the judge could exercise his discretion to grant relief. I would affirm his decision on this point also, if it were necessary to do so; but, as the forfeiture was waived, it seems to me that the action for possession fails. There is no need to exercise any relief.

BUCKLEY L.J. With regard to the other part of the case, that which relates to whether or not it would be right to permit relief from forfeiture if there were no waiver, the judge relied upon the circumstances which Lord Denning M.R. has already detailed in his judgment. For myself, I find it difficult to accept that those circumstances were sufficient ground for departing from the general principle that the court, in the exercise of its judicial discretion under s. 146 of the *Law of Property Act* 1925 (U.K.), ought not to grant relief to somebody who has been guilty of a breach of covenant in the lease of the kind which is involved in the present case. I feel myself to be in agreement with the views which were expressed by Hilbery J. in *Borthwick-Norton v. Romney Warwick Estates Ltd* [1950] 1 All E.R. 362 at 366, and what was said in the Court of Appeal by Lord Goddard C.J. in the same case reported in [1950] 1 All E.R. 798 at 801. In my judgment, exceptional circumstances need to be shown in a case in which the breach of covenant that is relied upon is a breach of covenant of this nature. But that, of course, is not to say that the section does not confer a discretion upon the court in such cases. It is merely an indication of the way in which courts in the past have thought it right to exercise that discretion in cases of this kind; and every case may be said to stand exclusively upon its own facts. Left to myself, I do not think I should have taken the course which the judge took in the present case: I would, I think, have concluded that this was a case in which it was not right to grant relief from forfeiture; but the judge was exercising a discretion: he was exercising a discretion in a case in which the covenant which was breached was not a covenant in terms not to use the property for immoral purposes, but was a covenant against using the property so as to occasion a nuisance; and in all the circumstances of the case and particularly having regard to the view which Lord Denning M.R. has already expressed, I think perhaps it would not be right for me to say that I think the judge's discretion should be overruled. I content myself, therefore, with saying that it was a discretion which I myself would have exercised otherwise had I been trying this case at first instance.

[Cairns L.J. delivered a separate judgment substantially in agreement with Lord Denning M.R.]

NOTES

1. In *Bathurst (Earl) v. Fine* [1974] 1 W.L.R. 905, Lord Denning M.R. (with whom Orr and Roskill L.JJ. agreed) expressed the view that "[i]n the ordinary way relief is almost always granted to a person who makes good the breach of covenant and is able and willing to fulfil his obligations in the future. That has been the position since *Hyman v. Rose* [1911] 2 K.B. 234". On the facts, the Court of Appeal refused relief because, having regard to the unique nature and value of the demised premises, the personal character of the tenant was an important factor, and, although all pecuniary loss to the lessor had been satisfied, the lessee had shown himself "not a fit person to be a tenant of this property". (The tenant, an American, had committed an offence while in France, and had been banned from re-entering Britain.) Compare *Lam Kee Ying Sdn. Bd. v. Lam Shes Tong* [1975] A.C. 247 at 258; *Pioneer Gravels (Qld) Pty Ltd v. T. & T. Mining Corp. Pty Ltd* [1975] Qd R. 151.

2. For a more recent case, where relief against forfeiture was refused on the ground of immoral user of the premises, see *G.M.S. Syndicate Ltd v. Gary Elliott Ltd* [1982] Ch. 1. Compare the comments of Hutley J.A. in *Seidler v. Schallhofer* [1982] 2 N.S.W.L.R. 80 at 98 et seq.; see also *Heglibiston Establishment v. Heyman* (1977) 121 Sol. J. 851.

3. The court often exercises its discretion upon terms: see, for example, the terms imposed in *Platt v. Ong* [1972] V.R. 197 at 201-202 and in *Duke of Westminster v. Swinton* [1948] 1 K.B. 524. The tenant, however, cannot be forced to accept the relief and is entitled to abandon his claim if he considers the terms too onerous: *Talbot v. Blindell* [1908] 2 K.B. 114 at 117.

4. The view traditionally has been that there could be no application by a tenant for relief against forfeiture unless the tenant was prepared to admit that the breach and forfeiture had occurred: *Lock v. Pearce* [1893] 2 Ch. 271 at 275; *David Jones Ltd v. Leventhal* (1927) 27 S.R. (N.S.W.) 350 at 357. But this view has come under challenge, it being said that there is no reason why a tenant cannot argue in the alternative that (1) no breach or forfeiture had occurred; and (2) if it had, relief against the forfeiture ought to be granted: *Consolidated Development Pty Ltd v. Holt* (1986) 6 N.S.W.L.R. 607.

5. By the terms of the legislation, the lessee may seek relief "where a lessor *is proceeding by action or otherwise*" to re-enter or forfeit, or where the lessor "*has re-entered without action*". Under the first alternative, strictly speaking, the lessee would need to apply for relief against forfeiture prior to the lessor's having obtained possession pursuant to a court order: *Rogers v. Rice* [1892] 2 Ch. 170 at 172. But the Privy Council has held that a court on appeal may grant relief against forfeiture even though the tenant has not claimed it in his pleadings at first instance (*Lam Kee Ying Sdn. Bd. v. Lam Shes Tong* [1975] A.C. 247 at 257); and there would be no need to keep within the statutory timetable if the subsection were seen as a supplement to or confirmation of the court's inherent jurisdiction to relieve against forfeiture rather than as the sole source of its jurisdiction: *Abbey National Building Society v. Maybeech Ltd* [1985] Ch. 190.

Under the second alternative (where the lessor has re-entered without taking court proceedings), no time limits are imposed by the subsection upon the lessee's claim to relief, although no doubt unwarranted delay in seeking relief will be a factor in deciding whether or not relief should be granted.

6. (1) As a general rule, where a head-lease is *forfeited*, any sub-lease falls with it. Legislation now empowers the court to grant relief to sub-tenants where the lessor "is proceeding, by action or otherwise, to enforce a right of re-entry of forfeiture" for breach of any covenant (including a covenant to pay rent) by the head-lessee. The court has a discretion to vest the lease in the sub-lessee on such terms as the court thinks fit: see *Conveyancing Act* 1919 (N.S.W.), s. 130. See generally, *Imray v. Oakshette* [1897] 2 Q.B. 218.

When acting under s. 130, the court grants a new leasehold or sub-leasehold interest in the sub-lessee; it is not merely a restoration of the former interest. In this respect, the position of the sub-lessee is different from that of a tenant who is granted relief against forfeiture under s. 129(2): see *Cadogan v. Dimovic* [1984] 2 All E.R. 168.

The court cannot grant relief to a sub-lessee under these provisions for a term extending beyond the date of determination of the head-lease: *Cannon Enterprises Ltd v. Ranchhod* [1975] 2 N.Z.L.R. 57.

(2) At common law, where a head-lease was *surrendered*, any sub-leases generally were not avoided (*Parker v. Jones* [1910] 2 K.B. 32), but the reversion of the sub-lease was destroyed and the sub-lessee's liability to the mesne lessor to pay rent and observe the covenants ceased (*Webb v. Russell* (1789) 3 Term R. 393; 100 E.R. 639); further, as there was no privity between sub-lessee and head-lessor, such liability was not replaced by any liability from the sub-lessee to the head-lessor. Legislation now provides that, upon surrender of a reversion, the estate which for the time being confers as against the tenant the next vested right is deemed the reversion expectant on the lease, to the extent and for the purpose of preserving incidents to and obligations on the reversion: see *Conveyancing Act* 1919 (N.S.W.), ss 121, 122.

VII.   RENT CONTROL AND SECURITY OF TENURE

The subject of leaseholds cannot be left without brief mention of important statutory controls on rent and security of tenure. In earlier sections of this chapter mention was made of some of the numerous statutory inroads into the general law of leases. None of these, however, goes so far as to undermine the essential contractual nature of the relationship of landlord and tenant.

In more recent times the freedom of landlord and tenant to contract as they wish (or, as more often occurs in practice, to contract as the landlord wishes) has been severely eroded. For example, substantial inroads into the contractual basis of leases in New South Wales were made by legislation now embodied in the *Landlord and Tenant (Amendment) Act* 1948 (N.S.W.). This Act had a precursor in rent control legislation of the First World War, namely, the *Fair Rents Act* 1915 (N.S.W.), in force from 1 January 1916 to 1 July 1933. That Act had been followed by the *Reduction of Rents Act* 1931 (N.S.W.), which provided for the reduction of existing rents by 22½ per cent. But its real genesis is to be found in the *National Security (Fair Rents) Regulations* of 1939 and 1941 (Cth) and the *National Security (Landlord and Tenant) Regulations* 1941 (Cth). These regulations, which placed controls on rent and on the powers of lessors to evict tenants, were passed following agreement by all States to co-operate with the Commonwealth in controlling wartime rents. The controls imposed under Commonwealth Regulations continued until 1948, when a referendum to give the Commonwealth permanent power over rent control was defeated. Thereafter, the New South Wales Parliament passed the *Landlord and Tenant (Amendment) Act* 1948, which introduced controls similar to those imposed under the Commonwealth Regulations. The 1948 Act remains in force, although over the last 20 years or so the ambit of its operation and the severity of many of its provisions have been considerably reduced. The Act has been substantially amended on numerous occasions since 1948, and has been the subject of a myriad of judicial decisions.

More recently yet again, the *Residential Tenancies Act* 1987 (N.S.W.) has imposed controls upon "residential tenancy agreements": as to which, see above p. 576. A number of the provisions of that Act have been referred to in this chapter.

INDEX

A

Abandonment, easement, of, 294-295, 296-301

Adverse possession
    prescription distinguished from, 258-259, 272-273, 286
    Torrens system, in, 209

Agricultural tenancy, tenant's fixtures, 13, 14

Air, easement for, 228-229

Aircraft, damage by, 1, 5

Air space, rights to, 1, 2, 3, 5, 8

Alienation
    severance of joint tenancy by, 51, 52, 60
    trust for sale and, 82ff

Annexation of covenants—*see* **Covenants affecting freehold land**

Annexation of fixtures, 12, 13, 15

Assignment, benefit of covenant, of, 322, 347-349

Assignment of lease—*see* **Leases**

Assurance fund—*see* **Torrens system**

Attornment clauses, mortgages, in, 440

B

Bankruptcy
    lessee, of, disclaimer by trustee, 14, 38
    official receiver, 14, 38, 112-113, 116, 118
    severs joint tenancy, 60

Building materials, annexure to land and buildings of, 12, 13

Buildings
    encroachment of,
        adjoining land, on, 1-3
        public road, on, 2
    pass by conveyance of land, 3, 12, 24
    support, whether right of, 244, 247, 258, 260-268, 273

Building schemes—*see* **Restrictive covenants**

C

Caveats—*see* **Torrens system**

Certificate of title, custody of and its effect, 147-151

Clogs on equity of redemption, 404-438
   —*see also* **Equity of redemption**

Collateral advantages in mortgages, 411-419

Competing interests, priorities between, 106ff
   —*see also* **Torrens system**

Concurrent interests
   types of, 44
   —*see also* **Joint tenancy, Tenancy in common**

Consideration, 110-111

Constructive Notice, 112
   —*see also* **Notice**

Co-ownership—*see* **Concurrent interests, Co-parcenary, Joint tenancy, Tenancy by entireties,
         Tenancy in common**

Co-parcenary, 44

Covenants affecting freehold land—*see also* **Forestry rights, Restrictive covenants**
   annexation of, at law, 322-327
         conditions necessary for, 322
         position in equity distinguished, 303, 322-340
         touch and concern land, must, 327-340
   benefit of
         annexation of benefit, 321, 322-340
         assignment of, 322
         equity, in—*see* **Restrictive covenants**
         identification of benefited land, 323
         implied annexation, 324-327
         land need not be subject to the burden, 323-324
         original covenantee, position of, 320-321
         successor in title, enforcement by, 322-327
         third parties, enforcement by, 321
         touch and concern land, 309, 322, 323, 325, 327-340
   burden of, 308-320
         chain of covenants, 308
         condition for taking benefit, 308
         enlarged long lease, 308
         equity, in—*see* **Restrictive covenants**
         not run with the land at law, 308-310
         rent charge, 309, 310
         right of re-entry for condition broken, 309
   easements, distinguished from, 303-304
   enforceability
         at law
               assignee, by, 303, 320-340
               covenantee, by, 320-321
               person entitled to benefit, by, 303, 320-340
               successors in title to covenantee, by, 303, 320-340
               successors in title to covenantor, not bound, 303, 308-320
         in equity—*see* **Restrictive covenants**
   forestry covenants, 307-308
   original covenantor, liability of, 303
   positive covenants, 223-227, 307-320
         forestry covenants, 307-308
         imposition at law, 308-320

Covenants affecting freehold land—*continued*
   positive covenants—*continued*
      public positive covenants, 307
   touch and concern land, must, 304
   Trade Practices Act 1974 (Cth), effect of, 304, 305-306

Covenants for title, 393

Covenants in leases—*see* **Leases**

Cujus est solum (etc.), 1

D

Dealing registrable, 164-165

Death, order of presumption, 45, 46, 48

Deposit of title deeds, 107, 147-152, 399-401

Derogation from grant, 242, 256, 257-258, 578-581

Description of land, 1, 2

Devise, fixtures pass under, 13

Distress for rent, 628

E

Easements—*see also* **Prescription**
   abandonment of, 294-295, 296-301
   accommodation of dominant tenement, 215, 216-221, 222-227
      positive obligations, 217, 223-227
      proximity, 217, 218, 222, 274
      related to user, 235-238
   acquisition, methods of
      estoppel, 273, 287-294
      express grant, 239-241, 252-257
      express reservation, 241
      implied by statute, 252-257
      implied grant or reservation, 242-252
      prescription, 258-273
      registered plan, 241-242
      statute, 241-242
   action for infringement of, 301-302
   air, of, 228-229, 257, 259, 270
   apparent easements—*see* Wheeldon v. Burrows, rule in
   common intention, of, 242, 246, 250-252
   continuous and apparent, 242, 243-248, 280-286
   dominant and servient tenements essential, 215, 221-227
   entry, whether right to carry out repair, 237
   equitable, 239-240
   essentials of, 214, 216-239
   extinguishment of, 294-301
      merger, by, 296
      order of court, by, 296-301
      release, by, 294-295
      Torrens title, under, 294, 295
      unity of ownership and possession, by, 295-296

Easements—*continued*
    fencing, 227, 231
    formal requirements for, 239-241
    implied by statute, 252-257
    implied grant of, 242-248, 280-286
    implied reservation, 242, 248-252, 286
    incidental rights under, 235-238
    infringement of, 301-302
    intended easements, 250-252, 286
    joint occupation, must not amount to, 219, 231-239
    jus spatiandi, 216-221
    light, for, 228, 230, 257, 259
    must be capable of forming subject matter of grant, 216, 218-221
    natural rights distinguished, 261
    necessity, of, 242, 243, 246, 248-252, 286, 296
    non-derogation from grant, effect of, 242, 243, 245, 247, 248, 257-258
    ownership and occupation of dominant and servient tenements, effect of on, 227, 295
    positive obligations imposed by, 217, 223-227, 231
    prescriptive, 258-273
    presumed grant, by, 242-252
    profit à prendre distinguished, 214-215
    proximity requirement, 217, 218, 222, 274
    quasi-easements, 242-252
    reciprocal easements, 244
    recreation, whether easement for, 216-221
    remedies for infringement of, 301-302
    repair
        easement requiring, 224-226
        whether right of entry for, 237, 245-247
    restrictive covenants distinguished, 303-304
    simultaneous conveyances, implied easements where, 242, 244, 248
    storage of goods, easement for, 234, 237, 238, 239, 253-255, 273
    subdivision of dominant tenement, effect of, 339, 340
    support
        easement for, 244, 247, 258, 260-268, 273
        natural rights for, 261
    Torrens title, easements under, 280-294
        creation, 280
            estoppel, by, 287-294
            express grant, by, 280, 283, 287,
            implied grant or reservation, by, 280-286
            necessity, by, 286
            prescription, by, 286, 287
        omission or misdescription on Register, 280-294
        recording of, under, 280
        statutory easements under, 286
        unrecorded easements under, 280-294
        user "as of right"—*see* **Prescription**
    user, extent of, 273-280
        excessive, 235-238, 273-279
        exclusive user, not an easement, 233, 238-239
        express grant, under, 273-279
        implied grant or reservation, under, 248-249, 279
        joint, 238
        limits on, 236-238, 248-249
        prescriptive easements, under, 272, 279-280
    view, no easement for, 228, 229, 258

Easements—*continued*
    water,
        easement imposing duty to contribute to cost, 223-226
        easement to take, 215, 272
    way, right of
        construction of grant of, 276, 277
        estoppel, arising by, 287-293
        excessive user of, 274-276, 277-278
        grant for all purposes, effect, 223, 277
        incidental rights under, 237, 279
        necessity, of, 248-250, 251
        prescriptive, 272
    weather, whether easement for protection from, 228-230, 257
    Wheeldon v. Burrows, rule in, 242-257, 280-286
        implied grant, 242-248
        implied reservation, 248-252
        non-derogation from grant, 242, 243, 257-258

Encroachment of buildings—*see* **Buildings**

Entireties, tenancy by, 44

Equitable interests—*see also* **Torrens system**
    better right to legal estate, 110
    expenditure on land of another, 3
    mere equities contrasted, 107
    priorities, 106ff
        legal and equitable interests, between, 109ff
        registration of deeds legislation, under, 110ff
        —*see also* **Priorities**
    purchaser without notice, 110
    tabula in naufragio, 110, 484-485
    where equities are equal, the first in time prevails, 106-107
    where equities are equal, the law prevails, 110

Equitable right to redeem, 389, 447-448
    —*see also* **Mortgages**

Equity of Redemption—*see also* **Mortgages**
    clogs on, 404-438
    collateral advantages and, 411-419
    mortgage of, 394
    nature of, 389, 404

Estoppel, easement acquired by, 273, 287-294

Exclusive possession, lessee's right to, 500-532

F

Fair wear and tear, 598-599

Fencing, easements of, 227, 231

Fixtures
    agricultural, 13-14
    annexation, test, 12-13
    annexure by
        devisee, 13
        life tenant, 15

Fixtures—*continued*
    annexure by—*continued*
        mortgagor, 13, 27, 29, 30
        owner, 13
        tenant, 13ff
    buildings, 12, 24
    chattels, distinguished from, 12ff, 15, 19, 23, 24, 27
    Credit Act 1984 (N.S.W.) and, 30-31
    definition, 12-13
    disclaimer on bankruptcy, 14, 38
    domestic, 13, 15
    executor, right to remove, 13
    landlord's, 13ff
    lessee's, 13ff
    mortgagee's, 13, 27
    nature of, 12ff
    ornamental, 13, 15
    purchaser's, 13
    quicquid plantatur solo (etc.), 12
        scope of maxim, 12ff
    removal of, 13-15, 31, 33, 37, 38, 40
        surrender of lease, effect of on right to remove, 14-15, 38, 40
    tenant for life's, 15
    tenant's, 13
    trade, 13, 15

Foreclosure—*see* **Mortgages**

Forestry covenants, 215, 307-308

Forestry rights, 215

Forfeiture of lease—*see* **Leases**

Fraud, 107, 109, 111, 112
    —*see also* **Torrens system**

Further advances—*see* **Priorities**

I

Incorporeal hereditaments—*see* **Easements, Profits à prendre**

Indefeasibility of title—*see* **Torrens system**

Interesse termini, 571

J

Joint Tenancy
    accounts between joint tenants, 90, 91
    alienation of share in, 51, 52
    characteristics of, 44, 45ff, 50
    creation of, 50-51
    determination of, 51, 69, 82, 85
    devolution of, 51
    dispositions of, 50, 51-52
    four unities, 50
    nature of, 44

Joint Tenancy—*continued*
  occupation rent, 86
  partition, 82
  per mie et per tout, 44
  presumption against, 50
  severance
      acquisition of other estate, by, 85
      agreement, by, 69
      alienation of share, by, 51
          involuntary, 60
          partial, 60
      conduct, by, 69, 74, 75, 80
      lease, effect of, 60, 66
      mortgage, effect of, 60, 63
      partition, by, 82
      property settlement, effect of, 68, 75-82
      will ineffective, 45
      words of, 50-51
  statutory trusts, 82-85
  survivorship, right of, 45
  survivor solely entitled, 51
  survivor, when doubtful, 45, 46, 48
      will, prevails over, 45
  trust for sale, 82ff
      no severance by, 85
  unity
      of interest, 50
      of possession, 44, 50
      of time, 50
      of title, 50
  will does not sever, 45

Joint tenant
  account by, 90ff
  improvements by, 93ff
  lease by, 60, 66
  mortgage by, 60, 63
  rents and profits, right to, 90ff
  rights against other joint tenants, 86ff
  sale in interest by, 51ff

Jus spatiandi, 216-221

L

Land
  definition and nature, 1, 2
  description of, 1
  fixtures included in, 12

Landlord—*see* **Lessor**

Leasehold—*see also* **Leases**
  mortgage of, 394

Leases
  assignment of, 603-604
      benefit of covenants upon, 625-627
      burden of covenants upon, 624-627

Leases—*continued*
　assignment of—*continued*
　　consent to, 604-606
　　　unreasonably withholding, 606-618
　　covenants against,
　　　absolute, 604-605
　　　qualified, 605-606
　　in breach of covenant, effect of, 618
　　indemnity for tenant, upon, 624-625
　　lease, 624-626, 627
　　reversion, 626-627
　　right to, 603-604
　certainty of term, necessity for, 532-536
　concurrent, 558
　condition in, distinguished from covenant, 630
　consent to assignment or sublease, 603-606
　　unreasonably withholding, 606-618
　covenants, 571-603
　　against assigning or sub-leasing, 604-618
　　assignment of lease, enforceability of upon, 624-626, 627
　　assignment of reversion, enforceability of upon, 626-627
　　benefit of, upon assignment of, 625-627
　　burden of, upon assignment of, 624-625, 627
　　conditions, distinguished from, 630
　　cultivate in husband-like manner, 585-586
　　definition, 571
　　fitness of furnished dwellings, 581-583
　　implied,
　　　by common law, 571-584
　　　by construction, 602
　　　by statute, 587-600
　　non-derogation from grant, 578-581
　　quiet enjoyment, for, 572-578
　　rent, to pay, 588
　　repair, to, 588-600
　　restraint of trade, and, 603
　　running with land, 619-624
　　short form (statutory), 603
　　tenant-like manner, to use in, 583-584
　　"touching and concerning" land, 620-624
　　usual, 600-602
　　yield up possession at termination of lease, to, 583
　creation of—*see also* **Torrens system**
　　entry, 571
　　statutory requirements for, 566-571
　　　not exceeding three years, 190-194, 566-571
　damages for breach of covenant to repair, 599-600
　derogation from grant, 578-581
　distress for rent, 628
　duration, required certainty of, 532-536
　easements by prescription, position where property tenanted, 271
　entry, 571
　equitable, 559-562
　　dependant on specific performance, 561-562
　　distinguished from legal, 561
　　Statute of Frauds, and, 562
　estoppel, by, 562-566
　exclusive possession, right to, 500-532

Leases—*continued*
    fitness of furnished premises, covenant for, 581-583
    forfeiture by re-entry, 629-655
        exercise of right, 629-632
        formal requirements, 632-638
            breach of covenant other than to pay rent, for, 633-638
            breach of covenant to pay rent, for, 632-633
        lessor's right to forfeit, 629-630
        notice requirements, 632-638
        of headlease, effect on sublease, 655
        relief against, 644-655
        waiver by lessor, 638-644
    holding over, 539
    "inherent defect", doctrine of, 596-598
    interesse termini, 571
    joint tenant, by, 60, 61
    licence distinguished from, 500-532
    mortgagee, by, 445-446
    mortgagor, by, 445-446
    peaceable re-entry, 629-630
    periodical, 557-558
    privity of contract and, 618-619
    privity of estate and, 619-620
        importance of, 620
    quiet enjoyment, covenant for, 572-578
    relief against forfeiture, 644-655
        breach of covenant other than to pay rent, for, 649-655
        effect of, 644
        non-payment of rent, for, 644-649
        of sublease, where headlease forfeited, 655
    rent
        covenant to pay, 588
        definition, 588
        landlord's duty to mitigate loss of, 588
        payment on periodic basis, effect of, 539-540, 557-558
    repair, 588-600
        contrasted with renewal, 594-598
        damages for breach of covenant to, 599-600
        "fair wear and tear", 598-599
        "good tenantable repair", 590-598
        "inherent defect" doctrine, 597-598
        "keeping in good repair", 588-590
        standard of, required, 590-594
    requirements for, 500-536
        —see also **Torrens system**
    reversion,
        assignment of, 626-627
    reversionary, 558-559
    short term (Torrens system), 190-196
    statutory (Conveyancing Act 1919, s. 127), 553-557
    sublease, 603-627
        consent to, 604-606
            unreasonably withholding, 606-618
        covenants against, 604-606
            absolute, 604-605
            qualified, 605-606
        in breach of covenant, effect of, 618
        right to grant, 603-604

Leases—*continued*
    sufferance, at, 536-539
    surrender of,
        effect on sublease, 655
    tenant-like manner, covenant to use in, 583-584
    term of years, for, 558
    Torrens title, under, 190-196, 567-571
    use and occupation, action for, 628-629
    waiver of forfeiture, 638-644
    waste by tenant, 583-584
    will, at, 539-546
    year to year, from, 546-553
    yield up possession at end of lease, covenant to, 585

Legal estates and interests, 106, 109, 110
    legislation, effect of on, 110ff
    priority between, 106
    registration of, 110ff
    —*see also* **Priorities**

Lessee—*see* **Tenant**

Lessor—*see also* **Leases**
    consent to assignment or sublease, 605-606
        unreasonably withholding, 606-618
    covenants by,
        fitness of furnished dwellings, 581-583
        non-derogation from grant, 578-581
        quiet enjoyment, 572-578
    easements,
        acquisition against, 271
        acquisition by, 271
    powers of, 587, 588, 618, 626-627
    remedies of, 628-655
        compensation for use of land, 628-629
        damages, 629
        distress for rent, 628
        forfeiture by re-entry, 629-655
            relief against, 644-655
            waiver of, 638-644
        injunction, 629

Licence, lease distinguished from, 500-536, 546

Licensee, tenant distinguished from, 500-536, 546

Light, easement of, 228, 230, 257, 259

Limitation of actions
    prescription, distinguished from, 258-259, 272-273, 286
    Torrens system, under, 209

Limited owners, 13-15

M

Mere equities, 107

Minerals, are land, 1

Mortgagee—*see also* **Mortgages**
    fixtures, right to, 13, 27, 30
    lease, power to grant, 445-446
    remedies of, 438-482
        foreclosure, 447-452
        improvement of mortgaged property, 443-445
        personal covenant of mortgagor, right to enforce, 438-439
        possession of mortgaged property, 439-442
        power of sale, 452-482
        receiver, power to appoint, 446-447

Mortgages
    agreement to grant, 395-399
        specific performance of, 396-399
    covenants for title in, 393
    creation of, 393-404
        old system title, 393-394
        Torrens title, 401-404
    deposit of title deeds, by, 107, 399-400
    equitable, 394-401
        duty of mortgagor under, 401
    equitable right to redeem, 389, 432, 447-448
    equity of redemption, 389, 404—*see also* **Equity of redemption**
        clogs on, 404-437
        mortgage of, 394
    foreclosure, 447-452
        effect of, 447-448
        nature of, 438, 447-448
        old system title, under, 448-451
        re-opening, 448-451, 452
        Torrens title, under, 451-452
    form of, 389-404
        old system title, under, 393-394
        Torrens title, under, 401-404
    improvements to mortgaged property,
        mortgagee's right to make, 443-445
    joint tenant, by, 60, 63
    lease, power to grant by mortgagor and mortgagee, 445-446
        old system title, 445
        Torrens title, 445-446
    leaseholds, of, 394
    nature of, 389-393
    "once a mortgage, always a mortgage", 404
    penalties in,
        interest, covenant to pay higher rate upon default, 422-423
        principal, covenant to repay larger amount upon default, 419-422
        principal and interest, covenant to pay whole upon default, 423-426
    personal covenant to repay, 389, 438-439
    possession under, 439-443
        mortgagee's liability when in, 440-443
        mortgagee's right to, 439-440
            under old system title, 439-440
            under Torrens title, 440
        mortgagor's right to, 439-440
    priorities—*see* **Priorities**
    property, improvements to while under mortgage, 443-445
    receiver
        duties of, 447

Mortgages—*continued*
    receiver—*continued*
        powers of, 446
        right to appoint, 446
    redemption of, 389
        after contractual date for repayment, 432-434
        before contractual date for repayment, 410-411, 427-432
        time limits on, 407-411
    remedies of mortgagees, 438-480—*see also* **Mortgagee**
    sale, power of, 452-482
        exercise of,
            duty of mortgagee, 458-478
            genuine sale, must be, 456-458
            injunction to restrain, 478-480
            proceeds of sale, application of, 482
            purchaser, protection of, 480-482
            self, mortgagee cannot sell to, 453-456
        source of, 452
    short form (statutory), 393
    "six months rule", 432-434
    unconscionable dealing, 426-427

N

Natural rights
    abutting ways, 287-294
    right to support, 261, 287-293

Notice—*see also* **Equitable interests, Registration of deeds, Torrens system**
    actual, 112
    bona fides and, 111, 112
        registered interest, 111, 112, 114
    constructive, 112, 192-193, 194-195
    imputed, 112, 193
    possession and, 111, 112, 113, 192-195
    priority and, 110, 111, 152-158, 161-163, 164
    purchaser from mortgagee exercising power of sale, by, 480-482
    purchaser without, 152, 154, 155, 156-157, 161-163, 164
    registration and, 110-114
    restrictive covenants, necessity for, 343
    statutory provisions concerning, 112

O

Official Receiver, 14, 38, 112-113, 116, 118

Old System title, 106, 125

P

Partition
    between co-owners, 82-85
    sale in lieu of, 82ff

Penalties—*see* **Mortgages**

Perpetuities—*see* **Rule against perpetuities**

Positive covenants—*see* **Covenants, Forestry rights**

Possession
   mortgages and—*see* **Mortgages**

Power of sale—*see* **Mortgages** (sale, power of)

Prescription
   adverse possession distinguished, 258-259, 272-273
   easements arising by,
      common law, at, 258-273
      continuous user, necessity for, 271-272
      lost modern grant, 259-268, 272

Priorities—*see also* **Torrens system**
   general law, at, 106ff
   mortgages, 483-499
      old system title, 483
      tacking, 483-499
         further advances, 111, 122, 485-499
         tabula in naufragio, 110, 152, 484-485
         Torrens title, 483
   registration of deeds legislation, under,
      bona fides, 111
      effect of, 110ff
      forgery, 112
      fraud, 112, 114, 116
      instruments, need for, 110, 111, 112, 113
      mistake, 112, 116

Privity of estate
   importance of, 620
   leases, and, 619-620

Profits à prendre
   appurtenant, 215, 222, 223
   creation, 215, 239, 240-241, 248, 253, 256, 260, 272
   defined, 214-215
   equitable profits, 239-240, 287
   extinguishment of, 227, 294-295, 296
   forestry rights deemed to be, 215
   formal requirements for creation, 239, 240-241
   in gross, 215, 222
   profits in common, 215
   registered plans, creation under, 241-242
   remedies for infringement, 301-302
   several profits, 215
   Torrens title, under, 215, 240, 280, 287

Protected tenancies, 655

Purchaser, fixtures, right to, 13

Purchaser without notice, 110-113
—*see also* **Equitable interests, Notice**

Q

Quicquid plantatur solo, solo cedit, 12

R

Receiver, appointed under mortgage, 446-447

Register—*see* **Torrens system**

Registrar-General—*see* **Torrens system**

Registration—*see* **Torrens system**

Registration of deeds—*see also* **Priorities**
    non-registration, effect of, 110-111
    registration,
        when amounts to notice, 110-111
        when does not amount to notice, 110-111, 122

Relief against forfeiture
    leases, of, 644-655

Rent—*see* **Leases**

Rent control, 655

Restraint of trade
    covenants and, 305
    leases and, 603
    mortgages and, 419, 434

Restrictive covenants—*see also* **Covenants affecting freehold land**
    annexation requirements, 349-351
    assignment of benefit, 347-349
    benefit of,
        assignment, 339, 347-349
        running of, 346, 347, 349-351
        schemes of development, 351-360
        successors in title to covenantee, 349-351
        third party enforcement, 321, 324, 332
        touch and concern land, must, 327-340
    building schemes—*see this entry* schemes of development
    burden, running of, 340-346
    covenantee's land, must benefit, 343-346
    creation,
        formal requirements, 331, 361-364
        statute, by, 364
        Torrens title, under, 364-376
    declaration as to enforceability of, 379
    easements distinguished from, 303-304
    equitable assignment, 347-349
    equitable basis, 304, 341, 343
    equitable interest in land, 303, 304
    essentials, 216-239
    extinguishment, 305, 331, 332, 376-388
    implied annexation, 324-327, 350-351
    limitations on usefulness, 307

Restrictive covenants—*continued*

modification, 378-388

negative, must be, 304, 307, 310, 342

notice requirement, 343

original covenantee, enforcement by, 346

original covenantor, liability of, 344, 346

planning considerations, relevance of, 304-305, 379-381

planning schemes, effect on, 304-305

positive covenants, 307-308, 342

    forestry covenants, 307-308

    public positive covenants, 307, 379

private planning schemes, as, 304, 307

public positive covenants, 307, 379

reforms recommended, 306-307, 342

release of, 376, 378

schemes of development,

    benefit may attach to land not owned by covenantee, 331, 332, 340, 352, 363

    formal requirements, 364-376

    Torrens title, under, 365-376

    unity of ownership, effect on, 376, 377-378

severance of covenants, 334, 335-340

subdivision of land benefited, effect, 335-336

successor to covenantee, enforcement by, 347, 349-351

—*see also this entry* schemes of development

successor to covenantor, liability of, 340-346

third parties, enforcement by, 321, 346

Torrens title under, 364-376, 377, 378

touch and concern covenantee's land, 327-340

town planning and, 304-305, 306-307

Trade Practices Act 1974 (Cth), effect of, 305-306

unity of ownership, effect on, 331, 376-378

Resumption, does not sever joint tenancy, 68

Right of survivorship—*see* **Survivorship, right of**

Rule against perpetuities, mortgages and, 410

S

Schemes of development—*see* **Restrictive covenants**

Security of tenure, 655

Sheriff, 118

Statutory trusts for sale or partition, 82-85

Subleases—*see* **Leases**

Survivorship, right of—*see also* **Joint tenancy**

determination of joint tenancy by, 45, 51

joint tenancy, under, 45

will, prevails against, 45

T

Tabula in naufragio—*see* **Priorities**

Tacking—*see* **Priorities**

Tenancy—*see also* **Leases**
    equitable, 559-562
    estoppel, by, 562-566
    licence, distinguished from, 500-536, 546
    periodical, 557-558
    statutory (Conveyancing Act 1919, s. 127), 553-557
    sufferance, at, 536-539
    term of years, for, 558
    will, at, 539-546
    year to year, from, 546-553

Tenancy by entireties, 44

Tenancy in common
    determination of, 85-86
    nature of, 44
    occupation rent, liability for, 86
    partition, 82ff
    presumption in favour of, 50
    purchase in unequal shares, 50
    severance of joint tenancy, by, 51, 60, 68, 69, 82, 85
    statutory trust for sale, 82ff
    survivorship, no right of, 45
    undivided shares, 44
    words of severance, 50-51

Tenant—*see also* **Leases**
    assignment of lease by, 603-618, 624-626
    covenants by
        to cultivate in a husband-like manner, 585-586
        to pay rent, 588
        to repair, 588-600
            damages for breach of, 599-600
        to use premises in tenant-like manner, 583-584
        to yield up possession at end of tenancy, 585
    equitable, 559-562
        dependent on specific performance, 561-562
        distinguished from legal, 561
    estoppel, by, 562-566
    exclusive possession, right to, 500-532
    holding over by, 536, 537, 539
    indemnity, right of upon assignment, 624-625
    licensee, distinguished from, 500-536, 546
    periodical, 557-558
    statutory (Conveyancing Act 1919, s. 127), 553-557
    sufferance at, 536-539
    term of years, for, 558
    will, at, 539-546
    year to year, from, 546-553

Tenant in common
    account, right to, 90
    improvements by, 93
    occupation rent, when payable by, 86

Timber
  forestry covenants, 215, 307-308
  forestry rights, 214, 215
  profit à prendre, 214, 215

Torrens system
  assurance fund, 126, 210-213
  caveats, 137-152
    failure to lodge, effect of, 138, 140-152
    form, 138
    interests protected by, 133, 137, 138-140
    lapsing, 140-144
    notice, as, 142, 148, 150
  Certificate of Title, 126
    custody of and its effect, 147-151
  curtain principle, 126
  dealing registrable, 152-164
  easements under—*see* **Easements**
  equitable interests
    failure to caveat,
      effect on, 140-152
    protection by caveat, 137-140
    unregistered interests, 140-163
  fraud, 127, 166-187
    by an agent, 184-187
    exception to indefeasibility, 166-187
    notice and, 166-184
  indefeasibility of title, 126, 127-130
    deferred indefeasibility rejected, 127-129, 130
    exceptions to, 165-208
      correction of errors, 200-201
      estates, interests, and other entries, 187-190
      fraud, 166-187
      omission or misdescription of easements, 280-294
      personal equities, 170-184, 196-200, 283, 285
      short term tenancies, 190-196, 567
      statutory charges, 201-204
  leases not exceeding three years, 190-196, 567
    notice and, 190-194
    registration requirements, 567-571
  mirror principle, 125, 126
  mortgages, 401-404
  notice
    caveats as, 142, 148, 150
    effect on pre-registration priority, 154, 155, 156-157, 161, 163, 164
    fraud and, 166-184
    short term leases and, 190-194
  overriding interests, 201-204, 284, 286
  priority
    caveats, effect on, 138, 140-152
    personal equities, effect on, 170-184, 196-200
    registration, by, 127-133
    unregistered interests, between, 127-129, 130, 152-165
  Register, 130
    correction of, 200-201
    effect of recording in, 187-190
  Registrar-General
    caveats, effect on, 138

Torrens system—*continued*
    Registrar-General—*continued*
        duty to register, 130-133
    registration and priority, 127-130
    registration of deeds, contrasted, 125
    restrictive covenants and—*see* **Restrictive covenants**
    title by registration, 125, 128
    unregistered interests, 129, 133-137, 152-163
        dealing registrable, 152-164
        notice of, 154, 155, 156-157, 161, 163, 164
        priority between, 127-129, 130, 152-165
        settlement, effect upon, 152-165
    volunteers, 204-208

"Touch and concern"
    covenants, necessity for passing benefit, 322, 327-340, 349
    leases, covenants in, 620-627

Town planning
    restrictive covenants, relationship to, 304-305, 306-307

U

Unconscionable dealing, mortgages and, 426-427

Unregistered interests—*see* **Torrens system**

"Usual" covenants in leases, 600-602

V

Volunteers—*see* **Torrens system**

W

Water—*see also* **Forestry covenants**
    easements of, imposing duty to share costs, 223-226
    easement to take, 215, 223-226, 254, 272

Wheeldon v. Burrows (rule in)—*see* **Easements**